# Creating America

## A History of the United States

**Beginnings
through
World War I**

**Zitkala-Ša**
Native American author

**Elizabeth Cady Stanton**
Leader of the women's rights movement in the 1800s

**Abigail Adams**
Supporter of women's rights; married to President John Adams

**Queen Liliuokalani**
Queen of Hawaii in the late 1800s

**Juan Seguín**
A hero of the Texas Revolution

**Andrew Jackson**
Seventh president of the United States

**Ida B. Wells**
Journalist and reformer who fought against discrimination

**Abraham Lincoln**
Sixteenth president of the
United States

**Crispus Attucks**
American colonist killed
in the Boston Massacre

**George Washington**
First president of
the United States

# Creating America

## A History of
## the United States

**Beginnings
through
World War I**

McDougal Littell
A DIVISION OF HOUGHTON MIFFLIN COMPANY

# Senior Consultants

**Jesus Garcia** is Professor of Social Studies at the University of Nevada at Las Vegas. A former social studies teacher, Dr. Garcia has co-authored many books and articles on subjects that range from teaching social studies in elementary school to seeking diversity in education. Dr. Garcia served as President of the National Council for the Social Studies in 2004–2005.

**Donna M. Ogle** is Professor of Reading and Language Arts at National-Louis University in Evanston, Illinois, and is a specialist in reading in the content areas with an interest in social studies. She is past president of the International Reading Association. A former social studies teacher, Dr. Ogle is also Director of a Goals 2000 grant for Reading and Thinking in the Content Areas for four Chicago high schools. She developed the K-W-L reading strategy that is so widely used in schools.

**C. Frederick Risinger** is Director of Professional Development and Coordinator for Social Studies Education at Indiana University. He is past president of the National Council for the Social Studies. Mr. Risinger also served on the coordinating committee for the National History Standards Project. He writes a monthly column on technology in the social studies classroom for *Social Education.*

**Joyce Stevos** recently retired from 36 years of service to the Providence, Rhode Island, Public Schools. For 15 of those years, she was the social studies area supervisor and developed programs on Holocaust studies, the Armenian genocide, character education, voter education, and government and law. Currently, she is a Ph.D. candidate in education focusing on how youth develop a citizen identity.

History-Social Science Content Standards for California Public Schools reproduced by permission, California Department of Education, CDE Press, 1430 N Street, Suite 3207, Sacramento, CA 95814

Maps on pages A1–A39 © Rand McNally & Company. All rights reserved.

Acknowledgments begin on page R100.

ISBN-13: 978-0-618-55949-7    ISBN-10: 0-618-55949-3

Printed in the United States of America
6 7 8 9 – DWO – 10 09 08 07 – Updated California Edition

# Consultants and Reviewers

## Content Consultants

The content consultants reviewed the manuscript for historical depth and accuracy and for clarity of presentation.

**Roger Beck**
Department of History
Eastern Illinois University
Charleston, Illinois

**David Farber**
Department of History
University of New Mexico
Albuquerque, New Mexico

**Cheryl Johnson-Odim**
Department of History
Loyola University
Chicago, Illinois

**Joseph Kett**
Department of History
University of Virginia
Charlottesville, Virginia

**Jack N. Rakove**
Department of History
Stanford University
Stanford, California

**Virginia Stewart**
Department of History
University of North Carolina,
    Wilmington
Wilmington, North Carolina

**Christopher Waldrep**
Department of History
Eastern Illinois University
Charleston, Illinois

**Clarence Walker**
Department of History
University of California, Davis
Davis, California

**Nancy Woloch**
Department of History
Barnard College
New York, New York

## Multicultural Advisory Board

The multicultural advisors reviewed the manuscript for appropriate historical content.

**Betty Dean**
Social Studies Consultant
Pearland, Texas

**Tyrone C. Howard**
College of Education
The Ohio State University
Columbus, Ohio

**Jose C. Moya**
Department of History
University of California
    at Los Angeles
Los Angeles, California

**Pat Payne**
Office of Multicultural Education
Indianapolis Public Schools
Indianapolis, Indiana

**Betto Ramirez**
Former Teacher, La Joya, Texas
Social Studies Consultant
Mission, Texas

**Jon Reyhner**
Department of Education
Northern Arizona University
Flagstaff, Arizona

**Ronald Young**
Department of History
Georgia Southern University
Statesboro, Georgia

# Consultants and Reviewers

## Teacher Consultants

The following educators contributed activity options for the Pupil's Edition and teaching ideas and activities for the Teacher's Edition.

**Paul C. Beavers**
J. T. Moore Middle School
Nashville, Tennessee

**Holly West Brewer**
Buena Vista Paideia Magnet School
Nashville, Tennessee

**Ron Campana**
Social Studies Consultant
New York, New York

**Patricia B. Carlson**
Swanson Middle School
Arlington, Virginia

**Ann Cotton**
Ft. Worth Independent School
    District
Ft. Worth, Texas

**Kelly Ellis**
Hamilton Junior High School
Cypress, Texas

**James Grimes**
Middlesex County Vocational–
Technical High School
Woodbridge, New Jersey

**Brent Heath**
De Anza Middle School
Ontario, California
NCSS 2004 Middle Level
    Teacher of the Year

**Suzanne Hidalgo**
Serrano Middle School
Highland, California

**Barbara Kennedy**
Sylvan Middle School
Citrus Heights, California

**Pamela Kniffin**
Navasota Junior High School
Navasota, Texas

**Tammy Leiber**
Navasota Junior High School
Navasota, Texas

**Lori Lesslie**
Cedar Bluff Middle School
Knoxville, Tennessee

**Brian McKenzie**
Dr. Charles R. Drew Science
    Magnet School
Buffalo, New York

**W. W. Bear Mills**
Goddard Junior High School
Midland, Texas

**Lindy Poling**
Millbrook High School
Raleigh, North Carolina

**Jean Price**
T. H. Rogers Middle School
Houston, Texas

**Meg Robbins**
Wilbraham Middle School
Wilbraham, Massachusetts

**Philip Rodriguez**
McNair Middle School
San Antonio, Texas

**Leslie Schubert**
Parkland School
McHenry, Illinois

**Robert Sisko**
Carteret Middle School
Carteret, New Jersey

**Marci Smith**
Hurst-Euless-Bedford Independent
    School District
Bedford, Texas

**James Sorenson**
Chippewa Middle School
Des Plaines, Illinois

**Nicholas G. Sysock**
Carteret Middle School
Carteret, New Jersey

**Lisa Williams**
Lamberton Middle School
Carlisle, Pennsylvania

**Michael Yell**
Hudson Middle School
Hudson, Wisconsin

## Teacher Panels

The following educators provided ongoing review during the development of prototypes, the table of contents, and key components of the program.

**Bill Albright**
Wilson Southern Junior High School
Sinking Spring, Pennsylvania

**Henry Assetto**
Gordon Middle School
Coatesville, Pennsylvania

**James Berry**
Kennedy Middle School
Grand Prairie, Texas

**Ralph Burnley**
Roosevelt Middle School
Philadelphia, Pennsylvania

**Mary Ann Canamar**
Garner Middle School
San Antonio, Texas

**Zoe Carter**
San Jacinto Junior High School
Midland, Texas

**Stephen Cicero**
Butler Area Junior High School
Butler, Pennsylvania

**Charles Crescenzi**
Dover Intermediate School
Dover, Pennsylvania

**Sharon McDonald**
Cook Junior High School
Houston, Texas

**Phil Mifsud**
Roosevelt Middle School
Erie, Pennsylvania

**Joel Mumma**
Centerville Middle School
Lancaster, Pennsylvania

**September Olson**
Richardson Middle School
El Paso, Texas

**Donald Roberts**
Frick International Studies Academy
Pittsburgh, Pennsylvania

**Mary Rogers**
Brookside Intermediate School
Friendswood, Texas

**Lucy Sanchez**
John F. Kennedy High School
San Antonio, Texas

**Steve Seale**
Hamilton Middle School
Houston, Texas

**Yolanda Villalobos**
Dallas Independent School District
Dallas, Texas

**Diane Williams**
Hill-Freedman Middle School
Philadelphia, Pennsylvania

**Lisa Williams**
Lamberton Middle School
Carlisle, Pennsylvania

## Student Board

The following students reviewed pages for the textbook.

**Adam Backhaus**
Parkland School
McHenry, Illinois

**Ben Barney**
Hamilton Junior High School
Cypress, Texas

**Amanda Berrier**
Lamberton Middle School
Carlisle, Pennsylvania

**Debra Hurwitz**
T. H. Rogers Middle School
Houston, Texas

**Reginald Jones**
Dr. Charles R. Drew Science
    Magnet School
Buffalo, New York

**Brendon Keinath**
Wilbraham Middle School
Wilbraham, Massachusetts

**Daniel MacDonald**
Carteret Middle School
Carteret, New Jersey

**Cameron Mote**
Serrano Middle School
Highland, California

**Kim Nguyen**
Sylvan Middle School
Citrus Heights, California

**Arianna G. Noriega**
De Anza Middle School
Ontario, California

**Nicholas Tofilon**
Burlington Middle School
Burlington, Wisconsin

**Emmanuel Zepeda**
Haven Middle School
Evanston, Illinois

# UNIT 1

# Three Worlds Meet  BEGINNINGS TO 1763

Pontiac

JOIN, or DIE.

George Washington

x

# UNIT 3

# The Early Republic   1789 – 1844

xii

# A Changing Nation
1810 – 1860

California gold miner

Frances Ellen
Watkins Harper

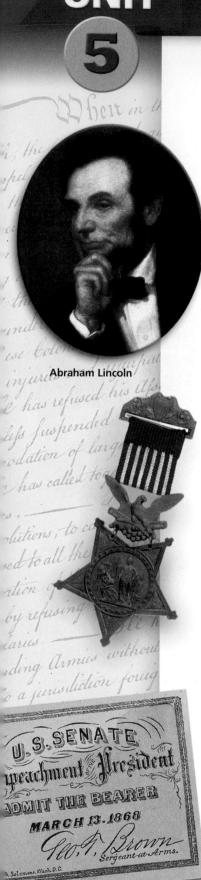

Abraham Lincoln

# UNIT 5

## The Nation Divided and Rebuilt    1846 – 1877

# America Transformed 1860 – 1914

THE JUNGLE

UPTON SINCLAIR

Queen Liliuokalani

WOMEN!
HELP AMERICA'S SONS
WIN THE WAR

I WANT YOU
FOR U.S. ARMY
NEAREST RECRUITING STATION

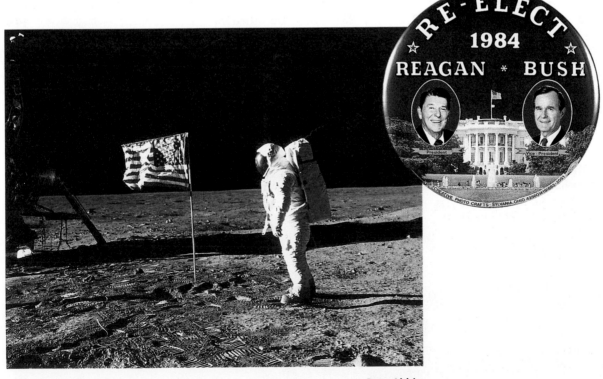

Buzz Aldrin

# Features

# Features

# Voices from the Past

**A VOICE FROM THE PAST**

The land is the finest for cultivation that I ever in my life set foot upon, and it also abounds in trees of every description.

**Henry Hudson,** quoted in *Discoverers of America*

**A VOICE FROM THE PAST**

These, with the pictures, busts [sculptures of the head and shoulders], and prints (of which copies upon copies are spread everywhere), have made your father's face as well known as that of the moon.

**Benjamin Franklin,** letter to his daughter Sally

# Voices from the Past

### A VOICE FROM THE PAST

I do not recollect of [remember] ever seeing my mother by the light of day. She was with me in the night. She would lie down with me, and get me to sleep, but long before I waked she was gone.

**Frederick Douglass,** *Narrative of the Life of Frederick Douglass*

# Voices from the Past

### A VOICE FROM THE PAST

[I was determined] to adopt an entirely contrary plan of proceedings from that of all others who had . . . visited Japan on the same errand.

**Commodore Matthew Perry,**
*Personal Journal*

### A VOICE FROM THE PAST

I have a dream that my four little children will one day live in a nation where they will not be judged by the color of their skin but by the content of their character. I have a dream today.

**Dr. Martin Luther King, Jr.,**
"I Have a Dream,"
August 28, 1963

# Historical Maps

# Charts and Graphs

**Causes of the War of 1812**

| Impressment of U.S. Citizens | Interference with American shipping | British support of Native-American resistance |

**WAR**

## Charts

## Graphs

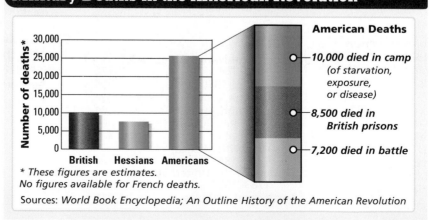

**CONNECTIONS TO MATH**

**Military Deaths in the American Revolution**

British · Hessians · Americans

Number of deaths*: 30,000 / 25,000 / 20,000 / 15,000 / 10,000 / 5,000 / 0

**American Deaths**

- 10,000 died in camp (of starvation, exposure, or disease)
- 8,500 died in British prisons
- 7,200 died in battle

\* These figures are estimates.
No figures available for French deaths.

Sources: *World Book Encyclopedia; An Outline History of the American Revolution*

# Time Lines and Infographics

## The Rise and Decline of Feudalism

In feudalism, nobles offered to protect peasants from invaders. In return, the peasants farmed the nobles' lands.

Feudalism made people feel safe enough to travel. Trade increased and towns grew.

Then many peasants ran away to towns, where they could live more freely. Feudalism declined. Trade continued to grow.

# THEMES of AMERICAN HISTORY

Imagine life in Jamestown, America's first permanent English settlement. The nation we inhabit now is a much different place than it was then, more than three centuries ago. Yet there are repeating themes—ideas and issues—in American history that tie the past and present together. This book focuses on nine significant themes in U.S. history. Understanding these themes will help you to make sense of American history.

## Democratic Ideals

From the day they declared themselves citizens of a new nation, Americans have built their society around the principles of democracy. In a democracy, power lies with the people, and every individual enjoys basic rights that cannot be taken away. Throughout the nation's history, however, some Americans—mainly women and minorities—have had to struggle to gain their full rights. Still, the ideals of democracy remain the guiding principles of this land.

*What right or freedom do you consider the most important? Why?*

## Citizenship

The citizens of the United States enjoy rights and freedoms found in very few other places in the world. Yet Americans know that with such freedoms come responsibilities and duties. Whether they stand in line to vote or spend a weekend to clean up a local river, Americans recognize that citizen participation is what keeps a democracy strong.

*How do citizens that you know contribute to your community?*

Dr. Martin Luther King, Jr.

## Impact of the Individual

The history of the United States is the story not only of governments and laws but of individuals. Indeed, individuals have made the United States what it is today through their extraordinary achievements. American history provides a variety of examples of the impact of the individual on society in both the United States and the world.

*Name several individuals who have an impact on American society today. What impact do they have?*

A young Asian immigrant

## Diversity and Unity

The United States has been a land of many peoples, cultures, and faiths. Throughout the nation's history, this blend of ethnic, racial, and religious groups has helped to create a rich and uniquely American culture. The nation's many different peoples are united in their belief in American values and ideals.

*What things do you enjoy that came to the United States from other cultures?*

## Immigration and Migration

The movement of people has played a vital role in American history. This country was settled by and has remained a magnet for immigrants. Even within the United States, large numbers of people have migrated to different regions of the country. However, movements to and within the United States have not always been voluntary. Africans were brought against their will to this country. Native Americans were forced from their homelands in order to make room for European settlers.

*Why do you think people continue to immigrate to the United States?*

## Expansion

When the United States declared its independence from Great Britain, it was only a collection of states along the Atlantic Ocean. But the new country would not remain that way for long. Many Americans shared a sense of curiosity, adventure, and a strong belief that their destiny was to expand all the way to the Pacific Ocean. Driven by this belief, they pushed westward. Americans' efforts to increase the size of their nation is a recurring theme in early U.S. history.

*Where do you predict that the exploration of space—the final frontier—will lead?*

**Poster for Buffalo Bill's Wild West show**

## America and the World

As the power and prestige of the United States have grown, the nation has played a much more active role in world affairs. Indeed, throughout the 20th century, the United States focused much of its energy on events beyond its borders. The nation fought in two world wars and tried to promote democracy, peace, and economic growth around the globe. As one of the world's political and economic leaders, the United States will continue to be a key player in world affairs throughout the new century.

*What do you think the role of the United States in the world should be today?*

## Science and Technology

Americans have always been quick to embrace inventions and new ways of doing things. After all, this country was settled by people who turned away from old ways and tried new ones. In the past two centuries, new inventions, new technologies, and scientific breakthroughs have transformed the United States—and will continue to do so in the new century.

*What recent inventions or innovations affect your life?*

## Economics in History

Economics has had a powerful impact on the course of U.S. history. For example, the desire for wealth led thousands to join the California Gold Rush in 1849. The nation as a whole has grown wealthy, thanks to its abundant resources and the hard work of its citizens. An important economic issue, however, has been how to make sure that all people have opportunities to share fully in the nation's wealth. This issue will continue to be important in the 21st century.

*What do you think are the most exciting economic opportunities for Americans today?*

**Thomas Edison's first light bulb**

# Student Guide to the
# California State Standards for Grade 8

The state of California has developed standards that guide the content taught in its public schools. At the beginning of every lesson in this book, you will see a listing of the California content standards and skills standards that are addressed in that lesson. The standards begin with a code that combines numbers and letters (such as 8.2.3 or HI 2), followed by the statement of the standard. These standards describe the knowledge and skills you are expected to have learned by the end of specific grades.

Standards that use numbers only (such as 8.2.3) are content standards, which describe the actual historical people and events that you will study in this book. Standards that combine letters and numbers (such as HI 2 or CST 3) refer to standards that cover the Historical and Social Sciences Analysis Skills that you will apply to the content standards for Grade 8.

The following charts contain the complete wording of the content and skills standards for Grade 8. These charts will help you keep track of what you learn throughout the year.

# History-Social Science Standards

## Grade 8 US History and Geography

**Standard 7.11**
Students analyze political and economic change in the sixteenth, seventeenth, and eighteenth centuries (the Age of Exploration, the Enlightenment, and the Age of Reason).

**7.11.1** Know the great voyages of discovery, the locations of the routes, and the influence of cartography in the development of a new European worldview.

**7.11.2** Discuss the exchanges of plants, animals, technology, culture, and ideas among Europe, Africa, Asia and the Americas in the 15th and 16th centuries and the major economic and social effects on each continent.

**7.11.3** Examine the origins of modern capitalism; the influence of mercantilism and cottage industry; the elements and importance of a market economy in seventeenth-century Europe; the changing international trading and marketing patterns, including their locations on a world map; and the influence of explorers and map makers.

**7.11.4** Explain how the main ideas of the Enlightenment can be traced back to such movements as the Renaissance, the Reformation, and the Scientific Revolution and to the Greeks, Romans, and Christianity.

**7.11.5** Describe how democratic thought and institutions were influenced by Enlightenment thinkers (e.g., John Locke, Charles-Louis Montesquieu, American founders).

**7.11.6** Discuss how principles in the Magna Carta were embodied in such documents as the English Bill of Rights and the American Declaration of Independence.

**Standard 8.1**
Students understand the major events preceding the founding of the nation and relate their significance to the development of American constitutional democracy.

**8.1.1** Describe the relationship between the moral and political ideas of the Great Awakening and the development of revolutionary fervor.

**8.1.2** Analyze the philosophy of government expressed in the Declaration of Independence, with an emphasis on government as a means of securing individual rights (e.g., key phrases such as "all men are created equal, that they are endowed by their Creator with certain unalienable Rights").

| | |
|---|---|
| **8.1.3** | Analyze how the American Revolution affected other nations, especially France. |
| **8.1.4** | Describe the nation's blend of civic republicanism, classical liberal principles, and English parliamentary traditions. |

| | |
|---|---|
| **Standard 8.2** | Students analyze the political principles underlying the U.S. Constitution and compare the enumerated and implied powers of the federal government. |
| **8.2.1** | Discuss the significance of the Magna Carta, the English Bill of Rights, and the Mayflower Compact.. |
| **8.2.2** | Analyze the Articles of Confederation and the Constitution and the success of each in implementing the ideals of the Declaration of Independence. |
| **8.2.3** | Evaluate the major debates that occurred during the development of the Constitution and their ultimate resolutions in such areas as shared power among institutions, divided state-federal power, slavery, the rights of individuals and states (later addressed by the addition of the Bill of Rights), and the status of American Indian nations under the commerce clause. |
| **8.2.4** | Describe the political philosophy underpinning the Constitution as specified in the *Federalist Papers* (authored by James Madison, Alexander Hamilton, and John Jay) and the role of such leaders as Madison, George Washington, Roger Sherman, Gouverneur Morris, and James Wilson in the writing and ratification of the Constitution. |
| **8.2.5** | Understand the significance of Jefferson's Statute for Religious Freedom as a forerunner of the First Amendment and the origins, purpose, and differing views of the founding fathers on the issue of the separation of church and state. |
| **8.2.6** | Enumerate the powers of government set forth in the Constitution and the fundamental liberties ensured by the Bill of Rights. |
| **8.2.7** | Describe the principles of federalism, dual sovereignty, separation of powers, checks and balances, the nature and purpose of majority rule, and the ways in which the American idea of constitutionalism preserves individual rights. |

| Standard 8.3 | Students understand the foundation of the American political system and the ways in which citizens participate in it. |
|---|---|
| 8.3.1 | Analyze the principles and concepts codified in state constitutions between 1777 and 1781 that created the context out of which American political institutions and ideas developed. |
| 8.3.2 | Explain how the ordinances of 1785 and 1787 privatized national resources and transferred federally owned lands into private holdings, townships, and states. |
| 8.3.3 | Enumerate the advantages of a common market among the states as foreseen in and protected by the Constitution's clauses on interstate commerce, common coinage, and full-faith and credit. |
| 8.3.4 | Understand how the conflicts between Thomas Jefferson and Alexander Hamilton resulted in the emergence of two political parties (e.g., view of foreign policy, Alien and Sedition Acts, economic policy, National Bank, funding and assumption of the revolutionary debt). |
| 8.3.5 | Know the significance of domestic resistance movements and ways in which the central government responded to such movements (e.g., Shays' Rebellion, the Whiskey Rebellion). |
| 8.3.6 | Describe the basic law-making process and how the Constitution provides numerous opportunities for citizens to participate in the political process and to monitor and influence government (e.g., function of elections, political parties, interest groups). |
| 8.3.7 | Understand the functions and responsibilities of a free press. |

| Standard 8.4 | Students analyze the aspirations and ideals of the people of the new nation. |
|---|---|
| 8.4.1 | Describe the country's physical landscapes, political divisions, and territorial expansion during the terms of the first four presidents. |
| 8.4.2 | Explain the policy significance of famous speeches (e.g., Washington's Farewell Address, Jefferson's 1801 Inaugural Address, John Q. Adams's Fourth of July 1821 Address). |

| | |
|---|---|
| **8.4.3** | Analyze the rise of capitalism and the economic problems and conflicts that accompanied it (e.g., Jackson's opposition to the National Bank; early decisions of the U.S. Supreme Court that reinforced the sanctity of contracts and a capitalist economic system of law). |
| **8.4.4** | Discuss daily life, including traditions in art, music, and literature, of early national America (e.g., through writings by Washington Irving, James Fenimore Cooper). |

| | |
|---|---|
| **Standard 8.5** | Students analyze U.S. foreign policy in the early Republic. |
| **8.5.1** | Understand the political and economic causes and consequences of the War of 1812 and know the major battles, leaders, and events that led to a final peace. |
| **8.5.2** | Know the changing boundaries of the United States and describe the relationships the country had with its neighbors (current Mexico and Canada) and Europe, including the influence of the Monroe Doctrine, and how those relationships influenced westward expansion and the Mexican-American War. |
| **8.5.3** | Outline the major treaties with American Indian nations during the administrations of the first four presidents and the varying outcomes of those treaties. |

| | |
|---|---|
| **Standard 8.6** | Students analyze the divergent paths of the American people from 1800 to the mid-1800s and the challenges they faced, with emphasis on the Northeast. |
| **8.6.1** | Discuss the influence of industrialization and technological developments on the region, including human modification of the landscape and how physical geography shaped human actions (e.g., growth of cities, deforestation, farming, mineral extraction). |
| **8.6.2** | Outline the physical obstacles to and the economic and political factors involved in building a network of roads, canals, and railroads (e.g., Henry Clay's American System). |
| **8.6.3** | List the reasons for the wave of immigration from Northern Europe to the United States and describe the growth in the number, size, and spatial arrangements of cities (e.g., Irish immigrants and the Great Irish Famine). |

**8.6.4** Study the lives of black Americans who gained freedom in the North and founded schools and churches to advance their rights and communities.

**8.6.5** Trace the development of the American education system from its earliest roots, including the roles of religious and private schools and Horace Mann's campaign for free public education and its assimilating role in American culture.

**8.6.6** Examine the women's suffrage movement (e.g., biographies, writings, and speeches of Elizabeth Cady Stanton, Margaret Fuller, Lucretia Mott, Susan B. Anthony).

**8.6.7** Identify common themes in American art as well as transcendentalism and individualism (e.g., writings about and by Ralph Waldo Emerson, Henry David Thoreau, Herman Melville, Louisa May Alcott, Nathaniel Hawthorne, Henry Wadsworth Longfellow).

**Standard 8.7** Students analyze the divergent paths of the American people in the South from 1800 to the mid-1800s and the challenges they faced.

**8.7.1** Describe the development of the agrarian economy in the South, identify the locations of the cotton-producing states, and discuss the significance of cotton and the cotton gin.

**8.7.2** Trace the origins and development of slavery; its effects on black Americans and on the region's political, social, religious, economic, and cultural development; and identify the strategies that were tried to both overturn and preserve it (e.g., through the writings and historical documents on Nat Turner, Denmark Vesey).

**8.7.3** Examine the characteristics of white Southern society and how the physical environment influenced events and conditions prior to the Civil War.

**8.7.4** Compare the lives of and opportunities for free blacks in the North with those of free blacks in the South.

| **Standard 8.8** | Students analyze the divergent paths of the American people in the West from 1800 to the mid-1800s and the challenges they faced. |
|---|---|
| 8.8.1 | Discuss the election of Andrew Jackson as president in 1828, the importance of Jacksonian democracy, and his actions as president (e.g., the spoils system, veto of the National Bank, policy of Indian removal, opposition to the Supreme Court). |
| 8.8.2 | Describe the purpose, challenges, and economic incentives associated with westward expansion, including the concept of Manifest Destiny (e.g., the Lewis and Clark expedition, accounts of the removal of Indians, the Cherokees' "Trail of Tears," settlement of the Great Plains) and the territorial acquisitions that spanned numerous decades. |
| 8.8.3 | Describe the role of pioneer women and the new status that western women achieved (e.g., Laura Ingalls Wilder, Annie Bidwell; slave women gaining freedom in the West; Wyoming granting suffrage to women in 1869). |
| 8.8.4 | Examine the importance of the great rivers and the struggle over water rights. |
| 8.8.5 | Discuss Mexican settlements and their locations, cultural traditions, attitudes toward slavery, land-grant system, and economies. |
| 8.8.6 | Describe the Texas War for Independence and the Mexican-American War, including territorial settlements, the aftermath of the wars, and the effects the wars had on the lives of Americans, including Mexican Americans today. |

| **Standard 8.9** | Students analyze the early and steady attempts to abolish slavery and to realize the ideals of the Declaration of Independence. |
|---|---|
| 8.9.1 | Describe the leaders of the movement (e.g., John Quincy Adams and his proposed constitutional amendment, John Brown and the armed resistance, Harriet Tubman and the Underground Railroad, Benjamin Franklin, Theodore Weld, William Lloyd Garrison, Frederick Douglass). |
| 8.9.2 | Discuss the abolition of slavery in early state constitutions. |
| 8.9.3 | Describe the significance of the Northwest Ordinance in education and in the banning of slavery in new states north of the Ohio River. |

| | |
|---|---|
| **8.9.4** | Discuss the importance of the slavery issue as raised by the annexation of Texas and California's admission to the union as a free state under the Compromise of 1850. |
| **8.9.5** | Analyze the significance of the States' Rights Doctrine, the Missouri Compromise (1820), the Wilmot Proviso (1846), the Compromise of 1850, Henry Clay's role in the Missouri Compromise and the Compromise of 1850, the Kansas-Nebraska Act (1854), the *Dred Scott* v. *Sandford* decision (1857), and the Lincoln-Douglas debates (1858). |
| **8.9.6** | Describe the lives of free blacks and the laws that limited their freedom and economic opportunities. |

| | |
|---|---|
| ▶**Standard 8.10** | Students analyze the multiple causes, key events, and complex consequences of the Civil War. |
| **8.10.1** | Compare the conflicting interpretations of state and federal authority as emphasized in the speeches and writings of statesmen such as Daniel Webster and John C. Calhoun. |
| **8.10.2** | Trace the boundaries constituting the North and the South, the geographical differences between the two regions, and the differences between agrarians and industrialists.. |
| **8.10.3** | Identify the constitutional issues posed by the doctrine of nullification and secession and the earliest origins of that doctrine. |
| **8.10.4** | Discuss Abraham Lincoln's presidency and his significant writings and speeches and their relationship to the Declaration of Independence, such as his "House Divided" speech (1858), Gettysburg Address (1863), Emancipation Proclamation (1863), and inaugural addresses (1861 and 1865). |
| **8.10.5** | Study the views and lives of leaders (e.g., Ulysses S. Grant, Jefferson Davis, Robert E. Lee) and soldiers on both sides of the war, including those of black soldiers and regiments. |
| **8.10.6** | Describe critical developments and events in the war, including the major battles, geographical advantages and obstacles, technological advances, and General Lee's surrender at Appomattox. |
| **8.10.7** | Explain how the war affected combatants, civilians, the physical environment, and future warfare. |

| | |
|---|---|
| **Standard 8.11** | Students analyze the character and lasting consequences of Reconstruction. |
| 8.11.1 | List the original aims of Reconstruction and describe its effects on the political and social structures of different regions. |
| 8.11.2 | Identify the push-pull factors in the movement of former slaves to the cities in the North and to the West and their differing experiences in those regions (e.g., the experiences of Buffalo Soldiers). |
| 8.11.3 | Understand the effects of the Freedmen's Bureau and the restrictions placed on the rights and opportunities of freedmen, including racial segregation and "Jim Crow" laws. |
| 8.11.4 | Trace the rise of the Ku Klux Klan and describe the Klan's effects. |
| 8.11.5 | Understand the Thirteenth, Fourteenth, and Fifteenth Amendments to the Constitution and analyze their connection to Reconstruction. |

| | |
|---|---|
| **Standard 8.12** | Students analyze the transformation of the American economy and the changing social and political conditions in the United States in response to the Industrial Revolution. |
| 8.12.1 | Trace patterns of agricultural and industrial development as they relate to climate, use of natural resources, markets, and trade and locate such development on a map. |
| 8.12.2 | Identify the reasons for the development of federal Indian policy and the wars with American Indians and their relationship to agricultural development and industrialization. |
| 8.12.3 | Explain how states and the federal government encouraged business expansion through tariffs, banking, land grants, and subsidies. |
| 8.12.4 | Discuss entrepreneurs, industrialists, and bankers in politics, commerce, and industry (e.g., Andrew Carnegie, John D. Rockefeller, Leland Stanford). |
| 8.12.5 | Examine the location and effects of urbanization, renewed immigration, and industrialization (e.g., the effects on social fabric of cities, wealth and economic opportunity, the conservation movement). |

**8.10.6** Discuss child labor, working conditions, and laissez-faire policies toward big business and examine the labor movement, including its leaders (e.g., Samuel Gompers), its demand for collective bargaining, and its strikes and protests over labor conditions.

**8.10.7** Identify the new sources of large-scale immigration and the contributions of immigrants to the building of cities and the economy; explain the ways in which new social and economic patterns encouraged assimilation of newcomers into the mainstream amidst growing cultural diversity; and discuss the new wave of nativism.

**8.12.8** Identify the characteristics and impact of Grangerism and Populism.

**8.12.9** Name the significant inventors and their inventions and identify how they improved the quality of life (e.g., Thomas Edison, Alexander Graham Bell, Orville and Wilbur Wright).

## Grades 6 Through 8  Historical and Social Sciences Analysis Skills

### Chronological and Spatial Thinking (CST)

1. Students explain how major events are related to one another in time.

2. Students construct various time lines of key events, people, and periods of the historical era they are studying.

3. Students use a variety of maps and documents to identify physical and cultural features of neighborhoods, cities, states, and countries and to explain the historical migration of people, expansion and disintegration of empires, and the growth of economic systems.

### Research, Evidence, and Point of View (REP)

1. Students frame questions that can be answered by historical study and research.

2. Students distinguish fact from opinion in historical narratives and stories.

3. Students distinguish relevant from irrelevant information, essential from incidental information, and verifiable from unverifiable information in historical narratives and stories.

4. Students assess the credibility of primary and secondary sources and draw sound conclusions from them.

5. Students detect the different historical points of view on historical events and determine the context in which the historical statements were made (the questions asked, sources used, author's perspectives).

## Historical Interpretation (HI)

1. Students explain the central issues and problems from the past, placing people and events in a matrix of time and place.

2. Students understand and distinguish cause, effect, sequence, and correlation in historical events, including the long- and short-term causal relations.

3. Students explain the sources of historical continuity and how the combination of ideas and events explains the emergence of new patterns.

4. Students recognize the role of chance, oversight, and error in history.

5. Students recognize that interpretations of history are subject to change as new information is uncovered.

6. Students interpret basic indicators of economic performance and conduct cost-benefit analyses of economic and political issues.

This section of the textbook helps you develop and practice the skills you need to study history and to take tests. Part 1, **Strategies for Studying History,** takes you through the features of the textbook and offers suggestions on how to use these features to improve your reading and study skills.

Part 2, **Test-Taking Strategies and Practice,** offers specific strategies for tackling many of the items you'll find on a test. It gives tips for answering multiple-choice, constructed-response, extended-response, and document-based questions. In addition, it offers guidelines for analyzing primary and secondary sources, maps, political cartoons, charts, graphs, and time lines. Each strategy is followed by a set of questions you can use for practice.

## CONTENTS

# Part 1: Strategies for Studying History

Reading is the central skill in the effective study of history or any other subject. You can improve your reading skills by using helpful techniques and through practice. The better your reading skills, the more you'll remember what you read. Below you'll find several strategies that involve built-in features of this textbook. Careful use of these strategies will help you learn and understand history more effectively.

## Preview Chapters Before You Read

Each chapter begins with a two-page chapter opener and a one-page **Reading Strategy** feature. Study the materials to help you get ready to read.

**1** Read the chapter and section titles and study the chapter-opening visual. Look for clues that indicate what will be covered in the chapter.

**2** Preview the time line. Note the years that the chapter covers. What important events took place during this time period?

**3** Study the **Interact with History** feature. Experience what it was like to live in the past by answering **What Do You Think?** questions.

**4** Read the **Reading Strategy** feature (see page S3). **What Do You Want to Know?** and the note taking chart will help focus your reading.

# Preview Sections Before You Read

Each chapter consists of three, four, or five sections. These sections focus on shorter periods of time or on particular historical themes. Use the section openers to help you prepare to read.

**5** Study the sentences under the headings **Main Idea** and **Why It Matters Now.** These tell you what's important in the material that you're about to read.

**6** Preview the **Terms & Names** list. This will give you an idea of the issues and personalities you will read about in the section.

**7** Read **One American's Story** and **A Voice from the Past**. These provide one individual's view of an important issue of the time.

**8** Notice how the section is divided into smaller chunks, each with a red headline. These headlines give you a quick outline of the section.

**9** Each section opener lists the California Standards covered in that section.

**TERMS & NAMES**

King George III          Stamp Act
Quartering Act          Patrick Henry
revenue                      boycott
Sugar Act                  Sons of Liberty

**4**

## What Do You Want to Know?

What questions do you have about the issues and events that pushed the American colonists toward rebellion? Record them in your notebook before you read the chapter.

# Use Active Reading Strategies As You Read

**Now you're ready to read the chapter. Read one section at a time, from beginning to end.**

**1** Ask and answer questions as you read. Look for the **Reading History** questions in the margin. Answering these will show whether you understand what you've just read.

**2** Try to visualize the people, places, and events you read about. Studying the pictures and any illustrated features will help you do this.

**3** Read to build your vocabulary. Use the marginal **Vocabulary** notes to find the meaning of unfamiliar terms.

**4** Look for the story behind the events. Read **Background** notes in the margin for additional information on people, places, events, and ideas.

---

*Reading* **History**

**A. Summarizing**
Who was upset by the Proclamation of 1763?

---

The first of Parliament's laws was the Proclamation of 1763. (See Chapter 5.) It said that colonists could not settle west of the Appalachian Mountains. Britain wanted this land to remain in the hands of its Native American allies to prevent another revolt like Pontiac's Rebellion.

The proclamation angered colonists who had hoped to move to the fertile Ohio Valley. Many of these colonists had no land of their own. It also upset colonists who had bought land as an investment. As a result, many ignored the law.

*Reading* **History**
A. Summarizing
Who was upset by the Proclamation of 1763?

### British Troops and Taxes

**King George III**, the British monarch, wanted to enforce the proclamation and also keep peace with Britain's Native American allies. To do this, he decided to keep 10,000 soldiers in the colonies. In 1765, Parliament passed the **Quartering Act**. This was a cost-saving measure that required the colonies to quarter, or house, British soldiers and provide them with supplies. General Thomas Gage, commander of these forces, put most of the troops in New York.

Britain owed a large debt from the French and Indian War. Keeping troops in the colonies would raise that debt even higher. Britain needed more **revenue**, or income, to meet its expenses. So it attempted to have the colonies pay part of the war debt. It also wanted them to contribute toward the costs of frontier defense and colonial government.

In the past, the king had asked the colonial assemblies to pass taxes to support military actions that took place in the colonies. This time, however, Parliament voted to tax the Americans directly.

In 1764, Parliament passed the **Sugar Act**. This law placed a tax on sugar, molasses, and other products shipped to the colonies. It also called for strict enforcement of the act and harsh punishment of smugglers.

Colonial merchants, who often traded in smuggled goods, reacted with anger.

Colonial leaders such as James Otis claimed that Parliament had no right to tax the colonies, since the colonists were not represented in Parliament. As Otis exclaimed, "Taxation without representation is tyranny!" British finance minister George Grenville disagreed. The colonists were subjects of Britain, he said, and enjoyed the protection of its laws. For that reason, they were subject to taxation.

**Vocabulary**
tyranny:
absolute power in the hands of a single ruler

### Britain Passes the Stamp Act

The Sugar Act was just the first in a series of acts that increased tension between the mother country and the colonies. In 1765, Parliament passed the **Stamp Act**. This law required all legal and commercial documents to carry an official stamp showing that a tax had been paid. All diplomas, contracts, and wills had to carry a stamp.

The colonial view of the hated stamp tax is shown by the skull and crossbones on this emblem (above); a royal stamp is pictured at right.

**160**

Even published materials such as newspapers had to be written on special stamped paper.

The Stamp Act was a new kind of tax for the colonies. The Sugar Act had been a tax on imported goods. It mainly affected merchants. In contrast, the Stamp Act was a tax applied within the colonies. It fell directly on all colonists. Even more, the colonists had to pay for stamps in silver coin—a scarce item in the colonies.

Colonial leaders vigorously protested. For them, the issue was clear. They were being taxed without their consent by a Parliament in which they had no voice. If Britain could pass the Stamp Act, what other taxes might it pass in the future? Samuel Adams, a leader in the Massachusetts legislature, asked, "Why not our lands? Why not the produce of our lands and, in short, everything we possess and make use of?" **Patrick Henry**, a member of Virginia's House of Burgesses, called for resistance to the tax. When another member shouted that resistance was treason, Henry replied, "If this be treason, make the most of it!"

### The Colonies Protest the Stamp Act

Colonial assemblies and newspapers took up the cry—"No taxation without representation!" In October 1765, nine colonies sent delegates to the Stamp Act Congress in New York City. This was the first time the colonies met to consider acting together in protest. Delegates drew up a petition to the king protesting the Stamp Act. The petition declared that the right to tax the colonies belonged to the colonial assemblies, not to Parliament. Later, colonial merchants organized a **boycott** of British goods. A boycott is a refusal to buy.

*Reading* **History**
B. Making Inferences Why did the colonists boycott goods?

Meanwhile, some colonists formed secret societies to oppose British policies. The most famous of these groups was the **Sons of Liberty**. Many Sons of Liberty were lawyers, merchants, and craftspeople—the colonists most affected by the Stamp Act. These groups staged protests against the act.

Background
To voice their protests, the Sons of Liberty in Boston met under a huge, 120-year-old elm tree that they called the Liberty Tree.

Not all of their protests were peaceful. The Sons of Liberty burned the stamped paper whenever they could find it. They also attacked customs officials, whom they covered with hot tar and feathers and paraded in public. Fearing for their safety, many customs officials quit their jobs.

The protests in the colonies had an effect in Britain. Merchants thought that their trade with America would be hurt. Some British political leaders, including

Colonists protest the Stamp Act.

**161**

---

**Vocabulary**
**tyranny:**
absolute power in the hands of a single ruler

---

**Background**
To voice their protests, the Sons of Liberty in Boston met under a huge, 120-year-old elm tree that they called the Liberty Tree.

# Review and Summarize What You Have Read

When you finish reading a section, review and summarize what you've read. If necessary, go back and reread information that was not clear the first time through.

**5** Reread the red headlines for a quick summary of the major points covered in the section.

**6** Study any charts, graphs, and maps in the section. These visual materials usually provide a condensed version of information in the section.

**7** Review the pictures and note how they relate to the section content.

**8** Complete all the questions in the **Section Assessment**. This will help you think critically about what you have just read.

---

immediately offered Massachusetts their support. They sent food and money to Boston. The committees of correspondence also called for a meeting of colonial delegates to discuss what to do next.

**5** ### The First Continental Congress Meets

In September 1774, delegates from all the colonies except Georgia met in Philadelphia. At this meeting, called the **First Continental Congress,** delegates voted to ban all trade with Britain until the Intolerable Acts were repealed. They also called on each colony to begin training troops. Georgia agreed to be a part of the actions of the Congress even though it had voted not to send delegates.

The First Continental Congress marked a key step in American history. Although most delegates were not ready to call for independence, they were determined to uphold colonial rights. This meeting planted the seeds of a future independent government. John Adams called it "a nursery of American statesmen." The delegates agreed to meet in seven months, if necessary. By that time, however, fighting with Britain had begun.

*Reading* **History**
**A. Evaluating**
Why do you think the First Continental Congress was important?

### Between War and Peace

The colonists hoped that the trade boycott would force a repeal of the Intolerable Acts. After all, past boycotts had led to the repeal of the Stamp Act and the Townshend Acts. This time, however, Parliament stood firm. It even increased restrictions on colonial trade and sent more troops.

By the end of 1774, some colonists were preparing to fight. In Massachusetts, John Hancock headed the Committee of Safety, which had the power to call out the militia. The colonial troops continued to train.

**6**

| CAUSE AND EFFECT: Growing Conflict Between Britain and America | | |
|---|---|---|
| DATE | BRITISH ACTION | COLONIAL REACTION |
| 1763 | Proclamation of 1763 issued | Proclamation leads to anger |
| 1765 | Stamp Act passed | Boycott of British goods; Stamp Act Resolves passed |
| 1766 | Stamp Act repealed; Declaration Act passed | Boycott ended |
| 1767 | Townshend Acts passed | New boycotts; Boston Massacre (March 1770) |
| 1770 | Townshend Acts repealed (April) | Tension between colonies and Britain reduced |
| 1773 | Tea Act passed | Boston Tea Party |
| 1774 | Intolerable Acts passed | First Continental Congress bans trade; militias organized |
| 1775 | Troops ordered to Lexington and Concord, Massachusetts | Militia fights British troops; Second Continental Congress; Continental Army established |

**SKILLBUILDER Interpreting Charts**
1. What British action caused the first violence in the growing conflict between Britain and America?
2. How might the Intolerable Acts be seen as a reaction as well as an action?

**171**

---

When the British moved, so did Revere and Dawes. They galloped over the countryside on their "midnight ride," spreading the news. In Lexington, they were joined by Dr. Samuel Prescott. When Revere and Dawes were stopped by a British patrol, Prescott broke away and carried the message to Concord.

### Lexington and Concord

At dawn on April 19, some 700 British troops reached Lexington. They found Captain John Parker and about 70 militiamen waiting. The British commander ordered the Americans to drop their muskets. They refused. No one knows who fired first, but within a few minutes eight militiamen lay dead. The British then marched to Concord, where they destroyed military supplies. A battle broke out at a bridge north of town, forcing the British to retreat.

C. Possible Answer
The American revolt stunned the world.

Nearly 4,000 Minutemen and militiamen arrived in the area. They lined the road from Concord to Lexington and peppered the retreating redcoats with musket fire. "It seemed as if men came down from the clouds," one soldier said. Only the arrival of 1,000 more troops saved the British from destruction as they scrambled back to Boston.

**Background**
British losses totaled 273 soldiers compared to 95 militiamen.

**Lexington and Concord** were the first battles of the Revolutionary War. As Ralph Waldo Emerson later wrote, colonial troops had fired the "shot heard 'round the world." Americans would now have to choose sides and back up their political opinions by force of arms. Those who supported the British were called **Loyalists.** Those who sided with the rebels were **Patriots.** The conflict between the two sides divided communities, families, and friends. The war was on!

*Reading* **History**
**C. Drawing Conclusions**
Why did Emerson call it the "shot heard 'round the world"?

**Now** *and* **then**

**PATRIOTS' DAY**
The "shot heard 'round the world" is celebrated every year in Massachusetts and Maine. Patriots' Day, as it is called, is the third Monday of April. In Concord and nearby towns, modern-day Minutemen like those below reenact the battle that began the Revolution on April 19, 1775. The Boston Marathon is also run on Patriots' Day.

**7**

**8** ### Section **3** Assessment

**1. Terms & Names**
**Explain the significance of:**
• militia
• Minuteman
• Intolerable Acts
• First Continental Congress
• Paul Revere
• Lexington and Concord
• Loyalist
• Patriot

**2. Using Graphics**
Use a diagram like the one below to show events that led to the Revolutionary War. (CST2)

[ ] → [ ] → [ ]

[ ] → Revolution

**3. Main Ideas**
**a.** Why did Britain pass the Intolerable Acts? (HI2)
**b.** Who took part in the First Continental Congress? (HI1)
**c.** What was the purpose of the "midnight ride"? (HI2)

**4. Critical Thinking**
**Supporting Opinions**
Do you think the fighting between Britain and the colonies could have been avoided? Why or why not? (REP5)

**THINK ABOUT**
• Britain's attitude toward the colonies
• colonial feelings about Britain

**ACTIVITY OPTIONS**
**GEOGRAPHY**
**MATH**
Research the Battles of Lexington and Concord. Draw a **map** of key events or create a **chart** showing statistics from the battles. (CST3)

# Part 2: Test-Taking Strategies and Practice

Improve your test-taking skills by practicing the strategies discussed in this section. Read the tips on the left-hand page. Then apply them to the practice items on the right-hand page.

## Multiple Choice

A multiple-choice question consists of a stem and a set of choices. The stem is usually in the form of a question or an incomplete sentence. One of the choices correctly answers the question or completes the sentence.

**1** Read the stem carefully and try to answer the question or complete the sentence without looking at the choices.

**2** Pay close attention to key words in the stem. They may direct you toward the correct answer.

**3** Read each choice with the stem. Don't jump to conclusions about the correct answer until you've read all of the choices.

**4** Think carefully about questions that include *All of the above* among the choices.

**5** After reading all of the choices, eliminate any that you know are incorrect.

**6** Use modifiers to help narrow your choice.

**7** Look for the best answer among the remaining choices.

stem

**1** 1. At the beginning of the Revolution, (most) **2** Americans were

*Most* is a key word here. Replacing it with *all* or *some* changes the sentence and calls for a different answer.

**3** choices

   A. united in support of the war.

   B. Patriots who wanted independence from Great Britain.

   C. against a war with Great Britain.

   D. Loyalists who supported the British point of view.

2. Which of the following weapons were first used effectively during World War I?

   A. Airplanes

   B. Machine guns

   C. Tanks

   D. All of the above **4**

If you select this answer, be sure that all of the choices are correct.

3. In the 1840s, many immigrants came to the United States to escape famine and revolutions in their homelands. A majority of these immigrants came from

   A. China and Japan. •———————— **5**

   B. Ireland and Germany. •————

   C. Eastern and southern Europe. •——

   D. (all) the countries of Latin America.

You can eliminate **A** if you remember that although many Chinese came during the California Gold Rush, which began in 1849, Japanese immigration began much later.

**6**

Absolute words, such as *all, never, always, every,* and *only,* often signal an incorrect choice.

**7**

**B** or **C** could be correct; however, most eastern and southern European immigrants came to the U.S. after 1900. In the mid-1800's, the Irish came because of famine and Germans came to escape revolutions; therefore, **B** is the best answer.

answers: 1 (C), 2 (D), 3 (B)

**Directions:** Read the following questions and choose the *best* answer from the four choices.

1. New inventions that helped open the Great Plains to farming included

   **A.** the steel windmill.

   **B.** barbed wire.

   **C.** the spring-tooth harrow.

   **D.** All of the above

2. Which of the following statements about the Constitution of the United States is *not* true?

   **A.** The Constitution provides for the election of a chief executive to serve for a term of four years.

   **B.** The Constitution establishes a bicameral legislature composed of the House of Representatives and the Senate.

   **C.** The Constitution gives the Senate the power to determine the constitutionality of laws passed by the Congress and state legislatures.

   **D.** The Constitution provides for change through an amendment process.

3. During the presidency of Thomas Jefferson, the United States was able to foster westward expansion when it acquired territory in what is known as

   **A.** Seward's Folly.

   **B.** the Missouri Compromise.

   **C.** the Kansas-Nebraska Act.

   **D.** the Louisiana Purchase.

4. Which of the following are correctly associated with the period of Reconstruction after the Civil War?

   **A.** California entered the Union as a free state.

   **B.** The Thirteenth, Fourteenth, and Fifteenth Amendments became part of the United States Constitution.

   **C.** The United States government took control of all the large plantations in the South and gave the land to former slaves.

   **D.** All of the above

# Primary Sources

Primary sources are materials written or made by people who took part in or witnessed historical events. Letters, diaries, speeches, newspaper articles, and autobiographies are all primary sources. So, too, are legal documents, such as wills, deeds, and financial records.

**1** Look at the source line and identify the author. Consider what qualifies the author to write about the events discussed in the passage.

**2** Skim the document to form an idea of what it is about.

**3** Note special punctuation. Ellipses indicate that words or sentences have been removed from the original passage. Brackets indicate words that were not in the original. Bracketed words often are replacements for difficult or unfamiliar terms.

**4** Carefully read the passage and distinguish between facts and the author's opinions. (That the groups of soldiers were wandering in all directions is a fact. The reasons for their wandering offered by Madison are her opinions.)

**5** Consider for whom the author was writing. The intended audience may influence what and how an author writes.

**6** Before rereading the passage, skim the questions to identify the information you need to find.

## The Flight from the White House

*Wednesday Morning, twelve o'clock.* Since sunrise I have been turning my spy-glass in every direction, . . but alas! I can see only groups of military, wandering in all directions, as if there was a lack of arms, or of spirit to fight for their own fireside. **3** **4**

**2** *Three o'clock.* Will you believe it, my sister? we have had a battle, or skirmish, near Bladensburg, and here I am still, within sound of the cannon!. . . Two messengers covered with dust come to bid me fly. . . . At this late hour a wagon has been [found], and I have had it filled with plate and the most valuable portable articles belonging to the house. Whether it will reach its destination . . . or fall into the hands of British soldiery, events must determine. Our kind friend, Mr. Carroll, has come to hasten my departure, and is in a very bad humor with me, because I insist on waiting until the large picture of General Washington is secured. . . . It is done! and the precious portrait placed in the hands of two gentlemen of New York, for safe keeping. And now, dear sister, I must leave this house. . . . When I shall again write to you, or where I shall be tomorrow, I cannot tell!

The author is Dolley Madison, the wife of President James Madison. She personally oversaw the evacuation of the White House in 1814. **1**

—Dolley Madison, in a letter to her sister describing her flight from the White House in August 1814

**5** This is a letter. If it were an official report to Congress, the style and content would be much different.

**6 1.** Dolley Madison's letter describes her preparations to flee the White House in advance of a British attack. In which war did this attack take place?

**A.** War of Jenkins' Ear

**B.** French and Indian War

**C.** Revolutionary War

**D.** War of 1812

**2.** Why might Dolley Madison be considered a good source of information on the British attack on Washington, D.C.?

**A.** She was the wife of President James Madison.

**B.** She was an eyewitness to the attack.

**C.** She helped her husband develop military policy.

**D.** She had intercepted British war plans.

**Directions:** Read the following excerpt from a letter on conservation. Use the passage to answer the questions.

> In the east, the States are now painfully, and at great expense, endeavoring to undo the effects of their former shortsighted policy in throwing away their forest lands. Congress has before it bills to establish by purchase great forest reserves in the White Mountains and the Southern Appalachians, and the only argument against the bills is that of their great expense. New York and Pennsylvania are now, late in the day, endeavoring themselves to protect the forests which guard the headwaters of their streams. Michigan and Wisconsin have already had their good timber stript from their forests by the great lumber companies. But the western States, far more fortunate than their eastern sisters in this regard, can now reserve their forests for the good of all their citizens, without expense, if they choose to show the requisite foresight.
>
> —President Theodore Roosevelt, in a private letter in 1907

1. According to President Roosevelt, forests not yet damaged by timber companies could be set aside at no expense in the

   A. Midwest.

   B. East.

   C. South.

   D. West.

2. You can tell from this letter that President Roosevelt

   A. favored changing forests to farmland.

   B. was a good president.

   C. supported environmental protection.

   D. was an owner of a large lumber company.

3. Which one of the following statements from the letter is most strictly a fact?

   A. "Congress has before it bills to establish by purchase great forest reserves in the White Mountains. . . ."

   B. "New York and Pennsylvania are now, late in the day, endeavoring themselves to protect the forests. . . . "

   C. ". . . States are now painfully, and at great expense, endeavoring to undo the effects of . . . throwing away their forest lands."

   D. "But the western States, far more fortunate than their eastern sisters . . . can now reserve their forests. . . ."

# Secondary Sources

Secondary sources are descriptions or interpretations of historical events made by people who were not at those events. The most common types of written secondary sources are history books, encyclopedias, and biographies. A secondary source often combines information from several primary sources.

**1** Read titles to preview what the passage is about.

**2** Look for topic sentences. These, too, will help you preview the content of the passage.

**3** As you read, use context clues to help you understand difficult or unfamiliar words. (You can tell from the description of the battle in the previous sentences that the word *fiasco* must mean something like "disaster," "failure," or "blunder.")

**4** As you read, ask and answer questions that come to mind. You might ask: Why would the Washington raid embarrass and anger Americans? Why did the Washington raid achieve little?

**5** Before rereading the passage, skim the questions to identify the information you need to find.

**1** **The British Offensive**

**2** Ironically, Britain's most spectacular success began as a diversion from [its main] offensive [in the North]. A British army that had come up from Bermuda entered Chesapeake Bay and on August 24, 1814, met a larger American force . . . at Bladensburg, Maryland. The Battle of Bladensburg deteriorated into the "Bladensburg Races" as the American troops fled, virtually without firing a shot. The British then descended on Washington, D.C. Madison, who had witnessed **3** the Bladensburg fiasco, fled into the Virginia hills. His wife, Dolley, loaded her silver, a bed, and a portrait of George Washington onto her carriage before joining him. British troops ate the supper prepared for the Madisons and then burned the presidential mansion **4** and other public buildings in the capital. Beyond embarrassing and angering Americans, the Washington raid accomplished little, for after a failed attack on Baltimore, the British broke off the operation.

—Paul S. Boyer, et al., *The Enduring Vision*

**5** **1.** Why do you think the authors refer to the Battle of Bladensburg as a "fiasco"?

   **A.** Because the American forces fled almost without a fight

   **B.** Because President Madison had to flee the White House

   **C.** Because it allowed the British to attack Washington, D.C.

   **D.** Because it was a famous victory for the British forces

**2.** What, according to the authors, did the British raid on Washington, D.C., accomplish?

   **A.** It paved the way for the British capture of Baltimore.

   **B.** It burned down all the public buildings in the city.

   **C.** It helped the British offensive in the North.

   **D.** It embarrassed and angered many Americans.

> Remember to be wary of choices that contain absolutes, such as *all, every,* or *only.*

answers: 1 (A), 2 (D)

**Directions:** Use the passage and your knowledge of U.S. history to answer the questions below.

### African-American Sailors

African Americans contributed greatly to the growth of maritime commerce in the United States. Beginning in colonial times, slaves, with their masters' permission, hired themselves out as sailors. Some served as translators on slave ships. Merchant ships also offered a means of escape for runaway slaves. A few escapees even took to the sea as pirates.

Seafaring was one of the few occupations open to free African Americans. They served on clippers, naval vessels, and whaling ships from the 1700s into the late 1800s. Federal crew lists from Atlantic seaports show that during this time African Americans made up 10 percent or more of sailors on American ships. Seafaring was an especially dangerous line of work for free blacks. They risked capture in southern ports, where they were often thrown in jail or sold into slavery.

1. What records show that African Americans made up 10 percent or more of sailors on American ships?

   A. Shipyard records

   B. Family Bibles

   C. Federal crew lists

   D. Ships' logs

2. The passage implies that free and enslaved African Americans went to sea for all of the following reasons *except* to

   A. escape slavery.

   B. live as pirates.

   C. earn wages as sailors.

   D. discover new lands.

3. The author states that life was especially dangerous for free African-American sailors because

   A. American prosperity depended on their work alone.

   B. the worst jobs on board ship were always assigned to them.

   C. they ran the risk of capture and enslavement in southern ports.

   D. they were more likely than white sailors to contract scurvy.

# Political Cartoons

Political cartoons are drawings that express views on political issues of the day. Cartoonists use symbols and such artistic styles as caricature—exaggerating a person's physical features—to get their message across.

**❶** Identify the subject of the cartoon. Titles and captions often indicate the subject matter.

**❷** Identify the main characters in the cartoon. Here, the main character is Horace Greeley, a candidate in the 1872 presidential election.

**❸** Note the symbols—ideas or images that stand for something else—used in the cartoon.

**❹** Study labels and other written information in the cartoon.

**❺** Analyze the point of view. How cartoonists use caricature often indicates how they feel. The exaggeration of Greeley's physical appearance—short and overweight—makes him appear comical.

**❻** Interpret the cartoonist's message.

The cartoonist shows Tammany Hall, New York's Democratic political machine, as a tiger. Uncle Sam, a symbol for the United States, is shown looking on.

The writing on the wall suggests that Tammany Hall wants reform. The "Whitewash" label on the bucket suggests that the tiger's true, corrupt, stripes are just being covered up.

Thomas Nast, *Harper's Weekly*, August 31, 1872

**❶** "What are you going to do about it, if 'Old Honesty' lets him loose again?"

1. Based on the cartoon, what do you think was Horace Greeley's major issue in the 1872 presidential campaign?

   **A.** Political reform

   **B.** States' rights

   **C.** Abolition

   **D.** Temperance

2. Which one of the following statements do you think *best* represents the cartoonist's point of view?

   **A.** Horace Greeley is an honest man.

   **B.** Tammany Hall supports political reform.

   **C.** Tammany Hall, regardless of Greeley's view, is still corrupt.

   **D.** Horace Greeley, like most Tammany politicians, is corrupt.

answers: 1 (A), 2 (C)

**Directions:** Use the cartoon and your knowledge of U.S. history to answer the questions below.

Rollin Kirby, *New York World*, 1917

"That's my fight, too!"

1. The cartoon character is a symbol of

   **A.** Americans opposed to war.

   **B.** the president of the United States.

   **C.** old soldiers retired from the United States Army.

   **D.** the United States as a whole.

2. The "fight" in the cartoon caption refers to

   **A.** the War of 1812.

   **B.** World War II in Europe.

   **C.** World War II in the Pacific.

   **D.** World War I in Europe.

3. The cartoonist's point of view is *best* described by which of the following statements?

   **A.** The United States believes it has an obligation to join in this foreign war.

   **B.** Uncle Sam is too old and too late for every battle.

   **C.** The United States should stay out of other countries' wars.

   **D.** A country should equip its soldiers with the best weapons and other supplies.

# Charts

Charts present information in a visual form. History textbooks use several types of charts, including tables, flow charts, Venn diagrams, and infographics. The type of chart most commonly found in tests is the table. It organizes information in columns and rows for easy viewing.

**❶** Read the title and identify the broad subject of the chart.

**❷** Read the column and row headings and any other labels. This will provide more details about the subject of the chart.

**❸** Compare and contrast the information from column to column and row to row.

**❹** Try to draw conclusions from the information in the chart. Ask yourself: What trends does the chart show?

**❺** Read the questions and then study the chart again.

Review difficult or unfamiliar words. Here, the term *nativity* means "place of birth."

**❶ United States Population by Region and Nativity, 1890–1920**

**❷**

| | 1890 | 1900 | 1910 | 1920 |
|---|---|---|---|---|
| **Northeast** | | | | |
| Total Population | 17,407,000 | 21,047,000 | 25,869,000 | 29,662,000 |
| % Native Born | 78 | 77 | 74 | 77 |
| % Foreign Born | 22 | 23 | 26 | 23 |
| **North Central** | | | | |
| Total Population | 22,410,000 | 26,333,000 | 29,889,000 | 34,020,000 |
| % Native Born | 82 | 84 | 84 | 86 |
| % Foreign Born | 18 | 16 | 16 | 14 |
| **South** | | | | |
| Total Population | 20,028,000 | 24,524,000 | 29,389,000 | 33,126,000 |
| % Native Born | 97 | 98 | 97 | 97 |
| % Foreign Born | 3 | 2 | 3 | 3 |
| **West** | | | | |
| Total Population | 3,134,000 | 4,309,000 | 7,082,000 | 9,214,000 |
| % Native Born | 76 | 79 | 79 | 82 |
| % Foreign Born | 24 | 21 | 21 | 18 |

**❹**

Compare changes in population over time and contrast statistics among regions.

**❸**

**Source:** *Historical Statistics of the United States*

**❺ 1.** The two regions with the highest percentage of foreign-born inhabitants are the

**A.** Northeast and the West.

**B.** West and the South.

**C.** South and the North Central.

**D.** North Central and the Northeast.

**2.** When did immigration to the Northeast peak?

**A.** Between 1910 and 1920

**B.** Before 1900

**C.** Between 1900 and 1910

**D.** After 1920

answers: 1 (A), 2 (C)

**Directions:** Use the charts and your knowledge of U.S. history to answer the questions below.

### Percentage of Population Free and Enslaved, by States and Territories, 1790

| North | | |
|---|---|---|
| State/Territory | Free | Enslaved |
| Connecticut | 98.9 | 1.1 |
| Delaware | 85.0 | 15.0 |
| Maine | 100.0 | 0.0 |
| Massachusetts | 100.0 | 0.0 |
| New Hampshire | 99.9 | 0.1 |
| New Jersey | 93.8 | 6.2 |
| New York | 93.8 | 6.2 |
| Pennsylvania | 99.1 | 0.9 |
| Rhode Island | 98.6 | 1.4 |
| Vermont | 100.0 | 0.0 |

| South | | |
|---|---|---|
| State/Territory | Free | Enslaved |
| Georgia | 64.5 | 35.5 |
| Kentucky | 83.1 | 16.9 |
| Maryland | 67.8 | 32.2 |
| North Carolina | 74.5 | 25.5 |
| South Carolina | 57.0 | 43.0 |
| Virginia | 60.9 | 39.1 |

**Source:** Inter-University Consortium for Political and Social Research

1. The state with the highest percentage of enslaved people was

   A. New Hampshire.

   B. North Carolina.

   C. Rhode Island.

   D. South Carolina.

2. Which of the following *best* describes most states in the North?

   A. The population was more than 98 percent free.

   B. More than 10 percent of the population was enslaved.

   C. Less than 60 percent of the population was free.

   D. The population was more than 20 percent enslaved.

3. Which statement about the percentage of enslaved people is true?

   A. It was much lower in the South.

   B. It was much higher in the South.

   C. There was no difference between the regions.

   D. There was a slight difference between the regions.

4. What economic factor *best* explains the population differences between the regions?

   A. The North focused on manufacturing.

   B. The North was wealthy enough to free enslaved people.

   C. The South focused on plantation agriculture.

   D. The South needed enslaved people for factory work.

# Line and Bar Graphs

Graphs show statistics in a visual form. Line graphs are particularly useful for showing changes over time. Bar graphs make it easy to compare numbers or sets of numbers.

**1** Read the title and identify the broad subject of the graph.

**2** Study the labels on the vertical and horizontal axes to see the kinds of information presented in the graph. Note the intervals between amounts and between dates. This will help you read the graph more efficiently.

**3** Look at the source line and evaluate the reliability of the information in the graph. Government statistics on education tend to be reliable.

**4** Study the information in the graph and note any trends.

**5** Draw conclusions and make generalizations based on these trends.

**6** Read the questions carefully and then study the graph again.

**1 High School Graduates, 1880–1920**

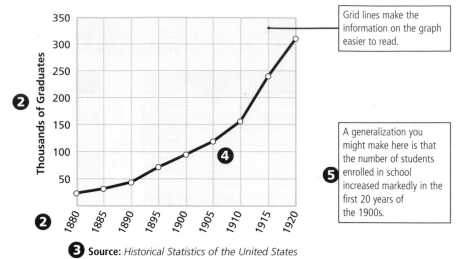

Grid lines make the information on the graph easier to read.

A generalization you might make here is that the number of students enrolled in school increased markedly in the first 20 years of the 1900s.

**3 Source:** *Historical Statistics of the United States*

**6 1.** How many students graduated from high school in 1905?

A. Exactly 100,000

B. About 125,000

C. About 150,000

D. Exactly 175,000

**1 Public Secondary School Enrollment, 1880–1920**

**3 Source:** *Historical Statistics of the United States*

**6 2.** Which one of the following sentences do you think *best* describes the trend shown in the bar graph?

A. The number of students enrolled steadily increased.

B. The number of students enrolled showed little change.

C. The number of students enrolled rose and fell.

D. The number of students enrolled steadily decreased.

answers: 1 (B), 2 (A)

**Directions**: Use the graphs and your knowledge of U.S. history to answer the questions below.

## Immigration from Southern and Eastern Europe, 1880–1920

**Source:** Historical Statistics of the United States

## Churches by Denomination, 1750

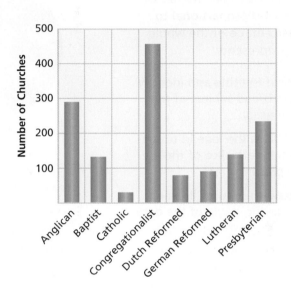

**Source**: Gilder Lehrman Institute of American History

1. During which five-year period did immigration from southern Europe and Eastern Europe reach its peak?

   A. 1890–1895

   B. 1895–1900

   C. 1905–1910

   D. 1910–1915

2. What caused the drastic decrease in immigration from these regions between 1914 and 1915?

   A. Anti-immigrant demonstrations by the "Know-Nothings"

   B. The Irish potato famine

   C. Immigration laws that prohibited immigration from Europe

   D. The outbreak of World War I in Europe

3. Which one of the following statements accurately reflects information in the graph?

   A. There were more Congregationalist churches than all other denominations combined.

   B. There were more Presbyterian churches than Anglican churches.

   C. The Baptists had the fewest churches.

   D. The Congregationalists had the most churches.

4. Which statement about religion in the colonies of the mid-18th century does the graph support?

   A. All of the colonists were Anglican.

   B. By 1750, there were many religions.

   C. The colonists of 1750 were not religious.

   D. Only immigrants from England established churches.

# Pie Graphs

A pie, or circle, graph shows relationships among the parts of a whole. These parts look like slices of a pie. The size of each slice is proportional to the percentage of the whole that it represents.

**1** Read the title and identify the broad subject of the pie graph.

**2** Look at the legend to see what each slice of the pie represents.

**3** Read the source line and note the origin of the data shown in the pie graph.

**4** Compare the slices of the pie and try to make generalizations and draw conclusions from your comparisons.

**5** Read the questions carefully and review difficult or unfamiliar terms.

**6** Eliminate choices that you know are wrong.

**1** The Electoral Vote in the 1824 Presidential Election

- John Quincy Adams
- Andrew Jackson
- William Crawford
- Henry Clay

**2** Sometimes the information in the legend is shown as labels around the outside of the pie graph.

**3** **Source:** Jordan, Litwack, et. al. *The United States*

Remember that pie graphs show proportions, or percentages, of the whole, not absolute quantities.

1. In the 1824 presidential election, which candidate held a (majority) of the Electoral College vote?

   **A.** Andrew Jackson

   **B.** Henry Clay

   **C.** William Crawford

   **D.** None of the candidates

   **6** You can eliminate **B** because Henry Clay received the lowest percentage of electoral votes.

   **5** In electoral terms, the word *majority* means "more than 50 percent," and *plurality* means "the most but less than 50 percent."

2. In the 1824 election, which candidate won a (plurality) of the electoral vote?

   **A.** Andrew Jackson

   **B.** John Quincy Adams

   **C.** Henry Clay

   **D.** William Crawford

answers: 1 (D), 2 (A)

Pie graph information from *The United States,* 6th ed., Jordan, Litwack, et. al., Englewood Cliffs, New Jersey: Prentice Hall, 1987.

**Directions:** Use the pie graphs and your knowledge of U.S. history to answer the questions below.

### Distribution of Workers in the United States, 1850 and 1900

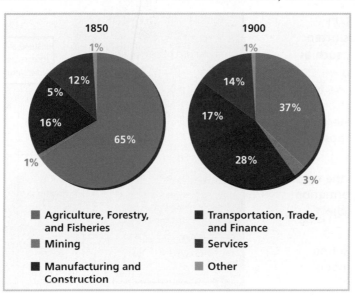

**Source:** *Historical Statistics of the United States*

1. In 1850, most people worked in

   A. agriculture, forestry, and fisheries.

   B. mining.

   C. services.

   D. transportation, trade, and finance.

2. In 1900, more people worked in manufacturing and construction than in

   A. agriculture, forestry, and fisheries.

   B. mining and agriculture, forestry, and fisheries combined.

   C. services and transportation, trade, and finance combined.

   D. transportation, trade, and finance.

3. Which occupation category showed an increase between 1850 and 1900?

   A. Manufacturing and construction

   B. Services

   C. Transportation, trade, and finance

   D. All of the above

4. What helped to bring about the changes reflected in the two pie graphs?

   A. The passage of new immigration laws

   B. The growth of industry

   C. The decline of world agricultural markets

   D. All of the above

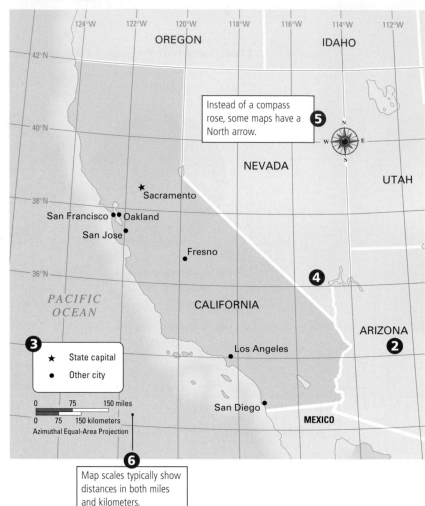

# Political Maps

Political maps show countries and the political divisions within countries—states, for example. They also show the location of major cities. In addition, political maps often show physical features, such as rivers, seas, oceans, and mountain ranges.

**1** Read the title to determine the subject and purpose of the map.

**2** Read the labels on the map. This will reveal information about the map's subject and purpose.

**3** Study the legend to find the meaning of symbols used on the map.

**4** Look at the lines of latitude and longitude. This grid makes locating places much easier.

**5** Use the compass rose to determine directions on the map.

**6** Use the scale to estimate the distances between places shown on the map.

**7** Read the questions and then carefully study the map to determine the answers.

**1** Political: California

Instead of a compass rose, some maps have a North arrow. **5**

**3**
★ State capital
● Other city

0    75    150 miles
0    75    150 kilometers
Azimuthal Equal-Area Projection

**6**
Map scales typically show distances in both miles and kilometers.

**7** **1.** Which of the following cities is located closest to 38° N 123° W?

**A.** Sacramento

**B.** San Francisco

**C.** Los Angeles

**D.** San Diego

**2.** If you took an airplane from San Diego to San Francisco, in which direction would you be traveling?

**A.** Northwest

**B.** Northeast

**C.** Southwest

**D.** Southeast

answers: 1 (B), 2 (A)

S20

**Directions:** Use the map and your knowledge of U.S. history to answer the questions below.

### New States, 1816–1848

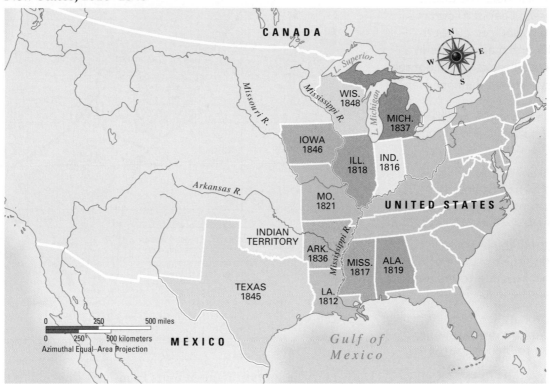

1.  Which state joined the Union in 1845?

    A. Iowa

    B. Illinois

    C. Wisconsin

    D. Texas

2.  The Mississippi River forms the western border of which of the following states?

    A. Missouri, Arkansas, and Louisiana

    B. Illinois and Mississippi

    C. Iowa and Missouri

    D. Iowa, Missouri, and Arkansas

3.  A barge filled with logs from Wisconsin is going to the Gulf of Mexico. It is most likely traveling

    A. south on the Mississippi River.

    B. west across the Great Plains.

    C. north on the Arkansas River.

    D. southwest through Indian Territory.

4.  The states admitted to the Union in the 1840s were

    A. Missouri, Wisconsin, and Illinois.

    B. Kansas, Texas, and Iowa.

    C. Texas, Wisconsin, and Iowa.

    D. Illinois, Texas, and Wisconsin.

# Thematic Maps

A thematic map, or special-purpose map, focuses on a particular topic. The location of baseball parks, a country's natural resources, election results, and major battles in a war are all topics you might see illustrated on a thematic map.

**1** Read the title to determine the subject and purpose of the map.

**2** Examine the labels on the map to find more information about the map's subject and purpose.

**3** Study the legend to find the meaning of the symbols and colors used on the map.

**4** Look at the colors and symbols on the map and try to identify patterns.

**5** Read the questions and then carefully study the map to determine the answers.

**1** **The Rush for California's Gold**

**1.** The shortest route in miles from New England to the gold fields of California was

A. the overland route across the Great Plains.

B. an ocean route around the South American continent.

C. a combination land and sea route by way of the Isthmus of Tehuantepec.

D. a combination land and sea route by way of the Isthmus of Panama.

**2.** Which of the following statements regarding the migration to California can be determined from the map?

A. Migrants who traveled through the Isthmus of Panama had the safest trip west.

B. Most migrants came to California on the transcontinental railroad.

C. Most migrants came from the southern states.

D. Migrants came from throughout the United States.

answers: 1 (A), 2 (D)

**Directions:** Use the map and your knowledge of U.S. history to answer the questions below.

### Presidential Election of 1860: Electoral Votes

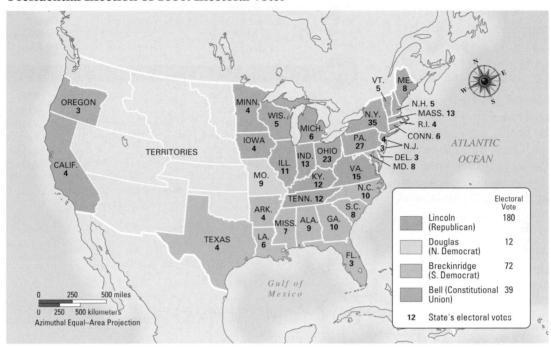

1. Abraham Lincoln received his greatest support in which region or regions of the country?

   A. the North and West

   B. the South and Southwest

   C. the Border States

   D. the territories

2. John Breckinridge received his greatest support in which region or regions of the country?

   A. the North and West

   B. the South

   C. the Border States

   D. the territories

3. Who won the presidential election of 1860?

   A. Constitutional Union Party candidate John Bell of Tennessee

   B. Southern Democratic Party candidate John Breckinridge of Kentucky

   C. Northern Democratic Party candidate Stephen A. Douglas of Illinois

   D. Republican Party candidate Abraham Lincoln of Illinois

4. Which state split its electoral vote in 1860?

   A. California

   B. New Jersey

   C. Missouri

   D. Pennsylvania

# Time Lines

A time line is a type of chart that lists events in the order in which they occurred. In other words, time lines are a visual method of showing what happened when.

**1** Read the title to discover the subject of the time line.

**2** Identify the time period covered by the time line by noting the earliest and latest dates shown. On vertical time lines, the earliest date is shown at the top. On horizontal time lines, it is on the far left.

**3** Read the events and their dates in sequence. Notice the intervals between events.

**4** Use your knowledge of history to develop a fuller picture of the events listed in the time line. For example, you might try to identify some of the leading individuals involved in the events.

**5** Note how events are related to one another. Look particularly for cause-effect relationships.

**6** Use the information you have gathered from the above strategies to answer the questions.

**1** Establishment of the American Government, 1775–1791

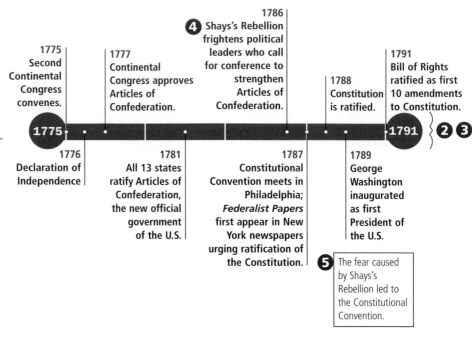

**6** **1.** The Articles of Confederation were the basis for the American government from

  **A.** 1776 to 1791.

  **B.** 1777 to 1781.

  **C.** 1777 to 1788.

  **D.** 1788 to 1791.

**2.** *The Federalist Papers* were originally written to

  **A.** urge public support for the Declaration of Independence.

  **B.** secure the adoption of the Articles of Confederation as the frame of government of the United States.

  **C.** convince the American people that the Constitution would give too much power to the national government.

  **D.** urge the ratification of the Constitution.

answers: 1 (C), 2 (D)

**Directions:** Use the time line and your knowledge of U.S. history to answer the questions below.

## Texas War for Independence and the Mexican-American War, 1835–1848

**1835**
Armed clashes between Mexicans and Texans

**1837**
Texas petitions for admission to U.S.; President Van Buren opposes annexation, fearing conflict over slavery and war with Mexico.

**1847**
Battle of Buena Vista in northern Mexico; U.S. troops land at Vera Cruz and march to Mexico City; Battle of Chapultepec.

**1845**
Texas annexed by U.S.

**1835** — **1848**

**1836**
Texas declares independence from Mexico; siege and fall of the Alamo; Texans massacred at Goliad; Santa Anna defeated at battle of San Jacinto.

**1846**
Mexican-American War begins; Bear Flag Revolt in California; Gen. Stephen Kearney invades California.

**1848**
Treaty of Guadalupe-Hidalgo ends Mexican War.

1. Texas won its independence following the defeat of Mexican forces at which one of the following battles?

   A. Alamo

   B. Goliad

   C. San Jacinto

   D. Buena Vista

2. What event led to the outbreak of the war between Mexico and the United States?

   A. Declaration of independence by Texas from Mexico

   B. The fall of the Alamo

   C. The Bear Flag Revolt in California

   D. Annexation of Texas by the United States

3. Texas first sought annexation by the U.S. in

   A. 1835.

   B. 1836.

   C. 1837.

   D. 1846.

4. By the Treaty of Guadalupe-Hidalgo, Mexico turned over to the United States lands that later became states. The Mexican Cession includes the current states of

   A. Texas and New Mexico.

   B. California, Nevada, Utah, and most of Arizona.

   C. Louisiana, Arkansas, and Oklahoma.

   D. California, Oregon, and Washington.

# Constructed Response

Constructed-response questions focus on various kinds of documents. Each document usually is accompanied by a series of questions. These questions call for short answers that, for the most part, can be found directly in the document. Some answers, however, require knowledge of the subject or time period addressed in the document.

**1** Read the title of the document to discover the subject addressed in the questions.

**2** Study and analyze the document. Take notes on what you see.

**3** Read the questions and then study the document again to locate the answers.

**4** Carefully write your answers. Unless the directions say otherwise, your answers need not be complete sentences.

**1** Joseph Glidden's Patent

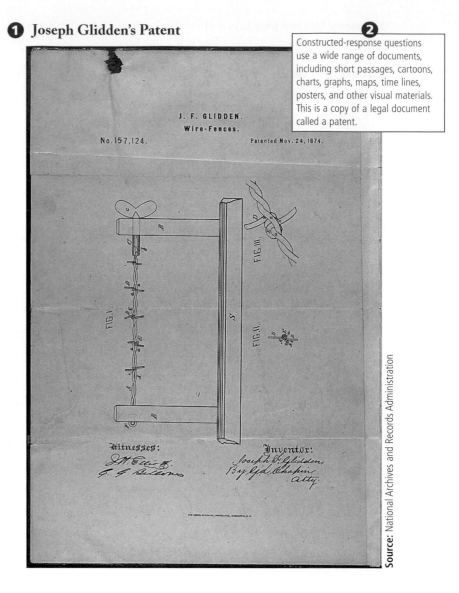

J. F. GLIDDEN.
Wire-Fences.
No. 157,124.
Patented Nov. 24, 1874.

Witnesses:

Inventor:
Joseph F. Glidden
By Gid. Chapin
Atty.

**2** Constructed-response questions use a wide range of documents, including short passages, cartoons, charts, graphs, maps, time lines, posters, and other visual materials. This is a copy of a legal document called a patent.

**Source:** National Archives and Records Administration

**3** **1.** What invention is illustrated on this patent?

**4** *barbed wire fence*

**2.** What suggests that this is a legal document?

*It is signed by witnesses and an attorney.*

**3.** What other developments had a major impact on farming on the plains in the 1800s?

*steel plows, reapers, threshers, dry farming*

**Directions:** Use the painting below and your knowledge of U.S. history to answer the questions. Your answers need not be in complete sentences.

### The Trail of Tears

*The Trail of Tears* painted by Robert Lindneux in 1942 is the portrayal of the 1838 removal of the Cherokee from their ancestral homelands to lands west of the Mississippi River.

1.  What in the painting suggests that the Cherokee were forcibly removed?

2.  How can you tell from the painting that the removal of the Cherokee was intended to be permanent?

3.  What action did the Cherokee take to prevent removal from their homes and how successful was it?

# Extended Response

Extended-response questions, like constructed-response questions, usually focus on one kind of document. However, they are more complex and require more time to complete than typical short-answer constructed-response questions. Some will ask you to complete a chart, graph, or diagram. Still others will ask you to write an essay, a report, or some other lengthier piece based on the document.

**❶** Read the title of the document to get an idea of the subject.

**❷** Study and analyze the document. Take notes on your ideas.

**❸** Carefully read the extended-response question or questions. (The question here asks you to write an essay by applying your knowledge of history to information in the map. A question could ask you to plot the map information as a bar graph or to present it in a time line.)

**❹** If the question requires an essay, jot down ideas in outline form. Use this outline to write your answer.

**❺** If the question calls for some type of diagram, make a rough sketch on scrap paper first. Then, make a final copy on the answer sheet.

**❶** Territorial Expansion of the United States, 1819–1853

**❷**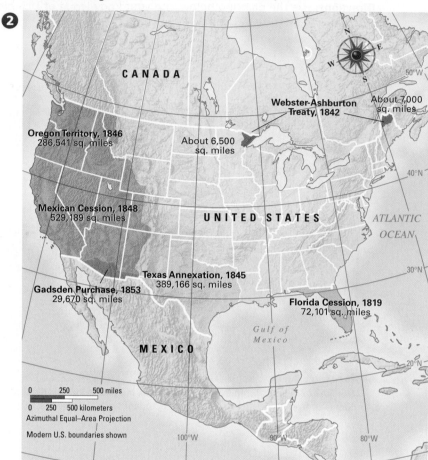

**❸** 1.   In a brief essay, explain how the United States acquired the three largest tracts of land and how these land acquisitions fulfilled the popular belief in manifest destiny.

**❹** **Essay Rubric**  The best essays will indicate how Texas came into the Union in 1845 as an independent republic and how the U.S. by a treaty with Britain, acquired the disputed Oregon territory and established the Northwest boundary of the U.S. at the 49th parallel. Essays will also explain that many Americans believed that the land acquisitions fulfilled the destiny of the U.S. to expand from ocean to ocean.

**Directions:** Read the following passage and study the chart. Then follow the directions beneath the chart to write a short essay.

### A Country Dividing

As the United States grew during the 1800s, Congress and the people argued about what form of government each new territory and state would have. The differences of opinion centered on one issue more than any other: slavery. Eventually, those sectional arguments led to the Civil War.

The chart below lists three acts of Congress that addressed the issue of slavery in the West. On the right are the provisions of each of these acts.

| Act | Provisions |
|---|---|
| **Missouri Compromise, 1820** | **1.** Slavery was to be prohibited in the Louisiana territory north of the 36° 30' parallel.<br>**2.** Missouri would enter the Union as a slave state.<br>**3.** Maine would enter the Union as a free state. |
| **Compromise of 1850** | **1.** The territories of New Mexico and Utah were created without restrictions on slavery.<br>**2.** California would enter the Union as a free state.<br>**3.** The slave trade would be prohibited in Washington, DC.<br>**4.** Congress would pass a strong fugitive slave law for mandatory return of escaped slaves. |
| **Kansas-Nebraska Act, 1854** | **1.** Two new territories, Kansas and Nebraska, were created.<br>**2.** The people residing in the Kansas and Nebraska territories would have the right to decide whether their territory would enter the Union as a free or slave state (Popular Sovereignty)<br>**3.** The Kansas-Nebraska Act repealed the Missouri Compromise of 1820 which prohibited slavery in territories north of 36° 30'. |

1. Write a brief essay explaining how the Missouri Compromise, the Compromise of 1850, and the Kansas-Nebraska Act promoted sectionalism.

# Document-Based Questions

A document-based question focuses on several documents—both visual and written. These documents often are accompanied by short-answer questions. You then use the answers to these questions and information from the documents to write an essay on a specified subject.

**1** Carefully read the "Historical Context" to get an indication of the issue addressed in the question.

**2** Note the action words used in the "Task" section. These words tell you exactly what the essay question requires.

**3** Study and analyze each document. Think about how the documents are connected to the essay question. Take notes on your ideas.

**4** Read and answer each of the document-specific questions.

## Introduction

**1** **Historical Context:** During President George Washington's first term, political parties started to develop around the beliefs of two members of Washington's cabinet, Secretary of the Treasury Alexander Hamilton and Secretary of State Thomas Jefferson. Despite Washington's opposition to political parties, they had a great influence in American domestic and foreign policy.

**2** **Task:** (Discuss) the role of the Federalist and the Democratic-Republican parties in the early Republic, and (explain) why George Washington believed that political parties were divisive.

## Part 1: Short Answer

Study each document carefully and answer the questions that follow.

### Document 1: A Warning on Political Parties

**3**

> Let me . . . warn you in the most solemn manner against the baneful [harmful] effects of the spirit of party generally. This spirit, unfortunately, is inseparable from our nature, having its root in the strongest passions of the human mind. . . .
>
> It serves always to distract the public councils and enfeeble [weaken] the public administration. It agitates the community with illfounded jealousies and false alarms; kindles the animosity [hatred] of one part against another; foments occasionally riot and insurrection. It opens the door to foreign influence and corruption, which find a facilitated access [easy entry] to the government itself through the channels of party passions.
>
> —George Washington, Farewell Address

**4** **Why did Washington believe that political parties would harm the nation?**

*He believed that political parties would have a bad effect on the nation by playing upon the jealousies of different factions and stirring up considerable trouble for the nation. Foreign governments might also find it easy to use political parties to influence our national affairs.*

## Document 2: Positions of the First United States Political Parties

| Federalist Party | Democratic-Republican Party |
|---|---|
| Strong central government | Weak central government |
| Loose interpretation of the Constitution | Strict interpretation of the Constitution |
| Government should pay states' Revolutionary War debts | Each state should pay its own debts |
| Favored a national bank | Opposed a national bank |
| Favored business interests | Favored agricultural interests |
| Pro-British foreign policy | Pro-French foreign policy |

**How were the policies favored by the Federalists different from those favored by the Democratic-Republicans?**

*The parties held opposite views on major policy issues.*

## Document 3: Policy Dispute in Congress Hall, Philadelphia

**The cartoon shows the two parties fighting over foreign policy. What does it imply about their ability to settle disagreements?**

*Their disputes, if not settled by debate, threaten to destroy the federal government.*

## Part 2: Essay

**5** Using information from the documents, your answers to the questions in Part 1, and your knowledge of U.S. history, write an essay in which you discuss the different views the first political parties held on major issues between 1789 and 1801 and explain why Washington believed that political parties were divisive. **6**

**5** Carefully read the essay question. Then write an outline for your essay.

**6** Write your essay. Be sure that it has an introductory paragraph that introduces your argument, main body paragraphs that explain it, and a concluding paragraph that restates your position. In your essay, include extracts or details from specific documents to support your ideas. Add other supporting facts or details that you know from your study of American history.

**Essay Rubric** The best essays will point out the differences between the Federalists and the Democratic-Republicans (Document 2), and will show how political disagreements, such as those portrayed in the cartoon (Document 3), supported Washington's warning in his Farewell Address (Document 1). Essays should draw upon information not specifically included in the documents that illustrates an understanding of the political debate during the Washington and Adams administrations. Students may also refer to the Alien and Sedition Acts passed by the Federalist Congress during Adams' presidency, and the opposing viewpoint expressed in the Kentucky and Virginia Resolutions authored by Jefferson and Madison, respectively.

## Introduction

**Historical Context:** In 1775, Great Britain had an army of 48,647 men located throughout the world, about 8,000 of them in the Americas. A rebellion by the small group of 13 colonies in America did not scare the keepers of such a large colonial empire.

**Task:** Discuss how the colonists' beliefs and military actions contributed to their victory in the Revolution. Include the significance of the American alliances with European nations.

## Part 1: Short Answer

Study each document carefully and answer the questions that follow.

### Document 1: First Georgia Regiment of Infantry Continental Line, 1777

The hunting shirt, or rifle dress, shown here was recommended by George Washington in his general order of July 24, 1776. Declaring it a practical item to be given to the troops, he also claimed that "... it is a dress justly supposed to carry no small terror to the enemy, who think every such person a complete marksman."

**Source:** New-York Historical Society

**What unusual military tactics did patriots like the man in the picture use to surprise and outsmart the British during the Revolution?**

Document 1: *Uniforms of the American Revolution: 1st Georgia Regiment Continental Infantry, 1777, Private Field Dress,* Charles Lefferts. Watercolor, gouache on paper. Copyright © Collection of the New-York Historical Society.

**Document 2: Philadelphia, September 12, 1777**

I close this paper with a short address to General Howe. . . . We know the cause which we are engaged in, and though a passionate fondness for it may make us grieve at every injury. . . . We are not moved by the gloomy smile of a worthless king, but by the ardent glow of generous patriotism. We fight not to enslave, but to set a country free, and to make room upon the earth for honest men to live in. In such a case we are sure that we are right; and we leave to you the despairing reflection of being the tool of a miserable tyrant.

—Thomas Paine, *The American Crisis No. IV*

**Although this excerpt is addressed to the British General Howe, how might it also have encouraged the colonists to continue their fight against the British?**

**Document 3: The Battle of Yorktown, 1781: Winning the American Revolution**

| Estimated American, French, and British Forces and Casualties | | |
|---|---|---|
| Generals and Their Divisions | Forces | Casualties |
| General Washington (American colonies) | 11,100 | 90 |
| General Rochambeau (France) | 7,800 | 250 |
| General Cornwallis (Britain) | 8,900 | 550 |

| Estimated French and British Naval Strength* | | |
|---|---|---|
| French and British Fleets | Ships | Guns on Board Ship |
| Admiral Graves (Britain) | 25 | 1,450 |
| Lieutenant General DeGrasse (France) | 35 | 2,610 |

*Does not include small craft or transport ships

**Source:** U.S. Army Center of Military History

**What support was provided by the French in the Battle of Yorktown?**

## Part 2: Essay

Using information from the documents, your answers to the questions in Part 1, and your knowledge of U.S. history, write an essay that discusses how the colonists' beliefs and military actions contributed to their victory in the Revolution. Include in your essay the significance of American alliances with European nations.

# RAND McNALLY
# World Atlas

# CONTENTS

## Complete Legend for Physical and Political Maps

### Symbols

Lake

Salt Lake

Seasonal Lake

River

Waterfall

Canal

△ Mountain Peak

▲ Highest Mountain Peak

### Cities

■ Los Angeles — City over 1,000,000 population

▣ Calgary — City of 250,000 to 1,000,000 population

• Haifa — City under 250,000 population

✹ Paris — National Capital

★ Vancouver — Secondary Capital (State, Province, or Territory)

### Type Styles Used to Name Features

**CHINA** — Country

ONTARIO — State, Province, or Territory

**PUERTO RICO (U.S.)** — Possession

ATLANTIC OCEAN — Ocean or Sea

*A l p s* — Physical Feature

*Borneo* — Island

### Boundaries

International Boundary

Secondary Boundary

### Land Elevation and Water Depths

**Land Elevation**

| Meters | | Feet |
|---|---|---|
| 3,000 and over -- | | -- 9,840 and over |
| 2,000 - 3,000 -- | | -- 6,560 - 9,840 |
| 500 - 2,000 -- | | -- 1,640 - 6,560 |
| 200 - 500 -- | | -- 656 - 1,640 |
| 0 - 200 -- | | -- 0 - 656 |

**Water Depth**

| | | |
|---|---|---|
| Less than 200 -- | | -- Less than 656 |
| 200 - 2,000 -- | | -- 656 - 6,560 |
| Over 2,000 -- | | -- Over 6,560 |

ARCTIC OCEAN

ATLANTIC
OCEAN

60°

Gagarino
Kiev

St. Acheul
Chelles          Hallstadt
Solutré          La Tène
Le Moustier     Villanova
Aurignac        Alps
Altamira   Pyrenees

Black Sea        Caucasus        Caspian Sea

40°

MEDITERRANEAN

Troy                                                    Anau

Mersin       Tell Halaf
Cnossus      Judeidah    Hassuna      Hissar
Gafsa                    Mt. Carmel   Jarmo       Sialk
SEA          Jericho                  Susa
Atlas   Mountains                     Al-Ubaid
                     Merimde          Eridu        Bakun
                                                   Kulli
SAHARA                Badari
                      Naqada
DESERT      Kharga Oasis              ARABIAN

                                       DESERT
20°

N

**La Tène**    European Iron Age Sites

**Judeidah**    Early Agricultural Communities

Le Moustier    Palaeolithic Sites

      Civilized areas in Third Millennium B.C.

      Civilized areas in Second Millennium B.C.

      Civilization 1000 B.C. - 200 A.D.

0    200    400    600    800 Miles

0    300    600    900    1200 Kilometers

Copyright by Rand McNally & Co.
Goodes Projection

20°                              40°                    60°

RAND McNALLY

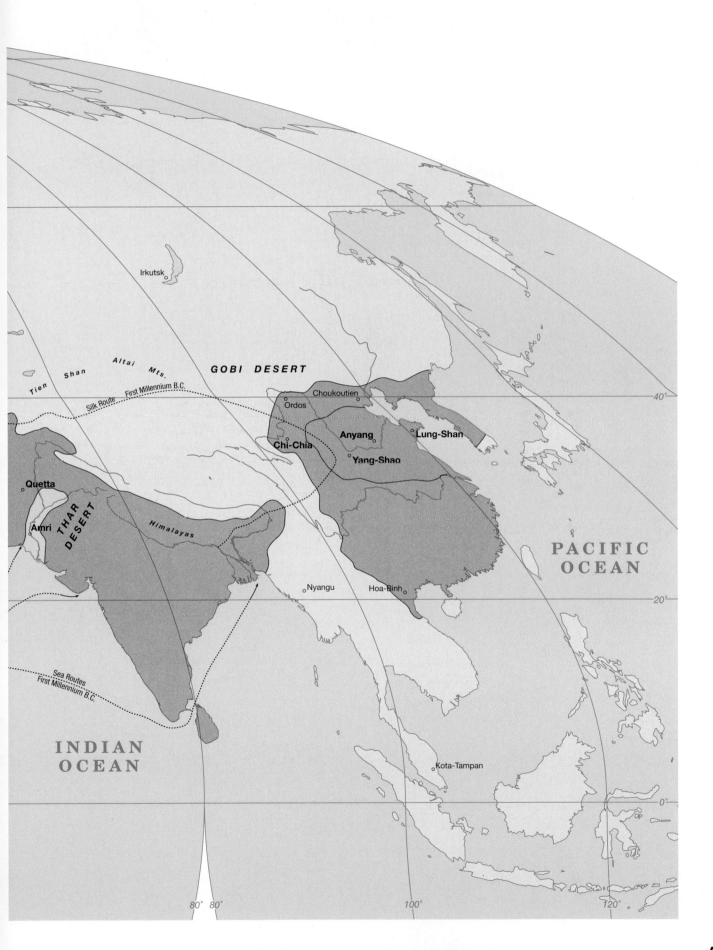

Irkutsk

Tien Shan

Altai Mts.

GOBI DESERT

Silk Route   First Millennium B.C.

Choukoutien

Ordos

Anyang

Chi-Chia

Yang-Shao

Lung-Shan

Quetta

THAR DESERT

Amri

Himalayas

Nyangu

Hoa-Binh

PACIFIC OCEAN

Sea Routes
First Millennium B.C.

INDIAN OCEAN

Kota-Tampan

40°

20°

0°

80°   80°

100°

120°

RAND McNALLY

ARCTIC OCEAN

Baffin Bay

GREENLAND (Den.)

Arctic Circle

ICELAND

FAROE IS. (Den.)

RUSSIA

ALASKA

Yukon (U.S.)

Anchorage

Aleutian Islands

CANADA

Hudson Bay

Newfoundland

UNITED KINGDOM

IRELAND

London

FRANCE

Vancouver

Missouri

Montréal

Ottawa

Chicago

New York

Washington D.C.

UNITED STATES

Colorado

Los Angeles

Houston

Mississippi

Gulf of Mexico

MEXICO

Mexico City

BAHAMAS

CUBA

HAITI

DOM. REP.

PUERTO RICO (U.S.)

JAMAICA

Caribbean Sea

BELIZE

GUAT.

HOND.

EL. SAL.

NIC.

COSTA RICA

PANAMA

Galapagos Islands (Ecuador)

ECUADOR

Caracas

VENEZUELA

GUYANA

SURINAME

FRENCH GUIANA

COLOMBIA

TRINIDAD AND TOBAGO

Amazon

PERU

Lima

BRAZIL

BOLIVIA

PARAGUAY

Rio de Janeiro

ARGENTINA

Santiago

URUGUAY

Buenos Aires

CHILE

ATLANTIC

OCEAN

Azores (Port.)

PORTUGAL

Madrid

SPAIN

Casablanca

MOROCCO

Canary Islands (Sp.)

W. SAHARA

CAPE VERDE

MAURITANIA

MALI

SENEGAL

Niger

GAMBIA

BURK. FASO

GUINEA-BISSAU

GUINEA

COTE D'IVOIRE

GHANA

SIERRA LEONE

LIBERIA

ST. HELENA (U.K.)

PACIFIC

OCEAN

MIDWAY IS. (U.S.)

Tropic of Cancer

Hawaiian Islands (U.S)

Equator

KIRIBATI

SAMOA

AMERICAN SAMOA

COOK ISLANDS (N.Z.)

TONGA

Tropic of Capricorn

FRENCH POLYNESIA

Easter Island (Chile)

FALKLAND IS. (U.K.)

South Georgia (U.K.)

South Orkney Is. (U.K.)

South Shetland Is. (U.K.)

Weddell Sea

Antarctic Circle

N

0       1000        2000 Miles
0   1000   2000   3000 Kilometers
Copyright by Rand McNally & Co.
Robinson Projection

ARCTIC OCEAN

Spitsbergen (Nor.)

Franz Josef Land

Novaya Zemlya

RUSSIA

NORWAY  FINLAND

SWEDEN

North Sea

DEN.

EST.
LAT.
LITH.

Volga

Moscow

Novosibirsk

Yenisey

Ob'

Lena

Bering Sea

Sea of Okhotsk

NETH.
BEL.

GERMANY

POLAND

BELARUS

UKRAINE

KAZAKHSTAN

MONGOLIA

SWITZ.

AUS.

CZ.
SLVK.
HUNG.

ROM.

MOLD.

ITALY

CRO.
BOS.
SERB.

BUL.

Black Sea

GEO.
ARM.  AZER.

UZBEKISTAN

KYRG.

CHINA

Beijing

NORTH KOREA

SOUTH KOREA

JAPAN

Tokyo

Rome

ALB.
MA.

GREECE

TURKEY

CYPRUS  LEB.

SYRIA

TURKMENISTAN

TAJIK.

Sea of Japan

Chang Jiang
Yangtze

Shanghai

PACIFIC

TUNISIA

Crete

Mediterranean Sea

ISRAEL  JORDAN

IRAQ

IRAN

AFGHANISTAN

NEPAL

BHU.

Cairo

KUWAIT

PAKISTAN

Kolkata (Calcutta)

BNGL.

Guangzhou

TAIWAN

Tropic of Cancer

ALGERIA

LIBYA

EGYPT

SAUDI ARABIA

QATAR

U.A.E.

OMAN

INDIA

MYANMAR

LAOS

South China Sea

NORTHERN MARIANA ISLANDS (U.S.)

WAKE ISLAND (U.S.)

NIGER

CHAD

SUDAN

Red Sea

YEMEN

Mumbai (Bombay)

Arabian Sea

Bay of Bengal

THAILAND

Bangkok

VIETNAM

CAMBODIA

PHILIPPINES

GUAM (U.S.)

OCEAN

NIGERIA

BENIN

CENTRAL AFRICAN REPUBLIC

ETHIOPIA

DJIBOUTI

SOMALIA

SRI LANKA

MALDIVES

BRUNEI

MALAYSIA

PALAU

FED. STATES OF MICRONESIA

MARSHALL ISLANDS

Addis Ababa

Lagos

CAMEROON

EQUATORIAL GUINEA

GABON

Congo

UGANDA

KENYA

SINGAPORE

Borneo

Equator

REP. OF CONGO

RWANDA

DEM. REP. OF CONGO

BURUNDI

TANZANIA

Sumatra

New Guinea

PAPUA NEW GUINEA

SOLOMON ISLANDS

Jakarta

INDONESIA

Java

EAST TIMOR

ANGOLA

ZAMBIA

COMOROS

SEYCHELLES

INDIAN

Darwin

Coral Sea

VANUATU

NAMIBIA

ZIMBABWE

MOZAMBIQUE

MADAGASCAR

MAURITIUS

REUNION (Fr.)

NEW CALEDONIA (Fr.)

FIJI

BOTSWANA

OCEAN

Tropic of Capricorn

SWAZILAND

AUSTRALIA

Darling

SOUTH AFRICA

LESOTHO

Perth

Sydney

Cape Town

Melbourne

NEW ZEALAND

Wellington

Tasmania

Kerguelen Islands (Fr.)

ANTARCTICA

Antarctic Circle

15°  30°  45°  60°  75°  90°  105°  120°  135°  150°  165°  180°

⊛ National Capital

• Major Cities

ARCTIC OCEAN

Baffin
Island
Baffin
Bay
Greenland
Jan Mayen

Arctic Circle
Iceland
Faroe Is.

Yukon
Mackenzie
Canadian Shield
Hudson
Bay

British
Isles

Mt. McKinley △
20,320 Ft.
6,194m

NORTH
AMERICA

St. Lawrence
Newfoundland
London

Aleutian Islands

Rocky Mountains
Great Plains
Appalachian Mts.

Vancouver

Iberian
Peninsula

Azores

Colorado
Washington D.C.

Los Angeles

Mississippi
Cape Hatteras

ATLANTIC

Atlas
Mts.

Midway Is.

Tropic of Cancer

Baja
California
Gulf of Mexico

Canary
Islands

Hawaiian
Islands

Yucatan
Peninsula
Cuba
Hispaniola
Puerto Rico

Cape
Verde
Islands

PACIFIC

Jamaica
Caribbean
Sea

Cape Verde

Niger

Palmyra

Trinidad
Orinoco

OCEAN

Equator
Galapagos Islands

Kiribati

Amazon
Amazon
Basin

SOUTH

Marquesas Is.

Andes

AMERICA

Samoa
Islands

Mato Grosso
Plateau

St. Helena

Tonga
Is.
Cook
Islands
Tahiti

Tropic of Capricorn

Rio de Janeiro

Easter Island

Andes
Paraná

Mt. Aconcagua △
22,831 Ft.
6,959m
Buenos Aires

N

Archipiélago
Juan Fernández

Chatham Is.

Patagonia

Falkland Is.
South
Georgia

0    1000    2000 Miles
0   1000   2000   3000 Kilometers
Copyright by Rand McNally & Co.
Robinson Projection

Tierra del Fuego
Cape Horn
South
Orkney Is.
South
Sandwich Is.

Antarctic Circle
South
Shetland Is.
Antarctic
Peninsula
Weddell
Sea

Ross
Sea
Marie
Byrd
Land
△ Vinson Massif
16,066 Ft.
4,897m

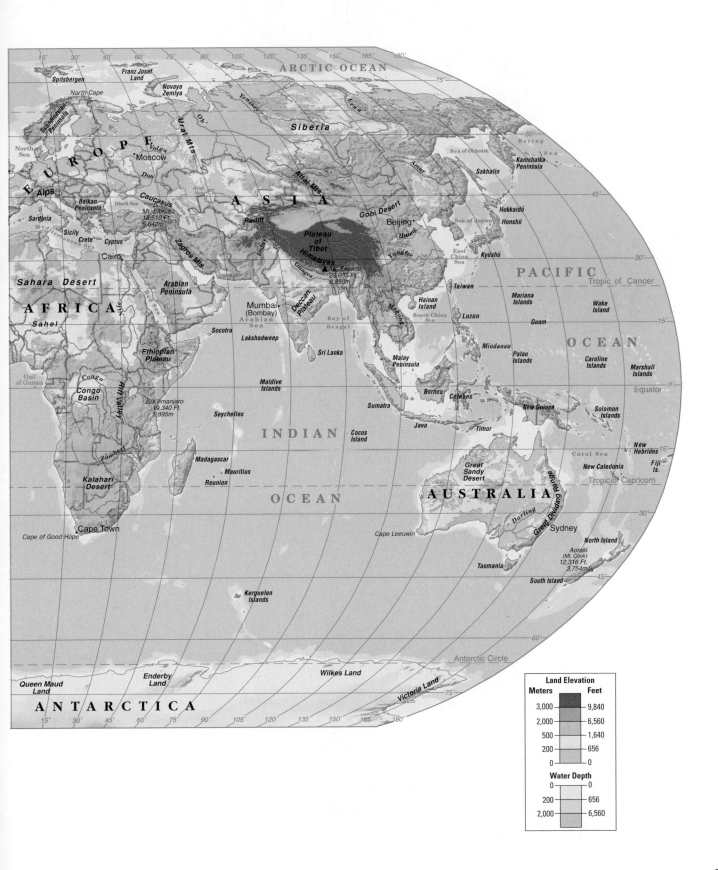

ARCTIC OCEAN

Spitsbergen
Franz Josef Land
North Cape
Novaya Zemlya
Scandinavian Peninsula
Yenisey
Lena
Siberia
Bering Sea
North Sea
EUROPE
Volga
Moscow
Ural Mts.
Ob'
Amur
Sea of Okhotsk
Kamchatka Peninsula
Sakhalin
Alps
Don
Caucasus
ASIA
Atlas Mts.
Sea of Japan
Hokkaidō
Balkan Peninsula
Black Sea
Mt. Elbrus
18,510 Ft.
5,642m
Aral Sea
Pamir
Gobi Desert
Honshū
Sardinia
Zagros Mts.
Plateau of Tibet
Beijing
Huang
East China Sea
Kyūshū
Sicily
Crete
Cyprus
Himalayas
Indus
Yangtze
PACIFIC
Cairo
Ganges
Mt. Everest
29,035 Ft.
8,850m
Sahara Desert
Arabian Peninsula
Deccan Plateau
Hainan Island
Taiwan
Tropic of Cancer
AFRICA
Nile
Red Sea
Mumbai (Bombay)
Arabian Sea
Bay of Bengal
Mekong
South China Sea
Mariana Islands
Wake Island
Sahel
Socotra
Luzon
Guam
OCEAN
Lakshadweep
Sri Lanka
Malay Peninsula
Mindanao
Palau Islands
Caroline Islands
Marshall Islands
Ethiopian Plateau
Maldive Islands
Borneo
Celebes
Gulf of Guinea
Congo
Congo Basin
Rift Valley
Kilimanjaro
19,340 Ft.
5,895m
Seychelles
Sumatra
Java
New Guinea
Solomon Islands
Equator
INDIAN
Cocos Island
Timor
New Hebrides
Zambezi
Madagascar
Mauritius
Reunion
Coral Sea
New Caledonia
Fiji Is.
Kalahari Desert
Great Sandy Desert
AUSTRALIA
Tropic of Capricorn
OCEAN
Darling
Great Dividing Range
Sydney
Cape Town
Cape of Good Hope
Cape Leeuwin
North Island
Aoraki (Mt. Cook)
12,316 Ft.
3,754m
Tasmania
South Island
Kerguelen Islands
Antarctic Circle
Queen Maud Land
Enderby Land
Wilkes Land
Victoria Land
ANTARCTICA

| Land Elevation | | |
|---|---|---|
| Meters | | Feet |
| 3,000 | | 9,840 |
| 2,000 | | 6,560 |
| 500 | | 1,640 |
| 200 | | 656 |
| 0 | | 0 |

| Water Depth | | |
|---|---|---|
| 0 | | 0 |
| 200 | | 656 |
| 2,000 | | 6,560 |

RAND McNALLY

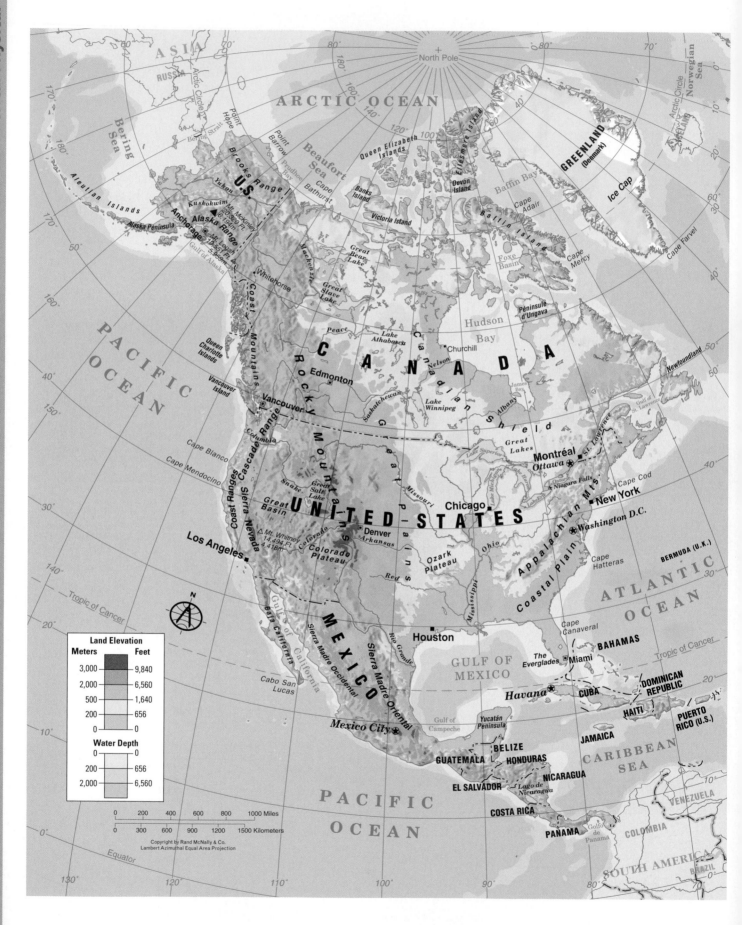

**Land Elevation**

| Meters | | Feet |
|---|---|---|
| 3,000 | | 9,840 |
| 2,000 | | 6,560 |
| 500 | | 1,640 |
| 200 | | 656 |
| 0 | | 0 |

**Water Depth**

| 0 | | 0 |
|---|---|---|
| 200 | | 656 |
| 2,000 | | 6,560 |

0 200 400 600 800 1000 Miles

0 300 600 900 1200 1500 Kilometers

Copyright by Rand McNally & Co.
Lambert Azimuthal Equal Area Projection

GULF OF MEXICO

NORTH AMERICA

MEXICO
BELIZE
GUATEMALA
HONDURAS
Gulf of Honduras
EL SALVADOR
NICARAGUA
COSTA RICA
PANAMA
Gulf of Panamá

CUBA
Greater Antilles
JAMAICA
HAITI
DOMINICAN REPUBLIC
PUERTO RICO (U.S.)
Lesser Antilles

CARIBBEAN SEA

ATLANTIC OCEAN

TRINIDAD AND TOBAGO

Cristóbal Colón Peak △ 18,948 Ft. 5,775m

Caracas ✪

Orinoco

Llanos

VENEZUELA

GUYANA

SURINAME

FRENCH GUIANA

Cape Orange

Galapagos Islands (Ec.)

ECUADOR

Bogotá ✪
COLOMBIA

Magdalena

△ Chimborazo 20,703 Ft. 6,310m

Putumayo

Japurá

Negro

Amazon

Manaus ■

Amazon

Ilha de Marajó

Belém ■

Equator

Amazon Basin

Selvas

Juruá

Madeira

Tapajós

BRAZIL

Tocantins

Mt. Huascarán 22,133 Ft. 6,746m ✪

PERU

Andes

Ucayali

Lima ✪

△ Mt. Illampu 21,066 Ft. 6,421m

Lake Titicaca

Cordillera Oriental

BOLIVIA

Mato Grosso Plateau

Brasília ✪

São Francisco

Recife ■

Serra do Espinhaço

△ Mt. Sajama 21,463 Ft. 6,542m

Atacama Desert

Gran Chaco

PARAGUAY

Paraná

São Paulo ■

Rio de Janeiro ■

Tropic of Capricorn

Isla San Ambrosio (Chile)

Mt. Ojos del Salado 22,615 Ft. 6,893m

Andes

ARGENTINA

Paraná

URUGUAY

Isla San Felix (Chile)

PACIFIC OCEAN

Archipiélago Juan Fernández (Chile)

Santiago ✪

CHILE

Mt. Aconcagua 22,831 Ft. 6,959m

Buenos Aires ✪

Río de la Plata

Pampas

N

ATLANTIC OCEAN

San Matías Gulf

Península Valdés

Chiloé

Patagonia

San Jorge Gulf

Point Medanoso

Grand Bay

West Falkland

FALKLAND ISLANDS (U.K.)

East Falkland

Strait of Magellan

Tierra del Fuego

Cape Horn

South Georgia (U.K.)

Drake Passage

South Shetland Islands (U.K.)

South Orkney Islands (U.K.)

South Sandwich Islands (U.K.)

## Land Elevation

| Meters | | Feet |
|---|---|---|
| 3,000 | | 9,840 |
| 2,000 | | 6,560 |
| 500 | | 1,640 |
| 200 | | 656 |
| 0 | | 0 |

## Water Depth

| 0 | | 0 |
|---|---|---|
| 200 | | 656 |
| 2,000 | | 6,560 |

0  200  400  600  800  1000 Miles
0  300  600  900  1200  1500 Kilometers

Copyright by Rand McNally & Co.
Lambert Azimuthal Equal Area Projection

Land Elevation

| Meters | | Feet |
|---|---|---|
| 3,000 | | 9,840 |
| 2,000 | | 6,560 |
| 500 | | 1,640 |
| 200 | | 656 |
| 0 | | 0 |

Water Depth

| 0 | | 0 |
|---|---|---|
| 200 | | 656 |
| 2,000 | | 6,560 |

0   200   400   600   800   1000 Miles

0   300   600   900   1200   1500 Kilometers

Copyright by Rand McNally & Co.
Lambert Azimuthal Equal Area Projection

**Land Elevation**

| Meters | Feet |
|---|---|
| 3,000 | 9,840 |
| 2,000 | 6,560 |
| 500 | 1,640 |
| 200 | 656 |
| 0 | 0 |

**Water Depth**

| | |
|---|---|
| 0 | 0 |
| 200 | 656 |
| 2,000 | 6,560 |

✪ National Capital

★ Secondary Capital
(State, Province, or Territory)

■ City over 1,000,000 population

▣ City of 250,000 to 1,000,000 population

• City under 250,000 population

PACIFIC OCEAN

Tropic of Cancer

Hawaiian Islands

Hawaii

Equator

Line Islands

Kiritimati

POLYNESIA

Marquesas Is.

FRENCH POLYNESIA

Tuamotu Archipelago

Society Islands

Tahiti

Austral Is.

Tropic of Capricorn

PITCAIRN (U.K.)

Northern Cook Islands

COOK ISLANDS (N.Z.)

Southern Cook Islands

TOKELAU (N.Z.)

AMERICAN SAMOA

SAMOA

NIUE (N.Z.)

WALLIS AND FUTUNA (FR.)

TONGA

Koro Sea

International Date Line

N

KIRIBATI

TUVALU

FIJI

Kermadec Islands (N.Z.)

Chatham Islands

MARSHALL ISLANDS

MICRONESIA

NAURU

MELANESIA

SOLOMON ISLANDS

Solomon Sea

VANUATU

NEW CALEDONIA (FR.)

New Caledonia

NORFOLK ISLAND (Austl.)

Auckland

North Island

New Zealand

Wellington

Cook Strait

South Island

Mt. Cook 12,316 Ft. 3,754m

Tasman Sea

NORTHERN MARIANA ISLANDS (U.S.)

GUAM (U.S.)

FEDERATED STATES OF MICRONESIA

PALAU

Halmahera

Bismarck Sea

Mount Wilhelm 14,793 Ft. 4,509m

PAPUA NEW GUINEA

New Guinea

Port Moresby

Torres Strait

Cape York Peninsula

Gulf of Carpentaria

Great Barrier Reef

Coral Sea

Brisbane

Sydney

Canberra

Mount Kosciuszko 7,310 ft. 2,229m

GREAT DIVIDING RANGE

Darling

Murray

Melbourne

Bass Strait

Tasmania

TAIWAN

Taipei

CHINA

Luzon Strait

South China Sea

Luzon

Manila

PHILIPPINES

Mindoro

Sulu Sea

Mindanao

Celebes Sea

Celebes

Philippine Sea

Moluccas

Ceram

Banda Sea

INDONESIA

EAST TIMOR

Timor

Timor Sea

Arafura Sea

Puncak Jaya 16,503 Ft. 5,030m

Kimberley Plateau

Great Sandy Desert

Gibson Desert

Great Victoria Desert

AUSTRALIA

Great Australian Bight

0 200 400 600 800 1000 Kilometers

0 200 400 600 800 Miles

Copyright by Rand McNally & Co.
Lambert Azimuthal Equal Area Projection

✪ RAND McNALLY

**A11**

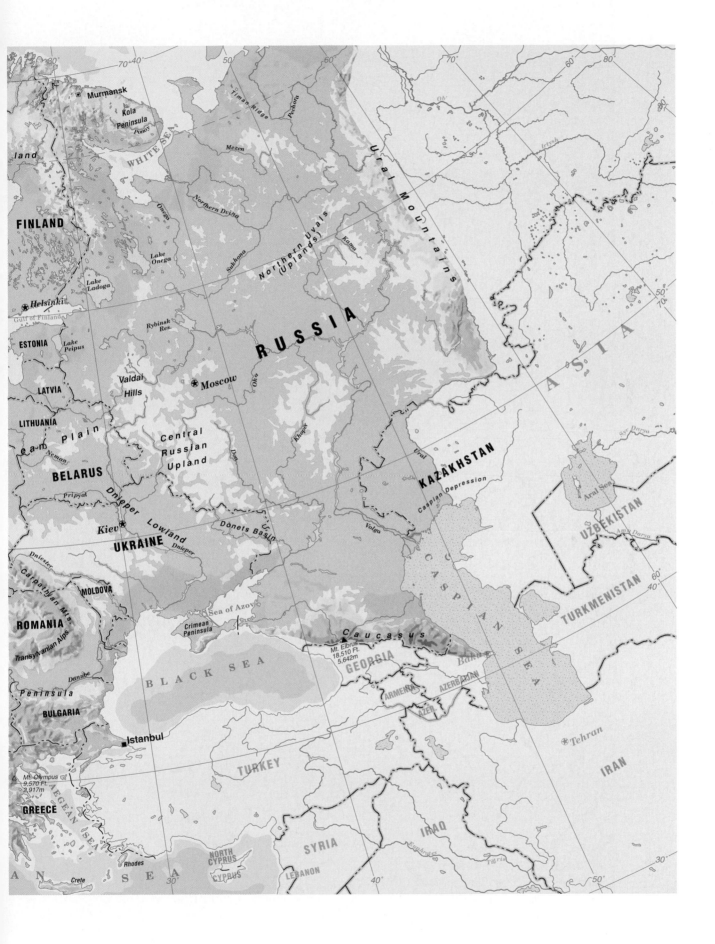

Murmansk

Kola
Peninsula

Ponoy

WHITE SEA

land

Mezen

Timan Ridge

Pechora

Ob'

FINLAND

Northern Dvina

Onega

Lake
Onega

Sukhona

Northern Uvals
(Uplands)

Kama

RUSSIA

Lake
Ladoga

Helsinki

Rybinsk
Res.

Gulf of Finland

ESTONIA

Lake
Peipus

Valdai

Hills

Moscow

Oka

ASIA

LATVIA

Don

Khopёr

LITHUANIA

e a m

P l a i n

Central
Russian
Upland

Neman

Ural

BELARUS

KAZAKHSTAN

Pripyat

Dnieper

Caspian Depression

Aral Sea

Kiev

Dnieper Lowland

Donets Basin

Volga

UZBEKISTAN

UKRAINE

Dnieper

Amu Darya

Dniester

Syr Darya

Carpathian Mts.

MOLDOVA

Sea of Azov

CASPIAN

ROMANIA

Crimean
Peninsula

Caucasus

TURKMENISTAN

Transylvanian Alps

Mt. Elbrus
18,510 Ft.
5,642m

Baku

SEA

Danube

BLACK SEA

GEORGIA

Peninsula

ARMENIA

AZERBAIJAN

BULGARIA

AZER.

Istanbul

Tehran

Mt. Olympus
9,570 Ft.
2,917m

TURKEY

IRAN

GREECE

IRAQ

AEGEAN SEA

SYRIA

A N

S E A

Rhodes

Crete

NORTH
CYPRUS

LEBANON

Euphrates

Tigris

CYPRUS

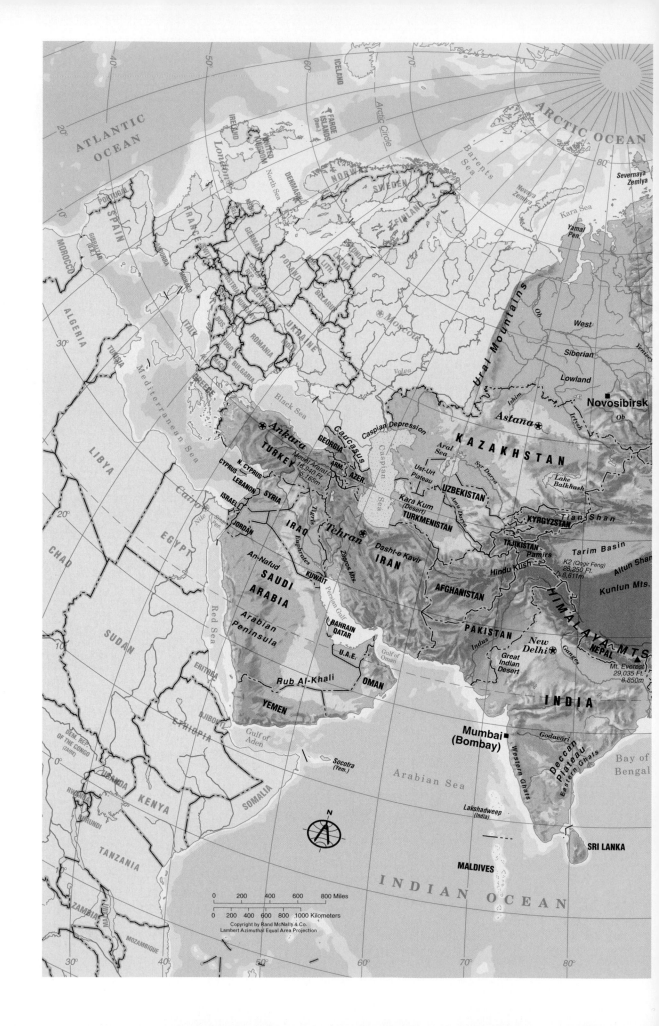

ATLANTIC OCEAN

ARCTIC OCEAN

ICELAND

IRELAND

UNITED KINGDOM

FARDE ISLANDS (Den.)

Arctic Circle

London

PORTUGAL

SPAIN

MOROCCO

GIBRALTAR

FRANCE

North Sea

DENMARK

NORWAY

SWEDEN

FINLAND

EST.

LATV.

LITH.

Barents Sea

Novaya Zemlya

Kara Sea

Yamal Pen.

Severnaya Zemlya

ALGERIA

ITALY

GERMANY

POLAND

BELARUS

Moscow

Ural Mountains

Ob

West

Siberian

Lowland

Yenisey

Novosibirsk

Irtysh

Ob

TUNISIA

AUST. HUNG.

SLOVAKIA

ROMANIA

UKRAINE

Volga

Astana

KAZAKHSTAN

Ishim

Irtysh

Mediterranean Sea

BULGARIA

GREECE

Black Sea

Ankara

TURKEY

Caucasus

GEORGIA

ARM.

AZER.

Caspian Depression

Aral Sea

Ust-Urt Plateau

Lake Balkhash

LIBYA

N. CYPRUS

CYPRUS

LEBANON

SYRIA

ISRAEL

JORDAN

IRAQ

Mt. Ararat 16,940 Ft. 5,165m

Tigris

Euphrates

Tehran

Zagros Mts.

Caspian Sea

Kara Kum (Desert)

UZBEKISTAN

TURKMENISTAN

Amu Darya

Syr Darya

KYRGYZSTAN

Tian Shan

TAJIKISTAN

Pamirs

Tarim Basin

K2 (Qogir Feng) 28,250 Ft. 8,611m

Altun Shan

EGYPT

Nile

Sinai Pen.

An-Nafud

SAUDI ARABIA

KUWAIT

Persian Gulf

IRAN

Dasht-e Kavir

AFGHANISTAN

Hindu Kush

Kunlun Mts.

HIMALAYA MTS.

CHAD

SUDAN

Red Sea

Arabian Peninsula

BAHRAIN

QATAR

U.A.E.

Gulf of Oman

PAKISTAN

Indus

New Delhi

Great Indian Desert

Ganges

NEPAL

Mt. Everest 29,035 Ft. 8,850m

ERITREA

Rub Al-Khali

OMAN

INDIA

DEM. REP. OF THE CONGO (Zaire)

DJIBOUTI

ETHIOPIA

YEMEN

Gulf of Aden

Mumbai (Bombay)

Godavari

Deccan Plateau

Western Ghats

Eastern Ghats

Bay of Bengal

UGANDA

RWANDA

BURUNDI

SOMALIA

Socotra (Yem.)

Arabian Sea

Lakshadweep (India)

SRI LANKA

KENYA

N

MALDIVES

INDIAN OCEAN

TANZANIA

0   200   400   600   800 Miles

0   200  400  600  800  1000 Kilometers

Copyright by Rand McNally & Co.
Lambert Azimuthal Equal Area Projection

ZAMBIA

MALAWI

MOZAMBIQUE

**Land Elevation**

| Meters | Feet |
|--------|------|
| 3,000 | 9,840 |
| 2,000 | 6,560 |
| 500 | 1,640 |
| 200 | 656 |
| 0 | 0 |

**Water Depth**

| | |
|--------|------|
| 0 | 0 |
| 200 | 656 |
| 2,000 | 6,560 |

Taymyr
Peninsula

New Siberian
Islands

East Siberian
Sea

Laptev Sea

Indigirka

Kolyma

Arctic Circle

Bering
Sea

Aleutian Islands (U.S.)

Central
Siberian
Uplands

Verkhoyansk Mts.

Lena

Sea of
Okhotsk

Kamchatka
Peninsula

R U S S I A

S i b e r i a

Angara

Lake
Baikal

Stanovoy Range

Amur

Greater Khingan Range

Sakhalin

Kuril Islands

P A C I F I C

Sayan Mountains

Sikhote-Alin Mts.

Trans Siberian

Sea of
Japan

Hokkaido

O C E A N

Altai Mts.

MONGOLIA

Gobi Desert

Beijing

NORTH
KOREA

SOUTH
KOREA

Honshu

Mt. Fuji △
12,388 ft.
3,776m

Tokyo

JAPAN

Shikoku

Kyushu

Tropic of Cancer

Qilian Shan

Huang

Yellow
Sea

C H I N A

Qinling Shandi

Chang (Yangtze)

Shanghai

East
China
Sea

NORTHERN MARIANA
ISLANDS (U.S.)

BHUTAN

Brahmaputra

Xi

TAIWAN

Philippine
Sea

GUAM (U.S.)

FEDERATED STATES OF
MICRONESIA

BNGL

MYANMAR

Irrawaddy

Salween

Red

Gulf of
Tonkin

Hainan Island

LAOS

Mekong

Luzon Strait

Luzon

PHILIPPINES

PALAU

THAILAND

VIETNAM

South
China
Sea

Manila

Mindanao

Equator

Bangkok

CAMBODIA

Andaman
Islands
(India)

Andaman
Sea

Gulf of
Thailand

Sulu Sea

Celebes
Sea

Nicobar
Islands
(India)

MALAY
PENINSULA

MALAYSIA

BRUNEI

MALAYSIA

Celebes

Ceram

Moluccas

New
Guinea

PAPUA NEW
GUINEA

Str. of Malacca

Singapore

Borneo

Banda Sea

Arafura Sea

Coral
Sea

Sumatra

Greater Sunda
Islands

I N D O N E S I A

EAST TIMOR

Gulf
of
Carpentaria

Jakarta

Java

Java Sea

Timor

Timor Sea

AUSTRALIA

RAND MᶜNALLY

**A15**

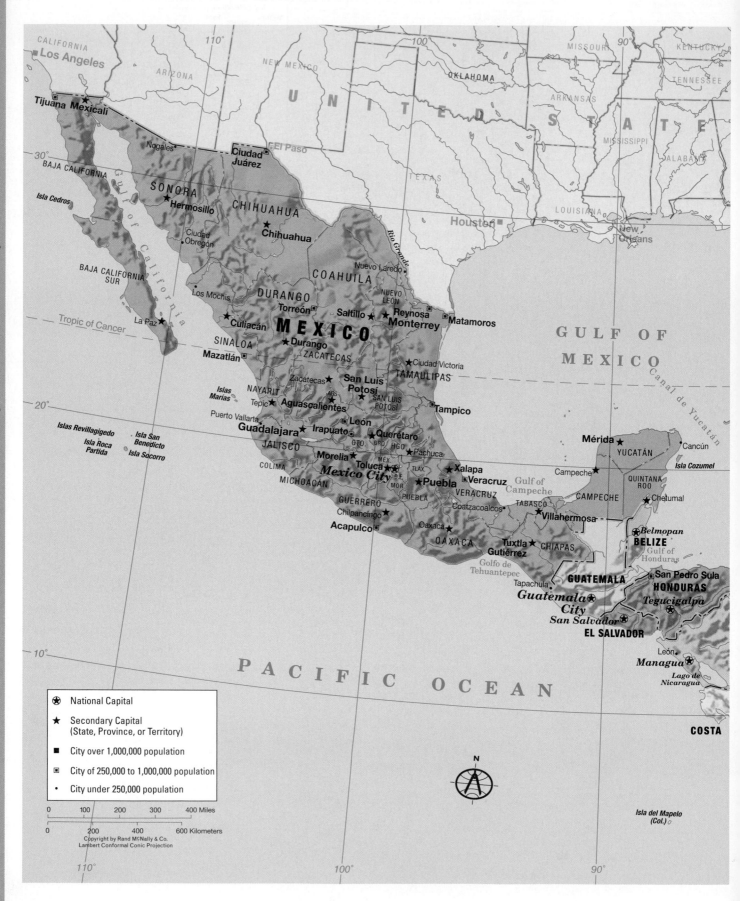

CALIFORNIA
**Los Angeles**

110°

NEW MEXICO

100°

MISSOURI

90°

KENTUCKY

ARIZONA

OKLAHOMA

ARKANSAS

TENNESSEE

**Tijuana** ★ **Mexicali**

MISSISSIPPI

ALABAMA

U N I T E D

S T A T E

30°

Nogales

El Paso

BAJA CALIFORNIA

**Ciudad
Juárez**

TEXAS

LOUISIANA

Isla Cedros

SONORA

**Hermosillo**

CHIHUAHUA

**Houston**

New
Orleans

Ciudad
Obregón

**Chihuahua**

BAJA CALIFORNIA
SUR

COAHUILA

Nuevo Laredo

Los Mochis

DURANGO

NUEVO
LEÓN

Tropic of Cancer

La Paz ★

**Culiacán**

**Torreón**

**Saltillo**

**Reynosa**

**Matamoros**

GULF OF

**MEXICO**

**Monterrey**

MEXICO

SINALOA

**Durango**

ZACATECAS

Ciudad Victoria

MEXICO

**Mazatlán**

Zacatecas

NAYARIT

**San Luis
Potosí**

TAMAULIPAS

Islas
Marías

Tepic

**Aguascalientes**

AGS

SAN LUIS
POTOSÍ

20°

Islas Revillagigedo

Isla San
Benedicto

Puerto Vallarta

**León**

**Tampico**

**Mérida** ★

Cancún

Isla Roca
Partida

Isla Socorro

**Guadalajara**

**Irapuato**

GTO

**Querétaro**

QRO

HGO

Pachuca

YUCATÁN

Isla Cozumel

JALISCO

COLIMA

**Morelia**

MEX

**Toluca** ★

MICHOACÁN

*Mexico City*

DF

TLAX

MOR

**Puebla**

**Xalapa**

**Veracruz**

Gulf of
Campeche

Campeche ★

QUINTANA
ROO

Chetumal ★

CAMPECHE

PUEBLA

VERACRUZ

Coatzacoalcos

TABASCO

GUERRERO

Chilpancingo

**Villahermosa**

Gulf of
Honduras

**Belmopan**

**BELIZE**

**Acapulco**

OAXACA

Oaxaca ★

**Tuxtla
Gutiérrez** ★

CHIAPAS

Golfo de
Tehuantepec

**San Pedro Sula**

**HONDURAS**

**Tegucigalpa** ★

Tapachula

**GUATEMALA**

*Guatemala
City*

*San Salvador*

**EL SALVADOR**

León ★

*Managua* ★

PACIFIC

OCEAN

Lago de
Nicaragua

**COSTA**

⊛  National Capital

★  Secondary Capital
    (State, Province, or Territory)

■  City over 1,000,000 population

▣  City of 250,000 to 1,000,000 population

•  City under 250,000 population

N

Isla del Mapelo
(Col.)

0    100    200    300    400 Miles

0        200        400        600 Kilometers

Copyright by Rand McNally & Co.
Lambert Conformal Conic Projection

110°

100°

90°

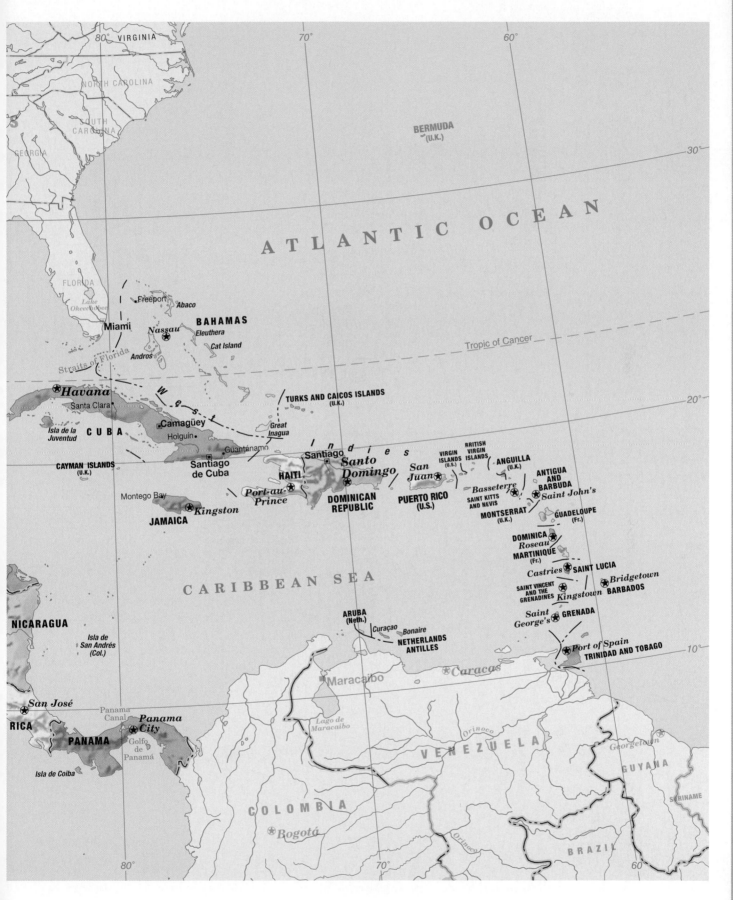

ATLANTIC OCEAN

BERMUDA
(U.K.)

30°

VIRGINIA

NORTH CAROLINA

SOUTH CAROLINA

GEORGIA

FLORIDA

*Lake Okeechobee*

**Miami**

Freeport • *Abaco*

**BAHAMAS**

*Nassau* ⊛
*Eleuthera*

*Cat Island*

*Andros*

Tropic of Cancer

20°

*Straits of Florida*

⊛**Havana**

Santa Clara •

*Isla de la Juventud*   **CUBA**

**Camagüey**

Holguín •

TURKS AND CAICOS ISLANDS
(U.K.)

*Great Inagua*

*W e s t*

CAYMAN ISLANDS
(U.K.)

Guantánamo

Santiago ■

Santiago de Cuba

**HAITI**

Port-au-Prince ⊛

*Santo Domingo*

**DOMINICAN REPUBLIC**

*I n d i e s*

San Juan ⊛

VIRGIN ISLANDS
(U.S.)

BRITISH VIRGIN ISLANDS

**PUERTO RICO**
(U.S.)

ANGUILLA
(U.K.)

**ANTIGUA AND BARBUDA**

*Basseterre* ⊛
SAINT KITTS AND NEVIS

*Saint John's* ⊛

Montego Bay •

**JAMAICA**

Kingston ⊛

MONTSERRAT
(U.K.)

GUADELOUPE
(Fr.)

**DOMINICA**

*Roseau* ⊛

**MARTINIQUE**
(Fr.)

*Castries* ⊛ **SAINT LUCIA**

CARIBBEAN SEA

**SAINT VINCENT AND THE GRENADINES**

*Kingstown* ⊛

*Bridgetown* ⊛
**BARBADOS**

**NICARAGUA**

*Isla de San Andrés*
(Col.)

**ARUBA**
(Neth.)

*Curaçao*

*Bonaire*

**NETHERLANDS ANTILLES**

*Saint George's* ⊛ **GRENADA**

⊛ *Port of Spain*
**TRINIDAD AND TOBAGO**

10°

⊛**Caracas**

**San José** ⊛

Panama Canal

*Panama City* ⊛

**RICA**

**PANAMA**

*Golfo de Panamá*

*Isla de Coiba*

⊛**Maracaibo**

*Lago de Maracaibo*

*Orinoco*

**V E N E Z U E L A**

*Georgetown* ⊛

**G U Y A N A**

**SURINAME**

**COLOMBIA**

⊛ *Bogotá*

*Orinoco*

**B R A Z I L**

80°                    70°                    60°

RAND M<sup>c</sup>NALLY

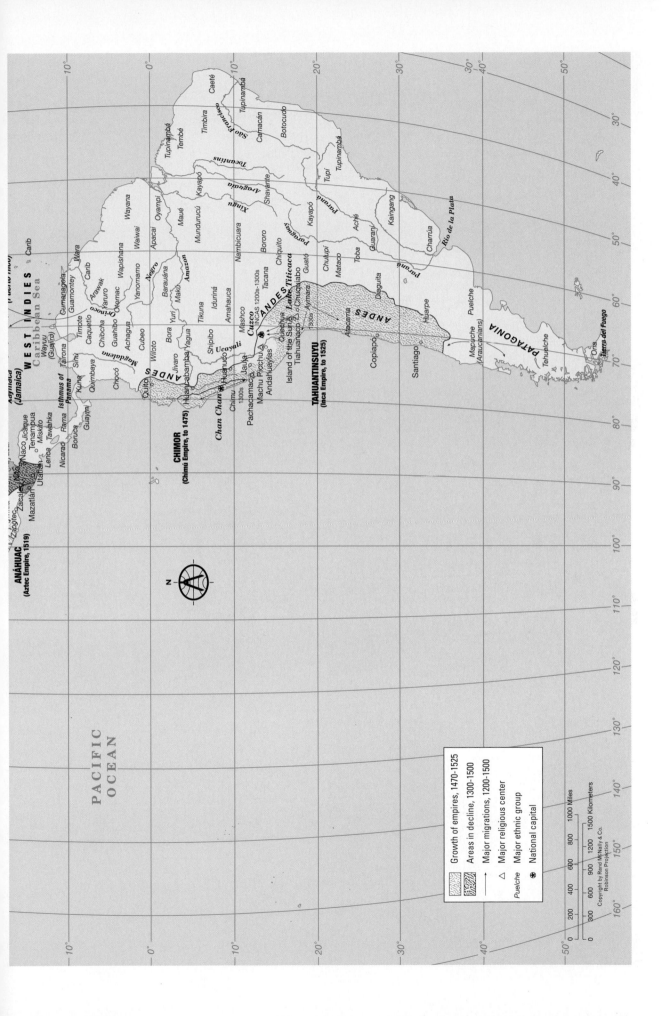

PACIFIC
OCEAN

WEST INDIES

Caribbean Sea

Isthmus of
Panama

**ANÁHUAC**
(Aztec Empire, 1519)

Aymara
(Jamaica)

Carib

**CHIMOR**
(Chimú Empire, to 1475)

**TAHUANTINSUYU**
(Inca Empire, to 1525)

ANDES

ANDES

PATAGONIA

Tierra del Fuego

**Chan Chan**

Cuzco
INCAS 1200s–1300s

Machu Picchu

Pachacamac

Andahuaylas

Lake Titicaca

Island of the Sun
Tiahuanaco
1300s

Quechua
Aymara

Chuquiabo

Orinoco

Negro

Amazon

Magdalena

Ucayali

Río de la Plata

Paraná

Puruná

Caetê

Tupinambá

Tembé

Timbira

São Francisco

Camacán

Botocudo

Tupinambá

Tupi

Tocantins

Araguaia

Kayapó

Xingu

Maué

Mundurucú

Apacaí

Oyampi

Wayana

Waiwai

Wapishana

Yanomamo

Otomac

Achagua

Guahibo

Chibcha

Caquetío

Timote

Sihu

Choco

Quimbaya

Guaymí

Boruca

Nicarao

Rama

Lenca

Utatlán

Mazatlán

Zacapu

Izquintepec

Zapotec

Tenampua

Naco

Jicaque

Miskito

Tawahka

Cumanagota

Guamontey

Wara

Arawak

Carib

Yaruro

Barauána

Makú

Yuri

Bora

Yagua

Shipibo

Idurinã

Amahuaca

Tikuna

Mashco

Tacana

Chiquito

Guató

Bororo

Shavante

Nambicuara

Paressí

Kayapó

Guaraní

Aché

Kaingang

Chamía

Toba

Mataco

Chulupi

Diaguita

Atacama

Copiapó

Santiago

Huarpe

Mapuche
(Araucanians)

Puelche

Tehuelche

Ona

Wiloto

Jivaro

Huánuco
1300s

Jauja

Chimu
1300s

Quito

Cubeo

Guajiro
(Wayúu)

Tairona

Timpe

Wiloto

*Puelche*

Growth of empires, 1470–1525
Areas in decline, 1300–1500
Major migrations, 1200–1500
△ Major religious center
*Puelche* Major ethnic group
⊛ National capital

0   200   400   600   800   1000 Miles
0   300   600   900   1200   1500 Kilometers

Copyright by Rand McNally & Co.
Robinson Projection

N

**Legend**

- ⊛ National Capital
- ★ Secondary Capital (State, Province, or Territory)
- ■ City over 1,000,000 population
- ▣ City of 250,000 to 1,000,000 population
- • City under 250,000 population

Copyright by Rand McNally & Co.
Alber's Conic Equal Area Projection

100   200   300 Miles
100   200   300   400 Kilometers

ATLANTIC OCEAN

PUERTO RICO (U.S.)

San Juan
Arecibo
Mayagüez   Caguas
Ponce

Caribbean Sea

0   25   50 Miles
0   25   50 Kilometers

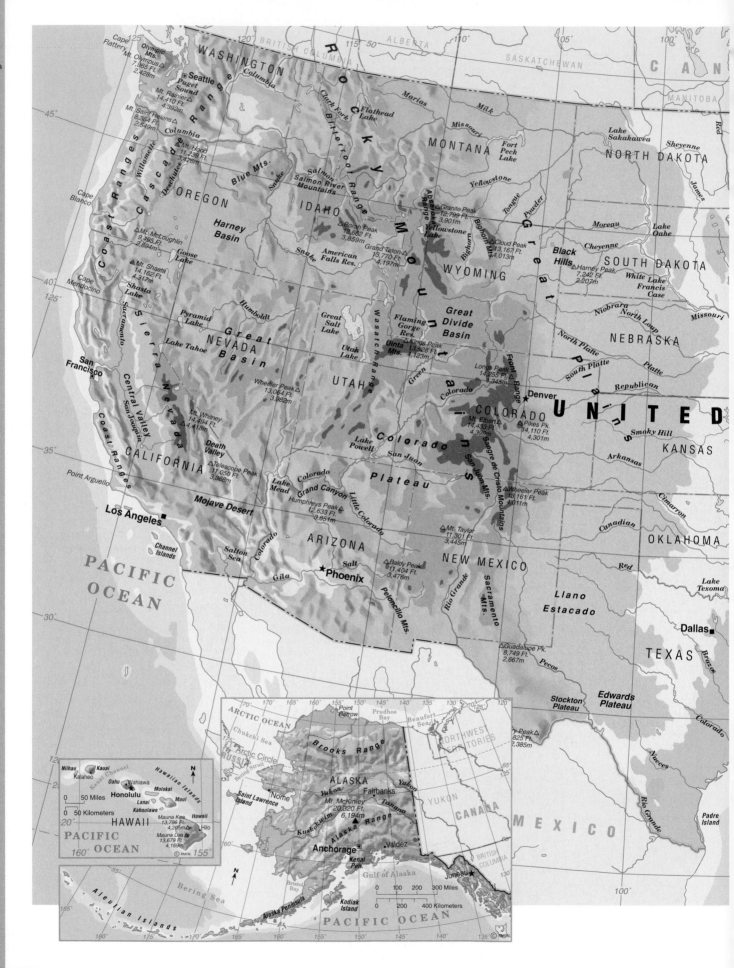

PACIFIC OCEAN

BRITISH COLUMBIA

ALBERTA

SASKATCHEWAN

MANITOBA

C A N

WASHINGTON

Cape Flattery
Mt. Olympus
7,965 Ft.
2,428m
Olympic Mts.
Seattle
Puget Sound
Mt. Rainier △
14,410 Ft.
4,392m
Mt. Saint Helens △
8,364 Ft.
2,549m
Columbia

Cascade Range

Mt. Hood △
11,239 Ft.
3,426m
Willamette
Deschutes
OREGON
Blue Mts.
Harney Basin

△ Mt. McLoughlin
9,495 Ft.
2,894m
Goose Lake

Cape Blanco

Cape Mendocino

Coast Ranges

Columbia
Clark Fork
Flathead Lake
Bitterroot Range
Snake
Salmon
Salmon River Mountains
IDAHO

ROCKY

Marias
Milk
MONTANA
Fort Peck Lake
Missouri
Yellowstone

Borah Peak
12,662 Ft.
3,859m
Snake
American Falls Res.
Grand Teton △
13,770 Ft.
4,197m
Absaroka Range
△ Granite Peak
12,799 Ft.
3,901m
Yellowstone Lake
Bighorn
Bighorn Mts.
△ Cloud Peak
13,167 Ft.
4,013m
WYOMING

MOUNTAINS

Tongue
Powder

Lake Sakakawea
NORTH DAKOTA
Moreau

Sheyenne
Red
James

Cheyenne
Lake Oahe

Black Hills
△ Harney Peak
7,242 Ft.
2,207m

Great Plains

SOUTH DAKOTA
White Lake Francis Case

△ Mt. Shasta
14,162 Ft.
4,317m
Shasta Lake
Sacramento

Pyramid Lake
Humboldt
Great
NEVADA
Basin
Lake Tahoe

Great Salt Lake
Utah Lake
Wasatch Range

Flaming Gorge Res.
Great Divide Basin
Uinta Mts.
△ Kings Peak
13,528 Ft.
4,123m
Green

Niobrara
North Loup
North Platte
NEBRASKA
Missouri

San Francisco

Sierra Nevada
San Joaquin
Central Valley
CALIFORNIA

Wheeler Peak △
13,064 Ft.
3,982m

Mt. Whitney △
14,494 Ft.
4,418m
Death Valley
△ Telescope Peak
11,050 Ft.
3,368m

UTAH

Colorado

Lake Powell
Colorado
Plateau
San Juan

Longs Peak △
14,255 Ft.
4,345m
Front Range
COLORADO
Denver ★
Mt. Elbert △
14,433 Ft.
4,399m
Pikes Pk. △
14,110 Ft.
4,301m

South Platte
Platte
Republican
Smoky Hill
Arkansas
KANSAS

UNITED

Point Arguello

Mojave Desert
Salton Sea
Colorado

Lake Mead
Grand Canyon
Humphreys Peak △
12,633 Ft.
3,851m
Little Colorado

Sangre de Cristo Mountains
△ Wheeler Peak
13,161 Ft.
4,011m

Cimarron

Los Angeles ■

Channel Islands

ARIZONA
Salt
Gila
Phoenix ★

△ Mt. Taylor
11,301 Ft.
3,445m
NEW MEXICO
△ Baldy Peak
11,404 Ft.
3,476m
Rio Grande
Sacramento Mts.
Pecos

Canadian
Red
OKLAHOMA
Lake Texoma

Dallas ■

PACIFIC OCEAN

Pelencillo Mts.

△ Guadalupe Pk.
8,749 Ft.
2,667m

Llano Estacado
TEXAS

Colorado

Stockton Plateau
Edwards Plateau

Rio Grande
MEXICO
Pecos
Nueces

Rio Grande
Padre Island
Brazos

ARCTIC OCEAN
Chukchi Sea
Point Barrow
Prudhoe Bay
Beaufort Sea

Arctic Circle
RUSSIA
Bering Strait
Saint Lawrence Island
Nome

Brooks Range
ALASKA
Yukon
Kuskokwim
Fairbanks
Tanana
Mt. McKinley
20,320 Ft.
6,194m
Alaska Range
Anchorage ■
Kenai Pen.
Valdez
Juneau ★

NORTHWEST TERRITORIES
ry Peak △
825 Ft.
2,385m

Yukon
CANADA
BRITISH COLUMBIA

Bering Sea
Bristol Bay
Kodiak Island
Aleutian Islands
Alaska Peninsula
Gulf of Alaska
PACIFIC OCEAN

0   100   200   300 Miles
0       200      400 Kilometers

Niihau
Kauai
Kalaheo
Oahu
Wahiawa
Honolulu ★
Molokai
Lanai
Maui
Kahoolawe
Kauai Channel
Hawaiian Islands
Mauna Kea
13,796 Ft.
4,205m △
Hawaii
Hilo
Mauna Loa △
13,679 Ft.
4,169m
HAWAII
PACIFIC OCEAN
0   50 Miles
0   50 Kilometers

N

N

© RMN.
155°

## Land Elevation

| Meters | | Feet |
|---|---|---|
| 3,000 | | 9,840 |
| 2,000 | | 6,560 |
| 500 | | 1,640 |
| 200 | | 656 |
| 0 | | 0 |

## Water Depth

| | |
|---|---|
| 0 | 0 |
| 200 | 656 |
| 2,000 | 6,560 |

0    100    200    300 Miles

0  100  200  300  400 Kilometers

Copyright by Rand McNally & Co.
Alber's Conic Equal Area Projection

### PUERTO RICO (U.S.)

ATLANTIC OCEAN

San Juan
Arecibo
Mayagüez
Ponce    Caguas

Caribbean Sea

0   25   50 Miles
0   25   50 Kilometers

RAND McNALLY

## Guam

Philippine Sea

144°45'    145°

13°30'    *Agana*  •Tamuning

GUAM
(U.S.)

PACIFIC
OCEAN

13°15'

144°45'    145°

0   2   4   6   8   10 Miles
0     5      10     15 Kilometers
Copyright by Rand McNally & Co.
Lambert Conformal Conic Projection

## Samoa

171°    170°

0   5   10  15  20  25 Miles
0    10   20   30   40 Kilometers
Copyright by Rand McNally & Co.
Lambert Conformal Conic Projection

PACIFIC
OCEAN

AMERICAN
SAMOA          *Ofu*⤙*Olosega*
                    *Tau*

14°

*Pago Pago*      Manua Islands
    *Aunuu*
*Tutuila*

## Pacific Islands

140°   150°   160°   170°   180°   20°   170°   160°   150°   140°   130°

PACIFIC          OCEAN          HAWAII

NORTHERN
MARIANA
ISLANDS
(U.S.)

GUAM (U.S.)

10°                                                                          10°

⊛*Koror*   CAROLINE ISLANDS     MARSHALL
                                ISLANDS
PALAU      FEDERATED STATES OF
           MICRONESIA

0°          NAURU        KIRIBATI                                    Equator    0°

INDON.                              PHOENIX
                                    ISLANDS
PAPUA NEW                SOLOMON
*Port*    GUINEA         ISLANDS   TUVALU   TOKELAU (N.Z.)
*Moresby*          ⊛*Honiara*                                 COOK
                        SANTA CRUZ        WALLIS AND  SAMOA   ISLANDS   FRENCH
10°  CORAL SEA          ISLANDS           FUTUNA              (N.Z.)    POLYNESIA   10°
                                          (Fr.)  ⊛*Apia*
Gulf of        VANUATU          FIJI      AMERICAN SAMOA
Carpentaria                               *Suva*
         Cairns         ⊛*Port Vila*  ⊛              NIUE
                                          TONGA       (N.Z.)
AUSTRALIA    NEW
             CALEDONIA
             (Fr.)   ⊛*Nouméa*
20°                                                                          20°

140°   150°   160°   170°   180°   170°   160°   150°   140°   130°

INTERNATIONAL DATE LINE

N

0   200  400  600  800  1000 Miles
0   300  600  900  1200 1500 Kilometers
Copyright by Rand McNally & Co.
Lambert Azimuthal Equal Area Projection

### (World map)

Arctic Circle

15°  0°  15°  30°  45°  60°  75°  90°  105°  120°  135°

75°  ICELAND                              R U S S I A
60°  NORWAY  FINLAND
     SWEDEN
     UNITED   DEN.
     KINGDOM
     IRELAND  NETH. GERMANY POLAND BELARUS  KAZAKHSTAN   MONGOLIA
     FRANCE  SWITZ.  UKRAINE
     SPAIN   ITALY   ROM.                  UZBEKISTAN  KYRG.
     PORTUGAL        BUL.      GEO. AZER.   TURKMENISTAN TAJIK.       NORTH
     MOROCCO  TUNISIA  GREECE  TURKEY   ARM.                   Beijing  KOREA  JAPAN
     GIBRALTAR        SYRIA  IRAQ  IRAN       AFGHANISTAN  C H I N A   Seoul  Tokyo
     ALGERIA  LIBYA  ISRAEL JORDAN KUWAIT              PAKISTAN  NEPAL  SOUTH  Osaka
              EGYPT   SAUDI   QATAR  OMAN  INDIA             BHU.  KOREA Shanghai
     MALI  NIGER  CHAD  SUDAN  ARABIA  U.A.E.          MYANMAR LAOS        Taipei
     NIGERIA  BENIN          ERITREA  YEMEN             (BURMA)       TAIWAN
     EQUATORIAL GUINEA CENTRAL AFRICAN DJIBOUTI  SRI LANKA  THAILAND Hong Kong NORTHERN
     CAMEROON  REPUBLIC  ETHIOPIA              VIETNAM           MARIANA
     SAO TOME  GABON CONGO DEM. REP.  UGANDA KENYA  CAMBODIA  Manila  ISLANDS (US)
     AND PRINCIPE  OF THE CONGO RWANDA BURUNDI  SOMALIA         PHILIPPINES GUAM (U.S.)
              ANGOLA  TANZANIA                  BRUNEI
                      ZAMBIA  MALAWI  COMOROS MALAYSIA           PALAU
     NAMIBIA  ZIMBABWE  MOZAMBIQUE MADAGASCAR SINGAPORE Borneo  New Guinea
     BOTSWANA  Tropic of Capricorn  MAURITIUS   Sumatra INDONESIA PAPUA
     LESOTHO           REUNION Jakarta EAST TIMOR  NEW GUINEA
                        (Fr.)              I N D O N E S I A

I N D I A N    O C E A N            A U S T R A L I A

                                                Melbourne

0    1000   2000 Miles
0  1000  2000  3000 Kilometers
Copyright by Rand McNally & Co.
Robinson Projection

A N T A R C T I C A

15°  0°  15°  30°  45°  60°  75°  90°  105°  120°  135°

| | |
|---|---|
| ⊛ | National Capital |
| ● | Major Cities |

## Puerto Rico and the U.S. Virgin Islands

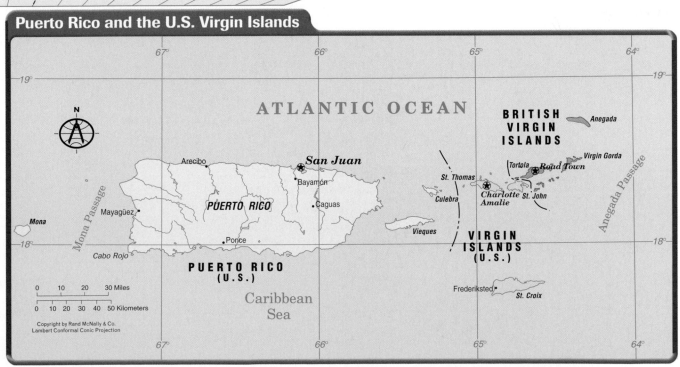

Copyright by Rand McNally & Co.
Lambert Conformal Conic Projection

RAND McNALLY

RAND MCNALLY

ATLANTIC OCEAN

Tropic of Cancer

GUADELOUPE (FR.)

DOMINICA (BR.)
MARTINIQUE (FR.)

TOBAGO (BR.)

ST. VINCENT (BR.)
GRENADA, (BR.)

PUERTO RICO (SP.)

HISPANIOLA

Santo
Domingo

CARIBBEAN SEA

HAITI (FR.)

N

NEWFOUNDLAND (BR.)

MIQUELON (FR.)
ST. PIERRE (FR.)

CAPE BRETON ISLAND (BR.)

St. Lawrence (in dispute)

JAMAICA (BR.)

CUBA (SP.)

Lake Ontario

Lake Erie

UNITED STATES

E. FLORIDA

Lake Huron

Lake Superior

Lake Michigan

(in dispute)
W. FLORIDA

GULF OF MEXICO

BRITISH

Mississippi

Rio Grande

SPANISH

PACIFIC OCEAN

UNEXPLORED

U.S.
Spanish
British
French
Other
Disputed

0   100   200   300   400 Miles
0   200   400   600 Kilometers

Copyright by Rand McNally & Co.
Lambert Azimuthal, Equal Area Projection

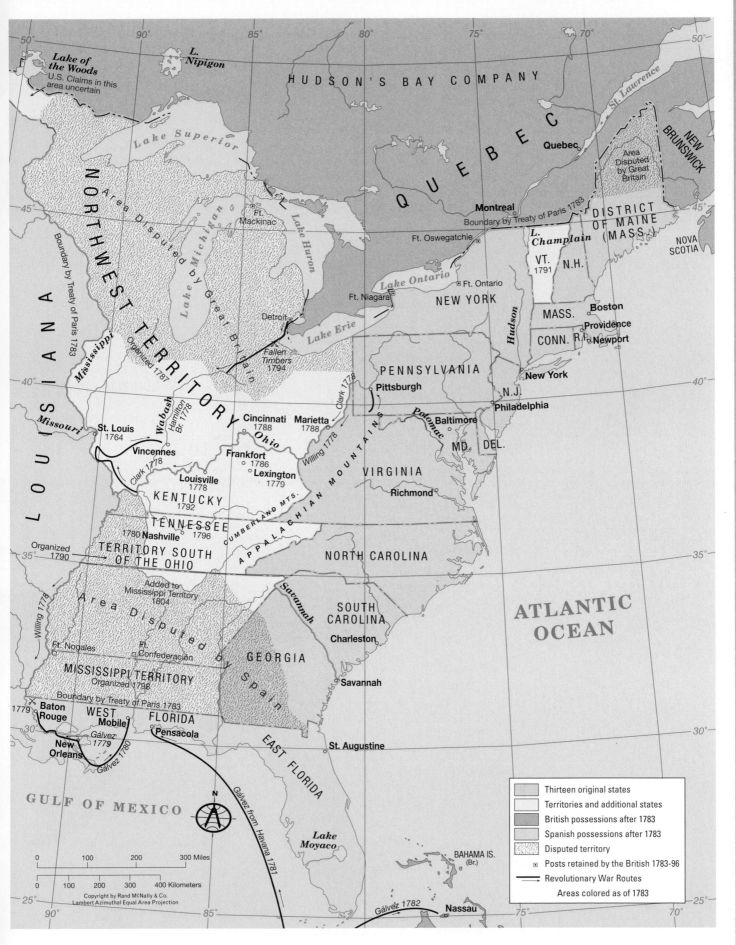

HUDSON'S BAY COMPANY

**Lake of the Woods**
U.S. Claims in this area uncertain

L. Nipigon

Lake Superior

QUEBEC

Quebec

St. Lawrence

NEW BRUNSWICK

Area Disputed by Great Britain

NORTHWEST TERRITORY

Area Disputed by Great Britain

Ft. Mackinac

Lake Michigan

Lake Huron

Montreal

Boundary by Treaty of Paris 1783

DISTRICT OF MAINE (MASS.)

NOVA SCOTIA

Ft. Oswegatchie

L. Champlain

VT. 1791

N.H.

Organized 1787

Boundary by Treaty of Paris 1783

Mississippi

Detroit

Lake Erie

Fallen Timbers 1794

Ft. Ontario

Ft. Niagara

NEW YORK

MASS.

Boston

Providence

CONN. R.I. Newport

LOUISIANA

Missouri

St. Louis 1764

Wabash

Hamilton Br. 1778

Vincennes

Clark 1778

Clark 1778

Cincinnati 1788

Ohio

Marietta 1788

Frankfort 1786

Louisville 1778

Lexington 1779

Willing 1778

PENNSYLVANIA

Pittsburgh

Potomac

New York

N.J.

Philadelphia

Baltimore

Hudson

MD. DEL.

APPALACHIAN MOUNTAINS

VIRGINIA

Richmond

KENTUCKY 1792

TENNESSEE 1796

CUMBERLAND MTS.

1780 Nashville

Organized 1790

TERRITORY SOUTH OF THE OHIO

NORTH CAROLINA

Added to Mississippi Territory 1804

Area Disputed by Spain

Savannah

SOUTH CAROLINA

Charleston

Willing 1778

Ft. Nogales

Ft. Confederación

GEORGIA

MISSISSIPPI TERRITORY
Organized 1798

Boundary by Treaty of Paris 1783

Baton Rouge
1779

WEST

Mobile

FLORIDA

Pensacola

Gálvez 1779

New Orleans

Gálvez 1780

EAST FLORIDA

Savannah

St. Augustine

ATLANTIC OCEAN

GULF OF MEXICO

Gálvez from Havana 1781

Lake Moyaco

N

BAHAMA IS. (Br.)

0    100    200    300 Miles

0   100   200   300   400 Kilometers

Copyright by Rand McNally & Co.
Lambert Azimuthal Equal Area Projection

Gálvez 1782    Nassau

| | Thirteen original states |
| | Territories and additional states |
| | British possessions after 1783 |
| | Spanish possessions after 1783 |
| | Disputed territory |
| ▫ | Posts retained by the British 1783-96 |
| → | Revolutionary War Routes |
| | Areas colored as of 1783 |

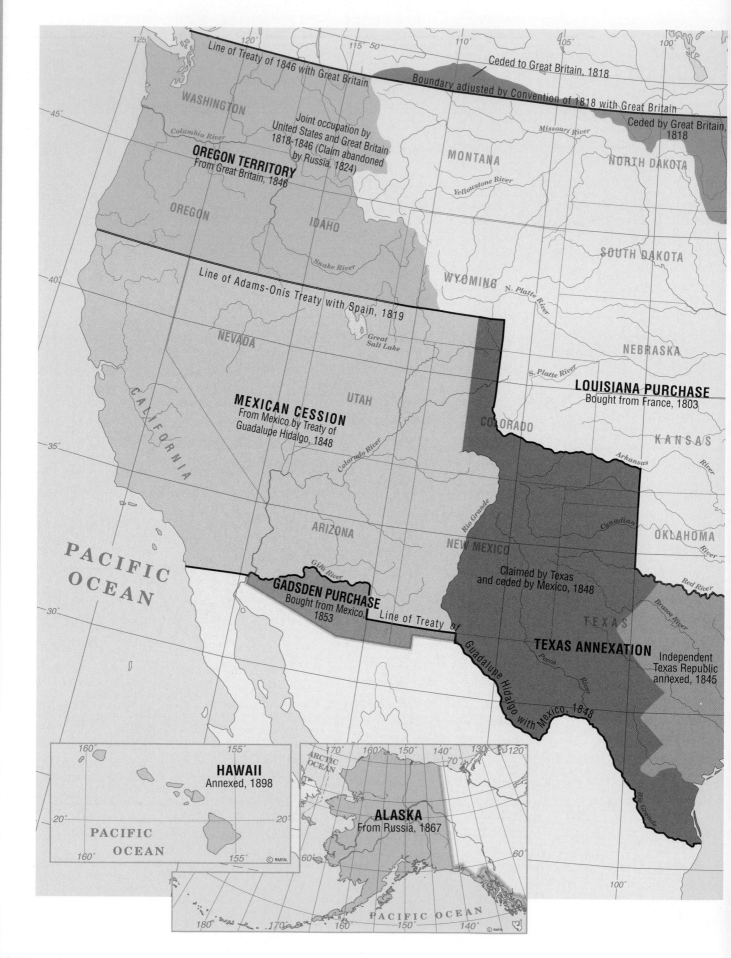

Line of Treaty of 1846 with Great Britain

Ceded to Great Britain, 1818

Boundary adjusted by Convention of 1818 with Great Britain

Ceded by Great Britain, 1818

WASHINGTON

Columbia River

Joint occupation by United States and Great Britain 1818-1846 (Claim abandoned by Russia, 1824)

MONTANA

NORTH DAKOTA

Missouri River

**OREGON TERRITORY**
From Great Britain, 1846

OREGON

IDAHO

Yellowstone River

SOUTH DAKOTA

Snake River

WYOMING

N. Platte River

Line of Adams-Onís Treaty with Spain, 1819

NEVADA

Great Salt Lake

UTAH

S. Platte River

NEBRASKA

**LOUISIANA PURCHASE**
Bought from France, 1803

**MEXICAN CESSION**
From Mexico by Treaty of Guadalupe Hidalgo, 1848

COLORADO

KANSAS

Arkansas

River

CALIFORNIA

Colorado River

ARIZONA

NEW MEXICO

Gila River

Rio Grande

Canadian

OKLAHOMA

River

**PACIFIC OCEAN**

**GADSDEN PURCHASE**
Bought from Mexico, 1853

Line of Treaty of

Claimed by Texas and ceded by Mexico, 1848

Red River

Pecos

Brazos River

TEXAS

Guadalupe Hidalgo with Mexico, 1848

**TEXAS ANNEXATION**
Independent Texas Republic annexed, 1845

River

Rio Grande

**HAWAII**
Annexed, 1898

**PACIFIC OCEAN**

ARCTIC OCEAN

**ALASKA**
From Russia, 1867

PACIFIC OCEAN

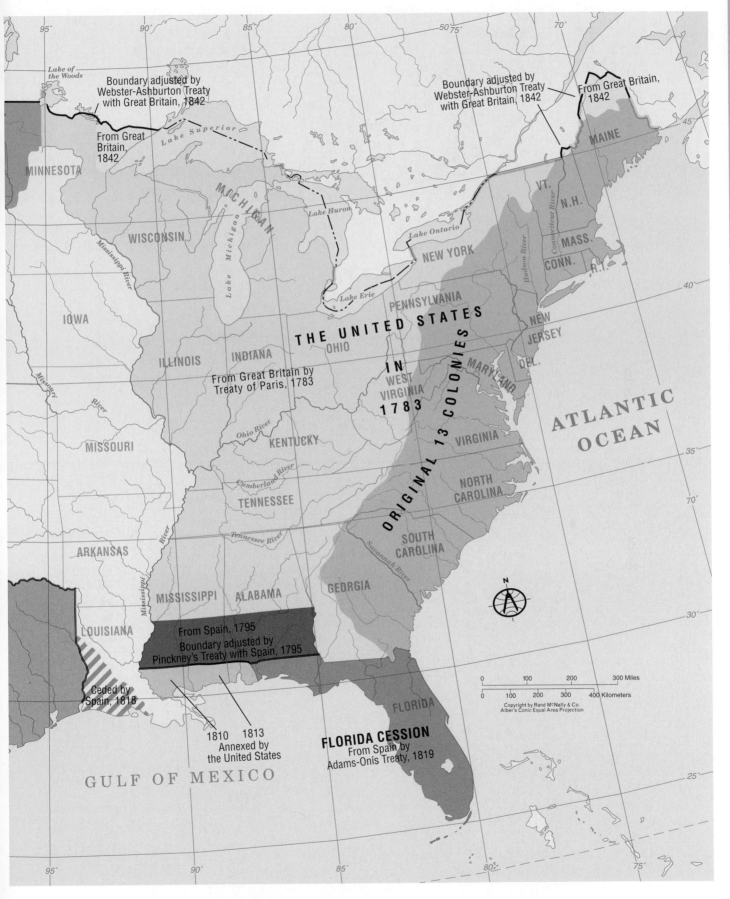

Boundary adjusted by
Webster-Ashburton Treaty
with Great Britain, 1842

Boundary adjusted by
Webster-Ashburton Treaty
with Great Britain, 1842

From Great Britain,
1842

*Lake of the Woods*

From Great
Britain,
1842

MINNESOTA

*Lake Superior*

MAINE

MICHIGAN

*Lake Huron*

VT.

N.H.

WISCONSIN

*Lake Michigan*

*Lake Ontario*

MASS.

NEW YORK

*Hudson River*

*Connecticut River*

CONN.

R.I.

*Lake Erie*

PENNSYLVANIA

NEW
JERSEY

IOWA

*Mississippi River*

THE UNITED STATES

OHIO

DEL.

INDIANA

IN

MARYLAND

*Missouri River*

ILLINOIS

From Great Britain by
Treaty of Paris, 1783

1783

WEST
VIRGINIA

*Ohio River*

KENTUCKY

VIRGINIA

ORIGINAL 13 COLONIES

MISSOURI

*Cumberland River*

NORTH
CAROLINA

ATLANTIC
OCEAN

TENNESSEE

*Tennessee River*

SOUTH
CAROLINA

ARKANSAS

*Savannah River*

*Mississippi River*

GEORGIA

N

MISSISSIPPI

ALABAMA

LOUISIANA

From Spain, 1795
Boundary adjusted by
Pinckney's Treaty with Spain, 1795

FLORIDA

Ceded by
Spain, 1818

0    100    200    300 Miles

0  100  200  300  400 Kilometers

Copyright by Rand McNally & Co.
Alber's Conic Equal Area Projection

1810    1813
Annexed by
the United States

FLORIDA CESSION
From Spain by
Adams-Onís Treaty, 1819

GULF OF MEXICO

**Slavery in the United States 1820–1860**

CANADA

ATLANTIC OCEAN

PACIFIC OCEAN

GULF OF MEXICO

MEXICO

WASHINGTON TERRITORY
Free by Oregon Act 1848
Open to Slavery by Dred Scott Decision 1857
Olympia

OREGON
Free by Oregon Act 1848
Salem

CALIFORNIA
Sacramento
San Francisco
Carson City
Los Angeles

UTAH TERRITORY
Open to Slavery by Compromise of 1850
Salt Lake City

NEBRASKA TERRITORY
Free by Missouri Compromise 1820
Open to Slavery by Kansas–Nebraska Act 1854
Yankton
Omaha
Denver City

(UNORGANIZED)
Free by Missouri Compromise 1820
Open to Slavery by Dred Scott Decision 1857

KANSAS TERRITORY
Free by Missouri Compromise 1820
Open to Slavery by Kansas–Nebraska Act 1854
Topeka
1855
1856
1856

NEW MEXICO TERRITORY
Open to Slavery by Compromise of 1850
Santa Fe
Tucson

Missouri Compromise line 1820 36° 30'

INDIAN TERRITORY

TEXAS
San Antonio

MINNESOTA
St. Paul

WISCONSIN
Milwaukee

IOWA
Des Moines
1850

MISSOURI
St. Louis
Jefferson City
1837

ILLINOIS
Chicago
1837

MICHIGAN
Detroit
1829

INDIANA
Indianapolis

OHIO
Cleveland
Cincinnati

KENTUCKY
Louisville
Lexington
1848

TENNESSEE
Nashville
Memphis

ARKANSAS
Little Rock
1837 1845
1840 1840
1840 1840
1845
Shreveport

MAINE
Portland

N.H.
VT.

MASS.
Boston

CONN.
R.I.
New York
1834
1835 1835
New Jersey

NEW YORK
Albany
Buffalo 1835

PENNSYLVANIA
Philadelphia
Pittsburgh
1859

DEL.
MARYLAND
Baltimore
1860

VIRGINIA
Washington
Richmond
Norfolk

NORTH CAROLINA
Wilmington

SOUTH CAROLINA
Charleston
1822

GEORGIA
Savannah
1849

FLORIDA
St. Augustine
1841

ALABAMA
Atlanta
Mobile

MISSISSIPPI
1840 1840
1840 1840

LOUISIANA
New Orleans

Lake Superior
Lake Michigan
Lake Huron
Lake Erie
Lake Ontario

Mississippi R.
Missouri R.
Columbia
Snake
Colorado

**Legend:**

| | |
|---|---|
| | 50% and over Slaves |
| | 1% to 50% Slaves |
| | Open to Slavery |
| | Free States |
| | Railroad |

| Symbol | |
|---|---|
| △ | Tobacco |
| ♣ | Cotton |
| ✦ | Sugar |
| □ | Rice |
| ✺ | Abolitionist Incidents |
| ✸ | Slave Revolts |

0 100 200 300 400 Miles
0 100 200 300 400 500 600 Kilometers

Copyright by Rand McNally & Co.
Alber's Conic Equal Area Projection

RAND McNALLY

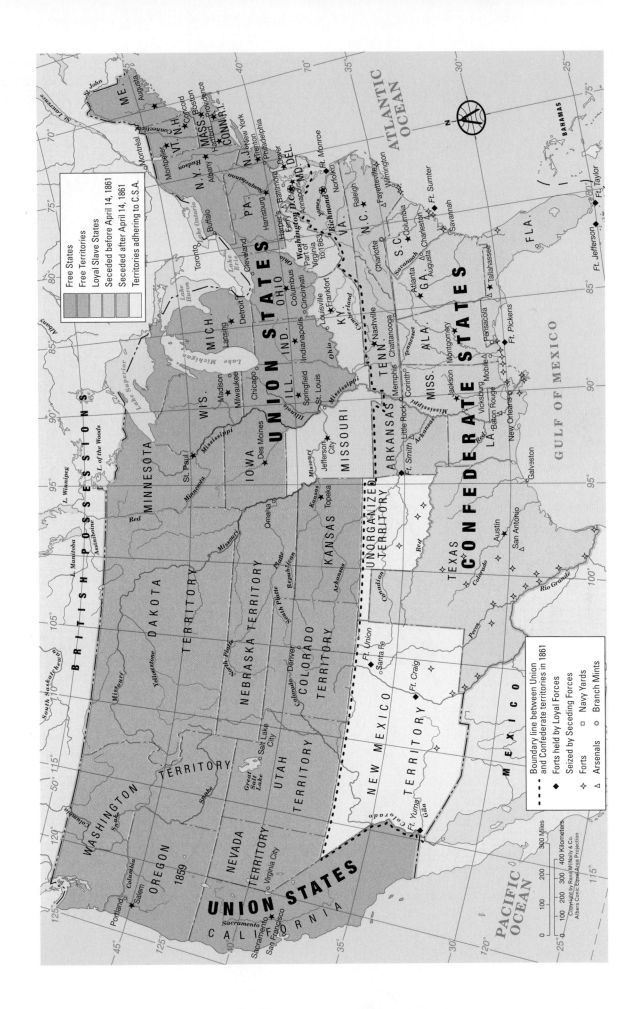

RAND McNALLY

**Secession 1860-1861**

Legend:
- Free States
- Free Territories
- Loyal Slave States
- Seceded before April 14, 1861
- Seceded after April 14, 1861
- Territories adhering to C.S.A.

- Boundary line between Union and Confederate territories in 1861
- ◆ Forts held by Loyal Forces
- ☆ Seized by Seceding Forces
- ✦ Forts
- △ Arsenals
- ◻ Navy Yards
- ○ Branch Mints

ATLANTIC OCEAN
PACIFIC OCEAN
GULF OF MEXICO
BRITISH POSSESSIONS
BAHAMAS
MEXICO

UNION STATES
CONFEDERATE STATES

Copyright by Rand McNally & Co.
Albers Conic Equal Area Projection

Scale: 0 100 200 300 Miles / 0 100 200 300 400 Kilometers

States and Territories labeled:
ME., N.H., VT., MASS., CONN., R.I., N.Y., PA., N.J., DEL., MD., VA., N.C., S.C., GA., FLA., ALA., MISS., TENN., ARKANSAS, LA., TEXAS, KY., OHIO, IND., ILL., MICH., WIS., MINNESOTA, IOWA, MISSOURI, KANSAS, NEBRASKA TERRITORY, DAKOTA TERRITORY, COLORADO TERRITORY, NEW MEXICO TERRITORY, UTAH TERRITORY, NEVADA TERRITORY, WASHINGTON TERRITORY, OREGON 1859, CALIFORNIA, UNORGANIZED TERRITORY

Cities: Augusta, Concord, Boston, Providence, Hartford, Montpelier, Montréal, New York, Trenton, Philadelphia, Dover, Baltimore, Annapolis, Washington D.C., Harper's Ferry, Richmond, Norfolk, Fort Monroe, Raleigh, Fayetteville, Wilmington, Charlotte, Columbia, Charleston, Savannah, Augusta, Atlanta, Montgomery, Tallahassee, Pensacola, Mobile, Jackson, Vicksburg, Baton Rouge, New Orleans, Galveston, San Antonio, Austin, Santa Fe, Ft. Union, Ft. Craig, Ft. Yuma, Salt Lake City, Virginia City, Sacramento, San Francisco, Salem, Portland, Columbia, Des Moines, St. Paul, Madison, Milwaukee, Chicago, Springfield, St. Louis, Jefferson City, Topeka, Omaha, Denver, Lansing, Detroit, Cleveland, Columbus, Cincinnati, Indianapolis, Louisville, Frankfort, Nashville, Chattanooga, Memphis, Corinth, Little Rock, Ft. Smith, Toronto, Buffalo, Harrisburg, Albany, Cumberland

Forts: Ft. Sumter, Ft. Pickens, Ft. Jefferson, Ft. Taylor, Ft. Monroe, Ft. Union, Ft. Craig, Ft. Yuma

Rivers and water: St. John, St. Lawrence, Hudson, Susquehanna, Lake Ontario, Lake Erie, Lake Huron, Lake Superior, Lake Michigan, Ohio, Mississippi, Missouri, Tennessee, Cumberland, Arkansas, Red, Platte, North Platte, South Platte, Republican, Kansas, Canadian, Pecos, Rio Grande, Colorado, Gila, Snake, Columbia, Yellowstone, L. Winnipeg, L. of the Woods, L. Manitoba, Great Salt Lake, Assiniboine, Saskatchewan, South Saskatchewan, Albany

Western Frontiers 1860–1890

**Legend**
- Settled by 1890
- Indian reservations 1880
- Railroads
- Trails west
- Extent of buffalo range 1870
- Cattle trails
- ✕ Mining
- ✳ Indian battle
- ✧ Incident of violence

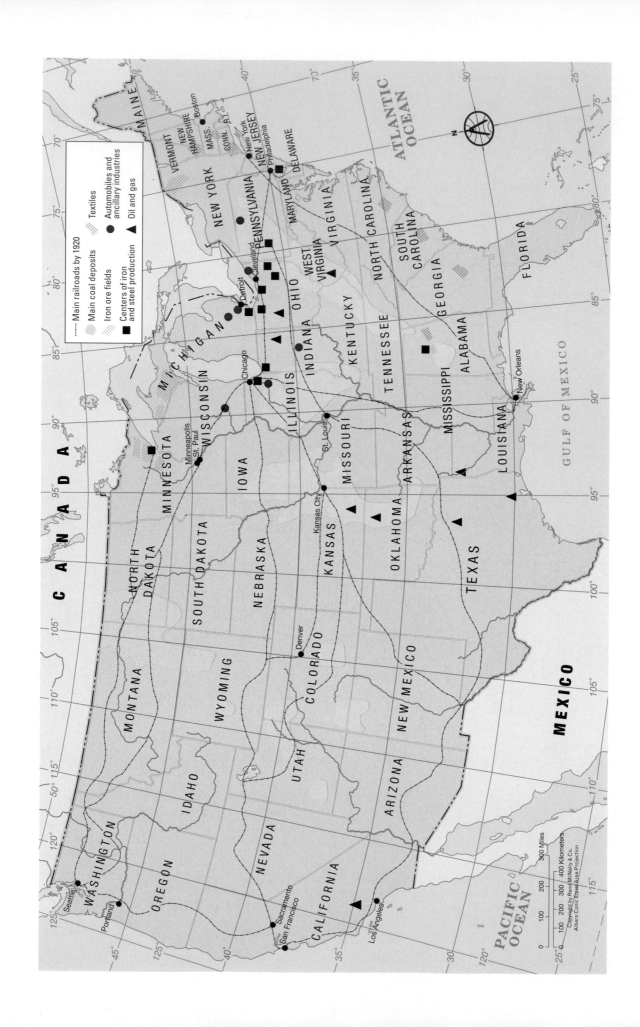

## U.S. Industries 1920

**Legend**

- Main railroads by 1920
- Main coal deposits
- Iron ore fields
- ■ Centers of iron and steel production
- Textiles
- ● Automobiles and ancillary industries
- ▲ Oil and gas

PACIFIC OCEAN

ATLANTIC OCEAN

GULF OF MEXICO

CANADA

MEXICO

MAINE
VERMONT
NEW HAMPSHIRE
MASS.
CONN. R.I.
NEW YORK
NEW JERSEY
PENNSYLVANIA
DELAWARE
MARYLAND
WEST VIRGINIA
VIRGINIA
OHIO
KENTUCKY
NORTH CAROLINA
SOUTH CAROLINA
TENNESSEE
GEORGIA
ALABAMA
MISSISSIPPI
FLORIDA
LOUISIANA
ARKANSAS
MISSOURI
INDIANA
ILLINOIS
MICHIGAN
WISCONSIN
IOWA
MINNESOTA
NORTH DAKOTA
SOUTH DAKOTA
NEBRASKA
KANSAS
OKLAHOMA
TEXAS
NEW MEXICO
COLORADO
WYOMING
MONTANA
IDAHO
UTAH
ARIZONA
NEVADA
CALIFORNIA
OREGON
WASHINGTON

Boston
New York
Philadelphia
Cleveland
Detroit
Chicago
St. Louis
Kansas City
Minneapolis
St. Paul
New Orleans
Denver
Seattle
Portland
Sacramento
San Francisco
Los Angeles

Copyright by Rand McNally & Co.
Albers Conic Equal Area Projection

0  100  200  300 Miles
0  100  200  300  400 Kilometers

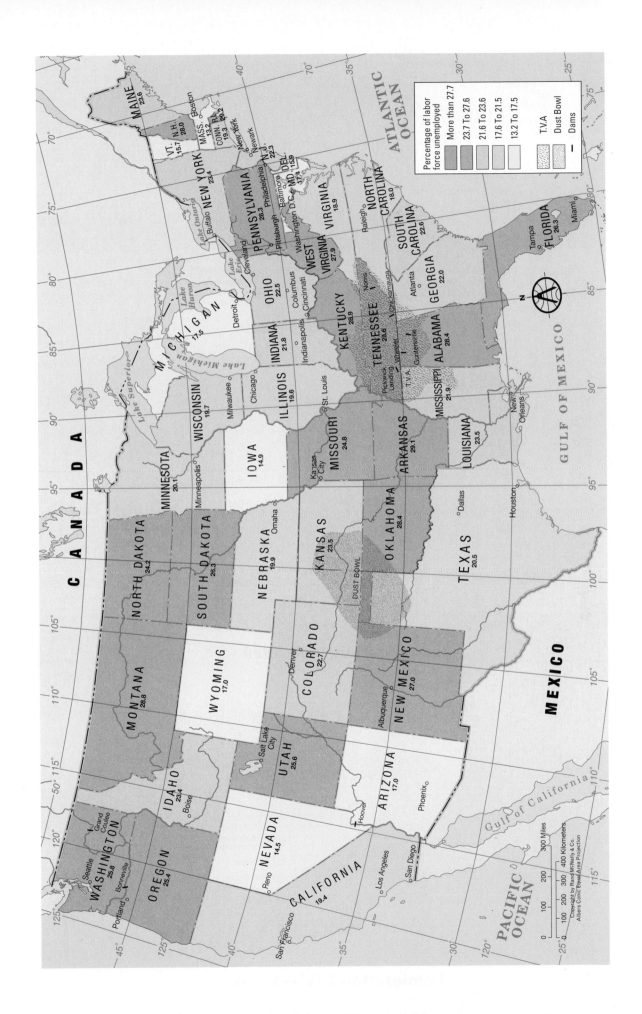

**Percentage of labor force unemployed**

- More than 27.7
- 23.7 To 27.6
- 21.6 To 23.6
- 17.6 To 21.5
- 13.2 To 17.5

- T.V.A
- Dust Bowl
- Dams

ATLANTIC OCEAN

GULF OF MEXICO

PACIFIC OCEAN

Gulf of California

MEXICO

CANADA

MAINE 23.6
VT. 15.7
N.H. 20.0
MASS. 13.2
CONN. R.I. 19.3 29.2
NEW YORK 23.4
PENNSYLVANIA 28.3
N.J. 22.3
DEL. 15.9
MD. 17.4
WEST VIRGINIA 27.9
VIRGINIA 18.9
NORTH CAROLINA 18.0
SOUTH CAROLINA 22.6
GEORGIA 22.0
FLORIDA 26.3
OHIO 22.5
MICHIGAN 17.5
INDIANA 21.8
KENTUCKY 28.9
TENNESSEE 23.6
ALABAMA 28.4
MISSISSIPPI 21.9
ILLINOIS 19.6
WISCONSIN 19.7
IOWA 14.9
MISSOURI 24.8
ARKANSAS 29.1
LOUISIANA 23.5
MINNESOTA 20.1
NORTH DAKOTA 24.2
SOUTH DAKOTA 26.3
NEBRASKA 19.9
KANSAS 23.5
OKLAHOMA 28.4
TEXAS 20.5
MONTANA 28.8
WYOMING 17.0
COLORADO 22.7
NEW MEXICO 27.0
IDAHO 23.4
UTAH 25.6
ARIZONA 17.0
NEVADA 14.5
WASHINGTON 25.8
OREGON 25.4
CALIFORNIA 19.4

Lake Superior
Lake Michigan
Lake Huron
Lake Erie
Lake Ontario

Boston
New York
Newark
Philadelphia
Washington D.C.
Baltimore
Pittsburgh
Raleigh
Atlanta
Tampa
Miami
Columbus
Cincinnati
Indianapolis
Detroit
Cleveland
Buffalo
Chicago
Milwaukee
St. Louis
Kansas City
Omaha
Minneapolis
Dallas
Houston
New Orleans
Denver
Albuquerque
Phoenix
Salt Lake City
Boise
Reno
San Francisco
Los Angeles
San Diego
Seattle
Portland
Grand Coulee
Bonneville
Hoover
Norris
Chickamauga
Wheeler
Guntersville
Pickwick Landing
T.V.A.

DUST BOWL

0 100 200 300 Miles
0 100 200 300 400 Kilometers
Albers Conic Equal Area Projection
Copyright by Rand McNally & Co.

RAND McNALLY

A35

## Immigration 1820–1870

4.3 million

2.5 million

UNITED STATES

Northwestern Europe
Central Europe

## Immigration 1880–1920

6.1 million
6.7 million
8.1 million

UNITED STATES

Northwestern Europe
Central Europe
Eastern and Southern Europe

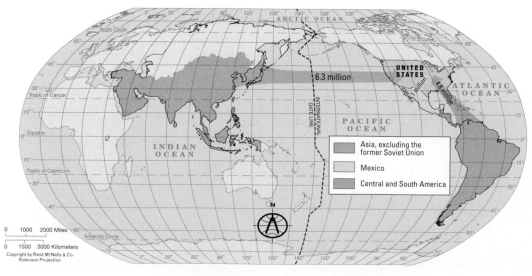

## Immigration 1960s–1990s

6.3 million
1 million
4.3 million

UNITED STATES

Asia, excluding the
former Soviet Union
Mexico
Central and South America

RAND McNALLY

Foreign born and first generation Americans;
by counties (source: *U.S. Decennial Census, 1910*)

Less than 10%
10% to 25%
25% to 50%
50% to 75%
75% and over

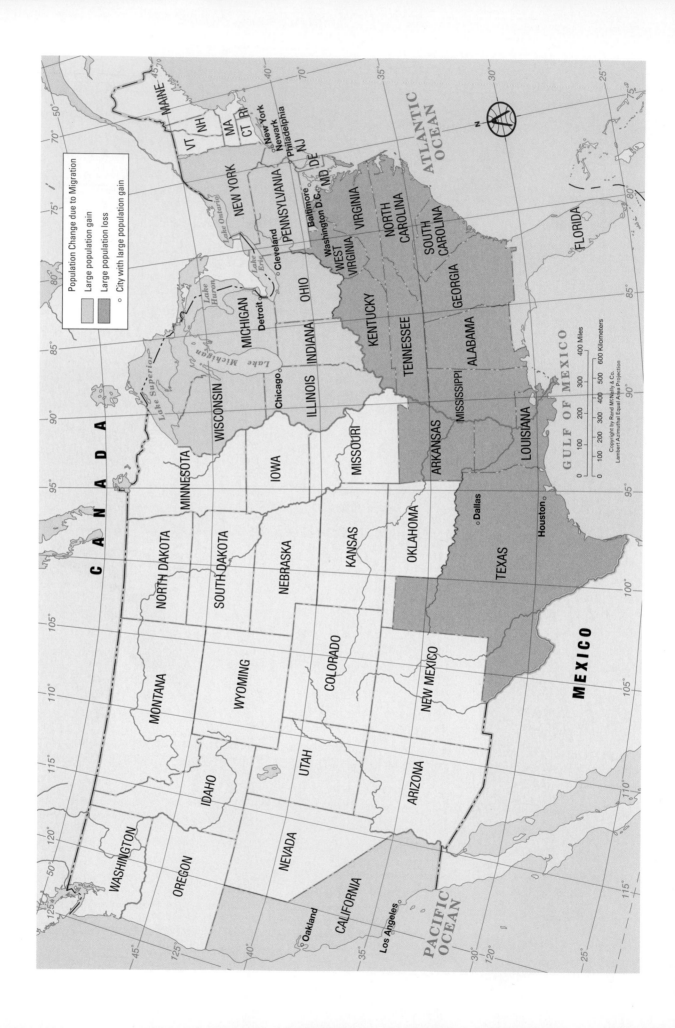

**Population Change due to Migration**

Large population gain

Large population loss

○ City with large population gain

GULF OF MEXICO

ATLANTIC OCEAN

PACIFIC OCEAN

MEXICO

CANADA

Copyright by Rand McNally & Co.
Lambert Azimuthal Equal Area Projection

**Per square mile**
*(per square kilometer)*

Under 2 *(Under 1)*
2-6 *(1-2)*
6-18 *(2-7)*
18-45 *(7-17)*
45-90 *(17-35)*
Over 90 *(Over 35)*
Urban Centers

N

ATLANTIC OCEAN

Boston
New York
Washington D.C.
Miami

Atlanta

Detroit

Chicago

St. Louis

Minneapolis

Kansas City

Dallas

Houston

GULF OF MEXICO

Denver

Seattle

San Francisco

Los Angeles

PACIFIC OCEAN

100    200    300 Miles
100 200 300 400 Kilometers
0

Copyright by Rand McNally & Co.
Lambert Azimuthal Equal Area Projection

Honolulu
PACIFIC OCEAN

Arctic Circle
Anchorage
PACIFIC OCEAN

RAND McNALLY

# The Landscape of America

The best place to begin your study of American history is with the geography of America. Geography is more than the study of the land and people. It also involves the relationship between people and their environment.

The United States is part of the North American continent. The United States ranks third in both total area and population in the world. It is filled with an incredible variety of physical features, natural resources, climatic conditions, and people. This handbook will help you to learn about these factors and to understand how they affected the development of the United States.

A timber company collects logs in the Northwest.

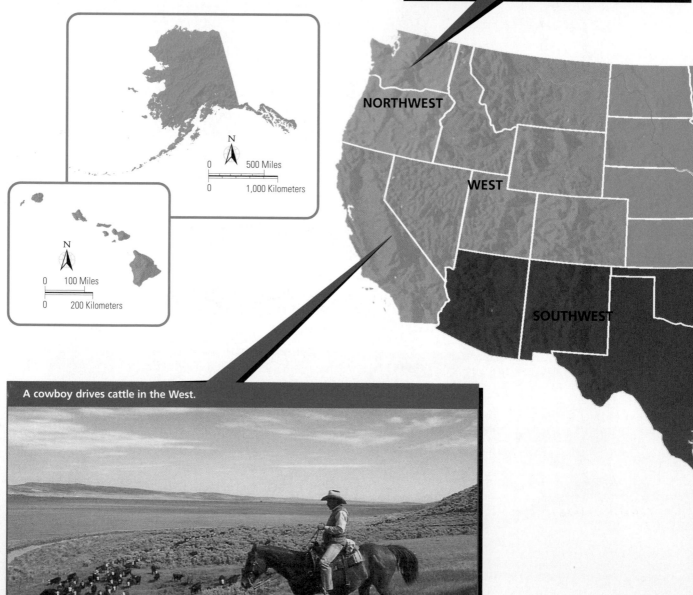

NORTHWEST

WEST

SOUTHWEST

N

0    500 Miles

0    1,000 Kilometers

N

0    100 Miles

0    200 Kilometers

A cowboy drives cattle in the West.

A combine harvests wheat in the Midwest.

## TABLE OF CONTENTS

Fishers haul their catch toward shore in the Northeast.

**NORTHEAST**

**MIDWEST**

**SOUTHEAST**

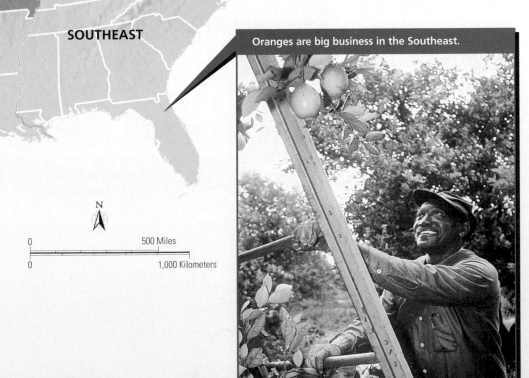
Oranges are big business in the Southeast.

N

| 0 | | 500 Miles |
| 0 | | 1,000 Kilometers |

*The Landscape of America* **3**

# Themes of Geography

One useful way to think about geography is in terms of major themes or ideas. These pages examine the five major themes of geography and show how they apply to Boston, Massachusetts. Recognizing and understanding these themes will help you to understand all the different aspects of geography.

## Location

"Where am I?" Your answer to this question is your *location*. One way to answer it is to use *absolute* location. That means you'll use the coordinates of longitude and latitude to give your answer (see page 8). For example, if you're in Boston, its absolute location is approximately 42° north latitude and 71° west longitude.

Like most people, however, you'll probably use *relative* location to answer the question. Relative location describes where a certain area is in relation to another area. For example, Boston lies in the northeast corner of the United States, next to the Atlantic Ocean.

**THINKING ABOUT GEOGRAPHY** What is the relative location of your school?

Boston is located on the shores of the Atlantic Ocean.

Boston has grown and changed since this 1722 map.

## Place

"What is Boston like?" *Place* can help you answer this question. Place refers to the physical and human factors that make one area different from another. Physical characteristics are natural features, such as physical setting, plants, animals, and weather. For example, Boston sits on a hilly peninsula.

Human characteristics include cultural diversity and the things people have made—including language, the arts, and architecture. For instance, Boston includes African Americans, as well as people of Irish, Italian, Chinese, and Hispanic ancestry.

**THINKING ABOUT GEOGRAPHY** What physical and human characteristics make where you live unique?

## Region

Geographers can't easily study the whole world at one time. So they break the world into regions. A *region* can be as large as a continent or as small as a neighborhood. A region has certain shared characteristics that set it apart. These characteristics might include political division, climate, language, or religion. Boston is part of the northeast region. It shares a climate—continental temperate—with the cities of New York and Philadelphia.

**THINKING ABOUT GEOGRAPHY** What characteristics does your city or town share with nearby cities or towns?

Airplanes from Boston's Logan International Airport move people and ideas around the globe.

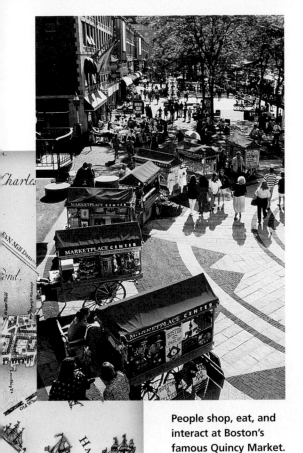

People shop, eat, and interact at Boston's famous Quincy Market.

## Movement

*Movement* refers to the shifting of people, goods, and ideas from one place to another. People constantly move in search of better places to live, and they trade goods with one another over great distances. Movement also causes ideas to travel from place to place. In recent years, technology has quickened the movement of ideas and goods.

Boston became known as the *Cradle of Liberty* because of the movement of ideas. The concepts of freedom and self-government that developed in Boston spread to the other colonies and helped to start the American Revolution.

**THINKING ABOUT GEOGRAPHY** What are some of the different ways you spread information and ideas?

## Human-Environment Interaction

*Human-environment interaction* refers to ways people interact with their environment, such as building a dam, cutting down a tree, or even sitting in the sun.

In Boston, human-environment interaction occurred when officials filled in swampy areas to make the city larger. In other ways, the environment has forced people to act. For example, people have had to invent ways to protect themselves from extreme weather and natural disasters.

**THINKING ABOUT GEOGRAPHY** What are ways that people in your city or town have changed their environment?

---

*Themes of Geography Assessment*

### 1. Main Ideas

**a.** What is the relative location of your home? (CST3)

**b.** What are three characteristics of the region in which you live? (CST3)

**c.** What are at least three ways in which you have recently interacted with the environment? (CST3)

### 2. Critical Thinking

**Forming and Supporting Opinions** Which aspect of geography described in these themes do you think has most affected your life? Explain. (HI1)

**THINK ABOUT**

• ways that you interact with your environment

• how you travel from place to place

# Map Basics

Geographers use many different types of maps, and these maps all have a variety of features. The map on the next page gives you information on a historical event—the War of 1812. But you can use it to learn about different parts of a map, too.

## Types of Maps

**Physical maps** Physical maps show mountains, hills, plains, rivers, lakes, oceans, and other physical features of an area.

**Political maps** Political maps show political units, such as countries, states, provinces, counties, districts, and towns. Each unit is normally shaded a different color, represented by a symbol, or shown with a different typeface.

**Historical maps** Historical maps illustrate such things as economic activity, migrations, battles, and changing national boundaries.

## Tools of Geography

The ancient Greeks developed some of the first ways to study geography. Today, geographers and map makers use advanced technology to study geography.

**GPS**
A Global Positioning System (GPS) is a navigational system that uses at least three satellites to identify a person's absolute location. It is also used to study other aspects of geography.

**Surveyors**
An American surveys the land in the 19th century.

**Computers**
Computers can create electronic maps in which geographers can quickly add or remove features that keep the map current. Computers can also be used to monitor environmental problems such as deforestation and global warming.

# Reading a Map

**A** **Lines** Lines indicate political boundaries, roads and highways, human movement, and rivers and other waterways.

**B** **Symbols** Symbols represent such items as capital cities, battle sites, or economic activities.

**C** **Labels** Labels are words or phrases that explain various items or activities on a map.

**D** **Compass Rose** A compass rose shows which way the directions north (N), south (S), east (E), and west (W) point on the map.

**E** **Scale** A scale shows the ratio between a unit of length on the map and a unit of distance on the earth. A typical one-inch scale indicates the number of miles and kilometers that length represents on the map.

**F** **Colors** Colors show a variety of information on a map, such as population density or the physical growth of a country.

**G** **Legend or Key** A legend or key lists and explains the symbols, lines, and colors on a map.

**H** **Lines of Longitude** These are imaginary, north-south lines that run around the globe.
**Lines of Latitude** These are imaginary, east-west lines that run around the globe. Together, latitude and longitude lines form a grid on a map or globe to indicate an area's absolute location.

**The War of 1812**

American forces
British forces
American victory
British victory
Fort

**Longitude Lines (Meridians)**

## Longitude lines

- are imaginary lines that run north to south around the globe and are known as meridians
- show the distance in degrees east or west of the prime meridian

The prime meridian is a longitude line that runs from the North Pole to the South Pole. It passes through Greenwich, England, and measures 0° longitude.

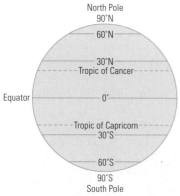

**Latitude Lines (Parallels)**

## Latitude lines

- are imaginary lines that run east to west around the globe and are known as parallels
- show distance in degrees north or south of the equator

The equator is a latitude line that circles the earth halfway between the North and South poles. It measures 0° latitude.

The tropics of Cancer and Capricorn are parallels that form the boundaries of the Tropics, a region that stays warm all year.

Latitude and longitude lines appear together on a map and allow you to pinpoint the absolute location of cities and other geographic features. You express this location through coordinates of intersecting lines. These are measured in degrees.

**Northern Hemisphere**

**Southern Hemisphere**

## Hemisphere

Hemisphere is a term for half the globe. The globe can be divided into Northern and Southern hemispheres (separated by the equator) or into Eastern and Western hemispheres. The United States is located in the Northern and Western hemispheres.

**Western Hemisphere**

**Eastern Hemisphere**

## Projections

A projection is a way of showing the curved surface of the earth on a flat map. Flat maps cannot show the size, shape, and direction of a globe all at once with total accuracy. As a result, all projections distort some aspect of the earth's surface. Some maps distort distances, while other maps distort angles. On the next page are four projections.

### Mercator Projection

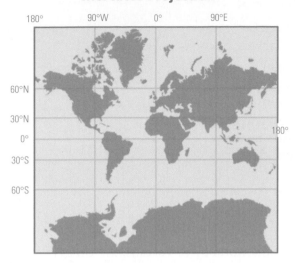

The Mercator projection shows most of the continents as they look on a globe. However, the projection stretches out the lands near the North and South poles. The Mercator is used for all kinds of navigation.

### Azimuthal Projection

An azimuthal projection shows the earth so that a straight line from the central point to any other point on the map gives the shortest distance between the two points. Size and shape of the continents are also distorted.

### Homolosine Projection

This projection shows the accurate shapes and sizes of the landmasses, but distances on the map are not correct.

### Robinson Projection

Textbook maps commonly use the Robinson projection. It shows the entire earth with nearly the true sizes and shapes of the continents and oceans. However, the shapes of the landforms near the poles appear flat.

---

## *Map Basics Assessment*

### 1. Main Ideas

**a.** What is the longitude and latitude of your city or town? (CST3)

**b.** What information is provided by the legend on the map on page 7? (CST3)

**c.** What is a projection? Compare and contrast Antarctica on the Mercator and the Robinson projections. (CST3)

### 2. Critical Thinking

**Making Inferences** Why do you think latitude and longitude are so important to sailors? (CST3)

**THINK ABOUT**
- the landmarks you use to find your way around
- the landmarks available to sailors on the ocean

# Physical Geography of the United States

From the heights of Mount McKinley (20,320 feet above sea level) in Alaska to the depths of Death Valley, California (282 feet below sea level), the geography of the United States is incredibly diverse. In between these extremes lie such varied features and conditions as scorching Arizona deserts, lush Oregon forests, freezing Vermont winters, and sunny Florida beaches. Physical geography involves all the natural features on the earth. This includes the land, resources, climate, and vegetation.

Flowers and brush cover the Coral Pink Sand Dunes in southern Utah.

## Land

Separated from much of the world by two oceans, the United States covers 3,717,796 square miles and spans the entire width of North America. To the west, Hawaii stretches the United States into the Pacific Ocean. To the north, Alaska extends the United States to the Arctic Circle. On the U.S. mainland, a huge central plain separates large mountains in the West and low mountains in the East. Plains make up almost half of the country, while mountains and plateaus make up a quarter each.

An abundance of lakes—Alaska alone has three million—and rivers also dot the landscape. Twenty percent of the United States is farmed, providing the country with a steady food supply. Urban areas cover only about two percent of the nation. Refer to the map on the next page for a complete look at the U.S. landscape.

**THINKING ABOUT GEOGRAPHY** What is the land like around your city or state?

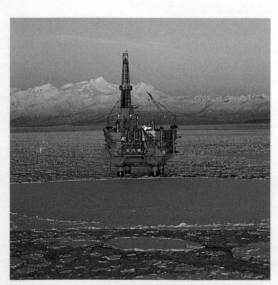

Oil drilled from Alaska helps power the nation's planes, trains, cars, and factories.

## Resources

The United States has a variety of natural resources. Vast amounts of coal, oil, and natural gas lie underneath American soil. Valuable deposits of lead, zinc, uranium, gold, and silver also exist. These resources have helped the United States become the world's leading industrial nation—producing nearly 21 percent of the world's goods and services.

These resources have also helped the United States become both the world's largest producer of energy (natural gas, oil, coal, nuclear power, and electricity) and the world's largest consumer of it. Other natural resources include the Great Lakes, which are shared with Canada. They contain about 20 percent of the world's total supply of fresh surface water. Refer to the map on the next page to examine the nation's natural resources.

**THINKING ABOUT GEOGRAPHY** What are the different natural resources that you and your family use in your daily lives?

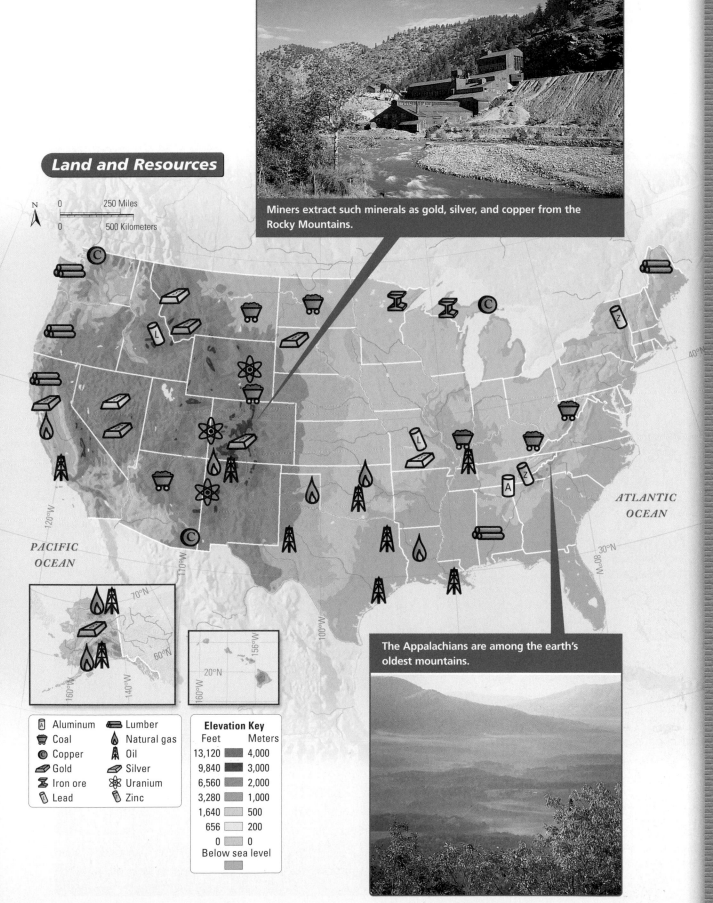

## Land and Resources

Miners extract such minerals as gold, silver, and copper from the Rocky Mountains.

The Appalachians are among the earth's oldest mountains.

PACIFIC OCEAN

ATLANTIC OCEAN

| | |
|---|---|
| 🅰 Aluminum | 🪵 Lumber |
| 🔥 Coal | 🔥 Natural gas |
| Ⓒ Copper | 🛢 Oil |
| 🪙 Gold | 🪙 Silver |
| ⚒ Iron ore | ⚛ Uranium |
| 🪙 Lead | 🧪 Zinc |

**Elevation Key**

| Feet | | Meters |
|---|---|---|
| 13,120 | | 4,000 |
| 9,840 | | 3,000 |
| 6,560 | | 2,000 |
| 3,280 | | 1,000 |
| 1,640 | | 500 |
| 656 | | 200 |
| 0 | | 0 |
| Below sea level | | |

*Physical Geography of the United States* **11**

## Climate

People brave the harsh winters in the continental temperate climate of the upper Midwest.

Mount Washington in New Hampshire has experienced one of the world's lowest recorded wind chills of over −100° F, one of the world's highest wind speeds at 231 miles per hour, and a three-day snow fall of 8 feet.

**Marine**
(mild year-round)

**Highland**
(cool year-round)

**Mediterranean**
(warm summers, and rainy, mild winters)

**Steppe**
(hot summers, cold winters, dry)

**Desert**
(very hot summers, with cold nights, very dry)

**Continental temperate**
(mild-to-hot summers, cold winters)

**Humid subtropical**
(hot summers, mild winters, rainy)

**Tropical**
(very hot summers, warm winters)

**Tundra**
(bitterly cold winters, freezing summers)

**Subarctic**
(very cold winters, cold summers)

Sequoia National Park in California contains the world's largest tree, the General Sherman, a giant sequoia. It measures 103 feet around at its base and is 275 feet high. It weighs about 6,167 tons—over 12 million pounds!

Rain and humidity nourish the lush forests in the humid subtropical climate of the Southeast.

CANADA

PACIFIC OCEAN

ATLANTIC OCEAN

Gulf of Mexico

Great Lakes

WASH.
OREGON
IDAHO
MONTANA
N. DAK.
S. DAK.
WYO.
NEV.
CALIF.
UTAH
COLO.
ARIZ.
N. MEX.
NEBR.
KANS.
OKLA.
TEXAS
MINN.
IOWA
MO.
ARK.
LA.
WIS.
ILL.
MICH.
IND.
OHIO
KY.
TENN.
MISS.
ALA.
GA.
W. VA.
VA.
N.C.
S.C.
FLA.
PA.
N.Y.
VT.
MAINE
N.H.
MASS.
R.I.
CONN.
N.J.
DEL.
MD.

ALASKA

HAWAII

N    0        500 Miles

0        1,000 Kilometers

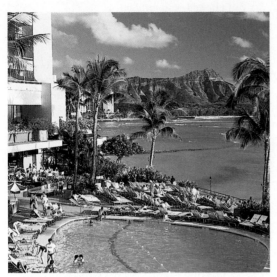

Tourists and residents bask in the sunshine of Waikiki Beach in Hawaii.

# Climate

The United States contains a variety of climates. For example, the mean temperature in January in Miami, Florida, is 67° F, while it is 11° F in Minneapolis, Minnesota. Most of the United States experiences a continental climate, or distinct change of seasons. Some regional climatic differences include hot and humid summers in the Southeast versus hot and dry summers in the Southwest. Harsh winters and heavy snow can blanket parts of the Midwest, the Northeast, and the higher elevations of the West and Northwest. Refer to the map on the previous page to see the nation's climatic regions.

Human activities have affected the climate, too. For example, pollution from cars and factories can affect local weather conditions and may be contributing to a dangerous rise in the earth's temperature.

**THINKING ABOUT GEOGRAPHY** How would you describe the climate where you live?

This mountainside burns with the autumn foliage of New Hampshire.

# Vegetation

Between 20,000 and 25,000 species and subspecies of plants and vegetation grow in the United States—including over 1,000 different kinds of trees. Climate often dictates the type of vegetation found in a region. For instance, cold autumns in the Northeast contribute to the brilliantly colored autumn leaves. Rain nourishes the forests in the Northwest and Southeast. The central plains, where rainfall is less heavy, are covered by grass. Cactus plants thrive in the dry southwestern deserts.

Along with natural vegetation, climate dictates the nation's variety of planted crops. For example, temperate weather in the Midwest helps wheat to grow, while warm weather nourishes citrus fruit in Florida and California.

**THINKING ABOUT GEOGRAPHY** What kinds of trees or plants grow in your region?

---

## Physical Geography Assessment

### 1. Main Ideas

**a.** What are the different aspects of physical geography? (CST3)

**b.** Which state contains the largest variety of climates? (CST3)

**c.** What two states contain most of the country's oil resources? (CST3)

### 2. Critical Thinking

**Drawing Conclusions** What do you think are the advantages of living in a country with diverse physical geography? (CST3)

**THINK ABOUT**

• the different resources available in your region
• the variety of recreational activities in your region

# Geographic Dictionary

**volcano**
an opening in the earth, usually raised, through which gasses and lava escape from the earth's interior

**strait**
a narrow strip of water connecting two large bodies of water

**cape**
a pointed piece of land extending into an ocean or lake

**sea level**
level of the ocean's surface, used as a reference point when measuring the height or depth of the earth's surface

**bay**
part of an ocean or lake partially enclosed by land

**harbor**
a sheltered area of water, deep enough for docking ships

**(river) mouth**
the place where a river flows into a lake or ocean

**marsh**
soft, wet, low-lying, grassy land that serves as a transition between water and land

**island**
a body of land surrounded by water

**flood plain**
flat land near the edges of rivers formed by mud and silt deposited by floods

**delta**
a triangular area of land formed from deposits at the mouth of a river

**swamp**
an area of land that is saturated by water

**desert**
a dry area where few plants grow

**butte**
a raised, flat area of land with steep cliffs, smaller than a mesa

**oasis**
a spot of fertile land in a desert, fed by water from wells or underground springs

**prairie**
a large, level area
of grassland with
few or no trees

**steppe**
a wide, treeless plain

**mountain**
natural elevation of the earth's
surface with steep sides and
greater height than a hill

**valley**
low land between hills or
mountains

**glacier**
a large ice mass that
moves slowly down a
mountain or over land

**mesa**
a wide, flat-topped mountain with
steep sides, larger than a butte

**cataract**
a large, powerful
waterfall

**canyon**
a narrow, deep valley
with steep sides

**cliff**
the steep, almost vertical edge
of a hill, mountain, or plain

**plateau**
a broad, flat area of
land higher than the
surrounding land

15

# Human Geography of the United States

Human geography focuses on people's relationships with each other and the surrounding environment. It includes two main themes of geography: human-environment interaction and movement. The following pages will help you to better understand the link between people and geography.

## Humans Adapt to Their Surroundings

Humans have always adapted to their environment. For example, in North America, many Native American tribes burned forest patches to create grazing area to attract animals and to clear area for farmland. In addition, Americans have adapted to their environment by building numerous dams, bridges, and tunnels. More recently, scientists and engineers have been developing building materials that will better withstand the earthquakes that occasionally strike California.

**THINKING ABOUT GEOGRAPHY** What are some of the ways in which you interact with your environment on a daily basis?

Early Americans of the Southwest protected themselves from the weather by building cliff dwellings.

The Hoover Dam, located on the Colorado River between Arizona and Nevada, provides electricity for Arizona, Nevada, and Southern California.

An oil spill from the ship *Exxon Valdez* harmed wildlife, such as this bird, in Prince William Sound, Alaska, in 1989.

## Humans Affect the Environment

When humans interact with the environment, sometimes nature suffers. In the United States, for example, major oil leaks or spills occur each year—fouling shorelines and harming wildlife. Building suburbs and strip malls has also destroyed forests, farmland, and valuable wetlands.

**THINKING ABOUT GEOGRAPHY** What are some of the environmental problems in your city or town?

### Destruction of Original Forests

*1620*

*1850*

*1926*

These maps show that, over the years, human beings have nearly cut down all the original forests in the United States. Each dot represents 25,000 acres.

Children plant trees along a Chicago expressway.

## Preserving and Restoring

Americans—as well as people all over the world—have been working hard to balance economic progress with conservation. For example, car companies in the United States and around the world are working to develop pollution-free vehicles. In 1994, the average American family of four recycled around 1,100 pounds of waste. And, in the 1990s, Americans have planted more than two million acres of new trees each year.

**THINKING ABOUT GEOGRAPHY** What are some of the ways in which you help the environment?

# Human Movement

In prehistoric times, people roamed the earth in search of food. Today in the United States, people move from place to place for many different reasons. Among them are cost of living, job availability, and climate. Since the 1970s, many Americans—as well as many new immigrants—moved to the Sunbelt. This region runs through the southern United States from Virginia to California. Between 1950 and 1990, that region's population soared from 52 million to 118 million.

**THINKING ABOUT GEOGRAPHY** Has your family ever moved? If so, what were some of the reasons?

This map shows human movement in the 1970s. The information below explains some of the results of this movement in the 1990s.

**Americans on the Move,** *1970s*

NORTHWEST

WEST

CALIFORNIA

**A**

•Phoenix

75,000

472,000

MIDWEST

SOUTHWEST

790,000

**B**

TEXAS

311,000

NORTHEAST
N.Y.

67,000

964,000

**C**

SOUTHEAST

**D**

FLORIDA

0       500 Miles
0       1,000 Kilometers

New home developments cover
the desert in Las Vegas, Nevada.

**A** By 1996, the Phoenix-Mesa metropolitan area reached a population of 2.75 million, more than the number of people living in the entire state in 1980.

**B** Between 1990 and 1994, Texas overtook New York as the nation's second most populous state, behind California.

**C** One of the nation's fastest growing areas was the Southeast, where population growth ranged from six to nine percent between 1990 and 1994. Jobs grew in the area by 14 percent.

**D** Florida's population is growing so much that it could become as populous as New York state by around 2020.

In the late 19th century, millions of immigrants arrived on the shores of the United States.

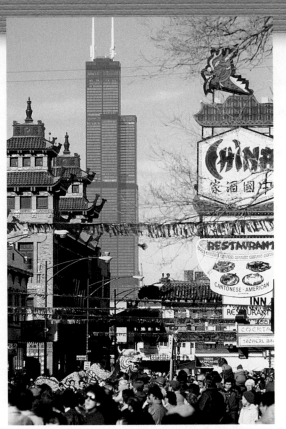

The Sears Tower overlooks Chinatown in Chicago.

## Humans Spread Ideas and Information

Throughout U.S. history, people from all over the world have come to the United States. They have brought with them food, music, language, technology, and other aspects of their culture. As a result, the United States is one of the most culturally rich and diverse nations in the world. Look around your town or city. You'll probably notice different people, languages, and foods.

Today, the spreading of ideas and customs does not rely solely on human movement. Technology—from the Internet to television to satellites—spreads ideas and information throughout the world faster than ever. This has created an ever-growing, interconnected world. As the 21st century opens, human geography will continue to play a key role in shaping the United States and the world.

**THINKING ABOUT GEOGRAPHY** How have computers and the Internet affected your life?

---

### *Human Geography Assessment*

#### 1. Main Ideas

**a.** What are some of the ways that people have helped to restore the environment? (CST3)

**b.** What are some of the ways that residents of your region have successfully modified their landscape? (CST3)

**c.** What are some of the reasons that people move from place to place? (CST3)

#### 2. Critical Thinking

**Recognizing Effects** In what ways has technology helped bring people in the world together? (CST3)

**THINK ABOUT**

• the different ways in which people communicate today

• the speed in which people today can communicate over long distances

# GEOGRAPHY HANDBOOK ASSESSMENT

## TERMS

Briefly explain the significance of each of the following.

1. physical map
2. political map
3. longitude
4. latitude
5. hemisphere
6. projection
7. flood plain
8. sea level
9. human geography
10. human movement

## REVIEW QUESTIONS

### Themes of Geography (pages 4–5)

1. What is the difference between *absolute* location and *relative* location? (CST3)
2. What is meant by the theme of place? (CST3)
3. What are the themes of movement and human-environment interaction? (CST3)

### Map Basics (pages 6–9)

4. What do you think are some of the benefits of using technology to study geography? (CST3)
5. What are the three major kinds of maps? (CST3)
6. What are latitude and longitude lines? (CST3)

### Physical Geography (pages 10–13)

7. How have the natural resources in the United States helped its economic development? (HI2)
8. What are the different climates within the United States? (CST3)

### Human Geography (pages 16–19)

9. How is human geography different from physical geography? (CST3)
10. What aspects of human geography might cause people to move? (HI2)

## CRITICAL THINKING

1. **Forming and Supporting Opinions** Which of the five themes of geography do you think has had the most impact on history? Why? (HI2)
2. **Analyzing Causes** How do the climate and natural resources of an area affect its economy? (HI6)
3. **Drawing Conclusions** How have computers helped geographers make more accurate maps? (CST3)
4. **Making Inferences** Why do you think the Mercator projection is used for all types of navigation? (HI2)
5. **Recognizing Effects** How does a diverse landscape help or hurt the economy of an area? (HI2)

## GEOGRAPHY SKILLS

### 1. INTERPRETING MAPS: Movement (CST3)

**Basic Map Elements**

a. What region of the United States is shown?
b. Compare the number of teams on the 1987 map and the 2000 map. How many more teams are on the 2000 map?

**Interpreting the Map**

c. What geographic theme(s) is most responsible for the increase in sports teams in this region?
d. According to the map, which sport enjoyed the biggest surge in popularity in this region?

**Major League Sports in Southeast Cities**

20

# GEOGRAPHY SKILLS

## 2. INTERPRETING MAPS: Region

Study the map and then answer the questions. (CST3)

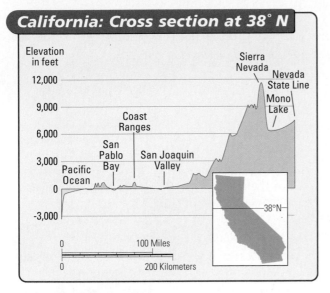

### California: Cross section at 38° N

Elevation in feet

Pacific Ocean, San Pablo Bay, Coast Ranges, San Joaquin Valley, Sierra Nevada, Nevada State Line, Mono Lake

38°N

0 — 100 Miles
0 — 200 Kilometers

### Basic Map Elements

a. What are the different landforms on the map?

### Interpreting the Map

b. What is the level of the San Joaquin Valley? How many miles does it take to get from there to the highest point in California at the 38th parallel?

## 3. INTERPRETING PRIMARY SOURCES

In 1803, President Thomas Jefferson appointed Meriwether Lewis to explore the lands of the Louisiana Purchase. Jefferson gave him these instructions: (REP4)

> The object of your mission is to explore the Missouri river . . . by its course & communication with the waters of the Pacific Ocean, may offer the most direct & practicable water communication across this continent, for the purposes of commerce. . . .
>   Other objects worthy of notice will be the soil & face of the country, its growth & vegetable productions . . . the mineral productions of every kind. . . . climate as characterized by the thermometer . . . the dates at which particular plants put forth or lose their flowers, or leaf, times of appearance of particular birds, reptiles, or insects.
>
> **Thomas Jefferson,** quoted in *The Journals of Lewis and Clark*

a. What was Jefferson expecting to find in the West?

b. Why might the president want to know about the land's soil and vegetable production?

c. What aspect of human geography might be of interest to the president?

# ALTERNATIVE ASSESSMENT

## 1. INTERDISCIPLINARY ACTIVITY: Math

**Plotting Latitude and Longitude** On a piece of graph paper, sketch a map of the United States. Be sure to draw in state boundaries, too. Then, using an atlas as a reference, draw and mark the latitude and longitude lines that cross the nation at five degree intervals. Plot the estimated longitude and latitude location of your city or town. Determine at which degrees the lines intersect where you live. Repeat this exercise for at least five different places you have visited or would like to visit within the United States. (CST3)

## 2. COOPERATIVE LEARNING ACTIVITY

**Making a Map** How well do you know the neighborhood around your school? Form groups of three to four students. Then work together to draw a map of the neighborhood around your school. Include:

- streets
- residences
- stores
- geographic features
- important landmarks

The map should be accurate but not too cluttered with unnecessary details. Compare your group's map with those of the other groups in the class. (CST3)

## 3. TECHNOLOGY ACTIVITY

**Writing Directions** Several Internet sites provide detailed maps of the United States. They also provide driving directions to most places in the country.

- Locate one of these map sites on the Internet.
- Think of a place in the United States that you would like to visit.
- Work with the computer to find the best route for reaching it.

Write out clear directions as well as the total mileage of your trip. Also, note the type of map it is and the features it highlights. (CST3)

For more important geography sites . . .

**INTERNET ACTIVITY**
CLASSZONE.COM

## 4. HISTORY PORTFOLIO

Review your alternative assessment activities. Use comments made by your teacher or classmates to improve your work.

Additional Test Practice, pp. S1–S33

**TEST PRACTICE**
CLASSZONE.COM

# Three Worlds Meet

The ruins of the Anasazi Cliff Palace, in modern-day Colorado, stand as a reminder of the Native American societies that existed before the arrival of Europeans.

"The story of my people and the story of this place are one single story."

—*Taos Pueblo man*

# The World in 1500

## Beginnings–1500

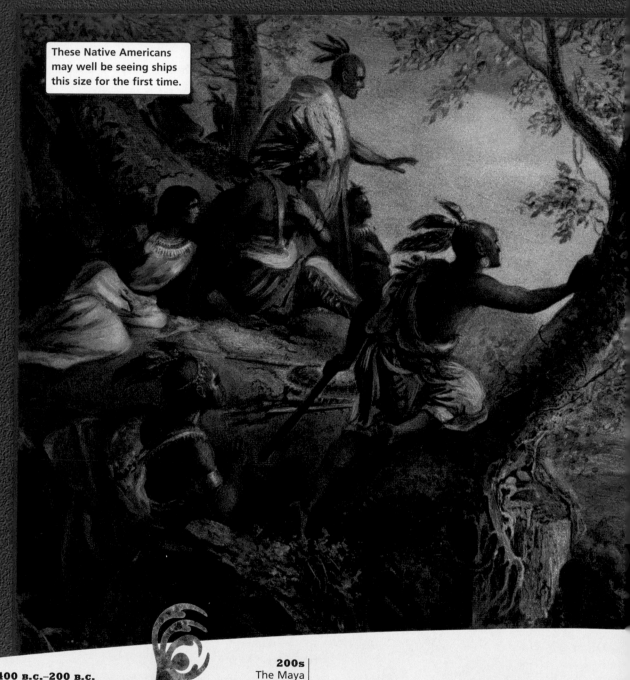

These Native Americans may well be seeing ships this size for the first time.

**400 B.C.–200 B.C.**
Hopewell culture, which created this mica birdclaw, flourishes in the Midwest.

**200s**
The Maya are using hieroglyphic writing.

Americas
World

200 B.C.

**About 6 B.C.**
Jesus of Nazareth is born. His teachings become the basis for Christianity.

**476**
Western Roman Empire ends. Over time, Europe splits into small kingdoms.

You are a Native American living on the northeastern coast of North America. One day you see a giant boat topped by strange white cloths. Men climb into smaller boats and row toward you. You have never seen men like this. They have pale skin and wear heavy, colorful clothing. You wonder what will happen when they land.

# What happens when different societies meet?

## What Do You Think?

- What can different societies learn from each other?
- What might they gain from each other?
- What positive and negative things might happen when they meet?

### RESEARCH LINKS
CLASSZONE.COM

Visit the Chapter 1 links for more information about the first Americans or European voyagers.

This European ship spent weeks at sea to reach the coast of North America.

**800s**
Maize is widely grown in what is now the utheastern United States.

**1000**
Viking Leif Erikson reaches what is now Newfoundland.

**1100s**
The city of Cahokia flourishes in what is now Illinois.

**1200s**
The Aztecs conquer much of central Mexico.

**1492**
The European explorer Columbus lands in the Americas.

A.D. 1500

**arly 600s**
uhammad begins e religion of Islam Arabia.

**1096**
Europeans begin the Crusades to capture the Holy Land from followers of Islam.

**1324**
Mansa Musa, emperor of Mali, travels to Islam's holy city. Word of his gold spreads to Europe.

*The World in 1500* **25**

# Reading Strategy: Categorizing Information

## What Do You Know?

What do you know about the history of the Americas, West Africa, and Europe? How advanced must a society be to build large structures?

### Think About

- what you know about other societies, such as Egypt, that built large structures
- what you've read in books
- your responses to the Interact with History about when different societies meet (see page 25)

## What Do You Want to Know?

What questions do you have about the past societies of the Americas, West Africa, and Europe? What do you want to know about how they met? Record those questions in your notebook before you read the chapter.

## Categorizing Information

One way to make better sense of what you read is to categorize. To categorize is to sort information into groups. The chart below will help you record information about the societies of the Americas, West Africa, and Europe. As you read, look for information relating to the categories of trade, technology, religion, and art. Record that information on your chart.

 See Skillbuilder Handbook, page R6.

 Taking Notes

|  | Trade | Technology | Religion | Art |
|---|---|---|---|---|
| **AMERICAS** |  |  |  |  |
| **WEST AFRICA** |  |  |  |  |
| **EUROPE** |  |  |  |  |

# Crossing to the Americas

| MAIN IDEA | WHY IT MATTERS NOW | TERMS & NAMES |
|---|---|---|
| Ancient peoples came from Asia to the Americas and over time developed complex civilizations. | Archaeologists and other scientists continue to make new discoveries about these ancient people. | archaeologist     domestication<br>artifact     civilization<br>migrate     irrigation<br>culture     Mound Builders |

## ONE AMERICAN'S STORY

For many years, Solveig Turpin has searched Texas for paintings that ancient people drew on rock walls. Turpin is an **archaeologist**. That is a scientist who studies the human past by examining the things people left behind. Turpin believes that one of the paintings she found shows a religious leader who turned himself into a panther.

### A VOICE FROM THE PAST

This is the Shaman [religious leader] who transforms into the largest and most powerful animal here. . . . I like to call [the shamans] supramen because they were over everything.

**Solveig Turpin,** quoted in *In Search of Ancient North America*

Archaeologists make theories about the past based on what they learn from bones and artifacts. **Artifacts** are tools and other objects that humans made. Section 1 discusses some theories about early Americans.

## The First People in America

As many societies do, many Native Americans have stories explaining the origin of their people. Some believe the gods created their ancestors. Others believe their ancestors were born of Mother Earth. In contrast, scientists think that the first Americans **migrated**, or moved, here from Asia. But scientists disagree about how and when this move took place.

Some ancient people may have crossed a land bridge that joined Asia and North America during the last Ice Age. The Ice Age was a time of extreme cold that lasted for thousands of years. Glaciers trapped so much water that ocean levels dropped. A bridge of land, now called Beringia, appeared where the Bering Strait is now. (See map, page 28.) When the earth grew warm again, the glaciers melted and flooded Beringia. Some scientists who hold this theory believe the earliest Americans arrived

**CALIFORNIA STANDARDS**

**CST1** Students explain how major events are related to one another in time.

**CST3** Students use a variety of maps and documents to identify physical and cultural features of neighborhoods, cities, states, and countries and to explain the historical migration of people, expansion and disintegration of empires, and the growth of economic systems.

**REP3** Students distinguish relevant information, essential from incidental information, and verifiable from unverifiable information in historical narratives and stories.

**REP4** Students assess the credibility of primary and secondary sources and draw sound conclusions from them.

**HI1** Students explain the central issues and problems from the past, placing people and events in a matrix of time and place.

### Taking Notes

Use your chart to take notes about the Americas.

| | Trade | |
|---|---|---|
| AMERICAS | | |
| WEST AFRICA | | |
| EUROPE | | |

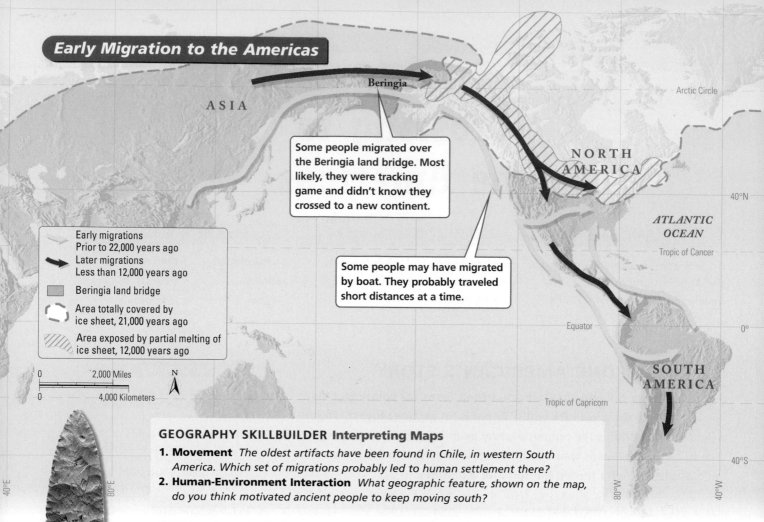

## Early Migration to the Americas

Some people migrated over the Beringia land bridge. Most likely, they were tracking game and didn't know they crossed to a new continent.

Some people may have migrated by boat. They probably traveled short distances at a time.

Early migrations
Prior to 22,000 years ago
Later migrations
Less than 12,000 years ago
Beringia land bridge
Area totally covered by ice sheet, 21,000 years ago
Area exposed by partial melting of ice sheet, 12,000 years ago

0    2,000 Miles
0    4,000 Kilometers

N

ASIA
Beringia
NORTH AMERICA
ATLANTIC OCEAN
SOUTH AMERICA
Arctic Circle
Tropic of Cancer
Equator
Tropic of Capricorn
40°N
0°
40°S

**GEOGRAPHY SKILLBUILDER Interpreting Maps**
1. **Movement** The oldest artifacts have been found in Chile, in western South America. Which set of migrations probably led to human settlement there?
2. **Human-Environment Interaction** What geographic feature, shown on the map, do you think motivated ancient people to keep moving south?

12,000 years ago. Other scientists believe humans came to the Americas much earlier. They have found artifacts in South America that tests show to be 30,000 years old. These scientists believe that people came to the Americas by many routes, over thousands of years. Some came by boat, sailing short distances from island to island. This theory may also change as scientists find more evidence of ancient Americans.

Ancient hunters used spear points such as this one, which is about 10,000 years old.

## Agriculture Leads to Civilization

A **culture** is a way of life shared by people with similar arts, beliefs, and customs. The first Americans lived in hunting and gathering cultures. They hunted small animals, such as rabbits, and large animals, such as the woolly mammoth. They gathered wild seeds, nuts, and berries.

In time, people started to plant the seeds they found. This was the beginning of agriculture. About 5,000 years ago, humans began domestication. **Domestication** is the practice of breeding plants or taming animals to meet human needs. By trial and error, people in central Mexico learned which seeds grew the best crops. By selecting the right seeds, they improved the quality of maize, or corn, until its ears were large. Dried and stored for future use, corn became a main food source.

Knowledge of agriculture spread throughout the Americas. Having a stable food supply changed the way people lived. Once they no longer had to travel to find food, they built permanent villages. Farmers were able to produce large harvests, so that fewer people needed to farm.

Vocabulary
woolly mammoth: a hairy ancestor of the elephant, now extinct

*Reading* **History**

**A. Drawing Conclusions** Why would a culture need to learn agriculture before it could develop a civilization?

Some people began to practice other crafts, such as weaving or making pots. A few people became religious leaders.

Slowly, some cultures grew complex and became civilizations. A **civilization** has five features: (1) cities that are centers of trade, (2) specialized jobs for different people, (3) organized forms of government and religion, (4) a system of record keeping, and (5) advanced tools.

## Early Mesoamerican Civilizations

About 1200 B.C., an advanced civilization arose in Mesoamerica, a region that stretches from central Mexico to present-day Nicaragua. For 800 years, a people called the Olmec thrived along the Gulf of Mexico. The Olmec set up a network of trade routes and constructed earthen mounds shaped like pyramids. They built large, busy cities like La Venta.

*A VOICE FROM THE PAST*

La Venta was not just an empty ceremonial spot visited by Olmec priests and nobles but a prosperous community of fishers, farmers, traders, and specialists, such as the artisans and the sculptors.

**Rebecca González,** quoted in "New Light on the Olmec," *National Geographic*

Around 400 B.C., the Olmec abandoned La Venta and other cities. Scientists don't know why. By then, Olmec culture had spread along trade routes and influenced others. Later people in Mesoamerica adapted Olmec religious practices and carved designs inspired by Olmec art.

By A.D. 250, about 650 years after the Olmec vanished, the Maya had developed a great civilization. Their cities were in southern Mexico and Guatemala, where they built pyramid mounds topped by temples. From artifacts, archaeologists know that the Maya had an accurate yearly calendar. They were the first people in the Americas to create a number system using zero. Their written language used picture symbols.

By 900, the Maya had abandoned many of their cities. Scientists think that revolts, disease, or crop failures may have caused their society to fail.

**Background**
Mathematicians in India also developed the idea of using a symbol for zero. Traders later carried the idea from Asia to Europe.

## The Hohokam and the Anasazi

During the Mayan period, an agricultural people inhabited the American Southwest. The Hohokam lived in what is now Arizona from about 300 B.C. to A.D. 1400. That desert region has little rain, so farming is difficult. But the Hohokam altered their dry environment. They dug hundreds of miles of canals to carry river water to their crops. The practice of bringing water to crops is called **irrigation.**

The Hohokam raised corn, beans, and squash. They also gathered wild plants and hunted animals. They traded widely—with people in Mexico, the Southwest, and California. Hohokam pottery and religious practices show the influence of Mesoamerican cultures, which they learned about through trade.

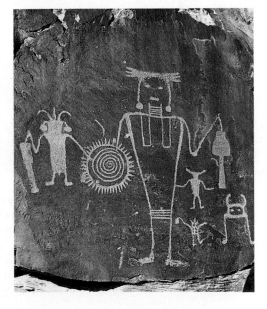

Ancient peoples of the American Southwest used images like this to communicate with each other. Such images are called petroglyphs.

# The Mound Builders

During the 1700s, Europeans discovered several mysterious earthen mounds in what is now the American Southeast and Midwest. They believed a lost civilization had built the mounds. Historians now know that different Native American groups, known as the Mound Builders, built these structures. The builders may have used the mounds for burial tombs, as a tribute to their gods, or for some other religious purpose. One famous mound is the Great Serpent Mound in present-day Ohio. The Adena, Fort Ancient, or Hopewell cultures possibly built it. An aerial photograph of the Great Serpent Mound is shown below.

**CALIFORNIA STANDARDS**

**REP1** Students frame questions that can be answered by historical study and research.

The ancient builders carefully outlined the shape of the serpent using rocks and clay mixed with ashes. This allowed them to design the image accurately and to give it a strong foundation.

Workers dug with large, flat stones and shoulder-blade bones from deer and elk. They used about 300,000 baskets of soil to build the mound. Construction most likely took between five and ten years and required hundreds of laborers.

The mound is a quarter mile long, averages 20 feet wide, and is about 5 feet high.

0          1/4 mile

## CONNECT TO HISTORY

1. **Drawing Conclusions** Review the five characteristics of a civilization on page 29. Which of these characteristics would a culture need to be able to build something like the Great Serpent Mound?

   **S** See Skillbuilder Handbook, page R13.

## CONNECT TO TODAY

2. **Researching** How do modern monuments to the dead differ from those constructed by the Mound Builders?

For more about Mound Builders . . .

**RESEARCH LINKS**
CLASSZONE.COM

Beginning about A.D. 100, the Anasazi lived in the area where Utah, Arizona, Colorado, and New Mexico now meet. Scientists don't know their origin. Like the Hohokam, the Anasazi were mainly farmers who also traded widely.

The Anasazi built houses with hundreds of rooms and many stories. For protection, they placed some buildings against overhanging canyon walls. The 800-room Pueblo Bonito in Chaco Canyon, New Mexico, housed perhaps 1,000 people. In the 1500s, when Spanish explorers first saw these houses, they called them *pueblos,* meaning villages. Around 1300, drought or warfare caused the Anasazi to leave their homes.

## The Mound Builders

In the eastern part of what is now the United States lived several groups of people called Mound Builders. The **Mound Builders** were early Native Americans who built large earthen structures.

The two oldest Mound Builder societies were the Adena and the Hopewell. Archaeologists know little about the Adena. The Hopewell, located in what is now the Midwest, lived from 400 B.C. to A.D. 400. Like the Hohokam, they grew corn. Artifacts show that they had a large trade network. It stretched from the Atlantic to the Rocky Mountains, and from the Great Lakes to Florida. Hopewell mounds served as burial sites. Their tombs contained jewelry and other gifts for the dead.

*Reading* **History**

**B. Comparing** What other ancient American cultures built pyramid-shaped mounds?

The last group of Mound Builders, the Mississippians, lived from A.D. 800 to 1700. They built some of the first cities in North America. For example, Cahokia in Illinois has more than 100 mounds. One of them, Monks Mound, rises 100 feet and covers 16 acres. In some cities, the Mississippians built flat-topped, pyramid-shaped temple mounds.

By the 1700s, most of the Mississippians had died from diseases they caught from Europeans. But many Native American groups continued to thrive throughout the United States, as you will read in Section 2.

---

**Section 1 Assessment**

### 1. Terms & Names

**Explain the significance of:**
- archaeologist
- artifact
- migrate
- culture
- domestication
- civilization
- irrigation
- Mound Builders

### 2. Using Graphics

Use a chart like the one below to list ancient cultures of Mesoamerica and North America and their locations.

| Ancient Culture | Location |
|---|---|
|  |  |

Which of these cultures was closest to where you live? (HI1)

### 3. Main Ideas

**a.** By what land bridge did some ancient people migrate to North America, and how was it created? (HI2)

**b.** How did the development of farming lead to the growth of civilization? (HI2)

**c.** How did trade help to spread culture? (HI2)

### 4. Critical Thinking

**Comparing** How did the Hohokam and the Anasazi adapt to living in their environment? (HI1)

**THINK ABOUT**
- Hohokam agriculture
- Anasazi dwellings

**ACTIVITY OPTIONS**

**SCIENCE**

**LANGUAGE ARTS**

Research the growing of corn. Draw a **diagram** of a corn plant with its parts labeled or write a **description** of how corn grows. (REP1)

# Societies of North America

| **MAIN IDEA** | **WHY IT MATTERS NOW** | **TERMS & NAMES** |
|---|---|---|
| By 1500, a variety of Native American groups—each with a distinct culture—lived in North America. | Many Americans today claim one or more of these cultures as part of their heritage. | technology · slash-and-burn agriculture · tundra · Deganawida · kayak · Iroquois League · matrilineal |

## ONE AMERICAN'S STORY

Many Native Americans today work to save their culture. Haida artist Bill Reid took part in this effort. When he was a teenager in the 1930s, few Haida artists were making totem poles or other Haida crafts. Reid began to learn about Haida arts from his grandfather.

Reid studied Northwest Coast native arts and jewelry making. Soon he created gold jewelry with Haida designs and carved sculptures. When Reid died, his work was praised.

*A VOICE FROM THE PAST*

Canada has lost one of its greatest artists. A descendant of a lineage of great Haida artists . . . , Bill Reid revived an artistic tradition that had survived only in museum collections.

**Dr. George MacDonald,** at Bill Reid's memorial service, March 24, 1998

Written records and people like Reid have preserved knowledge of the cultures that flourished in the Americas when Europeans arrived. This section explains the diversity of Native American groups in 1500.

## Native American Diversity

By 1500, Native Americans had divided into hundreds of cultural groups, speaking perhaps 2,000 languages. One reason Native Americans were so diverse was that each group adapted to its own environment—whether subzero ice fields, scorching deserts, or dense forests.

Environment shaped each group's economy, technology, and religion. **Technology** is the use of tools and knowledge to meet human needs. In some regions, Native Americans based their economy on farming. In others, they relied on hunting or fishing. Different environments caused technology to vary. In coastal areas, farmers made tools from shells. In

**Taking Notes**

Use your chart to take notes about the societies of North America.

| | Trade |
|---|---|
| AMERICAS | |
| WEST AFRICA | |
| EUROPE | |

**North America, 1500**

Cree

Kwakiutl

Blackfoot

Ojibwa

Nez Perce

Crow

Mandan

Algonquin

Ottawa

Chinook

PACIFIC OCEAN

Shoshone

Cheyenne

Dakota (Sioux)

Sauk

Potawatomi

Huron

Iroquois

Pomo

Arapaho

Pawnee

Iowa

Miami

Wampanoag Pequot

Paiute

Kansas

Delaware

ATLANTIC OCEAN

40°N

Miwok

Kiowa

Osage

Shawnee

Susquehanna

Powhatan

Navajo

Chumash

Hopi

Apache

Chickasaw

Tuscarora

Zuni Pueblo

Cherokee

Pima

Choctaw

Creek

**Native American Cultures**
- Subarctic
- Northwest Coast
- California
- Plateau
- Great Basin
- Mesoamerican
- Southwest
- Plains
- Eastern Woodlands
- Southeastern
- Caribbean
- — Major trade routes

N

0 — 500 Miles
0 — 1,000 Kilometers

Gulf of Mexico

Seminole

Tropic of Cancer

Huichol

Aztec

Taino

**GEOGRAPHY SKILLBUILDER**
**Interpreting Maps**
1. **Movement** Which Native American culture was able to trade directly with the Aztecs?
2. **Location** Which culture lived around the Great Lakes?

deserts, they used irrigation. Environment affected religion, too. Native Americans strongly believed that certain places were sacred—and that animals, plants, and natural forces had spiritual importance.

Although Native American groups had many differences, they all felt closely connected to nature, as shown in the following chant.

*A VOICE FROM THE PAST*

Earth's body has become my body
by means of these I shall live on.

Earth's mind has become my mind
by means of these I shall live on.

**Navajo Blessing Way,** quoted in *America in 1492*

In addition, trade linked Native Americans. Trading centers developed across North America, especially at points where two cultures met.

## Peoples of the North and Northwest Coast

**Background**
The Inuit are also called the Eskimo.

The Aleut (uh•LOOT) and the Inuit (IHN•yoo•iht) were peoples of the far North. The Aleut lived on islands off Alaska, and the Inuit lived near the coast on tundra. **Tundra** is a treeless plain that remains frozen under its top layer of soil. Ice and snow cover the ground most of the year.

Because their climate was too cold for farming, the Inuit and Aleut were hunters. They paddled **kayaks**, small boats made of animal skins, into icy seas to spear whales, seals, and walruses. They hunted these mammals for food, and they made seal and walrus skins into clothes. Some Inuit religious ceremonies honored the spirits of the whales and seals they caught. The Inuit also hunted such land animals as caribou. They made arrowheads and spear points from bones and antlers.

Farther south, Northwest Coast people also hunted sea mammals. But they mostly fished for salmon. Living by forests, Northwest Coast people used wood for houses, boats, and carved objects. They traded such coastal products as shells for items from the inland, such as furs.

*Reading***History**
**A. Making Inferences** Why would inland people trade for seashells?

Northwest Coast groups such as the Kwakiutl (KWAH•kee•OOT•uhl) and Haida had a special ceremony—the potlatch. Individuals would give away most or all of their goods as a way to claim status and benefit their community. They held potlatches to mark life events, such as naming a child or mourning the dead.

> *"The term [potlatch] comes from Chinook . . . and means 'to give.'"*
> Gloria Cranmer Webster, U'mista Cultural Centre

## Peoples of the West

Unlike the Native Americans of the Northwest Coast, those of the West did not rely mainly on the sea. The peoples of the West included tribes in California, the Columbia Plateau, and the Great Basin. Much of the West is desert or is not suitable for farming. The people who lived there existed mainly by hunting and gathering.

*Reading***History**
**B. Reading a Map** On the map on page 33, locate the cultures of California, the Plateau, and the Great Basin. Notice why these three together are called the peoples of the West.

The men hunted deer, elk, antelope, rabbits, and birds. They also fished, especially for salmon that swam up the western rivers. Women gathered such wild foods as nuts, seeds, and berries. Many western groups moved with the seasons to collect food.

The women of some western tribes became expert weavers. Pomo women wove beautiful baskets that they used to gather and store food. They wove some baskets tightly enough to be watertight.

The peoples of the West had strong spiritual beliefs, often linked to nature. Some held ceremonies to ensure a large food supply. Others held dances to ask for rain, for plant growth, and for good hunting. Still others believed that their religious leaders could contact the spirit world.

### The Aztec Calendar

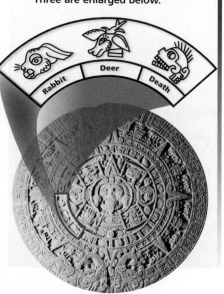

This stone is the Aztec calender wheel. In the center is the sun god. Around it are symbols for the 20 days of the Aztec month. Three are enlarged below.

Rabbit    Deer    Death

## Peoples of Mexico

Far to the south, the Aztecs ruled a great civilization in what is now central Mexico. The origin of the Aztecs is unclear. They may have been hunters and gatherers like the Native Americans of the West. Sometime during the 1100s, they migrated into the Valley of Mexico.

In 1325, they began to build their capital city, Tenochtitlán (teh•NAWCH•tee•TLAHN), on islands in Lake Texcoco. Two things helped the Aztecs become a strong empire. First, they drained swamps and built an irrigation system. This enabled them to grow plenty of food. Second, they were a warlike people who conquered most of their neighbors. The defeated people then had to send the Aztecs food and resources.

The Aztecs had a complex society. Rulers were the highest class. Priests and government workers ranked next. Slaves and servants were at the bottom. The Aztecs had elaborate religious ceremonies linked to their calendar and their study of the sun, moon, and stars. Many of their beliefs came from earlier Mesoamerican cultures.

The Aztecs' most important ritual involved feeding their sun god human blood. To do this, the Aztecs sacrificed prisoners of war by cutting out the person's heart while he was still alive. One reason the Aztecs fought so many wars was to capture prisoners to sacrifice.

## Peoples of the Southwest

North of the Aztec, in what is now the American Southwest, lived the Pueblo people. Their ancestors were the ancient Hohokam and Anasazi. Like their ancestors, the Pueblo used irrigation to alter their desert region for farming. They lived in many-storied houses of adobe—dried mud bricks. These large buildings sometimes held an entire village.

Pueblo Indian farmers raised corn, beans, and squash. For meat, they hunted game and raised turkeys. Men did most of the farming, hunting, weaving, and building. Women ground the corn and cooked the food, repaired the adobe houses, and crafted pottery.

_Reading_**History**

**C. Drawing Conclusions** Why do you think the Navajo adopted farming?

The Navajo and the Apache were nomadic, or wandering, hunter-gatherers who came to the region later than the Pueblo. For food, they relied mainly on game and on cactus, roots, and piñon nuts. Often, they traded these wild products for crops that the Pueblo had grown. Over time, the Navajo adopted farming and other Pueblo practices.

## Peoples of the Great Plains

Farther north, the Great Plains is a flat grassland region stretching from the Mississippi River west to the Rocky Mountains. Today, most people think of Plains Indians on horseback, but originally they had no horses. The Spanish first brought horses to the Americas in the 1500s.

**Background** Horses spread across North America through trade and by escaping from humans and wandering on their own.

Some Plains groups were nomads. Others lived in villages by rivers, where land was easier to farm. In summer, entire villages set out to track bison. Hunting bison on foot was difficult, but Plains tribes used their environment to help them. Working together, the villagers stampeded the herd over a cliff, so the fall would kill or disable the animals. Plains Indians not only ate the bison's meat. They also made its hide into clothes and its bones into tools.

**daily** *life*

**KACHINA DANCES**

Every year in summer the Hopi, Zuni, and other Pueblo Indians held a religious celebration. The ceremony called on the kachinas, or spirits of the ancestors. The Pueblo believed the kachinas had the power to bring a plentiful harvest. At the festival, masked dancers played the role of different kachinas. They danced and sang songs to bring rain in the year ahead. Today, the Pueblo also carve kachina dolls, shown below, as well as hold dances.

In winter such northern Plains groups as the Mandans and Pawnee lived in large circular lodges. Wooden beams held up the earthen walls. A hole at the top provided air, light, and an outlet for smoke from the fire. Buried partly underground, the earth lodge protected the people from the extreme cold and wind of the Plains climate.

Vocabulary
**lodge:** house

The spiritual beliefs of Plains tribes varied. Some felt a close tie to regional animals such as the bison or plants such as corn. Some honored sacred places, such as the Black Hills of South Dakota and Wyoming. Many Plains tribes held a ceremony called the Sun Dance, which involved making a vow and asking the Creator for aid.

## Peoples of the Southeast

The Southeast, which stretches from east Texas to the Atlantic Ocean, has mild winters and warm summers with plentiful rainfall. The long growing season led the Choctaw (CHAHK•taw), Chickasaw (CHIHK•uh•SAW), and other southeastern groups to become farmers. As many other Native Americans did, they grew corn, beans, squash, and pumpkins.

_Reading_**History**
**D. Analyzing Causes** Why would a long growing season lead people to become farmers?

Women did most of the farming, while men hunted, fished, and cleared land. The men spent months in the forest tracking deer. In the Southeast, people traced their family ties through the women. Societies in which ancestry is traced through the mother are called **matrilineal.**

In southeastern villages, people gathered at a central square for public meetings and such religious ceremonies as the Green Corn Festival. Held once a year, this festival offered thanks for the corn harvest and also served as a kind of New Year's celebration. People cleaned their houses, threw away old pots, and settled quarrels as a sign of a fresh start for the year.

## Peoples of the Eastern Woodlands

Many Native Americans in the Southeast and Eastern Woodlands played lacrosse using sticks like these. Modern Americans have adopted the game.

Like the Southeast, the Northeast had plenty of fish, game, and rain. But the climate was colder with snowy winters. Forests covered much of the region, so it is called the Eastern Woodlands. Most of the people living there spoke either an Iroquoian or Algonquian language.

Like all Native Americans, the Iroquois learned to live in their environment. They hunted wild game. They adapted the forest for farming by using slash-and-burn agriculture. In **slash-and-burn agriculture,** farmers chopped down and then burned trees on a plot of land. The ashes from the fire enriched the soil. When a field's soil became worn out, the farmer abandoned it and cleared a new field. The Iroquois lived in longhouses, bark-covered shelters as long as 300 feet. One longhouse held eight to ten families.

The Algonquin lived in wigwams, domelike houses covered with deerskin and slabs of bark. For protection, both the Iroquois and Algonquin surrounded their villages with high fences made of poles. Iroquois villagers often needed protection not only from the enemies of the Iroquois, but from each other. The Iroquois often raided neighboring villages for food and captives.

In the late 1500s, five northern Iroquois nations took the advice of a peace-seeking man named **Deganawida.** They stopped warring with each other and formed an alliance. This alliance of the Cayuga, Mohawk, Oneida, Onondaga, and Seneca was the **Iroquois League.** The League brought a long period of peace to the Iroquois. A council of leaders from each nation governed the League. They followed rules called the Great Law of Peace. The Iroquois were also a matrilineal society. If a leader did something wrong, the women of his clan could vote him out of office.

Across the Atlantic, the peoples of West Africa also adapted to their environment and engaged in trade. West Africa was the region from which most Africans were brought to the Americas. You will read about it in the next section.

## AMERICA'S HISTORY MAKERS

### DEGANAWIDA (THE PEACEMAKER)

Iroquois tradition honors Deganawida as the Peacemaker. Seeing how destructive warfare was for the Iroquois, Deganawida went from tribe to tribe and described his dream of peace. A poor speaker, he persuaded few warriors. Finally, an Iroquois chief named Hiawatha spoke for him. After long negotiations, the leaders of the warring nations made peace. However, Deganawida's own tribe, the Huron, did not join the League.

**How did both Deganawida and Hiawatha lead the Iroquois toward peace?**

---

## Section 2 Assessment

### 1. Terms & Names

**Explain the significance of:**
- technology
- tundra
- kayak
- matrilineal
- slash-and-burn agriculture
- Deganawida
- Iroquois League

### 2. Using Graphics

Use a cluster diagram to record how Native Americans from each region adapted to their environment. (HI1)

People of the North

Adapted to Environment

### 3. Main Ideas

**a.** What were some of the religious ceremonies of Native Americans? (HI1)

**b.** How were the Pueblo like their ancestors, the Hohokam? (HI1)

**c.** How did the formation of the Iroquois League benefit its member nations? (HI1)

### 4. Critical Thinking

**Drawing Conclusions**
How did trade benefit both groups that took part in it? (HI1)

**THINK ABOUT**
- who the Northwest Coast people traded with and what they exchanged
- what the Pueblo exchanged with nomadic groups

### ACTIVITY OPTIONS

**ART**

**LANGUAGE ARTS**

Reread the Navajo chant on page 33. Draw an **illustration** to go with the chant or write additional **verses**. (REP4)

# The Iroquois Great Law of Peace

**CALIFORNIA STANDARDS**

**Reading 2.0** Students read and understand grade-level-appropriate material. They describe and connect the essential ideas, arguments, and perspectives of the text by using their knowledge of text structure, organization, and purpose.

**REP4** Students assess the credibility of primary and secondary sources and draw sound conclusions from them.

**Setting the Stage** The five nations of the Iroquois League created a constitution, called the Great Law of Peace, that had 117 laws and customs. These laws governed all aspects of life and war. In this excerpt, Deganawida introduces the Great Law by describing a tree that symbolizes the permanence and stability of the league. **See Primary Source Explorer** ◎

**A CLOSER LOOK**

**THE COUNCIL FIRE**

The council fire of the Iroquois League was kept burning for about 200 years.

**1. What do you think it would mean if the council fire were allowed to die?**

**A CLOSER LOOK**

**THE GREAT WHITE ROOTS**

The roots of a tree help to anchor it in the ground, and they draw water and food from the soil.

**2. Why might Deganawida say the nature of the roots is "Peace and Strength"?**

**1** I am Deganawida and with the Five Nations' Confederate **Lords**[1] I plant the Tree of Great Peace. I plant it in your territory, **Adodarhoh,**[2] and the Onondaga Nation, in the territory of you who are Firekeepers.

I name the tree the Tree of the Great Long Leaves. Under the shade of this Tree of the Great Peace we spread the soft white feathery down of the globe thistle as seats for you, Adodarhoh, and your cousin Lords.

We place you upon those seats, spread soft with the feathery down of the globe thistle, there beneath the shade of the spreading branches of the Tree of Peace. There shall you sit and watch the Council Fire of the **Confederacy of the Five Nations,**[3] and all the affairs of the Five Nations shall be transacted at this place before you, Adodarhoh, and your cousin Lords, by the Confederate Lords of the Five Nations.

**2** Roots have spread out from the Tree of the Great Peace, one to the north, one to the east, one to the south, and one to the west. The name of these roots is The Great White Roots and their nature is Peace and Strength.

If any man or any nation outside the Five Nations shall obey the laws of the Great Peace and make known their disposition to the Lords of the Confederacy, they may trace the Roots to the Tree and if their minds are clean and they are obedient and promise to obey the wishes of the Confederate Council, they shall be welcomed to take shelter beneath the Tree of the Long Leaves.

1. **Lords:** chiefs.

2. **Adodarhoh:** the name of the office of the Onondaga chief.

3. **Confederacy of the Five Nations:** the Iroquois League.

## Interactive Primary Source Assessment

### 1. Main Ideas

**a.** In what territory was the Tree of the Great Peace planted? (REP4)

**b.** Where will the affairs of the Five Nations be conducted? (REP4)

**c.** Where have the Tree's roots spread? (REP4)

### 2. Critical Thinking

**Making Inferences** Were outsiders welcome to join the Iroquois League? Explain. (HI1)

**THINK ABOUT**

• the phrase *they may trace the Roots to the Tree*

• the phrase *take shelter beneath the Tree*

# Societies of West Africa

| **MAIN IDEA** | **WHY IT MATTERS NOW** | **TERMS & NAMES** |
|---|---|---|
| The peoples of West Africa developed sophisticated kingdoms, trade networks, and artistic achievements. | It was from this region that many Africans were brought to the Americas. | Ghana — Songhai<br>Muslims — Hausa<br>Islam — Yoruba<br>Mali — Benin |

## ONE AFRICAN'S STORY

King Tenkaminen (TEHN•kah•MEE•nehn) of the West African empire of **Ghana** was a powerful ruler. He grew rich by taxing gold traders who traveled through his land. In 1067, a geographer wrote a description of the royal court.

### A VOICE FROM THE PAST

The king adorns himself . . . wearing necklaces round his neck and bracelets on his forearms. . . . Behind the king stand ten pages holding shields and swords decorated with gold.

**al-Bakri,** quoted in *The Horizon History of Africa*

West Africa was the homeland of many of the enslaved Africans who were brought to the Americas after 1500. You will read about West Africa in this section.

## African Geography and World Trade

Africa is the world's second largest continent after Asia. (See the map on page 40.) Although Africa has a variety of land forms and climates, almost three quarters of it lies within the tropics. The equator runs east-west across the center of Africa. Dense rain forests stretch along the equator in central and western Africa. North and south of the rain forests are broad savannas, which are grassy plains with thorny bushes and scattered trees. Beyond the savanna in the North lies the Sahara, the world's largest desert. Beyond the savanna in the South lies the smaller Kalahari Desert.

By A.D. 1500, coastal ports had linked Africa with the rest of the world for many centuries. Ships from ports on the Mediterranean and the Red Sea carried goods to Arabia and Persia. On Africa's east coast, city-states carried on a brisk trade with ports across the Indian Ocean.

**CALIFORNIA STANDARDS**

**CST3** Students use a variety of maps and documents to identify physical and cultural features of neighborhoods, cities, states, and countries and to explain the historical migration of people, expansion and disintegration of empires, and the growth of economic systems.

**REP4** Students assess the credibility of primary and secondary sources and draw sound conclusions from them.

**REP5** Students detect the different historical points of view on historical events and determine the context in which the historical statements were made (the questions asked, sources used, author's perspectives).

**HI2** Students understand and distinguish cause, effect, sequence, and correlation in historical events, including the long- and short-term causal relations.

### Taking Notes

Use your chart to take notes about West Africa.

| | Trade | |
|---|---|---|
| AMERICAS | | |
| WEST AFRICA | | |
| EUROPE | | |

Like other parts of Africa, West Africa has rain forest along the equator and savanna to the north. The Niger River arcs across those grasslands and forests and then empties into the Atlantic Ocean. Along its northern edge, West Africa borders the Sahara.

## Ghana Grows Wealthy

On a map, the Sahara appears to be a barrier between West Africa and the ports on the Mediterranean coast. But by A.D. 500, camel caravans led by eager merchants made regular journeys across the great desert. This connected West Africa to the wider world.

Ghana became the first West African kingdom to grow rich through trade. From the 700s to the mid-1000s, Ghana prospered by controlling the busy trade in gold and salt. Located on the southern edge of the Sahara, Ghana became a marketplace for traders going north and south in search of salt and gold. (Ancient Ghana was northwest of modern Ghana.) Salt was important because it helps the human body retain water in hot weather. Traders carried salt from the Saharan salt mines in the north. In Ghana's markets, they met other traders offering gold from the forests of West Africa.

Ghana's king benefited from this trade. He imposed taxes on all gold and salt passing through his kingdom. The taxes had to be paid in gold. The king also claimed all gold nuggets found in his kingdom. Ghana's king used the resulting wealth to pay for an army and build an empire.

**Background**
The camel is used in the desert because it can travel up to 10 days without water.

*Reading***History**
**A. Analyzing Causes** Why did the king want taxes to be paid in gold and all gold nuggets to be given to him?

### West African Empires, 800–1500

The city of Timbuktu was famous not only for trade but also as a center of Islamic learning. This mosque was built in the 1300s and 1400s.

Legend:
- Ghana, 1000
- Mali, 1400
- Songhai, 1500
- Trade routes

### GEOGRAPHY SKILLBUILDER Interpreting Maps

1. **Place** Which of the three West African empires occupied the largest amount of territory?
2. **Movement** Describe the route that you would take from the port city of Tunis to the trade city of Timbuktu.

0          1,000 Miles

0          2,000 Kilometers

## Islam Enters Ghana

Many of the traders who came to Ghana from North Africa were Muslims. **Muslims** are followers of the religion of Islam. Founded by the prophet Muhammad in the 600s, **Islam** teaches that there is one God, named Allah. Muslims must perform such duties as praying five times a day and making a pilgrimage to the holy city of Mecca in Arabia. Muslim traders crossing the Sahara brought Islam from North Africa to West Africa. Ghana's rulers allowed those Muslims to build mosques, or houses of worship, in Ghana's capital, Kumbi Saleh. In time, Ghana's rulers employed Muslims as advisers.

**Vocabulary**
**pilgrimage:** a trip to a holy place

The Muslim empires of North Africa wanted to convert Ghana's people to Islam and to control Ghana's gold trade. In 1076, a Muslim army conquered Kumbi Saleh. This lessened Ghana's power. A number of local leaders took advantage of Ghana's weakness. They built up their own small states on the edges of the once mighty empire. Ghana never regained its former strength.

Over the next several centuries, more and more West Africans converted to Islam. In fact, many of the enslaved Africans who were brought to the Americas were Muslims.

## Mali Replaces Ghana

By the 1200s, another West African kingdom had taken over most of Ghana's territory. This kingdom, called **Mali,** became West Africa's most powerful state. Its wealth also came from control of the gold-salt trade. But because it was located farther south than Ghana, Mali was better able to control the trade on the upper Niger River. (Ancient Mali stretched farther west than modern Mali and not as far north.)

Mali's first great ruler, Sundiata (sun•JAHT•ah), reigned from about 1230 to 1255. He came to power by crushing a cruel, unpopular leader. Sundiata's armies conquered many important trading cities. This made Mali's hold on trade stronger and made Mali more prosperous. Sundiata was a Muslim, but he did not force his people to accept Islam. Most of the people of Mali retained their traditional African beliefs.

A European mapmaker placed this picture of Mansa Musa on a map in 1375. It was drawn from his imagination.

**Vocabulary**
**devout:** very religious

*Reading* **History**
**B. Making Inferences** How do you think the Egyptians reacted to Mansa Musa's caravan?

Mali's other great leader was Mansa Musa (MAHN•sah moo•SAH), who was a devout Muslim. Mansa Musa came to the throne in 1312. Under his leadership, the empire became one of the largest in the world.

Mansa Musa is best remembered for making the Muslim pilgrimage to Mecca in 1324 and 1325. On his way to Mecca, he stopped in Cairo, Egypt. According to some stories, Mansa Musa entered the city leading a huge caravan that included 500 servants who waved staffs decorated with gold. Each of the 80 camels in his caravan struggled under the weight of a 300-pound sack of gold. The legend of Mali's wealth spread all the way to Europe. This was one reason that Europeans began to trade with Africa about 150 years later.

On his return to Mali, Mansa Musa brought back many Muslim scholars, artists, and architects. They helped spread Islamic culture and learning throughout the empire. The city of Timbuktu (TIHM•buhk•TOO) in eastern Mali became a leading center of trade and Islamic learning. After Mansa Musa's death in 1337, Mali slowly grew weaker.

## The Empire of Songhai

As Mali's power decreased, the **Songhai** (SAWNG•HY) people living at the Great Bend in the Niger River broke away from its control. In 1464, under the leader Sunni Ali, they began their own empire. Sunni Ali was a Muslim, but he also practiced the traditional Songhai religion.

Under Sunni Ali, the Songhai captured the great city of Timbuktu. Then they put the important trading city of Djenné (jeh•NAY) under siege and captured it after seven years. In addition to conquering territory, Sunni Ali set up an organized system of government.

After Sunni Ali died in 1492, conflicts arose. Some Muslims began a rebellion because they wanted Islam to be the only religion of Songhai. The leader of the revolt was Askia Muhammad, a devoted Muslim.

Askia Muhammad won his fight and became Songhai's second great ruler. For 35 years, he ably governed the empire. He chose capable officials who made the government run smoothly. He also expanded trade and set up an efficient tax system. Askia Muhammad used his wealth to build mosques and support Muslim scholars.

After Askia Muhammad's reign, several weak rulers succeeded him. Even when a strong ruler took the throne again, the empire faced problems. In spite of Songhai's wealth and learning, it lacked modern weapons. In 1591, a Moroccan fighting force from North Africa invaded Songhai with gunpowder and cannon. They easily defeated Songhai's soldiers, who were defending their empire with swords and spears.

## Other West African Kingdoms

As empires rose and fell in some parts of West Africa, small city-states arose in other parts of the region. The **Hausa** (HOW•suh) states emerged after A.D. 1000 in what is now northern Nigeria. Hausa city-states, such as Katsina and Kano, thrived on trade. Although the Hausa people shared a language, their city-states were independent of each other.

The **Yoruba** (YAWR•uh•buh) lived in the forests southwest of the Niger River. Ife and Oyo, the largest Yoruba states, had kings

*Reading* **History**
**C. Recognizing Effects** How would Askia Muhammad's actions promote Islam in Songhai?

**AFRICAN HERITAGE**

One way many African Americans show pride in their heritage is by wearing kente cloth. Kente cloth, shown below, is a colorful fabric woven by the Akan and Ewe people of Ghana.

Some African Americans celebrate the holiday of Kwanzaa in December. Based on traditional African harvest festivals, Kwanzaa lasts a week. Each day honors a value held by Africans: unity, self-determination, collective responsibility, cooperative economics, purpose, creativity, and faith.

who were considered to be partly divine. The Yoruba were mostly farmers, but they also had gifted artists, who carved wood and ivory and cast metal sculptures. Yoruba statues are still considered great art.

Another kingdom famous for its art was Benin. **Benin,** located in the delta of the Niger River, lay on main trade routes and prospered because of that. The capital, Benin City, was large and surrounded by thick, earthen walls. About 1600, a Dutch visitor compared Benin City to his home city of Amsterdam in Europe.

*Reading***History**

**D. Analyzing Points of View** Do you think Dapper's view of Benin City is positive or negative? Explain.

### A VOICE FROM THE PAST

The houses in this town stand in good order, each one close and evenly placed with its neighbor, just as the houses in Holland stand. . . . The king's court is very great. It is built around many square-shaped yards.

**Olfert Dapper,** quoted in *Centuries of Greatness*

Benin artists produced sophisticated bronze statues such as this figure of a horn-blower.

In the late 1400s, Europeans reached Benin. Portuguese ships arrived, and the Portuguese set up a trade center near Benin City. Benin traders sold the Portuguese pepper, ivory, and leopard skins in exchange for copper and guns. In time, the Portuguese and other Europeans also began to trade for enslaved Africans. The Europeans who came to West Africa were not seeking information about its rich history or culture. They wanted a supply of laborers to work on large farms, called plantations. Chapter 2 explains more about plantations and slavery.

Trade was just one reason Europeans were sailing far beyond their lands. Social changes were also spurring them to explore the world. Those changes are discussed in Section 4.

---

## Section 3 Assessment

### 1. Terms & Names

**Explain the significance of:**
- Ghana
- Muslims
- Islam
- Mali
- Songhai
- Hausa
- Yoruba
- Benin

### 2. Using Graphics

Compare the Ghana Empire and the Mali Empire using a Venn diagram like the one shown.

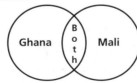

How was the influence of Islam different in each? (HI1)

### 3. Main Ideas

**a.** How did Ghana's ruler benefit from controlling the gold-salt trade? (HI2)

**b.** How did Islam spread within West Africa? (HI2)

**c.** For what artistic achievements are the Yoruba and the people of Benin known? (HI3)

### 4. Critical Thinking

**Identifying Facts and Opinions** Is the description of Benin City above mainly a statement of fact or opinion? (REP2)

**THINK ABOUT**
- whether Dapper's statement can be proven by measurement or observation
- whether his statement expresses his own bias

**ACTIVITY OPTIONS**

**SPEECH**

**GEOGRAPHY**

Retell Mansa Musa's famous journey as an **oral history** or create a **map** that shows the route you think he took from Mali to Mecca. (CST3)

# Societies of Europe

| MAIN IDEA | WHY IT MATTERS NOW | TERMS & NAMES |
|---|---|---|
| By 1500, Europe was going through a period of social change that sparked interest in learning and exploration. | The changes taking place in Europe led to the exploration of the Americas. | European Middle Ages     Renaissance<br>feudalism     printing press<br>manor system     Reformation<br>Crusades     profit |

**CALIFORNIA STANDARDS**

**7.11.1** Know the great voyages of discovery, the locations of the routes, and the influence of cartography in the development of a new European worldview.

**7.11.3** Examine the origins of modern capitalism; the influence of mercantilism and cottage industry; the elements and importance of a market economy in seventeenth-century Europe; the changing international trading and marketing patterns, including their locations on a world map; and the influence of explorers and map makers.

**REP4** Students assess the credibility of primary and secondary sources and draw sound conclusions from them.

**HI2** Students understand and distinguish cause, effect, sequence, and correlation in historical events, including the long- and short-term causal relations.

### Taking Notes

Use your chart to take notes about Europe.

| | Trade |
|---|---|
| AMERICAS | |
| WEST AFRICA | |
| EUROPE | |

## ONE EUROPEAN'S STORY

**Ermentrude gathered up a chicken and five eggs and went to see the steward. He was the man who managed the land where she lived for its owners. Ermentrude and her husband, Bodo, were farmers who worked on a small piece of a large estate owned by someone else.**

**Ermentrude gave the chicken and eggs to the steward as part of her rent. Then she hurried home to weave cloth and cook supper.**

**Ermentrude lived in the early 800s, but her life was typical of the way many Europeans lived for centuries. This section explains that way of life and how it had changed by 1500.**

## Feudalism in Europe

Ermentrude lived in the **European Middle Ages,** which lasted from the late 400s, when the Western Roman Empire ended, to about the 1300s. (In some parts of Europe, the Middle Ages lasted to the 1400s.) The Romans used written laws and a mighty army to keep order. But over time, the empire grew weak. Germanic tribes from the east and north invaded the empire and contributed to its fall. The rough, uneducated Germanic tribes destroyed the strong Roman government and trade networks, and the tribes set up small kingdoms. With no trade, people stopped using money. They paid in goods, such as chickens and eggs.

Other groups also disrupted Europe. During the 800s to 1000s, Vikings swept down from the north. From their warships, they carried out lightning raids, looting villages and then racing back out to sea. To survive such difficult times, Europeans turned to feudalism. **Feudalism** is a political system in which a king allows nobles, or lords, to use lands that belong to him. In return, the lords owe the king military service and protection for the people living on the land.

Along with feudalism, Europeans developed the **manor system.** In this system, lords divided their lands into manors, or large estates, that were farmed mostly by serfs. Serfs were landless peasants who weren't allowed to leave the manor. In return for the serfs' work, the lord promised to protect them.

The Roman Catholic Church also gained power during these uncertain times. Taking on the roles once filled by government officials, the Church collected taxes, aided the sick, and punished criminals. It became a powerful, unifying force throughout Europe.

*Reading***History**

**A. Identifying Problems** What problems were Europeans trying to solve with feudalism and the manor system?

## Revival of Trade and Towns

By the 1000s, feudalism had brought more stability to society. As strong lords gained more control over their lands, long periods of peace and security followed. Merchants once again felt safe to travel. New farming methods, such as better ways to plant and plow fields, led to a food surplus. With more to eat, the population increased. More people meant more demand for goods, which spurred trade. Old towns near busy trade routes revived, and new towns grew up near manor houses and churches. Money came back into use.

As the economy grew, many serfs ran away to towns. Some became craftspeople who practiced such trades as shoemaking. Others became merchants who sold the goods that craftspeople made. Merchants and craftspeople formed a new social class, the middle class. They had fewer riches, rights, and privileges than lords, but far more freedom than they had known as serfs.

**Vocabulary**
**craftspeople:** those who work in skilled trades

## Trade with the East

Trade increased, not only within Europe, but also with places outside Europe. Located on the Mediterranean, Italy had an advantage in this trade. Italian cities such as Venice traded with other port cities, such as Constantinople, located in what is now Turkey.

War also spurred trade. Many European Christians were angry that Muslims held the Holy Land, where Jesus had lived. In 1096, European Christians launched the **Crusades,** a series of wars to capture the Holy Land. They ultimately failed to keep the Holy Land, but the Crusades changed European life. Italians supplied the ships that carried Crusaders to the Middle East. On the return trip, the ships brought Asian goods to Europe. These goods had traveled across the Indian Ocean and then overland to the Mediterranean. After the Crusades, Italians continued to trade with Muslims in other Mediterranean cities.

An Italian merchant named Marco Polo also stirred European curiosity about distant lands. Polo had spent 24 years traveling in China and

*Reading***History**

**B. Recognizing Effects** What effect did the Crusades have on Italian trade?

### STRANGE *but* True

**PEPPER MILLIONAIRES**
Europeans were desperate to get spices, such as pepper and cloves. Before refrigeration, meat often spoiled. Spices helped disguise the taste of rotten meat.

In the 1500s, just one shipload of spices could make a merchant wealthy for life. The average working person would have to work at least 1,000 years to earn as much as a merchant could earn from one load of pepper!

In feudalism, nobles offered to protect peasants from invaders. In return, the peasants farmed the nobles' lands.

Feudalism made people feel safe enough to travel. Trade increased and towns grew.

Then many peasants ran away to towns, where they could live more freely. Feudalism declined. Trade continued to grow.

central Asia. A book written about Polo's travels described China's riches and wonders. It increased European interest in Asia.

## The Decline of Feudalism

The growth of trade and towns weakened feudalism because so many serfs left the manors for town life. The power of the lords shrank because they had fewer people under their control. Beginning in 1347, a deadly disease also weakened feudalism. The bubonic plague swept across Europe, killing about one-fourth of the population and reducing the number of workers. Lords competed for the laborers who survived, so they began to pay wages to peasants.

As feudal lords lost power, kings grew stronger. They won the support of townspeople because they could raise large armies to enforce order. In return, townspeople agreed to support their kings by paying taxes. The armies enforced order and imposed the king's authority over lesser lords. As countries became safer, trade flourished even more.

## The Renaissance and Reformation

Italy, which was thriving because of trade, became the birthplace of the **Renaissance**—a time of increased interest in art and learning. *Renaissance* is a French term meaning "rebirth." Lasting from the 1300s to 1600, the Renaissance spread from Italy throughout Europe.

Several forces led to this rebirth of learning. As feudalism weakened and the plague brought great suffering, Europeans began to question what life meant. In their search for new answers, some people turned to old sources. They read the writings and studied the art of the Greeks and Romans. The classical Greeks and Romans lived from about 750 B.C. to A.D. 476. As a result of these studies, European ideas changed.

1. The Greeks had praised human achievement. European scholars began humanism, the study of human worth, ideas, and potential.
2. Classical education stressed such subjects as history, philosophy, and literature. Europeans spent more time studying those subjects.
3. From classical art, European artists learned to make art more realistic. They created some of the world's finest paintings and statues.

*Reading***History**
**C. Analyzing Causes** What three causes led to the decline of feudalism?

4. Muslim scholars had saved classical manuscripts about science. Also, Muslim mathematicians had invented algebra. Contact with Muslim societies influenced European science and mathematics.

5. Cartography, or mapmaking, became more scientific. Resulting maps were based more on observations and calculations than on rumor and guesswork. Maps and globes became status symbols in Renaissance Europe. Their popularity encouraged European exploration, but also fostered a sense of superiority over the cultures Europeans encountered in their travels.

**Vocabulary**
**philosophy:** the study of the meaning of life

A new invention helped spread Renaissance ideas. In about 1455, a German named Johannes Gutenberg invented the **printing press,** a machine that mechanically prints pages. People no longer had to copy books by hand. Printers could make hundreds of copies of a book cheaply and accurately. More people read, and ideas spread quickly.

**Background**
A printing press uses movable type—blocks of metal or wood that have raised characters. The Chinese invented movable type in about 1045. Gutenberg re-invented it.

By the early 1500s, Renaissance ideas and other forces weakened the Catholic Church. Many church leaders were corrupt. Some claimed to grant God's forgiveness for money. Martin Luther, a German monk, publicly posted 95 statements that criticized such practices. This began the **Reformation,** a movement to correct problems in the Church.

The Reformation split the Church into two groups—Catholics and Protestants. In time, Protestants divided into many different churches. When European colonists came to America, they carried their religious disagreements and hopes for religious freedom with them.

## HISTORY through ART

This painting, _School of Athens_ by Raphael, shows many aspects of Renaissance art and culture.

- Like much Renaissance art, it looks more realistic than the art of the Middle Ages. (See page 44 for comparison.)
- It honors the Greek thinkers Aristotle and Plato, who are the two men in the center arch.
- It also honors Renaissance artists. Raphael himself is in the group to the right.

**Why might Raphael have wanted to include himself in a painting with famous Greeks?**

**After the Crusades, Europeans want Asian goods.**

*CAUSE*

*EFFECT*
**Italy dominates trade because it developed a network during the Crusades.**

*CAUSE*

*EFFECT*
**Other European nations want a share of Italy's profits.**

*CAUSE*

*EFFECT*
**Other nations seek water route to Asia.**

**SKILLBUILDER Interpreting Charts**

*What economic activity was the primary cause of exploration?*

# Changes in Trade

The Renaissance period saw not only changes in learning and religion, but also in trade. As trade grew, Italian merchants needed to improve the way they did business. They began to use more exact ways of keeping track of a business's income and its costs. By subtracting the costs from the income, the merchants determined the **profit**. Increased trade led to the formation of banks to store gold and silver for their owners. Soon bankers realized that they could lend that money to others before the owners needed it back. They charged interest fees on these loans. By collecting interest, bankers gained wealth and power.

Profit became increasingly important in the Renaissance economy. Italian merchants made huge profits by trading in Asian goods. Because Italians had done business with Muslims for centuries, they had a special relationship. In addition to that, the Italians used military strength to control the trade on the Mediterranean—and didn't allow other Europeans to take part in it.

Merchants in other European countries envied the profits made by Italian merchants. As a result, other Europeans began to want a share of the rich trade in Asian goods. They began to search for a non-Mediterranean water route to Asia, as you will read in Section 5.

*Reading* **History**
**D. Making Generalizations** If a country tries to completely dominate trade in a certain area, how will other countries respond?

---

## Section 4 Assessment

### 1. Terms & Names

**Explain the significance of:**
- European Middle Ages
- feudalism
- manor system
- Crusades
- Renaissance
- printing press
- Reformation
- profit

### 2. Using Graphics

On a chart like this one, list how the Renaissance changed art and learning. (HI3)

| Changes to Art and Learning |
|---|
| • |
| • |
| • |
| • |

### 3. Main Ideas

**a.** What caused feudalism to develop? (HI2)

**b.** What led to the revival of trade and towns? (HI2)

**c.** How did Italy come to control European trade with Asia? (HI2)

### 4. Critical Thinking

**Contrasting** How did the Renaissance differ from the European Middle Ages? (HI1)

**THINK ABOUT**
- the economy
- how power was distributed
- the authority of the church

**ACTIVITY OPTIONS**

**TECHNOLOGY**

**MUSIC**

Design a **Web site** or compose a **song** advertising the great new Renaissance invention—the printing press. (REP1)

# 5

# Early European Explorers

| MAIN IDEA | WHY IT MATTERS NOW | TERMS & NAMES |
|---|---|---|
| As Europeans searched for sea routes to Asia, Christopher Columbus reached the Americas. | Columbus's journey permanently linked the Americas to the rest of the world. | navigator      Christopher Columbus<br>caravel |

## ONE EUROPEAN'S STORY

Sailors seeking a route to Asia depended on the skill of their navigator. A **navigator** plans the course of a ship by using instruments to find its position. In the 1400s, Portugal had a famous prince called Henry the Navigator. Yet, Henry wasn't a navigator. He lived at Sagres, on the southwestern coast of Portugal. In this town, he began a school of navigation.

Henry decided to organize and pay for sailing expeditions to explore the Atlantic and the west coast of Africa. He was hoping to find African gold, to learn more about geography, and to spread Christianity. His ships traveled farther down the African coast than Europeans had ever gone. Because Henry sponsored the voyages, the English named him "the navigator." As you will read in this section, those voyages began Europe's age of discovery.

Henry the Navigator

CALIFORNIA STANDARDS

**7.11.1** Know the great voyages of discovery, the locations of the routes, and the influence of cartography in the development of a new European worldview.

**7.11.2** Discuss the exchanges of plants, animals, technology, culture, and ideas among Europe, Africa, Asia and the Americas in the 15th and 16th centuries and the major economic and social effects on each continent.

**REP5** Students detect the different historical points of view on historical events and determine the context in which the historical statements were made (the questions asked, sources used, author's perspectives).

**HI3** Students explain the sources of historical continuity and how the combination of ideas and events explains the emergence of new patterns.

**HI4** Students recognize the role of chance, foresight, and error in history.

**HI5** Students recognize that interpretations of history are subject to change as new information is uncovered.

## A Water Route to Asia

Under Prince Henry, the Portuguese developed an improved ship called the **caravel**. The caravel had triangular sails as well as square sails. Square sails carried the ship forward when the wind was at its back. Triangular sails allowed the caravel to sail into the wind. The caravel was better than other European ships of the time at sailing into the wind.

In January 1488, the Portuguese explorer Bartolomeu Dias (DEE•uhs) reached the southern tip of Africa. After sailing around it, he returned to Portugal at the urging of his crew. Portugal's king named the tip the Cape of Good Hope because he hoped they had found a route to Asia.

Ten years later, another Portuguese explorer, Vasco da Gama, followed Dias's route around the cape. He continued north along the eastern coast of Africa. Then he sailed east across the Indian Ocean to India. At last, someone had found an all-water route to Asia.

Taking Notes

Use your chart to take notes about European explorers.

| | Trade | |
|---|---|---|
| AMERICAS | | |
| WEST AFRICA | | |
| EUROPE | | |

**CHRISTOPHER COLUMBUS**

**1451–1506**

Christopher Columbus's son Ferdinand wrote that his father "took to the sea at the age of 14 and followed it ever after."

Columbus's early voyages nearly cost him his life. When he was 25, pirates off the coast of Portugal sank his ship. Columbus survived by grabbing a floating oar and swimming to shore.

But he also learned a lot from sailing on Portuguese ships. The sailors taught Columbus about Atlantic wind patterns. This knowledge later helped him on his history-making voyage.

**What character traits, shown in Columbus's early life, might have made him a good leader?**

That route meant that the Portuguese could now trade with Asia without dealing with the Muslims or Italians. Portugal took control of the valuable spice trade. The merchants of Lisbon, Portugal's capital, grew rich. Spain and other European rivals wanted to take part in this profitable trade. They began to look for their own water routes to Asia.

## Columbus's Plan

By the time of da Gama's voyage, an Italian sailor named **Christopher Columbus** thought he knew a faster way to reach Asia. Europeans had known for centuries that the earth is round. Columbus decided that instead of sailing around Africa and then east, he would sail west across the Atlantic. He calculated that it would be a short journey.

But Columbus made several mistakes. First, he relied on the writings of two people—Marco Polo and a geographer named Paolo Toscanelli—who were wrong about the size of Asia. They claimed that Asia stretched farther from west to east than it really did.

Second, Columbus underestimated the distance around the globe. He thought the earth was only two thirds as large as it actually is! Because of Polo and Toscanelli, Columbus thought that Asia took up most of that distance. Therefore, he believed that the Atlantic Ocean must be small. And a voyage west to Asia would be short.

In 1483, Columbus asked the king of Portugal to finance a voyage across the Atlantic. The king's advisers opposed the plan. They argued that Columbus had miscalculated the distance to Asia. They also reminded the king of the progress that Portuguese explorers had made sailing down the coast of Africa looking for a route to Asia. The advisers persuaded the king not to finance the voyage. So in 1486, Columbus turned to Portugal's rival, Spain.

## Help from Spain's Rulers

Spain's rulers, King Ferdinand and Queen Isabella, liked Columbus's plan because they wanted a share of the rich Asian trade. As a strong Catholic, the Queen also welcomed a chance to spread Christianity. But there were also reasons not to support Columbus. First, a royal council had doubts about Columbus's calculations and advised Ferdinand and Isabella not to finance him. Second, the Spanish monarchs were in the middle of a costly war to drive the Muslims out of Spain. Third, Columbus was asking a high payment for his services.

The years of waiting had made Columbus determined to profit from his explorations. As a reward for his efforts, he demanded the high title

_Reading_**History**

**A. Comparing**
Compare what happened after Portugal began to control the spice trade to what happened when Italy controlled it.

**Background**
As you read in Section 4, Marco Polo's book about his travels had increased European interest in Asia.

**Vocabulary**
**monarch:** a king or queen

Admiral of the Ocean Sea and a percentage of any wealth he brought from Asia. He also expected to be made the ruler of the lands he found.

Finally in January of 1492, the Spanish conquered the last Muslim stronghold in Spain. The Spanish monarchs could now afford to finance Columbus but still had doubts about doing so. Columbus left the palace to return home. But after listening to a trusted adviser, the king and queen changed their minds and sent a rider on horseback to bring Columbus back. He and the rulers finally reached an agreement.

*Reading* **History**

**B. Drawing Conclusions** Did this agreement give Columbus what he was asking for? Explain.

### A VOICE FROM THE PAST

Your Highnesses . . . accorded me great rewards and ennobled me so that from that time henceforth I might . . . be high admiral of the Ocean Sea and perpetual Governor of the islands and continent which I should discover.

**Christopher Columbus,** letter to King Ferdinand and Queen Isabella

Preparing to sail, Columbus assembled his ships—the *Niña*, the *Pinta*, and the *Santa María*—at the port of Palos de la Frontera in southern Spain.

## Setting Sail

At first, Columbus had trouble finding a crew. Then a respected local shipowner agreed to sign on as captain of the *Pinta*. Other crew members soon followed. About 90 men loaded the ships with enough food for one year, casks of fresh water, firewood, and other necessities.

## Exploration Leads to New Sea Routes, *1487–1504*

Route of Dias, 1487–1488
Route of da Gama, 1497–1498
Routes of Columbus:
1492–1493
1493–1496
1498–1500
1502–1504

EUROPE

NORTH AMERICA

ATLANTIC OCEAN

PORTUGAL SPAIN

SAN SALVADOR
CUBA
Tropic of Cancer

ASIA

HISPANIOLA

AFRICA

PACIFIC OCEAN

0° Equator

SOUTH AMERICA

INDIAN OCEAN

Tropic of Capricorn

0    1,000 Miles
0    2,000 Kilometers

### GEOGRAPHY SKILLBUILDER Interpreting Maps

1. **Movement** Approximately how many miles did Columbus sail before he reached San Salvador on his first voyage?
2. **Human-Environment Interaction** Why do you suppose that Dias stayed close to the west coast of Africa during his voyage, while da Gama sailed farther out?

**51**

The tiny fleet of wooden ships glided out of the harbor on August 3, 1492. First they sailed southwest toward the Canary Islands off the northwest coast of Africa. From there, Columbus was relying on trade winds that blew toward the west to speed his ships across the ocean.

Once aboard ship, Columbus kept a log, or daily record of each day's sailing. In fact, he kept two logs. One he showed to his men and one he kept secret. Columbus's secret log recorded the truth about the journey.

> **A VOICE FROM THE PAST**
>
> [We] made 15 leagues [this] day and . . . [I] decided to report less than those actually traveled so in case the voyage were long the men would not be frightened and lose courage.
>
> **Christopher Columbus,** quoted in *Columbus and the Age of Discovery*

*Reading***History**
C. Analyzing Causes What caused Columbus to decide to keep two logs?

By October 10, the men had lost both courage and confidence in their leader. They had been at sea for almost ten weeks and had not seen land for over a month. Afraid that they would starve if the trip went on longer, they talked of returning home. To avoid mutiny, Columbus and the crew struck a bargain. The men agreed to sail on for three more days, and Columbus promised to turn back if they had not sighted land by then. Two days later in the early morning hours of October 12, a sailor on the *Pinta* called out "Tierra, tierra" [Land, land].

## Reaching the Americas

By noon, the ships had landed on an island in the Caribbean Sea. Columbus believed that he had reached the Indies, islands in Southeast Asia where spices grew. The islanders who greeted Columbus and his men were Taino (TY•noh) people, but Columbus mistakenly called them Indians.

Columbus named the island San Salvador. After unfurling the royal banner and flags, he ordered his crew to "bear witness that I was taking possession of this island for the King and Queen." Eager to reach the rich country of Japan, which he believed was nearby, he left San Salvador. He took six or seven Taino with him as guides. For the next three months, he visited several of the Caribbean islands.

Finally, he reached an island that he named Española, which we call Hispaniola today. (See map on page 51.) On that island, Columbus and his men found some gold and precious objects such as pearls. This convinced Columbus that he had reached Asia. He decided to return home, leaving 39 of his men on Hispaniola. Even before Columbus left, his men had angered the Taino people by stealing from them and committing violence. By the time Columbus returned ten months later, the Taino had killed the men.

**Background**
Today, the Indies are called the East Indies. The islands of the Caribbean are called the West Indies.

**NATIVE AMERICAN VIEW OF COLUMBUS**

In 1992, many Native Americans protested the 500th anniversary of Columbus's voyage. Suzan Shown Harjo, who is Cheyenne and Creek, explained why.

*As Native American peoples in this red quarter of Mother Earth, we have no reason to celebrate an invasion that caused the demise [death] of so many of our people and is still causing destruction today.*

The Spanish enslaved the Taino, who nearly all died from disease and bad treatment. This statue is one of the few Taino artifacts left from the 1500s.

In January 1493, he sailed back to Spain. Firmly believing that he had found a new water route to Asia, he wrote to Ferdinand and Isabella. The Spanish rulers called him to the royal court to report on his voyage. Neither Columbus nor the king and queen suspected that he had landed near continents entirely unknown to Europeans.

A French mapmaker uses an instrument to learn his exact position on the globe.

## An Expanding Horizon

Columbus made three more voyages to the Americas, but never brought back the treasures he had promised Spain's rulers. He also failed to meet Queen Isabella's other goal. She wanted Christianity brought to new people. When she learned that Columbus had mistreated and enslaved the people of Hispaniola, she became angry.

After the fourth voyage, Spain's rulers refused to give Columbus any more help. He died in 1506, still believing he had reached Asia and bitter that he had not received the fame or fortune that he deserved.

In time, the geographic knowledge Columbus brought back changed European views of the world. People soon realized that Columbus had reached continents that had been unknown to them previously. And Europeans were eager to see if these continents could make them rich.

*Reading* **History**

**D. Making Inferences** How did the Atlantic become a bridge connecting Europe, Africa, and the Americas?

For centuries, Europeans had seen the ocean as a barrier. With one voyage, Columbus changed that. Instead of a barrier, the Atlantic Ocean became a bridge that connected Europe, Africa, and the Americas. As you will learn in Chapter 2, Columbus's explorations began an era of great wealth and power for Spain. As Spain grew rich, England, France, and other European countries also began to send ships to the Americas.

---

**Section 5 Assessment**

### 1. Terms & Names

**Explain the significance of:**
- navigator
- caravel
- Christopher Columbus

### 2. Using Graphics

On a diagram like the one shown, list the effects of Columbus's voyages.

Columbus's Voyages

| Effect | Effect | Effect | Effect |

Which effects were negative and which were positive? (HI2)

### 3. Main Ideas

**a.** Why was Prince Henry eager to find an all-water route to Asia? (HI2)

**b.** Why did Spain's king and queen decide to support Columbus's first voyage? (HI2)

**c.** Why was Columbus disappointed by the outcome of his four voyages to the Americas? (HI2)

### 4. Critical Thinking

**Analyzing Points of View** Explain how each of the following people might have viewed Columbus's first voyage. Give reasons for their points of view. (REP5)

**THINK ABOUT**
- Columbus
- Queen Isabella
- a Taino chief

**ACTIVITY OPTIONS**

**GEOGRAPHY**

**MATH**

Use the map on page 51. Create an enlarged **map** of Columbus's first voyage, or measure the distance of each voyage to list on a **table**. (CST3)

## The World in 1500 (CST2)

**476**
The city of Rome falls to Germanic tribes.

**500**

**500s**
Camel caravans are crossing the Sahara.

**800s**
The Mississippian culture arises.

**1076**
A Muslim army defeats Ghana.

**1096**
Europeans start the Crusades to win the Holy Land.

**1000**

**1230**
Sundiata starts the Mali Empire.

**1300**
The Anasazi abandon their homes.

**1325**
The Aztecs begin to build Tenochtitlán.

**1347**
The bubonic plague sweeps Europe, killing millions.

**1464**
The Songhai begin their own empire.

**1500**

**1492**
Seeking Asia, Christopher Columbus lands in the Americas.

Americas  West Africa  Europe

## TERMS & NAMES

Briefly explain the significance of each of the following.

1. migrate
2. civilization
3. technology
4. Iroquois League
5. Islam
6. feudalism
7. Crusades
8. Renaissance
9. navigator
10. Christopher Columbus

## REVIEW QUESTIONS

**Crossing to the Americas (pages 27–31)**

1. What are two theories about migration to the Americas? (HI1)
2. For what purposes did the Mound Builders construct earthen mounds? (HI2)

**Societies of North America (pages 32–38)**

3. What enabled the Aztecs to become a strong empire? (HI2)
4. How did the Iroquois League come about? (HI1)

**Societies of West Africa (pages 39–43)**

5. What enabled Ghana, Mali, and Songhai all to grow rich? (HI2)
6. How did Islam's influence in West Africa change from the 700s to the 1400s? (HI2)

**Societies of Europe (pages 44–48)**

7. How did the manor system work during the Middle Ages? (HI2)
8. How did the Crusades increase European interest in trade? (HI2)

**Early European Explorers (pages 49–53)**

9. Why did non-Italian Europeans seek new trade routes to Asia? (HI2)
10. How did Columbus miscalculate the distance to Asia? (HI4)

## CRITICAL THINKING

**1. USING YOUR NOTES: CATEGORIZING INFORMATION**

Using your completed chart, answer the questions below. (HI3)

| | Trade | Technology | Religion | Art |
|---|---|---|---|---|
| AMERICAS (Sections 1 and 2) | | | | |
| WEST AFRICA (Section 3) | | | | |
| EUROPE (Sections 4 and 5) | | | | |

a. What was one instance in which trade spread knowledge?

b. Which of the technologies that you listed are still used today?

c. What religions were practiced in each of the three regions?

**2. ANALYZING LEADERSHIP**

Do you think Columbus was a good leader or a bad one? Use details from the chapter to explain your answer. (HI1)

**3. THEME: DIVERSITY AND UNITY**

How have Native Americans, Africans, and Europeans all influenced American culture? Give examples from your own experience. (HI3)

**4. MAKING GENERALIZATIONS**

What types of goods are people most likely to seek through trade? Think about the trade goods mentioned in the chapter and why people wanted them. (HI2)

**5. APPLYING CITIZENSHIP SKILLS**

Compare the Iroquois League to what you know of the U.S. government. How are they similar? (HI3)

### Interact *with* History

Think about the various encounters between societies mentioned in the chapter. What do you think happened when more Europeans came to the Americas and met Native Americans?

Use the map and your knowledge of U.S. history to answer questions 1 and 2.

Additional Test Practice, pp. S1–S33.

**Columbus's First Voyage, 1492**

Westerly Winds

SPAIN

NORTH AMERICA

40°N

ATLANTIC OCEAN

Trade Winds

Columbus 1492

AFRICA

Trade Winds

N

SOUTH AMERICA

80°W  40°W  0°

**1.** How did the winds affect Columbus's journey? (7.11.1)

A. The westerly winds across the Atlantic made the voyage faster.

B. The trade winds across the Atlantic slowed down the voyage.

C. The trade winds across the Atlantic made the voyage faster.

D. The winds had little effect on Columbus's voyage.

**2.** If Columbus's route had been farther north, which of the following would have happened? (7.11.2)

A. The voyage would have taken less time.

B. The voyage would have taken more time.

C. The voyage would not have been different.

D. The voyage would not have been possible.

This quotation from Olfert Dapper is about Benin City in Africa. Use this quotation and your knowledge of West Africa to answer question 3.

### PRIMARY SOURCE

The houses in this town stand in good order, each one close and evenly placed with its neighbor, just as the houses in Holland stand . . . The king's court is very great. It is built around many square-shaped yards.

**Olfert Dapper,** *Centuries of Greatness*

**3.** The passage best supports which point of view? (7.11.2)

A. Benin City, and other African cities, should be unique, not modeled after European cities.

B. The king's court of Benin City was great in contrast to the rest of the city.

C. The design of Benin City made it an extremely valuable trade center.

D. The design of Benin City was appealing in its resemblance to European cities.

**TEST PRACTICE**
CLASSZONE.COM

## ALTERNATIVE ASSESSMENT

**1.** 📝 **WRITING ABOUT HISTORY**

Imagine you have been hired to write the **brochure** for a Native American exhibit at a museum. (HI1)

• Choose a Native American group discussed in the chapter. Use library resources to learn more about the group.

• Highlight their economy, religion and spiritual beliefs, or arts and crafts in your exhibit. Write a description of the exhibit for your brochure that would encourage people to come.

**2. COOPERATIVE LEARNING**

Work with a group to create a radio program of Columbus's first voyage. Group members can find his log in the library, select parts to record, or create sound effects to play in the background. (HI1)

## INTEGRATED TECHNOLOGY

**DOING INTERNET RESEARCH**

Countries and alliances often use a symbol to represent who they are. The Iroquois League chose a tree as their symbol. Use the Internet and library resources to research the Iroquois League and its symbol. (REP3)

• Research the beliefs and goals of the Iroquois League. Make a list of their beliefs and goals.

• Also search Native American museum sites and/or reservation sites in New York state.

• Describe why the tree was an appropriate symbol for the Iroquois League and explain how it represented the beliefs and goals of the alliance.

**For more about the Iroquois League . . .**

**INTERNET ACTIVITY**
CLASSZONE.COM

# Create and Decode a Pictograph

Native Americans of the Southwest created thousands of images to communicate with each other. These images, known as pictographs, helped people recall certain events, ideas, or information. Even if the people who created them were no longer present, others could read the messages. Most images were painted or carved on the surfaces of rock. There are three types of pictographs: petroglyphs, petrograms, and geoglyphs. (See HELP DESK on the next page.)

**ACTIVITY** Create a pictograph that other students will decode, or figure out. Then, acting as an anthropologist, interview students in one other group about their pictograph.

## TOOLBOX

Each group will need:

drawing paper or poster board

watercolor paints and brushes (optional)

markers

an envelope

regular and colored pencils

**The Fremont culture carved this petroglyph. It is currently located in Dinosaur National Monument—most of which sits in northwestern Colorado.**

## STEP BY STEP

**1** **Form a group of 4 or 5 students.** Together, think of a message to tell someone living in the future. What might you want future generations to know about your culture, or way of life? If you're having trouble coming up with a message, copy the chart below into your notebook. Write information for each category that you think would be interesting to future generations. Then choose one of these categories for your message.

| | |
|---|---|
| **Sports** | |
| **Politics** | |
| **Fashion** | |
| **Music** | |
| **Entertainment** | |
| **Weather** | |
| **Daily Life** | |

**2** **Examine reference materials.** In the library or on the Internet, research Native American pictographs. Use the information you find to help start your project. (See HELP DESK on the next page.)

**3** **Create your pictograph.**
Communicate your message with symbols like the ones that you have researched. Sketch your pictograph on the drawing paper or poster board with a pencil first. Make the pictograph simple so that the decoders will understand your message. Remember to use symbols—not letters.

**4** **Decorate your pictograph.**
Use markers or watercolor paints to finish your pictograph. Also, record the translation of your pictograph in your notebook.

**5** **Exchange your pictograph with another group of students.** Try to decode the message in the pictograph that the other group of students has given you. Write your translation and place it in your envelope. Give the envelope to the group whose pictograph you decoded.

## HELP DESK

For related information see Chapter 1, p. 29.

### Researching Your Project

• *On the Trail of Spider Woman: Petroglyphs, Pictographs, and Myths of the Southwest* by Carol Patterson-Rudolph. Shows variety of actual pictographs.

• *21 Kinds of American Folk Art and How to Make Each One* by Jean and Cle Kinney. Explains process of making pictographs.

For more about pictographs . . .

RESEARCH LINKS
CLASSZONE.COM

### Did You Know?

**Petroglyphs** are images carved into a rock using stone tools. **Petrograms** are images painted on a rock. **Geoglyphs** are images formed on the ground by scraping away soil or by arranging stones to form an image.

**6** **Compare the other students' translation with your actual message.** Did the other students understand your message? Let them know how accurate they were.

## WRITE AND SPEAK

Using the information in the pictograph that you decoded, write a description of the people who created the message. Use the symbols as well as the message itself to help you in your description. Explain to the class how you came to your conclusions.

### REFLECT & ASSESS

• Which symbols in your pictograph were clear to the decoders? Which were not clear?

• What methods did you use to decode the messages of others?

• What did you learn about language and communication from doing this pictograph decoding activity?

# European Exploration of the Americas 1492–1700

Ships in a harbor in Lisbon, Portugal, are preparing for a voyage of exploration.

Smaller boats ferry the crew to the sailing ships.

A crane loads supplies onto the ships, much like today.

**1497**
Cabot searches for Northwest Passage.

**1521**
Cortés conquers the Aztec Empire.

**1535**
Cartier leads expedition up St. Lawrence River.

**1539–1542**
Coronado, de Soto, and Cabrillo explore different parts of North America.

**1565**
Spanish found St. Augustine.

**N. America World** 1492

**1494**
Spain and Portugal agree to Treaty of Tordesillas.

**1534**
English Parliament declares Henry VIII head of the English Church.

**1542**
King of Spain issues the New Laws for better treatment of Native Americans.

**1588**
English navy defeats Spanish Armada.

The year is 1510. You live in a European port town and have heard exciting tales about mysterious lands across the sea. You decide to join a voyage of exploration in search of fortune.

# Would you join a voyage of exploration?

## What Do You Think?

- What do you think led Europeans to explore distant lands?
- What reasons would make you want to join a voyage of exploration?
- What reasons would keep you from joining such a voyage?

**RESEARCH LINKS**
CLASSZONE.COM

Visit the Chapter 2 links for more information about exploration of the Americas.

**1609**
Hudson searches for Northwest Passage.

**1626**
Dutch buy Manhattan Island.

**1680**
Popé leads Pueblo Revolt and forces Spanish from New Mexico.

1700

**1644**
Manchus establish Qing Dynasty in China.

**1651**
English Parliament passes Navigation Act.

# Reading Strategy: Finding Main Ideas

## What Do You Know?

What comes to mind when someone uses the word *explorer*? Why do you think people explored different territories?

### Think About

- what you've learned about explorers from movies, school, or your parents
- reasons that people travel throughout the world today
- your responses to the Interact with History about joining a voyage of exploration (see page 59)

(see page 59)

**CALIFORNIA STANDARDS**

**Reading 2.0** Students read and understand grade-level-appropriate material. They describe and connect the essential ideas, arguments, and perspectives of the text by using their knowledge of text structure, organization, and purpose.

## What Do You Want to Know?

What questions do you have about exploration or the early colonization of the Americas? Write those questions in your notebook before you read the chapter.

## Finding Main Ideas

To help you remember what you read, take notes about the events and ideas discussed in the chapter. Taking notes means writing down important information. The chart below lists the major events and ideas covered in the chapter. Use the chart to take notes about these important events and ideas.

**S** See Skillbuilder Handbook, page R3.

 **Taking Notes**

| Event/Idea | Notes |
|---|---|
| Exploration | |
| Establishing Colonies | |
| European Competition | |
| Columbian Exchange | |
| Origins of Slavery | |

# Spain Claims an Empire

| MAIN IDEA | WHY IT MATTERS NOW | TERMS & NAMES |
|---|---|---|
| Spain claimed a large empire in the Americas. | The influence of Spanish culture remains strong in modern America. | Treaty of Tordesillas  *conquistador*<br>missionary  Hernando Cortés<br>mercantilism  Montezuma<br>Amerigo Vespucci  Francisco Pizarro |

## ONE EUROPEAN'S STORY

In 1493, the rulers of Spain and Portugal wanted Pope Alexander VI to decide who would control the lands that sailors from their countries were exploring.

In May 1493, Alexander VI issued his ruling. He drew an imaginary line around the world. It was called the Line of Demarcation. Portugal could claim all non-Christian lands to the east of the line. Spain could claim the non-Christian lands to the west. In this section, you will learn how Spain and Portugal led Europe in the race to gain colonies in the Americas.

**Pope Alexander VI**

## Spain and Portugal Compete

King John II was unhappy with the pope's placement of the line. He believed that it favored Spain. So he demanded that the Spanish rulers meet with him to change the pope's decision. In June 1494, the two countries agreed to the **Treaty of Tordesillas** (TAWR•day•SEEL•yahs). This treaty moved the Line of Demarcation more than 800 miles farther west.

The change eventually allowed Portugal to claim much of eastern South America, which later became the Portuguese colony of Brazil. After making this agreement, Spain and Portugal increased their voyages of exploration in search of wealth, power, and glory.

European countries had three main goals during this age of exploration. First, they wanted to spread Christianity beyond Europe. Each expedition included **missionaries,** or people sent to convert the native peoples to Christianity. Second, they wanted to expand their empires. Third, they wanted to become rich.

By increasing their wealth, European countries could gain power and security. An economic system called **mercantilism** describes how

### Taking Notes

Use your chart to take notes about exploring and establishing colonies.

| Event/Idea | Notes |
|---|---|
| Exploration | |
| Establishing Colonies | |
| European Competition | |
| Columbian Exchange | |
| Origins of Slavery | |

# Mercantilism

The main goal of mercantilism was to increase the money in a country's treasury by creating a favorable balance of trade. A country had a favorable balance of trade if it had more exports than imports. Colonies helped a country have the goods to maintain a favorable balance of trade.

For example, say Spain sold $500 in sugar to France, and France sold $300 in cloth to Spain. France would also have to pay Spain $200 worth of precious metals to pay for all the sugar. Spain would then have a favorable balance of trade because the value of its exports (sugar) was greater than the value of its imports (cloth). Spain would become richer because of the precious metals it received from France.

Sugar
$500

Spain

France

Cloth
$300

Gold & Silver
$200

## CONNECT TO HISTORY

1. **Finding Main Ideas** Under mercantilism, what did a country need to do to become rich? Discuss the way colonies enriched a country according to mercantilism.

    See Skillbuilder Handbook, page R5.

## CONNECT TO TODAY

2. **Making Inferences** Think about your own family budget. What do you think would happen if your family collected less money than it paid for goods for several years? Do you think this situation would be the same for a nation as it would for a family?

   **For more about mercantilism . . .**

    **RESEARCH LINKS** CLASSZONE.COM

**CALIFORNIA STANDARDS**

**7.11.3** Examine the origins of modern capitalism; the influence of mercantilism and cottage industry; the elements and importance of a market economy in seventeenth-century Europe; the changing international trading and marketing patterns, including their locations on a world map; and the influence of explorers and map makers.

---

Europeans enriched their treasuries. (See *Economics in History*, above.) Colonies helped nations do this in several ways. They provided mines that produced gold and silver. They also produced goods such as crops that could be traded for gold and silver. Finally, they served as a market for the home country. The search for riches spurred European exploration.

> **Vocabulary**
> **colony:** a region or people that is politically and economically controlled by another country

## Europeans Explore Foreign Lands

After Columbus's first voyage, many explorers went to sea. **Amerigo Vespucci** (vehs•POO•chee) was one of the first. He was an Italian sailor who set out in 1501 to find a sea route to Asia. Vespucci realized that the land he saw on this voyage was not Asia. A German mapmaker was impressed by Vespucci's account of the lands, so he named the continent "America" after him.

Another famous explorer was the Spaniard Vasco Núñez de Balboa. Balboa heard Native American reports of another ocean. In 1513, he led an expedition through the jungles of Panama and reached the Pacific Ocean. Raising his sword, Balboa stepped into the surf and claimed the ocean and all the lands around it for Spain. (See page 59.)

Perhaps no explorer was more capable than the Portuguese sailor Ferdinand Magellan. He proposed to reach Asia by sailing west around South America. The Spanish king agreed to fund Magellan's voyage.

In 1519, Magellan set out from Spain with five ships and about 240 men. After a stormy passage around South America, Magellan entered the Pacific Ocean. For several months his crew crossed the Pacific, suffering great hardship. A member of the crew described what they ate.

**A VOICE FROM THE PAST**

We were three months and twenty days without . . . fresh food. We ate biscuit, which was no longer biscuit, but powder of biscuits swarming with worms. . . . We drank . . . water that had been putrid for many days.

**Antonio Pigafetta,** quoted in *The Discoverers*

*Reading***History**
**A. Finding Main Ideas** What were the main contributions of Vespucci, Balboa, and Magellan as explorers?

Eventually, Magellan reached the Philippines, where he became involved in a local war and was killed. But his crew traveled on. In 1522, the one remaining ship arrived back in Spain. The sailors in Magellan's crew became the first people to sail around the world.

## The Invasion of Mexico

While Magellan's crew was sailing around the world, the Spanish began their conquest of the Americas. Soldiers called ***conquistadors*** (kahn•KWIHS•tuh•DAWRZ), or conquerors, explored the Americas and claimed them for Spain. **Hernando Cortés** was one of these *conquistadors*. He landed on the Central American coast with 508 men in 1519.

The Spanish arrival shook the Aztec Empire, which dominated most

**European Exploration of the Americas, 1500–1550**

**Explorers' Routes**
- Spanish
- Portuguese
- French
- English
- Aztec Empire, 1519
- Inca Empire, 1525

Cabot 1497
Cartier
1535–1536
1534
ENGLAND
EUROPE
FRANCE
PORTUGAL
SPAIN
AZORES
CANARY ISLANDS
MADEIRA
AFRICA

NORTH AMERICA
Coronado 1540–1542
Santa Fe
De Soto 1539–1542
Cabrillo 1542–1543
Cabeza de Vaca 1528–1536
St. Augustine
Ponce de León 1512–1513
Cortés 1519
CUBA
HISPANIOLA
Santo Domingo
Gulf of Mexico
Tenochtitlán (Mexico City)
Veracruz
Caribbean Sea
Columbus 1502–1504
Verrazzano 1524
ATLANTIC OCEAN
40° N
Tropic of Cancer
Vespucci
Cabral 1500
Magellan 1519
Magellan's Crew 1522
0° Equator

PACIFIC OCEAN

N
0    1,000 Miles
0    2,000 Kilometers

Balboa 1510–1513
Pizarro 1530–1533
SOUTH AMERICA
1499–1500
1501–1502

**GEOGRAPHY SKILLBUILDER**
**Interpreting Maps**
1. **Movement** *How many years did it take Cabeza de Vaca to travel from Florida to Central Mexico?*
2. **Region** *Which continent did the English and French explore?*

of Mexico. The Aztec emperor **Montezuma** feared that Cortés had been sent by an Aztec god to rule Mexico. Montezuma sent Cortés gifts—including two disks of solid gold and silver—to get him to leave. But the gifts only excited Spanish dreams of riches.

The Spaniards marched inland and formed alliances (agreements with friendly peoples) with the native peoples who hated Aztec rule. After a few months, Cortés reached the Aztec capital, Tenochtitlán (teh•NAWCH•tee•TLAHN). Montezuma received Cortés with great ceremony and housed the *conquistadors* in a magnificent palace. But Cortés took Montezuma captive and tried to rule the Aztec Empire by giving commands through Montezuma. The Aztecs rebelled.

The Aztecs surrounded the Spaniards and their allies in their headquarters in Tenochtitlán. On the night of June 30, 1520, the Spaniards tried to sneak out of the city, but the Aztecs discovered them and vicious fighting broke out. About 800 Spaniards and more than 1,000 of their allies were killed that night. The Spaniards later called the event *La Noche Triste* (lah NAW•cheh TREES•teh)—the Sad Night.

Despite this defeat, the Spaniards and their allies regrouped. In May 1521, Cortés led his forces back to Tenochtitlán. At this point, the Spaniards got help from an invisible ally. Many Aztecs fell victim to an out-

**Background**
One of the people whom Cortés brought into his group was Malintzin. She was the daughter of a local chief and served as an interpreter for Cortés.

## AMERICA'S HISTORY MAKERS

**HERNANDO CORTÉS**

**1485–1547**

Hernando Cortés was born in Spain to a noble but poor family. In 1504, at the age of 19, he sailed to the Americas to seek his fortune. Although he became a wealthy landowner in Cuba, he was not satisfied. "I have come to win gold," he said, "not to plow the fields like a peasant." His great chance came when he was picked to lead the expedition to Mexico. Strongwilled, shrewd, and cruel, Cortés succeeded against great odds.

**MONTEZUMA**

**1466–1520**

Montezuma, ruler of the Aztec Empire, rose to the throne in 1502. His words carried weight with his subjects.

According to Juan de Tovar, a Jesuit, "When he spoke, he drew the sympathy of others by his subtle phrases and . . . by his profound reasoning." Montezuma lived in great luxury, receiving officials and commoners alike at his lavish palace. His subjects treated him almost as a god and were not allowed to look at him. Though brutal at times, he was said to be a just and effective ruler.

**Which man would you prefer to have as leader of your country? Why?**

**Vocabulary**
siege: surrounding of a city

break of smallpox, which severely weakened their ranks. The germs that caused this disease had been brought to America by the Europeans.

Cortés placed Tenochtitlán under siege for three months. When Tenochtitlán finally fell, the Aztec Empire lay in ruins. An Aztec poet described the scene.

> **A VOICE FROM THE PAST**
>
> Broken spears lie in the roads; we have torn our hair in our grief. The houses are roofless now, and their walls are red with blood. . . . We have pounded our hands in despair against the adobe walls, for our inheritance, our city, is lost and dead.
>
> **Aztec poet,** quoted in *Seeds of Change*

On the rubble of the Aztec capital, the Spanish built Mexico City. Over time, the populations and cultures of Spain and Mexico merged and produced a new society, that of the present-day nation of Mexico.

This Aztec mask represents Quetzalcoatl, the god that Montezuma feared had sent Cortés.

## The Conquest of the Incan Empire

*Reading*History
**B. Reading a Map** Use the map on page 63 to find the Incan Empire.

Despite the fall of the Aztecs, a people called the Inca still had a powerful empire centered in the Cuzco Valley in what is now Peru. By 1525, the Inca ruled a 2,000-mile-long territory in the Andes Mountains along the western coast of South America. The Inca also possessed much gold and silver.

Native American stories of Incan wealth reached the Spanish. In 1531, a *conquistador* named **Francisco Pizarro** led an expedition of 180 men into Peru. Like the Aztecs, the Incas feared that the Spanish might be gods. The Incan emperor Atahualpa (AH•tuh•WAHL•puh) ordered his troops not to fight. Then he went to meet the *conquistadors*. The Spanish attacked quickly. They killed thousands of Incas and took Atahualpa captive. In an attempt to free himself, the Incan emperor gave the Spanish a treasure of gold. The Spaniards strangled him anyway.

*Reading*History
**C. Drawing Conclusions** Why did the Incan Empire fall to the Spanish?

With Atahualpa dead, the Incan Empire collapsed. Having been ordered by Atahualpa not to fight, the Incas refused to defend themselves even after his death. Then Pizarro took control of this area for Spain. The Spanish called the area Peru.

## Reasons for Spanish Victories

People have long been amazed that the great Aztec and Incan empires fell to such small groups of Spanish *conquistadors*. But Spanish success can be explained by four major reasons.

1. The spread of European diseases killed millions of Native Americans and weakened their resistance to conquest.
2. The Spanish were excellent soldiers and sailors. They also had superior weapons, such as guns, that helped them defeat much larger Native American armies.

Estevanico was a slave who helped the Spanish explore parts of North America. He was killed during Coronado's search for golden cities.

3. Spain made alliances with Native Americans who were enemies of the Aztecs and Incas.
4. The Spanish *conquistadors* acted brutally toward the Native Americans under their control.

Having conquered the major Native American empires in Central and South America, the Spaniards began to explore other parts of North and South America.

*Reading*History
D. Drawing Conclusions
What was the most important reason for the Spanish success in conquering territory in the Americas?

## Other Spanish Explorers

The Spaniards hoped to collect treasures from North America as they had from Mexico and Peru. Rumors of golden cities kept Spanish hopes high. For example, a few men, including the Spaniard Álvar Núñez Cabeza de Vaca and Estevanico, a slave of North African descent, survived a shipwreck off the North American mainland. As the men wandered across the continent, they heard Native American stories about cities of gold. When they reached Mexico, Cabeza de Vaca and Estevanico thrilled the Spaniards with the rumors.

Between 1539 and 1542, three expeditions set out to find these cities. Francisco Vázquez de Coronado traveled through present-day Arizona and New Mexico. Hernando de Soto set out from Florida to explore the southeast. Juan Rodríguez Cabrillo sailed up the California coast. But all three failed to find the fabled cities of gold.

For a while, it seemed that the Spaniards would explore the Americas all by themselves. As you will read in the next section, however, the Spanish would soon face competition from other Europeans.

---

## Section 1 Assessment

### 1. Terms & Names

**Explain the significance of:**
- Treaty of Tordesillas
- missionary
- mercantilism
- Amerigo Vespucci
- *conquistador*
- Hernando Cortés
- Montezuma
- Francisco Pizarro

### 2. Using Graphics

Review the section and find four events to place on a time line that shows how Spain built its empire.

**Spain Builds an Empire**

Which event do you think is the most important? Why? (CST2)

### 3. Main Ideas

**a.** Why did Europeans explore different territories? (HI2)

**b.** Why did Spain succeed in conquering so much of the Americas? (HI2)

**c.** What was significant about the Magellan expedition? (HI2)

### 4. Critical Thinking

**Comparing** What was similar about the conquests of Mexico and Peru? (HI2)

**THINK ABOUT**
- the *conquistadors*
- the Incan and Aztec leaders

---

**ACTIVITY OPTIONS**

**ART**

**LANGUAGE ARTS**

Use the library or the Internet to find a photograph of an Aztec or Incan artifact. Create a **replica** or write a **description** of the object. (CST3)

# European Competition in North America

| MAIN IDEA | WHY IT MATTERS NOW | TERMS & NAMES |
|---|---|---|
| Other European countries competed with Spain for control over territory in the Americas. | European culture has strongly influenced American culture. | Henry Hudson    Jacques Cartier<br>John Cabot    Spanish Armada<br>Giovanni da Verrazzano    Samuel de Champlain<br>New France |

## ONE EUROPEAN'S STORY

In 1609, the Englishman **Henry Hudson** sailed under the Dutch flag from Europe. He hoped to find a route to China. Arriving at the coast of present-day New York, he sailed up the river that now bears his name. Hudson described what he saw.

*A VOICE FROM THE PAST*

The land is the finest for cultivation that I ever in my life set foot upon, and it also abounds in trees of every description. The natives are a very good people; for, when they saw that I would not remain, they . . . broke [their arrows] in pieces and threw them into the fire.

**Henry Hudson,** quoted in *Discoverers of America*

Hudson did not find a passage to Asia, but he led another expedition in 1610, this time for the English. In Canada, he disovered a large bay, today called Hudson Bay. After enduring a harsh winter, his crew rebelled. They put Hudson, his young son, and several loyal sailors in a small boat and set them adrift. Hudson's party was never heard from again.

## The Search for the Northwest Passage

Hudson's voyages showed that some European countries hoped to find a westward route to Asia as late as the 1600s. While Spain was taking control of the Americas, other Europeans were sending out expeditions to find the Northwest Passage, a water route through North America to Asia.

One of the first explorers to chart a northern route across the Atlantic in search of Asia was the Italian sailor **John Cabot**. In 1497, Cabot crossed the Atlantic Ocean to explore for the English. He landed in the area of Newfoundland, Canada. He was certain that he had reached Asia and claimed the land for England. The next year he set sail once more,

### CALIFORNIA STANDARDS

**7.11.2** Discuss the exchanges of plants, animals, technology, culture, and ideas among Europe, Africa, Asia and the Americas in the 15th and 16th centuries and the major economic and social effects on each continent.

**7.11.3** Examine the origins of modern capitalism; the influence of mercantilism and cottage industry; the elements and importance of a market economy in seventeenth-century Europe; the changing international trading and marketing patterns, including their locations on a world map; and the influence of explorers and map makers.

**CST3** Students use a variety of maps and documents to identify physical and cultural features of neighborhoods, cities, states, and countries and to explain the historical migration of people, expansion and disintegration of empires, and the growth of economic systems.

**HI2** Students understand and distinguish cause, effect, sequence, and correlation in historical events, including the long- and short-term causal relations.

### Taking Notes

Use your chart to take notes about European competition for colonies.

| Event/Idea | Notes |
|---|---|
| Exploration | |
| Establishing Colonies | |
| European Competition | |
| Columbian Exchange | |
| Origins of Slavery | |

*European Exploration of the Americas* **67**

hoping to reach Japan. He was never seen again. Even so, his voyages were the basis for future English colonies along North America's Atlantic shore.

In 1524, another Italian, **Giovanni da Verrazzano,** set out under the French flag to find the Northwest Passage. He explored the Atlantic coastline of North America, but there was no passage to be found.

France tried again between 1534 and 1536 with the voyages of **Jacques Cartier** (ZHAHK kahr•TYAY). Cartier traveled up the St. Lawrence River to the site of present-day Montreal. At that point, rapids blocked the way and ended his search for the Northwest Passage. It would be almost 75 years before the French would return to colonize the region.

*Reading* **History**

**A. Reading a Map** Use the maps on pages 63 and 67 to see the areas Cabot, Hudson, Verrazzano, and Cartier visited.

## Spain Responds to Competition

French and English claims to North America angered Spain, which had claimed the land under the Treaty of Tordesillas. The tensions between Spain, England, and France stemmed from religious conflicts in Europe, such as the Reformation, which you read about in Chapter 1. These conflicts also led to fighting in the Americas.

Florida was one of the battlegrounds between the Spanish and the French. In 1564, a group of French Protestants, called Huguenots (HYOO•guh•NAHTS), founded a colony called Fort Caroline. Before long, Spanish troops under the command of Pedro Menéndez de Avilés arrived in that area. "This is the armada of the King of Spain," he announced, "who has sent me [here] to burn and hang the Lutheran [Protestant] French." Menéndez built a fort, St. Augustine, a short distance away. Then he brutally massacred the French.

**Vocabulary**
**armada:** a fleet of warships

### America's HERITAGE

**ST. AUGUSTINE**
The thick stone walls of the fort at St. Augustine (shown below) still stand guard over the Florida coast today. Founded in 1565, St. Augustine is the oldest permanent European settlement in the United States. For more than two centuries, St. Augustine was an important outpost of Spain's empire in the Americas. Many Spanish colonial buildings remain at the site. The fort is now a national monument.

## Spain and England Clash

Religious differences and the quest for national power also led to conflict between Spain and England. In 1558, Queen Elizabeth I, a Protestant, came to the English throne. Spain, which was Catholic, plotted to remove the Protestant queen. But Elizabeth fought to defend England and challenge Spain's power at sea.

Although England's navy was not as powerful as Spain's, the English fleet had many speedy ships with skillful sailors. Daring sailors, known as sea dogs, used these ships to attack the bulky Spanish sailing ships—called galleons—that brought gold and silver from the Americas.

Sir Francis Drake became the most famous of the sea dogs because of his bold adventures and attacks against the Spanish. In 1577, Drake began a three-year voyage that took him around the world. During this voyage,

The English navy used its smaller, quicker ships to defeat the larger, slower galleons of the Spanish Armada.

he raided Spanish ports and ships in South America. He stole great amounts of treasure from them. When he arrived home in 1580, he was a national hero. Not only had Drake and his men hounded the Spanish, but they were also the first Englishmen to sail around the world.

## The Defeat of the Spanish Armada

The attacks of Drake and other sea dogs enraged Philip II, the Spanish king. Determined to teach the English a lesson, Philip sent the **Spanish Armada** to conquer England and restore Catholicism to that nation. This fleet, made up of 130 ships, set out for England in the summer of 1588.

The English and Spanish navies met in the English Channel, which separates England from the European continent. In their smaller but faster craft, the English darted among the Spanish warships, firing deadly rounds with their cannons. Confused and crippled, the armada was retreating when it was hit by a severe storm. With half of its ships destroyed, the armada barely made it home.

Spain was still quite strong after the defeat of the armada. It quickly rebuilt its navy and maintained its large colonial possessions. But Spain would never again be as powerful as it was in 1588.

The English victory over Spain had two important effects. First, England remained independent and Protestant. Although England was less powerful than Spain, it had shown that it could defend itself. Second, Spain's image suffered. The world saw that Spain could be beaten. Other nations joined England in challenging Spain.

*Reading* **History**
**B. Drawing Conclusions**
Why was the defeat of the Spanish Armada important?

English adventurers like Drake continued to attack Spanish interests abroad. In addition, England challenged Spanish claims to lands in North America, such as California and Newfoundland. Even so, England took a cautious approach to overseas expansion. The English government refused to provide money to start colonies. Instead, private citizens had to provide the money for colonization. As a result, England did not establish a successful colony in America until after 1600.

## The French and Dutch Seek Trade

France and the Netherlands were also looking for ways to gain wealth through exploration and colonization. At first, their goal in the Americas was to find the Northwest Passage to Asia. When that search failed, they began to focus on North America itself.

The Frenchman **Samuel de Champlain** (sham•PLAYN) explored the St. Lawrence River. In 1608, he founded a fur-trading post at Quebec. This post became the first permanent French settlement in North America. Champlain's activities opened a rich fur trade with local Native Americans. After a couple of decades, **New France,** as the colony was called, began to thrive.

At the same time, the Dutch were building a colony called New Netherland. It was located along the Hudson River in present-day New York. After Hudson's voyage up the river in 1609, the Dutch built Fort Nassau in 1614, near the site of the modern city of Albany.

In 1626, the Dutch bought Manhattan Island from Native Americans. The Dutch then founded the town of New Amsterdam on that site, where New York City is currently located. New Netherland was soon thriving from the fur trade with Native Americans.

These early French and Dutch colonies, however, were small compared to the large empire Spain was building in the Americas. You will read about the growth of Spain's American empire in the next section.

*Reading*History
C. Making Inferences Why do you think it took France and the Netherlands so long to set up colonies in the Americas?

Section 2 Assessment

### 1. Terms & Names

**Explain the significance of:**
- Henry Hudson
- John Cabot
- Giovanni da Verrazzano
- Jacques Cartier
- Spanish Armada
- Samuel de Champlain
- New France

### 2. Using Graphics

Use a chart like the one below to show how European nations competed for power. (REP1)

| England |  |
|---------|--|
| France |  |
| Netherlands |  |
| Spain |  |

### 3. Main Ideas

**a.** What were the English, French, and Dutch searching for in their early voyages of exploration? (HI1)

**b.** How did England defeat the Spanish Armada? (HI1)

**c.** Where did the French and Dutch set up their first American colonies? (HI1)

### 4. Critical Thinking

**Making Inferences** Why do you think England founded colonies later than Spain did? (HI1)

**THINK ABOUT**
- conditions in Spain and England
- the lands each country discovered

**ACTIVITY OPTIONS**

MUSIC

TECHNOLOGY

Research the life of one of the explorers discussed in this section. Compose a **song** or design a **Web page** about that person. (REP1)

# The Spanish and Native Americans

| MAIN IDEA | WHY IT MATTERS NOW | TERMS & NAMES |
|---|---|---|

**MAIN IDEA**

Spanish rule in the Americas had terrible consequences for Native Americans.

**WHY IT MATTERS NOW**

The destruction of Native American cultures created social problems that continue today.

**TERMS & NAMES**

viceroyalty
*encomienda*
*hacienda*
mission

Popé
plantation
Bartolomé de Las Casas
Columbian Exchange

## ONE AMERICAN'S STORY

Huamán Poma, a Peruvian Native American, wrote to King Philip III of Spain to complain about the abuse the Spanish heaped upon Native Americans.

### A VOICE FROM THE PAST

It is their [the Spanish] practice to collect Indians into groups and send them to forced labor without wages, while they themselves receive the payment.

**Huamán Poma,** *Letter to a King*

In his letter, Poma asked the king to help the Native Americans and uphold the rule of law in Peru. If the king actually read the letter, it made no difference. Spanish colonists continued to mistreat Native Americans as the Spanish Empire expanded in the Americas.

A Spanish priest forces a Native American woman to work at a loom.

**CALIFORNIA STANDARDS**

**7.11.2** Discuss the exchanges of plants, animals, technology, culture, and ideas among Europe, Africa, Asia and the Americas in the 15th and 16th centuries and the major economic and social effects on each continent.

**8.8.5** Discuss Mexican settlements and their locations, cultural traditions, attitudes toward slavery, land-grant system, and economies.

**CST3** Students use a variety of maps and documents to identify physical and cultural features of neighborhoods, cities, states, and countries and to explain the historical migration of people, expansion and disintegration of empires, and the growth of economic systems.

**HI2** Students understand and distinguish cause, effect, sequence, and correlation in historical events, including the long- and short-term causal relations.

## Spanish Colonies in the Americas

The Spanish Empire grew rapidly, despite efforts by other European countries to compete with Spain. By 1700, it controlled much of the Americas. Spain took several steps to establish an effective colonial government. First, it divided its American empire into two provinces called New Spain and Peru. Each province was called a **viceroyalty**. The top official of each viceroyalty was called the viceroy. He ruled in the king's name.

The Spanish also built new roads to transport people and goods across the empire. These roads stretched outward from the capitals at Mexico City and Lima. The roads helped Spain to control the colonies by allowing soldiers to move quickly from place to place. Roads also improved the Spanish economy because materials, such as gold and silver, could be transported efficiently to the coast and then to Spain.

**Taking Notes**

Use your chart to take notes about establishing colonies and the Columbian Exchange.

| Event/Idea | Notes |
|---|---|
| Exploration | |
| Establishing Colonies | |
| European Competition | |
| Columbian Exchange | |
| Origins of Slavery | |

## Spain's American Empire, 1700

NORTH AMERICA

ATLANTIC OCEAN

WEST INDIES

Mexico City

CENTRAL AMERICA

N 0 1,000 Miles
0 2,000 Kilometers

Viceroyalty of New Spain
Viceroyalty of Peru

Lima

SOUTH AMERICA

PACIFIC OCEAN

40°N
Tropic of Cancer
0° Equator
Tropic of Capricorn
40°S
120°W 80°W 40°W

**GEOGRAPHY SKILLBUILDER Interpreting Maps**
1. **Location** *Which viceroyalty included the West Indies?*
2. **Region** *Which viceroyalty covered more territory?*

# Life in Spanish America

Spanish colonists received *encomiendas* to help them make the colonies productive. An **_encomienda_** was a grant of Native American labor. Hernando Cortés received a grant of more than 100,000 Native Americans to work his estate.

The Spanish rulers also created large estates, called **_haciendas_**, to provide food for the colony. *Haciendas* usually became large farms where Native Americans worked to grow cash crops, such as coffee and cotton. The *encomienda* and *hacienda* systems put much of the power and land in the hands of a few people.

The Spaniards made sure that people with Spanish backgrounds held power in the colonies. Spanish-born colonists such as Cortés made up the top layer of colonial society. Just below the Spanish were the Creoles—people of Spanish descent who were born in the colonies. The next step down the social order were the *mestizos*. *Mestizos* are people of mixed Spanish and Native American ancestry. The people with the least power and fewest rights were Native Americans and enslaved Africans.

**Background**
The problem of unequal wealth, especially in land, continues to trouble Latin American societies today.

# The Role of the Church

The Catholic Church played an important role in Spanish colonial society. In places like New Mexico and California, the church built **missions,** settlements that included a church, a town, and farmlands. The goal of the missions was to convert Native Americans to Christianity. The missions also increased Spanish control over the land.

Missionaries helped the Native Americans to create a better supply of food. They also offered Native Americans protection against enemies. Many Native Americans learned how to read and write in the missions. Others developed skills such as carpentry and metalworking.

Over time, however, many Native Americans grew increasingly unhappy. The missionaries often worked them as if they were slaves. The missionaries also tried to replace Native American religions and traditions. As a result, some Native Americans ran away, while others rebelled. Some destroyed churches and killed missionaries.

In 1680, a man named **Popé** led the Pueblo Indians in a rebellion against the Spanish. His forces surrounded the Spanish settlement at

*Reading*History
**A. Summarizing** How did the Spanish missions change the lives of Native Americans?

Santa Fe, in present-day New Mexico, and forced the colonists to flee. Popé ordered the churches and other Spanish buildings to be destroyed. He then tried to revive native customs that had been lost under Spanish rule. But before long, attacks from neighboring tribes weakened Pueblo control. In 1692, the Spanish regained control of Santa Fe.

## Sugar Plantations Develop

The Spanish also forced Native Americans to work on **plantations**, large farms that raised cash crops. These crops were usually exported to Europe. The most important crop was sugar.

**Background**
Other plantation crops included tobacco, cotton, cochineal (a dye), and cacao.

Although sugar was in great demand in Europe, there was not much land there to grow it. The resulting demand led to the development of sugar plantations in the Americas. On his second voyage to the Americas, in 1493, Columbus brought sugar cane to Hispaniola, one of the Caribbean islands he had landed on in 1492. He found ideal conditions for sugar production there. Spanish planters soon expanded operations to the nearby islands that Spain colonized.

Sugar plantations required many workers, so the Spanish planters turned to native peoples, such as the Taino. Through *encomiendas*, the Spaniards forced thousands of Taino to work in the fields. The plantations thrived, but many of the Taino suffered and died.

## The Abuse of Native Americans

Most Spaniards treated the Native Americans as little more than beasts of burden. According to Fray Toribio de Benavente, a Catholic missionary, the Spanish "do nothing but command. They are the drones who suck the honey which is made by the poor bees, the Indians."

Not all Spaniards approved of this treatment. One man in particular fought for better treatment of Native

### HISTORY *through* ART

Theodore de Bry created this picture, *Sugar: the greatest gift of the Old World to the New,* in the 1600s. It shows workers processing sugar in the Americas. Europeans brought sugar production to the Americas from the Mediterranean.

**How does the picture help explain why the Europeans used slaves to make sugar?**

73

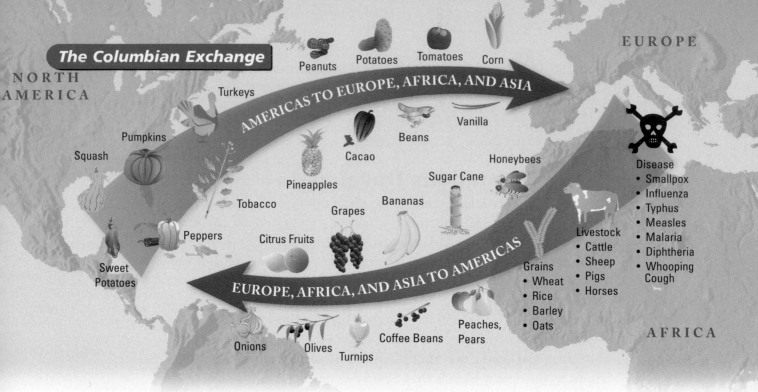

**The Columbian Exchange**

EUROPE

NORTH AMERICA

AMERICAS TO EUROPE, AFRICA, AND ASIA

Peanuts  Potatoes  Tomatoes  Corn

Turkeys

Pumpkins

Squash

Vanilla

Beans

Cacao

Honeybees

Sugar Cane

Pineapples

Tobacco

Bananas

Grapes

Peppers

Citrus Fruits

EUROPE, AFRICA, AND ASIA TO AMERICAS

Sweet Potatoes

Grains
• Wheat
• Rice
• Barley
• Oats

Livestock
• Cattle
• Sheep
• Pigs
• Horses

Disease
• Smallpox
• Influenza
• Typhus
• Measles
• Malaria
• Diphtheria
• Whooping Cough

Onions  Olives  Turnips  Coffee Beans  Peaches, Pears

AFRICA

Americans. His name was **Bartolomé de Las Casas**. Las Casas had come to Hispaniola in 1502 and taken part in the conquest of Cuba a decade later. For his part in the conquest, he received an *encomienda*. Las Casas was also a Catholic priest, however, and he soon faced a moral dilemma: How can a person serve God and enslave Native Americans at the same time?

In 1514, Las Casas gave up his claim to the Native Americans who worked for him. For the next 50 years, he fought against the abuse of Native Americans, earning the title "Protector of the Indians."

Because of his efforts, the Spanish king issued the New Laws in 1542. These laws ordered the gradual freeing of all enslaved Native Americans. Holders of *encomiendas* who were found guilty of mistreating Native Americans had their *encomiendas* taken away. However, Spanish colonists strongly protested against the New Laws, and the king eventually reversed many of them.

## The Columbian Exchange

The arrival of the Spanish in the Americas brought more than a clash of peoples and cultures. It also brought a movement of plants, animals, and diseases between the Eastern and Western hemispheres. This movement of living things between hemispheres is called the **Columbian Exchange**.

One result of the Columbian Exchange was the transfer of germs from Europe to the Americas. When Europeans came to America, they brought with them germs that caused diseases such as smallpox, measles, and influenza. Native Americans had no immunity to them.

Although exact numbers are unknown, historians estimate that diseases brought by Europeans killed more than 20 million Native Americans in Mexico in the first century after conquest. Many scholars agree that the population of Native Americans in Central America decreased by 90 to 95 percent between the years 1519 and 1619. The

*Reading*History
**B. Making Inferences** What might have happened if Native Americans had been immune to European diseases?

result was similar in Peru and other parts of the Americas. A Spanish missionary in Mexico described the effects of smallpox on the Aztecs.

### A VOICE FROM THE PAST

There was a great havoc. Very many died of it. They could not walk. . . . They could not move; they could not stir; they could not change position, nor lie on one side; nor face down, nor on their backs. And if they stirred, much did they cry out. Great was its destruction.

**Bernardino de Sahagún,** quoted in *Seeds of Change*

Other effects of the Columbian Exchange were more positive. The Spanish brought many plants and animals to the Americas. European livestock—cattle, pigs, and horses—all thrived in the Americas. Crops from the Eastern Hemisphere, such as grapes, onions, and wheat, also thrived in the Western Hemisphere.

The Columbian Exchange benefited Europe, too. Many American crops became part of the European diet. Two that had a huge impact were potatoes and corn, which are highly nutritious. They helped feed European populations that might otherwise have gone hungry. Potatoes, for example, became an important food in Ireland, Russia, and other parts of northern Europe. Without potatoes, Europe's population might not have grown as rapidly as it did.

By mixing the products of two hemispheres, the Columbian Exchange brought the world closer together. Of course, people were also moving from one hemisphere to the other, blending their cultures in the process. The next section focuses on one important aspect of the movement of peoples: the forced migration of enslaved Africans to the Americas.

**Background**
In Ireland, the population increased from 3.2 million in 1754 to more than 8 million in 1845, largely because of the high level of nutrients in potatoes.

## Now and then

**KILLER BEES**
Even today, plant and animal species continue to move from one hemisphere to the other. A recent example of this is the killer bee (shown below).

Killer bees were first brought to Brazil from Africa to help make honey in the 1950s. Killer bees are aggressive, however, and can kill large animals when they swarm. After some of these bees escaped from a Brazilian laboratory in 1957, they began to migrate. In recent years, they have been responsible for the deaths of a number of pets in the American Southwest.

---

## Section 3 Assessment

### 1. Terms & Names

**Explain the significance of:**
- viceroyalty
- *encomienda*
- *hacienda*
- mission
- Popé
- plantation
- Bartolomé de Las Casas
- Columbian Exchange

### 2. Using Graphics

Use a cluster diagram like the one below to show how Spain organized its colonies.

Spanish Colonies

How did these actions help the Spanish control the Americas? (HI1)

### 3. Main Ideas

**a.** What were the four levels of Spanish colonial society? (HI1)

**b.** What was the main crop grown on colonial plantations? (HI1)

**c.** How were Native Americans abused in the colonies? (HI1)

### 4. Critical Thinking

**Recognizing Effects**
What were the positive and negative effects of the Columbian Exchange? (REP5)

**THINK ABOUT**
- disease
- food
- livestock

**ACTIVITY OPTIONS**

**ART**
**LANGUAGE ARTS**

Make a **collage** that shows the plants and animals involved in the Columbian Exchange, or write a **story** that tells how Native Americans reacted to the animals. (HI2)

# Beginnings of Slavery in the Americas

| MAIN IDEA | WHY IT MATTERS NOW | TERMS & NAMES |
|---|---|---|
| Slavery in the Americas began in order to provide cheap labor for the colonies. | The effects of slavery, including racism, helped shape attitudes and social conditions in the United States. | slavery     slave codes<br>African Diaspora     racism<br>middle passage |

**CALIFORNIA STANDARDS**

**8.7.2** Trace the origins and development of slavery; its effects on black Americans and on the region's political, social, religious, economic, and cultural development; and identify the strategies that were tried to both overturn and preserve it (e.g., through the writings and historical documents on Nat Turner, Denmark Vesey).

**REP4** Students assess the credibility of primary and secondary sources and draw sound conclusions from them.

**HI1** Students explain the central issues and problems from the past, placing people and events in a matrix of time and place.

## ONE AMERICAN'S STORY

In 1546, Diego de Campo was the leader of 7,000 maroons, or runaway slaves on the island of Hispaniola. There were only about 1,000 European men on the island.

The Spanish planters greatly feared de Campo. When the Spanish attacked the maroons, de Campo and his followers defeated the Spanish.

Eventually the Spaniards captured de Campo. He offered to lead the fight against the maroons. The Spanish accepted the offer. With de Campo's help, the Spanish defeated the maroons, and slavery in Hispaniola grew. In this section, you will read how slave labor expanded in the Americas.

Colonial troops searched for communities of maroons to destroy them.

## The Origins of American Slavery

By the 1600s, <u>slavery,</u> the practice of holding a person in bondage for labor, was firmly established in the Americas. But slavery was not new. Its roots went back to the world's ancient civilizations.

Slavery took many different forms throughout history. In some societies, slaves were mainly domestic servants in wealthy households. Some slaves also labored in mines and fields.

People were often enslaved when they were captured in battle or sold to pay off debts. Some slaves were treated with respect. Some were allowed to marry and own property. The children of many slaves were allowed to go free.

Slavery began to change, however, with the rise of sugar plantations. Europeans had used slaves to grow sugar in the eastern Mediterranean since the 1100s. Then, in the 1400s and 1500s, Portugal and Spain set up sugar plantations on islands in the eastern Atlantic. To work these plantations, they used African slaves bought from traders in Africa.

**Taking Notes**

Use your chart to take notes about the origins of slavery.

| Event/Idea | Notes |
|---|---|
| Exploration | |
| Establishing Colonies | |
| European Competition | |
| Columbian Exchange | |
| Origins of Slavery | |

When the Spanish and Portuguese founded their colonies in the Americas, they brought the plantation system with them. At first they tried to enslave Native Americans to work in the fields and mines. But the Native Americans quickly died from overwork and disease. In some cases, they rebelled with the help of local allies.

The Spaniards then looked to other sources of slave labor, including Spanish slaves, black Christian slaves, and Asian slaves. But there was not enough of any of these groups to meet demand.

*Reading*History
**A. Drawing Conclusions** Why did colonists decide that African slaves were more useful than Native American slaves?

Finally, the Spanish and Portuguese enslaved Africans to provide labor. They enslaved Africans for four basic reasons. First, Africans were immune to most European diseases. Second, Africans had no friends or family in the Americas to help them resist or escape enslavement. Third, enslaved Africans provided a permanent source of cheap labor. Even their children could be held in bondage. Fourth, many Africans had worked on farms in their native lands.

## The Slave Trade

The slave trade grew slowly at first. In 1509, the Spanish governor of Hispaniola, Diego Colón—Columbus's son—wrote to King Ferdinand to complain about a labor shortage on the island. In response, the king sent 50 African slaves to Hispaniola. The slave trade increased with the demand for slaves to work in the colonies. Eventually the colonies came to depend on slave labor. As one Spanish official in Peru wrote, "The black slave is the basis of the *hacienda* and the source of all wealth which this realm produces."

European slave traders carried out the shipment of Africans to the Americas. The rulers of West African kingdoms participated in the trade, too. On the coast of Africa, local kings gathered captives from inland. The local kings then traded these captives for European goods, such as textiles, ironware, wine, and guns.

This trade made the coastal kingdoms rich while weakening inland African societies. In 1526, King Afonso, a West African ruler, protested against the slave trade in a letter to Portugal's king. Afonso wrote, "Everyday these [slave] merchants take our people. . . . So great is this corruption and evil that our country is becoming completely depopulated."

**Vocabulary**
**depopulated:** to lose population

**CONNECTIONS TO MATH**

**Slaves Imported to the Americas, *1493–1810***

Source: Philip D. Curtin, *The Atlantic Slave Trade*

**SKILLBUILDER Interpreting Graphs**

1. *About how many slaves were imported to the Americas between 1493 and 1810?*
2. *Why do you think the numbers increased?*

The diagram above shows how slave traders packed enslaved Africans onto slave ships for the middle passage. A British naval officer painted the picture on the right, which also shows the crowded conditions on slave ships.

# The Middle Passage

Afonso's protest did not stop the forced removal of people from Africa. This removal has become known as the **African Diaspora**. Before the slave trade ended in the late 1800s, approximately 12 million Africans had been enslaved and shipped to the Western Hemisphere. Of these, perhaps two million died during the voyage.

The voyage from Africa to the Americas was called the **middle passage**. The voyage was given this name because it was the middle leg of the triangular trade. The triangular trade refers to the movement of trade ships between Europe, Africa, and the Americas. You will learn more about the triangular trade in Chapter 4.

Olaudah Equiano (oh•LOW•duh EHK•wee•AHN•oh) was one of these kidnapped Africans. He made this journey in the 1700s. He was about 11 years old when he was taken from his home and sold into slavery. Later, after he bought his freedom, he wrote his life story and told what the middle passage was like.

> *A VOICE FROM THE PAST*
>
> The first object which saluted my eyes when I arrived on the coast, was the sea, and a slave ship . . . waiting for its cargo. These filled me with astonishment, which was soon converted into terror, when I was carried on board.
>
> **Olaudah Equiano,** quoted in *Great Slave Narratives*

Equiano saw a row of men shackled together in chains. He also saw a large boiling kettle. He feared that he was going to be cooked and eaten "by those white men with horrible looks, red faces, and long hair."

The scene on the slave deck below was even worse. Several hundred slaves were crammed into a space so small that there was not even enough room to stand up. Foul smells and disease, along with the shrieks and groans of the dying, made the middle passage a terrifying experience. The captives who did not die faced new horrors in the Americas.

**Vocabulary**
diaspora: the scattering of people outside their homeland

*Reading* **History**
B. Making Inferences Why would slave traders pack so many captives onto slave ships?

# Slavery in the Americas

Once the enslaved Africans arrived in the colonies, they were sold at auction. Some were taken to large homes where they worked as servants. Most were forced to do hard labor in *haciendas* or mines. They were also fed and housed poorly.

Many slaves resisted slavery by running away. Across Peru and New Spain, maroons formed communities, often with Native Americans. Sometimes enslaved Africans rebelled. To prevent rebellion, the Spanish government passed **slave codes,** laws to regulate the treatment of slaves. Some of these laws tried to soften the harsh conditions of slavery, but most were designed to punish slaves and keep them in bondage.

Over time, Europeans came to associate slavery with black Africans. To many Europeans, dark skin color became a sign of inferiority. Slavery, which developed to provide a labor force, led to racism. **Racism** is the belief that some people are inferior because of their race.

The slave trade lasted for nearly 400 years, from the early 1500s to the mid-1800s. This contact between Africa and the Americas also formed part of the Columbian Exchange that you read about in Section 3. Africans brought to the Americas a vast knowledge about farming and animals. At the same time, American crops such as sweet potatoes, peanuts, and chilies made their way to Africa.

Enslaved Africans also brought with them a strong artistic heritage of dance, music, and storytelling. The slave trade brought together people from different parts of Africa with different cultural traditions. The experience of slavery helped create a common African-based culture in the Americas. By the 1700s, all the American colonies of European countries had African slaves. As you will read in the next chapter, African culture would be one of the forces that shaped life in the American colonies.

*Reading* **History**

**C. Analyzing Causes** What could have caused slave traders to treat other humans with such cruelty?

---

## Section 4 Assessment

### 1. Terms & Names

**Explain the significance of:**
- slavery
- African Diaspora
- middle passage
- slave codes
- racism

### 2. Using Graphics

Use a diagram like the one below to compare the experience of Native Americans and Africans under slavery. (REP1)

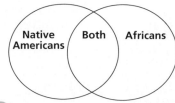

Native Americans — Both — Africans

### 3. Main Ideas

**a.** When did slavery begin? (8.7.2)

**b.** Why did Europeans bring Africans to the Americas? (8.7.2)

**c.** What are three examples of bad conditions faced by enslaved Africans? (8.7.2)

### 4. Critical Thinking

**Recognizing Effects** What were the long-term effects of slavery in the Americas? (HI2)

**THINK ABOUT**
- the economy in the Americas
- the African Diaspora
- cultural diversity in the Americas

**ACTIVITY OPTIONS**

**ART**

**MATH**

Research some aspect of the slave trade, such as the middle passage or the number of people enslaved. Paint a **picture** or draw a **graph** to show what you learned. (HI1)

# Chapter 2 ASSESSMENT

## TERMS & NAMES

Briefly explain the significance of each of the following.

1. mercantilism
2. Hernando Cortés
3. Montezuma
4. Spanish Armada
5. New France
6. *encomienda*
7. Columbian Exchange
8. slavery
9. African Diaspora
10. middle passage

## REVIEW QUESTIONS

### Spain Claims an Empire (pages 61–66)

1. What were three reasons for the European voyages of exploration in the 1400s and 1500s? (HI2)
2. Who conquered the Aztecs and Incas? (HI1)
3. What three reasons explain Spain's success in building an empire in the Americas? (HI2)

### European Competition in North America (pages 67–70)

4. What was the Northwest Passage? (HI1)
5. Why did the Spanish Armada attack England? (HI2)
6. What did the French and Dutch colonists trade? (HI1)

### The Spanish and Native Americans (pages 71–75)

7. How did Spanish rule affect Native Americans? (HI2)
8. How did the Columbian Exchange affect Europe? (HI2)

### Beginnings of Slavery in the Americas (pages 76–79)

9. Why did the Spanish and Portuguese use slave labor in their colonies? (HI2)
10. How did the slave trade work? (HI1)

## CRITICAL THINKING

### 1. USING YOUR NOTES: FINDING MAIN IDEAS

| Event/Idea | Notes |
|---|---|
| Exploration | |
| Establishing Colonies | |
| European Competition | |
| Columbian Exchange | |
| Origins of Slavery | |

Using your completed chart, answer the questions below. (HI2)

a. What causes did European competition and exploration have in common?
b. How did the establishment of colonies in the Americas lead to slavery?
c. Which concept in the chart contributed most to the Columbian Exchange?

### 2. ANALYZING LEADERSHIP

Think about the explorers and *conquistadors* discussed in this chapter. What qualities did they possess that made them successful in their efforts? (HI1)

### 3. THEME: IMMIGRATION AND MIGRATION

What were the causes and effects of the migration of Europeans and Africans to the Americas? (HI2)

### 4. APPLYING CITIZENSHIP SKILLS

What kind of values did Bartolomé de Las Casas demonstrate in his actions? How effective was he in improving his society? (HI1)

### Interact *with* History

Have your answers about whether or not you would join a voyage of exploration changed after reading the chapter? Explain.

## VISUAL SUMMARY

### European Exploration of the Americas (HI2)

Causes: National Competition, Desire for Wealth, Spread Christianity → European Exploration of the Americas → Effects: Destruction of Aztec and Incan Empires, The Columbian Exchange, European Colonies in the Americas, Slavery

## STANDARDS-BASED ASSESSMENT

Use the chart and your knowledge of U.S. history to answer questions 1 and 2.

Additional Test Practice, pp. S1–S33.

| Slaves Imported to the Americas (in thousands) | 1601–1810 | |
| REGION/COUNTRY | 1601–1700 | 1701–1810 |
| --- | --- | --- |
| British N. America | * | 348 |
| British Caribbean | 263.7 | 1,401.3 |
| French Caribbean | 155.8 | 1,348.4 |
| Spanish America | 292.5 | 578.6 |
| Dutch Caribbean | 40 | 460 |
| Danish Caribbean | 4 | 24 |
| Brazil (Portugal) | 560 | 1,891.4 |

*=less than 1,000

Source: Philip D. Curtin, *The Atlantic Slave Trade*

1. Which region or country imported the most slaves to the Americas? (8.7.2)
   A. British Caribbean
   B. French Caribbean
   C. Brazil (Portugal)
   D. Spanish Caribbean

2. Which region imported less than 1,000 slaves before 1700? (8.7.2)
   A. Brazil (Portugal)
   B. British North America
   C. Danish Caribbean
   D. Dutch Caribbean

This quotation is from Olaudah Equiano, an African slave. Use the quotation and your knowledge of U.S. history to answer question 3.

### PRIMARY SOURCE

The first object which saluted my eyes when I arrived on the coast, was the sea, and a slave ship . . . waiting for its cargo. These filled me with astonishment, which was soon converted into terror, when I was carried on board.

**Olaudah Equiano,** *Great Slave Narratives*

3. The passage supports which of the following conclusions? (8.7.2)
   A. Equiano and the others on board felt safe.
   B. The conditions on the ship were horrifying.
   C. Because he protested, Equiano was allowed to return home.
   D. Equiano's circumstances improved after he arrived in the colonies.

TEST PRACTICE
CLASSZONE.COM

## ALTERNATIVE ASSESSMENT

### 1. ✎ WRITING ABOUT HISTORY

Write a **newspaper article** about one of these events: *La Noche Triste* in Mexico or the murder of the Incan emperor Atahualpa. (HI1)

- Use library resources to research Mexican or Incan history.
- Your article should explain what happened and who was involved. Add details that explain when, where, why, and how the event occurred.
- Give your article an interesting headline.

### 2. COOPERATIVE LEARNING

With a group, create a diorama to depict one of the communities of Spanish America in the 1600s. Your diorama should include features such as a mission, a *hacienda*, roads, mines or sugar mills. Use drawings, maps, and written descriptions that depict daily life. (CST3)

## INTEGRATED TECHNOLOGY

### DOING INTERNET RESEARCH

The Columbian Exchange is the movement of plants and animals around the world as a result of exploration. Use the Internet and other library resources to research the movement of a plant or animal around the world. (CST3)

- Choose a specific plant or animal. You might choose corn, potatoes, chocolate, tea, coffee, sugar, or horses, cattle, or pigs.
- Use your plant or animal as a keyword. Search the Internet to find where the plant or animal first existed and where it moved.

**For more about the Columbian Exchange . . .**

INTERNET ACTIVITY
CLASSZONE.COM

# The English Establish 13 Colonies 1585–1732

The settlers at Jamestown, Virginia, built a fort with three walls rather than four to make it easier to defend.

These soldiers are training to defend the Jamestown fort and settlers.

**1585**
First English colony established at Roanoke.

**1607**
John Smith and other English settlers establish Jamestown.

**1620**
Pilgrims land at Plymouth.

**1630**
Puritans found Massachusetts Bay Colony.

N. America
World
1585

**1587**
Foreign missionaries are banished from Japan.

**1588**
England defeats Spanish Armada.

**1605**
Akbar, Mughal emperor of India, dies.

**1649**
Charles I of England is beheaded.

The settlers' houses were built inside the fort walls for protection.

The year is 1607. You have just sailed across the ocean and arrived in a strange land. Your family has traveled to the eastern coast of North America in search of freedom and prosperity. Your first task in the new land is to decide what you need to do to survive.

# What dangers would you face as a settler?

## What Do You Think?

- What do you need to survive in the wilderness?
- This settlement is actually a fort, with an armed force and high fences. What reasons might there be for building a fort?
- What kind of settlement would you build?

**RESEARCH LINKS**
CLASSZONE.COM
Visit the Chapter 3 links for more information about the English colonies.

**1664**
England takes New Amsterdam from Dutch.

**1675**
King Philip's War erupts.

**1681**
William Penn receives charter for Pennsylvania.

**1692**
Salem witchcraft trials are held.

**1732**
Colony of Georgia is founded by James Oglethorpe.

1732

**1660**
English monarchy is restored when Charles II returns from exile.

**1688**
William and Mary take power in Britain's Glorious Revolution.

*The English Establish 13 Colonies* **83**

# Reading Strategy: Sequencing Events

## What Do You Know?

What do you already know about the American colonies? What sort of person might choose to leave his or her native country and cross the ocean to settle in a new land?

**CALIFORNIA STANDARDS**

**Reading 2.7** Evaluate the unity, coherence, logic, internal consistency, and structural patterns of text.

### Think About

- what you've learned about American settlers from movies, television, historical fiction, or science fiction about space travel
- opportunities and challenges offered in a new land
- your responses to the Interact with History about facing dangers as a settler (see page 83)

## What Do You Want to Know?

What questions do you have about the Europeans who settled in North America? about those who were already here? Record your questions in your notebook before you read this chapter.

## Sequencing Events

Sequencing means putting events in order. In learning about the early colonies, for example, it will be useful to you to list the 13 original colonies and an important early date mentioned for each in the chapter. You might record the name and a date for each colony in a graphic organizer such as the one below. Copy this organizer in your notebook. Fill it in as you read the chapter.

**S** See Skillbuilder Handbook, page R4.

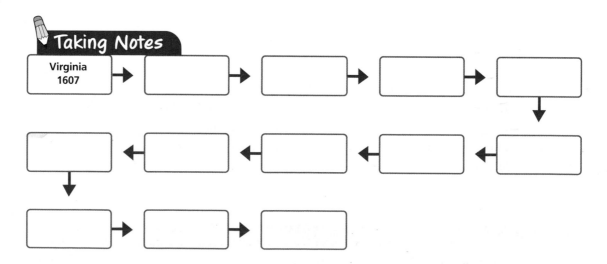

**Taking Notes**

Virginia
1607

# Early Colonies Have Mixed Success

| MAIN IDEA | WHY IT MATTERS NOW | TERMS & NAMES |
|---|---|---|
| Two early English colonies failed, but Jamestown survived—partly through individual effort and hard work. | Jamestown's survival led to more English colonies and a lasting English influence in the United States. | joint-stock company  indentured servant<br>charter  House of Burgesses<br>Jamestown  Bacon's Rebellion<br>John Smith |

## ONE AMERICAN'S STORY

In 1585, John White traveled with the first English expedition to Roanoke, an island off North Carolina. White sailed back to England in 1586 and then returned to Roanoke as governor the next year, bringing with him more than 100 settlers. Soon White's daughter Elinor gave birth to a baby girl. John White described the event.

Drawing by John White of a Pomeiock tribesman.

### A VOICE FROM THE PAST

On August 18 a daughter was born to Elinor, . . . wife of Ananias Dare. . . . The child was christened on the following Sunday and was named Virginia because she was the first Christian born in Virginia.

**John White,** *The New World*

In 1587, White was forced to sail back to England a second time to get needed supplies. He left the colonists, including his granddaughter, Virginia, in Roanoke. White was delayed and did not return to Roanoke until 1590.

To his shock and grief, he found no trace of the colonists or his granddaughter, all of whom had disappeared. The only clues to their whereabouts were the letters *CRO* carved in a tree and the word *Croatoan* carved in a doorpost. White never discovered the fate of his family and the other colonists. In this section, you will learn why English settlers such as White came to America despite such hardships.

## The English Plan Colonies

As you read in Chapter 2, religious and political rivalries increased between England and Spain in the late 1500s. Spain had many colonies in the Americas, but England had none. England began directing its resources toward establishing colonies after its defeat of the Spanish Armada in 1588.

**CALIFORNIA STANDARDS**

**7.11.3** Examine the origins of modern capitalism; the influence of mercantilism and cottage industry; the elements and importance of a market economy in seventeenth-century Europe; the changing international trading and marketing patterns, including their locations on a world map; and the influence of explorers and map makers.

**CST3** Students use a variety of maps and documents to identify physical and cultural features of neighborhoods, cities, states, and countries and to explain the historical migration of people, expansion and disintegration of empires, and the growth of economic systems.

**HI3** Students explain the sources of historical continuity and how the combination of ideas and events explains the emergence of new patterns.

**HI4** Students recognize the role of chance, foresight, and error in history.

**Taking Notes**

Use your chart to take notes about the early colonies.

| Virginia 1607 | → | |

Richard Hakluyt (HAK•LOOT), an English geographer, urged England to start a colony. Hakluyt thought that colonies would provide a market for English exports. They also would serve as a source of raw materials. By having colonies, England hoped to increase its trade and build up its gold supply. This is the economic theory of mercantilism (see page 62). In mercantilism, the state controls trade and attempts to transfer wealth from colonies to the parent country. Hakluyt also thought that English colonies would help to plant the Protestant faith in the Americas.

The earliest English colonists had many reasons for going to America. The lack of economic opportunity in England forced many to seek their fortunes abroad. Stories of gold mines lured some to leave England. Others left to escape religious persecution.

*Reading*History
**A. Summarizing**
Why did English colonists settle in America?

## Two Early Colonies Fail

Sir Walter Raleigh was a soldier, statesman, and adventurer who served under Queen Elizabeth I of England. She gave him permission to sponsor the colony at Roanoke. He named England's first colony Virginia after the unmarried, or virgin, queen. Financed by Raleigh, the colony began in 1585 on Roanoke Island. The colonists relied on the Native Americans for food. But when the Native Americans realized that the settlers wanted their land, they cut off the colonists' food supply. Those who survived returned to England in 1586.

**Vocabulary**
**financed:** paid for; raised funds for

In 1587, artist John White convinced Raleigh to try again to establish the Roanoke colony, with the disastrous results described in One American's Story (page 85). To this day, no one knows for sure what happened. Some historians think that the colonists mingled with the neighboring Native Americans. Others believe that they moved to Chesapeake Bay and were killed by Native Americans defending their land.

In 1607, the Plymouth Company sponsored the Sagadahoc colony at the mouth of the Kennebec River in Maine. Some of the settlers were English convicts. One colonist wrote of George Popham, the governor, "He stocked or planted [the colony] out of all the jails of England." Within the first year, arguments among colonists, a harsh winter, fights with Native Americans, and food shortages forced most of the colonists to return to England.

## Financing a Colony

Raleigh had financed the colony at Roanoke. When the colony failed, he lost his investment. The English learned from Raleigh's financial loss at Roanoke that one person could not finance a colony. To raise money, they turned to the **joint-stock company**. Joint-stock companies were backed by investors, people who put money into a project to earn profits. Each investor received pieces of ownership of the company called

### *Now and* then

**THE LUMBEE AND THE LOST COLONISTS**

The Lumbee tribe lives mainly in North Carolina. Some of the Lumbee believe they are descendants of the lost colonists of Roanoke. Among the evidence cited is the fact that 41 of the 95 last names of the Lumbee were last names of the colonists.

Other Lumbee don't believe that they are descended from English ancestors. The Lumbee are trying to win federal recognition as a Native American tribe. English ancestry might weaken their claim for federal financial support.

shares of stock. In this way, the investors split any profits and divided any losses.

Merchants organized the Virginia Company of London and the Virginia Company of Plymouth. King James I of England granted charters to both companies in 1606. A **charter** was a written contract, issued by a government, giving the holder the right to establish a colony.

## Jamestown Is Founded in 1607

In 1607, the Virginia Company of London financed an expedition to Chesapeake Bay that included more than 100 colonists. They sailed up the James River until they found a spot to settle. They named the first permanent English settlement **Jamestown** in honor of King James.

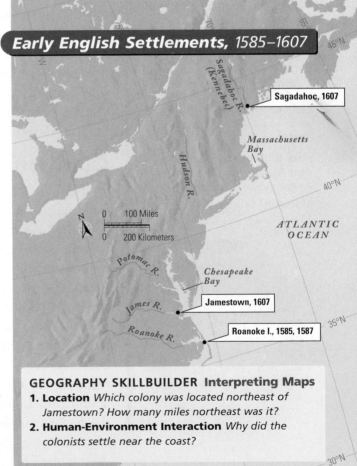

This is a computer reconstruction of the face of Mistress Forrest, believed to be the first English woman to come to Jamestown.

From the start, the Jamestown colonists endured terrible hardships. The site of the colony was swampy and full of malaria-carrying mosquitoes. This disease made the colonists sick with fever. Many also became ill from drinking the river water. To make matters worse, the London Company had incorrectly told the settlers that the colony would be rich in gold. They spent their days searching for gold rather than building houses and growing food.

The climate was also a hardship. The colonists soon learned that the summers were hot and humid and the winters bitter cold. As one colonist recalled, "There were never Englishmen left in a foreign country in such misery as we were in this newly discovered Virginia."

## Jamestown Grows

By January 1608, only 38 colonists remained alive. Later that year, **John Smith,** a soldier and adventurer, took control. To make sure the colonists worked, Smith announced, "He that will not work shall not eat." Smith's methods worked. He ordered an existing wall extended around Jamestown. He also persuaded the Powhatan tribe to trade their corn to the colonists. In 1609, Smith was injured in a gunpowder explosion and returned to England. That same year, 800 more English settlers arrived in Jamestown.

*Reading* **History**
**B. Solving Problems** If you had been John Smith, how would you have forced the colonists to work?

**Early English Settlements,** *1585–1607*

Sagadahoc (Kennebec) R.

Sagadahoc, 1607

*Massachusetts Bay*

Hudson R.

0   100 Miles
0   200 Kilometers

*ATLANTIC OCEAN*

Potomac R.

*Chesapeake Bay*

James R.

Jamestown, 1607

Roanoke R.

Roanoke I., 1585, 1587

**GEOGRAPHY SKILLBUILDER Interpreting Maps**
1. **Location** *Which colony was located northeast of Jamestown? How many miles northeast was it?*
2. **Human-Environment Interaction** *Why did the colonists settle near the coast?*

Because of growing tensions between the settlers and Native Americans, the Powhatan stopped trading food and attacked the settlers. The settlers did not dare leave the fort. During the "starving time," the colonists ate rats, mice, and snakes. Only 60 of the colonists were still alive when two ships arrived in 1610. Lord De La Warr, the new governor, imposed discipline, and the "starving time" ended.

In 1612, John Rolfe developed a high-grade tobacco that the colonists learned to grow. It quickly became very popular in England. The success of tobacco growing changed Jamestown in many ways. The Virginia Company thought of the colonists as employees. The colonists, however, wanted a share of the profits.

The company responded by letting settlers own land. Settlers worked harder when the land was their own. The company offered a 50-acre land grant for each man, woman, or child who could pay his or her way to the colony. In 1619, the first African Americans arrived in Jamestown. The population of Virginia jumped from about 600 in 1619 to more than 2,000 in 1621.

Even more laborers were needed. Those who could not afford passage to America were encouraged to become **indentured servants**. These men and women sold their labor to the person who paid their passage to the colony. After working for a number of years, they were free to farm or take up a trade of their own.

The colonists soon became annoyed at the strict rule of the governor, who represented the Virginia Company's interests back in London. To provide for more local control, the company decided that burgesses, or elected representatives, of the colonists would meet once a year in an assembly. The **House of Burgesses,** created in 1619, became the first representative assembly in the American colonies.

## Conflicts with the Powhatan

Cultural differences put the Powhatan and the English on a collision course. At first, the Powhatan traded food with the colonists. Then, as more colonists arrived and wanted land, relations grew worse. In an effort to improve relations between the English colonists and the Powhatan, John Rolfe married Chief Powhatan's daughter, Pocahontas, in 1614.

For a time, there was an uneasy peace. The colonists learned from the Powhatan how to grow corn, catch fish, and capture wild fowl. However, the expanding tobacco plantations took over more and more Powhatan land. In 1622, in response to land grabs by the colonists, the Powhatan killed hundreds of Jamestown's residents.

*Reading* **History**
C. Analyzing Causes What was the main reason for the various arrangements the Virginia Company came up with to bring people to America?

*Reading* **History**
D. Finding Main Ideas What was the central dispute between the Powhatan and the settlers?

## AMERICA'S HISTORY MAKERS

### POCAHONTAS
**1595?–1617**

Pocahontas met John Smith when she was about 12 years old. Smith taught her English and admired her spirit. She admired Smith's bravery and saved his life twice. After Smith returned to England, she married the colonist John Rolfe in 1614. Shown below is a portrait of Pocahontas, done in 1616.

Two years later, the Rolfes went to England to raise money for the Jamestown colony. While getting ready to sail home, Pocahontas died of smallpox.

**How did Pocahontas show that Native Americans and white settlers might live in peace?**

# Bacon's Rebellion in 1676

As you have seen, many of the English colonists who came to Virginia during the 1600s fought with the Native Americans. They also battled one another. By the 1670s, one-fourth of the free white men were former indentured servants. These colonists, who did not own land, resented the wealthy eastern landowners. The poor settlers lived mostly on Virginia's western frontier, where they battled the Native Americans for land.

Nathaniel Bacon and a group of landless frontier settlers opposed Governor William Berkeley. They complained about high taxes and Governor Berkeley's favoritism toward large plantation owners. Bacon demanded that Berkeley approve a war against the Native Americans to seize their land for tobacco plantations. Governor Berkeley's refusal of Nathaniel Bacon's demand sparked **Bacon's Rebellion** in 1676.

**Vocabulary**
**tyranny:** a government in which a single ruler has absolute power

Bacon marched into Jamestown, took control of the House of Burgesses, and burned Jamestown to the ground. Bacon's sudden illness and death ended the rebellion. Berkeley hanged Bacon's followers. Angered by Berkeley's actions, King Charles II recalled the governor to England. After that incident, the House of Burgesses passed laws to prevent a royal governor from assuming such power again. The burgesses had taken an important step against tyranny. In the next section, you will read about the New England colonies and their steps toward independence.

Nathaniel Bacon (right) confronts Virginia governor William Berkeley at Jamestown in 1676.

## Section 1 Assessment

### 1. Terms & Names

**Explain the significance of:**
- joint-stock company
- charter
- Jamestown
- John Smith
- indentured servant
- House of Burgesses
- Bacon's Rebellion

### 2. Using Graphics

Use a series-of-events chain to review events that led to the founding of Jamestown.

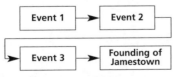

Event 1 → Event 2
Event 3 → Founding of Jamestown

What were reasons England wanted colonies in America? (CST2)

### 3. Main Ideas

**a.** Why did the first English settlement at Roanoke fail? (HI2)

**b.** How did the English finance their colonies after 1606? (HI2)

**c.** What was the outcome of Bacon's Rebellion? (HI2)

### 4. Critical Thinking

**Drawing Conclusions**
What were the main reasons that Jamestown survived and prospered? (HI1)

**THINK ABOUT**
- how, after the "starving time," Lord De La Warr took control
- John Rolfe's development of a high-grade tobacco plant

**ACTIVITY OPTIONS**

**ART**

**LANGUAGE ARTS**

You need indentured servants to work on your plantation. Draw a **poster** or write an **advertisement** that will attract people to your plantation. (REP5)

# Report from the New World

You are a settler who has landed on the wild eastern shore of North America. You and your 93 fellow colonists survived a frightening nine-week Atlantic voyage. Now you are struggling to build a new home in the wilderness. There are no roads, inns, or towns in this land. The game, berries, and fish here taste strange, sometimes unpleasant. Your only neighbors are small groups of Native Americans.

**COOPERATIVE LEARNING** On these pages are challenges you face as you put down roots in America. Working with a small group, decide how to deal with each challenge. Choose an option, assign a task to each group member, and do the activity. You will find useful information in the Data File. Be prepared to present your solutions to the class as part of a report to your sponsors back in England.

**CALIFORNIA STANDARDS**

**REP1** Students frame questions that can be answered by historical study and research.

**HI1** Students explain the central issues and problems from the past, placing people and events in a matrix of time and place.

**HI6** Students interpret basic indicators of economic performance and conduct cost-benefit analyses of economic and political issues.

**Reading 2.6** Use information from a variety of consumer, workplace, and public documents to explain a situation or decision and to solve a problem.

**Listening & Speaking 2.3** Deliver research presentations.

## CIVICS CHALLENGE

*"They had little or no care of any other thing, but to pamper their bellies."*

As your colony takes root, most members work hard to farm, cook, wash, mend, trade, and defend the colony. But a few colonists think only of their own comfort. You call a meeting to set some rules about work. Present your solution to this problem using one of these options:

- Make a poster for the meeting hall that states the new work rules and punishments.

- Write a report describing the problem and how the colony solved it.

## ECONOMICS CHALLENGE

### "A bright tin dish most pleased him."

By the time spring arrives, your stores of English foods are running low. You and your friends decide to try trading with the neighboring Native Americans. They could provide a steady supply of meat, fish, and vegetables until your harvest comes in. Develop a plan for opening trade. Present your plan using one of these options:

- As a group, role-play the meeting in which you create your trading plan.
- Write instructions for the team of colonists who will open trade with the Native Americans.

### ACTIVITY WRAP-UP

**Present to the class** As a group, review your solution to each challenge. Consider the following:

- How well each solution meets its particular challenge
- Which solution shows the most creativity

Once you have made your decision, present your solutions to the class. Each group member should take part in the presentation.

### The Journey

**Distance:** more than 5,000 nautical miles from Europe to the east coast of North America

**Length:** 6–14 weeks

**Dangers:** storms, scurvy, dysentery, malnutrition, seasickness, overcrowding

### Food and Livestock Taken

barrels of salted beef, oatmeal, dried grains, cheese, oil, vinegar, and salt; seeds for peas, barley, herbs, and other crops; cows, horses, goats, pigs, sheep, and chickens

### Equipment Taken

axes, hoes, nails, hooks for doors, hammers, chisels, hatchets, spades, pickaxes, iron pots, copper kettles, skillets, platters, dishes, wooden spoons, rugs

### Weapons Taken

swords, muskets, daggers, gunpowder, light armor, cannon

### Clothes Taken

shirts, several pairs of shoes, leather for mending, waistcoats, caps, skirts, jackets, trousers

### Dangers in America

**Biggest killers:** typhoid, dysentery, famine

**Other dangers:** pneumonia, malaria, and other diseases; exposure to harsh weather; fire; wild animals; attacks by Native Americans

### Benefits in America

religious and political freedom; opportunity to own land; abundant timber for shelters, forts, heat, ships, and trade; rich food resources

For more about the American colonies . . .

**RESEARCH LINKS**
CLASSZONE.COM

# New England Colonies

2

| MAIN IDEA | WHY IT MATTERS NOW | TERMS & NAMES |
|---|---|---|

**MAIN IDEA**

Religion influenced the settlement and government of the New England colonies.

**WHY IT MATTERS NOW**

The Puritan work ethic and religious beliefs influence American culture today.

**TERMS & NAMES**

Pilgrims

Mayflower Compact

Puritans

Great Migration

Fundamental Orders of Connecticut

Roger Williams

Anne Hutchinson

King Philip's War

**CALIFORNIA STANDARDS**

**8.2.1** Discuss the significance of the Magna Carta, the English Bill of Rights, and the Mayflower Compact.

**REP5** Students detect the different historical points of view on historical events and determine the context in which the historical statements were made (the questions asked, sources used, author's perspectives)

**HI2** Students understand and distinguish cause, effect, sequence, and correlation in historical events, including the long- and short-term causal relations.

## ONE AMERICAN'S STORY

In 1605, Englishmen captured and enslaved a Native American named Squanto and took him to England. Squanto returned to America in 1619. There he discovered that his Pawtuxet tribe had been killed by disease. In 1621, Squanto set about helping the English plant crops on tribal lands. Colonist William Bradford made the following comment.

### A VOICE FROM THE PAST

Squanto . . . was a special instrument sent of God for their [the colonists'] good beyond their expectation. . . . He directed them how to set their corn, where to take fish, and to procure other commodities, and was also their pilot to bring them to unknown places.

**William Bradford,** quoted in *The Pilgrim Reader*

Squanto teaches the Pilgrims how to grow corn.

In this section, you will learn about the Pilgrims and Puritans, their relations with the Native Americans, and their settlement of the New England colonies.

## The Voyage of the *Mayflower*

In the early 1500s, King Henry VIII of England broke that country's ties with the Catholic Church and established the Church of England, an official state church under his control. In the early 1600s, a religious group called the Separatists called for a total break with the Church of England. They thought it was too much like the Catholic Church.

The **Pilgrims** were a Separatist group. King James attacked them for rejecting England's official church. To escape this harsh treatment, the Pilgrims fled to Holland, a country known for its acceptance of different opinions. Eventually, the Pilgrims became dissatisfied with life in Holland. They approached the Virginia Company and asked if they could settle in America "as a distinct body by themselves." The Virginia

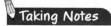

**Taking Notes**

Use your chart to take notes about the New England colonies.

Virginia 1607 ▶

The *Mayflower* brings the Pilgrims to Plymouth in 1620.

Company arranged for them to settle on land within its boundaries on the eastern coast of North America.

On a cold, raw November day in 1620, a ship called the *Mayflower* arrived off Cape Cod on the Massachusetts coast. Blown north of its course, the *Mayflower* landed in an area that John Smith had mapped and called New England. They landed at a site that had been named Plymouth.

Because the Pilgrims landed outside the limits of the Virginia Company, their charter did not apply. For the sake of order, the men aboard the *Mayflower* signed an agreement called the **Mayflower Compact**. In it, they vowed to obey laws agreed upon for the good of the colony. The Mayflower Compact helped establish the idea of self-government and majority rule. (See Interactive Primary Sources, page 98.)

## The Pilgrims Found Plymouth

Like the early settlers at Jamestown, the Pilgrims at Plymouth endured a starving time. That first winter, disease and death struck with such fury that "the living were scarce able to bury the dead." Half the group had died by spring.

However, energy, hope, and help returned. One day a Native American walked up to a group of colonists. To their astonishment, he called out, "Welcome, Englishmen." This was Samoset, a Pemaquid who had learned to speak English from European fishermen. Samoset introduced the settlers to another Native American named Squanto, a Pawtuxet, who also spoke English.

*"Welcome, Englishmen."*
Samoset

*Reading*History
**A. Making Inferences**
Why do you think Squanto was so helpful to the Pilgrims?

The Pilgrims had angered the Native Americans by taking their corn. Squanto acted as an interpreter between the Pilgrims and Chief Massasoit. He helped them to negotiate a peace treaty and showed them how to plant, hunt, and fish. While their crops grew, the colonists began trading with the Native Americans for furs and preparing lumber to ship back to England in order to make a profit.

Sometime in the fall—no one knows exactly when—the Plymouth settlement celebrated the blessings of a good harvest by holding a three-day feast. It was the first Thanksgiving. This Thanksgiving came to represent the peace that existed at that time between the Native Americans and Pilgrims.

Thanks to the help of Squanto and other Native Americans, the Pilgrims learned to survive in their new environment. Soon more people would sail to New England seeking religious freedom.

## The Puritans Come to Massachusetts Bay

Between about 1630 and 1640, a religious group called the **Puritans** left England to escape bad treatment by King James I. Unlike the Separatists, who wanted to break away from the Church of England, the Puritans wanted to reform, or "purify," its practices. By the thousands, Puritan families left for the Americas. Their leaving is known as the **Great Migration.** Many thousands of Puritans left their homeland to found new settlements around the world. Of these settlers, about 20,000 crossed the Atlantic Ocean to New England.

Many Puritan merchants had invested in the Massachusetts Bay Company. In 1629, the company received a royal charter to settle land in New England. In 1630, 11 well-supplied ships carried about 1,000 passengers to the Massachusetts Bay Colony. Unlike earlier colonists, the Puritans were well prepared and did not suffer through a starving time. John Winthrop was the colony's Puritan governor. He stated that the new colony would be a commonwealth, a community in which people work together for the good of the whole.

**Background**
During the Great Migration, the Puritans also went to Ireland, the Netherlands, the Rhineland, and the West Indies.

*Reading* **History**
**B. Making Inferences** After Winthrop, politicians sometimes spoke of America as "a city upon a hill." What does this phrase suggest about America's role in the world?

### A VOICE FROM THE PAST

So shall we keep the unity of the spirit, in the bond of peace. . . . Ten of us will be able to resist a thousand of our enemies. . . . For we must consider that we shall be as a City upon a Hill, the eyes of all people are on us.

**John Winthrop,** *"Model of Christian Charity"*

## The New England Way

The basic unit of the commonwealth was the congregation—a group of people who belong to the same church. Each Puritan congregation set up its own town. The meetinghouse was the most important building in each town. There people gathered for town meetings, a form of self-government in which people made laws and other decisions for the community. In the Massachusetts Bay Colony, only male church members could vote or hold office. They elected representatives to a lawmaking body called the General Court, which in turn chose the governor.

By law, everyone in town had to attend church services held in the meetinghouse. The sermon, the most important part of the church service, provided instruction in the "New England Way." This was a term

**THE FIRST THANKSGIVING**
It is hard to believe, but turkey was not on the menu at the first Thanksgiving. The Pilgrims and Native Americans ate venison (deer), roast duck, roast goose, clams and other shellfish, and eel (shown below). Other treats were white bread and corn bread, leeks, watercress, and salad herbs. The guests topped off their meal with wild plums and dried berries for dessert.

used by the Puritans to describe both their beliefs and their society, which emphasized duty, godliness, hard work, and honesty. The Puritans thought that amusements such as dancing and playing games would lead to laziness. They believed that God required them to work long and hard at their vocation.

The Puritan work ethic helped contribute to the rapid growth and success of the New England colonies. The New England Way also depended on education. Because the Puritans wanted everyone to be able to read the Bible, laws required that all children learn to read.

*Reading*History
C. Summarizing
What were some
important ele-
ments of the New
England Way?

Some Puritan congregations set up new colonies. In 1636, Thomas Hooker moved his congregation to the Connecticut Valley. There they wrote and adopted the **Fundamental Orders of Connecticut** in 1639 (see page 98). In effect, these laws were a constitution. The Fundamental Orders extended voting rights to non-church members and limited the power of the governor. They expanded the idea of representative government.

The first European settlement in New Hampshire was a village near Portsmouth in 1623. In 1638, John Wheelwright established the town of Exeter. The town's founders drew up the Exeter Compact, which was based on the Mayflower Compact.

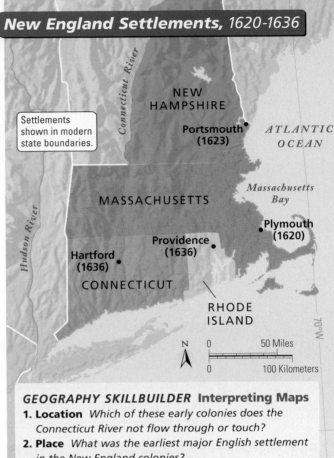

**New England Settlements, 1620–1636**

Settlements shown in modern state boundaries.

NEW HAMPSHIRE

Portsmouth (1623)

ATLANTIC OCEAN

Massachusetts Bay

MASSACHUSETTS

Plymouth (1620)

Providence (1636)

Hartford (1636)

CONNECTICUT

RHODE ISLAND

Connecticut River

Hudson River

N    0        50 Miles
     0        100 Kilometers

**GEOGRAPHY SKILLBUILDER Interpreting Maps**
1. **Location** *Which of these early colonies does the Connecticut River not flow through or touch?*
2. **Place** *What was the earliest major English settlement in the New England colonies?*

## Challenges to Puritan Leaders

Not everyone agreed with the New England Way. **Roger Williams** was a minister in Salem, Massachusetts, who founded the first Baptist church in America. He opposed forced attendance at church. He also opposed the English colonists' taking of Native American lands by force. Because of his beliefs, the General Court forced Williams to leave the colony. In 1636, he fled southward and founded the colony of Rhode Island, which guaranteed religious freedom and the separation of church and state.

**Anne Hutchinson** believed that a person could worship God without the help of a church, minister, or Bible. She conducted discussions in her home that challenged church authority. Hutchinson was brought to trial and forced to leave Massachusetts. In 1638, she fled to Rhode Island.

Anne Hutchinson preaches in her home in Boston.

Another religious group was the Quakers. Their name came from an early leader's statement that they should "tremble [quake] at the word of the Lord." Opponents coined the name as an insult. Quakers challenged the Massachusetts commonwealth. They believed that each person could know God directly through "an inner light." Neither ministers nor the Bible was needed. Quakers also believed in treating Native Americans fairly, which set them apart from other colonists. For such beliefs, Quakers were whipped, imprisoned, and hanged. Many left for Rhode Island.

*Reading* **History**

**D. Forming Opinions** Why is it odd that the Puritans persecuted certain individuals and groups for their religious beliefs?

## King Philip's War

The growing population of colonists began to force the Native Americans from their land. Europeans and Native Americans defined land ownership differently. To Europeans, land could be owned by individuals. To Native Americans, land belonged to everyone. Conflict over land resulted in warfare.

In 1675–1676, the Puritan colonies fought a brutal war with the Native Americans. This was known as **King Philip's War**. "King Philip" was the English name of Metacom, leader of the Wampanoag. To help fight the war, Metacom organized an alliance of tribes. The Wampanoag lost the war. Many were killed, while others were sold into slavery in the West Indies. Those who remained lost their land and were forced to become laborers. English settlers expanded even farther into Native American land.

**Background** Metacom was the son of Massasoit, friend of the Pilgrims.

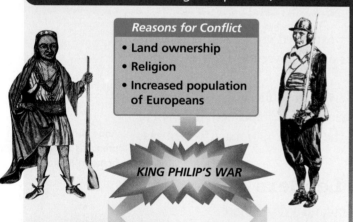

**CAUSE & EFFECT:** *King Philip's War, 1675–1676*

**Reasons for Conflict**
- **Land ownership**
- **Religion**
- **Increased population of Europeans**

**KING PHILIP'S WAR**

**Native American Losses**
- **Approximately 3,000 killed**
- **King Philip (Metacom) killed**
- **About 500 Native Americans enslaved**

**European Losses**
- **About 600 settlers killed**
- **More than 45 villages attacked**
- **About 12 villages destroyed**

Sources: *Encyclopedia Britannica, World Book Encyclopedia*

**SKILLBUILDER Interpreting Charts**

1. *Was there a greater loss of life among the settlers or the Native Americans?*
2. *How might the growing population of Europeans have created more conflict with the Native Americans?*

## The Salem Witchcraft Trials

Puritan New England was originally a society centered on the church. By the late 1600s, however, this had begun to change. Societal changes in Puritan New England had led to an atmosphere of fear and suspicion. Then, several Salem village girls were told frightening stories about witches by Tituba, a slave from the West Indies. Pretending to be bewitched, the girls falsely accused others of witchcraft. The witch-hunts began in 1692. The clergy viewed the Salem witch-hunts and trials as a sign from God for the village to return to a strict Puritan lifestyle.

This mid-nineteenth-century oil painting, *The Trial of George Jacobs, August 5, 1692,* was painted by T. H. Matteson in 1855. It captures the horrors of the Salem witch trials. As the young women cry out, the accused tries to defend himself against charges that he bewitched them.

Jacobs's own granddaughter testified against him. He was tried and convicted on August 5, 1692, and executed two weeks later along with four neighbors.

**How accurately do you think the painting shows the strong emotions in the courtroom?**

Hysteria spread through Salem. Those accused were forced to name others as witches. More than 100 people were arrested and tried. Of those, 20 were found guilty and put to death. Nineteen persons were hanged, and another was pressed to death by heavy stones when he refused to enter a plea in response to the charge of witchcraft. The panic was short-lived, and Salem came to its senses. The experience showed, however, how a society can create scapegoats for its problems.

In the next section, you will read about the Middle and Southern colonies, how they were founded, and how they provided the new settlers with economic opportunities.

**Vocabulary**
**scapegoat:** one that is made to bear the blame of others

---

## Section 2 Assessment

### 1. Terms & Names

**Explain the significance of:**
- Pilgrims
- Mayflower Compact
- Puritans
- Great Migration
- Fundamental Orders of Connecticut
- Roger Williams
- Anne Hutchinson
- King Philip's War

### 2. Using Graphics

Use a cluster diagram to review details about the New England Way.

New England Way

Which parts would you find easy to accept? Which difficult? (HI1)

### 3. Main Ideas

**a.** What is the Mayflower Compact? (HI1)

**b.** What is the meaning of the term the "Great Migration" (HI1)?

**c.** What were some of the causes of King Philip's War? (HI2)

### 4. Critical Thinking

**Recognizing Effects** What impact did the arrival of the English in New England have on the Native Americans? (HI2)

**THINK ABOUT**
- Squanto
- Chief Massasoit
- King Philip's War

---

**ACTIVITY OPTIONS**

**LANGUAGE ARTS**

**SPEECH**

Choose one of the Puritan dissenters from this section and retell his or her story. Either write a **newspaper article** about the person or give an **oral history.** (REP5)

# The Mayflower Compact

CALIFORNIA STANDARDS

**8.2.1** Discuss the significance of the Magna Carta, the English Bill of Rights, and the Mayflower Compact.

**Reading 2.3** Find similarities and differences between texts in the treatment, scope, or organization of ideas.

**Setting the Stage** In 1620, 41 of the colonists aboard the *Mayflower* drew up the Mayflower Compact. This document refers to the area where they landed as "Virginia" because the land grants of the Virginia Company extended into New England. The colonists provided for self-government under majority rule of the male voters. **See Primary Source Explorer**

### A CLOSER LOOK

**REASONS FOR VOYAGE**

The three reasons the colonists give for their voyage to the eastern seaboard of North America are the glory of God, the advancement of Christianity, and the honor of the king.

**1. Why might sailing to new lands advance Christianity?**

### A CLOSER LOOK

**GUIDING PURPOSE**

The general good of the colony is the guiding purpose of the colonists in signing the compact.

**2. What does this suggest about the relationship between the individual and the community?**

We, whose names are underwritten, . . . having undertaken for the glory of God, and advancement of the Christian faith, and the honor of our King and country, a voyage to plant the first colony in the northern parts of Virginia, do by these presents, solemnly and mutually in the presence of God and one another **covenant**[1] and combine ourselves together into a civil **body politic**,[2] for our better ordering and preservation; and furtherance of the ends aforesaid . . . do enact, constitute, and frame such just and equal laws, ordinances, acts, constitutions, and offices from time to time as shall be thought most [proper] and convenient for the general good of the colony unto which we promise all due submission and obedience. In witness whereof we have hereunto subscribed our names at Cape Cod the eleventh of November, in the year of our **sovereign**[3] lord King James of England . . . Anno Domini 1620.

From B. P. Poore, ed., *The Federal and State Constitutions*, Part I, p. 931.

1. **covenant:** promise in a binding agreement.

2. **body politic:** the people of a politically organized group.

3. **sovereign:** supreme.

# The Fundamental Orders of Connecticut

**Setting the Stage** In January 1639, male citizens of three townships in Connecticut (Hartford, Windsor, and Wethersfield) assembled and drew up the Fundamental Orders of Connecticut. This document is often called the first written constitution in America. It contains a preamble, or introduction, and a set of laws. **See Primary Source Explorer**

### Preamble

Forasmuch as it has pleased the Almighty God by the wise disposition of His Divine Providence so to order and dispose of things that we, the inhabitants and residents of Windsor, Hartford, and Wethersfield are now cohabiting and dwelling in and upon the river of Conectecotte [Connecticut] and the lands thereunto adjoining; and well knowing where a people are gathered together the Word of God requires that, to maintain the peace and union of such a people, there should be an orderly and decent government established according to God, to order and dispose of the affairs of the people at all seasons as occasion shall require; do therefore associate and **conjoin**[1] ourselves to be as one public state or commonwealth. . . . As also in our civil affairs to be guided and governed according to such laws, rules, orders, and decrees as shall be made, ordered and decreed, as follows:

## Laws, Rules, and Orders

**1.** It is ordered, sentenced, and decreed that there shall be yearly two general assemblies or courts. . . . The first shall be called the Court of Election, wherein shall be yearly chosen . . . so many magistrates and other public officers as shall be found **requisite**.[2] . . .

**4.** It is ordered . . . that no person be chosen governor above once in two years, and that the governor be always a member of some approved congregation. . . .

**5.** It is ordered . . . that to the aforesaid Court of Election the several towns shall send their deputies. . . . Also, the other General Court in September shall be for making of laws, and any other public occasion which concerns the good of the Commonwealth. . . .

**7.** It is ordered . . . that after there are warrants given out for any of the said General Courts, the constable or constables of each town shall forthwith give notice distinctly to the inhabitants of the same . . . that at a place and time . . . they meet and assemble themselves together to elect and choose certain deputies to be at the General Court then following to [manage] the affairs of the Commonwealth. . . .

1. **conjoin:** unite.
2. **requisite:** required.

## Interactive Primary Sources Assessment

### 1. Main Ideas

**a.** Whose rights did the Mayflower Compact protect? (REP4)

**b.** Why are written documents useful in setting up a government? (REP4)

**c.** How were the Fundamental Orders based on religion? (REP4)

### 2. Critical Thinking

**Supporting Opinions**
How do you think these documents reflect the English contribution to American democracy? (REP4)

**THINK ABOUT**
• self-government
• majority rule

# Founding the Middle and Southern Colonies

| MAIN IDEA | WHY IT MATTERS NOW | TERMS & NAMES |
|---|---|---|
| The founding of the Middle and Southern colonies provided settlers with many economic opportunities. | America is still a place where immigrants seek freedom and economic opportunity. | Peter Stuyvesant — William Penn<br>patroon — Quaker<br>Duke of York — royal colony<br>proprietary colony — James Oglethorpe |

**CALIFORNIA STANDARDS**

**8.7.1** Describe the development of the agrarian economy in the South, identify the locations of the cotton-producing states, and discuss the significance of cotton and the cotton gin.

**CST3** Students use a variety of maps and documents to identify physical and cultural features of neighborhoods, cities, states, and countries and to explain the historical migration of people, expansion and disintegration of empires, and the growth of economic systems.

**REP4** Students assess the credibility of primary and secondary sources and draw sound conclusions from them.

## ONE AMERICAN'S STORY

In 1624, the Dutch founded the colony of New Netherland (later New York) on the eastern coast of North America. **Peter Stuyvesant**, the new governor, arrived in the city of New Amsterdam in May 1647. Because of his rough manner, he lost the support of the Dutch colonists. In 1664, a British fleet ordered the city of New Amsterdam to surrender itself to British control. Unable to gain the support of the Dutch colonists, Stuyvesant surrendered. He then defended his decision to his superiors back in the Netherlands.

*A VOICE FROM THE PAST*

Powder and provisions failing, and no relief or reinforcements being expected, we were necessitated [forced] to come to terms with the enemy, not through neglect of duty or cowardice . . . but in consequence of an absolute impossibility to defend the fort.

Peter Stuyvesant, quoted in *Peter Stuyvesant and His New York*

Peter Stuyvesant, governor of the Dutch colony of New Netherland, lost his leg in 1644 during a military action against the island of St. Martin in the Caribbean.

In this section, you will read about the founding of the Middle Colonies (such as New York) and the Southern Colonies.

## The Middle Colonies

The Middle Colonies were New York, New Jersey, Pennsylvania, and Delaware. They were located between New England to the north and the Chesapeake region to the south. (See the map on page 102.) Swedes, Dutch, English, Germans, and Africans were among the groups who came to these colonies.

Religious freedom attracted many groups, including Protestants, Catholics, Quakers, and Jews. The Hudson and Delaware rivers supported shipping and commerce. The river valleys had rich soil and mild winters. These conditions were favorable for farming and raising livestock.

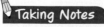

**Taking Notes**

Use your chart to take notes about the middle and southern colonies.

Virginia 1607 →

## New Netherland Becomes New York

In 1624, Dutch settlers financed by the Dutch West India Company founded the colony of New Netherland. New Netherland included the Hudson River valley, Long Island, and the land along the Delaware River.

To attract more settlers, the Dutch West India Company employed the patroon system. A **patroon** was a person who brought 50 settlers to New Netherland. As a reward, a patroon received a large land grant. He also received special privileges in hunting, fishing, and fur trading on his land.

In the early years, many different kinds of people settled in New Netherland. Twenty-three Jewish settlers arrived in 1654, and others soon followed. Later, Africans were brought to the colony as slaves and indentured servants. Many Puritans also came.

Peter Stuyvesant, the colony's governor, wanted to add land to New Netherland. He attacked the nearby charter colony of New Sweden in 1655. This colony was located along the Delaware River. The main settlement was Fort Christina (later named Wilmington, Delaware). It had been settled by Swedes in 1638. After an attack by the Dutch, the Swedes surrendered Fort Christina.

**Background**
The Duke of York became King James II in 1685.

England's King Charles II decided that his brother, the **Duke of York,** should drive the Dutch out of New Netherland. The Dutch colony was a threat to England because of its trade. It was also a threat because of its expanding settlements and its location. There were English colonies in New England to the north and Virginia to the south. As you have seen, when the duke's ships appeared off New Amsterdam in August 1664, the colony surrendered. New Netherland became the **proprietary colony** of New York. The Duke of York was now the proprietor, or owner, of the colony.

## New Jersey, Pennsylvania, and Delaware

The Duke of York had become the largest single landowner in America. He gave part of his claim, the province of New Jersey, to his friends Sir George Carteret and Lord John Berkeley in 1664. They encouraged settlers to come by promising freedom of religion. They also promised large grants of land and a representative assembly.

*Reading* **History**
A. Forming Opinions Why might the promise of religious freedom encourage a diverse population in a colony?

**William Penn** became another large landowner in America. Born into a wealthy English family, Penn joined the **Quakers,** to his father's disapproval. The young Penn was attacked for his Quaker beliefs. King Charles II owed the Penn family money. In repayment, in 1681 he gave Penn a large piece of land in America that came to be called Pennsylvania. The name means "Penn's woods."

### America's HERITAGE

**THE LOG CABIN**
Swedish colonists living in Delaware built the first log cabin in America in 1638. The log cabin was the perfect house to build where there were many trees. Settlers needed few tools to build such cabins, which were made of round logs with curved notches at the ends. After the ends were placed in the notches, the logs were secured. After 1780, the log cabin became the typical frontier home.

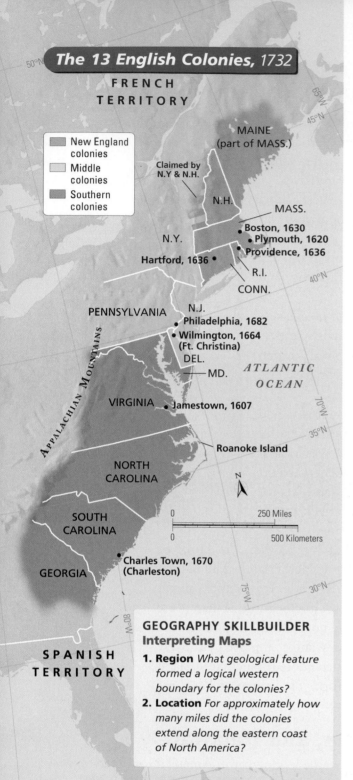

## The 13 English Colonies, 1732

FRENCH TERRITORY

New England colonies
Middle colonies
Southern colonies

MAINE (part of MASS.)

Claimed by N.Y & N.H.

N.H.

MASS.
• Boston, 1630
• Plymouth, 1620
• Providence, 1636

N.Y.

Hartford, 1636 •

R.I.

CONN.

N.J.

PENNSYLVANIA
• Philadelphia, 1682
• Wilmington, 1664 (Ft. Christina)
DEL.
MD.

ATLANTIC OCEAN

VIRGINIA • Jamestown, 1607

Roanoke Island

NORTH CAROLINA

SOUTH CAROLINA

GEORGIA

Charles Town, 1670 (Charleston)

APPALACHIAN MOUNTAINS

SPANISH TERRITORY

0 250 Miles
0 500 Kilometers

### GEOGRAPHY SKILLBUILDER
**Interpreting Maps**

1. **Region** What geological feature formed a logical western boundary for the colonies?
2. **Location** For approximately how many miles did the colonies extend along the eastern coast of North America?

Penn used this land to create a colony where Quakers could live according to their beliefs. Among other things, the Quakers believed that all people should live in peace and harmony. They welcomed different religions and ethnic groups. In Pennsylvania, Penn extended religious freedom and equality to all. He especially wanted the Native Americans to be treated fairly. In a letter to them in 1681, Penn said, "May [we] always live together as neighbors and friends."

Penn's policies helped make Pennsylvania one of the wealthiest of the American colonies. Many settlers came to Pennsylvania seeking religious freedom and a better life. In 1704, Penn granted the three lower counties of Delaware their own assembly. The counties later broke away to form the colony of Delaware.

*Reading* **History**
B. Comparing and Contrasting How did Penn's policies toward Native Americans compare with those of other colonies you have read about?

## The Southern Colonies

The new Southern Colonies were Maryland, the Carolinas, and Georgia. The Appalachian Mountains bordered parts of these colonies in the west. In the east, the colonies bordered the Atlantic Ocean. The soil and climate of this region were suitable for warm-weather crops such as tobacco, rice, and indigo.

## Maryland and the Carolinas

Lord Baltimore established Maryland in 1632 for Roman Catholics fleeing persecution in England. To attract other settlers besides Catholics, Lord Baltimore promised religious freedom. In 1649, Maryland passed the Toleration Act.

Maryland based its economy on tobacco, which required backbreaking work. Every three or four years, the tobacco crop used up the soil, and workers had to clear new land. Most laborers came as either servants or slaves. Maryland attracted few women as settlers.

In 1663, Carolina was founded as a colony. English settlers from Barbados built Charles Town, later called Charleston, in 1670. They busied themselves cutting timber, raising cattle, and trading with the Native Americans. After 1685, Charleston became a refuge for Huguenots, French Protestants seeking religious freedom.

Carolina's colonists needed laborers to grow rice and indigo. The English settlers encouraged the use of enslaved Africans. They also sold local Native Americans into slavery. As a result, wars broke out between the settlers and the Tuscarora and Yamasee tribes. The settlers' taking of tribal lands also fueled the wars.

Carolina's proprietors, or owners, refused to send help to stop a threatened Spanish attack on Charleston. Because of this, the colonists overthrew the colony's proprietary rule in 1719. In 1729, Carolina became a **royal colony.** Then it was ruled by governors appointed by the king. The colony was divided into North Carolina and South Carolina.

**Vocabulary**
**Carolina:** The name of the colony is based on a Latin form of "Charles," in honor of King Charles II.

# Georgia

In 1732, **James Oglethorpe** founded Georgia as a refuge for debtors. The English government wanted to use the colony as a military outpost against Spanish Florida to the south and French Louisiana to the west. In 1739, during a war between England and Spain, the Spanish tried to force the English colonists out of Georgia but were unsuccessful. English, German, Swiss, and Scottish colonists settled in Georgia. All religions were welcome. As the colony's leader, Oglethorpe set strict rules that upset the colonists. The king, in response to unrest, made Georgia a royal colony in 1752.

By the early 1700s, there were 13 English colonies along the eastern coast of North America. In the next chapter, you will read about how these colonies developed.

*Reading*History
**C. Reading a Map** Use the map on page 102 to check the location of Georgia in relation to the Spanish territory of Florida.

James Oglethorpe was the founder of Georgia.

---

## Section 3 Assessment

### 1. Terms & Names

**Explain the significance of:**
- Peter Stuyvesant
- patroon
- Duke of York
- proprietary colony
- William Penn
- Quaker
- royal colony
- James Oglethorpe

### 2. Using Graphics

Identify an effect for each cause listed in the chart below. (HI2)

| Cause | Effect |
|-------|--------|
| New Netherland threat to English | |
| English attacked Quakers | |
| Laborers needed in Carolinas | |
| Oglethorpe too strict in Georgia | |

### 3. Main Ideas

**a.** What were the goals of the patroon system? (HI1)

**b.** What three Middle Colonies offered religious freedom? (HI1)

**c.** What were three crops grown in the Southern Colonies? (HI1)

### 4. Critical Thinking

**Analyzing Causes** Why did colonists in Maryland and the Carolinas enslave Native Americans and use African slaves? (HI2)

**THINK ABOUT**
- the crops being grown
- the nature of farm work

### ACTIVITY OPTIONS

**LANGUAGE ARTS**

**SCIENCE**

What are the health effects of tobacco? Write a **news article** or give a **television report** for a science show about the effects of tobacco on the body. (REP4)

## TERMS & NAMES

Briefly explain the significance of each of the following.

1. joint-stock company
2. Jamestown
3. John Smith
4. House of Burgesses
5. Pilgrims
6. Mayflower Compact
7. Great Migration
8. Fundamental Orders of Connecticut
9. proprietary colony
10. William Penn

## REVIEW QUESTIONS

### Early Colonies Have Mixed Success (pages 85–91)

1. What were the reasons given by Richard Hakluyt that England should start a colony? (HI1)
2. Why were Jamestown and Plymouth financed by joint-stock companies? (HI1)
3. How did John Rolfe change the Virginia colony? (HI2)

### New England Colonies (pages 92–99)

4. What was John Winthrop's vision for Massachusetts Bay? (HI1)
5. What was the system of government in the Massachusetts Bay Colony? (HI1)
6. What were some effects of King Philip's War? (HI2)

### Founding the Middle and Southern Colonies (pages 100–103)

7. Why did Charles II want New Netherland? (HI2)
8. What were relations like between Native Americans and settlers in Pennsylvania? (HI1)
9. What was the Toleration Act of 1649? (HI1)
10. What ethnic and racial groups settled in the Middle Colonies and why did they do so? (HI2)

## CRITICAL THINKING

### 1. USING YOUR NOTES: SEQUENCING EVENTS

Using your completed chart, answer these questions: (CST2)

a. Which was the earliest successful settlement in Virginia?
b. Which colony was founded last?

### 2. ANALYZING LEADERSHIP

Why do you think William Penn was a more successful leader than Peter Stuyvesant? (REP4)

### 3. APPLYING CITIZENSHIP SKILLS

What were some of the common ideals that link the Mayflower Compact, the establishment of the House of Burgesses, and town meetings? (REP4)

### 4. THEME: IMPACT OF THE INDIVIDUAL

How did individual effort help ensure the success of England's colonies in America? (HI2)

### 5. ANALYZING CAUSES

What were the political, economic, and social causes for the founding of the different British colonies in North America? (HI2)

### Interact *with* History

How do the dangers you discussed before you read this chapter compare with the dangers people actually faced?

## VISUAL SUMMARY

## The 13 Colonies (CST1)

| | | Important Early Dates | Founder(s) |
|---|---|---|---|
| **New England Colonies** | Massachusetts | Plymouth, 1620; Mass. Bay, 1630 | Pilgrims; Puritans |
| | New Hampshire | Portsmouth, 1623 | Proprietors |
| | Rhode Island | Providence, 1636 | Roger Williams |
| | Connecticut | Hartford, 1636 | Thomas Hooker |
| **Middle Colonies** | New York (New Netherland) | Dutch settlers arrive, 1624 | Dutch West India Company |
| | Delaware | Fort Christina, 1638 | Swedes |
| | New Jersey | Duke of York establishes, 1664 | George Carteret, John Berkeley |
| | Pennsylvania | Charles II bestows land, 1681 | William Penn |
| **Southern Colonies** | Virginia | Jamestown, 1607 | Virginia Company of London |
| | Maryland | Founded as religious haven, 1632 | Lord Baltimore |
| | North Carolina | Founded, 1663 | Proprietors |
| | South Carolina | Founded, 1663 | Proprietors |
| | Georgia | Founded as debtors' refuge, 1732 | James Oglethorpe |

Use the graph and your knowledge of U.S. history to answer questions 1 and 2.

Additional Test Practice, pp. S1–S33.

### Population of the Colonies

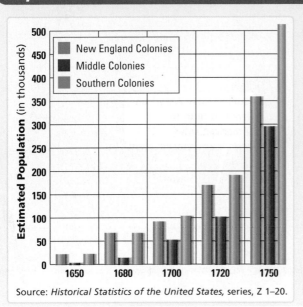

**Legend:**
- New England Colonies
- Middle Colonies
- Southern Colonies

Estimated Population (in thousands) — y-axis: 0, 50, 100, 150, 200, 250, 300, 350, 400, 450, 500

x-axis: 1650, 1680, 1700, 1720, 1750

Source: *Historical Statistics of the United States,* series, Z 1–20.

1. About how much did the population of the Southern colonies increase between 1720 and 1750? (8.1)

A. 100,000

B. 200,000

C. 300,000

D. 500,000

2. Between what time periods was the increase in the population of the New England colonies greatest? (8.1)

A. between 1650 and 1680

B. between 1680 and 1700

C. between 1700 and 1720

D. between 1720 and 1750

**This quotation is from Peter Stuyvesant, Dutch governor of New Amsterdam, about his encounter with British forces. Use the quotation and your knowledge of U.S. history to answer question 3.**

### PRIMARY SOURCE

Powder and provisions failing, and no relief or reinforcements being expected, we were necessitated [forced] to come to terms with the enemy, not through neglect of duty or cowardice . . . but in consequence of an absolute impossibility to defend the fort.

**Peter Stuyvesant,** *Peter Stuyvesant and His New York*

3. The passage best supports which conclusion? (8.1)

A. Stuyvesant surrendered to the British.

B. The citizens of New Amsterdam did not want to use their supplies.

C. Stuyvesant feared the British forces.

D. The people of New Amsterdam refused to surrender to the British.

**TEST PRACTICE**
CLASSZONE.COM

## ALTERNATIVE ASSESSMENT

### 1. WRITING ABOUT HISTORY

How would an attorney have defended an accused woman during the Salem witchcraft trials? Write a **statement** to the court defending the woman. (REP5)

- You can do research for your statement in books about the Salem witchcraft trials.
- Other sources of information include historical societies, archives, and museums.
- Your statement should persuade a jury of the time.

### 2. COOPERATIVE LEARNING

With a few of your classmates, write and perform a play about the "lost colonists" of Roanoke. Depict colonists dealing with food shortages, illness, and relations with Native Americans. (HI1)

## INTEGRATED TECHNOLOGY

### DOING INTERNET RESEARCH

The Mayflower Compact was devised in response to the need for some sort of government. Use it as a model for planning a government for your class. (REP4)

- Use the Internet or other library resources to learn more about the Mayflower Compact.
- Adapt ideas from the Mayflower Compact that might work for your class.
- Make decisions about what rules are needed, who will hold office, how they will be selected and how long they will serve, and whether or not there should be limits on majority rule.

**For more about the Mayflower Compact . . .**

**INTERNET ACTIVITY**
CLASSZONE.COM

# The Colonies Develop 1700–1753

In 1702, a vast countryside surrounded Philadelphia. Most colonists earned their living in the country. Fewer than one in ten lived in cities.

Some Native Americans lived close to the American cities.

**c. 1700**
Colonial population reaches 257,000.

**1712**
Slave uprising occurs in New York City.

**1718**
French found city of New Orleans at mouth of Mississippi River.

Spanish priests build Alamo in Texas.

USA
World 1700

**1701**
War of the Spanish Succession begins in Europe.

**1707**
Act of Union unites England with Scotland and creates Great Britain.

Philadelphia was a major center of commerce.

It is the early 1700s when you arrive in one of America's larger port cities. After nearly a month of ocean travel, you are thrilled to see land. As you leave the ship, you wonder where you will live and how you will earn a living.

# Would you settle on a farm or in a town?

## What Do You Think?

- Will you choose to live where other people from your homeland live? Or will you try somewhere new?

- How did you make a living in your old country? Will this influence your choice?

**RESEARCH LINKS**
CLASSZONE.COM

Visit the Chapter 4 links for more information about the development of the colonies.

**1733**
Benjamin Franklin publishes *Poor Richard's Almanac.*

**1739**
Enslaved Africans revolt in Stono Rebellion.

**1742**
First European settlement west of Allegheny Mountains is established.

**c. 1750** Population of the English colonies passes the one million mark.

**1727**
George II becomes King of Great Britain.

**1739**
Nadir Shah of Persia conquers Delhi, India.

**1752**
China suppresses Tibetan rebellion and forces Dalai Lama to accept its authority.

1753

# Reading Strategy: Analyzing Causes and Effects

## What Do You Know?

What ideas and pictures come to mind when you hear people talk about "the South" or "the North"? Why do you think these distinct regions developed?

### Think About
- what you have learned about these regions from books or movies
- the way geography affects people's choices
- your responses to the Interact with History about settling on a farm or in a town (see page 107)

**CALIFORNIA STANDARDS**

**Reading 2.0** Students read and understand grade-level-appropriate material. They describe and connect the essential ideas, arguments, and perspectives of the text by using their knowledge of text structure, organization, and purpose.

## What Do You Want to Know?

What questions do you have about how the four colonial regions developed? Record these questions in your notebook before you read the chapter.

## Analyzing Causes and Effects

As you read about history, it is important to understand not only what happened in the past, but also the reasons why it happened. Clue words that indicate cause—such as *because* and *since*—can help you look for causes of historical events. Use the chart below to list causes that contributed to the different economic developments in each of the colonial regions.

**S** See Skillbuilder Handbook, page R11.

###  Taking Notes

|  |  | NEW ENGLAND COLONIES | MIDDLE COLONIES | SOUTHERN COLONIES | BACKCOUNTRY |
|---|---|---|---|---|---|
| **CAUSES** | Climate |  |  |  |  |
|  | Resources |  |  |  |  |
|  | People |  |  |  |  |
| **EFFECT** | Economic Development |  |  |  |  |

# New England: Commerce and Religion

| MAIN IDEA | WHY IT MATTERS NOW | TERMS & NAMES |
|---|---|---|
| Fishing and trade contributed to the growth and prosperity of the New England Colonies. | Coastal cities in New England continue to engage in trade. | Backcountry     triangular trade<br>subsistence     Navigation Acts<br>farming     smuggling |

## ONE AMERICAN'S STORY

Peleg Folger, a New England sailor, kept a journal that describes what whaling was like in the 1750s. In one entry, he explained what happened after whales were sighted and small boats were launched to pursue them.

### A VOICE FROM THE PAST

So we row'd about a mile and a Half from the [ship], and then a whale come up under us, & [smashed in] our boat . . . and threw us every man overboard [except] one. And we all came up and Got Hold of the Boat & Held to her until the other boat (which was a mile and half off) came up and took us in, all Safe, and not one man Hurt.

**Peleg Folger,** quoted in *The Sea-Hunters*

When Folger and his mates killed a whale, they cut a hole in its head, and removed large amounts of oil from the animal. When the ship returned to port, this oil was sold to colonists, who used it as fuel in their lamps.

Many settlers in the New England Colonies—Massachusetts, New Hampshire, Connecticut, and Rhode Island—made a living from the sea. The majority of New Englanders, however, were farmers.

## Distinct Colonial Regions Develop

Between 1700 and 1750, the population of England's colonies in North America doubled and then doubled again. At the start of the century, the colonial population stood at about 257,000. By 1750, more than 1,170,000 settlers called the English colonies home.

By the 1700s, the colonies formed three distinct regions: the New England Colonies, the Middle Colonies, and the Southern Colonies. Another area was the **Backcountry**. It ran along the Appalachian Mountains through the far western part of the other regions.

**CALIFORNIA STANDARDS**

**8.6.1** Discuss the influence of industrialization and technological developments on the region, including human modification of the landscape and how physical geography shaped human actions (e.g., gowth of cities, deforestation, farming, mineral extraction).

**8.7.4** Compare the lives of and opportunities for free blacks in the North with those of free blacks in the South.

**8.10.2** Trace the boundaries constituting the North and the South, the geographical differences between the two regions, and the differences between agrarians and industrialists.

**REP4** Students assess the credibility of primary and secondary sources and draw sound conclusions from them.

**Taking Notes**

Use your chart to take notes about the New England colonies.

Several factors made each colonial region distinct. Some of the most important were each region's climate, resources, and people.

1. New England had long winters and rocky soil. English settlers made up the largest group in the region's population.
2. The Middle Colonies had shorter winters and fertile soil. The region attracted immigrants from all over Europe.
3. The Southern Colonies had a warm climate and good soil. There, some settlers used enslaved Africans to work their plantations.
4. The Backcountry's climate and resources varied, depending on the latitude. Many Scots-Irish immigrants settled there.

During the colonial era, the majority of people made their living by farming. However, the type of agriculture they practiced depended on the climate and resources in the region where they settled.

**Vocabulary**
**latitude:** the distance north or south of the equator, measured in degrees

## The Farms and Towns of New England

Life in New England was not easy. The growing season was short, and the soil was rocky. Most farmers practiced **subsistence farming**. That is, they produced just enough food for themselves and sometimes a little extra to trade in town.

Most New England farmers lived near a town. This was because colonial officials usually did not sell scattered plots of land to individual

**The New England Colonies, 1750**

MAINE (part of MASS.)

Claimed by N.Y. and N.H.

Cattle
Fish
Shipbuilding
Timber
Whaling

Falmouth
NEW HAMPSHIRE
Portsmouth
Salem
Boston
Plymouth
Newport
CONNECTICUT
New Haven
RHODE ISLAND
MASSACHUSETTS

Connecticut R.
Hudson R.
St. Lawrence R.
Lake Ontario

ATLANTIC OCEAN

0    100 Miles
0    200 Kilometers

**GEOGRAPHY SKILLBUILDER Interpreting Maps**
1. **Location** All of the New England Colonies are to the east of what major river?
2. **Region** What ocean-related products was colonial New England known for?

This New England meetinghouse is located in Sturbridge Village, Massachusetts.

farmers. Instead, they sold larger plots of land to groups of people—often to the congregation of a Puritan church. A congregation then settled the town and divided the land among the members of its church.

*Reading*History
A. Recognizing Effects How did the way land was sold in New England affect the way people lived?

This pattern of settlement led New England towns to develop in a unique way. Usually, a cluster of farmhouses surrounded a green—a central square where a meetinghouse was located and where public activities took place. Because people lived together in small towns, shopkeepers had enough customers to make a living. Also, if the townspeople needed a blacksmith or a carpenter, they could pool their money and hire one.

## Harvesting the Sea

New England's rocky soil made farming difficult. In contrast, the Atlantic Ocean offered many economic opportunities. In one story, a group of settlers was standing on a hill overlooking the Atlantic. One of them pointed out to sea and exclaimed, "There is a great pasture where our children's grandchildren will go for bread!"

The settler's prediction came true. Not far off New England's coast were some of the world's best fishing grounds. The Atlantic was filled with mackerel, halibut, cod, and many other types of fish.

New England's forests provided everything needed to harvest these great "pastures" of fish. The wood cut from iron-hard oak trees made excellent ship hulls. Hundred-foot-tall white pines were ideal for masts. Shipbuilders used about 2,500 trees to produce just one ship!

New England's fish and timber were among its most valuable articles of trade. Coastal cities like Boston, Salem, New Haven, and Newport grew rich as a result of shipbuilding, fishing, and trade.

**Background**
In 1742, over 16,000 people lived in Boston.

## Atlantic Trade

New England settlers engaged in three types of trade. First was the trade with other colonies. Second was the direct exchange of goods with Europe. The third type was the triangular trade.

**Triangular trade** was the name given to a trading route with three stops. For example, a ship might leave New England with a cargo of rum

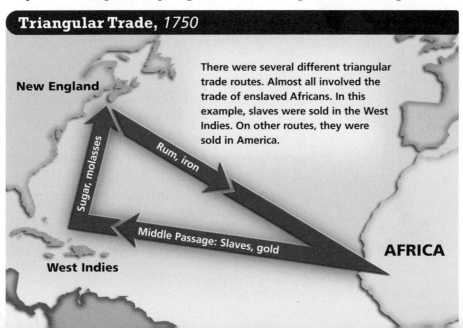

**Triangular Trade,** *1750*

There were several different triangular trade routes. Almost all involved the trade of enslaved Africans. In this example, slaves were sold in the West Indies. On other routes, they were sold in America.

New England

Sugar, molasses

Rum, iron

Middle Passage: Slaves, gold

West Indies

AFRICA

and iron. In Africa, the captain would trade his cargo for slaves. Slaves then endured the horrible Middle Passage to the West Indies, where they were exchanged for sugar and molasses. Traders then took the sugar and molasses back to New England. There, colonists used the molasses to make rum, and the pattern started over.

**Background**
See Olaudah Equiano's descriptions of the Middle Passage on page 78.

New England won enormous profits from trade. England wanted to make sure that it received part of those profits. So the English government began to pass the **Navigation Acts** in 1651. The Navigation Acts had four major provisions designed to ensure that England made money from its colonies' trade.

1. All shipping had to be done in English ships or ships made in the English colonies.
2. Products such as tobacco, wood, and sugar could be sold only to England or its colonies.
3. European imports to the colonies had to pass through English ports.
4. English officials were to tax any colonial goods not shipped to England.

But even after the passage of the Navigation Acts, England had trouble controlling colonial shipping. Merchants ignored the acts whenever possible. **Smuggling**—importing or exporting goods illegally— was common. England also had great difficulty preventing pirates—like the legendary Blackbeard—from interfering with colonial shipping.

## STRANGE *but* True

**BLACKBEARD THE PIRATE**

Of all the pirates who attacked colonial ships, Blackbeard (shown below) was the most famous. He was a fearsome man known to stick matches in his hair to light up his face during battle.

Blackbeard's pirate career finally came to an end in 1718, when Virginia's governor sent an expedition against him. Nearly half the expedition's men died in the key battle. Blackbeard himself did not fall until he had suffered nearly 25 wounds. Before sailing back to port, sailors cut off his head and put it on the front of their ship.

# African Americans in New England

There were few slaves in New England. Slavery simply was not economical in this region of small farms. Also, because the growing season was short, there was little work for slaves during the long winter months. Farmers could not afford to feed and house slaves who were not working.

*Reading*History
**B. Analyzing Causes** Why were there relatively few enslaved workers in New England?

Even so, some New Englanders in larger towns and cities did own slaves. They worked as house servants, cooks, gardeners, and stable-hands. In the 1700s, slave owners seldom had enough room to house more than one or two slaves. Instead, more and more slave owners hired out their slaves to work on the docks or in shops or warehouses. Slave owners sometimes allowed their slaves to keep a portion of their wages.

Occasionally, some enslaved persons were able to save enough to buy their freedom. In fact, New

England was home to more free blacks than any other region. A free black man might become a merchant, sailor, printer, carpenter, or landowner. Still, white colonists did not treat free blacks as equals.

## Changes in Puritan Society

The early 1700s saw many changes in New England society. One of the most important was the gradual decline of the Puritan religion. There were a number of reasons for this decline.

*Reading*History

**C. Making Inferences** Why might an interest in material things compete with the Puritan religion?

One reason was that the drive for economic success competed with Puritan ideas. Many colonists, especially those who lived along the coast, seemed to care as much about business and material things as they did about religion. One observer had this complaint.

*"[Boston] is so conveniently Situated for Trade."*

**An observer in 1713**

> *A VOICE FROM THE PAST*
>
> [Boston] is so conveniently Situated for Trade and the Genius of the people are so inclined to merchandise, that they seek no other Education for their children than writing and Arithmetick.
>
> **An observer in 1713,** quoted in *A History of American Life*

Another reason for the decline of the Puritan religion was the increasing competition from other religious groups. Baptists and Anglicans established churches in Massachusetts and Connecticut, where Puritans had once been the most powerful group.

Political changes also weakened the Puritan community. In 1691, a new royal charter for Massachusetts guaranteed religious freedom for all Protestants, not just Puritans. The new charter also granted the vote based on property ownership instead of church membership. This change put an end to the Puritan churches' ability to control elections.

To the south of New England were the Middle Colonies, which developed in quite different ways—as the next section shows.

---

### Section 1 Assessment

**1. Terms & Names**

**Explain the significance of:**
- Backcountry
- subsistence farming
- triangular trade
- Navigation Acts
- smuggling

**2. Using Graphics**

Use a chart like the one shown to record how New Englanders prospered from the Atlantic Ocean.

| Economic Activity | Benefits to Colonists |
|---|---|
| | |

How did some profit illegally from the ocean? (HI6)

**3. Main Ideas**

**a.** How did most people in New England earn a living? (HI1)

**b.** Why did England pass the Navigation Acts? (HI2)

**c.** What factors led to the decline of the Puritan religion in New England? (HI2)

**4. Critical Thinking**

**Making Inferences** What advantages might there be in living near other people in small towns, such as those in New England? (HI2)

**THINK ABOUT**
- the transportation options available to colonists
- why shopkeepers chose to open businesses in towns

---

**ACTIVITY OPTIONS**

**ART**

**TECHNOLOGY**

Read more about whaling. Make a **mobile** that shows different kinds of whales or plan a **multimedia presentation** on whaling today. (HI6)

# The Middle Colonies: Farms and Cities

| MAIN IDEA | WHY IT MATTERS NOW | TERMS & NAMES |
|---|---|---|
| The people who settled in the Middle Colonies made a society of great diversity. | States in this region still boast some of the most diverse communities in the world. | cash crop · artisan<br>gristmill · Conestoga wagon<br>diversity |

**CALIFORNIA STANDARDS**

**7.11.3** Examine the origins of modern capitalism; the influence of mercantilism and cottage industry; the elements and importance of a market economy in seventeenth-century Europe; the changing international trading and marketing patterns, including their locations on a world map; and the influence of explorers and map makers.

**8.6.1** Discuss the influence of industrialization and technological developments on the region, including human modification of the landscape and how physical geography shaped human actions (e.g., growth of cities, deforestation, farming, mineral extraction).

**8.7.4** Compare the lives of and opportunities for free blacks in the North with those of free blacks in the South.

**REP4** Students assess the credibility of primary and secondary sources and draw sound conclusions from them.

## ONE AMERICAN'S STORY

Elizabeth Ashbridge was only 19 years old when she arrived in America from England in the 1730s. Although she was an indentured servant, she hoped to earn her freedom and find a way to express her strong religious feelings.

After several years, Elizabeth did gain freedom. In Pennsylvania, she joined a religious group called the Society of Friends, or Quakers. The new Quaker longed to share her beliefs openly.

### A VOICE FROM THE PAST

I was permitted to see that all I had gone through was to prepare me for this day; and that the time was near, when it would be required of me, to go and declare to others what the God of mercy had done for my soul.

**Elizabeth Ashbridge,** *Some Account . . . of the Life of Elizabeth Ashbridge*

A woman speaks out at a Quaker meeting.

The Quakers believed that people of different beliefs could live together in harmony. They helped to create a climate of tolerance and acceptance in the Middle Colonies of New York, New Jersey, Pennsylvania, and Delaware, as you will read in this section.

## A Wealth of Resources

The Middle Colonies had much to offer in addition to a climate of tolerance. A Frenchman named Michel Guillaume Jean de Crèvecoeur (krehv•KUR) praised the region's "fair cities, substantial villages, extensive fields . . . decent houses, good roads, orchards, meadows, and bridges, where an hundred years ago all was wild, woody, and uncultivated."

The prosperity that Crèvecoeur described was typical of the Middle Colonies. Immigrants from all over Europe came to take advantage of this region's productive land. Their settlements soon crowded out Native Americans, who had lived in the region for thousands of years.

**Taking Notes**

Use your chart to take notes about the middle colonies.

| | NEW ENGLAND COLONIES | MIDD... |
|---|---|---|
| **CAUSES** Climate | | |
| Resources | | |
| People | | |
| **EFFECT** Economic Development | | |

Among the immigrants who came to the Middle Colonies were Dutch and German farmers. They brought the advanced agricultural methods of their countries with them. Their skills, knowledge, and hard work would soon result in an abundance of foods.

The Middle Colonies boasted a longer growing season than New England and a soil rich enough to grow **cash crops.** These were crops raised to be sold for money. Common cash crops included fruits, vegetables, and, above all, grain. The Middle Colonies produced so much grain that people began calling them the "breadbasket" colonies.

## The Importance of Mills

**Vocabulary**
**grist:** another name for grain, the one-seeded fruit of cereal grasses like wheat and rye

After harvesting their crops of corn, wheat, rye, or other grains, farmers took them to a **gristmill.** There, millers crushed the grain between heavy stones to produce flour or meal. Human or animal power fueled some of these mills. But water wheels built along the region's plentiful rivers powered most of the mills.

The bread that colonists baked with these products was crucial to their diet. Colonists ate about a pound of grain in some form each day—nearly three times more than Americans eat today. Even though colonists ate a great deal of grain, they had plenty left over to send to the region's coastal markets for sale.

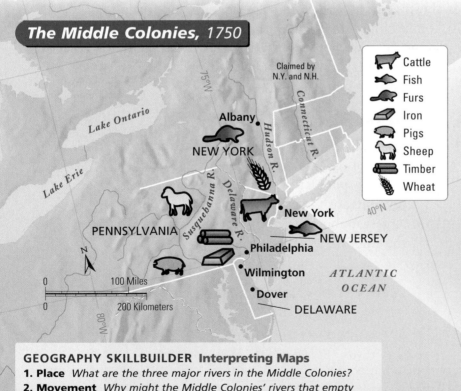

**The Middle Colonies, 1750**

Claimed by N.Y. and N.H.

Cattle
Fish
Furs
Iron
Pigs
Sheep
Timber
Wheat

Lake Ontario

Lake Erie

Albany

NEW YORK

Hudson R.

Connecticut R.

Susquehanna R.

Delaware R.

PENNSYLVANIA

New York

NEW JERSEY

Philadelphia

Wilmington

ATLANTIC OCEAN

Dover

DELAWARE

0    100 Miles
0    200 Kilometers

40°N

35°N

75°W

80°W

Philipsburg Manor, in Sleepy Hollow, New York, has a working 18th-century farm and a water-powered gristmill.

**GEOGRAPHY SKILLBUILDER Interpreting Maps**
1. **Place** *What are the three major rivers in the Middle Colonies?*
2. **Movement** *Why might the Middle Colonies' rivers that empty into the ocean be important for farmers?*

# The Cities Prosper

The excellent harbors along the coasts of the Middle Colonies were ideal sites for cities. New York City grew up at the mouth of the Hudson River, and Philadelphia was founded on the Delaware River. The merchants who lived in these growing port cities exported cash crops, especially grain, and imported manufactured goods.

Because of its enormous trade, Philadelphia was the fastest growing city in the colonies. The city owed its expansion to a thriving trade in wheat and other cash crops. By 1720, it was home to a dozen large shipyards—places where ships are built or repaired.

The city's wealth also brought many public improvements. Large and graceful buildings, such as Philadelphia's statehouse—which was later renamed Independence Hall—graced the city's streets. Streetlights showed the way along paved roads. In 1748, a Swedish visitor named Peter Kalm exclaimed that Philadelphia had grown up overnight.

*Reading* **History**

**A. Reading a Map** Locate New York and Philadelphia on the map on page 115. Note the rivers next to which they were built.

## daily *life*

### NAMES AND OCCUPATIONS

Many English colonists had names like Miller and Smith—names that reflected how their families had made a living in England. For example, a colonist named Miller probably had an ancestor who had operated a mill. Similarly, Smith probably had an ancestor who had been a blacksmith.

Sometimes colonists continued in the same occupations as their ancestors. But as time went on, colonists turned to other occupations, and their names no longer reflected how they earned a living. Yet names like Smith and Miller remain common in the United States, reflecting the country's past as English colonies.

### A VOICE FROM THE PAST

And yet its natural advantages, trade, riches and power, are by no means inferior to any, even of the most ancient towns in Europe.

**Peter Kalm,** quoted in *America at 1750*

New York could also thank trade for its rapid growth. This bustling port handled flour, bread, furs, and whale oil. At midcentury, an English naval officer admired the city's elegant brick houses, paved streets, and roomy warehouses. "Such is this city," he said, "that very few in England can rival it in its show."

## A Diverse Region

Many different immigrant groups arrived in the port cities of the Middle Colonies. Soon, the region's population showed a remarkable **diversity**, or variety, in its people. One of the largest immigrant groups in the region, after the English, was the Germans.

**Background** In 1742, New York City's population was about 11,000, and nearly 13,000 people lived in Philadelphia.

A. Cooper

A. Sawyer

A. Potter

Many of the Germans arrived between 1710 and 1740. Most came as indentured servants fleeing religious intolerance. Known for their skillful farming, these immigrants soon made a mark on the Middle Colonies. "German communities," wrote one historian, "could be identified by the huge barns, the sleek cattle, and the stout workhorses."

**Background**
By the second half of the 1700s, more than one in three colonists in Pennsylvania claimed German ancestry.

Germans also brought a strong tradition of craftsmanship to the Middle Colonies. For example, German gunsmiths first developed the long rifle. Other German **artisans**, or craftspeople, became ironworkers and makers of glass, furniture, and kitchenware. Cottage industries were common in the Middle Colonies and in Europe. Business people would hire people to work in their own homes performing tasks, such as spinning thread, or making goods. Cottage industries were the start of the factory system we know today.

**The Middle Colonies, 1750**

**Population Diversity**

French 2%
Swedish 3%
Welsh 3%
Scottish 4%
Irish 5%
African 7%
Scots-Irish 9%
Dutch 10%
German 18%
English 39%

Source: *Population of the British Colonies in America Before 1776*, 1975

**SKILLBUILDER Interpreting Graphs**
1. *What group made up nearly one-fifth of the population in the Middle Colonies?*
2. *What were the two main languages spoken in the Middle Colonies?*

Germans built **Conestoga wagons** to carry their produce to town. These wagons used wide wheels suitable for dirt roads, and the wagons' curved beds prevented spilling when climbing up and down hills. The wagons' canvas covers offered protection from rain. Conestoga wagons would later be important in settling the West.

*Reading* **History**
**B. Summarizing**
How would you describe the population of the Middle Colonies?

The Middle Colonies became home to many people besides the Germans. There were also the English, Dutch, Scots-Irish, African, Irish, Scottish, Welsh, Swedish, and French. Because of the diversity in the Middle Colonies, different groups had to learn to accept, or at least tolerate, one another.

## A Climate of Tolerance

While the English Puritans shaped life in the New England Colonies, many different groups contributed to the culture of the Middle Colonies. Because of the greater number of different groups, it was difficult for any single group to dominate the others. Thus, the region's diversity helped to create a climate of tolerance. Some of the region's religious groups also helped to promote tolerance.

The Middle Colonies' earliest settlers, the Dutch in New York and the Quakers in Pennsylvania, both practiced religious tolerance. That is, they honored the right of religious groups to follow their own beliefs without interference. Quakers also insisted on the equality of men and women. As a result, Quaker women served as preachers, and female missionaries traveled the world spreading the Quaker message.

## OBSERVATIONS

On the Inflaving, importing and purchafing of

# *Negroes;*

With fome Advice thereon, extracted from the Epiftle of the Yearly-Meeting of the People called Quakers, held at *London* in the Year 1758.

Anthony Benezet

*When ye fpread forth your Hands, I will hide mine Eyes from you, yea when ye make many Prayers I will not hear; your Hands are full of Blood. Wafh ye, make you clean, put away the Evil of your Doings from before mine Eyes* Ifai. 1, 15.

*Is not this the Faft that I have chofen, to loofe the Bands of Wickednefs, to undo the heavy Burden, to let the Oppreffed go free, and that ye break every Yoke,* Chap. 58, 7.

___

Second Edition.

GERMANTOWN:
Printed by CHRISTOPHER SOWER. 1760.

**Most Quakers were opposed to slavery. Shown here is a Quaker antislavery pamphlet printed in the Middle Colonies.**

Quakers were also the first to raise their voices against slavery. Quaker ideals influenced immigrants in the Middle Colonies—and eventually the whole nation.

## African Americans in the Middle Colonies

The tolerant attitude of many settlers in the Middle Colonies did not prevent slavery in the region. In 1750, about 7 percent of the Middle Colonies' population was enslaved. As in New England, many people of African descent lived and worked in cities.

New York City had a larger number of people of African descent than any other city in the Northern colonies. In New York City, enslaved persons worked as manual laborers, servants, drivers, and as assistants to artisans and craftspeople. Free African-American men and women also made their way to the city, where they worked as laborers, servants, or sailors.

Tensions existed between the races in New York City, sometimes leading to violence. In 1712, for example, about 24 rebellious slaves set fire to a building. They then killed nine whites and wounded several others who came to put out the fire. Armed colonists caught the suspects, who were punished horribly. Such punishments showed that whites would resort to force and violence to control slaves. Even so, the use of violence did little to prevent the outbreak of other slave rebellions.

Force would also be used in the South, which had far more enslaved Africans than the North. In the next section, you will learn how the South's plantation economy came to depend on the labor of enslaved Africans.

*Reading*History

**C. Forming Opinions** Why do you think that force was needed to keep Africans enslaved?

---

Section **2** Assessment

### 1. Terms & Names

**Explain the significance of:**
- cash crop
- gristmill
- diversity
- artisan
- Conestoga wagon

### 2. Using Graphics

Use a cluster diagram like the one shown to indicate where different immigrants in the Middle Colonies came from.

*(cluster diagram: center labeled "Middle Colonies' Population")*

What was the third largest group in the region? (REP1)

### 3. Main Ideas

**a.** What attracted settlers to the Middle Colonies? (HI1)

**b.** What service was performed at gristmills? (HI1)

**c.** Why might enslaved Africans be able to join in rebellion more easily in the city than the country? (HI1)

### 4. Critical Thinking

**Analyzing Causes** What factors allowed large coastal cities to develop in the Middle Colonies? (HI1)

**THINK ABOUT**
- geography
- people
- trade

**ACTIVITY OPTIONS**

**MATH**
**GEOGRAPHY**

Read more about Philadelphia. Create a **database** of the city's population growth in the 1700s or draw a **map** that shows its physical growth. (CST3)

# The Southern Colonies: Plantations and Slavery

| MAIN IDEA | WHY IT MATTERS NOW | TERMS & NAMES |
|---|---|---|

**MAIN IDEA**

The economy of the Southern Colonies relied heavily on slave labor.

**WHY IT MATTERS NOW**

The existence of slavery deeply affected the South and the nation.

**TERMS & NAMES**

indigo

Eliza Lucas

William Byrd II

overseer

Stono Rebellion

## ONE AMERICAN'S STORY

George Mason was born to a wealthy Virginia family in 1725. Mason—who later described the slave trade as "disgraceful to mankind"—wrote about the contributions of enslaved persons on his family's plantation.

George Mason

### A VOICE FROM THE PAST

My father had among his slaves carpenters, coopers [barrel makers], sawyers, blacksmiths, tanners, curriers, shoemakers, spinners, weavers and knitters, and even a distiller.

**George Mason,** quoted in *Common Landscape of America*

**CALIFORNIA STANDARDS**

**8.7.1** Describe the development of the agrarian economy in the South, identify the locations of the cotton-producing states, and discuss the significance of cotton and the cotton gin.

**8.7.2** Trace the origins and development of slavery; its effects on black Americans and on the region's political, social, religious, economic, and cultural development; and identify the strategies that were tried to both overturn and preserve it (e.g., through the writings and historical documents on Nat Turner, Denmark Vesey).

**8.7.3** Examine the characteristics of white Southern society and how the physical environment influenced events and conditions prior to the Civil War.

**8.7.4** Compare the lives of and opportunities for free blacks in the North with those of free blacks in the South.

**REP4** Students assess the credibility of primary and secondary sources and draw sound conclusions from them.

Because the Masons and other wealthy landowners produced all that they needed on their own plantations, they appeared to be independent. But their independence usually depended on the labor of enslaved Africans. Although planters were only a small part of the Southern population, the plantation economy and slavery shaped life in the Southern Colonies: Maryland, Virginia, the Carolinas, and Georgia.

## The Plantation Economy

The South's soil and almost year-round growing season were ideal for plantation crops like rice and tobacco. These valuable plants required much labor to produce, but with enough workers they could be grown as cash crops. Planters had no trouble transporting their crops because the region's many waterways made it easy for oceangoing ships to tie up at plantation docks.

Like George Mason's boyhood home, most plantations were largely self-sufficient. That is, nearly everything that planters, their families, and their workers needed was produced on the plantation. Because plantations were so self-sufficient, large cities like those in the North were rare

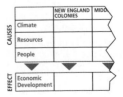

**Taking Notes**

Use your chart to take notes about the Southern colonies.

**Legend:**
- Corn
- Indigo
- Naval stores
- Pigs
- Rice
- Tobacco

Baltimore
MARYLAND
Potomac R.
Chesapeake Bay
VIRGINIA
Richmond
James R. Jamestown
Roanoke R.
NORTH CAROLINA
Wilmington
APPALACHIAN MOUNTAINS
SOUTH CAROLINA
ATLANTIC OCEAN
Savannah R.
GEORGIA
Charles Town (Charleston)
Altamaha R.
Savannah

0 100 Miles
0 200 Kilometers
N
40°N
35°N
85°W
75°W

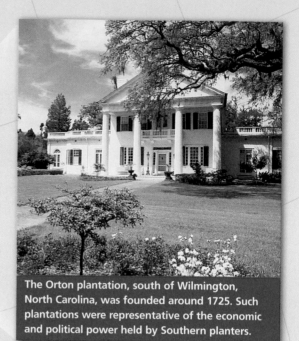

The Orton plantation, south of Wilmington, North Carolina, was founded around 1725. Such plantations were representative of the economic and political power held by Southern planters.

**GEOGRAPHY SKILLBUILDER Interpreting Maps**
1. **Location** The Southern Colonies were south of what latitude?
2. **Place** Which Southern Colonies grew crops of both rice and indigo?

in the Southern Colonies. The port city of Charles Town (later called Charleston) in South Carolina was an early exception.

As the plantation economy continued to grow, planters began to have difficulty finding enough laborers to work their plantations. Toward the end of the 1600s, the planters began to turn to enslaved Africans for labor.

**Background**
In 1742, Charles Town's population was 6,800.

# The Turn to Slavery

For the first half of the 1600s, there were few Africans in Virginia, whether enslaved or free. In 1665, fewer than 500 Africans had been brought into the colony. At that time, African and European indentured servants worked in the fields together.

Starting in the 1660s, the labor system began to change as indentured white servants started to leave the plantations. One reason they left was the large amount of land available in the Americas. It was fairly easy for white men to save enough money to buy land and start their own farms. White servants could not be kept on the plantations permanently. As Bacon's Rebellion showed, it was also politically dangerous for planters to try to keep them there (see page 89). As a result, the landowners had to find another source of labor.

**U.S. Slave Population**

Percentage of Population
40
30
20
10
0
1650 1670 1690 1710 1730 1750

■ North  ■ South

Source: Fogel and Engerman, *Time on the Cross,* 1974

*Reading* **History**
**A. Reading a Graph** Ask and answer a question about the geopgraphic pattern of changes in the slave population.

Planters tried to force Native Americans to work for them. But European diseases caused many Native Americans to die. Those who survived usually knew the country well enough to run away.

To meet their labor needs, the planters turned to enslaved Africans. As a result, the population of people of African descent began to grow rapidly. By 1750, there were over 235,000 enslaved Africans in America. About 85 percent lived in the Southern Colonies. Enslaved Africans made up about 40 percent of the South's population.

*Reading*History
B. Analyzing Causes What factors led to the importation of enslaved Africans into the South?

## Plantations Expand

The growth of slavery allowed plantation farming to expand in South Carolina and Georgia. Without slave labor, there probably would have been no rice plantations in the region's swampy lowlands.

Enslaved workers drained swamps, raked fields, burned stubble, and broke ground before planting. They also had to flood, drain, dry, hoe, and weed the same fields several times before the harvest.

The cultivation of rice required not only back-breaking labor but also considerable skill. Because West Africans had these skills, planters sought out slaves who came from Africa's rice-growing regions.

On higher ground, planters grew **indigo,** a plant that yields a deep blue dye. A young woman named **Eliza Lucas** had introduced indigo as a successful plantation crop after her father sent her to supervise his South Carolina plantations when she was 17.

## The Planter Class

Slave labor allowed planters, such as the Byrd family of Virginia, to become even wealthier. These families formed an elite planter class. They had money or credit to buy the most slaves. And because they had more slaves, they could grow more tobacco, rice, or indigo to sell.

Small landowners with just one or two slaves simply could not compete. Many gave up their land and moved westward. As a result, the powerful planter class gained control of the rich land along the coast. The planter class was relatively small compared to the rest of the population. However, this upper class soon took control of political and economic power in the South. A foreign traveler in the South commented that the planters "think and act precisely as do the nobility in other countries."

Some planters, following the traditions of nobility, did feel responsible for the welfare of their enslaved

*Reading*History
C. Recognizing Effects How did the growth of slavery affect political power in the South?

**AMERICA'S HISTORY MAKERS**

**WILLIAM BYRD II
1674–1744**

William Byrd II was one of the best known of the Southern planters. His family owned a large estate in Virginia. After his father died, Byrd took on his father's responsibilities, including membership in the House of Burgesses.

But Byrd is best remembered for his writing. His most famous work is *History of the Dividing Line betwixt Virginia and North Carolina.* In it, Byrd celebrates the land and climate of the South. At times, however, he is critical of its people. Even today, the book creates a vivid picture of life in the Southern Colonies.

**How did William Byrd II demonstrate his leadership abilities?**

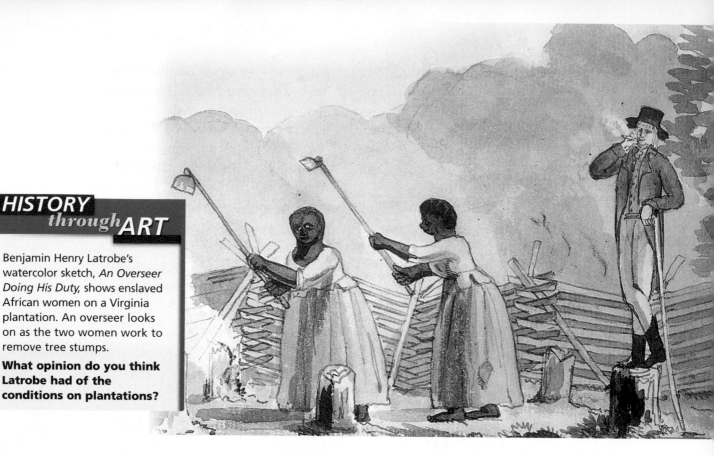

Benjamin Henry Latrobe's watercolor sketch, *An Overseer Doing His Duty,* shows enslaved African women on a Virginia plantation. An overseer looks on as the two women work to remove tree stumps.

**What opinion do you think Latrobe had of the conditions on plantations?**

workers. Power, they believed, brought with it the responsibility to do good. Many planters, though, were tyrants. They held complete authority over everyone in their households. Planters frequently used violence against slaves to enforce their will.

**Vocabulary**
**tyrant:** harsh ruler

## Life Under Slavery

On large Southern plantations, slaves toiled in groups of about 20 to 25 under the supervision of **overseers.** Overseers were men hired by planters to watch over and direct the work of slaves. Enslaved persons performed strenuous and exhausting work, often for 15 hours a day at the peak of the harvest season. If slaves did not appear to be doing their full share of work, they were often whipped by the overseer.

Enslaved people usually lived in small, one-room cabins that were furnished only with sleeping cots. For a week's food, a slave might receive only around a quarter bushel of corn and a pound of pork. Some planters allowed their slaves to add to this meager ration by letting them raise their own potatoes, greens, fruit, or chicken.

In spite of the brutal living conditions, Africans preserved many customs and beliefs from their homelands. These included music, dances, stories, and, for a time, African religions—including Islam. African kinship customs became the basis of African-American family culture. A network of kin was a source of strength even when families were separated.

*Reading* **History**
**D. Finding Main Ideas** What customs and beliefs from their homelands provided strength for enslaved Africans?

## Resistance to Slavery

At the same time that enslaved Africans struggled to maintain their own culture, they fought against their enslavement. They sometimes worked slowly, damaged goods, or purposely carried out orders the wrong way. A British traveler in 1746 noted that many slaves pretended not to understand tasks they often had performed as farmers in West Africa.

### A VOICE FROM THE PAST

You would really be surpriz'd at their Perseverance; let an hundred Men shew him how to hoe, or drive a wheelbarrow, he'll still take the one by the Bottom, and the other by the Wheel; and they often die before they can be conquer'd.

**Edward Kimber,** quoted in *White over Black*

At times, slaves became so angry and frustrated by their loss of freedom that they rose up in rebellion. One of the most famous incidents was the **Stono Rebellion.** In September 1739, about 20 slaves gathered at the Stono River just south of Charles Town. Wielding guns and other weapons, they killed several planter families and marched south, beating drums and loudly inviting other slaves to join them in their plan to seek freedom in Spanish-held Florida. By late that afternoon, however, a white militia had surrounded the group of escaping slaves. The two sides clashed, and many slaves died in the fighting. Those captured were executed.

**Background**
Slave codes were laws designed to control slaves and keep them in bondage.

Stono and similar revolts led planters to make slave codes even stricter. Slaves were now forbidden from leaving plantations without permission. The laws also made it illegal for slaves to meet with free blacks. Such laws made the conditions of slavery even more inhumane.

The Southern Colonies' plantation economy and widespread use of slaves set the region, and African-American culture in the region, on a very different path from that of the New England and Middle Colonies. In the next section, you will learn how settlers used the unique resources of the Backcountry to create settlements there.

---

## Section 3 Assessment

### 1. Terms & Names

**Explain the significance of:**
- indigo
- Eliza Lucas
- William Byrd II
- overseer
- Stono Rebellion

### 2. Using Graphics

Use a diagram like the one shown to review the factors that led to the use of slaves in the South.

| Causes | | Effect |
|---|---|---|
| ☐ | → | ☐ |
| ☐ | | |

Why didn't planters use Native American workers? (HI2)

### 3. Main Ideas

**a.** What percentage of the South's population was enslaved in 1750? (8.7.2)

**b.** What crops did plantations in Georgia and South Carolina grow? (8.7.2)

**c.** How did enslaved persons resist their slavery? (8.7.2)

### 4. Critical Thinking

**Contrasting** How did geographic differences between the Southern Colonies and the New England Colonies affect their labor systems? (8.7.1)

**THINK ABOUT**
- the climate of the regions
- the nature of the soil

### ACTIVITY OPTIONS

**ART**

**SCIENCE**

Do more research on rice plantations. Draw a **diagram** of a typical plantation or write a **report** on how rice is cultivated today. (CST3)

# Differences Among the Colonies

Many factors shape a region's economy and the way its settlers make a living. One of the most important is its physical geography—the climate, soil, and natural resources of the region. The geography of the American colonies varied from one colony to another. For example, in some areas, farmers could dig into rich, fertile soil. In others, they could not stick their shovels in the ground without hitting rocks.

**CALIFORNIA STANDARDS**

**8.6.1** Discuss the influence of industrialization and technological developments on the region, including human modification of the landscape and how physical geography shaped human actions (e.g., growth of cities, deforestation, farming, mineral extraction).

**8.7.1** Describe the development of the agrarian economy in the South, identify the locations of the cotton-producing states, and discuss the significance of cotton and the cotton gin.

## Major Regional Exports (by export value*)

### NEW ENGLAND COLONIES

New England had a short growing season and rocky soil. Colonists took advantage of other opportunities in the region, especially fishing and whaling.

| | |
|---|---|
| Dried Fish and Whale Oil | 44% |
| Livestock | 17% |
| Wood Products | 13% |
| Other | 26% |

### MIDDLE COLONIES

The longer growing season of the Middle Colonies—the "breadbasket colonies"—allowed farmers to grow cash crops of grain.

| | |
|---|---|
| Grain | 73% |
| Iron | 5% |
| Wood Products | 5% |
| Other | 17% |

### SOUTHERN COLONIES

The South had a nearly year-round growing season. The use of enslaved Africans allowed Southern planters to produce cash crops of tobacco and rice.

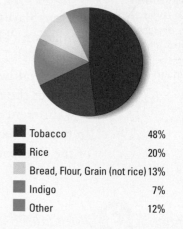

| | |
|---|---|
| Tobacco | 48% |
| Rice | 20% |
| Bread, Flour, Grain (not rice) | 13% |
| Indigo | 7% |
| Other | 12% |

*Export Value in Pounds Sterling (Five-Year Average, 1768–1772)

Source: James F. Shepherd and Gary M. Walton, *Shipping, Maritime Trade, and the Economic Development of Colonial North America* (Cambridge: Cambridge University Press, 1972.)

## ARTIFACT FILE

**Farmer's Plow** Middle colonists relied on the heavy blades of plows to cut seed rows into the region's fertile soil.

**Indigo** On some plantations in the South, planters grew crops of indigo plants—like the one pictured here—to produce the rich blue dyes used to color this yarn.

**Land Forms**

NEW ENGLAND
COLONIES

MIDDLE
COLONIES

SOUTHERN
COLONIES

■ Coastal plain
■ Piedmont
☐ Mountains
■ Rocky hills
■ Interior plain

**Soil**

NEW ENGLAND
COLONIES

MIDDLE
COLONIES

SOUTHERN
COLONIES

☐ Least fertile
■ Moderately
   fertile
■ Most fertile

**Growing Season**

NEW ENGLAND
COLONIES

MIDDLE
COLONIES

SOUTHERN
COLONIES

■ 3 to 5 months
■ 5 to 7 months
☐ 7 to 9 months
■ 9 to 12 months

**Physical Geography** The maps above show the different types of land forms, soil, and growing seasons that were found in the different colonial regions. These factors helped to shape the economies of each of the regions, which were quite different, as the pie graphs show on the previous page.

## On-Line Field Trip

**The New Bedford Whaling Museum**
in Massachusetts has many objects related to whaling, including bone or ivory objects called scrimshaws. A sailor carved this whale's tooth with a jackknife or sail needle and colored the design with ink.

For more about whaling . . .

RESEARCH LINKS
CLASSZONE.COM

## CONNECT TO GEOGRAPHY

1. **Region** How long was the growing season in most of the Southern Colonies?

2. **Human-Environment Interaction** How might the soil quality in the Middle Colonies have influenced the region's population?

   **G** See Geography Handbook, pages 10–13.

## CONNECT TO HISTORY

3. **Analyzing Causes** Why did the land forms and soil of New England cause many to turn to the Atlantic Ocean for a living?

# The Backcountry

| **MAIN IDEA** | **WHY IT MATTERS NOW** | **TERMS & NAMES** |
|---|---|---|
| Settlers moved to the Backcountry because land was cheap and plentiful. | Backcountry settlers established a rural way of life that still exists in certain parts of the country. | Appalachian Mountains, piedmont, fall line, clan |

## CALIFORNIA STANDARDS

**CST3** Students use a variety of maps and documents to identify physical and cultural features of neighborhoods, cities, states, and countries and to explain the historical migration of people, expansion and disintegration of empires, and the growth of economic systems.

**REP4** Students assess the credibility of primary and secondary sources and draw sound conclusions from them.

## ONE AMERICAN'S STORY

Alexander Spotswood governed Virginia from 1710 to 1722. He led a month-long expedition over the Blue Ridge Mountains in August 1716. During the 400-mile journey, adventurers braved dense thickets, muddy streams, and rattlesnakes. John Fontaine, who accompanied Spotswood, kept a diary of the trip.

Alexander Spotswood meets Native Americans in the Blue Ridge Mountains—a segment of the Appalachians Mountains.

### A VOICE FROM THE PAST

We had a rugged way; we passed over a great many small runs of water, some of which were very deep, and others very miry. Several of our company were dismounted, some were down with their horses, others under their horses, and some thrown off.

**John Fontaine,** quoted in *Colonial Virginia*

Spotswood's journey is considered a symbol of Virginia's westward expansion.

## Geography of the Backcountry

Just as Spotswood predicted, settlers soon began to move into the Backcountry. This was a region of dense forests and rushing streams in or near the **Appalachian Mountains.** The Appalachians stretch from eastern Canada south to Alabama.

In the South, the Backcountry began at the **fall line.** The fall line is where waterfalls prevent large boats from moving farther upriver. Beyond the fall line is the **piedmont.** Piedmont means "foot of the mountains." It is the broad plateau that leads to the Blue Ridge Mountains of the Appalachian range.

The Backcountry's resources made it relatively easy for a family to start a small farm. The region's many springs and streams provided water, and forests furnished wood that settlers could use for log cabins and fences.

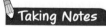

### Taking Notes

Use your chart to take notes about the backcountry.

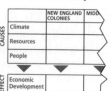

| | | NEW ENGLAND COLONIES | MIDD |
|---|---|---|---|
| CAUSES | Climate | | |
| | Resources | | |
| | People | | |
| EFFECT | Economic Development | | |

## Backcountry Settlers

The first Europeans in the Backcountry made a living by trading with the Native Americans. Backcountry settlers paid for goods with deerskins. A unit of value was one buckskin or, for short, a "buck."

Farmers soon followed the traders into the region, but they had to be cautious. As the number of settlements grew, the farmers often clashed with the Native Americans whose land they were taking.

Farmers sheltered their families in log cabins. They filled holes between the logs with mud, moss, and clay. Then they sawed out doors and windows. Lacking glass, settlers used paper smeared with animal fat to cover their windows.

William Byrd—on his expedition to establish the southern border of Virginia—described a long night that he spent in one such cabin. He complained that he and at least ten other people were "forct to pig together in a Room . . . troubled with the Squalling of peevish, dirty children into the Bargain."

Backcountry life may have been harsh, but by the late 1600s many families had chosen to move there. Some of them went to escape the plantation system, which had crowded out many small farmers closer to the seacoast. Then, in the 1700s, a new group of emigrants—the Scots-Irish—began to move into the Backcountry.

## The Scots-Irish

The Scots-Irish came from the borderland between Scotland and England. Most of them had lived for a time in northern Ireland. In 1707, England and Scotland merged and formed Great Britain. The merger caused many hardships for the Scots-Irish. Poverty and crop failures made this bad situation even worse.

As a result, Scots-Irish headed to America by the thousands. After they arrived, they quickly moved into the Backcountry. The Scots-Irish brought their clan system with them to the Backcountry. **Clans** are large groups of families—sometimes in the thousands—that claim a common ancestor. Clan members were suspicious of outsiders and banded together when danger threatened. These clans helped families to deal with the dangers and problems of the Backcountry.

**Vocabulary**
**buck:** an adult male deer; the adult female is called a *doe*

*Reading* **History**
**A. Analyzing Points of View**
What was William Byrd's attitude toward Backcountry settlers?

**Vocabulary**
**clan:** comes from an Old Irish word that means offspring, or descendants

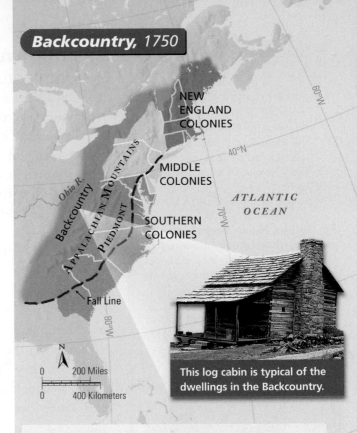

**Backcountry, 1750**

NEW ENGLAND COLONIES

MIDDLE COLONIES

SOUTHERN COLONIES

*ATLANTIC OCEAN*

Ohio R.

Backcountry

APPALACHIAN MOUNTAINS

PIEDMONT

Fall Line

60°W

40°N

70°W

80°W

0 200 Miles
0 400 Kilometers

This log cabin is typical of the dwellings in the Backcountry.

**GEOGRAPHY SKILLBUILDER Interpreting Maps**
**Region** *What geographical feature did the northern and southern areas of the Backcountry have in common?*

Three centuries ago, crowds in the Backcountry were thrilled by some of the same games that are now part of track and field competitions.

One of these games is the hammer throw. In this event, an athlete swings around a 16-pound metal ball on a wire-rope handle. After whirling around several times, the athlete lets go of the hammer, hoping it will travel the farthest distance.

The Scots-Irish brought other games to America, including the shotput, high jump, and long jump.

## Backcountry Life

Life in the Backcountry was very different from life along the seaboard. Settlers along the coast carried on a lively trade with England. But in the Backcountry, rough roads and rivers made it almost impossible to move goods.

As a result, Backcountry farmers learned quickly to depend on themselves. They built log cabins and furnished them with cornhusk mattresses and homemade benches and tables. They fed their families with the hogs and cattle they raised and with the fish and game they killed. They grew yellow corn to feed their livestock and white corn to eat. Popcorn was probably their only snack food. To protect their precious corn from pests, daytime patrols of women, children, and the elderly served as human scarecrows.

Women in the Backcountry worked in the cabin and fields, but they also learned to use guns and axes. An explorer who traveled in the region described one of these hardy Backcountry women.

*Reading*History
**B. Making Inferences** How would you describe the way people in the Backcountry lived?

### A VOICE FROM THE PAST

She is a very civil woman and shows nothing of ruggedness or Immodesty in her carriage, yett she will carry a gunn in the woods and kill deer, turkeys, etc., shoot doun wild cattle, catch and tye hoggs, knock down [cattle] with an ax and perform the most manfull Exercises.

**A visitor to the Backcountry,** quoted in *A History of American Life*

Settlers in the Backcountry often acted as if there were no other people in the region, but this was not so. In the woods and meadows that surrounded their cabins, settlers often encountered Native Americans and other groups that had made America their home.

## Other Peoples in North America

The Backcountry settlers started a westward movement that would play a critical role in American history. Most settlers' motivation to move west was simple—the desire for land.

Yet the push to the west brought settlers into contact with other peoples of North America. Native Americans had made their homes there for thousands of years. In addition, France and Spain claimed considerable territory in North America.

Sometimes this contact led to changes in people's cultures. For instance, North America had no horses until the Spanish colonists brought them into Mexico in the 1500s. Horses migrated north, and Native Americans caught them and made them an important part of their culture.

*Reading*History
**C. Summarizing** As England's colonies expanded westward, what groups did they encounter?

Contact also led to conflict. As English settlers pushed into the Backcountry, they put pressure on Native American tribes. Some tribes reacted by raiding isolated homesteads and small settlements. White settlers struck back, leading to more bloodshed.

This painting shows Native Americans catching wild horses. Many would later use the horses to hunt buffalo on the Great Plains.

The English colonists also came into conflict with the French. The French had colonized eastern Canada and had moved into the territories, rich with fur, along the Mississippi River. French fur traders wanted to prevent English settlers from moving west and taking away part of the trade. One Native American told an Englishman, "You and the French are like two edges of a pair of shears, and we are the cloth that is cut to pieces between them."

Spain also controlled large areas of North America—including territories that today form part or all of the states of Arizona, California, Colorado, Florida, Nevada, New Mexico, Texas, Utah, and Wyoming. Spanish settlers were farmers, ranchers, and priests. Priests, who established missions to convert Native Americans, built forts near the missions for protection. In 1718, Spaniards built Fort San Antonio de Bexar to guard the mission of San Antonio de Valero, later renamed the Alamo.

These different groups continued to compete—and sometimes fight—with one another. Frequently, England's colonies had to unite against these other groups. As a result, a common American identity began to take shape, as you will read in Chapter 5.

## Section 4 Assessment

### 1. Terms & Names

**Explain the significance of:**
- Appalachian Mountains
- fall line
- piedmont
- clan

### 2. Using Graphics

Use a chart like the one shown to list some of the geographic characteristics of the Backcountry. (CST3)

| Backcountry Geography |
|---|
| 1. |
| 2. |
| 3. |
| 4. |

### 3. Main Ideas

**a.** Which settlers migrated to the Backcountry? (HI1)

**b.** How did clans help the Scots-Irish survive? (HI1)

**c.** What economic activities did women carry out in the region? (HI1)

### 4. Critical Thinking

**Identifying Problems** As England's colonies expanded farther west, what problems would they face? (HI1)

**THINK ABOUT**
- other inhabitants of the Americas
- the resources desired by the colonists

**ACTIVITY OPTIONS**

**LANGUAGE ARTS**
**ART**

Read an account of the Backcountry written in the 1700s. Write a **newspaper article** or draw a series of **cartoons** that describe what you have read. (REP4)

# VISUAL SUMMARY

## The Colonies Develop (CST3)

### New England: Commerce and Religion

New England was distinguished by its small farming towns and profitable fishing and trade.

### The Middle Colonies: Farms and Cities

The Middle Colonies' farms produced large cash crops that fueled trade in its coastal cities.

### The Southern Colonies: Plantations and Slavery

The South's plantation economy and large number of enslaved Africans made it different from the other regions.

### The Backcountry

The Backcountry was distant from the denser coastal populations, so settlers there developed an independent and rugged way of life.

## TERMS & NAMES

Briefly explain the significance of the following.

1. Backcountry
2. subsistence farming
3. triangular trade
4. Navigation Acts
5. cash crop
6. gristmill
7. Conestoga wagon
8. overseer
9. Stono Rebellion
10. Appalachian Mountains

## REVIEW QUESTIONS

**New England: Commerce and Religion (pages 109–113)**

1. Describe the life of a New England farmer. (HI1)
2. In what ways did settlers in the region take advantage of the Atlantic Ocean? (HI1)
3. How were New England towns settled? (HI1)

**The Middle Colonies: Farms and Cities (pages 114–118)**

4. How were farms in the Middle Colonies different from those in New England? (CST3)
5. What characterized the population of the Middle Colonies? (HI1)

**The Southern Colonies: Plantations and Slavery (pages 119–125)**

6. Why did Southern planters infrequently travel to towns to sell their crops or to buy food and supplies? (HI2)
7. Why did planters turn to enslaved Africans for labor? (HI2)
8. In what ways did slaves resist? (HI1)

**The Backcountry (pages 126–129)**

9. Where was the Backcountry located in the 1700s? (HI1)
10. How was life in the Backcountry different from that along the coast? (HI1)

## CRITICAL THINKING

**1. USING YOUR NOTES: ANALYZING CAUSES AND EFFECTS**

Using your completed chart, answer the questions below. (CST1)

a. How was the Middle Colonies' climate different from the Backcountry's?
b. How did the South's labor system differ from the North's?
c. How did the resources of New England affect its economy?

**2. ANALYZING LEADERSHIP**

How did the South's plantation economy influence who became leaders in the region? (HI2)

**3. THEME: ECONOMICS IN HISTORY**

What factors influenced the economic development of each of the four colonial regions? (HI1)

**4. APPLYING CITIZENSHIP SKILLS**

How did the Quaker influence in the Middle Colonies contribute to the behavior of citizens of the region? (HI2)

**5. SEQUENCING EVENTS**

What changes took place in the population and treatment of African Americans between 1650 and 1750? (HI1)

### Interact with History

How would the choice that you made at the beginning of the chapter have varied according to the region in which you lived? Would you still make the same choice?

**Use the map and your knowledge of U.S. history to answer questions 1 and 2.**

Additional Test Practice, pp. S1–S33.

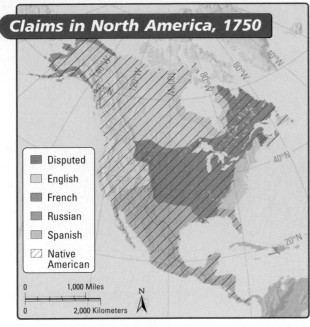

**Claims in North America, 1750**

Legend:
- Disputed
- English
- French
- Russian
- Spanish
- Native American

0       1,000 Miles
0       2,000 Kilometers

N

**1.** Which of the groups shown inhabited the largest area of North America? (8.1)

  **A.** English

  **B.** Native American

  **C.** Russian

  **D.** Spanish

**2.** Which European group claimed the northernmost territory? (8.1)

  **A.** English

  **B.** French

  **C.** Russian

  **D.** Spanish

**This quotation from Edward Kimber is about slaves in the United States. Use the quotation and your knowledge of U.S. history to answer question 3.**

*PRIMARY SOURCE*

You would really be surpriz'd at their Perseverance; let an hundred Men shew him how to hoe, or drive a wheelbarrow, he'll still take the one by the Bottom, and the other by the Wheel; and they often die before they can be conquer'd.

**Edward Kimber,** quoted in *White over Black*

**3.** The speaker uses the word *Perseverance* to emphasize which of the following? (8.7.2)

  **A.** the slave's belief in working hard at his or her tasks

  **B.** the slave's determination to resist enslavement

  **C.** the slave's confusion about what is expected of him or her

  **D.** the slave's submission to the condition of slavery

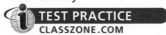

**TEST PRACTICE**
CLASSZONE.COM

# ALTERNATIVE ASSESSMENT

**1.** 📝 **WRITING ABOUT HISTORY**

Imagine that you are a Quaker living in colonial America. Write a **diary** entry about your typical day. (REP4)

- You can learn more about Quaker life in colonial times by reading primary sources found in the library.

- Before you begin to write, make a list of the ways in which you might spend a typical day as a Quaker. Use your notes to write your diary entry.

**2. COOPERATIVE LEARNING**

Work with a few of your classmates to design and construct a model of a log cabin. Group members can share the responsibilities for researching the history of log cabins, recording details about the location of your log cabin, and designing and building the cabin. (HI1)

# INTEGRATED TECHNOLOGY

**DOING INTERNET RESEARCH**

You can learn about different aspects of colonial farm life from primary sources. Use the Internet or library resources to begin your research. (REP4)

- Use the Internet to find primary sources such as diaries, journal entries, or letters.

- Another source of information might be historical or living history museums.

- Use your research to create a chart listing the differences between your family's lifestyle and a colonial family's.

**For more about colonial farming . . .**

**INTERNET ACTIVITY**
CLASSZONE.COM

CHAPTER
5

# Beginnings of an American Identity 1689–1763

**Section 1**
**Early American Culture**

**Section 2**
**Roots of Representative Government**

**Section 3**
**The French and Indian War**

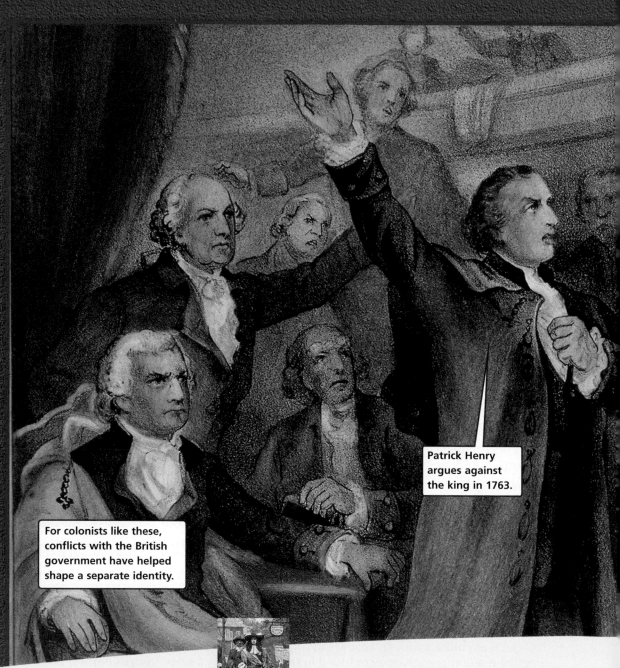

Patrick Henry argues against the king in 1763.

For colonists like these, conflicts with the British government have helped shape a separate identity.

**1689**
Massachusetts colonists overthrow royal governor Andros.

**1704**
*Boston Newsletter* is founded.

USA
World 1680

**1689**
William and Mary replace James II as rulers of England.

**1707**
England and Scotland join to form Great Britain.

**1709**
About 13,500 people leave the German states and emigrate to England.

You are outraged by the attacks on British traders and settlers. You wonder whether it is wise to join with other colonies, though. Will it mean that Virginians or New Englanders will be able to make laws for Pennsylvania?

# What do you have in common with other British colonists?

## What Do You Think?

• What are some good reasons to join with the other British colonies?

• How great are the differences between the British colonies?

• What separates British and French colonists?

**RESEARCH LINKS**
CLASSZONE.COM

Visit the Chapter 5 links for more information about early-American identity.

**1727**
George II becomes king of Great Britain.

**1735**
Decision in the Zenger trial supports freedom of the press.

**1738**
Minister George Whitefield arrives in Georgia.

**1754**
French and Indian War begins.

**1756**
Seven Years' War between France and Britain is declared.

**1759**
Quebec falls to the British.

**1763**
French and Indian War ends.

1763

# CHAPTER 5

# Reading Strategy: Finding Main Ideas

## What Do You know?

What beliefs do you consider American? How do you think people in Britain's American colonies saw themselves?

### Think About

- your own beliefs as an American
- what you know about the regions where the colonies were established
- what you know about the backgrounds and beliefs of colonists in different regions
- your responses to the Interact with History about what you have in common with other British colonists (see page 133)

## What Do You Want to Know?

What questions do you have about colonial America in the early and middle 1700s? Write them down in your notebook before you read this chapter.

JOIN, or DIE.

This cartoon was published by Benjamin Franklin in 1754. It urged the colonies to unite.

## Finding Main Ideas

To recognize a main idea, you must notice how smaller details are connected. In your notebook, copy a web like the one shown here. Write brief notes about the main things people in the British colonies had in common—the beliefs and experiences that formed an American identity.

- Read and remember the Main Idea at the beginning of each section.
- At the end of each group of paragraphs under a heading, ask yourself, "Have I learned about something that united the colonists?"

 See Skillbuilder Handbook, page R5.

### Taking Notes

Economy

Education

Religion

**American Identity**

Publishing

Political Ideas

War

# Early American Culture

| **MAIN IDEA** | **WHY IT MATTERS NOW** | **TERMS & NAMES** |
|---|---|---|
| The British colonies were shaped by prosperity, literacy, and new movements in religion and thought. | These forces began to create an American identity that is still developing today. | apprentice    Enlightenment<br>Great Awakening    Benjamin Franklin<br>Jonathan Edwards    John Locke<br>George Whitefield |

## ONE AMERICAN'S STORY

In 1704, Sarah Kemble Knight traveled on horseback from her home in Boston to New Haven, Connecticut. The journey took five days.

In her journal, Madam Knight described her travel hardships and commented on people she met.

*A VOICE FROM THE PAST*

We hoped to reach the french town and Lodg there that night, but unhapily lost our way about four miles short. . . . A surly old shee Creature, not worthy the name of woman, . . . would hardly let us go into her Door, though the weather was so stormy.

**Sarah Kemble Knight,** *The Journal of Madam Knight*

A 1920 reprint of *The Journal of Madam Knight*.

Knight's attitude toward people from other colonies was typical. In the early 1700s, people of the different British colonies did not think of themselves as living in one country. In this section, you will learn what began to draw the colonies together.

## Land, Rights, and Wealth

At the time of Madam Knight's journey, the colonies were thriving. Cheap farmland and plentiful natural resources gave colonists a chance to prosper. They would have had less opportunity in Europe. In England, fewer than 5 percent of the people owned land. In fact, land rarely went up for sale. By contrast, in the colonies, land was plentiful—once Native American groups were forced to give up their claims. Colonists who owned land were free to use or sell whatever it produced.

Land ownership gave colonists political rights as well as prosperity. Generally, only white male landowners or property owners could vote. There were some exceptions. City dwellers could vote by paying a fee.

**Taking Notes**

Use your chart to take notes about early American culture.

American Identity

| Colonial Social Ranks |
| --- |
| **HIGH** |
| • large landowners |
| • church officials |
| • government officials |
| • wealthy merchants |
| **UPPER MIDDLE** |
| • small farmers |
| • tradespeople |
| **LOWER MIDDLE** |
| • renters |
| • unskilled workers |
| **LOW** |
| • indentured servants |
| • slaves |

Land ownership also helped determine colonists' social position. Unlike England, America had no class of nobles whose titles passed from parent to child. But people were still divided into high, middle, and low ranks, as they were in England. Large landholders were high in rank. Small farmers who owned their land were in the middle rank. Most colonists fit this category. People who did not own land, such as servants, slaves, or hired workers, were low in rank. Colonial women held the same rank as their husbands or fathers.

Colonists showed respect to their "betters" by curtsying or tipping a hat, for example. Seats in church were assigned by rank, with wealthy families in the front pews and poor people in the back. Despite such divisions, the wealthy were expected to aid the poor.

*Reading*History
**A. Finding Main Ideas** What did colonists gain by owning land?

## Women and the Economy

Although women were not landholders, their work was essential to the colonial economy. As you learned in Chapter 4, enslaved African women helped raise cash crops such as tobacco and indigo. Most white women were farm wives who performed tasks and made products their families needed. They cooked, churned butter, made soap and candles, spun fibers, wove cloth, sewed and knitted clothes, and did many other chores. They usually tended a garden and looked after farm animals. At harvest time, they often worked in the fields alongside men and older children.

Because cash was scarce, farm wives bartered, or traded, with their neighbors for goods and services. For example, a woman who nursed a sick neighbor or helped deliver a baby might be paid in sugar or cloth.

Women in towns and cities usually did the same types of housework that rural women did. In addition, some urban women ran inns or other businesses. A few women, usually the wives or widows of tradesmen, practiced trades themselves.

*Reading*History
**B. Finding Main Ideas** In what ways was women's work essential to the economy?

Although women contributed to the colonial economy, they did not have many rights. Women could not vote. In most churches, they could not preach or hold office. (Quaker meetings were an exception.) A married woman could not own property without her husband's permission. By law, even the money a woman earned belonged to her husband.

## Young People at Work

Children's work also supported the colonial economy. Families were large. New England families, for example, had an average of six to eight children. More children meant more workers. Children as young as three or four were expected to be useful. They might help look after farm animals, gather berries, and watch younger children.

Around age six, boys were "breeched." This meant that they no longer wore the skirts or smocks of all young children but were given a pair of pants. They then began to help their fathers at work. Sons of farmers worked all day clearing land and learning to farm. Sons of craftsmen tended their fathers' shops and learned their fathers' trades.

Around age 11, many boys left their fathers to become apprentices. An **apprentice** learned a trade from an experienced craftsman. The apprentice received food, clothing, lodging, and a general education, as well as training in the specific craft or business. He worked for free, usually for four to seven years, until his contract was fulfilled. Then he could work for wages or start his own business.

Girls rarely were apprenticed. They learned sewing and other household skills from their mothers. In New England, girls of 13 or 14 often were sent away to other households to learn specialized skills such as weaving or cheese making. Orphaned girls and boys worked as servants for families who housed and fed them until adulthood.

*Reading* **History**
**C. Contrasting**
How did the training of boys and girls differ?

## Colonial Schooling

If land, wealth, and hard work were valued across the colonies, so was education. Most children were taught to read so that they could understand the Bible. Only children from wealthy families went beyond reading to learn writing and arithmetic. These children learned either from private tutors or in private schools. Poorer children sometimes learned to read from their mothers. Or they attended "dame schools," where women taught the alphabet and used the Bible to teach reading. Most children finished their formal education at age seven.

Children's textbooks emphasized religion. The widely used *New England Primer* paired the letter *A* with the verse "In *Adam's* fall / We Sinned all." Beside the letter *B* was a picture of the Bible. The primer contained the Lord's Prayer and *The Shorter Catechism,* more than 100 questions and answers about religion.

## HISTORY *through* ART

This drawing shows the inside of an 18th-century one-room schoolhouse.

**What does the picture suggest to you about colonial schooling?**

**THE SCHOOL OF MANNERS**

Colonial children learned proper behavior from *The School of Manners,* a book published in 1701. Here are examples of rules and an illustration from the book.

"Spit not in the Room, but in a corner, and rub it out with thy Foot, or rather go out and do it abroad."

"If thou meetest the scholars of any other School jeer not nor affront them, but show them love and respect and quietly let them pass along."

Colonial America had a high literacy rate, as measured by the number of people who could sign their names. In New England, 85 percent of white men were literate, compared with 60 percent of men in England. In the Middle Colonies, 65 percent of white men were literate, and in the South, about 50 percent were. In each region of the colonies, roughly half as many white women as men were literate. Most colonists thought schooling was more important for males. Educated African Americans were rare. If they were enslaved, teaching them to read was illegal. If they were free, they were often kept out of schools.

## Newspapers and Books

Colonial readers supported a publishing industry that also drew the colonies together. In the early 1700s, the colonies had only one local newspaper, the *Boston News-letter*. But over the next 70 years, almost 80 different newspapers appeared in America. Many were published for decades.

Most books in the colonies were imported from England, but colonists slowly began to publish their own books. Almanacs were very popular. A typical almanac included a calendar, weather predictions, star charts, farming advice, home remedies, recipes, jokes, and proverbs. In 1732, Benjamin Franklin began to publish *Poor Richard's Almanack*. It contained sayings that are still repeated today, such as "Haste makes waste."

Colonists also published poetry, regional histories, and autobiographies. Most personal stories told of struggles to maintain religious faith during hard times. A form of literature unique to the Americas was the captivity narrative. In it, a colonist captured by Native Americans described living among them.

Mary Rowlandson's 1682 captivity narrative, *The Sovereignty and Goodness of God,* was one of the first colonial bestsellers. Native Americans attacked Rowlandson's Massachusetts village in 1676, during King Philip's War. They held her hostage for 11 weeks. During that time, she was a servant to a Narragansett chieftain, knitting stockings and making shirts for his family and others. After townspeople raised money to ransom Rowlandson, she was released. Although she mourned a young daughter who had died in captivity, she praised God for returning her safely.

*Reading*History
**D. Contrasting**
How was colonial education different from education today?

*Reading*History
**E. Categorizing**
What were some types of colonial literature?

# The Great Awakening

**Vocabulary**
**ransom:** to pay for a captive's release

Mary Rowlandson's religious faith was central to her life. But in the early 1700s, many colonists feared they had lost the religious passion that had driven their ancestors to found the colonies. Religion seemed distant, even to regular churchgoers.

In the 1730s and 1740s, a religious movement called the **Great Awakening** swept through the colonies. The traveling ministers of this movement preached that inner religious emotion was more important than outward religious behavior. Their sermons appealed to the heart and drew large crowds. **Jonathan Edwards,** one of the best-known preachers, terrified listeners with images of God's anger but promised they could be saved.

> ### A VOICE FROM THE PAST
>
> And now you have an extraordinary opportunity, a day wherein Christ has thrown the door of mercy wide open, and stands in calling and crying with a loud voice to poor sinners. . . . How awful it is to be left behind at such a day!
>
> **Jonathan Edwards,** "Sinners in the Hands of an Angry God"

**Background**
Religious meetings with large, intensely emotional crowds remain part of American religious tradition.

The Great Awakening lasted for years and changed colonial culture. Congregations argued over religious practices and often split apart. People left their old churches and joined other Protestant groups such as Baptists. Some of these groups welcomed women, African Americans, and Native Americans. Overall, churches gained 20,000 to 50,000 new members. To train ministers, religious groups founded colleges such as Princeton and Brown.

The Great Awakening inspired colonists to help others. **George Whitefield** (HWIT•feeld) drew thousands of people with his sermons and raised funds to start a home for orphans. Other ministers taught Christianity and reading to Native Americans and African Americans. The Great Awakening encouraged ideas of equality and stressed the importance of the individual over the authority of the church. This encouraged colonists to also question the authority of the British government, and contributed to the revolutionary fervor of the colonists when they declared independence from England years later.

George Whitefield preaching to a crowd

*Reading*History

F. Recognizing Effects What were five effects of the Great Awakening?

## AMERICA'S HISTORY MAKERS

**BENJAMIN FRANKLIN**

**1706–1790**

As an Enlightenment thinker, Benjamin Franklin used reason to improve society. At 42, he retired from business to devote his life to science and public service. He proved that lightning was a form of electricity. Then he invented the lightning rod to protect buildings. The Franklin stove and bifocal eyeglasses were also his inventions. He organized a fire department, a lending library, and a society to discuss philosophy. Later he helped draft the Declaration of Independence.

**How did Franklin help improve colonial society?**

# The Enlightenment

Unlike the Great Awakening, which stressed religious emotion, the **Enlightenment** emphasized reason and science as the paths to knowledge. **Benjamin Franklin** was a famous American Enlightenment figure. This intellectual movement appealed mostly to wealthy, educated men. But it, too, had far-reaching effects on the colonies.

The Enlightenment began in Europe, as scientists discovered natural laws governing the universe. It drew on the Renaissance's value of Greek and Roman classical writings, as well as the Christian notion of individuals being equal under God, and the Reformation's challenge of the Catholic church's authority.

Enlightenment thinkers applied the idea of natural law to human societies. The English philosopher **John Locke** argued that people have natural rights to life, liberty, and property. People create governments to protect their natural rights, he claimed. If a government fails in this duty, people have the right to change it. Locke challenged the belief that kings had a God-given right to rule.

Charles-Louis Montesquieu, a French thinker, opposed monarchy altogether. He proposed a government with three branches, each keeping the power of the others in check. This idea of the separation of powers eventually became part of the U.S. government.

Enlightenment ideas of natural rights and government by agreement influenced leaders across Europe and the colonies. As you will see in Section 2, colonists began to wonder whether the British government protected their rights and freedoms.

**Background**
Locke argued against the idea that the kings had a God-given right to rule. But he still believed that the natural rights of individuals came from God.

---

## Section 1 Assessment

### 1. Terms & Names

**Explain the significance of:**
- apprentice
- Great Awakening
- Jonathan Edwards
- George Whitefield
- Enlightenment
- Benjamin Franklin
- John Locke

### 2. Using Graphics

Describe the parts of colonial culture in a chart.

| Economy | |
|---|---|
| Education | |
| Publishing | |
| Religion | |

Why was each important in colonial culture? (HI1)

### 3. Main Ideas

**a.** Why was land ownership so important to the colonists (HI1)?

**b.** How did women and young people contribute to the colonial economy? (HI2)

**c.** How did the Great Awakening affect the colonies? (HI2)

### 4. Critical Thinking

**Contrasting** How were the Great Awakening and the Enlightenment different? (CST1)

**THINK ABOUT**
- the ideas each movement promoted
- the people to whom each movement appealed

---

**ACTIVITY OPTIONS**

**LANGUAGE ARTS**

**ART**

Make up a **saying** that reflects some part of colonial culture, or draw an **illustration** of a saying from colonial times. (HI1)

# Roots of Representative Government

| **MAIN IDEA** | **WHY IT MATTERS NOW** | **TERMS & NAMES** |
|---|---|---|
| Colonists expected their government to preserve their basic rights as English subjects. | U.S. citizens expect these same rights, such as the right to a trial by jury. | Magna Carta · English Bill of Rights<br>Parliament · salutary neglect<br>Edmund Andros · John Peter Zenger<br>Glorious Revolution |

## ONE AMERICAN'S STORY

In 1688, the Puritan minister Increase Mather sailed to England to get relief for Massachusetts. The English government had canceled the charter of Massachusetts and sent a royal governor to rule.

The colonists thought the governor trampled their rights as English subjects. After four years in England, Mather came home with a new charter that he hoped would satisfy the colonists.

### A VOICE FROM THE PAST

For all English liberties are restored to them: No Persons shall have a Penny of their Estates taken from them; nor any Laws imposed on them, without their own Consent by Representatives chosen by themselves.

**Increase Mather,** quoted in *The Last American Puritan*

Mather called the new charter "a Magna Carta for New England." In this section, you will learn about the rights of English people set forth in the Magna Carta and later documents. These rights are the basis for the rights Americans enjoy today.

## The Rights of Englishmen

English colonists expected certain rights that came from living under an English government. These "rights of Englishmen" had developed over centuries.

The first step toward guaranteeing these rights came in 1215. That year, a group of English noblemen forced King John to accept the **Magna Carta** (Great Charter). The king needed the nobles' money to finance a war. This document guaranteed important rights to noblemen and freemen—those not bound to a master. They could not have their property seized by the king or his officials. They could not be taxed, in most

---

**CALIFORNIA STANDARDS**

**7.11.6** Discuss how principles in the Magna Carta were embodied in such documents as the English Bill of Rights and the American Declaration of independence.

**8.1.4** Describe the nation's blend of civic republicanism, classical liberal principles, and English parliamentary traditions.

**8.2.1** Discuss the significance of the Magna Carta, the English Bill of Rights, and the Mayflower Compact.

**8.3.7** Understand the functions and responsibilities of a free press.

**HI1** Students explain the central issues and problems from the past, placing people and events in a matrix of time and place.

---

**Taking Notes**

Use your chart to take notes about the roots of representative government in the American colonies.

American Identity

---

cases, unless a council of prominent men agreed. They could not be put to trial based only on an official's word, without witnesses. They could be punished only by a jury of their peers, people of the same social rank.

> **A VOICE FROM THE PAST**
>
> No freeman shall be seized, imprisoned, dispossessed, outlawed, or exiled, . . . nor will we proceed against or prosecute him except by the lawful judgment of his peers, or by the law of the land.
>
> **Magna Carta,** translated in *A Documentary History of England*

*Reading* **History**
**A. Comparing**
What rights from the Magna Carta remain rights in America today?

The Magna Carta limited the powers of the king. Over time, the rights it listed were granted to all English people, not just noblemen and freemen.

## Parliament and Colonial Government

One of the most important English rights was the right to elect representatives to government. **Parliament,** England's chief lawmaking body, was the colonists' model for representative government. Parliament was made up of two houses. Members of the House of Commons were elected by the people. Members of the House of Lords were nonelected nobles, judges, and church officials.

The king and Parliament were too far away to manage every detail of the colonies. Also, like the citizens of England, English colonists in America wanted to have a say in the laws governing them. So they formed

# CITIZENSHIP TODAY

# The Importance of Juries

The right to a trial by jury, established in the Magna Carta, is an important legal right. When you become an adult, you will likely be asked to serve on a jury.

Many young people in Knox County, Illinois, have already served as jurors on a teen court (shown below, with an advisor). They decide the best punishment for other teenagers who have admitted breaking a law. For example, shoplifters might be sentenced to write an apology to the store. Knox County is one of more than 500 U.S. communities that have teen courts.

Knox County Teen Court volunteers

## How Can You Serve on a Teen Court?

1. Search the library or Internet to learn more about teen courts.
2. Ask the police department whether your town has a teen court. If it does, volunteer.
3. If you want to start a teen court, seek advice from a community that has one.
4. Invite a lawyer to your class to talk about a juror's role.
5. Find a group to sponsor your court, and get support from youth officers and judges.

 See the Citizenship Handbook, page 280.

For more about courts and juries . . .

 **RESEARCH LINKS**
CLASSZONE.COM

**CALIFORNIA STANDARDS**

**8.2.6** Enumerate the powers of government set forth in the Constitution and the fundamental liberties ensured by the Bill of Rights.

their own elected assemblies, similar to the House of Commons. Virginia's House of Burgesses was the first of these. In Pennsylvania, William Penn allowed colonists to have their own General Assembly. These Virginia and Pennsylvania assemblies imposed taxes and managed the colonies.

Although the colonists governed themselves in some ways, England still had authority over them. The king appointed royal governors to rule some colonies on his behalf. Parliament had no representatives from the colonies. Even so, it passed laws that affected the colonies. The colonists disliked these laws, and they began to clash with royal governors over how much power England should have in America. These conflicts became more intense in the late 1600s.

*Reading*History
**B. Making Inferences** Why did the colonists dislike laws passed by Parliament?

## A Royal Governor's Rule

The reign of James II threatened the colonies' tradition of self-government. James became king in 1685. He wanted to rule England and its colonies with total authority. One of his first orders changed the way the Northern colonies were governed. These colonies, especially Massachusetts, had been smuggling goods and ignoring the Navigation Acts (see Chapter 4). When challenged, the people of Massachusetts had claimed that England had no right to make laws for them. The previous king, Charles II, had then canceled their charter.

King James combined Massachusetts and the other Northern colonies into one Dominion of New England, ruled by royal governor **Edmund Andros.** Andros angered the colonists by ending their representative assemblies and allowing town meetings to be held only once a year.

*Reading*History
**C. Recognizing Effects** How did James II weaken self-government in the colonies?

With their assemblies outlawed, some colonists refused to pay taxes. They said that being taxed without having a voice in government violated their rights. Andros jailed the loudest complainers. At their trial, they were told, "You have no more privileges left you than not to be Sould [sold] for Slaves."

The colonists sent Increase Mather to England to plead with King James (see One American's Story on page 141). However, a revolution in England swept King James and Governor Andros from power.

*"You have no more privileges left you."*

a Boston court official

The colonists hated Governor Andros.

**Background**
England had become Protestant in the 16th century. Catholics were kept out of high office.

## England's Glorious Revolution

The English Parliament had decided to overthrow King James for not respecting its rights. Events came to a head in 1688. King James, a Catholic, had been trying to pack his next Parliament with officials who would overturn anti-Catholic laws. He had dismissed the last Parliament in 1685. The Protestant leaders of Parliament were outraged. They offered the throne to James's Protestant daughter, Mary, and her husband, William of Orange. William was the ruler of the Netherlands. Having little support from the people, James fled the country at the end of 1688. Parliament named William and Mary the new monarchs of England. This change in leadership was called England's **Glorious Revolution.**

After accepting the throne, William and Mary agreed in 1689 to uphold the **English Bill of Rights.** This was an agreement to respect the rights of English citizens and of Parliament. Under it, the king or queen could not cancel laws or impose taxes unless Parliament agreed. Free elections and frequent meetings of Parliament must be held. Excessive fines and cruel punishments were forbidden. People had the right to complain to the king or queen in Parliament without being arrested.

**Background**
The English Bill of Rights was the model for the Bill of Rights in the U.S. Constitution.

The English Bill of Rights built upon the Magna Carta and established an important principle: the government was to be based on laws made by Parliament, not on the desires of a ruler. The rights of English people were strengthened.

The American colonists were quick to claim these rights. When the people of Boston heard of King James's fall, they jailed Governor Andros and asked Parliament to restore their old government.

## Shared Power in the Colonies

After the Glorious Revolution, the Massachusetts colonists regained some self-government. They could again elect representatives to an assembly. However, they still had a governor appointed by the crown.

**Background**
Massachusetts colonists also gained more religious freedom. They no longer had to be church members to vote.

The diagram on this page shows how most colonial governments were organized by 1700. Note how the royal governor, his council, and the colonial assembly shared power. The governor could strike down laws passed by the assembly, but the assembly paid the governor's salary. If he blocked the assembly, the assembly might refuse to pay him.

During the first half of the 1700s, England interfered very little in colonial affairs. This hands-off policy was called **salutary neglect.** Parliament passed many laws regulating trade, the use of money, and even apprenticeships in the colonies. But governors rarely enforced these laws. The colonists got used to acting on their own.

**Vocabulary**
salutary: healthful or beneficial

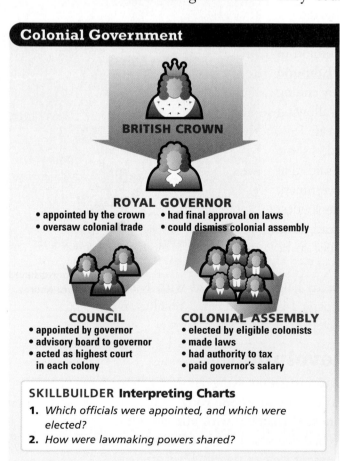

**Colonial Government**

**BRITISH CROWN**

**ROYAL GOVERNOR**
• appointed by the crown
• oversaw colonial trade
• had final approval on laws
• could dismiss colonial assembly

**COUNCIL**
• appointed by governor
• advisory board to governor
• acted as highest court in each colony

**COLONIAL ASSEMBLY**
• elected by eligible colonists
• made laws
• had authority to tax
• paid governor's salary

**SKILLBUILDER Interpreting Charts**
1. *Which officials were appointed, and which were elected?*
2. *How were lawmaking powers shared?*

Government officials burn the *New-York Weekly Journal.*

## The Zenger Trial

Colonists moved toward gaining a new right, freedom of the press, in 1735. That year, **John Peter Zenger,** publisher of the *New-York Weekly Journal,* stood trial for printing criticism of New York's governor. The governor had removed a judge and tried to fix an election.

### A VOICE FROM THE PAST

A Governor turns rogue [criminal], does a thousand things for which a small rogue would have deserved a halter [hanging], and because it is difficult . . . to obtain relief against him, . . . it is prudent [wise] to . . . join in the roguery.

***New-York Weekly Journal,*** quoted in *Colonial America, 1607–1763*

*Reading***History**
**D. Drawing Conclusions** Why was the Zenger trial a step toward freedom of the press?

At that time, it was illegal to criticize the government in print. Andrew Hamilton defended Zenger at his trial, claiming that people had the right to speak the truth. The jury agreed, and Zenger was released.

English rights were part of the heritage uniting people in the British colonies. In the next section, you will read about another unifying force—a war against the French and their Indian allies.

---

## Section 2 Assessment

### 1. Terms & Names

**Explain the significance of:**
- Magna Carta
- Parliament
- Edmund Andros
- Glorious Revolution
- English Bill of Rights
- salutary neglect
- John Peter Zenger

### 2. Using Graphics

In the boxes, show how the rights of English people developed in the three years mentioned.

```
        English Rights
   ┌────────┬────────┬────────┐
   │        │        │        │
  1215     1689     1735
```

Which right is most important to you? (8.2.1)

### 3. Main Ideas

**a.** What were three of the traditional rights expected by English colonists? (8.2.1)

**b.** In what ways did the English government anger the colonists in the late 1600s? (8.2.1)

**c.** How did England's policies toward the colonies change after the Glorious Revolution? (8.2.1)

### 4. Critical Thinking

**Supporting Opinions**
In your opinion, who had the most power—the royal governor, the council, or the assemblies? Defend your opinion. (8.2.1)

**THINK ABOUT**
- their roles in making laws
- their roles in raising money
- who had final approval in matters

### ACTIVITY OPTIONS

**SPEECH**
**ART**

Deliver **closing arguments** or create a **leaflet** defending John Peter Zenger and freedom of the press. (REP5)

# The French and Indian War

## MAIN IDEA

Britain's victory in the French and Indian War forced France to give up its North American colonies.

## WHY IT MATTERS NOW

British influence spread over North America, though French populations and place names still exist here.

## TERMS & NAMES

French and Indian War

Albany Plan of Union

Battle of Quebec

Treaty of Paris

Pontiac's Rebellion

Proclamation of 1763

**CALIFORNIA STANDARDS**

**CST1** Students explain how major events are related to one another in time.

**CST3** Students use a variety of maps and documents to identify physical and cultural features of neighborhoods, cities, states, and countries and to explain the historical migration of people, expansion and disintegration of empires, and the growth of economic systems.

**HI2** Students understand and distinguish cause, effect, sequence, and correlation in historical events, including the long- and short-term causal relations.

### ONE AMERICAN'S STORY

The Frenchman, Charles de Langlade, and his family controlled the fur trade around what is now Green Bay, Wisconsin.

In 1752, Charles commanded 250 Ottawa and Chippewa warriors in an attack on a village in present-day Ohio. His reason: the Miami people there had stopped trading with the French and were now trading with the British. Charles and his men destroyed the village's British trading post. This attack helped lead to the French and Indian War.

This section describes the war, in which French forces fought British forces in North America. Each side had Native American allies.

This 1903 painting by Edward Deming shows Charles de Langlade attacking British forces in 1755.

## France Claims Western Lands

As you learned in Chapters 2 and 4, the French were exploring the North American interior while English colonists were settling the eastern coast. By the late 1600s, French explorers had claimed the Ohio River valley, the Mississippi River valley, and the entire Great Lakes region. The French territory of Louisiana, claimed by the explorer La Salle in 1682, stretched from the Appalachian Mountains to the Rocky Mountains.

The French built their main settlements, Quebec and Montreal, along the St. Lawrence River in Canada. (See the map on page 148.) They also built forts along the Great Lakes and along rivers draining into the Mississippi. By 1760, the French colony, New France, had a European population of about 80,000. By contrast, the British colonies had more than a million settlers.

Some Europeans in New France were Jesuit priests. They wanted to convert Native Americans to Christianity. Other Europeans in New France worked as fur traders. Native Americans brought furs to French forts and

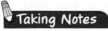

**Taking Notes**

Use your chart to take notes about the French and Indian War.

American Identity

Background
Often French
traders lived
among and
married Native
Americans.

exchanged them for goods such as iron pots and steel knives. Many French traders carried goods by canoe into remote parts of New France.

## Native American Alliances

The English competed with the French for furs. Also, different Native American groups competed to supply furs to the Europeans. The fur trade created economic and military alliances between the Europeans and their Native American trading partners. The Huron and Algonquin peoples of the Great Lakes region were allied with the French. The Iroquois of upper New York often were allied with the Dutch and, later, the English.

Background
The Iroquois
were a union of
six nations.

Alliances between Europeans and Native Americans led to their involvement in each other's wars. For example, by the mid-1600s, the Iroquois had trapped all the beavers in their own lands. To get more furs, they made war on their Huron and Algonquin neighbors, driving them

west. Eventually the Iroquois controlled an area ranging from Maine west to the Ohio Valley and north to Lake Michigan. Iroquois expansion threatened the French fur trade. In response, the French armed the Huron and Algonquin peoples to fight the Iroquois. The Iroquois were armed by the English.

Reading**History**
A. Recognizing
Effects How did
the fur trade lead
to wars?

When France and England declared war on each other in Europe in 1689, French and English colonists in America also began to fight. With their Native American allies, they attacked each other's settlements and forts. During the 1700s, two more wars between France and England fueled wars in their colonies. Neither side won a clear victory in these wars. A final war, the **French and Indian War** (1754–1763), decided which nation would control the northern and eastern parts of North America.

A French trader visits a Native American family.

## Conflict in the Ohio River Valley

The seeds for the French and Indian War were planted when British fur traders began moving into the Ohio River valley in the 1750s. British land companies were also planning to settle colonists there. The French and their Native American allies became alarmed. To keep the British out of the valley, Charles de Langlade destroyed the village of Pickawillany and its British trading post (see One American's Story on page 146).

The British traders left, and the French built forts to protect the region linking their Canadian and Louisiana settlements. This upset the Virginia colony, which claimed title to the land. In 1753, the lieutenant governor of Virginia sent a small group of soldiers to tell the French to

Reading**History**
B. Making
Inferences Why
was the Ohio
River Valley
important to the
French and British
governments?

leave. Their leader was a 21-year-old major named George Washington. Washington reported the French commander's reply.

**A VOICE FROM THE PAST**

He told me the Country belong'd to them, that no English Man had a right to trade upon them Waters; & that he had Orders to make every Person Prisoner that attempted it on the Ohio or the Waters of it.

**George Washington,** *"Journey to the French Commandant"*

Virginia's lieutenant governor sent about 40 men to build a fort at the head of the Ohio River, where Pittsburgh stands today. French and Native American troops seized the partially built fort in April 1754 and completed it themselves. The French named it Fort Duquesne (du•KAYN).

## War Begins and Spreads

George Washington was on his way to defend Fort Duquesne when he learned of its surrender. He and his men pushed on and built another small fort, Fort Necessity. Following Washington's surprise attack on a French force, the French and their allies attacked Fort Necessity on July 3, 1754. After Washington surrendered, the French let him march back to Virginia. The French and Indian War had begun. This war became part of the Seven Years' War (1756–1763), a worldwide struggle for empire between France and Great Britain.

**Background**
The Seven Years' War was fought not only in North America but also in the Caribbean, throughout Europe, and in India and Africa.

**French and Indian War, 1754–1763**

**GEOGRAPHY SKILLBUILDER**
**Interpreting Maps**

1. **Place** Which nation controlled territory along the St. Lawrence and Ohio rivers?
2. **Place** Which forts were the sites of British victories?

Legend:
- British territory
- French territory
- Disputed territory
- ✦ British victory
- ✧ French victory

0   100 Miles
0   200 Kilometers

While Washington was surrendering Fort Necessity, representatives from the British colonies and the Iroquois nations were meeting at Albany, New York. The colonists wanted the Iroquois to fight with them against the French. The Iroquois would not commit to this alliance.

Benjamin Franklin, who admired the union of the six Iroquois nations, suggested that the colonies band together for defense. His **Albany Plan of Union** was the first formal proposal to unite the colonies. The plan called for each colony to send representatives to a Grand Council. This council would be able to collect taxes, raise armies, make treaties, and start new settlements. The leaders in Albany supported Franklin's plan, but the colonial legislatures later defeated it because they did not want to give up control of their own affairs.

## Braddock's Defeat

Britain realized that to win the war, it could not rely solely on the colonists for funding or for troops. Therefore, the British sent General Edward Braddock and two regiments to Virginia. In 1755, Braddock marched toward the French at Fort Duquesne. George Washington was at his side. Their red-coated army of 2,100 moved slowly over the mountains, weighed down by a huge cannon.

On July 9, on a narrow trail eight miles from Fort Duquesne, fewer than 900 French and Indian troops surprised Braddock's forces. Washington suggested that his men break formation and fight from behind the trees, but Braddock would not listen. The general held his position and had four horses shot out from under him. Washington lost two horses. Four bullets went through Washington's coat, but, miraculously, none hit him. In the end, nearly 1,000 men were killed or wounded. General Braddock died from his wounds. American colonists were stunned by Braddock's defeat and by many other British losses over the next two years.

*Reading* **History**
**C. Drawing Conclusions** Why was Braddock defeated by a smaller enemy force?

## The British Take Quebec

In 1757, Britain had a new secretary of state, William Pitt, who was determined to win the war in the colonies. He sent the nation's best generals to America and borrowed money to pay colonial troops for fighting. The British controlled six French forts by August 1759, including Fort Duquesne (rebuilt as Fort Pitt). In late summer, the British began to attack New France at its capital, Quebec.

**Background** Because the British seemed likely to win the war, some Iroquois had joined them as allies.

## America's HERITAGE

**ACADIANS TO CAJUNS**
Braddock's defeat and other early losses in the war increased British concern about the loyalty of the French people in Acadia (now Nova Scotia). The British had won Acadia from France in 1713.

In 1755, British officers forced out 6,000 Acadians who would not take a loyalty oath. The British burned Acadian villages and spread the people to various British colonies, as shown. Eventually, some Acadians made their way to the French territory of Louisiana. There they became known as Cajuns.

149

Quebec sat on cliffs 300 feet above the St. Lawrence River. Cannon and thousands of soldiers guarded its thick walls. British general James Wolfe sailed around the fort for two months, unable to capture it. Then, in September, a scout found a steep, unguarded path up the cliffs to the plains just west of Quebec. At night, Wolfe and 4,000 of his men floated to the path and secretly climbed the cliffs.

When the French awoke, the British were lined up on the plains, ready to attack. In the short, fierce battle that followed, Wolfe was killed. The French commander, Montcalm, died of his wounds the next day. Quebec surrendered to the British. The **Battle of Quebec** was the turning point of the war. When Montreal fell the next year, all of Canada was in British hands.

*Reading***History**
D. Finding Main Ideas How were the British able to capture Quebec?

## The Treaty of Paris

Britain and France battled in other parts of the world for almost three more years. Spain made a pact in 1761 to aid France, but its help came too late. When the Seven Years' War ended in 1763, Britain had won.

By the **Treaty of Paris,** Britain claimed all of North America east of the Mississippi River. To reward Spain for its help, France gave it New Orleans and Louisiana, the French territory west of the Mississippi. Britain, which had seized Cuba and the Philippines from Spain, gave them back in exchange for Florida. The treaty ended French power in North America.

Background
France kept only a few islands near Newfoundland and in the West Indies.

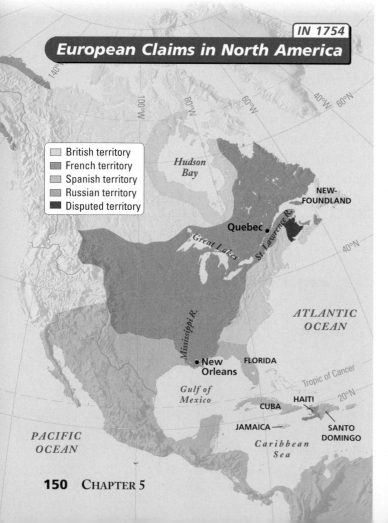

**IN 1754**
*European Claims in North America*

British territory
French territory
Spanish territory
Russian territory
Disputed territory

Hudson Bay

NEW-FOUNDLAND

Quebec

Great Lakes

St. Lawrence R.

ATLANTIC OCEAN

Mississippi R.

New Orleans    FLORIDA

Gulf of Mexico

Tropic of Cancer

20°N

CUBA    HAITI

JAMAICA    SANTO DOMINGO

PACIFIC OCEAN

Caribbean Sea

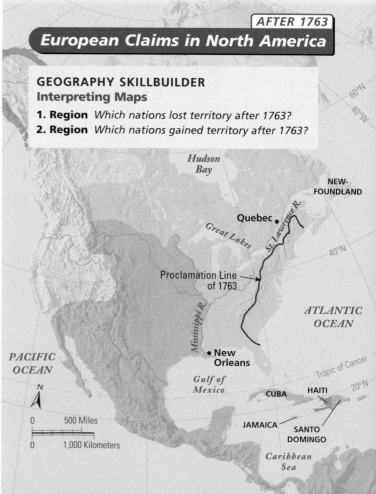

**AFTER 1763**
*European Claims in North America*

**GEOGRAPHY SKILLBUILDER**
**Interpreting Maps**

**1. Region** *Which nations lost territory after 1763?*
**2. Region** *Which nations gained territory after 1763?*

Hudson Bay

NEW-FOUNDLAND

Quebec

Great Lakes

St. Lawrence R.

Proclamation Line of 1763

ATLANTIC OCEAN

PACIFIC OCEAN

Mississippi R.

New Orleans

Gulf of Mexico

Tropic of Cancer

20°N

CUBA    HAITI

JAMAICA    SANTO DOMINGO

Caribbean Sea

N

0    500 Miles
0    1,000 Kilometers

# Pontiac's Rebellion

*Reading*History

E. Analyzing Points of View
Why did the Native Americans attack the British?

After French forces withdrew, the British took over their forts. They refused to give supplies to the Native Americans, as the French had. British settlers also moved across the mountains onto Native American land. In the spring and summer of 1763, Native American groups responded by attacking settlers and destroying almost every British fort west of the Appalachians. They surrounded the three remaining forts. This revolt was called **Pontiac's Rebellion,** although the Ottawa war leader Pontiac was only one of many organizers.

British settlers reacted with equal viciousness, killing even Indians who had not attacked them. British officers came up with a brutal plan to end the Delaware siege at Fort Pitt.

Pontiac

### A VOICE FROM THE PAST

Could it not be contrived to send the Small Pox among those disaffected [angry] tribes of Indians? We must on this occasion use every stratagem in our power to reduce them.

**Major General Jeffrey Amherst,** quoted in *The Conspiracy of Pontiac*

*Reading*History

F. Reading a Map
Find the Proclamation Line of 1763 on the map on page 150.

The officers invited Delaware war leaders in to talk and then gave them smallpox-infected blankets as gifts. This started a deadly outbreak.

By the fall, the Native Americans had retreated. Even so, the uprising made the British government see that defending Western lands would be costly. Therefore, the British issued the **Proclamation of 1763,** which forbade colonists to settle west of the Appalachians.

The colonists were angry. They thought they had won the right to settle the Ohio River Valley. The British government was angry at the colonists, who did not want to pay for their own defense. This hostility helped cause the war for American independence, as you will read.

---

## Section 3 Assessment

### 1. Terms & Names

**Explain the significance of:**

- French and Indian War
- Albany Plan of Union
- Battle of Quebec
- Treaty of Paris
- Pontiac's Rebellion
- Proclamation of 1763

### 2. Using Graphics

Write the month and year each battle occurred. Classify each as a French or British victory.

| Date | Incident | Victor |
|------|----------|--------|
|  | Seizure of Fort Duquesne |  |
|  | Surrender of Fort Necessity |  |
|  | Braddock's defeat |  |
|  | Battle of Quebec |  |

Which was most important? (CST2)

### 3. Main Ideas

**a.** How did the fur trade contribute to the French and Indian War? (HI2)

**b.** Why did the British begin to win the war after 1758? (HI2)

**c.** What were some causes and effects of Pontiac's Rebellion? (HI2)

### 4. Critical Thinking

**Analyzing Points of View**
Why did the French, British, and Native Americans fight over the Ohio River Valley? (REP5)

**THINK ABOUT**

- how the British viewed the valley
- how the French viewed it
- how the Native Americans viewed it

---

**ACTIVITY OPTIONS**

**GEOGRAPHY**

**MUSIC**

Learn more about the Battle of Quebec and its setting. Make a three-dimensional **model** of the battle or write a **song** about it. (HI1)

## Beginnings of an American Identity (CST3)

**Separate Colonies**

### Early American Culture

English colonists shared certain values, such as land ownership and hard work. The Great Awakening and the Enlightenment also drew colonists together.

### Roots of Representative Government

English colonists expected the right to elect representatives to government and other political rights that had developed in England over centuries.

### The French and Indian War

English colonists were also drawn together as they fought against common enemies—the French and their Native American allies.

**Common Identity**

## TERMS & NAMES

Briefly explain the significance of each of the following.

1. Great Awakening
2. Enlightenment
3. John Peter Zenger
4. Magna Carta
5. Parliament
6. Glorious Revolution
7. Edmund Andros
8. French and Indian War
9. Treaty of Paris
10. Proclamation of 1763

## REVIEW QUESTIONS

### Early American Culture (pages 135–140)

1. Why did colonists want to own land? (HI1)
2. What was women's role in the colonial economy? (HI1)
3. How did the Great Awakening create enthusiasm for revolution? (HI2)

### Roots of Representative Government (pages 141–145)

4. Why did colonies have representative assemblies? (HI1)
5. What was one important right granted in the Magna Carta? (REP4)
6. How did the Zenger trial help lead to freedom of the press? (HI2)
7. How was the English Bill of Rights related to the Glorious Revolution? (CST1)

### The French and Indian War (pages 146–151)

8. What was George Washington's role in the French and Indian War? (HI1)
9. What did England gain as a result of the French and Indian War? (HI2)
10. What was one reason for Pontiac's Rebellion? (HI2)

## CRITICAL THINKING

### 1. USING YOUR NOTES: FINDING MAIN IDEAS

Using your completed chart, answer the questions below. (CST3)

a. What were some political ideas shared by people in the American colonies?
b. How was religion important to American identity?
c. How did publishing help build an American identity?

### 2. THEME: DEMOCRATIC IDEALS

What democratic ideals did Americans inherit from England? (HI3)

### 3. APPLYING CITIZENSHIP SKILLS

Why is jury duty an example of responsible citizenship? (HI1)

### 4. CONTRASTING

How did colonial government differ from present-day government in the United States? (CST1)

### 5. ANALYZING CAUSES

What do you think was the most important cause of the French and Indian War? (HI2)

### 6. ANALYZING LEADERSHIP

Give an example of bad military or political leadership from the chapter. What mistake was made? (HI4)

### Interact with History

Now that you have read the chapter, what would you say British colonists in America had in common?

**Use the map and your knowledge of U.S. history to answer questions 1 and 2.**

Additional Test Practice, pp. S1–S33.

**French Explorers on the Mississippi**

Marquette and Joliet, 1673

La Salle 1679–1682

Present-day state boundary

**1.** Where did La Salle's journey begin? (8.8.2)

A. Lake Erie

B. Lake Huron

C. Lake Michigan

D. Lake Ontario

**2.** Along which river did both teams of explorers travel? (8.8.2)

A. Illinois River

B. Mississippi River

C. Ohio River

D. Wisconsin River

**This is a quotation from Increase Mather about colonial government. Use the quotation and your knowledge of U.S. history to answer question 3.**

### PRIMARY SOURCE

For all English liberties are restored to them: No Persons shall have a Penny of their Estates taken from them; nor any Laws imposed on them, without their own Consent by Representatives chosen by themselves.

**Increase Mather,** quoted in *The Last American Puritan*

**3.** The passage best represents which point of view? (8.1.2)

A. The colonists were entitled to the basic rights of English subjects.

B. The colonists' land belonged to the government.

C. Colonists did not have to pay taxes to the English government.

D. Colonists were not entitled to liberties granted to English subjects.

**TEST PRACTICE**
CLASSZONE.COM

## ALTERNATIVE ASSESSMENT

### 1. ▨ WRITING ABOUT HISTORY

During colonial times, children often had to learn work skills. Imagine that you were a young person during this time. Write a **letter** to your family describing your life and the work you do. (REP5)

• Use library resources to learn more about the roles of children during colonial times.

• Explain what you have learned about your work, and describe what you like or don't like about it.

### 2. COOPERATIVE LEARNING

Working in a group, hold a diplomatic council trying to prevent the French and Indian War. Group members can assume different roles: English and French officials, English settlers, French fur traders, English-allied Iroquois, French-allied Huron or Algonquin. (REP5)

## INTEGRATED TECHNOLOGY

### DOING INTERNET RESEARCH

Colonial American culture was not like modern American culture. Use the Internet to do research about life in 18th century colonial America. Then prepare a dramatic presentation featuring one of the important figures from the time, such as Benjamin Franklin, Madam Sarah Knight, or Pontiac. (REP4)

• On the Internet, find images, stories, poems, or novels, and articles about daily life, interests, or entertainment in the early and middle 1700s.

• Historical societies or living history museums in the original 13 states may also provide information about this period of time in American history.

**For more about colonial American culture . . .**

**INTERNET ACTIVITY**
CLASSZONE.COM

## Biographical Narratives:
### A Story About an Individual Who Made an Impact

**PURPOSE:** To write a biographical narrative for a class Web site called History Makers

**AUDIENCE:** Students around the world

In this unit, you read about many people who helped shape the early history of our country. Some are so famous that almost everyone knows their stories. Other people are less well known. For example, you may have read about the young indentured servant Elizabeth Ashbridge (page 114) for the first time. Yet she helped promote religious tolerance in the colonies, which would become a defining characteristic of American life.

Each person in Unit 1 made his or her own unique impact. Their biographical narratives, or life stories, are part of American history.

**CALIFORNIA STANDARDS**
**Writing 2.1** Write biographies, auto-biographies, short stories, or narratives.

A colonial woman expresses her religious freedom at a Quaker meeting.

## Organization & Focus

Your assignment is to write a biographical narrative about a key event in the life of one of the people you have read about in this unit. With such narrative strategies as dialogue and well-chosen details, you can bring the person to life. Your narrative, and those of your classmates, will be collected and published on a Web site called History Makers.

**CHOOSING A TOPIC** Review Unit 1 and look for individuals who made an impact on American history. You can search the stories that open each chapter, the chapters themselves, and the feature called *America's History Makers* for ideas. Choose the person who interests you the most as the subject of your biographical narrative. Research that person using library and Internet sources and select one event or incident from his or her life to relate in your narrative.

**IDENTIFYING PURPOSE AND AUDIENCE** Your purpose is to write a 500–700 word biographical narrative relating an event or incident in the life of a person who made an impact on American history. Your audience is made up of Internet users, especially other students, who are looking for information written in a lively style.

**FINDING DETAILS** Use questions like those in the chart below on Elizabeth Ashbridge to organize your biographical narrative. Include background description, physical description, and specific actions as you write answers to the questions. In addition, use dialogue to bring your subject to life. You should also reveal your own attitude toward your subject.

| Why is your subject important? | promoted religious tolerance |
|---|---|
| What background information do your readers need to know about your subject? | where she came from; what she experienced there |
| What event or incident in your subject's life do you want to describe? | joining the Quakers |
| When and where did the incident take place? | Pennsylvania, 1730s |
| Who else was involved? | other members |
| What do you think about your subject? | I admire her courage. |

## Research & Technology

If you need more background details for your story, look for them on the Internet. Search the name of your subject and the names of other people involved in the incident. You could also search the time and place the incident took place. Using key words such as *Middle Colonies, indentured servants* can help narrow your search.

**OUTLINING AND DRAFTING THE NARRATIVE** Use your planning chart as your outline. Draft a biographical narrative with dialogue and lifelike actions. Use transitions between sentences and paragraphs.

> **Technology Tip** Save or bookmark the Web sites you visit by selecting "Favorites" in your browser's tool bar and choosing "Add to Favorites."

## Evaluation & Revision

Don't forget to credit sources

Jeanine start writing work by her unive in 1927. still tor

When revising, check for strong word choice, clear organization, and smooth transitions. Read aloud dialogue to make sure it sounds natural, not stiff. Where possible, replace passive verbs with action verbs.

## Publish & Present

With your class, decide how to organize the History Makers menu. For example, should the History Makers be grouped according to time period or listed alphabetically? Once the class agrees on the design, create and upload the History Makers Web site.

### Self-Check

Does my biographical narrative have . . .

- ☐ a subject who made an impact on American history?
- ☐ background information on the subject?
- ☐ a clearly told incident about the subject?
- ☐ dialogue, specific actions, and physical descriptions?
- ☐ a viewpoint about the subject's impact?

# Creating a New Nation

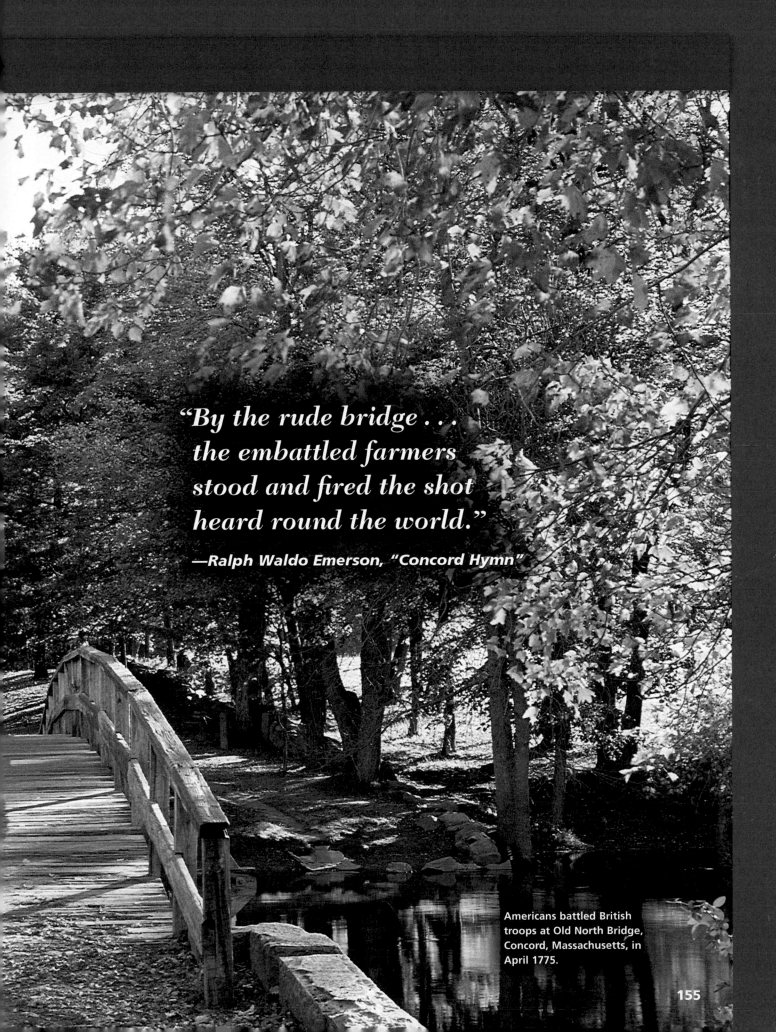

*"By the rude bridge . . . the embattled farmers stood and fired the shot heard round the world."*

**—Ralph Waldo Emerson, "Concord Hymn"**

Americans battled British troops at Old North Bridge, Concord, Massachusetts, in April 1775.

# The Road to Revolution 1763–1776

Angry confrontations between colonial protesters and British Red Coats became common as the colonies moved towards independence.

**1763**
Proclamation of 1763 becomes law.

**1765**
Stamp Act is passed.

**1767**
Townshend Acts are passed.

**1769**
Spanish begin to establish military posts and missions in California.

USA
World **1763**

**1763**
Treaty of Paris ends Seven Years' War in Europe.

**1765**
Chinese forces invade Burma.

**1769**
Scotland's James Watt patents a steam engine capable of running other machines.

The bayonets, or blades, on the soldiers' gun were very dangerous in close combat.

The fife and drum corps played music to keep soldiers at a steady march. During battle, the drummers beat out orders and the fifers carried messages and stretchers.

The year is 1765. Your neighbors are enraged by Britain's demand that British troops be housed in American cities at American expense. Britain has never done this before. There are protests in many cities. You have to decide what you would do.

# Would you join the protest?

## What Do You Think?

- What is the best way to show opposition to policies you consider unjust?

- Is there anything to be gained by protesting? Anything to be lost?

- Does government have the right to make demands without consent of the people? Why or why not?

**RESEARCH LINKS**
CLASSZONE.COM

Visit the Chapter 6 links for more information about the American Revolution.

**1770**
Boston Massacre

**1772**
Captain Cook explores the South Pacific.

**1773**
Boston Tea Party

**1774**
Intolerable Acts are passed; First Continental Congress meets.

**1774**
Reign of Louis XVI begins in France.

**1775**
Battles of Lexington and Concord

**1776**
Declaration of Independence is signed.

**1776**

# Reading Strategy: Sequencing Events

## What Do You Know?

What do you already know about the time before the Revolution? What were the issues that caused the colonists to choose independence?

CALIFORNIA STANDARDS

**Reading 2.7** Evaluate the unity, coherence, logic, internal consistency, and structural patterns of text.

**Think About**
- what you have learned about this period from movies, television, or historical fiction
- reasons people in history have chosen to fight for freedom from oppression
- your responses to the Interact with History about joining the protest (see page 157)

## What Do You Want to Know?

What questions do you have about the issues and events that pushed the American colonists toward rebellion? Record them in your notebook before you read the chapter.

## Sequencing Events

Sequencing means putting events in the order in which they happen in time. In learning about how the American colonies moved toward independence, it would be helpful to list the important events. Place them in the order in which they occurred. You might record the event and its date in a graphic organizer such as the one below. Copy this organizer in your notebook. Fill it in as you read the chapter.

**S** See Skillbuilder Handbook, page R4.

 **Taking Notes**

| Proclamation of 1763 | → | | → | | → | | |
| --- | --- | --- | --- | --- | --- | --- | --- |

| | ← | | ← | | ← | | |

| | → | | → | | → | Declaration of Independence, 1776 |

# Tighter British Control

| MAIN IDEA | WHY IT MATTERS NOW | TERMS & NAMES |
|---|---|---|
| Americans saw British efforts to tax them and to increase control over the colonies as violations of their rights. | Colonial protests were the first steps on the road to American independence. | King George III  Stamp Act<br>Quartering Act  Patrick Henry<br>revenue  boycott<br>Sugar Act  Sons of Liberty |

## ONE AMERICAN'S STORY

James Otis, Jr., a young Massachusetts lawyer, stormed through the streets of Boston one day in 1760. He was furious. His father had just been denied the post of chief justice of the Massachusetts colony by the royal governor. To Otis, this was one more example of Britain's lack of respect for colonial rights. Another example was its use of search warrants that allowed customs officers to enter any home or business to look for smuggled goods. Otis believed these searches were illegal.

In court in February 1761, Otis spoke with great emotion for five hours about the search warrant and its use.

James Otis, Jr.

*A VOICE FROM THE PAST*

It appears to me the worst instrument of arbitrary power, the most destructive of English liberty and the fundamental principles of law, that was ever found in an English law-book.

**James Otis, Jr.,** quoted in *James Otis: The Pre-Revolutionist* by J. C. Ridpath

In making the first public speech demanding English liberties for the colonists, James Otis planted a seed of freedom. In this section, you will read more about the early protests against Britain's policies in America.

## The Colonies and Britain Grow Apart

During the French and Indian War, Britain and the colonies fought side by side. Americans took great pride in being partners in the victory over the French. However, when the war ended, problems arose. Britain wanted to govern its 13 original colonies and the territories gained in the war in a uniform way. So the British Parliament in London imposed new laws and restrictions. Previously, the colonies had been allowed to develop largely on their own. Now they felt that their freedom was being limited.

Use your chart to take notes about the tightening of British control.

Proclamation of 1763 →

The first of Parliament's laws was the Proclamation of 1763. (See Chapter 5.) It said that colonists could not settle west of the Appalachian Mountains. Britain wanted this land to remain in the hands of its Native American allies to prevent another revolt like Pontiac's Rebellion.

The proclamation angered colonists who had hoped to move to the fertile Ohio Valley. Many of these colonists had no land of their own. It also upset colonists who had bought land as an investment. As a result, many ignored the law.

*Reading*History
**A. Summarizing**
Who was upset by the Proclamation of 1763?

## British Troops and Taxes

**King George III,** the British monarch, wanted to enforce the proclamation and also keep peace with Britain's Native American allies. To do this, he decided to keep 10,000 soldiers in the colonies. In 1765, Parliament passed the **Quartering Act.** This was a cost-saving measure that required the colonies to quarter, or house, British soldiers and provide them with supplies. General Thomas Gage, commander of these forces, put most of the troops in New York.

Britain owed a large debt from the French and Indian War. Keeping troops in the colonies would raise that debt even higher. Britain needed more **revenue,** or income, to meet its expenses. So it attempted to have the colonies pay part of the war debt. It also wanted them to contribute toward the costs of frontier defense and colonial government.

In the past, the king had asked the colonial assemblies to pass taxes to support military actions that took place in the colonies. This time, however, Parliament voted to tax the Americans directly.

In 1764, Parliament passed the **Sugar Act.** This law placed a tax on sugar, molasses, and other products shipped to the colonies. It also called for strict enforcement of the act and harsh punishment of smugglers. Colonial merchants, who often traded in smuggled goods, reacted with anger.

Colonial leaders such as James Otis claimed that Parliament had no right to tax the colonies, since the colonists were not represented in Parliament. As Otis exclaimed, "Taxation without representation is tyranny!" British finance minister George Grenville disagreed. The colonists were subjects of Britain, he said, and enjoyed the protection of its laws. For that reason, they were subject to taxation.

Vocabulary
**tyranny:**
absolute power in the hands of a single ruler

## Britain Passes the Stamp Act

The Sugar Act was just the first in a series of acts that increased tension between the mother country and the colonies. In 1765, Parliament passed the **Stamp Act.** This law required all legal and commercial documents to carry an official stamp showing that a tax had been paid. All diplomas, contracts, and wills had to carry a stamp.

The colonial view of the hated stamp tax is shown by the skull and crossbones on this emblem (above); a royal stamp is pictured at right.

**160**

Even published materials such as newspapers had to be written on special stamped paper.

The Stamp Act was a new kind of tax for the colonies. The Sugar Act had been a tax on imported goods. It mainly affected merchants. In contrast, the Stamp Act was a tax applied within the colonies. It fell directly on all colonists. Even more, the colonists had to pay for stamps in silver coin—a scarce item in the colonies.

Colonial leaders vigorously protested. For them, the issue was clear. They were being taxed without their consent by a Parliament in which they had no voice. If Britain could pass the Stamp Act, what other taxes might it pass in the future? Samuel Adams, a leader in the Massachusetts legislature, asked, "Why not our lands? Why not the produce of our lands and, in short, everything we possess and make use of?" **Patrick Henry,** a member of Virginia's House of Burgesses, called for resistance to the tax. When another member shouted that resistance was treason, Henry reportedly replied, "If this be treason, make the most of it!"

## The Colonies Protest the Stamp Act

Colonial assemblies and newspapers took up the cry—"No taxation without representation!" In October 1765, nine colonies sent delegates to the Stamp Act Congress in New York City. This was the first time the colonies met to consider acting together in protest. Delegates drew up a petition to the king protesting the Stamp Act. The petition declared that the right to tax the colonies belonged to the colonial assemblies, not to Parliament. Later, colonial merchants organized a **boycott** of British goods. A boycott is a refusal to buy.

Meanwhile, some colonists formed secret societies to oppose British policies. The most famous of these groups was the **Sons of Liberty.** Many Sons of Liberty were lawyers, merchants, and craftspeople—the colonists most affected by the Stamp Act. These groups staged protests against the act.

Not all of their protests were peaceful. The Sons of Liberty burned the stamped paper whenever they could find it. They also attacked customs officials, whom they covered with hot tar and feathers and paraded in public. Fearing for their safety, many customs officials quit their jobs.

The protests in the colonies had an effect in Britain. Merchants thought that their trade with America would be hurt. Some British political leaders, including

*Reading* **History**
**B. Making Inferences** Why did the colonists boycott goods?

**Background**
To voice their protests, the Sons of Liberty in Boston met under a huge, 120-year-old elm tree that they called the Liberty Tree.

Colonists protest the Stamp Act.

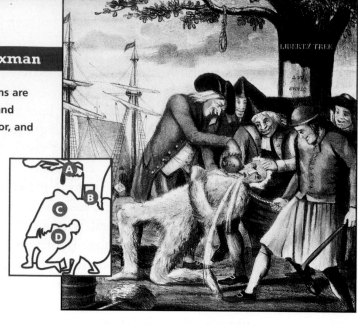

## Bostonians Paying the Taxman

In this British political cartoon, Americans are depicted as barbarians who would tar and feather a customs official, or tax collector, and pour hot tea down his throat.

**A** Liberty Tree as a gallows

**B** Stamp Act posted upside down

**C** Protesters in Boston

**D** Customs official tarred and feathered

the popular parliamentary leader William Pitt, agreed with American thinking about taxing the colonies. Pitt spoke out against the Stamp Act.

### A VOICE FROM THE PAST

The Americans have not acted in all things with prudence and [good] temper. They have been driven to madness by injustice. Will you punish them for the madness you have [caused]? . . . My opinion . . . is that the Stamp Act be repealed absolutely, totally and immediately.

**William Pitt,** quoted in *Patriots* by A. J. Langguth

Parliament finally saw that the Stamp Act was a mistake and repealed it in 1766. But at the same time, Parliament passed another law—the Declaratory Act. This law said that Parliament had supreme authority to govern the colonies. The Americans celebrated the repeal of the Stamp Act and tried to ignore the Declaratory Act. A great tug of war between Parliament and the colonies had begun. The central issue was control of the colonies, as you will learn in the next section.

*Reading*History
**C. Drawing Conclusions** Why was it important for Parliament to pass the Declaratory Act?

## Section 1 Assessment

### 1. Terms & Names

**Explain the significance of:**
- King George III
- Quartering Act
- revenue
- Sugar Act
- Stamp Act
- Patrick Henry
- boycott
- Sons of Liberty

### 2. Using Graphics

Use a cluster diagram like the one below to review points of conflict between Britain and the colonies. (HI1)

Points of Conflict

Which do you think was the most serious? Explain.

### 3. Main Ideas

**a.** Why did the Proclamation of 1763 anger colonists? (HI2)

**b.** How did colonists react to the Stamp Act? (HI2)

**c.** What was the goal of secret societies such as the Sons of Liberty? (HI2)

### 4. Critical Thinking

**Analyzing Points of View** What were the two sides in the debate over British taxation of the colonies? (REP5)

**THINK ABOUT**
- how Parliament viewed the colonies
- what concerned the colonists about taxes

### ACTIVITY OPTIONS

**ART**

**MUSIC**

Imagine that you are a colonial leader who wants to get your fellow colonists to protest British policy. Design a **poster** or write a **song of protest**. (REP5)

# Colonial Resistance Grows

| MAIN IDEA | WHY IT MATTERS NOW | TERMS & NAMES |
|---|---|---|
| Many Americans began to organize to oppose British policies. | Americans continue to protest what they view as wrongs and injustices. | Crispus Attucks Boston Massacre<br>Townshend Acts John Adams<br>writs of assistance committee of correspondence<br>Samuel Adams Boston Tea Party |

## ONE AMERICAN'S STORY

**Crispus Attucks** knew about the struggle for freedom. The son of an African-American father and a Native American mother, Attucks was born into slavery in Framingham, Massachusetts, around 1723. As a young man, Attucks escaped by running away to sea.

In March 1770, Attucks found himself in Boston, where feelings against British rule were hot. One night Attucks took part in a disturbance between colonists and British troops. He was about to play a key role in U.S. history—losing his life to a British bullet in a protest that came to be called the Boston Massacre. In Section 2, you will read how tension between Britain and its colonies led to violence.

## The Townshend Acts Are Passed

After the uproar over the Stamp Act, Britain hoped to avoid further conflict. Even so, it still needed to raise money to pay for troops and other expenses in America. The Quartering Act was not working. Most of the British army was in New York, and New York saw that as an unfair burden. Its assembly refused to pay to house the troops.

The king's finance minister, Charles Townshend, told Parliament that he had a way to raise revenue in the colonies. So in 1767, Parliament passed his plan, known as the **Townshend Acts**.

The first of the Townshend Acts suspended New York's assembly until New Yorkers agreed to provide housing for the troops. The other acts placed duties, or import taxes, on various goods brought into the colonies, such as glass, paper, paint, lead, and tea. Townshend thought that duties, which were collected before the goods entered the colonies, would anger the colonists less than the direct taxes of the Stamp Act. The money raised would be used to pay the salaries of British governors and other officials in the colonies. To enforce the acts, British officers

**CALIFORNIA STANDARDS**

**8.1** Students understand the major events preceding the founding of the nation and relate their significance to the development of American constitutional democracy.

**REP4** Students assess the credibility of primary and secondary sources and draw sound conclusions from them.

**REP5** Students detect the different historical points of view on historical events and determine the context in which the historical statements were made (the questions asked, sources used, author's perspectives).

**Taking Notes**

Use your chart to take notes about colonial resistance.

Proclamation of 1763 →

would use **writs of assistance,** or search warrants, to enter homes or businesses to search for smuggled goods.

## The Reasons for Protest

Protests immediately broke out at news of the Townshend Acts. New Yorkers were angry that their elected assembly had been suspended. People throughout the colonies were upset that Britain was placing new taxes on them. "The issue," said John Dickinson, an important Pennsylvania lawyer, was "whether Parliament can legally take money out of our pockets without our consent." He explained his opposition to the Townshend Acts in essays called *Letters from a Farmer in Pennsylvania,* published in 1767.

### A VOICE FROM THE PAST

Let these truths be . . . impressed on our minds—that we cannot be happy without being free—that we cannot be free without being secure in our property—that we cannot be secure in our property if without our consent others may . . . take it away—that taxes imposed on us by Parliament do thus take it away—that duties laid for the sole purpose of raising money are taxes—that attempts to lay such duties should be instantly and firmly opposed.

**John Dickinson,** quoted in *A New Age Now Begins* by Page Smith

*Reading***History**
**A. Making Inferences** Why does Dickinson believe that taxes interfere with happiness?

The colonists were also angry about the writs of assistance. Many believed, as James Otis had argued (see page 159), that the writs went against their natural rights. These rights had been described by English philosopher John Locke during the Enlightenment. The law of nature, said Locke, teaches that "no one ought to harm another in his life, health, liberty, or possessions." The colonists felt that the Townshend Acts were a serious threat to their rights and freedoms.

## Tools of Protest

To protest the Townshend Acts, colonists in Boston announced another boycott of British goods in October 1767. The driving force behind this protest was **Samuel Adams,** a leader of the Boston Sons of Liberty. Adams urged colonists to continue to resist British controls.

The boycott spread throughout the colonies. The Sons of Liberty pressured shopkeepers not to sell imported goods. The Daughters of Liberty called on colonists to weave their own cloth and use American products. As a result, trade with Britain fell sharply.

Colonial leaders asked for peaceful protests. Articles in the *Boston Gazette* asked the people to remain calm—

This engraving, *The Bloody Massacre Perpetrated in King Street* by Boston silversmith Paul Revere, appeared in the *Boston Gazette.*

"no mobs. . . . Constitutional methods are best." However, tempers were running high. When customs officers in Boston tried to seize the American merchant ship *Liberty,* which was carrying smuggled wine, a riot broke out. The rioters forced the customs officers to flee.

Fearing a loss of control, officials called for more British troops. A defiant Samuel Adams replied, "We will destroy every soldier that dares put his foot on shore. . . . I look upon them as foreign enemies."

For an activity about the Boston Massacre . . .

NET SIMULATION
CLASSZONE.COM

## The Boston Massacre

In the fall of 1768, 1,000 British soldiers (known as redcoats for their bright red jackets) arrived in Boston under the command of General Thomas Gage. With their arrival, tension filled the streets of Boston.

Since the soldiers were poorly paid, they hired themselves out as workers, usually at rates lower than those of American workers. Resentment against the redcoats grew. Soldiers and street youths often yelled insults at each other. "Lobsters for sale!" the youths would yell, referring to the soldiers' red coats. "Yankees!" the soldiers jeered. *Yankee* was supposed to be an insult, but the colonists soon took pride in the name.

On March 5, 1770, tensions finally exploded into violence. A group of youths and dockworkers—among them Crispus Attucks—started trading insults in front of the Custom House. A fight broke out, and the soldiers began firing. Attucks and four laborers were killed.

*Reading* **History**
B. Recognizing Propaganda How did the use of the word *massacre* show an anti-British view?

The Sons of Liberty called the shooting the **Boston Massacre.** They said that Attucks and the four others had given their lives for freedom. The incident became a tool for anti-British propaganda in newspaper articles, pamphlets, and posters. The people of Boston were outraged.

Meanwhile, the redcoats who had fired the shots were arrested for murder. **John Adams,** a lawyer and cousin of Samuel Adams, defended them in court. Adams was criticized for taking the case. He replied that the law should be "deaf . . . to the clamors of the populace." He supported

### SAMUEL ADAMS
#### 1722–1803

Samuel Adams was a Harvard graduate. But unlike his cousin John, also a Harvard graduate, he showed little skill for the law. Later, when he took control of the family business, he lost his father's fortune. Yet he succeeded in one important undertaking—moving America toward independence.

Adams's true talent lay in rousing people to action in support of a cause. A fiery orator and a master of propaganda, he used words as a weapon. One British official said that "every dip of his pen stings."

### JOHN ADAMS
#### 1735–1826

John Adams, unlike Samuel, was considered a moderate in the struggle against Britain. He was an important voice of reason and at first opposed resisting by force.

Adams believed in the rule of law. He called his defense of the soldiers in the Boston Massacre "one of the best pieces of service I ever rendered my country."

Eventually, Adams became convinced that only outright resistance would gain liberty for America. He said, "Britain has at last driven America, to the last Step, a compleat Seperation from her."

**How did the cousins John and Samuel Adams differ in the way they protested British actions?**

the colonial cause but wanted to show that the colonists followed the rule of law. Adams argued that the soldiers had acted in self-defense. The jury agreed. To many colonists, however, the Boston Massacre would stand as a symbol of British tyranny.

## The Tea Act

The colonists were unaware that on the day of the Boston Massacre, Parliament proposed the repeal of the Townshend Acts. One month later, all the acts except the tax on tea were repealed. The colonial boycott had been effective—British trade had been hurt. But Parliament kept the tea tax to show that it still had the right to tax the colonists. For most Americans, the crisis was over.

Samuel Adams, however, wanted to make sure people did not forget the cause of liberty. He started a drive to form **committees of correspondence** in various towns in Massachusetts. These groups exchanged letters on colonial affairs. Before long, committees throughout Massachusetts were corresponding with one another and with committees in other colonies.

Then, in 1773, Parliament opened up old wounds when it passed the Tea Act. Tea was very popular in the colonies, but much of it was smuggled in from Holland. The Tea Act gave the British East India Company control over the American tea trade. The tea would arrive in the colonies only in the trading company's ships and be sold there by its merchants. Colonists who had not been paying any tax on smuggled tea would now have to pay a tax on this regulated tea. This enraged colonial shippers and merchants. The colonists wondered what Parliament would do next.

*Reading*History

**C. Drawing Conclusions** Why did Samuel Adams think that the colonists might forget the cause of liberty?

## The Boston Tea Party

Protests against the Tea Act took place all over the colonies. In Charleston, South Carolina, colonists unloaded tea and let it rot on the docks. In New York City and Philadelphia, colonists blocked tea ships from landing. In Boston, the Sons of Liberty organized what came to be known as the **Boston Tea Party**.

*Reading*History

D. Reading a Map Find Boston Harbor on the map on page 172.

On the evening of December 16, 1773, a group of men disguised as Native Americans boarded three tea ships docked in Boston Harbor. One of the men, George Hewes, a Boston shoemaker, later recalled the events.

Colonists dumped hundreds of chests of tea into Boston Harbor in 1773 to protest the Tea Act.

### A VOICE FROM THE PAST

We then were ordered by our commander to open the hatches and take out all the chests of tea and throw them overboard. . . . In about three hours from the time we went on board, we had thus broken and thrown overboard every tea chest to be found on the ship, while those in the other ships were disposing of the tea in the same way, at the same time.

**George Hewes,** quoted in *A Retrospect of the Boston Tea-Party*

That night, Hewes and the others destroyed 342 chests of tea. Many colonists rejoiced at the news. They believed that Britain would now see how strongly colonists opposed taxation without representation.

Others doubted that destroying property was the best way to settle the tax debate. Some colonial leaders offered to pay for the tea if Parliament would repeal the Tea Act. Britain rejected the offer. It not only wanted repayment, but it also wanted the men who destroyed the tea to be brought to trial. The British reaction to the Boston Tea Party would fan the flames of rebellion in the 13 colonies, as you will read in the next section.

*Reading*History

E. Recognizing Effects How did Britain react to the Tea Party?

---

## Section 2 Assessment

### 1. Terms & Names

**Explain the significance of:**
- Crispus Attucks
- Townshend Acts
- writs of assistance
- Samuel Adams
- Boston Massacre
- John Adams
- committee of correspondence
- Boston Tea Party

### 2. Using Graphics

Create a time line like the one below to show the significant people and events described in this section.

1767                        1773

Which event do you think was the most important? Explain. (CST2)

### 3. Main Ideas

**a.** Why did colonists oppose the Townshend Acts? (HI2)

**b.** Why were British troops sent to Boston? (HI2)

**c.** What prompted the Boston Tea Party? (HI2)

### 4. Critical Thinking

**Drawing Conclusions** Do you think colonial outrage over the Boston Massacre was justified? Explain. (REP5)

**THINK ABOUT**
- how the British troops were taunted
- whether troops have the right to fire on citizens

### ACTIVITY OPTIONS

**SPEECH**

**TECHNOLOGY**

Read more about the Boston Massacre or the Boston Tea Party. Present an **oral report** or plan a **multimedia presentation** about the event. (HI1)

# Fight for Representative Government!

You are a colonist living in Boston on the eve of the American Revolution. Nearly a decade of protest against British policies has failed to secure American rights. Redcoats continue to be quartered in the city. The Tea Act still stands. Now the dumping of tea in Boston Harbor by some Patriots has charged the atmosphere with tension. Trouble lies ahead, but you are determined to fight for a government that will protect your rights.

**COOPERATIVE LEARNING** On this page are two challenges that you face as the conflict with Britain unfolds. Working with a small group, decide how to deal with each challenge. Choose an option, assign a task to each group member, and do the activity. You will find useful information in the Data File. Present your solutions to the class.

**CALIFORNIA STANDARDS**

**8.1.4** Describe the nation's blend of civic republicanism, classical liberal principles, and English parliamentary traditions.

**Writing 2.4** Write persuasive compositions.

**Listening and Speaking 1.0** Students deliver focused, coherent presentations that convey ideas clearly and relate to the background and interests of the audience. They evaluate the content of oral communication.

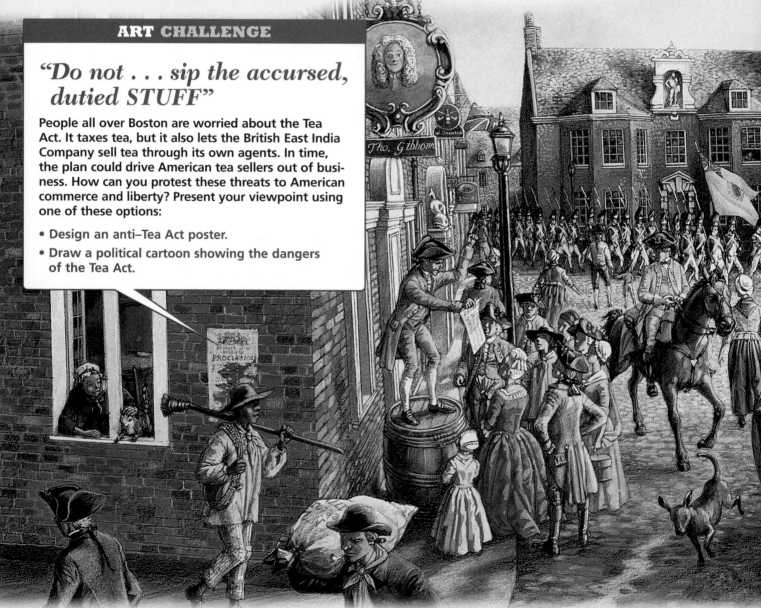

## ART CHALLENGE

### *"Do not . . . sip the accursed, dutied STUFF"*

People all over Boston are worried about the Tea Act. It taxes tea, but it also lets the British East India Company sell tea through its own agents. In time, the plan could drive American tea sellers out of business. How can you protest these threats to American commerce and liberty? Present your viewpoint using one of these options:

- Design an anti–Tea Act poster.
- Draw a political cartoon showing the dangers of the Tea Act.

## MATH CHALLENGE

# "Wear none but your own country linen"

Years of struggle have taken their toll on Boston. People are tired of soldiers and of boycotting British goods, such as clothing. But the Tea Act presents a huge threat. The Boston Tea Party took care of only one shipment. How can you help encourage the boycott of other British goods, such as clothing? Look at the Data File for help. Present your appeal using one of these options:

- Make a graph showing the effect of colonial boycotts on imports of British goods to America.
- Write an editorial using statistics to show how American boycotts have hurt the British.

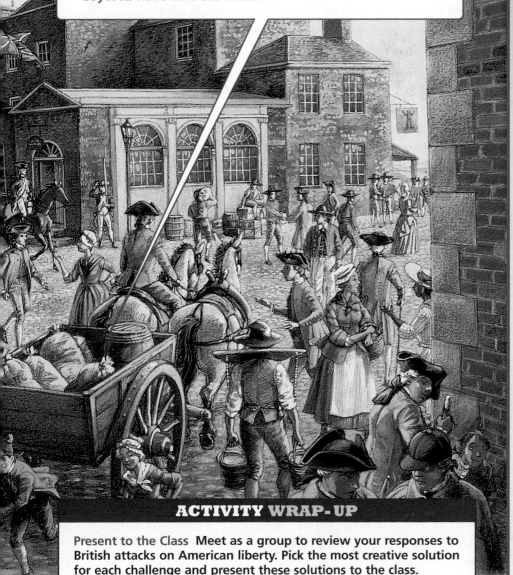

## ACTIVITY WRAP-UP

**Present to the Class** Meet as a group to review your responses to British attacks on American liberty. Pick the most creative solution for each challenge and present these solutions to the class.

## DATA FILE

### Population in 1774–1775
**Britain:** 7,860,000
**London:** 700,000

**The 13 colonies:** 2,350,000
**Philadelphia:** 33,000
**New York:** 22,000
**Boston:** 16,000

### North American Imports from Britain
(in millions of pounds sterling)

| Year | | Year | |
|---|---|---|---|
| 1763 | 1.6 | 1770 | 1.9 |
| 1764 | 2.3 | 1771 | 4.2 |
| 1765 | 1.9 | 1772 | 3.0 |
| 1766 | 1.8 | 1773 | 2.1 |
| 1767 | 1.9 | 1774 | 2.6 |
| 1768 | 2.2 | 1775 | 0.2 |
| 1769 | 1.3 | 1776 | 0.1 |

### North American Exports to Britain
(in millions of pounds sterling)

| Year | | Year | |
|---|---|---|---|
| 1763 | 1.1 | 1770 | 1.0 |
| 1764 | 1.1 | 1771 | 1.3 |
| 1765 | 1.2 | 1772 | 1.3 |
| 1766 | 1.0 | 1773 | 1.4 |
| 1767 | 1.1 | 1774 | 1.4 |
| 1768 | 1.3 | 1775 | 1.9 |
| 1769 | 1.1 | 1776 | 0.1 |

### Key Boycott Dates
1764 Boycott after passage of Sugar Act
1765 Boycott after passage of Stamp Act
1766 Boycott relaxed after Stamp Act repealed
1767 Boycott after passage of Townshend Acts
1770 Townshend Acts repealed
1774 Boycott after passage of Intolerable Acts

### Sales and Consumption of Tea at the Time of the Boston Tea Party
**British sales:** fourth most important product shipped to America
**American consumption:** 1.2 million pounds per year

For more on Revolutionary America . . .

**RESEARCH LINKS**
CLASSZONE.COM

# 3

# The Road to Lexington and Concord

| MAIN IDEA | WHY IT MATTERS NOW | TERMS & NAMES |
|---|---|---|
| The tensions between Britain and the colonies led to armed conflict in Massachusetts. | Americans at times still find themselves called upon to fight for their principles. | militia      Paul Revere<br>Minuteman    Lexington and<br>Intolerable Acts    Concord<br>First Continental    Loyalist<br>Congress      Patriot |

**CALIFORNIA STANDARDS**

**8.1** Students understand the major events preceding the founding of the nation and relate their significance to the development of American constitutional democracy.

**CST3** Students use a variety of maps and documents to identify physical and cultural features of neighborhoods, cities, states, and countries and to explain the historical migration of people, expansion and disintegration of empires, and the growth of economic systems.

**HI2** Students understand and distinguish cause, effect, sequence, and correlation in historical events, including the long- and short-term causal relations.

**HI3** Students explain the sources of historical continuity and how the combination of ideas and events explains the emergence of new patterns.

**Taking Notes**

Use your chart to take notes about the beginning of the American Revolution.

Proclamation of 1763 →

## ONE AMERICAN'S STORY

On April 19, 1775, some 70 militiamen led by Captain John Parker gathered in Lexington, Massachusetts, a town near Boston. A **militia** is a force of armed civilians pledged to defend their community. About one-third of the Lexington militia were **Minutemen**, trained to "act at a minute's warning." They had heard that the British were coming.

Parker's troops had never faced soldiers. Soon they would meet the British on Lexington Green in the first battle of the Revolutionary War. According to tradition, Parker told his men, "Stand your ground; don't fire unless fired upon, but if they mean to have war, let it begin here."

In this section, you will read how colonial protests led to revolution.

Statue of Captain John Parker in Lexington, Massachusetts

## The Intolerable Acts

The Boston Tea Party had aroused fury in Britain. One British official said that the people of Boston "ought to be knocked about their ears." King George III declared, "We must master them or totally leave them to themselves and treat them as aliens." Britain chose to "master" the colonies.

In 1774, Parliament passed a series of laws to punish the Massachusetts colony and to serve as a warning to other colonies. The British called these laws the Coercive Acts, but they were so harsh that the colonists called them the **Intolerable Acts**.

One of the acts would close the port of Boston until colonists paid for the destroyed tea. Others banned committees of correspondence, allowed Britain to house troops wherever necessary, and let British officials accused of crimes in the colonies stand trial in Britain. To enforce the acts, Parliament appointed General Thomas Gage governor of Massachusetts.

In 1773, Sam Adams had written, "I wish we could arouse the continent." The Intolerable Acts answered his wish. Other colonies immediately offered Massachusetts their support. They sent food and money to Boston. The committees of correspondence also called for a meeting of colonial delegates to discuss what to do next.

## The First Continental Congress Meets

In September 1774, delegates from all the colonies except Georgia met in Philadelphia. At this meeting, called the **First Continental Congress,** delegates voted to ban all trade with Britain until the Intolerable Acts were repealed. They also called on each colony to begin training troops. Georgia agreed to be a part of the actions of the Congress even though it had voted not to send delegates.

*Reading***History**
**A. Evaluating** Why do you think the First Continental Congress was important?

The First Continental Congress marked a key step in American history. Although most delegates were not ready to call for independence, they were determined to uphold colonial rights. This meeting planted the seeds of a future independent government. John Adams called it "a nursery of American statesmen." The delegates agreed to meet in seven months, if necessary. By that time, however, fighting with Britain had begun.

## Between War and Peace

The colonists hoped that the trade boycott would force a repeal of the Intolerable Acts. After all, past boycotts had led to the repeal of the Stamp Act and the Townshend Acts. This time, however, Parliament stood firm. It even increased restrictions on colonial trade and sent more troops.

By the end of 1774, some colonists were preparing to fight. In Massachusetts, John Hancock headed the Committee of Safety, which had the power to call out the militia. The colonial troops continued to train.

### CAUSE AND EFFECT: *Growing Conflict Between Britain and America*

| DATE | BRITISH ACTION | | COLONIAL REACTION |
|------|---------------|---|-------------------|
| 1763 | Proclamation of 1763 issued | ▶ | Proclamation leads to anger |
| 1765 | Stamp Act passed | ▶ | Boycott of British goods; Stamp Act Resolves passed |
| 1766 | Stamp Act repealed; Declaration Act passed | ▶ | Boycott ended |
| 1767 | Townshend Acts passed | ▶ | New boycotts; Boston Massacre (March 1770) |
| 1770 | Townshend Acts repealed (April) | ▶ | Tension between colonies and Britain reduced |
| 1773 | Tea Act passed | ▶ | Boston Tea Party |
| 1774 | Intolerable Acts passed | ▶ | First Continental Congress bans trade; militias organized |
| 1775 | Troops ordered to Lexington and Concord, Massachusetts | ▶ | Militia fights British troops; Second Continental Congress; Continental Army established |

**SKILLBUILDER Interpreting Charts**

1. *What British action caused the first violence in the growing conflict between Britain and America?*
2. *How might the Intolerable Acts be seen as a reaction as well as an action?*

Most colonial leaders believed that any fight with Britain would be short. They thought that a show of force would make Britain change its policies. Few expected a war. One who did was Patrick Henry.

*A VOICE FROM THE PAST*

Gentlemen may cry peace, peace—but there is no peace. The war is actually begun! The next gale that sweeps from the north will bring to our ears the clash of resounding arms! Our brethren are already in the field! Why should we idle here? . . . I know not what course others may take. But as for me, give me liberty or give me death.

**Patrick Henry,** quoted in *Patriots* by A. J. Langguth

Henry delivered what became his most famous speech in the Virginia House of Burgesses in March 1775.

## The Midnight Ride

Meanwhile, spies were busy on both sides. Sam Adams had built a spy network to keep watch over British activities. The British had their spies too. They were Americans who were loyal to Britain. From them, General Gage learned that the Massachusetts militia was storing arms and ammunition in Concord, about 20 miles northwest of Boston. He also heard that Sam Adams and John Hancock were in Lexington. On the night of April 18, 1775, Gage ordered his troops to arrest Adams and Hancock in Lexington and to destroy the supplies in Concord.

The Sons of Liberty had prepared for this moment. **Paul Revere,** a Boston silversmith, and a second messenger, William Dawes, were charged with spreading the news about British troop movements. Revere had arranged a system of signals to alert colonists in Charlestown, on the shore opposite Boston. If one lantern burned in the Old North Church steeple, the British troops were coming by land; if two, they were coming by water. Revere would go across the water from Boston to Charlestown and ride to Lexington and Concord from there. Dawes would take the land route.

*Reading* **History**

**B. Recognizing Effects** What effect might spying have had on the people of Boston?

**Background**
The signals were a backup system in case Revere was captured.

**The Revolution Begins,** *1775*

Concord R.

North Bridge

Concord

Revere captured.

Prescott joins Dawes and Revere.

Prescott goes forward.

Dawes escapes and turns back.

Lexington

Sudbury R.

Boston
MASS.

Mystic River

Old North Church

Charlestown

Cambridge

Charles River

Boston

Boston Harbor

N

0        2 Miles
0        4 Kilometers

**GEOGRAPHY SKILLBUILDER**
**Interpreting Maps**

1. **Location** *Where were battles fought?*
2. **Movement** *What was the distance between Lexington and Concord?*

— Revere's route
— Dawes's route
— Prescott's route
— British advance
- - British retreat
✹ Battle

When the British moved, so did Revere and Dawes. They galloped over the countryside on their "midnight ride," spreading the news. In Lexington, they were joined by Dr. Samuel Prescott. When Revere and Dawes were stopped by a British patrol, Prescott broke away and carried the message to Concord.

## Lexington and Concord

At dawn on April 19, some 700 British troops reached Lexington. They found Captain John Parker and about 70 militiamen waiting. The British commander ordered the Americans to drop their muskets. They refused. No one knows who fired first, but within a few minutes eight militiamen lay dead. The British then marched to Concord, where they destroyed military supplies. A battle broke out at a bridge north of town, forcing the British to retreat.

Nearly 4,000 Minutemen and militiamen arrived in the area. They lined the road from Concord to Lexington and peppered the retreating redcoats with musket fire. "It seemed as if men came down from the clouds," one soldier said. Only the arrival of 1,000 more troops saved the British from destruction as they scrambled back to Boston.

**Lexington and Concord** were the first battles of the Revolutionary War. As Ralph Waldo Emerson later wrote, colonial troops had fired the "shot heard 'round the world." Americans would now have to choose sides and back up their political opinions by force of arms. Those who supported the British were called **Loyalists**. Those who sided with the rebels were **Patriots**. The conflict between the two sides divided communities, families, and friends. The war was on!

**Background**
British losses totaled 273 soldiers compared to 95 militiamen.

*Reading*History
**C. Drawing Conclusions**
Why did Emerson call it the "shot heard 'round the world"?

### Now and then

**PATRIOTS' DAY**
The "shot heard 'round the world" is celebrated every year in Massachusetts and Maine. Patriots' Day, as it is called, is the third Monday of April. In Concord and nearby towns, modern-day Minutemen like those below reenact the battle that began the Revolution on April 19, 1775. The Boston Marathon is also run on Patriots' Day.

---

| Section 3 | Assessment |
|---|---|

### 1. Terms & Names

**Explain the significance of:**
- militia
- Minuteman
- Intolerable Acts
- First Continental Congress
- Paul Revere
- Lexington and Concord
- Loyalist
- Patriot

### 2. Using Graphics

Use a diagram like the one below to show events that led to the Revolutionary War. (CST2)

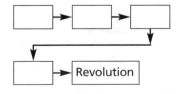

### 3. Main Ideas

**a.** Why did Britain pass the Intolerable Acts? (HI2)

**b.** Who took part in the First Continental Congress? (HI1)

**c.** What was the purpose of the "midnight ride"? (HI2)

### 4. Critical Thinking

**Supporting Opinions**
Do you think the fighting between Britain and the colonies could have been avoided? Why or why not? (REP5)

**THINK ABOUT**
- Britain's attitude toward the colonies
- colonial feelings about Britain

**ACTIVITY OPTIONS**

**GEOGRAPHY**
**MATH**

Research the Battles of Lexington and Concord. Draw a **map** of key events or create a **chart** showing statistics from the battles. (CST3)

*From*

# JOHNNY
# TREMAIN

*by Esther Forbes*

**CALIFORNIA STANDARDS**

**HI2** Students understand and distinguish cause, effect, sequence, and correlation in historical events, including the long- and short-term causal relations.

**Reading 3.2** Evaluate the structural elements of the plot (e.g., subplots, parallel episodes, climax), the plot's development, and the way in which conflicts are (or are not) addressed and resolved.

In 1775, 16-year-old Johnny Tremain lives in Boston and works as a delivery boy for a newspaper. Because he travels so much around the city, he is able to help the Patriots gather information about what the British are doing.

On the night of April 18, Johnny learns that British troops will be leaving on an expedition to seize the gunpowder at Lexington and Concord. He rushes to tell this news to Dr. Joseph Warren, who is a Patriot. Then Johnny goes to bed, wondering if the war has started and worried about his friend Rab, who has gone to join the Minutemen at Lexington.

So Johnny slept. It was daylight when he woke with Warren's hand upon his shoulder. Outside on Tremont Street he could hear the clumping of army boots. A sergeant was swearing at his men. The soldiers were paraded so close to the house, which stood **flush**[1] with the sidewalk-less street, that Johnny at first thought they must be in the room.

Doctor Warren dared speak no louder than a whisper.

"I'm going now."

"Something's happened?"

"Yes." He motioned Johnny to follow him into the kitchen. This room was on the back of the house. They could talk without danger of being overheard by the troops in the street.

Doctor Warren had on the same clothes as the day before. He had not been to bed. But now his hat was on his head. His black bag of instruments and medicines was packed and on the table. Silently he put milk, bread, herrings beside it, and gestured to Johnny to join him.

"Where did it begin?" asked Johnny.

"Lexington."

"Who won?"

"They did. Seven hundred against seventy. It wasn't a battle. It was . . . just target practice . . . for them. Some of our men were killed and the British **huzzaed**[2] and took the road to Concord."

"And did they get our supplies there?"

"I don't know. Paul Revere sent for me just after the firing on Lexington Green."

The young man's usually fresh-colored face was **haggard**[3]. He knew the seriousness of this day for himself and for his country.

"But everywhere the alarm is spreading. Men are grabbing their guns—marching for Concord. Paul Revere did get through in time last night. Billy Dawes a little later. Hundreds—maybe thousands—of Minute Men are on the march. Before the day's over, there'll be real fighting—not target practice. But Gage doesn't know that it's begun. You see, long before Colonel Smith got to Lexington—just as soon as he heard that Revere had warned the country—he sent back for reinforcements. For Earl Percy. You and I, Johnny, are just about the only people in Boston who know that blood has already been shed."

"Were many killed—at Lexington?"

"No, not many. They stood up—just a handful. The British fired on them. It was dawn."

Johnny licked his lips. "Did they tell you the names of those killed?"

---

1. **flush:** in a line with.

2. **huzzaed:** cheered.
3. **haggard:** tired.

"No. Did Rab get out in time?"

"Yes. Last Sunday."

The Doctor's clear blue eyes darkened. He knew what was in Johnny's mind. He picked up his bag. "I've got to get to them. They'll need surgeons. Then, too, I'd rather die fighting than on a gallows. Gage won't be so **lenient**[4] now—soon as he learns war has begun."

"Wait until I get my shoes on."

"No, Johnny, you are to stay here today. Pick up for me any information. For instance, out of my bedroom window I can see soldiers standing the length of the street 'way over to the Common. You find out what regiments are being sent—and all that. And today go about and listen to what folk are saying. And the names of any the British arrest. We know Gage expects to move his men back here tonight. If so, there'll be a lot of confusion getting them into town. You watch your chance and slip out to me."

"Where'll I find you?"

" . . . Ask about."

"I will do so."

"They've begun it. We'll end it, but this war . . . it may last quite a long time."

---

4. **lenient:** not strict.
5. **surgery:** operating room.

They shook hands silently. Johnny knew that Warren was always conscious of the fact that he had a crippled hand. Everybody else had accepted and forgotten it. The back door closed softly. Warren was gone.

Johnny went to the **surgery**,[5] put on his boots and jacket. The wall clock said eight o'clock. It was time to be about. There was no leaving by the front door. The soldiers were leaning against it. Through the curtains of the windows he could see the muskets. He noticed the facings on their uniforms. The Twenty-Third Regiment. The narrow course of Tremont Street was filled to the brim and overflowing with the waiting scarlet-coated men. Like a river of blood. He left by the kitchen.

**CONNECT TO HISTORY**

1. **Recognizing Effects** What was Johnny's reaction to the news about Lexington? Discuss what roles Johnny and Dr. Warren were to play in the early days of the Revolutionary War.

 See Skillbuilder Handbook, page R11.

**CONNECT TO TODAY**

2. **Researching** Where are there revolutions in the world today?

For more about revolutions . . .

RESEARCH LINKS
CLASSZONE.COM

British troops fire on the Lexington militia on April 19, 1775. The war begins here!

175

# Declaring Independence

**4**

| MAIN IDEA | WHY IT MATTERS NOW | TERMS & NAMES |
|---|---|---|
| Fighting between American and British troops led the colonies to declare their independence. | The United States of America was founded at this time. | Ethan Allen<br>artillery<br>Second Continental Congress<br>Continental Army | Benedict Arnold<br>Declaration of Independence<br>Thomas Jefferson |

**CALIFORNIA STANDARDS**

**7.11.6** Discuss how principles in the Magna Carta were embodied in such documents as the English Bill of Rights and the American Declaration of independence.

**8.1.2** Analyze the philosophy of government expressed in the Declaration of Independence, with an emphasis on government as a means of securing individual rights (e.g., key phrases such as "all men are created equal, that they are endowed by their Creator with certain unalienable Rights").

**CST1** Students explain how major events are related to one another in time.

**HI1** Students explain the central issues and problems from the past, placing people and events in a matrix of time and place.

**HI2** Students understand and distinguish cause, effect, sequence, and correlation in historical events, including the long- and short-term causal relations.

## ONE AMERICAN'S STORY

Abigail Adams and her husband, John Adams, would spend most of the Revolutionary War apart. He was often away in Philadelphia meeting with other Patriot leaders. In his absence, she ran the household and farm in Braintree, Massachusetts, and raised their four children. During their separation, they exchanged many letters. Abigail was a very sharp observer of the political scene. In one letter, she shared her concerns about the future of the American government.

*A VOICE FROM THE PAST*

If we separate from Britain, what Code of Laws will be established? How shall we be governed so as to retain our Liberties? Can any government be free which is not administered by general stated Laws? Who shall frame these Laws? Who will give them force and energy?

**Abigail Adams,** quoted in *Abigail Adams: Witness to a Revolution* by Natalie S. Bober

Abigail Adams was an early advocate of women's rights.

These questions would be answered later. First, a war had to be fought and won.

## The Continental Army Is Formed

After the fighting at Lexington and Concord, militiamen from Massachusetts and other colonies began gathering around Boston. Their numbers eventually reached some 20,000. General Gage decided to move his soldiers from the peninsula opposite Boston to the city itself. Boston was nearly surrounded by water. This fact, he thought, made a colonial attack by land almost impossible.

Not long after, on May 10, 1775, Americans attacked Britain's Fort Ticonderoga on the New York side of Lake Champlain. **Ethan Allen** led

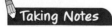

**Taking Notes**

Use your chart to take notes about the start of the Revolution and the Declaration of Independence.

Proclamation of 1763 →

this band of backwoodsmen known as the Green Mountain Boys. They captured the fort and its large supply of **artillery**—cannon and large guns. These guns would be used later to drive the British from Boston.

Also on May 10, the **Second Continental Congress** began meeting in Philadelphia. Delegates included John and Samuel Adams, John Hancock, Benjamin Franklin, George Washington, and Patrick Henry. They agreed to form the **Continental Army**. Washington, who was from Virginia, was chosen as its commanding general. He had served as a colonial officer with the British during the French and Indian War. Congress also authorized the printing of paper money to pay the troops. It was beginning to act as a government.

## The Battle of Bunker Hill

**Background**
The battle was called Bunker Hill because the original plan was to fight the battle there.

Meanwhile, tensions were building in Boston in June 1775. Militiamen seized Bunker Hill and Breed's Hill behind Charlestown. They built fortifications on Breed's Hill. Alarmed, the British decided to attack.

General William Howe crossed the bay with 2,200 British soldiers. Forming in ranks, they marched up Breed's Hill. On the hilltop, the militia waited. According to the legend, Colonel William Prescott ordered, "Don't fire until you see the whites of their eyes!" When the British got close, the militia unleashed murderous fire. The British fell back and then charged again. Finally, they forced the militia off the hill.

The redcoats had won the Battle of Bunker Hill, but at tremendous cost. More than 1,000 were killed or wounded, compared with some 400 militia casualties. "The loss we have sustained is greater than we can bear," wrote General Gage. The inexperienced colonial militia had held its own against the world's most powerful army.

*"Don't fire until you see the whites of their eyes!"*
**Colonel William Prescott**

The bloody fighting between militiamen and British troops is shown in *The Death of General Warren at Bunker Hill* by John Trumbull (1786).

**177**

## A Last Attempt at Peace

Despite this deepening conflict, most colonists still hoped for peace. Even some Patriot leaders considered themselves loyal subjects of the king. They blamed Parliament for the terrible events taking place.

In July 1775, moderates in Congress drafted the Olive Branch Petition and sent it to London. This document asked the king to restore harmony between Britain and the colonies. Some members opposed the petition but signed it anyway as a last hope.

The king rejected the petition, however, and announced new measures to punish the colonies. He would use the British navy to block American ships from leaving their ports. He also would send thousands of hired German soldiers, called Hessians, to fight in America. "When once these rebels have felt a smart blow, they will submit," he declared.

The colonial forces were not going to back down, though. They thought they were equal to the British troops. George Washington knew otherwise. The British soldiers were professionals, while the colonial troops had little training and were poorly equipped. The Massachusetts militia barely had enough gunpowder to fight one battle.

During the summer of 1775, Washington arrived at the militia camp near Boston. He immediately began to gather supplies and train the army. In the fall, Washington approved a bold plan. Continental Army troops would invade Quebec, in eastern Canada. They hoped to defeat British forces there and draw Canadians into the Patriot camp. One of the leaders of this expedition was **Benedict Arnold.** He was an officer who had played a role in the victory at Fort Ticonderoga.

After a grueling march across Maine, Arnold arrived at Quebec in November 1775. By that time, however, winter had set in. Under harsh conditions, the Americans launched their attack but failed. After several months, they limped home in defeat.

## The British Retreat from Boston

In Massachusetts, the Continental Army had surrounded British forces in Boston. Neither side was able or willing to break the standoff. However, help for Washington was on the way. Cannons were being hauled from Fort Ticonderoga. This was a rough job, since there were no roads across the snow-covered mountains. It took soldiers two months to drag the 59 heavy weapons to Boston, where they arrived in January 1776.

**Background**
The olive branch is considered a symbol of peace.

*Reading* **History**
**A. Analyzing Points of View** Why did King George reject the petition?

Armed with these cannons, Washington moved his troops to Dorchester Heights, overlooking Boston. The Americans threatened to bombard the city. General Howe, who was now in charge of the British forces, decided to withdraw his troops. On March 17, about 9,000 British soldiers departed Boston in more than 100 ships. Boston Patriots joyfully reclaimed their city. Although the British had damaged homes and destroyed possessions, Boston was still standing.

More than 1,000 Loyalist supporters left along with the British troops. Anti-British feeling in Boston was so strong that the Loyalists feared for their safety. Some Patriots even called for Loyalists to be hanged as traitors. This did not happen, but Loyalists' homes and property were seized.

*Reading*History

**B. Forming Opinions** Did the Loyalists deserve punishment? Explain.

## *Common Sense* Is Published

In early 1776, most Americans still wanted to avoid a final break with Britain. However, the publication of a pamphlet titled *Common Sense* helped convince many Americans that a complete break with Britain was necessary. Written by Thomas Paine, a recent immigrant from England, this pamphlet made a strong case for American independence.

Paine ridiculed the idea that kings ruled by the will of God. Calling George III "the Royal Brute," Paine argued that all monarchies were corrupt. He also disagreed with the economic arguments for remaining with Britain. "Our corn," he said, "will fetch its price in any market in Europe." He believed that America should follow its own destiny.

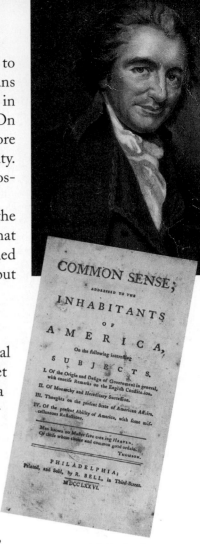

This is the front page of *Common Sense* by Thomas Paine (above). It was one of the most influential political documents in history.

---

### A VOICE FROM THE PAST

Everything that is right or natural pleads for separation. The blood of the slain, the weeping voice of nature cries, "'Tis time to part." Even the distance at which the Almighty has placed England and America is a strong and natural proof that the authority of the one over the other was never the design of heaven.

**Thomas Paine,** *Common Sense*

---

*Common Sense* was an instant success. Published in January, it sold more than 100,000 copies in three months. The call for independence had become a roar.

## A Time of Decision

The Continental Congress remained undecided. A majority of the delegates still did not support independence. Even so, in May 1776, Congress adopted a resolution authorizing each of the 13 colonies to establish its own government.

On June 7, Richard Henry Lee of Virginia introduced a key resolution. It called the colonies "free and independent states" and declared

### HISTORY through ART

The Declaration of Independence is presented for adoption to the Continental Congress by John Adams, Roger Sherman, Robert Livingston, Thomas Jefferson, and Benjamin Franklin (left to right). John Trumbull painted this work many years after the adoption of the Declaration on July 4, 1776.

**What is the artist trying to show about the mood of the American leaders as they declare independence?**

that "all political connection between them and the state of Great Britain is . . . totally dissolved."

Congress debated the resolution, but not all the delegates were ready to vote on it. They did, however, appoint a committee to draft a **Declaration of Independence**. The committee included Benjamin Franklin, John Adams, Roger Sherman, Robert Livingston, and **Thomas Jefferson**.

The group chose Jefferson to compose the Declaration. Two reasons for selecting Jefferson were that he was an excellent writer and that he came from Virginia. The members knew that no independence movement could succeed without Virginia's support. Jefferson immediately went to work. In two weeks, he had prepared most of the Declaration. (See pages 182–185.) On July 2, 1776, Congress considered Lee's resolution again. Despite some strong opposition, the measure passed. From this point forward, the colonies considered themselves independent.

## The Declaration Is Adopted

The Liberty Bell was rung to announce the first public reading of the Declaration of Independence, in Philadelphia on July 8, 1776.

Two days later, on July 4, 1776, Congress adopted the document that proclaimed independence—the Declaration of Independence. John Hancock, the president of the Congress, was the first to sign the Declaration. According to tradition, he wrote in large letters and commented, "There, I guess King George will be able to read that." The core idea of the Declaration is based on the philosophy of John Locke. This idea is that people have unalienable rights, or rights that government cannot take away. Jefferson stated this belief in what was to become the Declaration's best-known passage.

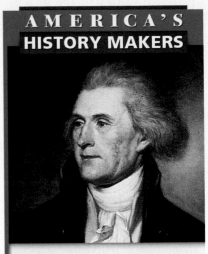

## AMERICA'S HISTORY MAKERS

### A VOICE FROM THE PAST

We hold these truths to be self-evident, that all men are created equal, that they are endowed by their Creator with certain unalienable Rights, that among these are Life, Liberty and the pursuit of Happiness.

**Thomas Jefferson,** The Declaration of Independence

*Reading* **History**

**C. Summarizing**
When does the Declaration say it is right to overthrow an established government?

If a government disregards these rights, Jefferson explained, it loses its right to govern. The people then have the right to abolish that government, by force if necessary. They can form a new government that will protect their rights. When Jefferson spoke of "the people," however, he meant only free white men. Women and enslaved persons were left out of the Declaration.

The Declaration also explained the reasons for breaking with Britain. It then declared the colonies to be free and independent states. This was a very serious action—treason from the British point of view—and the delegates knew it. John Hancock urged the delegates to stand together in mutual defense. Each realized that if the war were to be lost, they would most likely be hanged.

The Declaration closed with this pledge: "And for the support of this Declaration, with a firm reliance on the protection of divine Providence, we mutually pledge to each other our Lives, our Fortunes, and our sacred Honor."

Americans had declared independence. Now they had to win their freedom on the battlefield.

**THOMAS JEFFERSON**
**1743–1826**

Jefferson was just 33 when chosen to write the Declaration of Independence. He was already a brilliant thinker and writer and a highly respected political leader. Jefferson came from a wealthy Virginia family. As a child, he was interested in everything, and he became an inventor, scientist, and architect, among other things. In 1769, he began his political career in the House of Burgesses.

Jefferson felt that writing the Declaration was a major achievement of his life. He had that fact carved on his tombstone.

**Why do you think Jefferson felt the Declaration was one of his greatest achievements?**

## Section 4 Assessment

### 1. Terms & Names

**Explain the significance of:**
- Ethan Allen
- artillery
- Second Continental Congress
- Continental Army
- Benedict Arnold
- Declaration of Independence
- Thomas Jefferson

### 2. Using Graphics

Use the chart below to explain colonial views for and against independence.

**Views About Independence**

| | |
|---|---|
| For | |
| Against | |

What is the strongest reason for independence? against independence? (REP5)

### 3. Main Ideas

**a.** What challenges did George Washington face in forming the army? (HI1)

**b.** What forced the British to leave Boston? (HI1)

**c.** What is *Common Sense*? (HI1)

### 4. Critical Thinking

**Drawing Conclusions**
Why did it take colonists so long to declare independence? (REP1)

**THINK ABOUT**
- the colonists' British traditions
- the risk of revolution

### ACTIVITY OPTIONS

**ART**

**LANGUAGE ARTS**

Find out more about a person discussed in this section. Create a **trading card** or write a **biography** of that person. (REP3)

# The Declaration of Independence

**CALIFORNIA STANDARDS**

**8.1.2** Analyze the philosophy of government expressed in the Declaration of Independence, with an emphasis on government as a means of securing individual rights (e.g., key phrases such as "all men are created equal, that they are endowed by their Creator with certain unalienable Rights").

**Reading 2.2** Analyze text that uses proposition and support patterns.

**Setting the Stage** On July 4, 1776, the Second Continental Congress adopted what became one of America's most cherished documents. Written by Thomas Jefferson, the Declaration of Independence voiced the reasons for separating from Britain and provided the principles of government upon which the United States would be built. **See Primary Source Explorer**

## [Preamble]

When in the Course of human events, it becomes necessary for one people to dissolve the political bands which have connected them with another, and to assume among the powers of the earth, the separate and equal station to which the Laws of Nature and of Nature's God entitle them, a decent respect to the opinions of mankind requires that they should declare the causes which impel them to the separation.

## [The Right of the People to Control Their Government]

We hold these truths to be self-evident, that all men are created equal, that they are **endowed**[1] by their Creator with certain **unalienable**[2] Rights, that among these are Life, Liberty and the pursuit of Happiness; that, to secure these rights, Governments are instituted among Men, deriving their just powers from the consent of the governed; that whenever any Form of Government becomes destructive of these ends, it is the Right of the People to alter or to abolish it, and to institute new Government, laying its foundation on such principles and organizing its powers in such form, as to them shall seem most likely to effect their Safety and Happiness. Prudence, indeed, will dictate that Governments long established should not be changed for light and transient causes; and accordingly all experience hath shewn that mankind are more disposed to suffer, while evils are sufferable, than to right themselves by abolishing the forms to which they are accustomed. But when a long train of abuses and **usurpations**,[3] pursuing invariably the same Object, evinces a design to reduce them under absolute **Despotism**,[4] it is their right, it is their duty, to throw off such Government, and to provide new Guards for their future security.

Such has been the patient sufferance of these Colonies; and such is now the necessity which constrains them to alter their former Systems of Government. The history of the present King of Great Britain is a history of repeated injuries and usurpations, all having in direct object the establishment of an absolute Tyranny over these States. To prove this, let facts be submitted to a **candid**[5] world.

### A CLOSER LOOK

**RIGHTS OF THE PEOPLE**

The ideas in this passage reflect the views of John Locke. Locke was an English philosopher who believed that the natural rights of individuals came from God, but that a government's power comes from the consent of the governed. This belief is the foundation of modern democracy.

**1. In what way can American voters bring about changes in their government?**

---

1. **endowed:** provided.
2. **unalienable:** unable to be taken away.
3. **usurpations:** unjust seizures of power.
4. **Despotism:** rule by a tyrant with absolute power.
5. **candid:** fair, impartial.

## [Tyrannical Acts of the British King]

He has refused his Assent to Laws, the most wholesome and necessary for the public good.

He has forbidden his Governors to pass Laws of immediate and pressing importance, unless suspended in their operation till his assent should be obtained; and, when so suspended, he has utterly neglected to attend to them.

He has refused to pass other Laws for the accommodation of large districts of people, unless those people would **relinquish**[6] the right of Representation in the Legislature, a right inestimable to them, and formidable to tyrants only.

He has called together legislative bodies at places unusual, uncomfortable, and distant from the depository of their public Records, for the sole purpose of fatiguing them into compliance with his measures.

He has dissolved Representative Houses repeatedly, for opposing with manly firmness his invasions on the rights of the people.

He has refused for a long time, after such dissolutions, to cause others to be elected; whereby the Legislative powers, incapable of Annihilation, have returned to the people at large for their exercise; the State remaining in the mean time exposed to all the dangers of invasions from without, and **convulsions**[7] within.

He has endeavoured to prevent the population of these States; for that purpose obstructing the Laws for **Naturalization**[8] of Foreigners; refusing to pass others to encourage their migration hither, and raising the conditions of new Appropriations of Lands.

He has obstructed the Administration of Justice, by refusing his Assent to Laws for establishing Judiciary powers.

He has made Judges dependent on his Will alone, for the **tenure**[9] of their offices, and the amount and payment of their salaries.

He has erected a multitude of New Offices, and sent hither swarms of Officers to harass our people and **eat out their substance**.[10]

He has kept among us, in times of peace, Standing Armies, without the Consent of our legislatures.

He has affected to render the Military independent of and superior to the Civil power. He has combined with others to subject us to a jurisdiction foreign to our constitution and unacknowledged by our laws; giving his Assent to their Acts of pretended Legislation:

For **quartering**[11] large bodies of armed troops among us;

For protecting them, by a mock Trial, from punishment for any Murders which they should commit on the Inhabitants of these States;

For cutting off our Trade with all parts of the world;

### A CLOSER LOOK

**GRIEVANCES AGAINST BRITAIN**

The list contains 27 offenses by the British king and others against the colonies. Many offenses violate protections agreed to in 1215 in the Magna Carta. The list helps explain why it became necessary to seek independence.

**2. Which offense do you think was the worst? Why?**

### A CLOSER LOOK

**LOSS OF REPRESENTATIVE GOVERNMENT**

One of the Intolerable Acts of 1774 stripped the Massachusetts Legislature of many powers and gave them to the colony's British governor.

**3. Why was this action so "intolerable"?**

### A CLOSER LOOK

**QUARTERING TROOPS WITHOUT CONSENT**

The Quartering Act of 1765 required colonists to provide housing and supplies for British troops in America.

**4. Why did colonists object to this act?**

---

6. **relinquish:** give up.
7. **convulsions:** violent disturbances.
8. **Naturalization:** process of becoming a citizen.
9. **tenure:** term.
10. **eat out their substance:** drain their resources.
11. **quartering:** housing or giving lodging to.

**A CLOSER LOOK**

**TAXATION WITHOUT REPRESENTATION**

The colonists believed in the long-standing British tradition that Parliament could tax only those citizens it represented—and the colonists claimed to have no representation in Parliament.

**5. How do persons today give consent to taxation?**

For imposing Taxes on us without our Consent;

For depriving us, in many cases, of the benefits of Trial by Jury;

For transporting us beyond Seas to be tried for pretended offenses;

For abolishing the free System of English Laws in a neighboring Province, establishing therein an **Arbitrary**[12] government, and enlarging its Boundaries so as to render it at once an example and fit instrument for introducing the same absolute rule into these Colonies;

For taking away our Charters, abolishing our most valuable laws, and altering fundamentally the Forms of our Governments;

For suspending our own Legislatures, and declaring themselves invested with power to legislate for us in all cases whatsoever.

He has **abdicated**[13] Government here, by declaring us out of his Protection and waging War against us.

He has plundered our seas, ravaged our Coasts, burnt our towns, and destroyed the lives of our people.

He is at this time transporting large Armies of **foreign Mercenaries**[14] to compleat the works of death, desolation, and tyranny, already begun with circumstances of Cruelty & **perfidy**[15] scarcely paralleled in the most barbarous ages, and totally unworthy the Head of a civilized nation.

He has constrained our fellow Citizens, taken Captive on the high Seas, to bear Arms against their Country, to become the executioners of their friends and Brethren, or to fall themselves by their Hands.

He has excited **domestic insurrections**[16] amongst us, and has endeavoured to bring on the inhabitants of our frontiers the merciless Indian Savages, whose known rule of warfare is an undistinguished destruction of all ages, sexes and conditions.

## [Efforts of the Colonies to Avoid Separation]

In every stage of these Oppressions We have **Petitioned for Redress**[17] in the most humble terms; Our repeated Petitions have been answered only by repeated injury. A Prince, whose character is thus marked by every act which may define a Tyrant, is unfit to be the ruler of a free people.

Nor have We been wanting in attentions to our British brethren. We have warned them from time to time of attempts by their legislature to extend an unwarrantable jurisdiction over us. We have reminded them of the circumstances of our emigration and settlement here. We have appealed to their native justice and **magnanimity**,[18] and we have conjured them by the ties of our common kindred, to disavow these usurpations, which would inevitably interrupt our connections and correspondence. They too have been deaf to

**A CLOSER LOOK**

**PETITIONING THE KING**

The colonists sent many petitions to King George III. In the Olive Branch Petition of 1775, the colonists expressed their desire to achieve "a happy and permanent reconciliation." The king rejected the petition.

**6. Why did the colonists at first attempt to solve the dispute and remain loyal?**

12. **Arbitrary:** not limited by law.
13. **abdicated:** given up.
14. **foreign Mercenaries:** professional soldiers hired to serve in a foreign army.
15. **perfidy:** dishonesty, disloyalty.
16. **domestic insurrections:** rebellions at home.
17. **Petitioned for Redress:** asked for the correction of wrongs.
18. **magnanimity:** generosity, forgiveness.

the voice of justice and of **consanguinity**.[19] We must, therefore, **acquiesce**[20] in the necessity, which denounces our Separation, and hold them, as we hold the rest of mankind, Enemies in War, in Peace Friends.

## [The Colonies Are Declared Free and Independent]

We, therefore, the Representatives of the United States of America, in General Congress, Assembled, appealing to the Supreme Judge of the world for the **rectitude**[21] of our intentions, do, in the name, and by the Authority of the good People of these Colonies solemnly publish and declare, That these United Colonies are, and of Right ought to be, Free and Independent States; that they are Absolved from all Allegiance to the British Crown, and that all political connection between them and the State of Great Britain is, and ought to be, totally dissolved; and that as Free and Independent States, they have full Power to levy War, conclude Peace, contract Alliances, establish Commerce, and do all other Acts and Things which Independent States may of right do.

And for the support of this Declaration, with a firm reliance on the protection of divine Providence, we mutually pledge to each other our Lives, our Fortunes, and our sacred Honor. [Signed by]

John Hancock *President, from Massachusetts*

[**Georgia**] Button Gwinnett; Lyman Hall; George Walton

[**Rhode Island**] Stephen Hopkins; William Ellery

[**Connecticut**] Roger Sherman; Samuel Huntington; William Williams; Oliver Wolcott

[**North Carolina**] William Hooper; Joseph Hewes; John Penn

[**South Carolina**] Edward Rutledge; Thomas Heyward, Jr.; Thomas Lynch, Jr.; Arthur Middleton

[**Maryland**] Samuel Chase; William Paca; Thomas Stone; Charles Carroll

[**Virginia**] George Wythe; Richard Henry Lee; Thomas Jefferson; Benjamin Harrison; Thomas Nelson, Jr.; Francis Lightfoot Lee; Carter Braxton

[**Pennsylvania**] Robert Morris; Benjamin Rush; Benjamin Franklin; John Morton; George Clymer; James Smith; George Taylor; James Wilson; George Ross

[**Delaware**] Caesar Rodney; George Read; Thomas McKean

[**New York**] William Floyd; Philip Livingston; Francis Lewis; Lewis Morris

[**New Jersey**] Richard Stockton; John Witherspoon; Francis Hopkinson; John Hart; Abraham Clark

[**New Hampshire**] Josiah Bartlett; William Whipple; Matthew Thornton

[**Massachusetts**] Samuel Adams; John Adams; Robert Treat Paine; Elbridge Gerry

**A CLOSER LOOK**

**POWERS OF AN INDEPENDENT GOVERNMENT**

The colonists identified the ability to wage war and agree to peace; to make alliances with other nations; and to set up an economic system as powers of a free and independent government.

**7. What other powers are held by an independent government?**

**A CLOSER LOOK**

**DECLARATION SIGNERS**

The Declaration was signed by 56 representatives from the 13 original states.

**8. Which signers do you recognize? Write one line about each of those signers.**

19. **consanguinity:** relationship by a common ancestor; close connection.

20. **acquiesce:** accept without protest.

21. **rectitude:** moral uprightness.

## Interactive Primary Source Assessment

### 1. Main Ideas

**a.** What is the purpose of the Declaration of Independence as stated in the Preamble? (8.1.2)

**b.** What are the five main parts of the Declaration? (8.1.2)

**c.** What are three rights that all people have? (8.1.2)

### 2. Critical Thinking

**Drawing Conclusions** Why did the colonies feel that they had to declare their independence? (REP4)

**THINK ABOUT**

• colonial grievances against Britain

• Britain's response to these grievances

## The Road to Revolution (CST2)

**1763** — Proclamation of 1763

**1764** — Sugar Act

**1765** — Quartering Act; Stamp Act; Sons of Liberty; Stamp Act Congress

**1766** — Repeal of Stamp Act; Declaratory Act

**1767** — Townshend Acts; Suspension of New York Assembly

**1768** — Occupation of Boston by British troops

**1769** — Daughters of Liberty

**1770** — Boston Massacre; Repeal of all Townshend Acts except tea tax

**1772** — Committees of Correspondence

**1773** — Tea Act; Boston Tea Party

**1774** — Intolerable Acts; First Continental Congress; Boycott of British goods

**1775** — Battles of Lexington and Concord; Second Continental Congress; Appointment of Washington as commander of Continental Army; Battle of Bunker Hill; Olive Branch Petition

**1776** — *Common Sense;* Declaration of Independence

## TERMS & NAMES

Briefly explain the significance of each of the following.

1. Stamp Act
2. Sons of Liberty
3. writs of assistance
4. Samuel Adams
5. Boston Tea Party
6. militia
7. Lexington and Concord
8. Loyalist
9. Declaration of Independence
10. Thomas Jefferson

## REVIEW QUESTIONS

### Tighter British Control (pages 159–162)

1. How did relations between Britain and the colonies change after the Seven Years' War? (HI2)
2. Why did Britain try to tax the colonies? (HI1)
3. Why did the colonists cry, "No taxation without representation"? (HI1)

### Colonial Resistance Grows (pages 163–169)

4. How did the colonists protest the Townshend Acts? (HI2)
5. How was the Boston Massacre used for propaganda purposes? (HI1)
6. How did the committees of correspondence help keep people informed? (HI2)

### The Road to Lexington and Concord (pages 170–175)

7. Why was the First Continental Congress held? (HI2)
8. What was the Midnight Ride? (HI1)

### Declaring Independence (pages 176–185)

9. What was the Battle of Bunker Hill? (HI1)
10. What was the core idea of the Declaration of Independence? (REP4)

## CRITICAL THINKING

### 1. USING YOUR NOTES: SEQUENCING EVENTS

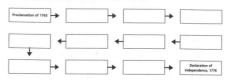

Using your completed chart, answer the questions below. (CST2)

a. What city was the site of early protest activity?

b. What event happened after the Tea Act?

### 2. ANALYZING LEADERSHIP

How did colonial leaders differ in their methods of defending and securing basic rights for the colonies? (HI1)

### 3. APPLYING CITIZENSHIP SKILLS

Did colonial leaders have a responsibility to include women, African Americans, and other groups in the Declaration of Independence? Explain. (REP4)

### 4. THEME: IMPACT OF THE INDIVIDUAL

How did John Adams's role as lawyer for the British soldiers involved in the Boston Massacre help set a tone for the Revolutionary cause? (HI1)

### 5. DRAWING CONCLUSIONS

What factors and events led the colonies to seek independence? (HI2)

### 6. SUPPORTING OPINIONS

Do you think the American Revolution would have occurred if Britain had not taxed the colonies? Why or why not? (HI4)

### Interact *with* History

Now that you have read about the road to revolution, do you consider your decision made at the beginning of the chapter to join or not join the protest a wise choice or a poor choice? Explain.

Use the map and your knowledge of U.S. history to answer questions 1 and 2.

Additional Test Practice, pp. S1–S33.

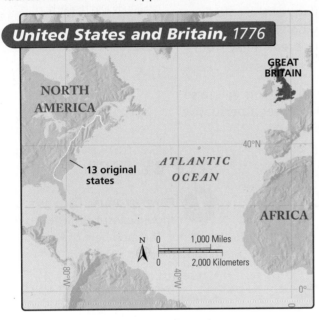

**United States and Britain, 1776**

GREAT BRITAIN

NORTH AMERICA

ATLANTIC OCEAN

13 original states

40°N

AFRICA

N

0        1,000 Miles

0        2,000 Kilometers

80°W    40°W    0°

1. What does the yellow shaded area on the map represent? (7.11.1)
   A. the original colonies
   B. Great Britain
   C. North America
   D. the United States

2. What is the approximate distance between the northernmost colony and Great Britain? (7.11.1)
   A. 1,000 miles
   B. 2,000 kilometers
   C. 3,000 miles
   D. 5,000 kilometers

This quotation from James Otis is about the use of search warrants by the British. Use the quotation and your knowledge of U.S. history to answer question 3.

### PRIMARY SOURCE

It appears to me the worst instrument of arbitrary power, the most destructive of English liberty and the fundamental principles of law, that was ever found in an English law-book.

**James Otis, Jr.,** quoted in *James Otis: The Pre-Revolutionist* by J. C. Ridpath

3. What conclusion can you draw about Otis's point of view? (8.1.2)
   A. Otis believed that the searches would benefit the colonists.
   B. Otis realized that British searches were more important than colonial liberties.
   C. Otis believed that colonists were entitled to certain liberties.
   D. Otis thought the searches were right.

**TEST PRACTICE**
CLASSZONE.COM

## ALTERNATIVE ASSESSMENT

### 1. 📝 WRITING ABOUT HISTORY

Colonists had divided opinions about the Boston Tea Party. Suppose you are a pollster, attempting to gather data about public opinion. Write **quotations** from five colonists who support the Tea Party and another five quotes from people who condemn the act. (REP5)

• You can write your quotations based on information found in books or on the Internet.

• Using a word processor, you can use different type sizes and fonts to emphasize the question you pose and the two opposing responses.

### 2. COOPERATIVE LEARNING

Participate in a class debate modeled after the discussions held by members of the Continental Congress concerning independence and the slave trade. (REP5)

## INTEGRATED TECHNOLOGY ACTIVITY

### PARTICIPATING IN A NET SIMULATION

Go to *NetSimulations: Boston Massacre* at **classzone.com** to participate in the jury trial of Captain Thomas Preston. He and the soldiers of the 29th British Regiment have been arrested for the murder of five citizens. (REP4)

• Use the information in this chapter and the simulation to review the events surrounding the Boston Massacre. Use the Juror's Journal to take notes.

• Read Captain Preston's statement, then begin questioning the prosecution and defense witnesses. Answer the questions in the Juror's Journal to record the evidence you hear.

• Listen to each attorney's closing arguments, then enter your verdict.

**NET SIMULATION**
CLASSZONE.COM

# Raise the Liberty Pole

In 1765, the Sons of Liberty gathered around a huge elm tree in Boston that they named the Liberty Tree. It became a meeting place where people voiced their protests against British policies. Replicas of the Liberty Tree—giant poles sometimes decorated with the flags of the colonies—were raised throughout the colonies. These liberty poles represented the unity of the American colonies as they struggled to break away from British rule.

**ACTIVITY** Like the American Patriots, each group of students will raise its own liberty pole. Each group also will write and deliver a persuasive speech supporting the cause of the American colonies.

**CALIFORNIA STANDARDS**

**REP1** Students frame questions that can be answered by historical study and research.

**Writing 2.4** Write persuasive compositions.

## TOOLBOX

Each group will need:

scissors

poster board

pencil

markers

masking tape

3 cardboard tubes from wrapping paper

construction paper

twine

stapler

## STEP BY STEP

**1 Form groups.** Each group should consist of four or five students. The members of your group will do the following jobs:

- research each colony
- design and create flags
- construct a pole
- write and deliver a speech

**2 Do research on the 13 colonies.** For each colony, your group should find a person, place, or object that represents that colony. For example, a Pilgrim's hat might represent Massachusetts. The 13 colonies are listed below.

| New England Colonies | Middle Colonies | Southern Colonies |
|---|---|---|
| Massachusetts (including Maine) | New York | North Carolina |
| New Hampshire | Delaware | Virginia |
| Connecticut | New Jersey | Maryland |
| Rhode Island | Pennsylvania | South Carolina |
| | | Georgia |

Members of the Sons of Liberty raise a liberty pole in July 1776 to celebrate America's independence.

**3** **Design and create 13 flags for the colonies.** Decide what person, place, or object you will use on your flag for each colony. Cut each flag out of the poster board. Sketch your design on the flag with a pencil. Then use markers to decorate it. On the back of each flag, explain how your design portrays the characteristics of that colony.

**4** **Construct the pole.** Using masking tape, fasten the three cardboard tubes together to form one long tube. Then reinforce the tube by taping construction paper around it.

**5** **String the flags on the pole.** Feed a piece of twine through the open ends of the long tube. Tie the ends of the twine together to form a tight loop. Now staple all 13 flags to the twine.

**6** **Raise your liberty pole.** Lean your liberty pole next to a small table or desk. Take turns with members of your group and visit other liberty poles. As students visit your station, explain the significance of your flag designs.

## WRITE AND SPEAK

Write a persuasive speech to recruit others to join the cause of liberty. In your speech, explain what is wrong with British policies. Give reasons why the colonies should become independent. Then read your speech to the other groups as part of the recruitment process.

## HELP DESK

For related information on the Liberty Tree, see pages 161–162 in Chapter 6.

### Researching Your Project

- *The Revolutionary War* by Bart McDowell

- *The American Revolutionaries* edited by Milton Meltzer

For more about the American Revolution . . .

**RESEARCH LINKS**
CLASSZONE.COM

### Did You Know?

The numbers 45 and 92 played an important part in the history of these liberty poles. The 45th issue of a British newspaper openly criticized the king in 1763 and was reprinted in the colonies. In 1768, 92 members of the Massachusetts General Assembly voted against canceling a letter to the other 12 colonies that called for action against Britain. To represent the numbers, 92 members of the Sons of Liberty would often raise liberty poles to a height of about 45 feet.

### REFLECT & ASSESS

- How well do your flags represent the colonies?

- How clearly does your speech explain grievances against the British?

- Why do you think the practice of raising liberty poles spread to many of the colonies?

# The American Revolution 1776–1783

This painting shows General Washington and his troops in their winter camp at Valley Forge.

**1776**
British capture New York, but Americans win a battle in New Jersey.

**1777**
Battles of Saratoga convince Europeans that America might win the war.

**1778**
France enters the war on the American side.

**1779**
American frontier soldiers take a British fort in what is now Indiana.

USA
World   1776

**1776**
Scotsman Adam Smith publishes a book saying that government shouldn't control the economy.

**1778**
Voltaire, who wrote about the rights of people, dies in Paris.

## Interact *with* History

It is 1777. Your brother is an American soldier. In his last letter to you, he wrote that the army has no shoes or bullets and little food. But he plans to keep fighting.

Now, a British army is coming toward your farm. You hear that the soldiers are stealing crops to feed themselves and their horses.

# What would you sacrifice to win freedom?

### What Do You Think?

• What sacrifices do civilians make during wartime?

• What sacrifices do soldiers make?

• Is it worth such sacrifices to win independence for your country? Why or why not?

**RESEARCH LINKS**
CLASSZONE.COM
Visit the Chapter 7 links for more information about the American Revolution.

---

**1780**
Moving south, the British capture Charles Town (Charleston).

**1781**
In the war's last big battle, the Americans and French defeat the British at Yorktown.

**1783**
Treaty of Paris ends the war.

**1783**

**1781**
Emperor Joseph II of Austria ends serfdom, which forced peasants to farm someone else's land for life.

**1783**
Simón Bolívar, who will become a revolutionary leader in South America, is born in what is now Venezuela.

# Reading Strategy: Sequencing Events

## What Do You Know?

What stories do you know about the people or events of the Revolution? How do people display courage and self-sacrifice during wartime?

### Think About

- what you've learned about American settlers from movies, television, historical fiction, or science fiction about space travel
- opportunities and challenges offered in a new land
- your responses to the Interact with History about sacrificing to win freedom (see page 191)

**CALIFORNIA STANDARDS**

**Reading 2.0** Students read and understand grade-level-appropriate material. They describe and connect the essential ideas, arguments, and perspectives of the text by using their knowledge of text structure, organization, and purpose.

## What Do You Want to Know?

 What would you like to learn about the steps that people took to win the American Revolution? In your notebook, record what you hope to learn from this chapter.

## Sequencing Events

To sequence is to put events in the order in which they happened. You learned this skill in Chapter 6 by sequencing the events that led to the American Revolution. Now as you read Chapter 7, practice sequencing again. Put the major battles and events of the war in order by recording them on a time line. Copy the time line below in your notebook. You may want to make it bigger.

 **See Skillbuilder Handbook, page R4.**

### Taking Notes

# The Early Years of the War

| MAIN IDEA | WHY IT MATTERS NOW | TERMS & NAMES |
|---|---|---|
| The American desire to gain rights and liberties led them to fight for independence from Britain. | Today those same rights and liberties are protected by the U.S. Constitution. | George Washington<br>mercenary<br>strategy<br>rendezvous<br>Battles of Saratoga |

## ONE AMERICAN'S STORY

In search of liberty, Haym Salomon moved from Europe to New York sometime between 1764 and 1775. He was a Jew from Poland. Salomon soon became a successful merchant and banker. During the war, Salomon supported the Patriot cause.

When the British captured New York in 1776, many Patriots fled but Salomon stayed. The British arrested him. Salomon spoke many languages. The British thought he could help them deal with foreign merchants, so they let him out of prison. Salomon used this opportunity to help other prisoners escape.

In 1778, the British wanted to arrest him again, so he fled to Philadelphia and continued to aid the Patriots. He loaned the new government more than $600,000, which was never repaid.

Like Salomon, many people made hard choices about which side to support during the Revolutionary War. This section discusses those choices and the obstacles Americans faced in the war's early years.

Haym Salomon sacrificed his health and his fortune to help his new country.

CALIFORNIA STANDARDS

**8.1** Students understand the major events preceding the founding of the nation and relate their significance to the development of American constitutional democracy.

**CST1** Students explain how major events are related to one another in time.

**HI1** Students explain the central issues and problems from the past, placing people and events in a matrix of time and place.

**HI2** Students understand and distinguish cause, effect, sequence, and correlation in historical events, including the long- and short-term causal relations.

**HI4** Students recognize the role of chance, foresight, and error in history.

## Americans Divided

The issue of separating from Great Britain divided American society. Opinion polls did not exist in the 1700s, so we don't know exactly how many people were on each side. But historians estimate that roughly 20 to 30 percent of Americans were Loyalists, roughly 40 to 45 percent were Patriots, and the rest remained neutral. Most Americans did not support the Revolution.

Both Patriots and Loyalists came from all walks of life and all parts of America. In general, New England and Virginia had high numbers of Patriots. Loyalists were numerous in cities, in New York State, and in the

**Taking Notes**

Use your chart to take notes about the early years of the American Revolution.

*The American Revolution* **193**

South. Many Loyalists worked for the British government or were clergy in the Church of England. Some Quakers were Loyalists, although many wanted peace. (Their faith taught that war was wrong.)

The war divided Native Americans, too. For instance, some Iroquois nations fought with the British and others with the Americans. Those Native Americans who joined the British feared that if the Americans won, they would take Native American land. Some Native Americans who lived near colonists and interacted with them sided with the Americans.

**Background**
The Iroquois League had generally kept peace among the Iroquois nations for about 200 years—until the American Revolution.

African Americans also fought on both sides. At first, slave owners feared that African Americans who had guns might lead slave revolts. Therefore, few states allowed African Americans to enlist, or sign up with the army. Then a British governor offered freedom to any enslaved person who joined the British army. Many slaves ran away to fight for the British. In response, most states began to accept African-American soldiers. In all, about 5,000 African Americans served in the Continental Army. Many African Americans who did so hoped that American independence would bring greater equality.

Differences over the war split families, too. For example, Benjamin Franklin's son William took Britain's side. The father and son stopped speaking.

## Creating an Army

Because not everyone supported the war, raising an army was difficult. The army also faced other problems. In June 1775, **George Washington** became the commander of the Continental Army. At first, this new national army was formed from state militias, made up of untrained and undisciplined volunteers.

After Congress created the Continental Army, men began to enlist, but most of them didn't stay long. At the start of the war, Congress asked men to enlist only for one year. Later Congress did lengthen the term of service. When the soldiers' time was up, they went home. As a result, Washington's army never numbered more than 17,000 men.

Congress's inability to supply the army also frustrated Washington. The soldiers needed everything—blankets, shoes, food, and even guns and ammunition. Angrily, Washington wrote, "Could I have foreseen what I have, and am likely to experience, no consideration upon earth should have induced [persuaded] me to accept this command."

Many women tried to help the army. Martha Washington and other wives followed their husbands to army camps. The women cooked, did laundry, and

*Reading*History
**A. Analyzing Causes** Why would the lack of agreement about the war make it hard to raise an army?

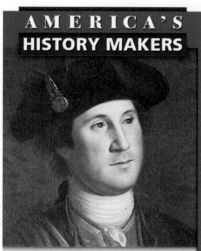

**AMERICA'S HISTORY MAKERS**

**GEORGE WASHINGTON**
**1732–1799**

At the age of 16, George Washington worked as a surveyor, setting land boundaries in the wilderness. He learned to handle hardship by hunting for food and sleeping outdoors.

In the French and Indian War, Washington had many brushes with death. Yet he wrote, "I heard the bullets whistle, and, believe me, there is something charming in the sound."

That war made him the most famous American officer. People loved him for his courage. As commander of the Continental Army, Washington's popularity helped unite Americans.

**How did Washington's early life prepare him to lead the army?**

nursed sick or wounded soldiers. A few women even helped fight. Mary Hays earned the nickname "Molly Pitcher" by carrying water to tired soldiers during a battle. Deborah Sampson dressed as a man, enlisted, and fought in several engagements.

Building an army was crucial to Washington's plan. To the British, the Americans were disorganized, inexperienced rebels. The British thought that if they won a decisive battle, the Americans would give up. By contrast, Washington's main goal was to survive. To do so, he needed to keep an army in the field, win some battles—no matter how small—and avoid a crushing defeat. He knew he could not hope to win a major battle until he had a large, well-equipped army.

*Reading*History
**B. Solving Problems** How did Washington try to solve the problem of leading a small, inexperienced force against a large professional army?

These Hessian boots weighed about 12 pounds a pair.

## Struggle for the Middle States

As Chapter 6 explains, Washington had forced the British to retreat from Boston in March 1776. He then hurried his army to New York City, where he expected the British to go next. One British goal was to occupy coastal cities so that their navy could land troops and supplies in those cities. From there, they could launch their military campaigns.

Washington's hunch was correct. In July 1776, Britain's General William Howe arrived in New York with a large army. Then in August, more soldiers arrived, including about 9,000 Hessian mercenaries. A **mercenary** is a professional soldier hired to fight for a foreign country. British soldiers usually signed up for life—which discouraged enlistment. So Britain needed mercenaries, whom it hired from the German states.

**Background**
The British-hired mercenaries came from a part of Germany called Hesse, which is the origin of the term *Hessian*.

For several months, the British and American armies fought for New York State. Finally, the British forced Washington to retreat through New Jersey. By December, when the American army crossed the Delaware River into Pennsylvania, it was in terrible condition. Charles Willson Peale, a Philadelphia painter who watched the crossing, saw one muddy soldier who "had lost all his clothes. He was in an old, dirty blanket jacket, his beard long, and his face so full of sores he could not clean it." To Peale's shock, the soldier called his name. He was Peale's brother!

Political writer Thomas Paine also witnessed the hard conditions and the soldiers' low spirits on the retreat. To

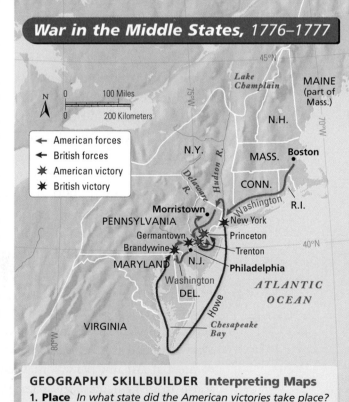

### War in the Middle States, 1776–1777

Legend:
← American forces
← British forces
✳ American victory
✳ British victory

0 100 Miles
0 200 Kilometers

Lake Champlain
MAINE (part of Mass.)
N.H.
N.Y.
MASS.   Boston
CONN.
R.I.
Morristown
PENNSYLVANIA
New York
Germantown
Princeton
Brandywine
Trenton
MARYLAND   N.J.
Philadelphia
Washington
DEL.
ATLANTIC OCEAN
VIRGINIA
Chesapeake Bay
Delaware R.
Hudson R.
Washington
Howe

**GEOGRAPHY SKILLBUILDER Interpreting Maps**
1. **Place** In what state did the American victories take place?
2. **Movement** How did the British general Howe travel from New York to Brandywine?

**Thomas Sully's** *Passage of the Delaware* **shows Washington at the Delaware River, leading to the American attack on the British at Trenton, New Jersey.**

urge them to keep fighting, Paine published the first in a series of pamphlets called *The American Crisis.*

> ### A VOICE FROM THE PAST
>
> These are the times that try men's souls. The summer soldier and the sunshine patriot will, in this crisis, shrink from the service of their country; but he that stands it *now,* deserves the love and thanks of man and woman.
>
> **Thomas Paine,** *The American Crisis*

*Reading* **History**
**C. Recognizing Propaganda** How does this passage promote the American cause?

Washington hoped a victory would encourage his weary men. He also knew that he must attack the British quickly because most of his soldiers would leave once their enlistments ended on December 31.

Late on December 25, 1776, Washington's troops rowed across the icy Delaware River to New Jersey. From there, they marched in bitter, early-morning cold to Trenton to surprise the Hessians, some of whom were sleeping after their Christmas celebration. The Americans captured or killed more than 900 Hessians and gained needed supplies. Washington's army won another victory at Princeton eight days later. These victories proved that the American general was better than the British had thought. The American army began to attract new recruits.

## Britain's Strategy

Meanwhile, the British were pursuing a **strategy**—an overall plan of action—to seize the Hudson River Valley. If successful, they would cut off New England from the other states. The strategy called for three armies to meet at Albany, New York. General John Burgoyne would lead a force south from Canada. Lieutenant Colonel Barry St. Leger would lead his army from Lake Ontario down the Mohawk Valley. Burgoyne expected General Howe to follow the Hudson north from New York City.

Burgoyne left Canada in June 1777 with an army that included British, Hessians, and Iroquois. In July, they captured Fort Ticonderoga.

Called "Gentleman Johnny" by his soldiers, Burgoyne enjoyed traveling slowly and throwing parties to celebrate victories. After Ticonderoga, his delays gave the Americans time to cut down trees to block his route. They also burned crops and drove off cattle, leaving the countryside bare of supplies for the British troops.

Things grew rougher during the last 25 miles of Burgoyne's march to Albany. On a map, the route looked easy, but it really crossed a swampy wilderness. The army had to build bridges and roads. Burgoyne took four weeks to reach the Hudson. Still confident, he looked forward to the **rendezvous,** or meeting, with St. Leger and Howe in Albany.

On August 4, Burgoyne received a message from Howe. He would not be coming north, Howe wrote, because he had decided to invade Pennsylvania to try to capture General Washington and Philadelphia—where the Continental Congress met. "Success be ever with you," wrote Howe. Yet Burgoyne needed Howe's soldiers, not his good wishes.

*Reading* **History**
**D. Evaluating**
Review Howe's two goals for his invasion of Pennsylvania. Was he successful?

Howe did invade Pennsylvania. In September 1777, he defeated but did not capture Washington at the Battle of Brandywine. Howe then occupied Philadelphia. In October, Washington attacked Howe at Germantown. Washington lost the battle, however, and retreated.

## Battles Along the Mohawk

As Burgoyne received Howe's message, St. Leger faced his own obstacle in reaching Albany. In the summer of 1777, he was trying to defeat a small American force at Fort Stanwix in the Mohawk River valley of New York. St. Leger's forces included Iroquois led by Mohawk chief Joseph Brant, also called Thayendanegea (THĪ•ehn•DAHG•ee).

Brant and his sister, Molly, had strong ties to the British. Molly was a British official's wife, and Joseph was a convert to the Church of England. Both Joseph and Molly tried to convince the Iroquois to fight for the British, who upheld Iroquois rights to their land.

**Vocabulary**
**convert:** a person who changes religions

During August 1777, American general Benedict Arnold led a small army up the Mohawk River. He wanted to chase the British away from

### War in the North, 1777

**GEOGRAPHY SKILLBUILDER Interpreting Maps**
1. **Place** *From which two cities did the British invade the United States?*
2. **Movement** *What did St. Leger want to capture by taking the longer route by way of Lake Ontario?*

The Iroquois chief Joseph Brant was a British ally.

Fort Stanwix. Arnold sent a captured Loyalist and some Iroquois who were American allies to spread the rumor that he had a large army.

The trick worked. St. Leger's troops were afraid they were about to be outnumbered. The army retreated so fast that it left behind tents, cannon, and supplies. Because of St. Leger's flight and Howe's refusal to follow the strategy, no one was left to rendezvous with Burgoyne.

## Saratoga: A Turning Point

By this time, Burgoyne's army was running out of supplies, and it needed horses. The general sent a raiding party into Vermont to see what it could find. The raiding party encountered New England troops, who badly defeated it at the Battle of Bennington on August 16, 1777.

Despite this setback, Burgoyne's army headed slowly toward Albany. On the way, it met a powerful Continental Army force led by General Horatio Gates. Gates's soldiers were waiting on a ridge called Bemis Heights, near Saratoga, New York. There the Americans had created fortifications, or built-up earthen walls, behind which to fight. The Polish engineer Tadeusz Kosciuszko (TAH•deh•oosh KAWSH•choosh•kaw) had helped the Americans do this.

Burgoyne would have to break through the fortifications to proceed to Albany. On September 19, he attacked. While Gates commanded the Americans on the ridge, Benedict Arnold led an attack on nearby

*Reading*History
**E. Reading a Map**
Find Saratoga on the map on page 197. Notice how close it is to Burgoyne's goal of Albany.

---

## CITIZENSHIP TODAY

# Exercising Free Speech

The British could have charged Thomas Paine with a crime for writing *The American Crisis.* The crime was sedition, or stirring up rebellion. By saying what he thought, Paine risked going to prison. Today U.S. citizens have the right to speak freely without fear of jail.

Like Thomas Paine, some students have used free speech to urge people to take action. For example, the Sidney Lanier Middle School in Houston, Texas, has published its school newspaper on the Internet. In October 1996, one writer urged other students to get involved in that year's election, saying, "Even though you will not be able to vote yet, you can still influence your parents to do so."

These students are working together to produce a school newspaper.

### How Do You Exercise Free Speech?

1. Working in a small group, choose an issue that you care about. Look through newsmagazines for ideas.

2. Use a cluster diagram to record your feelings and opinions about the issue.

3. As a group, decide what action you think people should take on the issue.

4. Write an article expressing the group's opinion. Each member should read the article and suggest changes. Revise the article.

5. Send the revised article to the editorial page of your school or local newspaper.

 See Citizenship Handbook, page 282.

For more about free speech . . .

 RESEARCH LINKS
CLASSZONE.COM

Freeman's Farm. His men repeatedly charged the British and inflicted heavy casualties. Still, the British held their position.

On October 7, another battle broke out. Again Arnold led daring charges against the British. Although hundreds of muskets were firing at him, he galloped through the battlefield "like a madman," a sergeant later said. Frightened, Burgoyne's Hessian mercenaries began to fall back. Eventually, a bullet tore into Arnold's leg and stopped him. Even so, the Americans forced Burgoyne to retreat.

Burgoyne's army moved slowly through heavy rain to a former army camp at Saratoga. By the time they arrived, the men were exhausted. Some fell in the mud and slept in their wet uniforms. The Continental Army then surrounded Burgoyne's army and fired on it day and night without stopping. Burgoyne decided to surrender. The series of conflicts that led to this surrender is known as the **Battles of Saratoga**.

The Battles of Saratoga had two very different consequences. As Benedict Arnold was recovering from his wound, he married a woman who was a Loyalist. Over time, Arnold came to feel that Congress had not rewarded him enough for his heroic actions at Saratoga and other battles. Influenced by his bitterness and his wife, he betrayed his army. In 1780, he agreed to turn over an American fort to the British. Although his plot was discovered before he could carry it out, he escaped. Even today, the name *Benedict Arnold* is used to mean traitor.

On the positive side, the victory at Saratoga was a turning point in the Revolution. It caused European nations to think that the Americans might win their war for independence. As you will read in Section 2, several European nations decided to help America in its struggle.

*Reading* **History**

**F. Forming and Supporting Opinions** Which of the two consequences of the Battles of Saratoga was more significant? Why?

## Section 1 Assessment

### 1. Terms & Names

**Explain the significance of:**
- George Washington
- mercenary
- strategy
- rendezvous
- Battles of Saratoga

### 2. Using Graphics

Use a cluster diagram like the one shown to list the difficulties Americans faced in the early years of the war.

American Difficulties

Which difficulty do you think was hardest to overcome? (HI1)

### 3. Main Ideas

**a.** How were Americans divided over the issue of separating from Great Britain? (HI1)

**b.** Why was it difficult for George Washington to form and keep a large army? (HI2)

**c.** How did the Battles of Saratoga mark a turning point in the war? (HI2)

### 4. Critical Thinking

**Contrasting** How did the British and American strategies differ during the early years of the war? (HI4)

**THINK ABOUT**
- what the British expected from the Americans
- Washington's main goals for the American army
- why Burgoyne invaded from Canada

**ACTIVITY OPTIONS**

**LANGUAGE ARTS**

**ART**

Learn more about a Revolutionary War leader. Write a brief **biography** or create a **trading card** with a picture on one side and important facts on the other. (REP3)

# The War Expands

| MAIN IDEA | WHY IT MATTERS NOW | TERMS & NAMES |
|---|---|---|
| Some Europeans decided to help America. As the war continued, it spread to the sea and the frontier. | This was the beginning of the United States' formal relationships with other nations. | ally<br>Marquis de Lafayette<br>bayonet<br>desert<br>privateer<br>James Forten<br>John Paul Jones |

**CALIFORNIA STANDARDS**

**8.1.3** Analyze how the American Revolution affected other nations, especially France.

**CST3** Students use a variety of maps and documents to identify physical and cultural features of neighborhoods, cities, states, and countries and to explain the historical migration of people, expansion and disintegration of empires, and the growth of economic systems.

**REP4** Students assess the credibility of primary and secondary sources and draw sound conclusions from them.

**HI1** Students explain the central issues and problems from the past, placing people and events in a matrix of time and place.

## ONE AMERICAN'S STORY

To defeat the British Empire, the United States needed a foreign ally. An **ally** is a country that agrees to help another country achieve a common goal. The ideal ally would share America's goal of defeating Britain. So the United States turned to France—Britain's long-time enemy.

In 1776, Congress sent Benjamin Franklin to France to persuade it to be the ally of the United States. Famous for his experiments with electricity, Franklin became a celebrity in Paris. He wrote to his daughter, saying that medallions with his likeness were popular there.

*Benjamin Franklin*

*A VOICE FROM THE PAST*

These, with the pictures, busts [sculptures of the head and shoulders], and prints (of which copies upon copies are spread everywhere), have made your father's face as well known as that of the moon.

**Benjamin Franklin,** letter to his daughter Sally

After America's victory at Saratoga, the French agreed to an alliance. This section explains how the war expanded with foreign aid.

## Help from Abroad

France was still bitter over its defeat by Britain in the French and Indian War, in which France lost its North American colonies. The French hoped to take revenge on the British by helping Britain's American colonies break free. In 1776, France began to give secret aid to the Americans. However, the French didn't want to lose to Britain a second time. That is why they didn't publicly ally themselves with the United States until after the Americans had proved they could win battles.

After hearing of the American victory at Saratoga, King Louis XVI of France recognized U.S. independence. In 1778, France signed two treaties of alliance with the United States. By doing so, France went to

**Taking Notes**

Use your chart to take notes about the expansion of the American Revolution.

| 1776 | 1777 | 1778 |
|---|---|---|

war with Britain. As part of its new alliance, France sent badly needed funds, supplies, and troops to America.

In 1779, France persuaded its ally Spain to help the Americans. Spain was also Britain's rival. The Spanish governor of Louisiana, General Bernardo de Gálvez, acted quickly. He captured the British strongholds of Natchez and Baton Rouge in the lower Mississippi Valley.

**Background**
Galveston, Texas, is named for Gálvez.

From there, his small army went on to take Mobile, and in 1781 Pensacola in West Florida. These victories prevented the British from attacking the United States from the southwest. In addition, Britain had to keep thousands of troops fighting Gálvez—instead of fighting the Americans. However, like France, Spain's motives were not simply to help the United States. Gálvez's victories helped extend Spain's empire in North America.

_Reading_**History**
**A. Recognizing Effects** How did America's allies prevent Britain from focusing all its might on the Americans?

By entering the war on America's side, France and Spain forced the British to fight a number of enemies on land and sea. The British had to spread their military resources over many fronts. For example, they were afraid they might have to fight the French in the West Indies, so they sent troops there. This prevented the British from concentrating their strength to defeat the inexperienced Americans.

## Europeans Help Washington

The Americans gained some of the military experience they needed from Europe. Several European military officers came to Washington's aid, including men from France, Poland, and the German states.

The **Marquis de Lafayette** (LAF•ee•EHT) was a 19-year-old French nobleman who volunteered to serve in Washington's army. He wanted a military career, and he believed in the American cause. He quickly gained Washington's confidence and was given the command of an army division. Lafayette won respect and love from his men by sharing their hardships. Called "the soldier's friend," he used his own money to buy warm clothing for his ragged troops. Washington regarded him almost as a son.

**Background**
Many of these European officers were professional soldiers looking for an army that would hire them. Some, like Lafayette, also believed in the American cause.

Lafayette fought in many battles and also persuaded the French king to send a 6,000-man army to America. He became a hero in both France and the United States. Later he took part in France's own revolution.

Along with Lafayette came the Baron de Kalb, a German officer who had served in the French army. He became one of Washington's generals and earned a reputation for bravery. In 1780, he received 11 wounds in the Battle of Camden and died.

Another German, Baron von Steuben, helped turn the inexperienced Americans

Lafayette stands with the slave James Armistead, whose owner allowed him to spy for Lafayette. After the war, the state of Virginia set Armistead free. Armistead then took Lafayette's last name as his own.

into a skilled fighting force. Washington asked him to train the army. In 1778, Steuben began by forming a model company of 100 men. Then he taught them how to move in lines and columns and how to handle weapons properly. Under Steuben's direction, the soldiers practiced making charges with **bayonets**—long steel knives attached to the ends of guns. Within a month, the troops were executing drills with speed and precision. Once the model company succeeded, the rest of the army adopted Steuben's methods.

## Winter at Valley Forge

Help from Europeans came at a time when the Americans desperately needed it. In late 1777, Britain's General Howe forced Washington to retreat from Philadelphia. Beginning in the winter of 1777–1778, Washington and his army camped at Valley Forge in southeast Pennsylvania.

On the march to Valley Forge, Washington's army was so short on supplies that many soldiers had only blankets to cover themselves. They also lacked shoes. The barefoot men left tracks of blood on the frozen ground as they marched. The soldiers' condition did not improve at camp. The Marquis de Lafayette described what he saw.

### A VOICE FROM THE PAST

The unfortunate soldiers were in want of everything; they had neither coats, nor hats, nor shirts, nor shoes; their feet and their legs froze till they grew black and it was often necessary to amputate them. . . . The Army frequently passed whole days without food.

**Marquis de Lafayette,** quoted in *Valley Forge: Pinnacle of Courage*

*Reading*History
B. Identifying Facts and Opinions Is Lafayette mainly recounting facts or expressing opinions? Explain.

Because of this, the name *Valley Forge* came to stand for the great hardships that Americans endured in the Revolutionary War. Over the winter, the soldiers at Valley Forge grew weak from not having enough food or warm clothing. Roughly a quarter of them died from malnutrition, exposure to the cold, or diseases such as smallpox and typhoid fever.

### daily*life*

**CAMP LIFE IN WINTER**

At Valley Forge, soldiers slept in small huts, 12 men to a hut. They slept in shifts so they could take turns using the scarce blankets. The men also shared clothing. If one went on guard duty, the others lent him their clothes and stayed by the fire in the hut until he came back. Guards had to stand in old hats to keep their shoeless feet warm.

The soldiers cooked on hot stones, in iron kettles, or on portable iron braziers. Often the only food they had was fire cakes— a bread made of flour and water paste.

These iron kettles were so heavy that soldiers often threw them away on a march.

This surgeon's kit includes a saw, used to perform amputations.

Soldiers would place burning coals in braziers like this. Braziers were used to cook food and heat huts.

Washington appealed to Congress to send the soldiers supplies, but it was slow in responding. Luckily, private citizens sometimes came to the soldiers' aid. According to one story, on New Year's Day 1778, a group of Philadelphia women drove ten teams of oxen into camp. The oxen were pulling wagons loaded with supplies and 2,000 shirts. The women had the oxen killed to provide food for the men.

*Reading* **History**
C. Analyzing Points of View
What are two different explanations for why American soldiers did not desert?

Despite the hardships, Washington and his soldiers showed amazing endurance. Under such circumstances, soldiers often **desert,** or leave military duty without intending to return. Some soldiers did desert, but Lieutenant Colonel John Brooks wrote that the army stayed together because of "Love of our Country." The men also stayed because of Washington. Private Samuel Downing declared that the soldiers "loved him. They'd sell their lives for him."

> *"If a country is not worth protecting, it is not worth claiming."*
> George Rogers Clark

## War on the Frontier

Elsewhere, other Americans also took on difficult challenges. In 1777, a 24-year-old frontiersman named George Rogers Clark walked into the office of Virginia's governor, Patrick Henry. Clark said he had come to take part in defending the Western frontier. He lived in Kentucky, which was claimed by Virginia. Clark wanted Virginia to defend that region against British soldiers and their Native American allies in what is now Indiana and Illinois. "If a country is not worth protecting," he said, "it is not worth claiming."

**Background**
In the late 1700s, the Western frontier was the region between the Appalachian Mountains and the Mississippi River.

Clark was difficult to ignore. He stood six feet tall, had red hair, and displayed a dramatic personality. He persuaded Governor Henry that he was right. The governor told Clark to raise an army to capture British posts on the Western frontier.

In May of 1778, Clark and a group of frontiersmen began to travel down the Ohio River. He recruited others on the way, until he had a force of 175 to 200. They went by boat and later on foot to Kaskaskia, a British post on the Mississippi River. They captured Kaskaskia without a fight.

Then they moved east to take Fort Sackville at Vincennes, in present-day Indiana. Earlier, a small force sent by Clark had taken Vincennes, but British forces under Henry Hamilton had recaptured it. Settlers called Hamilton the "Hair Buyer" because he supposedly paid rewards for American scalps.

## War on the Frontier, 1778

In 1778, George Rogers Clark captures British outposts on the American frontier without firing a shot. Though the British retake Vincennes, Clark regains it after a short battle in 1779.

L. Huron
L. Ontario
PROVINCE OF QUEBEC
Ft. Detroit
L. Erie
Hamilton
Wabash R.
Ft. Pitt
Vincennes (Ft. Sackville)
Clark
Ohio R.
Cahokia
Kaskaskia
Mississippi R.
40°N
80°W
85°W
90°W

← American forces
← British forces
✷ American victory
🏛 American fort
🏛 British fort

0   100 Miles
0   200 Kilometers
N

**GEOGRAPHY SKILLBUILDER** Interpreting Maps
1. **Movement** *From what fort did British general Hamilton travel to Vincennes?*
2. **Region** *What rivers form the boundaries of the region captured by Clark and his men?*

Determined to retake Fort Sackville, Clark and his men set out for Vincennes from Kaskaskia in February 1779. Hamilton wasn't expecting an attack because the rivers were overflowing their banks and the woods were flooded. Clark's men slogged through miles of icy swamps and waded through chest-deep water. They caught the British at Vincennes by surprise.

When Hamilton and his troops tried to remain in the fort, Clark pretended to have a larger force than he really had. He also found a way to frighten the British into leaving. Clark and his men had captured several Native Americans, who were allies of the British and had American scalps on their belts. Clark executed some of them in plain view of the fort. He promised to do the same to Hamilton and his men if they didn't surrender immediately. The British gave up.

*Reading*History
**D. Making Decisions** What factors do you think influenced Clark's decision to execute his prisoners?

Clark's victory gave the Americans a hold on the vast region between the Great Lakes and the Ohio River. This area was more than half the total size of the original 13 states. However, Fort Detroit on Lake Erie remained in the hands of the British.

## STRANGE *but* True

**THE FIRST COMBAT SUBMARINE**

During the Revolution, the Americans built the first combat submarine—the *Turtle,* shown below. It held only a pilot, who steered with one hand and cranked a propeller with the other. To submerge, the pilot used a foot pump to let in water.

In 1776, the *Turtle* failed on its mission to attach a bomb to a British warship in New York harbor. It reached the ship but couldn't drill through its copper-clad hull. The *Turtle* failed at later missions, too.

## War at Sea

The war expanded not only to the frontier but also to the sea. By 1777, Britain had about 100 warships off the American coast. This allowed Britain to control the Atlantic trade routes. There was no way the Americans could defeat the powerful British navy.

But American privateers attacked British merchant ships. A **privateer** is a privately owned ship that a wartime government gives permission to attack an enemy's merchant ships. After capturing a British merchant ship, the crew of a privateer sold its cargo and shared the money. As a result, a desire for profit as well as patriotism motivated privateers. The states and Congress commissioned more than 1,000 privateers to prey on the British. During the war, they captured hundreds of British ships. This disrupted trade, causing British merchants to call for the war to end.

Many men answered the privateers' call for volunteers. Among them was 14-year-old **James Forten,** who was the son of a free African-American sail maker. In 1780, Forten signed up to sail on the *Royal Louis* to earn money for his family after his father died. When a British ship captured the *Royal Louis* in 1781, the British offered Forten a free trip to England. Reportedly, Forten refused, saying he would never betray his country. Released from a British prison after the war, Forten walked barefoot from New York to his home in Philadelphia. He later became famous for his efforts to end slavery.

Vocabulary
**merchant ship:** a ship used in trade

## A Naval Hero

Though outnumbered, the Continental Navy scored several victories against the British. An officer named **John Paul Jones** won the most famous sea battle.

In 1779, Jones became the commander of a ship named *Bonhomme Richard*. With four other ships, he patrolled the English coast. In September, Jones's vessels approached a convoy in which two British warships were guarding a number of supply ships.

Jones closed in on the *Serapis*, the larger of the two warships. At one point, the *Bonhomme Richard* rammed the better-armed British vessel. As the two ships locked together, the confident British captain demanded that Jones surrender. In words that have become a famous U.S. Navy slogan, Jones replied, "I have not yet begun to fight!"

The two warships were so close together that the muzzles of their guns almost touched. They blasted away, each seriously damaging the other. On the shore, crowds of Britons gathered under a full moon to watch the fighting. After a fierce three-and-a-half-hour battle, the main mast of the *Serapis* cracked and fell. The ship's captain then surrendered. The *Bonhomme Richard* was so full of holes that it eventually sank, so Jones and his crew had to sail away in the *Serapis*!

Jones's success against the best navy in the world angered the British and inspired the Americans. Even so, the Americans knew that the war had to be won on land. The next section discusses the major land battles in the closing years of the war.

**Vocabulary**
**convoy:** a group of ships traveling together for safety

**JOHN PAUL JONES**
**1747–1792**

The most famous naval officer of the Revolution is known by a fake name. He was born John Paul in Scotland and first went to sea as a 12-year-old. By age 21, he had command of a merchant ship.

In 1773, Paul killed the leader of a mutiny on his ship. To avoid a murder trial, he fled to America and added Jones to his name.

Bold and daring, Jones scored many victories against the British. But his battle with the *Serapis* is what earned his place in history.

**What are the two words that you think best describe Jones's character? Explain.**

---

## Section 2 Assessment

### 1. Terms & Names

**Explain the significance of:**
- ally
- Marquis de Lafayette
- bayonet
- desert
- privateer
- James Forten
- John Paul Jones

### 2. Using Graphics

Use this diagram to list the effects of the entry of France and Spain into the war. (HI2)

Cause: France and Spain enter the war.

Effect → Effect → Effect

### 3. Main Ideas

**a.** What role did Benjamin Franklin play in helping America win the Revolution? (CST1)

**b.** How did European officers such as Lafayette aid America in the Revolutionary War? (CST1)

**c.** What was John Paul Jones's major contribution during the war, and why was it important? (CST1)

### 4. Critical Thinking

**Analyzing Points of View**
Why do you think George Rogers Clark thought the frontier was important to defend? (REP5)

**THINK ABOUT**
- why General Hamilton was called "Hair Buyer"
- why America might have wanted the frontier region after the war

### ACTIVITY OPTIONS

**ART**
**SPEECH**

Imagine yourself at Valley Forge in the winter of 1777–1778. Create a **comic strip** or give a **talk** describing your response to the harsh conditions. (HI1)

# The Path to Victory

<table>
<tr><td>MAIN IDEA</td><td>WHY IT MATTERS NOW</td><td>TERMS & NAMES</td></tr>
<tr><td>Seeking Loyalist support, the British invaded the South—but ultimately lost the war there.</td><td>For more than two centuries, the American Revolution has inspired other people to fight tyranny.</td><td>Lord Cornwallis   pacifist<br>guerrillas   Battle of Yorktown</td></tr>
</table>

**CALIFORNIA STANDARDS**

**8.1** Students understand the major events preceding the founding of the nation and relate their significance to the development of American constitutional democracy.

**CST3** Students use a variety of maps and documents to identify physical and cultural features of neighborhoods, cities, states, and countries and to explain the historical migration of people, expansion and disintegration of empires, and the growth of economic systems.

**HI3** Students explain the sources of historical continuity and how the combination of ideas and events explains the emergence of new patterns.

**HI4** Students recognize the role of chance, foresight, and error in history.

## ONE AMERICAN'S STORY

Patriot Nancy Hart glared at the five armed Loyalists who burst into her Georgia cabin. Tradition says that the men had shot her last turkey and ordered her to cook it for them. Raids like this were common in the South, where feuding neighbors used the war as an excuse to fight each other. Both Patriots and Loyalists took part in the raids.

As Hart prepared the food, she planned her attack. When dinner was ready, the men sat down to eat. Seizing one of their muskets, Hart shot and killed one man and wounded another. She aimed the gun at the others as her daughter ran for help. A group of Patriots arrived and hanged the Loyalists.

As Nancy Hart's story demonstrates, the fighting between Patriots and Loyalists in the South was vicious. In this section, you will learn why the British war effort shifted to the South and why it failed.

The state of Georgia named a county after Nancy Hart, who is shown here holding Loyalists prisoner.

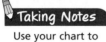

**Taking Notes**

Use your chart to take notes about the events that led to an American victory.

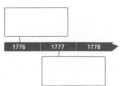

## Savannah and Charles Town

The British believed that most Southerners were Loyalists. Because of this, in 1778 the British decided to move the war to the South. After three years of fighting in the North, the British were no closer to victory. Although they had captured Northern cities, they couldn't control the countryside because they did not have enough troops to occupy it. The British believed that if they gained territory in the South, Southern Loyalists would hold it for them.

The British also expected large numbers of Southern slaves to join them because they had promised to grant the slaves freedom. Although thousands of African Americans did run away to join the British, not all of them were set free. Instead, some British officers sold African Americans into slavery in the West Indies.

*Reading* **History**

**A. Drawing Conclusions** Why was it an advantage to be able to move troops between the West Indies and the South?

Britain's West Indian colonies were a third reason the British invaded the South. Southern seaports were closer to the West Indies, where British troops were stationed. If the British captured Southern ports, they could move troops back and forth between the two regions.

In December 1778, the British captured the port of Savannah, Georgia. Using Savannah as a base, they then conquered most of Georgia. In 1780, a British army led by General Henry Clinton landed in South Carolina. They trapped American forces in Charles Town (now Charleston), which was the largest Southern city. When the city's 5,000 defenders surrendered, the Americans lost almost their entire Southern army. It was the worst American defeat of the war.

## The Swamp Fox and Guerrilla Fighting

After that loss, Congress assigned General Horatio Gates—the victor at Saratoga—to form a new Southern army. Continental soldiers led by Baron de Kalb formed the army's core. Gates added about 2,000 new and untrained militia. He then headed for Camden, South Carolina, to challenge the army led by the British general **Lord Cornwallis**.

On the way, a band of Patriots from South Carolina approached Gates. "Their number did not exceed 20 men and boys, some white, some black, and all mounted, but most of them miserably equipped," wrote an officer. Their leader was Francis Marion, called the "Swamp Fox." He provided Gates with helpful knowledge of South Carolina's coastal swamplands. Gates sent Marion to destroy boats on the Santee River behind Camden. (See the map on page 209.) This would cut off British communications with Charles Town.

In August 1780, Gates's army ran into British troops outside Camden. The Americans were in no condition to fight. They were out of supplies and half-starved. Even worse, Gates put the inexperienced militia along part of the frontline instead of behind the veterans. When the British attacked, the militia panicked and ran. Gates also fled, but Kalb remained with his soldiers and received fatal wounds. This second defeat in the South ended Gates's term as head of an army and caused American spirits to fall to a new low.

*Reading* **History**

**B. Evaluating** What do you think was most responsible for the American loss at Camden?

After Camden, a small British force set out for Charles Town with a column of American prisoners. Marion's band overwhelmed the British and freed the prisoners. Fighting from a base in the swamps, Marion's men cut the British supply line that led inland and north from Charles Town. Marion used the methods of a guerrilla. **Guerrillas** are small bands of fighters who weaken the enemy with surprise raids and hit-and-run attacks. Both Patriots and Loyalists formed guerrilla bands in the South. They carried out vicious raids.

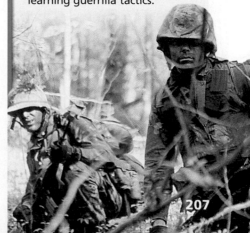

## *Now and* then

**BATTLE TACTICS**
A difference in battle tactics affected future warfare. British soldiers marched shoulder to shoulder in three rows. When they neared the enemy, the first row knelt, the second crouched, and the third remained standing. They all fired without aiming.

The Americans were better shots. They often marched in rows, but sometimes they hid in woods or behind walls to take aim. Guerrillas attacked swiftly, then fled into the countryside. Those tactics succeeded and are still used today. This photograph shows modern U.S. soldiers learning guerrilla tactics.

# Artillery of the Revolution

Artillery—large guns and cannon—played a key role in the American Revolution. The ability of these guns to kill and destroy from a distance made them essential in war. One witness of a battle described the destruction: "Many men were badly injured and mortally wounded by the fragments of bombs, . . . their arms and legs severed or themselves struck dead." Most cannon used in the Revolution were made of cast bronze. During the 1700s, artillery design did not change significantly. However, artillery became more mobile (more easily moved).

**CALIFORNIA STANDARDS**

**REP1** Students frame questions that can be answered by historical study and research.

After each shot, a soldier sponged the inside of the barrel. This put out sparks and cleaned away any dirt left from the last shot.

A soldier loaded the cannon with gunpowder and a cannonball. He did so by ramming them down the barrel.

Soldiers aimed the gun by turning the entire carriage. An instrument called a quadrant told them how high to raise the barrel to reach their target.

Cannon were classified by the weight of the iron ball they fired. American artillery ranged from 3-pounders to 32-pounders.

Soldiers lit the cannon by applying a red-hot wire or a tube of burning powder to a touchhole drilled through the back of the barrel, where the gunpowder lay. The gunpowder exploded, forcing the projectile out of the open end of the barrel.

In the 1700s, most cannon were accurate at ranges of up to 1,000 yards. That is the length of ten football fields laid end to end.

## CONNECT TO HISTORY

1. **Recognizing Effects** Why would it be an advantage to an army to have mobile artillery?

   [S] See Skillbuilder Handbook, page R11.

## CONNECT TO TODAY

2. **Researching** Find information about modern artillery in an encyclopedia or on the Internet. How did artillery change in the 20th century?

For more about artillery . . .

**RESEARCH LINKS**
CLASSZONE.COM

# The Tide Turns

Even battles in the South sometimes turned vicious. One example was the Battle of Kings Mountain, fought on the border of North and South Carolina in October 1780. After surrounding a force of about 1,000 Loyalist militia and British soldiers, the Americans slaughtered most of them. James P. Collins, a 16-year-old American, described the scene.

---

*A VOICE FROM THE PAST*

The dead lay in heaps on all sides, while the groans of the wounded were heard in every direction. I could not help turning away from the scene before me with horror and, though exulting in victory, could not refrain from shedding tears.

**James P. Collins,** quoted in *The Spirit of Seventy-Six*

---

Many of the dead had been shot or hanged after they surrendered. The Americans killed them in revenge for Loyalist raids and an earlier incident in which the British had butchered Americans. Kings Mountain was one of Britain's first losses in the South. It soon suffered more.

After Gates's defeat at Camden, Washington put a new general, Nathanael Greene, in charge of the Southern army. Greene was one of Washington's most able officers. He had been a Quaker, but his church had cast him out because of his belief in the armed struggle against the British. Most Quakers are **pacifist,** or opposed to war.

*Reading*History
C. Contrasting
How did Greene's strategy as a general differ from that of Gates at Camden?

Under Greene's command, the American army avoided full-scale battles, in which the British had the edge because of superior firepower. So the American forces let the British chase them around the countryside and wear themselves out. When the Americans did fight, they did their best to make sure the British suffered heavy losses.

As the fighting dragged on into its sixth year, opposition to the war grew in Britain. As a result, some British leaders began to think that American independence would not be so bad.

## The End of the War

In 1781, most of the fighting took place in Virginia. In July of that year, the British general Cornwallis set up his base at Yorktown, located on a peninsula in Chesapeake Bay. From there, his army could receive supplies by ship from New York.

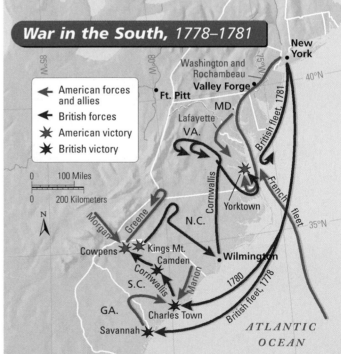

**War in the South,** *1778–1781*

American forces and allies
British forces
American victory
British victory

0    100 Miles
0    200 Kilometers

N

New York
Washington and Rochambeau
Valley Forge
Ft. Pitt
MD.
Lafayette
VA.
British fleet, 1781
French fleet
Cornwallis
Yorktown
N.C.
Morgan
Greene
Cowpens
Kings Mt.
Camden
Wilmington
Cornwallis
Marion
S.C.
1780
GA.
Charles Town
British fleet, 1778
1778
Savannah
ATLANTIC OCEAN

**GEOGRAPHY SKILLBUILDER Interpreting Maps**
1. **Place** *What ports did the British use to invade the South?*
2. **Movement** *Who traveled from Wilmington to Yorktown, and who traveled from New York?*

The victorious American forces accept the British surrender at Yorktown. George Washington is to the left of the American flag.

Washington saw Cornwallis's decision as a golden opportunity. In August 1781, a large French fleet arrived from the West Indies and blocked Chesapeake Bay. These ships prevented the British from receiving supplies—and from escaping. They also allowed Washington to come from the North and trap Cornwallis on the peninsula. Washington had enough men to do this because a large French force led by General Jean Rochambeau had joined his army.

Washington and Rochambeau moved south. When British ships tried to reach Cornwallis, French ships drove them back. In the **Battle of Yorktown,** the American and French troops bombarded Yorktown with cannon fire, turning its buildings to rubble. Cornwallis had no way out. On October 19, 1781, he surrendered his force of about 8,000.

Although some fighting continued, Yorktown was the last major battle of the war. When the British prime minister, Lord North, heard the news, he gasped, "It is all over!" Indeed, he and other British leaders were soon forced to resign. Britain's new leaders began to negotiate a peace treaty, which is discussed in the next section.

**Vocabulary**
**bombard:** to attack with artillery

## Section 3 Assessment

### 1. Terms & Names

**Explain the significance of:**
- Lord Cornwallis
- guerrillas
- pacifist
- Battle of Yorktown

### 2. Using Graphics

Use a chart like the one below to list the geographic factors that made the British move their war effort to the South.

| Physical factors, such as location | Human factors, such as who lived there |
|---|---|
| | |

Were the human factors as helpful as the British hoped? (HI2)

### 3. Main Ideas

**a.** Why did the fighting between Patriots and Loyalists in the South turn vicious? (HI1)

**b.** What type of warfare did Francis Marion and his men employ? (HI1)

**c.** How did Gates's errors in leadership contribute to the American loss at Camden? (HI4)

### 4. Critical Thinking

**Analyzing Causes** How did each of the following help bring about the British defeat at Yorktown? (HI2)

**THINK ABOUT**
- the location chosen by Cornwallis
- the French fleet
- the French troops under Rochambeau
- Washington's planning

**ACTIVITY OPTIONS**

**TECHNOLOGY**

**MUSIC**

Imagine that Congress has asked you to commemorate the Battle of Yorktown. Design a **Web page** or write a **song** celebrating the U.S. victory. (HI1)

# The Legacy of the War

| MAIN IDEA | WHY IT MATTERS NOW | TERMS & NAMES |
|---|---|---|
| After the war, the new nation faced issues such as a high national debt and calls for equality. | To promote liberty, some states passed laws outlawing slavery and protecting religious freedom. | Treaty of Paris of 1783  Elizabeth Freeman  republicanism  Richard Allen |

## ONE AMERICAN'S STORY

In 1776, 15-year-old Joseph Plumb Martin of Connecticut signed up to fight for the Americans. He stayed with the army until the war ended. Many years later, Martin wrote about leaving the army.

*A VOICE FROM THE PAST*

There was as much sorrow as joy. . . . We had lived together as a family of brothers for several years, . . . had shared with each other the hardships, dangers, and sufferings incident to a soldier's life; had sympathized with each other in trouble and sickness; . . . And now we were to be . . . parted forever.

**Joseph Plumb Martin,** quoted in *The Revolutionaries*

Joseph Plumb Martin may have dressed like this American soldier.

At war's end, Martin and his country faced an uncertain future. How would the United States recover from the war? What issues would confront the new nation? Section 4 discusses those questions.

## Why the Americans Won

In November 1783, the last British ships and troops left New York City, and American troops marched in. As Washington said good-bye to his officers in a New York tavern, he hugged each one. Tears ran down his face. He became so upset that he had to leave the room.

Earlier in the fall, Washington had written a farewell letter to his armies. In it, he praised them by saying that their endurance "through almost every possible suffering and discouragement for the space of eight long years, was little short of a standing miracle."

By their persistence, the Americans won independence even though they faced many obstacles. As you have read, they lacked training and experience. They were often short of supplies and weapons. By contrast, the British forces ranked among the best trained in the world. They were

**CALIFORNIA STANDARDS**

**7.11.3** Examine the origins of modern capitalism; the influence of mercantilism and cottage industry; the elements and importance of a market economy in seventeenth-century Europe; the changing international trading and marketing patterns, including their locations on a world map; and the influence of explorers and map makers.

**8.1.3** Analyze how the American Revolution affected other nations, especially France.

**8.1.4** Describe the nation's blend of civic republicanism, classical liberal principles, and English parliamentary traditions.

**8.4.3** Analyze the rise of capitalism and the economic problems and conflicts that accompanied it (e.g., Jackson's opposition to the National Bank; early decisions of the U.S. Supreme Court that reinforced the sanctity of contracts and a capitalist economic system of law).

**8.6.4** Study the lives of black Americans who gained freedom in the North and founded schools and churches to advance their rights and communities.

**Taking Notes**

Use your chart to take notes about the results of the American Revolution.

experienced and well-supplied professional soldiers. Yet the Americans had certain advantages that enabled them to win.

*Reading*History

**A. Evaluating**
What do you think was Washington's best characteristic as a leader?

1. **Better leadership.** British generals were overconfident and made poor decisions. By contrast, Washington learned from his mistakes. After early defeats, he developed the strategy of dragging out the war to wear down the British. Despite difficulties, he never gave up.
2. **Foreign aid.** Britain's rivals, especially France, helped America. Foreign loans and military aid were essential to America's victory.
3. **Knowledge of the land.** The Americans knew the land where the war took place and used that knowledge well. The British could control coastal cities but could not extend their control to the interior.
4. **Motivation.** The Americans had more reason to fight. At stake were not only their lives but also their property and their dream of liberty.

## The Treaty of Paris

As the winners, the Americans won favorable terms in the **Treaty of Paris of 1783,** which ended the Revolutionary War. The treaty included the following six conditions:

1. The United States was independent.
2. Its boundaries would be the Mississippi River on the west, Canada on the north, and Spanish Florida on the south.
3. The United States would receive the right to fish off Canada's Atlantic Coast, near Newfoundland and Nova Scotia.
4. Each side would repay debts it owed the other.
5. The British would return any enslaved persons they had captured.
6. Congress would recommend that the states return any property they had seized from Loyalists.

Neither Britain nor the United States fully lived up to the treaty's terms. Americans did not repay the prewar debts they owed British merchants or return Loyalist property. For their part, the British did not return

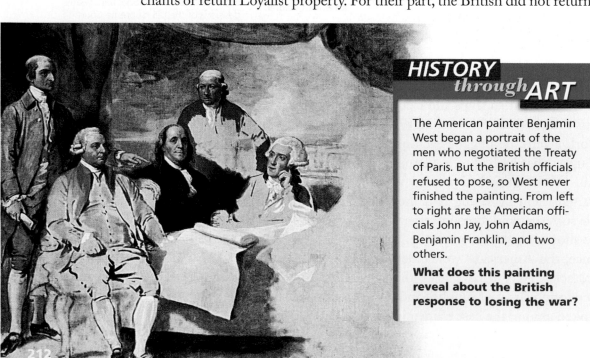

## HISTORY through ART

The American painter Benjamin West began a portrait of the men who negotiated the Treaty of Paris. But the British officials refused to pose, so West never finished the painting. From left to right are the American officials John Jay, John Adams, Benjamin Franklin, and two others.

**What does this painting reveal about the British response to losing the war?**

212

**Background**
Even after George Rogers Clark's Western victories, the British stayed at Fort Detroit.

runaway slaves. They also refused to give up military outposts in the Great Lakes area, such as Fort Detroit.

## Costs of the War

No one knows exactly how many people died in the war, but eight years of fighting took a terrible toll. An estimated 25,700 Americans died in the war, and 1,400 remained missing. About 8,200 Americans were wounded. Some were left with permanent disabilities, such as amputated limbs. The British suffered about 10,000 military deaths.

Many soldiers who survived the war left the army with no money. They had received little or no pay for their service. Instead of back pay, the government gave some soldiers certificates for land in the West. Many men sold that land to get money for food and other basic needs.

Both the Congress and the states had borrowed money to finance the conflict. The war left the nation with a debt of about $27 million—a debt that would prove difficult to pay off.

The losers of the war also suffered. Thousands of Loyalists lost their property. Between 60,000 and 100,000 Loyalists left the United States during and after the war. Among them were several thousand African Americans and Native Americans, including Joseph Brant. Most of the Loyalists went to Canada. There they settled new towns and provinces. They also brought English traditions to areas that the French had settled. Even today, Canada has both French and English as official languages.

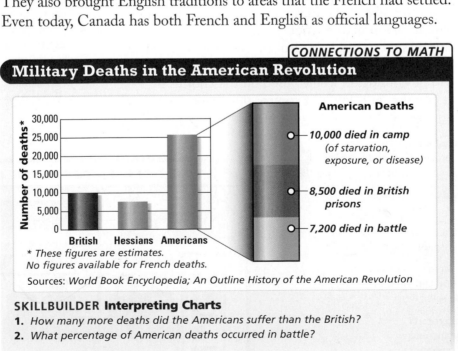

**Postwar Boundaries, *1783***

RUSSIAN TERRITORY

BRITISH TERRITORY

Hudson Bay

Claimed by Great Britain, Spain, and Russia

QUEBEC

Claimed by U.S and Great Britain

Claimed by U.S and Great Britain

SPANISH TERRITORY

UNITED STATES

ATLANTIC OCEAN

PACIFIC OCEAN

Claimed by U.S. and Spain

MEXICO    Gulf of Mexico

FRENCH TERRITORY

N

0    500 Miles

0    1,000 Kilometers

***Reading* History**
**B. Analyzing Causes** Why do you think the Loyalists left the United States?

**CONNECTIONS TO MATH**

### Military Deaths in the American Revolution

Number of deaths*

30,000
25,000
20,000
15,000
10,000
5,000
0

British    Hessians    Americans

* These figures are estimates.
No figures available for French deaths.

**American Deaths**

10,000 died in camp
(of starvation, exposure, or disease)

8,500 died in British prisons

7,200 died in battle

Sources: *World Book Encyclopedia; An Outline History of the American Revolution*

**SKILLBUILDER Interpreting Charts**
1. *How many more deaths did the Americans suffer than the British?*
2. *What percentage of American deaths occurred in battle?*

## Issues After the War

The American Revolution was not just a war, but a change in ideas about government. Before the war, Americans had demanded their rights as English citizens. But after declaring their independence, they replaced that goal with the idea of **republicanism.** This idea stated that instead of a king, the people would rule. The government would obtain its authority from the citizens and be responsible to them.

For this system to work, individuals would have to place the good of the country above their own interests. At first, only land-owning white males were allowed to take part in governing by voting or holding public office. However, women could help the nation by teaching their children the virtues that benefited public life. Such virtues included honesty, duty, and the willingness to make sacrifices.

As part of their liberty, Americans called for more religious freedom. Before the war, some laws discriminated against certain religions. Some states had not allowed Jews or Catholics to hold public office. After the

## Economics *in* History

# Free Enterprise

One cause of the Revolution was the colonists' resentment of British mercantilism. Parliament passed laws to discourage the colonists from developing their own manufacturing and to force them to buy British goods. During the war, British economic control weakened. British exports of woolens to the colonies dropped from £645,900 in 1774 to only £2,540 in 1776. As a result, the colonists were able to make more economic choices—for example, they could choose to manufacture wool clothing.

The end of Britain's mercantilist control allowed free enterprise to begin to develop in the United States. In a free-enterprise system, business can be conducted freely based on the choices of individuals. The government does not control the system, but only protects and regulates it.

**A** Competition encourages businesses to improve goods and services and to keep prices down.

**B** Property is owned by individuals and businesses.

**C** The desire to make a profit motivates businesspeople.

**D** Individuals, not the government, decide what to buy and what to manufacture and sell.

**E** The government protects private property and makes sure businesses operate fairly.

### CONNECT TO HISTORY

1. **Analyzing Causes** Why do you think the colonists were able to manufacture their own wool clothing during the war?

   **S** See Skillbuilder Handbook, page R11.

### CONNECT TO TODAY

2. **Comparing** Think about a mall where you shop. Name examples of businesses that compete with each other. Compare the methods they use to attract customers.

---

For more about free enterprise . . .

**RESEARCH LINKS** CLASSZONE.COM

THE FREE ENTERPRISE MALL

THE BARGAIN STORE

PAY LESS GET MORE STORE

war, states began to abolish those laws. They also ended the practice of using tax money to support churches.

Many people began to see a conflict between slavery and the ideal of liberty. Vermont outlawed slavery, and Pennsylvania passed a law to free slaves gradually. Individual African Americans also tried to end slavery. For example, **Elizabeth Freeman** sued for her freedom in a Massachusetts court and won. Her victory in 1781 and other similar cases ended slavery in that state. Freeman later described her desire for freedom.

**Background**
Only Northern states ended slavery after the war. In the North, slavery was not as important a part of the economy as in the South.

> ### A VOICE FROM THE PAST
>
> Anytime while I was a slave, if one minute's freedom had been offered to me, and I had been told I must die at the end of that minute, I would have taken it—just to stand one minute on God's earth a free woman.
>
> **Elizabeth Freeman,** quoted in *Notable Black American Women*

*Reading* **History**
**C. Solving Problems** How did free African Americans take on the responsibility of trying to improve their lives?

With freedom, African Americans began to form their own institutions. For example, the preacher **Richard Allen** helped start the Free African Society. That society encouraged African Americans to help each other. Allen also founded the African Methodist Episcopal Church, the first African-American church in the United States.

Elizabeth Freeman fought a court case that helped end slavery in Massachusetts.

The American Revolution also influenced people in other countries. The Declaration of Independence was widely circulated in France, and helped inspire the French Revolution in 1789. Revolutionaries in Latin America began to rise up against colonial powers in the late 1700s and early 1800s. By 1830, most of the former European colonies in Central and South America had won independence.

Perhaps the main issue facing Americans after the war was how to shape their national government. American anger over British taxes, violation of rights, and control of trade had caused the war. Now the United States needed a government that would protect citizens' rights and economic freedom. In Chapter 8, you will read how U.S. leaders worked to create such a government.

---

## Section 4 Assessment

### 1. Terms & Names

**Explain the significance of:**
- Treaty of Paris of 1783
- republicanism
- Elizabeth Freeman
- Richard Allen

### 2. Using Graphics

Use a chart like the one below to classify the terms of the Treaty of Paris according to which side they favored. (Do not list terms that don't favor either side.) (REP5)

| Terms of the Treaty of Paris | |
| --- | --- |
| **Favorable to America** | **Favorable to Britain** |
| | |

### 3. Main Ideas

**a.** What advantages helped the Americans win the Revolutionary War? (HI2)

**b.** How did the end of the war affect Loyalists? (HI2)

**c.** What were the economic costs of the war to individuals and to the government? (HI6)

### 4. Critical Thinking

**Recognizing Effects** How did republicanism shape the United States after the war? (CST1)

**THINK ABOUT**
- American ideas about government
- the roles men and women could play in public life
- religious freedom
- the antislavery movement

**ACTIVITY OPTIONS**

**SPEECH**

**MATH**

Look up the U.S. population in 1780. Calculate what percentage of American people died in the war. Report your findings in a **speech** or a **pie graph**. (REP3)

## TERMS & NAMES

Briefly explain the significance of each of the following.

1. George Washington
2. mercenary
3. Battles of Saratoga
4. ally
5. Marquis de Lafayette
6. John Paul Jones
7. Lord Cornwallis
8. Battle of Yorktown
9. Treaty of Paris of 1783
10. republicanism

## REVIEW QUESTIONS

**The Early Years of the War (pages 193–199)**

1. What motives led African Americans to fight for the British? The Americans? (HI2)
2. How did women help the American war effort? (HI1)
3. What events led to the British defeat at Saratoga? (HI2)

**The War Expands (pages 200–205)**

4. What foreign countries helped America? How? (HI1)
5. What were conditions like at Valley Forge? (HI1)

**The Path to Victory (pages 206–210)**

6. What two Southern ports did the British capture? (HI1)
7. How did America's ally France contribute to the victory at Yorktown? (HI2)

**The Legacy of the War (pages 211–215)**

8. For what did Washington praise his army in his farewell letter? (REP4)
9. What land did the United States acquire from Britain as a result of the Treaty of Paris? (HI2)
10. What three states outlawed slavery after the war? (HI2)

## CRITICAL THINKING

### 1. USING YOUR NOTES: SEQUENCING EVENTS

Using your completed time line, answer the questions below. (CST2)

a. What were the main events of 1776 and 1777?
b. While George Rogers Clark was capturing Kaskaskia, what was happening in the South?

### 2. ANALYZING LEADERSHIP

George Washington was the most beloved American leader of his time. What qualities do you think made him such a respected leader? (HI1)

### 3. THEME: CITIZENSHIP

What Revolutionary leaders displayed civic virtue by putting the good of the nation ahead of their own interests? Explain your answer. (HI1)

### 4. RECOGNIZING EFFECTS

How did Britain's loss in the war allow free enterprise to develop in the United States? (HI2)

### 5. APPLYING CITIZENSHIP SKILLS

How was the writing of *The American Crisis* an example of good U.S. citizenship? (REP4)

### Interact *with* History

How did the sacrifices you discussed before you read the chapter compare with what Patriots really did?

## VISUAL SUMMARY

# The American Revolution (CST2)

## People and Events of the Revolution

| Military | | Civilian | |
|---|---|---|---|
| George Washington | commanded the Continental Army. | Haym Salomon | helped finance the war for America. |
| Marquis de Lafayette | fought for the Americans. | Molly Pitcher | aided soldiers by bringing them water in battle. |
| John Burgoyne | surrendered to the Americans at Saratoga. | Thomas Paine | wrote *The American Crisis* to inspire Americans. |
| John Paul Jones | won a major naval victory for America. | Benjamin Franklin | was a diplomat to France and Britain. |
| George Rogers Clark | helped hold the Western frontier for America. | James Forten | was captured by the British but would not betray America. |
| Lord Cornwallis | surrendered at Yorktown, ending the war. | Nancy Hart | defended her Georgia home against Loyalist raiders. |

# STANDARDS-BASED ASSESSMENT

Use the map and your knowledge of U.S. history to answer questions 1 and 2.

Additional Test Practice, pp. S1–S33.

**Battle of Yorktown, 1781**

1. In what state was the Battle of Yorktown fought? (8.1)
   A. North Carolina
   B. Pennsylvania
   C. South Carolina
   D. Virginia

2. Which of the following describes the route of the forces led by Cornwallis? (8.1)
   A. south from York, PA to Yorktown, VA
   B. south from New York to Yorktown, VA
   C. north from Wilmington, NC to Richmond, VA
   D. north from Richmond, VA to Wilmington, NC

This quotation is from Thomas Paine discussing the Revolutionary War. Use the quotation and your knowledge of U.S. history to answer question 3.

### PRIMARY SOURCE

These are the times that try men's souls. The summer soldier and the sunshine patriot will, in this crisis, shrink from the service of their country; but he that stands it now, deserves the love and thanks of man and woman.

**Thomas Paine,** *The American Crisis*

3. Who is Paine referring to as "the summer soldier and the sunshine patriot"? (7.11.5)
   A. Americans who support the war only when it is going well
   B. Loyalists who never support the war efforts
   C. Americans who show continuous support for the war
   D. soldiers who perform best in good weather

**TEST PRACTICE** CLASSZONE.COM

# ALTERNATIVE ASSESSMENT

## 1. 📝 WRITING ABOUT HISTORY

Suppose you are a soldier at Valley Forge during the winter of 1777–1778. Write daily **journal** entries for one week, describing the harsh conditions of the camp and your physical and emotional state. (REP5)

- Research Valley Forge in books or encyclopedias.
- Try to locate primary sources such as letters, diaries, and journals of soldiers at Valley Forge.

## 2. COOPERATIVE LEARNING

Working in groups, prepare a talk show in which guests discuss which side to take in the Revolutionary War. One group member should be the host. Other members should be guests. Consider some of the following guests: the wife of an American soldier, an enslaved African American, an Iroquois chief, a Quaker minister, and an employee of the British government. (REP5)

# INTEGRATED TECHNOLOGY

## CREATING A MULTIMEDIA PRESENTATION

Choose a major battle of the Revolution. Then use the Internet and other library resources to research that battle. Gather information that represents the American and British points of view. (REP4)

- Locate details about the battle, as well as primary sources, such as quotations from participants on both sides. Make copies of any images you find, being careful to credit your sources.
- Find music of the time period and sound effects.
- Once you have collected these audio and visual materials, combine them to create a multimedia presentation.

For more about the battles . . .

**INTERNET ACTIVITY** CLASSZONE.COM

# Confederation to Constitution 1776–1791

Delegates kept the windows closed during meetings so that the proceedings would be secret.

Some of the most respected men in the nation served as delegates, including Alexander Hamilton and Benjamin Franklin.

**1777**
Patriots win Battles of Saratoga.
Continental Congress passes the Articles of Confederation.

**1781**
Articles of Confederation go into effect.
British surrender at Yorktown.

**1783**
Treaty of Paris formally ends the Revolutionary War.

USA
World **1776**

**1779**
Spain declares war on Britain.

**1781**
Joseph II allows religious freedom for Christians in Austria.

The delegates of the Constitutional Convention chose George Washington, hero of the Revolutionary War, to be president of the convention.

The year is 1787, and your young country needs to reform its government. Now everyone is wondering what the new government will be like. You have been called to a convention to decide how the new government should be organized.

# How do you form a government?

## What Do You Think?

- What will be your main goal in creating a new government?
- How will you get the people at the convention to agree on important issues?

**RESEARCH LINKS**
CLASSZONE.COM

Visit the Chapter 8 links for more information about America after the revolution.

**1786–1787**
Daniel Shays leads a rebellion of Massachusetts farmers.

**1787**
Constitutional Convention is held in Philadelphia.

**1788**
U.S. Constitution is ratified.

**1789**
George Washington becomes the first president of the United States.

**1791**
Bill of Rights is ratified.

**1791**

**1785**
Jean-Paul Blanchard and John Jefferies cross the English Channel in a balloon.

**1787**
Freetown, Sierra Leone, is made a home for freed slaves.

**1789**
French Revolution begins.

# Reading Strategy: Solving Problems

## What Do You Know?

What do you think of when people talk about the U.S. government? Why do nations have governments? What does the U.S. government do?

### Think About

- what you've learned about the U.S. government from the news or your teachers
- what the purpose of a government is
- how the government affects your everyday life
- your responses to the Interact with History about forming a government (see page 219)

**CALIFORNIA STANDARDS**

**Reading 2.0** Students read and understand grade-level-appropriate material. They describe and connect the essential ideas, arguments, and perspectives of the text by using their knowledge of text structure, organization, and purpose.

## What Do You Want to Know?

 What questions do you have about how the four colonial regions developed? Record these questions in your notebook before you read the chapter.

## Solving Problems

When you read history, look for how people solved problems they faced in the past. Copy the chart below in your notebook. Use it to identify the methods that Americans used to solve the problems faced by the nation after declaring its independence.

 See Skillbuilder Handbook, page R18.

 Taking Notes

| Problems | Solutions |
|---|---|
| Western lands | |
| Postwar depression | |
| Representation in the new government | |
| Slavery | |

# The Confederation Era

1

| MAIN IDEA | WHY IT MATTERS NOW | TERMS & NAMES |
|---|---|---|
| The Articles of Confederation were too weak to govern the nation after the war ended. | The weakness of the Articles of Confederation led to the writing of the U.S. Constitution. | Wilderness Road<br>republic<br>Articles of Confederation<br>Land Ordinance of 1785<br>Northwest Territory<br>Northwest Ordinance<br>Shays's Rebellion |

## ONE AMERICAN'S STORY

In 1775, Daniel Boone and 30 woodsmen cut a road over the Appalachian Mountains into Kentucky. After about 250 miles, they arrived in a meadow along the banks of the Kentucky River. Felix Walker, a member of Boone's party, described what they saw.

Detail of *Daniel Boone Escorting Settlers Through the Cumberland Gap* by George Caleb Bingham.

### A VOICE FROM THE PAST

On entering the plain we were permitted to view a very interesting and romantic sight. A number of buffaloes . . . between two and three hundred, made off. . . . Such a sight some of us never saw before, nor perhaps ever may again.

**Felix Walker,** quoted in *The Life and Adventures of Daniel Boone*

In the late 1700s, most Americans thought of Kentucky as the wild frontier. Some, like Boone, looked at the frontier and saw a world of opportunity. Exploring and governing these lands was one of the many challenges facing the new government of the United States.

## Moving West

The trail into Kentucky that Daniel Boone helped build was called the **Wilderness Road**. This road was not easy to travel. It was too narrow for carts or wagons, but it became the main road into Kentucky. The settlers came on foot or on horseback. Settlers were drawn to Kentucky's rich river valleys, where few Native Americans lived. But some Native Americans, such as the Shawnee, did live, hunt, and fish in the area.

Tensions between Native Americans and settlers led to violent confrontations. But the settlers did not stop coming. By the early 1790s, about 100,000 Americans lived there. While settlers headed into the Western territories, the people in the East began to create new state governments.

**CALIFORNIA STANDARDS**

**8.2.2** Analyze the Articles of Confederation and the Constitution and the success of each in implementing the ideals of the Declaration of Independence.

**8.3.1** Analyze the principles and concepts codified in state constitutions between 1777 and 1781 that created the context out of which American political institutions and ideas developed.

**8.3.2** Explain how the ordinances of 1785 and 1787 privatized national resources and transferred federally owned lands into private holdings, townships, and states.

**8.3.5** Know the significance of domestic resistance movements and ways in which the central government responded to such movements (e.g., Shays' Rebellion, the Whiskey Rebellion).

**8.9.2** Discuss the abolition of slavery in early state constitutions.

**8.9.3** Describe the significance of the Northwest Ordinance in education and in the banning of slavery in new states north of the Ohio River.

### Taking Notes

Use your chart to take notes about the western lands and postwar depression.

| Problems | |
|---|---|
| Western lands | |
| Postwar depression | |
| Representation in the new government | |
| Slavery | |

# New State Governments

Once the American colonies declared independence, each of the states set out to create its own government. The framers, or creators, of the state constitutions did not want to destroy the political systems that they had had as colonies. They simply wanted to make those systems more democratic. Some states experimented with creating separate branches of government, giving different powers to different branches. By creating separate branches, Americans hoped to prevent the government from becoming too powerful.

Nearly all states tried to weaken the executive branch. Terms of office were usually short, and elections were held frequently. Most states made property ownership a requirement for holding office or voting. Some states began passing laws gradually abolishing slavery. In 1783 a court decision ruled that Massachusetts's 1780 Constitution effectively outlawed slavery by declaring that "all men are born free and equal." By 1786 five states had abolished slavery.

Some states included a bill of rights in their constitutions as a way to keep the government under control. The idea of a bill of rights came from the English Bill of Rights of 1689. This was a list of rights that the government guaranteed to English citizens.

Although not all the states had a bill of rights, all of them did have a republican form of government. In a **republic,** the people choose representatives to govern them.

**Background**
Two states, Connecticut and Rhode Island, kept their old colonial charters as their constitutions. The other 11 states wrote new constitutions.

# The Articles of Confederation

While the states were setting up their governments, Americans also discussed the form of their national government. During the Revolutionary War, Americans realized that they needed to unite to win the war against Britain. As Silas Deane, a diplomat from Connecticut, wrote, "United we stand, divided we fall."

In 1776, the Continental Congress began to develop a plan for a national government. Congress agreed that the government should be a republic. But the delegates disagreed about whether each state should have one vote or voting should be based on population. They also disagreed about whether the national government or the individual states should control the lands west of the Appalachians.

The Continental Congress eventually arrived at a final plan, called the **Articles of Confederation.** In the Articles, the national government had few powers, because many Americans were afraid that a strong government would lead to tyranny, or oppressive rule. The national government was run by a Confederation Congress. Each state had only one vote in the Congress. The national government had the power to wage war, make peace, sign treaties, and issue money.

But the Articles left most important powers to the states. These powers included the authority to set taxes and enforce national laws. The Articles proposed to leave the states in control of the lands west of the Appalachian Mountains.

*Reading***History**
A. Reading a Map Look at the map on page 223 to see which states claimed territories in the West.

The Continental Congress passed the Articles of Confederation in November 1777. It then sent the Articles to the states for ratification, or approval. By July 1778, eight states had ratified the Articles. But some of the small states that did not have Western land claims refused to sign.

These states felt that unless the Western lands were placed under the control of the national government, they would be at a disadvantage. The states with Western lands could sell them to pay off debts left from the Revolution. But states without lands would have difficulty paying off the high war debts.

Over the next three years, all the states gave up their claims to Western lands. This led the small states to ratify the Articles. In 1781, Maryland became the 13th state to accept the Articles. As a result, the United States finally had an official government.

**Western Land Claims, 1781**

Legend:
☐ Original 13 states
■ Area of Western land claims

**GEOGRAPHY SKILLBUILDER Interpreting Maps**
1. **Location** Which of the original 13 states had Western land claims?
2. **Location** To what geographic feature did the Western land claims extend?

*Reading*History
B. Finding Main Ideas Why did the states without Western land claims want the other states to give up their claims?

## The Northwest Ordinance

One of the most important questions that the Confederation Congress faced was what to do with the Western lands that it now controlled. Congress passed important laws on how to divide and govern these lands—the Land Ordinance of 1785 and the Northwest Ordinance (1787). (See Geography in History on pages 226–227.)

The **Land Ordinance of 1785** called for surveyors to stake out six-mile-square plots, called townships, in the Western lands. Each township was to set aside a square-mile section of land for schools, marking the first time the national government promoted public education. These lands later became known as the **Northwest Territory**. The Northwest Territory included land that formed the states of Ohio, Indiana, Michigan, Illinois, and Wisconsin and part of Minnesota.

The **Northwest Ordinance** (1787) described how the Northwest Territory was to be governed. As the territory grew in population, it would gain rights to self-government. When there were 60,000 people, they could apply to become a new state.

The Northwest Ordinance also set conditions for settlement in the Northwest Territory and outlined the settlers' rights. Slavery was outlawed, but indentured servitude still existed, and slaves already in the territories were not automatically freed. Fugitives were to be returned. The rivers were to be open to navigation by all. Freedom of religion and trial by jury were guaranteed.

**Background**
As settlers moved into the Northwest Territory, they cleared thousands of acres of forest. See the Geography Handbook, page 17.

**Background**
According to the Northwest Ordinance, Native Americans were to be treated fairly, and their lands were not to be taken from them.

The Northwest Ordinance was important because it set a pattern for the orderly growth of the United States. As the nation grew, it followed this pattern in territories added after the Northwest Territory. The decision to ban slavery in the Northwest Territory contributed to the growing division between North and South over the practice.

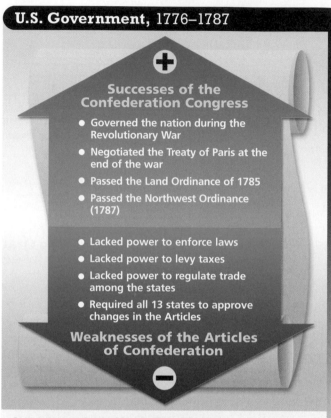

**U.S. Government, 1776–1787**

**Successes of the Confederation Congress**

- Governed the nation during the Revolutionary War
- Negotiated the Treaty of Paris at the end of the war
- Passed the Land Ordinance of 1785
- Passed the Northwest Ordinance (1787)

- Lacked power to enforce laws
- Lacked power to levy taxes
- Lacked power to regulate trade among the states
- Required all 13 states to approve changes in the Articles

**Weaknesses of the Articles of Confederation**

**SKILLBUILDER Interpreting Charts**
1. *What do you think was the greatest success of the Confederation Congress?*
2. *What do you think was the greatest weakness of the Articles of Confederation?*

## Weaknesses of the Articles

Aside from its handling of land issues, however, the Confederation Congress had few successes. By the end of the Revolutionary War, the United States faced serious problems, and the Confederation Congress did not have enough power to solve them.

Debt was a critical problem for the government. Congress had borrowed large sums to pay for the Revolutionary War. Much of that money was owed to soldiers of its own army. Upset at not being paid, several hundred soldiers surrounded the Pennsylvania State House where Congress was meeting in June 1783. The soldiers threatened the legislators, thrusting their bayonets through the windows. The delegates were forced to flee the city. The event was a clear sign of Congress's weakness.

Even if Congress wanted to pay the soldiers, it did not have the power to levy taxes. The national government depended on the states to send money to Congress. But the states sent very little money.

Congress was not alone in facing economic crises. People throughout the nation faced hard times. In Massachusetts, the economy was so bad that people rose up in arms against the government.

*Reading*History

C. Analyzing Causes How did debt cause problems for the U.S. government under the Articles of Confederation?

## Shays's Rebellion

In the mid-1780s, Massachusetts faced economic problems, as did other states. People had little money, but the state continued to levy high taxes. The average family owed $200 in taxes per year—more money than most farmers made. Many Massachusetts farmers fell deeply into debt. Debt laws at the time were strict. Anyone who could not repay his debts would have his property auctioned off. If the auction didn't raise enough money to settle the debts, the debtor could be put in jail. In western

Massachusetts, many jails were packed with debtors.

Farmers asked the Massachusetts legislature to provide debt relief. But the legislature refused—and the farmers rebelled. One of the leaders of the rebellion was a Revolutionary War veteran named Daniel Shays. He commanded a group of about 1,500 men.

In January 1787, Shays and his men marched on a federal arsenal, a place to store weapons. The arsenal was defended by 900 soldiers from the state militia. The militia quickly defeated Shays's men. But even though the militia put down **Shays's Rebellion,** as the uprising came to be known, the farmers won the sympathy of many people America's leaders realized that an armed uprising of common farmers spelled danger for the nation.

Some leaders hoped that the nation's ills could be solved by strengthening the national government. In the next section, you'll read how Americans held a convention to change the Articles of Confederation.

**Background**
In 1788, Daniel Shays was pardoned for his actions.

Shays's rebels take over a Massachusetts courthouse. A stone marker rests on the spot of the rebellion.

---

## Section 1 Assessment

### 1. Terms & Names

**Explain the significance of:**
- Wilderness Road
- republic
- Articles of Confederation
- Land Ordinance of 1785
- Northwest Territory
- Northwest Ordinance
- Shays's Rebellion

### 2. Using Graphics

Use a diagram like the one below to list some of the challenges Americans faced in shaping a new government.

Challenges

Which challenge do you think was the toughest? Why? (HI1)

### 3. Main Ideas

**a.** What issues affected the Western territories between 1775 and 1787? (8.2.2)

**b.** What were three successes of the Continental Congress? (8.2.2)

**c.** What were the strengths and weaknesses of the Articles of Confederation? (8.2.2)

### 4. Critical Thinking

**Forming and Supporting Opinions** Which side would you have supported during Shays's Rebellion—the farmers or the officials who called out the militia? Why? (REP4)

**THINK ABOUT**
- the farmers' problems
- the farmers' march on the arsenal
- the job of the government

**ACTIVITY OPTIONS**

**CIVICS**

**GEOGRAPHY**

Write an **opinion article** about how the United States should govern the Western territories or draw a **map** showing how you would have divided the lands. (REP5)

# The Northwest Territory

The Northwest Territory was officially known as "the Territory Northwest of the River Ohio." In the mid-1780s, Congress decided to sell the land in the territory to settlers. The sale of land solved two problems. First, it provided cash for the government. Second, it increased American control over the land.

The Land Ordinance of 1785 outlined how the land in the Northwest Territory would be divided. Congress split the land into grids with clearly defined boundaries. It created townships that could be divided into sections, as shown on the map below. Each township was six miles by six miles. This was an improvement over earlier methods of setting boundaries. Previously, people had used rocks, trees, or other landmarks to set boundaries. There had been constant fights over disputed claims.

**CALIFORNIA STANDARDS**

**8.3.2** Explain how the ordinances of 1785 and 1787 privatized national resources and transferred federally owned lands into private holdings, townships, and states.

## The Land Ordinance of 1785

(MINNESOTA)
Lake Superior
QUEBEC
45°N
(WISCONSIN)
Lake Huron
Lake Michigan
(MICHIGAN)
Lake Erie
Mississippi River
SPANISH POSSESSIONS
40°N
NORTHWEST TERRITORY
(ILLINOIS) (INDIANA) (OHIO)
Ohio River

(OHIO)
36 Miles
PA.
WEST VIRGINIA

Future state boundaries shown.
N
0      250 Miles
0      500 Kilometers
90°W   85°W   80°W   75°W

## TOWNSHIP, 1785

| 36 | 30 | 24 | 18 | 12 | 6 |
|----|----|----|----|----|---|
| 35 | 29 | 23 | 17 | 11 | 5 |
| 34 | 28 | 22 | 16 | 10 | 4 |
| 33 | 27 | 21 | 15 | 9  | 3 |
| 32 | 26 | 20 | 14 | 8  | 2 |
| 31 | 25 | 19 | 13 | 7  | 1 |

Each township contained 36 sections. Each section was one square mile.

## ARTIFACT FILE

**The Theodolite** The theodolite is a surveying tool. It consists of a telescope that can be moved from side to side and up and down. A theodolite measures angles and determines alignment. These functions are necessary for land surveyors to establish accurate boundaries for land claims.

**Township Map** Congress reserved several plots (outlined on map) for special purposes. A few were set aside for later sale to raise money for the government. One plot was reserved to support a local school.

**1** The first things settlers needed were food and shelter. Cutting trees provided fields for crops and wood for log cabins. The first crop most farmers planted was corn. Even if the land was not fully cleared of trees, farmers planted corn between the stumps.

**2** A shortage of labor meant that a farmer working alone was doing well if he cleared several acres a year. As a result, few farms were completely fenced in, and forest covered most of the property. Hogs were allowed to find food in the woods. Farmers collected apples from trees and used sap to make syrup.

**3** Over time, families planted fruits and vegetables. Cattle raising also became more common. Beef cattle supplied families with meat. Dairy cattle provided milk. Families could sell extra fruits, vegetables, and dairy products, such as butter and cheese.

## CONNECT TO GEOGRAPHY

1. **Region** What was the land in the Northwest Territory like before Americans settled there?

2. **Human-Environment Interaction** How did American settlers affect the landscape in the territory?

**G** See Geography Handbook, pages 4–5.

## CONNECT TO HISTORY

3. **Making Inferences** Why did so many people buy land in the new territory?

## On-Line Field Trip

**The Ohio Historical Society** is located in Columbus, Ohio. It maintains a Web site called Ohio History Central that includes information on the Ohio portion of the Northwest Territory.

For more about the Northwest Territory . . .

RESEARCH LINKS
CLASSZONE.COM

# Creating the Constitution

| MAIN IDEA | WHY IT MATTERS NOW | TERMS & NAMES |
|---|---|---|
| The states sent delegates to a convention to solve the problems of the Articles of Confederation. | The Constitutional Convention formed the plan of government that the United States still has today. | Constitutional Convention<br>James Madison<br>Virginia Plan<br>New Jersey Plan<br>Great Compromise<br>Three-Fifths Compromise |

**CALIFORNIA STANDARDS**

**8.2.3** Evaluate the major debates that occurred during the development of the Constitution and their ultimate resolutions in such areas as shared power among institutions, divided state-federal power, slavery, the rights of individuals and states (later addressed by the addition of the Bill of Rights), and the status of American Indian nations under the commerce clause.

**8.2.4** Describe the political philosophy underpinning the Constitution as specified in the Federalist Papers (authored by James Madison, Alexander Hamilton, and John Jay) and the role of such leaders as Madison, George Washington, Roger Sherman, Gouverneur Morris, and James Wilson in the writing and ratification of the Constitution.

**8.3.3** Enumerate the advantages of a common market among the states as foreseen in and protected by the Constitution's clauses on interstate commerce, common coinage, and full-faith and credit.

**Taking Notes**

Use your chart to take notes about the new government and slavery.

| Problems |
|---|
| Western lands |
| Postwar depression |
| Representation in the new government |
| Slavery |

## ONE AMERICAN'S STORY

On May 15, 1787, Virginia Governor Edmund Randolph arrived in Philadelphia. The young nation faced lawlessness, as Shays's Rebellion had shown. Now delegates from throughout the states were coming to Philadelphia to discuss reforming the government. Early in the convention Randolph rose to speak.

*A VOICE FROM THE PAST*

Let us not be afraid to view with a steady eye the [dangers] with which we are surrounded. . . . Are we not on the eve of [a civil] war, which is only to be prevented by the hopes from this convention?

**Edmund Randolph,** quoted in *Edmund Randolph: A Biography*

Edmund Randolph and the other delegates gathered in the Pennsylvania State House.

Over the next four months, the delegates debated how best to keep the United States from falling apart. In this section, you will read about the Convention of 1787 and the creation of the U.S. Constitution.

## A Constitutional Convention Is Called

In 1786, a series of events began that would eventually lead to a new form of government for the United States. In September of that year, delegates from five states met in Annapolis, Maryland, to discuss ways to promote trade among their states. At the time, most states placed high taxes on goods from other states. The delegates believed that creating national trade laws would help the economies of all the states.

Making such changes required amending the Articles of Confederation, because the national government had been granted no power to regulate trade among the states. The Annapolis delegates, led by Alexander Hamilton of New York, called for the states to send representatives to

Philadelphia the following May to discuss such changes.

At first, many Americans doubted that the national government needed strengthening. But news of Shays's Rebellion in late 1786 and early 1787 quickly changed many people's minds. Fearing that rebellion might spread, 12 states sent delegates to the meeting in Philadelphia in the summer of 1787. Only Rhode Island refused to participate.

**Background**
Rhode Island did not send delegates because it feared that a strong national government would force people to repay the war debts on difficult terms.

## The Convention's Delegates

The 55 delegates to the **Constitutional Convention,** as the Philadelphia meeting became known, were a very impressive group. About half were lawyers. Others were planters, merchants, and doctors. Three-fourths of them had been representatives in the Continental Congress. Many had been members of their state legislatures and had helped write their state constitutions. Along with other leaders of the time, these delegates are called the Founders, or Founding Fathers, of the United States.

America's most famous men were at the Constitutional Convention. George Washington, the hero of the Revolution, came out of retirement for the meeting. Benjamin Franklin, the famous scientist and statesman, lent his wit and wisdom to the convention. One of the ablest delegates was **James Madison.** Madison had read more than a hundred books on government in preparation for the meeting. When Thomas Jefferson, serving as ambassador to France, read the list of delegates, he wrote, "It is really an assembly of demigods."

*Reading*History
**A. Evaluating**
How well do the characteristics of the Founders serve as models of civic virtue?

Not everyone was at the Constitutional Convention. Thomas Jefferson and John Adams were overseas at their diplomatic posts. But they wrote home to encourage the delegates. Others had a less positive outlook on the convention. For example, Patrick Henry, who had been elected as a delegate from Virginia, refused to attend. He said he "smelled a rat in Philadelphia, tending toward monarchy."

Also, the convention did not reflect the diverse U.S. population of the 1780s. There were no Native Americans, African Americans, or women among the delegates. The nation's early leaders did not consider these groups of people to be citizens and did not invite any of them to attend. However, the framework of government the Founders established is the very one that would eventually provide full rights and responsibilities to all Americans.

## The Delegates Assemble

Most of the delegates arrived at the Constitutional Convention without a clear idea of what to expect. Some thought they would only draft amendments to the Articles of Confederation. Others thought they would design

*America's*
**HERITAGE**

**INDEPENDENCE HALL**
The Pennsylvania State House, where the Constitutional Convention took place, is now called Independence Hall. It is protected as part of a national park in Philadelphia.

The State House itself was the site where George Washington received his commission to lead the Continental Army and where the Declaration of Independence was signed. The Liberty Bell is nearby. Many visitors come to Philadelphia to stand in the building where much of America's early history as a nation was made.

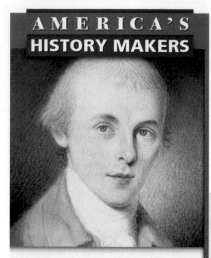

**JAMES MADISON**
**1751–1836**

James Madison was a short, soft-spoken man, but he may have made the greatest contribution of any of the Founders at the Constitutional Convention. He took thorough notes of the convention's proceedings. His notes are the most detailed picture we have of the debates and drama of the convention.

But Madison did not just observe the convention. He was perhaps the most important participant. One of the other delegates called him "the best informed Man of any point in debate." Madison was so important that he earned the title "Father of the Constitution."

**How did Madison contribute to the Constitutional Convention?**

an entirely new plan for the government. But they all agreed that the government should protect people's rights.

Back in 1776, many Americans thought that government was the main threat to people's rights. But by 1787, many realized that the people often came into conflict and needed a government that could maintain order. As a result, the government had to be strong enough to protect people's rights but not too strong to be controlled. Madison later wrote about this problem.

*A VOICE FROM THE PAST*

If men were angels, no government would be necessary. If angels were to govern men, neither external nor internal controls on government would be necessary. In framing a government which is to be administered by men over men, the great difficulty lies in this: you must first enable the government to control the governed; and in the next place oblige it [the government] to control itself.

**James Madison,** *The Federalist* "Number 51"

*Reading* **History**
**B. Using Primary Sources** According to Madison, what is the central problem in framing a government?

This was the challenge that faced the delegates: how to set up a strong but limited federal government. Some, such as Gouverneur Morris of New York, wanted the upper class to control the new government. Others, such as James Wilson of Pennsylvania, favored a direct democracy open to more people. By May 25, 1787, at least two delegates from each of seven states had arrived in Philadelphia. With 29 delegates in attendance, the convention was officially under way.

## The Convention Begins

The first order of business was to elect a president for the convention. Robert Morris of Pennsylvania nominated George Washington. Every delegate voted for him. Washington's quiet and dignified leadership set a solemn and serious tone for the convention.

At their next meeting, the delegates decided on the rules for the convention. They wanted to be able to consider all ideas and to be able to change sides in any debate. They did not want to be pressured by the politics of the day. For these reasons, they decided that their discussions would remain secret. To ensure privacy, the windows in their meeting room were kept shut even though it was summer. Guards were posted outside the door. With the secrecy rule approved, they got down to business.

*Reading* **History**
**C. Making Decisions** Do you agree with the Founders' decision to keep the convention secret? Why or why not?

## The Virginia Plan

On May 29, the delegates began the real work of designing a new national government. Presiding over the convention, George Washington recognized Edmund Randolph as the first speaker. Randolph offered a

The delegates at the Constitutional Convention debated the Constitution intensely.

plan for a whole new government. The plan became known as the **Virginia Plan.** Madison, Randolph, and the other Virginia delegates had drawn up the plan while they waited for the convention to open.

The Virginia Plan proposed a government that would have three branches. The first branch of government was the legislature, which made the laws. The second branch was the executive, which enforced the laws. The third branch was the judiciary, which interpreted the laws.

The Virginia Plan proposed a legislature with two houses. In both houses, the number of representatives from each state would be based on the state's population or its wealth. The legislature would have the power to levy taxes, regulate commerce, and make laws "in all cases where the separate states are incompetent [unable]."

*"If men were angels, no government would be necessary."*
**James Madison**

*Reading* **History**
**D. Summarizing** What was the Virginia Plan?

The Virginia Plan led to weeks of debate. Because they had larger populations, larger states supported the plan. It would give them greater representation in the legislature. The smaller states opposed this plan. They worried that the larger states would end up ruling the others. Delaware delegate John Dickinson voiced the concerns of the small states.

*A VOICE FROM THE PAST*

Some of the members from the small states wish for two branches in the general legislature and are friends to a good [strong] national government; but we would sooner submit [give in] to a foreign power than submit to be deprived, in both branches of the legislature, of an equal suffrage [vote], and thereby be thrown under the domination of the larger states.

**John Dickinson,** quoted in *Mr. Madison's Constitution*

## The Great Compromise

In response to the Virginia Plan, New Jersey delegate William Paterson presented an alternative on June 15. The **New Jersey Plan** called for a legislature with only one house. In it, each state would have one vote. In providing equal representation to each state, the New Jersey Plan was similar to the Articles of Confederation.

Even though the New Jersey Plan gave the legislature the power to regulate trade and to raise money by taxing foreign goods, it did not offer the broad powers proposed by the Virginia Plan. The delegates voted on these two plans on June 19. The Virginia Plan won and became the framework for drafting the Constitution.

## The Great Compromise

**VIRGINIA PLAN**

- The legislative branch would have two houses.
- Both houses in the legislature would assign representatives according to state population or wealth.

**NEW JERSEY PLAN**

- The legislature would have one house.
- Each state would have one vote in the legislature.

**THE GREAT COMPROMISE**

- The Senate would give each state equal representation.
- The legislature would have two houses.
- The House of Representatives would have representation according to state population.

**SKILLBUILDER Interpreting Charts**
1. Which plan appealed more to the small states?
2. Did the Great Compromise include more of what the large states wanted or more of what the small states wanted?

During the rest of June, the delegates argued over representation in the legislature. Emotions ran high as the delegates struggled for a solution. In desperation, the delegates selected a committee to work out a compromise in early July. The committee offered the **Great Compromise**. (Some people also refer to it as the Connecticut Compromise.)

To satisfy the smaller states, each state would have an equal number of votes in the Senate. To satisfy the larger states, the committee set representation in the House of Representatives according to state populations. More than a week of arguing followed the introduction of the plan, but on July 16, 1787, the convention passed it.

**Background**
Roger Sherman of Connecticut is widely credited with proposing the Great Compromise.

## Slavery and the Constitution

Because representation in the House of Representatives would be based on the population of each state, the delegates had to decide who would be counted in that population. The Southern states had many more slaves than the Northern states. Southerners wanted the slaves to be counted as part of the general population for representation but not for taxation. Northerners argued that slaves were not citizens and should not be counted for representation but should be counted for taxation.

On this issue, the delegates reached another compromise, known as the **Three-Fifths Compromise.** Under this compromise, three-fifths of the slave population would be counted when setting direct taxes on the states. This three-fifths ratio also would be used to determine representation in the legislature.

The delegates had another heated debate about the slave trade. Slavery had already been outlawed in several Northern states. All of the Northern states and several of the Southern states had banned the importation of slaves. Many Northerners wanted to see this ban extended to the rest of the nation. But Southern slaveholders strongly

**Reading History**

**E. Forming and Supporting Opinions** Did the delegates do the right thing in agreeing to the Three-Fifths Compromise? Explain.

disagreed. The delegates from South Carolina and Georgia stated that they would never accept any plan "unless their right to import slaves be untouched." Again, the delegates settled on a compromise. On August 29, they agreed that Congress could not ban the slave trade until 1808.

# Regulating Trade

Aside from delaying any ban on the slave trade, the Constitution placed few limits on Congress's power to regulate commerce. Most delegates were glad that Congress would regulate—and even promote—commerce. After all, commercial problems were the main cause of the Annapolis Convention in 1786. Southerners, however, succeeded in banning Congress from taxing exports because Southern economies depended on exports. The Constitution also gave Congress sole power to coin money. Congress could issue money under the Articles of Confederation, but so could the states, which led to economic conflicts.

The Articles of Confederation granted Congress and the states the power to make treaties with Native Americans, and this power was granted exclusively to Congress under the Constitution's Commerce Clause. But the status of Native Americans under the Constitution remained hazy. They were not citizens, nor were they considered foreign nations.

The Constitutional Convention continued to meet into September. On September 15, 1787, the delegates voted their support for the Constitution in its final form. All but three delegates signed the Constitution. It was then sent to the Confederation Congress, which sent it to the states for ratification, or approval. In the next section, you will read about the debate over ratification.

## Now and then

**PRESERVING THE CONSTITUTION**

The National Archives is responsible for preserving the 200-year-old sheets of parchment on which the original Constitution was first written.

The Archives stores the document in an airtight glass case enclosed in a 55-ton vault of steel and concrete. Every few years, scientists examine the pages with the latest technology. For the last examination in 1995, they used fiber-optic light sources and computer-guided electronic cameras designed for space exploration.

---

## Section 2 Assessment

### 1. Terms & Names

**Explain the significance of:**
- Constitutional Convention
- James Madison
- Virginia Plan
- New Jersey Plan
- Great Compromise
- Three-Fifths Compromise

### 2. Using Graphics

Use a chart like the one below to take notes on the contributions made by the leading delegates at the Constitutional Convention. (8.2.4)

| Delegate | Contribution |
|----------|--------------|
|          |              |
|          |              |
|          |              |
|          |              |

### 3. Main Ideas

**a.** What was the relationship between the Annapolis Convention and the Constitutional Convention? (CST1)

**b.** What is the significance of the date 1787? (CST1)

**c.** How did the Constitutional Convention reach a compromise on the issue of slavery? (CST1)

### 4. Critical Thinking

**Analyzing Points of View** How did the delegates at the convention differ on the issue of representation in the new government? (REP5)

**THINK ABOUT**
- the large states and the small states
- the Virginia Plan
- the New Jersey Plan
- the Great Compromise

**ACTIVITY OPTIONS**

**TECHNOLOGY**

**ART**

Think about the Three-Fifths Compromise. Make an **audio recording** of a speech or draw a **political cartoon** that expresses your views on the issue. (REP5)

# Ratifying the Constitution

| MAIN IDEA | WHY IT MATTERS NOW | TERMS & NAMES |
|---|---|---|
| Americans across the nation debated whether the Constitution would produce the best government. | American liberties today are protected by the U.S. Constitution, including the Bill of Rights. | federalism — *The Federalist* papers<br>Federalists — George Mason<br>Antifederalists — Bill of Rights |

**CALIFORNIA STANDARDS**

**8.1.4** Describe the nation's blend of civic republicanism, classical liberal principles, and English parliamentary traditions.

**8.2.3** Evaluate the major debates that occurred during the development of the Constitution and their ultimate resolutions in such areas as shared power among institutions, divided state-federal power, slavery, the rights of individuals and states (later addressed by the addition of the Bill of Rights), and the status of American Indian nations under the commerce clause.

**8.2.4** Describe the political philosophy underpinning the Constitution as specified in the Federalist Papers (authored by James Madison, Alexander Hamilton, and John Jay) and the role of such leaders as Madison, George Washington, Roger Sherman, Gouverneur Morris, and James Wilson in the writing and ratification of the Constitution.

**8.2.5** Understand the significance of Jefferson's Statute for Religious Freedom as a forerunner of the First Amendment and the origins, purpose, and differing views of the founding fathers on the issue of the separation of church and state.

**Taking Notes**

Use your chart to take notes about the new government.

| Problems |
|---|
| Western lands |
| Postwar depression |
| Representation in the new government |
| Slavery |

### ONE AMERICAN'S STORY

In 1788, in Hartford, Connecticut, 168 delegates met to decide whether their state should ratify the U.S. Constitution. Samuel Huntington, Connecticut's governor, addressed the assembly.

*A VOICE FROM THE PAST*

This is a new event in the history of mankind. Heretofore, most governments have been formed by tyrants and imposed on mankind by force. Never before did a people, . . . meet together by their representatives and . . . frame for themselves a system of government.

**Samuel Huntington,** quoted in *Original Meanings*

Samuel Huntington

In this section, you will learn about the ratification of the Constitution.

## Federalists and Antifederalists

By the time the convention in Connecticut opened, Americans had already been debating the new Constitution for months. The document had been printed in newspapers and handed out in pamphlets across the United States. The framers of the Constitution knew that the document would cause controversy. They immediately began to campaign for ratification, or approval, of the Constitution.

The framers suspected that people might be afraid the Constitution would take too much power away from the states. To address this fear, the framers explained that the Constitution was based on federalism. **Federalism** is a system of government in which power is shared between the central (or federal) government and the states. Linking themselves to the idea of federalism, the people who supported the Constitution took the name **Federalists**.

People who opposed the Constitution were called **Antifederalists**. They thought the Constitution took too much power away from the states and did not guarantee rights for the people. Some were afraid that a strong president might be declared king. Others thought the Senate might turn into a powerful aristocracy. In either case, the liberties won at great cost during the Revolution might be lost.

Antifederalists published their views about the Constitution in newspapers and pamphlets. They used logical arguments to convince people to oppose the Constitution. But they also tried to stir people's emotions by charging that it would destroy American liberties. As one Antifederalist wrote, "After so recent a triumph over British despots [oppressive rulers], . . . it is truly astonishing that a set of men among ourselves should have had the effrontery [nerve] to attempt the destruction of our liberties."

## The Federalist Papers

The Federalists did not sit still while the Antifederalists attacked the Constitution. They wrote essays to answer the Antifederalists' attacks. The best known of the Federalist essays are ***The Federalist* papers.** These essays first appeared as letters in New York newspapers. They were later published together in a book called *The Federalist*.

Three well-known politicians wrote *The Federalist* papers—James Madison, Alexander Hamilton, and John Jay, the secretary of foreign affairs for the Confederation Congress. Like the Antifederalists, the Federalists appealed to reason and emotion. In *The Federalist* papers, Hamilton described why people should support ratification.

*A VOICE FROM THE PAST*

Yes, my countrymen, . . . I am clearly of opinion it is in your interest to adopt it [the Constitution]. I am convinced that this is the safest course for your liberty, your dignity, and your happiness.

**Alexander Hamilton,** *The Federalist* "Number 1"

### Federalists and Antifederalists

| FEDERALISTS | ANTIFEDERALISTS |
|---|---|
| • Supported removing some powers from the states and giving more powers to the national government | • Wanted important political powers to remain with the states |
| • Favored dividing powers among different branches of government | • Wanted the legislative branch to have more power than the executive |
| • Proposed a single person to lead the executive branch | • Feared that a strong executive might become a king or tyrant |
| | • Believed a bill of rights needed to be added to the Constitution to protect people's rights |

**John Jay**

**George Mason**

**SKILLBUILDER Interpreting Charts**
1. *Which group wanted a stronger central government?*
2. *If you had been alive in 1787, would you have been a Federalist or an Antifederalist?*

**HISTORY** *through***ART**

Supporters of the Constitution turned out in parades like this one in New York in 1788. The "Ship of State" float has Alexander Hamilton's name on it to celebrate his role in creating the Constitution.

**What does the picture indicate about the importance of the Constitution in people's lives?**

The Federalists had an important advantage over the Antifederalists. Most of the newspapers supported the Constitution, giving the Federalists more publicity than the Antifederalists. Even so, there was strong opposition to ratification in Massachusetts, North Carolina, Rhode Island, New York, and Virginia. If some of these states failed to ratify the Constitution, the United States might not survive.

## The Battle for Ratification

The first four state conventions to ratify the Constitution were held in December 1787. It was a good month for the Federalists. Delaware, New Jersey, and Pennsylvania voted for ratification. In January 1788, Georgia and Connecticut ratified the Constitution. Massachusetts joined these states in early February.

By late June, nine states had voted to ratify the Constitution. That meant that the document was now officially ratified. But New York and Virginia had not yet cast their votes. There were many powerful Antifederalists in both of those states. Without Virginia, the new government would lack the support of the largest state. Without New York, the nation would be separated into two parts geographically.

Virginia's convention opened the first week in June. The patriot Patrick Henry fought against ratification. **George Mason,** perhaps the most influential Virginian aside from Washington, also was opposed to it. Mason had been a delegate to the Constitutional Convention in Philadelphia, but he had refused to sign the final document. Both Henry and Mason would not consider voting for the Constitution until a bill of rights was added. A bill of rights is a set of rules that defines people's rights.

James Madison was also at Virginia's convention. He suggested that Virginia follow Massachusetts's lead and ratify the Constitution, and he recommended the addition of a bill of rights. With the addition of a bill of rights likely, Virginia ratified the Constitution at the end of June.

*Reading* **History**

**B. Drawing Conclusions** How did the lack of a bill of rights endanger the Constitution?

The news of Virginia's vote arrived while the New York convention was in debate. The Antifederalists had outnumbered the Federalists when the convention had begun. But with the news of Virginia's ratification, New Yorkers decided to join the Union. New York also called for a bill of rights.

It was another year before North Carolina ratified the Constitution. In 1790, Rhode Island became the last state to ratify it. By then, the new Congress had already written a bill of rights and submitted it to the states for approval.

## The Bill of Rights

**Background**
The seven states that asked for a bill of rights were Massachusetts, South Carolina, New Hampshire, Virginia, New York, North Carolina, and Rhode Island.

At the same time that seven of the states ratified the Constitution, they asked that it be amended to include a bill of rights. Supporters of a bill of rights hoped that it would set forth the rights of all Americans. They believed it was needed to protect people against the power of the national government.

Madison, who was elected to the new Congress in the winter of 1789, took up the cause. He proposed a set of changes to the Constitution. Congress edited Madison's list and proposed placing the amendments at the end of the Constitution in a separate section.

The amendments went to the states for ratification. As with the Constitution, three-quarters of the states had to ratify the amendments for them to take effect. With Virginia's vote in 1791, ten of the amendments were ratified and became law. These ten amendments to the U.S. Constitution became known as the **Bill of Rights**. (See the Constitution Handbook, pages 266-268.)

The passage of the Bill of Rights was one of the first acts of the new government. In the next chapter, you will read about other issues that faced the new government.

### America's HERITAGE

**RELIGIOUS FREEDOM**
Jefferson and Madison believed that government enforcement of religious laws was the source of much social conflict. They supported freedom of religion as a way to prevent such conflict.

In 1777 Jefferson drafted the Virginia Statute for Religious Freedom, which Madison helped pass into law in 1786. The Statute, which became a basis of the First Amendment to the Constitution, assures that "no man shall be compelled to frequent or support any religious worship, place or ministry whatsoever," and that "all men shall be free to profess, and by argument to maintain, their opinion in matters of religion."

Jefferson was so proud of writing the Statute that he had it listed on his tombstone as one of his greatest achievements.

**Why might religious freedom be important in the new country?**

---

Section **3** Assessment

### 1. Terms & Names

**Explain the significance of:**
• federalism
• Federalists
• Antifederalists
• *The Federalist* papers
• George Mason
• Bill of Rights

### 2. Using Graphics

Use a diagram like the one below to compare and contrast the Federalists and the Antifederalists.

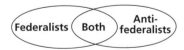

Which group do you think made the stronger argument about ratification? Why? (REP5)

### 3. Main Ideas

**a.** What were Patrick Henry's and George Mason's views on ratification? (8.2.3)

**b.** How did the Federalists and the Antifederalists try to convince people to take their sides in the debate over the Constitution? (8.2.3)

**c.** What was the significance of the Bill of Rights? (8.2.3)

### 4. Critical Thinking

**Recognizing Propaganda** Reread the quotation by Hamilton on page 235. Is it an example of propaganda? Why or why not? (REP4)

**THINK ABOUT**
• Hamilton's use of the word *countrymen*
• Hamilton's reference to liberty, dignity, and happiness

**ACTIVITY OPTIONS**

**SPEECH**
**LANGUAGE ARTS**

Review the major arguments for and against ratification of the Constitution. Hold a **press conference** or write a **news report** on the ratification debate. (REP5)

# The Federalist "Number 51"

**CALIFORNIA STANDARDS**

**Reading 2.3** Find similarities and differences between texts in the treatment, scope, or organization of ideas.

**Setting the Stage** James Madison wrote 29 essays in *The Federalist* papers to argue in favor of ratifying the Constitution. In *The Federalist* "Number 51," Madison explains how the government set up by the Constitution will protect the rights of the people by weakening the power of any interest, or group, to dominate the government. **See Primary Source Explorer**

---

**A CLOSER LOOK**

**MINORITY RIGHTS**

In the 1700s, people feared that democratic majorities could turn into mobs that would violate other people's rights. Madison had to explain how the Constitution would prevent this.

**1. What two methods does Madison suggest a society can use to protect minority rights?**

---

**A CLOSER LOOK**

**REPUBLICS IN LARGE SOCIETIES**

For centuries, people believed that only small societies could be republics. But Madison argues that large societies are more likely to remain republics.

**2. Why does Madison believe that a large republic is likely to protect justice?**

---

It is of great importance in a republic not only to guard the society against the oppression of its rulers, but to guard one part of the society against the injustice of the other part. Different interests necessarily exist in different classes of citizens. If a majority be united by a common interest, the rights of the minority will be insecure. There are but two methods of providing against this evil: the one by creating a will in the community independent of the majority—that is, of the society itself; the other, by **comprehending**[1] in the society so many separate descriptions of citizens as will render an unjust combination of a majority of the whole very improbable, if not **impracticable**.[2] . . .

**Whilst**[3] all authority in it will be derived from and dependent on the society, the society itself will be broken into so many parts, interests and classes of citizens, that the rights of individuals, or of the minority, will be in little danger from interested combinations of the majority. In a free government the security for civil rights must be the same as that for religious rights. It consists in the one case in the multiplicity of interests, and in the other in the **multiplicity of sects**.[4] . . .

In the extended republic of the United States, and among the great variety of interests, parties, and sects which it embraces, a **coalition**[5] of a majority of the whole society could seldom take place on any other principles than those of justice and the general good. . . .

It is no less certain than it is important . . . that the larger the society, provided it lie within a practicable sphere, the more duly capable it will be of self-government. And happily for the republican cause, the practicable sphere may be carried to a very great extent by a **judicious modification**[6] and mixture of the *federal principle*.

—*James Madison*

---

1. **comprehending:** understanding.
2. **impracticable:** not practical or realistic.
3. **whilst:** while.
4. **multiplicity of sects:** large number of groups.
5. **coalition:** alliance of groups.
6. **judicious modification:** careful change.

# Objections to the Constitution

**Setting the Stage** George Mason was one of the leading Antifederalists. In "Objections to the Constitution of Government Formed by the Convention," he listed his reasons for opposing ratification. Above all, he feared that the Constitution created a government that would destroy democracy in the young nation. **See Primary Source Explorer**

There is no Declaration of Rights; and the Laws of the general Government being **paramount**[1] to the Laws and Constitutions of the several States, the Declaration of Rights in the separate States are no Security. Nor are the people secured even in the Enjoyment of the Benefits of the common-Law. . . .

In the House of Representatives, there is not the Substance, but the Shadow only of Representation; which can never produce proper Information in the Legislature, or inspire Confidence in the People; the Laws will therefore be generally made by Men little concern'd in, and **unacquainted**[2] with their Effects and Consequences.

The Senate have the Power of altering all Money-Bills, and of originating Appropriations of Money and the **Sallerys**[3] of the Officers of their own Appointment in **Conjunction**[4] with the President of the United States; altho' they are not the Representatives of the People, or **amenable**[5] to them. . . .

The President of the United States has the unrestrained Power of granting Pardon for Treason; which may be sometimes exercised to screen from Punishment those whom he had secretly **instigated**[6] to commit the Crime, and thereby prevent a Discovery of his own Guilt.

This Government will **commence**[7] in a moderate **Aristocracy;**[8] it is at present impossible to foresee whether it will, in [its] Operation, produce a **Monarchy,**[9] or a corrupt oppressive Aristocracy; it will most probably vibrate some Years between the two, and then terminate in the one or the other.

—*George Mason*

1. **paramount:** most important.
2. **unacquainted:** unfamiliar.
3. **sallerys:** salaries.
4. **conjunction:** joining.
5. **amenable:** agreeable.
6. **instigated:** caused.
7. **commence:** begin.
8. **aristocracy:** rule by a few, usually nobles.
9. **monarchy:** rule by one, usually a king.

## A CLOSER LOOK

### DECLARATION OF RIGHTS

At the time of the ratification debate, Americans across the nation complained that the Constitution did not include a bill of rights.

**3. What arguments does Mason make about the lack of a Declaration of Rights?**

## A CLOSER LOOK

### ABUSE OF POWER

Mason believed that presidents might abuse the power to grant pardons for treason in order to protect the guilty.

**4. Can you think of any presidents who have granted pardons?**

## Interactive Primary Sources Assessment

### 1. Main Ideas

**a.** Why does Madison believe that a society broken into many parts will not endanger minority rights? (REP5)

**b.** What does Mason argue might happen if the president had the power to pardon people? (REP5)

**c.** For each writer, what is one example of a fact and one example of an opinion? (REP5)

### 2. Critical Thinking

**Drawing Conclusions** Who do you think makes the stronger argument? Explain your reasons. (REP4)

**THINK ABOUT**

• what you know about the history of the United States
• the evidence used by each writer

## VISUAL SUMMARY

# Confederation to Constitution (CST2)

*Articles of Confederation*

**1777**
Continental Congress passes the Articles of Confederation.

**1777–1781**
States debate ratification of the Articles of Confederation.

**1781**
Articles of Confederation go into effect.

**1786**
Annapolis Convention is held.

**1786–1787**
Shays's Rebellion occurs.

**1787**
Constitutional Convention is held in Philadelphia.

**1788**
U.S. Constitution is ratified.

**1789**
Government created by the new Constitution takes power.

**1791**
Bill of Rights is added to the Constitution.

*Constitution*

*Bill of Rights*

## TERMS & NAMES

Briefly explain the significance of each of the following.

1. republic
2. Articles of Confederation
3. Northwest Ordinance
4. Shays's Rebellion
5. Constitutional Convention
6. James Madison
7. Great Compromise
8. Federalists
9. George Mason
10. Bill of Rights

## REVIEW QUESTIONS

### The Confederation Era (pages 221–227)

1. What is the Wilderness Road, and where did it lead? (HI1)
2. What problems did the Confederation Congress successfully address? (HI1)
3. What powers did the government have under the Articles of Confederation? (REP4)
4. How did Shays's Rebellion affect people's views on the Articles of Confederation? (HI2)

### Creating the Constitution (pages 228–233)

5. What groups of people were not represented at the Constitutional Convention? (HI1)
6. What were some things the delegates agreed on at the convention? (HI1)
7. What compromises did the delegates make during the convention? (HI1)

### Ratifying the Constitution (pages 234–239)

8. What is federalism? (HI1)
9. Why were Virginia and New York important in the battle for ratification of the Constitution? (HI2)
10. Why did some states think that it was necessary to add a bill of rights to the Constitution? (HI1)

## CRITICAL THINKING

### 1. USING YOUR NOTES: SOLVING PROBLEMS

| Problems | Solutions |
|---|---|
| Western lands | |
| Postwar depression | |
| Representation in the new government | |
| Slavery | |

Using your completed chart, answer the questions below. (HI2)

a. What were the major problems facing the nation during the Confederation Era?
b. How well did the nation solve these problems? Explain.

### 2. ANALYZING LEADERSHIP

Think about the leaders discussed in this chapter. Based on their actions, which leader do you think made the greatest contribution to the Constitutional Convention? Why? (HI1)

### 3. THEME: DEMOCRATIC IDEALS

How do the Articles of Confederation and the Constitution each carry out democratic ideals? (REP4)

### 4. APPLYING CITIZENSHIP SKILLS

Do you think the Founders were right to make the compromises they did in the Constitution on the issues of representation and slavery? What might have happened if they had not compromised? (HI4)

### 5. RECOGNIZING EFFECTS

How might U.S. history be different if Virginia had refused to ratify the Constitution? If New York had refused? If both had refused? (HI4)

### Interact *with* History

How did your ideas about how you would form a government change after reading this chapter?

Use the map and your knowledge of U.S. history to answer questions 1 and 2.

Additional Test Practice, pp. S1–S33.

**Ratification in Middle States, 1790**

- Federalist majority
- Antifederalist majority
- Evenly divided
- Sparsely populated

NEW YORK

PENNSYLVANIA

New York

Philadelphia

NEW JERSEY

ATLANTIC OCEAN

DELAWARE

N 0 100 Miles

0 200 Kilometers

Source: *American Heritage Pictorial Atlas of United States History*

1. In which two states did the Federalists have statewide majorities? (8.2.4)

   A. Delaware and New Jersey

   B. Delaware and New York

   C. New Jersey and Pennsylvania

   D. New York and Pennsylvania

2. Which of the following is true? (8.2.4)

   A. Most of New York supported the Federalists.

   B. Most of Pennsylvania supported the Antifederalists.

   C. Philadelphia supported the Federalists.

   D. New Jersey supported both positions equally.

This quotation from John Dickinson describes his view of the Virginia Plan. Use the quotation and your knowledge of U.S. history to answer question 3.

*PRIMARY SOURCE*

Some of the members from the small states wish for two branches in the general legislature and are friends to a good [strong] national government; but we would sooner submit [give in] to a foreign power than submit to be deprived, in both branches of the legislature, of an equal suffrage [vote], and thereby be thrown under the domination of the larger states.

**John Dickinson,** quoted in *Mr. Madison's Constitution*

3. Which statement best summarizes his concern? (8.2.3)

   A. Large states should have more votes.

   B. Small states should have more votes.

   C. All states should have equal votes.

   D. The states should not have any votes.

**TEST PRACTICE**
CLASSZONE.COM

## ALTERNATIVE ASSESSMENT

### 1. WRITING ABOUT HISTORY

Suppose you are a reporter covering the Constitutional Convention. Write an **article** to inform readers about the Virginia Plan and the New Jersey Plan. (REP5)

- Conduct research about both plans in the library.
- Quote delegates in your article.
- Make your article objective.

### 2. COOPERATIVE LEARNING

Work with a group to stage a debate between a Federalist and an Antifederalist. In preparation, research arguments on each side of these issues: (REP5)

- the representation of people in Congress
- the strength of the president and Senate
- the need for a bill of rights

## INTEGRATED TECHNOLOGY

### DOING INTERNET RESEARCH

Conduct research to acquire biographical information about one of the following people highlighted in this chapter: Daniel Boone, John Jay, William Paterson, or George Mason. (REP3)

- On the Internet, locate Web sites that include details about the person's early life, family life, education, accomplishments, and historical significance.
- Take notes from your Internet sources, keeping track of the addresses of Web sites you find to be most informative. Then write a short biography about the person you chose.

For more about these individuals . . .

**INTERNET ACTIVITY**
CLASSZONE.COM

# The Living Constitution

The Framers of the Constitution created a flexible plan for governing the United States far into the future. They also described ways to allow changes in the Constitution. For over 200 years, the Constitution has guided the American people. It remains a "living document." The Constitution still thrives, in part, because it echoes the principles the delegates valued. Each generation of Americans renews the meaning of the Constitution's timeless ideas. These two pages show you some ways in which the Constitution has shaped events in American history. **See Primary Source Explorer** ◎

*"In framing a system which we wish to last for ages, we should not lose sight of the changes which ages will produce."*

—JAMES MADISON, CONSTITUTIONAL CONVENTION

## 1787

Delegates in Philadelphia sign the Constitution.

## 1965

Civil rights leaders protest to end the violation of their constitutional rights. Dr. Martin Luther King, Jr., Coretta Scott King, and others march from Selma toward Montgomery, Alabama, to gain voting rights.

## 1971

The 26th Amendment to the Constitution gives young people "18 years of age or older" the right to vote.

## 1981

A Supreme Court decision rules that Congress can exclude women from the draft. Still, many women who have joined the armed forces have served in combat.

## HOW TO READ THE CONSTITUTION

The complete text of the Constitution of the United States begins on page 248. The main column has the actual text. Some of the spellings and punctuation have been updated for easier reading. Headings and subheadings have been added to the Constitution to help you find specific topics. Those parts of the Constitution that are no longer in use have been crossed out. "A Closer Look" notes and charts will help you understand issues related to the Constitution.

### The New York Times

"All the News That's Fit to Print"

National Edition
Midwest: Mostly sunny, breezy and seasonable in the Great Lakes area and Ohio Valley. Becoming very warm after a cold start in the western Plains. Weather map is on page A8.

SATURDAY, FEBRUARY 13, 1999

ONE DOLLAR

VOL. CXLVIII.... No. 51,432

## CLINTON ACQUITTED DECISIVELY: NO MAJORITY FOR EITHER CHARGE

### President Says He Is Sorry And Seeks Reconciliation

**CENSURE IS BARRED**

But Rebuke From Both Sides of Aisle Dilutes President's Victory

By JAMES BENNET and JOHN M. BRODER

By ALISON MITCHELL

### The Fallout Of the Trial

Effects on the Office Are Far From Certain

By R. W. APPLE Jr.

## 1999

The Senate tries President Bill Clinton for the impeachment charges brought against him by the House of Representatives. As required by the Constitution, the Senate needs a two-thirds majority vote to convict him. This rule saves his presidency.

# Seven Principles of the Constitution

The Framers of the Constitution constructed a new system of government. Seven principles supported their efforts. To picture how these principles work, imagine seven building blocks. Together they form the foundation of the United States Constitution. In the pages that follow, you will find the definitions and main ideas of the principles shown in the graphic below.

**CALIFORNIA STANDARDS**

**8.1.4** Describe the nation's blend of civic republicanism, classical liberal principles, and English parliamentary traditions.

**8.2.7** Describe the principles of federalism, dual sovereignty, separation of powers, checks and balances, the nature and purpose of majority rule, and the ways in which the American idea of constitutionalism preserves individual rights.

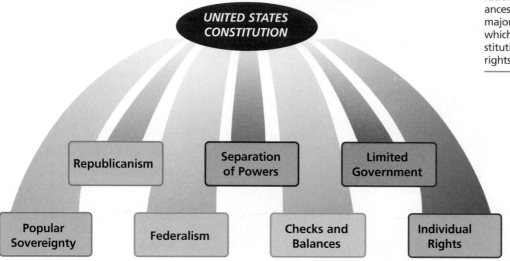

UNITED STATES CONSTITUTION

Republicanism • Separation of Powers • Limited Government

Popular Sovereignty • Federalism • Checks and Balances • Individual Rights

## 1 Popular Sovereignty
### *Who Gives the Government Its Power?*

"We the people of the United States . . . establish this Constitution for the United States of America." These words from the Preamble, or introduction, to the Constitution clearly spell out the source of the government's power. The American form of government comes from a school of political thought called classical liberalism, which emphasizes freedom, democracy, and the importance of the individual. The Constitution rests on the idea of **popular sovereignty**—a government in which the people rule. As the nation changed and grew, popular sovereignty took on new meaning. A broader range of Americans shared in the power to govern themselves.

In 1987, Americans gathered in Washington, D.C., to celebrate the 200th anniversary of the Constitution. The banner proudly displays that the power to govern belongs to the people.

In a republican government, voting citizens make their voices heard at the polls. The power of the ballot prompts candidates to listen to people's concerns.

## 2 Republicanism
### *How Are People's Views Represented in Government?*

The Framers of the Constitution wanted the people to have a voice in government. Yet the Framers also feared that public opinion might stand in the way of sound decision making. To solve this problem, they looked to republicanism as a model of government.

**Republicanism** is based on this belief: The people exercise their power by voting for their political representatives. According to the Framers, these lawmakers played the key role in making a republican government work. Article 4, Section 4, of the Constitution also calls for every state to have a "republican form of government." Civic Republicanism is the idea that citizens stay informed about politics and participate in the process.

## 3 Federalism
### *How Is Power Shared?*

The Framers wanted the states and the nation to become partners in governing. To build cooperation, the Framers turned to federalism. **Federalism** is a system of government in which power is divided between a central government and smaller political units, such as states. In the early years of the United States, federalism was closely related to *dual sovereignty,* the idea that the powers of the federal government and the states were clearly defined, and each had exclusive power over their own spheres with little overlap. This view of federalism led to states' rights conflicts, which were contributing factors in the Civil War.

The Framers used federalism to structure the Constitution. The Constitution assigns certain powers to the national government. These are *delegated powers.* Powers kept by the states are *reserved powers.* Powers shared or exercised by national and state governments are known as *concurrent powers.*

### Federalism

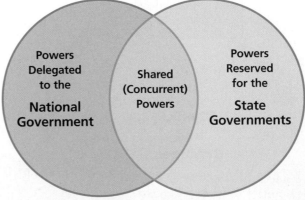

The overlapping spheres of power bind the American people together.

## 4 Separation of Powers
### *How Is Power Divided?*

CALIFORNIA STANDARDS

**8.2.7** Describe the principles of federalism, dual sovereignty, separation of powers, checks and balances, the nature and purpose of majority rule, and the ways in which the American idea of constitutionalism preserves individual rights.

The Framers were concerned that too much power might fall into the hands of a single group. To avoid this problem, they built the idea of **separation of powers** into the Constitution. This principle means the division of basic government roles into branches. No one branch is given all the power. Articles 1, 2, and 3 of the Constitution detail how powers are split among the three branches.

**Separation of Powers**

**UNITED STATES CONSTITUTION**

| **Article 1** | **Article 2** | **Article 3** |
|---|---|---|
| **Legislative Branch** | **Executive Branch** | **Judicial Branch** |
| Congress makes the laws. | President enforces the laws. | Supreme Court interprets the law. |

## 5 Checks and Balances
### *How Is Power Evenly Distributed?*

Checks and Balances

Executive Branch (President)
Checks on Courts
Checks on President
Checks on Congress
Checks on President
Judicial Branch (Supreme Court)
Legislative Branch (Congress)
Checks on Courts
Checks on Congress

Baron de Montesquieu, an 18th-century French thinker, wrote, "Power should be a check to power." His comment refers to the principle of **checks and balances.** Each branch of government can exercise checks, or controls, over the other branches. Though the branches of government are separate, they rely on one another to perform the work of government.

The Framers included a system of checks and balances in the Constitution to help make sure that the branches work together fairly. For example, only Congress can pass laws. Yet the president can check this power by refusing to sign a law into action. In turn, the Supreme Court can declare that a law, passed by Congress and signed by the president, violates the Constitution.

## ⑥ Limited Government
### *How Is Abuse of Power Prevented?*

The Framers restricted the power of government. Article 1, Section 9, of the Constitution lists the powers denied to the Congress. Article 1, Section 10, forbids the states to take certain actions.

The principle of **limited government** is also closely related to the "rule of law": In the American government everyone, citizens and powerful leaders alike, must obey the law. Individuals or groups cannot twist or bypass the law to serve their own interests.

'I AM THE LAW!'

In this political cartoon, President Richard Nixon shakes his fist as he defies the "rule of law." Faced with charges of violating the Constitution, Nixon resigned as president in 1974.

Students exercise their right to protest. They urge the community to protect the environment.

## ⑦ Individual Rights
### *How Are Personal Freedoms Protected?*

The first ten amendments to the Constitution shield people from an overly powerful government. These amendments are called the Bill of Rights. The Bill of Rights guarantees certain **individual rights,** or personal liberties and privileges. For example, government cannot control what people write or say. People also have the right to meet peacefully and to ask the government to correct a problem. Later amendments to the Constitution also advanced the cause of individual rights.

---

### *Assessment: Principles of the Constitution*

#### 1. Main Ideas

**a.** What are the seven principles of government? (8.2.7)

**b.** How does the Constitution reflect the principle of separation of powers? (8.2.7)

**c.** Why did the Framers include a system of checks and balances in the Constitution? (8.2.7)

#### 2. Critical Thinking

**Forming Opinions** How do the rights and responsibilities of U.S. citizenship reflect American national identity? (8.2.7)

**THINK ABOUT**

• what it means to be an American

• the rights and responsibilities of U.S. citizens

# The Constitution of the United States

**See Primary Source Explorer**

*" In 1787, I was not included in that 'We the people.' . . . But through the process of amendment, interpretation, and court decision, I have finally been included in 'We the people.'"*

—BARBARA JORDAN, 1974
The first African-American congresswoman from the South (Texas)

## Preamble. *Purpose of the Constitution*

We the people of the United States, in order to form a more perfect Union, establish justice, insure domestic tranquility, provide for the common defense, promote the general welfare, and secure the blessings of liberty to ourselves and our posterity, do ordain and establish this Constitution for the United States of America.

### A CLOSER LOOK  Goals of the Preamble

| PREAMBLE | EXPLANATION | EXAMPLES |
|---|---|---|
| "Form a more perfect Union" | Create a nation in which states work together | • U.S. Postal System<br>• U.S. coins, paper money |
| "Establish justice" | Make laws and set up courts that are fair | • Court system<br>• Jury system |
| "Insure domestic tranquility" | Keep peace within the country | • National Guard<br>• Federal marshals |
| "Provide for the common defense" | Safeguard the country against attack | • Army<br>• Navy |
| "Promote the general welfare" | Contribute to the happiness and well-being of all the people | • Social Security<br>• Food and drug laws |
| "Secure the blessings of liberty to ourselves and our posterity" | Make sure future citizens remain free | • Commission on Civil Rights<br>• National Council on Disability |

**SKILLBUILDER Interpreting Charts**
1. *Which goal of the Preamble do you think is most important? Why?*
2. *How does the Preamble reflect the principle of popular sovereignty?*

# Article 1. *The Legislature*

**MAIN IDEA** The main role of Congress, the legislative branch, is to make laws. Congress is made up of two houses—the Senate and the House of Representatives. Candidates for each house must meet certain requirements. Congress performs specific duties, also called delegated powers.

**WHY IT MATTERS NOW** Representatives in Congress still voice the views and concerns of the people.

**Section 1. Congress** All legislative powers herein granted shall be vested in a Congress of the United States, which shall consist of a Senate and House of Representatives.

## Section 2. The House of Representatives

**1. Elections** The House of Representatives shall be composed of members chosen every second year by the people of the several states, and the **electors** in each state shall have the qualifications requisite for electors of the most numerous branch of the state legislature.

**2. Qualifications** No person shall be a Representative who shall not have attained to the age of twenty-five years, and been seven years a citizen of the United States, and who shall not, when elected, be an inhabitant of that state in which he shall be chosen.

**3. Number of Representatives** Representatives and direct taxes shall be apportioned among the several states which may be included within this Union, according to their respective numbers, which shall be determined by adding to the whole number of free persons, including those bound to service for a term of years, and excluding Indians not taxed, three-fifths of all other Persons. The actual **enumeration** shall be made within three years after the first meeting of the Congress of the United States, and within every subsequent term of ten years, in such manner as they shall by law direct. The number of Representatives shall not exceed one for every thirty thousand, but each state shall have at least one Representative; and until such enumeration shall be made, the state of New Hampshire shall be entitled to choose three, Massachusetts eight, Rhode Island and Providence Plantations one, Connecticut five, New York six, New Jersey four, Pennsylvania eight, Delaware one, Maryland six, Virginia ten, North Carolina five, South Carolina five, and Georgia three.

**4. Vacancies** When vacancies happen in the representation from any state, the executive authority thereof shall issue writs of election to fill such vacancies.

**5. Officers and Impeachment** The House of Representatives shall choose their Speaker and other officers; and shall have the sole power of **impeachment.**

*A CLOSER LOOK*

**ELECTIONS**

Representatives are elected every two years. There are no limits on the number of terms a person can serve.

1. What do you think are the advantages of holding frequent elections of representatives?

*A CLOSER LOOK*

**REPRESENTATION**

Some delegates, such as Gouverneur Morris, thought that representation should be based on wealth as well as population. Others, such as James Wilson, thought representation should be based on population only. Ultimately, the delegates voted against including wealth as a basis for apportioning representatives.

2. How do you think the United States would be different today if representation were based on wealth?

**CALIFORNIA STANDARDS**

**8.2.6** Enumerate the powers of government set forth in the Constitution and the fundamental liberties ensured by the Bill of Rights.

**8.3.3** Enumerate the advantages of a common market among the states as foreseen in and protected by the Constitution's clauses on interstate commerce, common coinage, and full-faith and credit.

**8.3.6** Describe the basic lawmaking process and how the Constitution provides numerous opportunities for citizens to participate in the political process and to monitor and influence government (e.g., function of elections, political parties, interest groups).

## Section 3. The Senate

1. **Numbers** The Senate of the United States shall be composed of two Senators from each state, chosen by the legislature thereof, for six years; and each Senator shall have one vote.

2. **Classifying Terms** Immediately after they shall be assembled in consequence of the first election, they shall be divided as equally as may be into three classes. The seats of the Senators of the first class shall be vacated at the expiration of the second year, of the second class at the expiration of the fourth year, and of the third class at the expiration of the sixth year, so that one-third may be chosen every second year; and if vacancies happen by resignation, or otherwise, during the recess of the legislature of any state, the executive thereof may make temporary appointments until the next meeting of the legislature, which shall then fill such vacancies.

3. **Qualifications** No person shall be a Senator who shall not have attained to the age of thirty years, and been nine years a citizen of the United States, and who shall not, when elected, be an inhabitant of that state for which he shall be chosen.

### A CLOSER LOOK Federal Office Terms and Requirements

| POSITION | TERM | MINIMUM AGE | RESIDENCY | CITIZENSHIP |
|---|---|---|---|---|
| Representative | 2 years | 25 | state in which elected | 7 years |
| Senator | 6 years | 30 | state in which elected | 9 years |
| President | 4 years | 35 | 14 years in the U.S. | natural-born |
| Supreme Court Justice | unlimited | none | none | none |

**SKILLBUILDER Interpreting Charts**

*Why do you think the term and qualifications for a senator are more demanding than for a representative?*

4. **Role of Vice-President** The Vice-President of the United States shall be President of the Senate, but shall have no vote, unless they be equally divided.

5. **Officers** The Senate shall choose their other officers, and also a President **pro tempore**, in the absence of the Vice-President, or when he shall exercise the office of President of the United States.

6. **Impeachment Trials** The Senate shall have the sole power to try all impeachments. When sitting for that purpose, they shall be on oath or affirmation. When the President of the United States is tried, the Chief Justice shall preside: and no person shall be convicted without the concurrence of two-thirds of the members present.

7. **Punishment for Impeachment** Judgment in cases of impeachment shall not extend further than to removal from office, and disqualification to hold and enjoy any office of honor, trust or profit under the United States; but the party convicted shall nevertheless be liable and subject to **indictment**, trial, judgment and punishment, according to law.

## Section 4. Congressional Elections

**1. Regulations** The times, places and manner of holding elections for Senators and Representatives shall be prescribed in each state by the legislature thereof; but the Congress may at any time by law make or alter such regulations, except as to the places of choosing Senators.

**2. Sessions** The Congress shall assemble at least once in every year, ~~and such meeting shall be on the first Monday in December, unless they shall by law appoint a different day.~~

## Section 5. Rules and Procedures

**1. Quorum** Each house shall be the judge of the elections, returns and qualifications of its own members, and a majority of each shall constitute a **quorum** to do business; but a smaller number may adjourn from day to day, and may be authorized to compel the attendance of absent members, in such manner, and under such penalties as each house may provide.

**2. Rules and Conduct** Each house may determine the rules of its proceedings, punish its members for disorderly behavior, and, with the concurrence of two-thirds, expel a member.

**3. Congressional Records** Each house shall keep a journal of its proceedings, and from time to time publish the same, excepting such parts as may in their judgment require secrecy; and the yeas and nays of the members of either house on any question shall, at the desire of one-fifth of those present, be entered on the journal.

**4. Adjournment** Neither house, during the session of Congress, shall, without the consent of the other, adjourn for more than three days, nor to any other place than that in which the two houses shall be sitting.

## Section 6. Payment and Privileges

**1. Salary** The Senators and Representatives shall receive a compensation for their services, to be ascertained by law, and paid out of the treasury of the United States. They shall in all cases, except treason, felony and breach of the peace, be privileged from arrest during their attendance at the session of their respective houses, and in going to and returning from the same; and for any speech or debate in either house, they shall not be questioned in any other place.

**2. Restrictions** No Senator or Representative shall, during the time for which he was elected, be appointed to any civil office under the authority of the United States, which shall have been created, or the emoluments whereof shall have been increased during such time; and no person holding any office under the United States, shall be a member of either house during his continuance in office.

*A CLOSER LOOK*

**SENATE RULES**

Senate rules allow for debate on the floor. Using a tactic called filibustering, senators give long speeches to block the passage of a bill. Senator Strom Thurmond holds the filibustering record—24 hours, 18 minutes.

**4. Why might a senator choose filibustering as a tactic to block a bill?**

*A CLOSER LOOK*

**SALARIES**

Senators and representatives are paid $136,700 a year. The Speaker of the House is paid $175,400— the same as the vice-president.

**5. How do the salaries of members of Congress compare to those of adults you know?**

## Section 7. How a Bill Becomes a Law

**1. Tax Bills** All bills for raising **revenue** shall originate in the House of Representatives; but the Senate may propose or concur with amendments as on other Bills.

**2. Lawmaking Process** Every bill which shall have passed the House of Representatives and the Senate, shall, before it become a law, be presented to the President of the United States; if he approves he shall sign it, but if not he shall return it, with his objections to that house in which it shall have originated, who shall enter the objections at large on their journal, and proceed to reconsider it. If after such reconsideration two-thirds of that house shall agree to pass the bill, it shall be sent, together with the objections, to the other house, by which it shall likewise be reconsidered, and if approved by two-thirds of that house, it shall become a law. But in all such cases the votes of both houses shall be determined by yeas and nays, and the names of the persons voting for and against the bill shall be entered on the journal of each house respectively. If any bill shall not be returned by the President within ten days (Sundays excepted) after it shall have been presented to him, the same shall be a law, in like manner as if he had signed it, unless the Congress by their adjournment prevent its return, in which case it shall not be a law.

**3. Role of the President** Every order, resolution, or vote to which the concurrence of the Senate and House of Representatives may be necessary (except on a question of adjournment) shall be presented to the President of the United States; and before the same shall take effect, shall be approved by him, or being disapproved by him, shall be repassed by two-thirds of the Senate and House of Representatives, according to the rules and limitations prescribed in the case of a bill.

## A CLOSER LOOK  How a Bill Becomes a Law

### Introduction

The House introduces a bill and refers it to a committee.

The Senate introduces a bill and refers it to a committee.

### Committee Action

The House committee may approve, rewrite, or kill the bill.

The Senate committee may approve, rewrite, or kill the bill.

### Floor Action

The House debates and votes on its version of the bill.

House and Senate committee members work out the differences between the two versions.

The Senate debates and votes on its version of the bill.

## Section 8. Powers Granted to Congress

**1. Taxation** The Congress shall have power to lay and collect taxes, duties, imposts and excises, to pay the debts and provide for the common defense and general welfare of the United States; but all duties, imposts and excises shall be uniform throughout the United States;

**2. Credit** To borrow money on the credit of the United States;

**3. Commerce** To regulate commerce with foreign nations, and among the several states, and with the Indian tribes;

**4. Naturalization, Bankruptcy** To establish a uniform rule of **naturalization,** and uniform laws on the subject of bankruptcies throughout the United States;

**5. Money** To coin money, regulate the value thereof, and of foreign coin, and fix the standard of weights and measures;

**6. Counterfeiting** To provide for the punishment of counterfeiting the securities and current coin of the United States;

**7. Post Office** To establish post offices and post roads;

**8. Patents, Copyrights** To promote the progress of science and useful arts, by securing for limited times to authors and inventors the exclusive right to their respective writings and discoveries;

**9. Federal Courts** To constitute **tribunals** inferior to the Supreme Court;

**10. International Law** To define and punish piracies and **felonies** committed on the high seas, and offenses against the law of nations;

**11. War** To declare war, grant letters of marque and reprisal, and make rules concerning captures on land and water;

**12. Army** To raise and support armies, but no **appropriation** of money to that use shall be for a longer term than two years;

**13. Navy** To provide and maintain a navy;

**Final Approval**

**5** Both houses of Congress pass the revised bill.

**Enactment**

President signs the bill.

**OR**

President vetoes the bill.

**6**

**7** Two-thirds majority vote of Congress is needed to approve a vetoed bill.

**8** Bill Becomes Law.

LAW

**SKILLBUILDER Interpreting Charts**

1. *How can a president block a bill?*
2. *What examples of checks and balances are shown in the chart?*

**14. Regulation of Armed Forces** To make rules for the government and regulation of the land and naval forces;

**15. Militia** To provide for calling forth the **militia** to execute the laws of the Union, suppress insurrections and repel invasions;

**16. Regulations for Militia** To provide for organizing, arming, and disciplining the militia, and for governing such part of them as may be employed in the service of the United States, reserving to the states respectively the appointment of the officers, and the authority of training the militia according to the discipline prescribed by Congress;

**17. District of Columbia** To exercise exclusive legislation in all cases whatsoever, over such district (not exceeding ten miles square) as may, by cession of particular states, and the acceptance of Congress, become the seat of the government of the United States, and to exercise like authority over all places purchased by the consent of the legislature of the state in which the same shall be, for the erection of forts, magazines, arsenals, dockyards, and other needful buildings;—and

**18. Elastic Clause** To make all laws which shall be necessary and proper for carrying into execution the foregoing powers, and all other powers vested by this Constitution in the government of the United States, or in any department or officer thereof.

## A CLOSER LOOK  The Elastic Clause

**ELASTIC CLAUSE**

**1787** 13 states • agricultural • rural about 4 million people POP.

The elastic clause allows future generations to expand the meaning of the Constitution. Congress can take action on issues not spelled out in the Constitution.

**TODAY** 50 states • industrial • high-tech • urban POP. about 250 million people

## A CLOSER LOOK

**HABEAS CORPUS**

A writ of habeas corpus is a legal order. It protects people from being held in prison or jail without formal charges of a crime. In 1992, the Supreme Court recognized that "habeas corpus is the [basic] instrument for safeguarding individual freedom."

**8. How does habeas corpus help ensure fairness and justice?**

## Section 9. Powers Denied Congress

**1. Slave Trade** ~~The migration or importation of such persons as any of the states now existing shall think proper to admit, shall not be prohibited by the Congress prior to the year one thousand eight hundred and eight, but a tax or duty may be imposed on such importation, not exceeding ten dollars for each person.~~

**2. Habeas Corpus** The privilege of the writ of habeas corpus shall not be suspended, unless when in cases of rebellion or invasion the public safety may require it.

**3. Illegal Punishment** No <u>**bill of attainder**</u> or <u>**ex post facto law**</u> shall be passed.

**4. Direct Taxes** No capitation, ~~or other direct,~~ tax shall be laid, ~~unless in~~ ~~proportion to the census or enumeration herein before directed to be taken.~~

**5. Export Taxes** No tax or duty shall be laid on articles exported from any state.

**6. No Favorites** No preference shall be given by any regulation of commerce or revenue to the ports of one state over those of another: nor shall vessels bound to, or from, one state be obliged to enter, clear, or pay duties in another.

**7. Public Money** No money shall be drawn from the treasury, but in consequence of appropriations made by law; and a regular statement and account of the receipts and expenditures of all public money shall be published from time to time.

**8. Titles of Nobility** No title of nobility shall be granted by the United States: and no person holding any office of profit or trust under them shall, without the consent of the Congress, accept of any present, emolument, office, or title, of any kind whatever, from any king, prince, or foreign state.

## Section 10. Powers Denied the States

**1. Restrictions** No state shall enter into any treaty, alliance, or confederation; grant letters of marque and reprisal; coin money; emit bills of credit; make anything but gold and silver coin a <u>**tender**</u> in payment of debts; pass any bill of attainder, ex post facto law, or law impairing the obligation of contracts, or grant any title of nobility.

**2. Import and Export Taxes** No state shall, without the consent of the Congress, lay any imposts or duties on imports or exports, except what may be absolutely necessary for executing its inspection laws; and the net produce of all duties and imposts, laid by any state on imports or exports, shall be for the use of the treasury of the United States; and all such laws shall be subject to the revision and control of the Congress.

**3. Peacetime and War Restraints** No state shall, without the consent of Congress, lay any duty of tonnage, keep troops or ships of war in time of peace, enter into any agreement or compact with another state, or with a foreign power, or engage in war, unless actually invaded, or in such imminent danger as will not admit of delay.

---

### A CLOSER LOOK

**DIRECT TAX**

In 1913, the 16th Amendment allowed Congress to collect an income tax—a direct tax on the amount of money a person earns. Americans today pay much more in taxes than their ancestors would have imagined.

**9. Why do you think the issue of taxes is so important to people?**

---

### A CLOSER LOOK

**TITLES OF NOBILITY**

The Framers disapproved of titles of nobility. The list of grievances in the Declaration of Independence included numerous examples of King George III's abuses of power. Symbols of these abuses included English titles of nobility, such as "king," "queen," and "duke." The Framers said clearly that there would be no such titles in the new republic.

**10. How do TV news reporters address members of Congress and the president?**

---

## Article 1 Assessment

### 1. Main Ideas

**a.** What is the main job of the legislative branch? (8.2.6)

**b.** What role does the vice-president of the United States play in the Senate? (8.2.6)

**c.** Why are there more members in the House of Representatives than the Senate? (8.2.6)

**d.** What is one of the powers denied to Congress? (8.2.6)

### 2. Critical Thinking

**Drawing Conclusions** How does Article 1 show that the Constitution is a clearly defined yet flexible document? (8.2.6)

**THINK ABOUT**
• the powers of Congress
• the "elastic clause"

**natural-born citizen** a citizen born in the United States or a U.S. commonwealth, or to parents who are U.S. citizens living outside the country

**affirmation** a statement declaring that something is true

# Article 2. *The Executive*

> **MAIN IDEA** The president and vice-president are the leaders of the executive branch. Their main role is to enforce the laws. The president commands the military and makes foreign treaties with the Senate's approval.
>
> **WHY IT MATTERS NOW** As the United States has become a world power, the authority of the president has also expanded.

## Section 1. The Presidency

**1. Terms of Office** The executive power shall be vested in a President of the United States of America. He shall hold his office during the term of four years, and, together with the Vice-President, chosen for the same term, be elected, as follows:

**2. Electoral College** Each state shall appoint, in such manner as the Legislature thereof may direct, a number of electors, equal to the whole number of Senators and Representatives to which the State may be entitled in the Congress; but no Senator or Representative, or person holding an office of trust or profit under the United States, shall be appointed an elector.

### A CLOSER LOOK  Electoral College *(based on 2000 Census)*

American voters do not choose their president directly. Members of a group called the electoral college actually elect the president. Each state has electors. Together they form the electoral college. In most states, the winner takes all. Except for Maine and Nebraska, all the electoral votes of a state go to one set of candidates.

**number of electors for each state = total number of its senators and representatives**

WA 11, OR 7, MT 3, ND 3, MN 10, NH 4, ME 4, VT 3, NY 31, MA 12, RI 4, CT 7, NJ 15, DE 3, DC 3, MD 10, ID 4, WY 3, SD 3, WI 10, MI 17, PA 21, NV 5, UT 5, NE 5, IA 7, IL 21, IN 11, OH 20, WV 5, VA 13, CA 55, CO 9, KS 6, MO 11, KY 8, NC 15, AZ 10, NM 5, OK 7, AR 6, TN 11, SC 8, MS 6, AL 9, GA 15, HI 4, TX 34, LA 9, FL 27, AK 3

**SKILLBUILDER Interpreting Maps**

1. *How many electoral votes does your state have?*
2. *In which states would a presidential candidate campaign most heavily? Why?*

**3. Former Method of Electing President** ~~The electors shall meet in their respective states, and vote by ballot for two persons, of whom one at least shall not be an inhabitant of the same state with themselves. And they shall make a list of all the persons voted for, and of the number of votes for each; which list they shall sign and certify, and transmit sealed to the seat of the government of the United States, directed to the President of the Senate. The President of the Senate shall, in the presence of the Senate and House of Representatives, open all the certificates, and the votes shall then be counted. The person having the greatest number of votes shall be the~~

President, if such number be a majority of the whole number of electors appointed; and if there be more than one who have such majority, and have an equal number of votes, then the House of Representatives shall immediately choose by ballot one of them for President; and if no person have a majority, then from the five highest on the list the said House shall in like manner choose the President. But in choosing the President, the votes shall be taken by States, the representation from each state having one vote; a quorum for this purpose shall consist of a member or members from two-thirds of the states, and a majority of all the states shall be necessary to a choice. In every case, after the choice of the President, the person having the greatest number of votes of the electors shall be the Vice-President. But if there should remain two or more who have equal votes, the Senate shall choose from them by ballot the Vice-President.

**4. Election Day** The Congress may determine the time of choosing the electors, and the day on which they shall give their votes, which day shall be the same throughout the United States.

**5. Qualifications** No person except a **natural-born citizen,** or a citizen of the United States at the time of the adoption of this Constitution, shall be eligible to the office of President; neither shall any person be eligible to that office who shall not have attained to the age of thirty-five years, and been fourteen years a resident within the United States.

**6. Succession** In case of the removal of the President from office, or of his death, resignation, or inability to discharge the powers and duties of the said office, the same shall devolve on the Vice-President, and the Congress may by law provide for the case of removal, death, resignation or inability, both of the President and Vice-President, declaring what officer shall then act as President, and such officer shall act accordingly, until the disability be removed, or a President shall be elected.

**7. Salary** The President shall, at stated times, receive for his services, a compensation, which shall neither be increased nor diminished during the period for which he shall have been elected, and he shall not receive within that period any other emolument from the United States, or any of them.

**8. Oath of Office** Before he enter on the execution of his office, he shall take the following oath or **affirmation:**—"I do solemnly swear (or affirm) that I will faithfully execute the office of President of the United States, and will to the best of my ability, preserve, protect and defend the Constitution of the United States."

## Commander in Chief

As a military leader, President Abraham Lincoln meets with his generals during the Civil War.

## Chief Executive

Like a business executive, the president solves problems and makes key decisions. President John F. Kennedy is shown in the oval office in 1962.

## Chief Diplomat and Chief of State

As a foreign policy maker, President Richard M. Nixon visits the People's Republic of China in 1972.

## Legislative Leader

President Lyndon Johnson signs the Civil Rights Act of 1964. All modern presidents have legislative programs they want Congress to pass.

## Head of a Political Party

President Ronald Reagan rallies support at the 1984 Republican Convention. By this time, Reagan had put together a strong bloc of voters who supported the Republican Party's policies. During his presidency (1981–1989), Reagan helped build new unity among party members.

## Section 2. Powers of the President

**1. Military Powers** The President shall be commander in chief of the Army and Navy of the United States, and of the militia of the several states, when called into the actual service of the United States; he may require the opinion, in writing, of the principal officer in each of the executive departments, upon any subject relating to the duties of their respective offices, and he shall have power to grant **reprieves** and pardons for offenses against the United States, except in cases of impeachment.

**2. Treaties, Appointments** He shall have power, by and with the advice and consent of the Senate, to make treaties, provided two-thirds of the Senators present concur; and he shall nominate, and by and with the advice and consent of the Senate, shall appoint ambassadors, other public ministers and consuls, judges of the Supreme Court, and all other officers of the United States, whose appointments are not herein otherwise provided for, and which shall be established by law; but the Congress may by law vest the appointment of such inferior officers, as they think proper, in the President alone, in the courts of law, or in the heads of departments.

**3. Vacancies** The President shall have power to fill up all vacancies that may happen during the recess of the Senate, by granting commissions which shall expire at the end of their next session.

## Section 3. Presidential Duties

He shall from time to time give to the Congress information of the State of the Union, and recommend to their consideration such measures as he shall judge necessary and expedient; he may, on extraordinary occasions, **convene** both houses, or either of them, and in case of disagreement between them, with respect to the time of adjournment, he may adjourn them to such time as he shall think proper; he shall receive ambassadors and other public ministers; he shall take care that the laws be faithfully executed, and shall commission all the officers of the United States.

## Section 4. Impeachment

The President, Vice-President and all civil officers of the United States shall be removed from office on impeachment for, and conviction of, treason, bribery, or other high crimes and **misdemeanors**.

### VOCABULARY

**reprieves** delays or cancellations of punishment

**convene** call together

**misdemeanors** violations of the law

### A CLOSER LOOK

**SUPREME COURT APPOINTMENTS**

Recent presidents have used their power of appointment to add minorities and women to the Supreme Court. In 1967, President Lyndon Johnson appointed the first African-American justice, Thurgood Marshall. In 1981, President Ronald Reagan appointed the first woman, Sandra Day O'Connor.

**12. What do you think influences a president's choice for a Supreme Court justice?**

### A CLOSER LOOK

**STATE OF THE UNION**

Major TV networks broadcast the State of the Union address to the whole nation. In this yearly message, the president urges Congress to achieve certain lawmaking goals. The president's speech also must gain the attention of TV viewers.

**13. Why is the president's power to persuade an important political skill?**

---

### Article 2 Assessment

#### 1. Main Ideas

**a.** What is the chief purpose of the executive branch? (8.2.6)

**b.** What are the requirements for becoming president? (8.2.6)

**c.** How does the Constitution limit the president's power to make appointments and treaties? (8.2.6)

#### 2. Critical Thinking

**Analyzing Issues** Why do you think the Constitution states that the president must seek approval from the Senate for most political appointments and treaties? (8.2.6)

**THINK ABOUT**
• the abuse of power
• the will of the voters

**A CLOSER LOOK**

**ORGANIZING FEDERAL COURTS**

The Judiciary Act of 1789, passed by the First Congress, included establishing a Supreme Court with a chief justice and five associate justices and other lower federal courts.

**14. How many Supreme Court justices are there today?**

**A CLOSER LOOK**

**JUDICIAL POWER**

Judicial power gives the Supreme Court and other federal courts the authority to hear certain kinds of cases. These courts have the power to rule in cases involving the Constitution, national laws, treaties, and states' conflicts.

**15. What federal cases have you seen reported on TV?**

# Article 3. *The Judiciary*

> **MAIN IDEA** The judicial branch interprets the laws. This branch includes the Supreme Court, the highest court in the nation, and other federal courts.
>
> **WHY IT MATTERS NOW** Supreme Court rulings can shape government policies on hotly debated issues.

**Section 1. Federal Courts and Judges** The judicial power of the United States shall be vested in one Supreme Court, and in such **inferior courts** as the Congress may from time to time ordain and establish. The judges, both of the Supreme and inferior courts, shall hold their offices during good behavior, and shall, at stated times, receive for their services a compensation, which shall not be diminished during their continuance in office.

## Section 2. The Courts' Authority

**1. General Authority** The judicial power shall extend to all cases, in law and equity, arising under this Constitution, the laws of the United States, and treaties made, or which shall be made, under their authority;—to all cases affecting ambassadors, other public ministers and consuls;—to all cases of admiralty and maritime jurisdiction;—to controversies to which the United States shall be a party;—to controversies between two or more states;— between a state and citizens of another state;—between citizens of different states;—between citizens of the same state claiming lands under grants of different states, and between a state, or the citizens thereof, and foreign states, citizens or subjects.

**A CLOSER LOOK** **Judicial Review**

Judicial review allows the Supreme Court and other federal courts to play a key role in lawmaking. The judges examine a law or government activity. They then decide whether it violates the Constitution. The Supreme Court established this important right in the case of *Marbury* v. *Madison* (1803). (See Chapter 10.)

**2. Supreme Court** In all cases affecting ambassadors, other public ministers and consuls, and those in which a state shall be party, the Supreme Court shall have original jurisdiction. In all the other cases before mentioned, the Supreme Court shall have **appellate** jurisdiction, both as to law and fact, with such exceptions, and under such regulations, as the Congress shall make.

**CHECKS ON COURTS**
- Appoints federal judges
- Can grant reprieves and pardons for federal crimes

## Executive Branch (President)

**CHECKS ON CONGRESS**
- Can veto acts of Congress
- Can call special sessions of Congress
- Can suggest laws and send messages to Congress

**CHECKS ON PRESIDENT**
- Can impeach and remove the president
- Can override veto
- Controls spending of money
- Senate can refuse to confirm presidential appointments and to ratify treaties

## Legislative Branch (Congress)

**CHECKS ON COURT**
- Can impeach and remove federal judges
- Establishes lower federal courts
- Can refuse to confirm judicial appointments

**CHECKS ON PRESIDENT**
- Can declare executive acts unconstitutional
- Judges, appointed for life, are free from executive control

## Judicial Branch (Supreme Court)

**CHECKS ON CONGRESS**
- Judicial review—Can declare acts of Congress unconstitutional

**SKILLBUILDER Interpreting Charts**
1. *Why is judicial review an important action of the Supreme Court?*
2. *Which check do you think is most powerful? Why?*

**3. Trial by Jury** The trial of all crimes, except in cases of impeachment, shall be by jury; and such trial shall be held in the state where the said crimes shall have been committed; but when not committed within any state, the trial shall be at such place or places as the Congress may by law have directed.

## Section 3. Treason

**1. Definition** Treason against the United States shall consist only in levying war against them, or in adhering to their enemies, giving them aid and comfort. No person shall be convicted of treason unless on the testimony of two witnesses to the same overt act, or on confession in open court.

**2. Punishment** The Congress shall have power to declare the punishment of treason, but no attainder of treason shall work corruption of blood, or forfeiture except during the life of the person attained.

*Article 3 Assessment*

### 1. Main Ideas

**a.** What is the main purpose of the judicial branch? (8.2.6)

**b.** What is judicial review? (8.2.6)

**c.** What are two kinds of cases that can begin in the Supreme Court? (8.2.6)

### 2. Critical Thinking

**Drawing Conclusions** Why might the Supreme Court feel less political pressure than Congress in making judgments about the Constitution? (8.2.6)

**THINK ABOUT**
- the appointment of Supreme Court justices
- Congress members' obligation to voters

### A CLOSER LOOK  Federalism

## Americans live under both national and state governments.

**NATIONAL POWERS**
- Maintain military
- Declare war
- Establish postal system
- Set standards for weights and measures
- Protect copyrights and patents

**SHARED POWERS**
- Collect taxes
- Establish courts
- Regulate interstate commerce
- Regulate banks
- Borrow money
- Provide for the general welfare
- Punish criminals

**STATE POWERS**
- Establish local governments
- Set up schools
- Regulate state commerce
- Make regulations for marriage
- Establish and regulate corporations

**SKILLBUILDER Interpreting Charts**
*What do you think is the purpose of dividing the powers between national and state governments?*

# Article 4. *Relations Among States*

> **MAIN IDEA** States must honor one another's laws, records, and court rulings.
>
> **WHY IT MATTERS NOW** Article 4 promotes cooperation, equality, and fair treatment of citizens from all the states.

**Section 1. State Acts and Records** Full faith and credit shall be given in each state to the public acts, records, and judicial proceedings of every other state. And the Congress may by general laws prescribe the manner in which such acts, records and proceedings shall be proved, and the effect thereof.

## Section 2. Rights of Citizens

**1. Citizenship** The citizens of each state shall be entitled to all privileges and **immunities** of citizens in the several states.

**2. Extradition** A person charged in any state with treason, felony, or other crime, who shall flee from justice, and be found in another state, shall on demand of the executive authority of the state from which he fled, be delivered up, to be removed to the state having jurisdiction of the crime.

**3. Fugitive Slaves** No person held to service or labor in one state, under the laws thereof, escaping into another, shall, in consequence of any law or regulation therein, be discharged from such service or labor, but shall be delivered up on claim of the party to whom such service or labor may be due.

### A CLOSER LOOK

**EXTRADITION**

Persons charged with serious crimes cannot escape punishment by fleeing to another state. They must be returned to the first state and stand trial there.

**16. Why do you think the Framers included the power of extradition?**

## Section 3. New States

**1. Admission** New states may be admitted by the Congress into this Union; but no new state shall be formed or erected within the jurisdiction of any other state; nor any state be formed by the junction of two or more states, or parts of states, without the consent of the legislatures of the states concerned as well as of the Congress.

**2. Congressional Authority** The Congress shall have power to dispose of and make all needful rules and regulations respecting the territory or other property belonging to the United States; and nothing in this Constitution shall be so construed as to prejudice any claims of the United States, or of any particular state.

## Section 4. Guarantees to the States

The United States shall guarantee to every state in this Union a republican form of government, and shall protect each of them against invasion; and on application of the legislature, or of the executive (when the legislature cannot be convened) against domestic violence.

# Article 5. *Amending the Constitution*

> **MAIN IDEA** The Constitution can be amended, or formally changed.
>
> **WHY IT MATTERS NOW** The amendment process allows the Constitution to adapt to modern times.

The Congress, whenever two-thirds of both houses shall deem it necessary, shall propose amendments to this Constitution, or, on the application of the legislatures of two-thirds of the several states, shall call a convention for proposing amendments, which, in either case, shall be valid to all intents and purposes, as part of this Constitution, when ratified by the legislatures of three-fourths of the several states, or by conventions in three-fourths thereof, ¹as the one or the other mode of ratification may be proposed by the Congress; ~~provided that no amendment which may be made prior to the year one thousand eight hundred and eight shall in any manner affect the first and fourth clauses in the ninth section of the first article~~; and that no state, without its consent, shall be deprived of its equal **suffrage** in the Senate.

**A CLOSER LOOK**

**ADMISSION TO STATEHOOD**

In 1998, Puerto Ricans voted against their island becoming the 51st state. A lawyer in Puerto Rico summed up a main reason: "Puerto Ricans want to have ties to the U.S., but they want to protect their language and culture." Also, as a U.S. commonwealth, Puerto Rico makes its own laws and handles its own finances.

**17. Do you think Puerto Rico should become a state? Why or why not?**

**A CLOSER LOOK** Process for Amending the Constitution

**Proposing Amendments**

| **2/3** vote of both houses of Congress | **2/3** state legislatures' call for a national convention |

**Ratifying Amendments**

| **3/4** approval of state legislatures | **3/4** approval at a state convention |

**SKILLBUILDER Interpreting Charts**
*Why do you think more votes are needed to ratify an amendment than to propose one?*

**PAYING DEBTS**

The U.S. government agreed to pay all debts held under the Articles of Confederation. For example, the United States still owed money from the costs of the Revolutionary War.

**18. What problems might arise in a country that has a huge national debt?**

# Article 6. *Supremacy of the National Government*

> **MAIN IDEA** The Constitution, national laws, and treaties are the supreme, or highest, law of the land. All government officials must promise to support the Constitution.
>
> **WHY IT MATTERS NOW** The authority of federal laws over state laws helps keep the nation unified.

**Section 1. Valid Debts** All debts contracted and engagements entered into, before the adoption of this Constitution, shall be as valid against the United States under this Constitution, as under the Confederation.

**Section 2. Supreme Law** This Constitution, and the laws of the United States which shall be made in pursuance thereof; and all treaties made, or which shall be made, under the authority of the United States, shall be the supreme law of the land; and the judges in every state shall be bound thereby, anything in the constitution or laws of any state to the contrary notwithstanding.

In 1957, the "supreme law of the land" was put to a test. The governor of Arkansas defied a Supreme Court order. The Court ruled that African-American students could go to all-white public schools. President Dwight D. Eisenhower then sent federal troops to protect the first African-American students to enroll in Central High School in Little Rock, Arkansas.

**Section 3. Loyalty to Constitution** The Senators and Representatives before mentioned, and the members of the several state legislatures, and all executive and judicial officers, both of the United States and of the several states, shall be bound by oath or affirmation to support this Constitution; but no religious test shall ever be required as a qualification to any office or public trust under the United States.

REDEUNT SATURNIA REGNA.

On the erection of the Eleventh PILLAR of the great National DOME, we beg leave most sincerely to felicitate "OUR DEAR COUNTRY."

Rise it will.

The foundation good—it may yet be SAVED.

The FEDERAL EDIFICE.

**A CLOSER LOOK**

This political cartoon shows that New York was the 11th state to ratify the Constitution. Each of the 13 states is represented by a pillar.

# Article 7. *Ratification*

**MAIN IDEA** Nine of the 13 states had to ratify, or approve, the Constitution before it could go into effect.

**WHY IT MATTERS NOW** The approval of the Constitution launched a new plan of government still followed today.

The **ratification** of the conventions of nine states shall be sufficient for the establishment of this Constitution between the states so ratifying the same. Done in convention by the **unanimous consent** of the states present, the seventeenth day of September in the year of our Lord one thousand seven hundred and eighty-seven and of the independence of the United States of America the twelfth. In witness whereof we have hereunto subscribed our names.

*George Washington—President and deputy from Virginia*

**New Hampshire:** *John Langdon, Nicholas Gilman*

**Massachusetts:** *Nathaniel Gorham, Rufus King*

**Connecticut:** *William Samuel Johnson, Roger Sherman*

**New York:** *Alexander Hamilton*

**New Jersey:** *William Livingston, David Brearley, William Paterson, Jonathan Dayton*

**Pennsylvania:** *Benjamin Franklin, Thomas Mifflin, Robert Morris, George Clymer, Thomas FitzSimons, Jared Ingersoll, James Wilson, Gouverneur Morris*

**Delaware:** *George Read, Gunning Bedford, Jr., John Dickinson, Richard Bassett, Jacob Broom*

**Maryland:** *James McHenry, Dan of St. Thomas Jenifer, Daniel Carroll*

**Virginia:** *John Blair, James Madison, Jr.*

**North Carolina:** *William Blount, Richard Dobbs Spaight, Hugh Williamson*

**South Carolina:** *John Rutledge, Charles Cotesworth Pinckney, Charles Pinckney, Pierce Butler*

**Georgia:** *William Few, Abraham Baldwin*

**A CLOSER LOOK**

**THE SIGNERS**

The 39 men who signed the Constitution were wealthy and well-educated. About half of them were trained in law. Others were doctors, merchants, bankers, and slaveholding planters. Missing from the list of signatures are the names of African Americans, Native Americans, and women. These groups reflected the varied population of the United States in the 1780s.

**19. How do you think the absence of these groups affected the decisions made in creating the Constitution?**

## Articles 4–7 Assessment

### 1. Main Ideas

**a.** What rights does Article 4 guarantee to citizens if they go to other states in the nation? (8.2.6)

**b.** What are two ways of proposing an amendment to the Constitution? (8.2.6)

**c.** What makes up "the supreme law of the land"? (8.2.6)

### 2. Critical Thinking

**Forming and Supporting Opinions** Should the Framers of the Constitution have allowed the people to vote directly for ratification of the Constitution? Why or why not? (HI1)

**THINK ABOUT**

• the idea that the government belongs to the people
• the general public's ability to make sound political decisions

# The Bill of Rights
# and Amendments 11–27

**CALIFORNIA STANDARDS**

**8.2.3** Evaluate the major debates that occurred during the development of the Constitution and their ultimate resolutions in such areas as shared power among institutions, divided state-federal power, slavery, the rights of individuals and states (later addressed by the addition of the Bill of Rights), and the status of American Indian nations under the commerce clause.

**8.2.6** Enumerate the powers of government set forth in the Constitution and the fundamental liberties ensured by the Bill of Rights.

**8.2.7** Describe the principles of federalism, dual sovereignty, separation of powers, checks and balances, the nature and purpose of majority rule, and the ways in which the American idea of constitutionalism preserves individual rights.

**8.3.7** Understand the functions and responsibilities of a free press.

In 1787, Thomas Jefferson sent James Madison a letter about the Constitution. Jefferson wrote, "I will now add what I do not like . . . [there is no] bill of rights." He explained his reasons: "A bill of rights is what the people are entitled to against every government on earth . . . and what no just government should refuse." Jefferson's disapproval is not surprising. In writing the Declaration of Independence, he spelled out basic individual rights that cannot be taken way. These are "life, liberty, and the pursuit of happiness." The Declaration states that governments are formed to protect these rights.

Several states approved the Constitution only if a list of guaranteed freedoms was added. While serving in the nation's first Congress, James Madison helped draft the Bill of Rights. In 1791, these first ten amendments became part of the Constitution.

## AMENDMENTS 1–10. *The Bill of Rights*

> **MAIN IDEA** The Bill of Rights protects citizens from government interference.
> **WHY IT MATTERS NOW** Issues related to the Bill of Rights are still being applied, tested, and interpreted.

### AMENDMENT 1. Religious and Political Freedom (1791)

Congress shall make no law respecting an establishment of religion, or prohibiting the free exercise thereof; or **abridging** the freedom of speech, or of the press; or the right of the people peaceably to assemble, and to petition the Government for a redress of grievances.

### A CLOSER LOOK  The Five Freedoms

**Freedom of Religion**
Right to worship

**Freedom of Speech**
Right to state ideas

**Freedom of the Press**
Right to publish ideas

**Freedom of Assembly**
Right to meet peacefully in groups

**Freedom to Petition**
Right to protest the government

**SKILLBUILDER** Interpreting Charts
1. *Why is freedom of speech and the press important in a democratic society?*
2. *What impact has religious freedom had on the American way of life?*

## AMENDMENT 2. Right to Bear Arms (1791) A well-regulated militia, being necessary to the security of a free state, the right of the people to keep and bear arms, shall not be infringed.

## AMENDMENT 3. Quartering Troops (1791) No soldier shall, in time of peace be **quartered** in any house, without the consent of the owner, nor in time of war, but in a manner to be prescribed by law.

## AMENDMENT 4. Search and Seizure (1791) The right of the people to be secure in their persons, houses, papers, and effects, against unreasonable searches and seizures, shall not be violated, and no warrants shall issue, but upon probable cause, supported by oath or affirmation, and particularly describing the place to be searched, and the persons or things to be seized.

## AMENDMENT 5. Rights of Accused Persons (1791) No person shall be held to answer for a capital, or otherwise infamous crime, unless on a presentment or indictment of a Grand Jury, except in cases arising in the land or naval forces, or in the militia, when in actual service in time of war or public danger; nor shall any person be subject for the same offense to be twice put in jeopardy of life or limb; nor shall be compelled in any criminal case to be a witness against himself, nor be deprived of life, liberty, or property, without **due process of law;** nor shall private property be taken for public use, without just compensation.

## AMENDMENT 6. Right to a Speedy, Public Trial (1791)
In all criminal prosecutions, the accused shall enjoy the right to a speedy and public trial, by an impartial jury of the State and district wherein the crime shall have been committed, which district shall have been previously ascertained by law, and to be informed of the nature and cause of the accusation; to be confronted with the witnesses against him; to have **compulsory process** for obtaining witnesses in his favor, and to have the assistance of **counsel** for his defense.

### A CLOSER LOOK

#### SEARCHES

Metal detectors at airports search passengers. Airline workers search all carry-on luggage. Do these actions violate the 4th Amendment? The courts say no. They have cited many situations that allow for searches without a warrant, or written order. A person's right to privacy is balanced against the government's need to prevent crime.

**20. What does the right to privacy mean to you at home and at school?**

### A CLOSER LOOK

In 1966, the Supreme Court made a decision based on the 5th and 6th Amendments. The warnings outlined in this ruling are often called "Miranda rights." Miranda rights protect suspects from giving forced confessions. Police must read these rights to a suspect they are questioning. For example:
- "You have the right to remain silent."
- "Anything that you say can and will be used against you in a court of law."
- "You have the right to an attorney."

A CLOSER LOOK

Protesters such as the young woman at left claim that the death penalty violates the 8th Amendment, which protects people against "cruel and unusual punishment." Supporters (above) believe that the death penalty is a justly deserved punishment.

ABOLISH THE DEATH PENALTY

**A CLOSER LOOK**

**STATES' POWERS**

The 10th Amendment gives the states reserved powers. Any powers not clearly given to the national government by the U.S. Constitution or denied to the states in Article I, Section 10, belong to the states. State constitutions sometimes assume authority in unexpected areas. For example, California's constitution sets rules for governing the use of fishing nets.

**21. What are some common areas in which states have authority?**

**AMENDMENT 7. Trial by Jury in Civil Cases (1791)** In suits at **common law,** where the value in controversy shall exceed twenty dollars, the right of trial by jury shall be preserved, and no fact tried by a jury, shall be otherwise reexamined in any court of the United States, than according to the rules of the common law.

**AMENDMENT 8. Limits of Fines and Punishments (1791)** Excessive **bail** shall not be required, nor excessive fines imposed, nor cruel and unusual punishments inflicted.

**AMENDMENT 9. Rights of People (1791)** The enumeration in the Constitution of certain rights shall not be construed to deny or disparage others retained by the people.

**AMENDMENT 10. Powers of States and People (1791)** The powers not delegated to the United States by the Constitution, nor prohibited by it to the States, are reserved to the States respectively, or to the people.

## Bill of Rights Assessment

### 1. Main Ideas

**a.** Which amendment protects your privacy? (8.2.6)

**b.** Which amendments guarantee fair legal treatment? (8.2.6)

**c.** Which amendment prevents the federal government from taking powers away from the states and the people? (8.2.6)

### 2. Critical Thinking

**Forming and Supporting Opinions** The 4th, 5th, 6th, 7th, and 8th Amendments protect innocent people accused of crimes. Do you think these five amendments also favor the rights of actual criminals? Explain. (8.2.6)

**THINK ABOUT**

• criminals who go free if valuable evidence is found after their trials

• criminals released on bail

# Amendments 11–27

> **MAIN IDEA** The Constitution has adapted to social changes and historical trends.
> **WHY IT MATTERS NOW** Amendments 11–27 show that the Constitution is a living document.

## AMENDMENT 11. Lawsuits Against States (1798)

**Passed by Congress March 4, 1794. Ratified February 7, 1795. Proclaimed 1798.**
**Note: Article 3, Section 2, of the Constitution was modified by Amendment 11.**

The Judicial power of the United States shall not be construed to extend to any suit in law or **equity**, commenced or prosecuted against one of the United States by citizens of another state, or by citizens or subjects of any foreign state.

## AMENDMENT 12. Election of Executives (1804)

**Passed by Congress December 9, 1803. Ratified June 15, 1804.**
**Note: Part of Article 2, Section 1, of the Constitution was replaced by the 12th Amendment.**

The electors shall meet in their respective states and vote by ballot for President and Vice-President, one of whom, at least, shall not be an inhabitant of the same state with themselves; they shall name in their ballots the person voted for as President, and in distinct ballots the person voted for as Vice-President, and they shall make distinct lists of all persons voted for as President, and of all persons voted for as Vice-President, and of the number of votes for each, which lists they shall sign and certify, and transmit sealed to the seat of the government of the United States, directed to the President of the Senate;—the President of the Senate shall, in the presence of the Senate and House of Representatives, open all the certificates and the votes shall then be counted;—the person having the greatest number of votes for President, shall be the President, if such number be a majority of the whole number of electors appointed; and if no person have such majority, then from the persons having the highest numbers not exceeding three on the list of those voted for as President, the House of Representatives shall choose immediately, by ballot, the President. But in choosing the President, the votes shall be taken by states, the representation from each state having one vote; a quorum for this purpose shall consist of a member or members from two-thirds of the states, and a majority of all the states shall be necessary to a choice. And if the House of Representatives shall not choose a President whenever the right of choice shall devolve upon them, before the fourth day of March next following, then the Vice-President shall act as President, as in the case of the death or other constitutional disability of the President. The person having the greatest number of votes as Vice-President, shall be the Vice-President, if such number be a majority of the whole number of Electors appointed, and if no person have a majority, then from the two highest numbers on the list, the Senate shall choose the Vice-President; a quorum for the purpose shall consist of two-thirds of the whole number of Senators, and a majority of the whole number shall be necessary to a choice. But no person constitutionally ineligible to the office of President shall be eligible to that of Vice-President of the United States.

**A CLOSER LOOK**

### SEPARATE BALLOTS

The presidential election of 1800 ended in a tie between Thomas Jefferson and Aaron Burr. At this time, the candidate with the most votes became president. The runner-up became vice-president. The 12th Amendment calls for separate ballots for the president and vice-president. The vice-president is specifically elected to the office, rather than being the presidential candidate with the second-most votes.

**22. Why do you think it's important for a presidential election to result in a clear-cut winner?**

# AMENDMENT 13. Slavery Abolished (1865)

**Passed by Congress January 31, 1865. Ratified December 6, 1865.**

**Note: A portion of Article 4, Section 2, of the Constitution was superseded by the 13th Amendment.**

**Section 1.** Neither slavery nor involuntary **servitude**, except as a punishment for crime whereof the party shall have been duly convicted, shall exist within the United States, or any place subject to their jurisdiction.

**Section 2.** Congress shall have power to enforce this article by appropriate legislation.

# AMENDMENT 14. Civil Rights (1868)

**Passed by Congress June 13, 1866. Ratified July 9, 1868.**

**Note: Article 1, Section 2, of the Constitution was modified by Section 2 of the 14th Amendment.**

**Section 1.** All persons born or **naturalized** in the United States, and subject to the jurisdiction thereof, are citizens of the United States and of the state wherein they reside. No state shall make or enforce any law which shall abridge the privileges or immunities of citizens of the United States; nor shall any state deprive any person of life, liberty, or property, without due process of law; nor deny to any person within its jurisdiction the equal protection of the laws.

**Section 2.** Representatives shall be apportioned among the several states according to their respective numbers, counting the whole number of persons in each state, excluding Indians not taxed. But when the right to vote at any election for the choice of electors for President and Vice-President of the United States, Representatives in Congress, the executive and judicial officers of a state, or the members of the legislature thereof, is denied to any of the male inhabitants of such state, being twenty-one years of age, and citizens of the United States, or in any way abridged, except for participation in rebellion, or other crime, the basis of representation therein shall be reduced in the proportion which the number of such male citizens shall bear to the whole number of male citizens twenty-one years of age in such state.

## A CLOSER LOOK

The 14th Amendment laid the groundwork for many civil rights laws, such as the Americans with Disabilities Act (1990). This act gave people with mental or physical disabilities "equal protection of the laws." For example, public places had to be designed for wheelchair use. Wider doors and ramps allow disabled people to go in and out of buildings.

**Section 3.** No person shall be a Senator or Representative in Congress, or elector of President and Vice-President, or hold any office, civil or military, under the United States, or under any state, who, having previously taken an oath, as a member of Congress, or as an officer of the United States, or as a member of any state legislature, or as an executive or judicial officer of any state, to support the Constitution of the United States, shall have engaged in **insurrection** or rebellion against the same, or given aid or comfort to the enemies thereof. But Congress may, by a vote of two-thirds of each house, remove such disability.

**Section 4.** The validity of the public debt of the United States, authorized by law, including debts incurred for payment of pensions and **bounties** for services in suppressing insurrection or rebellion, shall not be questioned. But neither the United States nor any state shall assume or pay any debt or obligation incurred in aid of insurrection or rebellion against the United States, or any claim for the loss or emancipation of any slave; but all such debts, obligations and claims shall be held illegal and void.

**Section 5.** The Congress shall have power to enforce, by appropriate legislation, the provisions of this article.

## AMENDMENT 15. Right to Vote (1870)

**Passed by Congress February 26, 1869. Ratified February 3, 1870.**

**Section 1.** The right of citizens of the United States to vote shall not be denied or abridged by the United States or by any state on account of race, color, or previous condition of servitude.

**Section 2.** The Congress shall have power to enforce this article by appropriate legislation.

**A CLOSER LOOK**

**VOTING RIGHTS**

The Voting Rights Act of 1965 extended the 15th Amendment. To qualify as voters, African Americans were no longer required to take tests proving that they could read and write. Also, federal examiners could help register voters. As a result, the number of African-American voters rose sharply.

**23.** What effect do you think the Voting Rights Act had on candidates running for office?

## A CLOSER LOOK Reconstruction Amendments

The 13th, 14th, and 15th Amendments are often called the Reconstruction Amendments. They were passed after the Civil War during the government's attempt to rebuild the Union and to grant rights to recently freed African Americans.

**Amendment 13**

**Amendment 14**

**Amendment 15**

**1865**
• Ended slavery in the United States

**1868**
• Defined national and state citizenship
• Protected citizens' rights
• Promised "equal protection of the laws"

**1870**
• Designed to protect African Americans' voting rights

**SKILLBUILDER Interpreting Charts**
*What problems did these amendments try to solve?*

## A CLOSER LOOK

### INCOME TAX

People below the poverty level, as defined by the federal government, do not have to pay income tax. In 1997, the poverty level for a family of four was $16,400 per year. About 13.3 percent of all Americans were considered poor in 1997.

**24. Why do you think people below the poverty level do not pay any income tax?**

# AMENDMENT 16. Income Tax (1913)

**Passed by Congress July 12, 1909. Ratified February 3, 1913.**

**Note: Article 1, Section 9, of the Constitution was modified by the 16th Amendment.**

The Congress shall have power to lay and collect taxes on incomes, from whatever source derived, without apportionment among the several states, and without regard to any census or enumeration.

# AMENDMENT 17. Direct Election of Senators (1913)

**Passed by Congress May 13, 1912. Ratified April 8, 1913.**

**Note: Article 1, Section 3, of the Constitution was modified by the 17th Amendment.**

**Section 1.** The Senate of the United States shall be composed of two Senators from each state, elected by the people thereof, for six years; and each Senator shall have one vote. The electors in each state shall have the qualifications requisite for electors of the most numerous branch of the state legislatures.

**Section 2.** When vacancies happen in the representation of any state in the Senate, the executive authority of such state shall issue writs of election to fill such vacancies: Provided, that the legislature of any state may empower the executive thereof to make temporary appointments until the people fill the vacancies by election as the legislature may direct.

**Section 3.** This amendment shall not be so construed as to affect the election or term of any Senator chosen before it becomes valid as part of the Constitution.

# AMENDMENT 18. Prohibition (1919)

**Passed by Congress December 18, 1917. Ratified January 16, 1919. Repealed by the 21st Amendment.**

**Section 1.** After one year from the ratification of this article the manufacture, sale, or transportation of intoxicating liquors within, the importation thereof into, or the exportation thereof from the United States and all territory subject to the jurisdiction thereof for beverage purposes is hereby prohibited.

**Section 2.** The Congress and the several states shall have concurrent power to enforce this article by appropriate legislation.

**Section 3.** This article shall be inoperative unless it shall have been ratified as an amendment to the Constitution by the legislatures of the several states, as provided in the Constitution, within seven years from the date of the submission hereof to the states by the Congress.

## A CLOSER LOOK

Under Prohibition, people broke the law if they made, sold, or shipped alcoholic beverages. Powerful crime gangs turned selling illegal liquor into a big business. This photo shows federal agents getting ready to smash containers of illegal whiskey. The 21st Amendment ended Prohibition.

I WISH MA COULD VOTE

## AMENDMENT 19. Woman Suffrage (1920)

Passed by Congress June 4, 1919. Ratified August 18, 1920.

**Section 1.** The right of citizens of the United States to vote shall not be denied or abridged by the United States or by any state on account of sex.

**Section 2.** Congress shall have power to enforce this article by appropriate legislation.

## AMENDMENT 20. "Lame Duck" Sessions (1933)

Passed by Congress March 2, 1932. Ratified January 23, 1933.

Note: Article 1, Section 4, of the Constitution was modified by Section 2 of this amendment. In addition, a portion of the 12th Amendment was superseded by Section 3.

**Section 1.** The terms of the President and Vice-President shall end at noon on the 20th day of January, and the terms of Senators and Representatives at noon on the 3rd day of January, of the years in which such terms would have ended if this article had not been ratified; and the terms of their successors shall then begin.

**Section 2.** The Congress shall assemble at least once in every year, and such meeting shall begin at noon on the 3rd day of January, unless they shall by law appoint a different day.

**Section 3.** If, at the time fixed for the beginning of the term of the President, the President elect shall have died, the Vice-President elect shall become President. If a President shall not have been chosen before the time fixed for the beginning of his term, or if the President elect shall have failed to qualify, then the Vice-President elect shall act as President until a President shall have qualified; and the Congress may by law provide for the case wherein neither a President elect nor a Vice-President elect shall have qualified, declaring who shall then act as President, or the manner in which one who is to act shall be selected, and such person shall act accordingly until a President or Vice-President shall have qualified.

**Section 4.** The Congress may by law provide for the case of the death of any of the persons from whom the House of Representatives may choose a President whenever the right of choice shall have devolved upon them, and for the case of the death of any of the persons from whom the Senate may choose a Vice-President whenever the right of choice shall have devolved upon them.

**Section 5.** Sections 1 and 2 shall take effect on the 15th day of October following the ratification of this article.

**Section 6.** This article shall be **inoperative** unless it shall have been ratified as an amendment to the Constitution by the legislatures of three-fourths of the several states within seven years from the date of its submission.

## AMENDMENT 21. Repeal of Prohibition (1933)

**Passed by Congress February 20, 1933. Ratified December 5, 1933.**

**Section 1.** The eighteenth article of amendment to the Constitution of the United States is hereby repealed.

**Section 2.** The transportation or importation into any state, territory, or possession of the United States for delivery or use therein of intoxicating liquors, in violation of the laws thereof, is hereby prohibited.

**Section 3.** This article shall be inoperative unless it shall have been ratified as an amendment to the Constitution by conventions in the several states, as provided in the Constitution, within seven years from the date of the submission hereof to the states by the Congress.

## AMENDMENT 22. Limit on Presidential Terms (1951)

**Passed by Congress March 21, 1947. Ratified February 27, 1951.**

**Section 1.** No person shall be elected to the office of the President more than twice, and no person who has held the office of President, or acted as President, for more than two years of a term to which some other person was elected President shall be elected to the office of the President more than once. But this article shall not apply to any person holding the office of President when this article was proposed by the Congress, and shall not prevent any person who may be holding the office of President, or acting as President, during the term within which this article becomes operative from holding the office of President or acting as President during the remainder of such term.

**Section 2.** This article shall be inoperative unless it shall have been ratified as an amendment to the Constitution by the legislatures of three-fourths of the several states within seven years from the date of its submission to the states by the Congress.

**A CLOSER LOOK**

George Washington set the tradition of limiting the presidency to two terms. Franklin Roosevelt broke this custom when he was elected president four terms in a row—1932, 1936, 1940, and 1944. His record-long presidency led to the 22nd Amendment. A two-term limit, written into the Constitution, checks the president's power.

# AMENDMENT 23. Voting in District of Columbia (1961)

**Passed by Congress June 17, 1960. Ratified March 29, 1961.**

**Section 1.** The district constituting the seat of government of the United States shall appoint in such manner as Congress may direct: a number of electors of President and Vice-President equal to the whole number of Senators and Representatives in Congress to which the district would be entitled if it were a state, but in no event more than the least populous state; they shall be in addition to those appointed by the states, but they shall be considered, for the purposes of the election of President and Vice-President, to be electors appointed by a state; and they shall meet in the district and perform such duties as provided by the twelfth article of amendment.

**Section 2.** The Congress shall have power to enforce this article by appropriate legislation.

# AMENDMENT 24. Abolition of Poll Taxes (1964)

**Passed by Congress August 27, 1962. Ratified January 23, 1964.**

**Section 1.** The right of citizens of the United States to vote in any **primary** or other election for President or Vice-President, for electors for President or Vice-President, or for Senator or Representative in Congress, shall not be denied or abridged by the United States or any state by reason of failure to pay any poll tax or other tax.

**Section 2.** The Congress shall have power to enforce this article by appropriate legislation.

# AMENDMENT 25. Presidential Disability, Succession (1967)

**Passed by Congress July 6, 1965. Ratified February 10, 1967.**

**Note: Article 2, Section 1, of the Constitution was affected by the 25th Amendment.**

**Section 1.** In case of the removal of the President from office or of his death or resignation, the Vice-President shall become President.

**Section 2.** Whenever there is a vacancy in the office of the Vice-President, the President shall nominate a Vice-President who shall take office upon confirmation by a majority vote of both houses of Congress.

**Section 3.** Whenever the President transmits to the President pro tempore of the Senate and the Speaker of the House of Representatives his written declaration that he is unable to discharge the powers and duties of his office, and until he transmits to them a written declaration to the contrary, such powers and duties shall be discharged by the Vice-President as Acting President.

## A CLOSER LOOK

### POLL TAX

The poll tax was aimed at preventing African Americans from exercising their rights. Many could not afford to pay this fee required for voting.

**26. How do you think the 24th Amendment affected elections?**

## A CLOSER LOOK

### PRESIDENTIAL DISABILITY

President John F. Kennedy's death in 1963 signaled the need for the 25th Amendment. The Constitution did not explain what to do in the case of a disabled president. James Reston, a writer for *The New York Times,* summed up the problem: Suppose Kennedy was "strong enough to survive [the bullet wounds], but too weak to govern." The 25th Amendment provides for an orderly transfer of power.

**27. What do you think can happen in a country where the rules for succession are not clear?**

**Section 4.** Whenever the Vice-President and a majority of either the principal officers of the executive departments or of such other body as Congress may by law provide, transmit to the President pro tempore of the Senate and the Speaker of the House of Representatives their written declaration that the President is unable to discharge the powers and duties of his office, the Vice-President shall immediately assume the powers and duties of the office as Acting President. Thereafter, when the President transmits to the President pro tempore of the Senate and the Speaker of the House of Representatives his written declaration that no inability exists, he shall resume the powers and duties of his office unless the Vice-President and a majority of either the principal officers of the executive department[s] or of such other body as Congress may by law provide, transmit within four days to the President pro tempore of the Senate and the Speaker of the House of Representatives their written declaration that the President is unable to discharge the powers and duties of his office. Thereupon Congress shall decide the issue, assembling within forty-eight hours for that purpose if not in session. If the Congress, within twenty-one days after receipt of the latter written declaration, or, if Congress is not in session, within twenty-one days after Congress is required to assemble, determines by two thirds vote of both houses that the President is unable to discharge the powers and duties of his office, the Vice-President shall continue to discharge the same as Acting President; otherwise, the President shall resume the powers and duties of his office.

---

**A CLOSER LOOK  Amendments Time Line** *1791–1992*

Use the key below to help you categorize the amendments.

■ **Voting Rights**

■ **Social Changes**

■ **Overturned Supreme Court Decisions**

■ **Election Procedures and Conditions of Office**

**Amendment 15**
**1870**
Stops national and state governments from denying the vote based on race.

**Bill of Rights**
**Amendments 1–10**
**1791**

**Amendment 13**
**1865**
Bans slavery.

**1790**

**Amendment 11**
**1798**
Protects state from lawsuits filed by citizens of other states or countries.

**Amendment 12**
**1804**
Requires separate electoral ballots for president and vice-president.

**Amendment 14**
**1868**
Defines American citizenship and citizens' rights.

## AMENDMENT 26. 18-year-old Vote (1971)

**Passed by Congress March 23, 1971. Ratified July 1, 1971.**

**Note: Amendment 14, Section 2, of the Constitution was modified by Section 1 of the 26th Amendment.**

**Section 1.** The right of citizens of the United States, who are eighteen years of age or older, to vote shall not be denied or abridged by the United States or by any state on account of age.

**Section 2.** The Congress shall have power to enforce this article by appropriate legislation.

## AMENDMENT 27. Congressional Pay (1992)

**Passed by Congress September 25, 1789. Ratified May 7, 1992.**

No law, varying the compensation for the services of the Senators and Representatives, shall take effect, until an election of Representatives shall have intervened.

**A CLOSER LOOK**

Members of the recording industry founded Rock the Vote. They urge young people to vote in elections.

---

## Amendments 11–27 Assessment

### 1. Main Ideas

**a.** Which amendments affected the office of president? (8.2.6)

**b.** Which pair of amendments shows the failure of laws to solve a social problem? (8.2.6)

**c.** Which amendments corrected unfair treatment toward African Americans and women? (8.2.6)

### 2. Critical Thinking

**Summarizing** What is the purpose of amending the Constitution? (8.2.6)

**THINK ABOUT**

• the purpose of the Constitution

• problems and issues that Americans have faced throughout U.S. history

---

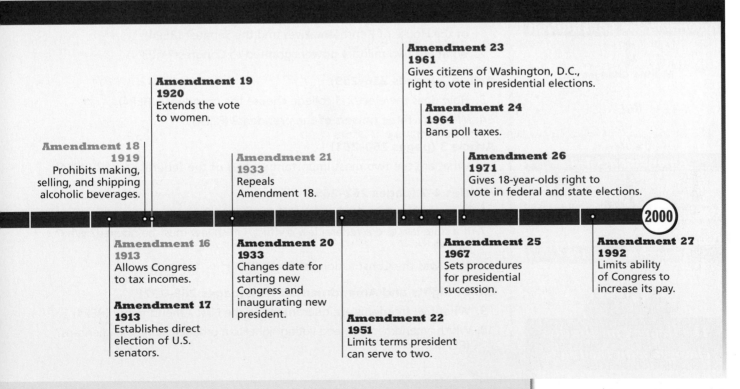

**Amendment 18**
**1919**
Prohibits making, selling, and shipping alcoholic beverages.

**Amendment 19**
**1920**
Extends the vote to women.

**Amendment 21**
**1933**
Repeals Amendment 18.

**Amendment 23**
**1961**
Gives citizens of Washington, D.C., right to vote in presidential elections.

**Amendment 24**
**1964**
Bans poll taxes.

**Amendment 26**
**1971**
Gives 18-year-olds right to vote in federal and state elections.

**2000**

**Amendment 16**
**1913**
Allows Congress to tax incomes.

**Amendment 17**
**1913**
Establishes direct election of U.S. senators.

**Amendment 20**
**1933**
Changes date for starting new Congress and inaugurating new president.

**Amendment 22**
**1951**
Limits terms president can serve to two.

**Amendment 25**
**1967**
Sets procedures for presidential succession.

**Amendment 27**
**1992**
Limits ability of Congress to increase its pay.

## VISUAL SUMMARY

### The Constitution of the United States (8.2.6)

**Preamble**

WE THE PEOPLE

**Article 1    Article 2    Article 3**

**The Branches of Government**

**Executive**
President

**Judicial**
Supreme Court

**Legislative**

Senate    House of Representatives

**Article 4                    Article 6**

**The Federal System**

**Powers of the State**

**Powers of the National Government**

"Supreme law of the land"

**Article 5**

**Amending the Constitution**

**Making Changes**

*Bill of Rights*

**Amendments 1–10**

**Personal Freedoms**    **Personal Security**    **Rights of the Accused**

**Amendments 11–27**

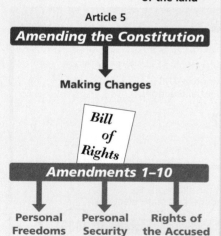

*The living Constitution changes with the times.*

## VOCABULARY

Briefly explain the significance of each of the following.

1. electors
2. impeachment
3. naturalization
4. felonies
5. bill of attainder
6. ex post facto law
7. suffrage
8. due process of law
9. servitude
10. primary

## SEVEN PRINCIPLES OF THE CONSTITUTION

Make a chart like the one shown. Then fill it in with a definition of each principle and an example from the Constitution. (REP4)

| Principle | Definition | Example |
|---|---|---|
| 1. popular sovereignty | | |
| 2. republicanism | | |
| 3. federalism | | |
| 4. separation of powers | | |
| 5. checks and balances | | |
| 6. limited government | | |
| 7. individual rights | | |

## REVIEW QUESTIONS

**Article 1 (pages 249–255)**

1. What are the requirements for becoming a member of the House of Representatives and the Senate? (REP4)
2. What are two military powers granted to Congress? (REP4)

**Article 2 (pages 256–259)**

3. How does the electoral college choose the president? (REP4)
4. What are three powers of the president? (REP4)

**Article 3 (pages 260–261)**

5. What are the two most important powers of the federal courts? (REP4)

**Articles 4–7 (pages 262–265)**

6. How can the Constitution be changed? (REP4)
7. If a state law and a federal law conflict, which law must be obeyed? Why? (REP4)
8. How was the Constitution ratified? (REP4)

**Bill of Rights and Amendments 11–27 (pages 266–277)**

9. What five freedoms are guaranteed in the First Amendment? (REP4)
10. Which amendments extend voting rights to a broader range of Americans? (REP4)

# CRITICAL THINKING

## 1. DRAWING CONCLUSIONS

In a two-column chart, summarize the processes for changing the Constitution. Then use your completed chart to answer the questions below. (REP4)

| Proposing Amendments | Ratifying Amendments |
|---|---|
| 1. | 1. |
| 2. | 2. |

a. What role can citizens play in proposing amendments?

b. What do you think are the main reasons for changing the Constitution?

## 2. MAKING INFERENCES

Explain how the "elastic clause" in Article 1 gives Congress the authority to take action on other issues unknown to the Framers of the Constitution. (REP4)

## 3. ANALYZING LEADERSHIP

Think about the president's roles described in the Constitution. What qualities does a president need to succeed as a leader in so many different areas? (REP4)

## 4. RECOGNIZING EFFECTS

How would you describe the impact of the 14th, 15th, and 16th Amendments on life in the United States? (REP4)

## 5. APPLYING CITIZENSHIP

Suppose you and your family go on a road trip across several states. According to Article 4 of the Constitution, what citizens' rights do you have in the states you are visiting? (REP4)

# HISTORY SKILLS

## INTERPRETING PRIMARY SOURCES

In 1937, President Franklin D. Roosevelt gave a speech over the radio. He used interesting comparisons to explain how the government works. (REP4)

> I described the American form of government as a three-horse team provided by the Constitution to the American people so that their field might be plowed. The three horses are, of course, the three branches of government—the Congress, the Executive, and the Courts. . . . It is the American people themselves who are in the driver's seat. It is the American people themselves who want the furrow plowed.
>
> **Franklin D. Roosevelt,** Radio Address

- How does Roosevelt describe the separation of powers?

- How does Roosevelt explain popular sovereignty?

# ALTERNATIVE ASSESSMENT

## 1. INTERDISCIPLINARY ACTIVITY: Government

**Creating a Database** Review the grievances against King George III listed in the Declaration of Independence. Then create a database that shows how specific sections of the U.S. Constitution addressed those grievances. Write a brief summary stating how well the Constitution addressed the grievances. (REP4)

## 2. COOPERATIVE LEARNING ACTIVITY

**Drafting a Constitution** Imagine you are asked to write a constitution for a newly formed country. Working with a group, use the outline below to organize and write your constitution. (HI1)

   I. Purpose of the Constitution (Preamble)

   II. Making Laws (Legislative Branch)

   III. Carrying Out the Laws (Executive Branch)

   IV. Making Laws Fair (Judicial Branch)

   V. Choosing Leaders

   VI. Citizens' Rights (Bill of Rights)

## 3. 🖸 PRIMARY SOURCE EXPLORER

**Making a Learning Center** Creating the U.S. Constitution was one of the most important events in the nation's history. Use the CD-ROM and the library to collect information on different topics related to the Constitution. (REP3)

Create a learning center featuring the suggestions below.

- Find biographies and portraits of the Framers.

- Collect important primary sources such as James Madison's notes and *The Federalist* papers.

- Gather recent pictures and news articles about the Congress, the president, the Supreme Court, and the Bill of Rights.

## 4. HISTORY PORTFOLIO

Review your draft of the constitution you wrote for the assessment activity. Choose one of these options below. (HI1)

 **Option 1** Use comments made by your teacher or classmates to improve your work.

 **Option 2** Illustrate your constitution. Add your work to your history portfolio.

---

Additional Test Practice, pp. S1–S33      **TEST PRACTICE** CLASSZONE.COM

# The Role of the Citizen

Citizens of the United States enjoy many basic rights and freedoms. Freedom of speech and religion are examples. These rights are guaranteed by the Constitution, the Bill of Rights, and other amendments to the Constitution. Along with these rights, however, come responsibilities. Obeying rules and laws, voting, and serving on juries are some examples.

Active citizenship is not limited to adults. Younger citizens can help their communities become better places. The following pages will help you to learn about your rights and responsibilities. Knowing them will help you to become an active and involved citizen of your community, state, and nation.

In this book you will find examples of active citizenship by young people like yourself. **Look for the Citizenship Today features.**

**CALIFORNIA STANDARDS**

**8.2.6** Enumerate the powers of government set forth in the Constitution and the fundamental liberties ensured by the Bill of Rights.

**8.2.7** Describe the principles of federalism, dual sovereignty, separation of powers, checks and balances, the nature and purpose of majority rule, and the ways in which the American idea of constitutionalism preserves individual rights.

**8.3.6** Describe the basic law-making process and how the Constitution provides numerous opportunities for citizens to participate in the political process and to monitor and influence government (e.g., function of elections, political parties, interest groups).

President John F. Kennedy urged all Americans to become active citizens and work to improve their communities.

The weather was sunny but cold on January 20, 1961—the day that John F. Kennedy became the 35th president of the United States. In his first speech as president, he urged all Americans to serve their country. Since then, Kennedy's words have inspired millions of Americans to become more active citizens.

*"Ask not what your country can do for you—ask what you can do for your country!"*

—JOHN F. KENNEDY

## What Is a Citizen?

A citizen is a legal member of a nation and pledges loyalty to that nation. A citizen has certain guaranteed rights, protections, and responsibilities. A citizen is a member of a community and wants to make it a good place to live.

Today in the United States there are a number of ways to become a citizen. The most familiar are citizenship by birth and citizenship by naturalization. All citizens have the right to equal protection under the law.

**CITIZENSHIP BY BIRTH** A child born in the United States is a citizen by birth. Children born to U.S. citizens traveling or living outside the country, such as military personnel, are citizens. Even children born in the United States to parents who are not citizens of the United States are considered U.S. citizens. These children have dual citizenship. This means they are citizens of two countries—both the United States and the country of their parents' citizenship. At the age of 18, the child may choose one of the countries for permanent citizenship.

**CITIZENSHIP BY NATURALIZATION** A person who is not a citizen of the United States may become one through a process called naturalization. The steps in this process are shown below. To become a naturalized citizen, a person must meet certain requirements.

- Be at least 18 years old. Children under the age of 18 automatically become naturalized citizens when their parents do.
- Enter the United States legally.
- Live in the United States for at least five years immediately prior to application.
- Read, write, and speak English.
- Show knowledge of American history and government.

**See Citizenship Today: Becoming a Citizen, p. 427**

### Steps in the Naturalization Process

1. File an application.
2. Take an examination.
3. File a legal petition for naturalization.
4. Appear at a court hearing.
5. Take an oath of allegiance.

Hundreds of people become new citizens at a single ceremony in San Antonio, Texas.

# What Are Your Rights?

Citizens of the United States are guaranteed rights by the U.S. Constitution, state constitutions, and state and federal laws. All citizens have three kinds of rights: basic freedoms, protection from unfair government actions, and equal treatment under the law.

Citizens' basic rights and freedoms are sometimes called **civil rights**. Some of these rights are personal, and others are political.

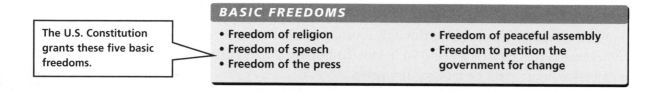

The U.S. Constitution grants these five basic freedoms.

**BASIC FREEDOMS**
- Freedom of religion
- Freedom of speech
- Freedom of the press
- Freedom of peaceful assembly
- Freedom to petition the government for change

The second category of rights is intended to protect citizens from unfair government actions.

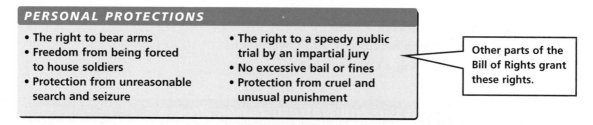

**PERSONAL PROTECTIONS**
- The right to bear arms
- Freedom from being forced to house soldiers
- Protection from unreasonable search and seizure
- The right to a speedy public trial by an impartial jury
- No excessive bail or fines
- Protection from cruel and unusual punishment

Other parts of the Bill of Rights grant these rights.

The third category is the right to equal treatment under the law. The government cannot treat one individual or group differently from another.

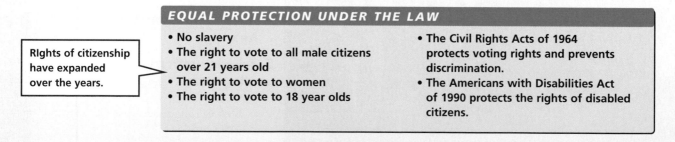

Rights of citizenship have expanded over the years.

**EQUAL PROTECTION UNDER THE LAW**
- No slavery
- The right to vote to all male citizens over 21 years old
- The right to vote to women
- The right to vote to 18 year olds
- The Civil Rights Acts of 1964 protects voting rights and prevents discrimination.
- The Americans with Disabilities Act of 1990 protects the rights of disabled citizens.

**LIMITS TO RIGHTS** The rights guaranteed to citizens have sensible limits. For example, the right to free speech does not allow a person to falsely shout, "Fire!" at a crowded concert. The government may place limits on certain rights to protect national security or to provide equal opportunities for all citizens. And rights come with responsibilities.

# What Are Your Responsibilities?

For American democracy to work, citizens must carry out important responsibilities. There are two kinds of responsibilities—personal and civic. Personal responsibilities include taking care of yourself, helping your family, knowing right from wrong, and behaving in a respectful way.

Civic responsibilities are those that involve your government and community. They include obeying rules and laws, serving on juries, paying taxes, and defending your country when called upon. One of the most important responsibilities is voting. When you turn 18, you will have that right.

As a young person, you can be a good citizen in a number of ways. You might work with other people in your community to make it a fair and just place to live. Working for a political party or writing to your elected officials about issues that concern you are some other examples.

The chart below shows how responsibilities change with a citizen's age. Notice that all citizens share the responsibility to obey the laws of their communities.

**See Citizenship Today: Obeying Rules and Laws, p. 300**

**CALIFORNIA STANDARDS**

**8.3.6** Describe the basic law-making process and how the Constitution provides numerous opportunities for citizens to participate in the political process and to monitor and influence government (e.g., function of elections, political parties, interest groups).

**Reading 2.6** Use information from a variety of consumer, workplace, and public documents to explain a situation or decision and to solve a problem.

**Writing 2.3** Write research reports.

## Responsibilities of a Citizen

**UNDER 18**
- Receive an education, either at school or at home.
- Take responsibility for one's behavior.
- Help one's family.

**ALL AGES**
- Obey rules and laws.
- Be tolerant of others.
- Pay taxes.
- Volunteer for a cause.
- Stay informed about issues.

**OVER 18**
- Vote.
- Serve on a jury.
- Serve in the military to defend country.

> Currently both men and women can serve in the military. Only men must register for the draft.

## CITIZENSHIP ACTIVITIES

**1.** Interview a recently naturalized citizen. Ask about the test he or she took to become a U.S. citizen. Write a report of your findings.

**2.** Using newspapers or magazines, find examples of citizens using their unalienable rights or practicing responsible citizenship. Cut out five articles to illustrate the points. Mount them and write a one-sentence explanation of each article.

# Building Citizenship Skills

Good citizenship skills include **staying informed, solving problems** or **making decisions,** and **taking action.** Every citizen can find ways to build citizenship skills. By showing respect for the law and for the rights of others in your daily life, you promote democracy. You can also work to change conditions in your community to make sure all citizens experience freedom and justice.

## How Do You Stay Informed?

Americans can sometimes feel that they have access to too much information. It may seem overwhelming. Even so, you should stay informed on issues that affect your life. Staying informed gives you the information you need to make wise decisions and helps you find ways to solve problems.

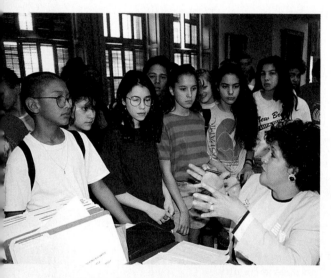

These Texas middle school students are staying informed by talking to their Texas state representative. Many public officials enjoy having students visit and ask them questions about their jobs, and about issues students think are important.

### Watch, Listen, and Read

The first step in practicing good citizenship is to know how to find information that you need.

Sources of information include broadcast and print media and the Internet. Public officials and civic organizations are also good sources for additional information. Remember as you are reading to evaluate your sources.

See Citizenship Today:
Debating Points of View, p. 469

### Evaluate

As you become informed, you will need to make judgments about the accuracy of your news sources. You must also be aware of those sources' points of view and biases. (A bias is a judgment formed without knowing all of the facts.)

You should determine if you need more information. If you do, then decide where to find it. After gathering information, you may be ready to form an opinion or a plan of action to solve a problem.

See Citizenship Today:
Detecting Bias in the Media, p. 664

### Communicate

To bring about change in their communities, active citizens may need to contact public officials. In today's world, making contact is easy.

You can reach most public officials by telephone, voice mail, fax, or letter. Many public officials also have Internet pages or e-mail that encourages input from the public.

# How Do You Make Wise Decisions?

Civic life involves making important decisions. As a voter, whom should you vote for? As a juror, should you find the defendant guilty or not guilty? As an informed citizen, should you support or oppose a proposed government action? Unlike decisions about which video to rent, civic decisions cannot be made by a process as easy as tossing a coin. Instead, you should use a problem-solving approach like the one shown in the chart below. Decision making won't always proceed directly from step to step. Sometimes it's necessary to backtrack a little. For example, you may get to the "Analyze the Information" step and realize that you don't have enough information to analyze. Then you can go back a step and gather more information.

## Problem-Solving and Decision-Making Process

Problem-solving and decision-making involves many steps. This diagram shows you how to take those steps. Notice that you may have to repeat some steps depending on the information you gather.

**EVALUATE THE SOLUTION**
Review the results of putting your solution into action. Did the solution work? Do you need to adjust the solution in some way?

**IMPLEMENT THE SOLUTION**
Take action or plan to take action on a chosen solution.

**CHOOSE A SOLUTION**
Choose the solution you believe will best solve the problem and help you reach your goal.

**CONSIDER OPTIONS**
Think of as many ways as possible to solve the problem. Don't be afraid to include ideas that others might think are unacceptable.

**ANALYZE THE INFORMATION**
Look at the information and determine what it reveals about solving the problem.

**GATHER INFORMATION**
Get to know the basics of the problem. Find out as much as possible about the issues.

**IDENTIFY THE PROBLEM**
Decide what the main issues are and what your goal is.

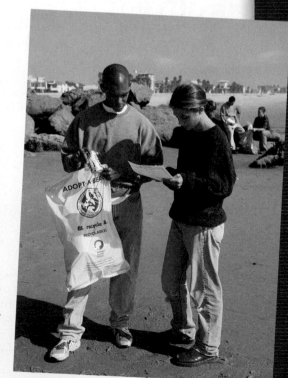

Students working on an environmental project are gathering and analyzing information to help them make decisions.

# How Do You Participate in Your Community?

Across the country many young people have come up with ways to make their communities better places to live. Thirteen-year-old Aubyn Burnside of Hickory, North Carolina, is just one example. Aubyn felt sorry for foster children she saw moving their belongings in plastic trash bags. She founded Suitcases for Kids. This program provides used luggage for foster children who are moving from one home to another. Her program has been adopted by other young people in several states. Below are some ways in which you can participate in your community.

**See Citizenship Today: Community Service, p. 612**

**CALIFORNIA STANDARDS**

**8.3.6** Describe the basic law-making process and how the Constitution provides numerous opportunities for citizens to participate in the political process and to monitor and influence government (e.g., function of elections, political parties, interest groups).

**Reading 2.6** Use information from a variety of consumer, workplace, and public documents to explain a situation or decision and to solve a problem.

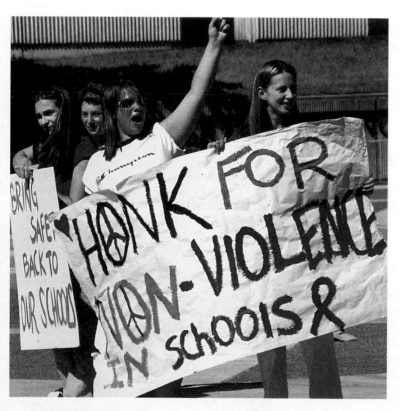

Students participate in a rally to promote safety in their school.

## Find a Cause

How can you become involved in your community? First, select a community problem or issue that interests you. Some ideas from other young people include starting a support group for children with cancer, publishing a neighborhood newspaper with children's stories and art, and putting on performances to entertain people in shelters and hospitals.

## Develop Solutions

Once you have found a cause on which you want to work, develop a plan for solving the problem. Use the decision-making or problem-solving skills you have learned to find ways to approach the problem. You may want to involve other people in your activities.

## Follow Through

Solving problems takes time. You'll need to be patient in developing a plan. You can show leadership in working with your group by following through on meetings you set up and plans you make. When you finally solve the problem, you will feel proud of your accomplishments.

## CITIZENSHIP ACTIVITIES

1. Use the telephone directory to make a list of names, addresses, and phone numbers of public officials or organizations that could provide information about solving problems in your community.

2. Copy the steps in the problem-solving and decision-making diagram and show how you followed them to solve a problem or make a decision. Be sure to clearly state the problem and the final decision.

# Practicing Citizenship Skills

CALIFORNIA STANDARDS

**8.3.6** Describe the basic law-making process and how the Constitution provides numerous opportunities for citizens to participate in the political process and to monitor and influence government (e.g., function of elections, political parties, interest groups).

**Reading 2.6** Use information from a variety of consumer, workplace, and public documents to explain a situation or decision and to solve a problem.

**Listening and Speaking 1.0** Students deliver focused, coherent presentations that convey ideas clearly and relate to the background and interests of the audience. They evaluate the content of oral communication.

You have learned that good citizenship involves three skills: staying informed, solving problems, and taking action. Below are some activities to help you improve your citizenship skills. By practicing these skills you can work to make a difference in your own life and in the lives of those in your community.

Citizen ➤ KNOW YOUR RIGHTS ➤ BE RESPONSIBLE ➤ STAY INFORMED ➤ MAKE GOOD DECISIONS ➤ PARTICIPATE IN YOUR COMMUNITY ➤ Model Citizen

## CITIZENSHIP ACTIVITIES

### Stay Informed

**CREATE A PAMPHLET OR RECRUITING COMMERCIAL**

Ask your school counselors or write to your state department of education to get information on state-run colleges, universities, or technical schools. Use this information to create a brochure or recruiting commercial showing these schools and the different programs and degrees they offer.

**KEEP IN MIND**

**What's there for me?** It may help you think about what areas students are interested in and may want to pursue in later life.

**Where is it?** You may want to have a map showing where the schools are located in your state.

**How can I afford it?** Students might want to know if financial aid is available to attend the schools you have featured.

### Make Wise Decisions

**CREATE A GAME BOARD OR SKIT**

Study the decision-making diagram on page 285. With a small group, develop a skit that explains the steps in problem solving. Present your skit to younger students in your school. As an alternative, create a game board that would help younger students understand the steps in making a decision.

**KEEP IN MIND**

**What do children this age understand?** Be sure to create a skit or game at an age-appropriate level.

**What kinds of decisions do younger students make?** Think about the kinds of decisions that the viewers of your skit or players of the game might make.

**How can I make it interesting?** Use visual aids to help students understand the steps in decision making.

### Take Action

**CREATE A BULLETIN BOARD FOR YOUR CLASS**

Do some research on the Internet or consult the yellow pages under "Social Services" to find the names of organizations that have volunteer opportunities for young people. Call or write for more information. Then create a bulletin board for your class showing groups that would like volunteer help.

**KEEP IN MIND**

**What kinds of jobs are they?** You may want to list the types of skills or jobs volunteer groups are looking for.

**How old do I have to be?** Some groups may be looking for younger volunteers; others may need older persons.

**How do I get there?** How easy is it to get to the volunteer group's location?

# Writing about History

## Response to Literature:
### Feelings about a War Poem

CALIFORNIA STANDARDS
**Writing 2.2** Write responses to literature.

**PURPOSE:** To write a response to a literary work
**AUDIENCE:** Classmates in your history and language arts classes

Historians and authors of novels and poetry have different purposes for writing. The historian's purpose is to convey information. The author's purpose is to create a world as vividly as possible and invite the reader into it. Every word chosen affects how the reader imagines that world. The author also uses word choice to try to influence the reader's feelings about the subject. You can explore your feelings and understanding of a literary work by writing a response to it.

The author of the poem below would have disapproved of the colonial woman shown here with her "rifle gun" raised against the British.

## Organization & Focus

Your assignment is to write an essay on how an author's choice of words, literary style, and techniques affects you. Read the two verses from the poem here called "The Rebels," which was written by John Ferdinand Dalzell Smyth and published in 1778. Smyth was a captain in the Queens Rangers, a group of loyalists who fought against the colonial revolutionaries. As you read the verses, ask yourself how the author makes you feel about the rebels and the loyalists.

In your notebook, write a sentence expressing your overall impression of both the rebels and the loyalists from this poem. You can use this sentence to help you draft the **thesis statement,** or main idea, of your response.

### from "The Rebels"

Ye brave honest subjects who dare to be loyal,
And have stood the brunt of every trial,
Of hunting shirts and rifle guns;
Come listen awhile and I'll tell you a song;
I'll show you those Yankees are all in the wrong,
Who, with blustering look and most awkward gait,[1]
'Gainst their lawful sovereign dare for to prate,[2]
With their hunting shirts and rifle guns.
Forgetting the mercies of Great Britain's King,
Who saved their forefathers' necks from the string,
With hunting shirts and rifle guns,
They renounce all allegiance and take up their arms,
Assemble together like hornets in swarms,
So dirty their backs, and so wretched their show,
That carrion-crow[3] follows wherever they go,
With their hunting shirts and rifle guns.

1 **gait:** manner of walking
2 **prate:** to rant or shout about
3 **carrion-crow:** a bird of prey that feeds on the dead

**IDENTIFYING PURPOSE AND AUDIENCE** Your purpose is to write a 500–700 word essay explaining your response to the poem. Support your judgments using references to the text. You should also make inferences about the effect of the poem on a larger audience. The audience for your response is made up of your classmates in both your history and your language arts class. Keep in mind that your language arts classmates probably will not have read the selections from this poem.

**FINDING DETAILS** Reread the verses and complete this chart. List details from the poem about the loyalists and the rebels and write down your response to them. Samples are provided.

| Details about Loyalists | Response | Details about Rebels | Response |
|---|---|---|---|
| Brave, honest, loyal | Strongly positive | Blustering look | Makes rebels seem noisy and rude |

**OUTLINING AND DRAFTING THE ESSAY** Express the main idea about your response to the poem in your thesis statement. Then use your chart to outline and provide supporting details for your response.

## Research & Technology

You can find the whole text of "The Rebels" online. Enter the title of the poem and the author's name in a search engine. If you like, you can analyze the other verses to find more supporting details for your response.

**Technology Tip** Use the thesaurus in your word processor to help you find words that exactly express your response.

## Evaluation & Revision

When you are satisfied with *what* you have said in your essay, reread it to see where you can improve *how* you said it. Pay special attention to your thesis statement, your choice of words, and your organization and transitions.

## Publish & Present

Exchange essays with your history and language arts classmates and talk about your responses to other war literature you have read.

**Self-Check**

Does my response to literature have . . .

☐ a clear thesis statement that expresses my response?

☐ references to the text that support my judgment?

☐ inferences about the effect of the poem on a larger audience?

☐ good organization and smooth transitions?

☐ a strong, clear conclusion?

# The Early Republic

> *"Our country! May she always be in the right; but our country, right or wrong."*
>
> **—Stephen Decatur**

Known as "Old IronsIdes," the U.S.S. *Constitution* won more battles than any other early American warship. Today it rests in Boston Harbor.

# CHAPTER 9

# Launching a New Republic 1789–1800

**Section 1**
**Washington's Presidency**

**Section 2**
**Challenges to the New Government**

**Section 3**
**The Federalists in Charge**

George Washington's first cabinet. Left to right: Secretary of War Henry Knox, Secretary of State Thomas Jefferson, Attorney General Edmund Randolph, Secretary of the Treasury Alexander Hamilton, and President George Washington.

**1789**
George Washington inaugurated as president.

**1791**
The first Bank of the United States is established.

**1792**
**Washington reelected president.**

**1794**
Whiskey Rebellion occurs.

**USA World** 1789

**1789**
French Revolution begins.

**1791**
Slaves revolt in Santo Domingo.

**1793**
French king Louis XVI executed; Reign of Terror begins in France

290

The year is 1789, and George Washington has been inaugurated as the first president of the United States. It quickly becomes obvious to you and to others that the president will need help. He chooses people with different talents and experience to help him govern.

# What kind of person would you choose to help you govern?

## What Do You Think?

- Why might you want people with different viewpoints in your government?

- What do you think your biggest challenges would be?

**RESEARCH LINKS**
CLASSZONE.COM

Visit the Chapter 9 links for more information about the new republic.

**1796**
John Adams elected president.

**1797**
Britain appoints Richard Wellesley Governor-General of India.

**1798**
Alien and Sedition Acts

**1798**
French Expedition to Egypt

**1800**
Thomas Jefferson elected president.

**1800**

**1800**
Napoleon becomes First Consul of France.

# Reading Strategy: Identifying and Solving Problems

## What Do You Know?

What do you think of when you hear the words *democracy* and *republic*? Why do you think the citizens and leaders of the new country wanted to establish a republic governed by laws?

**Think About**
- the experience of the colonists under British rule
- the effect of the Revolutionary War and the period immediately after the war
- your responses to the Interact with History about choosing people to govern (see page 291)

## What Do You Want to Know?

What questions do you have about the people who created the U.S. government? Record your questions in your notebook before you read the chapter.

**CALIFORNIA STANDARDS**

**Reading 2.7** Evaluate the unity, coherence, logic, internal consistency, and structural patterns of text.

This early American flag has 13 stars representing the original 13 colonies.

## Identifying and Solving Problems

As you read history, try to identify problems in past times and the solutions that people came up with to solve their problems. A graphic organizer such as the chart below can help you to keep track of problems and their solutions. In the middle of the chart, four headings categorize the major issues faced by the young nation. Copy the chart into your notebook and then record problems and the proposed solutions in each category.

**S** See Skillbuilder Handbook, page R18.

### Taking Notes

| PROBLEMS | | SOLUTIONS |
|---|---|---|
| | Economics | |
| | Politics | |
| | Foreign Affairs | |
| | Relations with Native Americans | |

# Washington's Presidency

| MAIN IDEA | WHY IT MATTERS NOW | TERMS & NAMES |
|---|---|---|
| The president and the Congress began to set up the new government. | The strength of the U.S. today is due to the decisions of the Founders about how to organize the government. | inaugurate     cabinet <br> Federal Judiciary    tariff <br> Act |

## ONE AMERICAN'S STORY

Charles Thomson had served as secretary of the Continental Congress in 1774. Now, on April 14, 1789, he came to Mount Vernon in Virginia with a letter for George Washington. Washington knew the reason for the visit. Thomson's letter was to tell him that he had been elected the nation's first president. Before giving Washington the letter, Thomson made a short speech.

Charles Thomson delivers the news to Washington.

*A VOICE FROM THE PAST*

I have now Sir to inform you that . . . your patriotism and your readiness to sacrifice . . . private enjoyments to preserve the liberty and promote the happiness of your Country [convinced the Congress that you would accept] this important Office to which you are called not only by the unanimous votes of the Electors but by the voice of America.

**Charles Thomson,** quoted in Washington's Papers, Library of Congress

As you will read in this section, Washington accepted the honor and the burden of his new office. He guided the nation through its early years.

## Washington Takes Office

Washington had been elected only a few months before. Each member of the electoral college had written down two names. The top vote-getter, Washington, became president. The runner-up, John Adams, became vice-president. Washington left Mount Vernon on April 16, 1789. He traveled north through Baltimore and Philadelphia to New York City, the nation's capital. On April 30 at Federal Hall, Washington was **inaugurated,** or sworn in, as president. John Adams of Massachusetts was his vice-president.

**CALIFORNIA STANDARDS**

**8.3.4** Understand how the conflicts between Thomas Jefferson and Alexander Hamilton resulted in the emergence of two political parties (e.g., view of foreign policy, Alien and Sedition Acts, economic policy, National Bank, funding and assumption of the revolutionary debt).

**8.4.1** Describe the country's physical landscapes, political divisions, and territorial expansion during the terms of the first four presidents.

**8.4.3** Analyze the rise of capitalism and the economic problems and conflicts that accompanied it (e.g., Jackson's opposition to the National Bank; early decisions of the U.S. Supreme Court that reinforced the sanctity of contracts and a capitalist economic system of law).

**HI1** Students explain the central issues and problems from the past, placing people and events in a matrix of time and place.

**HI3** Students explain the sources of historical continuity and how the combination of ideas and events explains the emergence of new patterns.

**Taking Notes**

Use your chart to take notes about Washington's presidency.

- Economics
- Politics
- Foreign Affairs
- Relations with Native Americans

As the nation's first president, Washington faced a difficult task. He knew that all eyes would be on him. His every action as president would set a precedent—an example that would become standard practice. People argued over what to call him. Some, including John Adams, suggested "His Excellency" or "His Highness." Others argued that such titles would suggest that he was a king. The debate tied up Congress for a month. Finally, "Mr. President" was agreed upon. Congress had to settle other differences about how the new government should be run.

*Reading*History
A. Making Inferences Why were people so concerned about how to address the president?

## Setting Up the Courts

The writers of the Constitution had left many matters to be decided by Congress. For example, the Constitution created a Supreme Court but left it to Congress to decide the number of justices. Leaders also argued about how much power the Supreme Court should have. One reason for disagreement was that the states already had their own courts. How would authority be divided between the state and federal courts?

To create a court system, Congress passed the **Federal Judiciary Act** of 1789. This act gave the Supreme Court six members: a chief justice, or judge, and five associate justices. Over time, that number has grown to nine. The act also provided for other lower, less powerful federal courts. Washington appointed John Jay, the prominent New York lawyer and diplomat, as chief justice.

Vocabulary
judiciary: system of courts and judges

### THE PRESIDENT'S CABINET

The president's cabinet has more than tripled in size since it began with the secretaries of state, war, and treasury, and the attorney general. As the nation has faced new challenges, the government has added new departments. In 1977, concerns about oil shortages led to the creation of the Department of Energy. The Department of Veterans' Affairs was added in 1989. Today the cabinet (shown below) includes the heads of 14 departments.

## Washington's Cabinet

The Constitution also gave Congress the task of creating departments to help the president lead the nation. The president had the power to appoint the heads of these departments, who were to assist the president with the many issues and problems he had to face. These heads of departments became his **cabinet.**

The Congress created three departments. In his first major task as president, Washington chose talented people to run them. For secretary of war, he picked Henry Knox, a trusted general during the Revolution. It was Knox's job to oversee the nation's defenses. For secretary of state, Washington chose Thomas Jefferson. He had been serving as U.S. minister to France. The State Department oversaw relations between the United States and other countries. Washington turned to the brilliant Alexander Hamilton to be the secretary of the treasury. Hamilton had to manage the government's money. The secretary's ties to the president began during the war when he had served as one of Washington's aides. To advise the government on legal matters, Washington picked Edmund Randolph as attorney general.

These department heads and the attorney general made up Washington's cabinet. The Constitution made no mention of a cabinet. However, Washington began the practice of calling his department heads together to advise him.

## Economic Problems

As secretary of the treasury, Alexander Hamilton faced the task of straightening out the nation's finances. First of all, the new government needed to pay its war debts. During the Revolution, the United States had borrowed millions of dollars from France, the Netherlands, and Spain. Within the United States, merchants and other private citizens had loaned money to the government. State governments also had wartime debts to pay back. By 1789, the national debt totaled more than $52 million.

Most government leaders agreed that the nation must repay its debts to win the respect of both foreign nations and its own citizens. Hamilton saw that the new nation must assure other countries that it was responsible about money. These nations would do business with the United States if they saw that the country would pay its debts. If the nation failed to do so, no country would lend it money in the future.

Hamilton came up with a financial plan that reflected his belief in a strong central government. He thought the power of the national government should be stronger than that of the state governments. Hamilton also believed that government should encourage business and industry. He sought the support of the nation's wealthy merchants and manufacturers. He thought that the nation's prosperity depended on them. The government owed money to many of these rich men. By paying them back, Hamilton hoped to win their support for the new government.

**ALEXANDER HAMILTON**
**1755?–1804**
Alexander Hamilton was born into poverty in the British West Indies. When he was ten years old, the young Alexander went to work as a clerk. He so impressed his employers that they helped to send him to school at King's College (now Columbia University) in New York.

During the Revolutionary War, he became an aide to General Washington. Hamilton moved up quickly in the army and later in political life. Although of humble origins, Hamilton had little faith in the common people and put his trust in the wealthy and educated to govern.

**Why is it odd that Hamilton distrusted the common people to govern?**

*Reading*History
**B. Making Inferences** Why might merchants and manufacturers support a strong central government?

## Hamilton's Financial Plan

In 1790, Hamilton presented his plan to Congress. He proposed three steps to improve the nation's finances.

1. paying off all war debts
2. raising government revenues
3. creating a national bank

Hamilton wanted the federal government to pay off the war debts of the states. However, sectional differences arose over repayment of state debts. Virginia, Georgia, and many other Southern states had already repaid their debts and did not like being asked to help Northern states pay theirs.

Hamilton asked Thomas Jefferson of Virginia to help him gain Southern support. They reached a compromise. In exchange for Southern support of the plan, Northerners agreed to place the new nation's capital in the South. The location chosen was on the Potomac River between Virginia and Maryland.

The secretary of the treasury favored tariffs. A **tariff** is a tax on imported goods. It serves two purposes: raising money for the government and encouraging the growth of American industry. The government placed the highest tariffs on foreign goods—such as shoes and textiles—that Americans bought in great quantities. This ensured a steady flow of income to the government. In addition, since tariffs made foreign goods more expensive, they encouraged people to buy American goods.

Hamilton also called for the creation of a national bank. Such a bank would meet many needs. It would give the government a safe place to keep

# Economics *in* History

## How Banks Work

Why did Hamilton want to create a national bank? He believed that such a bank could help the economy of the new nation. It would create a partnership between the federal government and American business.

Let's say you deposited money into a bank account. Then you went back another day to withdraw some of the money. What happened in the meantime? Did the money just sit in the bank until you wanted it back? No—the bank used your money, and in doing so, helped fuel economic growth. In this way, money flows in a circular path from people like you into the general economy and back to you again. In the process, money can create goods and services, jobs, and profits, as the diagram explains.

### CONNECT TO HISTORY
1. **Analyzing Points of View**
   Do you think that the people who feared a strong central government supported Hamilton's idea of a national bank? Why or why not?

   **S** See Skillbuilder Handbook, page R9.

### CONNECT TO TODAY
2. **Making Inferences** How do banks make money?

For more about banking . . .

RESEARCH LINKS
CLASSZONE.COM

**1** Workers use their wages to buy the goods and services they want. They deposit some money in banks as savings because banks pay them interest.

**2** Banks use much of the money they receive in deposits. They lend money to people who want to buy cars or homes or to businesses that want to expand operations. Banks charge interest—a fee for a loan—to those who borrow the money.

**3** Businesses use the loans to create new products and services. As they sell more, they hire more workers and raise wages.

H&M Co.

goods and services

money. It would also make loans to businesses and government. Most important, it would issue bank notes—paper money that could be used as currency. Overall, Hamilton's plan would strengthen the central government. However, this worried Jefferson and Madison.

**Two of the first U.S. coins, 1792**

## Interpreting the Constitution

Jefferson and Madison believed that the Constitution discouraged the concentration of power in the federal government. The Constitution's writers had tried to make the document general enough so that it would be flexible. As a result, disagreements sometimes arose over the document's meaning.

The debate over Hamilton's plan for a national bank exposed differences about how to interpret the Constitution. Madison and Jefferson argued that the Constitution did not give the government the power to set up a bank. They believed in the strict construction—narrow or strict interpretation—of the Constitution. They stated that the government has only those powers that the Constitution clearly says it has. Therefore, since the Constitution does not mention a national bank, the government cannot create one.

Hamilton disagreed. He favored a loose construction—broad or flexible interpretation—of the Constitution. Pointing to the elastic clause in the document, he argued that the bank was "necessary and proper" to carry out the government's duties. (See The Living Constitution, page 254.) According to this view, when the Constitution grants a power to Congress, it also grants Congress the "necessary and proper" means to carry out that power. Jefferson and Hamilton argued their positions to Washington. Hamilton won, and the Bank of the United States was set up in 1791. The president, meanwhile, was dealing with other challenges at home and abroad, which you will read about in Section 2.

*Reading* **History**
**C. Contrasting**
What is the main difference between strict and loose interpretations of the Constitution?

---

**Section 1 Assessment**

### 1. Terms & Names

**Explain the significance of:**
- inaugurate
- Federal Judiciary Act
- cabinet
- tariff

### 2. Using Graphics

In a chart, list members of Washington's cabinet and their responsibilities.

| Cabinet member | Responsibilities |
|---|---|
|  |  |

Which cabinet member had the greatest responsibilities? Explain. (REP1)

### 3. Main Ideas

**a.** What was the purpose of Washington's cabinet? (8.3.4)

**b.** What economic problems did the new government face? (8.3.4)

**c.** How did Hamilton's financial plan attempt to solve the nation's economic problems? (8.3.4)

### 4. Critical Thinking

**Contrasting** How did Hamilton and Jefferson differ in their interpretation of the Constitution? (REP5)

**THINK ABOUT**
- views on the national bank
- views on the role of government

---

**ACTIVITY OPTIONS**

**LANGUAGE ARTS**

**ART**

Imagine you oppose or support Hamilton's plan for the nation's finances. Write a **letter to the editor** or draw a **political cartoon** expressing your opinion. (REP5)

# 2

# Challenges to the New Government

| MAIN IDEA | WHY IT MATTERS NOW | TERMS & NAMES |
|---|---|---|
| Washington established central authority at home and avoided war with European powers. | Washington's policies at home and abroad set an example for later presidents. | Battle of Fallen Timbers   French Revolution<br>Treaty of Greenville   neutral<br>Whiskey Rebellion   Jay's Treaty<br>Pinckney's Treaty |

**CALIFORNIA STANDARDS**

**8.3.5** Know the significance of domestic resistance movements and ways in which the central government responded to such movements (e.g. Shay's Rebellion , the Whiskey Rebellion).

**8.4.1** Describe the country's physical landscapes, political divisions, and territorial expansion during the terms of the first four presidents.

**8.5.2** Know the changing boundaries of the United States and describe the relationships the country had with its neighbors (current Mexico and Canada) and Europe, including the influence of the Monroe Doctrine, and how those relationships influenced westward expansion and the Mexican-American War.

**8.5.3** Outline the major treaties with American Indian nations during the administrations of the first four presidents and the varying outcomes of those treaties.

**Taking Notes**

Use your chart to take notes about challenges to the new government.

Economics

Politics

Foreign Affairs

Relations with Native Americans

## ONE AMERICAN'S STORY

In the West, American settlers met fierce resistance from Native Americans. Chief Little Turtle of the Miami tribe of Ohio had won decisive victories against U.S. troops.

In 1793, the Miami again faced attack by American forces. Little Turtle warned his people about the troops led by General Anthony Wayne.

### A VOICE FROM THE PAST

We have beaten the enemy twice under different commanders. . . . The Americans are now led by a chief [Wayne] who never sleeps. . . . We have not been able to surprise him. Think well of it. . . . It would be prudent [wise] to listen to his offers of peace.

**Little Turtle,** quoted in *The Life and Times of Little Turtle*

While the council members weighed Little Turtle's warning, President Washington was making plans to secure—guard or protect—the western borders of the new nation.

## Securing the Northwest Territory

As a general, Washington had skillfully waged war. As the nation's president, however, he saw that the country needed peace in order to prosper. But in spite of his desire for peace, he considered military action as trouble brewed in the Trans-Appalachian West, the land between the Appalachian Mountains and the Mississippi River. The 1783 Treaty of Paris had attempted to resolve the claims. The source of the trouble was competing claims for these lands. Some years later, however, Spain, Britain, the United States, and Native Americans claimed parts of the area as their own.

Spain held much of North America west of the Mississippi. It also claimed Florida and the port of New Orleans at the mouth of the

Mississippi. For American settlers in the West, this port was key to trade. They carried their goods to market by flatboat down the Mississippi to New Orleans. They took Spanish threats to close the port very seriously. The Spanish also stirred up trouble between the white settlers and the Creeks, Choctaws, and other Native American groups in the Southeast.

The strongest resistance to white settlement came from Native Americans in the Northwest Territory. This territory was bordered by the Ohio River to the south and Canada to the north. Native Americans in that territory hoped to join together to form an independent Native American nation. In violation of the Treaty of Paris, the British still held forts north of the Ohio River. The British supported Native Americans in order to maintain their access to fur in these territories. Eventually, Native Americans and white settlers clashed over the Northwest Territory.

*Reading*History
A. Making Inferences What expectations might the Native Americans have had of the British as the tribes came into conflict with white settlers?

## Battle of Fallen Timbers

Believing the Northwest Territory was critical to the security and growth of the new nation, Washington sent troops to the Ohio Valley. As you read in One American's Story, this first federal army took a beating from warriors led by Little Turtle in 1790. The chief's force came from many tribes, including the Shawnee, Ottawa, and Chippewa, who joined in a confederation to defeat the federal army.

After a second defeat in 1791 of an army headed by General Arthur St. Clair, Washington ordered another army west. This time Anthony Wayne, known as "Mad Anthony" for his reckless courage, was at its head.

The other chiefs ignored Little Turtle's advice to negotiate. They replaced him with a less able leader. Expecting British help, Native American warriors gathered at British-held Fort Miami. On August 20, 1794, a fighting force of around 2,000 Native Americans clashed with Wayne's troops. The site was covered with trees that had been struck down by a storm. The Native Americans were defeated in what became known as the **Battle of Fallen Timbers**.

The Battle of Fallen Timbers memorial sculpture below shows two American soldiers and a Native American.

### The Trans-Appalachian West, *1791–1795*

Mississippi R.

L. Michigan

L. Ontario

CANADA

Detroit

Battle of Fallen Timbers

L. Erie

Ft. Miami

Ft. Wayne

Wabash R.

PENNSYLVANIA

Illinois R.

NORTHWEST TERRITORY

St. Clair's Defeat

Ft. Greenville

•Pittsburgh

Ohio R.

VIRGINIA

KENTUCKY

0    100 Miles

0    200 Kilometers

Land ceded (surrendered) by Native Americans in Treaty of Greenville (1795)

★ Battle

U.S.-held fort

British-held fort

**GEOGRAPHY SKILLBUILDER**
**Interpreting Maps**

1. **Region** What does the yellow area of the map represent?
2. **Location** Why might the British forts be located near water?

The Native Americans retreated to Fort Miami. The British, not wanting war with the United States, refused to help them. The Battle of Fallen Timbers crushed Native American hopes of keeping their land in the Northwest Territory. Twelve tribes signed the **Treaty of Greenville** in 1795. They agreed to cede, or surrender, much of present-day Ohio and Indiana to the U.S. government.

*Reading***History**

**B. Reading a Map**
Use the map on page 299 to see which two states to the south bordered the land ceded by Native Americans.

### The Whiskey Rebellion

Not long after the Battle of Fallen Timbers, Washington put another army into the field. The conflict arose over the government's tax on whiskey, part of Hamilton's financial plan. From Pennsylvania to Georgia, outraged farmers resisted the tax. For them, whiskey—and the grain it was made from—were important products.

Because of poor roads, backcountry farmers had trouble getting their grain to market. Crops such as wheat and rye were more easily carried to market in liquid form, so farmers made their grain into whiskey. A farmer's horse could haul only two bushels of rye but could carry two barrels of rye whiskey. This was an amount equal to 24 bushels of the grain. In addition, their customers paid more for whiskey than grain. With little cash to buy goods, let alone pay the tax, farmers often traded whiskey for salt, sugar, and other goods. The farmers used whiskey as money to get whatever supplies they needed.

## CITIZENSHIP TODAY

# Obeying Rules and Laws

As the Whiskey Rebellion shows, since the earliest days of the republic our government has made laws and punished those who broke them. These laws affect not only adult citizens, but young people as well.

Today, for example, communities across the country are trying to control the problem of juvenile crime by imposing curfews on young people. These laws require minors to be off the streets after a certain time, often ten or eleven at night. Penalties can be harsh. In certain communities, minors who break curfew laws can be detained, and their parents can be fined.

People who favor curfews believe such laws cut crime. Those who oppose curfews think such limits are the responsibility of parents and not the government.

## Why Should You Obey Rules and Laws?

1. What are some arguments in favor of curfew laws? What are arguments against them? Make a list of each.

2. Poll your classmates to see how many agree with each position.

3. Write an essay expressing your opinion on this issue.

4. Brainstorm changes or adaptations to curfew laws that you think would make them more flexible.

 See Citizenship Handbook, page 283.

**For more about young people and the law . . .**

 RESEARCH LINKS
CLASSZONE.COM

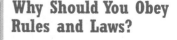

In the summer of 1794, a group of farmers in western Pennsylvania staged the **Whiskey Rebellion** against the tax. One armed group beat up a tax collector, coated him with tar and feathers, and stole his horse. Others threatened an armed attack on Pittsburgh.

Washington, urged on by Hamilton, was prepared to enforce the tax and crush the Whiskey Rebellion. They feared that not to act might undermine the new government and weaken its authority. Hamilton condemned the rebels for resisting the law.

*"Such a resistance is treason."*
Alexander Hamilton

### A VOICE FROM THE PAST

Such a resistance is treason against society, against liberty, against everything that ought to be dear to a free, enlightened, and prudent people. To tolerate it were to abandon your most precious interests. Not to subdue it were to tolerate it.

**Alexander Hamilton,** *The Works of Alexander Hamilton*

In October 1794, General Henry Lee, with Hamilton at his side, led an army of 13,000 soldiers into western Pennsylvania to put down the uprising. As news of the army's approach spread, the rebels fled. After much effort, federal troops rounded up 20 barefoot, ragged prisoners. Washington had proved his point. He had shown that the government had the power and the will to enforce its laws. Meanwhile, events in Europe gave Washington a different kind of challenge.

## The French Revolution

In 1789, a financial crisis led the French people to rebel against their government. Inspired by the American Revolution, the French revolutionaries demanded liberty and equality, and set out to create a government based on the will of the people. At first, Americans supported the **French Revolution**. By 1792, however, the revolution had become very violent. Thousands of French citizens were massacred. Then, in 1793, Louis XVI, the king of France, was executed.

Other European monarchs believed the revolution threatened their own thrones. France soon declared war on Britain, Holland, and Spain. Britain led the fight against France.

The war between France and Britain put the United States in an awkward position. France had been America's ally in the Revolution against the British.

## Connections TO WORLD HISTORY

### EYEWITNESS TO REVOLUTION

In 1789, an American citizen with a strange first name, Gouverneur Morris, went to Paris as a private business agent. Three years later, President Washington appointed him U.S. minister to France. An eyewitness to the French Revolution, Morris kept a detailed record of what he saw, including the execution of the king and queen by guillotine, as shown below.

Here is part of a letter he wrote on October 18, 1793:

"Terror is the order of the Day. . . . The Queen was executed the Day before yesterday. Insulted during her Trial and reviled in her last Moments, she behav'd with Dignity throughout."

A 1778 treaty still bound the two nations together. In addition, many saw France's revolution as proof that the American cause had been just. Jefferson felt that a move to crush the French Revolution was an attack on liberty everywhere. Hamilton, though, pointed out that Britain was the United States' most important trading partner, and British trade was too important to risk war.

In April 1793, Washington declared that the United States would remain **neutral,** not siding with one country or the other. He stated that the nation would be "friendly and impartial" to both sides. Congress then passed a law forbidding the United States to help either side.

*Reading*History
C. Drawing Conclusions
What sort of U.S. obligation to France did the wartime alliance and treaty of 1778 create?

## Remaining Neutral

Britain made it hard for the United States to remain neutral. Late in 1792, the British began seizing the cargoes of American ships carrying goods from the French West Indies.

Washington sent Chief Justice John Jay to England for talks about the seizure of U.S. ships. Jay also hoped to persuade the British to give up their forts on the Northwest frontier. During the talks in 1794, news came of the U.S. victory at the Battle of Fallen Timbers. Fearing another entanglement, the British agreed to leave the Ohio Valley by 1796. In **Jay's Treaty,** the British also agreed to pay damages for U.S. vessels they had seized. Jay failed, however, to open up the profitable British West Indies trade to Americans. Because of this, Jay's Treaty was unpopular.

Like Jay, Thomas Pinckney helped the United States reduce tensions along the frontier. In 1795, **Pinckney's Treaty** with Spain gave Americans the right to travel freely on the Mississippi River. It also gave them the right to store goods at the port of New Orleans without paying customs duties. In addition, Spain accepted the 31st parallel as the northern boundary of Florida and the southern boundary of the United States.

Meanwhile, more American settlers moved west. As you will read in the next section, change was coming back east as Washington stepped down.

*Reading*History
D. Evaluating
What were some of the advantages to the new nation of remaining neutral?

Section **2** Assessment

### 1. Terms & Names

**Explain the significance of:**

• Battle of Fallen Timbers
• Treaty of Greenville
• Whiskey Rebellion
• French Revolution
• neutral
• Jay's Treaty
• Pinckney's Treaty

### 2. Using Graphics

Use a chart to record U.S. responses to various challenges.

| Challenge | Response |
|-----------|----------|
| From Spain | |
| From Britain | |
| From France | |

Which challenge seemed greatest? Why? (HI2)

### 3. Main Ideas

**a.** What military and other actions secured the West for the United States? (HI2)

**b.** Why did Washington consider it important to put down the Whiskey Rebellion? (HI2)

**c.** How did the French Revolution create problems for the United States? (HI2)

### 4. Critical Thinking

**Drawing Conclusions**
Why was neutrality a difficult policy for the United States to maintain? (HI1)

**THINK ABOUT**

• ties with France
• ties with Britain
• restrictions on trade

**ACTIVITY OPTIONS**

**GEOGRAPHY**

**ART**

Make a **map** that describes the Battle of Fallen Timbers, or draw a **scene** from that battle. (HI1)

# The Federalists in Charge

| MAIN IDEA | WHY IT MATTERS NOW | TERMS & NAMES |
|---|---|---|
| The split between Hamilton and Jefferson led to the growth of political parties. | The two-party system is still a major feature of politics in the United States. | foreign policy    Alien and Sedition Acts<br>political party    states' rights<br>XYZ Affair |

## ONE AMERICAN'S STORY

In 1796, President George Washington decided that two terms in office was enough. But as he left office, he feared the growth of political parties would split the nation into enemy camps. In 1796, he wrote a final address to the nation.

### A VOICE FROM THE PAST

Let me now . . . warn you . . . against the [harmful] effects of the spirit of party. . . . This spirit, unfortunately . . . exists in different shapes in all governments . . . but in those of the popular form, it is seen in its greatest rankness and is truly their worst enemy.

**George Washington,** Farewell Address

This painting portrays Mount Vernon in 1792.

In his address, Washington warned of the dangers of political division, or what he termed "the spirit of party." As you will see in this section, few people took his advice.

## Washington Retires

Washington had come to the presidency greatly admired by the American people. Throughout his eight years in office (1789–1797), he had tried to serve as a symbol of national unity. In large part, he succeeded. During his second term, however, opponents of Jay's Treaty led attacks on the president. Thomas Paine called Washington "treacherous in private friendship . . . and a hypocrite in public life" because he failed to support the French Revolution.

Washington saw such attacks as the outcome of political disagreements. In his farewell address, he warned that such differences could weaken the nation. Despite his advice, political parties became a part of American politics.

**CALIFORNIA STANDARDS**

**8.3.4** Understand how the conflicts between Thomas Jefferson and Alexander Hamilton resulted in the emergence of two political parties (e.g., view of foreign policy, Alien and Sedition Acts, economic policy, National Bank, funding and assumption of the revolutionary debt).

**8.3.7** Understand the functions and responsibilities of a free press.

**8.4.2** Explain the policy significance of famous speeches (e.g., Washington's Farewell Address, Jefferson's 1801 Inaugural Address, John Q. Adams's Fourth of July 1821 Address).

**8.5.2** Know the changing boundaries of the United States and describe the relationships the country had with its neighbors (current Mexico and Canada) and Europe, including the influence of the Monroe Doctrine, and how those relationships influenced westward expansion and the Mexican-American War.

**8.10.3** Identify the constitutional issues posed by the doctrine of nullification and secession and the earliest origins of that doctrine.

**Taking Notes**

Use your chart to take notes about the Federalists and the establishment of a two-party system.

- Economics
- Politics
- Foreign Affairs
- Relations with Native Americans

Americans listened more closely to Washington's parting advice on **foreign policy**—relations with the governments of other countries. He urged the nation's leaders to remain neutral and "steer clear of permanent alliances with any portion of the foreign world." He warned that agreements with foreign nations might work against U.S. interests. His advice served to guide U.S. foreign policy into the twentieth century.

## Growth of Political Parties

Despite Washington's warning against political parties, Americans were deeply divided over how the nation should be run. During Washington's first term (1789–1792), Hamilton and Jefferson had hotly debated the direction the new nation should take. Then Jefferson returned to Virginia in 1793. During Washington's second term, Madison took Jefferson's place in the debates with Hamilton.

Both sides disagreed on how to interpret the Constitution and on economic policy. Hamilton favored the British government and opposed the French Revolution. Jefferson and Madison were the opposite. Hamilton fought for a strong central government. Jefferson and Madison feared such a government might lead to tyranny. They had different visions of what the nation should become. Hamilton wanted a United States in which trade, manufacturing, and cities grew. Jefferson and Madison pictured a rural nation of planters and farmers.

These differences on foreign and domestic policy led to the nation's first political parties. A **political party** is a group of people that tries to promote its ideas and influence government. It also backs candidates for office. Together, Jefferson and Madison founded the Democratic-Republican Party. The party name reflected their strong belief in democracy and the republican system. Their ideas drew farmers and workers to the new party. Hamilton and his friends formed the Federalist Party. Many Northern merchants and manufacturers became Federalists.

*Reading*History
**A. Summarizing**
What were the major beliefs of each party?

| The First Political Parties | |
| --- | --- |
| **FEDERALISTS** | **DEMOCRATIC-REPUBLICANS** |
| Strong national government | Limited national government |
| Fear of mob rule | Fear of rule by one person or a powerful few |
| Loose construction (interpretation) of the Constitution | Strict construction (interpretation) of the Constitution |
| Favored national bank | Opposed national bank |
| Economy based on manufacturing and shipping | Economy based on farming |
| Supporters: lawyers, merchants, manufacturers, clergy | Supporters: farmers, tradespeople |

**SKILLBUILDER Interpreting Charts**
1. *Which economic interests were served by the Federalists?*
2. *Which party favored a ruling elite? Which put more trust in the common people?*

**WASHINGTON, D.C., AND BENJAMIN BANNEKER**

Benjamin Banneker was a free African-American farmer. He was a self-taught mathematician and astronomer. He also wrote an almanac (see below). He was named to the survey commission appointed to lay out the boundaries of the nation's new capital. Working with chief planner Pierre L'Enfant, Banneker helped to decide where the White House and Capitol would be located. Their final design is shown at the left.

## John Adams Takes Office

In 1796, the United States held its first elections in which political parties competed. The Federalists picked Washington's vice-president, John Adams, as their candidate for president. An experienced public servant, Adams had been a leader during the Revolution and at the Continental Congress. He had also been a diplomat in France, the Netherlands, and Britain before serving with Washington. The Democratic-Republicans chose Jefferson.

In the electoral college, Adams received 71 votes and Jefferson 68. The Constitution stated that the runner-up should become vice-president. Therefore, the country had a Federalist president and a Democratic-Republican vice-president. Adams became president in 1797. His chief rival, Jefferson, entered office as his vice-president. In 1800, Adams became the first president to govern from the nation's new capital city, Washington, D.C.

## Problems with France

When Washington left office in 1797, relations between France and the United States were tense. With Britain and France still at war, the French began seizing U.S. ships to prevent them from trading with the British. Within the year, the French had looted more than 300 U.S. ships.

Although some Federalists called for war with France, Adams hoped talks would restore calm. To this end, he sent Charles Pinckney, Elbridge Gerry, and John Marshall to Paris. Arriving there, they requested a meeting with the French minister of foreign affairs. For weeks, they were

American newspapers fueled public anger over the XYZ Affair by publishing editorials and cartoons like this one. Here the five-man group ruling France demands money at dagger point from the three Americans. The American diplomats respond, "Cease bawling, monster! We will not give you sixpence!"

**What attitude does the cartoonist have toward France's role in this affair? How can you tell?**

ignored. Then three French agents—later referred to as X, Y, and Z—took the Americans aside to tell them the minister would hold talks. However, the talks would occur only if the Americans agreed to loan France $10 million and to pay the minister a bribe of $250,000. The Americans refused. "No, no, not a sixpence," Pinckney shot back.

Adams received a full report of what became known as the **XYZ Affair**. After Congress and an outraged public learned of it, the press turned Pinckney's words into a popular slogan: "Millions for defense, not one cent for tribute!" In 1798, Congress canceled its treaties with France and allowed U.S. ships to seize French vessels. Congress also set aside money to expand the navy and the army.

*Reading* **History**
**B. Drawing Conclusions** How did the XYZ Affair show the young nation's growing confidence?

## The Alien and Sedition Acts

The conflict with France made Adams and the Federalists popular with the public. Many Democratic-Republicans, however, were sympathetic to France. One Democratic-Republican newspaper called Adams "the blasted tyrant of America." In turn, Federalists labeled Democratic-Republicans "democrats, mobcrats, and other kinds of rats."

Angered by criticism in a time of crisis, Adams blamed the Democratic-Republican newspapers and new immigrants. Many of the immigrants were Democratic-Republicans. To silence their critics, the Federalist Congress passed the **Alien and Sedition Acts** in 1798. These acts targeted aliens—immigrants who were not yet citizens. One act increased the waiting period for becoming a U.S. citizen from 5 to 14 years. Other acts gave the president the power to arrest disloyal aliens or order them out of the country during wartime. A fourth act outlawed sedition, saying or writing anything false or harmful about the government.

With these acts, the Federalists clamped down on freedom of speech and the press. About 25 Democratic-Republican newspaper editors were charged under this act, and 10 were convicted of expressing opinions damaging to the government. A Vermont congressman, Matthew Lyon, was also locked up for saying that the president should be sent "to a mad house." The voters re-elected Lyon while he was in jail.

*Reading*History
**C. Making Inferences** How might the theory of states' rights undermine the federal government?

The Democratic-Republicans, led by Jefferson and Madison, searched for a way to fight the Alien and Sedition Acts. They found it in a theory called **states' rights**. According to this theory, states had rights that the federal government could not violate. Jefferson and Madison wrote resolutions (or statements) passed by the Kentucky and Virginia legislatures in 1798 and 1799. In the Kentucky Resolutions, Jefferson proposed nullification, the idea that a state could nullify a federal law within the state. In the Virginia Resolutions, Madison said a state could interpose, or place, itself between the federal government and its citizens. These resolutions declared that the Alien and Sedition Acts violated the Constitution. No other states supported Kentucky and Virginia. However, within two years the Democratic-Republicans won control of Congress, and they either repealed the Alien and Sedition Acts or let them expire.

## Peace with France

While Federalists and Democratic-Republicans battled at home, Adams reopened talks with France. This time the two sides quickly signed the Convention of 1800, an agreement to stop all naval attacks.

Adams's actions made him enemies among the Federalists, but he spoke proudly of having saved the nation from bloodshed. Adams lost the presidential election of 1800 to Thomas Jefferson. You will read more about Jefferson in the next chapter.

### *America's* HERITAGE

**FREEDOM OF THE PRESS**

Since the Alien and Sedition Acts, the Supreme Court has ruled many times that a free press had the right to publish information critical of or harmful to the government or government officials.

A free press has a responsibility to remain independent, not just from the government, but from individuals or groups which might influence its reporting. For instance, a newspaper or television network must be unafraid to cover a heavy advertiser accurately, even if a critical or negative story causes the company to pull its advertising. Editors and reporters must frequently report gifts they are given and financial holdings they may have.

To demonstrate accountability, most media outlets run corrections, when necessary, and letters from viewers or readers.

---

**Section ❸ Assessment**

**1. Terms & Names**

**Explain the significance of:**
- foreign policy
- political party
- XYZ Affair
- Alien and Sedition Acts
- states' rights

**2. Using Graphics**

Use a cluster diagram to review details about the Alien and Sedition Acts.

What was the worst effect of the Alien and Sedition Acts? Why? (HI2)

**3. Main Ideas**

**a.** What two pieces of advice did Washington give in his Farewell Address? (8.3.4)

**b.** What led to the rise of political parties? (8.3.4)

**c.** Why did Congress pass the Alien and Sedition Acts? How did Kentucky and Virginia respond? (8.3.4)

**4. Critical Thinking**

**Evaluating** Do you think Washington's warning about political parties was good advice? Explain. (REP4)

**THINK ABOUT**
- roles of political parties
- advantages of parties
- disadvantages of parties

**ACTIVITY OPTIONS**

**TECHNOLOGY**

**SPEECH**

Read more about Benjamin Banneker. Plan part of a **video presentation** on him or present **dramatic readings** of excerpts from the almanac he wrote. (REP4)

## TERMS & NAMES

Briefly explain the significance of each of the following.

1. inaugurate
2. cabinet
3. tariff
4. Battle of Fallen Timbers
5. Whiskey Rebellion
6. neutral
7. foreign policy
8. political party
9. Alien and Sedition Acts
10. states' rights

## REVIEW QUESTIONS

### Washington's Presidency (pages 293–297)

1. What questions about the judiciary were left open by the Constitution? How were they answered? (HI1)
2. What financial problems did the new nation face? (HI1)
3. How did Hamilton and Jefferson interpret the Constitution differently? (REP5)

### Challenges to the New Government (pages 298–302)

4. What did Washington do to secure the West? (HI1)
5. What were the major arguments regarding taxation under the new government? (REP5)
6. Why did Washington favor neutrality in the conflict between France and Britain? (HI1)
7. What problems did the Jay and Pinckney treaties address? (HI1)

### The Federalists in Charge (pages 303–307)

8. Why did Washington oppose political parties? (HI1)
9. What was the XYZ Affair? (HI1)
10. Why did Federalists pass the Alien and Sedition Acts? How did Republicans respond? (HI2)

## CRITICAL THINKING

### 1. USING YOUR NOTES: IDENTIFYING AND SOLVING PROBLEMS

PROBLEMS

Economics
Politics
Foreign Affairs
Relations with Native Americans

SOLUTIONS

Using your completed chart, answer the questions. (HI2)

a. What were the problems that characterized the Federalist era?

b. What do the solutions to these problems reveal about the characteristics of the era?

### 2. ANALYZING LEADERSHIP

How did Washington's efforts to serve as a symbol of national unity help the new nation? (HI1)

### 3. APPLYING CITIZENSHIP SKILLS

How might the farmers in the Whiskey Rebellion have expressed their disapproval of the whiskey tax while staying within the law? (HI4)

### 4. THEME: DEMOCRATIC IDEALS

Did the formation of political parties make the nation more or less democratic? (HI1)

### Interact with History

How did the challenges of setting up a government that you discussed before you read the chapter compare with the actual challenges you read about?

## VISUAL SUMMARY

# The First Presidents (8.4.1)

**WASHINGTON PRESIDENCY 1789–1797**

Strong Government
• Cabinet
• Judiciary

Remaining Neutral
• Jay's Treaty
• Pinckney's Treaty

Secure the West
• Battle of Fallen Timbers
• Treaty of Greenville

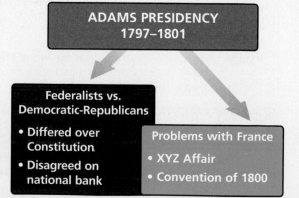

**ADAMS PRESIDENCY 1797–1801**

Federalists vs. Democratic-Republicans
• Differed over Constitution
• Disagreed on national bank

Problems with France
• XYZ Affair
• Convention of 1800

# STANDARDS-BASED ASSESSMENT

Use the chart and your knowledge of U.S. history to answer questions 1 and 2.

Additional Test Practice, pp. S1–S33.

## Financial Problems, 1789–1791

| DEBTS | EXPENSES | INCOME |
|---|---|---|
| $77,230,000 = total public debt | $4,270,000 budget to run government | $4,400,000 from duties or taxes imposed on imported and exported goods |

Source: *Historical Statistics of the United States*

**1.** How much money did the government owe during the period shown on the chart? (8.3.4)

- A. $4,270,000
- B. $4,400,000
- C. $77,000,000
- D. $77,230,000

**2.** What could the government do to increase income? (8.3.4)

- A. decrease duties and taxes
- B. increase duties and taxes
- C. increase the national budget
- D. pay off the public debt

This quotation from George Washington's Farewell Address is a warning to future leaders. Use this quotation and your knowledge of U.S. history to answer question 3.

### PRIMARY SOURCE

Let me now . . . warn you . . . against the [harmful] effects of the spirit of party. . . . This spirit, unfortunately . . . exists in different shapes in all governments . . . but in those of the popular form, it is seen in its greatest rankness and is truly their worst enemy.

**George Washington,** Farewell Address

**3.** What danger was Washington warning Americans about in his Farewell Address? (8.3.4)

- A. foreign governments
- B. Antifederalists
- C. political parties
- D. taxation

TEST PRACTICE
CLASSZONE.COM

---

# ALTERNATIVE ASSESSMENT

## 1. ✎ WRITING ABOUT HISTORY

Imagine that you are a U.S. citizen during the French Revolution. Write a **letter** to the secretary of state giving reasons why you think the United States should aid the French, aid the British, or remain neutral. (REP5)

- Use library resources to research the different sides.
- Use your research to persuade the secretary of state to your point of view.

## 2. COOPERATIVE LEARNING

Work with other students to research the Alien and Sedition Acts and the positions taken by both political parties. Consider these questions: Were the acts constitutional or an abuse of basic rights? Should criticism of the government be allowed in a time of possible war? Choose two group members to debate the Federalist and Democratic-Republican positions. (REP4)

# INTEGRATED TECHNOLOGY

## CREATING A CAMPAIGN COMMERCIAL

Create a 30-second television commercial for either John Adams, the Federalist party candidate, or Thomas Jefferson, the Democratic-Republican party candidate. (REP5)

- On the Internet, find information about your candidate that shows why he is a good choice.
- Locate at least two pictures that reveal different images of the candidate. Also, use the Internet to find suitable background music for the commercial.
- Use your resource materials to create a 30-second campaign commercial.

For more about the 1796 election . . .

INTERNET ACTIVITY
CLASSZONE.COM

# The Jefferson Era 1800–1816

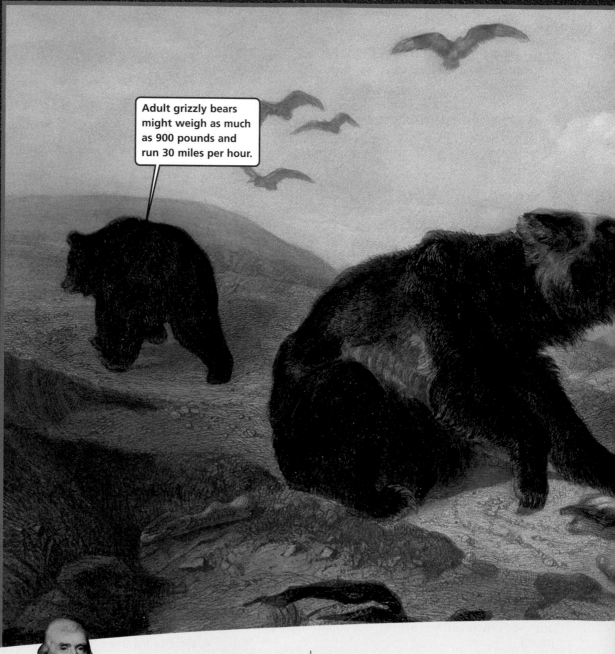

Adult grizzly bears might weigh as much as 900 pounds and run 30 miles per hour.

**1801**
Thomas Jefferson is elected president.

**1803**
Louisiana Purchase is made.

**1804**
Jefferson is reelected.
Lewis and Clark expedition begins.

**1807**
Embargo Act is passed.

USA
World   1800

**1801**
Tripoli declares war on the United States.

**1803**
Europe's Napoleonic wars resume after brief peace.

**1805**
British win at Trafalgar.
French win at Austerlitz.

# Interact *with* History

You have been chosen to participate in an expedition to the West in the early 1800s. You are excited and curious, but also a little scared. You know that you will see and experience many new things. But you know there are risks involved, too.

# What dangers will you face on an expedition west?

In the early 1800s, it took about 20 seconds to load and fire a gun.

## What Do You Think?

- Notice the land features in these scenes. What problems might they hold for an explorer?
- What other people might you meet on the expedition?

**RESEARCH LINKS**
CLASSZONE.COM
Visit the Chapter 10 links for more information about the Jefferson Era.

**808** ames Madison elected resident.

**1811** Battle of Tippecanoe is fought.

**1812** War of 1812 begins.

**1814** British attack Washington, D.C.

**1815** Battle of New Orleans is fought.

**1816**

**1810** Father Hidalgo calls for Mexican independence.

**1814** Napoleon is defeated and exiled to Elba.

**1815** Napoleon returns and is defeated at Waterloo.

*The Jefferson Era* **311**

# Reading Strategy: Summarizing

## What Do You Know?

What parts of the United States today were not part of the country in 1800? What should leaders consider before they buy land for their countries?

### Think About
- where the money for the purchase will come from
- what should be done if people already live on the land
- your responses to the Interact with History about facing dangers on an expedition west (see page 311)

## What Do You Want to Know?

 What details do you need to help you understand the nation's expansion in the early 1800s? Make a list of information you need in your notebook before you read the chapter.

**CALIFORNIA STANDARDS**

**Reading 2.4** Compare the original text to a summary to determine whether the summary accurately captures the main ideas, includes critical details, and conveys the underlying meaning.

United States in 1800

United States in 1816

## Summarizing

When you study history, it is important to clearly understand what you read. One way to achieve a clear understanding is to summarize. When you summarize, you restate what you have read into fewer words, stating only the main ideas and essential details. It is important to use your own words in a summary. Use the chart below to record your summaries of the main ideas and essential details in Chapter 10.

**S** See Skillbuilder Handbook, page R2.

### Taking Notes

| The Jefferson Era |
| --- |
| Summaries |
| **Main Idea:** Thomas Jefferson is elected president.<br>**Details:** Jefferson replaces Federalist policies with his own but has problems with the judiciary. |
| **Main Idea:**<br>**Details:** |
| **Main Idea:**<br>**Details:** |
| **Main Idea:**<br>**Details:** |

# Jefferson Takes Office

| MAIN IDEA | WHY IT MATTERS NOW | TERMS & NAMES |
|---|---|---|
| When Jefferson became president in 1801, his party replaced Federalist programs with its own. | Today's Democratic Party traces its roots to the party of Jefferson, the Democratic-Republicans. | radical<br>Judiciary Act of 1801<br>John Marshall<br>*Marbury* v. *Madison*<br>unconstitutional<br>judicial review |

## ONE AMERICAN'S STORY

In the election of 1800, backers of John Adams and Thomas Jefferson fought for their candidates with nasty personal attacks. For instance, James Callender warned voters not to reelect President John Adams.

### A VOICE FROM THE PAST

In the fall of 1796 . . . the country fell into a more dangerous juncture than almost any the old confederation ever endured. The tardiness and timidity of Mr. Washington were succeeded by the rancour [bitterness] and insolence [arrogance] of Mr. Adams. . . . Think what you have been, what you are, and what, under [Adams], you are likely to become.

**James Callender,** quoted in *American Aurora*

Adams's defenders were just as vicious. Yet, in spite of the campaign's nastiness, the election ended with a peaceful transfer of power from one party to another. The 1800 election was a contest between two parties with different ideas about the role of government.

## The Election of 1800

The two parties contesting the election of 1800 were the Federalists, led by President John Adams, and the Democratic-Republicans, represented by Thomas Jefferson. Each party believed that the other was endangering the Constitution and the American republic.

The Democratic-Republicans thought they were saving the nation from monarchy and oppression. They argued, again and again, that the Alien and Sedition Acts supported by the Federalists violated the Bill of Rights. (See pages 306–307.) The Federalists thought that the nation was about to be ruined by **radicals**—people who take extreme political positions. They remembered the violence of the French Revolution, in which radicals executed thousands in the name of liberty.

**CALIFORNIA STANDARDS**

**8.3.4** Understand how the conflicts between Thomas Jefferson and Alexander Hamilton resulted in the emergence of two political parties (e.g., view of foreign policy, Alien and Sedition Acts, economic policy, National Bank, funding and assumption of the revolutionary debt).

**8.4.1** Describe the country's physical landscapes, political divisions, and territorial expansion during the terms of the first four presidents.

**8.4.2** Explain the policy significance of famous speeches (e.g., Washington's Farewell Address, Jefferson's 1801 Inaugural Address, John Q. Adams's Fourth of July 1821 Address).

**8.4.3** Analyze the rise of capitalism and the economic problems and conflicts that accompanied it (e.g., Jackson's opposition to the National Bank; early decisions of the U.S. Supreme Court that reinforced the sanctity of contracts and a capitalist economic system of law).

**Taking Notes**

Use your chart to take notes about Jefferson's presidency.

| The Jefferson Era |
|---|
| Summaries |
| Main Idea: .<br>Details: |
| Main Idea:<br>Details: |
| Main Idea:<br>Details: |
| Main Idea:<br>Details: |

When election day came, the Democratic-Republicans won the presidency. Jefferson received 73 votes in the electoral college, and Adams earned 65. But there was a problem. Aaron Burr, whom the Democratic-Republicans wanted as vice president, also received 73 votes.

**Background**
In 1804, the Twelfth Amendment solved this problem by creating separate ballots for president and vice president.

## Breaking the Tie

According to the Constitution, the House of Representatives had to choose between Burr and Jefferson. The Democratic-Republicans clearly intended for Jefferson to be president. However, the new House of Representatives, dominated by Jefferson's party, would not take office for some months. Federalists still held a majority in the House, and their votes would decide the winner.

The Federalists were divided. Some feared Jefferson so much that they decided to back Burr. Others, such as Alexander Hamilton, considered Burr an unreliable man and urged the election of Jefferson. Hamilton did not like Jefferson, but he believed that Jefferson would do more for the good of the nation than Burr. "If there be a man in the world I ought to hate," he said, "it is Jefferson. . . . But the public good must be [more important than] every private consideration."

Over a period of seven days, the House voted 35 times without determining a winner. Finally, two weeks before the inauguration, Alexander Hamilton's friend James A. Bayard persuaded several Federalists not to vote for Burr. On the thirty-sixth ballot, Jefferson was elected president. Aaron Burr, who became vice president, would never forget Hamilton's insults.

People were overjoyed by Jefferson's election. A Philadelphia newspaper reported that bells rang, guns fired, dogs barked, cats meowed, and children cried over the news of Jefferson's victory.

*Reading* **History**
**A. Analyzing Points of View**
Why did Hamilton think that Jefferson was the better choice for president?

## The Talented Jefferson

In over 200 years, the United States has had more than 40 presidents. Many of them were great leaders. But no president has ever matched Thomas Jefferson in the variety of his achievements.

Jefferson's talents went beyond politics. He was still a young lawyer when he became interested in the architecture of classical Greece and Rome. The look of our nation's capital today reflects that interest. When Washington, D.C., was being built during the 1790s, Jefferson advised its architects and designers.

Jefferson's passion for classical styles can also be seen in his plan of Monticello, his Virginia home. For this elegant mansion, Jefferson designed storm windows, a seven-day clock, and a dumbwaiter—a small elevator that brought bottles of wine from the cellar.

Jefferson was a skilled violinist, horseman, amateur scientist, and a devoted reader, too. His book collection later became the core of the Library of Congress. After his election, Jefferson applied his many talents and ideas to the government of the United States.

## Jefferson's Philosophy

The new president had strong opinions about what kind of country the United States ought to be. But his first order of business was to calm the nation's political quarrels.

*A VOICE FROM THE PAST*

Let us, then, fellow-citizens, unite with one heart and one mind. . . . Every difference of opinion is not a difference of principle. . . . We are all Republicans, we are all Federalists.

**Thomas Jefferson,** First Inaugural Address

*Reading***History**

**B. Summarizing**
How did Thomas Jefferson try to unite the nation after he was elected?

One way Jefferson tried to unite Americans was by promoting a common way of life. He wanted the United States to remain a nation of small independent farmers. Such a nation, he believed, would uphold the strong morals and democratic values that he associated with country living. He hoped that the enormous amount of available land would prevent Americans from crowding into cities, as people had in Europe.

As president, Jefferson behaved more like a gentleman farmer than a privileged politician. Instead of riding in a fancy carriage to his inauguration, Jefferson walked the two blocks from his boarding house to the Capitol. Though his chef served elegant meals, the president's guests ate at round tables so that no one could sit at the head of the table.

To the end, Jefferson refused to elevate himself because of his office. For his tombstone, he chose this simple epitaph: "Here was buried

**The Talented Jefferson**

For his Virginia home, Jefferson designed a dumbwaiter to bring bottles from his wine cellar.

Thomas Jefferson was a man of extraordinary talent. His architectural skill can be seen in the design of Monticello, shown here.

Jefferson improved the design of this early copy machine. As a user of the device wrote with one pen, a second pen made an exact copy.

315

Thomas Jefferson, author of the Declaration of American Independence, of the statute of Virginia for religious freedom, and father of the University of Virginia." Jefferson chose not to list his presidency. His belief in a modest role for the central government is reflected in the changes he made during his presidency.

**Background**
In addition to founding the University of Virginia in 1819, Jefferson designed its buildings and supervised their construction.

## Undoing Federalist Programs

Jefferson believed that the federal government should have less power than it had had under the Federalists. During his term of office, he sought to end many Federalist programs.

At the president's urging, Congress—now controlled by Democratic-Republicans—allowed the Alien and Sedition Acts to end. Jefferson then released prisoners convicted under the acts—among them, James Callender. Congress also ended many taxes, including the unpopular whiskey tax. Because the loss of tax revenue lowered the government's income, Jefferson reduced the number of federal employees to cut costs. He also reduced the size of the military.

Jefferson next made changes to the Federalists' financial policies. Alexander Hamilton had created a system that depended on a certain amount of public debt. He believed that people who were owed money by their government would make sure the government was run properly. But Jefferson opposed public debt. He used revenues from tariffs and land sales to reduce the amount of money owed by the government.

**AMERICA'S HISTORY MAKERS**

**JOHN MARSHALL**
**1755–1835**

John Marshall was born, the first of 15 children, in Virginia's backcountry. He had little formal schooling. He received most of his education from his parents and a minister who lived with the family one year.

Even so, the lasting strength of the U.S. Constitution is partly due to Marshall's brilliant legal mind. In his long tenure as Chief Justice, John Marshall participated in more than 1,000 decisions and wrote 519 of them himself.

**How does Marshall's record as Chief Justice demonstrate his decision-making abilities?**

## Marshall and the Judiciary

Though Jefferson ended many Federalist programs, he had little power over the courts. John Adams had seen to that with the **Judiciary Act of 1801**. Under this act, Adams had appointed as many Federalist judges as he could between the election of 1800 and Jefferson's inauguration in 1801. These last-minute appointments meant that the new Democratic-Republican president would face a firmly Federalist judiciary.

Jefferson often felt frustrated by Federalist control of the courts. Yet because judges received their appointments for life, the president could do little.

Before he left office in 1801, President Adams also appointed a new Chief Justice of the Supreme Court. He chose a 45-year-old Federalist, **John Marshall**. He guessed that Marshall would be around for a long time to check the power of the Democratic-Republicans. He was right. Marshall served as Chief Justice for over three decades. Under Marshall, the Supreme Court upheld federal authority and strengthened federal

*Reading* **History**
**C. Analyzing Causes** Why did the Federalists retain a great deal of power even after they were defeated by the Democratic-Republicans?

courts. One of the most important decisions of the Marshall Court was ***Marbury v. Madison*** (1803).

## *Marbury v. Madison*

**Vocabulary**
**justice of the peace:** a low-level official with limited authority, including the power to perform marriages

William Marbury was one of Adams's last-minute appointments. Adams had named him as a justice of the peace for the District of Columbia.

Marbury was supposed to be installed in his position by Secretary of State James Madison. When Madison refused to give him the job, Marbury sued. The case went to the Supreme Court, which ruled that the law under which Marbury sued was **unconstitutional**—that is, it contradicted the law of the Constitution.

**HISTORIC DECISIONS**
*OF THE SUPREME COURT*

For more information on *Marbury v. Madison*, see pp. 740–741.

Although the Court denied Marbury's claim, it did establish the principle of **judicial review**. This principle states that the Supreme Court has the final say in interpreting the Constitution. In his decision, Marshall declared, "It is emphatically the province and duty of the Judicial Department to say what the law is." If the Supreme Court decides that a law violates the Constitution, then that law cannot be put into effect.

Jefferson and Madison were angry when Marshall seized this new power for the Supreme Court, but they could hardly fight his decision. After all, he had decided *Marbury* v. *Madison* in their favor.

By establishing judicial review, Marshall helped to create a lasting balance among the three branches of government. The strength of this balance would be tested as the United States grew. In the next section, you will read about a period of great national growth.

### Now and then

**THE SUPREME COURT TODAY**

The principle of judicial review is still a major force in American society. In June 1999, the Supreme Court used this power to restrict the ability of the federal government to enforce its laws in the 50 states.

In one case, *Alden* v. *Maine*, the Court ruled that employees of a state government cannot sue their state even when the state violates federal labor laws—such as those that set guidelines for overtime wages.

---

**Section 1 Assessment**

### 1. Terms & Names

**Explain the significance of:**
• radical
• Judiciary Act of 1801
• John Marshall
• *Marbury* v. *Madison*
• unconstitutional
• judicial review

### 2. Using Graphics

Use a chart like the one below to list some of the changes made by Jefferson and his party.

| Changes made by Democratic-Republicans |
|---|
| 1. |

What branch of government gave Jefferson trouble? (HI1)

### 3. Main Ideas

**a.** How was the tie between Jefferson and Burr settled after the election of 1800? (HI1)

**b.** In what ways did Jefferson's talents reach beyond politics? (HI1)

**c.** How did the opinions of Jefferson and Hamilton regarding the public debt differ? (HI1)

### 4. Critical Thinking

**Making Generalizations**
How was Thomas Jefferson's philosophy reflected in his personal life? (HI1)

**THINK ABOUT**
• how he behaved after being elected
• how he felt about his presidency later in life

**ACTIVITY OPTIONS**

**TECHNOLOGY**

**ART**

Read more about Thomas Jefferson. Design Jefferson's **Internet home page** showing his inventions or create a **model** of a building he designed. (HI1)

# The Louisiana Purchase and Exploration

| MAIN IDEA | WHY IT MATTERS NOW | TERMS & NAMES |
|---|---|---|
| Jefferson purchased the Louisiana Territory in 1803 and doubled the size of the United States. | Thirteen more states were eventually organized on the land acquired by the Louisiana Purchase. | Louisiana Purchase · Lewis and Clark expedition · Meriwether Lewis · Sacagawea · William Clark · Zebulon Pike |

**CALIFORNIA STANDARDS**

**8.4.1** Describe the country's physical landscapes, political divisions, and territorial expansion during the terms of the first four presidents.

**8.5.2** Know the changing boundaries of the United States and describe the relationships the country had with its neighbors (current Mexico and Canada) and Europe, including the influence of the Monroe Doctrine, and how those relationships influenced westward expansion and the Mexican-American War.

**8.8.2** Describe the purpose, challenges, and economic incentives associated with westward expansion, including the concept of Manifest Destiny (e.g., the Lewis and Clark expedition, accounts of the removal of Indians, the Cherokees' "Trail of Tears," settlement of the Great Plains) and the territorial acquisitions that spanned numerous decades.

**8.8.4** Examine the importance of the great rivers and the struggle over water rights.

**Taking Notes**

Use your chart to take notes about the exploration of the West.

| The Jefferson Era |
|---|
| Summaries |
| Main Idea: . Details: |
| Main Idea: Details: |
| Main Idea: Details: |
| Main Idea: Details: |

## ONE AMERICAN'S STORY

In 1790, Captain Robert Gray became the first American to sail around the world. Two years later, Gray explored a harbor in what is now Washington state. New England merchants like Captain Gray had to sail all the way around South America to reach the profitable trading regions of the Oregon Country. (See the map on page 320.) In spite of the long trip, merchants from Boston soon began to appear there frequently.

Gray's explorations helped to establish U.S. claims to the Pacific Northwest. In this section, you will learn how a lucky land purchase and a daring expedition further hastened westward expansion.

Robert Gray sailed his ship *Columbia* on voyages to the Northwest and China.

## The West in 1800

In 1800, when Americans talked about the "West," they meant the area between the Appalachian Mountains and the Mississippi River. Thousands of settlers were moving westward across the Appalachians to settle in this region. Many moved onto land long inhabited by Native Americans. Even so, several U.S. territories soon declared statehood. Kentucky and Tennessee had become states by 1800, and Ohio entered the union in 1803.

Although the Mississippi River was the western border of the United States, there was a great deal of activity further west. In 1800, France and Spain were negotiating for ownership of the Louisiana Territory—the vast region between the Mississippi River and the Rocky Mountains.

The Pacific coast region and the Oregon Country, as you read in One American's Story, also attracted increasing attention. In California, Spain had a chain of 21 missions stretching from San Diego to San Francisco. Starting just north of San Francisco, Russian settlements dotted the Pacific coast all the way to Alaska. Great Britain also claimed land in the region.

## *Reading*History
A. Reading a Map Use the map on page 320 to find the location of New Orleans.

As the number of Westerners grew, so did their political influence. A vital issue for many settlers was the use of the Mississippi River. Farmers and merchants used the river to move their products to the port of New Orleans, and from there to east coast markets. Threats to the free navigation of the Mississippi and the use of the port at New Orleans brought America to the brink of war.

## Napoleon and New Orleans

"There is on the globe one single spot the possessor of which is our natural and habitual enemy," President Jefferson wrote. That spot was New Orleans. This strategic port was originally claimed by France. After losing the French and Indian War, France turned over the Louisiana Territory—including New Orleans—to Spain. But in a secret treaty in 1800, Spain returned Louisiana and the port to France's powerful leader, Napoleon. Now Napoleon planned to colonize the American territory.

Background
In 1799, Napoleon was made the top official of the French Republic. In 1804, he became emperor.

In 1802, these developments nearly resulted in war. Just before turning Louisiana over to France, Spain closed New Orleans to American shipping. Angry Westerners called for war against both Spain and France. To avoid hostilities, Jefferson offered to buy New Orleans from France. He received a surprising offer back. The French asked if the United States wanted to buy all of the Louisiana Territory—a tract of land even larger than the United States at that time.

## Connections TO WORLD HISTORY

### TOUSSAINT L'OUVERTURE

Toussaint L'Ouverture was born in Hispaniola, an island in the West Indies once colonized by both France and Spain. In 1791, L'Ouverture helped to lead a slave revolt against the French-controlled part of Hispaniola. A natural leader, L'Ouverture won admiration when he preached harmony between former slaves and planters.

In 1801, L'Ouverture overran the Spanish part of the island. He then freed all the slaves and put himself in charge of the entire island.

Hoping to regain their territory, the French invaded in 1802. They arrested L'Ouverture but failed to end the rebellion.

## The Louisiana Purchase

A number of factors may have led Napoleon to make his surprising offer. He was probably alarmed by America's fierce determination to keep the port of New Orleans open. Also, his enthusiasm for a colony in America may have been lessened by events in a French colony in the West Indies. There, a revolt led by Toussaint L'Ouverture (too•SAN loo•vehr•TOOR) had resulted in disastrous losses for the French. Another factor was France's costly war against Britain. America's money may have been more valuable to Napoleon than its land.

## *Reading*History
B. Making Inferences Why did Jefferson purchase Louisiana even though the Constitution said nothing about the president's right to buy land?

Jefferson was thrilled by Napoleon's offer. However, the Constitution said nothing about the president's right to buy land. This troubled Jefferson, who believed in the strict interpretation of the Constitution. But he also believed in a republic of small farmers, and that required land. So, on April 30, 1803, the **Louisiana Purchase** was approved for $15 million—about three cents per acre. The purchase doubled the size of the United States. At the time, Americans knew little about the territory. But that would soon change.

# Lewis and Clark Explore

Since 1802, Thomas Jefferson had planned an expedition to explore the Louisiana country. Now that the Louisiana Purchase had been made, learning about the territory became even more important.

Jefferson chose a young officer, Captain **Meriwether Lewis,** to lead the expedition. In Jefferson's map-lined study, the two men eagerly planned the trip. Lewis turned to his old friend, Lieutenant **William Clark,** to select and oversee a volunteer force, which they called the Corps of Discovery. Clark was a skilled mapmaker and outdoorsman and proved to be a natural leader. The Corps of Discovery soon became known as the **Lewis and Clark expedition.**

Clark was accompanied by York, his African-American slave. York's hunting skills won him many admirers among the Native Americans met by the explorers. The first black man that many Indians had ever seen, York became something of a celebrity among them.

Lewis and Clark set out in the summer of 1803. By winter, they reached St. Louis. Located on the western bank of the Mississippi River, St. Louis would soon become the gateway to the West. But in 1803, the city was a sleepy town with just 180 houses. Lewis and Clark spent the winter at St. Louis and waited for the ceremony that would mark the transfer of Louisiana to the United States. In March 1804, the American flag flew over St. Louis for the first time.

**Vocabulary**
**corps** (kor): a number of people acting together for a similar purpose

## The Louisiana Purchase and Explorations, *1804–1807*

The Rocky Mountain summit of Pikes Peak is 14,110 feet high.

**GEOGRAPHY SKILLBUILDER Interpreting Maps**
**1. Location** *What two rivers met at the starting point of the Lewis and Clark expedition?*
**2. Movement** *How were Lewis and Clark's return routes different from each other?*

**MERIWETHER LEWIS**

**1774–1809**

Meriwether Lewis was well qualified for the first overland expedition to the Pacific Northwest. In Virginia, he had become an expert hunter. From 1801 to 1803, he worked for President Jefferson, who had him trained in geography, mineralogy, and astronomy.

The journals Lewis kept tell what the West was like in the early 1800s and are still exciting to read. In one entry, dated September 17, 1804, Lewis describes the "immense herds of Buffaloe, deer Elk and Antelopes which we saw in every direction feeding on the hills and plains."

**WILLIAM CLARK**

**1770–1838**

William Clark was an army friend of Meriwether Lewis. Lewis personally chose him to be co-captain of the Corps of Discovery.

Clark's experience in his state militia and the U.S. Army had taught him how to build forts, draw maps, and lead expeditions through enemy territory.

He had less formal training than Lewis, but with his six feet of height and muscular build, he was a more rugged explorer.

Clark's leadership skills smoothed disputes. Also, his artistic skills made the expedition's maps and drawings both accurate and beautiful.

**What were the different skills of Lewis and Clark that qualified them as co-leaders of the expedition?**

# Up the Missouri River

*Reading*History

C. Making Inferences Why did Lewis and Clark travel on the Missouri River?

The explorers, who numbered about 40, set out from St. Louis in May of 1804. They headed up the Missouri River in one shallow-bottomed riverboat and two pirogues—canoes made from hollowed-out tree trunks. They had instructions from President Jefferson to explore the river and hoped to find a water route across the continent. Lewis and Clark were also told to establish good relations with Native Americans and describe the landscape, plants, and animals they saw.

The explorers inched up the Missouri. The first afternoon, they traveled only about three miles. Sometimes the men had to pull, rather than row or sail, their boats against the current. In late October, they reached the Mandan Indian villages in what is now North Dakota.

The explorers built a small fort and spent the winter with the friendly Mandan. There, they also met British and French-Canadian trappers and traders. They were not happy to see the Americans. They suspected that the Americans would soon compete with them for the rich trade in beaver furs—and they were right.

In the spring of 1805, the expedition set out again. A French trapper, his 17-year-old-wife, **Sacagawea** (SAK•uh•juh•WEE•uh), and their baby went with them. Sacagawea was a Shoshone woman whose language skills and knowledge of geography would be of great value to Lewis and Clark—especially when they reached the area where she was born.

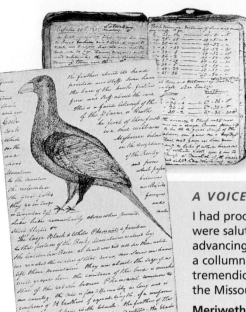

## On to the Pacific Ocean

On their way west, the expedition had to stop at the Great Falls of the Missouri. Lewis called this ten-mile-long series of waterfalls "the grandest sight I ever beheld." He described his approach to the falls.

### A VOICE FROM THE PAST

I had proceeded on this course about two miles . . . whin my ears were saluted with the agreeable sound of a fall of water and advancing a little further I saw the spray arrise above the plain like a collumn of smoke. . . . (It) soon began to make a roaring too tremendious to be mistaken for any cause short of the great falls of the Missouri.

**Meriwether Lewis,** quoted in *Undaunted Courage*

**Lewis and Clark kept beautiful journals that provided priceless information about the West.**

To get around the Great Falls, the explorers had to carry their boats and heavy supplies for 18 miles. They built wheels from cottonwood trees to move the boats. Even with wheels, the trek took nearly two weeks. Rattlesnakes, bears, and even a hailstorm slowed their steps.

As they approached the Rocky Mountains, Sacagawea excitedly pointed out Shoshone lands. Eager to make contact with the tribe, Lewis and a small party made their way overland. Lewis soon found the Shoshone, whose chief recognized Sacagawea as his sister. The chief traded horses to Lewis and Clark, and the Shoshone helped them cross the Rocky Mountains.

The explorers then journeyed to the mighty Columbia River, which leads to the Pacific Ocean. In November 1805, Clark wrote in his journal, "Ocian in view! O! The joy." They soon arrived at the Pacific Coast. There, they spent a rain-soaked winter before returning to St. Louis the following year.

The Lewis and Clark expedition brought back a wealth of scientific and geographic information. Though they learned that an all-water route across the continent did not exist, Americans received an exciting report of what lay to the west.

*Reading*History
**D. Finding Main Ideas** Why was the Lewis and Clark expedition valuable?

## Pike's Expedition

Lewis and Clark explored the northern part of the Louisiana Purchase. In 1806, an expedition led by **Zebulon Pike** left St. Louis on a southerly route. (Refer to the map on page 320.) Pike's mission was to find the sources of the Arkansas and Red rivers. The Red River formed a boundary between Spanish territory and Louisiana.

Pike's party of two dozen men headed westward across the Great Plains. When they reached the Arkansas River, they followed it toward the Rocky Mountains. From 150 miles away, Pike spied the Rocky Mountain peak that would later bear his name—Pikes Peak. However, he failed in his attempt to climb it. Then they turned south, hoping that they would eventually run into the Red River. Instead, they ran into the

**Background**
The previous year, Pike had led a 5,000-mile expedition to search for the source of the Mississippi River.

▶ 1. **Accurate maps**
Lewis and Clark and Pike produced the first good maps of the Louisiana Territory. Later travelers would use these maps to make their way west.

▶ 2. **Growth of fur trade**
Exploration boosted interest in the fur trade. Hunters and trappers would add to the knowledge of the West.

▶ 3. **Mistaken view of Great Plains**
Pike inaccurately described the treeless Great Plains as a desert. This led many Americans to believe that the Plains were useless for farming.

**SKILLBUILDER Interpreting Charts**
*Why might Pike's description of the Great Plains have led to the idea that Native Americans east of the Mississippi should be moved there?*

**Compass used by Lewis and Clark**

**Vocabulary**
**Rio Grande:** Spanish for *big river*

Rio Grande, which was in Spanish territory. There, they were arrested by Spanish troops.

The explorers returned to the United States after being released by Spanish officials in 1807. Though Pike and his men never explored the Red River, they did bring back valuable descriptions of the Great Plains and the Rio Grande River Valley.

## The Effects of Exploration

The first American explorers of the West brought back tales of adventure as well as scientific and geographical information. As the chart above shows, this information would have long-lasting effects.

Early in Jefferson's presidency, events at home occupied much of the new president's time. In the next section, you will learn about foreign affairs during the same time period.

---

**Section 2 Assessment**

### 1. Terms & Names

**Explain the significance of:**
- Louisiana Purchase
- Meriwether Lewis
- William Clark
- Lewis and Clark expedition
- Sacagawea
- Zebulon Pike

### 2. Using Graphics

Use a chart like the one below to record the factors that might have led Napoleon to sell the Louisiana Territory. (HI2)

Causes

Effect

Napoleon sells Louisiana Territory

### 3. Main Ideas

**a.** What groups might dispute European land claims in the West? (HI1)

**b.** Why was New Orleans important to Americans? (HI1)

**c.** How did Sacagawea help Lewis and Clark? (HI1)

### 4. Critical Thinking

**Recognizing Effects** What were some of the effects of the explorations of the West in the 1800s? (HI2)

**THINK ABOUT**
- how other people might use the information brought back by the explorers
- the economic effects of the expedition

**ACTIVITY OPTIONS**

**WORLD HISTORY**
**GEOGRAPHY**

Read more about New Orleans. Make an illustrated **time line** of the French, Spanish, and U.S. ownership of the city or create a **map** of its port. (CST2)

# Native Americans on the Explorers' Route

When Thomas Jefferson bought the Louisiana Territory, Native Americans had already been living in that area for thousands of years. Before Lewis and Clark began their trip, Jefferson instructed them to deal with Native Americans in a peaceful manner and to make it clear that the United States wished to be "friendly and useful to them." On their journey, Lewis and Clark met almost 50 different tribes.

**① Oto**

In 1804, Lewis and Clark met the Oto, a buffalo-hunting people. This was the first formal meeting of U.S. representatives with western Native Americans. Lewis told the Oto that they were "children" of a new great "father"—President Thomas Jefferson.

**Sacagawea**

In 1805, the explorers arrived in Shoshone territory near the Rocky Mountains. A Shoshone chief, Cameahwait, confirmed that there was no all-water route to the Pacific. Later, when Cameahwait recognized Sacagawea as his sister, he agreed to sell the explorers the horses they needed to cross the mountains.

> **CALIFORNIA STANDARDS**
>
> **8.4.1** Describe the country's physical landscapes, political divisions, and territorial expansion during the terms of the first four presidents.
>
> **8.8.2** Describe the purpose, challenges, and economic incentives associated with westward expansion, including the concept of Manifest Destiny (e.g., the Lewis and Clark expedition, accounts of the removal of Indians, the Cherokees' "Trail of Tears," settlement of the Great Plains) and the territorial acquisitions that spanned numerous decades.

## ARTIFACT FILE

**Buffalo Robe** Pictured to the right is a section of a Mandan buffalo robe. On it, a Mandan painted a battle scene between the Mandan and the Sioux.

Map labels:

50°N

Chinook
Columbia R.
Palouse
Ft. Clatsop
Lewis and Clark 1806
Umatilla
Walla-Walla
Yakima
Flatheads
Shoshone
Bannock
ROCKY MOUNTAINS

Blackfoot
Nez Perce
Atsina
Lewis's return
Clark's return
Northern Cheyenne
Mandan ②
Lewis's return

Teton Sioux ③

Southern Cheyenne

Pawnee
Oto ①

Kansa

Lewis and Clark 1804–1805
Missouri R.
Mississippi R.

N

0        250 Miles
0        500 Kilometers

40°N

St. Louis

120°W
110°W

PACIFIC OCEAN

30°N

Gulf of Mexico

② **Mandan**
Neighboring tribes as well as exploring Europeans relied on the mainstay of Mandan culture—corn. The Mandan also crafted beautiful leatherwork and pottery. Lewis and Clark spent an entire winter with the Mandan.

③ **Teton Sioux**
Upon meeting the Teton Sioux, Lewis and Clark showed off an air gun. Known for their aggressiveness, the Teton already viewed the Americans as competitors for trade in this region. As a result, confrontation marked Lewis and Clark's visit.

## On-Line Field Trip

**The Peabody Museum** in Cambridge, Massachusetts, holds an important collection of Native American artifacts. This rain hat was worn by Chinook whalers of the Northwest. The Chinook made these water-repellent hats out of cedar bark and bear grass.

For more about Native American artifacts . . .

RESEARCH LINKS
CLASSZONE.COM

## CONNECT TO GEOGRAPHY

1. **Place** What fort was built where the Columbia River empties into the Pacific Ocean?
2. **Location** In what mountain range did the Shoshone tribe live?

G See Geography Handbook, page 4.

## CONNECT TO HISTORY

3. **Forming Opinions** What do you think the Native Americans that Lewis and Clark met thought about the explorers?

# 3

# Problems with Foreign Powers

| MAIN IDEA | WHY IT MATTERS NOW | TERMS & NAMES |
|---|---|---|
| Jefferson tried to avoid involvement in the problems of other nations. | British interference with the affairs of the United States led to the War of 1812. | impressment     Tecumseh<br>Embargo Act    War Hawk<br>of 1807 |

**CALIFORNIA STANDARDS**

**8.5.1** Understand the political and economic causes and consequences of the War of 1812 and know the major battles, leaders, and events that led to a final peace.

**8.5.2** Know the changing boundaries of the United States and describe the relationships the country had with its neighbors (current Mexico and Canada) and Europe, including the influence of the Monroe Doctrine, and how those relationships influenced westward expansion and the Mexican-American War.

**8.5.3** Outline the major treaties with American Indian nations during the administrations of the first four presidents and the varying outcomes of those treaties.

**HI2** Students understand and distinguish cause, effect, sequence, and correlation in historical events, including the long- and short-term causal relations.

## ONE AMERICAN'S STORY

In 1804, the United States was at war with Tripoli, a state on the North African coast. The war was the result of repeated attacks on American merchant ships by African pirates. U.S. Navy Lieutenant Stephen Decatur was sent to destroy the U.S. warship *Philadelphia*—which had been captured by Tripoli—so that it could not be used by the enemy.

Decatur set fire to the *Philadelphia* and then escaped under enemy fire with only one man wounded. Decatur later issued this rallying cry for all Americans.

### A VOICE FROM THE PAST

Our country! In her [relationships] with foreign nations may she always be in the right; but our country, right or wrong.
**Stephen Decatur,** 1816

The conflict with Tripoli showed how hard it was for the United States to stay out of foreign affairs while its citizens participated so heavily in overseas trade. In this section, you will learn how President Jefferson handled problems with other nations.

Stephen Decatur struggles in hand-to-hand combat with African pirates.

**Taking Notes**

Use your chart to take notes about problems with foreign powers.

| The Jefferson Era |
|---|
| Summaries |
| Main Idea:<br>Details: |
| Main Idea:<br>Details: |
| Main Idea:<br>Details: |
| Main Idea:<br>Details: |

## Jefferson's Foreign Policy

When Thomas Jefferson took office in 1801, he wanted to focus on domestic concerns. In his inaugural address, he noted that America was "kindly separated by nature and a wide ocean from the exterminating havoc [wars] of one quarter of the globe." He advised the United States to seek the friendship of all nations, but to enter into "entangling alliances with none."

However, the president's desire to keep the United States separated from other nations and their problems was doomed to fail. For one thing, American merchants were busily engaged in trade all over the world. For another, the Louisiana Purchase and the Lewis and Clark expedition were about to open the country to westward expansion. Expansion would bring Americans into closer contact with people from other nations who had already established settlements in the West.

Finally, the United States had little control over the actions of foreign nations—as North African interference with U.S. shipping had shown. Staying out of the ongoing conflict between France and England would be just as difficult.

*Reading*History
A. Analyzing Causes Why was it hard for the United States to avoid other nations' problems?

## Problems with France and England

For a long time, the United States managed not to get involved in the European wars that followed the French Revolution. At times, the nation even benefited from the conflict. Busy with affairs in Europe, France sold the Louisiana Territory to the United States. And American shippers eagerly took over the trade interrupted by the war.

By 1805, however, the British began to clamp down on U.S. shipping. They did not want Americans to provide their enemies with food and supplies. After the United States threatened to take action, the British decided to set up a partial blockade. This would only allow some American ships to bring provisions to Europe.

This partial blockade angered France, which enacted its own laws to control foreign shipping. These changes put American merchants in a difficult position. If they obeyed the British rules, their ships could be seized by the French. If they obeyed the French rules, their ships could be seized by the British.

Britain also interfered with U.S. trade by the **impressment,** or kidnapping, of American sailors to work on British ships. Between 1803 and 1812, the British impressed about 6,000 American sailors.

One of the most famous incidents occurred in 1807. The British ship *Leopard* attacked an American naval ship, the *Chesapeake,* off the coast of Virginia. Three Americans lost their lives in the battle. The attack aroused widespread anger. Had Congress been in session, America might have declared war. But Jefferson, who had been re-elected in 1804, decided against it. One critic, furious at the president's caution, called Jefferson a "dish of skim milk curdling at the head of our nation."

British officers seize an American sailor at gunpoint.

## Trade as a Weapon

Vocabulary
coercion: the practice of forcing someone to act in a certain way by use of pressure or threats

Instead of declaring war, Jefferson asked Congress to pass legislation that would stop all foreign trade. "Peaceable coercion," as the president described his policy, would prevent further bloodshed.

In December, Congress passed the **Embargo Act of 1807**. Now American ships were no longer allowed to sail to foreign ports. The act also closed American ports to British ships.

Jefferson's policy was more harmful to the United States than to the British and French. American farmers and merchants were especially hard hit. Southern and Western farmers, for example, lost important markets for their grain, cotton, and tobacco. Shippers lost income, and many violated the embargo by making false claims about where they were going.

The embargo became a major issue in the election of 1808. Jefferson's old friend James Madison won the election. By the time he took office, Congress had already repealed the embargo.

Madison's solution to the problem was a law that allowed merchants to trade with any country except France and Britain. Trade with these countries would start again when they agreed to respect U.S. ships. But this law proved no more effective than the embargo.

*Reading*History

**B. Recognizing Effects** What were the results of the Embargo Act?

## Tecumseh and Native American Unity

The Shawnee chief Tecumseh led Native American resistance to white rule in the Ohio River Valley.

British interference with American shipping and impressment of U.S. citizens made Americans furious. They also were angered by Britain's actions in the Northwest. Many settlers believed that the British were stirring up Native American resistance to frontier settlements.

Since the Battle of Fallen Timbers in 1794 (see page 299), Native Americans continued to lose their land. Thousands of white settlers had swarmed into Ohio and then into Indiana. Jefferson's Native American policy promoted what he called "civilization," getting Native Americans to farm the land, convert to Christianity, and live as white settlers lived. Instead of having Indian agents take land by force, Jefferson increased the number of trading posts on the frontier. Jefferson hoped Native Americans would buy goods on credit, fall into debt, and sell off lands to repay the debts.

**Tecumseh,** a Shawnee chief, vowed to stop the loss of Native American land. He believed that the reason Native Americans continued to lose their land was because they were separated into many different tribes. He concluded that Native Americans had to do what white Americans had done: unite. Events in 1809 proved him right.

That September, William Henry Harrison, governor of the Indiana Territory, signed the Treaty of Fort Wayne with chiefs of the Miami, Delaware, and Potawatomi tribes. They agreed to sell over three million acres of land. But Tecumseh declared the treaty meaningless.

*Reading*History

**C. Forming Opinions** Why did Tecumseh declare the Treaty of Fort Wayne meaningless?

> *A VOICE FROM THE PAST*
>
> [Whites] have taken upon themselves to say this [land] belongs to the Miamis, this to the Delawares and so on. But the Great Spirit intended [Native American land] to be the common property of all the tribes, [and it cannot] be sold without the consent of all.
>
> **Tecumseh,** quoted in *Tecumseh and the Quest for Indian Leadership*

After the Treaty of Fort Wayne, many Native Americans began to answer Tecumseh's call for unity. But his efforts ultimately failed. In

November 1811, while Tecumseh was away recruiting tribes for his alliance, the Shawnee were defeated by Harrison's forces at the Battle of Tippecanoe. It was a severe setback for Tecumseh's movement.

## War Hawks

After the battle of Tippecanoe, Tecumseh and his warriors found a warm welcome with the British in Canada. At that point, the Native Americans and the British became allies, which raised even higher the anti-British feelings in the West.

Leaders such as Congressman Henry Clay of Kentucky angrily demanded war against Britain. Westerners who called for war were known as **War Hawks.** They wanted British aid to Native Americans stopped, and they wanted the British out of Canada. Conquering Canada would open up a vast new empire for Americans.

Other Americans sought war because of the British violations of American rights at sea. Future president Andrew Jackson said hostilities were necessary to protect "our maritime citizens impressed on board British ships of war," and to "open a market for the productions of our soil."

Urged on by Jackson and the War Hawks, Congress declared war on Britain on June 18, 1812. In the next section, you will read about the second—and final—war between the United States and Great Britain.

**Vocabulary**
**hawk:** a person who favors the use of military force to carry out foreign policy

### Causes of the War of 1812

| Impressment of U.S. Citizens | Interference with American shipping | British support of Native-American resistance |

*WAR*

**SKILLBUILDER Interpreting Charts**
*Which cause of the War of 1812 was not related to activities on the sea?*

---

Section **3** Assessment

### 1. Terms & Names

**Explain the significance of:**
- impressment
- Embargo Act of 1807
- Tecumseh
- War Hawk

### 2. Using Graphics

Use a chart like the one below to record the effects of Jefferson's Embargo Act.

Causes

| Embargo Act |

Effects

Why didn't the act work? (HI2)

### 3. Main Ideas

**a.** How did the British and French interfere with American shipping? (HI1)

**b.** How did Jefferson respond to the interference? (HI1)

**c.** Why did the War Hawks favor war? (HI1)

### 4. Critical Thinking

**Analyzing Points of View**
Why did Tecumseh think it was important for Native Americans to unite? (REP5)

**THINK ABOUT**
- what he learned about white men
- what Native Americans would lose if they did not act together

---

**ACTIVITY OPTIONS**

**ART**

**SPEECH**

Do research on the Battle of Tippecanoe. Draw a **comic strip story** of the battle or hold a **press conference** to describe the battle's outcome. (HI1)

# The War of 1812

| MAIN IDEA | WHY IT MATTERS NOW | TERMS & NAMES |
|---|---|---|
| Angered by Britain's interference in the nation's affairs, the United States went to war. | The War of 1812 showed that the United States was willing and able to protect its national interests. | Oliver Hazard Perry<br>Battle of the Thames<br>Francis Scott Key<br>Treaty of Ghent |

**CALIFORNIA STANDARDS**

**8.5.1** Understand the political and economic causes and consequences of the War of 1812 and know the major battles, leaders, and events that led to a final peace.

**CST3** Students use a variety of maps and documents to identify physical and cultural features of neighborhoods, cities, states, and countries and to explain the historical migration of people, expansion and disintegration of empires, and the growth of economic systems.

**HI2** Students understand and distinguish cause, effect, sequence, and correlation in historical events, including the long- and short-term causal relations.

## ONE AMERICAN'S STORY

The war between the United States and Britain had begun in 1812. Two years later, British troops were marching toward Washington, D.C. Dolley Madison, the president's wife, stayed behind until the last minute to save important historical objects from the White House.

### A VOICE FROM THE PAST

I have had [a wagon] filled with . . . the most valuable portable articles belonging to the house. . . . I insist on waiting until the large picture of General Washington is secured.

**Dolley Madison,** from a letter sent to her sister

When the British troops arrived in the city, they set fire to many public buildings, including the White House and the Capitol. You will learn about other events of the War of 1812 in this section.

Before British troops set fire to the president's mansion, Dolley Madison saved priceless historical objects.

**Taking Notes**

Use your chart to take notes about the War of 1812.

| The Jefferson Era | | |
|---|---|---|
| Summaries | | |
| Main Idea: .<br>Details: | | |
| Main Idea:<br>Details: | | |
| Main Idea:<br>Details: | | |
| Main Idea:<br>Details: | | |

## The War Begins

Britain did not really want a war with the United States because it was already involved in another war with France. To try to avoid war, the British announced that they would no longer interfere with American shipping. But the slow mails of the day prevented this news from reaching the United States until weeks after June 18th, when Congress approved Madison's request for a declaration of war.

The War of 1812 had two main phases. From 1812 to 1814, Britain concentrated on its war against France. It devoted little energy to the conflict in North America, although it did send ships to blockade the American coast. The second phase of the war began after the British defeated France in April 1814. With their European war nearly at an end, the British could turn their complete attention to the United States.

The United States military was weak when the war was declared. Democratic-Republicans had reduced the size of the armed forces. When the war began, the Navy had only about 16 ships. The army had fewer than 7,000 men. These men were poorly trained and equipped, and were often led by inexperienced officers. A young Virginia army officer complained that the older officers were victims of "sloth, ignorance, or habits of [excessive] drinking."

## The First Phase of the War

In spite of its small size, the United States Navy rose to the challenge. Its warships were the fastest afloat. American naval officers had gained valuable experience fighting pirates in the Mediterranean Sea. Early in the war, before the British blockaded the coast, ships such as the *Constitution* and the *United States* won stirring victories. These victories on the high seas boosted American confidence.

The most important U.S. naval victory took place on Lake Erie. In the winter of 1812-1813, the Americans had begun to build a fleet on the shores of Lake Erie. **Oliver Hazard Perry,** an experienced officer, took charge of this infant fleet. In September 1813, the small British force on the lake set out to attack the American ships. Commodore Perry, who had predicted that this would be "the most important day of my life," sailed out to meet the enemy. Perry's ship, the *Lawrence*, flew a banner declaring, "Don't give up the ship."

**The War of 1812**

0 — 250 Miles
0 — 500 Kilometers

**BATTLES OF THE WAR**

1. **Atlantic Ocean.** British navy blockades American coast, 1813

2. **Lake Erie.** Perry's fleet defeats a British fleet, 1813

3. **Thames River.** Harrison defeats British in Canada, killing Tecumseh, 1813

4. **Washington, D.C.** British burn the capital but later fail to capture nearby Baltimore, 1814

5. **Lake Champlain.** American ships defeat British, who retreat to Canada, 1814

6. **New Orleans.** Jackson's army defeats British in Battle of New Orleans, 1815

← American forces
← British forces
✳ American victory
✳ British victory
🏰 Fort

**GEOGRAPHY SKILLBUILDER**
**Interpreting Maps**

1. **Location** *Where was Fort McHenry located?*
2. **Movement** *Which battle required American troops to march into Canada?*

For two hours, the British and Americans exchanged cannon shots. Perry's ship was demolished and the guns put out of action. He grabbed his ship's banner and leaped into a rowboat. Under British fire, he and four companions rowed to another ship. In command of the second ship, Perry destroyed two of the enemy's ships and soon forced the British to surrender. After the battle, Perry sent a message to General Harrison: "We have met the enemy and they are ours."

> **"Don't give up the ship."**
> Banner on Perry's ship, the *Lawrence*

When General Harrison received Perry's note, he set out to attack the British. But when Harrison transported his army across Lake Erie to Detroit, he discovered that the British had retreated into Canada. Harrison pursued the British forces and defeated them at the **Battle of the Thames** in October. This victory put an end to the British threat to the Northwest—and also claimed the life of Tecumseh, who died in the battle fighting for the British.

*Reading* **History**
A. Drawing Conclusions
What was the overall result of the Battle of the Thames?

## The Second Phase of the War

After defeating Napoleon in April 1814, Britain turned its full attention to the United States. As you read in One American's Story, British forces burned the Capitol building and the president's mansion in August. The British then attacked Fort McHenry at Baltimore.

The commander of Fort McHenry had earlier requested a flag "so large that the British will have no difficulty in seeing it." Detained on a British ship, a Washington lawyer named **Francis Scott Key** watched the all-night battle. At dawn, Key discovered that the flag was still flying. He expressed his pride in what became the U.S. national anthem.

### America's HERITAGE

**THE STAR-SPANGLED BANNER**

The "Star-Spangled Banner," inspired by the flag that flew over Fort McHenry (see below), continues to move Americans. On hearing this national anthem, patriotic listeners stand, take off their hats, and put their hands over their hearts. These actions pay respect to the American flag and the song that celebrates it.

Francis Scott Key's song enjoyed widespread popularity for more than 100 years before an act of Congress made it the national anthem in 1931.

*A VOICE FROM THE PAST*

Oh say can you see by the dawn's early light
What so proudly we hail'd at the twilight's last gleaming,
Whose broad stripes and bright stars through the perilous fight
O'er the ramparts we watch'd were so gallantly streaming?
And the rockets' red glare, the bombs bursting in air,
Gave proof through the night that our flag was still there.
Oh, say does that star-spangled banner yet wave
O'er the land of the free and the home of the brave?

**Francis Scott Key,** *Star-Spangled Banner*

Meanwhile, in the north, the British sent a force from Canada across Lake Champlain. Its goal was to push south and cut off New England. The plan failed when the American fleet defeated the British in the Battle of Lake Champlain in September 1814.

In the south, the British moved against the strategic port of New Orleans. In December 1814, dozens of ships carrying 7,500 British troops approached Louisiana. To fight them, the Americans patched together an army under the command of General Andrew Jackson.

*Reading* **History**
B. Reading a Map
Locate the battles of the second phase of the war on the map on page 331. Note how far apart the sites were.

*Reading*History

**C. Making Inferences** Why did Jackson fight the British at New Orleans after a peace treaty was signed?

The British attacked Jackson's forces on January 8, 1815. Protected by earthworks, American riflemen mowed down the advancing redcoats. It was a great victory for Jackson. American casualties totaled 71, compared to Britain's 2,000. Though the Battle of New Orleans made Jackson a hero, it was unnecessary. Slow mails from Europe had delayed news of the **Treaty of Ghent,** which ended the War of 1812. It had been signed two weeks earlier, on December 24, 1814.

## The Legacy of the War

The treaty showed that the war had no clear winner. No territory changed hands, and trade disputes were left unresolved. Still, the war had important consequences. First, the heroic exploits of men such as Andrew Jackson and Oliver Perry increased American patriotism. Second, the war broke the strength of Native Americans, who had sided with the British. Finally, when war interrupted trade, the Americans were forced to make many of the goods they had previously imported. This encouraged the growth of U.S. manufactures.

The United States had also proved that it could defend itself against the mightiest military power of the era. For perhaps the first time, Americans believed that the young nation would survive and prosper. You will learn about the country's growing prosperity in Chapter 11.

**The Effects of the War**

**WAR**

| Increased American patriotism | Weakened Native American resistance | U.S. manufacturing grew |

**SKILLBUILDER Interpreting Charts**
*Which effect do you think resulted from the war's interruption of U.S. trade?*

---

**Section 4 Assessment**

### 1. Terms & Names

**Explain the significance of:**
- Oliver Hazard Perry
- Battle of the Thames
- Francis Scott Key
- Treaty of Ghent

### 2. Using Graphics

Use a chart like the one shown to record military events of the War of 1812.

| First Phase of War | Second Phase of War |
|---|---|
| 1. | 2. |

Why was the war divided into two phases? (CST1)

### 3. Main Ideas

**a.** What was the state of the U.S. military when the war began? (HI1)

**b.** What were the results of General Harrison's victory at the Battle of the Thames? (HI2)

**c.** Where did the British focus their attacks during the second phase of the war? (HI1)

### 4. Critical Thinking

**Recognizing Effects** What was the legacy of the War of 1812? (HI2)

**THINK ABOUT**
- Americans' feelings toward their country
- U.S. relations with Native Americans
- possible economic effects

**ACTIVITY OPTIONS**

**LANGUAGE ARTS**

**ART**

Research the U.S.S. *Constitution.* Write a **poem** to commemorate one of its victories or design a **model** to show its parts. (REP1)

# The Jefferson Era

(CST2)

## Jefferson Takes Office

Thomas Jefferson and his party, the Democratic-Republicans, win control of the government from the Federalists.

## The Louisiana Purchase and Exploration

After Jefferson purchases Louisiana from France, Lewis and Clark are sent to explore the new American territory.

## Problems with Foreign Powers

Other countries' interference makes it difficult for Jefferson to stay out of foreign affairs.

## The War of 1812

When Britain continues to interfere in American affairs, the two nations battle in the War of 1812.

---

## TERMS & NAMES

Briefly explain the significance of each of the following:

1. *Marbury* v. *Madison*
2. judicial review
3. Louisiana Purchase
4. Lewis and Clark expedition
5. impressment
6. Embargo Act of 1807
7. Tecumseh
8. War Hawk
9. Oliver Hazard Perry
10. Treaty of Ghent

## REVIEW QUESTIONS

**Jefferson Takes Office
(pages 313–317)**

1. What were the main parties in the election of 1800, and how did their views differ? (HI1)
2. How did Jefferson envision the future of America? (HI1)

**The Louisiana Purchase and Exploration (pages 318–325)**

3. What was the extent of U.S. territory after the Louisiana Purchase? (CST3)
4. What difficulties did the Lewis and Clark expedition face? (HI1)
5. What troubles did Zebulon Pike have on his 1806-1807 trip? (HI1)

**Problems with Foreign Powers (pages 326–329)**

6. Why did Jefferson have difficulty staying out of foreign affairs? (HI2)
7. How did Tecumseh intend to prevent the loss of Native American land? (HI1)
8. What were some of the causes of the War of 1812? (HI2)

**The War of 1812
(pages 330–333)**

9. Which battle ended the British threat to the U.S. Northwest? (HI2)
10. What event preceded the second phase of the war? (HI2)

---

## CRITICAL THINKING

### 1. USING YOUR NOTES: SUMMARIZING

Using your completed chart, answer the questions below. (HI1)

| The Jefferson Era |
|---|
| Summaries |
| **Main Idea:** Thomas Jefferson is elected president. **Details:** Jefferson replaces Federalist policies with his own but has problems with the judiciary. |
| **Main Idea:** **Details:** |
| **Main Idea:** **Details:** |
| **Main Idea:** **Details:** |

a. What were the major events of the Jefferson era?
b. Based on these events, how would you describe the characteristics of the era?

### 2. ANALYZING LEADERSHIP

How do you think Thomas Jefferson's behavior as president might have affected the way future presidents viewed the office? (CST1)

### 3. THEME: EXPANSION

How did the expansion of the United States affect its foreign policy? (HI2)

### 4. RECOGNIZING PROPAGANDA

Before elections, supporters of different candidates sometimes make outrageous claims. How was the election of 1800 an example of this? (REP4)

### 5. APPLYING CITIZENSHIP SKILLS

In what ways did Jefferson's behavior as president reflect his idea of good citizenship? (HI1)

### Interact *with* History

How did the dangers you predicted before you read the chapter compare to those experienced by people on expeditions west?

## STANDARDS-BASED ASSESSMENT

Use the graph and your knowledge of U.S. history to answer questions 1 and 2.

Additional Test Practice, pp. S1–S33.

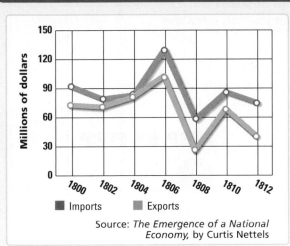

Foreign Trade, 1800–1812

■ Imports   ■ Exports

Source: *The Emergence of a National Economy,* by Curtis Nettels

**1.** What was the value of imports in 1812? (8.4.3)

   **A.** about 30 million dollars

   **B.** about 40 million dollars

   **C.** about 60 million dollars

   **D.** about 70 million dollars

**2.** Between which years did the value of U.S. trade decrease dramatically? (8.4.3)

   **A.** 1800–1802

   **B.** 1804–1806

   **C.** 1806–1808

   **D.** 1810–1812

This quotation from Thomas Jefferson is about political parties. Use the quotation and your knowledge of U.S. history to answer question 3.

### PRIMARY SOURCE

Let us, then, fellow-citizens, unite with one heart and one mind. . . . Every difference of opinion is a difference of principle. . . . We are all Republicans, we are all Federalists.

**Thomas Jefferson,** First Inaugural Address

**3.** Which of the following statements best summarizes Jefferson's point of view? (8.4.2)

   **A.** Political parties are divisive and should be dissolved.

   **B.** A new party, the Republican-Federalist party, should be formed.

   **C.** Political parties should cooperate on issues of government.

   **D.** The Republican party should be dissolved.

TEST PRACTICE
CLASSZONE.COM

## ALTERNATIVE ASSESSMENT

### 1. ✍ WRITING ABOUT HISTORY

Suppose you are John Adams and the year is 1800. Thomas Jefferson is ending many of the Federalist programs that you initiated while president. Write a **letter** to a friend that describes your distress. (REP5)

- Use library resources to find the programs that Jefferson eliminated and write about them.

- Find quotations that convey Adams's emotions.

### 2. COOPERATIVE LEARNING

Work with two other students to develop a plan to end British interference with U.S. shipping. Have one student represent shippers, another represent farmers, and the third represent citizens who are demanding war. Discuss the interests of these groups and possible compromises. Then write a policy statement. (HI1)

## INTEGRATED TECHNOLOGY

### CREATING A MULTIMEDIA PRESENTATION

Use the Internet, books, and other reference materials to create a multimedia presentation about one of the major battles of the War of 1812. (HI1)

- Using the Internet and resources in the library, find written descriptions of the battle, paintings of the battle, pictures of weaponry, battle statistics, and music from the time period.

- Present your findings to the class in a multimedia presentation. Consider adding sound effects to enhance the presentation.

**For more about the War of 1812 . . .**

INTERNET ACTIVITY
CLASSZONE.COM

# Making Explorers' Field Notes

On their expedition in the early 1800s, Lewis and Clark filled their journals with field notes—detailed observations and scientific illustrations of the land, plants, and wildlife they saw. Lewis made drawings of plants and animals. Clark drew detailed maps. For many years, their journals were the main source of information about the West.

**ACTIVITY** Create a journal of field notes that includes illustrations of plants, animals, and terrain found in your neighborhood. Then write a comparison article between your field notes and those of Lewis and Clark.

**CALIFORNIA STANDARDS**

**HI3** Students explain the sources of historical continuity and how the combination of ideas and events explains the emergence of new patterns.

**Writing 2.6** Write technical documents.

## TOOLBOX

Each group will need:

| | |
|---|---|
| drawing paper | ruler |
| poster board for covers | string |
| pencil and pen | hole punch and hole reinforcers |
| scissors | |

## STEP BY STEP

**1** **Form groups.** Each group should consist of 3 to 4 students. The members of your group will do the following tasks:

- design and create a handmade journal
- take a walk in your neighborhood and record observations as field notes
- compare the field notes you have created with those of Lewis and Clark

**2** **Make your journal.** Your group will need a journal to make field notes on the nature walk. Each page of the journal should be six inches wide and roughly eight inches long, approximately the size of the one used by Lewis and Clark. Cut 10–15 sheets of that size out of the drawing paper. Create a front and back cover for the journal using the poster board.

The scientific and artistic skills of Lewis and Clark made their journals both accurate and beautiful.

**3** **Put your journal together.** Punch three holes in the left side of the pages, including the covers. Place hole reinforcers around the holes to ensure that the pages won't tear. Bind the pages and the covers together with string.

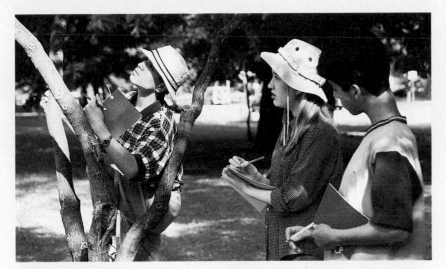

**4** **Explore your neighborhood.** Take a walk in your neighborhood, in the area around your school, or in a nearby woods. You might want to divide the tasks of observing, drawing, describing, and mapping among the members of the group.

**5** **Model your field notes on those of Lewis and Clark.** In their journals, Lewis and Clark included drawings of animals and plants, as well as detailed observations about them. Remember to draw the plants, insects, and animals as if you have never seen them before.

**6** **Make a map of your route.** In addition to the drawings, create a map of your walk. Include any interesting landmarks as well as a detailed description of the terrain. Remember to sketch the route as if it's unexplored territory.

## WRITE AND SPEAK

Write and present a paper that compares and contrasts Lewis and Clark's journal with the one your group has completed. Also, explain how your journal might help someone who has just moved to your school or neighborhood.

## HELP DESK

For related information, see pages 320–325 in Chapter 10.

### Researching Your Project

• You can find copies of Lewis and Clark's journals in many libraries.

• *Undaunted Courage* by Stephen Ambrose gives a fascinating account of the expedition.

For more about Lewis and Clark . . .

**RESEARCH LINKS**
CLASSZONE.COM

### Did You Know?

• The Corps of Discovery sent Jefferson six live specimens of animals, including a prairie dog.

• At one point, the men on the expedition consumed nine pounds of buffalo meat a day.

• Swarms of mosquitoes plagued the expedition. The explorers often found it impossible to eat without inhaling some of the pesky insects.

• Clark estimated that the expedition traveled 4,162 miles. His guess was only 40 miles off the actual distance.

### REFLECT & ASSESS

• What process did your group use to observe, draw, and describe your route?

• How did you decide what information to include in your journal?

• How important are the illustrations to understanding the area in which your group took its walk?

# National and Regional Growth 1800–1844

Robert Fulton made the steamboat a commercial success.

The steam locomotive helped build U.S. industry.

The telegraph could quickly send messeges over great distances.

This Currier and Ives print, *Progress of the Century,* shows some inventions of the 1800s.

**1807**
Robert Fulton launches a steamboat on the Hudson River.

**1808**
Congress bans the African slave trade.

**1812**
War of 1812 disrupts U.S. shipping.

**1816**
James Monroe is elected President.

**1820**
Missouri Compromise balances number of slave and free states.

USA
World · 1800

**1804**
Haiti wins independence from France.

**1815**
Napoleon defeated at Waterloo.

**1821**
Peru and Mexico gain independence from Spain.

The rotary printing press was made for high volume printing.

From 1790 to 1840, you have seen an explosion of new inventions. These include the cotton gin, the steamboat, the steel plow, and the telegraph. You have also seen neighbors leave their farms to run machines in new factories. You sense that the country is changing.

# How will new inventions change your country?

## What Do You Think?

- What would it mean to be able to grow more grain and cotton?
- What would it mean to communicate and travel more quickly?
- How might it feel to do factory work instead of farm work?

### RESEARCH LINKS
**CLASSZONE.COM**

Visit the Chapter 11 links for more information about the growing nation.

**1823**
Monroe Doctrine issued.

**1825**
Erie Canal completed.

**1825**
First public railroad operates in England.

**1831**
Nat Turner leads slave rebellion in Virginia.

**1833**
Slavery is abolished in British Empire.

**1838**
Frederick Douglass flees to New York City to escape slavery.

**1839**
Louis Daguerre is recognized for his photographic process.

**1844**
Telegraph line connects Washington, D.C., and Baltimore.

1844

# Reading Strategy: Analyzing Causes and Effects

## What Do You Know?

What connects you to someone who lives in the same region? When have you felt a bond with someone from a different region?

**Think About**

- the activities of people in different regions
- the things that unite people as a nation
- your responses to the Interact with History about how inventions change your country (see page 339)

## What Do You Want to Know?

 What would you ask people from different regions—a factory worker, wheat farmer, plantation owner, or field slave—about their lives in the 1800s? Write these questions in your notebook. Read to see if they are answered in Chapter 11.

**CALIFORNIA STANDARDS**

**Reading 2.0** Students read and understand grade-level-appropriate material. They describe and connect the essential ideas, arguments, and perspectives of the text by using their knowledge of text structure, organization, and purpose.

Midwestern farms

Northeastern factories

Southern cotton plantations

## Analyzing Causes and Effects

To help you understand the development of regional growth, sectional tensions, and national unity in Chapter 11, pay attention to causes and effects. Growth, tensions, and unity each had more than one cause. As you read, identify different causes and note them on the chart below. Often a topic sentence at the beginning of a paragraph will state a cause and effect. Be alert for such clue words as "led to," "as a result," and "changed."

**S** See Skillbuilder Handbook, page R10.

### Taking Notes

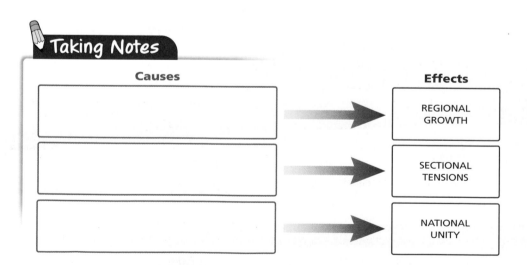

| Causes | | Effects |
|---|---|---|
| | → | REGIONAL GROWTH |
| | → | SECTIONAL TENSIONS |
| | → | NATIONAL UNITY |

# Early Industry and Inventions

| MAIN IDEA | WHY IT MATTERS NOW | TERMS & NAMES |
|---|---|---|
| New machines and factories changed the way people lived and worked in the late 1700s and early 1800s. | The industrial development that began more than 200 years ago continues today. | Samuel Slater<br>Industrial Revolution<br>factory system<br>Lowell mills<br>interchangeable parts<br>Robert Fulton<br>Samuel F. B. Morse |

## ONE AMERICAN'S STORY

In 1789, the Englishman **Samuel Slater** sailed to the United States under a false name. It was illegal for textile workers like him to leave the country. Britain wanted no other nation to copy its new machines for making thread and cloth. But Slater was going to bring the secret to America.

With the backing of investor Moses Brown, Slater built the first successful water-powered textile mill in America. You will learn in Section 1 how the development of industries changed the ways Americans lived and worked.

Samuel Slater's mill was located in Pawtucket, Rhode Island.

**CALIFORNIA STANDARDS**

**8.5.1** Understand the political and economic causes and consequences of the War of 1812 and know the major battles, leaders, and events that led to a final peace.

**8.6.1** Discuss the influence of industrialization and technological developments on the region, including human modification of the landscape and how physical geography shaped human actions (e.g., growth of cities, deforestation, farming, mineral extraction).

**8.10.2** Trace the boundaries constituting the North and the South, the geographical differences between the two regions, and the differences between agrarians and industrialists.

**8.12.1** Trace patterns of agricultural and industrial development as they relate to climate, use of natural resources, markets, and trade and locate such development on a map.

**HI2** Students understand and distinguish cause, effect, sequence, and correlation in historical events, including the long- and short-term causal relations.

### Taking Notes

Use your chart to take notes about early industry and inventions.

Causes

## Free Enterprise and Factories

The War of 1812 brought great economic changes to the United States. It sowed the seeds for an Industrial Revolution like the one begun in Britain during the late 18th century. During the **Industrial Revolution,** factory machines replaced hand tools, and large-scale manufacturing replaced farming as the main form of work. For example, before the Industrial Revolution, women spun thread and wove cloth at home in cottage industries. The invention of such machines as the spinning jenny and the power loom made it possible for unskilled workers to produce cloth. These workers, who were often children, could produce more cloth, more quickly.

The **factory system** brought many workers and machines together under one roof. Most factories were built near a source of water to power the machines. People left their farms and crowded into cities where the factories were. They worked for wages, on a set schedule. Their way of life changed, and not always for the better.

Many Americans did not want the United States to industrialize. But the War of 1812 led the country in that direction. Because the British naval blockade kept imported goods from reaching U.S. shores, Americans had to start manufacturing their own goods. The blockade also stopped investors from spending money on shipping and trade. Instead, they invested in new American industries. Taking advantage of the country's free enterprise system, American businessmen built their own factories, starting in New England. These businessmen and their region grew wealthier.

**Vocabulary**
**industrialize:** to develop factories

*Reading***History**
**A. Recognizing Effects** How did the War of 1812 cause economic changes in America?

## Factories Come to New England

New England was a good place to set up factories for several reasons. Factories needed water power, and New England had many fast-moving rivers. For transportation, it also had ships and access to the ocean. In addition, New England had a willing labor force. The area's first factory workers were families who were tired of scraping a living from their stony fields.

Samuel Slater built his first spinning mill in Pawtucket, Rhode Island, in 1790. He hired eight children between the ages of 7 and 12, paying them a low wage. Later, he built a larger mill and employed whole families. As Slater influenced others to start mills, his family system of employment spread through Rhode Island, Connecticut, and southern Massachusetts.

## The Lowell Mills Hire Women

**Lowell girls published a literary magazine.**

In 1813, the American textile industry leaped forward when Francis Cabot Lowell built a factory in Waltham, in eastern Massachusetts. This factory not only spun raw cotton into yarn, but wove it into cloth on power looms. Lowell had seen power looms in English mills and had figured out how to build them. Like Samuel Slater, he had brought secrets to America.

The Waltham factory was so successful that Lowell and his partners built a new factory town, Lowell, near the Merrimack and Concord rivers. The **Lowell mills,** textile mills in the village, employed farm girls who lived in company-owned boardinghouses. "Lowell girls" worked 12½-hour days in deafening noise.

**Background** Founded in 1826, the town was named for Lowell, who died in 1817.

### A VOICE FROM THE PAST

At first the hours seemed very long . . . and when I went out at night the sound of the mill was in my ears . . . . You know that people learn to sleep with the thunder of Niagara [falls] in their ears, and a cotton mill is no worse, though you wonder that we do not have to hold our breath in such a noise.

**"Letters from Susan,"** quoted in the *Lowell Offering*

**New England Textile Mill**

1. Moving water turns a wheel, which powers the machines through a system of gears and belts.

2. Carding and drawing machines straighten raw cotton fibers and twist them loosely.

3. Spinning machines spin the fibers into yarn, or thread.

4. Power looms weave yarn into cloth.

In 1835, Lowell had 22 mills. In 1855, it had 52 mills employing more than 13,000 workers and producing 2.25 million yards of cotton cloth a week.

Young women came to Lowell in spite of the noise. In the early years, wages were high—between two and four dollars a week. Older women supervised the girls, making them follow strict rules and attend church. Girls read books, went to lectures, and even published a literary magazine—the *Lowell Offering*. Usually they worked for only a few years, until they married. By the 1830s, however, falling profits meant that wages dropped and working conditions worsened for the Lowell girls.

The Lowell mills and other early factories ran on water power. Factories built after the 1830s were run by more powerful steam engines. Because steam engines used coal and wood, not fast-moving water, factories could be built away from rivers and beyond New England.

*Reading***History**
**B. Contrasting** How did the Lowell mills differ from Slater's mill?

## A New Way to Manufacture

New manufacturing methods changed the style of work in other industries besides the textile industry. In 1797, the U.S. government hired the inventor Eli Whitney to make 10,000 muskets for the army. He was to have the guns ready in two years. Before this time, guns were made one at a time by gunsmiths, from start to finish. Each gun differed slightly. If a part broke, a new part had to be created to match the broken one.

Whitney sought a better way to make guns. In 1801, he went to Washington with a box containing piles of musket parts. He took a part from each pile and assembled a musket in seconds. He had just demonstrated the use of **interchangeable parts**, parts that are exactly alike.

Robert Fulton invented the *Clermont*, a steamboat.

Machines that produced exactly matching parts soon became standard in industries. Interchangeable parts speeded up production, made repairs easy, and allowed the use of lower-paid, less-skilled workers. But the new system also required a new style of management, with inspectors to make sure each piece was uniform. Workers who were used to more independence disliked such close supervision.

*Reading*History

C. Recognizing Effects What were the effects of using interchangeable parts?

## Moving People, Goods, and Messages

New inventions increased factory production. They also improved transportation and communication. Steamboats carried people and goods farther and faster and led to the growth of cities like New Orleans and St. Louis. **Robert Fulton** invented a steamboat that could move against the current or a strong wind. He launched the *Clermont* on the Hudson River in 1807. Its steam engine turned two side paddle wheels, which pulled the boat through the water.

The *Clermont* was dubbed "Fulton's Folly" and described as "looking precisely like a backwoods saw-mill mounted on a scow [boat] and set on fire." But it made the 300-mile trip from New York to Albany and back in a record 62 hours. Even Fulton had not expected to travel so quickly.

### A VOICE FROM THE PAST

I overtook many sloops and schooners, beating to the windward, and parted with them as if they had been at anchor. The power of propelling boats by steam is now fully proved.

**Robert Fulton,** quoted in *Robert Fulton and the "Clermont"*

In 1811, the first steamship traveled down the Mississippi and Ohio rivers. But its engine was not powerful enough to return upriver, against the current. Henry Miller Shreve, a trader on the Mississippi, designed a more powerful engine. He installed it on a double-decker boat with a paddle wheel in the back. In 1816, he sailed this boat up the Mississippi and launched a new era of trade and transportation on the river.

In 1837, **Samuel F. B. Morse** first demonstrated his telegraph. This machine sent long and short pulses of electricity along a wire. These pulses could be translated into letters of a message. With the telegraph, it took only seconds to communicate with someone in another city. In 1844, the first long-distance telegraph line carried news from Baltimore to Washington, D.C., about who had been nominated for president. Telegraph lines spanned the country by 1861, bringing people closer as a nation. Both the telegraph and the steamboat brought more national unity.

*Reading*History
D. Recognizing Effects What made the steamboat and telegraph such important inventions?

# Technology Improves Farming

Other new inventions increased farm production. In 1836, the blacksmith John Deere invented a lightweight plow with a steel cutting edge. Older cast-iron plows were designed for the light, sandy soil of New England. But rich, heavy Midwestern soil clung to the bottom of these plows and slowed farmers down. Deere's new plow made preparing ground much less work. As a result, more farmers began to move to the Midwest.

The mechanical reaper and the threshing machine were other inventions that improved agriculture. Cyrus McCormick's reaper, patented in 1834, cut ripe grain. The threshing machine separated kernels of wheat from husks.

**Vocabulary
patented:** protected by a patent, which gives an inventor the sole right to make, use, or sell an invention

John Deere invented the steel plow.

New technologies linked regions and contributed to national unity. With new farm equipment, Midwestern farmers grew food to feed Northeastern factory workers. In turn, Midwestern farmers became a market for Northeastern manufactured goods. The growth of Northeastern textile mills increased demand for Southern cotton. This led to the expansion of slavery in the South, as you will learn in Section 2.

## Section 1 Assessment

### 1. Terms & Names

**Explain the significance of:**
- Samuel Slater
- Industrial Revolution
- factory system
- Lowell mills
- interchangeable parts
- Robert Fulton
- Samuel F. B. Morse

### 2. Using Graphics

On a chart like the one below, note new inventions, their dates, and their effects on the United States.

| Invention | Date | Effects |
|-----------|------|---------|
|           |      |         |
|           |      |         |
|           |      |         |

Which inventions did most to link the nation? Explain. (HI3)

### 3. Main Ideas

**a.** Why was New England a good place to build early factories? (HI1)

**b.** What were working conditions like in Lowell mills? (HI1)

**c.** How were different U.S. regions linked economically? (HI1)

### 4. Critical Thinking

**Evaluating** How would you judge Samuel Slater and Francis Lowell, who brought secrets to the United States illegally? (HI1)

**THINK ABOUT**
- what they gained
- how they affected the United States and England
- what you believe about keeping technology secret

**ACTIVITY OPTIONS**

**SCIENCE**

**SPEECH**

Explain how an invention from this chapter works, either in an **oral report** or a **labeled diagram**. (REP1)

# Run a Mill Town

You are the owner of a new water-powered textile mill that will soon open in New England. Mills have been around for more than 20 years, and you have studied their operations closely. Even so, you face many problems as you start your business. Machinery failures, labor problems, demanding investors—all will be part of your life from now on.

**COOPERATIVE LEARNING** On this page are two challenges you face as the owner of a textile mill. Working with a small group, decide how to deal with each challenge. Choose an option, assign a task to each group member, and do the activity. You will find useful information in the Data File. Be prepared to present your solutions to the class.

**CALIFORNIA STANDARDS**

**8.6.1** Discuss the influence of industrialization and technological developments on the region, including human modification of the landscape and how physical geography shaped human actions (e.g., growth of cities, deforestation, farming, mineral extraction).

**HI6** Students interpret basic indicators of economic performance and conduct cost-benefit analyses of economic and political issues.

**Reading 2.6** Use information from a variety of consumer, workplace, and public documents to explain a situation or decision and to solve a problem.

## HEALTH CHALLENGE

### *"Anna Tripp lost three fingers today."*

A neighboring mill owner has just left after sharing some bad news. Today 12-year-old Anna Tripp lost three fingers in one of his machines. Last week, one of his workers was hit and nearly killed by the flying end of a broken belt. Several girls went home because they had trouble breathing. They blamed the closed, damp machine rooms with lint-filled air. How will you reduce the number of costly health problems like these in your mill? Present your plan using one of these options:

• Write a speech to workers outlining the company's safety measures.

• Design a sign for each floor of the mill stating the company's safety rules.

## MATH CHALLENGE

# "So many applicants for employment"

To make a profit, you must operate at top capacity for the lowest cost. Your mill generates 2 mill power. This dictates how many spinners you can hire. You need about two-and-a-half times that many weavers. What will be your weekly payroll for spinners and weavers? How many men will you hire? Women? Look at the Data File for help. Present your hiring plan for spinners and weavers using one of these options:

- Write a report telling investors whom you plan to hire.
- Design want-ad posters aimed at the workers you are looking for.

## ACTIVITY WRAP-UP

**Present to the Class** Meet as a group to review your responses to running a mill town. Pick the most creative solution for each challenge and present these solutions to the class.

## DATA FILE

### Water Power

**Potential energy:** energy released when water falls from a height.

**Kinetic energy:** energy provided by fast-moving water.

**1 mill power:** power produced by 25 cubic feet of water per second dropping over a 30-foot fall; about 60 horsepower.

**1 mill power:** runs 3,584 spindles.

### Waterwheels

Overshot

Undershot

Mid-wheel

### Wage Rates

**Men:** $.85–$2.09 per day, depending on skill

**Women:** $.52–$.78 per day, depending on skill

### Positions

**Pickers:** clean raw cotton.

**Carders:** feed cotton into machine that makes a thick strand of fibers.

**Spinners:** operate a machine that twists thick fibers into yarn and winds it on bobbins fastened to moving spindles. One worker operates 128 spindles.

**Dressers:** treat finished yarn with a starch paste.

**Drawing-in hands:** attach dressed yarn to the mechanical loom for weavers.

**Weavers:** weave dressed yarn into finished cloth. One worker operates two looms.

### Work Hours

12 hours per day, 6 days per week, 309 days per year with holidays on Fast Day (spring), the Fourth of July, and Thanksgiving

For more about textile mills . . .

RESEARCH LINKS
CLASSZONE.COM

# Plantations and Slavery Spread

| **MAIN IDEA** | **WHY IT MATTERS NOW** | **TERMS & NAMES** |
|---|---|---|
| The invention of the cotton gin and the demand for cotton caused slavery to spread in the South. | The spread of slavery created lasting racial and sectional tensions. | Eli Whitney    spirituals<br>cotton gin    Nat Turner |

**CALIFORNIA STANDARDS**

**8.6.1** Discuss the influence of industrialization and technological developments on the region, including human modification of the landscape and how physical geography shaped human actions (e.g., growth of cities, deforestation, farming, mineral extraction).

**8.7.1** Describe the development of the agrarian economy in the South, identify the locations of the cotton-producing states, and discuss the significance of cotton and the cotton gin.

**8.7.2** Trace the origins and development of slavery; its effects on black Americans and on the region's political, social, religious, economic, and cultural development; and identify the strategies that were tried to both overturn and preserve it (e.g., through the writings and historical documents on Nat Turner, Denmark Vesey).

**8.9.6** Describe the lives of free blacks and the laws that limited their freedom and economic opportunities.

**8.10.2** Trace the boundaries constituting the North and the South, the geographical differences between the two regions, and the differences between agrarians and industrialists.

**Taking Notes**

Use your chart to take notes about plantations and the spread of slavery.

**Causes**

## ONE AMERICAN'S STORY

**Catherine Beale was born into slavery in 1838. In 1929, she recalled her childhood on a plantation.**

*A VOICE FROM THE PAST*

We had to work in the field in the day and at night we had to pick out the seed before we went to bed. And we had to clean the wool, we had to pick the burrs and sticks out so it would be clean and could be carded and spun and wove.

**Catherine Beale,** quoted in *Slave Testimony*

Enslaved workers labor in the cotton fields.

Catherine had to clean cotton by hand because the plantation didn't have a cotton gin. This machine made it easier for enslaved workers to clean cotton. But it also made cotton growing and slave owning more profitable. In this section, you will learn how slavery expanded in the South and how it affected the lives of people living under it.

## The Cotton Boom

**Eli Whitney** invented a machine for cleaning cotton in 1793, after visiting the Georgia plantation of Catherine Greene, the widow of a Revolutionary War general. Mrs. Greene was struggling to make her plantation profitable. English textile mills had created a huge demand for cotton, but the short-fibered cotton that grew in most parts of the South was hard to clean by hand. A worker could clean just one pound of this cotton in a day.

Whitney's **cotton gin** (short for "engine") made the cotton-cleaning process far more efficient. With the new machine, one worker could now clean as much as 50 pounds of cotton a day. The cotton gin helped set the South on a different course of development from the North. It made

## The Cotton Gin

1. A hand crank turns a series of rollers.

2. A roller with wire teeth pulls the cotton through slots too narrow for the seeds.

3. The cotton seeds fall into a hopper.

4. A roller with brushes removes the cleaned cotton from the first roller.

5. The cleaned cotton leaves the gin.

short-fibered cotton a commercial product and changed Southern life in four important ways.

1. It triggered a vast move westward. Cotton farming moved beyond the Atlantic coastal states, where long-fibered, easy-to-clean cotton grew. Cotton plantations began to spread into northern Florida, Alabama, and Mississippi. Then they crossed into Louisiana and Arkansas. After 1840, they reached Texas.

2. Because cotton was valuable, planters grew more cotton rather than other goods, and cotton exports increased.

3. More Native American groups were driven off Southern land as it was taken over for cotton plantations.

4. Growing cotton required a large work force, and slavery continued to be important as a source of labor. Many slaves from the east were sold south and west to new cotton plantations.

*Reading*History

**A. Reading a Map** Use the map on page 350 to find cotton-growing areas in 1840.

*Reading*History

**B. Recognizing Effects** What impact did the cotton gin have on the South?

## Slavery Expands

From 1790 to 1860, cotton production rose greatly. So did the number of enslaved people in the South. Using slave labor, the South raised millions of bales of cotton each year for the textile mills of England and the American Northeast. (See the graph on page 350.) In 1820, the South earned $22 million from cotton exports. By the late 1830s, earnings from cotton exports were nearly ten times greater, close to $200 million.

As cotton earnings rose, so did the price of slaves. A male field hand sold for $300 in the 1790s. By the late 1830s, the price had jumped to

## The Cotton Kingdom, 1840

Cotton-growing areas, 1840

ATLANTIC OCEAN

Gulf of Mexico

### Cotton Production, 1800–1860

Bales of cotton (in millions)

1800  1820  1840  1860

Source: *Historical Statistics of the United States*

**GEOGRAPHY SKILLBUILDER Interpreting Maps**

1. **Human-Environment Interaction** *Which five states had the largest areas devoted to growing cotton?*
2. **Human-Environment Interaction** *How far north did people grow cotton?*

$1,000. After 1808, when it became illegal to import Africans for use as slaves, the trading of slaves already in the country increased.

The expansion of slavery had a major impact on the South's economy. But its effect on the people living there was even greater.

## Slavery Divides the South

Slavery divided white Southerners into those who held slaves and those who did not. Slaveholders with large plantations were the wealthiest and most powerful people in the South, but they were relatively few in number. Only about one-third of white families owned slaves in 1840. Of these slave-owning families, only about one-tenth had large plantations with 20 or more slaves.

Most white Southern farmers owned few or no slaves. Still, many supported slavery anyway. They worked their small farms themselves and hoped to buy slaves someday, which would allow them to raise more cotton and earn more money. For both small farmers and large planters, slavery had become necessary for increasing profits.

*Reading* **History**

C. Analyzing Points of View Why did many white farmers without slaves still support slavery?

## African Americans in the South

Slavery also divided black Southerners into those who were enslaved and those who were free. Enslaved African Americans formed about one-third of the South's population in 1840. About half of them worked on large plantations with white overseers. Decades later, a former slave described the routine in an interview.

**A VOICE FROM THE PAST**

The overseer was 'straddle his big horse at three o'clock in the mornin', roustin' the hands off to the field. . . . The rows was a mile long and no matter how much grass [weeds] was in them, if you [left] one sprig on your row they [beat] you nearly to death.

**Wes Brady,** quoted in *Remembering Slavery*

*Reading***History**

**D. Contrasting** How was plantation slavery different from slavery in cities?

Not all slaves faced the back-breaking conditions of plantations. In cities, enslaved persons worked as domestic servants, skilled craftsmen, factory hands, and day laborers. Sometimes they were hired out and allowed to keep part of their earnings. Frederick Douglass, an African-American speaker and publisher, once commented, "A city slave is almost a freeman, compared with a slave on the plantation." But they were still enslaved.

In 1840, about 8 percent of African Americans in the South were free. They had either been born free, been freed by an owner, or bought their own freedom. A significant number of free blacks in the South overcame great obstacles to become skilled workers. Some did well enough to become planters. Many others lived in cities such as Baltimore and Washington, D.C.

Though not enslaved, free blacks faced many problems. Some states made them leave once they gained their freedom. Most states did not permit them to vote or receive an education. Many employers refused to hire them. But their biggest threat was the possibility of being captured and sold into slavery.

## Finding Strength in Religion

An African-American culture had emerged on plantations by the early 1800s. Slaves relied on that culture—with its strong religious convictions, close personal bonds, and abundance of music—to help them endure the brutal conditions of plantation life.

*Reading***History**

**E. Making Inferences** Why would enslaved African Americans be inspired by the biblical story of Moses?

Some slaveholders tried to use religion to make slaves accept their treatment. White ministers stressed such Bible passages as "Servants, obey your masters." But enslaved people took their own messages from the Bible. They were particularly inspired by the story of Moses leading the Hebrews out of bondage in Egypt.

Enslaved people expressed their religious beliefs in **spirituals,** religious folk songs. Spirituals often contained coded

**daily** *life*

**SPIRITUALS**

Singing spirituals offered comfort for pain, bound people together at religious meetings, and eased the boredom of daily tasks. This verse came from a spiritual sung by slaves in Missouri.

*Dear Lord, dear lord,*
*    when slavery'll cease*
*Then we poor souls*
*    will have our peace;—*
*There's a better day a coming,*
*Will you go along with me?*
*There's a better day a coming,*
*Go sound the jubilee!*

Detail of *Plantation Burial*, (1860), John Antrobus.

messages about a planned escape or an owner's unexpected return. African-American spirituals later influenced blues, jazz, and other forms of American music.

## Families Under Slavery

Perhaps the cruelest part of slavery was the sale of family members away from one another. Although some slaveholders would not part mothers from children, many did, causing unforgettable grief. When enslaved people ran away, it was often to escape separation or to see family again.

When slave families could manage to be together, they took comfort in their family life. They married, though their marriages were not legally recognized. They tried to raise children, despite interference from owners. Most slave children lived with their mothers, who tried to protect them from punishment. Parents who lived on other plantations often stole away to visit their children, even at the cost of a whipping. Frederick Douglass recalled visits from his mother, who lived 12 miles away.

*Reading***History**
F. Recognizing Effects How did slavery harm family life?

### A VOICE FROM THE PAST

I do not recollect of [remember] ever seeing my mother by the light of day. She was with me in the night. She would lie down with me, and get me to sleep, but long before I waked she was gone.

**Frederick Douglass,** *Narrative of the Life of Frederick Douglass*

Douglass's mother resisted slavery by the simple act of visiting her child. Douglass later rebelled by escaping to the North. Other enslaved people rebelled in more violent ways.

A slave auction threatens to split a family apart.

# Slave Rebellions

Armed rebellion was an extreme form of resistance to slavery. Gabriel Prosser planned an attack on Richmond, Virginia, in 1800. In 1822, a free minister named Denmark Vesey planned a revolt in Charleston, South Carolina. Both plots were betrayed, and the leaders were hanged. At Vesey's trial, witnesses said between 6,000 and 9,000 slaves were to be involved, which would have made it the largest slave rebellion in the United States.

The most famous rebellion was led by **Nat Turner** in Virginia in 1831. On August 21, Turner and 70 followers killed 55 white men, women, and children. Later, witnesses claimed that he spoke these words.

> ### A VOICE FROM THE PAST
>
> We do not go forth for the sake of blood and carnage; . . . Remember that ours is not a war for robbery, . . . it is a struggle for freedom.
>
> **Nat Turner,** quoted in *Nat Turner,* by Terry Bisson

*Reading* **History**

**G. Recognizing Effects** How did Nat Turner's rebellion affect white Southerners?

Most of Turner's men were captured when their ammunition ran out, and 16 were killed. When Turner was caught, he was tried and hanged.

Turner's rebellion spread fear in the South. Whites killed more than 200 African Americans in revenge. State legislatures passed harsh laws that kept free blacks and slaves from having weapons or buying liquor. Slaves could not hold religious services unless whites were present.

After Turner's rebellion, the grip of slavery grew even tighter in the South. Tension over slavery increased between the South and the North, as you will see in the next section.

## AMERICA'S HISTORY MAKERS

**NAT TURNER**
**1800–1831**

Nat Turner was born on a plantation in Virginia. As a child, Turner learned to read and write. He became an enthusiastic reader of the Bible. Slaves gathered in forest clearings to listen to his powerful sermons. Turner believed that God wanted him to free the slaves, even if by armed rebellion. He defended the justice of his cause in what came to be known as *Confessions of Nat Turner,* which he dictated to a white lawyer before his execution.

**How did Turner justify his rebellion?**

---

## Section 2 Assessment

### 1. Terms & Names

**Explain the significance of:**
- Eli Whitney
- cotton gin
- spirituals
- Nat Turner

### 2. Using Graphics

In a chart like the one below, note facts about each group of Southerners.

| Group | Facts |
|---|---|
| slaveholding whites | |
| nonslaveholding whites | |
| enslaved blacks | |
| free blacks | |

Why do you think many free blacks lived in cities? (REP3)

### 3. Main Ideas

**a.** How did the cotton gin lead to the spread of slavery? (8.7.2)

**b.** How was life different for plantation slaves, city slaves, and free blacks in the South? (8.7.4)

**c.** What were three ways that enslaved people resisted slavery? (8.7.2)

### 4. Critical Thinking

**Forming Opinions** How do you think slave rebellions affected the institution of slavery? (HI2)

**THINK ABOUT**
- Nat Turner's reasons for rebelling
- the reaction of white Southerners and slave owners to Turner's rebellion

---

**ACTIVITY OPTIONS**

**LANGUAGE ARTS**

**SPEECH**

Write a **book report** on a slave narrative, or perform an **oral interpretation** of a passage from one. (REP4)

# Nationalism and Sectionalism

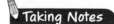

| MAIN IDEA | WHY IT MATTERS NOW | TERMS & NAMES |
|---|---|---|

**MAIN IDEA**

Patriotic pride united the states, but tension between the North and South emerged.

**WHY IT MATTERS NOW**

The tension led to the Civil War, and regional differences can still be found in the United States today.

**TERMS & NAMES**

nationalism    James Monroe
Henry Clay    sectionalism
American System    Missouri Compromise
Erie Canal    Monroe Doctrine

**CALIFORNIA STANDARDS**

**8.4.1** Describe the country's physical landscapes, political divisions, and territorial expansion during the terms of the first four presidents.

**8.4.2** Explain the policy significance of famous speeches (e.g., Washington's Farewell Address, Jefferson's 1801 Inaugural Address, John Q. Adams's Fourth of July 1821 Address).

**8.5.2** Know the changing boundaries of the United States and describe the relationships the country had with its neighbors (current Mexico and Canada) and Europe, including the influence of the Monroe Doctrine, and how those relationships influenced westward expansion and the Mexican-American War.

**8.6.1** Discuss the influence of industrialization and technological developments on the region, including human modification of the landscape and how physical geography shaped human actions (e.g., growth of cities, deforestation, farming, mineral extraction).

**8.6.2** Outline the physical obstacles to and the economic and political factors involved in building a network of roads, canals, and railroads (e.g., Henry Clay's American System).

**Taking Notes**

Use your chart to take notes about nationalism and sectionalism.

Causes

## ONE AMERICAN'S STORY

The War of 1812 sent a wave of nationalist feeling through the United States. **Nationalism** is a feeling of pride, loyalty, and protectiveness toward your country. Representative **Henry Clay**, from Kentucky, was a strong nationalist. After the war, President James Madison supported Clay's plan to strengthen the country and unify its regions.

*A VOICE FROM THE PAST*

Every nation should anxiously endeavor to establish its absolute independence, and consequently be able to feed and clothe and defend itself. If it rely upon a foreign supply that may be cut off . . . it cannot be independent.

**Henry Clay,** quoted in *The Annals of America*

Henry Clay

In this section, you will learn how nationalism affected U.S. economic growth and foreign policy. You'll also see how Americans were beginning to be torn between the interests of their own regions and those of the country as a whole.

## Nationalism Unites the Country

In 1815, President Madison presented a plan to Congress for making the United States economically self-sufficient. In other words, the country would prosper and grow by itself, without foreign products or foreign markets.

The plan—which Henry Clay promoted as the **American System**—included three main actions.

1. **Establish a protective tariff,** a tax on imported goods that protects a nation's businesses from foreign competition. Congress passed a tariff in 1816. It made European goods more expensive and encouraged Americans to buy cheaper American-made products.

*Reading*History

**A. Recognizing Effects** How would the three parts of the American System help to make the country self-sufficient?

2. **Establish a national bank** that would promote a single currency, making trade easier. (Most regional banks issued their own money.) In 1816, Congress set up the second Bank of the United States.
3. **Improve the country's transportation systems,** which were important for a strong economy. Poor roads made transportation slow and costly.

## Roads and Canals Link Cities

Representative John C. Calhoun of South Carolina also called for better transportation systems. "Let us bind the Republic together with a perfect system of roads and canals," he declared in 1817. Earlier, in 1806, Congress had funded a road from Cumberland, Maryland, to Wheeling, Virginia. By 1841, the National Road, designed as the country's main east-west route, had been extended to Vandalia, Illinois.

Water transportation improved, too, with the building of canals. In fact, the period from 1825 to 1850 is often called the Age of Canals. Completed in 1825, the massive **Erie Canal** created a water route between New York City and Buffalo, New York. The canal opened the upper Ohio Valley and the Great Lakes region to settlement and trade. It also fueled nationalism by unifying these two sections of the country.

The Erie Canal allowed farm products from the Great Lakes region to flow east and people and manufactured goods from the East to flow west. Trade stimulated by the canal helped New York City become the nation's largest city. Between 1820 and 1830, its population swelled from less than 125,000 to more than 200,000.

**Major Canals, 1840**

Legend: — Canal · National Road

**GEOGRAPHY SKILLBUILDER Interpreting Maps**
1. **Movement** By what water route could goods from Cleveland reach New York City?
2. **Region** Which region benefited more from canals—the North or the South?

The Erie Canal was 4 feet deep, 40 feet wide, and 360 miles long.

Around the 1830s, the nation began to use steam-powered trains for transportation. In 1830, only about 30 miles of track existed in the United States. But by 1850, the number had climbed to 9,000 miles. Improvements in rail travel led to a decline in the use of canals.

## The Era of Good Feelings

**HISTORIC DECISIONS** *OF THE SUPREME COURT*

For more information on *McCulloch* v. *Maryland*, see pp. 742–743.

For more information on *Gibbons* v. *Ogden*, see pp. 744–745.

As nationalist feelings spread, people slowly shifted their loyalty away from state governments and more toward the federal government. Democratic-Republican **James Monroe** won the presidency in 1816 with a large majority of electoral votes. The Federalist Party provided little opposition to Monroe and soon disappeared. Political differences gave way to what one Boston newspaper called the Era of Good Feelings.

During the Monroe administration, several landmark Supreme Court decisions promoted national unity by strengthening the federal government. For example, in *McCulloch* v. *Maryland* (1819), the state of Maryland wanted to tax its branch of the national bank. If this tax were allowed, the states could claim to have power over the federal government. The Court upheld federal authority by ruling that a state could not tax a national bank.

**James Monroe**

**Background**
Maryland also argued that Congress had no power to create the bank, but the Court ruled that it did have such power.

### A VOICE FROM THE PAST

The States have no power, by taxation or otherwise, to retard, impede, burden, or in any manner control the operations of the constitutional laws enacted by Congress.

**Chief Justice John Marshall,** *McCulloch* v. *Maryland* (1819)

Another Court decision that strengthened the federal government was *Gibbons* v. *Ogden* (1824). Two steamship operators fought over shipping rights on the Hudson River in New York and New Jersey. The Court ruled that interstate commerce could be regulated only by the federal government, not the state governments. The Court also weakened the states' control over business and financial transactions by extending the range of the "contract clause" in the Constitution to forbid states from passing laws "impairing the obligation of contracts." The 1819 decision *Dartmouth College* v. *Woodward* established that states could not interfere with or nullify corporate contracts. This ruling built on an earlier one, *Fletcher* v. *Peck* (1810), which extended the contract clause to include public and private contracts.

The Supreme Court under John Marshall clearly stated important powers of the federal government. A stronger federal government reflected a growing nationalist spirit.

*Reading* **History**
**B. Finding Main Ideas** How did the Supreme Court strengthen the federal government?

## Settling National Boundaries

This nationalist spirit also made U.S. leaders want to define and expand the country's borders. To do this, they had to reach agreements with Britain and Spain.

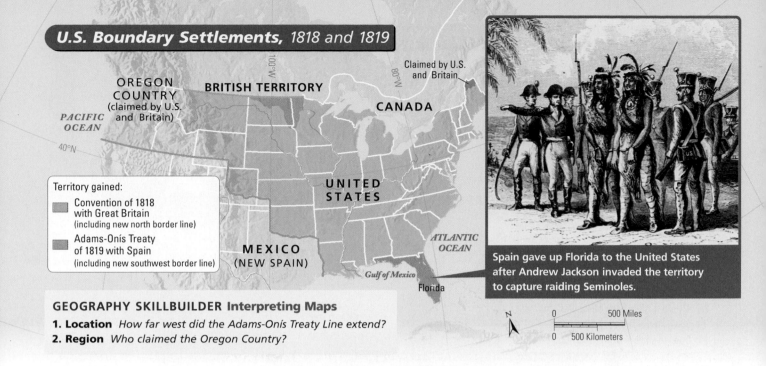

## U.S. Boundary Settlements, 1818 and 1819

OREGON COUNTRY
(claimed by U.S. and Britain)

BRITISH TERRITORY

Claimed by U.S. and Britain

CANADA

PACIFIC OCEAN

40°N

100°W

80°W

UNITED STATES

Territory gained:

Convention of 1818 with Great Britain (including new north border line)

Adams-Onís Treaty of 1819 with Spain (including new southwest border line)

MEXICO (NEW SPAIN)

Gulf of Mexico

Florida

ATLANTIC OCEAN

N

0        500 Miles

0      500 Kilometers

Spain gave up Florida to the United States after Andrew Jackson invaded the territory to capture raiding Seminoles.

**GEOGRAPHY SKILLBUILDER Interpreting Maps**
1. **Location** How far west did the Adams-Onís Treaty Line extend?
2. **Region** Who claimed the Oregon Country?

Two agreements improved relations between the United States and Britain. The Rush-Bagot Agreement (1817) limited each side's naval forces on the Great Lakes. In the Convention of 1818, the two countries set the 49th parallel as the U.S.-Canadian border as far west as the Rocky Mountains.

But U.S. relations with Spain were tense. The two nations disagreed on the boundaries of the Louisiana Purchase and the ownership of West Florida. Meanwhile, pirates and runaway slaves used Spanish-held East Florida as a refuge. In addition, the Seminoles of East Florida raided white settlements in Georgia to reclaim lost lands.

*Reading* **History**

**C. Analyzing Causes** Why did Andrew Jackson invade East Florida?

In 1817, President Monroe ordered General Andrew Jackson to stop the Seminole raids, but not to confront the Spanish. Jackson followed the Seminoles into Spanish territory and then claimed the Floridas for the United States.

Monroe ordered Jackson to withdraw but gave Spain a choice. It could either police the Floridas or turn them over to the United States. In the Adams-Onís Treaty of 1819, Spain handed Florida to the United States and gave up claims to the Oregon Country. The map above shows boundaries drawn and territories gained in 1818 and 1819.

## Sectional Tensions Increase

At the same time nationalism was unifying the country, sectionalism was threatening to drive it apart. **Sectionalism** is loyalty to the interests of your own region or section of the country, rather than to the nation as a whole. Economic changes had created some divisions within the United States. As you have seen, white Southerners were relying more on cotton and slavery. In the Northeast, wealth was based on manufacturing and trade. In the West, settlers wanted cheap land and good transportation. The interests of these sections were often in conflict.

## The Missouri Compromise, 1820–1821

BRITISH TERRITORY

CANADA

Claimed by U.S. and Great Britain

Free state, 1820 MAINE

PACIFIC OCEAN

OREGON COUNTRY (Claimed by U.S. and Great Britain)

UNORGANIZED TERRITORY

MICHIGAN TERRITORY

VT.
N.H.
N.Y.
MASS.
CONN.
R.I.
PA.
N.J.
OHIO
MD.
DEL.
VA.
ATLANTIC OCEAN

ILL. IND.

36°30' Missouri Compromise Line

MISSOURI Slave state, 1821

KY.

N.C.

NEW SPAIN (MEXICO)

ARKANSAS TERRITORY

TENN.

S.C.

Free states and territories
Closed to slavery by Missouri Compromise
Slave states and territories
Open to slavery by Missouri Compromise

MISS. ALA. GA.

LA.

FLORIDA TERRITORY

Gulf of Mexico

500 Miles
1,000 Kilometers

### GEOGRAPHY SKILLBUILDER Interpreting Maps

1. **Location** At what latitude was the Missouri Compromise Line?
2. **Region** What territory was opened to slavery by the Missouri Compromise?

Sectionalism became a major issue when Missouri applied for statehood in 1817. People living in Missouri wanted to allow slavery in their state. At the time, the United States consisted of 11 slave states and 11 free states. Adding Missouri as a slave state would upset the balance of power in Congress. The question of Missouri soon divided the nation.

## The Missouri Compromise

For months, the nation argued over admitting Missouri as a slave state or a free state. Debate raged in Congress over a proposal to ban slavery in Missouri. Angry Southerners claimed that the Constitution did not give Congress the power to ban slavery. They worried that free states could form a majority in Congress and ban slavery altogether.

Meanwhile, Maine, which had been part of Massachusetts, also wanted statehood. Henry Clay, the Speaker of the House, saw a chance for compromise. He suggested that Missouri be admitted as a slave state and Maine as a free state. Congress passed Clay's plan, known as the **Missouri Compromise**, in 1820. It kept the balance of power in the Senate between the slave states and free states. It also called for slavery to be banned from the Louisiana Territory north of the parallel 36° 30', Missouri's southern border.

## The Monroe Doctrine

The nation felt threatened not only by sectionalism, but by events elsewhere in the Americas. In Latin America, several countries had

*Reading* **History**

D. Analyzing Points of View Why was it so important to Southerners to admit Missouri as a slave state?

successfully fought for their independence from Spain and Portugal. Some European monarchies planned to help Spain and Portugal regain their colonies. U.S. leaders feared that if this happened, their own government would be in danger. Russian colonies in the Pacific Northwest also concerned Americans. The Russians entered Alaska in 1784. By 1812, their trading posts reached almost to San Francisco.

John Quincy Adams, at the time James Monroe's secretary of state, spoke out against colonialism. In an 1821 speech, he declared that American foreign policy would not include colonization.

**Background**
*Latin America* refers to the Spanish- and Portugese-speaking nations of the Western Hemisphere south of the United States.

### A VOICE FROM THE PAST

[America] has, in the lapse of nearly half a century, without a single exception, respected the independence of other nations while asserting and maintaining her own.

She has abstained from interference in the concerns of others, even when conflict has been for principles to which she clings, as to the last vital drop that visits the heart.

**John Quincy Adams,** speech before House of Representatives, July 4, 1821

In December 1823, President Monroe issued a statement that became known as the **Monroe Doctrine.** (See Interactive Primary Source, page 360.) Monroe said that the Americas were closed to further colonization. He also warned that European efforts to reestablish colonies would be considered "dangerous to our peace and safety." Finally, he promised that the United States would stay out of European affairs. The Monroe Doctrine showed that the United States saw itself as a world power and protector of Latin America.

In Chapter 12, you will learn how a new democratic spirit grew—and how Native Americans suffered—during Andrew Jackson's presidency.

---

**Section**  **Assessment**

### 1. Terms & Names

**Explain the significance of:**
- nationalism
- Henry Clay
- American System
- Erie Canal
- James Monroe
- sectionalism
- Missouri Compromise
- Monroe Doctrine

### 2. Using Graphics

On a diagram like the one below, name things that contributed to national unity in the early 1800s.

Which of these are still important for national unity? (HI3)

### 3. Main Ideas

**a.** How did the Erie Canal help the nation grow? (HI3)

**b.** How did the Missouri Compromise resolve a conflict between the North and South? (HI3)

**c.** What was the main message of the Monroe Doctrine, and toward whom was it directed? (HI3)

### 4. Critical Thinking

**Recognizing Effects** If the Supreme Court had decided differently in *Gibbons* v. *Ogden* or *McCulloch* v. *Maryland,* what might be one result today? (REP4)

**THINK ABOUT**
- if states could interfere with federal laws
- if states controlled interstate commerce

**ACTIVITY OPTIONS**

**LANGUAGE ARTS**

**ART**

In an **editorial** or a **political cartoon,** give your opinion of either the Missouri Compromise or the Monroe Doctrine. (HI5)

# The Monroe Doctrine

**CALIFORNIA STANDARDS**

**8.5.2** Know the changing boundaries of the United States and describe the relationships the country had with its neighbors (current Mexico and Canada) and Europe, including the influence of the Monroe Doctrine, and how those relationships influenced westward expansion and the Mexican-American War.

**Reading 2.2** Analyze text that uses proposition and support patterns.

**Setting the Stage** On December 6, 1823, President James Monroe gave a State of the Union address. Part of the speech became known as the Monroe Doctrine. The "allied powers" Monroe refers to are Russia, Prussia, Austria, and France. Earlier in the year, these European monarchies had crushed a revolution in Spain and restored the Spanish king to his throne. They were threatening to help Spain regain its Latin American colonies. See **Primary Source Explorer**

**A CLOSER LOOK**

**NO FUTURE COLONIES**

Monroe declares that European countries may not start any new colonies in the Americas.

**1. Why might it threaten the United States to have new European colonies near them?**

**A CLOSER LOOK**

**NEUTRALITY TOWARD EUROPE**

Monroe says that the United States will not take sides in European wars.

**2. Why might the United States want to remain neutral toward conflicts in Europe?**

[T]he occasion has been judged proper for asserting, as a principle in which the rights and interests of the United States are involved, that the American continents, by the free and independent condition which they have assumed and maintain, are henceforth not to be considered as subjects for future colonization by any European powers. . . .

It was stated at the commencement of the last session that great effort was then making in Spain and Portugal to improve the condition of the people of those countries and that it appeared to be conducted with extraordinary moderation. It need scarcely be remarked that the result has been so far very different from what was then anticipated. . . . The citizens of the United States cherish sentiments the most friendly in favor of the liberty and happiness of their fellowmen on that side of the Atlantic. In the wars of the European powers in matters relating to themselves we have never taken any part, nor does it **comport**[1] with our policy so to do. It is only when our rights are invaded or seriously **menaced**[2] that we resent injuries or make preparation for our defense.

With the movements in this hemisphere we are of necessity more immediately connected, and by causes which must be obvious to all enlightened and impartial observers. The political system of the allied powers is essentially different in this respect from that of America. This difference proceeds from that which exists in their respective governments; and to the defense of our own, which has been achieved by the loss of so much blood and treasure, and matured by the wisdom of their most enlightened citizens, and under which we have enjoyed **unexampled felicity,**[3] this whole nation is devoted. We owe it, therefore, to **candor**[4] and to the **amicable**[5] relations existing between the

---

1. **comport:** agree with.
2. **menaced:** threatened.
3. **unexampled felicity:** the greatest happiness.
4. **candor:** honesty.
5. **amicable:** friendly.

United States and those powers to declare that we should consider any attempt on their part to extend their system to any portion of this hemisphere as dangerous to our peace and safety.

With the existing colonies or dependencies of any European power we have not interfered and shall not interfere. But with the governments who have declared their independence and maintained it, and whose independence we have, on great consideration and on just principles, acknowledged, we could not view any **interposition**[6] for the purpose of oppressing them, or controlling in any other manner their destiny, by any European power in any other light than as the manifestation of an unfriendly disposition toward the United States. In the war between those new governments and Spain we declared our neutrality at the time of their recognition, and to this we have adhered and shall continue to adhere, provided no change shall occur which, in the judgment of the competent authorities of this government, shall make a corresponding change on the part of the United States indispensable to their security.

The late events in Spain and Portugal show that Europe is still unsettled. Of this important fact no stronger proof can be adduced than that the allied powers should have thought it proper, on any principle satisfactory to themselves, to have interposed by force in the internal concerns of Spain. To what extent such interposition may be carried, on the same principle, is a question in which all independent powers whose governments differ from theirs are interested, even those most remote, and surely none more so than the United States.

—*James Monroe*

6. **interposition:** interference.

*A CLOSER LOOK*

**A DIFFERENT SYSTEM**

Monroe states that the United States will defend its republican form of government and would be threatened if Europeans set up monarchies in the Americas.

**3. Why would U.S. citizens want their government to be a republic and not an absolute monarchy?**

*A CLOSER LOOK*

**NO INTERFERENCE**

Monroe warns that if Europeans invade the newly independent republics in Latin America, this would be considered hostile to the United States as well.

**4. What would the United States have to fear if these republics were overthrown?**

## Interactive Primary Source Assessment

### 1. Main Ideas

**a.** Why might the United States want no more European colonies in the Americas, particularly in Latin America? (REP4)

**b.** How would staying neutral in European wars protect the United States? (REP4)

**c.** How might the U.S. system of government be threatened if Europeans regained control of former colonies in the Americas? (REP4)

### 2. Critical Thinking

**Making Inferences** For decades, the United States lacked the military power to enforce the Monroe Doctrine and depended on the British navy to keep other European powers out of Latin America. Why, then, did the United States proclaim the Monroe Doctrine? (REP4)

**THINK ABOUT**

• what the doctrine shows about the values and wishes of the United States

• what it shows about how the country saw itself or wanted to be seen

(CST1)

## Early Industry and Inventions

New machines allowed the Northeast to industrialize and the Midwest to increase farm production.

## Plantations and Slavery Spread

The cotton gin led to the expansion of plantations and slavery in the South.

## Nationalism and Sectionalism

Nationalism drew regions together. At the same time, economic differences created tension between regions.

## TERMS & NAMES

Briefly explain the significance of each of the following.

1. Samuel Slater
2. Industrial Revolution
3. Robert Fulton
4. Eli Whitney
5. cotton gin
6. Nat Turner
7. nationalism
8. sectionalism
9. Missouri Compromise
10. Monroe Doctrine

## REVIEW QUESTIONS

### Early Industry and Inventions (pages 341–347)

1. How did the War of 1812 push the United States to build factories? (HI2)
2. How did the War of 1812 and free enterprise affect the U.S. economy? (HI2)
3. What was one effect of the steamboat? (HI2)
4. How did interchangeable parts transform the manufacturing process? (HI2)

### Plantations and Slavery Spread (pages 348–353)

5. Why did slavery spread in the South? (HI2)
6. What were three hardships faced by enslaved people on plantations? (HI1)
7. How did religion help people endure or resist slavery? (HI2)

### Nationalism and Sectionalism (pages 354–361)

8. How did the Supreme Court's ruling in *McCulloch* v. *Maryland* strengthen the federal government? (HI2)
9. How did the United States gain the territory of Florida? (HI1)
10. What were the terms of the Missouri Compromise? (HI1)

## CRITICAL THINKING

### 1. USING YOUR NOTES: ANALYZING CAUSES AND EFFECTS

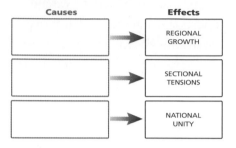

Using your completed chart, answer the questions. (HI2)

a. What were three causes leading to national unity?
b. What was one cause of sectional tension?

### 2. THEME: SCIENCE AND TECHNOLOGY

Of all the new inventions mentioned in the chapter, which do you think was most important and why? (HI1)

### 3. ANALYZING CAUSES

How did geographic differences between regions lead to economic differences between them? (HI2)

### 4. APPLYING CITIZENSHIP SKILLS

Do you think the Missouri Compromise was a wise decision? Consider what might have happened without it, and also why it made Jefferson so uneasy. (HI4)

### 5. ANALYZING LEADERSHIP

Think about the Monroe Doctrine and the boundary settlements achieved during the Monroe administration. How would you judge Monroe's foreign policy? (REP4)

## Interact *with* History

Did you predict the ways that new inventions would change the country? What surprised you?

Use the map and your knowledge of U.S. history to answer questions 1 and 2.

Additional Test Practice, pp. S1–S33.

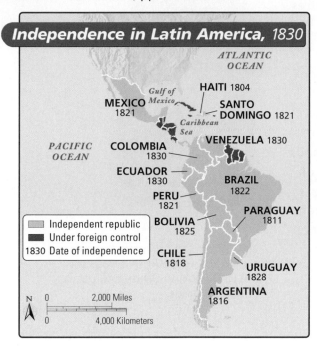

**Independence in Latin America, 1830**

ATLANTIC OCEAN

Gulf of Mexico

HAITI 1804

MEXICO 1821

SANTO DOMINGO 1821

Caribbean Sea

PACIFIC OCEAN

COLOMBIA 1830

VENEZUELA 1830

ECUADOR 1830

BRAZIL 1822

PERU 1821

PARAGUAY 1811

BOLIVIA 1825

CHILE 1818

URUGUAY 1828

ARGENTINA 1816

Independent republic
Under foreign control
1830 Date of independence

N

0 ———— 2,000 Miles
0 ———— 4,000 Kilometers

**1.** Which Latin American countries became independent the same year as Mexico? (8.1.3)

  **A.** Argentina and Brazil

  **B.** Chile and Haiti

  **C.** Peru and Santo Domingo

  **D.** Peru and Uruguay

**2.** Which Latin American country was the first to gain independence? (8.1.3)

  **A.** Argentina

  **B.** Haiti

  **C.** Mexico

  **D.** Paraguay

Henry Clay is talking about the United States in this quotation. Use the quotation and your knowledge of U.S. history to answer question 3.

**PRIMARY SOURCE**

Every nation should anxiously endeavor to establish its absolute independence, and consequently be able to feed and clothe and defend itself. If it rely upon a foreign supply that may be cut off . . . it cannot be independent.

**Henry Clay,** quoted in *The Annals of America*

**3.** What idea was Henry Clay supporting in this speech? (8.6.2)

  **A.** separatism

  **B.** nationalism

  **C.** sectionalism

  **D.** patriotism

**TEST PRACTICE**
CLASSZONE.COM

## ALTERNATIVE ASSESSMENT

**1.** 📝 **WRITING ABOUT HISTORY**

Write the dialogue for a one-act **play** about the slave rebellion led by Nat Turner. (REP4)

• Use library resources to learn about Nat Turner.

• Include the events that led up to the rebellion.

• Explain the lasting effects of the rebellion.

**2. COOPERATIVE LEARNING**

Participate in a class project to plan an exhibit depicting what slavery was like on cotton plantations. Choose one of the following topics: what enslaved people wore; what their living conditions were like; what rules they lived under; or what stories they told. Work with other students to research that subject. Discuss how to exhibit your findings. (REP3)

## INTEGRATED TECHNOLOGY

**FINDING PRIMARY SOURCES ON THE INTERNET**

There are many first-hand accounts of factory life at the Lowell mills. Use the Internet to find at least two of the following on-line primary sources. Read the excerpts and articles, write five interesting facts that you learned from these sources, and then share them with the class. (REP4)

• "Tales of Factory Life" an excerpt from *Lowell Offering*

• "The Spirit of Discontent" an excerpt from *Lowell Offering*

• "Harriet Robinson: Lowell Mill Girls"

• Factory Rules from the *Handbook to Lowell*, 1848

For more about the Lowell mills . . .

**INTERNET ACTIVITY**
CLASSZONE.COM

**Writing Model**
ClassZone.com

# Research Reports:
## Forces Affecting the Growing Nation

**CALIFORNIA STANDARDS**
**Writing 2.3** Write research reports.

**PURPOSE:** To write a research report exploring forces that unified and divided the new nation

**AUDIENCE:** Your classmates

In Unit 3, you read about the huge changes that took place between 1789 and 1844 as the new nation grew from the original 13 colonies to a single nation. During those years of growth, some forces brought the nation together while others caused division and disagreement. How strong was the nation's sense of unity? Were the forces of discord strong enough to pose a real threat? You can find answers to questions like these by writing a **research report**, a composition that pulls together information from primary and secondary sources.

The War of 1812 divided Americans. During the war, British troops set fire to the White House and other public buildings.

## Organization & Focus

Your assignment is to write a 500–700 word research report on the forces that unified and divided the growing nation during the years covered in this unit. Your report should have an introduction, a body, and a conclusion, plus a **bibliography**—a list of the sources used in preparing the report. Define your **thesis,** or controlling main idea, in your introduction. The body of your report should support this thesis. Your conclusion should restate or summarize your thesis.

**CHOOSING A TOPIC** Review chapters 9, 10, and 11, looking for examples or incidents that reveal either a unifying or a dividing force in the nation. Keep track of this information in a two-column chart. When you have reviewed all three chapters, look over your chart and decide which examples or incidents you want to research further.

**IDENTIFYING PURPOSE AND AUDIENCE** Even today, there are forces that unify and divide Americans. The roots of some of these forces date back to the early years of our nation. Your purpose, then, is to research and explain some of these forces so that your audience—your classmates—can understand how these forces affect them today.

## Research & Technology

Keep track of your sources on note cards. At the top of each card, write a heading, such as *Dividing Force*. Below the heading, write the source's title, author, publisher, date, page number, or Web address. Record important ideas, concepts, and direct quotations for each source. You will use the cards to write your footnotes and bibliography. A sample note card is shown below.

**Technology Tip** Keep in mind that Web sites sponsored by educational institutions *(.edu)* and government agencies *(.gov)* are generally most reliable.

> Dividing Force
>
> <u>The American Spirit</u> , Volume 1, by Thomas A. Bailey and David M. Kennedy. Published by D.C. Heath and Company in 1994, pages 228–244.
>
> War of 1812: War Hawks in Congress supported it; pro-British Federalists of New England opposed it. The war divided the nation.
>
> Quote: Called "Mr. Madison's war" by those opposed to it.

**OUTLINING AND DRAFTING YOUR REPORT** Use the headings on your note cards to outline your report. Use the information on the cards to draft it. As you write your report, paraphrase and summarize the ideas taken from your sources. Whenever you use a fact or quotation from a source, indicate that with a footnote. Illustrate and enhance your information using charts, graphs, and maps.

## Evaluation & Revision

A good research report should reflect a balance between ideas taken from sources and your own ideas. Try reading your first draft aloud to a "test reader." Add, take out, or replace any information based on your reader's reaction.

When you are satisfied with your report, prepare your bibliography and footnotes. Your language arts textbook or school handbook will help you use the correct form.

**Self-Check**

Does my report have . . .

- [ ] a clearly defined thesis?
- [ ] supporting details drawn from a variety of sources?
- [ ] quotation marks to show borrowed words?
- [ ] a strong conclusion?
- [ ] footnotes and bibliography in the proper form?

## Publish & Present

After editing your report, prepare and print a final copy. Present your report to the class. After all the presentations, discuss the forces that continue to unify and divide the nation today.

# A Changing Nation

Scotts Bluff in Nebraska became a landmark for settlers migrating west on the Oregon Trail.

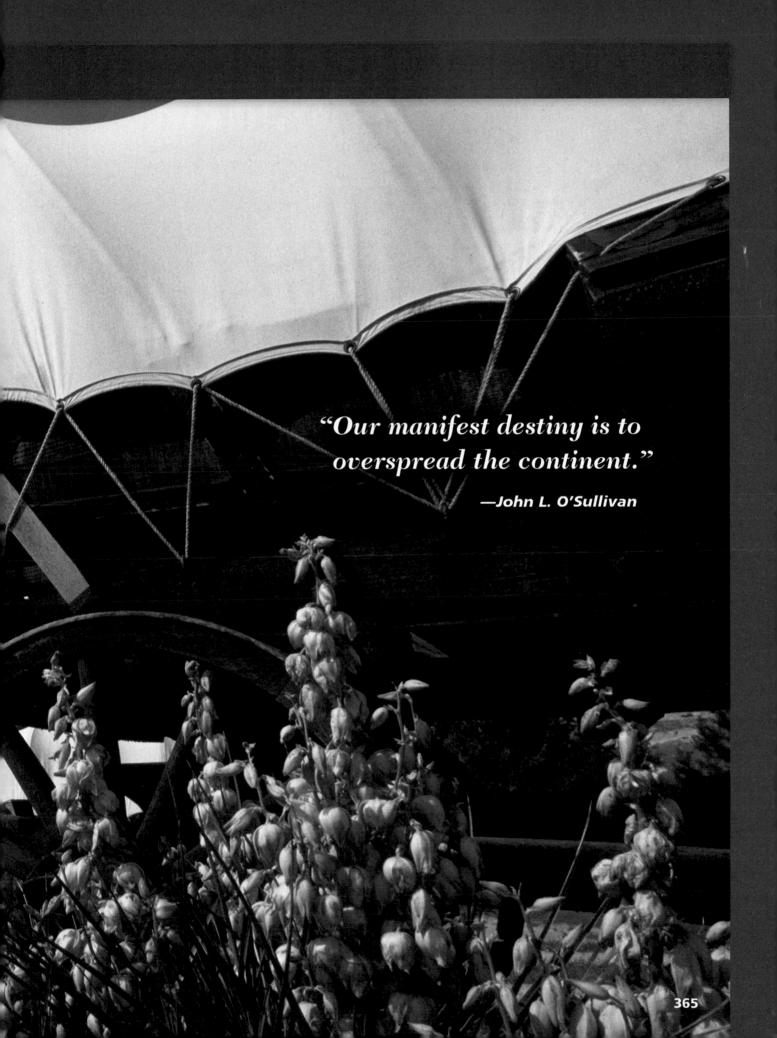

"Our manifest destiny is to overspread the continent."

—John L. O'Sullivan

# The Age of Jackson 1824–1840

President-elect Andrew Jackson is on his way to Washington in this painting.

As a general, Andrew Jackson was a hero of the War of 1812, defeating the British at the Battle of New Orleans.

**1828**
Tariff of Abominations signed into law.

**Andrew Jackson is elected president.**

**1830**
Indian Removal Act is passed.

**1824**
John Quincy Adams is elected president.

USA
World 1824

**1824**
Simón Bolívar becomes president of Peru.

**1828**
Uruguay gains independence.

**1830**
Revolutions occur in Belgium, France, and Poland.

The year is 1828. You will vote for president for the first time. Important economic, social, and political issues face the country. The favored candidate is Andrew Jackson, a military hero. Before you vote, you should decide what you are looking for in a leader.

# What qualities do you think make a strong leader?

## What Do You Think?

- Which earlier presidents would you consider strong leaders and which not?

- Would qualities that make a military leader also make a good president? Why or why not?

**RESEARCH LINKS**
CLASSZONE.COM

Visit the Chapter 12 links for more information about the Age of Jackson.

**1832**
Jackson vetoes charter of Bank of the United States.

South Carolina nullifies tariffs.

**Jackson is reelected.**

**1836**
**Martin Van Buren is elected president.**

**1838**
Cherokees begin to travel the Trail of Tears.

**1840**
**William Henry Harrison is elected president.**

1840

**1832**
Reform Act increases number of voters in Britain.

**1837**
Victoria becomes queen of Great Britain.

**1838**
Zulu clash with Boer settlers in South Africa.

# Reading Strategy: Finding Main Ideas

## What Do You Know?

What do you already know about the issues that faced the nation in the first half of the 19th century? How did presidents before Jackson deal with problems?

### Think About

- what you have learned about Andrew Jackson from books and movies
- how American life is affected by the actions of a president, by conflicts among different parts of the country, and by the will of the people
- your responses to the Interact with History about qualities that make a strong leader (see page 367)

## What Do You Want to Know?

 What questions do you have about Jackson and his presidency? Record them in your notebook before reading the chapter.

## Finding Main Ideas

To make it easier for you to understand what you read, learn to find the main idea of each paragraph, topic heading, and section. Remember that the supporting details help explain the main ideas. On the chart below, write down the main ideas about the political, economic, and social changes during Jackson's presidency.

 See Skillbuilder Handbook, page R5.

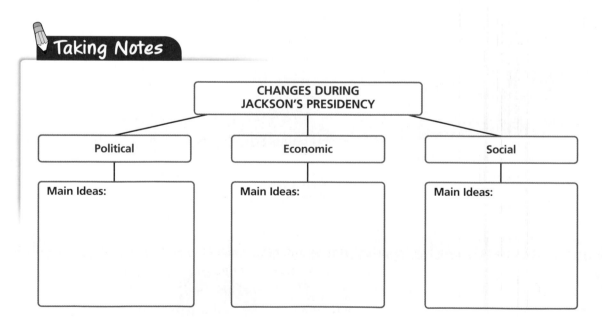

**Taking Notes**

CHANGES DURING
JACKSON'S PRESIDENCY

| Political | Economic | Social |
|---|---|---|
| Main Ideas: | Main Ideas: | Main Ideas: |

# Politics of the People

| MAIN IDEA | WHY IT MATTERS NOW | TERMS & NAMES |
|---|---|---|
| Andrew Jackson's election to the presidency in 1828 brought a new era of popular democracy. | Jackson's use of presidential powers laid the foundation of the modern presidency. | John Quincy Adams  Andrew Jackson  Jacksonian democracy  spoils system |

## ONE AMERICAN'S STORY

For 40 years, Margaret Bayard Smith and her husband, a government official, were central figures in the political and social life of Washington. In 1824, Smith described how John Quincy Adams reacted to his election as president.

*A VOICE FROM THE PAST*

When the news of his election was communicated to Mr. Adams by the Committee . . . the sweat rolled down his face—he shook from head to foot and was so agitated that he could scarcely stand or speak.

**Margaret Bayard Smith,** *The First Forty Years of Washington Society*

**Margaret Bayard Smith**

Adams had reason to be shaken by his election. It had been hotly contested, and he knew that he would face much opposition as he tried to govern. In this section, you will learn how Adams defeated Andrew Jackson in 1824, only to lose to him four years later.

## The Election of 1824

In 1824, regional differences led to a fierce fight over the presidency. The Democratic-Republican Party split apart, with four men hoping to replace James Monroe as president. **John Quincy Adams,** Monroe's secretary of state, was New England's choice. The South backed William Crawford of Georgia. Westerners supported Henry Clay, the "Great Compromiser," and **Andrew Jackson,** a former military hero from Tennessee.

Jackson won the most popular votes. But he did not receive a majority of electoral votes. According to the Constitution, if no person wins a majority of electoral votes, the House of Representatives must choose the president. The selection was made from the top three vote getters.

Clay had come in fourth and was out of the running. In the House vote, he threw his support to Adams, who then won. Because Adams

**CALIFORNIA STANDARDS**

**8.2.7** Describe the principles of federalism, dual sovereignty, separation of powers, checks and balances, the nature and purpose of majority rule, and the ways in which the American idea of constitutionalism preserves individual rights.

**8.3.6** Describe the basic law-making process and how the Constitution provides numerous opportunities for citizens to participate in the political process and to monitor and influence government (e.g., function of elections, political parties, interest groups).

**8.8.1** Discuss the election of Andrew Jackson as president in 1828, the importance of Jacksonian democracy, and his actions as president (e.g., the spoils system, veto of the National Bank, policy of Indian removal, opposition to the Supreme Court).

**REP4** Students assess the credibility of primary and secondary sources and draw sound conclusions from them.

**Taking Notes**

Use your chart to take notes about political changes.

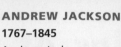
**JOHN QUINCY ADAMS**
**1767–1848**

John Quincy Adams was born into wealth and social position. He was the son of President John Adams. Like his father, he had a sharp mind, spoke eloquently, worked tirelessly in public service, and had high principles. But he was sometimes vain, and unwilling to compromise. This made him unpopular with many people and often ineffective. After his presidency, he served with distinction in Congress.

**ANDREW JACKSON**
**1767–1845**

Andrew Jackson was the son of a poor farm couple from South Carolina. Orphaned by age 14, he was a wild and reckless youth.

Jackson moved on to become a successful lawyer and plantation owner in Tennessee. But his quick temper still got him into brawls and duels. Bullets in his body from two duels frequently caused him pain.

Jackson's humble background and reputation for toughness endeared him to voters. They considered him one of their own.

**Why do you think Jackson was popular but Adams was not?**

later named Clay as his secretary of state, Jackson's supporters claimed that Adams gained the presidency by making a deal with Clay. Charges of a "corrupt bargain" followed Adams throughout his term.

Adams had many plans for his presidency. He wanted to build roads and canals, aid education and science, and regulate the use of natural resources. But Congress, led by Jackson supporters, defeated his proposals.

*Reading* **History**
**A. Analyzing Causes** What was the main reason John Quincy Adams was not effective as president?

## Jacksonian Democracy

Jackson felt that the 1824 election had been stolen from him—that the will of the people had been ignored. Jackson and his supporters were outraged. He immediately set to work to gain the presidency in 1828.

For the next four years, the split in the Democratic-Republican Party between the supporters of Jackson and of Adams grew wider. Jackson claimed to represent the "common man." He said Adams represented a group of privileged, wealthy Easterners. This division eventually created two parties. The Democrats came from among the Jackson supporters, while the National Republicans grew out of the Adams camp.

The election of 1828 again matched Jackson against Adams. It was a bitter campaign—both sides made vicious personal attacks. Even Jackson's wife, Rachel, became a target. During the campaign, Jackson crusaded against control of the government by the wealthy. He promised to look out for the interests of common people. He also promoted the concept of majority rule. The idea of spreading political power to all the people and ensuring majority rule became known as **Jacksonian democracy**.

Actually, the process of spreading political power had begun before Jackson ran for office. When Jefferson was president in the early 1800s, additional people had gained the right to vote as states reduced restrictions on who could vote. Before, for example, only those who owned property or paid taxes could vote in many states. This easing of voting restrictions increased the number of voters. But voting was still limited to adult white males.

The expansion of voting rights helped Jackson achieve an overwhelming win in the 1828 presidential election. Jackson's triumph was hailed as a victory for common people. Large numbers of Western farmers as well as workers in the nation's cities supported him. Their vote put an end to the idea that the government should be controlled by an educated elite. Now, the common people would be governed by one of their own. (See chart "Changes in Ideas About Democracy," page 373.)

*Reading* **History**
**B. Recognizing Effects** What factor made Jackson's appeal to the "common man" especially important in the election of 1828?

## The People's President

Jackson's humble background, and his reputation as a war hero, helped make him president. Many saw his rise above hardship as a real American success story. He was the first president not from an aristocratic Massachusetts or Virginia family, and the first from the West.

Jackson indeed had had a hard life. His father died shortly before his birth, and Jackson grew up on a frontier farm in South Carolina. At 13, he joined the militia with his older brother to fight in the Revolutionary War. In 1781, they were taken prisoner by the British. While captive, he allegedly refused when commanded to shine an officer's boots. The officer struck Jackson with a sword, leaving scars on his hand and head. Later, Jackson's mother obtained her sons' release from a military prison, where they had become ill with smallpox. Jackson's brother died, but his mother nursed Jackson back to health. A short time later, she also died. Jackson's experiences during the Revolution left him with a lifelong hatred of the British.

After the war, Jackson moved to the Tennessee frontier. In 1784, he began to study law. He built a successful legal practice and also bought and sold land. Jackson then purchased a plantation near Nashville and ran successfully for Congress. After the War of 1812 broke out, he was appointed a general in the army. At the Battle of New Orleans in 1815, Jackson soundly defeated the British even though his troops were greatly outnumbered. He became a national war hero. He earned the nickname "Old Hickory," after a soldier claimed that he was "tough as hickory."

## Jackson Takes Office

Jackson's success in the presidential election of 1828 came at a high price. Shortly after he won, his wife, Rachel, died of a heart attack. Jackson believed that the campaign attacks on her reputation had killed her. She was a private woman who preferred a quiet life. In fact, she had

## STRANGE *but* True

**ADAMS AND JEFFERSON**

John Adams and Thomas Jefferson died on the same day—the Fourth of July, 1826, the 50th anniversary of the adoption of the Declaration of Independence.

Both Adams and Jefferson were founders of the nation, signers of the Declaration, and presidents. They were also political enemies who had become friends late in life.

Adams was 90; Jefferson, 83. Adams's last words were "Jefferson still survives." He was unaware that Jefferson had died hours earlier.

Jackson usually wore this miniature oil portrait of his beloved wife, Rachel, around his neck.

said that she would "rather be a doorkeeper in the house of God than . . . live in that palace at Washington." Margaret Bayard Smith described Rachel's importance to Jackson, saying she "not only made him a happier, but a better man."

Jackson looked thin, pale, and sad at his inauguration on March 4, 1829. But the capital was full of joy and excitement. Thousands of people were there. Senator Daniel Webster wrote about the inauguration.

### A VOICE FROM THE PAST

I have never seen such a crowd before. Persons have come five hundred miles to see General Jackson, and they really seem to think that the country has been rescued from some dreadful danger.

**Daniel Webster,** *Correspondence*

*Reading***History**
**C. Drawing Conclusions** Why did Jackson's supporters react with such enthusiasm at his inauguration?

At the inauguration ceremony, the crowd shouted, waved, applauded, and saluted its hero. He bowed low to the people in turn. A throng followed Jackson to the White House reception. One person described the crowd as containing "all sorts of people, from the highest and most polished, down to the most vulgar and gross in the nation."

The crowd grew rowdy. People broke china and glasses as they grabbed for the food and drinks. The pushing and shoving finally drove the new president to flee the White House. As Supreme Court Justice Joseph Story observed, "The reign of King Mob seemed triumphant."

## CITIZENSHIP TODAY

# Exercising the Vote

During the Age of Jackson, rules on who could vote were eased. This increased the number of voters. But voting was still limited to adult white males. Over the years, other groups gained the right to vote, including African Americans, women, and Native Americans. Today's elections are open to all citizens aged 18 and over.

Future voters can practice casting their votes in mock, or pretend, elections. The National Student/Parent Mock Election teaches students to be informed voters. Mock presidential elections attract coverage by the media. Television stations may even broadcast live from schools, interviewing student voters.

Students register to vote in a mock election.

One high school student, Charlie Tran from San Jose, California, said, "Students seem to catch the important political events surrounding them. Some students are taking their views . . . to a new level by campaigning for the candidate they support."

### How Do You Set Up a Mock Election?

1. Choose issues and candidates and then set up a mock election in your classroom. (You could focus on the national, state, or local level.)

2. Create the materials of an election, such as the polling place, ballots, and posters.

3. Campaign for the candidates or the issues you support.

4. Conduct the voting.

5. Prepare mock media reports on the election's outcome. You may want to interview voters.

 See Citizenship Handbook, page 283.

**For more about citizenship and voting . . .**

 RESEARCH LINKS
CLASSZONE.COM

## Changes in Ideas About Democracy

| JEFFERSONIAN DEMOCRACY | JACKSONIAN DEMOCRACY |
| --- | --- |
| government for the people by capable, well-educated leaders | government by the people |
| democracy in political life | democracy in social, economic, and political life |
| championed the cause of the farmer in a mainly agricultural society | championed the cause of the farmer and the laborer in an agricultural and industrial society |
| limited government | limited government, but with a strong president |

**SKILLBUILDER Interpreting Charts**

1. *What do you think was the most important change in democracy?*
2. *Did Jefferson or Jackson exercise more power?*

# A New Political Era Begins

Jackson's inauguration began a new political era. In his campaign, he had promised to reform government. He started by replacing many government officials with his supporters. This practice of giving government jobs to political backers became known as the **spoils system**. The name comes from a statement that "to the victor belong the spoils [possessions] of the enemy." Jackson's opponents charged that the practice was corrupt. But he defended it, noting that it broke up one group's hold on government.

As president, Jackson would face three major issues—the status of Native Americans, the rights of the states, and the role of the Bank of the United States. In the next section, you will learn how Jackson's policies affected Native Americans.

---

## Section 1 Assessment

### 1. Terms & Names

**Explain the significance of:**
- John Quincy Adams
- Andrew Jackson
- Jacksonian democracy
- spoils system

### 2. Using Graphics

Use a chart to identify important biographical information about Andrew Jackson. (REP3)

| Life of Andrew Jackson | |
| --- | --- |
| Youthful life | |
| Road to Congress | |
| War hero | |
| Appeal to voters | |

### 3. Main Ideas

**a.** How did Andrew Jackson react to the election of 1824? Why? (HI2)

**b.** What factors helped Jackson win the presidency in 1828? (HI2)

**c.** What was the effect of expanding voting rights? (HI2)

### 4. Critical Thinking

**Analyzing Points of View**
What are reasons for and against the spoils system? (REP5)

**THINK ABOUT**
- the effects of giving government workers lifetime jobs
- the effects of rewarding political supporters

---

**ACTIVITY OPTIONS**

**GEOGRAPHY**

**MATH**

Find out which states Jackson and Adams won in the 1828 election. Show the results on a **map** or **chart** that includes vote totals and percentages. (CST3)

# Jackson's Policy Toward Native Americans

| MAIN IDEA | WHY IT MATTERS NOW | TERMS & NAMES |
|---|---|---|
| During Jackson's presidency, Native Americans were forced to move west of the Mississippi River. | This forced removal forever changed the lives of Native Americans in the United States. | Sequoya<br>Indian Removal Act<br>Indian Territory<br>Trail of Tears<br>Osceola |

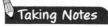

**Taking Notes**

Use your chart to take notes about social changes.

## ONE AMERICAN'S STORY

In 1821, a brilliant Cherokee named **Sequoya** (sih KWOY uh) invented a writing system for the Cherokee language. Using this simple system, the Cherokees soon learned to read and write. A traveler in 1828 marveled at how many Cherokees had learned to read and write without schools or even paper and pens.

*A VOICE FROM THE PAST*

I frequently saw as I rode from place to place, Cherokee letters painted or cut on the trees by the roadside, on fences, houses, and often on pieces of bark or board, lying about the houses.

**Anonymous traveler,** quoted in the *Advocate*

Sequoya hoped that by gaining literacy—the ability to read and write—his people could share the power of whites and keep their independence. But even Sequoya's invention could not save the Cherokees from the upheaval to come. In this section, you will learn about President Jackson's policy toward Native Americans and its effects.

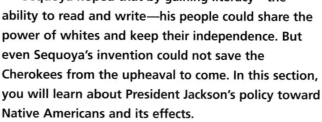

Sequoya invented a writing system of 86 characters, shown here, for the Cherokee language.

## Native Americans in the Southeast

Since the 1600s, white settlers had pushed Native Americans westward as they took more and more of their land. However, there were still many Native Americans in the East in the early 1800s. Some whites hoped that the Native Americans could adapt to the white people's way of life. Others wanted the Native Americans to move. They believed this was the only way to avoid conflict over land. Also, many whites felt that Native Americans were "uncivilized" and did not want to live near them.

By the 1820s, about 100,000 Native Americans remained east of the Mississippi River. The majority were in the Southeast. The major tribes

Reading**History**

**A. Reading a
Map** Use the map
on page 376 to
locate Native
American lands
in the Southeast.

were the Cherokee, Chickasaw, Choctaw, Creek, and Seminole. Whites called them the Five Civilized Tribes because they had adopted many aspects of white culture. They held large areas of land in Georgia, the Carolinas, Alabama, Mississippi, and Tennessee.

## The Cherokee Nation

More than any other Southeastern tribe, the Cherokee had adopted white customs, including their way of dressing. Cherokees owned prosperous farms and cattle ranches. Some even had slaves. From Sequoya, they acquired a written language, and they published their own newspaper, the *Cherokee Phoenix*. Some of their children attended missionary schools. In 1827, the Cherokees drew up a constitution based on the U.S. Constitution and founded the Cherokee Nation.

A year after the Cherokees adopted their constitution, gold was discovered on their land in Georgia. Now, not only settlers but also miners wanted these lands. The discovery of gold increased demands by whites to move the Cherokees. The federal government responded with a plan to remove all Native Americans from the Southeast.

## Jackson's Removal Policy

Andrew Jackson had long supported a policy of moving Native Americans west of the Mississippi. He first dealt with the Southeastern tribes after the War of 1812. The federal government ordered Jackson, then acting as Indian treaty commissioner, to make treaties with the Native Americans of the region. Through these treaties forced on the tribes, the government gained large tracts of land.

Jackson believed that the government had the right to regulate where Native Americans could live. He viewed them as conquered subjects who lived within the borders of the United States. He thought that Native Americans had one of two choices. They could adopt white culture and become citizens of the United States. Or they could move into the Western territories. They could not, however, have their own governments within the nation's borders.

After the discovery of gold, whites began to move onto Cherokee land. Georgia and other Southern states passed laws that gave them the right to take over Native American lands. When the Cherokee and other tribes protested, Jackson supported the states.

To solve the problem, Jackson asked Congress to pass a law that would require Native Americans to either move west or submit to state laws. Many Americans objected to Jackson's proposal. Massachusetts congressman Edward Everett opposed removing Native Americans against their will to a distant land. There, he said, they would face "the

**Now** *and* **then**

**CHEROKEE PEOPLE TODAY**

Today, there are more than 300,000 Cherokees. They are part of three main groups—the Cherokee Nation of Oklahoma, the United Keetoowah Band in Oklahoma, and the Eastern Band of Cherokee Indians of North Carolina.

Wilma Mankiller, shown below, was the first woman elected principal chief of the Cherokee Nation of Oklahoma. She has said that the "Cherokee people possess an extraordinary ability to face down adversity and continue moving forward. We are able to do that because our culture, though certainly diminished, has sustained us since time immemorial."

## Removal of Native Americans, 1820–1840

Removal Routes:
← Cherokee  ← Creek
← Chickasaw  ← Seminole
← Choctaw  ← Other tribes

### Southeastern People Relocated

Cherokees
Chickasaws
Choctaws
Creeks
Seminoles

0  2  4  6  8  10  12  14  16
(in thousands)

🐎 = 2,000 Native Americans

**GEOGRAPHY SKILLBUILDER Interpreting Maps**
1. **Movement** *How long was the Trail of Tears?*
2. **Location** *What states bordered Indian Territory?*

perils and hardships of a wilderness." Religious groups such as the Quakers also opposed forced removal of Native Americans. After heated debate, Congress passed the **Indian Removal Act** in 1830. The act called for the government to negotiate treaties that would require Native Americans to relocate west.

Jackson immediately set out to enforce the law. He thought his policy was "just and liberal" and would allow Native Americans to keep their way of life. Instead, his policy caused much hardship and forever changed relations between whites and Native Americans.

*Reading* **History**

B. Drawing Conclusions
What were reasons for and against the Indian Removal Act?

## The Trail of Tears

As whites invaded their homelands, many Native Americans saw no other choice but to sign treaties exchanging their land for land in the West. Under the treaties, Native Americans would be moved to an area that covered what is now Oklahoma and parts of Kansas and Nebraska. This area came to be called **Indian Territory.**

Beginning in the fall of 1831, the Choctaw and other Southeast tribes were removed from their lands and relocated to Indian Territory. The Cherokees, however, first appealed to the U.S. Supreme Court to protect their land from being seized by Georgia. In 1832, the Court, led by Chief Justice John Marshall, ruled that only the federal government, not the states, could make laws governing the Cherokees. This ruling meant that the Georgia laws did not apply to the Cherokee Nation. However, both Georgia and President Jackson ignored the Supreme Court. Jackson said, "John Marshall has made his decision. . . . Now let him enforce it."

A small group of Cherokees gave up and signed a treaty to move west. But the majority of the Cherokees, led by John Ross, opposed the treaty. Jackson refused to negotiate with these Cherokees.

In 1838, federal troops commanded by General Winfield Scott rounded up about 16,000 Cherokees and forced them into camps. Soldiers took people from their homes with nothing but the clothes on their backs. Over the fall and winter of 1838–1839, these Cherokees set out on the long journey west. Forced to march in the cold, rain, and snow without adequate clothing, many grew weak and ill. One-fourth died. The dead included John Ross's wife. One soldier never forgot what he witnessed on the trail.

*Reading* **History**

**C. Recognizing Effects** What happened to the Cherokees as a result of the Indian Removal Act?

### A VOICE FROM THE PAST

Murder is murder and somebody must answer, somebody must explain the streams of blood that flowed in the Indian country in . . . 1838. Somebody must explain the four-thousand silent graves that mark the trail of the Cherokees to their exile. I wish I could forget it all, but the picture of six-hundred and forty-five wagons lumbering over the frozen ground with their Cargo of suffering humanity still lingers in my memory.

**John G. Burnett,** quoted in *The Native Americans,* edited by Betty and Ian Ballantine

This harsh journey of the Cherokee from their homeland to Indian Territory became known as the **Trail of Tears**.

## HISTORY *through* ART

In 1838, the Cherokees left their homeland by wagon, horse, donkey, and foot, forced to travel hundreds of miles along the Trail of Tears. This painting is by Robert Lindneux, a 20th-century artist.

**How does this portrayal of the Trail of Tears reflect continuity and change in 19th-century American life?**

Osceola led the Seminoles in their fight against removal.

# Native American Resistance

Not all the Cherokees moved west in 1838. That fall, soldiers had rounded up an old Cherokee farmer named Tsali and his family, including his grown sons. On the way to the stockade, they fought the soldiers. A soldier was killed before Tsali fled with his family to the Great Smoky Mountains in North Carolina. There they found other Cherokees. The U.S. Army sent a message to Tsali. If he and his sons would give themselves up, the others could remain. They surrendered, and all except the youngest son were shot. Their sacrifice allowed some Cherokees to stay in their homeland.

Other Southeast tribes also resisted relocation. In 1835, the Seminoles refused to leave Florida. This refusal led to the Second Seminole War. One elderly Seminole explained why he could not leave: "If suddenly we tear our hearts from the homes around which they are twined [wrapped around], our heart strings will snap."

One of the most important leaders in the war was **Osceola** (AHS ee OH luh). Hiding in the Everglades, Osceola and his band used surprise attacks to defeat the U.S. Army in many battles. In 1837, Osceola was tricked into capture when he came to peace talks during a truce. He later died in prison. But the Seminoles continued to fight. Some went deeper into the Everglades, where their descendants live today. Others moved west. The Second Seminole War ended in 1842.

Some tribes north of the Ohio River also resisted relocation. The Shawnee, Ottawa, Potawatomi, Sauk, and Fox were removed to Indian Territory. But in 1832, a Sauk chief named Black Hawk led a band of Sauk and Fox back to their lands in Illinois. In the Black Hawk War, the Illinois militia and the U.S. Army crushed the uprising.

In the next section, you will learn about other issues Jackson faced, especially increasing tensions between various sections of the country.

**Background**
The Seminoles fought three wars against the U.S. government between 1817 and 1858, when their resistance ended.

## Section 2 Assessment

### 1. Terms & Names
**Explain the significance of:**
- Sequoya
- Indian Removal Act
- Indian Territory
- Trail of Tears
- Osceola

### 2. Using Graphics
Use a chart to list the reasons for Jackson's Native American removal policy.

| Reasons Native Americans Were Forced West | | |
|---|---|---|
| Economic | Political | Social |
| | | |

What do you think was the main reason? (HI2)

### 3. Main Ideas
**a.** How did President Jackson justify the Indian Removal Act? (HI1)

**b.** In what ways did Native Americans resist the Indian Removal Act? (HI1)

**c.** What were the consequences of the Indian Removal Act? (HI1)

### 4. Critical Thinking
**Recognizing Effects**
What were some economic effects of the Indian Removal Act on Native Americans? On whites? (HI2)

**THINK ABOUT**
- what the Native Americans lost
- what the white settlers gained

**ACTIVITY OPTIONS**

**GEOGRAPHY**

**MATH**

Use the map on page 376 to estimate the distance traveled by each of the five Southeastern tribes. Show your calculation on a **map** or **chart**. (CST3)

# Conflicts Over States' Rights

| MAIN IDEA | WHY IT MATTERS NOW | TERMS & NAMES |
|---|---|---|
| Jackson struggled to keep Southern states from breaking away from the Union over the issue of tariffs. | Disputes about states' rights and federal power remain important in national politics. | John C. Calhoun  Webster-Hayne debate<br>Tariff of Abominations  Daniel Webster<br>doctrine of nullification  secession |

## ONE AMERICAN'S STORY

Raised in South Carolina, **John C. Calhoun** was elected to the U.S. Congress at the age of 28. He soon became one of its leaders. Calhoun supported the need for a strong central government and also spoke out against sectionalism.

### A VOICE FROM THE PAST

What is necessary for the common good may apparently be opposed to the interest of particular sections. It must be submitted to [accepted] as the condition of our [nation's] greatness.

**John C. Calhoun,** quoted in *John C. Calhoun: American Portrait* by Margaret L. Coit

But Calhoun's concern for the economic and political well-being of his home state of South Carolina, and the South in general, later caused him to change his beliefs. He became a champion of states' rights.

In this section, you will learn how two strong-willed men—Calhoun and Jackson—came in conflict over the issue of states' rights.

## Rising Sectional Differences

Andrew Jackson had taken office in 1829. At the time, the country was being pulled apart by conflicts among its three main sections—the Northeast, the South, and the West. Legislators from these regions were arguing over three major economic issues: the sale of public lands, internal improvements, and tariffs.

The federal government had acquired vast areas of land through conquests, treaties, and purchases. It raised money partly by selling these public lands. However, Northeasterners did not want public lands in the West to be sold at low prices. The cheap land would attract workers who were needed in the factories of the Northeast. But Westerners wanted

**CALIFORNIA STANDARDS**

**8.9.5** Analyze the significance of the States' Rights Doctrine, the Missouri Compromise (1820), the Wilmot Proviso (1846), the Compromise of 1850, Henry Clay's role in the Missouri Compromise and the Compromise of 1850, the Kansas-Nebraska Act (1854), the Dred Scott v. Sandford decision (1857), and the Lincoln-Douglas debates (1858).

**8.10.1** Compare the conflicting interpretations of state and federal authority as emphasized in the speeches and writings of statesmen such as Daniel Webster and John C. Calhoun.

**8.10.2** Trace the boundaries constituting the North and the South, the geographical differences between the two regions, and the differences between agrarians and industrialists.

**8.12.3** Explain how states and the federal government encouraged business expansion through tariffs, banking, land grants, and subsidies.

**Taking Notes**

Use your chart to take notes about political changes.

CHANGES DURING JACKSON'S PRESIDENCY

POLITICAL

low land prices to encourage settlement. The more people who moved West, the more political power the section would have.

The issue of internal improvements also pulled the sections apart. Business leaders in the Northeast and West backed government spending on internal improvements, such as new roads and canals. Good transportation would help bring food and raw materials to the Northeast and take manufactured goods to Western markets. Southerners opposed more federal spending on internal improvements because the government financed these projects through tariffs, which were taxes on imported goods. The South did not want any increase in tariffs.

Since 1816, tariffs had risen steadily. They had become the government's main source of income. Northerners supported high tariffs because they made imported goods more expensive than American-made goods. The Northeast had most of the nation's manufacturing. Tariffs helped American manufacturers sell their products at a lower price than imported goods.

The South opposed rising tariffs because its economy depended on foreign trade. Southern planters sold most of their cotton to foreign buyers.

## Economics *in* History

# How Tariffs Work

Tariffs are taxes added to the cost of goods imported from another country. There are two kinds of tariffs—revenue tariffs and protective tariffs. **Revenue tariffs** are used to raise money, like the sales taxes that states add to purchases today. These tariffs tend to be fairly low. **Protective tariffs** usually are much higher. They have another goal: to persuade consumers to buy goods made in their own country instead of purchasing foreign-made products. Congress passed a protective tariff in 1828 to help American companies.

The illustration shows how a protective tariff works. A British-made teapot sells for $3.50, and a similar teapot made in the United States sells for $4.00. Most shoppers will buy the British teapot and save 50 cents. But when the government adds a 40 percent tariff to British goods, the price of the British teapot soars to $4.90. The result: consumers buy the now-cheaper American teapots.

**CONNECT TO HISTORY**
1. **Recognizing Effects** Do consumers benefit from high tariffs? Why or why not?

**S** See Skillbuilder Handbook, page R11.

**CONNECT TO TODAY**
2. **Making Inferences** Today, many leaders around the world promote the idea of "free trade." What do you think "free trade" means?

For more about tariffs . . .

 **RESEARCH LINKS** CLASSZONE.COM

$2.50 to produce in Britain    $1.00 profit    + tariff    $4.90

 $3.50 + TARIFF 40% → $4.90

$3.00 to produce in the U.S.    $4.00

$1.00 profit    $4.00

They were not paid in money but were given credit. They then used the credit to buy foreign manufactured goods. Because of higher tariffs, these foreign goods cost more. Eventually, the tariff issue would lead to conflict between North and South.

## Tariff of Abominations

In 1828, in the last months of John Quincy Adams's presidency, Congress passed a bill that significantly raised the tariffs on raw materials and manufactured goods. Southerners were outraged. They had to sell their cotton at low prices to be competitive. Yet tariffs forced them to pay high prices for manufactured goods. Southerners felt that the economic interests of the Northeast were determining national policy. They hated the tariff and called it the **Tariff of Abominations** (an abomination is a hateful thing).

Differences over the tariff helped Jackson win the election of 1828. Southerners blamed Adams for the tariff, since it was passed during his administration. So they voted against him.

## Crisis over Nullification

The Tariff of Abominations hit South Carolinians especially hard because their economy was in a slump. Some leaders in the state even spoke of leaving the Union over the issue of tariffs. John C. Calhoun, then Jackson's vice-president, understood the problems of South Carolina's farmers because he was one himself. But he wanted to find a way to keep South Carolina from leaving the Union. The answer he arrived at was the **doctrine of nullification.** A state, Calhoun said, had the right to nullify, or reject, a federal law that it considers unconstitutional.

Calhoun was not the first person to propose the doctrine of nullification. Thomas Jefferson developed it in 1799 in the Kentucky Resolutions to defeat the Alien and Sedition Acts. He argued that the Union was a league of sovereign, or self-governing, states that had the right to limit the federal government. Calhoun extended the doctrine. He said that any state could nullify, or make void, a federal law within its borders. He believed that Congress had no right to impose a tariff that favored one section of the country. Therefore, South Carolina had the right to nullify the tariff. Calhoun's doctrine was an extreme form of states' rights—the theory that states have the right to judge whether a law of Congress is unconstitutional. Nullification challenged the "Supremacy Clause" of the Constitution, which declared that the Constitution and federal laws were the supreme law of the land. Also, at the time of Jefferson's doctrine of nullification, the Supreme Court had not yet established itself as the interpreter of federal laws in *Marbury* v. *Madison*.

In the summer of 1828, Calhoun wrote a document called the "South Carolina Exposition and Protest." It stated his theory. Calhoun allowed the document to be published, but he did not sign his name. He knew his ideas would cause controversy.

*Reading*History
A. Analyzing Causes Why did the three sections of the country differ on the sale of public lands, internal improvements, and tariffs?

*Reading*History
B. Summarizing How did the issue of tariffs threaten to tear the Union apart?

A South Carolina woman sews a palmetto emblem (inset) to her hat to show her support for nullification. The palmetto is a South Carolina symbol.

Vocabulary
controversy: a public dispute

"Liberty and Union, now and forever, one and inseparable!"

Daniel Webster of
Massachusetts

"The measures of the federal
government . . . will soon involve
the whole South in . . . ruin."

Robert Y. Hayne of South Carolina

Daniel Webster
(standing) and
Robert Y. Hayne
(seated, with
hands extended)
debated nullifica-
tion in the U.S.
Senate in 1830.

## The States' Rights Debate

Calhoun was right. His ideas added fuel to the debate over the nature of
the federal union. This debate had been going on since independence
from Britain. More and more people took sides. Some supported a
strong federal government. Others defended the rights of the states.
This question would be a major political issue from this time until the
Civil War was fought to resolve it some 30 years later.

One of the great debates in American history took place in the U.S.
Senate over the doctrine of nullification—the **Webster-Hayne debate**
of 1830. On one side was **Daniel Webster,** a senator from
Massachusetts and the most powerful speaker of his time. On the other
was Robert Y. Hayne, a senator from South Carolina. Hayne defended
nullification. He argued that it gave the states a lawful way to protest
and to maintain their freedom. He also said that the real enemies of the
Union were those "who are constantly stealing power from the States,
and adding strength to the Federal Government."

Webster argued that it was the people and not the states that made
the Union. In words that were printed and spread across the country,
Webster declared that freedom and the Union go together.

### A VOICE FROM THE PAST

When my eyes shall be turned to behold for the last time the sun in heaven,
may I not see him shining on the broken and dishonored fragments of a once
glorious Union. . . . Liberty and Union, now and forever, one and inseparable!

**Daniel Webster,** a speech in the U.S. Senate, January 26, 1830

Jackson had not yet stated his position on the issue of states' rights, even
though Calhoun was his vice-president. He got his chance in April at a
dinner in honor of the birthday of Thomas Jefferson. Calhoun and other

*Reading* **History**
**C. Analyzing Points of View** What do you think Calhoun meant by "the benefits and burdens of the Union" should be equally distributed?

supporters of nullification planned to use the event to win support for their position. Jackson learned of their plans and went to the dinner prepared.

After dinner, Jackson was invited to make a toast. He stood up, looked directly at Calhoun, and stated bluntly, "Our Federal Union—it must be preserved." As Calhoun raised his glass, his hand trembled. Called on to make the next toast, Calhoun stood slowly and said, "The Union—next to our liberty, the most dear; may we all remember that it can only be preserved by respecting the rights of the states and distributing equally the benefits and burdens of the Union." From that time, the two men were political enemies.

## South Carolina Threatens to Secede

Even though Jackson made it clear that he opposed the doctrine of nullification, he did not want to drive the South out of the Union. He asked Congress to reduce the tariff, and Congress did so in 1832. But Southerners thought the reduced rates were still too high. South Carolina nullified the tariff acts of 1828 and 1832 and voted to build its own army. South Carolina's leaders threatened **secession,** or withdrawal from the Union, if the federal government tried to collect tariffs.

Jackson was enraged. He told a South Carolina congressman that if the state's leaders defied federal laws, he would "hang the first man of them I can get my hands on." Jackson ran for reelection in 1832, this time without Calhoun as his running mate. After he won, he made it clear that he would use force to see that federal laws were obeyed and the Union preserved.

In the Senate, Henry Clay came forward with a compromise tariff in 1833. He hoped that it would settle the issue and prevent bloodshed. Congress quickly passed the bill, and the crisis ended. South Carolina stayed in the Union. In the next section, you will read about another issue of Jackson's presidency—his war on the national bank.

---

### Section 3 Assessment

**1. Terms & Names**

**Explain the significance of:**
- John C. Calhoun
- Tariff of Abominations
- doctrine of nullification
- Webster-Hayne debate
- Daniel Webster
- secession

**2. Using Graphics**

Use a chart to indicate how each section stood on these issues. (REP5)

| | North-east | West | South |
|---|---|---|---|
| Sale of public lands | | | |
| Internal improvements | | | |
| High tariffs | | | |

**3. Main Ideas**

**a.** Why did the South oppose high tariffs? (HI1)

**b.** What were Calhoun's reasons for proposing the doctrine of nullification? (HI1)

**c.** Why did South Carolina threaten secession, and how was the crisis resolved? (HI2)

**4. Critical Thinking**

**Recognizing Effects** In what ways would the doctrine of nullification have made it difficult for the federal government to operate? (HI2)

**THINK ABOUT**
- its effect on the enforcement of laws
- its effect on the power of the federal government

**ACTIVITY OPTIONS**

**SPEECH**
**TECHNOLOGY**

Research Daniel Webster's speech; a part of it appears on page 382. Deliver a **speech** for or against nullification to the class, or record it on an **audiocassette.** (REP4)

# Prosperity and Panic

| MAIN IDEA | WHY IT MATTERS NOW | TERMS & NAMES |
|---|---|---|
| Jackson's policies caused the economy to collapse after he left office and affected the next election. | The condition of the economy continues to affect the outcomes of presidential elections. | inflation<br>Martin Van Buren<br>Panic of 1837<br>depression<br>Whig Party<br>William Henry Harrison<br>John Tyler |

**CALIFORNIA STANDARDS**

**8.4.3** Analyze the rise of capitalism and the economic problems and conflicts that accompanied it (e.g., Jackson's opposition to the National Bank; early decisions of the U.S. Supreme Court that reinforced the sanctity of contracts and a capitalist economic system of law).

**8.8.1** Discuss the election of Andrew Jackson as president in 1828, the importance of Jacksonian democracy, and his actions as president (e.g., the spoils system, veto of the National Bank, policy of Indian removal, opposition to the Supreme Court).

**REP4** Students assess the credibility of primary and secondary sources and draw sound conclusions from them.

**REP5** Students detect the different historical points of view on historical events and determine the context in which the historical statements were made (the questions asked, sources used, author's perspectives).

**HI6** Students interpret basic indicators of economic performance and conduct cost-benefit analyses of economic and political issues.

**Taking Notes**

Use your chart to take notes about economic changes.

## ONE AMERICAN'S STORY

Nicholas Biddle was the president of the powerful Second Bank of the United States—the bank that Andrew Jackson believed to be corrupt. Jackson declared war on Biddle and the bank. But Biddle felt sure of his political power.

### A VOICE FROM THE PAST

I have always deplored making the Bank a [political] question, but since the President will have it so, he must pay the penalty of his own rashness. . . . [M]y hope is that it will contribute to relieve the country of the domination of these miserable [Jackson] people.

**Nicholas Biddle,** from a letter to Henry Clay dated August 1, 1832

Nicholas Biddle

In this section, you will read about Jackson's war on the bank.

## Mr. Biddle's Bank

The Second Bank of the United States was the most powerful bank in the country. It held government funds and issued money. As its president, Nicholas Biddle set policies that controlled the nation's money supply.

Although the bank was run efficiently, Jackson had many reasons to dislike it. For one thing, he had come to distrust banks after losing money in financial deals early in his career. He also thought the bank had too much power. The bank made loans to members of Congress, and Biddle openly boasted that he could influence Congress. In addition, Jackson felt the bank's lending policies favored wealthy clients and hurt the average person.

To operate, the bank had to have a charter, or a written grant, from the federal government. In 1832, Biddle asked Congress to renew the bank's charter, even though it would not expire until 1836. Because 1832 was an election year, he thought Jackson would agree to renewal rather than risk angering its supporters. But Jackson took the risk.

# Jackson's War on the Bank

**Vocabulary**
**monopoly:** a company or group with complete control over a product or service

When Congress voted to renew the bank's charter, Jackson vetoed the renewal. In a strongly worded message to Congress, Jackson claimed the bank was unconstitutional. He said the bank was a monopoly that favored the few at the expense of the many. The Supreme Court earlier had ruled that the bank was constitutional. But Jackson claimed elected officials had to judge the constitutionality of a law for themselves. They did not need to rely on the Supreme Court. His veto message also contained this attack on the bank.

### A VOICE FROM THE PAST

It is to be regretted that the rich and powerful too often bend the acts of government to their selfish purposes. . . . Distinctions in society will always exist under every just government. . . . [B]ut when the laws undertake to . . . make the rich richer and the potent more powerful, the humble members of society . . . have a right to complain of the injustice of their Government.

**Andrew Jackson,** veto message, July 10, 1832

*Reading* **History**

**A. Analyzing Points of View**
What reasons did Jackson have for wanting to destroy the Second Bank of the United States?

Jackson's war on the bank became the main issue in the presidential campaign of 1832. The National Republican Party and its candidate, Henry Clay, called Jackson a tyrant. They said he wanted too much power as president. The Democrats portrayed Jackson as a defender of the people. When he won reelection, Jackson took it as a sign that the public approved his war on the bank.

In his second term, Jackson set out to destroy the bank before its charter ended in 1836. He had government funds deposited in state banks, which opponents called Jackson's "pet banks." Biddle fought back by making it harder for people to borrow money. He hoped the resulting economic troubles would force Jackson to return government deposits to the bank. Instead, the people rallied to Jackson's position. Eventually, the bank went out of business. Jackson had won the war, but the economy would be a victim.

## Jackson Fights the Second Bank

In this political cartoon, Jackson fights the many-headed monster—the Second Bank of the United States and its branches—with a cane labeled "VETO."

**A** President Jackson

**B** Cane labeled "VETO"

**C** Nicholas Biddle

**D** Vice-President Van Buren

## Prosperity Becomes Panic

Most of the nation prospered during Jackson's last years in office. Because it was easier to borrow money, people took out loans to buy public lands, and the economy boomed. But the "pet banks" issued too much paper money. The rise in the money supply made each dollar worth less. As a result, prices rose. **Inflation,** which is an increase in prices and decrease in the value of money, was the outcome. To fight inflation, Jackson issued an order that required people to pay in gold or silver for public lands.

Jackson left office proud of the nation's prosperity. But it was a puffed-up prosperity. Like a balloon, it had little substance. Because of Jackson's popularity, his vice-president, **Martin Van Buren,** was elected president in 1836. Within a few months after Van Buren took office, a panic—a widespread fear about the state of the economy—spread throughout the country. It became known as the **Panic of 1837.**

People took their paper money to the banks and demanded gold or silver in exchange. The banks quickly ran out of gold and silver. When the government tried to get its money from the state banks, the banks could not pay. The banks defaulted, or went out of business. A **depression,** or severe economic slump, followed.

The depression caused much hardship. Because people had little money, manufacturers no longer had customers for their goods. Almost 90 percent of factories in the East closed in 1837. Jobless workers had no way of buying food or paying rent. People went hungry. They lived in shelters or on the streets, where many froze in the winter. Every section of the country suffered, but the depression hit hardest in the cities. Farmers were hurt less because they could at least grow their own food. The depression affected politics, too.

*Reading*History

**B. Recognizing Effects** What were the short-term and long-term effects of Jackson's war on the bank?

## The Rise of the Whig Party

In the depths of the depression, Senators Henry Clay and Daniel Webster argued that the government needed to help the economy. Van Buren disagreed. He believed that the economy would improve if left alone. He argued that "the less government interferes with private pursuits the better for the general prosperity." Many Americans blamed Van Buren for the Panic, though he had taken office only weeks before it started. The continuing depression made it almost impossible for him to win reelection in 1840.

Van Buren faced a new political party in that election. During Jackson's war on the national bank, Clay, Webster, and other Jackson opponents had formed the **Whig Party.** It was named after a British party that opposed royal power. The Whigs opposed the concentration of power in the chief executive—whom they mockingly called "King Andrew" Jackson. In 1840, the Whigs chose **William Henry Harrison** of Ohio to run for president and **John Tyler** of Virginia to run for vice-president.

*Reading*History

**C. Making Inferences** Why did the Whigs want to nominate a candidate like Harrison, who did not have strong political views?

The Whigs nominated Harrison largely because of his military record and his lack of strong political views. Harrison had led the army that defeated the Shawnees in 1811 at the Battle of Tippecanoe. He also had been a hero during the War of 1812. The Whigs made the most of Harrison's military record and his nickname, "Old Tippecanoe." The phrase "Tippecanoe and Tyler too" became the Whig election slogan.

## The Election of 1840

During the 1840 election campaign, the Whigs emphasized personalities more than issues. They tried to appeal to the common people, as Andrew Jackson had done. Harrison was the son of a Virginia plantation owner. However, because he had settled on a farm in Ohio, the Whigs said Harrison was a true Westerner. They used symbols of the frontier, such as a log cabin, to represent Harrison. The Whigs contrasted Harrison with the wealthy Van Buren. Harrison won in a close election.

At his inauguration, the 68-year-old president spoke for nearly two hours in cold March weather with no hat or coat. Later, he was caught in the rain. He came down with a cold that developed into pneumonia. On April 4, 1841, one month after being inaugurated, Harrison died—the first president to die in office. Vice-President Tyler became president.

The election of 1840 showed the importance of the West in American politics. In the next chapter, you'll learn more about the lure of the West and the westward expansion of the United States.

---

Section **4** Assessment

### 1. Terms & Names

**Explain the significance of:**
- inflation
- Martin Van Buren
- Panic of 1837
- depression
- Whig Party
- William Henry Harrison
- John Tyler

### 2. Using Graphics

Use a diagram to list the events that led to the closing of the Second Bank of the United States.

What was the most significant event? (CST2)

### 3. Main Ideas

**a.** Why did Jackson declare war on the Second Bank of the United States? (CST1)

**b.** How did Jackson kill the bank? (CST1)

**c.** What role did Jackson's popularity play in the elections of 1836 and 1840? (CST1)

### 4. Critical Thinking

**Comparing** What strategy did the Whig Party use in the 1840 election? (HI1)

**THINK ABOUT**
- how Harrison was portrayed
- what group of voters it was trying to attract

**ACTIVITY OPTIONS**

**LANGUAGE ARTS**

**ART**

Imagine yourself as a presidential candidate in 1840. Focusing on the economy as an issue, write a campaign **slogan** or create a **banner** to rally support. (HI1)

## TERMS & NAMES

Briefly explain the significance of each of the following.

1. John Quincy Adams
2. Jacksonian democracy
3. spoils system
4. Sequoya
5. Indian Removal Act
6. Trail of Tears
7. secession
8. inflation
9. depression
10. Whig Party

## REVIEW QUESTIONS

### Politics of the People (pages 369–373)

1. How was Jackson different from earlier presidents? (HI1)
2. How did Jackson appeal to voters in his election campaign of 1828? (HI1)

### Jackson's Policy Toward Native Americans (pages 374–378)

3. What were Georgia's policies toward Native Americans? (HI1)
4. What was Jackson's position on Native Americans in the United States? (HI1)
5. How did the Indian Removal Act affect Native Americans? (HI2)

### Conflicts over States' Rights (pages 379–383)

6. How did the issue of tariffs divide the country? (HI2)
7. Why did nullification threaten the nation? (HI1)
8. How was the nullification crisis resolved? (HI1)

### Prosperity and Panic (pages 384–387)

9. Why did Jackson oppose the Second Bank of the United States? (HI1)
10. What were the effects of Jackson's war on the bank? (HI1)

## VISUAL SUMMARY

## CRITICAL THINKING

### 1. USING YOUR NOTES: FINDING MAIN IDEAS

Use your completed chart to answer the questions. (HI2)

a. What do you think was the most positive change of the Jackson era? Explain.
b. What was the most negative change? Explain.
c. Based on these changes, how would you describe the characteristics of the Jackson era?

### 2. ANALYZING LEADERSHIP

What was the basis of Andrew Jackson's power as president? (HI1)

### 3. APPLYING CITIZENSHIP SKILLS

How did the majority of voters in the presidential elections of 1828 and 1840 exercise their vote in a similar way? (CST1)

### 4. THEME: ECONOMICS IN HISTORY

Based on its economic effects, was Jackson's decision to end the national bank a good one? Explain. (HI6)

### 5. MAKING INFERENCES

In what ways did Andrew Jackson's policy toward Native Americans reflect bias? (REP5)

### Interact *with* History

Now that you have read the chapter, do you think the qualities that made Jackson a strong military leader made him a good president? Explain your answer.

# Major Issues of Jackson's Presidency (8.8.1)

| POLICY TOWARD NATIVE AMERICANS | CONFLICT OVER STATES' RIGHTS | WAR ON BANK OF THE UNITED STATES |
|---|---|---|
| White settlers wanted Native American lands. | Sectional differences developed. | Second Bank of the United States had economic and political power. |
| Jackson proposed Indian Removal Act of 1830. | Jackson supported strong central government. | Jackson opposed bank and vetoed renewal of its charter. |
| Thousands of Native Americans removed to Indian Territory. | South Carolina threatened to secede over tariff issue, but compromise reached. | Bank driven out of business, but Jackson's policies eventually led to inflation and depression. |

Use the graph and your knowledge of U.S. history to answer questions 1 and 2.

Additional Test Practice, pp. S1–S33.

**Voter Participation,** *1824 & 1828 Elections*

Voters (in millions)

Source: *Historical Statistics of the United States*

= 0.25 million (250,000) eligible voters

= 0.1 million (100,000) actual votes

**1.** What does the red body figure represent on the graph? (8.8.1)

   **A.** .01 million eligible voters

   **B.** .25 million eligible voters

   **C.** .01 million actual voters

   **D.** .25 million actual voters

**2.** Approximately what percentage of eligible voters cast their ballots in 1828? (8.8.1)

   **A.** 15 percent

   **B.** 30 percent

   **C.** 60 percent

   **D.** 90 percent

In this speech Daniel Webster is speaking out against nullification. Use the quotation and your knowledge of U.S. history to answer question 3.

### PRIMARY SOURCE

When my eyes shall be turned to behold for the last time the sun in heaven, may I not see him shining on the broken and dishonored fragments of a once glorious Union. . . . Liberty and Union, now and forever, one and inseparable!

**Daniel Webster,** a speech in the U.S. Senate, January 26, 1830

**3.** Which sentence sums up Webster's point of view? (8.10.1)

   **A.** A divided Union would be an impressive sight.

   **B.** Webster has much to do before he dies.

   **C.** Environmental protection laws are important.

   **D.** A strong federal government is best for all states.

**TEST PRACTICE**
CLASSZONE.COM

## ALTERNATIVE ASSESSMENT

### 1. ✎ WRITING ABOUT HISTORY

Write an **editorial** to convince voters to select the Whig candidate in 1840, William Henry Harrison. Focus on the beliefs and image of the Whig party as well as on personal characteristics of Harrison. (REP4)

- A good editorial supports an opinion with facts.
- Read editorials from a local newspaper to become familiar with the persuasive language.

### 2. COOPERATIVE LEARNING

Working in a small group, help plan and write a proposal outlining a solution to the problems between white settlers and Native Americans in the southeast in the early 1800s. List ideas and identify their positives and negatives. Divide the tasks of outlining, writing, revising, and presenting your plan to the class. (REP3)

## INTEGRATED TECHNOLOGY

### DESIGNING A POLITICAL CAMPAIGN WEB SITE

Plan a Web site for candidate Andrew Jackson for the 1828 presidential campaign. Use the Internet and library resources to locate information about Jackson's personal and political life. (REP4)

- Design the Web site to include biographical facts and photographs.
- Locate quotations from speeches and other primary sources. Include them to present Jackson's views on the major issues surrounding the campaign.
- Locate appropriate links for visitors to the Web site.

**For more about Andrew Jackson . . .**

**INTERNET ACTIVITY**
CLASSZONE.COM

# Manifest Destiny 1810–1853

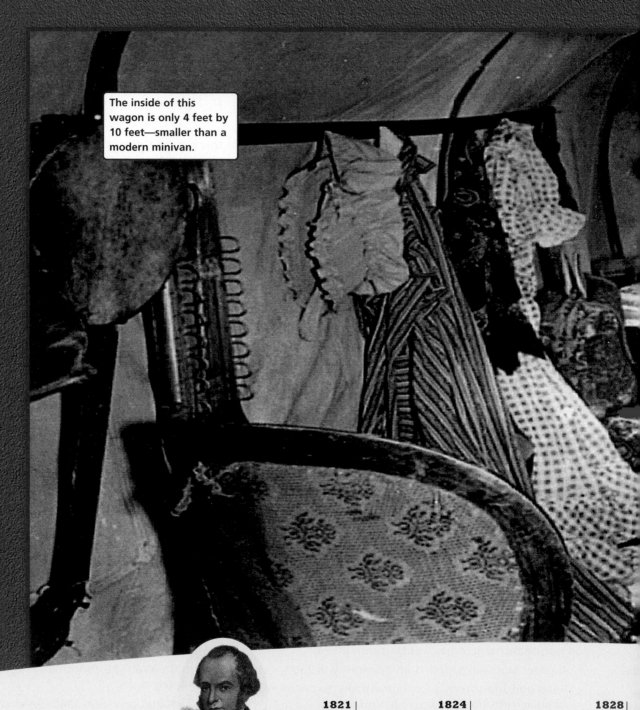

The inside of this wagon is only 4 feet by 10 feet—smaller than a modern minivan.

USA World 1810

**1815**
Napoleon defeated at Waterloo.

**1821**
Stephen Austin settles in Texas.

**1821**
Mexico gains independence from Spain.

**1824**
Jedediah Smith finds South Pass.

**1828**
Andrew Jackson is elected president.

canvas roof with patch

kerosene lamp

butter churn

spinning wheel

chest of silverware

The year is 1844, and you live on a small rocky farm in Massachusetts. Your family has decided to move to Oregon to gain cheap, fertile land. Your father says this move will make your family better off—and give you a better future.

# What might you gain or lose by going west?

## What Do You Think?

- What do you think daily life on the trail west might be like?

- What might be the greatest obstacles that you face?

- Notice the necessities packed in this crowded wagon. What might have been left behind?

**RESEARCH LINKS**
CLASSZONE.COM

Visit the Chapter 13 links for more information about the westward movement.

**832**
hief Black
awk leads Sauk
bellion.
ndrew Jackson
reelected.

**1836**
Martin Van
Buren is
elected
president.

**1841**
John Tyler
becomes
president.

**1844**
James
Polk is
elected
president.

**1847**
Mormons
migrate to Utah.

**1848**
Zachary Taylor
is elected
president.

**1853**
United States
makes Gadsden
Purchase.

**1853**

**1839**
Opium War
fought in China.

**1840**
Benito Juárez
leads reform
movement
in Mexico.

**1847**
Liberia, established
by a former American slave,
proclaimed an independent nation.

# Reading Strategy: Categorizing Information

## What Do You Know?

What do you think of when you hear the phrase "the West"? Who do you think moved west in the early 1800s? What do you think drew them to the West?

### Think About
- what you've learned about the West from movies or travel
- reasons that people move to new places today
- your responses to the Interact with History about going West (see page 391)

## What Do You Want to Know?

What questions do you have about the westward movement of the 1800s? Write those questions in your notebook before you read the chapter.

**CALIFORNIA STANDARDS**

**Reading 2.0** Students read and understand grade-level-appropriate material. They describe and connect the essential ideas, arguments, and perspectives of the text by using their knowledge of text structure, organization, and purpose.

## Categorizing Information

To help you understand and remember historical information, learn to categorize. Categorizing means organizing information into groups. The chart below will help you categorize the information in this chapter about the westward movement. Use the chart to categorize information about what groups went west, why they went, and what events brought each territory into the United States.

**S** See Skillbuilder Handbook, page R6.

 Taking Notes

|  | Types of people who traveled there | Why they went there | Key events that brought the territory into the United States |
|---|---|---|---|
| New Mexico |  |  |  |
| Utah |  |  |  |
| Oregon |  |  |  |
| Texas |  |  |  |
| California |  |  |  |

# Trails West

| MAIN IDEA | WHY IT MATTERS NOW | TERMS & NAMES |
|---|---|---|

**MAIN IDEA**

Thousands of settlers followed trails through the West to gain land and a chance to make a fortune.

**WHY IT MATTERS NOW**

This migration brought Americans to the territories that became New Mexico, Oregon, and Utah.

**TERMS & NAMES**

Jedediah Smith
mountain man
Jim Beckwourth
land speculator

Santa Fe Trail
Oregon Trail
Mormon
Brigham Young

## ONE AMERICAN'S STORY

The mountain man <u>Jedediah Smith</u> was leading an expedition to find a route through the Rocky Mountains when a grizzly bear attacked. The bear seized Smith's head in its mouth, shredded his face, and partially tore off one ear. Smith's men chased the bear away. Jim Clyman recalled the scene.

Jedediah Smith

*A VOICE FROM THE PAST*

I asked [Smith] what was best. He said, "One or two go for water and if you have a needle and thread get it out and sew up my wounds around my head." . . . I told him I could do nothing for his ear. " Oh, you must try to stitch it up some way or other," said he. Then I put in my needle and stitched it through and through.

**Jim Clyman,** quoted in *The West,* by Geoffrey C. Ward

Ten days after this attack, Jedediah Smith was ready to continue exploring. Smith was one of the daring fur trappers and explorers known as <u>**mountain men**</u>. The mountain men opened up the West by discovering the best trails through the Rockies. In this section, you will learn about the trails—and why pioneers followed them west.

## Mountain Men and the Rendezvous

Mountain men spent most of the year alone, trapping small animals such as beavers. Easterners wanted beaver furs to make the men's hats that were in fashion at the time. To obtain furs, mountain men roamed the Great Plains and the Far West, the regions between the Mississippi River and the Pacific Ocean, and set traps in icy mountain streams.

Because of their adventures, mountain men such as Jedediah Smith and <u>**Jim Beckwourth**</u> became famous as rugged loners. However, they were not as independent as the legends have portrayed them. Instead, they were connected economically to the businessmen who bought their furs.

CALIFORNIA STANDARDS

**8.8.2** Describe the purpose, challenges, and economic incentives associated with westward expansion, including the concept of Manifest Destiny (e.g., the Lewis and Clark expedition, accounts of the removal of Indians, the Cherokees' "Trail of Tears," settlement of the Great Plains) and the territorial acquisitions that spanned numerous decades.

**8.8.3** Describe the role of pioneer women and the new status that western women achieved (e.g., Laura Ingalls Wilder, Annie Bidwell; slave women gaining freedom in the West; Wyoming granting suffrage to women in 1869).

**CST3** Students use a variety of maps and documents to identify physical and cultural features of neighborhoods, cities, states, and countries and to explain the historical migration of people, expansion and disintegration of empires, and the growth of economic systems.

**REP4** Students assess the credibility of primary and secondary sources and draw sound conclusions from them.

**Taking Notes**

Use your chart to take notes about New Mexico, Oregon, and Utah.

| | Types of people who traveled there |
|---|---|
| New Mexico | |
| Utah | |
| Oregon | |
| Texas | |
| California | |

One businessman, William Henry Ashley, created a trading arrangement called the rendezvous system. Under this system, individual trappers came to a pre-arranged site for a rendezvous with traders from the east. The trappers bought supplies from those traders and paid them in furs. The rendezvous took place every summer from 1825 to 1840. In that year, silk hats replaced beaver hats as the fashion, and the fur trade died out.

## Mountain Men Open the West

During the height of the fur trade, mountain men worked some streams so heavily that they killed off the animals. This forced the trappers to search for new streams where beaver lived. The mountain men's explorations provided Americans with some of the earliest firsthand knowledge of the Far West. This knowledge, and the trails the mountain men blazed, made it possible for later pioneers to move west.

For example, thousands of pioneers used South Pass, the wide valley through the Rockies that Jedediah Smith had publicized. Smith learned of this pass, in present-day Wyoming, from Native Americans. Unlike the high northern passes used by Lewis and Clark, South Pass was low, so snow did not block it as often as it blocked higher passes. Also, because South Pass was wide and less steep, wagon trails could run through it.

Smith wrote to his brother that he wanted to help people in need: "It is for this that I go for days without eating, and am pretty well satisfied if I can gather a few roots, a few snails, . . . a piece of horseflesh, or a fine roasted dog."

*Reading*History
**A. Reading a Map** Find South Pass on the map on page 395. Notice which two trails used that pass.

## The Lure of the West

Few of the people who went west shared Smith's noble motive. To many, the West with its vast stretches of land offered a golden chance to make money. The Louisiana Purchase had doubled the size of the United States, and some Americans wanted to take the land away from Native Americans who inhabited this territory.

People called **land speculators** bought huge areas of land. To speculate means to buy something in the hope that it will increase in value. If land value did go up, speculators divided their land holdings into smaller sections. They made great profits by selling those sections to the thousands of settlers who dreamed of owning their own farms.

Manufacturers and merchants soon followed the settlers west. They hoped to earn money by making and selling items that farmers needed. Other people made the trip to find jobs or to escape people to whom they owed money.

**Trails West, 1850**

Blackfoot

Nez Perce

Crow

OREGON TERRITORY

UNORGANIZED TERRITORY

CASCADE RANGE

Ft. Hall

Sublette Cutoff

South Pass

Cheyenne

Pawnee

Chimney Rock, Nebraska, was an important landmark on the Oregon Trail.

CALIFORNIA

Pomo

Sacramento

San Francisco

Salt Lake City

UTAH TERRITORY

ROCKY MOUNTAINS

Great Plains

Chimney Rock

IOWA

Mississippi R.

Council Bluffs

Nauvoo

ILLINOIS

St. Louis

Independence

MISSOURI

SIERRA NEVADA

Ute

PACIFIC OCEAN

N

Los Angeles

Navajo

NEW MEXICO TERRITORY

Santa Fe

Cimarron Cutoff

TEXAS

Cherokee
Creek
Seminole
Choctaw
Chickasaw

0    200 Miles
0    200 Kilometers

■ Oregon Trail
■ California Trail
  Santa Fe Trail
■ Old Spanish Trail
■ Mormon Trail
*Crow*  Native Americans
🏛 Fort

**GEOGRAPHY SKILLBUILDER Interpreting Maps**

1. **Place** *What is the length in miles of the Oregon Trail from Independence, Missouri, to Fort Vancouver?*
2. **Human-Environment Interaction** *Why do you think some of the trails ran along rivers?*

## The Trail to Santa Fe

Traders also traveled west in search of markets. After Mexico gained independence from Spain in 1821, it opened its borders to American traders, whom Spain had kept out. In response, the Missouri trader William Becknell set out with hardware, cloth, and china for Santa Fe, capital of the Mexican province of New Mexico. By doing so, he opened the **Santa Fe Trail,** which led from Missouri to Santa Fe. Once in Santa Fe, he made a large profit because the New Mexicans were eager for new merchandise.

When Becknell returned to Missouri weeks later, a curious crowd met him. One man picked up one of Becknell's bags and slit it open with a knife. As gold and silver coins spilled onto the street, the onlookers gasped. The news spread that New Mexico was a place where traders could become rich.

The following spring, Becknell headed to Santa Fe again. This time he loaded his trade goods into covered wagons, which Westerners called prairie schooners. Their billowing white canvas tops made them look like schooners, or sailing ships.

Becknell could not haul wagons over the mountain pass he had used on his first trip to Santa Fe. Instead, he found a cutoff, a shortcut that avoided steep slopes but passed through a deadly desert to the south. As his traders crossed the burning sands, they ran out of water. Crazed by

*Reading* **History**

**B. Making Inferences** What do you think other Missourians might decide to do after seeing Becknell's wealth?

thirst, they lopped off mules' ears and killed their dogs to drink the animals' blood. Finally, the men found a stream. The water saved them from death, and they reached Santa Fe.

Becknell returned home with another huge profit. Before long, hundreds of traders and prairie schooners braved the cutoff to make the 800-mile journey from Missouri to New Mexico each year.

## Oregon Fever

Hundreds of settlers also began migrating west on the **Oregon Trail,** which ran from Independence, Missouri, to the Oregon Territory. The first whites to cross the continent to Oregon were missionaries, such as Marcus and Narcissa Whitman in 1836. At that time, the United States and Britain were locked in an argument about which country owned Oregon. To the Whitmans' great disappointment, they made few converts among the Native Americans. However, their glowing reports of Oregon's rich land began to attract other American settlers.

Amazing stories spread about Oregon. The sun always shone there. Wheat grew as tall as a man. One tale claimed that pigs were "running about, . . . round and fat, and already cooked, with knives and forks sticking in them so you can cut off a slice whenever you are hungry."

Such stories tempted many people to make the 2,000-mile journey to Oregon. In 1843, nearly 1,000 people traveled from Missouri to Oregon. The next year, twice as many came. "The Oregon Fever has broken out," observed a Boston newspaper, "and is now raging."

## One Family Heads West

The experiences of the Sager family show how difficult the trail could be. In 1844, Henry Sager, his wife, and six children left Missouri to find cheap, fertile land in Oregon. They had already moved four times in the past four years. Henry's daughter Catherine explained her family's moves.

### A VOICE FROM THE PAST

Father was one of those restless men who are not content to remain in one place long at a time. . . . [He] had been talking of going to Texas. But mother, hearing much said about the healthfulness of Oregon, preferred to go there.

**Catherine Sager,** quoted in *The West,* by Geoffrey C. Ward

The Oregon Trail was dangerous, so pioneers joined wagon trains. They knew their survival would depend on cooperation. Before setting out, the wagon train members agreed on rules and elected leaders to enforce them.

Even so, life on the trail was full of hardship. The Sagers had barely begun the trip when Mrs. Sager gave birth to her seventh child. Two

**Vocabulary**
**converts:** people who accept a new religious belief

months later, nine-year-old Catherine fell under a moving wagon, which crushed her left leg. Later, "camp fever" killed both of the Sager parents.

Even though the Sager parents had died, the other families in the train cooperated to help the Sager orphans make it to Oregon. There, the Whitmans agreed to adopt them. When Narcissa met them, Catherine recalled, "We thought as we shyly looked at her that she was the prettiest woman we had ever seen."

*Reading* **History**

C. **Finding Main Ideas** What difficulties did families like the Sagers face?

## The Mormon Trail

While most pioneers went west in search of wealth, one group migrated for religious reasons. The **Mormons**, who settled Utah, were members of the Church of Jesus Christ of Latter-Day Saints. Joseph Smith had founded this church in upstate New York in 1830. The Mormons lived in close communities, worked hard, shared their goods, and prospered.

The Mormons, though, also made enemies. Some people reacted angrily to the Mormons' teachings. They saw the Mormon practice of polygamy—allowing a man to have more than one wife at a time—as immoral. Others objected to their holding property in common.

*Reading* **History**

D. **Analyzing Causes** Why did Brigham Young lead the Mormons to Utah?

In 1844, an anti-Mormon mob in Illinois killed Smith. **Brigham Young,** the next Mormon leader, moved his people out of the United States. His destination was Utah, then part of Mexico. In this desolate region, he hoped his people would be left to follow their faith in peace.

In 1847, about 1,600 Mormons followed part of the Oregon Trail to Utah. There they built a new settlement by the Great Salt Lake. Because Utah has little rainfall, the Mormons had to work together to build dams and canals. These structures captured water in the hills and carried it to the farms in the valleys below. Through teamwork, they made their desert homeland bloom.

In the meantime, changes were taking place in Texas. As you will read in Section 2, Americans had been moving into that Mexican territory, too.

Section **1** Assessment

### 1. Terms & Names

**Explain the significance of:**
- Jedediah Smith
- mountain man
- Jim Beckwourth
- land speculator
- Santa Fe Trail
- Oregon Trail
- Mormon
- Brigham Young

### 2. Using Graphics

Use a cluster diagram like the one shown to review details about the trails west.

Trails West

Which trail would you have wanted to travel? Why? (CST3)

### 3. Main Ideas

**a.** How did the mountain men open up the West for later settlement? (HI1)

**b.** What are two examples of pioneer groups who used cooperation to overcome hardship? (HI1)

**c.** What economic and social forces drew people to the West? (HI1)

### 4. Critical Thinking

**Drawing Conclusions** Of all the hardships faced by people who went west, what do you think was the worst? Explain. (REP3)

**THINK ABOUT**
- the mountain men
- William Becknell
- the Sagers
- the Mormons

**ACTIVITY OPTIONS**

**LANGUAGE ARTS**

**ART**

Research a pioneer from this section and either write a **letter** from his or her point of view to a friend or illustrate a **journal entry** with sights from your journey. (REP5)

# Survive the Oregon Trail!

You are part of a wagon train heading west on the Oregon Trail. During your journey, you will cross endless flat prairies and mountains that climb more steeply than a staircase. You will suffer through blazing heat and icy snowstorms. Food is scarce in the land you travel through—and human settlements are even more scarce.

**COOPERATIVE LEARNING** On this page are three challenges you will face on your journey. Working with a small group, create a solution for each challenge. To help your group work together, assign a task to each group member. You will find helpful information in the Data File. Be prepared to present your solutions to the class.

## SCIENCE CHALLENGE

### *"The most terrible mountains"*

One pioneer called the Rockies "the most terrible mountains for steepness." Your oxen have struggled for hours to pull your wagon up a steep slope. Now you have to go down the other side without crashing—and wagon wheels have no brakes. How will you slow your descent? Use the Data File for help. Present your ideas using one of these options:

• Write instructions for climbing and descending the mountain.

• Illustrate your solution in a how-to diagram.

## CIVICS CHALLENGE

### *"A thieving scoundrel"*

You wake one morning to the sound of shouting. One of the men in the wagon train has been caught stealing another family's ox—to replace an ox that died from drinking bad water. The wagon train leader asks you to help decide how to punish the thief. Present your decision using one of these options:

• As a group, role-play a discussion of what the punishment should be.

• Write an explanation of a punishment to the wagon train leader.

## HEALTH CHALLENGE

### *"A grand blow-out"*

On July 4, your wagon train stops near Independence Rock for "a grand blow-out" to celebrate your progress. Each family will bring a dish to the party. What will you cook that is tasty and nutritious? You might use supplies from your wagon and berries or animals from the area. Look at the Data File for help. Present your choice using one of these options:

- Draw a picture of your dish and describe it.
- Write an original recipe.

### The Journey

**Distance:** 2,000 miles

**Length:** 4–6 months

**Average daily distance:** 12–15 miles

**Best time to travel:** April–September

### The Wagon

**Size of box:** 4 x 10 feet

**Load:** 1,600–2,500 pounds

**Oxen needed per wagon:** 4–8

### Animals Taken

oxen, horses, dairy cows, cattle, chickens, mules, pigs, dogs, cats

### Food Supplies

flour, corn meal, salt, baking soda, sugar, crackers, dried beans, rice, dried fruit, bacon, coffee, vinegar

### Cooking Equipment

Dutch oven, large kettle, frying pan, bread pan, coffee grinder, rolling pin, tin cups and plates, water kegs, knives, spoons

### Other Equipment

bedding, spare wagon parts, tar, rope, chains, pulleys, tools, fishing poles, guns, ammunition, matches, soap, medicines

### Trail Hazards

**Worst discomforts:** heat, cold, wind, rain, dust, mud, mosquitoes, hunger, thirst

**Biggest killer:** disease

**Most common accidents:** shooting, drowning, crushing by wagon wheels, injuries from animals

For more about the Oregon Trail . . .

**RESEARCH LINKS**
CLASSZONE.COM

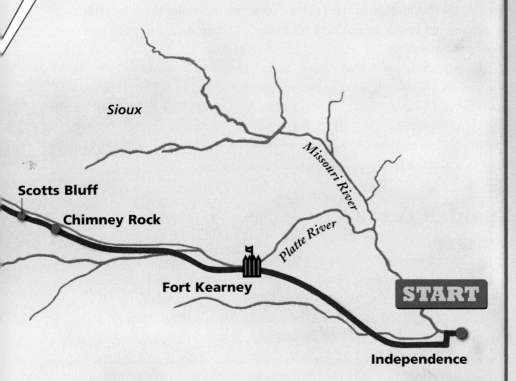

Sioux

Missouri River

Scotts Bluff

Chimney Rock

Platte River

Fort Kearney

**START**

Independence

## ACTIVITY WRAP-UP

**Present to the class** Using the model shown here, ask and answer questions about geographic patterns in the West. Choose the best questions to present to the class.

# The Texas Revolution

| MAIN IDEA | WHY IT MATTERS NOW | TERMS & NAMES |
|---|---|---|

**MAIN IDEA**

American and Tejano citizens led Texas to independence from Mexico.

**WHY IT MATTERS NOW**

The diverse culture of Texas has developed from the contributions of many different groups.

**TERMS & NAMES**

Stephen Austin

Tejano

Antonio López de Santa Anna

Sam Houston

William Travis

Juan Seguín

Battle of the Alamo

Lone Star Republic

## CALIFORNIA STANDARDS

**8.5.2** Know the changing boundaries of the United States and describe the relationships the country had with its neighbors (current Mexico and Canada) and Europe, including the influence of the Monroe Doctrine, and how those relationships influenced westward expansion and the Mexican-American War.

**8.8.5** Discuss Mexican settlements and their locations, cultural traditions, attitudes toward slavery, land-grant system, and economies.

**8.8.6** Describe the Texas War for Independence and the Mexican-American War, including territorial settlements, the aftermath of the wars, and the effects the wars had on the lives of Americans, including Mexican Americans today.

**CST1** Students explain how major events are related to one another in time.

**Taking Notes**

Use your chart to take notes about Texas.

| | Types of people who traveled there |
|---|---|
| New Mexico | |
| Utah | |
| Oregon | |
| Texas | |
| California | |

## ONE AMERICAN'S STORY

Son of a bankrupt Missouri mine owner, **Stephen Austin** read his mother's letter, written in 1821, in stunned silence. His father, Moses Austin, was dead. In his last moments, she told her son, "He called me to his bedside, . . . he begged me to tell you to take his place . . . to go on . . . in the same way he would have done."

Stephen knew what that meant. Moses Austin had spent the last years of his life chasing a crazy dream. He had hoped to found a colony for Americans in Spanish Texas. A week after his father's death, Stephen Austin was standing on Texas soil. His father's dream would become his destiny.

This section explains how Stephen Austin, along with others, worked hard to make the lands of Texas a good place to live.

## Spanish Texas

The Spanish land called *Tejas* (Tay•HAHS) bordered the United States territory called Louisiana. The land was rich and desirable. It had forests in the east, rich soil for growing corn and cotton, and great grassy plains for grazing animals. It also had rivers leading to natural ports on the Gulf of Mexico. It was home to Plains and Pueblo Native Americans. Even though *Tejas* was a state in the Spanish colony of New Spain, it had few Spanish settlers. The Spanish mission system you learned about in Chapter 2 was still common. Missions raised crops and livestock, traded with other missions, and were largely self-sufficient. Around 1819, Spanish soldiers drove off Americans trying to claim those lands as a part of the Louisiana Purchase.

In 1821, only about 4,000 *Tejanos* (Tay•HAH•nohs) lived in Texas. *Tejanos* are people of Spanish heritage who consider Texas their home. The Comanche, Apache, and other tribes fought fiercely against Spanish settlement of Texas. Also, the mission system began to decline. The Spanish officials wanted many more settlers to move to Texas. They hoped that new colonists would help to defend against Native Americans and Americans who illegally sneaked into Texas.

Vocabulary
*empresarios:*
individuals who
agreed to recruit
settlers for the
land

To attract more people to Texas, the Spanish government offered huge tracts of land to *empresarios*. But they were unable to attract Spanish settlers. So, when Moses Austin asked for permission to start a colony in Texas, Spain agreed. Austin was promised a large section of land. He had to agree that settlers on his land had to follow Spanish laws.

TEXAS!!

Emigrants who are desirous of assisting Texas at this important crisis of her affairs may have a free passage and equipments, by applying at the
NEW-YORK and PHILADELPHIA HOTEL,
On the Old Levee, near the Blue Stores.

Now is the time to ensure a fortune in Land:
To all who remain in Texas during the War will be allowed 1280 Acres.
To all who remain Six Months, 640 Acres.
To all who remain Three Months, 320 Acres.
And as Colonists, 4600 Acres for a family and 1470 Acres for a Single Man.
New Orleans, April 23d, 1836.

## Mexican Independence Changes Texas

Shortly after Stephen Austin arrived in Texas in 1821, Mexico successfully gained its independence from Spain. *Tejas* was now a part of Mexico. With the change in government, the Spanish land grant given to Austin's father was worthless. Stephen Austin traveled to Mexico City to persuade the new Mexican government to let him start his colony. It took him almost a year to get permission. And the Mexican government would consent only if the new settlers agreed to become Mexican citizens and members of the Roman Catholic Church.

Between 1821 and 1827, Austin attracted 297 families to his new settlement. These original Texas settler families are known as the "Old Three Hundred." He demanded evidence that each family head was moral, worked hard, and did not drink. So law-abiding were his colonists that Austin could write to a new settler, "You will be astonished to see all our houses with no other fastening than a wooden pin or door latch."

The success of Austin's colony attracted more land speculators and settlers to Texas from the United States. Some were looking for a new life, some were escaping from the law, and others were looking for a chance to grow rich. By 1830, the population had swelled to about 30,000, with Americans outnumbering the *Tejanos* six to one.

Posters such as the one above encouraged Americans from the East to settle in Texas. Some people scrawled G.T.T. on their doors to indicate they had "gone to Texas."

## Rising Tensions in Texas

As more and more Americans settled in Texas, tensions between them and the *Tejanos* increased. Used to governing themselves, Americans resented following Mexican laws. Since few Americans spoke Spanish, they were unhappy that all official documents had to be in that language. Slave owners were especially upset when Mexico outlawed slavery in 1829. They wanted to maintain slavery so they could grow cotton. Austin persuaded the government to allow slave owners to keep their slaves.

On the other hand, the *Tejanos* found the Americans difficult to live with, too. *Tejanos* thought that the Americans believed they were superior and deserved special privileges. The Americans seemed unwilling to adapt to Mexican laws, and few converted to Catholicism.

*Reading* **History**
A. Analyzing
Causes Why was
there growing
tension between
Americans and
*Tejanos?*

The Mexican government sent an official to Texas to investigate the tensions. He was not happy with what he found. In 1829, he reported to his government, "I am warning you to take timely measures . . . Texas could throw this whole nation into revolution." His advice turned out to be right.

Responding to the warnings, the Mexican government cracked down on Texas. First, it closed the state to further American immigration. Next, it required Texans to pay taxes for the first time. Finally, to enforce these new laws, the government sent more Mexican troops to Texas.

*Reading*History

**B. Summarizing**
What three actions did the Mexican government take to control Texas?

## Texans Revolt Against Mexico

These actions caused angry protests. Some Texans even talked of breaking away from Mexico. Most, however, listened to Austin, who remained loyal to Mexico. In 1833, Austin set off for Mexico City with a petition. This document listed reforms supported by both Americans and *Tejanos*. The most important request was that Texas become a self-governing state within Mexico.

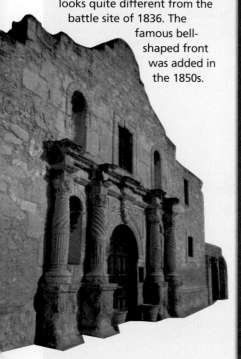

### America's HERITAGE

**REMEMBER THE ALAMO!**
Today the Alamo, shown below, is again under siege. Moisture seeps into the limestone walls and causes them to crumble. Many people view the mission as a memorial to Americans' willingness to fight for freedom, so a Texas group has begun attempts to preserve the Alamo from further damage. The Alamo looks quite different from the battle site of 1836. The famous bell-shaped front was added in the 1850s.

In Mexico City, Austin met General **Antonio López de Santa Anna,** the Mexican president. At first, the general agreed to most of the reforms in Austin's petition. But then Santa Anna learned of a letter Austin had written. The letter said that if the changes weren't approved Austin would support breaking away from Mexican rule. This was rebellion! The general had Austin jailed for an entire year. The Texans were furious and ready to rebel.

Santa Anna's answer to talk of rebellion was to send more troops to Texas. In late September 1835, Mexican soldiers marched to the town of Gonzales. They had orders to seize a cannon used by the Texans for protection against Native Americans. Texas volunteers had hung a flag on the big gun that said, "Come and Take It."

The Mexican troops failed to capture the cannon. Two months later, Texans drove Mexican troops out of an old mission in San Antonio that was used as a fortress. It was called the Alamo. Among the Texas volunteers were free African Americans such as Hendrick Arnold and Greenbury Logan. Angered by these insults, Santa Anna and 6,000 troops headed for Texas.

*Reading*History

**C. Analyzing Causes** What Texan actions moved Santa Anna to head toward Texas?

## The Fight for the Alamo

On March 1–2, 1836, Texans met at a settlement called Washington-on-the-Brazos to decide what to do about Santa Anna's troops. They believed they could do only one thing: to declare Texas a free and independent republic. **Sam Houston,** the only man at the meeting with military experience, was placed in command of the Texas army.

The Texas army hardly existed. At that moment, there were two small forces ready to stand up to Santa Anna's army. One was a company of 420 men, led by James Fannin, stationed at Goliad, a fort in southeast Texas. The second was a company of 183 volunteers at the Alamo. Headed by **William Travis,** this small force included such famous frontiersmen as Davy Crockett and Jim Bowie. In addition, **Juan Seguín** (wahn seh•GEEN) led a band of 25 *Tejanos* in support of revolt.

On February 23, 1836, Santa Anna's troops surrounded San Antonio. The next day, Mexicans began their siege of the Alamo. Two nights later, Travis scrawled a message to the world.

*Reading* **History**

**D. Making Inferences** Why would William Travis address his message to all Americans?

> **A VOICE FROM THE PAST**
>
> The enemy has demanded a surrender. . . . I have answered the demand with a cannon shot, and our flag still waves proudly from the walls. I shall never surrender or retreat.
>
> **William Travis,** "To the People of Texas and all the Americans in the World"

Because Juan Seguín spoke Spanish, he was chosen to carry the plea through enemy lines. Seguín got the message through to other Texas defenders. But when he returned, he saw the Alamo in flames.

The Alamo's defenders held off the Mexican attack for 12 violent days. Travis and the defenders stubbornly refused to surrender. On the 13th day, Santa Anna ordered more than 1,800 men to storm the fortress. The Texans met the attackers with a hailstorm of cannon and gun fire. Then suddenly it became strangely quiet. The Texans had run out of ammunition. At day's end, all but five Texans were dead. The **Battle of the Alamo** was over.

## HISTORY through ART

The Battle of the Alamo was so intense that Davy Crockett did not have time to reload his gun, which he called "Betsy." He used it as a club. This print is by a 20th-century illustrator, Frederick Yohn.

**What does the print reveal about the battle?**

**JUAN SEGUÍN**
**1806–1890**

Juan Seguín was a *Tejano* hero of the Texas Revolution. It was Seguín who dashed through enemy lines at the Alamo with a last desperate attempt for aid.

And after the war, it was Seguín who arranged for the remains of the Alamo defenders to be buried with full military honors.

Newcomers to Texas who disliked all *Tejanos* falsely accused Seguín of planning rebellion. Fearing for his life, he fled to Mexico in 1842, there "to seek a refuge amongst my enemies."

**SAM HOUSTON**
**1793–1863**

Raised by a widowed mother, Sam Houston grew up in Tennessee. He lived with the Cherokee for about three years. Later, he served in the U.S. Army, in Congress, and as the governor of Tennessee.

"I was a General without an army," wrote Houston, after taking command of the Texas forces in 1836. Yet by the time the war was over, he and his troops had defeated Santa Anna's larger army.

Houston was elected the first president of the Republic of Texas. When Texas became a state, he served as a U.S. senator.

**In what ways did the experiences of Seguín and Houston differ?**

Those men who had not died in the fighting were executed at Santa Anna's command. A total of 183 Alamo defenders died. A few women and children were not killed. Susanna Dickinson, one of the survivors, was ordered by Santa Anna to tell the story of the Alamo to other Texans. He hoped the story would discourage more rebellion. The slaughter at the Alamo shocked Texans—and showed them how hard they would have to fight for their freedom from Mexico.

## Victory at San Jacinto

With Santa Anna on the attack, Texans—both soldiers and settlers—fled eastward. Houston sent a message to the men at Goliad, ordering them to retreat. They were captured by Mexican forces, who executed more than 300. The Texans would not soon forget the massacre at Goliad. But even in retreat and defeat, Houston's army doubled. Now it was a fighting force of 800 angry men. It included *Tejanos*, American settlers, volunteers from the United States, and many free and enslaved African Americans.

In late April, Santa Anna caught up with Houston near the San Jacinto (san juh•SIN•toh) River. Late in the afternoon of April 21, 1836, the Texans advanced on the Mexican army "with the stillness of death." When close to Santa Anna's camp, they raced forward, rifles ready, screaming "Remember the Alamo!" "Remember Goliad!"

In just 18 minutes, the Texans killed more than half of the Mexican army. Santa Anna was forced to sign a treaty giving Texas its freedom. With the Battle of San Jacinto, Texas was now independent.

*Reading* **History**
**E. Reading a Map**
Use the map on page 405 to see where battles were taking place.

## Lone Star Republic

In September 1836, Texans raised a flag with a single star. They adopted a nickname—**Lone Star Republic**—and proclaimed Texas an independent nation. The new nation set up its own army and navy. Sam Houston was elected president of the Lone Star Republic by a landslide.

Many Texans did not want Texas to remain independent for long. They considered themselves Americans and wanted to be a part of the United States. In 1836, the Texas government asked Congress to annex Texas to the Union.

**Vocabulary**
**annex:** to join territory to an existing country

Many Northerners objected. They argued that Texas would become a slave state, and they opposed any expansion of slavery. If Texas joined the Union, slave states would outnumber free states and have a voting advantage in Congress. Other people feared that annexing Texas would lead to war with Mexico.

*Reading* **History**
**F. Analyzing Causes** Why didn't Congress annex Texas?

In response, Congress voted against annexation. Texas remained an independent republic for almost ten years. In the next section, you will learn that the question of annexing Texas did lead to a war between the United States and Mexico.

**UNITED STATES**
**The Texas Revolution,** *1836*

Boundary Claimed by Mexico

Brazos River
Trinity River
Sabine River

**REPUBLIC OF TEXAS**

Colorado River

Land disputed by Texas and Mexico
Washington-on-the-Brazos
San Jacinto, Apr. 21, 1836

Nueces River
San Antonio, Dec. 10, 1835
Gonzales, Oct. 2, 1835
Houston
Galveston
Santa Anna
Alamo, Mar. 6, 1836
Urrea
Brazoria
Goliad, Mar. 20, 1836
Matagorda
Rio Grande
Refugio, Mar. 14, 1836
*Gulf of Mexico*

**MEXICO**
N
Santa Anna
Boundary Claimed by Texas
Urrea

0   100 Miles
0   200 Kilometers

→ Texan forces
→ Mexican forces
✦ Texan victory
✸ Mexican victory
— Modern Texas border

30°N
25°N
100°W
96°W

**GEOGRAPHY SKILLBUILDER Interpreting Maps**
1. **Movement** *About how many total miles did Santa Anna travel from Mexico to San Jacinto?*
2. **Movement** *Look at the distances traveled by Mexican forces and those traveled by the Texans. Which side do you think had an advantage? Explain.*

---

**Section 2 Assessment**

### 1. Terms & Names

**Explain the significance of:**
- Stephen Austin
- *Tejano*
- Antonio López de Santa Anna
- Sam Houston
- William Travis
- Juan Seguín
- Battle of the Alamo
- Lone Star Republic

### 2. Using Graphics

Use a diagram like the one shown to review events that led to Texan independence and put them in order. (CST2)

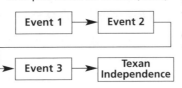

Event 1 → Event 2
Event 3 → Texan Independence

### 3. Main Ideas

**a.** Why did Americans want to move to Texas? (HI2)

**b.** How did the Mexican government respond to the Texas rebellion? (HI2)

**c.** Why did Congress refuse to annex Texas? (HI2)

### 4. Critical Thinking

**Recognizing Effects** How did losing the Battle of the Alamo help the Texans win their independence? (CST1)

**THINK ABOUT**
- the Texans' and Americans' shock over the loss of the battle to the Mexicans
- the need to recruit more forces to fight with the Texas army

**ACTIVITY OPTIONS**

**ART**
**TECHNOLOGY**

Research a figure from the Texas Revolution. Create a **trading card** or design that person's **Web page** for the Internet. (HI1)

# The War with Mexico

**3**

| MAIN IDEA | WHY IT MATTERS NOW | TERMS & NAMES |
|---|---|---|
| The United States expanded its territory westward to stretch from the Atlantic to the Pacific coast. | Today, one-third of all Americans live in the areas added to the United States in 1848. | James K. Polk<br>manifest destiny<br>Zachary Taylor<br>Bear Flag Revolt<br>Winfield Scott<br>Treaty of Guadalupe Hidalgo<br>Mexican Cession |

**CALIFORNIA STANDARDS**

**8.5.2** Know the changing boundaries of the United States and describe the relationships the country had with its neighbors (current Mexico and Canada) and Europe, including the influence of the Monroe Doctrine, and how those relationships influenced westward expansion and the Mexican-American War.

**8.8.2** Describe the purpose, challenges, and economic incentives associated with westward expansion, including the concept of Manifest Destiny (e.g., the Lewis and Clark expedition, accounts of the removal of Indians, the Cherokees' "Trail of Tears," settlement of the Great Plains) and the territorial acquisitions that spanned numerous decades.

**8.8.6** Describe the Texas War for Independence and the Mexican-American War, including territorial settlements, the aftermath of the wars, and the effects the wars had on the lives of Americans, including Mexican Americans today.

**Taking Notes**

Use your chart to take notes about Oregon, New Mexico, and California.

| | Types of people who traveled there |
|---|---|
| New Mexico | |
| Utah | |
| Oregon | |
| Texas | |
| California | |

## ONE AMERICAN'S STORY

Henry Clay sneered, "Who is **James K. Polk**?" Clay had just learned the name of the man nominated by Democrats to run against him for president in 1844. "A mistake!" answered Washington insiders.

News of Polk's nomination was flashed to the capital by the newly invented telegraph machine. People were convinced that the machine didn't work. How could the Democrats choose Polk? A joke!

Polk was America's first "dark horse," a candidate who received unexpected support. The Democrats had nominated this little-known man only when they could not agree on anyone else.

James Polk

Still, Polk wasn't a complete nobody. He had been governor of Tennessee and served seven terms in Congress. Polk was committed to national expansion. He vowed to annex Texas and take over Oregon.

When the votes were counted, James Knox Polk became the 11th president of the United States. As you will read in this section, after his election Polk looked for ways to expand the nation.

## Americans Support Manifest Destiny

The abundance of land in the West seemed to hold great promise for Americans. Although populated with Native Americans and Mexicans, those lands were viewed by white settlers as unoccupied. Many Americans wanted to settle those lands themselves, and they worried about competition from other nations. Mexico occupied the southwest lands, and Britain shared the northwest Oregon Territory with the United States. Many Americans believed that the United States was destined to stretch across the continent from the Atlantic Ocean to the Pacific Ocean. In 1845, a newspaper editor named John O'Sullivan gave a name to that belief.

> **A VOICE FROM THE PAST**
>
> Our manifest destiny [is] to overspread and possess the whole of the continent which Providence [God] has given us for the development of the great experiment of liberty and . . . self-government.
>
> **John O'Sullivan,** *United States Magazine and Democratic Review*

*Reading*History

**A. Drawing Conclusions**
What were the positives and negatives of the idea of manifest destiny?

John O'Sullivan used the word *manifest* to mean clear or obvious. The word *destiny* means events sure to happen. Therefore, **manifest destiny** suggested that expansion was not only good but bound to happen—even if it meant pushing Mexicans and Native Americans out of the way. After Polk's election in 1844, manifest destiny became government policy.

The term "manifest destiny" was new, but the idea was not. By the 1840s, thousands of Americans had moved into the Oregon Territory. Since 1818, Oregon had been occupied jointly by the United States and Britain. In his campaign, Polk had talked of taking over all of Oregon. "Fifty-four forty or fight!" screamed one of his slogans. The parallel of 54° 40' N latitude was the northern boundary of the shared Oregon Territory.

Rather than fight for all of Oregon, however, Polk settled for half. In 1846, the United States and Great Britain agreed to divide Oregon at the 49th parallel. This agreement extended the boundary line already drawn between Canada and the United States. Today this line still serves as the border between much of the United States and Canada.

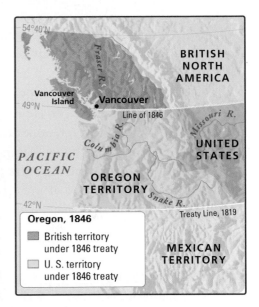

*"Our manifest destiny [is] to . . . possess the whole of the continent."*
John O'Sullivan

## Troubles with Mexico

Polk had good reason for avoiding war with Britain over Oregon. By 1846, he had much bigger troubles brewing with Mexico over Texas.

In 1845, Congress admitted Texas as a slave state, in spite of Northern objections to the spread of slavery. However, Mexico still claimed Texas as its own. Mexico angrily viewed this annexation as an act of war. To make matters worse, Texas and Mexico could not agree on the official border between them. Texas claimed the Rio Grande, a river south of San Antonio, as its southern boundary. Mexico insisted on the Nueces (noo•AY•sis) River as the border of Texas. The difference in the distance between the two rivers was more than 100 miles at some points. Many thousands of miles of territory were at stake.

*Reading*History

**B. Reading a Map**
Use the map on page 408 to find the locations of the disputed border between Texas and Mexico.

Mexico said it would fight to defend its claim. Hoping to settle the dispute peacefully, Polk sent John Slidell, a Spanish-speaking ambassador, to offer Mexico $25 million for Texas, California, and New Mexico. But Slidell's diplomacy failed.

Believing that the American people supported his expansion plans, Polk wanted to force the issue with Mexico. He purposely ordered General **Zachary Taylor** to station troops on the northern bank of the Rio Grande. This river bank was part of the disputed territory. Viewing this as an act of war, Mexico moved an army into place on the southern bank. On April 25, 1846, a Mexican cavalry unit crossed the Rio Grande. They ambushed an American patrol and killed or wounded 16 American soldiers.

When news of the attack reached Washington, Polk sent a rousing war message to Congress, saying, "Mexico has invaded our territory and shed American blood upon American soil." Two days later, Congress declared war. The War with Mexico had begun. Thousands of volunteers, mostly from western states, rushed to enlist in the army. Santa Anna, who was president of Mexico, built up the Mexican army.

However, Americans had mixed reactions to Polk's call for war. Illinois representative Abraham Lincoln questioned the truthfulness of the president's message and the need to declare war. Northeasterners questioned the justice of men dying in such a war. Slavery became an issue in the debates over the war. Southerners saw expansion into Texas as an opportunity to extend slavery and to increase their power in Congress. To

*Reading*History
C. Analyzing Causes How did the War with Mexico start?

**The War with Mexico, 1846–1847**

A symbol of the Bear Flag Revolt, this flag has a grizzly bear and a star made with blackberry juice. The revolt declared California independent from Mexico.

CALIFORNIA REPUBLIC

OREGON TERRITORY

UNORGANIZED TERRITORY

UNITED STATES

Sonoma • Bear Flag Revolt
• San Francisco
• Monterey (seized, July 7, 1846)
Santa Barbara
Los Angeles, Jan. 8–10, 1847
San Diego, Dec. 6, 1846
Kearny

Ft. Leavenworth
Bent's Fort
Santa Fe

Fort
→ U.S. forces
➡ Mexican forces
✶ U.S. victory
✹ Mexican victory
— Modern Texas border

PACIFIC OCEAN

DISPUTED TERRITORY

TEXAS

New Orleans

San Antonio
Corpus Christi
Taylor
MEXICO
Saltillo
Buena Vista, Feb. 22–23, 1847
Monterrey, Sept. 21–24, 1846
Matamoros
Gulf of Mexico

Tropic of Cancer

• Mazatlán
Tampico
Veracruz, Mar. 9–27, 1847
Mexico City, Sept. 13–14, 1847
Santa Anna
Scott

**GEOGRAPHY SKILLBUILDER Interpreting Maps**
1. **Movement** *About how far did General Kearny's troops move to reach San Diego?*
2. **Location** *Why would defending Texas be much easier than defending Mexico?*

prevent this from happening, antislavery representatives introduced a bill to prohibit slavery in any lands taken from Mexico. Frederick Douglass, the abolitionist, summarized the arguments.

### A VOICE FROM THE PAST

The determination of our slaveholding President to prosecute the war, and the probability of his success in wringing from the people men and money to carry it on, is made evident, . . . None seem willing to take their stand for peace at all risks; and all seem willing that the war should be carried on in some form or other.

**Frederick Douglass** in *The North Star,* January 21, 1848

Despite opposition, the United States plunged into war. In May 1846, General Taylor led troops into Mexico. Many Americans thought it would be easy to defeat the Mexicans, and the war would end quickly.

## Capturing New Mexico and California

Not long after the war began, General Stephen Kearny (KAHR•nee)— a U.S. Army officer—and his men left Fort Leavenworth, Kansas, with orders to occupy New Mexico. Then they were to continue west to California. As his troops marched along the Santa Fe Trail, they sang songs like this one.

*Reading* **History**

**D. Making Inferences**
How does this song support the idea of manifest destiny?

### A VOICE FROM THE PAST

Old Colonel Kearny, you can bet,
Will keep the boys in motion,
Till Yankee Land includes the sand
On the Pacific Ocean.

Six weeks and 650 hot and rugged miles later, Kearny's army entered New Mexico. Using persuasion instead of force, he convinced the Mexican troops that he meant to withdraw. This allowed him to take New Mexico without firing a shot. Then Kearny and a small force of soldiers marched on toward California, which had only 8,000 to 12,000 Mexican residents. The remaining force moved south toward Mexico.

In California, Americans led by the explorer John C. Frémont rebelled against Mexican rule in the **Bear Flag Revolt**. They arrested the Mexican commander of Northern California and raised a crude flag showing a grizzly bear sketched in blackberry juice. The rebels declared California independent of Mexico and named it the Republic of California. In the fall, U.S. troops reached California and joined forces with the rebels. Within weeks, Americans controlled all of California.

## The Invasion of Mexico

The defeat of Mexico proved far more difficult. The Mexican army was much larger, but the U.S. troops

## STRANGE *but* True

**SANTA ANNA'S LOST LEG**
Santa Anna lost his left leg in a battle with the French. In 1842, he held a funeral for his severed limb. On that day, church and political officials followed the dictator's leg through the streets of Mexico City to its final resting place—an urn placed on a column.

Two years later, an angry mob broke the urn and threw the leg away. The leg was rescued by a loyal soldier who took it home and hid it.

Thirty years later, that soldier visited Santa Anna and returned the bones of his long-lost leg.

were led by well-trained officers. American forces invaded Mexico from two directions.

General Taylor battled his way south from Texas toward the city of Monterrey in northern Mexico. On February 22, 1847, his 4,800 troops met General Santa Anna's 15,000 Mexican soldiers near a ranch called Buena Vista. After the first day of fighting, Santa Anna sent Taylor a note offering him a chance to surrender. Taylor declined. At the end of the second bloody day of fighting, Santa Anna reported that "both armies have been cut to pieces." However, it was Santa Anna who retreated after the Battle of Buena Vista. The war in the north of Mexico was over.

In southern Mexico, fighting continued. A second force led by General **Winfield Scott** landed at Veracruz on the Gulf of Mexico and battled inland toward Mexico City. Outside the capital, Scott met fierce resistance at the castle of Chapultepec (chuh•POOL•tuh•pek). About 1,000 soldiers and 100 young military cadets bravely defended the fortress. Despite their determined resistance, Mexico City fell to Scott in September 1847. As he watched, a Mexican officer sighed and said, "God is a Yankee."

**Background**
General Winfield Scott had become a national hero during the War of 1812.

## The Mexican Cession

On February 2, 1848, the war officially ended with the **Treaty of Guadalupe Hidalgo** (gwah•duh•LOOP•ay hih•DAHL•go). In this treaty, Mexico recognized that Texas was part of the United States, and the Rio Grande was the border between the nations. Mexico also ceded, or gave up, a vast region

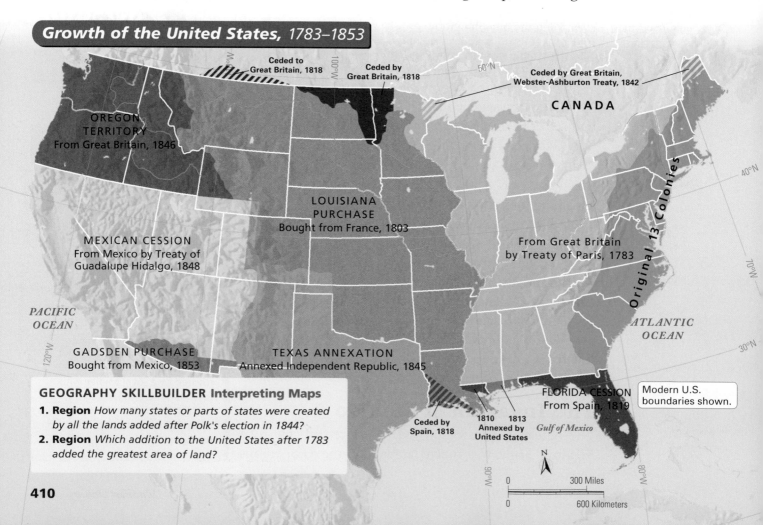

### Growth of the United States, *1783–1853*

Ceded to Great Britain, 1818

Ceded by Great Britain, 1818

Ceded by Great Britain, Webster-Ashburton Treaty, 1842

CANADA

**OREGON TERRITORY**
From Great Britain, 1846

**LOUISIANA PURCHASE**
Bought from France, 1803

Original 13 Colonies

**MEXICAN CESSION**
From Mexico by Treaty of Guadalupe Hidalgo, 1848

From Great Britain by Treaty of Paris, 1783

*PACIFIC OCEAN*

*ATLANTIC OCEAN*

**GADSDEN PURCHASE**
Bought from Mexico, 1853

**TEXAS ANNEXATION**
Annexed Independent Republic, 1845

**FLORIDA CESSION**
From Spain, 1819

Modern U.S. boundaries shown.

Ceded by Spain, 1818

1810  1813
Annexed by United States

*Gulf of Mexico*

N

0        300 Miles

0        600 Kilometers

**GEOGRAPHY SKILLBUILDER Interpreting Maps**

1. **Region** How many states or parts of states were created by all the lands added after Polk's election in 1844?
2. **Region** Which addition to the United States after 1783 added the greatest area of land?

*Reading* **History**

**E. Finding Main Ideas** What were the three main parts of the Treaty of Guadalupe Hidalgo?

known as the **Mexican Cession.** (See the map on page 410.) Together with Texas, this land amounted to almost one-half of Mexico. The loss was a bitter defeat for Mexico, particularly because many Mexicans felt that the United States had provoked the war in the hope of gaining Mexican territory.

In return, the United States agreed to pay Mexico $15 million. The United States would also pay the $3.25 million of claims U.S. citizens had against Mexico. Finally, it also promised to protect the approximately 80,000 Mexicans living in Texas and the Mexican Cession.

Mexicans living in the United States saw the conquest of their land differently. Suddenly they were a minority in a nation with a strange language, culture, and legal system. At the same time, they would make important contributions to their new country. A rich new culture resulted from the blend of many cultures in the Mexican Cession.

## "From Sea to Shining Sea"

*Reading* **History**

**F. Making Inferences** Why did the United States pay a large price for the Gadsden Purchase?

The last bit of territory added to the continental United States was a strip of land across what is now southern New Mexico and Arizona. The government wanted the land as a location for a southern transcontinental railroad. In 1853, Mexico sold the land—called the Gadsden Purchase—to the United States for $10 million.

On July 4, 1848, in Washington, President Polk laid the cornerstone of a monument to honor George Washington. In Washington's day, the western border of the United States was the Mississippi River. The United States in 1848 now stretched "from sea to shining sea." In August, Polk learned that gold had been found in California. Next, you will read about the California gold rush.

### Now and then

**MEXICAN LAND RIGHTS**

The treaty of Guadalupe Hidalgo was intended to preserve Mexican land rights in areas that Mexico ceded to the United States, but common land grants, or land given to a community, remained in dispute. In 1891 the U.S. Government established a special court to decide land grant claims. The court's rulings left many Mexican Americans on small farms landless. In addition, many Mexican Americans lost their land in shady business deals.

Some of their descendents continue to dispute the claims, and have had some court victories in recent years. In 2000, a family in Texas was awarded oil royalties from land it lost in 1938. In 2002 the heirs to a land grant in Colorado won a 21-year court case allowing grazing and timber rights on a 77,000-acre ranch.

---

## Section 3 Assessment

### 1. Terms & Names

**Explain the significance of:**
- James K. Polk
- manifest destiny
- Zachary Taylor
- Bear Flag Revolt
- Winfield Scott
- Treaty of Guadalupe Hidalgo
- Mexican Cession

### 2. Using Graphics

Review the chapter and find five key events to place on a time line as shown. (CST2)

**War with Mexico**

1846 ———————————— 1848

### 3. Main Ideas

**a.** How did the acquisitions of Oregon and the Mexican Cession relate to the idea of manifest destiny? (HI3)

**b.** Why were some people opposed to the War with Mexico? (HI3)

**c.** What does the phrase "sea to shining sea" mean? (HI3)

### 4. Critical Thinking

**Comparing** Compare the different ways land was acquired by the United States in the period of manifest destiny from 1844 to 1853. (HI1)

**THINK ABOUT**
- the acquisition of the Oregon Territory
- lands in the Southwest

---

**ACTIVITY OPTIONS**

**MATH**

**GEOGRAPHY**

In an almanac, find the current population of the states formed from the Mexican Cession. Create a **graph** or a **map** to display the information. (CST3)

# The California Gold Rush

| MAIN IDEA | WHY IT MATTERS NOW | TERMS & NAMES |
|---|---|---|
| Gold was found in California, and thousands rushed to that territory. California quickly became a state. | The gold rush made California grow rapidly and helped bring about California's cultural diversity. | forty-niner<br>*Californio*<br>Mariano Vallejo<br><br>John Sutter<br>James Marshall<br>California gold rush |

**CALIFORNIA STANDARDS**

**8.8.2** Describe the purpose, challenges, and economic incentives associated with westward expansion, including the concept of Manifest Destiny (e.g., the Lewis and Clark expedition, accounts of the removal of Indians, the Cherokees' "Trail of Tears," settlement of the Great Plains) and the territorial acquisitions that spanned numerous decades.

**8.8.3** Describe the role of pioneer women and the new status that western women achieved (e.g., Laura Ingalls Wilder, Annie Bidwell; slave women gaining freedom in the West; Wyoming granting suffrage to women in 1869).

**REP4** Students assess the credibility of primary and secondary sources and draw sound conclusions from them.

**HI2** Students understand and distinguish cause, effect, sequence, and correlation in historical events, including the long- and short-term causal relations.

## ONE AMERICAN'S STORY

Luzena Wilson said of the year 1849, "The gold excitement spread like wildfire." The year before, James Marshall had discovered gold in California. Luzena's husband decided to become a **forty-niner**—someone who went to California to find gold, starting in 1849.

Most forty-niners left their families behind, but Luzena traveled to California with her husband. She soon discovered that women—and their homemaking skills—were rare in California. Shortly after she arrived, a miner offered her five dollars for the biscuits she was baking. Shocked, she just stared at him. He quickly doubled his offer and paid in gold. Luzena realized she could make money by feeding miners, so she opened a hotel.

In this section, you will read about the forty-niners like the Wilsons and what their mining experiences were like. You will also discover how the gold rush boosted California's economy and changed the nation's history.

This woman is carrying food to miners, just as Luzena Wilson did.

**Taking Notes**

Use your chart to take notes about California.

| | Types of people who traveled there |
|---|---|
| New Mexico | |
| Utah | |
| Oregon | |
| Texas | |
| California | |

## California Before the Rush

Before the forty-niners came, California was populated by as many as 150,000 Native Americans and 8,000 to 12,000 *Californios*—settlers of Spanish or Mexican descent. Most *Californios* lived on huge cattle ranches. They had acquired their estates when the Mexican government took away the land that once belonged to the California missions.

One important *Californio* was **Mariano Vallejo** (mah•RYAH•noh vah•YEH•hoh). A member of one of the oldest Spanish families in America, he owned 250,000 acres of land. Proudly describing the accomplishments of the *Californios*, Vallejo wrote, "We were the pioneers of the Pacific coast . . . while General Washington was carrying on the war of the Revolution." Vallejo himself had been the commander of Northern California when it belonged to Mexico.

**Vocabulary**
immigration:
the movement
of people into a
country or region
where they were
not born

When Mexico owned California, its government feared American immigration and rarely gave land to foreigners. But **John Sutter,** a Swiss immigrant, was one exception. Dressed in a secondhand French army uniform, Sutter had visited the Mexican governor in 1839. A charming man, Sutter persuaded the governor to grant him 50,000 acres in the unsettled Sacramento Valley. Sutter built a fort on his land and dreamed of creating his own personal empire based on agriculture.

In 1848, Sutter sent a carpenter named **James Marshall** to build a sawmill on the nearby American River. One day Marshall inspected the canal that brought water to Sutter's Mill. He later said, "My eye was caught by a glimpse of something shining. . . . I reached my hand down and picked it up; it made my heart thump for I felt certain it was gold."

## Rush for Gold

News of Marshall's thrilling discovery spread rapidly. From all over California, people raced to the American River—starting the **California gold rush.** A gold rush occurs when large numbers of people move to a site where gold has been found. Throughout history, people have valued gold because it is scarce, beautiful, easy to shape, and resistant to tarnish.

Miners soon found gold in other streams flowing out of the Sierra Nevada Mountains. Colonel R. B. Mason, the military governor of California, estimated that the region held enough gold to "pay the cost of the present war with Mexico a hundred times over." He sent this news to Washington with a box of gold dust as proof.

The following year thousands of gold seekers set out to make their fortunes. A forty-niner who wished to reach California from the East had a choice of three routes, all of them dangerous:

1. Sail 18,000 miles around South America and up the Pacific coast—suffering from storms, seasickness, and spoiled food.
2. Sail to the narrow Isthmus of Panama, cross overland (and risk catching a deadly tropical disease), and then sail to California.
3. Travel the trails across North America—braving rivers, prairies, mountains, and all the hardships of the trail.

*Reading***History**
**A. Categorizing**
What were the three different types of transportation that people took to get to California?

Because the adventure was so difficult, most gold seekers were young men. "A gray beard is almost as rare as a petticoat," observed one miner. Luzena Wilson said that during the six months she lived in the mining city of Sacramento, she saw only two other women.

**HISTORY** *through***ART**

Clipper ship companies used advertising cards such as this one to convince Easterners that their line provided the fastest, most pleasant voyages.

**How has the artist tried to project a positive image for sailing west?**

Nearly everyone in the United States owns at least one pair of faded, comfortable blue jeans. The first jeans were invented for California miners.

In 1873, a man named Levi Strauss wanted to sell sturdy pants to miners. Strauss made his pants out of the strongest fabric he could buy—cotton denim. He reinforced the pockets with copper rivets so that they could hold heavy tools without ripping.

For more than 125 years, jeans have remained popular. Levi Strauss's pants have proved to be durable in more ways than one.

# Life in the Mining Camps

The mining camps had colorful names like Mad Mule Gulch, Hangtown, and Coyote Diggings. They began as rows of tents along the streams flowing out of the Sierra Nevada. Gradually, the tents gave way to rough wooden buildings that housed stores and saloons.

Mining camps could be dangerous. One woman who lived in the region wrote about camp violence.

*A VOICE FROM THE PAST*

In the short space of twenty-four days, we have had murders, fearful accidents, bloody deaths, a mob, whippings, a hanging, . . . and a fatal duel.

**Louise Clappe**, quoted in *Frontier Women*

The mining life was hard for other reasons. Camp gossip told of miners who grew rich overnight by finding eight-pound nuggets, but in reality, such easy pickings were rare. Miners spent their days standing knee-deep in icy streams, where they sifted through tons of mud and sand to find small amounts of gold. Exhaustion, poor food, and disease all damaged the miners' health.

Not only was acquiring gold brutally difficult, but the miners had to pay outrageously high prices for basic supplies. In addition, gamblers and con artists swarmed into the camps to swindle the miners of their money. As a result, few miners grew rich.

*Reading* **History**

**B. Making Inferences** Why do you think life in the mining camps was so rough?

# Miners from Around the World

About two-thirds of the forty-niners were Americans. Most of these were white men—many from New England. However, Native Americans, free blacks, and enslaved African Americans also worked the mines.

Thousands of experienced miners came from Sonora in Mexico. Other foreign miners came from Europe, South America, Australia, and China. Most of the Chinese miners were peasant farmers who fled from a region that had suffered several crop failures. By the end of 1851, one of every ten immigrants was Chinese.

Used to backbreaking labor in their homeland, the Chinese proved to be patient miners. They would take over sites that American miners had abandoned because the easy gold was gone. Through steady, hard work, the Chinese made these "played-out" sites yield profits. American miners resented the success of the Chinese and were suspicious of their different foods, dress, and customs. As the numbers of Chinese miners grew, American anger toward them also increased.

*Reading* **History**

**C. Analyzing Causes** Why did some Americans resent Chinese miners?

# Surface Mining

Gold is found in cracks, called veins, in the earth's rocky crust. As mountains and other outcrops of rock erode, the gold veins come to the surface. The gold breaks apart into nuggets, flakes, and dust. Flood waters then wash it downhill into stream beds. To mine this surface gold, forty-niners had to use tools designed to separate it from the mud and sand around it. American miners learned some technology from Mexicans who came from the mining region of Sonora.

**CALIFORNIA STANDARDS**

**8.6.1** Discuss the influence of industrialization and technological developments on the region, including human modification of the landscape and how physical geography shaped human actions (e.g., growth of cities, deforestation, farming, mineral extraction).

Miners shoveled dirt into the sluice. The rushing water carried lightweight materials along with it. Heavy gold sank to the bottom and was trapped between the ridges.

A sluice was a series of long boxes with ridges on the bottom. Water ran through the sluice, which angled downward.

Although this photograph shows American and Chinese miners working together, in many places Americans chased the Chinese away.

Mexican miners introduced the use of the pan. A miner would fill a pan with dirt and water. Then he would swirl the pan. Water sloshed over the sides, carrying lightweight minerals with it. Gold settled in the bottom.

## CONNECT TO HISTORY

1. **Drawing Conclusions**
   Which mining method could be used by an individual miner and which needed a group of miners? Explain your answer.

   **S** See Skillbuilder Handbook, page R13.

## CONNECT TO TODAY

2. **Researching** How is gold mined today?

For more about the California gold rush . . .

**RESEARCH LINKS**
CLASSZONE.COM

**415**

## Conflicts Among Miners

A mixture of greed, anger, and prejudice caused some miners to cheat others. For example, I. B. Gilman promised to free an enslaved African American named Tom if he saved enough gold. For more than a year, Tom mined for himself after each day's work was done. When he finally had $1,000, Gilman gave him a paper saying he was free. The next day, the paper suspiciously disappeared. Even though Tom was certain he had been robbed, he couldn't prove it. He had to work for another year before Gilman would free him.

Once the easy-to-find gold was gone, American miners began to force Native Americans and foreigners such as Mexicans and Chinese out of the gold fields to reduce competition. This practice increased after California became a state in 1850. One of the first acts of the California state legislature was to pass the Foreign Miners Tax, which imposed a tax of $20 a month on miners from other countries. That was more than most could afford to pay. As the tax collectors arrived in the camps, most foreigners left.

Driven from the mines, the Chinese opened shops, restaurants, and laundries. So many Chinese owned businesses in San Francisco that their neighborhood was called Chinatown, a name it still goes by today.

*Reading***History**

D. Analyzing Causes How did the state government make mining harder for foreigners?

## The Impact of the Gold Rush

By 1852, the gold rush was over. While it lasted, about 250,000 people flooded into California. This huge migration caused economic growth that changed California permanently. The port city of San Francisco grew to become a center of banking, manufacturing, shipping, and trade. Its population exploded from around 400 in 1845 to 35,000 in 1850. Sacramento became the center of a productive farming region.

However, the gold rush ruined many *Californios*. The newcomers did not respect *Californios*, their customs, or their legal rights. In many cases,

### CAUSE AND EFFECT: U.S. Expansion, 1846–1853

| CAUSE | | EFFECT |
|-------|---|--------|
| Westward trails move thousands to new territories. | ▶ | Oregon Territory acquired by the United States. |
| Austin and others colonize Texas. | ▶ | Texas Revolution |
| United States annexes Texas. | ▶ | War with Mexico |
| Mexican Cession acquired by the United States. | ▶ | United States expands "sea to sea." |
| Transcontinental railroad route needed. | ▶ | Gadsden Purchase |
| Thousands of gold seekers rush to California. | ▶ | California becomes a state. |

**SKILLBUILDER Interpreting Charts**

1. Which two causes are related to transportation?
2. Which cause fulfilled the nation's "manifest destiny"?

<u>Reading</u>**History**

**E. Recognizing Effects** What impact did the gold rush have on the people who lived in California before the forty-niners came?

Americans seized their property. For example, Mariano Vallejo lost all but 300 acres of his huge estate. Even so, their Spanish heritage became an important part of California culture.

Native Americans suffered even more. Thousands of them died from diseases brought by the newcomers. The miners hunted down and killed thousands more. The reason was the Anglo-American belief that Native Americans stood in the way of progress. By 1870, California's Native American population had fallen from 150,000 to only about 58,000.

A final effect of the gold rush was that by 1849 California had enough people to apply for statehood. Skipping the territorial stage, California applied to Congress for admission to the Union and was admitted as a free state in 1850. Although its constitution outlawed slavery, it did not grant African Americans the vote.

For some people, California's statehood proved to be the opportunity of a lifetime. The enslaved woman Nancy Gooch gained her freedom because of the law against slavery. She then worked as a cook and washerwoman until she saved enough money to buy the freedom of her son and daughter-in-law in Missouri. Nancy Gooch's family moved to California to join her. Eventually, they became so prosperous that they bought Sutter's sawmill, where the gold rush first started.

On a national level, California's statehood created turmoil. Before 1850, there was an equal number of free states and slave states. Southerners feared that because the statehood of California made free states outnumber slave states, Northerners might use their majority to abolish slavery. As Chapter 15 explains, conflict over this issue threatened the survival of the Union.

Mariano Vallejo, unhappy that *Californio* culture was ignored in the new American California, named his home "Tear of the Mountain."

---

## Section 4 Assessment

### 1. Terms & Names

**Explain the significance of:**

- forty-niner
- *Californio*
- Mariano Vallejo
- John Sutter
- James Marshall
- California gold rush

### 2. Using Graphics

Use a chart like the one shown to review and record hardships faced by the forty-niners.

| HARDSHIPS | |
|---|---|
| In the camps | |
| At work mining | |

Which hardships would you have found most difficult?

### 3. Main Ideas

**a.** How did the California gold rush get started?

**b.** Why didn't many forty-niners become rich?

**c.** How did women and people of different racial, ethnic, or national groups contribute to the California gold rush?

### 4. Critical Thinking

**Recognizing Effects** What were some of the effects of the California gold rush?

**THINK ABOUT**

- changes in San Francisco
- California's bid for statehood

---

**ACTIVITY OPTIONS**

**SCIENCE**

**TECHNOLOGY**

Research the hazards of mining gold and either plan a **science exhibit** or give an **electronic presentation**.

## VISUAL SUMMARY

### Manifest Destiny
(8.5.2)

**United States in 1810**

### Trails West

Mountain men and traders opened trails in the Far West. Pioneers then went west to gain land, wealth, or religious freedom.

### The Texas Revolution

Americans moved into the Mexican territory of Texas. Conflicts led those Americans to revolt, and Texas gained independence.

### The War with Mexico

President Polk wanted to expand the nation. He negotiated to gain Oregon. The United States fought Mexico to gain much of the Southwest.

### The California Gold Rush

The discovery of gold lured thousands of people to California. California's economy and population grew, resulting in statehood.

**United States in 1853**

## TERMS & NAMES

Briefly explain the significance of each of the following.

1. mountain man
2. Oregon Trail
3. Stephen Austin
4. *Tejano*
5. Antonio López de Santa Anna
6. manifest destiny
7. Bear Flag Revolt
8. Mexican Cession
9. forty-niner
10. California gold rush

## REVIEW QUESTIONS

### Trails West (pages 393–399)

1. What were three reasons why people moved west? (HI2)
2. What were the three main trails that led to the West? (HI1)
3. How did the Mormons make the land in Utah productive? (HI1)

### The Texas Revolution (pages 400–405)

4. Why were Texans unhappy with Mexican rule? (HI1)
5. Why were the battles of the Alamo and San Jacinto important to the Texas Revolution? (CST1)

### The War with Mexico (pages 406–411)

6. What areas did the United States gain as a result of Americans' belief in manifest destiny? (HI1)
7. What links the Bear Flag Revolt to the War with Mexico? (CST1)
8. What lands did the United States acquire as a result of the Treaty of Guadalupe Hidalgo? (HI1)

### The California Gold Rush (pages 412–417)

9. Who were four groups of people who became forty-niners? (HI1)
10. What were three ways California changed because of the gold rush? (HI2)

## CRITICAL THINKING

### 1. USING YOUR NOTES: CATEGORIZING INFORMATION

| | Types of people who traveled there | Why they went there | Key events that allowed the U.S. to take ownership of the territory |
|---|---|---|---|
| New Mexico | | | |
| Utah | | | |
| Oregon | | | |
| Texas | | | |
| California | | | |

Using your completed chart, answer the questions below. (HI2)

a. In what ways were the reasons people went west similar?
b. Which of the five regions listed on your chart entered the United States peacefully?
c. Which event added the most territory to the United States?

### 2. ANALYZING LEADERSHIP

Think about the leaders discussed in this chapter. What characteristics did they have that made them good leaders? (HI1)

### 3. THEME: EXPANSION

How did the idea of manifest destiny help bring about the expansion of the United States? (HI2)

### 4. DRAWING CONCLUSIONS

How did the War with Mexico and the California gold rush contribute to the cultural diversity of the United States? (HI3)

### 5. APPLYING CITIZENSHIP SKILLS

What were the different viewpoints that people held about the War with Mexico? (REP5)

### Interact *with* History

Based on this chapter, what do you think you would have gained or lost by going west?

Use the map and your knowledge of U.S. history to answer questions 1 and 2.

Additional Test Practice, pp. S1–S33.

**Settlement of Texas**

Legend:
- Before 1800
- Between 1800 and 1850
- Between 1850 and 1870
- Between 1870 and 1890
- After 1890

**1.** The area around which city in Texas was settled first? (8.8.6)

**A.** Houston

**B.** Dallas

**C.** San Antonio

**D.** El Paso

**2.** In what general direction was Texas settled? (8.8.6)

**A.** north to south

**B.** east to west

**C.** west to east

**D.** south to north

John O'Sullivan describes settling the United States in this quotation. Use the quotation and your knowledge of U.S. history to answer question 3.

**PRIMARY SOURCE**

Our manifest destiny[is] to overspread and possess the whole of the continent which Providence has given us for the development of the great experiment of liberty and . . . self-government.

**John O'Sullivan**, *United States Magazine and Democratic Review*

**3.** The passage supports which of the following points of view? (8.8.2)

**A.** Continental expansion by the United States is bound to happen.

**B.** Continental expansion is limited by self-government.

**C.** The claims of other countries to the same territory must be respected.

**D.** Expansion across the entire continent will require some limits on liberty.

**TEST PRACTICE**
CLASSZONE.COM

# ALTERNATIVE ASSESSMENT

## 1. WRITING ABOUT HISTORY

Suppose that you are a reporter for a newspaper in northern California in 1849. Write a **news article** about the discovery of gold. The article should follow the basic organization of a news article by answering the questions *Who? What? Where? When? And How?* (REP3)

- You can research your article by looking in books about the California gold rush, in general histories of California, and on the Internet.

## 2. COOPERATIVE LEARNING

Work with a group of three or four other students to create a panel discussion that explores the different viewpoints surrounding the Mexican War. Research attitudes toward the war. Then outline and participate in the panel discussion for the class. (REP5)

# INTEGRATED TECHNOLOGY ACTIVITY

## DOING INTERNET RESEARCH

Life on the wagon trains was not like life "back east." (REP4)

- On the Internet or in other sources, find primary sources about life on the wagon trains, such as letters, diaries, journals, newspaper articles, and books.

- Once you have collected a number of primary sources, present your findings to your class.

**INTERNET ACTIVITY**
CLASSZONE.COM

# A New Spirit of Change 1820–1860

The poverty and overcrowding of the urban slums is the focus of this sketch.

Children found simple ways of entertaining themselves.

**1828**
Noah Webster publishes the *American Dictionary of the English Language*.

**1829**
David Walker prints *Appeal*, a pamphlet urging slaves to revolt.

**1836**
The Lowell mill girls go on strike to demand better conditions.

USA
World    1820

**1824**
The British Parliament makes trade unions illegal.

**1827**
Ludwig van Beethoven dies.

**1829**
Louis Braille invents a raised type that allows blind people to read.

You are a writer who moves to New York in the mid-1800s. A newspaper hires you to write about reform. One day, you hear a speaker call for the end of slavery. Another day you talk to a factory worker whose pay has been cut. In the city, you see great poverty and suffering.

# What reforms do you think will most benefit American society?

## What Do You Think?

- How might you persuade Americans to change life in the city?
- Should reform come about through new laws or through individual actions?

**RESEARCH LINKS**
CLASSZONE.COM
Visit the Chapter 14 links for more information about the changing nation.

**1843**
Dorothea Dix asks the Massachusetts legislature to improve the care of the mentally ill.

**1848**
The Seneca Falls Convention demands women's rights.

**1851**
Maine passes a law banning the sale of alcohol.

**1860**

**1845**
Ireland's potato crop fails, causing famine. Thousands flee to America.

**1848**
A revolution in Germany fails. Some Germans move to America.

**1854**
Brazil's first railway opens.

# Reading Strategy: Comparing

**CALIFORNIA STANDARDS**

**Reading 3.3** Compare and contrast motivations and reactions of literary characters from different historical eras confronting similar situations or conflicts.

## What Do You Know?

What do you think were the worst problems in the United States in the mid-1800s? How do you think people tried to solve them?

**Think About**
- stories or films that are set in this period
- problems that exist now
- the actions people take to solve today's problems
- your responses to the Interact with History about reforms that will benefit American society (see page 421)

## What Do You Want to Know?

What would you like to learn about the way individuals changed the United States in the mid-1800s? Record your questions in your notebook before you read the chapter.

A young Frederick Douglass learns to read.

## Comparing

To understand the many influences on U.S. culture, learn to compare. Comparing means examining the similarities between people, actions, or ideas. The chart below will help you compare the influences that various people had upon America in the middle of the 19th century. Use the chart to take notes about how people changed America. Also take notes about people who tried to have an influence but failed.

See Skillbuilder Handbook, page R10.

 **Taking Notes**

| | How People Influenced America in the Mid-1800s |
| --- | --- |
| Immigrants | |
| Writers | |
| Reformers | |
| Abolitionists | |
| Women | |

# The Hopes of Immigrants

| MAIN IDEA | WHY IT MATTERS NOW | TERMS & NAMES |
|---|---|---|
| In the mid-1800s, millions of Europeans came to the United States hoping to build a better life. | These Germans, Irish, and Scandinavians had a strong influence on American culture. | emigrant     famine<br>immigrant     prejudice<br>steerage     nativist<br>push-pull factor |

## ONE AMERICAN'S STORY

In June 1831, Gjert Hovland (YEHRT HAHV•LIHND) and his family left Norway for America. After a few years, Hovland wrote to a friend in Norway.

*A VOICE FROM THE PAST*

It would greatly please me to learn that all of you who are in need and have little chance of supporting yourselves and your families have decided to leave Norway and come to America; for, even if many more come, there will still be room here for all. Those who are willing to work will not lack employment or business here.

**Gjert Hovland,** letter to Torjuls Maeland, April 22, 1835

Advertisements for land attracted immigrants.

**CALIFORNIA STANDARDS**

**8.2.7** Describe the principles of federalism, dual sovereignty, separation of powers, checks and balances, the nature and purpose of majority rule, and the ways in which the American idea of constitutionalism preserves individual rights.

**8.6.3** List the reasons for the wave of immigration from Northern Europe to the United States and describe the growth in the number, size, and spatial arrangements of cities (e.g., Irish immigrants and the Great Irish Famine).

**8.12.1** Trace patterns of agricultural and industrial development as they relate to climate, use of natural resources, markets, and trade and locate such development on a map.

**8.12.5** Examine the location and effects of urbanization, renewed immigration, and industrialization (e.g., the effects on social fabric of cities, wealth and economic opportunity, the conservation movement).

Millions of people like Hovland decided to become **emigrants,** or people who leave a country. Arriving in the United States, they became **immigrants,** or people who settle in a new country. This section explains how immigrants enriched the United States with their work and their cultures.

## Why People Migrated

Most immigrants endured hardships to come to America. Although some, like Hovland, brought their families, many immigrant men came alone and suffered loneliness. Nearly all immigrants made the ocean voyage in **steerage,** the cheapest deck on a ship. In steerage, hundreds of people lived jammed together for ten days to a month. Conditions were filthy. Many passengers became ill or died on the journey.

Despite the hard passage, immigrants flocked to the United States during the mid-1800s. They came from Britain, Ireland, Germany, Scandinavia (Sweden, Denmark, and Norway), and China. Most came from Europe. What made them come to America? Historians talk about

**Taking Notes**

Use your chart to take notes about the influence of immigrants.

| | How People |
|---|---|
| Immigrants | |
| Writers | |
| Reformers | |
| Abolitionists | |
| Women | |

*A New Spirit of Change* **423**

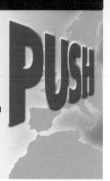

**PULL**

1. **Freedom**
2. **Economic opportunity**
3. **Abundant land**

**PUSH**

1. **Population growth**
2. **Agricultural changes**
3. **Crop failures**
4. **Industrial Revolution**
5. **Religious and political turmoil**

<u>push-pull factors</u>. These forces push people out of their native lands and pull them toward a new place. **Push factors** included the following:

1. **Population growth.** Better food and sanitation caused Europe's population to boom after 1750, and the land became overcrowded.
2. **Agricultural changes.** As Europe's population grew, so did cities. Landowners wanted to make money selling food to those cities. New methods made it more efficient to farm large areas of land than to rent small plots to tenants. So landlords forced tenants off the land.
3. **Crop failures.** Poor harvests made it difficult for small farmers to pay their debts. Some of these farmers chose to start over in America. Crop failures also led to hunger, causing people to emigrate.
4. **Industrial Revolution.** Goods produced in factories became cheaper than goods produced by artisans. Suddenly out of work, some artisans took factory jobs. Others emigrated.
5. **Religious and political turmoil.** To escape religious persecution, Quakers fled Norway and Jews left Germany. Also, many Germans came to America after a revolution in Germany failed in 1848.

Immigrants chose the United States because of three main **pull factors**:

1. **Freedom.** As Gjert Hovland wrote, "Everyone has the freedom to practice the teaching and religion he prefers."
2. **Economic opportunity.** Immigrants sought a land where they could support their families and have a better future. Immigration often rose during times of U.S. prosperity and fell during hard times.
3. **Abundant land.** The acquisition of the Louisiana Purchase and the Mexican Cession gave the United States millions more acres of land. To land-starved Europeans, America was a land of opportunity.

**Vocabulary**
tenant: renter

**Vocabulary**
artisan: skilled worker

*Reading* **History**
**A. Solving Problems** Many of the push factors were problems. Which pull factors were solutions to which problems?

## Scandinavians Seek Land

Public land in America was sold for $1.25 an acre, which lured thousands of Scandinavians. At first, their governments tried to keep them at home. A Swedish law of 1768 restricted the right to emigrate. But growing poverty in Scandinavia caused officials to cancel this law in 1840.

Scandinavian clergymen also tried to halt the emigration. At first, they warned their church members against leaving the homeland. Eventually, though, the preachers realized their words had little effect. Some of them even went to America themselves.

*Reading*History

**B. Making Inferences** Why do you think Scandinavians moved to places that felt familiar?

In the United States, Scandinavians chose regions that felt familiar. Many settled in the Midwest, especially Minnesota and Wisconsin. These states had lakes, forests, and cold winters like their homelands. A high proportion of Scandinavian immigrants became farmers.

# Germans Pursue Economic Opportunity

Like the Scandinavians, many Germans moved to the Midwest. Germans especially liked Wisconsin because the climate allowed them to grow their traditional crop of oats. Some moved to Milwaukee, Wisconsin, because the Catholic bishop there was German. (In the 1800s, German Christian immigrants included both Catholics and Protestants.)

Germans also settled in Texas. In New Braunfels, a group of German nobles bought land and sold it in parcels to German immigrants. The town had to survive poor harvests and conflicts with Native Americans, but it eventually prospered. Germans also founded Fredericksburg, Texas, which still retains its German culture today.

Immigrants from Germany settled in cities as well as on farms or the frontier. German artisans opened businesses as bakers, butchers, carpenters, printers, shoemakers, and tailors. Many German immigrants achieved great success. For instance, in 1853 John Jacob Bausch and Henry Lomb started a firm to make eyeglasses and other lenses. Their company became the world's largest lens maker.

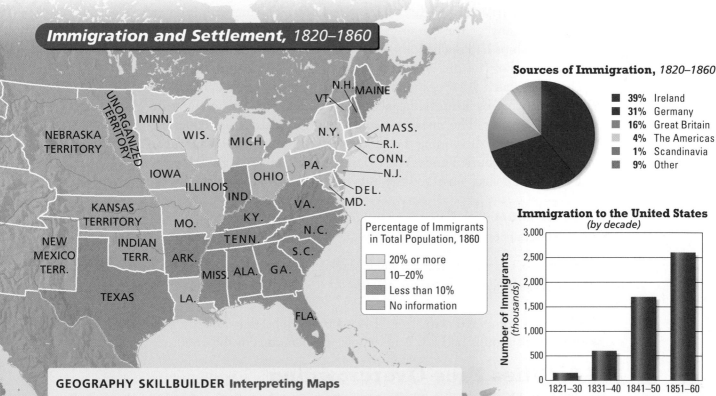

**Immigration and Settlement,** *1820–1860*

**Sources of Immigration,** *1820–1860*

- **39%** Ireland
- **31%** Germany
- **16%** Great Britain
- **4%** The Americas
- **1%** Scandinavia
- **9%** Other

Percentage of Immigrants in Total Population, 1860

- 20% or more
- 10–20%
- Less than 10%
- No information

**Immigration to the United States**
*(by decade)*

Number of Immigrants *(thousands)*

1821–30  1831–40  1841–50  1851–60

**GEOGRAPHY SKILLBUILDER Interpreting Maps**
1. **Place** *Which states had the highest percentage of immigrants in 1860?*
2. **Region** *Compare the settlement of immigrants in the North and the South. What do you know about the South that might account for this difference?*

Source: *Historical Statistics of the United States*

Some German immigrants were Jews. Many of them worked as traveling salespeople. They brought pins, needles, pots—and news—to frontier homes and mining camps. In time, some opened their own general stores. Other Jews settled in cities, where many found success. For example, Alexander Rothschild worked as a grocer upon arriving in Hartford, Connecticut, in the 1840s. By 1851, he ran a popular hotel.

The Germans were the largest immigrant group of the 1800s and strongly influenced American culture. Many things we think of as originating in America came from Germany—the Christmas tree, gymnasiums, kindergartens, and the hamburger and frankfurter.

## The Irish Flee Hunger

Most Irish immigrants were Catholic. Protestant Britain had ruled Ireland for centuries—and controlled the Catholic majority by denying them rights. Irish Catholics could not vote, hold office, own land, or go to school. Because of the poverty produced by Britain's rule, some Irish came to America in the early 1800s.

Then, in 1845, a disease attacked Ireland's main food crop, the potato, causing a severe food shortage called a **famine**. The Irish Potato Famine killed 1 million people and forced many to emigrate. By 1854, between 1.5 and 2 million Irish had fled their homeland.

In America, Irish farmers became city-dwellers. Arriving with little or no savings, many of these immigrants had to settle in the port cities where their ships had docked. By 1850, the Irish made up one-fourth of the population of Boston, New York, Philadelphia, and Baltimore.

The uneducated Irish immigrants arrived with few skills and had to take low-paying, back-breaking jobs. Irish women took in washing or worked as servants. The men built canals and railroads across America. So many Irishmen died doing this dangerous work that people said there was "an Irishman buried under every [railroad] tie." In 1841, British novelist Charles Dickens observed the huts in which railroad workers lived.

*A VOICE FROM THE PAST*

The best were poor protection from the weather; the worst let in the wind and rain through the wide breaches in the roofs of sodden grass and in the walls of mud; some had neither door nor window; some had nearly fallen down.

**Charles Dickens,** quoted in *To Seek America*

The Irish competed with free blacks for the jobs that nobody else wanted. Both groups had few other choices in America in the 1800s.

## U.S. Cities Face Overcrowding

Immigrants like the Irish and Germans flocked to American cities. So did native-born Americans, who hoped for the chance to make a better living. Between 1800 and 1830, New York's population jumped from 60,489 to 202,589. St. Louis doubled its population every nine years. Cincinnati grew even faster, doubling every seven years.

Rapid urban growth brought problems. Not enough housing existed for all the newcomers. Greedy landlords profited from the housing shortage by squeezing large apartment buildings onto small lots. Using every inch of space for rooms, these cramped living quarters lacked sunlight and fresh air. Their outdoor toilets overflowed, spreading disease. In such depressing urban neighborhoods, crime flourished.

American cities were unprepared to tackle these problems. In fact, before 1845, New York City had no public police force. Until the 1860s, it had only a volunteer fire department. And in 1857, the rapidly growing city had only 138 miles of sewers for 500 miles of streets.

_Reading_**History**
D. Identifying Problems What problems were politicians trying to solve by offering to help new immigrants?

Most immigrant groups set up aid societies to help newcomers from their country. Many city politicians also offered to assist immigrants in exchange for votes. The politicians set up organizations to help new arrivals find housing and work.

## Some Americans Oppose Immigration

Some native-born Americans feared that immigrants were too foreign to learn American ways. Others feared that immigrants might come to outnumber natives. As a result, immigrants faced anger and prejudice. **Prejudice** is a negative opinion that is not based on facts. For example,

# CITIZENSHIP TODAY

## Becoming a Citizen

Most immigrants who came to America in the 1800s shared one thing: an appreciation for the nation's values and laws. As a result, many chose to become U.S. citizens.

This trend continues today. In recent decades, more than half a million Vietnamese have immigrated to the United States. Many became citizens of their new country. One of them was Lam Ton, who is a successful restaurant owner in Chicago. Ton viewed U.S. citizenship as both a privilege and a duty. "We have to stick to this country and help it do better," he said.

Each year, immigrants from around the world are sworn in as U.S. citizens on Citizenship Day, September 17. But first they must pass a test on English, the U.S. political system, and the rights and duties of citizenship.

**This young immigrant proudly holds up his certificate of citizenship.**

### How Does Someone Become a Citizen?

1. In a small group, discuss what questions you would ask those seeking to become U.S. citizens.

2. Create a citizenship test using your questions.

3. Have another group take the test and record their scores.

4. Use the McDougal Littell Internet site to link to the actual U.S. citizenship test. Compare it to your test.

   **See Citizenship Handbook, page 281.**

For more about becoming a U.S. citizen . . .

RESEARCH LINKS

CLASSZONE.COM

In 1844, a riot took place between Catholics and non-Catholics in Philadelphia. Several people were killed.

some Protestants in the 1800s believed that Catholics threatened democracy. Those Protestants feared that the Pope, the head of the Roman Catholic Church, was plotting to overthrow democracy in America.

Native-born Americans who wanted to eliminate foreign influence called themselves **nativists.** Some nativists refused to hire immigrants and put up signs like "No Irish need apply." In cities like New York and Boston, nativists formed a secret society. Members promised not to vote for any Catholics or immigrants running for political office. If asked about their secret group, they said, "I know nothing about it."

In the 1850s, nativists started a political party. Because of the members' answers to questions about their party, it was called the Know-Nothing Party. It wanted to ban Catholics and the foreign-born from holding office. It also called for a cut in immigration and a 21-year wait to become an American citizen. The Know-Nothings did elect six governors. But they disappeared quickly as a national party. Their northern and southern branches couldn't agree on the issue of slavery.

In spite of such barriers as prejudice, the immigrants of the 1800s had a strong impact on American culture. Writers and artists of the 1800s also shaped American culture. Section 2 discusses their influence.

**Background**
Protestants feared the Pope because in many European countries, the Catholic Church worked closely with the ruling monarchs.

---

## Section 1 Assessment

### 1. Terms & Names

**Explain the significance of:**
- emigrant
- immigrant
- steerage
- push-pull factor
- famine
- prejudice
- nativist

### 2. Using Graphics

Use a cluster diagram like the one below to record details about immigration, such as which groups came, where they settled, and how they influenced America. (HI1)

Immigration

### 3. Main Ideas

**a.** What were the push-pull factors that led to immigration? (HI2)

**b.** How did the arrival of so many immigrants affect U.S. cities? (HI2)

**c.** What was the Know-Nothing Party, and what was its point of view about immigration? (HI5)

### 4. Critical Thinking

**Analyzing Causes** How did the rapid increase in immigration cause conflict? (HI2)

**THINK ABOUT**
- why Irish immigrants and free blacks competed for jobs
- the growth of cities and the problems it created
- the prejudices of nativists
- religious differences

**ACTIVITY OPTIONS**

**TECHNOLOGY**
**ART**

Plan a **multimedia presentation** or design a **Web page** that shows immigrants the advantages of settling in the United States. (HI6)

# American Literature and Art

| MAIN IDEA | WHY IT MATTERS NOW | TERMS & NAMES |
|---|---|---|
| Inspired by nature and democratic ideals, writers and artists produced some of America's greatest works. | Nineteenth-century writers such as Hawthorne and Thoreau laid the foundation for American literature. | romanticism · transcendentalism<br>Hudson River school · civil disobedience |

## ONE AMERICAN'S STORY

Washington Irving wrote some of the first stories to describe America. For example, "Rip Van Winkle" tells of a man in New York State. Rip wakes up after a 20-year nap to find many changes. He goes to the inn, which once had a picture of King George on its sign.

*A VOICE FROM THE PAST*

The red coat was changed for one of blue and buff, a sword was held in the hand instead of a sceptre [staff of authority], the head was decorated with a cocked hat, and underneath was painted in large characters, GENERAL WASHINGTON.

**Washington Irving,** "Rip Van Winkle"

In another Irving tale, "The Legend of Sleepy Hollow," a spooky creature chases a teacher.

**CALIFORNIA STANDARDS**

**8.4.4** Discuss daily life, including traditions in art, music, and literature, of early national America (e.g., through writings by Washington Irving, James Fenimore Cooper).

**8.6.6** Examine the women's suffrage movement (e.g., biographies, writings, and speeches of Elizabeth Cady Stanton, Margaret Fuller, Lucretia Mott, Susan B. Anthony).

**8.6.7** Identify common themes in American art as well as transcendentalism and individualism (e.g., writings about and by Ralph Waldo Emerson, Henry David Thoreau, Herman Melville, Louisa May Alcott, Nathaniel Hawthorne, Henry Wadsworth Longfellow).

**REP4** Students assess the credibility of primary and secondary sources and draw sound conclusions from them.

While Rip slept, the Americans had fought and won their revolution!

Irving's work helped to win European respect for American writing for the first time. This section discusses other individuals of the 1800s who created uniquely American literature and art.

## Writing About America

Irving and other writers were influenced by a style of European art called **romanticism**. It stressed the individual, imagination, creativity, and emotion. It drew inspiration from nature. American writers turned their interest in nature into a celebration of the American wilderness.

Many books featured the wilderness. James Fenimore Cooper wrote five novels about the dramatic adventures of wilderness scout Natty Bumppo. One that remains popular is *The Last of the Mohicans*. Francis Parkman wrote a travel book, *The Oregon Trail*, about the frontier trail.

*Taking Notes*

Use your chart to take notes about the influence of writers.

|  | How People |
|---|---|
| Immigrants |  |
| Writers |  |
| Reformers |  |
| Abolitionists |  |
| Women |  |

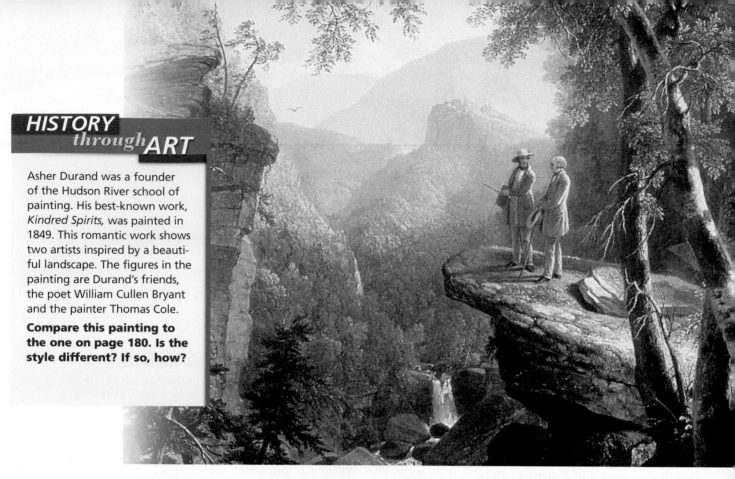

## HISTORY through ART

Asher Durand was a founder of the Hudson River school of painting. His best-known work, *Kindred Spirits,* was painted in 1849. This romantic work shows two artists inspired by a beautiful landscape. The figures in the painting are Durand's friends, the poet William Cullen Bryant and the painter Thomas Cole.

**Compare this painting to the one on page 180. Is the style different? If so, how?**

In addition, writers began to use a more American style. A teacher and lawyer named Noah Webster gave guidelines to that style in his *American Dictionary of the English Language.* Webster first published his dictionary in 1828. He later revised it in 1840. The dictionary gave American, not British, spellings and included American slang.

Other writers besides Irving celebrated America's past. Henry Wadsworth Longfellow wrote many poems that retold stories from history. For example, "Paul Revere's Ride" depicted the Revolutionary hero's ride to warn of a British attack. Generations of students memorized lines from the poem, such as, "One if by land, and two if by sea; / And I on the opposite shore will be."

## Creating American Art

European styles continued to influence American artists, but some took these styles in new directions. One group of painters influenced by romanticism worked near the Hudson River in New York State. **Hudson River school** artists painted lush natural landscapes. Several members of this school went west for a change of scenery. For example, Albert Bierstadt took several trips to America's mountainous West. He produced huge paintings that convey the majesty of the American landscape. (See page 310.)

Other artists also went west. John James Audubon came to the United States from France at age 18. Traveling across the continent, Audubon sketched the birds and animals of his adopted country.

Enslaved African Americans also contributed to American art. They made beautiful baskets, quilts, and pottery. Most of these slaves

**Background**
The National Audubon Society, whose goal is the protection of wildlife today, is named for John James Audubon.

remained anonymous, but one did not. David Drake worked in a South Carolina pottery factory and signed the pottery he created. He was the only factory worker to do so.

## Following One's Conscience

By the 1840s, Americans took new pride in their emerging culture. Ralph Waldo Emerson, a New England writer, encouraged this pride. He urged Americans to cast off European influence and develop their own beliefs. His advice was to learn about life from self-examination and from nature as well as books.

> *"No law can be sacred to me but that of my nature."*
> **Ralph Waldo Emerson**

Emerson's student, Henry David Thoreau, followed that advice. In 1845, Thoreau moved to a simple cabin he had built by Walden Pond near the town of Concord, Massachusetts. Thoreau furnished it with only a bed, a table, a desk, and three chairs. He wrote about his life in the woods in *Walden*. Thoreau said that people should live by their own individual standards.

---

*A VOICE FROM THE PAST*

If a man does not keep pace with his companions, perhaps it is because he hears a different drummer. Let him step to the music which he hears, however measured or far away.

**Henry David Thoreau,** *Walden*

---

*Reading* **History**

**A. Making Inferences** What do you think it means to "hear a different drummer"?

Emerson and Thoreau belonged to a group of thinkers with a new philosophy called **transcendentalism**. It taught that the spiritual world is more important than the physical world. It also taught that people can find the truth within themselves—through feeling and intuition.

Because Thoreau believed in the importance of individual conscience, he urged people not to obey laws they considered unjust. Instead of protesting with violence, they should peacefully refuse to obey those laws. This form of protest is called **civil disobedience**. For example, Thoreau did not want to support the U.S. government, which allowed slavery and fought the War with Mexico. Instead of paying taxes that helped to finance the war, Thoreau went to jail.

Louisa May Alcott began her writing career as a transcendentalist poet in the 1850s, but achieved her greatest fame in 1868 with her book *Little Women*, which became popular with children as well as adults. Alcott was active in abolition and suffrage movements. Another New England transcendentalist, Margaret Fuller, also called for change. In her magazine, *The Dial*, and in her book, *Woman in the Nineteenth Century*, Fuller argued for women's rights.

**Connections TO LITERATURE**

**"CIVIL DISOBEDIENCE"**
In his essay "Civil Disobedience," Thoreau wrote that "Under a government which imprisons any unjustly the true place for a just man is also a prison."

Thoreau did land in prison when he refused to pay his taxes. According to legend, Emerson visited Thoreau in jail and asked, "Why are you here?" Thoreau replied, "Why are you not here?"

In the 20th century, Mohandas K. Gandhi of India and Martin Luther King, Jr., of the United States both used civil disobedience to fight injustice.

# Exploring the Human Heart

Like Thoreau, other writers broke with tradition. In 1855, poet Walt Whitman published *Leaves of Grass,* a book that changed American poetry. His bold, unrhymed poems praised ordinary people. Emily Dickinson lived in her family's home almost her entire life. She wrote poems on small pieces of paper that she sewed into booklets. Her subjects include God, nature, love, and death. Most of her 1,775 poems were published only after her death. Both Whitman and Dickinson shaped modern poetry by experimenting with language.

Fiction writers of the 1800s also shaped American literature. Edgar Allan Poe wrote terrifying tales that influence today's horror story writers. He also wrote the first detective story, "The Murders in the Rue Morgue."

Nathaniel Hawthorne depicted love, guilt, and revenge during Puritan times in *The Scarlet Letter.* The novel shows that harsh judgment without mercy can lead to tragedy. Hawthorne may have learned that lesson from his family history. One of his ancestors condemned people at the Salem witchcraft trials.

Herman Melville won fame by writing thrilling novels about his experiences as a sailor. In 1851, Melville published his masterpiece, *Moby Dick.* This novel tells about a man's destructive desire to kill a white whale. Although the novel was not popular when it was published, it is widely read now. Several movie versions exist.

These fiction writers portrayed the harmful effects of cruel actions. Other people thought that individuals could alter society for good. Section 3 describes those reformers.

*Reading* **History**

**B. Recognizing Effects** How did Poe influence the fiction that people read today?

---

## Section ② Assessment

### 1. Terms & Names

**Explain the significance of:**
- romanticism
- Hudson River school
- transcendentalism
- civil disobedience

### 2. Using Graphics

Use a chart like the one below to list important individual writers and artists. For each one, name or describe one of his or her works.

| Writer or artist | His or her work |
|---|---|
| | |
| | |

Which one would you like to learn more about? Why? (8.6.7)

### 3. Main Ideas

**a.** What was romanticism and how did Americans adapt it? (8.6.7)

**b.** What is civil disobedience and what did Thoreau do that is an example of it? (8.6.7)

**c.** How did the writers of the mid-1800s shape modern literature? (8.6.7)

### 4. Critical Thinking

**Evaluating** Why do you think the literature and art of the mid-1800s are still valued? (CST3)

**THINK ABOUT**
- the way they feature U.S. history and culture
- their universal themes—themes that relate to all people in all time periods
- the way they reflect changes happening at that time

**ACTIVITY OPTIONS**

**ART**

**TECHNOLOGY**

Choose an American painting, sketch it, and make it into a **jigsaw puzzle;** or make an **audio recording** of a museum guide's description of it. (8.6.7)

# Reforming American Society

| MAIN IDEA | WHY IT MATTERS NOW | TERMS & NAMES |
|---|---|---|
| In the mid-1800s, several reform movements worked to improve American education and society. | Several laws and institutions, such as public schools, date back to this period. | revival / Second Great Awakening / temperance movement / labor union / strike / Horace Mann / Dorothea Dix |

## ONE AMERICAN'S STORY

Anne Newport Royall wrote about America's growing interest in religion. She also described a preacher at a Tennessee **revival**, or meeting to reawaken religious faith.

### A VOICE FROM THE PAST

His text was, "He that hath ears to hear, let him hear." The people must have been deaf indeed that could not have heard him. . . . He began low but soon bawled to deafening. He spit in his hands, rubbed them against each other, and then would smite them together, till he made the woods ring.

**Anne Newport Royall,** *Letters from Alabama*

Section 3 explains how, in the mid-1800s, many individuals called on Americans to reform, or to improve themselves and their society.

**CALIFORNIA STANDARDS**

**8.6.5** Trace the development of the American education system from its earliest roots, including the roles of religious and private schools and Horace Mann's campaign for free public education and its assimilating role in American culture.

**8.7.4** Compare the lives of and opportunities for free blacks in the North with those of free blacks in the South.

**8.9.6** Describe the lives of free blacks and the laws that limited their freedom and economic opportunities.

**REP4** Students assess the credibility of primary and secondary sources and draw sound conclusions from them.

## A Spirit of Revival

The renewal of religious faith in the 1790s and early 1800s is called the **Second Great Awakening**. Revivalist preachers said that anyone could choose salvation. This appealed to equality-loving Americans. Revivals spread quickly across the frontier. Settlers eagerly awaited the visits of preachers like Peter Cartwright. At the age of 16, Cartwright had given up a life of gambling and joined a Methodist Church. He became a minister and spent more than 60 years preaching on the frontier.

The revival also traveled to Eastern cities. There, former lawyer Charles Grandison Finney held large revival meetings. He preached that "all sin consists in selfishness" and that religious faith led people to help others. Such teaching helped awaken a spirit of reform. Americans began to believe that they could act to make things better.

**Taking Notes**

Use your chart to take notes about the influence of reformers.

| | How People |
|---|---|
| Immigrants | |
| Writers | |
| Reformers | |
| Abolitionists | |
| Women | |

Temperance pledges often displayed inspiring pictures and mottoes.

## Temperance Societies

Led by churches, some Americans began the **temperance movement,** which is a campaign to stop the drinking of alcohol. Heavy drinking was common in the early 1800s. Some workers spent most of their wages on alcohol—leaving their families without enough money to live on. As a result, many women joined the temperance movement. "There is no reform in which women can act better or more appropriately than temperance," said Mary C. Vaughan.

Some temperance workers handed out pamphlets urging people to stop drinking. Others produced dramas, such as one entitled *The Drunkard,* to dramatize the evils of alcohol. In addition, temperance speakers traveled widely, asking people to sign a pledge to give up alcohol. By 1838, a million people had signed.

Temperance also won the support of business owners. Industry needed workers who could keep schedules and run machines. Alcohol made it hard for workers to do either. New England businessman Neal Dow led the fight to make it illegal to sell alcohol. In 1851, Maine banned the sale of liquor. By 1855, 13 other states passed similar laws. But many people opposed these laws, and most were repealed. Still, the movement to ban alcohol remained strong, even into the 20th century.

*Reading* **History**
**A. Evaluating**
How did the temperance movement affect the development of drama?

**Vocabulary**
**repeal:** to cancel

## Fighting for Workers' Rights

As business owners tried to improve workers' habits, workers called for improvements in working conditions. Factory work was noisy, boring, and unsafe. In the 1830s, American workers began to organize.

The young women mill workers in Lowell, Massachusetts, started a labor union. A **labor union** is a group of workers who band together to seek better working conditions. In 1836, the mill owners raised the rent of the company-owned boarding houses where the women lived. About 1,500 women went on **strike,** stopping work to demand better conditions. Eleven-year-old Harriet Hanson helped lead the strikers.

### A VOICE FROM THE PAST

I . . . started on ahead, saying, . . . "I don't care what you do, I am going to turn out, whether anyone else does or not," and I marched out, and was followed by the others. As I looked back at the long line that followed me, I was more proud than I have ever been since.

**Harriet Hanson,** quoted in *A People's History of the United States*

Other workers called for shorter hours and higher wages. In 1835 and 1836, 140 strikes took place in the eastern United States. Then the Panic of 1837 brought hard times. Jobs were scarce, and workers were afraid to cause trouble. The young labor movement fell apart. Even so, workers achieved a few goals. For example, in 1840 President Martin Van Buren ordered a ten-hour workday for government workers.

**Background**
President Van Buren's order reduced the workweek from 70 to 60 hours.

## Improving Education

Schools had played an important role in colonial society, especially in New England, since the 1600s. (See Chapter 5.) But education was uneven. In the 1830s, Americans began to demand better schools. In 1837, Massachusetts set up the first state board of education in the United States. Its head was **Horace Mann**. Mann called public education "the great equalizer." He also argued that "education creates or develops new treasures—treasures never before possessed or dreamed of by any one." By 1850, many Northern states had opened public elementary schools.

Boston opened the first public high school in 1821. A few other Northern cities followed suit. In addition, churches and other groups founded hundreds of private colleges in the following decades. Many were located in states carved from the Northwest Territory. These included Antioch and Oberlin Colleges in Ohio, the University of Notre Dame in Indiana, and Northwestern University in Illinois.

There were few educational opportunities for girls beyond elementary school. Emma Willard opened the Troy Female Seminary in Troy, New York in 1821. Her school was one of the first to teach women science, social studies, and mathematics. Mary Lyon founded Mount Holyoke College in South Hadley, Masschusetts, in 1837. Oberlin became the first college to accept women as well as men. In 1849, English immigrant Elizabeth Blackwell became the first woman to earn a medical degree in the United States. Despite such individual efforts, it was rare for a woman to attend college until the late 1800s.

*Reading*History
B. Making Inferences Why do you think women and African Americans had a hard time getting an education?

African Americans also faced obstacles to getting an education. This was especially true in the South. There, teaching an enslaved person to read had been illegal since the Nat Turner Rebellion in 1831. Enslaved African Americans who tried to learn were brutally punished. Even in the North, most public schools barred African-American children.

Few colleges accepted African Americans. Those that did often took only one or two blacks at a time. The first African American to receive a college degree was Alexander Twilight in 1823. John Russwurm received one in 1826 and later began the first African-American newspaper.

**Mary Jane Patterson was the first African-American woman to earn a college degree. She graduated from Oberlin in 1862 and went on to work as a teacher.**

## Caring for the Needy

As some people promoted education, others tried to improve society's care for its weakest members. In 1841, **Dorothea Dix**, a reformer from Boston, was teaching Sunday school at a women's jail. She discovered

## AMERICA'S HISTORY MAKERS

### HORACE MANN
**1796–1859**

Horace Mann once said in a speech to students, "Be ashamed to die until you have won some victory for humanity." Mann had no reason to be ashamed. As a child, he knew poverty and hardship. He educated himself and later fought for public education for other people.

Toward the end of his life, Mann became president of Antioch College. It committed itself to education for both men and women and equal rights for African Americans.

### DOROTHEA DIX
**1802–1887**

At the age of 12, Dorothea Dix left an unhappy home to go live with her grandparents in Boston. Just two years later, she began teaching little children.

In 1841, Dix saw the harsh treatment of mentally ill women. Society frowned upon women traveling alone, but Dix defied custom. She went by train to several places where the mentally ill were housed.

Dix wrote a report about her research. (See page 438.) That report changed the care of the mentally ill.

**How might their backgrounds have motivated Dorothea Dix and Horace Mann to become leaders in reform movements?**

some women who were locked in cold, filthy cells simply because they were mentally ill. Visiting other jails, Dix learned that the mentally ill often received no treatment. Instead, they were chained and beaten. Dix pleaded with the Massachusetts Legislature to improve the care of the mentally ill. Later, she traveled all over the United States on behalf of the mentally ill. Her efforts led to the building of 32 new hospitals.

Some reformers worked to improve life for people with other disabilities. Thomas H. Gallaudet started the first American school for deaf children in 1817. Samuel G. Howe founded the Perkins School for the Blind in Boston in the 1830s.

Reformers also tried to improve prisons. In the early 1800s, debtors, lifelong criminals, and child offenders were put in the same cells. Reformers demanded that children go to special jails. They also called for the rehabilitation of adult prisoners. Rehabilitation means preparing people to live useful lives after their release from prison.

*Reading*History
**C. Recognizing Effects** How did reformers change the treatment of the mentally ill, the disabled, and prisoners?

## Spreading Ideas Through Print

During this period of reform, Americans began to receive more information about how they should lead their lives. In the 1830s, cheaper newsprint and the invention of the steam-driven press lowered the price of a newspaper to a penny. Average Americans could afford to buy the "penny papers." Penny papers were also popular because, in addition to serious news, they published gripping stories of fires and crimes.

Hundreds of new magazines also appeared. One was the *Ladies' Magazine.* Its editor was Sarah Hale, a widow who used writing to support her family. The magazine advocated education for women. It also suggested that men and women were responsible for different, but equally important, areas of life. The magazine taught that a woman's area was the home and the world of "human ties." A man's area was politics and the business of earning a living for his family. Later, Hale edited *Godey's Lady's Book,* which published poems and stories as well as articles.

## Creating Ideal Communities

While magazines sought to tell people how to live and reform movements tried to change society, some individuals decided to start over. They aimed to build an ideal society, called a **utopia.**

*Reading*History
D. Forming and Supporting Opinions Why do you think it was hard for utopias to succeed? Give reasons.

Two attempts at utopias were New Harmony, Indiana, and Brook Farm, Massachusetts. In both, residents received food and other necessities of life in exchange for work. However, both utopias experienced conflicts and financial difficulties. They ended after only a few years.

Religious belief led to some utopias. For example, the Shakers followed the beliefs of Ann Lee. She preached that people should lead holy lives in communities that demonstrate God's love to the world. When a person became a Shaker, he or she vowed not to marry or have children. Shakers shared their goods with each other, believed that men and women are equal, and refused to fight for any reason. Shakers set up communities in New York, New England, and on the frontier.

People called them *Shakers* because they shook with emotion during church services. Otherwise, Shaker life was calm. Shakers farmed and built simple furniture in styles that remain popular today. The childless Shakers depended on converts and adopting children to keep their communities going. In the 1840s, the Shakers had 6,000 members—their highest number. In 1999, only seven Shakers remained.

In the 1840s and 1850s, reform found a new direction. Many individuals began to try to win rights for two oppressed groups—women and enslaved persons. Section 4 discusses these efforts.

---

## Section 3 Assessment

### 1. Terms & Names

**Explain the significance of:**
- revival
- Second Great Awakening
- temperance movement
- labor union
- strike
- Horace Mann
- Dorothea Dix

### 2. Using Graphics

Create a chart like the one below. Use it to list problems identified by reformers and their solutions to them. (HI2)

| Problem | Reformer's Solution |
|---------|---------------------|
|         |                     |

### 3. Main Ideas

**a.** How did the Second Great Awakening influence the reform movement? (HI1)

**b.** How did labor unions try to force business owners to improve working conditions? (HI1)

**c.** What were women's contributions to the reform movement? (HI1)

### 4. Critical Thinking

**Recognizing Effects** What was the long-term impact of the reform movement that took place in the mid-1800s? (HI2)

**THINK ABOUT**
- the changes reformers made in education, temperance, prisons, and the care of the disabled
- which of those changes are still in effect today

### ACTIVITY OPTIONS

**SPEECH**

**CIVICS**

Think of a modern problem that is similar to an issue discussed in this section. Give a **speech** or write a **letter** to a government official suggesting a reform. (HI1)

# Report to the Massachusetts Legislature

**CALIFORNIA STANDARDS**

**Reading 2.7** Evaluate the unity, coherence, logic, internal consistency, and structural patterns of text.

**REP4** Students assess the credibility of primary and secondary sources and draw sound conclusions from them.

**Setting the Stage** After traveling to several places where the mentally ill were kept, Dorothea Dix wrote a report describing the conditions she had discovered. In 1843, she presented her report to lawmakers to alert them to the horrible treatment of the mentally ill. This report has been called the "first piece of social research ever conducted in America." An excerpt from Dorothea Dix's report follows. **See Primary Source Explorer** ◉

**A CLOSER LOOK**

**ADVOCATE OF THE HELPLESS**

In earlier times, the term *idiotic* did not mean stupid. It was used to describe someone who was mentally retarded.

**1. For what groups of people is Dix pleading for help?**

**A CLOSER LOOK**

**JUDICIOUS CARE**

Dix describes a woman who needs only some care and a useful task to do.

**2. What did the woman's keeper say when Dix pointed that out?**

## Report to the Massachusetts Legislature

Gentlemen: . . . I come to present the strong claims of suffering humanity. I come to place before the Legislature of Massachusetts the condition of the miserable, the desolate, the outcast. I come as the **advocate**[1] of helpless, forgotten, insane, and idiotic men and women; of beings sunk to a condition from which the most unconcerned would start with real horror; of beings wretched in our prisons, and more wretched in our **almshouses**.[2]

I must confine myself to a few examples, but am ready to furnish other and more complete details, if required.

I proceed, gentlemen, briefly to call your attention to the *present* state of insane persons confined within this **Commonwealth**,[3] in *cages, closets, cellars, stalls, pens! Chained, naked, beaten with rods*, and *lashed* into obedience.

I offer the following extracts from my notebook and journal.

*Springfield*: In the jail, one lunatic woman, furiously mad, a state **pauper**,[4] improperly situated, both in regard to the prisoners, the keepers, and herself. It is a case of extreme self-forgetfulness and oblivion to all the decencies of life, to describe which would be to repeat only the grossest scenes. She is much worse since leaving Worcester. In the almshouse of the same town is a woman apparently only needing **judicious**[5] care and some well-chosen employment to make it unnecessary to confine her in solitude in a dreary unfurnished room. Her appeals for employment and companionship are most touching, but the mistress replied "she had no time to attend to her."

*Lincoln*: A woman in a cage. *Medford*: One idiotic subject chained, and one in a close stall for seventeen years. *Pepperell*: One often doubly chained, hand and foot; another violent; several peaceable now. *Brookfield*: One man caged, comfortable. *Granville*: One often closely confined, now losing the use of his

---

1. **advocate**: a person who pleads another person's cause.
2. **almshouses**: homes for poor people.

3. **Commonwealth**: one of four U.S. states whose constitution uses this term to describe their form of self-government; in this case, Massachusetts.

4. **pauper**: a person who lives on the state's charity.
5. **judicious**: wise and careful.

limbs from want of exercise. *Charlemont:* One man caged. *Savoy:* One man caged. *Lenox:* Two in the jail, against whose unfit condition there the jailer protests.

*Dedham:* The insane **disadvantageously**[6] placed in the jail. In the almshouse, two females in stalls, situated in the main building, lie in wooden bunks filled with straw; always shut up. One of these subjects is supposed curable. The overseers of the poor have declined giving her a trial at the hospital, as I was informed, on account of expense.

Besides the above, I have seen many who, part of the year, are chained or caged. The use of cages is all but universal. Hardly a town but can refer to some not distant period of using them; chains are less common; **negligences**[7] frequent; willful abuse less frequent than sufferings proceeding from ignorance, or want of consideration. I encountered during the last three months many poor creatures wandering reckless and unprotected through the country. . . . But I cannot **particularize.**[8] In traversing the state, I have found hundreds of insane persons in every variety of circumstance and condition, many whose situation could not and need not be improved; a less number, but that very large, whose lives are the saddest pictures of human suffering and degradation.

I give a few illustrations; but description fades before reality. . . .

Men of Massachusetts, I beg, I implore, I demand pity and protection for these of my suffering, outraged sex. . . . Become the benefactors of your race, the just guardians of the solemn rights you hold in trust. Raise up the fallen, **succor**[9] the desolate, restore the outcast, defend the helpless, and for your eternal and great reward receive the benediction, "Well done, good and faithful servants, become rulers over many things!"

**A CLOSER LOOK**

**I HAVE SEEN MANY**

Notice that Dix cites evidence from many different towns.

**3. Why do you think she includes so many specific details in her report?**

**A CLOSER LOOK**

**MEN OF MASSACHUSETTS**

When Dix says "Men of Massachusetts," she is still speaking to the members of the state legislature.

**4. What does Dix want the Massachusetts Legislature to do?**

6. **disadvantageously:** harmfully.

7. **negligences:** careless actions.

8. **particularize:** to name in detail.

9. **succor:** to give help during a time of need.

---

*Interactive Primary Source Assessment*

### 1. Main Ideas

**a.** On what evidence did Dorothea Dix base her report about "suffering humanity"? (REP4)

**b.** How were the mentally ill treated in Massachusetts? (REP4)

**c.** Who did Dorothea Dix ask to help to improve the care of the mentally ill? (REP4)

### 2. Critical Thinking

**Evaluating** Dix succeeded in convincing the legislature to provide funds for new hospitals. What do you think made her report so persuasive? (REP4)

**THINK ABOUT**

• the details included in the report

• how Dix got the information to write her report

• the techniques you would use to persuade someone

# 4

# Abolition and Women's Rights

**CALIFORNIA STANDARDS**

**8.6.6** Examine the women's suffrage movement (e.g., biographies, writings, and speeches of Elizabeth Cady Stanton, Margaret Fuller, Lucretia Mott, Susan B. Anthony).

**8.7.4** Compare the lives of and opportunities for free blacks in the North with those of free blacks in the South.

**8.9.1** Describe the leaders of the movement (e.g., John Quincy Adams and his proposed constitutional amendment, John Brown and the armed resistance, Harriet Tubman and the Underground Railroad, Benjamin Franklin, Theodore Weld, William Lloyd Garrison, Frederick Douglass).

**8.9.6** Describe the lives of free blacks and the laws that limited their freedom and economic opportunities.

## ONE AMERICAN'S STORY

African-American poet Frances Ellen Watkins Harper often wrote about the suffering of enslaved persons, such as enslaved mothers.

*A VOICE FROM THE PAST*

They tear him from her circling arms,
Her last and fond embrace.
Oh! never more may her sad eyes
Gaze on his mournful face.

No marvel, then, these bitter shrieks
Disturb the listening air:
She is a mother, and her heart
Is breaking in despair.

**Frances Ellen Watkins Harper, "The Slave Mother"**

Frances Ellen Watkins Harper

As this section explains, many individuals in the mid-1800s demanded equal rights for African Americans and women.

## Abolitionists Call for Ending Slavery

**Abolition,** the movement to end slavery, began in the late 1700s. In the years before his death in 1790, Benjamin Franklin became an outspoken abolitionist, although he previously owned slaves. By 1804, most Northern states had outlawed slavery. In 1807, Congress banned the importation of African slaves into the United States. Abolitionists then began to demand a law ending slavery in the South.

David Walker, a free African American in Boston, printed a pamphlet in 1829 urging slaves to revolt. Copies of the pamphlet appeared in the South. This angered slaveholders. Shortly afterward, Walker died mysteriously. Another free black in Massachusetts, Charles Remond, became the Anti-Slavery Society's first African-American speaker in 1838.

**Taking Notes**

Use your chart to take notes about the influence of abolitionists and women.

| | How People |
|---|---|
| Immigrants | |
| Writers | |
| Reformers | |
| Abolitionists | |
| Women | |

A few Northern whites also fought slavery. In 1831, William Lloyd Garrison began to publish an abolitionist newspaper, *The Liberator*, in Boston. Of his antislavery stand, he wrote, "I will not retreat a single inch—AND I WILL BE HEARD." Many people hated his views. In 1834, a furious mob in Boston grabbed Garrison and dragged him toward a park to hang him. The mayor stepped in and saved his life.

Two famous abolitionists were Southerners who had grown up on a plantation. Sisters Sarah and Angelina Grimké believed that slavery was morally wrong. They moved north and joined an antislavery society. At the time, women were not supposed to lecture in public. But the Grimkés lectured against slavery anyway. Theodore Weld, Angelina's husband, was also an abolitionist. He led a campaign to send antislavery petitions to Congress. Proslavery congressmen passed gag rules to prevent the reading of those petitions in Congress.

John Quincy Adams ignored the gag rules and read the petitions. He also introduced an amendment to abolish slavery. Proslavery congressmen tried to stop him. Such efforts, however, only weakened the proslavery cause by showing them to be opponents of free speech. Adams also defended a group of Africans who had rebelled on the slave ship *Amistad*. He successfully argued their case before the U.S. Supreme Court in 1841, and in 1842, the Africans returned home.

## Eyewitnesses to Slavery

Two moving abolitionist speakers, **Frederick Douglass** and **Sojourner Truth**, spoke from their own experience of slavery. Douglass's courage and talent at public speaking won him a career as a lecturer for the Massachusetts Anti-Slavery Society.

People who opposed abolition spread rumors that the brilliant speaker could never have been a slave. To prove them wrong, in 1845 Douglass published an autobiography that vividly narrated his slave experiences. Afterwards, he feared recapture by his owner, so he left America for a two-year speaking tour of Great Britain and Ireland. When Douglass returned, he bought his freedom. He began to publish an antislavery newspaper.

Sojourner Truth also began life enslaved. Originally named Isabella, Sojourner Truth was born in New York State. In 1827, she fled her owners and went to live with Quakers, who set her free. They also helped her win a court battle to recover her young son. He had been sold illegally into slavery in the South. A devout Christian, Truth changed her name in 1843 to reflect her life's work: to sojourn (or stay temporarily in a place) and "declare the truth to the people." Speaking for abolition, she drew huge crowds throughout the North.

**AMERICA'S HISTORY MAKERS**

**FREDERICK DOUGLASS**
**1817–1895**

Douglass, born Frederick Bailey, was the son of a black mother and a white father. When he was eight, his owner sent him to be a servant for the Auld family. Mrs. Auld defied state law and taught young Frederick to read.

At the age of 16, Douglass returned to the plantation as a field hand. He endured so many whippings he later wrote, "I was seldom free from a sore back."

In 1838, he escaped to the North by hopping a train with a borrowed pass. To avoid recapture, he changed his last name.

**How did Mrs. Auld unknowingly help Douglass become an abolitionist leader? Explain.**

# The Underground Railroad

Some abolitionists wanted to do more than campaign for laws ending slavery. Some brave people helped slaves escape to freedom along the Underground Railroad. Neither underground nor a railroad, the **Underground Railroad** was actually an aboveground series of escape routes from the South to the North. On these routes, runaway slaves traveled on foot. They also took wagons, boats, and trains.

Still, the lives of free African Americans in the North were not easy. While there was more social and political freedom than in the South, racism was still common, and led to job and housing discrimination. Many free blacks were unskilled, and had to compete for jobs with recent immigrants from Europe. Many states prohibited free African Americans from voting, while New York used property requirements to restrict access. By 1860, only five New England states allowed free African Americans to vote.

On the Underground Railroad, the runaways usually traveled by night and hid by day in places called stations. Stables, attics, and cellars all served as stations. Free blacks such as Frederick Douglass and Philadelphia's Robert Purvis hid runaways in their homes.

# Harriet Tubman

The people who led the runaways to freedom were called conductors. One of the most famous conductors was **Harriet Tubman.** Born into slavery in Maryland, the 13-year-old Tubman once tried to save another slave from punishment. The angry overseer fractured Tubman's skull with a two-pound weight. She suffered fainting spells for the rest of her life but did not let that stop her from working for freedom. In 1849, Tubman learned that her owner was about to sell her. Instead, she escaped. She later described her feelings as she crossed into the free state of Pennsylvania: "I looked at my hands to see if I was the same person now that I was free. There was such a glory over everything."

After her escape, Harriet Tubman made 19 dangerous journeys to free enslaved persons. The tiny woman carried a pistol to frighten off slave

*Reading* **History**

C. Reading a Map
The map on page 447 shows the routes of the Underground Railroad. Notice that most of these routes led to Canada.

## Free African Americans in the North and South

| | NORTH | SOUTH |
|---|---|---|
| Job opportunities | Domestic work, farming, sailing. Some skilled positions in cities | Tradespeople, laborers, servants |
| Economic status | Middle-class communities in New York City, Philadelphia, but most free blacks live in poverty | Many free blacks in middle class, a few become planters |
| Social rights | Free to gather in groups and form social organizations | Heavy discrimination. Travel and meeting in groups restricted |
| | Discrimination still common, travel restricted | Danger of being recaptured and enslaved |

*Reading* **History**

D. Forming and Supporting Opinions Why do you think escaped slaves such as Douglass and Tubman risked their lives to help free others?

**William Lloyd Garrison**

Even after being threatened with hanging, Garrison continued to publish his antislavery newspaper, *The Liberator*.

**Sojourner Truth and Harriet Tubman**

Truth spoke out for both abolition and women's rights. Tubman risked her life leading people to freedom on the Underground Railroad.

**Lucretia Mott and Susan B. Anthony**

An abolitionist, Mott also helped lead the movement for women's rights. Anthony fought for women's suffrage into the 20th century.

hunters and medicine to quiet crying babies. Her enemies offered $40,000 for her capture, but no one caught her. "I never run my train off the track and I never lost a passenger," she proudly declared. Among the people she saved were her parents.

## Women Reformers Face Barriers

**Vocabulary**
delegation: a group that represents a larger group

Other women besides the Grimké sisters and Sojourner Truth were abolitionists. Two of these were **Lucretia Mott** and **Elizabeth Cady Stanton**. Mott and Stanton were part of an American delegation that attended the World Anti-Slavery Convention in London in 1840. These women had much to say about their work. Yet when they tried to enter the convention, they were not allowed to do so. Men angrily claimed that it was not a woman's place to speak in public. Instead, the women had to sit silent behind a heavy curtain.

To show his support, William Lloyd Garrison joined them. He said, "After battling so many long years for the liberties of African slaves, I can take no part in a convention that strikes down the most sacred rights of all women."

Stanton applauded Garrison for giving up his chance to speak on abolition, the cause for which he had fought so long. "It was a great act of self-sacrifice that should never be forgotten by women."

However, most people agreed with the men who said that women should stay out of public life. Women in the 1800s enjoyed few legal or political rights. They could not vote, sit on juries, or hold public office. Many laws treated women—especially married women—as children. Single women enjoyed some freedoms, such as being able to manage their own property. But in most states, a husband controlled any property his wife inherited and any wages she might earn.

As the convention ended, Stanton and Mott decided it was time to demand equality for women. They made up their minds to hold a convention for women's rights when they returned home.

**ELIZABETH CADY STANTON**
**1815–1902**

Elizabeth Cady Stanton's first memory was the birth of a sister when she was four. So many people said, "What a pity it is she's a girl!" that Stanton felt sorry for the new baby. She later wrote, "I did not understand at that time that girls were considered an inferior order of beings."

When Stanton was 11, her only brother died. Her father said, "Oh, my daughter, I wish you were a boy!" That sealed Stanton's determination to prove that girls were just as important as boys.

**How did Stanton's childhood experiences motivate her to help other people besides herself?**

# The Seneca Falls Convention

Inspired by their bad experience at the World Anti-Slavery Convention and by Margaret Fuller's early feminist book *Woman in the Nineteenth Century,* Stanton and Mott held the **Seneca Falls Convention** for women's rights in Seneca Falls, New York, on July 19 and 20, 1848. The convention attracted between 100 and 300 women and men, including Frederick Douglass.

Before the meeting opened, a small group of planners debated how to present their complaints. One woman read aloud the Declaration of Independence. This inspired the planners to write a document modeled on it. The women called their document the Declaration of Sentiments and Resolutions. Just as the Declaration of Independence said that "All men are created equal," the Declaration of Sentiments stated that "All men and women are created equal." It went on to list several complaints or resolutions. Then it concluded with a demand for rights.

### A VOICE FROM THE PAST

Now, in view of this entire disenfranchisement [denying the right to vote] of one-half the people of this country, their social and religious degradation—in view of the unjust laws above mentioned, and because women do feel themselves aggrieved, oppressed, and fraudulently deprived of their most sacred rights, we insist that they have immediate admission to all the rights and privileges which belong to them as citizens of the United States.

Seneca Falls Declaration of Sentiments and Resolutions, 1848

*Reading*History
**E. Using Primary Sources** Why did the women at the Seneca Falls Convention believe they deserved rights and privileges?

Every resolution won unanimous approval from the group except **suffrage,** or the right to vote. Some argued that the public would laugh at women if they asked for the vote. But Elizabeth Cady Stanton and Frederick Douglass fought for the resolution. They argued that the right to vote would give women political power that would help them win other rights. The resolution for suffrage won by a slim margin.

The women's rights movement was ridiculed. In 1852, the *New York Herald* poked fun at women who wanted "to vote, and to hustle with the rowdies at the polls" and to be men's equals. The editorial questioned what would happen if a pregnant woman gave birth "on the floor of Congress, in a storm at sea, or in the raging tempest of battle."

# Continued Calls for Women's Rights

In the mid-1800s, three women lent powerful voices to the growing women's movement. Sojourner Truth, Maria Mitchell, and Susan B. Anthony each offered a special talent.

In 1851, Sojourner Truth rose to speak at a convention for women's rights in Ohio. Some participants hissed their disapproval. Because

Truth supported the controversial cause of abolition, they feared her appearance would make their own cause less popular. But Truth won applause with her speech that urged men to grant women their rights.

> **A VOICE FROM THE PAST**
>
> I have heard much about the sexes being equal. I can carry as much as any man, and can eat as much too, if I can get it. I am as strong as any man. . . . If you have woman's rights give it to her and you will feel better. You will have your own rights, and they won't be so much trouble.
>
> **Sojourner Truth,** quoted by Marius Robinson, convention secretary

The scientist Maria Mitchell fought for women's equality by helping to found the Association for the Advancement of Women. Mitchell was an astronomer who discovered a comet in 1847. She became the first woman elected to the American Academy of Arts and Sciences.

Susan B. Anthony was a skilled organizer who worked in the temperance and antislavery movements. She built the women's movement into a national organization. Anthony argued that a woman must "have a purse [money] of her own." To this end, she supported laws that would give married women rights to their own property and wages. Mississippi passed the first such law in 1839. New York passed a property law in 1848 and a wages law in 1860. By 1865, 29 states had similar laws. (Anthony also fought for suffrage. See Chapter 22.)

But women's suffrage stayed out of reach until the 1900s, and the U.S. government did not fully abolish slavery until 1865. As you will read in the next chapter, the issue of slavery began to tear the nation apart in the mid-1800s.

This drawing shows a husband and wife fighting over who will "wear the pants in the family"— that is, who will rule the household.

THE DISCORD.

---

## Section 4 Assessment

### 1. Terms & Names

**Explain the significance of:**
- abolition
- Frederick Douglass
- Sojourner Truth
- Underground Railroad
- Harriet Tubman
- Lucretia Mott
- Elizabeth Cady Stanton
- Seneca Falls Convention
- suffrage

### 2. Using Graphics

On a time line like the one below, record significant individuals and events in the historical development of the abolition movement. (CST2)

1807                    1865

Why does the time line end in 1865?

### 3. Main Ideas

**a.** Why were freedom of speech and freedom of the press important to the abolitionist movement? (HI3)

**b.** What were Frederick Douglass's contributions to the abolitionist movement? (HI3)

**c.** What were Elizabeth Cady Stanton's contributions to the women's rights movement? (HI3)

### 4. Critical Thinking

**Drawing Conclusions**
Why do you think that many of the people who fought for abolition also fought for women's rights? (HI2)

**THINK ABOUT**
- why they opposed slavery
- the social and economic position of women
- what the two causes had in common

### ACTIVITY OPTIONS

**TECHNOLOGY**

**DRAMA**

With a partner, act out a meeting between a reformer from Section 3 and one from Section 4. **Videotape** their conversation or **perform** it for the class. (REP5)

# The Underground Railroad

The Underground Railroad was a network of people and places that hid escaping slaves and helped them reach safety in the North or in Canada. One reason slaves often went to Canada is that a U.S. federal law required people to return runaway slaves to their owners. Defying this law, both whites and blacks helped slaves to escape.

The map on page 447 shows the main escape routes. As the map shows, most of the slaves who escaped came from states bordering free states, such as Kentucky and Virginia. Distances from there to the North were relatively short, increasing the chances of reaching freedom. However, the number of slaves who escaped from the Deep South, such as Georgia and South Carolina, was very small, because of the long distances that had to be traveled. While no one knows the exact number, historians estimate that 40,000 to 100,000 people may have used the Underground Railroad on their journey from slavery to freedom.

**CALIFORNIA STANDARDS**

**8.7.2** Trace the origins and development of slavery; its effects on black Americans and on the region's political, social, religious, economic, and cultural development; and identify the strategies that were tried to both overturn and preserve it (e.g., through the writings and historical documents on Nat Turner, Denmark Vesey).

**8.9.1** Describe the leaders of the movement (e.g., John Quincy Adams and his proposed constitutional amendment, John Brown and the armed resistance, Harriet Tubman and the Underground Railroad, Benjamin Franklin, Theodore Weld, William Lloyd Garrison, Frederick Douglass).

**Among the many people who helped slaves to freedom was former slave Harriet Tubman (far left). She became a well-known guide on the Underground Railroad. She is pictured with her husband (third from left), along with other formerly enslaved people.**

# ARTIFACT FILE

**Identity Tag** Enslaved persons were forced to wear tags that identified to whom they belonged.

**Freedom Marker** The "P" on the rock shown here told slaves that they were in Pennsylvania, a free state.

Free States
Slave states
Routes of the
Underground Railroad

BRITISH TERRITORY

UNORGANIZED TERRITORY

*Lake Superior*

CANADA

Montreal

MAINE

45°N

MINNESOTA
(Statehood
in 1858)

WISCONSIN

*Lake Michigan*

*Lake Huron*

Collingwood

VT.

N.H.

MICHIGAN

Detroit

*Lake Ontario*

Niagara Falls

NEW YORK

MASS.

Boston

CONN. R.I.

40°N

Erie

New York City

Brooklyn

IOWA

Chicago

Sandusky

PENNSYLVANIA

N.J.

ILLINOIS

INDIANA

OHIO

Baltimore

MD.

DEL.

KANSAS TERRITORY

St. Louis

MISSOURI

Cincinnati
Ripley

Washington, D.C.

35°N

Evansville

*Ohio River*

VIRGINIA

Cairo

KENTUCKY

INDIAN
TERRITORY

ARKANSAS

*Mississippi River*

TENNESSEE

NORTH
CAROLINA

ATLANTIC
OCEAN

SOUTH
CAROLINA

TEXAS

MISSISSIPPI

ALABAMA

GEORGIA

30°N

LOUISIANA

New Orleans

FLORIDA

25°N

*Gulf of Mexico*

N

0      200 Miles
0      400 Kilometers

100°W   95°W   90°W   85°W

## On-Line Field Trip

**The National Underground Railroad Freedom Center** opened in 2004 in Cincinnati, Ohio. Its collections include artifacts and primary sources like this poster, which shows that substantial rewards were offered for the recapture of slaves.

**For more about the Underground Railroad . . .**

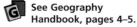

STOP THE THIEF!
One Hundred Dollars Reward.
Stolen from the Plantation of Mrs. E. S.
FARRAR, on the night of Saturday-last, two Negro Girls.
One, MARY, low stature, heavy and squarely formed, very straight,
black hair—a very bright Mulatto.
The other named CINTA or CINDERILLA, dark Copper, common
height, has a flesh mole, near the left ear, and is well formed. Mary is
twenty years old and CINTA nineteen.
I will pay a reward of $25 for the apprehension of each, if taken in
the State, and $50 if taken out of it.
My address is Howardsville, Albemarle County, or Rockfish Depot,
Nelson County.
September 15, 1862.              RICHARD T. FARRAR.

## CONNECT TO GEOGRAPHY

1. **Place** What geographic feature made it more likely that a slave in Missouri would escape to Michigan than to New York?
2. **Movement** In what way did the Underground Railroad differ from other migrations?

**G** See Geography Handbook, pages 4–5.

## CONNECT TO HISTORY

3. **Drawing Conclusions** How did the Underground Railroad reflect the American people's division over slavery?

## TERMS & NAMES

Briefly explain the significance of each of the following.

1. immigrant
2. push-pull factors
3. civil disobedience
4. revival
5. Second Great Awakening
6. labor union
7. abolition
8. Underground Railroad
9. Seneca Falls Convention
10. suffrage

## REVIEW QUESTIONS

### The Hopes of Immigrants (pages 423–428)

1. What factors influenced so many immigrants to come to America in the 1800s? (HI2)
2. What did Germans contribute to U.S. identity? (HI1)
3. How did the potato famine affect Irish emigration? (HI2)

### American Literature and Art (pages 429–432)

4. How did American artists display the love of nature in their paintings? (HI1)
5. What did the transcendentalists believe? (HI1)

### Reforming American Society (pages 433–439)

6. Why did many business owners support the temperance movement? (HI2)
7. Why was it hard for African Americans to receive an education? (HI2)

### Abolition and Women's Rights (pages 440–447)

8. Who published antislavery writings? (HI1)
9. How did the Underground Railroad work? (HI1)
10. What was the Seneca Falls Declaration of Sentiments and Resolutions? (HI1)

## CRITICAL THINKING

### 1. USING YOUR NOTES: COMPARING

| How People Influenced America in the mid-1800s | |
| --- | --- |
| Immigrants | |
| Writers | |
| Reformers | |
| Abolitionists | |
| Women | |

Using your chart, answer the questions below. (HI3)

a. Who influenced America to make reforms?

b. Compare the goals of abolitionists and women. How are they alike?

### 2. ANALYZING LEADERSHIP

Who is someone from this chapter who exercised leadership by standing up for an unpopular position? (HI1)

### 3. THEME: IMPACT OF THE INDIVIDUAL

Judging from what you read in this chapter, what methods can individuals use to influence their society? (HI1)

### 4. APPLYING CITIZENSHIP SKILLS

Who in this chapter displayed good citizenship by taking responsibility for their own behavior or by providing for their families? Give examples. (HI1)

### 5. FORMING AND SUPPORTING OPINIONS

If someone asked you what was the most important reform of this period, what would you say? Why? (HI1)

### Interact with History

Think about the laws you proposed before you read the chapter. Has your opinion changed since you read the chapter?

## VISUAL SUMMARY

# A New Spirit of Change (HI1)

**The Hopes of Immigrants**
Immigrants came to America from many European countries. They strongly influenced American life and culture.

**IMPACT OF THE INDIVIDUAL**

**Reforming American Society**
Inspired by a religious revival, a reform movement swept the country. It aided schools, the workplace, and the disabled.

**American Literature and Art**
American writers and artists of the 1800s produced some of America's greatest works, which are still studied.

**Abolition and Women's Rights**
Whites and blacks united to fight slavery. Women abolitionists expanded their fight to include women's rights as well.

Use the graph and your knowledge of U.S. history to answer questions 1 and 2.

Additional Test Practice, pp. S1–S33.

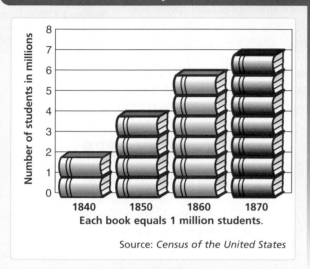

**School Enrollment,** *1840–1870*

Each book equals 1 million students.

Source: *Census of the United States*

**1.** On the graph, what does each book stand for? (8.6.5)

   **A.** 100 students

   **B.** 1,000 students

   **C.** 100,000 students

   **D.** 1,000,000 students

**2.** What is the difference in school enrollment between 1840 and 1870? (8.6.5)

   **A.** 2 million students

   **B.** 4 million students

   **C.** 5 million students

   **D.** 7 million students

**Henry David Thoreau is discussing individuality in this quotation. Use the quotation and your knowledge of U.S. history to answer question 3.**

### PRIMARY SOURCE

If a man does not keep pace with his companions, perhaps it is because he hears a different drummer. Let him step to the music which he hears, however measured or far away.

**Henry David Thoreau,** *Walden*

**3.** Which sentence best states Thoreau's perspective? (8.6.7)

   **A.** People should be able to enjoy whatever type of music they want.

   **B.** People should do what they believe is right, regardless of what others think.

   **C.** People should always comply with the wishes of those around them.

   **D.** People should understand that there is only one right way to behave.

**TEST PRACTICE**
CLASSZONE.COM

## ALTERNATIVE ASSESSMENT

**1.** 📝 **WRITING ABOUT HISTORY**

You are a reporter interviewing immigrants as they arrive in the United States after an ocean voyage. Decide what country your interviewee is from, and write questions and answers that would come from an **interview**. Ask questions about the voyage, as well as questions that reveal why they immigrated. (REP4)

• Use books about U.S. immigrants to research your interview.

**2. COOPERATIVE LEARNING**

Working with other students, make an annotated map of the Underground Railroad. Divide the work of researching to find accounts of slaves who escaped along the Underground Railroad. Type short summaries of their stories and identify their location on the map. (REP4)

## INTEGRATED TECHNOLOGY

**DOING BIOGRAPHICAL INTERNET RESEARCH**

Biographical information can be obtained from many on-line sources. Use the Internet to find facts about one of the following people: Horace Mann, Elizabeth Blackwell, Alexander Twilight, or Maria Mitchell. (REP4)

• Use your subject's name as a keyword in your research.

• Use a minimum of three different online sources and record the Web sites you used in your research.

• Once you have conducted your research, write a fact sheet about the person you chose.

**For more about these individuals . . .**

**INTERNET ACTIVITY**
CLASSZONE.COM

# Pack Your Trunk

For immigrants, packing up to go to a new land required making hard decisions. Wealthy people could ship belongings ahead. Most immigrants, though, carried their belongings in burlap bags, knotted sheets, large baskets, or small trunks. Even children carried small bundles. Only the very basic items or very precious ones could be taken to the United States. Baggage contained practical items such as tools and household items. But some had personal items such as portraits of loved ones. A few people even carried bags of dirt from their home country!

**ACTIVITY** Pack a trunk with items needed for a new life in the United States. Explain why you chose the items that you have packed. Finally, write a letter to a friend or relative back in Europe about your journey to the United States.

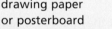

**CALIFORNIA STANDARDS**

**REP1** Students frame questions that can be answered by historical study and research.

**Writing 2.1** Write biographies, autobiographies, short stories, or narratives.

## TOOLBOX

Each group will need:

| | |
|---|---|
| a shoebox | markers or colored pencils |
| assorted magazines (optional) | 3 x 5 note cards |
| craft sticks | masking tape |
| drawing paper or posterboard | styrofoam (optional) |

## STEP BY STEP

**1** **Form groups.** Each group should consist of about four or five students. Assign group members the following tasks:

- Do research on what people brought with them when immigrating to the United States.
- Choose ten items that you will need for your new life.
- Present your items in class and give reasons for selecting them.

**2** **Research what immigrants brought with them.** In the library or on the Internet (see Researching Your Project on the next page), research what immigrants brought with them to the United States. Make a list of everything you think you'll need for a new life in the United States. Some basic items included

- books
- favorite or special clothing
- toys
- important documents

Real immigrants brought these items to the United States: a mortar and pestle (used to grind spices or medicines), a shoe brush, a coffee grinder, and a paisley shawl.

**3** **Create your items.** From your list, choose ten items that you think will be most important to starting a new life. Then draw pictures of the selected items or cut pictures of them out of a magazine. Attach a craft stick to the back of the picture with masking tape.

**4** **Write reasons.** Think of why you selected each of the ten items. Write the reasons for each item on a separate 3 x 5 note card. Attach each note card to the back of the corresponding picture.

**5** **Decorate the shoebox to look like a trunk.** Using the masking tape, affix your pictures to the rim of the shoebox, or use styrofoam in the bottom of the box to insert the pictures.

**6** **Examine other groups' trunks.** Walk around the room and examine the contents of the other groups' trunks. Compare your trunk with that of your classmates. Share your reasons for selecting certain items.

## WRITE AND SPEAK

**Write a descriptive letter.** Use the point of view of an immigrant. Write a letter to someone in your homeland describing your journey to the United States. Your letter might also describe what you miss most (personal belongings or people, for example) since the move. Read the letters to others in your class.

 **HELP DESK**

For related information, see pages 423–428 in Chapter 14.

### Researching Your Project

• *They Sought a New World* by William Kurdek and Margaret S. Englehart

• *American Immigration* by Edward G. Hartmann

For more about immigration . . .

**RESEARCH LINKS**
CLASSZONE.COM

### Did You Know?

Most immigrants traveled in **steerage** or third class. It was the lowest area of the ship, where a steering mechanism was located. A family "berth," or space allotted, in steerage was about six feet square.

Before World War I, fares in steerage to the United States from Europe were never more than $35 and by 1900 were as low as $10.

Shipping companies often fed herring (a kind of fish) to the immigrants. Herring was cheap and nourishing. It was also thought to help prevent seasickness.

### REFLECT & ASSESS

• What priorities did you use in selecting items for your trunk?

• Which items would have to be left behind if you only had a small bag for your belongings?

• Why do you think other groups selected items different from yours?

## Persuasive Writing:
### In Defense of an Important Cause

**Writing Model**
ClassZone.com

**CALIFORNIA STANDARDS**
**Writing 2.4** Write persuasive compositions.

**PURPOSE:** To argue for a cause you read about in Unit 4

**AUDIENCE:** Americans who lived between 1810 and 1860

Persuasive writing is writing whose purpose is to convince another person to adopt your opinion or viewpoint. Throughout this unit, you have read about people who used persuasion to advance their ideas. For example, the Cherokee argued before the Supreme Court that they should be allowed to hold onto their land in Georgia. Dorothea Dix tried to convince Massachusetts lawmakers to improve the care of the mentally ill.

Dorothea Dix traveled all over the United States on behalf of the mentally ill.

## Organization & Focus

Your assignment is to write a 500–700 word persuasive essay on a topic that stirred strong conflicting viewpoints in the years between 1810 and 1860. Imagine yourself living in those times. Which issue do you feel most strongly about? Which issue affects you personally?

**CHOOSING A TOPIC** Review chapters 12, 13, and 14 and look for causes that divided the nation. Choose the cause that interests you the most and that affects you most deeply as the subject of your persuasive essay.

**IDENTIFYING PURPOSE AND AUDIENCE** Your purpose is to persuade others to adopt your opinion. Americans living when the cause was being debated will be your audience. As you develop your argument, keep your audience in mind. What do they stand to gain from adopting your opinion?

**FINDING SUPPORTING EVIDENCE** Look through the unit and other sources for details, examples, and reasons you can use to support your argument. As you search for evidence, be aware of the difference between facts and opinions. A fact is a statement that can be proved. An opinion is a belief of the writer or speaker. The following statements illustrate the difference between a fact and an opinion.

**Fact:** Dorothea Dix helped found 32 mental hospitals and a school for the blind.

**Opinion:** According to historian David Wahler, Dorothea Dix was one of the most effective reformers of the 19th century.

Here are some other kinds of evidence you can use to support your argument.

| Statistics | Facts that are stated in numbers |
|------------|----------------------------------|
| Examples | Specific instances that explain your point |
| Observations | Events or situations you yourself have seen |
| Anecdotes | Brief stories that illustrate your point |
| Quotations | Direct statements from authorities |

**OUTLINING AND DRAFTING** Outline the three main parts of your persuasive essay. The **introduction** should grab the reader's interest and define your **thesis,** or controlling main idea. The **body** of your essay should provide supporting evidence for your argument. It should also address your audience's concerns and possible counterarguments. Counterarguments are any objections that others have raised. The **conclusion** should tie everything together and make a strong appeal.

## Research & Technology

Find out more about your cause and the people who supported and opposed it using library and Internet sources. Enter the names of the supporters and opponents on a search engine. You could also enter the name or description of your cause.

**Technology Tip** Before you go online, have a search strategy. For example, using key words such as *Massachusetts Legislature, Dix report* can help narrow your search. Ask a librarian to recommend search engines and directories.

## Evaluation & Revision

Before evaluating and revising your essay, put yourself in the shoes of someone who disagrees with you and ask these questions:

- What do I believe about this issue, and why?
- Why have arguments failed to convince me before?
- What evidence and reasoning do I need before I will be persuaded to change my mind?

Revise your writing until you feel confident you have addressed all these questions.

### Self-Check
Does my essay have . . .

- [ ] awareness of my audience and purpose?
- [ ] an introduction that defines my thesis?
- [ ] evidence, examples, and reasoning that support my argument?
- [ ] a strong conclusion with a final appeal?

## Publish & Present

Make a neat final copy of your persuasive essay. Include a sketch or drawing that illustrates your issue or position. If possible, read your essay aloud to your classmates and display it on a bulletin board.

# A Nation Divided and Rebuilt

"*Government of the people, by the people, for the people, shall not perish from the earth.*"

—*Abraham Lincoln, Gettysburg Address*

Gettysburg, Pennsylvania, was the site of the most decisive battle of the Civil War.

# The Nation Breaking Apart 1846–186

ILLINOIS BORN UNDER THE ORDINANCE OF '87.

Lincoln's eloquent speaking style often made him a crowd favorite.

Abraham Lincoln and Stephen A. Douglas debate the issue of slavery in the 1858 Senate campaign in Illinois.

**1846**
War with Mexico begins.
Wilmot Proviso is introduced.

**1848**
Zachary Taylor is elected president.

**1850**
President Taylor dies.
Millard Fillmore becomes president.
Congress passes the Compromise of 1850.

**1852**
*Uncle Tom's Cabin* is published.
**Franklin Pierce is elected president.**

175,000 SETS. 270,000 VOLUMES SOLD.
UNCLE TOM'S CABIN
FOR SALE HERE.
The Greatest Book of the Age.

USA
World  1846

**1848**
Rebellions erupt across Europe.

**1850**
Taiping Rebellion begins in China.

**1853**
Crimean W begins.

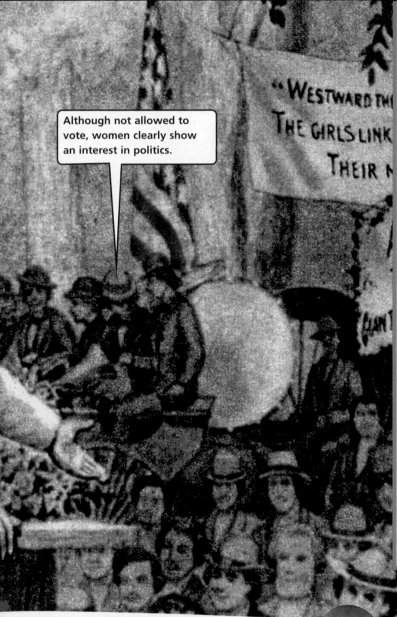

Although not allowed to vote, women clearly show an interest in politics.

"WESTWARD TH[E]
THE GIRLS LINK
THEIR [...]

You are a reporter following Abraham Lincoln and Stephen A. Douglas on the campaign trail in 1858. The issue of slavery is causing heated debates. Respectable men have turned to violence to settle their differences. You worry that soon this violence may affect the entire nation.

# How would you keep the nation together?

## What Do You Think?

- Why do you think people feel so strongly about slavery?

- Do you think debates, such as those between Lincoln and Douglas, could settle emotional issues without leading to violence?

**RESEARCH LINKS**
CLASSZONE.COM

Visit the Chapter 15 links for more information about pre-war tension.

**1854**
Congress passes the Kansas–Nebraska Act.

**1856**
James Buchanan is elected president.

**1857**
Chief Justice Roger B. Taney delivers his opinion in the *Dred Scott* case.

**1860**
Abraham Lincoln is elected president.

**1861**
The Confederate States of America is formed.

1861

**1856**
War breaks out between Britain and Persia.

**1861**
Czar Alexander II frees the serfs in Russia.

# CHAPTER 15

# Reading Strategy: Analyzing Causes

## What Do You Know?

What do you think about when you hear the terms *slavery* and *abolition?* Why do you think the issue of slavery caused so much anger and resentment?

### Think About

- what you've learned about differences between the North and the South from books, travel, television, or movies
- reasons people have violent conflicts today
- your responses to the Interact with History about keeping the nation together (see page 455)

## What Do You Want to Know?

What questions do you have about the sectional crisis that led to the Civil War? Record them in your notebook before you read this chapter.

**CALIFORNIA STANDARDS**

**Reading 2.0** Students read and understand grade-level-appropriate material. They describe and connect the essential ideas, arguments, and perspectives of the text by using their knowledge of text structure, organization, and purpose.

Slavery caused such strong emotions that fights sometimes broke out between members of Congress.

## Analyzing Causes

Analyzing causes means looking closely at events and describing why they happened. The diagram below will help you analyze some of the causes of secession. Use the diagram to take notes on how each issue drove the North and the South farther apart.

**S** See Skillbuilder Handbook, page R11.

### Taking Notes

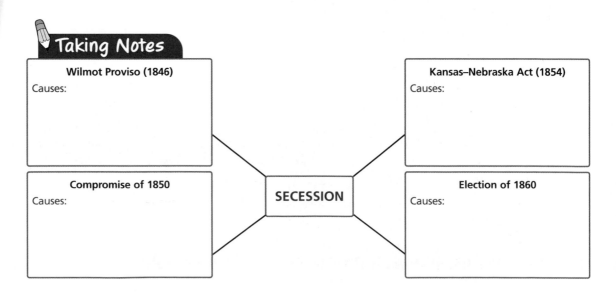

| Wilmot Proviso (1846)  Causes: | | Kansas–Nebraska Act (1854)  Causes: |
|---|---|---|
| | **SECESSION** | |
| Compromise of 1850  Causes: | | Election of 1860  Causes: |

# Growing Tensions Between North and South

| MAIN IDEA | WHY IT MATTERS NOW | TERMS & NAMES |
|---|---|---|
| Disagreements between the North and the South, especially over the issue of slavery, led to political conflict. | Regional differences can make national problems difficult to resolve. | Wilmot Proviso    Daniel Webster<br>Free-Soil Party    Stephen A. Douglas<br>Henry Clay    Compromise of 1850 |

## ONE EUROPEAN'S STORY

During the 1830s, a French government official named Alexis de Tocqueville [TOHK•vihl] traveled down the Ohio River. The river was the border between Ohio, a free state, and Kentucky, a slave state. Tocqueville noted what he saw on both sides of the river.

**Alexis de Tocqueville**

*A VOICE FROM THE PAST*

The State of Ohio is separated from Kentucky just by one river; on either side of it the soil is equally fertile, and the situation equally favourable, and yet everything is different. Here [on the Ohio side] a population devoured by feverish activity, trying every means to make its fortune. . . . There [on the Kentucky side] are people who make others work for them and show little compassion, a people without energy, mettle or the spirit of enterprise. . . . These differences cannot be attributed to any other cause but slavery.

**Alexis de Tocqueville,** *Journey to America*

In this section, you will read about the differences between the North and the South.

## North and South Take Different Paths

As you read in Chapter 11, the economies of the North and the South developed differently in the early 1800s. Although both economies were mostly agricultural, the North began to develop more industry and commerce. By contrast, the Southern economy relied on plantation farming.

The growth of industry in the North helped lead to the rapid growth of Northern cities. Much of this population growth came from immigration. In addition, immigrants and Easterners moved west and built farms in the new states formed from the Northwest Territory. Most canals and railroads ran east and west, helping the Eastern and Midwestern states develop strong ties with each other.

**CALIFORNIA STANDARDS**

**8.7.1** Describe the development of the agrarian economy in the South, identify the locations of the cotton-producing states, and discuss the significance of cotton and the cotton gin.

**8.7.2** Trace the origins and development of slavery; its effects on black Americans and on the region's political, social, religious, economic, and cultural development; and identify the strategies that were tried to both overturn and preserve it (e.g., through the writings and historical documents on Nat Turner, Denmark Vesey).

**8.9.4** Discuss the importance of the slavery issue as raised by the annexation of Texas and California's admission to the union as a free state under the Compromise of 1850.

**8.9.6** Describe the lives of free blacks and the laws that limited their freedom and economic opportunities.

**8.10.1** Compare the conflicting interpretations of state and federal authority as emphasized in the speeches and writings of statesmen such as Daniel Webster and John C. Calhoun.

**8.10.2** Trace the boundaries constituting the North and the South, the geographical differences between the two regions, and the differences between agrarians and industrialists.

**Taking Notes**

Use your chart to take notes about the Wilmot Proviso and the Compromise of 1850.

SECESSION

# Economics *in* History

## Trade

Trade is based on a simple idea. If you have something someone else needs or wants, and that person has something you need or want, you exchange, or trade, those two things. After the trade, you should both be better off than before.

The concept of trade works similarly for groups of people. For example, in the early 1800s, the South had few factories. Planters who wanted manufactured goods usually had to buy them from manufacturers in the North or in Europe. To have the cash to buy those goods, Southerners sold other goods, such as cotton, to the North and other countries. Each sold the goods they could produce in order to get money to buy the goods they could not make.

**CONNECT TO HISTORY**

**1. Solving Problems** What problem does trade help a country solve? How else could a country solve this problem?

See Skillbuilder Handbook, page R18.

**CONNECT TO TODAY**

**2. Comparing** What goods do Americans sell to other countries today? What goods do Americans buy from other countries?

For more about trade . . .

**RESEARCH LINKS**
CLASSZONE.COM

Northern States and Other Countries

Southern States

The South developed differently than the North. A few wealthy planters controlled Southern society. They made great profits from the labor of their slaves. Much of this profit came from trade. Planters relied on exports, especially cotton. Because these plantations were so profitable, planters invested in slaves instead of industry. As a result, the South developed little industry.

Most Southern whites were poor farmers who owned no slaves. But even many of the nonslaveholding whites supported slavery because it kept them off the bottom of society.

*Reading* **History**

**A. Making Generalizations** How did the economies of the North and the South differ?

## Antislavery and Racism

The issue of slavery caused tension between the North and the South. In the North, the antislavery movement had slowly been gaining strength since the 1830s. Abolitionists believed that slavery was unjust and should be abolished immediately. Many Northerners who opposed slavery took a less extreme position. Some Northern workers and immigrants opposed slavery because it was an economic threat to them. Because slaves did not work for pay, free workers feared that managers would employ slaves rather than them. Some workers were even afraid that the expansion of slavery might force workers into slavery to find jobs.

Despite their opposition to slavery, most Northerners, even abolitionists, were racist by modern standards. Many whites refused to go to school with, work with, or live near African Americans. In most states, even free African Americans could not vote.

When Northern attacks on slavery increased, slaveholders defended slavery. Most offered the openly racist argument that white people were superior to blacks. Many also claimed that slavery helped slaves by introducing them to Christianity, as well as providing them with food, clothing, and shelter throughout their lives. Slaveholders were determined to defend slavery and their way of life. In this way, the different ideas about slavery brought the North and the South into conflict.

**Vocabulary**
**racist:** having prejudice based on race

## The Wilmot Proviso

After the Missouri Compromise in 1820, political disagreements over slavery seemed to go away. But new disagreements arose with the outbreak of the War with Mexico in 1846. Many Northerners believed that Southerners wanted to take territory from Mexico in order to extend slavery. To prevent that, Representative David Wilmot of Pennsylvania proposed a bill, known as the **Wilmot Proviso,** to outlaw slavery in any territory the United States might acquire from the War with Mexico.

But slaveholders believed that Congress had no right to prevent them from bringing slaves into any of the territories. They viewed slaves as property. The Constitution, they claimed, gave equal protection to the property rights of all U.S. citizens. The Wilmot Proviso removed the right of slaveholders to take their slaves, which they regarded as property, anywhere in the United States or its territories. Southerners claimed that the bill was unconstitutional.

The Wilmot Proviso divided Congress along regional lines. The bill passed the House of Representatives. But Southerners prevented it from passing the Senate.

Even though the Wilmot Proviso never became law, it had important effects. It led to the creation of the **Free-Soil Party,** a political party dedicated to stopping the expansion of slavery. The party's slogan expressed its ideals—"Free Soil, Free Speech, Free Labor, and Free Men." The Free-Soil Party won more than ten seats in Congress in the election of 1848. More important, the party made slavery a key issue in national politics. Politicians could ignore slavery no longer.

*Reading* **History**
**B. Recognizing Effects** What were the effects of the Wilmot Proviso?

### Connections TO WORLD HISTORY

**EXPANDING SLAVERY**

While the Wilmot Proviso upset slavery defenders, the Ostend Manifesto of 1854 angered anti-slavery forces. On the instruction of Secretary of State William Marcy, ambassadors to England, France, and Spain met in Ostend, Belgium to discuss plans to purchase Cuba from Spain. This purchase would increase the slave territory in the United States, and would reduce the risk of a Cuban slave revolt similar to the one in Haiti.

The diplomats wrote a document which offered to buy Cuba, but also warned that the United States would take the island by force if negotiations failed. The Ostend Manifesto became a political disaster for President Franklin Pierce's administration, and widened the divide over slavery.

## Controversy over Territories

By 1848, the nation's leaders had begun to debate how to deal with slavery in the lands gained from the War with Mexico. The proposed addition of new states threatened the balance in Congress between North and South. The discovery of gold in California brought thousands of people into that territory. There would soon be enough people in California for it to apply for statehood. Most California residents wanted their state to be a free state. But this would tip the balance of power clearly in favor of the North. Southerners wanted to divide California in half, making the northern half a free state and the southern half a slave state.

In 1849, President Zachary Taylor—who opposed the extension of slavery—proposed that California submit a plan for statehood that year, without going through the territorial stage. Taylor's plan gave Southern slaveholders little time to move to California with their slaves.

In March 1850, California applied to be admitted as a free state. With California as a free state, slave states would become a minority in the Senate just as they were in the House. Jefferson Davis, a senator from Mississippi, warned, "For the first time, we are about permanently to destroy the balance of power between the sections."

## The Compromise of 1850

California could not gain statehood, however, without the approval of Congress. And Congress was divided over the issue. Behind the scenes, statesmen sought compromise. Taking the lead was Senator **Henry Clay**

**Background**
U.S. land gains from the War with Mexico included all or parts of the future states of California, Nevada, Utah, Arizona, New Mexico, and Colorado.

This engraving dramatically portrays the Senate debate over the Compromise of 1850.

John C. Calhoun of South Carolina opposed the Compromise of 1850. He believed the South had no reason to compromise on the issue of slavery.

Henry Clay led the Congress in creating compromises on several important issues during his long career.

Daniel Webster spoke eloquently in favor of the compromise.

of Kentucky. Clay had helped create the Missouri Compromise in 1820. Now Clay crafted a plan to settle the California problem.

*Reading*History
C. Reading a Map
Look at the map on page 464 to see how the Compromise of 1850 affected the territories open to slavery.

1. To please the North, California would be admitted as a free state, and the slave trade would be abolished in Washington, D.C.
2. To please the South, Congress would not pass laws regarding slavery for the rest of the territories won from Mexico, and Congress would pass a stronger law to help slaveholders recapture runaway slaves.

Many people on both sides felt they had to give up too much in this plan. But others were tired of the regional bickering. They wanted to hold the Union together. **Daniel Webster,** senator from Massachusetts, supported the compromise for the sake of the Union.

### A VOICE FROM THE PAST

I wish to speak today, not as a Massachusetts man, nor as a Northern man, but as an American. . . . I speak today for the preservation of the Union. Hear me for my cause.

**Daniel Webster,** quoted in *The Annals of America*

The job of winning passage of the plan fell to Senator **Stephen A. Douglas** of Illinois. By the end of September, Douglas succeeded, and the plan, now known as the **Compromise of 1850,** became law.

Some people celebrated the compromise, believing that it had saved the Union. But the compromise would not bring peace. In the next section, you will learn how sectional tensions continued to rise.

## AMERICA'S HISTORY MAKERS

**STEPHEN A. DOUGLAS**
**1813–1861**

Stephen A. Douglas was one of the most powerful members of Congress in the mid-1800s. In fact, he was called the "Little Giant" because he commanded great respect even though he was only five feet four inches tall.

Perhaps the most important issue that Douglas faced during his career was the expansion of slavery into the territories. Douglas privately hated slavery. But he did not believe a debate on morality would do any good. He suggested that the people of each territory should decide whether or not to allow slavery.

**What groups of Americans agreed with Douglas's position on slavery?**

---

## Section  1 Assessment

### 1. Terms & Names

**Explain the significance of:**

- Wilmot Proviso
- Free-Soil Party
- Henry Clay
- Daniel Webster
- Stephen A. Douglas
- Compromise of 1850

### 2. Using Graphics

Use a chart like the one below to explain the effects of each cause.

| Causes | Effects |
|---|---|
| Abolitionism | |
| Wilmot Proviso | |
| California's application for statehood | |

Which issue do you think most threatened national unity? (HI2)

### 3. Main Ideas

**a.** What were two ways that the North and the South differed by the mid-1800s? (HI1)

**b.** In what ways was racism common in both the North and the South? (HI1)

**c.** How did the War with Mexico lead to conflict between the North and the South? (HI1)

### 4. Critical Thinking

**Comparing and Contrasting** How was the Compromise of 1850 similar to and different from the Missouri Compromise? (CST1)

**THINK ABOUT**

- the regional tensions at the time the compromises were proposed
- who proposed each bill
- the provisions of the bills

---

### ACTIVITY OPTIONS

**TECHNOLOGY**

**SPEECH**

Imagine you are a television news director. Plan a five-minute **documentary** or organize a **panel discussion** on the Compromise of 1850. (HI1)

# The Crisis Deepens

| MAIN IDEA | WHY IT MATTERS NOW | TERMS & NAMES |
|---|---|---|
| Turmoil over slavery led to acts of violence. | Violence can make compromise more difficult. | Harriet Beecher Stowe / popular sovereignty<br>*Uncle Tom's Cabin* / Kansas–Nebraska Act<br>Fugitive Slave Act / John Brown |

### Taking Notes

Use your chart to take notes about the Kansas-Nebraska Act.

SECESSION

## ONE AMERICAN'S STORY

**Harriet Beecher Stowe** was outraged when she heard about the part of the Compromise of 1850 that would help slaveholders recapture runaway slaves. She stated that the Christian men who passed this law "cannot know what slavery is."

Stowe's anger motivated her to write ***Uncle Tom's Cabin,*** a novel that portrayed slavery as brutal and immoral. In this section, you will learn how the Compromise of 1850 deepened the division between the North and the South.

**Harriet Beecher Stowe**

## The Fugitive Slave Act

The 1850 law to help slaveholders recapture runaway slaves was called the **Fugitive Slave Act.** People accused of being fugitives under this law could be held without an arrest warrant. In addition, they had no right to a jury trial. Instead, a federal commissioner ruled on each case. The commissioner received five dollars for releasing the defendant and ten dollars for turning the defendant over to a slaveholder.

Southerners felt that the Fugitive Slave Act was justified because they considered slaves to be property. But Northerners resented the Fugitive Slave Act. It required Northerners to help recapture runaway slaves. It placed fines on people who would not cooperate and jail terms on people who helped the fugitives escape. In addition, Southern slave catchers roamed the North, sometimes capturing free African Americans.

The presence of slave catchers throughout the North brought home the issue of slavery to Northerners. They could no longer ignore the fact that, by supporting the Fugitive Slave Act, they played an important role in supporting slavery. They faced a moral choice. Should they obey the law and support slavery, or should they break the law and oppose slavery?

## Uncle Tom's Cabin

Stowe published *Uncle Tom's Cabin* in 1852. It dramatically portrayed the moral issues of slavery. In fact, a play based on the book increased the popularity of drama as well as abolitionism. The book's main character was Uncle Tom, a respected older slave. The plot centers on Tom's life under three owners. Two of the owners were kind, but the third was cruel. The novel includes dramatic scenes, such as the dangerous escape of a slave named Eliza and her baby across the Ohio River.

*Reading* **History**
A. Analyzing Points of View How did the play *Uncle Tom's Cabin* affect the development of drama in the United States?

> *A VOICE FROM THE PAST*
>
> Eliza made her desperate retreat across the river just in the dusk of twilight. The gray mist of evening, rising slowly from the river, enveloped her as she disappeared up the bank, and the swollen current and floundering masses of ice presented a hopeless barrier between her and her pursuer.
>
> **Harriet Beecher Stowe,** *Uncle Tom's Cabin*

Stowe's book was wildly popular in the North. But white Southerners believed the book falsely criticized the South and slavery.

## The Kansas–Nebraska Act

While the Fugitive Slave Act and *Uncle Tom's Cabin* heightened the conflicts between the North and the South, the issue of slavery in the territories brought bloodshed to the West. In 1854, Senator Stephen A. Douglas of Illinois drafted a bill to organize territorial governments for the Nebraska Territory. He proposed that it be divided into two territories—Nebraska and Kansas.

To get Southern support for the bill, he suggested that the decision about whether to allow slavery in each of these territories be settled by popular sovereignty. **Popular sovereignty** is a system where the residents vote to decide an issue. If this bill passed, it would result in getting rid of the Missouri Compromise by

**Background** The Nebraska Territory was part of the Louisiana Purchase. It lay north of the 36° 30' line, so the Missouri Compromise banned slavery there.

In 1854, Bostonians protested the capture of an African American by federal marshals under the Fugitive Slave Act.

463

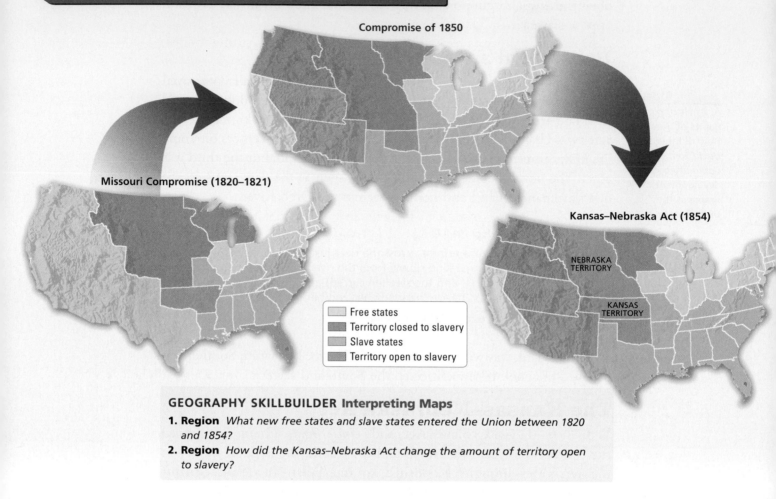

## Free and Slave States and Territories, *1820–1854*

**Compromise of 1850**

**Missouri Compromise (1820–1821)**

**Kansas–Nebraska Act (1854)**

NEBRASKA TERRITORY

KANSAS TERRITORY

- ☐ Free states
- ☐ Territory closed to slavery
- ☐ Slave states
- ☐ Territory open to slavery

**GEOGRAPHY SKILLBUILDER Interpreting Maps**

1. **Region** *What new free states and slave states entered the Union between 1820 and 1854?*
2. **Region** *How did the Kansas–Nebraska Act change the amount of territory open to slavery?*

allowing people to vote for slavery in territories where the Missouri Compromise had banned it.

As Douglas hoped, Southerners applauded the repeal of the Missouri Compromise and supported the bill. Even though the bill angered opponents of slavery, it passed. It became known as the **Kansas–Nebraska Act**. Few people realized that the act would soon turn Kansas into a battleground over slavery.

## "Bleeding Kansas"

Proslavery and antislavery settlers rushed into the Kansas Territory, just west of Missouri, to vote for the territorial legislature. At the time of the election in March 1855, there were more proslavery settlers than antislavery settlers in the territory. But the proslavery forces did not want to risk losing the election. Five thousand Missourians came and voted in the election illegally. As a result, the official Kansas legislature was packed with proslavery representatives.

Antislavery settlers boycotted the official government and formed a government of their own. With political authority in dispute, settlers on both sides armed themselves. In May, a proslavery mob attacked the town of Lawrence, Kansas. The attackers destroyed offices and the

**Vocabulary**
**boycott:** refuse to participate in

house of the governor of the antislavery government. This attack came to be known as the Sack of Lawrence.

Onto this explosive scene came **John Brown,** an extreme abolitionist. To avenge the Sack of Lawrence, Brown and seven other men went to the cabins of several of his proslavery neighbors and murdered five people. This attack is known as the Pottawatomie Massacre, after the creek near where the victims were found. As news of the violence spread, civil war broke out in Kansas. It continued for three years, and the territory came to be called "Bleeding Kansas."

*Reading*History

**B. Sequencing Events** What events in Kansas preceded the Pottawatomie Massacre?

## Violence in Congress

While violence was spreading in Kansas in the spring of 1856, blood was also being shed in the nation's capital. In late May, Senator Charles Sumner of Massachusetts delivered a speech attacking the proslavery forces in Kansas. His speech was packed with insults. Sumner even made fun of A. P. Butler, a senator from South Carolina.

Preston Brooks, a relative of Butler, heard about Sumner's speech. To defend Butler and the South, he attacked Sumner, who was sitting at his desk. Brooks hit Sumner over the head with his cane. Sumner tried to defend himself, but his legs were trapped. Brooks hit him 30 times or more, breaking his cane in the assault. (The painting on page 455 shows this event.)

Many Southerners cheered Brooks's defense of the South. But most Northerners were shocked at the violence in the Senate. "Bleeding Kansas" and "Bleeding Sumner" became rallying cries for antislavery Northerners and slogans for a new political party. In the next section, you will learn about the creation of the Republican Party.

## STRANGE *but* True

**PRESTON BROOKS'S CANE**

Many Americans, Northerners and Southerners alike, were ashamed of the behavior of Sumner and Brooks. But sectional tensions were so high at the time that a large number of Southerners cheered Brooks for his actions.

A number of Brooks's supporters sent him new canes to replace the one he had broken while hitting Sumner on the head. Some of the canes were inscribed with mottoes such as "Hit Him Again."

---

**Section 2 Assessment**

### 1. Terms & Names

**Explain the significance of:**
- Harriet Beecher Stowe
- *Uncle Tom's Cabin*
- Fugitive Slave Act
- popular sovereignty
- Kansas–Nebraska Act
- John Brown

### 2. Using Graphics

Use a chart like the one below to compare Northern and Southern views of the issues listed. (REP5)

| Northern View | Issue | Southern View |
|---|---|---|
| | Fugitive Slave Act | |
| | Kansas–Nebraska Act | |
| | "Bleeding Kansas" | |

### 3. Main Ideas

**a.** How did the book *Uncle Tom's Cabin* influence national politics? (HI2)

**b.** Why was the Kansas–Nebraska Act so controversial? (HI2)

**c.** What was the cause of "Bleeding Kansas"? (HI2)

### 4. Critical Thinking

**Solving Problems** What would you have done to prevent the violence in Kansas? (REP1)

**THINK ABOUT**
- the repeal of the Missouri Compromise
- popular sovereignty
- the actions of John Brown

**ACTIVITY OPTIONS**

**LITERATURE**

**ART**

Read a chapter of *Uncle Tom's Cabin.* Write a **book review** or make a series of **drawings** illustrating the story. (REP4)

# 3

# Slavery Dominates Politics

| MAIN IDEA | WHY IT MATTERS NOW | TERMS & NAMES |
|---|---|---|
| Disagreement over slavery led to the formation of the Republican Party and heightened sectional tensions. | The Democrats and the Republicans are the major political parties of today. | Republican Party<br>John C. Frémont<br>James Buchanan<br>*Dred Scott* v. *Sandford* · Roger B. Taney<br>Abraham Lincoln<br>Harpers Ferry |

**CALIFORNIA STANDARDS**

**8.7.2** Trace the origins and development of slavery; its effects on black Americans and on the region's political, social, religious, economic, and cultural development; and identify the strategies that were tried to both overturn and preserve it (e.g., through the writings and historical documents on Nat Turner, Denmark Vesey).

**8.9.5** Analyze the significance of the States' Rights Doctrine, the Missouri Compromise (1820), the Wilmot Proviso (1846), the Compromise of 1850, Henry Clay's role in the Missouri Compromise and the Compromise of 1850, the Kansas-Nebraska Act (1854), the Dred Scott v. Sandford decision (1857), and the Lincoln-Douglas debates (1858).

**8.10.4** Discuss Abraham Lincoln's presidency and his significant writings and speeches and their relationship to the Declaration of Independence, such as his "House Divided" speech (1858), Gettysburg Address (1863), Emancipation Proclamation (1863), and inaugural addresses (1861 and 1865).

**Taking Notes**

Use your chart to take notes about the election of 1860.

SECESSION

## ONE AMERICAN'S STORY

Joseph Warren, editor of the Detroit *Tribune,* wanted the antislavery parties of Michigan to join forces.

### A VOICE FROM THE PAST

[A convention should be called] irrespective of the old party organizations, for the purpose of agreeing upon some plan of action that shall combine the whole anti-Nebraska, anti-slavery sentiment of the State, upon one ticket [set of candidates endorsed by a political party].

**Detroit *Tribune,*** quoted in *The Origins of the Republican Party*

On July 6, 1854, antislavery politicians from various parties met to form a new party and called themselves Republicans. In this section, you will learn why the Republican Party was formed and how it changed American politics in the 1850s.

This medal shows an early Republican Party motto. It also makes clear the connection to the Free-Soil Party's antislavery position.

## The Republican Party Forms

The creation of the Republican Party grew out of the problems caused by the Kansas–Nebraska Act of 1854. The law immediately caused a political crisis for the Whig Party. Southern Whigs had supported the bill for the same reason that Northern Whigs had opposed it: the bill proposed to open new territories to slavery. There was no room for compromise, so the party split.

The Southern Whigs were destroyed by the split. A few joined the Democratic Party. But most searched for leaders who supported slavery and the Union. The Northern Whigs, however, joined with other opponents of slavery and formed the **Republican Party.**

The Republicans quickly gained strength in the North. "Bleeding Kansas" was the key to the Republican rise. Many people blamed the violence on the Democrats. With the 1856 elections nearing, the

Republicans believed that they had an excellent opportunity to gain seats in Congress and win the presidency.

The Republicans needed a strong presidential candidate in 1856 to strengthen their young party. They nominated **John C. Frémont**. Young and handsome, Frémont was a national hero for his explorations in the West, which earned him the nickname the "Pathfinder."

Republicans liked Frémont for a couple of reasons. He had spoken in favor of admitting both California and Kansas as free states. Also, he had little political experience and did not have a controversial record to defend. Even so, the Republican position on slavery was so unpopular in the South that Frémont's name did not appear on the ballot there.

*Reading*History

A. Summarizing Why did the Republicans nominate Frémont for president in 1856?

## The Election of 1856

The Democrats nominated **James Buchanan** to run for the presidency in 1856. As minister to Great Britain, he had been in England since 1853 and had spoken neither for nor against the Kansas–Nebraska Act.

Buchanan took advantage of his absence from the country. He said little about slavery and claimed that his goal was to maintain the Union. Buchanan appealed to Southerners, to many people in the upper South and the border states, and to Northerners who were afraid that Frémont's election could tear the nation apart.

The American, or Know-Nothing, Party also nominated a presidential candidate in 1856. They chose Millard Fillmore, who had been president, following the death of Zachary Taylor, from 1850 until 1853. But the Know-Nothings were divided over slavery and had little strength.

The 1856 presidential election broke down into two separate races. In the North, it was Buchanan against Frémont. In the South, it was Buchanan against Fillmore. Buchanan won. He carried all the slave states except Maryland, where Fillmore claimed his only victory. Buchanan also won several Northern states.

Although he lost the election, Frémont won 11 Northern states. These results showed two things. First, the Republican Party was a major force in the North. Second, the nation was sharply split over slavery.

HISTORIC
DECISIONS
*OF THE SUPREME COURT*

For more information on *Dred Scott* v. *Sandford*, see pp. 746–747.

## The Case of Dred Scott

The split in the country was made worse by the Supreme Court decision in the case of Dred Scott. Scott had been a slave in Missouri. His owner took him to live in territories where slavery was illegal. Then they returned to Missouri. After his owner's death, Scott sued for his freedom. He argued that he was a free man because he had lived in territories where slavery was illegal. His case, **_Dred Scott_ v. _Sandford_**, reached the Supreme Court in 1856.

## Now and then

**THIRD-PARTY CANDIDATES**

American politics has usually been dominated by two parties. Most third-party candidates, such as the Republican Frémont in 1856, lose elections. Still, third parties are important. Women's right to vote, child labor laws, and the Social Security Act all began as third-party initiatives.

Modern third parties such as the Libertarian, Reform, and Green parties, continue to run candidates for office. In 1998, Reform Party candidate Jesse Ventura was elected governor of Minnesota. In the 2000 presidential election, Ralph Nader (below) ran for the Green Party and received nearly 3 million votes.

In 1857, the Court ruled against Scott. Chief Justice **Roger B. Taney** [TAW•nee] delivered his opinion in the case. In it, he said that Dred Scott was not a U.S. citizen. As a result, he could not sue in U.S. courts. Taney also ruled that Scott was bound by Missouri's slave code because he lived in Missouri. As a result, Scott's time in free territory did not matter in his case.

In addition, Taney argued that Congress could not ban slavery in the territories. To do so would violate the slaveholders' property rights, protected by the Fifth Amendment. In effect, Taney declared legislation such as the Missouri Compromise unconstitutional.

Southerners cheered the Court's decision. Many Northerners were outraged and looked to the Republican Party to halt the growing power of Southern slaveholders.

*Reading* **History**

**B. Recognizing Effects** How did Taney's opinion affect the Missouri Compromise?

**Dred Scott (above) first sued for his freedom in 1846. The Supreme Court, led by Chief Justice Roger B. Taney (right), did not rule on the case until 1857.**

## Lincoln and Douglas Debate

After the *Dred Scott* decision, the Republicans charged that the Democrats wanted to legalize slavery not only in all U.S. territories but also in all the states. They used this charge to attack individual Democrats. Stephen A. Douglas, sponsor of the Kansas–Nebraska Act, was one of their main targets in 1858. That year, Illinois Republicans nominated **Abraham Lincoln** to challenge Douglas for his U.S. Senate seat. In his first campaign speech, Lincoln expressed the Northern fear that Southerners wanted to expand slavery to the entire nation. He set the stage for his argument by using a metaphor from the Bible.

> *A VOICE FROM THE PAST*
>
> "A house divided against itself cannot stand." I believe this government cannot endure, permanently half slave and half free. I do not expect the Union to be dissolved—I do not expect the house to fall—but I do expect it will cease to be divided. It will become all one thing, or all the other.
>
> **Abraham Lincoln,** Springfield, Illinois, June 16, 1858

Later in the year, the two men held formal debates across Illinois. The Lincoln–Douglas debates are now seen as models of political debate. At the time, the debates allowed people to compare the short, stocky, well-dressed Douglas with the tall, thin, gawky Lincoln.

The two men squarely addressed the nation's most pressing issue: the expansion of slavery. For Lincoln, slavery was "a moral, a social and a political wrong," and he suggested that African Americans had rights under the Declaration of Independence. But he did not suggest abolishing slavery where it already existed. He argued only that slavery should not be expanded.

Douglas did not share Lincoln's belief that it was the national government's role to prevent the expansion of slavery. Instead, he argued

## Debating Points of View

Debate has long been an important method of exploring public issues. The Lincoln-Douglas debates drew crowds from all over Illinois to hear Lincoln and Douglas discuss the issues of the day. Debates such as these can help people find out about candidates' views.

Today, the National Forensic League (NFL) sponsors Lincoln-Douglas Debates, competitions for high school students. Many judges, actors, news commentators, and talk show hosts began to develop their debating skills in such competitions.

High school students can benefit from learning to defend their positions in debates. One student explained what she learned from NFL debates. "I learned about how to think really fast and how to respond."

Jessica Bailey of Apple Valley High School in Minnesota won second place in the national Lincoln-Douglas Debates competition in 1998.

### How Do You Debate an Issue?

1. Choose a debate opponent and an issue to debate. (One NFL topic for national competition was whether the federal government should establish an educational policy to increase academic achievement in secondary schools in the United States.)

2. Research the topic you chose.

3. Agree on a format for your debate—how many minutes for presentation, rebuttal, and closing.

4. Debate your opponent in front of the class.

5. Find out how many students in the audience agree with each side, then ask for their reasons.

 See Citizenship Handbook, page 285.

For more about debating . . .

 **RESEARCH LINKS** CLASSZONE.COM

---

that popular sovereignty was the best way to address the issue because it was the most democratic method to do so.

But popular sovereignty was a problem for Douglas. The Supreme Court decision in the *Dred Scott* case had made popular sovereignty unconstitutional. Why? It said that people could not vote to ban slavery, because doing so would take away slaveholders' property rights. In the debates, Lincoln asked Douglas if he thought people in a territory who were against slavery could legally prohibit it—despite the *Dred Scott* decision.

Douglas replied that it did not matter what the Supreme Court might decide about slavery because "the people have the lawful means to introduce it or exclude it as they please." Douglas won reelection. Lincoln, despite his loss, became a national figure and strengthened his standing in the Republican Party.

*Reading* **History**
**C. Making Inferences** Why were popular sovereignty and the opinion in the *Dred Scott* case inconsistent?

## John Brown Attacks Harpers Ferry

In 1859, John Brown, who had murdered proslavery Kansans three years before, added to the sectional tensions. Brown had a plan. He wanted to inspire slaves to fight for their freedom. To do this, he planned to capture the weapons in the U.S. arsenal at **Harpers Ferry,** Virginia.

On October 16, 1859, Brown and 18 followers—13 whites and 5 blacks—captured the Harpers Ferry arsenal. They killed four people in the raid. Brown then sent out the word to rally and arm local slaves.

**Vocabulary**
**arsenal:** stock of weapons

# HISTORY through ART

John Steuart Curry painted *The Tragic Prelude* between 1937 and 1942. He shows a wild-eyed John Brown standing on the bodies of Civil War soldiers.

**What do you think Curry's views were on John Brown's role in U.S. history?**

But no slaves joined the fight. The U.S. Marines attacked Brown at Harpers Ferry. Some of his men escaped. But Brown and six others were captured, and ten men were killed.

Brown was then tried for murder and treason. He was convicted and sentenced to hang. On the day he was hanged, abolitionists tolled bells and fired guns in salute. Southerners were enraged by Brown's actions and horrified by Northern reactions to his death.

As the nation headed toward the election of 1860, the issue of slavery had raised sectional tensions to the breaking point. In the next section, you will read about the election of 1860 and its effect on the nation.

---

## Section  Assessment

### 1. Terms & Names

**Explain the significance of:**

- Republican Party
- John C. Frémont
- James Buchanan
- *Dred Scott* v. *Sandford*
- Roger B. Taney
- Abraham Lincoln
- Harpers Ferry

### 2. Using Graphics

Use a chart like the one below to take notes on the major events discussed in this section. (REP3)

| Election of 1856 | |
|---|---|
| *Dred Scott* v. *Sandford* | |
| Lincoln–Douglas debates | |
| Harpers Ferry | |

### 3. Main Ideas

**a.** What issues led to the creation of the Republican Party? (HI2)

**b.** What consequences did the *Dred Scott* decision have for free blacks? (HI2)

**c.** How did John Brown's attack on Harpers Ferry increase tensions between the North and the South? (HI2)

### 4. Critical Thinking

**Identifying Facts and Opinions** How did Lincoln and Douglas disagree about slavery? Which of their views were facts, and which were opinions? (REP2)

**THINK ABOUT**

- Lincoln's speech at Springfield in 1858
- Douglas's support of popular sovereignty

---

**ACTIVITY OPTIONS**

**MATH**

**GEOGRAPHY**

Do research to find election returns from the 1856 presidential election. Make **graphs** or draw a **map** to illustrate the results. (CST3)

# Lincoln's Election and Southern Secession

| MAIN IDEA | WHY IT MATTERS NOW | TERMS & NAMES |
|---|---|---|
| The election of Lincoln led the Southern states to secede from the Union. | This was the only time in U.S. history that states seceded from the Union. | platform      Jefferson Davis<br>secede      Crittenden Plan<br>Confederate States<br>    of America |

## ONE AMERICAN'S STORY

In 1860, most people assumed that William Seward of New York would win the Rebublican party's presidential nomination.

However, throughout the Republican convention, other candidates tried to win away Seward's delegates. Abraham Lincoln, a lesser-known candidate from Illinois, gained strength. The reporter Murat Halstead described the scene as Lincoln received the winning votes.

In 1860, the Republican delegates met in Chicago at a convention hall known as the Wigwam.

### A VOICE FROM THE PAST

There was a moment's silence. The nerves of the thousands, which through the hours of suspense had been subjected to terrible tension, relaxed, and as deep breaths of relief were taken, there was a noise in the Wigwam [convention hall] like the rush of a great wind [just before] a storm—and in another breath, the storm was there. There were thousands cheering with the energy of insanity.

**Murat Halstead,** *Caucuses of 1860*

**CALIFORNIA STANDARDS**

**8.9.5** Analyze the significance of the States' Rights Doctrine, the Missouri Compromise (1820), the Wilmot Proviso (1846), the Compromise of 1850, Henry Clay's role in the Missouri Compromise and the Compromise of 1850, the Kansas-Nebraska Act (1854), the Dred Scott v. Sandford decision (1857), and the Lincoln-Douglas debates (1858).

**8.10.2** Trace the boundaries constituting the North and the South, the geographical differences between the two regions, and the differences between agrarians and industrialists.

**8.10.4** Discuss Abraham Lincoln's presidency and his significant writings and speeches and their relationship to the Declaration of Independence, such as his "House Divided" speech (1858), Gettysburg Address (1863), Emancipation Proclamation (1863), and inaugural addresses (1861 and 1865).

Having won the nomination, Lincoln could turn his attention to winning the general election. In this section, you will learn about the election of 1860 and its role in pushing the nation toward civil war.

**Taking Notes**

Use your chart to take notes about the election of 1860.

SECESSION

## Political Parties Splinter

In April, a few weeks before the Republicans nominated Abraham Lincoln, the Democrats held their convention in Charleston, South Carolina. Northern and Southern Democrats disagreed over what to say about slavery in the party's **platform,** or statement of beliefs.

The Southerners wanted the party to defend slavery in the platform.

But Northerners wanted the platform to support popular sovereignty as a way of deciding whether a territory became a free state or a slave state. The Northerners won the platform vote, causing 50 Southern delegates to walk out of the convention.

The remaining delegates tried to nominate a presidential candidate. Stephen A. Douglas was the leading contender, but the Southerners who stayed refused to back him because of his support for popular sovereignty. Douglas could not win enough votes to gain the nomination.

Finally, the Democrats gave up and decided to meet again in Baltimore in June to choose a candidate. But as the Baltimore convention opened, Northerners and Southerners remained at odds. This time, almost all the Southerners left the meeting.

With the Southerners gone, the Northern Democrats nominated Douglas. Meanwhile, the Southern Democrats decided to nominate their own candidate. They chose John Breckinridge of Kentucky, the current vice-president and a supporter of slavery.

As you read in One American's Story on page 471, the Republicans had already nominated Abraham Lincoln. In addition to Lincoln, Douglas, and Breckinridge, a candidate from a fourth party entered the race. This party was called the Constitutional Union Party, and its members had one aim—to preserve the Union. They nominated John Bell of Tennessee to run for president.

*Reading*History
A. Recognizing Effects How did slavery affect U.S. political parties in 1860?

## The Election of 1860

The election of 1860 turned into two different races for the presidency, one in the North and one in the South. Lincoln and Douglas were the only candidates with much support in the North. Breckinridge and Bell competed for Southern votes.

Lincoln and Breckinridge were considered to have the most extreme views on slavery. Lincoln opposed the expansion of slavery into the territories. Breckinridge insisted that the federal government be required to protect slavery in any territory. Douglas and Bell were considered moderates because neither wanted the federal government to pass new laws on slavery.

The outcome of the election made it clear that the nation was tired of compromise. Lincoln defeated Douglas in the North. Breckinridge carried most of the South. Douglas and Bell managed to win only in the states between the North and the Deep South. Because the North had more people in it than the South, Lincoln won the election.

This cartoon of the long-legged Abe Lincoln shows him to be the fittest candidate in the 1860 presidential election.

## The Election of 1860

| | | Electoral Vote | Popular Vote |
|---|---|---|---|
| | Lincoln (Republican) | 180 | 1,865,593 |
| | Douglas (N. Democrat) | 12 | 1,382,713 |
| | Breckinridge (S. Democrat) | 72 | 848,356 |
| | Bell (Constitutional Union) | 39 | 592,906 |

**GEOGRAPHY SKILLBUILDER Interpreting Maps**

1. **Region** *Which state split its vote, and which candidates received those votes?*
2. **Region** *How many states did Lincoln win?*

Despite Lincoln's statements that he would do nothing to abolish slavery in the South, white Southerners did not trust him. Many were sure that he and the other Republicans would move to ban slavery. As a result, white Southerners saw the Republican victory as a threat to the Southern way of life.

## Southern States Secede

Before the 1860 presidential election, many Southerners had warned that if Lincoln won, the Southern states would **secede**, or withdraw from the Union. Supporters of secession based their arguments on the idea of states' rights. They argued that the states had voluntarily joined the Union. Consequently, they claimed that the states also had the right to leave the Union.

On December 20, 1860, South Carolina became the first state to secede. Other states in the Deep South, where slave labor and cotton production were most common, also considered secession. During the next six weeks, Mississippi, Florida, Alabama, Georgia, Louisiana, and Texas joined South Carolina in secession.

In early February 1861, the states that had seceded met in Montgomery, Alabama. They formed the **Confederate States of America**. The convention named **Jefferson Davis** president of the Confederacy.

**Background**
Before becoming president of the Confederacy, Davis had been a hero during the War with Mexico and a U.S. senator.

In his First Inaugural Address, Lincoln argued passionately for the North and the South to preserve the Union.

Along with naming Davis president, the convention drafted a constitution. The Confederate Constitution was modeled on the U.S. Constitution. But there were a few important differences. For example, the Confederate Constitution supported states' rights. It also protected slavery in the Confederacy, including any territories it might acquire.

Having formed its government, the Confederate states made plans to defend their separation from the Union. Some believed that war between the states could not be avoided. But everyone waited to see what the Union government would do in response.

## The Union Responds to Secession

Northerners considered the secession of the Southern states to be unconstitutional. During his last months in office, President James Buchanan argued against secession. He believed that the states did not have the right to withdraw from the Union because the federal government, not the state governments, was sovereign. If secession were permitted, the Union would become weak, like a "rope of sand." He believed that the U.S. Constitution was framed to prevent such a thing from happening.

In addition to these issues, secession raised the issue of majority rule. Southerners complained that Northerners intended to use their majority to force the South to abolish slavery. But Northerners responded that Southerners simply did not want to live by the rules of democracy. They complained that Southerners were not willing to live with the election results. As Northern writer James Russell Lowell

**Vocabulary**
**sovereign:** supreme, self-governing authority

wrote, "[The Southerners'] quarrel is not with the Republican Party, but with the theory of Democracy."

## Efforts to Compromise Fail

With the states in the lower South forming a new government in Montgomery, Alabama, some people continued to seek compromise. Senator John J. Crittenden of Kentucky developed a compromise plan. The **Crittenden Plan** was presented to Congress in late February 1861, but it did not pass.

*"We must not be enemies."*

Abraham Lincoln

With the hopes for compromise fading, Americans waited for Lincoln's inauguration. What would the new president do about the crisis? On March 4, Lincoln took the oath of office and gave his First Inaugural Address. Citing the Constitution many times, as well as the Declaration of Independence, he assured the South that he had no intention of abolishing slavery there. But he spoke forcefully against secession. Then he ended his speech with an appeal to friendship.

*Reading* **History**

**B. Making Inferences** What do you think Lincoln meant by "mystic chords of memory"?

### A VOICE FROM THE PAST

We are not enemies, but friends. We must not be enemies. Though passion may have strained, it must not break our bonds of affection. The mystic chords of memory, stretching from every battle-field and patriot grave, to every living heart and hearthstone, all over this broad land, will yet swell the chorus of the Union, when again touched, as surely they will be, by the better angels of our nature.

**Abraham Lincoln,** *First Inaugural Address*

Lincoln would not press the South. He wanted no invasion. But he would not abandon the government's property there. Several forts in the South, including Fort Sumter in South Carolina, were still in Union hands. These forts would soon need to be resupplied. Throughout March and into April, Northerners and Southerners waited anxiously to see what would happen next. You will find out in the next chapter.

---

Section  **4** Assessment

### 1. Terms & Names

**Explain the significance of:**
- platform
- secede
- Confederate States of America
- Jefferson Davis
- Crittenden Plan

### 2. Using Graphics

Use a time line to fill in the main events that occurred between April 1860 and March 1861.

| April 1860 | June 1860 | Feb. 1861 |
| --- | --- | --- |
| May 1860 | Nov. 1860 | March 1861 |

Do you think secession could have been avoided? Why? (CST2)

### 3. Main Ideas

**a.** Who were the candidates in the 1860 presidential election, and what policies did each candidate stand for? (HI1)

**b.** Which states seceded right after Lincoln's election? How did they justify this action? (HI2)

**c.** What attempts did the North and the South make to compromise? What were the results? (HI2)

### 4. Critical Thinking

**Analyzing Points of View** Do you think the Southern states seceded to protect slavery or states' rights? (REP5)

**THINK ABOUT**
- the Southern view of the Fugitive Slave Act
- the Confederate Constitution
- slaveholders' views of the Republican Party

**ACTIVITY OPTIONS**

**SPEECH**

**TECHNOLOGY**

Read Lincoln's First Inaugural Address. Deliver a section of the **speech** before the class or plan an **electronic presentation** about that day and Lincoln's message. (REP4)

## VISUAL SUMMARY

### The Nation Breaking Apart (CST2)

**SLAVERY**

**1846**
Wilmot Proviso

Compromise of **1850**

**1854**
Kansas–Nebraska Act

**1855**
"Bleeding Kansas"

**1856**
Caning of Sumner

**1857**
*Dred Scott* v. *Sandford*

**1859**
Attack on Harpers Ferry

Election of **1860**

**Secession**

## TERMS & NAMES

Briefly explain the significance of each of the following.

1. Wilmot Proviso
2. Compromise of 1850
3. *Uncle Tom's Cabin*
4. popular sovereignty
5. Kansas–Nebraska Act
6. John Brown
7. John C. Frémont
8. *Dred Scott* v. *Sandford*
9. secede
10. Confederate States of America

## REVIEW QUESTIONS

### Growing Tensions Between North and South (pages 457–461)

1. How did the North and the South differ in the 1840s? (HI1)
2. How did Southerners react to the Wilmot Proviso? (HI2)
3. What was Stephen A. Douglas's role in passing the Compromise of 1850? (HI1)

### The Crisis Deepens (pages 462–465)

4. How did Northerners react to the Fugitive Slave Act? (HI2)
5. Why did most Northerners and Southerners disagree about the Kansas–Nebraska Act? (HI1)
6. How did "Bleeding Kansas" cause problems for Democrats? (HI2)

### Slavery Dominates Politics (pages 466–470)

7. Where did Lincoln and Douglas each stand on slavery? (REP5)
8. What was the result of John Brown's raid on Harpers Ferry? (HI2)

### Lincoln's Election and Southern Secession (pages 471–475)

9. What were the results of the election of 1860, and what did these results show? (HI1)
10. How did Southerners justify secession? (REP5)

## CRITICAL THINKING

### 1. USING YOUR NOTES: ANALYZING CAUSES

Using your completed diagram, answer the questions below. (HI2)

Wilmot Proviso (1846) — Kansas–Nebraska Act (1854)

SECESSION

Compromise of 1850 — Election of 1860

a. What did the Compromise of 1850 and the Kansas–Nebraska Act have in common?
b. Which event do you think caused the most damage to the relationship between the North and the South? Explain.

### 2. ANALYZING LEADERSHIP

Why were the nation's leaders in 1860 unable to compromise like the leaders in 1820 and 1850? Does their failure to compromise in 1860 mean that they were not as capable as earlier leaders? (CST1)

### 3. APPLYING CITIZENSHIP SKILLS

What alternatives did the states in the lower South have to secession? Which of these alternatives do you think would have been the best choice? (HI4)

### 4. SOLVING PROBLEMS

How did slavery divide Americans in the 1850s? (HI1)

### 5. THEME: DIVERSITY AND UNITY

What could have been done in the 1850s to prevent the Southern states from seceding? What did Americans have in common that could have overcome their differences over slavery? (HI4)

### Interact *with* History

Now that you have read about the sectional crisis of the 1850s, do you think the solution you came up with at the start of the chapter would have helped keep the Union together? Explain.

Use the map and your knowledge of U.S. history to answer questions 1 and 2.

Additional Test Practice, pp. S1–S33.

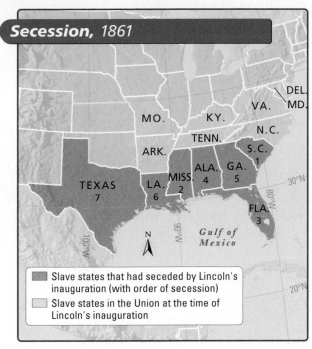

Secession, 1861

Gulf of Mexico

N

30°N

20°N

80°W

90°W

100°W

DEL.
MD.
VA.
MO.
KY.
N.C.
TENN.
ARK.
S.C.
1
ALA.
4
GA.
5
TEXAS
7
LA.
6
MISS.
2
FLA.
3

- ■ Slave states that had seceded by Lincoln's inauguration (with order of secession)
- ■ Slave states in the Union at the time of Lincoln's inauguration

**1.** Of the following states, which was the last to secede before Lincoln's Inauguration? (8.10.2)

- **A.** South Carolina
- **B.** Texas
- **C.** Georgia
- **D.** Louisiana

**2.** How many slave states were in the Union at the time of Lincoln's inauguration? (8.10.2)

- **A.** 6
- **B.** 7
- **C.** 8
- **D.** 9

**Abraham Lincoln is discussing the future of the United States regarding slavery in this quotation. Use the quotation and your knowledge of U.S. history to answer question 3.**

### PRIMARY SOURCE

"A house divided against itself cannot stand." I believe this government cannot endure, permanently half slave and half free. I do not expect the Union to be dissolved—I do not expect the house to fall—but I do expect it will cease to be divided. It will become all one thing, or all the other.

**Abraham Lincoln,** Springfield, Illinois, June 16, 1858

**3.** Which of the following best states Lincoln's point of view? (8.10.4)

- **A.** The states of the Union will be all free.
- **B.** The states of the Union will be all slave.
- **C.** The Union will remain intact.
- **D.** The Union will be divided.

TEST PRACTICE
CLASSZONE.COM

## ALTERNATIVE ASSESSMENT

### 1. ✒ WRITING ABOUT HISTORY

Imagine you work for a popular magazine and have been assigned to write an **article** about one of the important figures in this chapter. You might choose such figures such as Harriet Beecher Stowe or Stephen A. Douglas. (REP4)

- Write a series of questions to ask this person.
- Use library resources to see how he or she might answer your questions.

### 2. COOPERATIVE LEARNING

Work with a small group to research the Dred Scott case and conduct a mock trial. In your research, look for information about the roles of Taney, the other justices, Scott, and other major participants. After you conduct the trial, have your class decide on a verdict. (REP5)

## INTEGRATED TECHNOLOGY

### DOING INTERNET RESEARCH

Political parties in America changed a great deal during the 1840s and 1850s. Using the Internet or other library resources, research the election returns of the presidential elections from 1848 to 1860. (REP4)

- Use an online or standard encyclopedia to find the election results.
- Prepare a presentation for your class. Create pie charts to show the percentage of votes that went to each political party in each election. Or use bar graphs to show the growth in total popular vote for each party for each election.

For more about these elections . . .

INTERNET ACTIVITY
CLASSZONE.COM

# The Civil War Begins 1861–1862

In this vivid engraving, South Carolina shore guns fire on Fort Sumter in Charleston's harbor.

**March 4, 1861**
Abraham Lincoln inaugurated as president.

**April 12, 1861**
Confederate forces fire on Fort Sumter.

**July 21, 1861**
First Battle of Bull Run (Manassas) occurs.

USA
World  **1861**

**March, 1861**
Italy unified under King Victor Emmanuel II.

**May 13, 1861**
Britain declares neutrality in American Civil War.

The battle rages in the harbor.

People watch the bombardment from their rooftops.

The date is April 12, 1861. You and other residents of Charleston, South Carolina, watch the bombardment of Fort Sumter by Confederate forces. This event signals the beginning of the Civil War—a war between factions or regions of the same country.

# How might a civil war be worse than other wars?

## What Do You Think?

- What social, political, and economic problems might be likely to occur in a civil war?

- What might happen when a civil war breaks out?

**RESEARCH LINKS**
CLASSZONE.COM

Visit the Chapter 16 links for more information about the beginning of the Civil War.

---

**March 9, 1862**
The warships
*Monitor* and
*Merrimack* (or
*Virginia*) clash.

**April 6, 1862**
Battle of Shiloh
takes place.

**April 25, 1862**
New Orleans falls
to Union forces.

**September 17, 1862**
Battle of Antietam
(Sharpsburg) occurs.

**April 13, 1862**
France annexes
Cochin China
(southern Vietnam).

**May 5, 1862**
French troops are
defeated at
Puebla, Mexico.

**June 25, 1862**
Imperial decree
expels foreigners
from Japan.

**September, 1862**
Bismarck becomes
prime minister
of Prussia.

1862

*The Civil War Begins* **479**

# Reading Strategy: Comparing and Contrasting

## What Do You Know?

What do you think of when you hear the phrase *civil war*? What would it be like to fight in a war of brother against brother? Where and how did the Civil War begin?

### Think About

- what a civil war is
- what you've learned about the Civil War from movies, television, and books
- reasons that countries threaten to break apart in today's world
- your responses to the Interact with History about how a civil war is worse than other wars (see page 479)

**CALIFORNIA STANDARDS**

**Reading 2.0** Students read and understand grade-level-appropriate material. They describe and connect the essential ideas, arguments, and perspectives of the text by using their knowledge of text structure, organization, and purpose.

## What Do You Want to Know?

 What details do you need to help you understand the outbreak of the Civil War? Make a list of those details in your notebook before you read the chapter.

## Comparing and Contrasting

When you compare, you look for similarities between two or more objects, ideas, events, or people. When you contrast, you look for differences. Comparing and contrasting can be a useful strategy for studying the two sides in a war. Use the chart shown here to compare and contrast the North and the South in the early years of the Civil War.

 **See Skillbuilder Handbook, page R10.**

### Taking Notes

|  | North | South |
|---|---|---|
| **Reasons for fighting** |  |  |
| **Advantages** |  |  |
| **Disadvantages** |  |  |
| **Military strategy** |  |  |
| **Battle victories** |  |  |

# War Erupts

1

| MAIN IDEA | WHY IT MATTERS NOW | TERMS & NAMES |
|---|---|---|
| The secession of the Southern states quickly led to armed conflict between the North and the South. | The nation's identity was in part forged by the Civil War. | Fort Sumter    Anaconda Plan<br>Robert E. Lee    blockade<br>border state    First Battle of<br>King Cotton        Bull Run |

## ONE AMERICAN'S STORY

Like other South Carolinians, Emma Holmes got caught up in the passions that led her state to secede. In her diary, she wrote about South Carolina's attack on Fort Sumter, a federal fort in Charleston's harbor.

### A VOICE FROM THE PAST

[A]t half past four this morning, the heavy booming of cannons woke the city from its slumbers. . . . Every body seems relieved that what has been so long dreaded has come at last and so confident of victory that they seem not to think of the danger of their friends. . . . With the telescope I saw the shots as they struck the fort and [saw] the masonry crumbling.

**Emma Holmes,** *The Diary of Emma Holmes 1861–1866*

This photograph of Emma Holmes was taken in 1900.

**CALIFORNIA STANDARDS**

**8.10.2** Trace the boundaries constituting the North and the South, the geographical differences between the two regions, and the differences between agrarians and industrialists.

**8.10.4** Discuss Abraham Lincoln's presidency and his significant writings and speeches and their relationship to the Declaration of Independence, such as his "House Divided" speech (1858), Gettysburg Address (1863), Emancipation Proclamation (1863), and inaugural addresses (1861 and 1865).

**8.10.5** Study the views and lives of leaders (e.g., Ulysses S. Grant, Jefferson Davis, Robert E. Lee) and soldiers on both sides of the war, including those of black soldiers and regiments.

**8.10.6** Describe critical developments and events in the war, including the major battles, geographical advantages and obstacles, technological advances, and General Lee's surrender at Appomattox.

Many Southerners expected a short war that they would easily win. Northerners expected the same. In this section, you will learn how the war started, how the states divided, and how each side planned to win.

## First Shots at Fort Sumter

As they seceded from the Union (the states loyal to the United States of America during the Civil War), the Southern states took over most of the federal forts inside their borders. President Abraham Lincoln had to decide what to do about the forts that remained under federal control. Major Robert Anderson and his garrison held on to **Fort Sumter** in the harbor of Charleston, South Carolina, but they were running out of supplies.

If Lincoln supplied the garrison, he risked war. If he ordered the troops to leave the fort, he would be giving in to the rebels. Lincoln informed South Carolina that he was sending supply ships to Fort Sumter. Leaders of the Confederacy (the nation formed by Southern states in 1861) decided to prevent the federal government from holding onto the fort by attacking before the supply ships arrived.

**Taking Notes**

Use your chart to take notes about military strategies and the advantages and disadvantages for both sides.

| Reasons for fighting | |
|---|---|
| Advantages | |
| Disadvantages | |
| Military strategy | |
| Battle victories | |

At 4:30 A.M. on April 12, 1861, shore guns opened fire on the island fort. For 34 hours, the Confederates fired shells into the fort until Anderson was forced to surrender. No one was killed, but the South's attack on Fort Sumter was the beginning of the Civil War.

## Lincoln Calls Out the Militia

Two days after the surrender of Fort Sumter, President Lincoln asked the Union states to provide 75,000 militiamen for 90 days to put down the uprising in the South. Citizens of the North responded with enthusiasm to the call to arms. A New York woman wrote, "It seems as if we never were alive till now; never had a country till now."

In the upper South, however, state leaders responded with anger. The governor of Kentucky said that the state would "furnish no troops for the wicked purpose of subduing her sister Southern States." In the weeks that followed, Virginia, North Carolina, Tennessee, and Arkansas voted to join the Confederacy.

As each state seceded, volunteers rushed to enlist, just as citizens did in the North. A young Arkansas enlistee wrote, "So impatient did I become for starting that I felt like ten thousand pins were pricking me in every part of the body, and started off a week in advance of my brothers." Some feared the war would be over before they got the chance to fight.

With Virginia on its side, the Confederacy had a much better chance for victory. Virginia was wealthy and populous, and the Confederacy in May of 1861 moved its capital to Richmond. Virginia also was the home of **Robert E. Lee,** a talented military leader. When Virginia seceded, Lee resigned from the United States Army and joined the Confederacy. Although Lee opposed slavery and secession, he explained, "I cannot raise my hand against my birthplace, my home, my children." He eventually became the commanding general of the Army of Northern Virginia.

## Choosing Sides

After Virginia seceded, both sides knew that the border states would play a key role in the war's outcome. The **border states**—Delaware, Maryland, Kentucky, and Missouri—were slave states that bordered states in which slavery was illegal. Because of their location and resources, the border states could tip the scales toward one side.

Keeping Maryland in the Union was important for the North. If Maryland seceded, then Washington, D.C., would be cut off from the Union. To hold on to the state, Lincoln ordered the arrest of Maryland lawmakers who backed the South. Union forces arrested 31 secessionist

**AMERICA'S HISTORY MAKERS**

**ABRAHAM LINCOLN**
**1809–1865**
Today, Abraham Lincoln is considered one of the great men of all time. Yet early in his presidency, he was widely criticized and ridiculed. Critics labeled him ignorant, incompetent, and socially crude. As Lincoln grew into his job, however, he gained the respect and affection of many Northerners.

Even as a youth, Lincoln had displayed a gift for public speaking. During the Civil War, through his speeches and writings, Lincoln inspired fellow Americans to "dare to do our duty as we understand it."

**Why would the ability to inspire people be important in a wartime leader?**

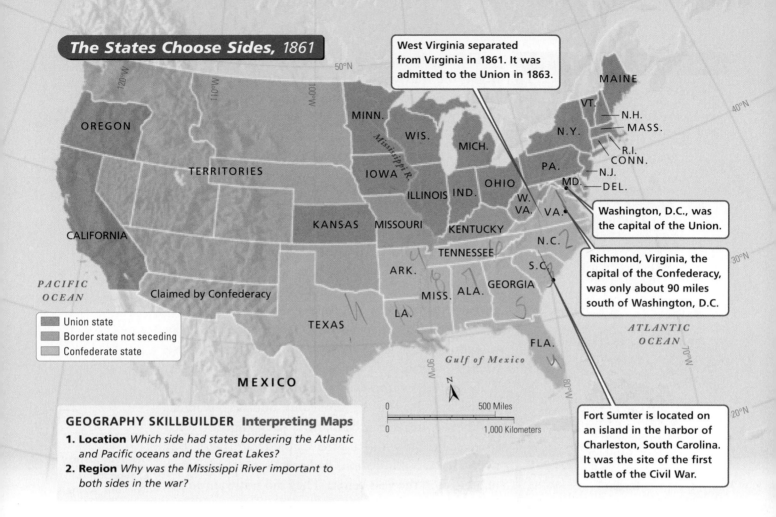

**The States Choose Sides, 1861**

West Virginia separated from Virginia in 1861. It was admitted to the Union in 1863.

Washington, D.C., was the capital of the Union.

Richmond, Virginia, the capital of the Confederacy, was only about 90 miles south of Washington, D.C.

Fort Sumter is located on an island in the harbor of Charleston, South Carolina. It was the site of the first battle of the Civil War.

Claimed by Confederacy

- Union state
- Border state not seceding
- Confederate state

PACIFIC OCEAN

ATLANTIC OCEAN

Gulf of Mexico

MEXICO

0          500 Miles
0          1,000 Kilometers

**GEOGRAPHY SKILLBUILDER Interpreting Maps**
1. **Location** Which side had states bordering the Atlantic and Pacific oceans and the Great Lakes?
2. **Region** Why was the Mississippi River important to both sides in the war?

members of the legislature. They were held for at least two months—after the election of a new legislature.

Kentucky was also important to both sides because of its rivers. For the Union, the rivers could provide an invasion route into the South. For the South, the rivers could provide a barrier. Kentuckians were deeply divided over secession. However, a Confederate invasion in 1861 prompted the state to stay in the Union.

*Reading* **History**

**B. Summarizing**
Why were the border states critical to the war's outcome?

Both Missouri and Delaware also stayed in the Union. In Virginia, federal troops helped a group of western counties break away. These counties formed the state of West Virginia and returned to the Union. In the end, 24 states made up the Union and 11 joined the Confederacy.

## Strengths and Weaknesses

The Union had huge advantages in manpower and resources. The North had about 22 million people. The Confederacy had roughly 9 million, of whom about 3.5 million were slaves. About 85 percent of the nation's factories were located in the North. The North had more than double the railroad mileage of the South. Almost all the naval power and shipyards belonged to the North.

The Union's greatest asset, however, was President Abraham Lincoln. He developed into a remarkable leader. Lincoln convinced Northerners that democracy depended on preserving the Union.

The pie charts show the relative strength of the Union and the Confederacy in population and industry.

**Total U.S. Population**

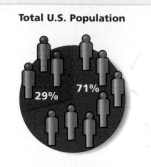

29%  71%

■ Union   ■ Confederacy

**Total U.S. Railroad Mileage**

29%  71%

**Total U.S. Manufacturing Plants**

15%

85%

**Total U.S. Industrial Workers**

8%

92%

Source: *Encyclopedia Americana*

**SKILLBUILDER**
**Interpreting Charts**
1. *Which side had more resources?*
2. *How might the North's railways and factories have helped its armies?*

---

The Confederacy had some advantages, too. It began the war with able generals, such as Robert E. Lee. It also had the advantage of fighting a defensive war. This meant Northern supply lines would have to be stretched very far. In addition, soldiers defending their homes have more will to fight than invaders do.

## The Confederate Strategy

At first, the Confederacy took a defensive position. It did not want to conquer the North—it only wanted to be independent. "All we ask is to be let alone," said Confederate President Jefferson Davis. Confederate leaders hoped the North would soon tire of the war and accept Southern independence.

The South also depended on **King Cotton** as a way to win foreign support. Cotton was king because Southern cotton was important in the world market. The South grew most of the cotton for Europe's textile mills. When the war broke out, Southern planters withheld cotton from the market. They hoped to force France and Britain to aid the Confederate cause. But in 1861, European nations had surplus cotton because of a big crop the year before. They did not want to get involved in the American war.

As the war heated up, the South soon moved away from its cautious plans. It began to take the offensive and try for big victories to wreck Northern morale.

## The Union Strategy

The North wanted to bring the Southern states back into the Union. To do this, the North developed an offensive strategy based on General Winfield Scott's **Anaconda Plan.** This plan was designed to smother the South's economy like a giant anaconda snake squeezing its prey.

The plan called for a naval blockade of the South's coastline. In a **blockade,** armed forces prevent the transportation of goods or people into or out of an area. The plan also called for the Union to gain control of the Mississippi River. This would split the Confederacy in two.

One of the drawbacks of Scott's plan was that it would take time to work. But many people, eager for action, were calling for an immediate attack on Richmond, the Confederate capital. Lincoln ordered an invasion of Virginia in the summer of 1861.

*Reading* **History**
**C. Supporting Opinions** At the beginning of the Civil War, which side would you have predicted to win? Why?

# Battle of Bull Run

To take Richmond, the Union army would first have to defeat the Confederate troops stationed at the town of Manassas, Virginia. This was a railway center southwest of Washington, D.C.

On July 21, 1861, Union forces commanded by General Irvin McDowell clashed with Confederate forces headed by General Pierre Beauregard near a little creek called Bull Run north of Manassas. In the North, this battle came to be known as the **First Battle of Bull Run**.

At one point in the battle, a Confederate officer rallied his troops by pointing his sword toward Southern General Thomas J. Jackson. The officer cried, "There is Jackson standing like a stone wall! Rally behind the Virginians!" From this incident, Jackson won the nickname "Stonewall" Jackson. His men held fast against the Union assault.

As fresh troops arrived, the Confederates equaled the Union forces in number and launched a countercharge. Attacking the Union line, they let out a blood-curdling scream. This scream, later called the "rebel yell," caused the Union troops to panic. They broke ranks and scattered.

The Confederate victory in the First Battle of Bull Run thrilled the South and shocked the North. Many in the South thought the war was won. The North realized it had underestimated its opponent. Lincoln sent the 90-day militias home and called for a real army of 500,000 volunteers for three years. In the next section, you will learn what army life was like.

The Confederate Army passes in review before General Pierre Beauregard.

---

## Section 1 Assessment

### 1. Terms & Names

**Explain the significance of:**
- Fort Sumter
- Robert E. Lee
- border state
- King Cotton
- Anaconda Plan
- blockade
- First Battle of Bull Run

### 2. Using Graphics

Use a Venn diagram to compare and contrast the strengths of the North and the South. (8.10.6)

North — Strengths in common — South

### 3. Main Ideas

**a.** How did citizens in the North and the South respond to the outbreak of the Civil War? (HI2)

**b.** Why were the border states important to both sides in the Civil War? (HI1)

**c.** What kind of military strategy did each side develop? (HI1)

### 4. Critical Thinking

**Comparing** How was the South's situation in the Civil War similar to the situation of the Patriots in the Revolutionary War? (REP5)

**THINK ABOUT**
- their reasons for fighting
- their opponents' strengths

**ACTIVITY OPTIONS**

**LANGUAGE ARTS**
**TECHNOLOGY**

Read an account of the First Battle of Bull Run. Use the information to write a **news article** or plan the battle's **home page** for the Internet. (REP4)

## from

# Across Five Aprils

### by Irene Hunt

**CALIFORNIA STANDARDS**

**8.10.7** Explain how the war affected combatants, civilians, the physical environment, and future warfare.

**Reading 3.4** Analyze the relevance of the setting (e.g., place, time, customs) to the mood, tone, and meaning of the text.

**At the beginning of the Civil War, nine-year-old Jethro Creighton and his family live on a farm in southern Illinois. Although Illinois is a free state that remains in the Union, many people in the area have ties to states where slavery is legal. For example, the Creightons have relatives in "Kaintuck," or Kentucky. When this excerpt begins, Jethro has already seen his brother Tom and his cousin Eb go off to fight for the Union. His other brothers, John and Bill, are trying to decide which side to fight for.**

A line of wild geese flew southward far overhead, and Jethro stood motionless as he watched them disappear from sight. So **engrossed**[1] he was with the flight of the geese that he did not hear Bill's footsteps until his brother was quite near. He caught his breath at sight of Bill's face, which was swollen and beginning to grow discolored from a deep cut and many bruises.

"What's hurt you, Bill?" he asked, his voice barely **audible**,[2] for he was pretty sure he knew.

"We had a fight, Jeth, about an hour ago. We fit like two madmen, I guess."

"You and John?"

Bill's sigh was almost a moan. "Yes, me and John. Me and my brother John."

Jethro could not answer. He stared at the cut above Bill's right eye, from which blood still trickled down his cheek. Somewhere, far off in another field, a man shouted to his horses, and the shout died away in a cry that ran frightened over the brown water of the creek and into the darkening woods.

He had heard cries often that autumn, all through the countryside. They came at night, wakened him, and then lapsed into silence, leaving him in fear and **perplexity**.[3] Sounds once familiar were no longer as they had seemed in other days—his father calling cattle in from the pasture, the sheep dog's bark coming through the fog, the distant creak of the pulley as Ellen drew water for her chickens—all these once familiar sounds had taken on overtones of wailing, and he seemed to hear an echo of that wailing now. He shivered and looked away from his brother's face.

Bill sat down on the ground beside him. "Did ever Ma tell you, Jeth, about when John and me was little and was goin' to school fer the first time? At night I'd git a book and I'd say to Pa, 'What air that word, Pa?' and when he would tell me, I'd turn to John, jest a scant year older, and I'd say, 'Did Pa call it right, Johnny?' Ma and Pa used to laugh at that, but they was pleased to talk about it. They was always set up at John and me bein' so close."

"I know it." Jethro's words came from a tight throat. "What made you fight, Bill?"

"Hard feelin's that have been buildin' up fer weeks, hard feelin's that fin'ly come out in hard words." He held his hand across his eyes for a minute and then spoke quickly. "I'm leavin', Jeth; it ain't that I want to, but it's that I must. The day is comin' when I've got to fight, and I won't fight fer **arrogance**[4] and big money aginst the southern farmer. I won't do it. You tell Pa that. Tell him, too, that I'm takin' my brown mare—she's mine, and I hev the right. Still, it will leave him short, so you tell him that I'm leavin' money I

---

1. **engrossed:** absorbed; occupied.
2. **audible:** able to be heard.
3. **perplexity:** confusion.
4. **arrogance:** overbearing pride.

made at the sawmill and at corn shuckin'; it's inside the cover of his Bible. You tell him to take it and buy another horse."

Jethro was crying unashamedly in the face of his grief. "Don't go, Bill. Don't do it," he begged.

"Jeth . . ."

"I don't want you to go, Bill. I don't think I kin stand it."

"Listen to me, Jeth; you're gittin to be a sizable boy. There's goin' to be a lot of things in the years ahead that you'll have to stand. There'll be things that tear you apart, but you'll have to stand 'em. You can't count on cryin' to make 'em right."

The colors were beginning to fade on Walnut Hill. A light wind bent the dried grass and weeds. Jethro felt choked with grief, but he drew a sleeve across his eyes and tried to look at his brother without further weeping.

"Where will you go, Bill?"

"To Kaintuck. I'll go to Wilse's place first. From there—I don't know."

"Will you fight fer the Rebs?"

Bill hesitated a few seconds. "I've studied this thing, Jeth, and I've hurt over it. My heart ain't in this war; I've told you that. And while I say that the right ain't all on the side of the North, I know jest as well that it ain't all on the side of the South either. But if I hev to fight, I reckon it will be fer the South."

Jethro nodded. There were things you had to endure. After a while he asked, "Air you goin' tonight, Bill?"

"Right away. I've had things packed in that holler tree fer a couple days. I've knowed that this was comin' on, but I couldn't make myself leave. Now I'm goin'. The little mare is saddled and tied down at the molasses press. I'll go as fur as Newton tonight; in the morning I'll take out early."

He got to his feet. "There's lots of things I want to say, but I reckon I best not talk." Without looking at Jethro he laid his hand on the boy's shoulder. "Git all the larnin' you kin— and take keer of yoreself, Jeth," he said and turned abruptly away.

"Take keer of yoreself, Bill," Jethro called after him.

Across the prairies, through the woods, over the brown water of the creek, there was a sound of crying. Jethro ran to a tree and hid his face. He had heard his mother say that if you watch a loved one as he leaves you for a long journey, it's like as not to be the last look at him that you'll ever have.

Like the Creighton brothers, the Terrill brothers had different loyalties. William Rufus Terrill (left) fought for the Union as an artillery officer at Shiloh. His brother, James Terrill (right), was the commanding officer of a Virginia infantry regiment. Both men died in the war. William was killed at Perryville, Kentucky, in 1862; James was killed in battle in 1864. After the war, the family built a memorial to the brothers, which contained the words, "God Alone Knows Which Was Right."

## CONNECT TO HISTORY

1. **Recognizing Effects** How has the Civil War affected the Creighton family? Discuss how the effect reflects what is happening in the country.

   See Skillbuilder Handbook, page R11.

## CONNECT TO TODAY

2. **Researching** Where have civil wars or internal rebellions taken place in the recent past?

For more about other civil wars . . .

RESEARCH LINKS
CLASSZONE.COM

# Life in the Army

| **MAIN IDEA** | **WHY IT MATTERS NOW** | **TERMS & NAMES** |
|---|---|---|
| Both Union and Confederate soldiers endured many hardships serving in the army during the Civil War. | The hardships endured led to long-lasting bitterness on both sides. | hygiene  minié ball  rifle  ironclad |

**CALIFORNIA STANDARDS**

**8.10.5** Study the views and lives of leaders (e.g., Ulysses S. Grant, Jefferson Davis, Robert E. Lee) and soldiers on both sides of the war, including those of black soldiers and regiments.

**8.10.6** Describe critical developments and events in the war, including the major battles, geographical advantages and obstacles, technological advances, and General Lee's surrender at Appomattox.

**8.10.7** Explain how the war affected combatants, civilians, the physical environment, and future warfare.

**REP4** Students assess the credibility of primary and secondary sources and draw sound conclusions from them.

## ONE AMERICAN'S STORY

In 1862, Peter Vredenburgh, Jr., answered President Lincoln's call for an additional 300,000 soldiers. Nearly 26 years old, Vredenburgh became a major in the 14th Regiment New Jersey Volunteer Infantry. Less than two months after joining the regiment, he wrote a letter urging his parents to keep his 18-year-old brother from enlisting.

### A VOICE FROM THE PAST

I am glad that Jim has not joined any Regt. [regiment] and I hope he never will. I would not have him go for all my pay; it would be very improbable that we could both go through this war and come out unharmed. Let him come here and see the thousands with their arms and legs off, or if that won't do, let him go as I did the other day through the Frederick hospitals and see how little account a man's life and limbs are held in by others.

**Major Peter Vredenburgh, Jr.,** quoted in *Upon the Tented Field*

*Major Peter Vredenburgh, Jr., was an officer in the Union army.*

On September 19, 1864, Vredenburgh was killed in battle. In this section, you will learn more about other soldiers and what their experiences were like.

## Those Who Fought

✏️ **Taking Notes**

Use your chart to take notes about the reasons for fighting the Civil War.

| Reasons for fighting |
|---|
| Advantages |
| Disadvantages |
| Military strategy |
| Battle victories |

Like Peter Vredenburgh, the majority of soldiers in the Civil War were between 18 and 30 years of age. But both the Confederate and Union armies had younger and older soldiers. Charles Carter Hay was just 11 years old when he joined an Alabama regiment. William Wilkins was 83 when he became one of the Pennsylvania Home Guards.

Farmers made up the largest group among Civil War soldiers. About half the soldiers on both sides came from farms. Having rarely traveled far from their fields, many viewed going off to war as an exciting adventure. Some rode a train for the first time.

Although the majority of soldiers in the war were born in the United States, immigrants from other countries also served. German and Irish immigrants made up the largest ethnic groups. One regiment from New York had soldiers who were born in 15 foreign countries. The commanding officer gave orders in seven languages.

At the beginning of the war, African Americans wanted to fight. They saw the war as a way to end slavery. However, neither the North nor the South accepted African Americans into their armies. As the war dragged on, the North finally took African Americans into its ranks. Native Americans served on both sides.

*Reading* **History**
**A. Summarizing**
How did most men in the North and the South feel about going off to war?

In all, about 2 million American soldiers served the Union, and fewer than 1 million served the Confederacy. The vast majority were volunteers. Why did so many Americans volunteer to fight? Many sought adventure and glory. Some sought an escape from the boredom of farm and factory work. Some signed up because their friends and neighbors were doing it. Others signed up for the recruitment money offered by both sides. Soldiers also fought because they were loyal to their country or state.

## Turning Civilians into Soldiers

After enlisting, a volunteer was sent to a nearby army camp for training. A typical camp looked like a sea of canvas tents. The tents were grouped by company, and each tent held from two to twenty men. In winter, the soldiers lived in log huts or in heavy tents positioned on a log base. In the Civil War, Confederate soldiers and soldiers in volunteer units in the Union Army elected their company officers. Both the Union and Confederate armies followed this practice.

A soldier in training followed a set schedule. A bugle or drum awakened the soldier at dawn. After roll call and breakfast, the soldier had the first of several drill sessions. In between drills and meals, soldiers performed guard duty, cut wood for the campfires, dug trenches for latrines (outdoor toilets), and cleaned up the camp.

Shortly after they came to camp, new recruits were given uniforms and equipment. Union soldiers wore blue uniforms, and Confederate soldiers wore gray or

**daily** *life*

**DRILL SESSIONS**

"The first thing in the morning is drill. Then drill, then drill again. Then drill, drill, a little more drill. Then drill, and lastly drill." That is the way one soldier described his day in camp.

A soldier in training might have as many as five drill sessions a day, each lasting up to two hours. The soldiers learned to stand straight and march in formation. They also learned to load and fire their guns. Shown drilling below are soldiers of the 22nd New York State Militia near Harpers Ferry, Virginia, in 1862.

yellowish-brown uniforms. Getting a uniform of the right size was a problem, however. On both sides, soldiers traded items to get clothing that fit properly.

Early in the war, Northern soldiers received clothing of very poor quality. Contractors took advantage of the government's need and supplied shoddy goods. Shoes made of imitation leather, for example, fell apart when they got wet. In the Confederacy, some states had trouble providing uniforms at all, while others had surpluses. Because the states did not always cooperate and share supplies, Confederate soldiers sometimes lacked shoes. Like soldiers in the Revolutionary War, they marched over frozen ground in bare feet. After battles, needy soldiers took coats, boots, and other clothing from the dead.

At the beginning of the war, most soldiers in army camps received plenty of food. Their rations included beef or salt pork, flour, vegetables, and coffee. But when they were in the field, the soldiers' diet became more limited. Some soldiers went hungry because supply trains could not reach them.

**Background**
Before uniforms became standardized, soldiers dressed in outfits supplied from home. This caused confusion on the battlefield.

## STRANGE *but* True

### DEADLIER THAN BULLETS

"Look at our company—21 have died of disease, 18 have become so unhealthy as to be discharged, and only four have been killed in battle." So a Louisiana officer explained the high death rate in the Civil War.

More than twice as many men died of disease as died of battle wounds. Intestinal disorders, including typhoid fever, diarrhea, and dysentery, killed the most. Pneumonia, tuberculosis, and malaria killed many others. Bad water and food, poor diet, exposure to cold and rain, unsanitary conditions, and disease-carrying insects all contributed to the high rate of disease.

# Hardships of Army Life

Civil War soldiers in the field were often wet, muddy, or cold from marching outdoors and living in crude shelters. Many camps were unsanitary and smelled from the odors of garbage and latrines. One Union soldier described a camp near Washington. In the camp, cattle were killed to provide the troops with meat.

### A VOICE FROM THE PAST

The hides and [waste parts] of the [cattle] for miles upon miles around, under a sweltering sun and sultry showers, would gender such swarms of flies, armies of worms, blasts of stench and oceans of filth as to make life miserable.

**William Keesy,** quoted in *The Civil War Infantryman*

Not only were the camps filthy, but so were the soldiers. They often went weeks without bathing or washing their clothes. Their bodies, clothing, and bedding became infested with lice and fleas.

Poor **hygiene**—conditions and practices that promote health—resulted in widespread sickness. Most soldiers had chronic diarrhea or other intestinal disorders. These disorders were caused by contaminated water or food or by germ-carrying insects. People did not know that germs cause diseases. Doctors failed to wash their hands or their instruments. An observer described how surgeons "armed with long, bloody knives and saws, cut and sawed away with frightful rapidity, throwing the mangled limbs on a pile nearby as soon as removed."

*Reading* **History**
**B. Making Inferences** What changes could have helped lower the spread of disease among soldiers?

The naval duel between the Union *Monitor* and the Confederate *Merrimack* (or *Virginia*) took place on March 9, 1862.

# Changes in Military Technology

While camp life remained rough, military technology advanced. Improvements in the weapons of war had far-reaching effects. Battle tactics changed, and casualties soared.

Rifles that used minié balls contributed to the high casualty rate in the Civil War. A **rifle** is a gun with a grooved barrel that causes a bullet to spin through the air. This spin gives the bullet more distance and accuracy. The **minié ball** is a bullet with a hollow base. The bullet expands upon firing to fit the grooves in the barrel. Rifles with minié balls could shoot farther and more accurately than old-fashioned muskets. As a result, mounted charges and infantry assaults did not work as well. Defenders using rifles could shoot more of the attackers before they got close.

**Ironclads,** warships covered with iron, proved to be a vast improvement over wooden ships. In the first ironclad battle, the Confederate *Virginia* (originally named the *Merrimack*) battled the Union *Monitor* off the coast of Virginia in 1862. After hammering away for about four hours, the battle ended in a draw. (See page 492 for more information on ironclads.)

Despite new technology and tactics, neither side gained a decisive victory in the first two years of the war, as you will see in the next section.

**Vocabulary**
**casualties:** number of people killed or injured

*Reading* **History**
**C. Drawing Conclusions** Which changes in military technology had an effect on the average soldier? Why?

---

## Section 2 Assessment

### 1. Terms & Names

**Explain the significance of:**
• hygiene
• rifle
• minié ball
• ironclad

### 2. Using Graphics

Complete the chart below.

| The Typical Civil War Soldier | |
| --- | --- |
| Age | |
| Occupation | |
| Training | |
| Hardships | |

Which hardship do you think would have been most difficult to endure? Why? (REP3)

### 3. Main Ideas

**a.** How were the wartime experiences of Northern and Southern soldiers alike? (HI1)

**b.** What factors contributed to the spread of disease among soldiers? (HI2)

**c.** How did the use of the rifle and minié ball change combat tactics in the Civil War? (HI3)

### 4. Critical Thinking

**Forming and Supporting Opinions** What were the motives that led individual soldiers to fight in the Civil War? (REP3)

**THINK ABOUT**
• the multiple reasons that people had for enlisting
• what you consider valid reasons for fighting

---

**ACTIVITY OPTIONS**

**LANGUAGE ARTS**

**ART**

Imagine you are a soldier in the Civil War. Write a **letter** home to your parents about your experience or draw an **illustrated map** of your training camp. (HI1)

# Ironclads

They moved through the water, as one observer put it, "like a huge, half-submerged crocodile." To crew members of traditional wooden ships, the ironclads indeed may have seemed like horrible mechanical monsters.

With a powerful iron hull almost entirely under water and a rotating gun turret, or short tower, an ironclad easily destroyed the older vessels it met. When the *Monitor* and the *Merrimack* (or *Virginia*) clashed during the Civil War in the first battle ever waged between ironclads, a new era of naval warfare had begun. Below is a closer look at the Union's *Monitor*.

**CALIFORNIA STANDARDS**

**8.10.7** Explain how the war affected combatants, civilians, the physical environment, and future warfare.

Steam engines powered the ship. They were connected by a propeller shaft to a four-blade propeller. Behind the propeller sat the vessel's rudder. This entire area was heavily protected so the ship could keep moving under heavy fire or ramming.

The pilothouse, where the captain steered the ship, was a rectangular, reinforced iron box-like structure. A small opening all around the top allowed for full visibility.

The ship's weapons—two large cannons—were enclosed in a rotating iron turret. This allowed the guns to fire at an enemy from all directions. Ammunition was passed up to the gunners through a hatch in the floor.

| SCALE AND SIZE OF WARSHIPS | | | | |
|---|---|---|---|---|
| Class, Name, Launch Date | Length | Weight | Number of Crew | Weaponry |
| **Ironclad** (USS *Monitor*) 1862 | 172 ft. | 987 tons | 49 | two 11-inch smoothbore cannons |
| **Battleship** (USS *Maine*) 1889 | 319 ft. | 6,682 tons | 374 | four 10-inch guns, six 6-inch guns, seven rapid-fire 6-pounders, four torpedo tubes |
| **Nuclear Submarine** (USS *Nautilus*) 1954 | 324 ft. | 4,092 tons | 105 | six torpedo tubes |
| **Aircraft Carrier** (USS *Nimitz*) 1972 | 1,092 ft. | 95,000 tons | 6,000 | 24 F-14A Tomcat warplanes, 16 radar guided missiles, six-barrel, 20-millimeter Gatling gun |

## CONNECT TO HISTORY

1. **Drawing Conclusions** Why would a rotating gun be an advantage in a naval battle?

**S** See Skillbuilder Handbook, page R13.

## CONNECT TO TODAY

2. **Researching** Find out more about modern battleships or aircraft carriers, and write a brief report about their capabilities in battle.

For more about military ships . . .

**RESEARCH LINKS** CLASSZONE.COM

# No End in Sight

| MAIN IDEA | WHY IT MATTERS NOW | TERMS & NAMES |
|---|---|---|
| In the first two years of the war, neither side gained a decisive victory over the other. | A long war can cause much death and destruction and leave a bitter legacy. | Ulysses S. Grant · Seven Days' Battles · Battle of Shiloh · Battle of Antietam · cavalry |

## ONE AMERICAN'S STORY

In the summer of 1861, President Lincoln gave George McClellan command of the Union army in the East. The army had recently been defeated at Bull Run. Within months, McClellan restored the soldiers' confidence and organized and trained an army that could defeat the Confederates. But while Lincoln kept urging him to attack Richmond, McClellan kept drilling his troops.

### A VOICE FROM THE PAST

[S]oon as I feel that my army is well organized and well disciplined and strong enough, I will advance and force the Rebels to a battle on a field of my own selection. A long time must elapse before I can do that.

**General George McClellan,** quoted in *Civil War Journal: The Leaders*

Lincoln said McClellan had "the slows." While McClellan was stalling in the East, another general was winning victories in the West.

## Union Victories in the West

That victorious Union general in the West was **Ulysses S. Grant**. In civilian life, he had failed at many things. But Grant had a simple strategy of war: "Find out where your enemy is, get at him as soon as you can, strike at him as hard as you can, and keep moving on."

In February 1862, Grant made a bold move to take Tennessee. Using ironclad gunboats, Grant's forces captured two Confederate river forts. These were Fort Henry on the Tennessee and Fort Donelson on the nearby Cumberland. (See map on next page.) The seizure of Fort Henry opened up a river highway into the heart of the South. Union gunboats could now travel on the river as far as northern Alabama. When the people of Nashville, Tennessee, heard the forts were lost, they fled the city in panic. A week later, Union troops marched into Nashville.

**CALIFORNIA STANDARDS**

**8.10.4** Discuss Abraham Lincoln's presidency and his significant writings and speeches and their relationship to the Declaration of Independence, such as his "House Divided" speech (1858), Gettysburg Address (1863), Emancipation Proclamation (1863), and inaugural addresses (1861 and 1865).

**8.10.5** Study the views and lives of leaders (e.g., Ulysses S. Grant, Jefferson Davis, Robert E. Lee) and soldiers on both sides of the war, including those of black soldiers and regiments.

**8.10.6** Describe critical developments and events in the war, including the major battles, geographical advantages and obstacles, technological advances, and General Lee's surrender at Appomattox.

**CST1** Students explain how major events are related to one another in time.

**HI1** Students explain the central issues and problems from the past, placing people and events in a matrix of time and place.

**Taking Notes**

Use your chart to take notes about the battle victories for both sides.

| Reasons for fighting | |
|---|---|
| Advantages | |
| Disadvantages | |
| Military strategy | |
| Battle victories | |

# The Battle of Shiloh

After Grant's river victories, Albert S. Johnston, Confederate commander on the Western front, ordered a retreat to Corinth, Mississippi. Grant followed. By early April, Grant's troops had reached Pittsburg Landing on the Tennessee River. There he waited for more troops from Nashville. Johnston, however, decided to attack before Grant gained reinforcements. Marching his troops north from Corinth on April 6, 1862, Johnston surprised the Union forces near Shiloh Church. The **Battle of Shiloh** in Tennessee turned into the fiercest fighting the Civil War had yet seen.

Commanders on each side rode into the thick of battle to rally their troops. One Union general, William Tecumseh Sherman, had three horses shot out from under him. General Johnston was killed, and the command passed to General Pierre Beauregard. By the end of the day, each side believed that dawn would bring victory.

That night, there was a terrible thunderstorm. Lightning lit up the battlefield, where dead and dying soldiers lay in water and mud. During the night, Union boats ran upriver to ferry fresh troops to Grant's camp. Grant then led an attack at dawn and forced the exhausted Southern troops to retreat.

The cost of the Union victory was staggering. Union casualties at Shiloh numbered over 13,000, about one-fourth of those who had fought. The Confederates lost nearly 11,000 out of 41,000 soldiers. Describing

*Reading*History

**A. Contrasting**
How did Grant differ from McClellan as a military leader?

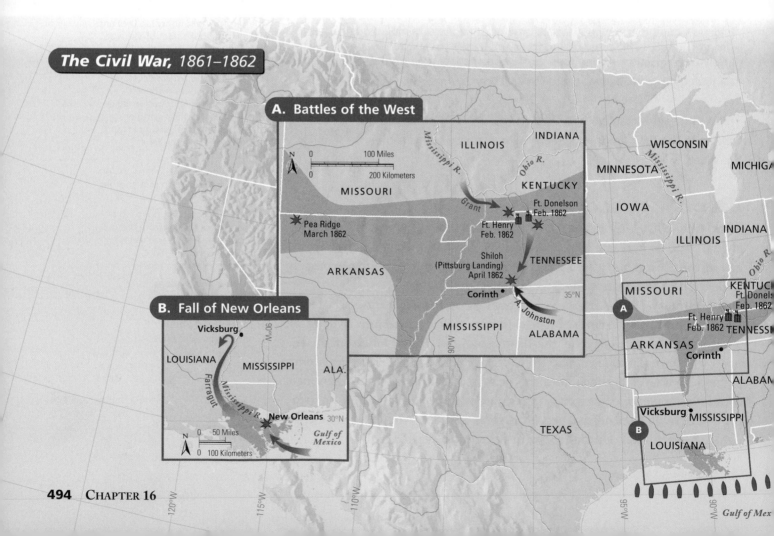

**The Civil War, 1861–1862**

**A. Battles of the West**

**B. Fall of New Orleans**

the piles of mangled bodies, General Sherman wrote home, "The scenes on this field would have cured anybody of war." Congressmen criticized Grant for the high casualties and urged Lincoln to replace him. But Lincoln replied, "I can't spare this man—he fights."

## The Fall of New Orleans

The spring of 1862 brought other bad news for the Confederacy. On April 25, a Union fleet led by David Farragut captured New Orleans, the largest city in the South. Rebel gunboats tried to ram the Union warships and succeeded in sinking one. Farragut's ships had to run through cannon fire and then dodge burning rafts in order to reach the city. Residents stood on the docks and cursed the Yankee invaders, but they were powerless to stop them.

The fall of New Orleans was a heavy blow to the South. Mary Chesnut of South Carolina, the wife of an aide to President Davis, wrote in her diary, "New Orleans gone—and with it the Confederacy. Are we not cut in two?" Indeed, after the victories of General Grant and Admiral Farragut, only a 150-mile stretch of the Mississippi remained in Southern hands. The Union was well on its way to achieving its goal of cutting the Confederacy in two. But guarding the remaining stretch of the river was the heavily armed Confederate fort at Vicksburg, Mississippi.

*Reading* **History**

**B. Recognizing Effects** Why was the fall of New Orleans significant?

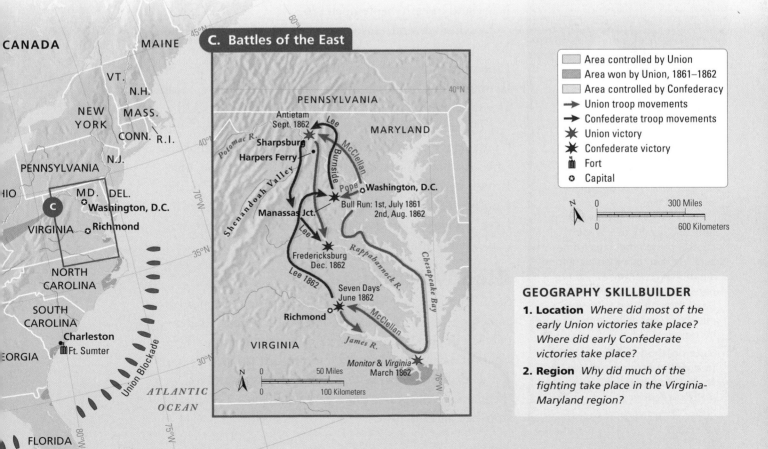

**C. Battles of the East**

Area controlled by Union
Area won by Union, 1861–1862
Area controlled by Confederacy
→ Union troop movements
→ Confederate troop movements
✳ Union victory
✳ Confederate victory
🏛 Fort
✛ Capital

**GEOGRAPHY SKILLBUILDER**

1. **Location** *Where did most of the early Union victories take place? Where did early Confederate victories take place?*

2. **Region** *Why did much of the fighting take place in the Virginia-Maryland region?*

*The Civil War Begins* **495**

## Lee Claims Victories in the East

Meanwhile, also in the spring of 1862, McClellan finally made his move to try to capture Richmond. He planned to attack the Confederate capital by way of a stretch of land between the York and James rivers. McClellan succeeded in bringing his troops within a few miles of Richmond.

But in June 1862, Robert E. Lee took charge of the Army of Northern Virginia and proceeded to turn the situation around. Lee sent Jeb Stuart and his **cavalry**—soldiers on horseback—to spy on McClellan. With about 1,000 men, Stuart rode around the whole Union army in a few days and reported its size back to Lee. Lee then attacked McClellan's army. The two sides clashed for a week, from June 25 to July 1, 1862, in what became known as the **Seven Days' Battles**. The Army of Northern Virginia suffered heavier losses, but it forced McClellan's army to retreat.

In late August, the Confederates won a second victory at Bull Run, and Union troops withdrew back to Washington. Within just a few months, Lee had ended the Union threat in Virginia.

*Reading*History

C. Making Inferences How was Lee's appointment fortunate for the South?

## Lee Invades the North

Riding a wave of victories, General Lee decided to invade the Union. He wrote to tell President Davis of his plan. Lee thought it was a crucial time, with the North at a low point. Without waiting for Davis's response, Lee crossed the Potomac with his army and invaded Maryland in early September 1862.

Lee had several reasons for taking the war to the North. He hoped a victory in the North might force Lincoln to talk peace. The invasion would give Virginia farmers a rest from war during the harvest season. The Confederates could plunder Northern farms for food.

Lee hoped the invasion would show that the Confederacy could indeed win the war, which might convince Europe to side with the South. By this time, both Britain and France were leaning toward recognizing the Confederacy as a separate nation. They were impressed by Lee's military successes, and their textile industry was now hurting from the lack of Southern cotton.

*Reading*History

D. Reading a Map Use the map on page 495 to follow Lee's movements into the North.

## Bloody Antietam

Soon after invading Maryland, Lee drew up a plan for his campaign in the North. A Confederate officer accidentally left a copy of Lee's battle plans wrapped around three cigars at a campsite. When Union troops stopped to rest at the abandoned campsite, a Union soldier stumbled on the plans. The captured plans gave McClellan a chance to stop Lee and his army.

### AMERICA'S HISTORY MAKERS

**JEFFERSON DAVIS**
**1808–1889**

Jefferson Davis expected to be given a military command when the Confederacy was formed in 1861. But Davis was chosen President of the Confederacy instead, which stunned and saddened him.

Because of his strong sense of duty and loyalty to the South, Davis accepted the unwelcome post. He had to immediately form a national government and prepare for war at the same time. Davis found it hard to compromise or accept disagreement with his opinions.

**How do the qualities required in a military leader differ from those required in a political leader?**

McClellan went on the attack, though he moved slowly as always. On September 17, 1862, at Antietam Creek near Sharpsburg, Maryland, McClellan's army clashed with Lee's. The resulting **Battle of Antietam** was the bloodiest day in all of American history. A Confederate officer later described the battle.

*Confederate artillery soldiers lie dead after the Battle of Antietam.*

### A VOICE FROM THE PAST

Again and again . . . by charges and counter-charges, this portion of the field was lost and recovered, until the green corn that grew upon it looked as if it had been struck by a storm of bloody hail. . . . From sheer exhaustion, both sides, like battered and bleeding athletes, seemed willing to rest.

**John B. Gordon,** quoted in *Voices of the Civil War*

After fighting all day, neither side had gained any ground by nightfall. The only difference was that about 25,000 men were dead or wounded. Lee, who lost as much as one-third of his fighting force, withdrew to Virginia. The cautious McClellan did not follow, missing a chance to finish off the crippled Southern army. Lincoln was so fed up that he fired McClellan in November, 1862. In the next chapter, you will learn about the historic action Lincoln took after the Battle of Antietam.

---

Section **3** Assessment

### 1. Terms & Names

**Explain the significance of:**
- Ulysses S. Grant
- Battle of Shiloh
- cavalry
- Seven Days' Battles
- Battle of Antietam

### 2. Using Graphics

Review the section and find five key events to place on a time line as shown.

Which of these events do you think was most important? (CST2)

### 3. Main Ideas

**a.** Why were Union victories in the West and the fall of New Orleans significant to the Union cause? (HI2)

**b.** Why did Lee go on the offensive against the North? (HI2)

**c.** How did the South's fortunes change after Lee took command of the Army of Northern Virginia? (HI2)

### 4. Critical Thinking

**Making Inferences** What does Lee's invasion of the North suggest about his qualities as a general and a leader? (REP4)

**THINK ABOUT**
- Lee's military skills and style
- the North's resources

**ACTIVITY OPTIONS**

GEOGRAPHY
ART

Develop a new military strategy for either the North or the South. Show your strategy on a **map** or in a **diagram** of troop movements. (HI4)

# Chapter 16 ASSESSMENT

## TERMS & NAMES

Briefly explain the significance of each of the following.

1. Fort Sumter
2. Robert E. Lee
3. border state
4. blockade
5. hygiene
6. rifle
7. ironclad
8. Ulysses S. Grant
9. Battle of Shiloh
10. Battle of Antietam

## REVIEW QUESTIONS

### War Erupts (pages 481–487)

1. How and when did the Civil War start? (HI1)
2. What advantages did the North have at the beginning of the war? (HI1)
3. What were the war strategies of the two sides? (HI1)

### Life in the Army (pages 488–492)

4. What was the typical Civil War soldier like? (HI1)
5. Why did so many people volunteer to fight in the Civil War? (HI1)
6. Why was the incidence of disease so high among Civil War soldiers? (HI2)
7. How did the use of rifles and minié balls change war tactics? (HI2)

### No End in Sight (pages 493–497)

8. What goal of the Union strategy did Grant further, and how did he do it? (HI1)
9. Why did the North have such a hard time capturing Richmond, Virginia? (HI2)
10. How did Lee's appointment to head the Army of Northern Virginia affect the course of the war? (HI2)

## CRITICAL THINKING

### 1. USING YOUR NOTES: COMPARING AND CONTRASTING

|  | North | South |
|---|---|---|
| Reasons for fighting |  |  |
| Advantages |  |  |
| Disadvantages |  |  |
| Military strategy |  |  |
| Battle victories |  |  |

Using your completed chart, answer the questions. (HI2)

a. Which side seemed likelier to win the war? Why?

b. Which side followed more closely its original strategy in the first two years of the war?

### 2. ANALYZING LEADERSHIP

Think about the leaders discussed in this chapter. Choose one. What character traits helped make him an effective leader? (HI1)

### 3. APPLYING CITIZENSHIP SKILLS

Which individuals or groups of people demonstrated good and poor citizenship during the war? Explain your choices. (HI1)

### 4. THEME: CITIZENSHIP

How could people on both sides of the Civil War believe that they were being good citizens by fighting? (REP5)

### 5. MAKING DECISIONS

In your opinion, was Lincoln correct in deciding to go to war to save the Union? Explain your answer. (HI5)

### Interact with History

How did the consequences and effects of civil war that you predicted before you read the chapter compare with the actual conditions you read about?

## VISUAL SUMMARY

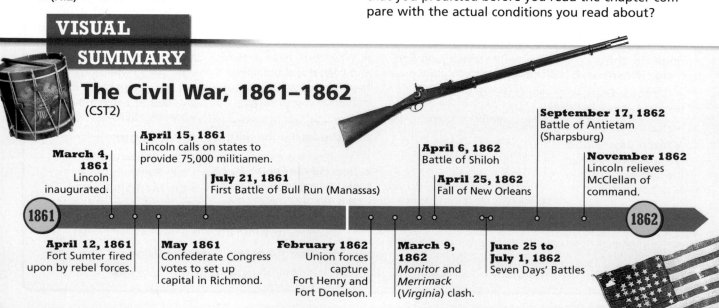

### The Civil War, 1861–1862
(CST2)

**March 4, 1861**
Lincoln inaugurated.

**April 15, 1861**
Lincoln calls on states to provide 75,000 militiamen.

**July 21, 1861**
First Battle of Bull Run (Manassas)

**April 6, 1862**
Battle of Shiloh

**April 25, 1862**
Fall of New Orleans

**September 17, 1862**
Battle of Antietam (Sharpsburg)

**November 1862**
Lincoln relieves McClellan of command.

**April 12, 1861**
Fort Sumter fired upon by rebel forces.

**May 1861**
Confederate Congress votes to set up capital in Richmond.

**February 1862**
Union forces capture Fort Henry and Fort Donelson.

**March 9, 1862**
*Monitor* and *Merrimack* (*Virginia*) clash.

**June 25 to July 1, 1862**
Seven Days' Battles

1861     1862

**Use the map and your knowledge of U.S. history to answer questions 1 and 2.**

Additional Test Practice, pp. S1–S33.

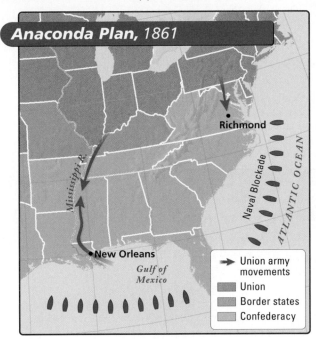

**Anaconda Plan,** 1861

Richmond

Mississippi R.

Naval Blockade

ATLANTIC OCEAN

New Orleans

Gulf of Mexico

→ Union army movements
■ Union
■ Border states
■ Confederacy

**1.** What does the arrow in the east indicate? (8.10.6)

   **A.** movement of Union troops toward Richmond

   **B.** movement of resisting Confederate troops

   **C.** movement of Confederate troops to take New Orleans

   **D.** movement of Union troops up the Mississippi

**2.** Which of the following did the blockade prevent access to? (8.10.6)

   **A.** border states

   **B.** Confederate states

   **C.** Union states

   **D.** Union troops

**General George McClellan discusses his battle plan in this quotation. Use the quotation and your knowledge of U.S. history to answer question 3.**

### PRIMARY SOURCE

[S]oon as I feel that my army is well organized and well disciplined and strong enough, I will advance and force the Rebels to a battle on a field of my own selection. A long time must elapse before I can do that.

**General George McClellan,** quoted in *Civil War Journal: The Leaders*

**3.** Which of the following summarizes McClellan's priority in leading his army into battle? (8.10.6)

   **A.** He will lead his troops into battle quickly.

   **B.** He refuses to go into battle without more troops.

   **C.** He wants to feel confident in his army's readiness for battle.

   **D.** He intends to make a surprise attack.

**TEST PRACTICE**
CLASSZONE.COM

## ALTERNATIVE ASSESSMENT

**1.** ✍ **WRITING ABOUT HISTORY**

Assume the role of a soldier during the Civil War, either Union or Confederate, and write a **letter** home to your family. (REP4)

• Use library resources to find written accounts from soldiers during the Civil War.

• Use what you learn to write your own letter. Include details about your daily life and your feelings about the war.

**2. COOPERATIVE LEARNING**

Work in a small group to develop a compromise that would have resolved the conflict between the North and the South. Have one member of your group take the position of a Northerner, another a Southerner, and a third the mediator between the two. (REP5)

## INTEGRATED TECHNOLOGY

**DOING INTERNET RESEARCH**

Life in the army training camps during the Civil War was difficult. Use the Internet to research army life. Then create a presentation about an aspect army life. (REP4)

• Find primary sources about life in the army, such as diaries, letters, photographs, and news articles.

• Choose a specific topic for your presentation. For example, you might focus on drawings, maps, and photos that show the design of a typical army camp, items used for cooking, lodging, sanitation, military drilling, and recreation, or firsthand accounts of camp life from letters and diaries.

For more about Civil War armies . . .

**INTERNET ACTIVITY**
CLASSZONE.COM

# The Tide of War Turns 1863–1865

**CHAPTER 17**

Confederate and Union cavalry clash at Yellow Tavern, Virginia, on May 11, 1864.

The slight curve of the cavalry sword provided a better slashing motion when fighting on horseback.

**January 1863**
Lincoln issues the Emancipation Proclamation after presenting it to his cabinet.

**July 1863**
Battle of Gettysburg takes place.
Union takes Vicksburg.

**March 1864**
Grant is put in charge of all Union armies.

**USA World** 1863

**January 1863**
Polish nationalists revolt against Russian rule.

**July 1863**
Source of Nile River is found at Lake Victoria in present-day Uganda.

**June 1864**
Archduke Maximilian of Austria becomes emperor of Mexico.

The Confederate uniforms were gray and the Union's were blue. The two sides are often referred to by these colors.

In 1863, you have been a Civil War soldier for two years. The life of a soldier is a hard one. The food is awful. Disease is common. Worst of all is the horrible violence and death. Often you feel the urge to run away and go home.

# What would inspire you to keep fighting?

## What Do You Think?

- What would you be willing to sacrifice for your country? What if your country fought for something you did not believe in?

- How would the attitudes of fellow soldiers influence your decision?

 **RESEARCH LINKS**
CLASSZONE.COM
Visit the Chapter 17 links for more information about the Civil War.

**November 1864**
Lincoln is reelected.

 **April 1865**
Union takes Richmond.
Lee surrenders at Appomattox Court House.
Lincoln is assassinated.

1866

 **September 1864**
First International Workingmen's Association is established, and Karl Marx becomes its leader.

**September 1865**
English officials arrest *Fenian* leaders of planned uprising in Ireland.

# Reading Strategy: Comparing and Contrasting

## What Do You Know?

What advantages and disadvantages did the North and the South have? Did particular individuals give either side an advantage during the Civil War?

### Think About

- what qualities contribute to the success of military leaders
- the importance of obeying orders for soldiers even if it might mean death
- your responses to the Interact with History about what would inspire you to keep fighting (see page 502)

## What Do You Want to Know?

What questions do you have about the later part of the Civil War and how it ended? Make a list of those questions before you read the chapter.

## Comparing and Contrasting

When you study historical events, it is important to compare and contrast the effects that events had on different individuals and groups. A single event might affect two groups of people in completely different ways. Use the chart below to compare and contrast the impact of events on the Union and the Confederacy in the later years of the Civil War.

**S** See Skillbuilder Handbook, page R10.

### ✎ Taking Notes

|  | North | South |
|---|---|---|
| Emancipation Proclamation |  |  |
| War's Impact |  |  |
| Northern Victories in Battle |  |  |
| Union Wins Civil War |  |  |

# The Emancipation Proclamation

| MAIN IDEA | WHY IT MATTERS NOW | TERMS & NAMES |
|---|---|---|
| In 1863, President Lincoln issued the Emancipation Proclamation, which helped to change the war's course. | The Emancipation Proclamation was an important step in ending slavery in the United States. | Emancipation Proclamation    54th Massachusetts Regiment |

## ONE AMERICAN'S STORY

During the Civil War, abolitionists like Frederick Douglass continued their bitter fight against slavery. Douglass urged President Lincoln to emancipate, or free, enslaved Americans.

**Frederick Douglass**

### A VOICE FROM THE PAST

To fight against slaveholders, without fighting against slavery, is but a half-hearted business, and paralyzes the hands engaged in it. . . . Fire must be met with water. . . . War for the destruction of liberty [by the South] must be met with war for the destruction of slavery.

**Frederick Douglass,** quoted in *Battle Cry of Freedom*

**CALIFORNIA STANDARDS**

**8.10.4** Discuss Abraham Lincoln's presidency and his significant writings and speeches and their relationship to the Declaration of Independence, such as his "House Divided" speech (1858), Gettysburg Address (1863), Emancipation Proclamation (1863), and inaugural addresses (1861 and 1865).

**8.10.5** Study the views and lives of leaders (e.g., Ulysses S. Grant, Jefferson Davis, Robert E. Lee) and soldiers on both sides of the war, including those of black soldiers and regiments.

**8.10.7** Explain how the war affected combatants, civilians, the physical environment, and future warfare.

**REP4** Students assess the credibility of primary and secondary sources and draw sound conclusions from them.

**HI3** Students explain the sources of historical continuity and how the combination of ideas and events explains the emergence of new patterns

Douglass pointed out that the Confederate war effort depended on slave labor. For both practical and moral reasons, Douglass said, Lincoln should free the slaves. In this section, you will learn how ending slavery became an important goal of the Civil War.

## Calls for Emancipation

Throughout the war, abolitionists had been urging Lincoln to emancipate enslaved persons. Many criticized the president for being too cautious. Some even charged that Lincoln's lack of action aided the Confederate cause.

Still, Lincoln hesitated. He did not believe he had the power under the Constitution to abolish slavery where it already existed. Nor did he want to anger the four slave states that remained in the Union. He also knew that most Northern Democrats, and many Republicans, opposed emancipation.

Lincoln did not want the issue of slavery to divide the nation further than it already had. Although he disliked slavery, the president's first priority was to preserve the Union. "If I could save the Union without freeing

**Taking Notes**

Use your chart to take notes about the effects of the Emancipation Proclamation.

| Emancipation Proclamation |
|---|
| War's Impact |
| Northern Victories in Battle |
| Union Wins Civil War |

*any* slave I would do it," he declared. "If I could save it by freeing *all* the slaves I would do it; and if I could save it by freeing some and leaving others alone, I would also do that."

By the summer of 1862, however, Lincoln had decided in favor of emancipation. The war was taking a terrible toll. If freeing the slaves helped weaken the South, then he would do it. Lincoln waited, however, for a moment when he was in a position of strength. After General Lee's forces were stopped at Antietam, Lincoln decided to act.

## The Emancipation Proclamation

On January 1, 1863, Lincoln issued the **Emancipation Proclamation,** which freed all slaves in Confederate territory. The proclamation had a tremendous impact on the public. However, it freed very few slaves. Most of the slaves that Lincoln intended to liberate lived in areas distant from the Union troops that could enforce his proclamation.

**Background**
In September 1862, Lincoln issued an early proclamation that gave rebellious states a chance to preserve slavery by rejoining the Union.

Lincoln presents the Emancipation Proclamation to his cabinet.

### A VOICE FROM THE PAST

On the first day of January, in the year of our Lord one thousand eight hundred and sixty-three, all persons held as slaves within any State or designated part of a State, the people whereof shall then be in rebellion against the United States, shall be then, [thenceforth], and forever free.

**Abraham Lincoln,** from the *Emancipation Proclamation*

Why, critics charged, did Lincoln free slaves only in the South? The answer was in the Constitution. Because freeing Southern slaves weakened the Confederacy, the proclamation could be seen as a military action. As commander-in-chief, Lincoln had this authority. Yet the Constitution did not give the president the power to free slaves within the Union. But Lincoln did ask Congress to abolish slavery gradually throughout the land.

Although the Emancipation Proclamation did not free many enslaved people at the time it was issued, it was important as a symbolic measure. For the North, the Civil War was no longer a limited war whose main goal was to preserve the Union. It was a war of liberation.

*Reading*History
**A. Drawing Conclusions** Why did Lincoln choose to limit his proclamation mostly to rebellious states?

## Response to the Proclamation

Abolitionists were thrilled that Lincoln had finally issued the Emancipation Proclamation. "We shout for joy that we live to record this righteous decree," wrote Frederick Douglass. Still, many believed the law should have gone further. They were upset that Lincoln had not freed *all* enslaved persons, including those in the border states.

*Reading*History
B. Summarizing
Why did
Northern
Democrats
oppose the
Emancipation
Proclamation?

Other people in the North, especially Democrats, were angered by the president's decision. Northern Democrats, the majority of whom were against emancipating even Southern slaves, claimed that the proclamation would only make the war longer by continuing to anger the South. A newspaperman in Ohio called Lincoln's proclamation "monstrous, impudent, and heinous . . . insulting to God as to man."

Most Union soldiers, though, welcomed emancipation. One officer noted that, although few soldiers were abolitionists, most were happy "to destroy everything that . . . gives the rebels strength."

White Southerners reacted to the proclamation with rage. Although it had limited impact in areas outside the reach of Northern armies, many slaves began to run away to Union lines. At the same time that these slaves deprived the Confederacy of labor, they also began to provide the Union with soldiers.

## African-American Soldiers

In addition to freeing slaves, the Emancipation Proclamation declared that African-American men willing to fight "will be received into the armed service of the United States."

Frederick Douglass had argued for the recruitment of African-American soldiers since the start of the war. He declared, "Once [you] let the black man get upon his person the brass letters, U.S. . . . there is no power on earth which can deny that he has earned the right to citizenship."

Before the proclamation, the federal government had discouraged the enlistment of African Americans, and only a few regiments were formed. After emancipation, African Americans rushed to join the army. By war's end, about 180,000 black soldiers wore the blue uniform of the Union army.

African-American soldiers were organized in all-black regiments, usually led by white officers. They were often given the worst jobs

Thousands
of African
Americans, such
as these men of
the 4th U.S.
Colored Troops,
fought for the
Union during the
Civil War.

to do and were paid less than white soldiers. Despite these obstacles, African-American soldiers showed great courage on the battlefield and wore their uniforms with pride. More than one regiment insisted on fighting without pay rather than accepting lower pay than the white soldiers.

## The 54th Massachusetts

One unit that insisted on fighting without pay was the **54th Massachusetts Regiment,** one of the first African-American regiments organized in the North. The soldiers of the 54th—among whom were two sons of Frederick Douglass—soon made the regiment the most famous of the Civil War.

The 54th Massachusetts earned its greatest fame in July 1863, when it led a heroic attack on Fort Wagner in South Carolina. The soldiers' bravery at Fort Wagner made the 54th a household name in the North and increased African-American enlistment.

The soldiers of the 54th Massachusetts and other African-American regiments faced grave dangers if captured. Rather than take African Americans as prisoners, Confederate soldiers often shot them or returned them to slavery.

The war demanded great sacrifices, not only from soldiers and prisoners, but also from people back home. In the next section, you will read about the hardships that the Civil War placed on the civilian populations in both the North and the South.

*Reading*History

**C. Identifying Facts** How did many black soldiers protest when they were offered lower pay than white soldiers?

---

## Section 1 Assessment

### 1. Terms & Names

**Explain the significance of:**
- Emancipation Proclamation
- 54th Massachusetts Regiment

### 2. Using Graphics

Use a chart to record responses to the Emancipation Proclamation.

Responses to Proclamation

How did the proclamation change Northerners' views of the war? (HI2)

### 3. Main Ideas

**a.** What was Lincoln's reason for not emancipating slaves when the war began? (HI2)

**b.** Why was the immediate impact of the Emancipation Proclamation limited? (HI2)

**c.** Why did black soldiers often face greater hardships than white soldiers? (HI2)

### 4. Critical Thinking

**Recognizing Effects** How did the Emancipation Proclamation change the role of African Americans in the war? (CST1)

**THINK ABOUT**
- how the proclamation changed military policy
- the response of many Southern slaves to the proclamation

---

**ACTIVITY OPTIONS**

**TECHNOLOGY**

**MUSIC**

Do research on the 54th Massachusetts Regiment. Create a **Web site** for the regiment or write a **song** about the soldiers' heroism at Fort Wagner. (HI1)

# War Affects Society

2

| MAIN IDEA | WHY IT MATTERS NOW | TERMS & NAMES |
|---|---|---|
| The Civil War caused social, economic, and political changes in the North and the South. | Some changes, like the growth of industry, affected Americans long after the end of Civil War. | Copperhead  income tax<br>conscription  greenback<br>bounty  Clara Barton |

## ONE AMERICAN'S STORY

As the Civil War moved into its third year, the constant demand for men and resources began to take its toll back home. Sometimes, the hardships endured by civilians resulted in angry scenes. On April 3, 1863, a resident of Richmond, Virginia, named Agnes came upon a group of hungry women and children, who had gathered in front of the capitol. She described the scene as these women and children were joined by other people who were upset by the shortage of food.

*A VOICE FROM THE PAST*

The crowd now rapidly increased, and numbered, I am sure, more than a thousand women and children. It grew and grew until it reached the dignity of a mob—a bread riot.

**Agnes,** quoted in *Reminiscences of Peace and War*

Food became scarce in many places during the Civil War. Here, women demand milk for their hungry families.

CALIFORNIA STANDARDS

**8.10.6** Describe critical developments and events in the war, including the major battles, geographical advantages and obstacles, technological advances, and General Lee's surrender at Appomattox.

**8.10.7** Explain how the war affected combatants, civilians, the physical environment, and future warfare.

**REP4** Students assess the credibility of primary and secondary sources and draw sound conclusions from them.

**HI6** Students interpret basic indicators of economic performance and conduct cost-benefit analyses of economic and political issues.

The mob then went out of control. It broke into shops and stole food and other goods. Only the threat of force ended the riot. In this section, you will read more about hardships that the Civil War caused on the home front.

## Disagreement About the War

In the spring of 1863, riots like the one in Richmond broke out in a number of Southern towns. Southerners were growing weary of the war and the constant sacrifices it demanded.

Confederate soldiers began to leave the army in increasing numbers. By the end of the year, the Confederate army had lost nearly 40 percent of its men. Some of these men were on leave, but many others were deserters.

Taking Notes

Use your chart to take notes about the effects of the Civil War.

Emancipation Proclamation
War's Impact
Northern Victories in Battle
Union Wins Civil War

In this political cartoon, the Union defends itself against "Copperheads." This was the name given to Northerners who sympathized with the South.

Faced with the difficulties of waging war, the Confederate states fell into disagreement. The same principle of states' rights that led them to break with the Union kept them from coordinating their war effort. As one Southern governor put it, "I am *still* a rebel . . . no matter who may be in power."

Disagreements over the conduct of the war also arose in the North. Lincoln's main opponents were the **Copperheads,** Northern Democrats who favored peace with the South. (A copperhead is a poisonous snake that strikes without warning.) Lincoln had protesters arrested. He also suspended the writ of habeas corpus, which prevents the government from holding citizens without a trial.

Vocabulary
**writ:** a written order issued by a court of law

## The Draft Laws

As the war dragged on, both the North and the South needed more soldiers. As a result, both sides passed laws of **conscription,** also known as the draft. These laws required men to serve in the military.

The Confederates had been drafting soldiers since the spring of 1862. By 1863, all able-bodied white men between the ages of 18 and 45 were required to join the army. However, there were a number of exceptions. Planters who owned 20 or more slaves could avoid military service. In addition, wealthy men could hire substitutes to serve in their place. By 1863, substitutes might cost as much as $6,000. The fact that wealthy men could avoid service caused poor Southerners to complain that it was a "rich man's war but a poor man's fight."

The Union draft law was passed in March 1863. Like the Confederacy, the Union allowed draftees to hire substitutes. However, the North also offered $300 **bounties,** or cash payments, to men who volunteered to serve. As a result, only a small percentage of men in the North were drafted. Most men volunteered and received the bounty.

*Reading* **History**
**A. Drawing Conclusions** Why were many soldiers dissatisfied with the draft laws?

Even so, the draft was extremely unpopular. In July 1863, anger over the draft and simmering racial tensions led to the New York City draft riots. For four days, rioters destroyed property and attacked people on the streets. Over 100 people were killed—many of them African Americans.

## Economic Effects of the War

Many people suffered economic hardship during the war. The suffering was severe in the South, where most battles were fought, but the North also experienced difficulties.

Food shortages were very common in the South, partly because so many farmers were fighting in the Confederate army. Moreover, food sometimes could not get to market because trains were now being used to carry war materials. The Confederate army also seized food and other supplies for its own needs.

*Reading*History
**B. Analyzing Causes** Why were economic problems particularly bad in the South?

Another problem, especially in the South, was inflation—an increase in price and decrease in the value of money. The average family food bill in the South increased from $6.65 a month in 1861 to $68 by mid–1863. Over the course of the war, prices rose 9,000 percent in the South.

Inflation in the North was much lower, but prices still rose faster than wages, making life harder for working people. Some people took advantage of wartime demand and sold goods for high prices.

Overall, though, war production boosted Northern industry and fueled the economy. In the short term, this gave the North an economic advantage over the South. In the long term, industry would begin to replace farming as the basis of the national economy.

During the war, the federal government passed two important economic measures. In 1861, it established the first **income tax**—a tax on earnings. The following year, the government issued a new paper currency, known as **greenbacks** because of their color. The new currency helped the Northern economy by ensuring that people had money to spend. It also helped the Union to pay for the war.

Some Southerners in the border states took advantage of the stronger Union economy by selling cotton to Northern traders, in violation of Confederate law. "Yankee gold," wrote one Confederate officer, "is fast accomplishing what Yankee arms could never achieve—the subjugation of our people."

**Vocabulary**
**subjugate:** to bring under control or to conquer

## Resistance by Slaves

Another factor that affected the South was the growing resistance from slaves. To hurt the Southern economy, slaves slowed their pace of work or stopped working altogether. Some carried out sabotage, destroying crops and farm equipment to hurt the plantation economy. When white

**daily**_life_

**INFLATION IN THE SOUTH**
During the Civil War, inflation caused hardship in the North and the South. But inflation was especially severe in the Confederacy, where prices could become outrageously high.

The food prices shown below are from 1864. Consider how many days it took a Confederate soldier to earn enough money to buy each of these foods.

**$6.00**
Dozen Eggs

**$6.25**
Pound of Butter

**$10.00**
Quart of Milk

**$12.00**
Pound of Coffee

**$18.00**

Confederate Soldier's Monthly Pay

planters fled advancing Union armies, slaves often refused to go along. They stayed behind, waiting for Union soldiers to free them.

Some enslaved people even rose up in rebellion against their overseers. More commonly, though, slaves ran away from plantations to join the Union forces as they pushed farther into Confederate territory. One Union officer described a common sight.

### A VOICE FROM THE PAST

It was very touching to see the vast numbers of colored [African-American] women following after us with babies in their arms, and little ones like our Anna clinging to their tattered skirts. One poor creature, while nobody was looking, hid two boys, five years old, in a wagon, intending, I suppose that they should see the land of freedom if she couldn't.

**Union officer,** quoted in *The Civil War*

## AMERICA'S HISTORY MAKERS

### CLARA BARTON
#### 1821–1912

Trained as a schoolteacher, <u>Clara Barton</u> was working for the government when the Civil War began. She organized a relief agency to help with the war effort. "While our soldiers stand and fight," she said, "I can stand and feed and nurse them."

She also made food for soldiers in camp and tended to the wounded and dying on the battlefield. At Antietam, she held a doctor's operating table steady as cannon shells burst all around them. The doctor called her "the angel of the battlefield." After the war, Barton founded the American Red Cross.

**How did Clara Barton demonstrate her leadership abilities?**

After Lincoln issued the Emancipation Proclamation, the number of slaves fleeing Southern plantations greatly increased. By the end of the war, as many as half a million had fled to Union lines.

## Women Aid the War Effort

With so many men away at war, women in both the North and the South assumed increased responsibilities. Women plowed fields and ran farms and plantations. They also took over jobs in offices and factories that had previously been done only by men.

Other social changes came about because of the thousands of women who served on the front lines as volunteer workers and nurses. Susie King Taylor was an African-American woman who wrote an account of her experiences as a volunteer with an African-American regiment. She asked her readers to remember that "many lives were lost,—not men alone but noble women as well."

Relief agencies put women to work washing clothes, gathering supplies, and cooking food for soldiers. Also, nursing became a respectable profession for many women. By the end of the war, around 3,000 nurses had worked under the leadership of Dorothea Dix in Union hospitals. Southern women were also active as nurses and as volunteers on the front.

Women also played a key role as spies in both the North and the South. Harriet Tubman served as a spy for Union forces along the coast of South Carolina. The most famous Confederate spy was Belle Boyd. Although she was arrested six times, she continued her work through much of the war. At one point, she even sent messages from her jail cell by putting them in little rubber balls and tossing them out the window.

*Reading*History
C. Summarizing
How did women participate in the Civil War?

# Civil War Prison Camps

Women caught spying were thrown into jail, but soldiers captured in battle suffered far more. At prison camps in both the North and the South, prisoners of war faced terrible conditions.

One of the worst prison camps in the North was in Elmira, New York. Perhaps the harshest feature of a prisoner's life at the camp was the New York winter. One prisoner called Elmira "an excellent summer prison for southern soldiers, but an excellent place for them to find their graves in the winter." In just one year, more than 24 percent of Elmira's 12,121 prisoners died of sickness and exposure to severe weather.

*Reading*History

**D. Making Inferences** Why were death rates so high at many Civil War prison camps?

Conditions were also horrible in the South. The camp with the worst reputation was at Andersonville, Georgia. Built to hold 10,000 prisoners, at one point it housed 33,000. Inmates had little shelter from the heat or cold. Most slept in holes scratched in the dirt. Drinking water came from one tiny creek that also served as a sewer. As many as 100 men per day died at Andersonville from starvation, disease, and exposure.

People who saw the camps were shocked by the condition of the soldiers. The poet Walt Whitman—who served as a Union nurse—described a group of soldiers who returned from a prison camp. He exclaimed, "Can those be *men?* . . . are they not really mummied, dwindled corpses?"

Around 50,000 men died in Civil War prison camps. But this number was dwarfed by the number of dead on the battlefronts and even more from disease in army camps. In the next section, you will read about the bloody battles that led to the end of the Civil War.

The terrible conditions at Civil War prison camps caused much suffering and death.

---

## Section 2 Assessment

### 1. Terms & Names

**Explain the significance of:**
- Copperhead
- conscription
- bounty
- income tax
- greenback
- Clara Barton

### 2. Using Graphics

Use a diagram like the one below to compare conditions in the North and South during the later years of war. (8.10.6)

**Conditions During the War**

North   Both   South

### 3. Main Ideas

**a.** How did the South's principle of states' rights undermine the Confederate war effort? (HI1)

**b.** How did the draft laws in the North and South differ? (HI1)

**c.** What conditions at prison camps caused so many to suffer behind enemy lines? (HI2)

### 4. Critical Thinking

**Making Generalizations** What economic changes took place during the Civil War? (HI2)

**THINK ABOUT**
- the war's effect on prices
- industry and agriculture
- new economic measures begun by the government

**ACTIVITY OPTIONS**

**GEOGRAPHY**

**SPEECH**

Study Civil War prison camps. Make a **map** showing where they were located or give a **speech** explaining why prisoners should be treated better. (CST3)

# 3

# The North Wins

| MAIN IDEA | WHY IT MATTERS NOW | TERMS & NAMES |
|---|---|---|

**MAIN IDEA**

Thanks to victories, beginning with Gettysburg and ending with Richmond, the Union survived.

**WHY IT MATTERS NOW**

If the Union had lost the war, the United States might look very different now.

**TERMS & NAMES**

Battle of Gettysburg

Pickett's Charge

Ulysses S. Grant

Robert E. Lee

Siege of Vicksburg

William Tecumseh Sherman

Appomattox Court House

**CALIFORNIA STANDARDS**

**8.10.4** Discuss Abraham Lincoln's presidency and his significant writings and speeches and their relationship to the Declaration of Independence, such as his "House Divided" speech (1858), Gettysburg Address (1863), Emancipation Proclamation (1863), and inaugural addresses (1861 and 1865).

**8.10.5** Study the views and lives of leaders (e.g., Ulysses S. Grant, Jefferson Davis, Robert E. Lee) and soldiers on both sides of the war, including those of black soldiers and regiments.

**8.10.6** Describe critical developments and events in the war, including the major battles, geographical advantages and obstacles, technological advances, and General Lee's surrender at Appomattox.

**8.10.7** Explain how the war affected combatants, civilians, the physical environment, and future warfare.

**CST1** Students explain how major events are related to one another in time.

**Taking Notes**

Use your chart to take notes about the military victories of the North.

Emancipation Proclamation

War's Impact

Northern Victories in Battle

Union Wins Civil War

## ONE AMERICAN'S STORY

Joshua Lawrence Chamberlain left his job as a college professor and took command of troops from his home state of Maine. His description of the aftermath of one battle shows how soldiers got used to the war's violence.

### A VOICE FROM THE PAST

It seemed best to [put] myself between two dead men among the many left there by earlier assaults, and to draw another crosswise for a pillow out of the trampled, blood-soaked sod, pulling the flap of his coat over my face to fend off the chilling winds, and still more chilling, the deep, many voiced moan [of the wounded] that overspread the field.

**Joshua Lawrence Chamberlain,** quoted in *The Civil War*

Chamberlain is best remembered for his courageous actions at the Battle of Gettysburg. In this section, you will read about that battle and others that led to the end of the Civil War.

## The Road to Gettysburg

In September 1862, General McClellan stopped General Lee's Northern attack at the Battle of Antietam. But the cautious McClellan failed to finish off Lee's army, which retreated safely to Virginia.

President Lincoln, who was frustrated by McClellan, replaced him with Ambrose Burnside. But Burnside also proved to be a disappointment. At the Battle of Fredericksburg, Virginia, in December 1862, Burnside attacked Confederate troops who had dug trenches. The bloody result was 12,600 Union casualties. This disastrous attack led General Lee to remark, "It is well that war is so terrible—we should grow too fond of it!"

Lincoln replaced Burnside with General Joseph Hooker, who faced Lee the following May at Chancellorsville, Virginia. The result was yet another Union disaster. With half as many men as Hooker, Lee still managed to cut the Union forces to pieces. However, the South paid a high price for its victory. As General "Stonewall" Jackson returned from a patrol on May 2, Confederate guards thought he was a Union soldier and shot him in the arm. Shortly after a surgeon amputated the arm, Jackson caught pneumonia. On May 10, Lee's prized general was dead.

In spite of Jackson's tragic death, Lee decided to head North once again. He hoped that a Confederate victory in Union territory would fuel Northern discontent with the war and bring calls for peace. He also hoped a Southern victory would lead European nations to give diplomatic recognition and aid to the Confederacy.

## The Battle of Gettysburg

In late June 1863, Lee crossed into southern Pennsylvania. The Confederates learned of a supply of shoes in the town of Gettysburg and went to investigate. There, on July 1, they ran into Union troops. Both sides called for reinforcements, and the **Battle of Gettysburg** was on.

The fighting raged for three days. On the rocky hills and fields around Gettysburg, 90,000 Union troops, under the command of General George Meade, clashed with 75,000 Confederates.

During the struggle, Union forces tried to hold their ground on Cemetery Ridge, just south of town, while rebel soldiers tried to dislodge them. At times, the air seemed full of bullets. "The balls were whizzing so thick," said one Texan, "that it looked like a man could hold out a hat and catch it full."

The turning point came on July 3, when Lee ordered General George Pickett to mount a direct attack on the middle of the Union line. It was a deadly mistake. Some 13,000 rebel troops charged up the ridge into heavy Union fire. One soldier recalled "bayonet thrusts, sabre strokes, pistol shots . . . men going down on their hands and knees, spinning round like tops . . . ghastly heaps of dead men."

**Pickett's Charge,** as this attack came to be known, was torn to pieces. The Confederates retreated and waited for a Union counterattack. But once again, Lincoln's generals failed to finish off Lee's army. The furious Lincoln wondered when he would find a general who would defeat Lee once and for all.

Even so, the Union rejoiced over the victory at Gettysburg. Lee's hopes for a Confederate victory in the North were crushed. The North had lost 23,000 men, but Southern losses were even greater. Over one-third of Lee's army, 28,000 men, lay dead or wounded. Sick at heart, Lee led his army back to Virginia.

*Reading***History**

**A. Reading a Map** Use the map and illustration on pages 514–515 to study Gettysburg's geography.

*Reading***History**

**B. Making Inferences** Why might Lincoln have been disappointed after the Union victory at Gettysburg?

### *America's* HERITAGE

**THE GETTYSBURG ADDRESS**

On November 19, 1863, President Lincoln spoke at the dedication of a cemetery in Gettysburg for the 3,500 soldiers buried there. His speech was short, and few who heard it were impressed. Lincoln himself called it "a flat failure."

Even so, the Gettysburg Address has since been recognized as one of the greatest speeches of all time. In it, Lincoln declared that the nation was founded on "the proposition that all men are created equal." He ended with a plea to continue the fight for democracy so that "government of the people, by the people, for the people shall not perish from the earth."

*See page 524 for the full text of the Gettysburg Address.*

# Battle of Gettysburg

A monument stands today near a ridge at the Gettysburg battlefield. Labeled the "High Water Mark of the Rebellion," it shows how far Confederate troops advanced against Union lines. There, on July 3, 1863, the South came closest to winning the Civil War.

The fighting began on July 1. When a Confederate force captured Gettysburg, Union defenders took up new positions in the hills south of town. The next day, Confederate troops attacked across a wheat field and peach orchard in an attempt to seize the hill called Little Round Top. But Union forces held their ground.

July 3 was the decisive day. Lee, having failed to crack the side of General Meade's Union line, attacked its center. In an assault that came to be known as Pickett's Charge, some 13,000 men charged uphill across an open field toward the Union lines along Cemetery Ridge. Union soldiers covered the field with rifle and cannon fire. "Pickett's Charge" was a Confederate disaster.

> **CALIFORNIA STANDARDS**
>
> **8.10.6** Describe critical developments and events in the war, including the major battles, geographical advantages and obstacles, technological advances, and General Lee's surrender at Appomattox.

Before beginning the charge named for him, Major General Pickett wrote to his fiancée, "My brave Virginians are to attack in front. Oh, may God in mercy help me."

## ARTIFACT FILE

**Soldiers' Diaries**
Many Civil War soldiers wrote about their wartime experiences in personal diaries, such as this one belonging to Sergeant Alfred S. Rowe of Maryland.

**Regimental Flag** Flags helped soldiers to identify the different sides during battle. Often, a regiment's flag would show the names of battles it had fought. This flag, which belonged to the 28th North Carolina, was captured at Pickett's Charge.

Gettysburg

Culp's Hill

Cemetery Hill

Cemetery Ridge

As in many battles of the Civil War, the outcome at Gettysburg was affected by the landscape. Both sides fought for control of the high ground. Union control of the two "Round Top" hills, Cemetery Ridge and Culp's Hill, gave Meade the advantage.

Peach Orchard

Wheat Field

Devil's Den

Little Round Top

Big Round Top

## On-Line Field Trip

**The Gettysburg National Military Park Museum** contains many objects relating to the Battle of Gettysburg, including this federal bass drum. This heavy drum—two feet in diameter—was harnessed to the neck of a soldier, who beat time with leather-covered wooden mallets.

For more about Gettysburg . . .

## CONNECT TO GEOGRAPHY

1. **Place** How might Confederate positions on low ground have put them at a disadvantage?

2. **Human-Environment Interaction** How might the attitudes of Union soldiers have been affected by fighting in their own territory?

See Geography Handbook, pages 4–5.

## CONNECT TO HISTORY

3. **Asking Questions** Ask and answer a question about how the geographic patterns of the Gettysburg area affected the battle.

*The Tide of War Turns* **515**

**ULYSSES S. GRANT**
**1822–1885**

<u>General Ulysses S. Grant</u> was an unlikely war hero. Although educated at West Point Military Academy, he was a poor student and showed little interest in an army career. With his quiet manner and rumpled uniform, he often failed to impress his fellow officers.

Yet on the battlefield, Grant proved to be a brilliant general. Highly focused and cool under fire, he won the first major Union victories of the war.

Grant was willing to fight Lee—even if the costs were high. He told his generals, "Wherever Lee goes, there you will go also."

**ROBERT E. LEE**
**1807–1870**

<u>Robert E. Lee</u> seemed destined for greatness. In his crisp uniform and trim, white beard, Lee was a dashing figure on the battlefield.

Born to a leading Virginia family, Lee was a top student at West Point and won praise for his actions in the Mexican War. General Winfield Scott called him "the very best soldier I have ever seen in the field."

Lee did not want to fight the Union, but he felt he had to stand by Virginia. "I did only what my duty demanded," Lee said. "I could have taken no other course without dishonor."

**How did the tough decisions made by Grant and Lee affect the Civil War?**

## The Siege of Vicksburg

On July 4, 1863, the day after Pickett's Charge, the Union received more good news. In Mississippi, General Ulysses S. Grant had defeated Confederate troops at the **Siege of Vicksburg**.

The previous year, Grant had won important victories in the West that opened up the Mississippi River for travel deep into the South. Vicksburg was the last major Confederate stronghold on the river. Grant had begun his attack on Vicksburg in May 1863. But when his direct attacks failed, he settled in for a long siege. Grant's troops surrounded the city and prevented the delivery of food and supplies. Eventually, the Confederates ran out of food. In desperation, they ate mules, dogs, and even rats. Finally, after nearly a month and a half, they surrendered.

The Union victory fulfilled a major part of the Anaconda Plan. The North had taken New Orleans the previous spring. Now, with complete control over the Mississippi River, the South was split in two.

With the victories at Vicksburg and Gettysburg, the tide of war turned in favor of the North. Britain gave up all thought of supporting the South. And, in General Grant, President Lincoln found a man who was willing to fight General Lee.

**Vocabulary**
siege: the surrounding of a city, town, or fortress by an army trying to capture it

**Background**
The Anaconda Plan called for blockading Southern ports, taking control of the Mississippi, and capturing Richmond.

## Sherman's Total War

In March 1864, President Lincoln named General Grant commander of all the Union armies. Grant then developed a plan to defeat the Confederacy. He would pursue Lee's army in Virginia, while Union forces under General **William Tecumseh Sherman** pushed through the Deep South to Atlanta and the Atlantic coast.

Battling southward from Tennessee, Sherman took Atlanta in September 1864. He then set out on a march to the sea, cutting a path of destruction up to 60 miles wide and 300 miles long through Georgia.

Sherman waged total war: a war not only against enemy troops, but against everything that supports the enemy. His troops tore up rail lines, destroyed crops, and burned and looted towns.

*Reading*History

C. Drawing Conclusions How might the political situation in the North have been different if Sherman had not taken Atlanta?

Sherman's triumph in Atlanta was important for Lincoln. In 1864, the president was running for reelection, but his prospects were not good. Northerners were tired of war, and Democrats—who had nominated George McClellan—stood a good chance of winning on an antiwar platform.

Sherman's success changed all that. Suddenly, Northerners could sense victory. Lincoln took 55 percent of the popular vote and won re-election. In his second inaugural speech, Lincoln hoped for a speedy end to the war: "With malice towards none; with charity for all; . . . let us strive on to finish the work we are in; to bind up the nation's wounds; . . . to do all which may achieve and cherish a just, and a lasting peace." (See page 525 for more of Lincoln's Second Inaugural Address.)

In December, Sherman took Savannah, Georgia. He then sent a telegram to Lincoln: "I beg to present you, as a Christmas gift, the city of Savannah, with 150 heavy guns and . . . about 25,000 bales of cotton."

> ## "Let us strive . . . to bind up the nation's wounds."
> **Abraham Lincoln**

## The Civil War, 1863–1865

- Area controlled by Union
- Area won by Union, 1863–1865
- Area controlled by Confederacy
- → Union troop movements
- → Confederate troop movements
- ✹ Union victory
- ✷ Confederate victory

**NEW YORK**
**CONN.**
**PENNSYLVANIA**
Gettysburg July 1863 ✷
**N.J.**
**OHIO**
**MD.**
**DEL.**
Washington, D.C.
Chancellorsville May 1863 ✷✷ Fredericksburg Dec. 1862
**W.V.**
Richmond ✹
**VIRGINIA**
**KENTUCKY**
**MISSOURI**
**ARKANSAS**
Nashville
**TENNESSEE** Chattanooga Nov. 1863 ✹
Corinth
Grant
**NORTH CAROLINA** Raleigh
**SOUTH CAROLINA** Wilmington
Columbia
**ATLANTIC OCEAN**
**MISSISSIPPI**
Vicksburg ✹ July 1863
Montgomery
**ALABAMA**
Atlanta
Sherman
Charleston
✷ Ft. Wagner July 1863
**GEORGIA**
Savannah occupied Dec. 1864
Union Blockade
Jacksonville
**LOUISIANA** Mobile Pensacola
St. Augustine
New Orleans
**FLORIDA**
Gulf of Mexico

N
0 ____ 200 Miles
0 ____ 400 Kilometers

### Inset map
**MARYLAND**
Washington, D.C.
Potomac River
Grant
Wilderness, May 5–6, 1864
Lee
Rappahannock R.
Spotsylvania May 8–19, 1864
Cold Harbor, June 1864
James River
**VIRGINIA**
Richmond
Lee
Appomattox Court House, Apr. 9, 1865 Lee surrenders to Grant
Petersburg, June 1864– Apr. 1865
Grant

**GEOGRAPHY SKILLBUILDER Interpreting Maps**
1. **Movement** About how many miles did Sherman's troops have to march to get from Atlanta to Savannah?
2. **Location** At what location did Grant and Lee face off for nearly ten months?

In 1861, Congress created the Medal of Honor to reward individual bravery in combat.

# Grant's Virginia Campaign

After taking Savannah, Sherman moved north through the Carolinas seeking to meet up with Grant's troops in Virginia. Since May 1864, Grant and his generals had been fighting savage battles against Lee's forces. In battle after battle, Grant would attack, rest, then attack again, all the while moving south toward Richmond.

At the Battle of the Wilderness in May 1864, Union and Confederate forces fought in a tangle of trees and brush so thick that they could barely see each other. Grant lost over 17,000 men, but he pushed on. "Whatever happens," he told Lincoln, "we will not retreat."

At Spotsylvania and Cold Harbor, the fighting continued. Again, the losses were staggering. Grant's attack in June, at Cold Harbor, cost him 7,000 men, most in the first few minutes of battle. Some Union troops were so sure they would die in battle that they pinned their names and addresses to their jackets so their bodies could be identified later.

In June 1864, Grant's armies arrived at Petersburg, just south of Richmond. Unable to break through the Confederate defenses, the Union forces dug trenches and settled in for a long siege. The two sides faced off for ten months.

In the end, though, Lee could not hold out. Grant was drawing a noose around Richmond. So Lee pulled out, leaving the Confederate capital undefended. The Union army marched into Richmond on April 3. One Richmond woman recalled, "Exactly at eight o'clock the Confederate flag that fluttered above the Capitol came

*Reading* **History**

D. Reading a Map Use the map on page 517 to find the locations of the major battles of Grant's Virginia campaign.

## HISTORY *through* ART

This photograph shows Union officers before the Battle of the Wilderness. Next to the tree on the right is the photographer Mathew Brady. Photography was still a new art when the Civil War began. Brady's Civil War photos represent one of the first examples of photojournalism.

**How might people's attitudes toward war be affected when they can see pictures from the front lines?**

down and the Stars and Stripes were run up. . . . We covered our faces and cried aloud."

## Surrender at Appomattox

From Richmond and Petersburg, Lee fled west, while Grant followed in pursuit. Lee wanted to continue fighting, but he knew that his situation was hopeless. He sent a message to General Grant that he was ready to surrender.

On April 9, 1865, Lee and Grant met in the small Virginia town of **Appomattox Court House** to arrange the surrender. Grant later wrote that his joy at that moment was mixed with sadness.

### A VOICE FROM THE PAST

I felt like anything rather than rejoicing at the downfall of a foe who had fought so long and valiantly, and had suffered so much for a cause, though that cause was, I believe, one of the worst for which a people ever fought, and one for which there was the least excuse. I do not question, however, the sincerity of the great mass of those who were opposed to us.

**Ulysses S. Grant,** *Personal Memoirs*

Grant offered generous terms of surrender. After laying down their arms, the Confederates could return home in peace, taking their private possessions and horses with them. Grant also gave food to the hungry Confederate soldiers.

After four long years, the Civil War was coming to a close. Its effects would continue, however, changing the country forever. In the next section, you will learn about the long-term consequences of the Civil War.

## Section 3 Assessment

### 1. Terms & Names

**Explain the significance of:**
- Battle of Gettysburg
- Pickett's Charge
- Ulysses S. Grant
- Robert E. Lee
- Siege of Vicksburg
- William Tecumseh Sherman
- Appomattox Court House

### 2. Using Graphics

Use a time line like the one below to record key events from Section 3.

1862                    1866
|———|———|———|———|

Which event is considered the turning point of the war? (CST2)

### 3. Main Ideas

**a.** Why was the Battle of Gettysburg important? (8.10.6)

**b.** Why was Northern success in the Siege of Vicksburg important? (8.10.6)

**c.** How did Grant treat Confederate soldiers after the surrender at Appomattox Court House? (8.10.6)

### 4. Critical Thinking

**Contrasting** How was the Civil War different from wars that Americans had previously fought? (HI3)

**THINK ABOUT**
- the role of civilians
- Sherman's military strategy

### ACTIVITY OPTIONS

**GEOGRAPHY**
**LANGUAGE ARTS**

Research the Siege of Vicksburg. Make a **topographic map** of the area or write an **article** describing the soldiers' hardships during the siege. (CST3)

# The Legacy of the War

| MAIN IDEA | WHY IT MATTERS NOW | TERMS & NAMES |
|---|---|---|
| The Civil War brought great changes and new challenges to the United States. | The most important change was the liberation of 4 million enslaved persons. | Thirteenth Amendment    John Wilkes Booth |

### CALIFORNIA STANDARDS

**8.10.7** Explain how the war affected combatants, civilians, the physical environment, and future warfare.

**8.12.1** Trace patterns of agricultural and industrial development as they relate to climate, use of natural resources, markets, and trade and locate such development on a map.

**8.12.3** Explain how states and the federal government encouraged business expansion through tariffs, banking, land grants, and subsidies.

**REP4** Students assess the credibility of primary and secondary sources and draw sound conclusions from them.

**HI2** Students understand and distinguish cause, effect, sequence, and correlation in historical events, including the long- and short-term causal relations.

## ONE AMERICAN'S STORY

In the spring of 1864, a year before the end of the Civil War, the Union army was running out of cemetery space to bury its war dead. The secretary of war ordered Quartermaster General Montgomery Meigs to find a new site for a cemetery. Without hesitation, Meigs chose Robert E. Lee's plantation in Arlington, Virginia, just across the Potomac River from Washington, D.C.

Meigs's decision to turn Lee's plantation into a Union cemetery was highly symbolic. The Union soldiers who died fighting Lee's army would be buried in Lee's front yard. That site became Arlington National Cemetery.

During the Civil War, the government turned Robert E. Lee's Virginia plantation into a graveyard.

## Costs of the War

Many Northerners shared Montgomery Meigs's bitter feelings toward the South. At the same time, many Southerners felt great resentment toward the North. After the war, President Lincoln hoped to heal the nation and bring North and South together again. The generous terms of surrender offered to Lee were part of that effort. Hard feelings remained, however, in part because the costs of the war were so great.

The Civil War was the deadliest war in American history. In four years of fighting, approximately 620,000 soldiers died—360,000 for the Union and 260,000 for the Confederacy. Another 275,000 Union soldiers and 260,000 Confederate soldiers were wounded. Many suffered from their wounds for the rest of their lives.

Altogether, some 3,000,000 men served in the armies of the North and South—around 10 percent of the population. Along with the soldiers, many other Americans had their lives disrupted by the war.

**Taking Notes**

Use your chart to take notes about the effects of the Union's victory in the Civil War.

| Emancipation Proclamation |
|---|
| War's Impact |
| Northern Victories in Battle |
| Union Wins Civil War |

The war also had great economic costs. Together, the North and South spent more than five times the amount spent by the government in the previous eight decades. Many years after the fighting was over, the federal government was still paying interest on loans taken out during the war.

## The Thirteenth Amendment

One of the greatest effects of the war was the freeing of millions of enslaved persons. As the Union army moved through the South during and after the war, Union soldiers released African Americans from bondage. One of those released was Booker T. Washington, who later became a famous educator and reformer. He recalled the day a Union officer came to his plantation to read the Emancipation Proclamation.

> **A VOICE FROM THE PAST**
>
> After the reading we were told that we were all free, and could go when and where we pleased. My mother, who was standing by my side, leaned over and kissed her children, while tears of joy ran down her cheeks. She explained to us what it all meant, that this was the day for which she had been so long praying, but fearing that she would never live to see.
>
> **Booker T. Washington,** quoted in his autobiography, *Up from Slavery*

The Emancipation Proclamation applied primarily to slaves in the Confederacy, however. Many African Americans in the border states were still enslaved. In 1864, with the war still under way, President Lincoln had approved of a constitutional amendment to end slavery entirely, but it failed to pass Congress.

In January 1865, Lincoln urged Congress to try again to end slavery. This time, the measure—known as the **Thirteenth Amendment**—passed. By year's end, 27 states, including eight in the South, had ratified the amendment. From that point on, slavery was banned in the United States.

## Lincoln's Assassination

Lincoln did not live to see the end of slavery, however. Five days after Lee's surrender at Appomattox, the president and his wife went to see a play at Ford's Theatre in Washington, D.C. During the play, a Confederate supporter, **John Wilkes Booth,** crept into the balcony where the president sat and shot him in the back of the head. Booth then jumped over the railing and landed on the stage. Although he broke his leg in the leap, he managed to escape the theater.

CONFEDERATE CASUALTIES

UNION CASUALTIES

Source: *World Book; Historical Statistics of the United States; The United States Civil War Center*

**ECONOMIC COSTS**

- Federal loans and taxes to finance the war totaled $2.6 billion.
- Federal debt on June 30, 1865, rose to $2.7 billion.
- Confederate debt ran over $700 million.
- Union inflation reached 182% in 1864 and 179% in 1865.
- Confederate inflation rose to 9,000% by the end of the war.

**SKILLBUILDER**
**Interpreting Graphs**
1. *About how many Confederate soldiers were killed in the Civil War?*
2. *Approximately how many soldiers were wounded in the war?*

That same evening, an accomplice of Booth stabbed Secretary of State William Seward, who later recovered. Another man was supposed to assassinate Vice-President Johnson, but he failed to carry out the attack.

Although Booth had managed to escape after shooting the president, Union troops found and killed him several days later. Soldiers also hunted down Booth's accomplices, whom they either hanged or imprisoned.

After Lincoln was shot, he was carried to a house across the street from the theater. The bullet in his brain could not be removed, however. The next morning, April 15, 1865, the president died. He was the first American president to be assassinated.

Lincoln's murder stunned the nation and caused intense grief. In Washington, D.C., people wept in the streets. One man who mourned the nation's loss was the poet Walt Whitman. In one poem, Whitman considered the president's legacy.

> **A VOICE FROM THE PAST**
> This dust was once the man,
> Gentle, plain, just and resolute, under whose cautious hand,
> Against the foulest crime in history known in any land or age,
> Was saved the Union of these States.
> **Walt Whitman,** *This Dust Was Once the Man*

The loss of Lincoln's vast experience and great political skills was a terrible setback for a people faced by the challenge of rebuilding their nation. In both the North and the South, life would never be the same after the Civil War.

## Consequences of the War

In the North, the war changed the way people thought about the country. In fighting to defend the Union, people came to see the United States as a single nation rather than a collection of states. After 1865, people no longer said "the United States *are*" but "the United States *is*."

The war also caused the national government to expand. Before the war, the government was relatively small and had limited powers. With the demands of war, however, the government grew larger and more powerful. Along with a new paper currency and income tax, the government established a new federal banking system. It also funded railroads, gave western land to settlers, and provided for state colleges. This growth of federal power continued long after the war was over.

The war also changed the Northern economy. New industries such as steel, petroleum, food processing, and manufacturing grew rapidly. By

**Vocabulary**
**accomplice:** someone who aids a lawbreaker

*Reading* **History**
**C. Summarizing** How did Americans react to the assassination of Lincoln?

**Background**
In the 1850s, an improved way of making steel—the Bessemer process—had been perfected, allowing for the mass production of steel.

## CAUSE AND EFFECT: *The Civil War, 1861–1865*

| CAUSES | IMMEDIATE EFFECTS |
|---|---|
| Conflict over slavery in territories | Abolition of slavery |
| Economic differences between North and South | Devastation of South |
| | Reconstruction of South |
| Failure of Congress to compromise | **LONG-TERM EFFECTS** |
| Election of Lincoln as president | Growth of industry |
| Secession of Southern states | Government more powerful |
| Firing on Fort Sumter | Nation reunited |

**SKILLBUILDER Interpreting Charts**
1. *What military event is among the causes of the Civil War?*
2. *What effect did the Civil War have on the federal government?*

**Background**
Some people have called the Civil War the first modern war because of the use of machines, the destructiveness, and the effects on civilians, which would be repeated in later wars.

the late 1800s, industry had begun to replace farming as the basis of the national economy.

For the South, however, the war brought economic disaster. Farms and plantations were destroyed. About 40 percent of the South's livestock was killed. Fifty percent of its farm machinery was wrecked. Factories were also demolished, and thousands of miles of railroad tracks were torn up. Also gone was the labor system that the South had used—slavery.

Before the war, the South accounted for 30 percent of the nation's wealth. After the war it accounted for only 12 percent. These economic differences between the North and the South would last for decades.

The country faced difficult challenges after the war. How would the South be brought back into the Union, and how would four million former slaves be integrated into national life? You will read more about these challenges in the next chapter.

---

## Section 4 Assessment

### 1. Terms & Names

**Explain the significance of:**
- Thirteenth Amendment
- John Wilkes Booth

### 2. Using Graphics

Use a chart like the one below to record the social, economic, and political legacy of the Civil War.

**Legacy of the Civil War**

| Society | Economy | Politics |
|---|---|---|
| | | |

Is the legacy of the Civil War still apparent today? How? (HI2)

### 3. Main Ideas

**a.** What were some of the human costs of the Civil War? (HI1)

**b.** What did the Thirteenth Amendment achieve? (HI1)

**c.** What was the state of the Southern economy after the Civil War? (HI1)

### 4. Critical Thinking

**Making Inferences** How do you think the assassination of President Lincoln affected the nation? (HI2)

**THINK ABOUT**
- the reaction of ordinary citizens
- its impact on government

---

**ACTIVITY OPTIONS**

**MATH**

**TECHNOLOGY**

Read about the postwar economy. Create a **database** on industry in the North or make a **storyboard** for a video on the problems in the South. (HI6)

# The Gettysburg Address (1863)

**Setting the Stage** On November 19, 1863, officials gathered in Gettysburg, Pennsylvania. They were there to dedicate a national cemetery on the ground where the decisive Battle of Gettysburg had taken place nearly five months earlier. Following the ceremony's main address, which lasted nearly two hours, President Lincoln delivered his Gettysburg Address in just over two minutes. In this famous speech, Lincoln expressed his hopes for the nation. **See Primary Source Explorer**

**A CLOSER LOOK**

**LINCOLN'S MODESTY**

Lincoln claimed that what he said at Gettysburg would not be long remembered. However, the address soon came to be recognized as one of the best speeches of all time.

**1. What features of Lincoln's address make it so memorable?**

**A CLOSER LOOK**

**FIGHTING FOR A CAUSE**

Different people fought for different causes during the Civil War. Sometimes, the causes for which people fought changed over the course of the war.

**2. What cause is Lincoln referring to in the Gettysburg Address?**

Four **score**[1] and seven years ago our fathers brought forth on this continent a new nation, conceived in liberty, and dedicated to the proposition that all men are created equal.

Now we are engaged in a great civil war, testing whether that nation or any nation so conceived and so dedicated, can long endure. We are met on a great battlefield of that war. We have come to dedicate a portion of that field, as a final resting place for those who here gave their lives that that nation might live. It is altogether fitting and proper that we should do this.

But, in a larger sense, we cannot dedicate—we can not **consecrate**[2]—we can not hallow—this ground. The brave men, living and dead, who struggled here, have consecrated it, far above our poor power to add or **detract.**[3] The world will little note, nor long remember what we say here, but it can never forget what they did here. It is for us the living, rather, to be dedicated here to the unfinished work which they who fought here have thus far so nobly advanced. It is rather for us to be here dedicated to the great task remaining before us—that from these honored dead we **take increased devotion to**[4] that cause for which they **gave the last full measure of devotion**[5]—that we here highly resolve that these dead shall not have died **in vain**[6]—that this nation, under God, shall have a new birth of freedom—and that government of the people, by the people, for the people, shall not perish from the earth.

1. **score:** a group of 20.
2. **consecrate:** to declare as sacred.
3. **detract:** to take away from.
4. **take increased devotion to:** work harder for.
5. **gave the last full measure of devotion:** sacrificed their lives.
6. **in vain:** for nothing.

# Second Inaugural Address (1865)

**Setting the Stage** President Lincoln delivered his Second Inaugural Address just before the end of the Civil War. In this excerpt, he recalled the major cause of the war and vowed to fight for the restoration of peace and unity. **See Primary Source Explorer** 💿

**CALIFORNIA STANDARDS**

**Reading 2.2** Analyze text that uses proposition and support patterns.

One-eighth of the whole population were colored slaves. . . . These slaves constituted a peculiar and powerful interest. All knew that this interest was somehow the cause of the war. To strengthen, perpetuate, and extend this interest was the object for which the **insurgents**[1] would rend the Union even by war, while the Government claimed no right to do more than to restrict the territorial enlargement of it. Neither party expected for the war the magnitude or the duration which it has already attained. Neither anticipated that the cause of the conflict might cease with or even before the conflict itself should cease. Each looked for an easier triumph, and a result less fundamental and astounding. Both read the same Bible and pray to the same God, and each invokes His aid against the other. . . . Fondly do we hope, fervently do we pray, that this mighty **scourge**[2] of war may speedily pass away. Yet, if God wills that it continue until all the wealth piled by the **bondsman's**[3] two hundred and fifty years of **unrequited**[4] toil shall be sunk, and until every drop of blood drawn with the lash shall be paid by another drawn with the sword, as was said three thousand years ago, so still it must be said "the judgments of the Lord are true and righteous altogether."

With malice toward none, with charity for all, with firmness in the right as God gives us to see the right, let us strive on to finish the work we are in, to bind up the nation's wounds, to care for him who shall have borne the battle and for his widow and his orphan, to do all which may achieve and cherish a just and lasting peace among ourselves and with all nations.

1. **insurgent:** one that revolts against civil authority.
2. **scourge:** a source of suffering and devastation.
3. **bondsman:** enslaved person.
4. **unrequited:** not paid for.

## A CLOSER LOOK

### SLAVERY IN TERRITORIES

Before the Civil War, Northern states wanted to prohibit slavery in territories that would eventually become new states. Southern states fought to expand slavery, fearing the prohibition would threaten slavery where it already existed.

**1. Why did the Southerners fear that prohibiting slavery in new territories might threaten slavery where it already existed?**

## A CLOSER LOOK

### MALICE TOWARD NONE

As Northerners became more confident in victory, many looked forward to punishing Southerners, whom they blamed for the war. Lincoln, however, urged citizens to care for one another and work for a just and lasting peace.

**2. Why do you think that Lincoln believed it would be wiser for Americans not to place blame or seek revenge on one another?**

## Interactive Primary Sources Assessment

### 1. Main Ideas

**a.** Why might President Lincoln have begun the Gettysburg Address by noting that the country was "dedicated to the proposition that all men are created equal"? (REP4)

**b.** According to Lincoln's Second Inaugural Address, why did the Confederacy go to war? (REP4)

**c.** To what did Lincoln refer with the phrase "the bondsman's two hundred and fifty years of unrequited toil?" (REP4)

### 2. Critical Thinking

**Making Inferences** In 1865, if the South had asked to rejoin the Union without ending slavery, do you think Lincoln would have agreed? (REP4)

**THINK ABOUT**

• what Lincoln identifies as the cause of the war
• what might happen if the war ended but slavery did not

## TERMS & NAMES

Briefly explain the significance of each of the following.

1. Emancipation Proclamation
2. 54th Massachusetts Regiment
3. conscription
4. Battle of Gettysburg
5. Ulysses S. Grant
6. Robert E. Lee
7. Siege of Vicksburg
8. William Tecumseh Sherman
9. Appomattox Court House
10. Thirteenth Amendment

## REVIEW QUESTIONS

**The Emancipation Proclamation (pages 503–506)**

1. Why did Lincoln issue the Emancipation Proclamation? (HI2)
2. How did black soldiers aid the war effort? (HI1)

**War Affects Society (pages 507–511)**

3. How did events on the home front show the toll that war was taking there? (HI1)
4. Why did some people say the Civil War was a "rich man's war but a poor man's fight"? (HI1)
5. How did enslaved persons help the Union? (HI2)

**The North Wins (pages 512–519)**

6. Why was the Battle of Gettysburg so important? (HI2)
7. How did Sherman's march help the Union? (HI2)
8. How did Grant defeat Lee? (HI1)

**The Legacy of the War (pages 520–523)**

9. How was the Thirteenth Amendment different from the Emancipation Proclamation? (HI1)
10. How did the war change the national economy? (HI2)

## CRITICAL THINKING

**1. USING YOUR NOTES: COMPARING AND CONTRASTING (HI2)**

|  | North | South |
|---|---|---|
| Emancipation Proclamation |  |  |
| War's Impact |  |  |
| Northern Victories in Battle |  |  |
| Union Wins Civil War |  |  |

a. How did white and black Southerners react to the Emancipation Proclamation?
b. How did inflation affect the North and the South?

**2. ANALYZING LEADERSHIP**

What qualities made Lincoln an effective leader? (HI1)

**3. THEME: IMPACT OF THE INDIVIDUAL**

How did General Grant's actions in the war make a crucial difference to the outcome? (HI2)

**4. FORMING AND SUPPORTING OPINIONS**

One Union relief worker said, "The suffering of men in battle is nothing next to the agony that women feel sending forth their loved ones to war." Do you agree with this statement? Explain why or why not. (REP4)

**5. APPLYING CITIZENSHIP SKILLS**

How might the behavior of General Grant and President Lincoln toward the Confederacy have helped to begin healing the war-torn nation? (HI2)

### Interact *with* History

Having read about the ferocity of battle during the Civil War, do you still believe that you would be inspired to continue the fighting? Why or why not?

## VISUAL SUMMARY

# The Civil War, 1863–1865 (CST2)

**January 1863**
Emancipation Proclamation is issued.

**July 1863**
Battle of Gettysburg takes place.
Union takes Vicksburg.

**September 1864**
Sherman takes Atlanta, Georgia.

**May 1864**
Battle of the Wilderness and Spotsylvania occur.

**December 1864**
Sherman takes Savannah, Georgia.

**April 1865**
Lee surrenders at Appomattox Court House.
Lincoln is assassinated.

1863 — 1866

**March 1863**
Union passes the draft law.

**March 1864**
Grant is put in charge of all Union armies.

**November 1864**
Lincoln is reelected.

**January 1865**
Thirteenth Amendment is passed by Congress.

**June 1864**
Battle of Cold Harbor occurs.

## STANDARDS-BASED ASSESSMENT

Use the map and your knowledge of U.S. history to answer questions 1 and 2.

Additional Test Practice, pp. S1–S33.

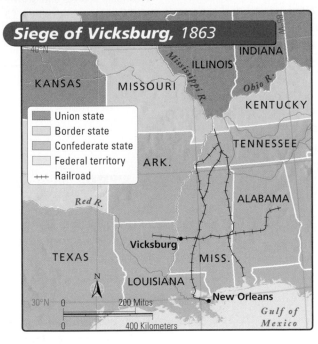

Siege of Vicksburg, 1863

Legend:
- Union state
- Border state
- Confederate state
- Federal territory
- +++ Railroad

KANSAS, MISSOURI, ILLINOIS, INDIANA, KENTUCKY, TENNESSEE, ARK., ALABAMA, TEXAS, MISS., LOUISIANA, Vicksburg, New Orleans, Mississippi R., Ohio R., Red R., Gulf of Mexico, 40°N, 30°N

0 200 Miles
0 400 Kilometers

**1.** Vicksburg was built next to which of the following bodies of water? (8.10.6)

A. Red River

B. Ohio River

C. Mississippi River

D. Gulf of Mexico

**2.** Why might Vicksburg be important for Southerners supplying the Confederacy from Texas? (8.10.6)

A. Vicksburg was on a river and a rail line.

B. Vicksburg was located in a border state.

C. Vicksburg was an ocean port city.

D. Vicksburg was located in Texas.

Frederick Douglass explains his views on the efforts to end slavery in this quotation. Use the quotation and your knowledge of U.S. history to answer question 3.

### PRIMARY SOURCE

To fight against slaveholders, without fighting against slavery, is but a half-hearted business, and paralyzes the hands engaged in it . . . Fire must be met with water . . . War for the destruction of liberty [by the South] must be met with war for the destruction of slavery.

**Frederick Douglass,** quoted in *Battle Cry of Freedom*

**3.** What do you think Frederick Douglass meant when he said "Fire must be met with water?" (8.9.1)

A. He was referring to new military weapons.

B. The Civil War must wipe out slavery just as water puts out a fire.

C. Fire and water were symbols of the war against the Confederacy.

D. He wanted an end to the "flames" of warfare.

TEST PRACTICE
CLASSZONE.COM

## ALTERNATIVE ASSESSMENT

### 1. ✍ WRITING ABOUT HISTORY

Write a **report** about the advances of military technology during the Civil War. Your report should give a detailed description of the new or improved weapons that were used during the war. (REP4)

• Research your report by reading books about military technology or books about the Civil War.

### 2. COOPERATIVE LEARNING

Work with a group to produce a newspaper that covers a specific period of the Civil War. Choose the period you want to cover and decide whether you will take a Northern or Southern viewpoint. Then, group members can select topics, such as important battles and military strategies, social or economic conditions, or important figures, to research and write about. (REP5)

## INTEGRATED TECHNOLOGY

### DOING INTERNET RESEARCH

The Battle at Gettysburg was a turning point in the Civil War. Use the Internet and other library resources to create a presentation on the Battle at Gettysburg. (REP3)

• Find primary sources about the battle, such as letters, diary entries, and journals.

• Another source of information might be Web sites for Civil War museums or archives.

• You might consider focusing your presentation on paintings or written descriptions of the battle, images of destruction caused by conflict, music from the time period, or statistics on casualties.

**For more about the Battle of Gettysburg . . .**

INTERNET ACTIVITY
CLASSZONE.COM

# Create a Medal of Honor

In 1782, George Washington established the nation's first award to recognize the bravery of American soldiers. It was a purple heart made of cloth and was called the Badge of Military Merit. But the award was not used much after the Revolutionary War. Then, in 1861, Congress created a new award—the Medal of Honor. In the Civil War, 1,520 Union soldiers, including 20 African Americans, received the medal. Today, that medal is the highest United States military award for individual bravery and is commonly referred to as the Congressional Medal of Honor.

**ACTIVITY** Create a medal of honor for a hero or heroine from either side of the Civil War. Write a letter recommending your hero for the medal. Then read a speech in class as you award your medal to the deserving individual.

**CALIFORNIA STANDARDS**

**REP4** Students assess the credibility of primary and secondary sources and draw sound conclusions from them.

**Writing 2.1** Write biographies, autobiographies, short stories, or narratives.

## TOOLBOX

Each group will need:

tops of juice cans or cardboard

aluminum foil

pieces of ribbon

safety pins

glue

markers

scissors

writing paper

## STEP BY STEP

**1** **Form groups.** Each group should consist of three or four students. Each group will:

- identify a Civil War hero or heroine
- create a medal
- write a letter explaining why your group considers that person a hero
- award the medal and read a speech in class

**2** **Research a hero.** First, brainstorm characteristics that you think a hero should have. Then, using this chapter, books on the Civil War, or the Internet, select an individual who you think was a hero for either side of the Civil War. Take notes on the actions of the person you selected. The actions should show how that person meets your standards for being a hero.

The Congressional Medal of Honor rewards military personnel who risked their lives, "above and beyond the call of duty." In the Civil War, 1,520 Union soldiers, including 20 African Americans, received the Medal of Honor.

## HELP DESK

For related information, see page 518 in Chapter 17.

### Researching Your Project

Visit the library to learn more about the history of military awards or go to your local historical museum to examine actual medals.

**For more about military awards . . .**

**RESEARCH LINKS**
CLASSZONE.COM

### Did You Know?

Since the Congressional Medal of Honor was created in 1861, 3,408 persons have received the award. Nineteen persons have received two such awards. Only one woman has received the award.

The Confederate States of America also awarded 43 of its finest men with the Confederate Medal of Honor.

The practice of awarding medals began in Europe during the Middle Ages. Kings realized that giving land to valued knights was too costly, so they gave medals instead.

**③ Design your medal.** Think about the shape, images, and words that you will use to make your medal of honor. You may want to look at the example from Chapter 17 and in Civil War books. Sketch a design of your medal in pencil.

**④ Construct your medal.** Using art supplies, construct a medal based on your design. First, construct the medal itself by using a juice can lid or a cardboard pattern. Decorate the medal by using foil and markers. Then add a ribbon and pin.

**⑤ Write a letter.** The letter should be addressed to the Congress of the United States of America or the Congress of the Confederate States of America. Your letter should give reasons for recommending your hero based on the person's actions. Carefully recopy your letter after you have made any corrections.

**⑥ Pin up the medal.** Create a Medal of Honor board with other groups in your class. Pin up all the medals you have created. Discuss with other groups the standards your group set for calling a person a hero.

## REFLECT & ASSESS

- What requirements did you set for awarding a medal of honor?

- What reasons did your letter and speech give for awarding the medal?

- What symbols did you use for your medal? Why did you select them?

## WRITE AND SPEAK

**Write a Speech** As a Civil War military leader, write a speech praising the courage and bravery of the individual who is receiving the medal. Choose another member of your group to act as the recipient of the award. Read your speech to the class as you award the medal to that person.

# Reconstruction
## 1865–1877

Notice the two churches in this image appear largely undamaged from the battle.

Reconstruction meant rebuilding the government, economy, and cities of the South.

**1865**
Andrew Johnson becomes president after Lincoln's assassination.

**1866**
Civil Rights Act is passed.

**1867**
Reconstruction Acts are passed.

**1868**
Fourteenth Amendment extends full citizenship to African Americans.

**Ulysses S. Grant is elected president.**

**1870**
Fifteenth Amendment guarantees voting rights to African Americans.

USA
World  1865

**1865**
Joseph Lister pioneers antiseptic surgery.

**1867**
Emperor Maximilian is executed in Mexico.

**1870**
Unification of Italy is completed.

The Civil War has just ended, and the Southern economy is in ruins. Slavery has been abolished. Northerners and Southerners feel deep anger toward one another. As a member of Congress, you must help the nation recover.

Freed African Americans sit in the ruins of Charleston, South Carolina, after the Civil War.

# How would you rebuild the Union?

## What Do You Think?

- What problems would you face in rebuilding the nation?
- How would you ease tensions between North and South?
- How would you help freed African Americans?

**RESEARCH LINKS**
CLASSZONE.COM
Visit the Chapter 18 links for more information about Reconstruction.

**1872**
Grant is reelected president.

**1873**
Financial panic leads to an economic depression.

**1877**
Rutherford B. Hayes is inaugurated as president and ends Reconstruction.

1877

**1871**
Unification of Germany is completed by Kaiser Wilhelm I.

**1874**
In England, the Factory Act limits the working week to 56.5 hours.

**1876**
Korea becomes an independent nation.

# Reading Strategy: Identifying and Solving Problems

## What Do You Know?

What do you think it means to reconstruct something? What kinds of things did the U.S. government need to reconstruct after the Civil War? Which of these issues do you think was most important?

### Think About
- what you learned about the Civil War in the last two chapters
- what you've learned about civil rights in the United States from television and movies
- your responses to the Interact with History about rebuilding the Union (see page 531)

**CALIFORNIA STANDARDS**

**Reading 2.6** Use information from a variety of consumer, workplace, and public documents to explain a situation or decision and to solve a problem.

## What Do You Want to Know?

What questions do you have about Reconstruction? Record those questions in your notebook before you read this chapter.

## Identifying and Solving Problems

Sometimes, to understand what you read, you must learn to identify problems and solutions. As you read through this chapter, use a diagram like the one below to take notes on the problems the United States faced during Reconstruction and the actions the nation took to solve them.

**S** See Skillbuilder Handbook, page R18.

### Taking Notes

| Problems | Solutions |
|---|---|
| Black codes | |
| President Johnson | |
| Education | |
| Economy | |
| Ku Klux Klan | |
| Voting | |

# Rebuilding the Union

| MAIN IDEA | WHY IT MATTERS NOW | TERMS & NAMES |
|---|---|---|
| During Reconstruction, the president and Congress fought over how to rebuild the South. | Reconstruction was an important step in the African-American struggle for civil rights. | Radical Republicans  Reconstruction  Freedmen's Bureau  Andrew Johnson  black codes  civil rights  Fourteenth Amendment |

## ONE AMERICAN'S STORY

After the Civil War, Pennsylvania congressman Thaddeus Stevens became a leader of the Radical Republicans. This group of congressmen favored using federal power to create a new order in the South and to promote full citizenship for freed African Americans. Stevens stated that "the whole fabric of southern society must be changed."

In this section, you will learn how political leaders battled over how to bring the Southern states back into the Union.

Thaddeus Stevens addresses Congress.

**CALIFORNIA STANDARDS**

**8.11.1** List the original aims of Reconstruction and describe its effects on the political and social structures of different regions.

**8.11.3** Understand the effects of the Freedmen's Bureau and the restrictions placed on the rights and opportunities of freedmen, including racial segregation and "Jim Crow" laws.

**8.11.5** Understand the Thirteenth, Fourteenth, and Fifteenth Amendments to the Constitution and analyze their connection to Reconstruction.

**REP4** Students assess the credibility of primary and secondary sources and draw sound conclusions from them.

## Reconstruction Begins

After the Civil War ended in 1865, the South faced the challenge of building a new society not based on slavery. The process the federal government used to readmit the Confederate states to the Union is known as **Reconstruction**. Reconstruction lasted from 1865 to 1877.

In his Second Inaugural Address, in March 1865, Lincoln promised to reunify the nation "with malice [harm] toward none, with charity for all." Lincoln's plan included pardoning Confederate officials. It also called for allowing the Confederate states to quickly form new governments and send representatives to Congress.

To assist former slaves, the president established the **Freedmen's Bureau.** This federal agency set up schools and hospitals for African Americans and distributed clothes, food, and fuel throughout the South.

When Lincoln was killed in April 1865, Vice-President **Andrew Johnson** became president. Johnson was a Democrat. The Republicans

### Taking Notes

Use your chart to take notes about black codes and President Johnson.

**Problems**

| Black codes | ➤ |
| President Johnson | ➤ |
| Education | ➤ |
| Economy | ➤ |
| Ku Klux Klan | ➤ |
| Voting | ➤ |

**ANDREW JOHNSON**
**1808–1875**

Andrew Johnson was a self-educated man whose strong will led to trouble with Congress.

As a former slaveholder from Tennessee, Johnson called for a mild program for bringing the South back into the Union. In particular, he let states decide whether to give voting rights to freed African Americans.

Johnson's policies led to a break with the Radical Republicans in Congress and, finally, to his impeachment trial (see page 537).

**Why might Johnson have chosen not to punish the South?**

had put him on the ticket in 1864 to help win support in the nation's border states. Johnson was a former slaveholder and, unlike Lincoln, a stubborn, unyielding man.

Johnson believed that Reconstruction was the job of the president, not Congress. His policies were based on Lincoln's goals. He insisted that the new state governments ratify the Thirteenth Amendment, which prohibited slavery. He also insisted that they accept the supreme power of the federal government.

Johnson offered amnesty, or official pardon, to most white Southerners. He promised to return their property. In return, they had to pledge loyalty to the United States. At first, the large plantation owners, top military officers, and ex-Confederate leaders were not included in this offer. But they, too, eventually won amnesty.

## Rebuilding Brings Conflict

As the Southern states rebuilt, they set up new state governments that seemed very much like the old ones. Some states flatly refused to ratify the Thirteenth Amendment. "This is a white man's government," said the governor of South Carolina, "and intended for white men only."

The Southern states passed laws, known as **black codes,** which limited the freedom of former slaves. In Mississippi, for instance, one law said that African Americans had to have written proof of employment. Anyone without such proof could be put to work on a plantation. African Americans were forbidden to meet in unsupervised groups or carry guns. Because of such laws, many people in the North suspected that white Southerners were trying to bring back the "old South."

When Congress met in December 1865, its members refused to seat representatives from the South. Many of these Southern representatives had been Confederate leaders only months before.

Under the Constitution, Congress has the right to decide whether its members are qualified to hold office. So instead of admitting the Southerners, Congress set up a committee to study conditions in the South and decide whether the Southern states should be represented. By taking such action, Congress let the president know that it planned to play a role in Reconstruction.

Republicans outnumbered Democrats in both houses of Congress. Most Republicans were moderates who believed that the federal government should stay out of the affairs of individuals and the states.

The Radical Republicans, however, wanted the federal government to play an active role in remaking Southern politics and society. Led by Thaddeus Stevens and Massachusetts senator Charles Sumner, the

**Background**
Not all Confederate leaders were pardoned. Former Confederate president Jefferson Davis, for example, was imprisoned for two years awaiting trial for treason. But he was never tried.

*Reading* **History**
**A. Analyzing Causes** What was the main reason Southern states passed black codes?

**Vocabulary**
**moderates:** people opposed to extreme views

group also demanded full and equal citizenship for African Americans. Their aim was to destroy the South's old ruling class and turn the region into a place of small farms, free schools, respect for labor, and political equality for all citizens.

Radical Republicans pose for a formal portrait. Standing (left to right): James F. Wilson, George S. Boutwell, and John A. Logan. Seated: Benjamin F. Butler, Thaddeus Stevens, Thomas Williams, and John A. Bingham.

## The Civil Rights Act

Urged on by the Radicals, Congress passed a bill promoting **civil rights**—those rights granted to all citizens. The Civil Rights Act of 1866 declared that all persons born in the United States (except Native Americans) were citizens. It also stated that all citizens were entitled to equal rights regardless of their race.

Republicans were shocked when President Johnson vetoed the bill. Johnson argued that federal protection of civil rights would lead "towards centralization" of the national government. He also insisted that making African Americans full citizens would "operate against the white race." Congress voted to override Johnson's veto. That is, two-thirds of the House and two-thirds of the Senate voted for the bill after the president's veto, and the bill became law.

## The Fourteenth Amendment

*Reading* **History**

**B. Making Inferences** How did the Fourteenth Amendment encourage states to give African Americans the vote?

Republicans were not satisfied with passing laws that ensured equal rights. They wanted equality to be protected by the Constitution itself. To achieve this goal, Congress proposed the **Fourteenth Amendment** in 1866. It stated that all people born in the United States were citizens and had the same rights. All citizens were to be granted "equal protection of the laws." However, the amendment did not establish black suffrage. Instead, it declared that any state that kept African Americans from voting would lose representatives in Congress. This meant that the Southern states would have less power if they did not grant black men the vote.

Johnson refused to support the amendment. So did every former Confederate state except Tennessee. This rejection outraged both moderate and Radical Republicans. As a result, the two groups agreed to join forces and passed the Reconstruction Acts of 1867. The passage of these acts began a period known as Radical Reconstruction. From this point on, Congress controlled Reconstruction.

One of the Reconstruction Acts of 1867 divided the South into five military districts, each run by an army commander. Members of the ruling class before the war lost their voting rights. The law also stated that before the Southern states could reenter the Union, they would have to do two things:

1. They must approve new state constitutions that gave the vote to all adult men, including African Americans.
2. They must ratify the Fourteenth Amendment.

**Background**
Attempts to secure voting rights for African Americans applied only to men. Women were not allowed to vote until 1919.

## The New Southern Governments

In 1867, Southern voters chose delegates to draft their new state constitutions. About three-fourths of the delegates were Republicans. Many of the Republicans were poor white farmers. Angry at planters for starting what they called the "rich man's war," these delegates were called scalawags (scoundrels) for going along with Radical Reconstruction.

Another one-fourth of the Republican delegates were known as carpetbaggers—white Northerners who had rushed to the South after the war. Many Southerners accused them, often unfairly, of seeking only to get rich or gain political power.

**Background**
Carpetbaggers were said to have headed south carrying only a cheap suitcase, known as a carpetbag.

African Americans made up the rest of the Republican delegates. Of these, half had been free before the war. Most were ministers, teachers, or skilled workers. About 80 percent of them could read.

The new constitutions written by these delegates set up public schools and gave the vote to all adult males. By 1870, voters in all the Southern states had approved their new constitutions. As a result, the former Confederate states were let back into the Union and allowed to send representatives to Congress.

During Reconstruction, more than 600 African Americans served in state legislatures throughout the South, and 14 of the new U.S. congressmen from the South were African Americans. Two African Americans served as U.S. senators during this time. One was Hiram Revels of Mississippi, a minister in the African Methodist Episcopal Church. He had recruited African Americans to fight for the Union during the Civil War.

*Reading* **History**
C. Finding Main Ideas What political gains did African Americans make during Reconstruction?

### HISTORY *through* ART

*His First Vote*, an 1868 oil painting by Thomas Waterman Wood, shows a new African-American voter.

**How do you think the man felt about voting?**

536

For an activity
about Johnson's
impeachment . . .

NET SIMULATION
CLASSZONE.COM

# Johnson Is Impeached

President Johnson fought against many of
Congress's reform efforts during Radical
Reconstruction. For instance, he chose
people friendly to ex-Confederates to
serve as military commanders in the
South. The conflict between Johnson and
Congress soon brought a showdown.

In 1867, Congress passed the Tenure
of Office Act, which prohibited the president from firing government
officials without the Senate's approval. In February 1868, Johnson fired
his secretary of war, Edwin Stanton, over disagreements about
Reconstruction. Three days later, the House of Representatives voted to
impeach the president. This means that the House formally accused him
of improper conduct while in office. By removing Johnson from office,
they hoped to strengthen Congress's role in Reconstruction.

The case moved to the Senate for a trial. After several weeks of testimony, the senators prepared to vote. George Julian, a 20-year congressman
from Indiana, recalled the tension in the air.

*This is a ticket
to the 1868
impeachment
trial of President
Johnson.*

**Reading History**

**D. Drawing
Conclusions** Why
did Congress
decide to impeach
President
Johnson?

### A VOICE FROM THE PAST

The galleries were packed, and an indescribable anxiety was written on
every face. Some of the members of the House near me grew pale and sick
under the burden of suspense. Such stillness prevailed that the breathing in
the galleries could be heard at the announcement of each Senator's voice.

**George Julian,** quoted in *Grand Inquests*

**Vocabulary
acquitted:** cleared
of a charge

In the end, President Johnson was acquitted by a single vote. But much
work remained to be done in rebuilding the South. In the next section, you
will learn how African Americans in the South worked to improve their lives.

---

## Section 1 Assessment

### 1. Terms & Names

**Explain the
significance of:**

• Radical Republicans
• Reconstruction
• Freedmen's Bureau
• Andrew Johnson
• black codes
• civil rights
• Fourteenth
  Amendment

### 2. Using Graphics

Use a diagram to review the
events that led to Johnson's
impeachment.

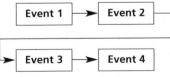

Which event seems most
important and why? (CST2)

### 3. Main Ideas

**a.** What was Lincoln's
Reconstruction plan? (8.11.1)

**b.** How did white
Southerners plan to restore
the "old South"? (8.11.1)

**c.** What impact did the
Reconstruction Acts of 1867
have on the South? (8.11.1)

### 4. Critical Thinking

**Evaluating** Do you think
the House was justified in
impeaching President
Johnson? Why or why not?
(REP5)

**THINK ABOUT**

• the clash over
  Reconstruction policies
• Congress's motives for
  impeaching Johnson

**ACTIVITY OPTIONS**

**TECHNOLOGY**

**SPEECH**

Research an African American who served in Congress during Reconstruction.
Design his Internet **home page,** or make a **speech** about his accomplishments. (HI1)

# Rebuilding Richmond

You live in Richmond, Virginia, the capital of the Confederacy. It is 1865, and the South faces defeat in the Civil War. On April 2, Confederate officials set fire to supplies in Richmond to prevent the approaching Union army from using them. The fire spreads out of control and destroys downtown Richmond. The next day, Union troops march into the city and take command. You must now help rebuild the city.

**This picture shows a street in Richmond before the fire.**

**COOPERATIVE LEARNING** On this page are two challenges you face as a resident of Richmond. Working with a small group, decide how to solve one of these problems. Divide the work among the group members. You will find useful information in the Data File. Be prepared to present your solutions to the class.

**CALIFORNIA STANDARDS**

**HI4** Students recognize the role of chance, foresight, and error in history.

**Reading 2.6** Use information from a variety of consumer, workplace, and public documents to explain a situation or decision and to solve a problem.

**Listening and Speaking 2.3** Deliver research presentations.

## ARTS CHALLENGE

### *"We want the burnt district of Richmond to . . . sit proudly again."*

The smell of charred wood still floats in the breeze. However, spirit and determination fill the air. Warehouses are opening. Newly cleared streets bustle with activity. The rebuilding of Richmond has begun. How would you design one block of Richmond's new downtown business district? Use the Data File for help. Then present your plan using one of these options:

• Make a model of your new city block.

• Ask and answer questions about how buildings and services should be distributed on the model block.

### THE BURNT DISTRICT

- about $30 million damage
- 20 city blocks destroyed, including 900 buildings

**Destroyed Property**

all banks, 20 law offices, 24 grocery stores, 36 merchant shops, 2 carriage factories, 2 paper mills, 7 book and stationery stores, 2 train depots, 3 bridges, a church, a machine shop, a tin shop, a pottery factory, several flour mills and printing offices

**Surviving Property**

capitol and city hall, residential areas, ironworks

### EMERGENCY SERVICES

**Union Army**

- distributes 13,000 food rations
- provides medical help
- guards homes; patrols streets

**American Union Commission**

- hands out food tickets
- distributes 80,000 pounds of flour; feeds soup to 800 people a day
- provides garden seeds and sells shovels at cost to farmers

### REBUILDING

**April 1865**

- rubble is cleared
- markets sell meat, fish, produce
- hotels and bakeries open
- one bridge is rebuilt

**May 1865**

- two banks open
- gas and telegraph service is restored
- river opens to steamboat traffic

**Summer 1865**

- horse-drawn buses operate
- city government is reinstated

**Fall 1865**

- ironworks reopens
- 100 buildings are now under construction

For more about Reconstruction . . .

RESEARCH LINKS
CLASSZONE.COM

---

## CIVICS CHALLENGE

# "Open robberies have been perpetrated."

Robberies and assaults are commonplace, especially in the burnt area of the downtown. Groups of orphaned children also roam the city, picking pockets to support themselves. Union military police supposedly protect the public. However, soldiers sometimes commit crimes themselves. What would you do to improve public safety? Use the Data File for help. Present your ideas using one of these options:

- Hold a town meeting to explore possible solutions.
- Create a set of emergency laws, with plans for publicizing them.

## ACTIVITY WRAP-UP

Meet as a group to review your responses to rebuilding Richmond. Pick your most creative solution and present it to the class.

# 2

# Reconstruction and Daily Life

| MAIN IDEA | WHY IT MATTERS NOW | TERMS & NAMES |
|---|---|---|
| As the South rebuilt, millions of newly freed African Americans worked to improve their lives. | Many important African-American institutions, including colleges, began during Reconstruction. | freedmen's school  Ku Klux Klan<br>sharecropping  lynch |

CALIFORNIA STANDARDS

**8.11.1** List the original aims of Reconstruction and describe its effects on the political and social structures of different regions.

**8.11.3** Understand the effects of the Freedmen's Bureau and the restrictions placed on the rights and opportunities of freedmen, including racial segregation and "Jim Crow" laws.

**8.11.4** Trace the rise of the Ku Klux Klan and describe the Klan's effects.

**REP4** Students assess the credibility of primary and secondary sources and draw sound conclusions from them.

## ONE AMERICAN'S STORY

One day, as the Civil War came to a close, two enslaved women named Mill and Jule saw a fleet of Union gunboats coming up the Mississippi River. Yankee soldiers came ashore and offered them and other slaves passage aboard their boats. On that day, Mill and Jule left the plantation.

*A VOICE FROM THE PAST*

An' we all got on the boat in a hurry . . . we all give three times three cheers for the gunboat boys, and . . . three times three cheers for gov'ment.

**Mill and Jule,** quoted in *We Are Your Sisters*

The Union's victory in the Civil War spelled the end of slavery in America. In this section, you will learn about the gains and setbacks of former slaves during Reconstruction.

Freed people and a federal soldier pose on a South Carolina plantation.

## Responding to Freedom

African Americans' first reaction to freedom was to leave the plantations. No longer needing passes to travel, they journeyed throughout the region. "Right off colored folks started on the move," recalled one freedman. "They seemed to want to get closer to freedom, so they'd know what it was—like it was a place or a city." Some former slaves returned to the places where they were born. Others went looking for more economic opportunity in the North and West. Still others traveled just because they could.

African Americans also traveled in search of family members separated from them during slavery. One man walked 600 miles from Georgia to North Carolina to find his family. To locate relatives, people placed advertisements in newspapers. The Freedmen's Bureau helped many families reunite. A Union officer wrote in 1865, "Men are taking

**Taking Notes**

Use your chart to take notes about education, the economy, and the Ku Klux Klan.

**Problems**

- Black codes
- President Johnson
- Education
- Economy
- Ku Klux Klan
- Voting

*Reading* **History**

**A. Analyzing Causes** For what reasons did former slaves move?

their wives and children, families which had been for a long time broken up are united and oh! such happiness."

Freedom allowed African Americans to strengthen their family ties. Former slaves could marry legally. They could raise families without fearing that their children might be sold. Many families adopted children of dead relatives and friends to keep family ties strong.

## Starting Schools

With freedom, African Americans no longer had to work for an owner's benefit. They could now work to provide for their families. To reach their goal of economic independence, however, most had to learn to read and write. As a result, children and adults flocked to **freedmen's schools** set up to educate newly freed African Americans. Such schools were started by the Freedmen's Bureau, Northern missionary groups, and African-American organizations. Freed people in cities held classes in warehouses, billiard rooms, and former slave markets. In rural areas, classes were held in churches and houses. Children who went to school often taught their parents to read at home.

*Reading* **History**

**B. Finding Main Ideas** Why did freed people desire an education?

In the years after the war, African-American groups raised more than $1 million for education. However, the federal government and private groups in the North paid most of the cost of building schools and hiring teachers. Between 1865 and 1870, the Freedmen's Bureau spent $5 million for this purpose.

**Background** Most African Americans were illiterate because teaching slaves to read and write had been illegal.

More than 150,000 African-American students were attending 3,000 schools by 1869. About 10 percent of the South's African-American adults could read. A number of them became teachers. Northern teachers, black and white, also went South to teach freed people. Many white Southerners, however, worked against these teachers' efforts. White racists even killed teachers and burned freedmen's schools in some parts of the South. Despite these setbacks, African Americans kept working toward an education.

## America's HERITAGE

### BLACK COLLEGES
Some of today's African-American colleges and universities date back to Reconstruction. The Freedmen's Bureau and other societies raised funds to build many of the schools. Howard University, shown in this photograph, opened in 1867. It was named for General Oliver Otis Howard, head of the Freedmen's Bureau. During Reconstruction, these colleges offered courses ranging from basic reading and writing to medicine and law. They also trained much-needed teachers.

African–American families hoped to own land but were often disappointed.

# 40 Acres and a Mule

More than anything else, freed people wanted to own land. As one freedman said, "Give us our own land and we take care of ourselves, but without land, the old masters can hire us or starve us, as they please."

As the Civil War ended, General William T. Sherman suggested that abandoned land in coastal South Carolina be split into 40-acre parcels and given to freedmen. The rumor then spread that all freedmen would get 40 acres and a mule. Most African Americans thought they deserved at least that much. In the end, however, most freedmen never received land. Those who did often had to return it to its former owners after the owners were pardoned by President Johnson. One freedman, Bayley Wyat, protested.

### A VOICE FROM THE PAST

Our wives, our children, our husbands, [have] been sold over and over again to purchase the lands we now [locate] upon; for that reason we have a divine right to the land. . . . And then didn't we clear the land, and raise the crops of corn, of cotton, of tobacco, of rice, of sugar, of everything.

**Bayley Wyat,** quoted in *Reconstruction: America's Unfinished Revolution*

Radical Republican leaders Thaddeus Stevens and Charles Sumner pushed to make land reform part of the Reconstruction Acts of 1867. Stevens proposed a plan to Congress that would have taken land from plantation owners and given it to freed people.

Many moderate Republicans and even some Radicals were against the plan. They believed that new civil and voting rights were enough to give African Americans a better life.

Supporters of the plan argued that civil rights meant little without economic independence. Land could provide that independence, they claimed. However, Congress did not pass the land-reform plan.

*Reading* **History**
C. Analyzing Points of View
What were some arguments in favor of giving land to freed people?

# The Contract System

Without their own property, many African Americans returned to work on plantations. They returned not as slaves but as wage earners. They and the planters both had trouble getting used to this new relationship. "It seems humiliating to be compelled to bargain and haggle with our own servants about wages," wrote the daughter of a Georgia plantation owner. For their part, many freed workers assumed that wages were extra. They thought that the planters still had to house and feed them.

After the Civil War, planters desperately needed workers to raise cotton, still the South's main cash crop. African Americans reacted to this demand for labor by choosing the best contract offers. The contract system was far better than slavery. African Americans could decide whom to work for, and planters could not abuse them or split up families.

The contract system still had drawbacks, however. Even the best contracts paid very low wages. Workers often could not leave the plantations

**Background**
Civil War deaths and the departure of slaves from plantations created a labor shortage in the South.

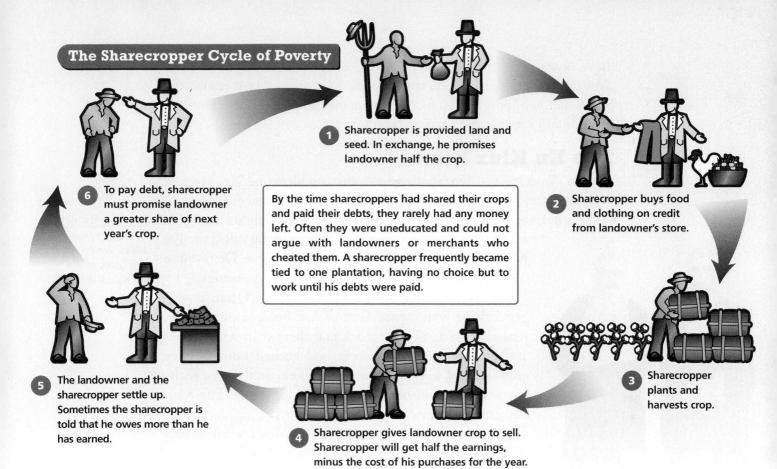

**The Sharecropper Cycle of Poverty**

1. Sharecropper is provided land and seed. In exchange, he promises landowner half the crop.

2. Sharecropper buys food and clothing on credit from landowner's store.

3. Sharecropper plants and harvests crop.

4. Sharecropper gives landowner crop to sell. Sharecropper will get half the earnings, minus the cost of his purchases for the year.

5. The landowner and the sharecropper settle up. Sometimes the sharecropper is told that he owes more than he has earned.

6. To pay debt, sharecropper must promise landowner a greater share of next year's crop.

By the time sharecroppers had shared their crops and paid their debts, they rarely had any money left. Often they were uneducated and could not argue with landowners or merchants who cheated them. A sharecropper frequently became tied to one plantation, having no choice but to work until his debts were paid.

without permission. Many owners cheated workers out of wages and other benefits. Worse yet, laws punished workers for breaking their contracts, even if the plantation owners were abusing or cheating them. These drawbacks made many African Americans turn to sharecropping.

## Sharecropping and Debt

Under the **sharecropping** system, a worker rented a plot of land to farm. The landowner provided the tools, seed, and housing. When harvest time came, the sharecropper gave the landowner a share of the crop. This system gave families without land a place to farm and gave landowners cheap labor.

But problems soon arose with the sharecropping system. One cause of these problems was that farmers and landowners had opposite goals. Farmers wanted to grow food to feed their families, but landowners forced them to grow cash crops, such as cotton. As a result, farmers had to buy food from the local store—which was usually owned by the landlord. Most farmers did not have the money to pay for goods. As a result, many were caught in a cycle of debt, as shown in the diagram above. Often farmers had to use one year's harvest to pay the previous year's bills.

White farmers also became sharecroppers. Many had lost their land in the war. Others had lost it to taxes. By 1880, one-third of the white farmers in the Deep South worked someone else's land.

No matter who worked the plantations, much of what they grew was cotton. After the war, the value of cotton dropped. Southern planters responded by trying to produce more of the cash crop—a move that

*Reading*History
**D. Recognizing Effects** What were some problems with the sharecropping system?

drove down prices even further. Growing cotton exhausted the soil and reduced the amount of land available for food crops. As a result, the South had to import half its food. Relying on cotton was one reason the Deep South experienced years of rural poverty.

## The Ku Klux Klan

African Americans in the South faced other problems besides poverty. They also faced violent racism. Many planters and former Confederate soldiers did not want African Americans to have more rights. In 1866, such feelings spurred the rise of a secret group called the **Ku Klux Klan.** The Klan's goals were to restore Democratic control of the South and keep former slaves powerless.

These Ku Klux Klan members were arrested after an 1868 riot in Alabama.

The Klan attacked African Americans. Often it targeted those who owned land or had become prosperous. Klansmen rode on horseback and dressed in white robes and hoods. They beat people and burned homes. They even **lynched** some victims, killing them on the spot without a trial as punishment for a supposed crime. The Klan also attacked white Republicans.

Klan victims had little protection. Military authorities in the South often ignored the violence. President Johnson had appointed most of these authorities, and they were against Reconstruction.

The Klan's terrorism served the Democratic Party. As gun-toting Klansmen kept Republicans away from the polls, the Democrats increased their power.

In the next section you will see how planters took back control of the South. You also will learn how they blocked African Americans' attempts to win more rights.

*Reading***History**
**E. Finding Main Ideas** What were the goals of the Ku Klux Klan?

---

Section **2** Assessment

### 1. Terms & Names

**Explain the significance of:**
• freedmen's school
• sharecropping
• Ku Klux Klan
• lynch

### 2. Using Graphics

Use a cluster diagram like the one below to review details about sharecropping.

For farmers, what were the advantages and disadvantages of sharecropping? (CST3)

### 3. Main Ideas

**a.** How did freedom help strengthen African-American families? (HI2)

**b.** How were African Americans educated during Reconstruction? (HI1)

**c.** What were the main reasons African Americans wanted their own land? (HI1)

### 4. Critical Thinking

**Analyzing Causes**
Despite greater civil rights, why did African Americans still face difficulty in improving their lives? (REP5)

**THINK ABOUT**
• the defeat of the land-reform bill
• the Ku Klux Klan's rise
• the attitude of military authorities in the South

**ACTIVITY OPTIONS**

**SPEECH**
**ART**

Make a **speech** to President Johnson or design a **mural** explaining why land should be given to newly freed African Americans. (HI1)

# End of Reconstruction

| MAIN IDEA | WHY IT MATTERS NOW | TERMS & NAMES |
|---|---|---|
| As white Southerners regained power, Reconstruction ended, as did black advances toward equality. | Reforms made during Reconstruction made later civil rights gains possible. | Fifteenth Amendment     Compromise of 1877<br>Panic of 1873 |

## ONE AMERICAN'S STORY

Robert B. Elliott was a U.S. congressman from South Carolina during Reconstruction. In 1874, he made a speech in favor of a civil rights bill that would outlaw racial discrimination in public service.

### A VOICE FROM THE PAST

The passage of this bill will determine the civil status, not only of the negro but of any other class of citizens who may feel themselves discriminated against. It will form the capstone of that temple of liberty begun on this continent.

**Robert B. Elliott,** quoted in *The Glorious Failure*

Robert B. Elliott

In 1877, federal troops left the South. White Southerners took back control of the region. Quickly, they forced African Americans, including Elliott, out of office. In Section 3, you will learn about the events that ended Reconstruction. You will also see how Reconstruction's end meant setbacks in the fight for civil rights.

## The Election of Grant

The Republican Party seemed stronger than ever in 1868. That year, its candidate, General Ulysses S. Grant, won the presidency. During the campaign, the Democrats attacked the Republicans' Reconstruction policies. They blamed the party for granting rights to African Americans.

On Election Day, however, the Republicans won. Grant received 214 electoral votes. His Democratic opponent received only 80. The popular count was much closer. Grant had a majority of only 306,000 votes.

Grant would not have had such a majority without the freedmen's vote. Despite attacks by the Ku Klux Klan, about 500,000 African Americans voted in the South. Most cast their ballots for Grant.

**Taking Notes**

Use your chart to take notes about voting.

**Problems**

- Black codes →
- President Johnson →
- Education →
- Economy →
- Ku Klux Klan →
- Voting →

# Now and then

## The Fifteenth Amendment

After Grant's victory, Radical Republicans worried that the Southern states might try to keep African Americans from voting in future elections. To prevent this, Radical leaders proposed a new constitutional amendment.

The **Fifteenth Amendment** stated that citizens could not be stopped from voting "on account of race, color, or previous condition of servitude." (This amendment, like the Fourteenth Amendment, did not apply to Native Americans on tribal lands.) The amendment was ratified in 1870.

The Fifteenth Amendment was not aimed only at the South. African-American men could not vote in 16 states. "We have no moral right to impose an obligation on one part of the land which the rest will not accept," one Radical wrote. With the Fifteenth Amendment, the nation again turned toward democracy.

The Fifteenth Amendment did not apply to women. This made many white women angry. Why couldn't they vote when black men—former slaves—could? Suffragist Elizabeth Cady Stanton protested the idea of uneducated immigrants and freedmen "who never read the Declaration of Independence" making laws for educated white women. Most African-American women were not as angry. To Frances E. W. Harper, a black suffragist and writer, it was important for African Americans to gain voting rights, even if that meant only men at first.

*Reading* **History**

**A. Comparing** How was the Fifteenth Amendment a step beyond the Fourteenth Amendment?

**Vocabulary**
**suffragist:** someone who favors equal voting rights, especially for women

## Grant Fights the Klan

Despite gaining the vote, African Americans in the South continued to be terrorized by the Ku Klux Klan. In 1871, to stop the terror, President Grant asked Congress to pass a tough law against the Klan. Joseph Rainey, a black congressman from South Carolina, had received death threats from the Klan. He urged his fellow lawmakers to support the bill.

> *A VOICE FROM THE PAST*
>
> When myself and colleagues shall leave these Halls and turn our footsteps toward our southern home we know not but that the assassin may await our coming. Be it as it may we have resolved to be loyal and firm, and if we perish, we perish! I earnestly hope the bill will pass.
>
> **Joseph Rainey,** quoted in *The Trouble They Seen*

Congress approved the anti-Klan bill. Federal marshals then arrested thousands of Klansmen. Klan attacks on African-American voters declined. As a result, the 1872 presidential election was both fair and peaceful in the South. Grant won a second term.

# Scandal and Panic Weaken Republicans

Under the Grant administration, support for the Republicans and Reconstruction weakened. Scandals hurt the administration and caused divisions in the Republican Party. A financial panic further hurt the Republicans and turned the country's attention away from Reconstruction.

President Grant did not choose his advisers well. He put his former army friends and his wife's relatives in government positions. Many of these people were unqualified. Some Grant appointees took bribes. Grant's private secretary, for instance, took money from whiskey distillers who wanted to avoid paying taxes. Grant's secretary of war, General William Belknap, left office after people accused him of taking bribes.

*Reading*History
**B. Making Inferences** How did Republican scandals hurt Reconstruction?

Such scandals deeply outraged many Republicans. In 1872, some Republican officials broke away and formed the new Liberal Republican Party. The Republicans, no longer unified, became less willing to impose tough Reconstruction policies on the South.

In 1873, political corruption and Republican quarreling gave way to a more serious problem. When several powerful Eastern banks ran out of money after making bad loans, a financial panic swept the country. In the **Panic of 1873**, banks across the land closed. The stock market temporarily collapsed. The panic caused an economic depression, a time of low business activity and high unemployment. The railroad industry, which relied on banks for loans, suffered. Within a year, 89 of the country's 364 railroads went broke. Railroad failures left Midwestern farmers with no way to move their crops, and many farmers were ruined.

This cartoon from *Puck* magazine shows President Grant weighed down by corruption in his administration.

The depression, which lasted about five years, touched nearly all parts of the economy. By 1875, more than 18,000 companies had folded. Hundreds of workers had lost their jobs. Many Americans blamed the crisis on the Republicans—the party in power. As a result, Democrats won victories in the 1874 congressional and state elections. In the middle of the depression, Americans grew tired of hearing about the South's problems. The nation was losing interest in Reconstruction.

*Reading*History
**C. Recognizing Effects** What resulted from the Panic of 1873?

## Supreme Court Reversals

To make matters worse for the Republicans, the Supreme Court began to undo some of the changes that had been made in the South. In an 1876 case, *U.S.* v. *Cruikshank,* the Court ruled that the federal government could not punish individuals who violated the civil rights of African Americans. Only the states had that power, the Court declared. Southern state officials often would not punish those who attacked African Americans. As a result, violence against them increased.

In the 1876 case *U.S.* v. *Reese,* the Court ruled in favor of white Southerners who barred African Americans from voting. The Court stated that the Fifteenth Amendment did not give everyone the right to vote—it merely listed the grounds on which states could not deny the vote. In other words, states could prevent African Americans from voting for other reasons. States later imposed poll taxes and literacy tests to restrict the vote. These Court decisions weakened Reconstruction and blocked African-American efforts to gain full equality.

*Reading* **History**

**D. Recognizing Effects** How did the Reese and Cruikshank rulings affect African Americans' efforts to gain civil rights?

## Reconstruction Ends

The final blow to Reconstruction came with the 1876 presidential election. The Democrats nominated Samuel J. Tilden, governor of New York. The Republicans chose Rutherford B. Hayes, governor of Ohio. The race was very close. Victory depended on the electoral votes of South Carolina, Louisiana, and Florida. The votes in those states were so close that both the Democrats and the Republicans claimed victory. A special commission of eight Republicans and seven Democrats made a deal. Under the **Compromise of 1877,** Hayes became president. In return, the Republicans compromised with the Southern Democrats on several issues.

**This cartoon from** *Harper's Weekly* **shows a federal soldier as the freedman's only defense against white Southerners.**

1. The government would remove federal troops from the South.
2. The government would provide land grants and loans for the construction of railroads linking the South to the West Coast.
3. Southern officials would receive federal funds for construction and improvement projects.
4. Hayes would appoint a Democrat to his cabinet.
5. The Democrats promised to respect African Americans' civil and political rights.

*Reading* **History**

**E. Summarizing** What events led to a weakening of support for Reconstruction?

Abolitionist Wendell Phillips was against the compromise. He doubted that the South would respect black rights. "The whole soil of the South is hidden by successive layers of broken promises," he said. "To trust a Southern promise would be fair evidence of insanity."

After the 1876 presidential election, the Reconstruction governments in the South collapsed. The Democrats returned to power, believing that they were the redeemers, or rescuers, of the South.

## Reconstruction: Civil Rights Amendments and Laws

| Civil Rights Act of 1866 | • Granted citizenship and equal rights to all persons born in the United States (except Native Americans) |
|---|---|
| Fourteenth Amendment (1868) | • Granted citizenship and equal protection of the laws to all persons born in the United States (except Native Americans) |
| Fifteenth Amendment (1870) | • Protected the voting rights of African Americans |
| Civil Rights Act of 1875 | • Outlawed racial segregation in public services<br>• Ensured the right of African Americans to serve as jurors |

**SKILLBUILDER Interpreting Charts**
1. *Which amendment and law are most similar?*
2. *Which amendment specifically protects voting rights?*

# The Legacy of Reconstruction

Historians still argue about the success of Reconstruction. The nation did rebuild and reunite. However, Reconstruction did not achieve equality for African Americans.

After Reconstruction, most African Americans still lived in poverty. Legally, they could vote and hold public office. But few took part in politics. They continued to face widespread violence and prejudice.

During this period, however, African Americans did make lasting gains. Protection of civil rights became part of the U.S. Constitution. The Fourteenth and Fifteenth amendments would provide a legal basis for civil rights laws of the 20th century. Black schools and churches begun during Reconstruction also endured. Reconstruction changed society, putting African Americans on the path toward full equality. In the next unit, you will learn about other changes in American society after the Civil War.

## Section 3 Assessment

### 1. Terms & Names

**Explain the significance of:**
• Fifteenth Amendment
• Panic of 1873
• Compromise of 1877

### 2. Using Graphics

Review the chapter and find five significant individuals and events to place on a time line as shown.

```
1865    event    event    1877
 |_____|_____|_____|
    event    event    event
```

Which event or person was most important and why? (CST2)

### 3. Main Ideas

**a.** What did the Fifteenth Amendment declare? (HI1)

**b.** What effect did scandals in the Grant administration have on the Republican Party? (HI2)

**c.** What demands did Southern Democrats make in the Compromise of 1877? (HI1)

### 4. Critical Thinking

**Drawing Conclusions**
Why do you think the Republicans were willing to agree to the Compromise of 1877 and end Reconstruction? (REP5)

**THINK ABOUT**
• the election of 1876
• the Panic of 1873
• the Supreme Court rulings

**ACTIVITY OPTIONS**

**LANGUAGE ARTS**
**CIVICS**

Research Ku Klux Klan activities barring African Americans from voting. Then write a protest **letter to the editor** or propose a **law** to protect voting rights. (HI1)

## TERMS & NAMES

Briefly explain the significance of each of the following.

1. Reconstruction
2. Andrew Johnson
3. black codes
4. civil rights
5. Fourteenth Amendment
6. sharecropping
7. lynch
8. Fifteenth Amendment
9. Panic of 1873
10. Compromise of 1877

## REVIEW QUESTIONS

### Rebuilding the Union (pages 533–539)

1. What was the Freedmen's Bureau? (HI1)
2. What were the main parts of President Johnson's Reconstruction plan? (HI1)
3. Who were scalawags and carpetbaggers? (HI1)
4. What reason did the House give for impeaching President Johnson?(HI2)

### Reconstruction and Daily Life (pages 540–544)

5. Why did Congress not pass a land-reform plan? (HI1)
6. What new systems of labor developed in the South after the Civil War? (HI1)
7. How did the Ku Klux Klan serve the Democratic Party? (HI2)

### End of Reconstruction (pages 545–549)

8. Why did the Fifteenth Amendment arouse anger in many women? (HI2)
9. What caused an economic depression in the 1870s? (HI2)
10. How did Supreme Court rulings during Reconstruction help weaken African Americans' civil rights? (HI2)

## VISUAL SUMMARY

## CRITICAL THINKING

### 1. USING YOUR NOTES: IDENTIFYING AND SOLVING PROBLEMS

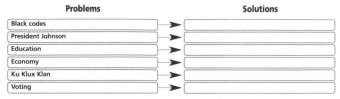

| Problems | | Solutions |
|---|---|---|
| Black codes | ➤ | |
| President Johnson | ➤ | |
| Education | ➤ | |
| Economy | ➤ | |
| Ku Klux Klan | ➤ | |
| Voting | ➤ | |

Using your diagram, answer the following questions. (HI2)

a. What was the solution to the problem of educating African Americans?

b. What was the solution to the problem of Ku Klux Klan violence?

### 2. ANALYZING LEADERSHIP

Why might Reconstruction be considered a time in which the presidency was weak? (HI1)

### 3. THEME: DEMOCRATIC IDEALS

How did the Fourteenth and Fifteenth amendments promote greater equality for African Americans? How were the amendments limited? (HI1)

### 4. APPLYING CITIZENSHIP SKILLS

What were the different viewpoints of Elizabeth Cady Stanton and Frances E. W. Harper regarding the Fifteenth Amendment's failure to give women an important right of citizenship—the right to vote? (REP5)

### 5. ANALYZING CAUSES

What aspect of the Compromise of 1877 likely played the greatest role in ending Reconstruction? (HI2)

### Interact *with* History

How did your solutions to rebuilding the nation compare with the actual solutions carried out?

# Reconstruction (8.11)

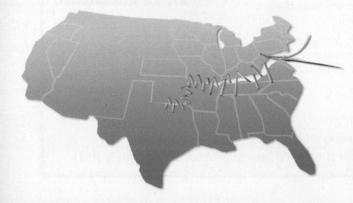

### Rebuilding the Union

During Reconstruction, Congress decided how the Southern states would be readmitted to the Union and passed laws to improve conditions for freed people.

### Reconstruction and Daily Life

After slavery ended, freed African Americans reunited their families, attended school, and began working for pay. Racist violence and lack of land slowed their progress.

### End of Reconstruction

In the 1870s, hostile Supreme Court decisions, the Southern Democrats' return to power, and the withdrawal of federal troops from the South ended Reconstruction.

## STANDARDS-BASED ASSESSMENT

**Use the map and your knowledge of U.S. history to answer questions 1 and 2.**

Additional Test Practice, pp. S1–S33.

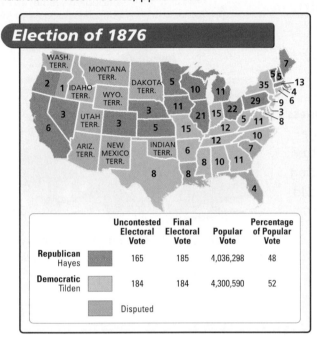

### Election of 1876

|  | | Uncontested Electoral Vote | Final Electoral Vote | Popular Vote | Percentage of Popular Vote |
|---|---|---|---|---|---|
| **Republican** Hayes | | 165 | 185 | 4,036,298 | 48 |
| **Democratic** Tilden | | 184 | 184 | 4,300,590 | 52 |
| | Disputed | | | | |

**1.** In what region of the country were most of the disputed votes located? (8.11.1)

**A.** the North

**B.** the South

**C.** the Northeast

**D.** the Southwest

**2.** What regions voted mostly Republican? (8.11.1)

**A.** the North and East

**B.** the South and East

**C.** the South and West

**D.** the North and West

**Robert B. Elliott gives his views of the civil rights bill in this quotation. Use the quotation and your knowledge of U.S. history to answer question 3.**

*PRIMARY SOURCE*

The passage of this bill will determine the civil status, not only of the negro but of any other class of citizens who may feel themselves discriminated against. It will form the capstone of that temple of liberty begun on this continent.

**Robert B. Elliott,** quoted in *The Glorious Failure*

**3.** This passage supports which point of view? (8.11.5)

**A.** African Americans would never gain freedom without the passage of the civil rights bill.

**B.** The passage of the civil rights bill would be important to southern states only.

**C.** The passage of the civil rights bill would help any group subject to discrimination.

**D.** Failure to pass the civil rights bill would mean renewed war in the United States.

**TEST PRACTICE**
CLASSZONE.COM

## ALTERNATIVE ASSESSMENT

**1.** 📝 **WRITING ABOUT HISTORY**

Write a **letter** to the editor of a newspaper stating your opinion of the freedmen's schools. You might write from the perspective of a plantation owner, or from that of a recently-freed African American. (REP5)

- Use library resources to research the schools.
- Support your opinion with facts from your research.
- Try to persuade your reader to support your position.

**2. COOPERATIVE LEARNING**

Work with two classmates to research sharecropping. Each group member can choose a different perspective to research: a land owner; a white sharecropper, or an African-American sharecropper. Explain how their perspectives differ from each other. (REP5)

## INTEGRATED TECHNOLOGY

**PARTICIPATING IN A NET SIMULATION**

Go to *NetSimulations: The Impeachment of Andrew Johnson* at **classzone.com** to participate in the impeachment trial of the president. You must evaluate the evidence against President Johnson and vote to retain or remove him from office. (REP5)

- Use the simulation to learn about the impeachment process, the conflicts between Congress and the president, and the events that led to the trial.
- Answer questions in the Senator's Journal, and use it to take notes.
- Before you cast your vote, carefully consider the closing arguments of each attorney.

**NET SIMULATION**
CLASSZONE.COM

# Business Writing:
## A Letter to Your Employer

**Writing Model**
ClassZone.com

**CALIFORNIA STANDARDS**
**Writing 2.5** Write documents related to career development, including simple business letters and job applications.

**PURPOSE:** To convey information in a business letter

**AUDIENCE:** Your employer, a magazine editor

Many of the most moving documents from the Civil War era are letters. Some are personal letters, from sons to mothers, brothers to brothers, husbands to wives. Others are more formal. These include **business letters,** which are written with a tone and language suited to their audience. For example, a letter written from a sergeant on the battlefield to his commanding officer would be respectful in tone. The writer would present only the necessary information and would avoid using slang or jargon.

A letter about an important development during the Civil War might refer to food shortages. Here, women demand more milk.

## Organization & Focus

You write for a magazine during the Civil War era. Your assignment is to write a simple business letter to your managing editor about a story you would like to cover. In the letter, you will present information purposefully and clearly and explain why the story should be included in your magazine.

**IDENTIFYING PURPOSE AND AUDIENCE** Your purpose is to both inform and persuade. You will inform your managing editor about an important event, person, or development from the Civil War era. You will try to convince him or her that this subject is worth writing about. Your audience is your supervisor, the managing editor of the magazine you work for.

**CHOOSING A TOPIC** Review the chapters in Unit 5. As you scan each one, note the events, people, and developments that interest you. Jot down details about what makes each one newsworthy. When you have finished, review your notes and decide which event, person, or development you think should be included in your magazine.

**FINDING SUPPORTING EVIDENCE** After making your choice, gather the facts and reasons you need to explain to your editor why the story you have chosen is the most important one to cover. Use this book and library and Internet resources for any additional support.

## OUTLINING AND DRAFTING

A business letter has five key elements: a heading; an inside address; a salutation, or greeting; a body; and a closing. This standard format is modeled in the letter to the right.

Use your own real address in the heading. Make up a name and address for the inside address. In the body of your letter, identify the subject you want to develop for the magazine and explain why you think it is important. Remember to maintain a respectful tone.

**Heading** Where the letter comes from and when

**Inside Address** To whom the letter is sent

Sergeant Joseph Snow
3rd Battalion
Vicksburg, Mississippi

April 10, 1863

Captain John Simon
Washington, D.C.

Dear Sir: **Salutation** Greeting

The men and I have arrived and have set up camp on the outskirts of Vicksburg. As instructed, we are preparing for a long siege.

An inventory of our supplies reveals that we are well stocked with weapons and clothing. However, rations are low. The soldiers do not complain but show definite signs of fatigue. Therefore, I respectfully request that a shipment of salt pork, vegetables, and coffee be sent as soon as possible.

Thank you for your attention to this matter. I await your further orders.

**Closing** Sincerely yours,
Joseph Snow

**Body** Text of the message

---

## Research & Technology

For a vivid sense of life during the Civil War, search for letters from the period on the Internet. There are many collections online that present original documents.

**Technology Tip** When you start typing your letter, your word processor will ask if you want help formatting it. Experiment with letting the computer help you.

## Evaluation & Revision

Exchange letters with a classmate for feedback on the format, tone, and content of your letter. Revise your letter until you are satisfied with it.

**Self-Check**

Does my letter have . . .

☐ the five key elements of a business letter?

☐ information presented simply and clearly?

☐ the proper tone for a business letter?

## Publish & Present

If possible, print your letter on paper that resembles parchment and share it with your class.

# America
# Transformed

> *"Give me your tired, your poor,
> Your huddled masses, yearning
> to breathe free..."*
> —*Emma Lazarus*

European immigrants such as those shown in this photograph (taken around 1900) streamed into Ellis Island at the turn of the century.

# Growth in the West 1860–1900

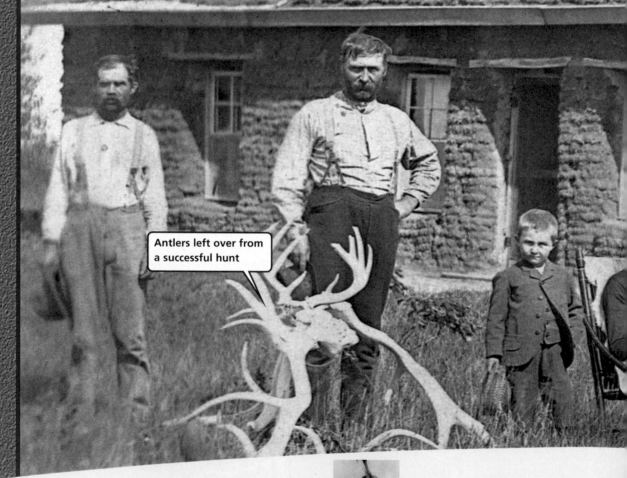

A Nebraska "sodbuster" family takes time away from their chores to pose in front of their sod house.

Antlers left over from a successful hunt

**1862**
Congress passes the Homestead Act.

**1864**
Sand Creek Massacre

**1867**
The Grange is founded.

**1876**
Sitting Bull leads Native American warriors at the Battle of the Little Bighorn.

**1880**
James Garfield is elected president

USA
World 1860

**1861**
Serfs are freed in Russia.

**1871**
Franco-Prussian War ends.

**1876**
Japan recognizes Korean independence.

The windows in this sod house are a real luxury.

It is 1865, and the Civil War has just ended. You are drawn to the West by stories of gold, silver, fertile soil, and free land, and by tales of adventure and new opportunities. Yet you know there would be hardships and unknown dangers. Your life would never be the same.

# How might your life change in the West?

## What Do You Think?

- What might be some of the ways to make a living in the West?
- What do you think your daily life would be like in the West?
- What would be the biggest difference in your life?

**RESEARCH LINKS**
CLASSZONE.COM

Visit the Chapter 19 links for more information about the American West.

---

**1881**
Chester Arthur becomes president after Garfield is assassinated.

**1884**
Grover Cleveland is elected president.

**1889**
Oklahoma land rush begins.

**1890**
Wounded Knee Massacre

**1891**
Farmers organize the Populist Party.

**1896**
William McKinley is elected president.

**1900**

**1885**
in Conference on African airs divides Africa among European nations.

**1889**
First Pan-American Conference is held.

**1893**
France takes over Indochina.

**1900**
Boxer Rebellion takes place in China.

# Reading Strategy: Finding Main Ideas

## What Do You Know?

What do you think about when you hear terms like *cowboy* and *Wild West?* What do you already know about the people, places, and events in the West in the last half of the 19th century?

### Think About

- what you have learned about the West from books, movies, and television
- what happens when different cultures clash
- your responses to the Interact with History about how the West might change your life (see page 555)

## What Do You Want to Know?

 What details do you need to help you understand the settling of the West? Make a list of those details in your notebook before you read the chapter.

**CALIFORNIA STANDARDS**

**Reading 2.0** Students read and understand grade-level-appropriate material. They describe and connect the essential ideas, arguments, and perspectives of the text by using their knowledge of text structure, organization, and purpose.

The West

## Finding Main Ideas

To make it easier for you to understand what you read, learn to find the main idea of each paragraph, topic heading, and section. Remember that the supporting details help to explain the main ideas. On the chart below, write down the main ideas about the many diverse people who settled the West.

**S** See Skillbuilder Handbook, page R5.

### Taking Notes

- Cowhands/Ranchers
- Miners
- Native Americans
- African Americans
- **Many diverse people settled the West!**
- Women
- Farmers
- Mexican Americans

# Miners, Ranchers, and Cowhands

| **MAIN IDEA** | **WHY IT MATTERS NOW** | **TERMS & NAMES** |
|---|---|---|
| Miners, ranchers, and cowhands settled in the West seeking economic opportunities. | The mining and cattle industries that developed then still contribute to American economic growth. | frontier     long drive<br>Great Plains     *vaquero*<br>boomtown     vigilante |

## ONE AMERICAN'S STORY

Nat Love was born a slave in Tennessee in 1854. After the Civil War, he was one of thousands of African Americans who left the South and went west. In 1869, Love headed for Dodge City, Kansas

Love's horse taming skills landed him a job as a cowhand. He became well known for his expert horsemanship and rodeo riding and roping. In his 1907 autobiography, Love offered a lively but exaggerated account of his life.

### A VOICE FROM THE PAST

I carry the marks of fourteen bullet wounds on different parts of my body, most any one of which would be sufficient to kill an ordinary man. . . . Horses were shot from under me, men killed around me, but always I escaped with a trifling wound at the worst.

**Nat Love,** *The Life and Adventures of Nat Love*

Nat Love was an African-American cowhand who became a rodeo star.

As you will read in this section, few cowhands led lives as exciting as that described by Nat Love, but they all helped to open a new chapter in the history of the American West.

## Geography and Population of the West

In the mid-1800s, towns such as St. Joseph and Independence, Missouri, were jumping-off places for settlers going west. They were the last cities and towns before the frontier. The **frontier** was the unsettled or sparsely settled area of the country occupied largely by Native Americans.

Many white settlers thought of the **Great Plains**—the area from the Missouri River to the Rocky Mountains—as empty. (See map on page 558.) Few had been attracted to its rolling plains, dry plateaus, and deserts. However, west of the Rockies, on the Pacific Coast, settlers had followed miners streaming into California after the 1849 gold rush. By 1850, California had gained statehood. Oregon followed in 1859.

**Taking Notes**

Use your chart to take notes about miners, ranchers, and cowhands.

Many diverse people settled the West!

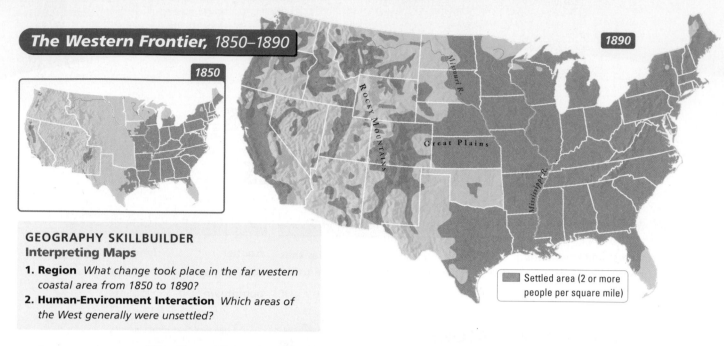

1850

1890

Settled area (2 or more people per square mile)

**GEOGRAPHY SKILLBUILDER**
**Interpreting Maps**

1. **Region** What change took place in the far western coastal area from 1850 to 1890?
2. **Human-Environment Interaction** Which areas of the West generally were unsettled?

The Great Plains had few trees, but its grasslands were home to about 300,000 Native Americans in the mid-1800s. Most followed the buffalo herds that rumbled across the open plains. Despite the presence of these peoples, the United States claimed ownership of the area.

Railroads played a key role in settling the western United States. Trains carried the natural resources of the West—minerals, timber, crops, and cattle—to eastern markets. In turn, trains brought miners, ranchers, and farmers west to develop these resources further. As the railroads opened new areas to white settlement, they also helped to bring an end to the way of life of the West's first settlers—the Native Americans.

*Reading* **History**

**A. Making Inferences** Why were railroads so important to the West?

## Mining in the West

In 1859, gold and silver strikes drew fortune seekers to Colorado and Nevada. As many as 100,000 miners raced to the Rocky Mountains in Colorado after gold was discovered near Pikes Peak. Also in 1859, prospectors hit "pay dirt" at the Comstock Lode in western Nevada. (A lode is a deposit of a valuable mineral buried in layers of rock.) From 1859 to 1880, the Comstock mine produced some $300 million in silver and gold.

Nearby Virginia City, Nevada, became a **boomtown,** a town that has a sudden burst of economic or population growth. Population jumped from 3,000 in the 1860s to over 20,000 in the 1870s. The writer Samuel Clemens, better known as Mark Twain, captured the excitement of life there.

**Vocabulary**
**strike:** valuable discovery of a precious mineral

*A VOICE FROM THE PAST*

The sidewalks swarmed with people. . . . Money was as plenty as dust; [everyone] considered himself wealthy. . . . There were . . . fire companies, brass bands, banks, hotels, theaters . . . gambling palaces . . . street-fights, murders, . . . riots, . . . and a half dozen jails . . . in full operation.

**Mark Twain,** *Roughing It*

Other major strikes took place in the Black Hills of South Dakota in 1874 and at Cripple Creek, Colorado, in 1891. In 1896, gold was discovered in

Miners brought ore, like the gold nugget shown, from underground mines that dotted the hillsides.

Canada's Yukon Territory. News of the strike set off a fresh epidemic of gold fever. Prospectors rushed to the Yukon's Klondike region.

The chance to strike it rich drew Americans from both East and West coasts. Gold fever also attracted miners from other parts of the world, including Europe, South America, Mexico, and China. Unfortunately, few prospectors became rich. Most left, disappointed and broke.

Early miners used panning and sluicing to wash sand and gravel from a stream to separate out any bits of precious metal, as you read in Chapter 13. Large mining companies moved in after surface mines no longer yielded gold or silver. Only they could buy the costly, heavy equipment needed to take the precious metals from underground. Water cannons blasted away hillsides to expose gold deposits. In other places, workers sank shafts thousands of feet into the ground to create underground mines. These new methods recovered more precious metals, but in the process stripped hillsides of vegetation and left rivers polluted.

Paid workers in company mines replaced independent prospectors. The work was hard and dangerous. Dust caused lung problems, and deadly cave-ins could trap miners hundreds of feet below the surface.

By the 1890s, the mining boom was over. Many mines closed because the costs had become too high, and the quality of the ore had dropped. Jobless workers moved elsewhere. Once-thriving communities became ghost towns. Still, the mining boom had lasting effects. Nevada, Colorado, and South Dakota all grew so rapidly that they soon gained statehood.

*Reading* **History**

**B. Recognizing Effects** Why did large mining companies replace individual prospectors?

## The Rise of the Cattle Industry

The cattle trade had existed in the Southwest since the Spanish arrived there in the 1500s. But cattle herds remained small until the Civil War. There were few buyers for Western beef because there was no efficient way to get the beef to markets in the more heavily populated cities of the East. The ranchers mostly sold their cattle locally.

The extension of railroad lines from Chicago and St. Louis into Kansas by the 1860s brought changes. An Illinois livestock dealer named Joseph McCoy realized that railroads could bring cattle from Texas ranches to meat-hungry Eastern cities. Cowhands had only to drive cattle herds north from Texas to his stockyards in Abilene, Kansas. From there, the beef could be shipped to Chicago and points east by rail car.

McCoy's plan turned cattle ranching into a very profitable business. Cattle fed on the open range for a year or two and cost the rancher nothing. Ranchers then hired cowhands to round up the cattle and take them to Abilene. There they were sold for as much as ten times their original price. The success of the Abilene stockyards spurred the growth of other Kansas cow towns, including Wichita and Dodge City. The cattle drives to cow towns along the railways were called the **long drives.**

Over time, cowhands followed specific trails across the plains. The first was the Chisholm Trail, which stretched from San Antonio, Texas, to Abilene, Kansas. It was named for Jesse Chisholm, a trader who marked the northern part of the route. From 1867 to 1884, about four million cattle were driven to market on this trail. As cattle raising became more profitable, ranching spread north across the plains from Texas to Montana.

## *Vaqueros* and Cowhands

The first cowhands, or **_vaqueros,_** as they were known in Spanish, came from Mexico with the Spaniards in the 1500s. They settled in the Southwest. The *vaqueros* helped Spanish, and later Mexican, ranchers manage their herds. From the *vaquero,* the American cowhand learned to rope and ride. Cowhands also adapted the saddle, spurs, lariat (which they used to rope a calf or steer), and chaps of the *vaqueros.*

About one in three cowhands in the West was either Mexican or African-American. Many Mexican cowhands were descendants of the *vaqueros.* Some African-American cowhands were former slaves. They came west at the end of Reconstruction because the enactment of Black Codes in the South put restrictions on their freedom. Also among the cowhands were a large number of former Confederate and Union soldiers.

## The "Wild West"

At first, the rapidly growing cow towns had no local governments. There were no law officers to handle the fights that broke out as cowhands drank and gambled after a long drive. A more serious threat to law and order came from "con men." These swindlers saw new towns as places to get rich quick by cheating others.

Some Union and Confederate veterans were led to crime by hard feelings left over from the Civil War.

*Reading* **History**

C. Reading a Map
Use the map on page 581 to locate the Chisholm Trail.

**Background**
Chaps, from the Spanish word *chaperejos,* were seatless leather pants worn over trousers to protect legs from scrub brush, snakes, and cactus.

**Vocabulary**
con man: a person who cheats victims by first gaining their confidence

daily *life*

**LIFE OF A COWHAND: THE ROUNDUP**

During some parts of the year, the cowhand's life was downright dull. While cattle grazed on the open range, cowhands sat around the ranch, repairing their gear and doing odd jobs. The pace quickened at roundup time in the spring and fall.

For several weeks, 150 to 250 cowhands from nearby ranches rode hundreds of miles locating cattle. Cowhands from each ranch collected their cattle, removed sick or weak animals, and branded new calves. Then the cowhands were ready for the long drive. A roundup by *vaqueros* is shown in this painting by James Walker.

Outlaws like "Billy the Kid" and Jesse and Frank James made crime a way of life. Some women, such as Belle Starr, became outlaws, too.

For protection, citizens formed vigilante groups. **Vigilantes** were people who took the law into their own hands. They caught suspected criminals and punished them without a trial. Vigilante justice often consisted of hanging suspects from the nearest tree or shooting them on the spot. As towns became more settled, citizens elected a local sheriff or asked the federal government for a marshal. These law officers would arrest lawbreakers and hold them in jail until the time of trial.

## End of the Long Drives

For about 20 years, the cattle industry boomed. As the railroads extended farther west and south into Texas, the long drives grew shorter. The future looked bright. But by 1886, several developments had brought the cattle boom to an end. First, the price of beef dropped sharply as the supply increased in the early 1880s. Then came the newly invented barbed wire. As more settlers moved to the Great Plains to farm or raise sheep, they fenced in their lands with barbed wire. The open range disappeared, and cattle could no longer pass freely over the trails. Finally, in the harsh winter of 1886–1887, thousands of cattle on the northern Plains froze to death. Many ranchers were put out of business.

*Reading*History
**D. Analyzing Causes** What caused the decline of cattle ranching on the open range?

Meanwhile, as the mining and cattle industries were developing, the Native Americans of the Great Plains were being pushed off their land, as you will read in the next section.

## STRANGE *but* True

**FENCE-CUTTING WARS**

Barbed-wire fences solved some problems in the west but created others. Some ranchers put up fences that blocked other farmers' access to resources. During an 1883 drought in Texas, individuals and groups began cutting fences. As damage across the state rose, clashes between fence-cutters and ranchers became violent. In 1884 the Texas legislature made fence-cutting a felony but also placed restrictions on fence placement.

The right to water was an important cause of the fence-cutting wars. Water rights in the West are based on a principle called prior appropriation, or "first in time, first in right." The first to use water from a source gets "senior" water rights. In times of drought, those with junior water rights may not get any water from a source. Several western states have "water courts" specifically to review disputed water claims.

---

**Section 1 Assessment**

**1. Terms & Names**

**Explain the significance of:**
- frontier
- Great Plains
- boomtown
- long drive
- *vaquero*
- vigilante

**2. Using Graphics**

Use a diagram to review the rise and fall of the cattle industry. (CST3)

**3. Main Ideas**

**a.** What economic opportunities drew large numbers of people to the West beginning in the 1860s? (HI3)

**b.** How did the transcontinental railroad spur Western settlement? (HI3)

**c.** What did cowhands learn from the *vaqueros?* (HI3)

**4. Critical Thinking**

**Evaluating** Could cattle ranchers have stopped the decline of the cattle industry that occurred in the late 1880s? (HI4)

**THINK ABOUT**
- economic causes
- impact of weather
- changing settlement patterns

**ACTIVITY OPTIONS**

**LANGUAGE ARTS**

**MUSIC**

Do research on a legendary figure of the West such as Wyatt Earp, "Calamity Jane," or Nat Love. Then write a **biographical sketch** or **song** about the person. (HI1)

# Native Americans Fight to Survive

| MAIN IDEA | WHY IT MATTERS NOW | TERMS & NAMES |
|---|---|---|
| The Native Americans of the Great Plains fought to maintain their way of life as settlers poured onto their lands. | The taking of their lands led to social and economic problems for Native Americans that continue to this day. | reservation    Battle of the Little Bighorn<br>Sand Creek Massacre    Wounded Knee Massacre<br>Sitting Bull<br>George A. Custer    Dawes Act |

## ONE AMERICAN'S STORY

Buffalo Bird Woman was a Hidatsa who lived almost 100 years. She was born in 1840. As a child, she and her family made their home along the Missouri River. Later the federal government forced her family onto a reservation. A **reservation** is land set aside for Native American tribes.

The federal government attempted to "Americanize" Native American children, including Buffalo Bird Woman, by sending them away to boarding schools. But Buffalo Bird Woman struggled to hold on to Hidatsa customs. As an old woman, she looked back on her early years.

**Buffalo Bird Woman**

### A VOICE FROM THE PAST

Sometimes at evening I sit, looking out on the . . . Missouri [River]. . . . In the shadows I seem . . . to see our Indian village, with smoke curling upward from the earth lodges; and in the river's roar I hear the yells of the warriors, the laughter of . . . children as of old.

**Buffalo Bird Woman,** quoted in *Native American Testimony*, edited by Peter Nabokov

As white settlers claimed Native American lands, Plains peoples fought a losing battle to save not only their homes but their way of life.

## Native American Life on the Plains

Before the arrival of Europeans in the 1500s, most Plains tribes lived in villages along rivers and streams. The women tended crops of beans, corn, and squash. The men hunted deer and elk and in the summer stalked the vast buffalo herds that inhabited the Plains.

In the early 1540s, the Spanish brought the first horses to the Great Plains. The arrival of horses changed the way of life of the Plains people. They quickly became expert riders. By the late 1700s, most Plains tribes kept their own herds of horses. Mounted on horseback, hunters traveled far from their villages seeking buffalo.

**Taking Notes**

Use your chart to take notes about Native Americans.

Many diverse people settled the West!

The buffalo was central to the life of Plains tribes. Its meat became the chief food in their diet, while its skins served as portable shelters called tepees. Plains women turned buffalo hides into clothing, shoes, and blankets and used buffalo chips (dried manure) as cooking fuel. Bones and horns became tools and bowls. Over time, many Plains tribes developed a nomadic way of life tied to buffalo hunting.

**Vocabulary**
**nomadic:** wandering from place to place

# A Clash of Cultures

When the federal government first forced Native American tribes of the Southeast to move west of the Mississippi in the 1830s, it settled them in Indian Territory. This territory was a huge area that included almost all of the land between the Missouri River and Oregon Territory. Most treaties made by the government with Native Americans promised that this land would remain theirs "as long as Grass grows or water runs."

Unfortunately, these treaty promises would be broken. Government policy was based on the belief that white settlers were not interested in the Plains. The land was considered too dry for farming. However, as wagon trains bound for Oregon and California crossed the Great Plains in the 1850s, some pioneers saw possibilities for farming and ranching on its grasslands. Soon white settlers moved onto the prairies.

*Reading* **History**

**A. Analyzing Causes** What was the major source of conflict between white settlers and Native Americans?

Spurred by the ranching and mining booms mentioned in Section 1, settlers pressured the federal government for more land. They also wanted protection from Native Americans in the area. In 1851, the government responded by calling the Sioux, Cheyenne, Arapaho, and other

## Native American Lands in the West, 1850–1890

**MAJOR EVENTS OF THE INDIAN WARS**

1. Sand Creek Massacre, 1864
2. Fetterman Massacre, 1866
3. Battle of the Little Bighorn, 1876
4. Geronimo surrenders, 1886
5. Wounded Knee Massacre, 1890

**GEOGRAPHY SKILLBUILDER**
**Interpreting Maps**

1. **Location** In which area of the West did most of the major battles take place?
2. **Movement** What was the major change that took place in the West between 1850 and 1890?

Land lost by Native Americans
- Before 1850
- 1850–1870
- 1870–1890
- Native American reservations in 1890
- Never formally ceded by treaty

0   400 Miles
0   800 Kilometers

PACIFIC OCEAN

**563**

Plains tribes together near Fort Laramie in present-day Wyoming. Government officials tried to buy back some Native American land and also set boundaries for tribal lands. Many Plains tribes signed the First Treaty of Fort Laramie (1851)—they saw no other choice. From 1853 to 1856, the United States entered 52 different treaties with various Native American nations.

But some Cheyennes and Sioux resisted. They preferred conflict with settlers and soldiers to the restrictions of reservation life. In southeastern Colorado, bands of Cheyenne warriors attacked miners and soldiers. In response, about 1,200 Colorado militia led by Colonel John Chivington opened fire on a peaceful Cheyenne village along Sand Creek in 1864. More than 150 Cheyenne men, women, and children were killed in what came to be known as the **Sand Creek Massacre.**

The Plains tribes reacted to such attacks by raiding white settlements. One of the fiercest battles took place in Montana. There the government had begun to build a road called the Bozeman Trail across Sioux hunting grounds. To stop construction, the Sioux attacked construction workers. In 1866, Captain W. J. Fetterman and 80 troopers stumbled into a deadly ambush set by the Sioux. All the soldiers were killed in what was called the Fetterman Massacre.

Such incidents finally forced the government to try to find a way to end the fighting. In 1868, U.S. officials signed the Second Treaty of Fort Laramie with the Sioux, Northern Cheyenne, and Arapaho. The treaty gave these tribes a large reservation in the Black Hills of South Dakota.

*Reading*History

**B. Reading a Map**
Locate the site of the Sand Creek Massacre on the map on page 563.

## Battle of the Little Bighorn

The Second Treaty of Fort Laramie did not end the trouble between the Sioux and white settlers, though. In 1874, white prospectors discovered gold in the Black Hills. Paying no attention to the Fort Laramie treaty, thousands of miners rushed onto Sioux land. Tribal leaders angrily rejected a government offer to buy back the land. Many Sioux warriors fled the reservation during the

### HISTORY *through*ART

Artist Edgar S. Paxson researched the Battle of the Little Bighorn for 20 years to try to accurately re-create the last moments of the fighting. Custer is at the center clutching at a bullet wound in his chest.

**What do you think this painting shows about the fighting at the Little Bighorn?**

winter of 1875–1876. They united under the leadership of two Sioux chiefs—**Sitting Bull** and Crazy Horse—to push back the intruders.

The Seventh Cavalry set out to return the Sioux to the reservations. It was commanded by Lieutenant Colonel **George A. Custer,** a hero of the Civil War and of other campaigns against Plains tribes. On June 25, his forces met several thousand Sioux and Cheyennes near the Little Bighorn River in Montana in the **Battle of the Little Bighorn**. In less than two hours, Custer and his men—211 in all—were wiped out.

News of Custer's defeat shocked the nation. The government responded by stepping up military action. As a result, Little Bighorn was the last major Native American victory. In 1877, Crazy Horse surrendered and Sitting Bull and his followers fled to Canada. In 1881, Sitting Bull's starving band surrendered to U.S. troops and were returned to the reservation.

*Reading*History

C. Recognizing Effects What were the results of the Battle of the Little Bighorn?

## Resistance in the Northwest and Southwest

Background

Nez Perce means "pierced nose" in French. French-Canadian trappers gave this name to these Native American people because some of them wore jewelry in their noses.

The Nez Perce (nehz PURS) was a Northwest tribe that lived in eastern Oregon and Idaho. Until the 1860s, the Nez Perce lived peacefully on land guaranteed to them by an 1855 treaty. However, as white settlement increased, the government forced them to sell most of their land and move to a narrow strip of territory in Idaho. Most reluctantly agreed, but a group of Nez Perce led by Chief Joseph refused.

In 1877, Chief Joseph and his followers fled north to seek refuge in Canada. For four months, the Nez Perce traveled across 1,000 miles of rugged terrain with army troops in pursuit. About 40 miles from the Canadian border, the army caught up with them. Greatly outnumbered, the Nez Perce surrendered. Chief Joseph spoke for his people when he said, "I will fight no more, forever."

In the Southwest, both the Navajos and Apaches fought against being removed to reservations. U.S. troops ended Navajo resistance in Arizona in 1863 by burning Navajo homes and crops. Most Navajos surrendered. Nearly 8,000 took what they called the "Long Walk," a brutal journey of 300 miles to a reservation in eastern New Mexico. Hundreds died on the way. Their new home was a parched strip of land near the Pecos River. After four years, the government allowed the Navajos to return to Arizona, where many live today.

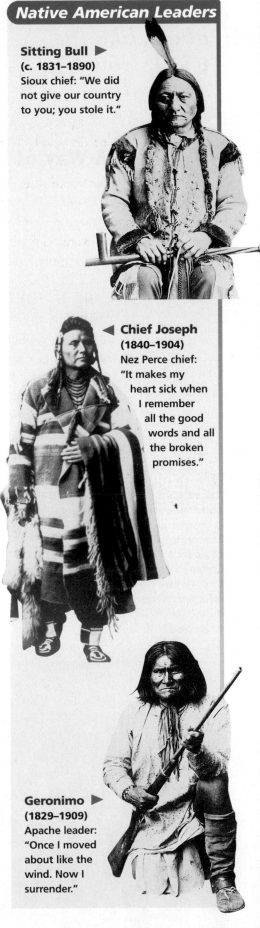

**Native American Leaders**

**Sitting Bull** ▶
(c. 1831–1890)
Sioux chief: "We did not give our country to you; you stole it."

◀ **Chief Joseph**
(1840–1904)
Nez Perce chief: "It makes my heart sick when I remember all the good words and all the broken promises."

**Geronimo** ▶
(1829–1909)
Apache leader: "Once I moved about like the wind. Now I surrender."

*"Once I moved about like the wind. Now I surrender."*

Geronimo

In the early 1870s, the government forced many Apaches to settle on a barren reservation in eastern Arizona. But a group led by Geronimo refused to remain. Escaping the reservation, these Apaches survived by raiding settlers' homes. Geronimo was captured many times but always managed to escape. In 1886, however, he finally surrendered and was sent to prison.

## A Way of Life Ends

As the Native Americans of the Plains battled to remain free, the buffalo herds that they depended upon for survival dwindled. At one time, 30 million buffalo roamed the Plains. However, hired hunters killed the animals to feed crews building railroads. Others shot buffalo as a sport or to supply Eastern factories with leather for robes, shoes, and belts. From 1872 to 1882, hunters killed more than one million buffalo each year.

**Background**
In 1889, fewer than 100 buffalo remained.

By the 1880s, most Plains tribes had been forced onto reservations. With their hunting grounds fast disappearing, some turned in despair to a Paiute prophet named Wovoka. He preached a vision of a new age in which whites would be removed and Native Americans would once again freely hunt the buffalo. To prepare for this time, Wovoka urged Native Americans to perform the chants and movements of the Ghost Dance. Wovoka's hopeful vision quickly spread among the Plains peoples.

Many of Wovoka's followers, especially among the Sioux, fled their reservations and gathered at the Pine Ridge Reservation in South Dakota. White settlers and government officials began to fear that they were preparing for war. The army was sent to track down the Ghost Dancers. They rounded them up, and a temporary camp was made along Wounded Knee Creek in South Dakota, on December 28, 1890. The next day, as the Sioux were giving up their weapons, someone fired a shot. The troopers responded to the gunfire, killing about 300 men, women, and children. The **Wounded Knee Massacre,** as it was called, ended armed resistance in the West.

These Native American students in Oklahoma Territory in 1901 posed for a class picture at the school where they were sent to learn the culture of white people.

*Reading* **History**
D. Drawing Conclusions
What was the most important factor in the defeat of the Native Americans?

## The Dawes Act Fails

Some white Americans had been calling for better treatment of Native Americans for years. In 1881, Helen Hunt Jackson published *A Century of Dishonor*, which listed the failures of the federal government's policies toward Native Americans. About the same time, Sarah Winnemucca, a Paiute reformer, lectured in the East about the injustices of reservation life.

*Reading*History

**E. Analyzing Points of View** Why did reformers support assimilation?

Many well-meaning reformers felt that assimilation was the only way for Native Americans to survive. Assimilation meant adopting the culture of the people around them. Reformers wanted to make Native Americans like whites—to "Americanize" them.

The **Dawes Act,** passed in 1887, was intended to encourage Native Americans to give up their traditional ways and become farmers. The act divided reservations into individual plots of land for each family. The government sold leftover land to white settlers. The government also sent many Native American children to special boarding schools where they were taught white culture. In "One American's Story," you read about the effort to Americanize Buffalo Bird Woman. But these attempts to Americanize the children still did not make them part of white society.

In the end, the Dawes Act did little to benefit Native Americans. Not all of them wanted to be farmers. Those who did lacked the tools, training, and money to be successful. Over time, many sold their land for a fraction of its real value to white land promoters or settlers.

The situation of Native Americans at the end of the 1800s was tragic. Their lands had been taken and their culture treated with contempt. Not until decades later would the federal government recognize the importance of their way of life. In the next section, you will read about some of the people who settled on Native American lands.

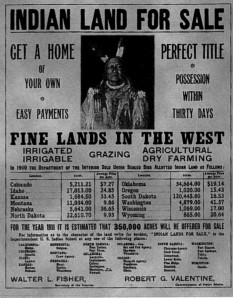

This poster advertised the sale of Native American lands to white settlers.

---

## Section 2 Assessment

### 1. Terms & Names

**Explain the significance of:**
- reservation
- Sand Creek Massacre
- Sitting Bull
- George A. Custer
- Battle of the Little Bighorn
- Wounded Knee Massacre
- Dawes Act

### 2. Using Graphics

Use a chart to compare the life of Plains people before and after the arrival of white settlers. (HI2)

|  | Before | After |
|---|---|---|
| Meeting survival needs |  |  |
| Customs |  |  |
| Land use |  |  |

### 3. Main Ideas

**a.** How did federal government policy toward Native Americans change as white settlers moved to the West? (HI2)

**b.** How did the destruction of the buffalo affect Plains peoples? (HI2)

**c.** Why was Wounded Knee a turning point in relations between Native Americans and the government? (HI2)

### 4. Critical Thinking

**Recognizing Effects** How were the effects of the Dawes Act different from what was intended? (HI2)

**THINK ABOUT**
- goals of the act
- impact on the land use, culture, and independence of the Plains peoples

---

**ACTIVITY OPTIONS**

**TECHNOLOGY**

**SPEECH**

Research the life of a Native American leader discussed in this section. Create that person's **Web page** or give a **speech** from this person's perspective. (HI1)

# Life in the West

| MAIN IDEA | WHY IT MATTERS NOW | TERMS & NAMES |
|---|---|---|
| Diverse groups of people helped to shape both the reality and the myth of the West. | The myth of the West continues to be a part of our culture. | homestead<br>Mexicano<br><br>buffalo soldier<br>William "Buffalo Bill" Cody |

**Taking Notes**

Use your chart to take notes about women and Mexican Americans.

Many diverse people settled the West!

## ONE AMERICAN'S STORY

Abigail Scott was born in Illinois in 1834. At 17, she moved to Oregon by wagon train with her family. Her mother died on the journey. In Oregon, Abigail taught school until she married a farmer named Benjamin Duniway in 1853. When he was disabled in an accident, Abigail assumed the support of her family. She wrote about a day on a pioneer farm with its endless chores.

*A VOICE FROM THE PAST*

[W]ashing, scrubbing, churning . . . preparing . . . meals in our lean-to kitchen . . . [having] to bake and clean and stew and fry; to be in short, a general pioneer drudge, with never a penny of my own, was not pleasant business.

**Abigail Scott Duniway,** in her autobiography, *Path Breaking*

Like Abigail Scott Duniway, this pioneer woman worked long and hard. She is shown here with buffalo chips she has collected to use as fuel.

Later, Duniway grew committed to the cause of women's rights. Oregon honored Duniway for her part in the suffrage struggle by registering her as the state's first woman voter. As you will read in this section, women like Duniway helped to shape the West.

## Women in the West

Women often were not given recognition for their efforts to turn scattered Western farms and ranches into settled communities. In their letters and diaries, many women recorded the harshness of pioneer life. Others talked about the loneliness. While men went to town for supplies or did farm chores with other men, women rarely saw their neighbors. Mari Sandoz lived in Nebraska on a **homestead,** a piece of land and the house on it. She wrote that women "had only the wind and the cold and the problems of clothing [and] shelter." Living miles from others, women were their family's doctors—setting broken bones and delivering babies—as well as cooks.

Despite its challenges, Western life provided opportunities for women. Most who worked held traditional jobs. They were teachers or servants or gave their families financial support by taking in sewing or laundry. However, a few became sheriffs, gamblers, and even outlaws. In mining camps and cow towns, some even ran dance halls and boarding houses.

Western lawmakers recognized the contributions women made to Western settlement by giving them more legal rights than women had in the East. In most territories, women could own property and control their own money. In 1869, Wyoming Territory led the nation in giving women the vote. Esther Morris, who headed the suffrage fight there, convinced lawmakers women would bring law and order to the territory.

**Reading History**

**A. Making Inferences** Why were women in the West the first to win the right to vote?

When Wyoming sought statehood in 1890, many in Congress demanded that the state repeal its woman suffrage law. But Wyoming lawmakers stood firm. They told Washington, "We may stay out of the Union for 100 years, but we will come in with our women." Congress backed down. By 1900, women had also won the right to vote in Colorado, Utah, and Idaho.

## The Rise of Western Cities

Cities seemed to grow overnight in the West. Gold and silver strikes made instant cities of places like Denver in Colorado Territory and brought new life to sleepy towns like San Francisco in California. These cities prospered, while much of the area around them remained barely settled. San Francisco grew from a small town to a city of about 25,000 in just one year after the 1849 gold rush.

Miners who flocked to the "Pikes Peak" gold rush of 1859 stopped first in Denver to buy supplies. Not even a town in 1857, Denver was the capital of Colorado Territory by 1867. A decade later, it became the state capital when Colorado was admitted into the Union. The decision by Denver citizens to build a railroad to link their city with the transcontinental railroad sent population soaring. In 1870, it had about 4,800 residents. In 1890, it had nearly 107,000.

The railroads also brought rapid growth to other towns in the West. Omaha, Nebraska, flourished as a meat-processing center for cattle ranches in the area. Portland, Oregon, became a regional

| Population of Western Cities | | |
|---|---|---|
| CITY | 1860 | 1890 |
| Denver | 2,603* | 106,713 |
| Omaha | 1,883 | 140,452 |
| Portland | 2,874 | 46,385 |
| San Francisco | 56,802 | 298,997 |

**SKILLBUILDER Interpreting Charts**

*Which city had the largest increase in numbers of people, 1860–1890?*

*1861 Territorial Census
Sources: *Population Abstract of the United States; Colorado Republic*

San Francisco, 1847

San Francisco, 1850

569

**"Billy the Kid"** ▶
(Henry McCarty,
1859–1881)
He was an outlaw and
hired gun who called
himself William
Bonney and was
killed at 21.

▲ **Wyatt Earp**
(1848–1929)
He was a frontier peace officer,
gunfighter, and gambler in towns
such as Dodge City, Kansas, and
Tombstone, Arizona.

◀ **"Calamity Jane"**
(Martha Jane
Canary, c. 1852–
1903)
She had a legendary
career as a wagon
driver, scout, and
Wild West Show
performer.

market for fish, grain, and lumber. While these cities were growing on the Great Plains and Pacific coast, the Southwest was also developing.

## Mexicanos and Buffalo Soldiers

The Southwest included what are now New Mexico, Texas, Arizona, and California. For centuries, it had been home to people of Spanish descent whose ancestors had come from Mexico. These Spanish-speaking southwesterners called themselves **Mexicanos**.

In the 1840s, the annexation of Texas and Mexico's defeat in the Mexican War brought much of the Southwest under the control of the United States. Soon after, English-speaking white settlers—called Anglos by the Mexicanos—began arriving. These pioneers were attracted to the Southwest by opportunities in ranching, farming, and mining. Their numbers grew in the 1880s and 1890s, as railroads connected the region with the rest of the country.

As American settlers crowded into the Southwest, the Mexicanos lost economic and political power. Many also lost land. They claimed their land through grants from Spain and Mexico. But American courts did not usually recognize these grants. Only in New Mexico Territory did Hispanic society survive despite Anglo-American settlement.

In 1866 the U.S. Army created African-American regiments to serve mainly in the West and Southwest, where Native Americans nicknamed them **"buffalo soldiers."** African-American troops helped keep the peace on the frontier but were also called on to fight in campaigns against Native Americans. Although there were still racial conflicts within the military and among civilians, army life provided opportunity and a basic education for many African Americans.

## The Myth of the Old West

America's love affair with the West began just as the cowboy way of life was vanishing in the late 1800s. To most Americans, the West had become a larger-than-life place where brave men and women tested themselves against hazards of all kinds and won. Easterners eagerly bought "dime novels" filled with tales of daring adventures. Sometimes the hero was a real person like Wyatt Earp or "Calamity Jane." But the plots were fiction or exaggerated accounts of real-life incidents.

*Reading* **History**
**B. Summarizing**
Who were the
Mexicanos?

**Background**
From 1866 to
1898, some 12,500
African Americans
served in the West
in the 9th and
10th Cavalry and
the 24th and
25th Infantry
regiments.

Also adding to the myth were more serious works of fiction, like Owen Wister's *The Virginian* (1902). Such works showed little of the drabness of daily life in the West. White settlers played heroic roles not only in novels but also in plays and, later, in movies. Native Americans generally appeared as villains. African Americans were not even mentioned.

**William "Buffalo Bill" Cody,** a buffalo hunter turned showman, brought the West to the rest of the world through his Wild West show. Cody recognized people's fascination with the West. His show, with its reenactments of frontier life, played before enthusiastic audiences across the country and in Europe.

## The Real West

The myth of the Old West overlooked the contributions of many peoples. The first cowhands, as you read earlier, were the Mexican *vaqueros*. Native Americans and African Americans played a role in cattle ranching, too. And the railroads would not have been built without Chinese immigrant labor.

Western legends often highlighted the attacks by Native Americans on soldiers or settlers. But the misunderstandings and broken treaties that led to the conflicts were usually overlooked.

Historians also say that the image of the self-reliant Westerner who tames the wild frontier ignores the important role played by the government in Western settlement. Settlers needed the help of the army to remove Native Americans. The government also aided in the building of the railroads and gave the free land that drew homesteaders to the West. You will read about these homesteaders and the problems that they faced in the next section.

*Reading* **History**

**C. Comparing**
How does the real West compare to the myth of the West?

## Section 3 Assessment

### 1. Terms & Names

**Explain the significance of:**
- homestead
- Mexicano
- buffalo soldier
- William "Buffalo Bill" Cody

### 2. Using Graphics

Use a chart to compare Wild West myths with the realities of Western life.

| Myth | Real life |
|------|-----------|
|      |           |
|      |           |
|      |           |

What do you think is the most well-known myth about the West? (REP3)

### 3. Main Ideas

**a.** How were women's contributions to the West recognized by Western lawmakers? (HI3)

**b.** Which factors led to the growth of such Western cities as Denver, Omaha, and San Francisco? (HI3)

**c.** How did the arrival of Anglo-Americans change life for Spanish-speaking residents of the Southwest? (HI3)

### 4. Critical Thinking

**Making Inferences** What changed the attitudes of Western lawmakers about giving women voting rights? (HI2)

**THINK ABOUT**
- new roles for women
- need for stability in Western communities
- part played by women in settlement

**ACTIVITY OPTIONS**

**MATH**

**SPEECH**

Pick a Western city mentioned in this section. Create a **database** of information about the city or give a **short speech** describing its growth. (HI1)

# Stage a Wild West Show!

You are the manager of Buffalo Bill's Wild West, the biggest and most famous of the 50 outdoor circuses and shows performing in the United States in the 1880s. Your job is to keep the show running smoothly. You oversee publicity and keep performers and livestock housed, fed, and supplied with the gear they need. You also manage finances.

**COOPERATIVE LEARNING** On this page are three challenges you face as the manager of Buffalo Bill's Wild West show. Working with a small group, decide how to deal with each challenge. Choose an option, assign a task to each group member, and do the activity. You will find useful information in the Data File.

---

**CALIFORNIA STANDARDS**

**HI6** Students interpret basic indicators of economic performance and conduct cost-benefit analyses of economic and political issues.

**Reading 2.6** Use information from a variety of consumer, workplace, and public documents to explain a situation or decision and to solve a problem.

---

## MATH CHALLENGE

### "over $280,000"

What a season you had from May to September of 1886! The show took in more than $280,000. But you had big expenses, too. You want to compare income and expenses so you can make changes to increase profits. Use the Data File for more statistics. Then present your summary using one of these options:

• Make a line graph comparing income and expenses.

• Make a pie chart showing how you spent the income—that is, what your expenses were. Include one sector for profit (the difference between total income and total expenses). Label each sector with the percentage.

---

## LANGUAGE ARTS CHALLENGE

### "the thunder of hoofs"

Over the last three days, attendance at the show has slacked off. To meet expenses and generate a profit, you need to fill 15,000 seats. You decide to stir up interest using the local newspaper. Use the Data File for information. Then promote the show.

• Write an article dramatizing the Wild West show.

• Write a script to be used by the master of ceremonies.

**BUFFALO BILL'S WILD WEST**
AND CONGRESS OF ROUGH RIDERS OF THE WORLD.

## ART CHALLENGE

### *"History . . . in Living Legends"*

You need more posters right away because splashy posters are your best advertising. They dazzle people with thrilling Western scenes. They also give show times and admission fees. Use the Data File for help. Then present your ideas using one of these options:

- Design a 2' x 3' poster showing the excitement of the Wild West show.
- Sketch two small action posters, each showing one event, for shop windows.

## ACTIVITY WRAP-UP

**Present to the class** Meet as a group to review your methods of promoting and charting the success of your Wild West show. Evaluate which of your solutions is the best for each challenge. Once you have chosen one solution for each, make a class presentation. Each group member should take part.

## DATA FILE

### WILD WEST SHOW
- 3-hour show; admission, 50¢

**Major Show Acts**
- "Star-Spangled Banner" Overture
- Grand Review of Buffalo Bill Cody and cast on horseback
- Annie Oakley shoots card targets, apple off her poodle's head
- Reenactments of covered wagons crossing the prairie; a Native American buffalo hunt; outlaws attacking a mail coach; a battle between army and Native Americans
- Sharpshooting by Buffalo Bill

**Show Crew and Gear**
- crew of 700—including Buffalo Bill, Annie Oakley, Sitting Bull, cowhands, Native Americans, 36-piece band, cooks, blacksmiths, teams to set up grandstand and tents
- animals—including 500 horses, 10 mules, 5 steers, 18 buffalo
- gear—including covered wagons and tepees, guns and ammunition, living and dressing room tents, dining tents, booths selling popcorn, souvenirs, and canvas scenery backdrops, 26-car train for transport

### INCOME AND EXPENSES
May 9–September 25, 1886

**Total income:** $287,000 (from attendance)

**Total expenses:** $285,000

Owners', managers', key performers' salaries: $55,000

Rents: $58,000

Advertising: $17,000

Printing: $4,000

Groceries/ammunition: $7,000

Miscellaneous expenses: $144,000 (other wages, livestock feed, electricity, medical, security, etc.)

For more about the Old West . . .

 **RESEARCH LINKS** CLASSZONE.COM

# Farming and Populism

| MAIN IDEA | WHY IT MATTERS NOW | TERMS & NAMES |
|---|---|---|
| A wave of farmers moved to the Plains in the 1800s and faced many economic problems. | Farmers are facing similar economic problems today. | Homestead Act    cooperative<br>Exoduster    Populist Party<br>sodbuster    gold standard<br>Grange    William Jennings Bryan |

## CALIFORNIA STANDARDS

**8.11.2** Identify the push-pull factors in the movement of former slaves to the cities in the North and to the West and their differing experiences in those regions (e.g., the experiences of Buffalo Soldiers).

**8.12.1** Trace patterns of agricultural and industrial development as they relate to climate, use of natural resources, markets, and trade and locate such development on a map.

**8.12.3** Explain how states and the federal government encouraged business expansion through tariffs, banking, land grants, and subsidies.

**8.12.8** Identify the characteristics and impact of Grangerism and Populism.

### ONE AMERICAN'S STORY

From 1865 to 1900, about 800,000 Swedes left their homeland in northern Europe. Most Swedes were drawn to the United States by the promise of more and better land.

For Olaf Olsson, the acres of free land offered to settlers by the U.S. government was an unbelievable opportunity. Shortly after he arrived in 1869, Olsson wrote home to tell friends and family what awaited them in America.

#### A VOICE FROM THE PAST

We do not dig gold with pocket knives, we do not expect to become . . . rich in a few days or in a few years, but what we aim at is to own our own homes. . . . The advantage which America offers is not to make everyone rich at once, without toil or trouble, but . . . that the poor . . . can work up little by little.

**Olaf Olsson,** quoted in *The Swedish Americans,* by Allyson McGill

As you will read in this section, many Americans as well as immigrants from all parts of Europe shared Olsson's optimism.

## U.S. Government Encourages Settlement

For years, people had been calling on the federal government to sell Western land at low prices. Before the Civil War, Southern states fought such a policy. They feared that a big westward migration would result in more nonslave states. Once the South left the Union, however, the way was clear for a new land policy. To interest both American and immigrant families like the Olssons in going west, the federal government passed the **Homestead Act** in 1862. This law offered 160 acres of land free to anyone who agreed to live on and improve the land for five years.

After Reconstruction ended in 1877, African Americans in the South faced harsh new forms of discrimination. (See Chapter 18.) By 1879,

**Taking Notes**

Use your chart to take notes about farmers and African Americans.

Many diverse people settled the West!

leaders like Benjamin "Pap" Singleton of Tennessee had convinced thousands to migrate to new homes in Kansas. They compared themselves to the biblical Hebrews led out of slavery in Egypt and called themselves **Exodusters**. One of them, John Solomon Lewis, remarked, "When I landed on the soil of Kansas, I looked on the ground and I says this is free ground." In all, some 50,000 African Americans settled in Kansas, Missouri, Indiana, and Illinois.

Thousands of European immigrants also sought a new start in the West. Swedes, like Olaf Olsson, joined Germans, Norwegians, Ukrainians, and Russians on the Great Plains. They often first learned about the West from land agents for American railroad companies. These salesmen traveled throughout Europe with pamphlets proclaiming "Land for the Landless! Homes for the Homeless."

From 1850 to 1870, the government gave millions of acres of public land to the railroads to promote railroad expansion. The railroads resold much of the land to settlers. This not only made the railroad companies rich, but it also supplied new customers for railroad services. The railroads' sales pitch worked. In the 1860s, so many Swedes and Norwegians settled in Minnesota that a local editor wrote, "It seems as if the Scandinavian Kingdoms were being emptied into this state."

*Reading* **History**

A. Analyzing Causes How did the railroads help to settle the West?

## Life on the Farming Frontier

Once pioneers reached their new homes on the plains, they faced many challenges never mentioned by the land agents. The plains were nearly treeless. So farmers were forced to build their first homes from blocks of sod. Sod is the top layer of prairie soil that is thickly matted with grass roots.

For fuel, the **sodbusters,** as the farmers were called, burned corn cobs or "cow chips" (dried manure). In many places, sodbusters had to dig wells more than 280 feet deep to reach the only water. Blizzards, prairie fires, hailstorms, tornadoes, grasshoppers, and drought added to the misery of life on the plains. Many settlers, such as Katherine Kirk of South Dakota, wondered whether they had the courage "to stick it out."

## Connections TO SCIENCE

### SOD HOUSES

To build their dwellings, Plains farmers, or sodbusters, like the Nebraska family pictured here, cut the tough buffalo grass of the prairie into two-or three-foot strips. Then they laid chunks of sod into two rows as walls. The walls were often 36 inches thick.

Prairie grass was thick. Its roots grew outward under the soil, often connecting with one another. This held the sod together. The roots also provided a layer of insulation. So sod houses, or soddies, stayed warm in the winter and cool in the summer. But their roofs leaked rain and dirt, and the walls housed mice, snakes, and insects.

New inventions helped farmers to meet some of these challenges. A steel plow invented by John Deere in 1838 and improved upon by James Oliver in 1868 sliced through the tough sod. Windmills adapted to the plains pumped water from deep wells to the surface. Barbed wire allowed farmers to fence in land and livestock. Reapers made the harvesting of crops much easier, and threshers helped farmers to separate grain or seed from straw. These inventions also made farm work more efficient. From 1860 to 1890, farmers doubled their production of wheat.

## The Problems of Farmers

As farmers became more efficient, they grew more and more food. The result was that farmers in the West and South watched with alarm as prices for farm crops began to drop lower and lower in the 1870s.

## Economics *in* History

# Supply and Demand

Farmers in the West were having economic problems in the 1880s. The supply of food was increasing rapidly, but consumer demand was growing slowly. To attract more consumers, farmers had to drop the prices of their products.

The farmers were experiencing the **law of supply and demand.** The amount of economic goods available for sale is the **supply.** The willingness and ability of consumers to spend money for goods and services is **demand.** The price of goods is set by the supply of that good and the demand for that good.

At a lower price, businesses produce less of a good because they will make less money. As the price rises, they produce more. Consumer demand works in the opposite way. Consumers want to buy more of the good when the price is lower—after all, it costs them less. They buy less when the price is higher. The actual price of a good results from a compromise—how much consumers are willing to pay and how little businesses are willing to take for the good.

**CONNECT TO HISTORY**

1. **Recognizing Effects** Suppose farmers found a new market for their wheat—the people in another country, for instance. What effect would that have on price? Why?

   **S** See Skillbuilder Handbook, page R11.

**CONNECT TO TODAY**

2. **Comparing** How does the price of blue jeans show the law of supply and demand?

For more about supply and demand . . .

**RESEARCH LINKS** CLASSZONE.COM

1 Prices are high.

2 Producers want to increase supply.

3 More goods push price down.

4 Demand increases.

5 Producer increases supply.

6 Price decreases again.

7 Producer supplies less.

8 Prices increase and demand falls

(See "Economics in History" on page 576.) Wheat that sold for $1.45 a bushel after the Civil War was 49 cents 30 years later. One reason for lower prices was overproduction. Farmers were growing more food because additional farmland had been opened up and farming methods and machines had improved.

Receiving less money for their crops was bad enough. But at the same time farmers had to spend more to run a farm. New farm machinery and railroad rates were especially costly. Railroads charged the farmers high fees to carry their crops to market. The railroads also usually owned the

"The Grange Awakening the Sleepers" (1873) shows a farmer trying to warn the country about the menace of the railroads.

grain elevators where crops were stored until shipment. Farmers had no choice but to pay the high costs of storage that railroads charged.

Farmers were angry. They began to work together to seek solutions to their problems. In 1867, farmers had formed the **Grange,** officially known as the Patrons of Husbandry. The group's main purpose at first had been to meet the social needs of farm families who lived great distances from one another. However, as economic conditions got worse, Grange members took action. They formed **cooperatives.** These are organizations owned and run by their members. The cooperatives bought grain elevators and sold crops directly to merchants. This allowed farmers to keep more of their profits.

Farmers also began to demand action from the government to change their circumstances. For example, Grangers asked states to regulate railroad freight rates and storage charges. Illinois, Minnesota, Wisconsin, and Iowa did so. In 1877, the Supreme Court backed the farmers in their fight against the railroads. In *Munn* v. *Illinois,* the Court ruled that states and the federal government could regulate the railroads because they were businesses that served the public interest.

## The Rise of Populism

In 1890, several farm groups joined together to try to gain political power. They formed the **Populist Party,** or People's Party. The Populists wanted the government to adopt a free silver policy, that is, the unlimited coining of silver. Since silver was plentiful, more money would be put in circulation. They believed that increasing the money supply would cause inflation. Inflation, in turn, would result in rising prices. Higher prices for crops would help farmers pay back the money that they had borrowed to improve their farms.

Opponents of free silver wanted to keep the gold standard. Under the **gold standard,** the government backs every dollar with a certain amount

*Reading*History

**B. Summarizing** What steps did farmers take to seek solutions to their problems?

of gold. Since the gold supply is limited, fewer dollars are in circulation. Inflation is less likely. This protects the value of money by keeping prices down.

In 1892, the Populist Party platform called for free silver to expand the money supply, government ownership of railroads, shorter working hours, and other political reforms. The Populist presidential candidate, James B. Weaver, lost to Grover Cleveland. But he won more than a million votes—a good showing for a third-party candidate.

## The Election of 1896

By the next presidential campaign, money issues mattered much more to voters. The nation had suffered through a serious depression, the Panic of 1893. The Republican candidate, William McKinley, favored the gold standard. He warned that "free silver" would mean higher prices for food and other goods.

The Populists joined the Democratic Party in supporting **William Jennings Bryan** of Nebraska. Bryan urged the Democratic convention to support free silver in his stirring "Cross of Gold" speech.

### A VOICE FROM THE PAST

Burn down your cities and leave our farms, and your cities will spring up again as if by magic; but destroy our farms and the grass will grow in the street of every city in the country. . . . [We] . . . answer . . . their demand for a gold standard by saying . . . : You shall not press down upon the brow of labor this crown of thorns. You shall not crucify mankind upon a cross of gold.

**William Jennings Bryan,** Democratic Convention speech, July 8, 1896

*Reading* **History**

C. Analyzing Points of View What point was William Jennings Bryan making about the importance of farms?

Farmers in the South and the West voted overwhelmingly for Bryan. But McKinley, who was backed by industrialists, bankers, and other business leaders, won the East and the election by about half a million votes. This election was the beginning of the end for the Populist Party.

## The Closing of the Frontier

By the late 1880s, fenced-in fields had replaced open plains. The last remaining open land was in Indian Territory. The Oklahoma land rush of 1889 symbolized the closing of the frontier. At the blast of the starting gun on April 22, thousands of white settlers rushed to claim two million acres of land that had once belonged to Native Americans. In May 1890, this part of Indian Territory officially became Oklahoma Territory. In 1890, 17 million people lived between the Mississippi and the Pacific. That year the Census Bureau declared that the country no longer had a continuous frontier line—the frontier no longer existed.

To many, the frontier was what had made America unique. In 1893, historian Frederick Jackson Turner wrote an influential essay on the frontier. Turner said that the frontier was a promise to all Americans, no matter how poor, that they could advance as far as their abilities allowed. To Turner the frontier meant opportunity, and its closing marked the end of an era.

Thousands of settlers rushed into Oklahoma Territory in 1889 to claim the last open land on the frontier.

*Reading*History

**D. Using Secondary Sources** What did Frederick Jackson Turner believe about the frontier?

*A VOICE FROM THE PAST*

Up to our own day American history has been in a large degree the history of the colonization of the Great West. The existence of an area of free land, its continuous recession, and the advance of American settlement westward, explain American development.

**Frederick Jackson Turner,** "The Significance of the American Frontier"

Today many historians question Turner's view. They think he gave too much importance to the frontier in the nation's development and in shaping a special American character. These historians point out that the United States remains a land of opportunity long after the frontier's closing.

In the next chapter, you will learn how an industrial society developed in the East during the same period that the West was settled.

---

*Section*  *Assessment*

### 1. Terms & Names

**Explain the significance of:**
- Homestead Act
- Exoduster
- sodbuster
- Grange
- cooperative
- Populist Party
- gold standard
- William Jennings Bryan

### 2. Using Graphics

Review the chapter and find five key events to place on a time line as shown.

1860   event   event   1890

event   event   event

What do you think was the most important event? (CST2)

### 3. Main Ideas

**a.** How did the federal government encourage and support settlement of the Plains? (HI2)

**b.** Which groups of people moved onto the Plains in the late 1800s? Why did they come? (HI2)

**c.** Which problems in the 1890s led farmers to take political action? (HI2)

### 4. Critical Thinking

**Drawing Conclusions** Why did the Grange favor government regulation of the railroads? (REP5)

**THINK ABOUT**
- powers of monopolies
- importance of railroads to farmers
- railroad freight and storage rates

**ACTIVITY OPTIONS**

**TECHNOLOGY**

**SPEECH**

Pick one invention that helped farmers on the Plains. Plan an **electronic presentation** on the invention or deliver a **sales pitch** to potential buyers. (HI1)

## Growth of the West (8.8)

The West

### Miners

Miners were attracted to the West by gold and silver strikes. Mining contributed to the population growth of many Western territories.

### Cowhands & Ranchers

Ranchers and cowhands established a thriving cattle industry. New settlement, barbed wire, and bad weather ended the cattle boom.

### Native Americans

Government policies, wars, and the destruction of the buffalo led to the defeat of the Plains peoples and to their placement on reservations.

### Homesteaders

Hundreds of thousands of homesteaders settled on the Plains. Their life was hard, but they used new technologies to increase their output.

## TERMS & NAMES

Briefly explain the significance of each of the following.

1. frontier
2. long drive
3. reservation
4. Battle of the Little Bighorn
5. Dawes Act
6. homestead
7. Mexicano
8. Homestead Act
9. sodbuster
10. Populist Party

## REVIEW QUESTIONS

### Miners, Ranchers, and Cowhands (pages 557–561)

1. What role did miners play in the settlement of the West? (HI1)
2. What made cattle ranching so profitable in the late 1800s? (HI2)
3. What ended the boom in the cattle business? (HI2)

### Native Americans Fight to Survive (pages 562–567)

4. What caused conflict between Native Americans and white settlers on the Great Plains? (HI1)
5. How did Native Americans resist white settlement? (HI1)

### Life in the West (pages 568–573)

6. What rights did women in the West gain before women in Eastern states? (HI1)
7. How has the myth of the "Wild West" been revised? (HI5)

### Farming and Populism (pages 574–579)

8. How did the federal government encourage people to settle on the Great Plains? (HI2)
9. What were the goals of the Grange? (HI1)
10. What marked the closing of the frontier? (HI1)

## CRITICAL THINKING

### 1. USING YOUR NOTES: FINDING MAIN IDEAS

Using your completed chart, answer the questions below. (HI1)

a. What were the main reasons that drew people to the West?
b. Which groups do you think benefited from being in the West and which groups did not? Explain.

### 2. APPLYING CITIZENSHIP SKILLS

What are the dangers of vigilante justice? (HI1)

### 3. THEME: DIVERSITY AND UNITY

Why might the contributions of women and Native Americans, African Americans, and other ethnic groups have been overlooked in early books and films on the West? (HI1)

### 4. ANALYZING LEADERSHIP

Why did the Nez Perce Chief Joseph decide to surrender? What other choices might he have made? (HI5)

### 5. CONTRASTING

How did ranchers and sodbusters differ over land use? Why did these differences lead to conflict? (HI2)

### 6. FORMING AND SUPPORTING OPINIONS

What do you think would be the most difficult challenge in starting a new life on the Great Plains? Give reasons for your answer (HI1).

### Interact with History

Now that you have read the chapter, would you still make the same statements about how your life would change in the West? Explain.

## STANDARDS-BASED ASSESSMENT

Use the map and your knowledge of U.S. history to answer questions 1 and 2.

Additional Test Practice, pp. S1–S33.

**1.** What is the longest cattle trail? (8.12.1)

  **A.** Chisholm Trail

  **B.** Goodnight-Loving Trail

  **C.** Shawnee Trail

  **D.** Western Trail

**2.** How many miles did the longest trail cover? (8.12.1)

  **A.** about 600 miles

  **B.** about 800 miles

  **C.** about 1,000 miles

  **D.** about 1,200 miles

This quotation from Olaf Olsson describes the advantage of America. Use the quotation and your knowledge of U.S. history to answer question 3.

### PRIMARY SOURCE

We do not dig gold with pocket knives, we do not expect to become . . . rich in a few days or in a few years, but what we aim at is to own our own homes. . . . The advantage which America offers is not to make everyone rich at once, without toil or trouble, but . . . that the poor . . . [can] secure a large piece of good land almost without cost, that they can work up little by little.

**Olaf Olsson,** quoted in *The Swedish Americans,* by Alison McGill

**3.** What type of person is described in the passage? (8.6.3)

  **A.** a person who has inherited land

  **B.** a person who hopes for instant wealth

  **C.** a person who has a strong work ethic

  **D.** a person who works well as part of a team

**TEST PRACTICE**
CLASSZONE.COM

## ALTERNATIVE ASSESSMENT

### 1. ✍ WRITING ABOUT HISTORY

You are a biographer writing about Native American leaders of the West. Write a **biography** of a leader, such as Sitting Bull, Chief Joseph, or Geronimo. (REP4)

- Use library resources to research your subject.
- Persuade your reader that your subject is an important historical figure.

### 2. COOPERATIVE LEARNING

Work with a small group to create a play based on the life of the sodbusters. Choose a topic, such as "the journey west," "first impressions," or "women's work and worries." Research and choose quotations related to your topic. Some group members can compose lines to introduce and make transitions between topics and others can perform the readings. (REP3)

## INTEGRATED TECHNOLOGY

### DOING INTERNET RESEARCH

The "Wild West" of the late 1800s was a land of myth and legend. Use the Internet or library resources to find information in order to create a "Wild West" Web site. (REP4)

- Find newspaper articles, advertisements, and stories about the "Wild West."
- You can also learn about this era from books, and from documentary films.
- Select legendary personalities to be featured in your Web site, and choose musical selections to add background.

For more about the "Wild West" . . .

**INTERNET ACTIVITY**
CLASSZONE.COM

# An Industrial Society 1860–1914

At the turn of the century, industrial strikes for better conditions often erupted in violence, as this illustration shows.

Most of the workers have only bricks, stones, or sticks for weapons.

There were no laws protecting children from dangerous work or long hours.

**1863**
Two companies begin to build a transcontinental railroad across the United States.

**1879**
Thomas Edison invents a practical lightbulb.

**1882**
Thomas Edison installs electric lights in New York City.

USA
World 1860

**1869**
Suez Canal opens in Egypt.

The year is 1894. You work in a factory that is unheated and badly lit. The machine that you operate is dangerous. The economy is doing poorly, so the factory has cut your wages. Some of your coworkers have gone out on strike. They want better pay and working conditions.

# Would you join the strike? Why or why not?

## What Do You Think?

- What are some risks you would be taking if you join the strike?

- What might you gain if you take part in the strike?

- What other methods might you use to persuade your employer to meet your demands?

**RESEARCH LINKS**
CLASSZONE.COM
Visit the Chapter 20 links for more information about U.S. industry.

**1888**
jamin
son is
lected
ident.

**1892**
Grover Cleveland is elected president for the second time.

**1894**
Pullman Strike halts rail traffic across the nation.

**1901**
Oil drillers discover a huge oil field in Texas.

**1905**
Supreme Court overturns a New York law establishing a 60-hour workweek for bakers.

1914

**1889**
The world's tallest structure to date, the Eiffel Tower in Paris, is built of iron.

**1896**
The Italian engineer Guglielmo Marconi patents the radio.

**1904**
Russia finishes building the first Trans-Siberian railway across Asia.

# Reading Strategy: Analyzing Causes and Effects

## What Do You Know?

Do you know of any businesses that started back in the 1800s? How do businesses grow?

### Think About

- businesses that you see in your community
- businesses that are advertised on television, in magazines or newspapers, or on the Internet
- your responses to the Interact with History about conflict with workers (see page 583)

## What Do You Want to Know?

 What facts and details would help you understand how a nation of small businesses became a nation of giant corporations? In your notebook, list the facts and details you hope to learn from this chapter.

## Analyzing Causes and Effects

The conditions or actions that lead to a historical event are its causes. The consequences of an event are its effects. As you read the chapter, look for the causes and effects of industrial and railroad growth. Causes include geographical factors and actions by individuals and the government. Effects include both benefits and problems. Use the diagram below to record both causes and effects.

**S** See Skillbuilder Handbook, page R11.

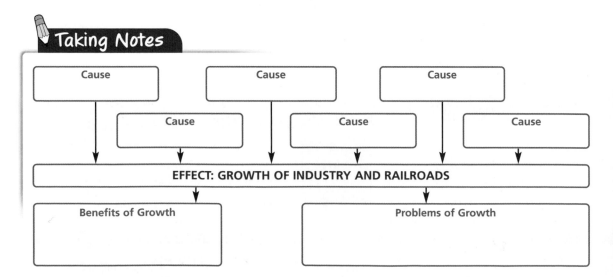

Taking Notes

| Cause | Cause | Cause |
|---|---|---|

| Cause | Cause | Cause |
|---|---|---|

**EFFECT: GROWTH OF INDUSTRY AND RAILROADS**

| Benefits of Growth | Problems of Growth |
|---|---|

# The Growth of Industry

| MAIN IDEA | WHY IT MATTERS NOW | TERMS & NAMES |
|---|---|---|
| The growth of industry during the years 1860 to 1914 transformed life in America. | Modern businesses rely on many of the inventions and products developed during that time. | petroleum    generator<br>patent    **Thomas Edison**<br>business cycle    **Alexander Graham Bell**<br>**Bessemer steel process**    **Centennial Exhibition** |

## ONE AMERICAN'S STORY

In the 1850s, most Americans lit their homes with oil lamps. They could have used kerosene, an oil made from coal, but it was expensive. Then, in 1855, a chemist reported that kerosene could be made more cheaply from an oily liquid called <u>petroleum</u>. However, people didn't know how to obtain petroleum from underground. They just gathered it slowly when it seeped to the surface.

In 1857, Edwin Drake visited a site in Pennsylvania where petroleum oozed to the surface.

Drake began drilling in 1859. He struck oil in August. This event launched the oil industry—one of many new industries that developed in the late 1800s, as this section explains.

The wooden structure is Drake's first oil well.

## The Industrial Revolution Continues

Throughout the 1800s, factory production expanded in the United States. By the Civil War, factory production had spread beyond New England textiles to other regions and industries. Several factors encouraged this growth.

1. **Plentiful natural resources.** America had immense forests and large supplies of water. It also had vast mineral wealth, including coal, iron, copper, silver, and gold. Industry used these resources to manufacture a variety of goods.
2. **Growing population.** From 1860 to 1900, the U.S. population grew from 31.5 million to 76 million. This led to a growing need for goods. The demand for goods spurred the growth of industry.

**Taking Notes**

Use your chart to take notes about the growth of industry.

Background
Some of these
canals were built
because of Henry
Clay's American
System. (See
Chapter 11.)

3. **Improved transportation.** In the early 1800s, steamboats, canals, and railroads made it possible to ship items long distances more quickly. Railroad building boomed after the Civil War. As shipping raw materials and finished goods became easier, industry grew.

4. **High immigration.** Between 1860 and 1900, about 14 million people immigrated to the United States. Many of them knew specialized trades, such as metalworking. In addition, unskilled immigrants supplied the labor that growing industry needed.

5. **New inventions.** New machines and improved processes helped industry produce goods more efficiently. Inventors applied for patents for the machines or processes they invented. A **patent** is a government document giving an inventor the exclusive right to make and sell his or her invention for a specific number of years.

6. **Investment capital.** When the economy was thriving, many businesses made large profits. Hoping to share in those profits, banks and wealthy people lent businesses money. The businesses used this capital to build factories and buy equipment.

7. **Government assistance.** Between 1860 and 1900 the United States imposed several tariffs on imported goods. State and federal governments also used land grants and subsidies to help businesses grow.

## The Business Cycle

American industry did not grow at a steady pace; it experienced ups and downs. This pattern of good and bad times is called the **business cycle**.

**The Business Cycle**

Change in volume of what businesses produce

Peak (high point)

Expansion (growth)

Contraction (decrease)

Expansion

Peak

Trough (low point)

Passage of time

**SKILLBUILDER Interpreting Charts**
1. *How does the amount of goods produced at the peak compare to the amount at the trough?*
2. *Are all peaks equally prosperous? Explain.*

During good times, called booms, people buy more, and some invest in business. As a result, industries and businesses grow. During bad times, called busts, spending and investing decrease. Industries lay off workers and make fewer goods. Businesses may shrink—or even close. Such a period of low economic activity is a depression.

America experienced depressions in 1837 and 1857. Both were eventually followed by periods of strong economic growth. In the late 1800s, there were two harsh depressions, also called panics. The depression of 1873 lasted five years. At its height, three million people were out of work. During the depression that began in 1893, thousands of businesses failed, including more than 300 railroads.

*Reading*History
**A. Recognizing
Effects** How do
you think
depressions
affect ordinary
people?

Even with these economic highs and lows, industries in the United States grew tremendously between 1860 and 1900. Overall, the amount of manufactured goods increased six times during these years.

## Steel: The Backbone of Industry

The steel industry contributed to America's industrial growth. Before the mid-1800s, steel was very expensive to manufacture because the steel-making process used huge amounts of coal. In the 1850s, William Kelly in the United States and Henry Bessemer in England independently developed a new process for making steel. It used less than one-seventh of the coal that the older process used. This new manufacturing technique was called the **Bessemer steel process.**

Because the Bessemer process cut the cost of steel, the nation's steel output increased 500 times between 1867 and 1900. Industry began to make many products out of steel instead of iron. These products included plows, barbed wire, nails, and beams for buildings. But the main use of steel throughout the late 1800s was for rails for the expanding railroads. (See Section 2.)

## Edison and Electricity

Another industry that grew during the late 1800s was the electric-power industry. By the 1870s, inventors had designed efficient generators. A **generator** is a machine that produces electric current. As a result, people grew eager to tap the power of electricity.

The inventor who found the most ways to use electricity was **Thomas Edison.** In 1876, he opened a laboratory in Menlo Park, New Jersey. He employed many assistants, whom he organized into teams to do research. Edison's laboratory invented so many things that Edison received more than 1,000 U.S. patents, more than any other individual inventor.

Edison would start with an idea for a possible invention. Then he would work hard to make that idea a reality—even if problems arose.

*A VOICE FROM THE PAST*

It has been just so in all my inventions. The first step is an intuition—and comes with a burst, *then* difficulties arise. . . . "Bugs"—as such little faults and difficulties are called—show themselves and months of anxious watching, study and labor are requisite [needed] before commercial success—or failure—is certainly reached.

**Thomas Edison,** quoted in *Edison* by Matthew Josephson

Edison's most famous invention was practical electric lighting. Other inventors had already created electric lights, but they were too bright and

*Reading* **History**

**B. Drawing Conclusions**
Which industries benefited from the steel products mentioned here?

*Reading* **History**

**C. Finding Main Ideas** According to Edison, is inventing easy?

**Connections** TO **SCIENCE**

**IRON VS. STEEL**

Why is the comic book hero Superman also called the man of steel? People often use the word *steel* as a synonym for strength.

Steel is an iron alloy—a blend of iron and other materials such as carbon. But steel is stronger and more durable than iron. That is why steel replaced iron in many industries in the late 1800s. A giant ladle (bucket) used to pour melted steel is pictured below.

Stainless steel, invented in the early 1900s, has an additional benefit: it doesn't rust. Stainless steel is used in tools, machines, and many household items, such as pots, pans, and utensils.

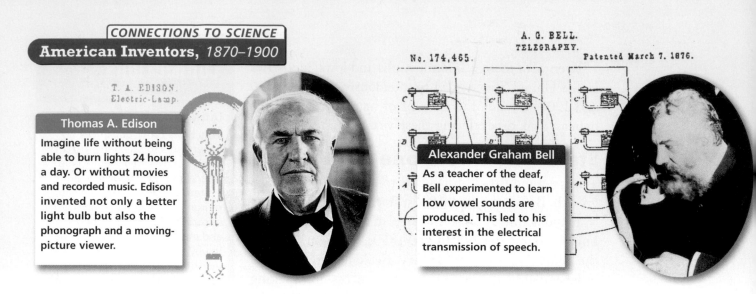

T. A. EDISON.
Electric-Lamp.

A. G. BELL.
TELEGRAPHY.
No. 174,465.    Patented March 7, 1876.

**Thomas A. Edison**

Imagine life without being able to burn lights 24 hours a day. Or without movies and recorded music. Edison invented not only a better light bulb but also the phonograph and a moving-picture viewer.

**Alexander Graham Bell**

As a teacher of the deaf, Bell experimented to learn how vowel sounds are produced. This led to his interest in the electrical transmission of speech.

flickery for home use. Edison figured out how to make a safe, steady light bulb. He also invented a system to deliver electricity to buildings.

By 1882, he had installed electric lighting in a half-mile-square area of New York City. Electric lighting quickly replaced gaslights. By the late 1880s, Edison's factory produced about a million light bulbs a year.

## Bell and the Telephone

Electricity played a role in communications devices invented during the 1800s. In 1835, Samuel Morse developed the telegraph. It allowed people to use electrical impulses to send messages over long distances.

The next step in communications was the telephone, invented by **Alexander Graham Bell.** He was a Scottish immigrant who taught deaf students in Boston. At night, Bell and his assistant, Thomas Watson, tried to invent a device to transmit human speech using electricity.

After years of experiments, Bell succeeded. One day in March 1876, he was adjusting the transmitter in the laboratory in his apartment. Watson was in another room with the receiver. The two doors between the rooms were shut. According to Watson's memoirs, Bell accidentally spilled acid on himself and said, "Mr. Watson, come here. I want you." Watson rushed down the hall. He burst into the laboratory, exclaiming that he had heard and understood Bell's words through the receiver.

Bell showed his telephone at the **Centennial Exhibition** in June 1876. That was an exhibition in Philadelphia to celebrate America's 100th birthday. There, several of the world's leading scientists and the emperor of Brazil saw his demonstration. Afterward, they declared, "Here is the greatest marvel ever achieved in electrical science."

## Inventions Change Industry

The telephone industry grew rapidly. By 1880, more than 50,000 telephones had been sold. The invention of the switchboard allowed more and more people to connect into a telephone network. Women commonly worked in the new job of switchboard operator.

The typewriter also opened jobs for women. Christopher Latham Sholes helped invent the first practical typewriter in 1867. He also

*Reading*History
**D. Analyzing Points of View**
Why do you think the scientists said this about the telephone?

J. E. MATZELIGER.
LASTING MACHINE.

Patented Mar. 20, 1883.

### Jan Matzeliger

An immigrant from Dutch Guiana, Matzeliger worked in a shoe factory. To reduce the time needed to fasten shoe leather to the sole by hand, he invented a machine to do the job. It increased production by 1,400 percent!

**U.S. Patents Issued,** *1860–1909*

Source: *Historical Statistics of the United States*

**SKILLBUILDER Interpreting Graphs**

1. *How many more patents were issued from 1900 to 1909 than from 1860 to 1869?*
2. *Was this a time of increasing or decreasing inventiveness?*

improved the machine and sold his rights to it to a manufacturer who began to make typewriters in the 1870s.

The sewing machine also changed American life. Elias Howe first patented it in 1846. In the next few years, the sewing machine received many design improvements. Isaac Singer patented a sewing machine in 1851 and continued to improve it. It became a bestseller and led to a new industry. In factories, people produced ready-made clothes. Instead of being fitted to each buyer, clothes came in standard sizes and popular styles. Increasingly, people bought clothes instead of making their own.

Other inventors helped industry advance. African-American inventor Granville T. Woods patented devices to improve telephone and telegraph systems. Margaret Knight invented machines for the packaging and shoemaking industries and also improved motors and engines.

Of all the up-and-coming industries of the middle 1800s, one would have a larger impact on American life than any other. That was the railroad industry. You will read about railroads in Section 2.

---

## Section 1 Assessment

### 1. Terms & Names

**Explain the significance of:**
- petroleum
- patent
- business cycle
- Bessemer steel process
- generator
- Thomas Edison
- Alexander Graham Bell
- Centennial Exhibition

### 2. Using Graphics

Use a cluster diagram like the one below to list some of the inventions of the late 1800s.

Inventions

How has one of these inventions recently been improved? (HI1)

### 3. Main Ideas

**a.** What factors contributed to industrial growth in the United States? (HI2)

**b.** What is the business cycle? (HI2)

**c.** What caused the steel-making industry to boom and why? (HI2)

### 4. Critical Thinking

**Recognizing Effects** How did the inventions of the late 1800s make it easier to do business? (HI3)

**THINK ABOUT**
- electric generators and light bulbs
- the telephone
- the typewriter

### ACTIVITY OPTIONS

**SCIENCE**

**TECHNOLOGY**

Choose an invention and learn more about it. Create a **display** explaining how it works or design a **Web page** linking to sites with more information. (REP1)

# Railroads Transform the Nation

| **MAIN IDEA** | **WHY IT MATTERS NOW** | **TERMS & NAMES** |
|---|---|---|
| The railroads tied the nation together, speeded industrial growth, and changed U.S. life. | The railroad first made possible our modern system of shipping goods across the country. | transcontinental railroad<br>standard time |

**CALIFORNIA STANDARDS**

**8.6.2** Outline the physical obstacles to and the economic and political factors involved in building a network of roads, canals, and railroads (e.g., Henry Clay's American System).

**8.12.1** Trace patterns of agricultural and industrial development as they relate to climate, use of natural resources, markets, and trade and locate such development on a map.

**8.12.3** Explain how states and the federal government encouraged business expansion through tariffs, banking, land grants, and subsidies.

**8.12.4** Discuss entrepreneurs, industrialists, and bankers in politics, commerce, and industry (e.g., Andrew Carnegie, John D. Rockefeller, Leland Stanford).

**CST3** Students use a variety of maps and documents to identify physical and cultural features of neighborhoods, cities, states, and countries and to explain the historical migration of people, expansion and disintegration of empires, and the growth of economic systems.

## ONE AMERICAN'S STORY

Ah Goong was one of thousands of Chinese workers on the Western railroads in the late 1800s. In some places, the workers had to blast rock from a cliff wall. The lightest Chinese were lowered in wicker baskets hundreds of feet to the blasting site. Years later, Ah Goong's granddaughter described her grandfather's job.

*A VOICE FROM THE PAST*

Swinging near the cliff, Ah Goong . . . dug holes, then inserted gunpowder and fuses. . . . The basketmen signaled one another to light the fuses. He struck match after match and dropped the burnt matches over the sides. At last his fuse caught; he waved, and the men above pulled hand over hand hauling him up, pulleys creaking.

**Maxine Hong Kingston,** *China Men*

Chinese immigrants—like the one at the lower left—helped build several railroads in the West.

This section discusses the building of the railroads.

## Deciding to Span the Continent

Americans had talked about building a **transcontinental railroad**—one that spanned the entire continent—for years. Such a railroad would encourage people to settle the West and develop its economy. In 1862, Congress passed a bill that called for two companies to build a transcontinental railroad across the center of the United States.

The Central Pacific, led by Leland Stanford, was to start in Sacramento, California, and build east. The Union Pacific was to start in Omaha, Nebraska, and build west. To build the railroad, these two companies had to raise large sums of money. The government lent them millions of dollars. It also gave them 20 square miles of public land for every mile of track they laid. The railroad companies could then sell the land to raise money.

With the guarantees of loans and land, the railroads attracted many investors. The Central Pacific began to lay its first track in 1863. The

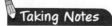

**Taking Notes**

Use your chart to take notes about the growth of railroads.

Union Pacific laid its first rail in July 1865 (after the Civil War had ended).

## Building the Railroad

The Central Pacific faced a labor shortage because most men preferred to try to strike it rich as miners. Desperate for workers, the Central Pacific's managers overcame the widespread prejudice against the Chinese and hired several dozen of them. The Chinese were small and weighed, on average, no more than 110 pounds. But they were efficient, fearless, and hard working.

They also followed their own customs, which led to an unexpected benefit for the railroad company. The Chinese drank tea instead of unboiled water, so they were sick less often than other workers. Pleased with the Chinese workers, the company brought more men over from China. At the peak of construction, more than 10,000 Chinese worked on the Central Pacific.

The Union Pacific hired workers from a variety of backgrounds. After the Civil War ended in 1865, former soldiers from both North and South flocked to work on the railroad. Freed slaves came, too. But one of the largest groups of Union Pacific workers was immigrants, many from Ireland.

Both railroads occasionally hired Native Americans. Washos, Shoshones, and Paiutes all assisted the race of the rails across the deserts of Nevada and Utah.

*Background*
Boiling water kills germs.

*Reading*History
**A. Drawing Conclusions** Why did the Union Pacific have a larger supply of workers?

## Railroads Tie the Nation Together

Only short, undergrown trees dotted the vast open space. To the south shimmered the Great Salt Lake. In the east rose the bluish shapes of the Rocky Mountains. Across that space, from opposite directions, the workers of the Central Pacific and the Union Pacific toiled. By May 10, 1869, Central Pacific workers had laid 690 miles of track. Union Pacific workers had laid 1,086 miles. Only one span of track separated the two lines at their meeting point at Promontory, Utah.

Hundreds of railroad workers, managers, spectators, and journalists gathered on that cool, windy day to see the transcontinental railroad completed. Millions of Americans waited to hear the news by telegraph. A band played as a Chinese crew and an Irish crew laid the last rails. The last spike, a golden one, was set in place. First, the president of the Central Pacific raised a hammer to drive in the spike. After he swung the hammer down, the crowd roared with laughter. He had missed. The vice-president of the Union Pacific took a turn and also missed. But the telegraph operator couldn't see and had already sent the message: "done." People across the nation celebrated.

*Reading*History
**B. Reading a Map** Using the map on page 592, find the Union Pacific and Central Pacific Railroads. Notice how they connect Omaha to Sacramento.

**This golden spike united the Central Pacific and Union Pacific Railroads.**

The Union Pacific-Central Pacific line was the first transcontinental railroad. By 1895, four more U.S. lines had been built across the continent. Between 1869 and 1890, the amount of money railroads earned carrying freight grew from $300 million to $734 million per year.

**Background**
Canada had also built a transcontinental railroad, so there were six altogether.

## Railroad Time

The railroads changed America in a surprising way: they altered time. Before the railroads, each community determined its own time, based on calculations about the sun's travels. This system was called "solar time." Solar time caused problems for people who scheduled trains crossing several time zones and for travelers.

### A VOICE FROM THE PAST

I have been annoyed and perplexed by the changes in the time schedules of connecting railroads. My watch could give me no information as to the arrival and departure of trains, nor of the time for meals.

**John Rodgers,** quoted in *Passage to Union*

To solve this problem, the railroad companies set up **standard time**. It was a system that divided the United States into four time zones. Although the plan went into effect on November 18, 1883, Congress did not adopt standard time until 1918. By then, most Americans saw its benefit because following schedules had become part of daily life.

### Railroads of the Transcontinental Era, 1865–1900

**Time Zones**
- Eastern
- Central
- Mountain
- Pacific

**GEOGRAPHY SKILLBUILDER Interpreting Maps**
1. **Region** *Were there more railroads in the Eastern or Western half of the country?*
2. **Place** *What do you think each of the four time zones was named for?*

# Economic and Social Changes

The railroads changed people's lives in many other important ways. They helped create modern America.

1. **Linked the economies of the West and East.** From the West, the railroads carried eastward raw materials such as lumber, livestock, and grain. Materials like these were processed in Midwestern cities such as Chicago and Cleveland. (See Geography in History on pages 598–599.) From Eastern cities, in turn, came manufactured goods, which were sold to Westerners.

2. **Helped people settle the West.** Railroads were lifelines for settlers. Trains brought them lumber, farm equipment, food, and other necessities and hauled their crops to market.

3. **Weakened the Native American hold on the West.** As Chapter 19 explained, the railroads carried hunters who killed off the herds of buffalo. They also brought settlers and miners who laid claim to Native American land.

4. **Gave people more control of the environment.** Before railroads, people lived mainly where there were waterways, such as rivers. Roads were primitive. Railroads made possible cities such as Denver, Colorado, which had no usable waterways.

Just as railroads changed life for many Americans in the late 1800s, so did big business. You will read about big business in Section 3.

*Reading***History**

**C. Evaluating** Which of these four changes do you think were positive, and which were negative?

## Connections TO ART & MUSIC

**RAILROAD HEROES**

Several American songs celebrate railroad heroes. One tells of Casey Jones, an engineer who saved lives. He slammed on the brakes as his train rounded a bend and plowed into a stalled freight train. He died but slowed the train enough to save his passengers.

Another song tells of a mythical worker named John Henry, shown below. This ballad celebrates an African American's strength in a track-laying race against a steam-driven machine.

---

## Section 2 Assessment

### 1. Terms & Names

**Explain the significance of:**
- transcontinental railroad
- standard time

### 2. Using Graphics

Using a chart like the one below, record which groups of people helped build the transcontinental railroad.

| Central Pacific | Union Pacific |
|---|---|
|  |  |

Which group worked on both railroads? (HI1)

### 3. Main Ideas

**a.** Why did the federal government want a transcontinental railroad built? (HI2)

**b.** How did the government encourage the building of the railroad? (HI2)

**c.** Why was standard time created? (HI2)

### 4. Critical Thinking

**Recognizing Effects** Which of the trends started by railroads are still part of the modern business world? (HI2)

**THINK ABOUT**
- railroads' effect on time
- the way they linked the economy
- the way they changed where people settled

**ACTIVITY OPTIONS**

**ART**

**TECHNOLOGY**

You have been asked to honor those who built the transcontinental railroad. Design a **memorial** or create the opening screen of a **multimedia presentation**. (REP1)

# The Rise of Big Business

| MAIN IDEA | WHY IT MATTERS NOW | TERMS & NAMES |
|---|---|---|
| Business leaders guided industrial expansion and created new ways of doing business. | These leaders developed the modern corporation, which dominates business today. | robber baron monopoly<br>corporation trust<br>John D. Rockefeller philanthropist<br>Andrew Carnegie Gilded Age |

## ONE AMERICAN'S STORY

In 1853, when Jay Gould was 17, he visited New York. Big-city wealth impressed Gould. After returning to his small hometown, he told a friend, "Crosby, I'm going to be rich. I've seen enough to realize what can be accomplished by means of riches, and I tell you I'm going to be rich."

Gould achieved his goal. By the time he died in 1892, he was worth $77 million. He made a lot of his money using methods that are illegal today—such as bribing officials and selling fake stock. Most of his deals involved railroads.

Jay Gould was a robber baron. A **robber baron** was a business leader who became wealthy through dishonest methods. This section discusses other business leaders and their companies.

Jay Gould used methods such as trickery and false reports to "bowl over" his competition.

## The Growth of Corporations

Until the late 1800s, most businesses were owned directly by one person or by a few partners. Then advances in technology made many business owners want to buy new equipment. One way to raise money to do so was to turn their businesses into corporations. A **corporation** is a business owned by investors who buy part of the company through shares of stock. A corporation has advantages over a privately owned business:

1. By selling stock, a corporation can raise large amounts of money.
2. A corporation has a special legal status and continues to exist after its founders die. Banks are more likely to lend a corporation money.
3. A corporation limits the risks to its investors, who do not have to pay off the corporation's debts.

In the late 1800s, few laws regulated corporations. This led to the growth of a few giant corporations that dominated American industry. The oil and steel industries are examples of this process.

**Taking Notes**

Use your chart to take notes about the growth of big business.

# The Oil and Steel Industries

As Section 1 explained, the oil and steel industries began to grow in the late 1800s. Two men dominated these industries. **John D. Rockefeller** led the oil industry, and **Andrew Carnegie** controlled the steel industry.

John D. Rockefeller built his first refinery in 1863. He decided that the best way to make money was to put his competitors out of business. A company that wipes out its competitors and controls an industry is a **monopoly**. Rockefeller bought other refineries. He made secret deals with railroads to carry his oil at a lower rate than his competitors' oil. He also built and purchased his own pipelines to carry oil.

Rockefeller's most famous move to end competition was to develop the trust in 1882. A **trust** is a legal body created to hold stock in many companies, often in the same industry. Rockefeller persuaded other oil companies to join his Standard Oil Trust. By 1880, the trust controlled 95 percent of all oil refining in the United States—and was able to set a high price for oil. The public had to pay that price because they couldn't buy oil from anyone else. As head of Standard Oil, Rockefeller earned millions of dollars. He also gained a reputation as a ruthless robber baron.

Businessmen in other industries began to follow Rockefeller's example. Trusts were formed in the sugar, cottonseed oil, and lead-mining industries. Many people felt that these monopolies were unfair and hurt the economy. But the government was slow to regulate them.

Rockefeller tried to control all the companies in his industry. By contrast, Andrew Carnegie tried to beat his competition in the steel industry

**Vocabulary**
refinery: a plant that purifies oil

*Reading* **History**

**A. Analyzing Points of View**
Why do you think people thought monopolies were unfair?

## AMERICA'S HISTORY MAKERS

### JOHN D. ROCKEFELLER
**1839–1937**

John D. Rockefeller was born to a poor family in upstate New York. From his mother, he learned the habit of frugality— he avoided unnecessary spending. "Willful waste makes woeful want" was a saying that Rockefeller's mother passed down to him.

By 1897, he had made millions and millions of dollars. Instead of keeping all that vast fortune for himself and his family, he spent the rest of his life donating money to several worthy causes.

### ANDREW CARNEGIE
**1835–1919**

When Andrew Carnegie was 12, he and his family moved from Scotland to Pennsylvania. Carnegie's first job was in a cotton mill.

Later he worked in a telegraph office. There he was noticed by a railroad superintendent, who hired Carnegie as his assistant. Carnegie learned not only about running a big business but also about investing money. Eventually, he quit to start his own business.

Despite his fortune, Carnegie once wrote that none of his earnings gave him as much happiness as his first week's pay.

**Compare the characters of Rockefeller and Carnegie. What do you think made each of them successful?**

by making the best and cheapest product. To do so, he sought to control all the processes related to the manufacture of steel. He bought the mines that supplied his iron ore, and the ships and railroads that carried that ore to his mills. Carnegie's company dominated the U.S. steel industry from 1889 to 1901, when he sold it to J.P. Morgan, the nation's most prominent banker.

Rockefeller and Carnegie were multimillionaires. They also were both **philanthropists,** people who give large sums of money to charities. Rockefeller donated money to the University of Chicago and Rockefeller University in New York. Carnegie also gave money to universities, and he built hundreds of public libraries. During his life, Rockefeller gave away more than $500 million. Carnegie gave away more than $350 million.

*Reading* **History**

**B. Contrasting**
How did the methods that Carnegie and Rockefeller used to eliminate competition differ?

## The Gilded Age

The rags-to-riches stories of people such as Rockefeller and Carnegie inspired many Americans to believe that they too could grow rich. Stories like theirs also inspired writer Horatio Alger. He wrote popular stories about poor boys who worked hard and became quite successful.

Inspiring as these stories were, they hid an important truth. Most people who made millions of dollars had not been raised in poverty. Many belonged to the upper classes and had attended college. Most began their careers with the advantage of money or family connections.

For the rich, the late 1800s was a time of fabulous wealth. Writers Mark Twain and Charles Warner named the era the **Gilded Age.** To

# HISTORY *through* ART

Artist Eastman Johnson painted this portrait of Alfredrick Smith Hatch's family, one of the wealthiest families in America, in 1870–1871. It shows the family in their New York mansion. Notice the expensive furnishings.

Photographer Jessie Tarbox Beals shot this photograph of a poor family in a tenement in 1910. A tenement is an apartment house that is usually rundown and overcrowded. This family probably had only this tiny space.

**How do these two images reflect continuity and change in American life during the Gilded Age?**

gild is to coat an object with gold leaf. Gilded decorations were popular during the era. But the name has a deeper meaning. Just as gold leaf can disguise an object of lesser value, so did the wealth of a few people mask society's problems, including corrupt politics and widespread poverty.

# The South Remains Agricultural

One region that knew great poverty was the South. The Civil War had left the South in ruins. Industry did grow in some Southern areas, such as Birmingham, Alabama. Founded in 1871, Birmingham developed as an iron- and steel-producing town. In addition, cotton mills opened from southern Virginia to Alabama. Compared with the Northern economy, however, the Southern economy grew very slowly after the war.

Most of the South remained agricultural. As you have read, many Southern landowners rented their land to sharecroppers who paid a large portion of their crops as rent. Often sharecroppers had to buy their seed and tools on credit. The price of cotton, the South's main crop, was very low. Sharecroppers made little money from selling cotton and had difficulty paying what they owed. And because most sharecroppers had little education, merchants cheated them, increasing their debt.

*Reading* **History**
C. Making Inferences What is Fortune implying about the storekeeper?

**A VOICE FROM THE PAST**

My father once kept an account . . . of the things he "took up" at the store as well as the storekeeper. When the accounts were footed [added] up at the end of the year the thing became serious. The storekeeper had $150 more against my father than appeared on the latter's book. . . . It is by this means that [sharecroppers] are swindled and kept forever in debt.

**T. Thomas Fortune,** testimony to a Senate committee, 1883

At the same time that sharecroppers struggled to break free of debt, workers in the industrial North also faced injustices. In the next section, you will learn how labor unions tried to fight back.

---

**Section 3 Assessment**

### 1. Terms & Names

**Explain the significance of:**
- robber baron
- corporation
- John D. Rockefeller
- Andrew Carnegie
- monopoly
- trust
- philanthropist
- Gilded Age

### 2. Using Graphics

Use a Venn diagram like the one shown to compare and contrast Rockefeller and Carnegie.

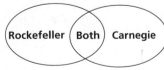

Whose business methods do you agree with more? (8.12.4)

### 3. Main Ideas

**a.** Why did the number of corporations grow in the late 1800s? (8.12.4)

**b.** Who is an example of a robber baron? Why? (8.12.4)

**c.** Why was the South so much less industrial than the North? (8.12.4)

### 4. Critical Thinking

**Forming and Supporting Opinions** Do you think that wealthy people have a duty to become philanthropists? Explain your opinion. (8.12.4)

**THINK ABOUT**
- Carnegie and Rockefeller
- how most wealthy people gain their money
- the differences between the rich and the poor

**ACTIVITY OPTIONS**

**MATH**

**SPEECH**

In your local or school library, look up the business cycle. Create a **graph** of the cycle for the last century or prepare an **oral report** to Congress on the trends. (HI6)

# Industry in the Midwest

The Midwest is the region around the Great Lakes and the Upper Mississippi Valley. The region saw explosive growth during the 1800s. The first wave came after 1825, when the Erie Canal linked the East with the Great Lakes region. The second wave, caused by investments in products related to the Civil War (1861–1865), saw a boom in mining, farming, forestry, and meat-packing. By 1890, 29 percent of the country's manufacturing employment was in the Midwest, and the next big wave of growth was just beginning. New industries included steel and steel products, such as train rails and skyscraper beams.

Transportation and resources spurred the region's growth. Coal, oil, iron ore, limestone, and lumber were abundant, and the land was fertile. Trains, rivers, and lakes connected the Midwest to markets in the East and South and brought in raw materials from the West. The map on page 599 shows the resources of the lower Great Lakes and how transportation by rail and water joined regions.

The industries of the Midwest used raw materials that came both from their own region and from other regions of the country. For example, the cattle in this photograph of the Chicago stockyards came by rail from the ranches of the West. In contrast, the logs being floated down the river came from the pine forests of Michigan and Wisconsin.

**CALIFORNIA STANDARDS**

**8.12.1** Trace patterns of agricultural and industrial development as they relate to climate, use of natural resources, markets, and trade and locate such development on a map.

## ARTIFACT FILE

**A Quick Dinner** Midwestern meat-packing companies advertised canned meats as a way to save time feeding a hungry family.

ARMOUR'S
*Veribest*
CANNED MEATS

**Affordable Housing** People began to build with wooden siding over a frame of wooden two-by-fours. These homes were cheap and quick to construct.

Lake Superior

CANADA

MAINE

VERMONT

NEW HAMPSHIRE

Lake Huron

MASS.

WISCONSIN

St. Paul

Minneapolis

MINNESOTA

Green Bay

MICHIGAN

Lake Michigan

Milwaukee

Madison

Grand Rapids

Lansing

Detroit

*Lake Erie*

Lake Ontario

*Erie Canal*

Buffalo

NEW YORK

CONN.    R.I.

New York

IOWA

Dubuque

Galena

Chicago

South Bend

Toledo

Cleveland

Youngstown

PENNSYLVANIA

NEW JERSEY

Philadelphia

Titusville

Pittsburgh

MARYLAND

DELAWARE

ILLINOIS

Springfield

INDIANA

Indianapolis

Cincinnati

OHIO

Columbus

*Ohio R.*

WEST VIRGINIA

VIRGINIA

MISSOURI

St. Louis

*Illinois R.*

*Mississippi R.*

KENTUCKY

N

0        100 Miles

0        200 Kilometers

NORTH CAROLINA

**Legend**
- Timbered region
- Prairie region
- Petroleum
- Sawmill center
- Iron and steel center
- Meatpacking
- Shipping
- Canal
- Railroad

Iron ore from the Lake Superior region and coal from southern Illinois were used to manufacture steel.

## On-Line Field Trip

**The Chicago Historical Society** in Chicago, Illinois, contains photographs, documents, and artifacts such as this Western Electric typewriter, made in 1900. Typewriters enabled office workers to produce neat, clean documents quickly.

For more about the Midwest . . .

## CONNECT TO GEOGRAPHY

1. **Region** What advantages did the Midwest have that helped it become highly industrialized?

2. **Human-Environment Interaction** How did the development of railroads add to the region's advantages?

See Geography Handbook, pages 4–5.

## CONNECT TO HISTORY

3. **Analyzing Causes** Chicago was a big meatpacking center. Why do you think that industry chose to locate there?

# Workers Organize

**④**

| MAIN IDEA | WHY IT MATTERS NOW | TERMS & NAMES |
|---|---|---|
| To increase their ability to bargain with management, workers formed labor unions. | Many of the modern benefits that workers take for granted were won by early unions. | sweatshop  Pullman Strike<br>Knights of Labor  Eugene V. Debs<br>socialism  Samuel Gompers<br>Haymarket affair  American Federation of Labor (AFL) |

**CALIFORNIA STANDARDS**

**8.12.4** Discuss entrepreneurs, industrialists, and bankers in politics, commerce, and industry (e.g., Andrew Carnegie, John D. Rockefeller, Leland Stanford).

**8.12.6** Discuss child labor, working conditions, and laissez-faire policies toward big business and examine the labor movement, including its leaders (e.g., Samuel Gompers), its demand for collective bargaining, and its strikes and protests over labor conditions.

**REP4** Students assess the credibility of primary and secondary sources and draw sound conclusions from them.

**HI3** Students explain the sources of historical continuity and how the combination of ideas and events explains the emergence of new patterns.

## ONE AMERICAN'S STORY

In 1867, Mary Harris Jones lost her husband and four children to yellow fever. Moving to Chicago, she started a dressmaking business. But the great Chicago fire of 1871 destroyed everything she owned. Instead of giving up in despair, Jones found a cause to fight for.

*A VOICE FROM THE PAST*

From the time of the Chicago fire I . . . decided to take an active part in the efforts of the working people to better the conditions under which they worked and lived.

**Mary Harris Jones,** *Autobiography of Mother Jones*

Jones became an effective labor leader. Workers loved her so much that they called her Mother Jones. In this section, you will learn about the labor movement of the late 1800s.

## Workers Face Hardships

Business owners of the late 1800s wanted to keep their profits high, so they ran their factories as cheaply as possible. Some cut costs by requiring workers to buy their own tools or to bring coal to heat the factories. Others refused to buy safety equipment. For example, railroads would not buy air brakes or automatic train-car couplers. Because of this, 30,000 railroad workers were injured and 2,000 killed every year.

If a factory became too crowded, the owner rarely built a larger one. Instead, the owner sent part of the work to be done by smaller businesses that critics called sweatshops. **Sweatshops** were places where workers labored long hours under poor conditions for low wages. Often children—some as young as five years old—worked alongside adults.

Factory and sweatshop workers did the same jobs, such as sewing collars or making buttonholes, all day long. They grew bored and did not

**Taking Notes**

Use your chart to take notes about organized labor.

GROWTH OF INDUSTRY AND RAILROADS

experience the satisfaction that came from making an entire product themselves. Further, both factory and sweatshop owners kept wages low. In the 1880s, the average weekly wage was less than $10. This barely paid a family's expenses. If a worker missed work due to illness or had any unexpected bills, the family went into debt. Most families could not survive unless everyone had a job. Between 1890 and 1910, 20 percent of boys and 10 percent of girls under age 15 had full-time jobs. Workers began to feel that only other working people could understand their troubles.

### A VOICE FROM THE PAST

They know what it is to bring up a family on ninety cents a day, to live on beans and corn meal week in and week out, to run in debt at the stores until you cannot get trusted [credit] any longer, to see the wife breaking down . . . , and the children growing sharp and fierce like wolves day after day because they don't get enough to eat.

**A railroad worker,** quoted in the *Philadelphia Inquirer,* July 23, 1877

Child labor was common in the late 1800s, and as this boy's bare feet demonstrate, safety practices were rare.

So discontented workers joined together to try to improve their lives. They formed labor unions—groups of workers that negotiated with business owners to obtain better wages and working conditions.

## Early Unions

As you read in Chapter 14, the first labor unions began in the mid-1800s but were unable to win many improvements for workers. After the Civil War, some unions started to form national organizations. One of these was the **Knights of Labor.** This was a loose federation of workers from all different trades. Unlike many labor organizations, the Knights allowed women and, after 1878, African-American workers to join their union. They inspired many people to support their cause.

Then, beginning in 1873, the United States fell into a serious economic depression. Over the next four years, millions of workers took pay cuts, and about one-fifth lost their jobs. In July 1877, the Baltimore and Ohio (B & O) Railroad declared a wage cut of 10 percent. The day the pay cut was to go into effect, B & O workers in Martinsburg, West Virginia, refused to run the trains. No labor union had called the strike. The workers themselves had stopped working on their own.

This work stoppage was the Railroad Strike of 1877. As the news spread, workers in many cities and in other industries joined in. This threw the country into turmoil. In several cities, state militias battled angry mobs. President Rutherford B. Hayes called out federal troops. Before the two-week strike ended, dozens of people were killed.

The strike did not prevent the railroad pay cut, but it showed how angry American workers had become. In 1884–1885, railroaders again went out on strike. This time they went on strike against the Union

Pacific and two other railroads. The strikers, who were members of the Knights of Labor, gained nationwide attention when they won their strike. Hundreds of thousands of new workers joined the union.

## Union Setbacks

The growth of labor unions scared many business leaders. They blamed the labor movement on socialists and anarchists. Socialists believe in **socialism**. In that economic system, all members of a society are equal owners of all businesses—they share the work and the profits. Anarchists are far more extreme. They want to abolish all governments.

Business and government leaders feared that unions might spread such ideas, so they tried to break union power. In Chicago in 1886, the McCormick Harvester Company locked out striking union members and hired strikebreakers to replace them. On May 3, union members, strikebreakers, and police clashed. One union member was killed.

The next day, a protest meeting was held at Haymarket Square. Held on a rainy evening, the rally was small. As police moved in to end the meeting, an unknown person threw a bomb. It killed 7 police and wounded about 60. The police then opened fire on the crowd, killing several people and wounding about a hundred. This conflict was called the **Haymarket affair**.

Afterward, the Chicago police arrested hundreds of union leaders, socialists, and anarchists. Opposition to unions increased. The membership in the Knights of Labor dropped rapidly—even though that wasn't the union that had called the meeting at Haymarket Square.

*Reading* **History**
**B. Recognizing Effects** Did the action of the bomber make it seem more or less likely that anarchists were behind union activity? Explain.

## The Homestead and Pullman Strikes

Labor conflicts grew more bitter. In 1892, Andrew Carnegie reduced wages at his steel mills in Homestead, Pennsylvania, but the union refused to accept the cut. The company responded by locking out union workers from the mills and announcing that it would hire nonunion labor. The company also hired 300 armed guards. In response, the locked-out workers gathered weapons. The guards arrived on July 6, and a battle broke out that left ten people dead. The Pennsylvania state militia began to escort the nonunion workers to the mills. After four months, the strike collapsed, breaking the union.

Workers lost another dispute in 1894. In that depression year, many railroad companies went bankrupt. To stay in business, the Pullman Palace Car Company, which made railroad cars,

**One night during the Pullman Strike, some 600 freight cars were burned.**

*Reading* **History**
**C. Analyzing Causes** Why was it so difficult for early unions to win against big business?

cut workers' pay 25 percent. But Pullman did not lower the rent it charged workers to live in company housing. After their rent was deducted from the lower pay, many Pullman workers took home almost nothing.

The Pullman workers began the **Pullman Strike,** a strike which spread throughout the rail industry in 1894. When the Pullman Company refused to negotiate, American Railway Union president **Eugene V. Debs** called on all U.S. railroad workers to refuse to handle Pullman cars. Rail traffic in much of the country came to a halt. President Grover Cleveland called out federal troops, which ended the strike. Debs was put in jail.

## Gompers Founds the AFL

Not all companies treated workers as harshly as Carnegie and Pullman did. For instance, in the 1880s, the soap company Procter & Gamble began to give its employees an extra half day off a week. It also began a profit-sharing plan, in which a company gives part of its profits to workers.

However, workers at most companies received low wages and few benefits. So in spite of the opposition to unions, the labor movement did not die. In 1886, labor leader **Samuel Gompers** helped found a new national organization of unions called the **American Federation of Labor (AFL).** Gompers served as AFL president for 37 years.

*Reading* **History**

**D. Identifying Problems** What problems did the AFL try to solve?

The AFL focused on improving working conditions. By using strikes, boycotts, and negotiation, the AFL won shorter working hours and better pay for workers. By 1904, it had about 1.7 million members.

In the next few decades, labor unions helped change the way all Americans worked. At the same time, city growth and immigration transformed America. You will read about that in Chapter 21.

*Now* **and then**

**MODERN BENEFITS WON BY UNIONS**

Today, many Americans work 40 hours per week—perhaps 9-to-5, Monday through Friday. Contrast this situation with the 10-to12-hour days of most 19th-century workers. The 8-hour day was one benefit won by labor unions. Other benefits unions won include workers' compensation (insurance that pays for injuries received on the job), pensions, and paid vacation.

Unions continue to fight to improve the lives of working Americans. In recent years they have tried to increase benefits for part-time and temporary workers. They have also fought for safety standards to prevent injuries, such as carpal tunnel syndrome, which affects many workers who use computers.

---

*Section* **4** *Assessment*

### 1. Terms & Names

**Explain the significance of:**
- sweatshop
- Knights of Labor
- socialism
- Haymarket affair
- Pullman Strike
- Eugene V. Debs
- Samuel Gompers
- American Federation of Labor (AFL)

### 2. Using Graphics

Review this section and find five key events to place on a time line like the one below.

1870   event   event   1910

event   event   event

What individuals played significant roles in these events? (CST2)

### 3. Main Ideas

**a.** What hardships did workers face in the late 1800s? (HI1)

**b.** What happened to unions after the protest at Haymarket Square? (HI2)

**c.** How did Carnegie's company break the union at the Homestead mills? (HI2)

### 4. Critical Thinking

**Drawing Conclusions** In your opinion, was the government more supportive of unions or business in the late 1800s? Explain. (REP4)

**THINK ABOUT**
- the Railroad Strike of 1877
- the Homestead Strike
- the Pullman Strike

**ACTIVITY OPTIONS**

**LANGUAGE ARTS**

**ART**

Decide whether unions should be encouraged. Write an **editorial** or create a **public message poster** expressing your opinion. (REP5)

## VISUAL SUMMARY

### An Industrial Society (8.12)

**Long-Term Causes**
- plentiful natural resources
- building of canals and railroads in early 1800s

**Immediate Causes**
- continued building of railroads in late 1800s
- growing population and high immigration
- new inventions and industrial processes
- investment capital and development of corporations

**GROWTH of INDUSTRY**

**Immediate Effects**
- increased amount of manufactured goods
- growth of large corporations, monopolies, and trusts
- poor conditions for workers in factories and sweatshops
- labor unions and strikes

STRIKE

**Long-Term Effects**
- economies of East and West linked together
- labor movement wins permanent changes, such as reduced working hours

## TERMS & NAMES

Briefly explain the significance of each of the following.

1. patent
2. business cycle
3. transcontinental railroad
4. standard time
5. corporation
6. John D. Rockefeller
7. Andrew Carnegie
8. Haymarket affair
9. Pullman Strike
10. American Federation of Labor (AFL)

## REVIEW QUESTIONS

### The Growth of Industry (pages 585–589)

1. How do inventors protect their rights to what they invent? (HI1)
2. What did Thomas Edison and Alexander Graham Bell invent? (HI1)

### Railroads Transform the Nation (pages 590–593)

3. What geographic feature made building the Central Pacific difficult? (HI2)
4. What took place when workers connected the Central Pacific and the Union Pacific? (HI1)

### The Rise of Big Business (pages 594–599)

5. What is a monopoly? (HI1)
6. What are trusts, and why did some people think they were bad for the country? (HI1)
7. Why did writers Mark Twain and Charles Warner name the late 1800s the Gilded Age? (HI1)

### Workers Organize (pages 600–603)

8. What ideas did businesses fear that unions would spread? (HI1)
9. How did the Pullman Strike begin and end? (HI2)
10. Which unions were led by Eugene V. Debs and Samuel Gompers? (HI1)

## CRITICAL THINKING

### 1. USING YOUR NOTES: ANALYZING CAUSES AND EFFECTS

Using your completed chart, answer the questions below. (HI2)

| Cause | Cause | Cause |
| --- | --- | --- |
| Cause | Cause | Cause |

**GROWTH OF INDUSTRY AND RAILROADS**

| Benefits of Growth | Problems of Growth |
| --- | --- |

a. How did the growth of railroads act as a cause of industrial growth?
b. Who do you think benefited most from the growth of industry? Explain.

### 2. THEME: ECONOMICS IN HISTORY

Who is someone from this chapter that might view the United States as a land of economic opportunity? Explain your answer. (REP5)

### 3. ANALYZING LEADERSHIP

What characteristics of a good leader did Mother Jones possess? (HI1)

### 4. APPLYING CITIZENSHIP SKILLS

Were John D. Rockefeller and Andrew Carnegie good citizens? Support your answer with details from this chapter. (HI1)

### 5. COMPARING

How were the problems of sharecroppers, described on page 597, similar to those of Pullman workers, described on pages 602–603? (CST1)

### 6. DRAWING CONCLUSIONS

Why do you think unions were more successful at attracting members in the late 1800s than in the early 1800s? (HI1)

### Interact with History

Now that you have read the chapter, would you change your mind about joining the strike? Explain.

Use the graph and your knowledge of U.S. history to answer questions 1 and 2.

Additional Test Practice, pp. S1–S22.

**U.S. Rails Produced,** *1860–1909*

Source: *Historical Statistics of the United States*

**1.** Which decade saw the biggest change in rail production? (8.12.1)

A. 1870–1879

B. 1880–1889

C. 1890–1899

D. 1900–1909

**2.** What does this graph indicate about what was happening in the railroad industry? (8.12.1)

A. The industry grew quickly and leveled off.

B. The industry was booming.

C. The industry was failing.

D. The industry grew in very small increments.

**Thomas Edison describes the process of inventing in this quotation. Use the quotation and your knowledge of U.S. history to answer question 3.**

*PRIMARY SOURCE*

It has been just so in all my inventions. The first step is an intuition—and comes with a burst, then difficulties arise. . . . "Bugs"—as such little faults and difficulties are called—show themselves and months of anxious watching, study and labor are requisite [needed] before commercial success—or failure—is certainly reached.

**Thomas Edison,** quoted in *Edison* by Matthew Josephson

**3.** According to Edison, what elements are common to the creation of his inventions? (8.12.9)

A. idea, observation, study, and work

B. observation, energy, study, and work

C. study, observation, work, and energy

D. work, idea, energy, and luck

**TEST PRACTICE**
CLASSZONE.COM

## ALTERNATIVE ASSESSMENT

### 1. ✒ WRITING ABOUT HISTORY

Assume the role of a labor leader, such as Mother Jones, and write a **speech** informing workers of their rights and urging them to unite. (REP5)

- Use library resources to write your speech.
- Focus your speech by addressing one major issue, such as safe working conditions, shorter working hours, or increased wages.

### 2. COOPERATIVE LEARNING

With your group, research the life of a business or labor leader from this chapter. Write and perform a monologue in which the leader discusses his or her life. Group members can share the responsibilities for researching and writing the monologue, finding costumes and props, and acting out the monologue. (REP3)

## INTEGRATED TECHNOLOGY

### DOING INTERNET RESEARCH

During different periods of U.S. history, scientific ideas have influenced technological developments. Use the Internet and the library to research how scientific ideas affected industrialization in the 19th century. (HI3)

- Use keywords such as *industrialization + electricity* to do research on the Internet.
- Look for Web sites for museums of science and industry.
- In your research, consider how the Bessemer process affected industrialization. Compile your research into a report.

For more about science and technology . . .

**INTERNET ACTIVITY**
CLASSZONE.COM

# Changes in American Life 1880–1914

Crowds of people walk, work, and shop on Mulberry Street in New York's Lower East Side.

Vendors sell an assortment of fruits and vegetables.

**1882**
Congress passes the Chinese Exclusion Act.

**1889**
The first electric elevator is installed.
Jane Addams founds Hull House.

**1888**
Electric trolleys are set up in Richmond, Virginia.

**1892**
Immigration center opens on Ellis Island.

**1893**
Columbian Exposition opens in Chicago.

**USA**
**World** 1880

**1889**
Brazil becomes a republic.
Barnum & Baily circus opens in London.

**1893**
Karl Benz invents the modern automobile.

East Coast cities like New York developed large immigrant neighborhoods.

Horse drawn carts are the most popular method for moving people and goods through the streets.

It is 1900, and you have decided to leave your native country. After a long and difficult voyage, you arrive in the United States. Now you need to find a new home and a job. You have to create a new life in a strange land.

# How will you make a home in your new country?

## What Do You Think?

- What caused you to leave your native country?
- What problems did you face on your voyage?
- What do you hope to find in the United States?

**RESEARCH LINKS**
CLASSZONE.COM

Visit the Chapter 21 links for more information about the changing American society.

**96**
preme Court
ablishes
eparate-but-
ual" doctrine
*Plessy* v.
*rguson* case.

**1906**
Earthquake
and fire
devastate
San Francisco.

**1909**
National Association for the
Advancement of Colored People
(NAACP) is founded.

1914

**96**
st modern
ympic Games
e held in
hens, Greece.

**1910**
Mexican
Revolution
begins.

*Changes in American Life* **607**

# Reading Strategy: Categorizing Information

## What Do You Know?

What do you think about when you hear the term *immigration?* Why do people move to different countries? What kinds of challenges might immigrants face in their new country?

### Think About

- what you know about immigration from the experience of your family
- what would make you want to move away from your home
- your responses to the Interact with History about making a home in a new country (see page 607)

**CALIFORNIA STANDARDS**

**Reading 2.0** Students read and understand grade-level-appropriate material. They describe and connect the essential ideas, arguments, and perspectives of the text by using their knowledge of text structure, organization, and purpose.

## What Do You Want to Know?

 What questions do you have about American life around 1900? Write them in your notebook before you read the chapter.

## Categorizing Information

To help you make sense of what you read, learn to categorize. Categorizing means sorting information into groups. The chart below will help you take notes and categorize the changes in American life that occurred during the late 19th and early 20th centuries.

 **See Skillbuilder Handbook, page R6.**

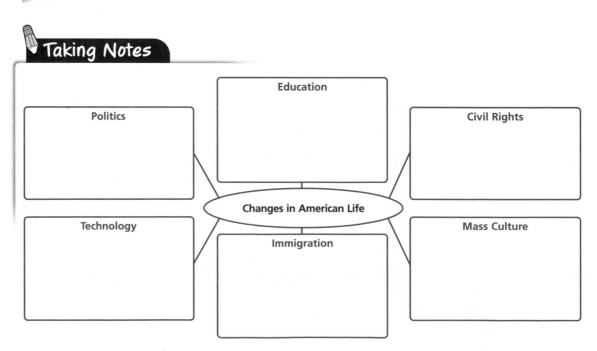

Taking Notes

- Politics
- Education
- Civil Rights
- Technology
- Changes in American Life
- Immigration
- Mass Culture

# Cities Grow and Change

| MAIN IDEA | WHY IT MATTERS NOW | TERMS & NAMES |
|---|---|---|

**MAIN IDEA**
Industrialization and immigration caused American cities to grow rapidly.

**WHY IT MATTERS NOW**
Modern American city life first emerged during this period.

**TERMS & NAMES**
urbanization
tenement
slum
social gospel

Jane Addams
Hull House
political machine
Tammany Hall

## ONE AMERICAN'S STORY

Carl Jensen came to the United States from Denmark in 1906. Like most of the millions of immigrants who came to America around the turn of the century, he immediately began to look for work.

### A VOICE FROM THE PAST

I wandered in search of work . . . waiting through rain and sleet and snow with gangs of longshoremen [dockworkers] to reach the boss before he finished picking the men he wanted. . . . Strong men crushed each other to the ground in their passion for work.

**Carl Jensen,** quoted in *A Sunday Between Wars*

Shipyards in growing cities

At the turn of the century, the promise of work drew millions of people like Carl Jensen from around the world to American cities. In this section, you will read about the rapid growth of American cities.

## Industrialization Expands Cities

The Industrial Revolution, which had been changing how people worked, also changed *where* people worked. Since colonial days, most Americans had lived and worked in rural areas. But in the late 1800s, that began to change as more and more people moved to cities to find jobs.

Industries were drawn to cities because cities offered good transportation and plentiful workers. Increasing numbers of factory jobs appeared in America's cities, followed by more workers to fill those jobs. The growth of cities that resulted from these changes is called **urbanization**.

Many of the people who moved to American cities were immigrants like Carl Jensen. People also migrated from America's farms to the cities. Once there, even workers with few skills could usually find steady work.

**Taking Notes**
Use your chart to take notes about changes in technology and politics.

Changes in American Life

Modern cities depend on skyscrapers to increase the space for people to live and work. Steel, electricity, and elevators make skyscrapers possible.

**1** **STEEL FRAMES** Steel beams can carry much more weight than brick or stone walls. The strength of the steel allows architects to design extremely tall buildings.

**2** **WINDOWS** In skyscrapers, the outer walls do not support the weight of the building; the steel beams do. As a result, many skyscrapers have outer walls made of glass to allow sunlight inside.

**3** **ELEVATOR** Tall buildings would be useless if people could not reach all of the floors. Elevators powered by electricity make such tall buildings practical.

# Technology Changes City Life

New technologies helped cities absorb the millions of people who flocked there. For example, new technologies made possible the construction of skyscrapers, buildings that looked tall enough to scrape the sky. Skyscrapers helped cities grow and made modern city life possible.

The elevator was a key invention for constructing tall buildings that could hold greater numbers of people. Before the 1860s, buildings rarely rose higher than four stories because it was hard for people to climb to the top. In 1889, the Otis Elevator Company installed the first electric elevator. Now buildings could be more than a few stories tall because people no longer had to walk up to the higher floors. As a result, buildings could hold more people.

The use of steel also helped to increase the height of buildings. In 1885, the Home Insurance Building in Chicago boasted an iron and steel skeleton that could hold the immense weight of the skyscraper's floors and walls. The building climbed to ten stories. Skyscrapers changed city skylines forever.

*Reading***History**
**A. Recognizing Effects** How did industry and technology help cities grow?

# The Streetcar City

As electricity helped change the way people traveled inside buildings, it also changed how people traveled around cities. Before industrialization, people walked or used horse-drawn vehicles to travel over land. But by 1900, electric streetcars in American cities were carrying more than 5 billion passengers a year. Streetcars and trains changed the walking city into the streetcar city.

**Background**
Streetcars are also called trolleys.

In 1888, Richmond, Virginia, became the first American city to have a transportation system powered by electricity. Other cities soon installed their own electric streetcars. The streetcars could quickly carry people to work and play all over the city. Some cities, such as Chicago, moved their electric streetcars above the street level, creating elevated, or "el," lines. Other cities, like New York, placed their city rail lines in underground tunnels, making subways.

The streetcar city spread outward from the city's center in ways the walking city never could. The ability to live farther away from work helped new suburbs to develop around cities. Some people in the suburbs wanted to become part of the city they bordered. That way they also could be served by the city's transportation system. Largely due to public transportation, cities expanded. For example, in 1889, Chicago annexed several suburbs and more than doubled its population as well as its area.

**Vocabulary**
annex: to add

## Urban Disasters and Slums

The concentration of people in cities increased the danger of disasters because people and buildings were packed closely together. For example, in 1906, a powerful earthquake rocked San Francisco. The tremors caused large fires to tear through the city. The central business district was destroyed. About 700 people died, and nearly $400 million in property was damaged. But natural disasters were not the only source of danger for the people of the cities. Poverty and disease also threatened their lives.

As people flocked to cities, overcrowding became a serious problem. It was especially serious for families who could not afford to buy a house. Such families usually lived in rented apartments or tenements. A **tenement** is an apartment house that is usually run-down and overcrowded.

Old buildings, landlord neglect, poor design, and little government control led to dangerous conditions in many tenements. Poor families who could not afford to rent a place of their own often needed to move in with other families. This resulted in severely overcrowded tenements. Inadequate garbage pick-up also caused problems. Tenants sometimes dumped their garbage into the narrow air shafts between tenements. There was little fresh air, and the smell was awful.

Many tenements had no running water. Residents had to collect water

*Reading*History
**B. Summarizing**
What was it like to live in a turn-of-the-century tenement?

**HISTORY** *through* ART

This photograph by Lewis Hine shows a family of Italian immigrants in their cramped, decaying tenement in New York City in 1912. Often photographers, such as Hine, had their subjects pose for their pictures to create the strongest effect.

**What effect do you think Hine wanted this photograph to have?**

611

from a faucet on the street. The water could be heated for bathing. But it was often unsafe for drinking. Sewage flowed in open gutters and threatened to spread disease among tenement dwellers.

A neighborhood with such overcrowded, dangerous housing was called a **slum.** The most famous example was New York City's Lower East Side. But every city had slums. Jacob Riis emigrated to New York from Denmark in 1870. His job as a police reporter took him to the city's worst slums. In 1890, he published How the Other Half Lives, which drew attention to the poor conditions in these neighborhoods.

## Reformers Attack Urban Problems

Many Americans were also disgusted by poverty and slums. Some people fought to reform, or create changes, that would solve these problems. They were known as urban reformers.

The social gospel movement provided one basis for these beliefs. The **social gospel** movement aimed to improve the lives of the poor. Led by Protestant ministers, the ideas of the movement were based on Christian values. The most important concerns of the social gospel movement were labor reforms, such as abolishing child labor. Some reformers inspired by the movement opened settlement houses. They helped the poor and immigrants improve their lives. Settlement houses offered services such as daycare, education, and health care to needy people in slum neighborhoods.

*Reading* **History**
C. Making Inferences How did Christian values support the social gospel movement?

# CITIZENSHIP TODAY

## Community Service

Since the United States began, citizens have shared concerns about their communities. Many citizens, such as Jane Addams in 1889, have identified problems and proposed solutions to them.

In 1993, sixth-grader David Levitt asked his principal if the leftover food from the school cafeteria could be sent to a program to feed needy people. David was told that many restrictions prevented giving away the food.

Determined to get food to people who needed it, David talked to the school board, the state health department, and private companies to convince them to back his program. Today, more than 500,000 pounds of food from schools has been given to hungry people in the Seminole, Florida, area.

**David Levitt carries supplies for his food pantry program.**

### How Do You Participate in Your Community?

1. In a small group, think about problems within your community. Make a list of those problems.

2. Choose one problem to work on.

3. Gather information about the problem. Keep a log of your sources to use again.

4. After you gather information, brainstorm solutions to the problem. Create a plan to carry out one solution.

5. Present the problem and your plan to the class.

   **See the Citizenship Handbook, page 286.**

For more about community service . . .

**RESEARCH LINKS**
CLASSZONE.COM

Many settlement house founders were educated middle-class women. **Jane Addams** founded Chicago's **Hull House** in 1889 with Ellen Gates Starr. Hull House soon became a model for other settlement houses, including New York's Henry Street Settlement House, which Lillian D. Wald established in 1889.

## Political Machines Run Cities

Political machines were another type of organization that addressed the problems of the city. A **political machine** is an organization that influences enough votes to control a local government.

Political machines gained support by trading favors for votes. For example, machine bosses gave jobs or food to supporters. In return, supporters worked and voted for the machine. Political machines also did many illegal things. They broke rules to win elections. They accepted bribes to affect government actions.

The most famous political machine was **Tammany Hall** in New York City. It was led by William Marcy Tweed. Along with his greedy friends, "Boss" Tweed stole enormous amounts of money from the city.

*Reading History*
**D. Comparing and Contrasting** How were settlement houses and political machines similar? How were they different?

Despite such corruption, political machines did a number of good things for cities. They built parks, sewers, schools, roads, and orphanages in many cities. In addition, machine politicians often helped immigrants get settled in the United States by helping them find jobs or homes. Many immigrants gratefully supported the political machine after this kind of help. In the next section, you will learn more about immigration.

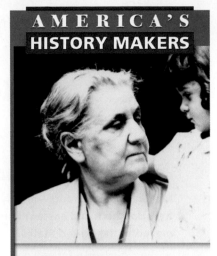

---

### Section 1 Assessment

**1. Terms & Names**

**Explain the significance of:**
• urbanization
• tenement
• slum
• social gospel
• Jane Addams
• Hull House
• political machine
• Tammany Hall

**2. Using Graphics**

Use a chart like the one below to show the causes and effects of urban growth. (HI2)

| Cause | Effect |
|---|---|
| Steel | |
| Elevators | |
| Streetcars | |
| Immigration | |

**3. Main Ideas**

**a.** Why did immigrants and farmers settle in big cities at the end of the 19th century? (HI1)

**b.** What are two inventions that made modern city life possible? (HI1)

**c.** What urban problems did reformers try to solve? (HI1)

**4. Critical Thinking**

**Evaluating** What were some of the advantages and disadvantages of machine politics? (HI1)

**THINK ABOUT**
• the problems faced by immigrants and cities
• Tammany Hall and "Boss" Tweed

**ACTIVITY OPTIONS**

**LANGUAGE ARTS**

**ART**

It is 1900, and you have just moved to an American city. Write a **letter** to friends back home or draw a **picture** that describes your new home. (HI1)

# The New Immigrants

| MAIN IDEA | WHY IT MATTERS NOW | TERMS & NAMES |
| --- | --- | --- |
| Millions of immigrants—mostly from southern and eastern Europe—moved to the United States. | The new immigrants had an important role in shaping American culture in the 20th century. | new immigrants<br>Ellis Island<br>Angel Island<br>melting pot<br>assimilation<br>Chinese Exclusion Act |

**CALIFORNIA STANDARDS**

**8.12.5** Examine the location and effects of urbanization, renewed immigration, and industrialization (e.g., the effects on social fabric of cities, wealth and economic opportunity, the conservation movement).

**8.12.7** Identify the new sources of large-scale immigration and the contributions of immigrants to the building of cities and the economy; explain the ways in which new social and economic patterns encouraged assimilation of new-comers into the mainstream amidst growing cultural diversity; and discuss the new wave of nativism.

**REP4** Students assess the credibility of primary and secondary sources and draw sound conclusions from them.

## ONE AMERICAN'S STORY

In 1907, 10-year-old Edward Corsi left Italy to come to America. After two weeks at sea, he caught sight of the Statue of Liberty.

### A VOICE FROM THE PAST

This symbol of America . . . inspired awe in the hopeful immigrants. Many older persons among us, burdened with a thousand memories of what they were leaving behind, had been openly weeping. . . . Now somehow steadied, I suppose, by the concreteness of the symbol of America's freedom, they dried their tears.

**Edward Corsi,** *In the Shadow of Liberty*

In this section, you will learn about the immigrants who came to the United States around 1900 and their effect on the nation.

The Statue of Liberty and Ellis Island were two of the first things many immigrants saw of the United States.

## The New Immigrants

Until the 1890s, most immigrants to the United States had come from northern and western Europe. But after 1900, fewer northern Europeans immigrated, and more southern and eastern Europeans did. This later group of immigrants came to be known as the **new immigrants.** Southern Italy sent large numbers of immigrants. Many Jews from eastern Europe and Slavic peoples, such as Poles and Russians, also immigrated.

**Ellis Island** was the first stop for most immigrants from Europe. There, they were processed before they could enter the United States. First, they had to pass a physical examination. Those with serious health problems or diseases were sent home. Next, they were asked a series of questions: Name? Occupation? How much money do you have?

Slovenian immigrant Louis Adamic described the night he spent on Ellis Island. He and many other immigrants slept in a huge hall. Lacking a warm blanket, the young man "shivered, sleepless, all night, listening to snores" and dreams "in perhaps a dozen different languages."

**Taking Notes**

Use your chart to take notes about changes in immigration.

Changes in American Life

## U.S. Immigration, *1841–1900*

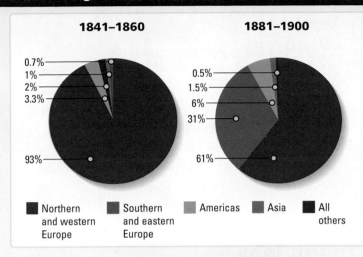

**1841–1860**

- 0.7%
- 1%
- 2%
- 3.3%
- 93%

**1881–1900**

- 0.5%
- 1.5%
- 6%
- 31%
- 61%

■ Northern and western Europe ■ Southern and eastern Europe ■ Americas ■ Asia ■ All others

**1841–1900**

Immigrants (in millions)

Years

Source: *Historical Statistics of the United States*

**SKILLBUILDER Interpreting Graphs**

1. *About how many immigrants came to the United States from 1841 to 1860?*
2. *About how many southern and eastern European immigrants came to the United States from 1881 to 1900?*

While European immigrants passed through Ellis Island on the East Coast, Asians landed at **Angel Island** in San Francisco Bay. In Angel Island's filthy buildings, most Chinese immigrants were held for several weeks. One unhappy prisoner carved in the wall, "For what reason must I sit in jail? It is only because my country is weak and my family poor."

Many Mexican immigrants entered the United States through Texas. Jesús [heh•SOOS] Garza recalled how simple his journey was. "I paid my $8, passed my examination, then changed my Mexican coins for American money and went to San Antonio, Texas."

## Settling in America

Immigrants settled where they could find jobs. Many found work in American factories. The immigrants contributed to the growth of cities such as New York, Boston, Philadelphia, Pittsburgh, and Chicago. About half of the new immigrants settled in four industrial states: Massachusetts, New York, Pennsylvania, and Illinois.

Once in America, newer immigrants looked for people from the same village in the old country to help them find jobs and housing. People with similar ethnic backgrounds often moved to the same neighborhoods. As a result, ethnic neighborhoods with names like "Little Italy" and "Chinatown" became common in American cities.

The immigrants living in these communities pooled money to build places of worship for their neighborhoods. They published newspapers in their native languages. They commonly supported political machines, often led by politicians who had also come from their country of origin. Such politicians could speak the native language and help new arrivals feel comfortable. Most importantly, politicians could help immigrants find jobs.

*Reading*History
**A. Identifying Problems** How did immigrants show creativity in solving problems?

*"I paid my $8, passed my examination, . . . and went to San Antonio."*

**Jesús Garza**

*Changes in American Life* **615**

Labor unions helped immigrants fit into American life. The various languages on the signs at this rally show the ethnic diversity in the labor movement.

## Immigrants Take Tough Jobs

Immigrants took whatever jobs they could get. Many immigrants worked in Northern factories. As you read in Chapter 20, most factories offered low wages, long hours, and unsafe conditions. Many European immigrants who had settled in the East found jobs in sweatshops for about $10 a week. One observer of textile sweatshops noted, "The faces, hands, and arms to the elbows of everyone in the room are black with the color of the cloth on which they are working."

While European immigrants settled mostly in the East and Midwest, Asian immigrants settled mostly in the West. Many Chinese immigrants worked on the railroad. Others settled in Western cities where they set up businesses such as restaurants and stores. Large numbers of Japanese immigrants first came to Hawaii in 1885 to work on sugar plantations. Others settled on the mainland, where they fished, farmed, and worked in mines.

Immigrants from Mexico came to the Southwest. Mexican immigration increased after 1910 when revolution in that country forced people to flee. Growers and ranchers in California and Texas used the cheap labor Mexican immigrants offered. Owners of copper mines in Arizona hired Mexicans as well.

*Reading* **History**

**B. Making Inferences** What did all the immigrants seem to have in common?

## Becoming Americans

Some Americans have described the United States as a **melting pot,** or a place where cultures blend. The new immigrants blended into American society as earlier immigrants had. This process of blending into society is called **assimilation.** Most new immigrants were eager to assimilate. To do so, they studied English and how to be American citizens.

Many workers began to assimilate at work. Employers and labor unions both tried to "Americanize" immigrant workers by offering classes in citizenship and English. A Lithuanian worker explained that his labor union helped him learn to "read and speak and enjoy life like an American." He then became an interpreter for the union to help other Lithuanians become Americans.

At the same time the immigrants were learning about America, they were also *changing* America. Immigrants did not give up their cultures right away. Bits and pieces of immigrant languages, foods, and music worked their way into the rest of American culture.

Despite their efforts to assimilate, immigrants faced prejudice from native-born Americans. Many Protestants feared the arrival of Catholics and Jews. Other native-born Americans thought immigrants would not fit into democratic society because they would be controlled by political machines. Such prejudices led some native-born Americans to push for restrictions to reduce the numbers of new immigrants coming to America.

## Restrictions on Immigration

Many native-born Americans also feared they would have to compete with immigrants for jobs. Immigrants were desperate for jobs and would often take work for lower wages in worse conditions than other Americans. Some Americans worried that there would not be enough jobs for everyone. These fears led to an upsurge in nativist opposition to immigration. In 1882, Congress began to pass laws to restrict immigration. They placed taxes on new immigrants and banned specific groups, such as beggars and people with diseases. Nonwhites faced deeper prejudice than European immigrants, and Asians faced some of the worst. In 1882, Congress passed the **Chinese Exclusion Act**. It banned Chinese immigration for ten years. It was renewed twice and lasted until 1942.

The Chinese Exclusion Act was not the only example of prejudice in America around 1900. As you will read in the next section, racial discrimination was common throughout the United States.

**Background**
The Chinese Exclusion Act was renewed in 1892. In 1902, the ban was made permanent. It was not repealed until 1943.

**Now** *and* **then**

**LATE 20TH-CENTURY IMMIGRATION**

Historians refer to the people who came to the United States around 1900 as the "new immigrants." But an even newer wave of immigrants has been coming to the United States since the 1980s.

From 1981 to 1996, nearly 13.5 million people immigrated to the United States. About 6.5 million came from other nations in the Western Hemisphere. In the same period, 4.8 million people came from Asia.

---

*Section* **2** *Assessment*

### 1. Terms & Names

**Explain the significance of:**
- new immigrants
- Ellis Island
- Angel Island
- melting pot
- assimilation
- Chinese Exclusion Act

### 2. Using Graphics

Use a chart to take notes on immigrant experiences in the United States.

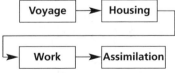

Which part of the immigrant experience was the most difficult? (8.12.7)

### 3. Main Ideas

**a.** How were the new immigrants different from earlier immigrants? (8.12.7)

**b.** How did immigrants support one another? (8.12.7)

**c.** Why did nonwhite immigrants have a harder time assimilating than European immigrants did? (8.12.7)

### 4. Critical Thinking

**Making Generalizations**
How well does the idea of the melting pot reflect U.S. immigration around 1900? (8.12.7)

**THINK ABOUT**
- assimilation
- immigrant languages and cultures
- ethnic neighborhoods

---

**ACTIVITY OPTIONS**

**MATH**

**GEOGRAPHY**

Research immigration to your city or state. Create a **spreadsheet** of this information or draw a **map** showing immigration routes. (CST3)

from

# Dragonwings

## by Laurence Yep

**CALIFORNIA STANDARDS**

**Reading 3.2** Evaluate the structural elements of the plot (e.g., subplots, parallel episodes, climax), the plot's development, and the way in which conflicts are (or are not) addressed and resolved.

In 1903, eight-year-old Moon Shadow makes the long journey from China to join his father in San Francisco. After living for a time in Chinatown, the two move into a white neighborhood where Moon Shadow's father takes a job as a handyman working for Miss Whitlaw, who runs a boarding house for elderly people. Moon Shadow makes friends with Miss Whitlaw's niece Robin. In April of 1906, their world is turned upside down. As Moon Shadow goes outside to fetch water from the pump, an earthquake hits San Francisco, endangering rich and poor, young and old, American and immigrant alike.

The morning was filled with that soft, gentle twilight of spring, when everything is filled with soft, dreamy colors and shapes; so when the earthquake hit, I did not believe it at first. It seemed like a nightmare where everything you take to be the rock-hard, solid basis for reality becomes unreal.

Wood and stone and brick and the very earth became fluidlike. The pail beneath the pump jumped and rattled like a spider dancing on a hot stove. The ground deliberately seemed to slide right out from under me. I landed on my back hard enough to drive the wind from my lungs. The whole world had become unglued. Our stable and Miss Whitlaw's house and the tenements to either side heaved and bobbed up and down, riding the ground like ships on a heavy sea. Down the alley mouth, I could see the cobblestone street **undulate**[1] and twist like a red-backed snake.

From inside our stable, I could hear the cups and plates begin to rattle on their shelves, and the equipment on Father's work table clattered and rumbled **ominously**.[2]

Suddenly the door banged open and Father stumbled out with his clothes all in a bundle. "It's an earthquake, I think," he shouted. He had washed his hair the night before and had not had time to twist it into a **queue**,[3] so it hung down his back long and black.

He looked around in the back yard. It was such a wide, open space that we were fairly safe there. Certainly more safe than in the frame doorway of our stable. He got into his pants and shirt and then his socks and boots.

"Do you think one of the mean dragons is doing all this?" I asked him.

"Maybe. Maybe not." Father had sat down to stuff his feet into his boots. "Time to wonder about that later. Now you wait here."

He started to get to his feet when the second tremor shook and he fell forward flat on his face. I heard the city bells ringing. They were rung by no human hand—the earthquake had just shaken them in their steeples. The second tremor was worse than the first. From all over came an immense wall of noise: of metal tearing, of bricks crashing, of wood breaking free from wood nails, and all. Everywhere, what man had built came undone. I was looking at a tenement house to our right and it just seemed to shudder and then collapse. One moment there were solid wooden walls and the next moment it had fallen with the cracking of wood and the tinkling of glass and the screams of people inside.

---

1. **undulate:** to move like a wave.
2. **ominously:** threateningly.
3. **queue:** a long braid of hair hanging down the back.

Mercifully, for a moment, it was lost to view in the cloud of dust that rose up. The debris surged against Miss Whitlaw's fence and toppled it over with a creak and a groan and a crash. I saw an arm sticking up from the mound of rubble and the hand was twisted at an impossible angle from the wrist. Coughing, Father pulled at my arm. "Stay here now," he ordered and started for Miss Whitlaw's.

I turned. Her house was still standing, but the tenement house to the left had partially collapsed; the wall on our side and part of the front and back had just fallen down, revealing the apartments within: the laundry hanging from lines, the old brass beds, and a few lucky if astonished people just looking out dazedly on what had once been walls. I could see Jack sitting up in bed with his two brothers. His mother and father were standing by the bed holding on to Maisie. Their whole family crowded into a tiny two-room apartment. Then they were gone, disappearing in a cloud of dust and debris as the walls and floor collapsed. Father held me as I cried.

Miss Whitlaw came out onto her porch in her nightdress and a shawl. She pulled the shawl tighter about her shoulders. *"Are you all right?"*

*"Yes,"* Father said, patting me on the back.

*"Aren't we, Moon Shadow?"*

"Yes." I wiped my eyes on my sleeves.

*"Is everyone okay inside?"* Father asked Miss Whitlaw.

She nodded. We joined her on the porch and walked with her into her house. Robin was sitting on the stairs that led up to the second floor. She huddled up, looking no longer like the noisy, **boisterous**[4] girl I knew. The front door was open before her. She must have gone outside to look. *"Just about the whole street's gone."*

From up the stairs we could hear the **querulous**[5] old voices of the boarders demanding to know what had happened. Miss Whitlaw shouted up the stairs, "Everything's all right."

*"Are you sure?"* Father asked quietly.

Miss Whitlaw laughed. *"From top to bottom. Papa always built well. He said he wanted a house that could hold a herd of thundering elephants—that was what he always called Mama's folks. He never liked them much."*

*"It's gone,"* Robin repeated. *"Just about the whole street's gone."*

"Oh, really now." Miss Whitlaw walked past Robin. We followed her out the front door to the front porch. Robin was right.

---

4. **boisterous:** loud, noisy.

5. **querulous:** complaining.

San Franciscans watch the destruction caused by the 1906 earthquake and the resulting fire.

## CONNECT TO HISTORY

1. **Finding Main Ideas** How does the earthquake affect the neighborhood that Moon Shadow lives in?

 **See Skillbuilder Handbook, page R5.**

## CONNECT TO TODAY

2. **Researching** What happened in San Francisco after the quake? Did it affect the immigrants differently than others?

For more about the San Francisco earthquake . . .

 RESEARCH LINKS
CLASSZONE.COM

# Segregation and Discrimination

**CALIFORNIA STANDARDS**

**8.11.2** Identify the push-pull factors in the movement of former slaves to the cities in the North and to the West and their differing experiences in those regions (e.g., the experiences of Buffalo Soldiers).

**8.11.3** Understand the effects of the Freedmen's Bureau and the restrictions placed on the rights and opportunities of freedmen, including racial segregation and "Jim Crow" laws.

**8.12.5** Examine the location and effects of urbanization, renewed immigration, and industrialization (e.g., the effects on social fabric of cities, wealth and economic opportunity, the conservation movement).

**8.12.7** Identify the new sources of large-scale immigration and the contributions of immigrants to the building of cities and the economy; explain the ways in which new social and economic patterns encouraged assimilation of newcomers into the mainstream amidst growing cultural diversity; and discuss the new wave of nativism.

**Taking Notes**

Use your chart to take notes about changes in civil rights.

Changes in American Life

## ONE AMERICAN'S STORY

African-American sisters Bessie and Sadie Delany grew up in North Carolina in the early 20th century. Almost 100 years later, they described their first taste of <u>racial discrimination</u>, different treatment on the basis of race.

Bessie (left) and Sadie Delany

### A VOICE FROM THE PAST

We were about five and seven years old. . . . Mama and Papa used to take us to Pullen Park . . . and that particular day, the trolley driver told us to go to the back. We children objected loudly, because we always liked to sit in the front. . . . But Mama and Papa just gently told us to hush and took us to the back.

**Sarah L. Delany and A. Elizabeth Delany,** *Having Our Say*

As you will read in this section, racial discrimination was common throughout the United States.

## Racism Causes Discrimination

As you read in earlier chapters, racist attitudes had been developing in America since the introduction of slavery. The low social rank held by slaves led many whites to believe that whites were superior to blacks. Most whites held similar attitudes toward Asians, Native Americans, and Latin Americans. Even most scientists of the day believed that whites were superior to nonwhites. However, no scientists believe this today.

Such attitudes led whites to discriminate against nonwhites across the country. The most obvious example of racial discrimination was in the South. Southern blacks had their first taste of political power during Reconstruction. (See Chapter 18.) But when Reconstruction ended in 1877, Southern states began to restrict African Americans' rights.

## Segregation Expands in the South

One way for whites to weaken African-American political power was to restrict their voting rights. For example, Southern states passed laws that set up literacy, or reading, tests and poll taxes to prevent African Americans from voting. White officials made sure that blacks failed literacy tests by giving unfair exams. For example, white officials sometimes gave blacks tests written in Latin. Poll taxes kept many blacks from voting because they didn't have enough cash to pay the tax.

_Reading_**History**

**A. Recognizing Effects** What was the purpose behind literacy tests, poll taxes, and grandfather clauses?

Such laws threatened to prevent poor whites from voting, too. To keep them from losing the vote, several Southern states added grandfather clauses to their constitutions. Grandfather clauses stated that a man could vote if he or an ancestor, such as a grandfather, had been eligible to vote before 1867. Before that date, most African Americans, free or enslaved, did not have the right to vote. Whites could use the grandfather clause to protect their voting rights. Blacks could not.

In addition to voting restrictions, African Americans faced Jim Crow laws. **Jim Crow** laws were extensions of the "black codes" of Reconstruction meant to enforce **segregation,** or separation, of white and black people in public places. As a result, separate schools, trolley seats, and restrooms were common throughout the South.

## *Plessy v. Ferguson*

**HISTORIC DECISIONS**
_OF THE SUPREME COURT_

For more information on *Plessy* v. *Ferguson,* see pp. 748–749.

African Americans resisted segregation, but they had little power to stop it. In 1892, Homer Plessy, an African American, sued a railroad company, arguing that segregated seating violated his Fourteenth Amendment right to "equal protection of the laws."

In 1896, the case of ***Plessy v. Ferguson*** reached the Supreme Court. The Court ruled against Plessy. It argued that "separate but equal" facilities did not violate the Fourteenth Amendment. This decision allowed Southern states to maintain segregated institutions.

_Reading_**History**

**B. Identifying Problems** Why was a policy of "separate but equal" unfair?

But the separate facilities were not equal. White-controlled governments and companies allowed the facilities for African Americans to decay. African Americans would have to organize to fight for equality.

Segregation forced African Americans to use separate entrances from whites and to attend separate, usually inferior, schools like the one shown below.

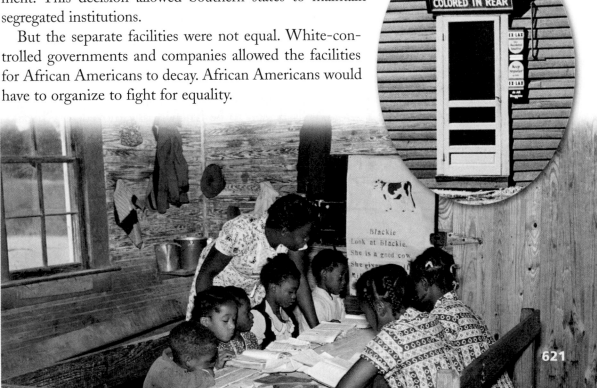

## African Americans Organize

<u>Booker T. Washington</u> was an early leader in the effort to achieve equality. He had been born into slavery. But after the Civil War, he became a teacher. In 1881, he founded the Tuskegee Institute in Alabama to help African Americans learn trades and gain economic strength. Washington hired talented teachers and scholars, such as George Washington Carver.

To gain white support for Tuskegee, Washington did not openly challenge segregation. As he said in an 1895 speech in Atlanta, in "purely social matters" whites and blacks "can be as separate as the fingers, yet one as the hand in all things essential to mutual progress."

However, some blacks disagreed with Washington's views. <u>W. E. B. Du Bois</u> (doo•BOYS) encouraged African Americans to reject segregation.

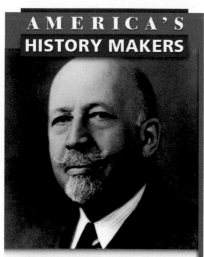

### AMERICA'S HISTORY MAKERS

**W. E. B. DU BOIS**

**1868–1963**

W. E. B. Du Bois grew up in a middle-class home. He went to college and earned his doctorate at Harvard. Du Bois became one of the most distinguished scholars of the 20th century.

Du Bois fought against segregation. He believed that the best way to end it would be to have educated African Americans lead the fight. He referred to this group of educated African Americans as the "Talented Tenth"—the most educated 10 percent of African Americans.

**Why do you think Du Bois believed the Talented Tenth should lead the fight against segregation?**

*A VOICE FROM THE PAST*

Is it possible . . . that nine millions of men can make effective progress in economic lines if they are deprived of political rights? . . . If history and reason give any distinct answer to these questions, it is an emphatic *No.*

**W. E. B. Du Bois,** *The Souls of Black Folk*

In 1909, Du Bois and other reformers founded the National Association for the Advancement of Colored People, or the <u>NAACP</u>. The NAACP played a major role in ending segregation in the 20th century.

*Reading*History

**C. Making Inferences** In what way did Washington and Du Bois disagree about how to achieve African-American progress?

## Violence in the South and North

Besides discrimination, African Americans in the South also faced violence. The Ku Klux Klan, which first appeared during Reconstruction, used violence to keep blacks from challenging segregation. More than 2,500 African Americans were lynched between 1885 and 1900.

<u>Ida B. Wells,</u> an African-American journalist from Memphis, led the fight against lynching. After three of her friends were lynched in 1892, she mounted an anti-lynching campaign in her newspaper. When whites called for Wells herself to be lynched, she moved to Chicago. But she continued her work against lynching. (See Interactive Primary Sources, page 624.)

Like Wells, many blacks moved north to escape discrimination. Public facilities there were not segregated by law. But Northern whites still discriminated against blacks. Blacks could not get housing in white neighborhoods and usually were denied good jobs. Anti-black feelings among whites sometimes led to violence. In 1908, whites in Springfield, Illinois, attacked blacks who had moved there. The whites lynched two blacks within a half mile of Abraham Lincoln's home.

# Racism in the West

Chinese immigrants who came to the West in the 1800s also faced severe discrimination as part of the new wave of nativism against recent immigrants.

Chinese laborers received lower wages than whites for the same work. Sometimes, Chinese workers faced violence. In 1885, white workers in Rock Springs, Wyoming, refused to work in the same mine as Chinese workers. The whites stormed through the Chinese part of town, shooting Chinese people and burning buildings. During the attack, 28 Chinese people were killed and 15 were wounded.

At the same time, Mexicans and African Americans who came to the American Southwest were forced into peonage (PEE•uh•nihj). In this system of labor, people are forced to work until they have paid off debts. Congress outlawed peonage in 1867, but some workers were still forced to work to repay debts. In 1911, the U.S. Supreme Court declared such labor to be the same as peonage. As a result, the Court struck down such forms of labor as a violation of the Thirteenth Amendment.

Despite the problems caused by racism, many Americans had new opportunities to enjoy their lives at the turn of the century. In the next section, you will learn about changes in people's daily lives.

The Workingmen's Party of California produced this anti-Chinese poster during the 1880s.

**Background**
The Thirteenth Amendment banned "involuntary servitude"—another term for slavery.

---

## Section 3 Assessment

### 1. Terms & Names

**Explain the significance of:**
- racial discrimination
- Jim Crow
- segregation
- *Plessy* v. *Ferguson*
- Booker T. Washington
- W. E. B. Du Bois
- NAACP
- Ida B. Wells

### 2. Using Graphics

Use a chart to identify people and events related to racial discrimination at the turn of the century.

| People | |
|--------|--|
| Events | |

Which person do you think did the most to end racial discrimination? (HI1)

### 3. Main Ideas

**a.** What were Jim Crow laws? (8.12.7)

**b.** How did discrimination against African Americans in the North differ from discrimination in the South? (8.12.7)

**c.** What did Chinese immigrants and Mexican immigrants have in common? (8.12.7)

### 4. Critical Thinking

**Solving Problems** What could have been done to end racial discrimination against nonwhites in the United States at the turn of the century? (8.12.7)

**THINK ABOUT**
- attitudes of whites about nonwhites
- the efforts of nonwhites to find jobs and security
- competition for jobs

### ACTIVITY OPTIONS

**LANGUAGE ARTS**

**TECHNOLOGY**

Research a civil rights leader from the turn of the century. Write a short **biography** of that person or design a **Web site** devoted to the work of that person. (HI1)

# from *Crusade for Justice* (1892)

**CALIFORNIA STANDARDS**

**REP4** Students assess the credibility of primary and secondary sources and draw sound conclusions from them.

**Reading 2.3** Find similarities and differences between texts in the treatment, scope, or organization of ideas.

**Setting the Stage** Ida B. Wells was the editor of the *Free Speech and Headlight,* a small Baptist newspaper in Memphis, Tennessee. She used the paper to attack the evils of Jim Crow, especially lynching. In her autobiography, *Crusade for Justice,* she described the events that led to the lynching of three of her friends. **See Primary Source Explorer**

**A CLOSER LOOK**

**ECONOMIC COMPETITION**

Moss, McDowell, and Stewart were African Americans who opened a grocery store near a white-owned store in a black neighborhood.

**1. Why might the opening of the black-owned grocery store lead to problems?**

**A CLOSER LOOK**

**LYNCHINGS**

There was a sharp increase in the number of lynchings in the United States in the 1890s. From 1891 to 1900, more than 1,100 African Americans were lynched.

**2. Why do you think the number of lynchings increased in this period?**

**A CLOSER LOOK**

**THE GREAT MIGRATION**

Between 1890 and 1920, hundreds of thousands of African Americans left the South to escape racism. This movement is called the Great Migration.

**3. Why does Wells's newspaper advise African Americans to move away in the wake of the lynching?**

While I was thus carrying on the work of my newspaper . . . there came the lynching in Memphis which changed the whole course of my life. . . .

Thomas Moss, Calvin McDowell, and Henry Stewart owned and operated a grocery store. . . . There was already a grocery owned and operated by a white man who **hitherto**[1] had had a **monopoly**[2] on the trade of this thickly populated colored suburb. Thomas's grocery changed all that, and he and his **associates**[3] were made to feel that they were not welcome by the white grocer. . . .

About ten o'clock that [one Saturday] night, . . . shots rang out in the back room of the store. The men stationed there had seen several white men stealing through the rear door and fired on them without a moment's pause. Three of these men were wounded, and others fled and gave the alarm.

Sunday morning's paper came out with **lurid**[4] headlines telling how officers of the law had been wounded while in the **discharge**[5] of their duties. . . . The same newspaper told of the arrest and jailing of the **proprietor**[6] of the store and many of the colored people. . . .

On Tuesday following, . . . a body of picked [white] men was admitted to the jail. . . . This mob took out of their cells Thomas Moss, Calvin McDowell, and Henry Stewart. . . . They were loaded on a switch engine of the railroad which ran back of the jail, carried a mile north of the city limits, and horribly shot to death.

Although stunned by the events of that hectic week, the *Free Speech* [Wells's newspaper] felt that it must carry on. Its [lead article] for that week said:

The city of Memphis has demonstrated that neither character nor standing **avails**[7] the Negro if he dares to protect himself against the white man or become his rival. There is nothing we can do about the lynching now, as we are out-numbered and without arms. The white mob could help itself to ammunition without pay, but the order was rigidly enforced against the selling of guns to Negroes. There is therefore only one thing left that we can do; save our money and leave a town which will neither protect our lives and property, nor give us a fair trial in the courts, but takes us out and murders us in cold blood when accused by white persons.

---

1. **hitherto:** until this time.
2. **monopoly:** exclusive control by one person or group.
3. **associates:** friends or partners.
4. **lurid:** causing shock or horror.
5. **discharge:** performance of duty.
6. **proprietor:** owner.
7. **avails:** helps.

# Like Country Pretty Much

**Setting the Stage** Kee Low was a Chinese immigrant. He had come to the United States in 1876. He was interviewed in 1924 as part of a project by scholars to create a "Survey of Race Relations." This is an excerpt from that interview. In it, Kee Low tells his story. Despite the racism, he still "like country pretty much." **See Primary Source Explorer**

I arrived in San Francisco in 1876, 49 years ago. Come to San Francisco when country one hundred years old. People treat Chinese rotten then. Don't blame people much at that time. Chinese and European not educated as much then as today. More civilized today. People drive Chinese out of country. . . .

I was living on the waterfront, and they told me to get out one day. Sunday morning, they come together and drive Chinese out. . . . They want to get us out to San Francisco, to go on steamer, and we stayed on the **wharf**[1] all night, and they bring us little black coffee and little bread in morning. We pretty hungry. The last day, some of the citizens, Judge Greene, Judge Hanford, United States Attorney, nice fellow want to help us. . . . Judge Greene told the Chinese that those who wanted to stay and make good citizens could stay, and those who wanted to go could go. One half wanted to go, and one half wanted to stay. . . .

There were so many around the streets that they had to have somebody to protect these people. Some of the **hobos**[2] tried to make them go back to the wharf, but volunteers tried to keep these fellows away. They **commenced**[3] shooting and kill one of them. So Chinese people get excited when gun begin to sound, so they throw shoes, blankets and everything and run. I was uptown myself. I didn't intend to go. I ran outside to see what happened because I was so excited. . . . Call up one or two friends of mine and tell them get killed, and we better get out of the way. We run out in woods. Build fire. Pretty cold. I told friends, we got to protect ourselves. We got to get out of here.

1. **wharf:** landing place for ships.   2. **hobos:** homeless people.   3. **commenced:** began.

## A CLOSER LOOK

**RACIST ATTITUDES**

Some people believe that racism is caused by ignorance.

4. Why does Kee Low believe that discrimination against the Chinese was worse in the 1870s than in the 1920s?

## A CLOSER LOOK

**REASONS TO STAY**

Despite the violence that they faced for having Asian ancestry, half of the Chinese with Kee Low wanted to stay in the United States.

5. Why do you think Asian-Americans stayed in the United States despite discrimination?

---

## Interactive Primary Sources Assessment

### 1. Main Ideas

**a.** What do the accounts of Wells and Low have in common? (REP4)

**b.** How did the officers of the law behave differently in the report by Low than in the one by Wells? (REP4)

**c.** What conclusions do Wells and Low come to about how someone should respond to discrimination? (REP4)

### 2. Critical Thinking

**Forming and Supporting Opinions** Do you think Wells and Low were right to flee racism? Why? (REP4)

**THINK ABOUT**
• the causes of racism
• the threat of violence to Wells and Low

# Society and Mass Culture

④

| MAIN IDEA | WHY IT MATTERS NOW | TERMS & NAMES |
|---|---|---|
| Industrialization and new technologies created a mass culture in the United States. | Modern American mass culture had its beginnings during this period. | mass culture    mail-order catalog<br>Joseph Pulitzer    leisure<br>William Randolph Hearst    vaudeville<br>department store    ragtime |

### CALIFORNIA STANDARDS

**8.12.5** Examine the location and effects of urbanization, renewed immigration, and industrialization (e.g., the effects on social fabric of cities, wealth and economic opportunity, the conservation movement).

**8.12.9** Name the significant inventors and their inventions and identify how they improved the quality of life (e.g., Thomas Edison, Alexander Graham Bell, Orville and Wilbur Wright).

**HI1** Students explain the central issues and problems from the past, placing people and events in a matrix of time and place.

## ONE AMERICAN'S STORY
Mary Ellen Chase dreaded her first day of teaching, but she did her best to control the class.

### A VOICE FROM THE PAST
I stormed up and down. . . . This pathetic pretense of courage, aided by the mad flourishing of my razor strop, brought forth . . . the expression of respectful fear on the faces of the young giants.

**Mary Ellen Chase,** quoted in *The Good Old Days—They Were Terrible!*

Students work on their lessons in this New York City classroom in 1906.

In this section, you will learn how education helped create an American **mass culture**—a common culture experienced by large numbers of people.

**Taking Notes**
Use your chart to take notes about changes in education and mass culture.

Changes in American Life

## Education and Publishing Grow
Immigration caused enormous growth in American schools. To teach citizenship and English to immigrants, new city and state laws required children to attend school. Between 1880 and 1920, the number of children attending school more than doubled. To serve the growing number of students, the number of public high schools increased from 2,526 in 1890 to 14,326 in 1920.

The growth of education increased American literacy. Reading became more popular. Americans read large numbers of novels. Dime novels were especially popular. They sold for ten cents each and told exciting tales of romance and adventure, often set in the West or on the high seas.

Americans also read more newspapers. Tough competition pushed newspaper publishers to try all sorts of gimmicks to outsell their rivals. For example, **Joseph Pulitzer,** owner of the *New York World,* and

**William Randolph Hearst,** owner of the *New York Morning Journal,* were fierce competitors. They filled the pages of their papers with spectacular stories. They also added special features, such as comics and sports.

## Modern Advertising and New Products

Newspapers had a wide influence on American life, including the rise of modern advertising. Advertisers used images of celebrities in newspapers and magazines to tempt people to buy products. They advertised everything from cereal to jewelry to soap. Some ads played on people's fears. For example, advertisers might scare a young woman concerned about her appearance into buying a particular brand of face cream. Advertising was effective in turning brand names into household words.

Advertisements also helped people learn about new products. At the turn of the century, new inventions, such as the electric washing machine, promised to help people do their household chores more easily. Because women did most of these chores as well as most of the shopping, manufacturers marketed these new devices to women.

One of the places people could buy these—and many other—goods was in department stores. **Department stores** sold everything from clothing to furniture to hardware. The Chicago businessman Marshall Field discovered as a sales clerk that he could increase his sales by paying close attention to each woman customer. Field opened his own department store in downtown Chicago with the motto, "Give the lady what she wants."

People who did not live near a department store could order goods through the mail. Companies like Montgomery Ward and Sears Roebuck sent catalogs to customers. These **mail-order catalogs** included pictures and descriptions of merchandise. People could place their orders by mail, and the company would deliver the product. Richard Sears claimed that he sold 10,000 items a minute.

In 1896, the post office made it easier for people to receive goods through the mail by establishing a new delivery system. Rural free delivery brought packages directly to homes in rural areas. Now people in these areas could get the same goods as people in the cities.

### STRANGE *but* True

#### BICYCLES TO AIRPLANES

At the turn of the century, two bicycle mechanics invented a machine that would help advertisers and businessmen reach new customers. In 1892, Orville and Wilbur Wright opened a bicycle shop in Ohio. They used the profits to fund experiments in aeronautics, the construction of aircraft.

In 1903, the Wright brothers took a gasoline-powered airplane that they had designed to a sandy hill outside Kitty Hawk, North Carolina. On December 17 of that year, Orville made the first successful flight of a powered aircraft in history. By 1918, the U.S. Postal Service began airmail service that made it faster and easier for people to get goods.

## Urban Parks and World's Fairs

Advertising and shopping were not the only daily activities changing at this time. **Leisure,** or free time, activities also changed. In cities, new parks provided people with entertainment. The increasing number of people working in factories and offices liked going to parks to get some sunshine and fresh air. Parks helped bring grass and trees back into city landscapes.

▼ **Coney Island**
Visitors to New York's Coney Island cool off in the Steeple-chase Pool.

▼ **World's Fair**
Visitors to the 1893 world's fair in Chicago saw exotic sights, such as elephants.

▼ **Football**
Excited fans watch the 1881 Harvard–Yale football game at the Polo Grounds in New York.

Central Park in New York City is the nation's best-known urban park. Opened in 1876, Central Park looked like the country. Trees and shrubs dotted its gently rolling landscape. Winding walkways let city dwellers imagine they were strolling in the woods. People could also ride bicycles and play sports in the park.

In addition to urban parks, amusement parks provided a place people could go for fun. The most famous amusement park was Coney Island in New York City. Completed in 1904, Coney Island had shops, food vendors, and exciting rides like roller coasters. One immigrant woman said Coney Island "is just like what I see when I dream of heaven!"

World's fairs provided another wildly popular form of entertainment for Americans. Between 1876 and 1916, several U.S. cities, including Philadelphia, Chicago, St. Louis, and San Francisco, hosted world's fairs. The fairs were designed to show off American technology. The 1876 fair in Philadelphia displayed Alexander Graham Bell's newly invented telephone. Millions of people attended these fairs. Nearly 10 million attended the Philadelphia fair alone. Visitors were drawn to foods, shows, and amusements. The historian Thomas Schlereth described the giant wheel built by George Ferris at the 1893 Chicago fair.

*Reading* **History**
**B. Comparing and Contrasting** What did urban parks and world's fairs have in common?

**A VOICE FROM THE PAST**

Chicago's answer to Paris's 1889 Eiffel Tower, Ferris's 264-foot bicycle wheel in the sky dominated the landscape. With thirty-six cars, each larger than a Pullman coach and capable of holding 60 people, the wheel, when fully loaded, rotated 2,160 people in the air.

**Thomas Schlereth,** *Victorian America*

# Spectator Sports

During this time, spectator sports also became popular entertainment. Baseball, football, boxing, and many other sports drew thousands of people to fields and gyms around the country.

Baseball was the most popular sport. Summer games drew crowds of enthusiastic fans. By the 1890s, baseball had standardized rules and a published schedule of games. Racial discrimination kept African-American baseball players out of baseball's American and National Leagues. In order to compete, African Americans formed their own teams in the Negro American League and the Negro National League.

## Going to the Show

In addition to sports, other forms of live entertainment attracted large audiences. **Vaudeville,** for example, featured a mixture of song, dance, and comedy. A show would have a series of acts leading up to an exciting end, which advertisers billed as the "wow finish."

New types of music also began to be heard. **Ragtime,** a blend of African-American songs and European musical forms, was an important new musical form. African-American composer Scott Joplin heard ragtime while he traveled through black communities from New Orleans to Chicago. Joplin's "Maple Leaf Rag," published in 1899, became a hit in the first decade of the 20th century.

Early in the 20th century, movies began to compete with live entertainment. The first movies were silent and were added as the final feature of a vaudeville show. Soon storefront theaters appeared that showed only movies. After 1905, these movie theaters were called nickelodeons because they charged just a nickel for admission.

Movies, music, sports, and advertising contributed to shaping modern American mass culture. People across the nation experienced many of these things. In the next chapter, you will learn about different nationwide changes—the reform movements of the Progressive era.

*Reading*History
C. Making Inferences How do you think movies contributed to mass culture?

---

## Section 4 Assessment

### 1. Terms & Names

**Explain the significance of:**
- mass culture
- Joseph Pulitzer
- William Randolph Hearst
- department store
- mail-order catalog
- leisure
- vaudeville
- ragtime

### 2. Using Graphics

Use a diagram like the one below to note the changes that created a mass culture at the turn of the century. (HI3)

### 3. Main Ideas

**a.** What did dime novels and newspapers have in common? (HI3)

**b.** How did new technologies change the way people bought goods? (HI3)

**c.** What did visitors see at world's fairs? (HI3)

### 4. Critical Thinking

**Making Inferences** Why did mass culture emerge during this period? (HI2)

**THINK ABOUT**
- the impact of newspapers
- advertising and catalogs
- the development of leisure time

**ACTIVITY OPTIONS**

**ART**

**LANGUAGE ARTS**

Research a world's fair from the turn of the century. Then make a **poster** or write a **newspaper advertisement** that will attract people to the fair. (HI1)

*Changes in American Life* **629**

## TERMS & NAMES

Briefly explain the significance of each of the following.

1. urbanization
2. Jane Addams
3. political machine
4. Ellis Island
5. assimilation
6. Jim Crow
7. *Plessy* v. *Ferguson*
8. W. E. B. Du Bois
9. Joseph Pulitzer
10. leisure

## REVIEW QUESTIONS

### Cities Grow and Change (pages 609–613)

1. How did public transportation change city life? (HI2)
2. What dangers did urban overcrowding pose to tenement dwellers? (HI1)
3. How did big-city political machines keep their power? (HI1)

### The New Immigrants (pages 614–619)

4. Where did most American immigrants come from around 1900? (CST3)
5. How did immigrants enter the United States? (HI1)
6. Why have some people described the United States as a melting pot? (HI1)

### Segregation and Discrimination (pages 620–625)

7. Why was *Plessy* v. *Ferguson* an important Supreme Court decision? (HI1)
8. What did African-American leaders do to fight discrimination? (HI1)

### Society and Mass Culture (pages 626–629)

9. What is mass culture? (HI1)
10. How did city parks improve city life? (HI2)

## CRITICAL THINKING

### 1. USING YOUR NOTES: CATEGORIZING INFORMATION

Using your completed chart, answer the questions below: (CST1)

a. What changes did increased immigration cause?
b. How did the growing popularity of spectator sports and movies help bring about mass culture?
c. Which changes helped immigrants assimilate into American life?

### 2. ANALYZING LEADERSHIP

Think about the actions of Booker T. Washington and W. E. B. Du Bois. What approach did each take against discrimination? Whose approach do you think was the most likely to be effective? (HI1)

### 3. THEME: DIVERSITY AND UNITY

How do you think the emergence of mass culture around 1900 affected immigrants and nonwhites? (HI1)

### 4. APPLYING CITIZENSHIP SKILLS

What kinds of things prevented African Americans and immigrants from having full citizenship? How did they attempt to participate in American politics? (HI1)

### Interact *with* History

Have your ideas about how you'll make a home in the United States changed after reading the chapter? Explain.

## VISUAL SUMMARY

# Changes in American Life (8.12)

**Cities Grow and Change**
Industrialization caused American cities to grow.

**The New Immigrants**
Large numbers of immigrants, especially from southern and eastern Europe, came to the United States.

American Life Around 1900

**Segregation and Discrimination**
Racial and ethnic minorities faced discrimination across the country.

only whites allowed
Whites Only

**Society and Mass Culture**
New leisure activities and mass culture emerged at this time.

## STANDARDS-BASED ASSESSMENT

**Use the graph and your knowledge of U.S. history to answer questions 1 and 2.**

Additional Test Practice, pp. S1–S33.

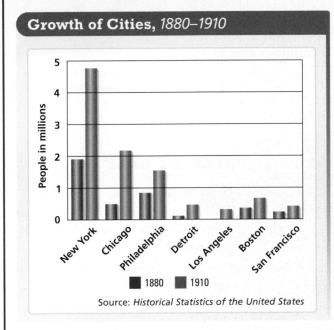

### Growth of Cities, *1880–1910*

Source: *Historical Statistics of the United States*

1. Which city's population increased by the greatest amount between 1880 and 1910? (8.12.5)
   - **A.** Boston
   - **B.** Chicago
   - **C.** New York
   - **D.** Philadelphia

2. For which city is no 1880 population information provided? (8.12.5)
   - **A.** Chicago
   - **B.** Detroit
   - **C.** Los Angeles
   - **D.** New York

**This quotation from teacher Mary Ellen Chase is about how she controlled a classroom. Use the quotation and your knowledge of U.S. history to answer question 3.**

### PRIMARY SOURCE

I stormed up and down. . . . This pathetic pretense of courage, aided by the mad flourishing of my razor strop, brought forth . . . the expression of respectful fear on the faces of the young giants.

**Mary Ellen Chase,** quoted in *The Good Old Days—They Were Terrible!*

3. Based on this passage, which of the following best states Mary Ellen Chase's view of what was important in a classroom? (8.12.5)
   - **A.** fear and punishment
   - **B.** large classrooms
   - **C.** a physically-strong teacher
   - **D.** respect and discipline

**TEST PRACTICE**
CLASSZONE.COM

## ALTERNATIVE ASSESSMENT

### 1. 📝 WRITING ABOUT HISTORY

Write a **guide** for new immigrants coming to the United States at the beginning of the 20th century. (HI1)

- Include information about life in the cities, job opportunities, discrimination, and leisure activities.
- Include icons or other illustrations where possible as an aid to people who are just learning English.

### 2. COOPERATIVE LEARNING

Work with a few of your classmates to research city parks built in the late 1800s and design your own park. Include sports fields, areas for rest, places for nature and wildlife, and buildings for food and restrooms. Divide responsibilities for researching and designing the park. (REP4)

## INTEGRATED TECHNOLOGY

### DOING INTERNET RESEARCH

Racial discrimination has been a tragic feature of American history. Conduct research to create a museum exhibit about discrimination and civil rights. (REP4)

- Use the Internet to locate primary sources such as newspaper articles or autobiographies.
- Look for information on racial or ethnic groups that faced discrimination, as well as biographies of important civil rights leaders. Then prepare a presentation for your class that illustrates how beliefs and practices have changed.

**For more about racial discrimination . . .**

**INTERNET ACTIVITY**
CLASSZONE.COM

# Create an Exhibit

In 1904 the Louisiana Purchase Exposition, better known as the St. Louis World's Fair, opened to great fanfare. The event celebrated the 100th anniversary of the U.S. purchase of the Louisiana Territory from France in 1803. Taking five years to plan and opening a year late, the fair focused on education and American technology. The automobile was among the most notable attractions at the fair. People from 63 countries and 43 states gathered in St. Louis.

**People stroll down The Great Pike at the St. Louis World's Fair.**

**ACTIVITY** Create an exhibit that reflects some aspect of technology at the end of the 19th century. Then make a classroom fair. Write an article about it and give a speech describing your favorite exhibit.

## TOOLBOX

Each group will need:

| | |
|---|---|
| bifold (type of poster board that folds open) | scissors |
| | pencils |
| poster board | glue |
| drawing paper | cardboard |
| markers | |

### CALIFORNIA STANDARDS

**REP1** Students frame questions that can be answered by historical study and research.

**Listening and Speaking 2.0** Students deliver well-organized formal presentations employing traditional rhetorical strategies (e.g., narration, exposition, persuasion, description).

## STEP BY STEP

**1** **Form groups.** Each group should consist of three or four students. During the workshop, each group will be expected to:

- research technology and inventions just prior to 1904
- design and create an exhibit for a classroom fair
- write a news report about the fair
- give a speech in praise of a favorite exhibit at the fair

**2** **Research the fair.** Using this chapter, books on the St. Louis fair, or the Internet, find out what kinds of exhibits were displayed. Also research the technology and inventions of the time. Some themes of the fair's massive exhibit halls are listed below. Pick one theme on which to focus. Then brainstorm ideas for your exhibit and choose the best one.

| World's Fair Themes | |
|---|---|
| transportation | education |
| technology | the arts |

The New York-to-St. Louis Automobile Parade arrives at the St. Louis World's Fair.

**HELP DESK**

For related information, see pages 627–628 in Chapter 21.

## Researching Your Project

- *The Song of the Molimo* by Jane Cutler

For more about world's fairs . . .

**RESEARCH LINKS**
CLASSZONE.COM

**③ Design your exhibit.** Think about what your group wants to create. Using drawing paper, sketch a design of the exhibit in pencil. Next to your sketch, list all the items you'll need for the exhibit. Assign each person in your group certain items to bring for the next class period.

**④ Lay out your display.** Use the images and text you found to visually organize the three-panel display. Vary the size of the images, type-size of the text, and include color to make your layout clear and interesting. Remember to create a title.

## Did You Know?

One vender at the fair had difficulty selling tea in the hot St. Louis summer. As a result, he began putting ice cubes in the tea, and sales of his "iced tea" soared.

Though there has been some controversy over who invented the ice-cream cone, the St. Louis World's Fair was the place it became popular. One story states that a vendor at the fair rolled a waffle into a cone-shaped holder when another vendor ran out of dishes. However, Italo Marchiony of New York City claimed to have been selling ice-cream cones since 1896.

A Machine for the New Century

**⑤ Create a mini St. Louis fair.** Along with the other groups, arrange the exhibits around the classroom. Walk around the room and look at the other groups' exhibits. Discuss with other groups how you created your exhibit.

## REFLECT & ASSESS

- How did your group come up with its idea?
- How does your design fit into the theme of the St. Louis fair?
- What criteria did you use when judging the exhibits?

## WRITE AND SPEAK

**Write a newspaper article.** Cover the fair as a journalist from another city. Write an article about the classroom fair, describing the atmosphere as well as the exhibits. Then give a speech in praise of the outstanding exhibit of the fair.

# Technical Writing:
## A Transforming Innovation

**Writing Model**
ClassZone.com

**CALIFORNIA STANDARDS**
**Writing 2.6** Write technical documents.

**PURPOSE:** To write a technical document on an invention or organization that transformed the nation

**AUDIENCE:** Your classmates

The many transformations you read about in Unit 6 came about because people worked tirelessly to solve problems. Inventors and manufacturers worked on new industrial methods, such as the Bessemer steel process. Business owners and workers found new ways to get along. Transportation experts designed railway systems that connected the country. These people all shared their knowledge in **technical documents,** writing that conveys information about a system, product, or organization.

By the early 1900s, the Wright brothers had designed a gasoline-powered airplane that would transform the nation and the world.

## Organization & Focus

Your assignment is to write a technical document on an invention, system, or organization developed between 1860 and 1900 that transformed American life. For example, you could write a detailed description on how to operate a sewing machine for new seamstresses. Or you could write a description of the bylaws, or rules, of a labor union for new workers.

**IDENTIFYING PURPOSE AND AUDIENCE** Your purpose is to identify the sequence of activities needed to design a system, operate a tool, or explain the bylaws of an organization. Your audience is your classmates.

**CHOOSING A TOPIC** Skim chapters 20 and 21, paying special attention to the Terms & Names and Review Questions in the chapter assessments. Look for a technology, invention, or organization that transformed the nation. Perhaps you would like to explain how a telephone works or tell how to build a skyscraper. Maybe you want to describe the new labor laws of the AFL. Take notes on two or three subjects that interest you. When you have finished, review your notes and make your choice.

**FINDING DETAILS** The kinds of details you need for your technical document include steps in a process and a discussion of how parts relate to a whole. The information in this textbook can get you started, but you will need to do research to gather enough information to write a good technical document.

## Research & Technology

Use the Internet and library sources to find information on your subject. Remember that you will need to find information on the tool, system, or organization you have selected shortly after it was invented or developed. Search key words such as *telephone, invention* to find information in the appropriate time period.

**OUTLINING AND DRAFTING** After you have gathered the information you need, divide it into manageable chunks for your reader. Too much technical information at once is hard to absorb. You might want to break the information down into steps as shown below.

> **Technology Tip** Use your word processor or a graphics program to make diagrams, flow charts, and other graphics that will make your technical document easier to understand. Use the Help menu if necessary.

**Step 1**
Describe the parts of the telephone.

**Step 2**
Explain how to operate a telephone.

**Step 3**
Briefly tell how the telephone works.

**Step 4**
Conclude by saying how the telephone will transform American life.

Use headings and different font sizes to break up the text. Include diagrams or other graphics to illustrate the steps of an activity or process. Also, be sure to define technical terms that may be unfamiliar to your readers.

## Evaluation & Revision

Ask a classmate to review your document and to jot down any questions he or she might have about the information or detailed steps it contains. Try to answer those questions as you revise your document.

### Self-Check

Does my technical document . . .

- [ ] explain a sequence of activities or the bylaws of an organization?
- [ ] seem readable and clear?
- [ ] define technical terms?
- [ ] use headings and graphics to aid comprehension?

## Publish & Present

Design a cover for your technical document and present the information to your classmates. Discuss how the innovation transformed American life.

# Modern America Emerges

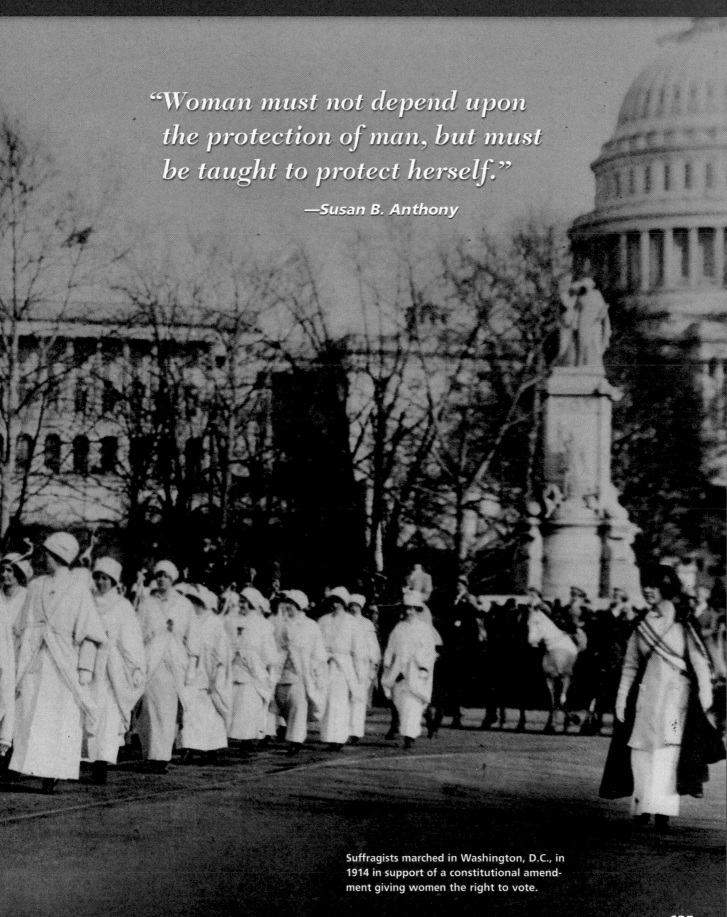

"Woman must not depend upon
the protection of man, but must
be taught to protect herself."

—Susan B. Anthony

Suffragists marched in Washington, D.C., in
1914 in support of a constitutional amendment giving women the right to vote.

# The Progressive Era 1890–1920

A family earns money by making artificial flowers in its tenement.

**1890**
Congress passes Sherman Antitrust Act.

**1896**
William McKinley is elected president.

**1901**
McKinley is assassinated, and Theodore Roosevelt becomes president.

**1904**
Roosevelt is reelected president.

USA
World   **1890**

**1890**
German leader Bismarck is dismissed by Kaiser Wilhelm II.

**1894**
Uganda becomes a British protectorate.

**1898**
Marie Curie discovers radium.

**1900**
Boxer uprising against foreigners begins in China.

Children play in the filth of the gutter.

It is 1901, and Theodore Roosevelt has suddenly become president. You and all Americans are counting on him to help end child labor, poverty, business abuses, and political corruption. You're anxious to see what actions the new president will take to address these problems.

# How would you solve one of these problems?

## What Do You Think?

- What problems do the photographs show?
- What qualities would a leader need to tackle such problems?
- What might be the cause of these problems?

**RESEARCH LINKS**
CLASSZONE.COM

Visit the Chapter 22 links for more information about the Progressive Era.

**1908**
William Howard Taft is elected president.

enry Ford introduces the Model T automobile.

**1910**
Union of South Africa is established.

**1912**
Woodrow Wilson is elected president.

**1913**
17th Amendment provides for direct election of senators.

**1913**
Gandhi, leader of Indian resistance movement, is arrested.

**1919**
18th Amendment outlaws alcohol.

**1920**
19th Amendment grants women the right to vote.

1920

*The Progressive Era* **637**

# Reading Strategy: Identifying and Solving Problems

## What Do You Know?

What do you know about life in American cities in the early 1900s? What problems plagued the cities? How have people living in cities overcome obstacles?

### Think About
- what you've learned in previous chapters
- what you know about urban problems today
- your responses to the Interact with History about solving social problems (see page 637)

## What Do You Want to Know?

What questions do you have about the reform movements of the early 1900s? Record your questions in your notebook before you read the chapter.

**CALIFORNIA STANDARDS**

**Reading 2.0** Students read and understand grade-level-appropriate material. They describe and connect the essential ideas, arguments, and perspectives of the text by using their knowledge of text structure, organization, and purpose.

A social worker pays a visit to a poor family.

## Identifying and Solving Problems

This chapter focuses on the problems that Americans faced at the turn of the century and how they worked to solve those problems. A graphic organizer can help you keep track of problems and solutions. Major problems faced by the nation at the turn of the century are listed in the first column of the chart below. As you read, record solutions for these problems in the second column of the chart.

**S** See Skillbuilder Handbook, page R18.

 Taking Notes

| PROBLEM | SOLUTION |
|---------|----------|
| **Political:** patronage; limited suffrage and democracy | |
| **Social:** poverty; alcohol abuse | |
| **Economic:** power of big corporations; unemployment | |
| **Environmental:** impure food and water; diminishing natural resources | |

# Roosevelt and Progressivism

1

| MAIN IDEA | WHY IT MATTERS NOW | TERMS & NAMES |
|---|---|---|
| Reformers tried to solve the problems of the cities. They gained a champion in Theodore Roosevelt. | Many of the reforms of the Progressive Era have had an effect on life in America today. | progressivism    referendum<br>muckrakers    recall<br>direct primary    Sherman Antitrust Act<br>initiative    Theodore Roosevelt |

## ONE AMERICAN'S STORY

In 1887, journalist Nellie Bly investigated an asylum—a place where people with mental illness can get help. She faked mental illness so that she could become a patient. Afterwords, Bly wrote about what she had witnessed. She described being forced to take ice cold baths.

### A VOICE FROM THE PAST

My teeth chattered and my limbs were goose-fleshed and blue with cold. Suddenly I got, one after the other, three buckets of water over my head—ice-cold water, too—into my eyes, my ears, my nose and my mouth.

**Nellie Bly,** quoted in *Nellie Bly: Daredevil, Reporter, Feminist*

She reported that nurses choked and beat patients. Shortly after Bly's stories appeared, conditions at the asylum improved.

Like other reformers, Bly wanted to correct the wrongs in American society. All of these reformers made up the Progressive movement around the turn of the century.

## The Rise of Progressivism

As you saw in Chapter 21, the rapid growth of cities and industries in the United States at the turn of the century brought many problems. Among them were poverty, the spread of slums, and poor conditions in factories. A depression in the 1890s made problems worse. In addition, corrupt political machines had won control of many city and state governments. Big corporations had gained power over the economy and government.

To attack these problems, individuals organized a number of reform movements. These reformers believed in the basic goodness of people. They also believed in democracy. The reformers were mostly native born and middle-class. They could be found in either political party. Their reform movements came to be grouped under the label **progressivism.**

**CALIFORNIA STANDARDS**

**8.8.3** Describe the role of pioneer women and the new status that western women achieved (e.g., Laura Ingalls Wilder, Annie Bidwell; slave women gaining freedom in the West; Wyoming granting suffrage to women in 1869).

**8.12.1** Trace patterns of agricultural and industrial development as they relate to climate, use of natural resources, markets, and trade and locate such development on a map.

**8.12.5** Examine the location and effects of urbanization, renewed immigration, and industrialization (e.g., the effects on social fabric of cities, wealth and economic opportunity, the conservation movement).

**REP4** Students assess the credibility of primary and secondary sources and draw sound conclusions from them.

**HI1** Students explain the central issues and problems from the past, placing people and events in a matrix of time and place.

**Taking Notes**

Use your chart to take notes about problems faced by Americans and their attempted solutions.

| PROBLEM |
|---|
| **Political:** patronage; limited suffrage and der |
| **Social:** poverty; alcohol abuse |
| **Economic:** power of big corporations; unemploy |
| **Environmental:** impure food and water; diminishing |

About 1900, a new group of writers began to expose corruption in American society. They were called **muckrakers**. The muckrakers created a public demand for reform. Muckraker Ida Tarbell, for example, accused Standard Oil of using unfair tactics to force small companies out of business.

The progressive reformers shared at least one of three basic goals: first, to reform government and expand democracy; second, to promote social welfare; third, to create economic reform.

## Reforming Government and Expanding Democracy

In the 1870s and 1880s, elected officials often handed out government jobs and contracts. In return, they won political support. This practice was called patronage. It became a hot political issue during the presidencies of Rutherford B. Hayes, James Garfield, and Chester Arthur. Finally, Congress passed the Pendleton Civil Service Act in 1883. This law required people to take civil service exams for certain government jobs. It also prevented elected officials from firing civil service workers for political reasons.

In the 1890s and early 1900s, progressive leaders in a number of states sought to expand democracy. They wanted to give voters more control over their government. In 1903, under progressive governor Robert M. La Follette, Wisconsin became the first state to establish a direct primary. In a **direct primary**, voters, rather than party conventions, choose candidates to run for public office.

*Reading*History

**A. Finding Main Ideas** What was the main goal behind the progressive reforms of government?

In Oregon, newspaper editor William S. U'Ren promoted three reforms besides the direct primary.

1. **Initiative**—This reform allowed voters to propose a law directly.
2. **Referendum**—In this reform, a proposed law was submitted to the vote of the people.
3. **Recall**—This reform allowed people to vote an official out of office.

In the years that followed, many other states adopted one or more of these progressive reforms.

## Promoting Social Welfare

This goal addressed such problems as poverty, unemployment, and poor working conditions. You read about the social gospel and settlement house movements in Chapter 21. Leaders in these movements promoted many social-welfare reforms. For example, Jane Addams provided social services to the poor at Hull House. She also worked to help the unemployed. Florence Kelley, also from Hull House, pushed for minimum wage laws and limits on women's working hours.

Another group of reformers who wanted to improve social welfare were the prohibitionists. They worked to prevent alcohol from ruining people's lives. The prohibitionists built on the temperance movement of the 1800s. Annie Kennedy married John Bidwell, the wealthy founder of Chico, California, in 1868. Annie was active in the suffrage and prohibition movements, and strongly influenced her husband's politics. John ran for governor of California in 1875 and 1890, and for president on the Prohibition Party ticket in 1892. The Bidwells also supported election reform, an income tax, and regulation of monopolies.

This photograph shows an immigrant family in a crowded tenement at the turn of the century.

## Creating Economic Reform

*Reading* **History**

**B. Summarizing**
How did progressives pursue their three basic goals?

The third progressive goal was to create economic reform. This meant limiting the power of big business and regulating its activities. By the late 1800s, business leaders in some major industries had formed trusts. These were combinations of businesses. The business firms in a trust worked together to cut prices and squeeze out competitors. Then the trust would raise prices and make larger profits.

The **Sherman Antitrust Act** of 1890 made it illegal for corporations to gain control of industries by forming trusts. However, the government did not enforce the law at first. Enforcement required a strong president.

## Roosevelt and the Square Deal

**Theodore Roosevelt**—the first progressive president—provided this strength and leadership. He came to the presidency by accident. In 1898, Roosevelt won fame fighting in the Spanish-American War in Cuba. He returned as a war hero and was elected governor of New York. In 1900, Roosevelt ran on the Republican ticket as President McKinley's vice president.

Then an assassin shot McKinley, just six months after his inauguration. Roosevelt became president when McKinley died on September 14, 1901. At age 42, Roosevelt was the youngest person ever to become president. He brought his boundless energy to the office. Americans admired Roosevelt's zest for living. He gained the public's support for reform.

Roosevelt began his reforms with an effort to break up the corporate trusts. He thought industries should be regulated for the public interest.

---

*A VOICE FROM THE PAST*

When I say I believe in a square deal I do not mean, and nobody who speaks the truth can mean, that he believes it possible to give every man the best hand. If the cards do not come to any man, or if they do come, and he has not got the power to play them, that is his affair. All I mean is that there shall not be any crookedness in the dealing.

**Theodore Roosevelt,** speech on April 5, 1905

---

Roosevelt saw government as an umpire. Its purpose was to ensure fairness, or a "square deal," for workers, consumers, and big business. To root out "crookedness," Roosevelt used the Sherman Antitrust Act. Since its passage in 1890, many corporations had ignored the law, which was intended to regulate the trusts. No one had enforced it—no one, that is, until Roosevelt became president in 1901.

At the end of 1901, the nation's railroads were run by a handful of companies. The power of railroads continued to grow. It was not surprising, therefore, that one of Roosevelt's first targets was the railroads. He used the Sherman Antitrust Act to bust up a railroad trust.

Roosevelt was not against big business as such. However, he opposed any trust he thought worked against the national interest. In addition to the railroad trust, Roosevelt broke up the Standard Oil Company and a tobacco trust. In all, the government filed suit against 44 corporations during Roosevelt's presidency.

*Reading*History
**C. Making Inferences** How do you think big business leaders regarded President Roosevelt? Why?

## Roosevelt Leads Progressive Reforms

As president, Roosevelt had a great deal of power to push progressive ideas. To make such ideas into law, however, he needed help. Roosevelt got it as voters began pressuring their senators and representatives. As a result, Congress passed laws that helped change American society.

Roosevelt acted to regulate the meat-packing industry after reading Upton Sinclair's *The Jungle.* The novel describes a packing plant in which dead rats end up in the sausage. Sinclair focused attention on the poor sanitary conditions under which the meat-packers worked. "I aimed at the public's heart, and by accident I hit it in the stomach," he noted. By this, Sinclair meant he hoped to promote socialism, but had ended up promoting safety regulations.

Roosevelt launched an investigation of the meat-packing industry. In 1906, he signed the Meat Inspection Act. This act created a government meat inspection program. Roosevelt also signed the Pure Food and Drug Act. This law banned the sale of impure foods and medicines.

While Roosevelt tried to win a square deal for most Americans, he did not push for civil rights for African Americans. He believed that discrimination was morally wrong. However, he did not take the political risk of leading a fight for civil rights.

**Shown at the left is the cover of Upton Sinclair's novel, *The Jungle.* The photograph shows immigrant workers stuffing sausages in a Chicago meat-packing house.**

THE JUNGLE

UPTON SINCLAIR

# Conservation

Roosevelt was a strong crusader for conservation—controlling how America's natural resources were used. As an outdoorsman and hunter, he had observed the gradual loss of natural resources. He camped with naturalist John Muir for four days in Yosemite, California. Because he loved the Yosemite Valley so much, he set out to preserve Yosemite and other areas for people's "children and their children's children."

Roosevelt preserved more than 200 million acres of public lands. He established the nation's first wildlife refuge at Pelican Island, Florida. He doubled the number of national parks in the United States. At one point, Congress refused to establish any more national parks. Roosevelt used the Antiquities Act to create national monuments instead. In this way, he preserved the Grand Canyon and the Petrified Forest in Arizona. Roosevelt spoke of the glories of the Grand Canyon while visiting the site in 1903.

*Reading*History

**D. Finding Main Ideas** Why did President Roosevelt bypass Congress?

### A VOICE FROM THE PAST

Leave it as it is. You cannot improve on it. The ages have been at work on it, and man can only mar it.

**Theodore Roosevelt**, quoted in *Yellowstone*

Both the Grand Canyon and the Petrified Forest have since become national parks. America's next president, William Howard Taft, was not as interested in conservation. However, he did continue Roosevelt's progressive reforms, as you will read in the next section.

## AMERICA'S HISTORY MAKERS

**THEODORE ROOSEVELT**
**1858–1919**

From his youth on, Theodore Roosevelt lived what he called the "strenuous life." He rode horses, hiked, boxed, wrestled, and played tennis. In winter, he swam in the icy Potomac River. He hunted rhinoceros in Africa, harpooned devilfish in Florida, and boated down the Amazon.

Americans loved reading of his exploits and affectionately referred to him as "Teddy" or "T.R." Once, on a hunting trip, he refused to shoot a bear cub. News of the event resulted in a new toy—the teddy bear.

**How did Roosevelt's active style of living carry over into his presidency?**

---

## Section 1 Assessment

### 1. Terms & Names

**Explain the significance of:**
- progressivism
- muckrakers
- direct primary
- initiative
- referendum
- recall
- Sherman Antitrust Act
- Theodore Roosevelt

### 2. Using Graphics

Use a chart to list examples of progressive reforms.

| Goals | Reforms |
|---|---|
| To expand democracy | |
| To protect social welfare | |
| To create economic reform | |

Which reform was most important? Explain. (HI2)

### 3. Main Ideas

**a.** What kinds of problems did progressives attempt to solve? (HI1)

**b.** What did President Roosevelt mean by a "square deal," and how did he try to achieve it? (HI1)

**c.** What were Roosevelt's achievements in the field of conservation? (HI1)

### 4. Critical Thinking

**Recognizing Effects** In what ways do the reforms that President Roosevelt promoted affect your life today? (HI2)

**THINK ABOUT**
- the quality of the food you eat
- natural resources that have been preserved

### ACTIVITY OPTIONS

**ART**

**GEOGRAPHY**

Do research on one of the natural areas that President Roosevelt preserved. Create a **travel brochure** or an illustrated **map** of the area. (CST3)

# The National Parks Movement

As the United States expanded westward, two things became evident. First, this was a land of astonishing beauty. Second, this unspoiled beauty would not last if it wasn't protected.

President Theodore Roosevelt may have given the conservation movement its most significant boost. An outdoorsman, naturalist, and visionary, he established the U.S. Forest Service and set aside more than 200 million acres of public lands as national parks, forests, monuments, and wildlife refuges.

Creating parks was just the first step in protecting these lands. Problems arose that had not been foreseen. These problems included a lack of funds and growing numbers of tourists and researchers. In 1916, the National Park Service was established with the goal of saving the parks for future generations.

**Alaska**

In 1903, Teddy Roosevelt (left) joined conservationist John Muir (right) for a camping trip. Their trip took them from the "big trees" of the Sequoia forest to the wonders of the Yosemite Valley. This photo of Roosevelt and Muir was taken at Glacier Point in Yosemite. Both men wanted to protect the magnificent beauty of America's most spectacular regions.

**Hawaii**

## ARTIFACT FILE

**Sequoia National Park** is a land of giants. In a forest where many trees are more than 250 feet high, it is difficult to get a sense of scale when looking at the biggest of these giants. The General Sherman Tree, shown here, is the largest tree by volume in the world. A number of trees in Sequoia National Park are named for Civil War generals.

GENERAL SHERMAN

**Everglades National Park** in Florida is part of the approximately 1,500,000-acre Everglades region. This wetland habitat is home to birds, especially waders such as herons, egrets, and ibis, and is famous for its alligators.

## The National Parks Today

Olympic
North Cascades
Mount Rainier
Glacier
Crater Lake
Redwood
Yellowstone
Grand Teton
Lassen Volcanic
Theodore Roosevelt
Voyageurs
Isle Royale
Acadia
Wind Cave
Badlands
Yosemite
Great Basin
Capitol Reef
Arches
Rocky Mountain
Shenandoah
Kings Canyon
Zion
Black Canyon of the Gunnison
Canyonlands
Sequoia
Bryce Canyon
Death Valley
Mesa Verde
Mammoth Cave
Channel Islands
Grand Canyon
Joshua Tree
Petrified Forest
Great Smoky Mountains
Saguaro
Carlsbad Caverns
Hot Springs
ATLANTIC OCEAN
Guadalupe Mountains
Big Bend
Gulf of Mexico
N
Everglades
Biscayne
PACIFIC OCEAN
500 Miles
Dry Tortugas
0
1000 Kilometers
0

50°N
40°N
30°N
110°W

National parks are identified on the map above. The National Park System includes many areas, all of which are under the management of the National Park Service (NPS).

## On-Line Field Trip

**Yellowstone National Park** was designated the world's first national park in 1872. Covering about 2,200,000 acres, Yellowstone is still the largest national park in the United States. There are many geysers in Yellowstone, including Old Faithful (at right).

For more about national parks . . .

**RESEARCH LINKS**
CLASSZONE.COM

### CONNECT TO GEOGRAPHY

1. **Region** What might be two reasons the national parks are concentrated where they are?

2. **Human-Environment Interaction** What effects might visits from many tourists have on a national park?

**G** See Geography Handbook, page 17.

### CONNECT TO HISTORY

3. **Analyzing Causes** What general mood of the era made the late 1800s a likely time for successfully starting a national park?

# Taft and Wilson as Progressives

| MAIN IDEA | WHY IT MATTERS NOW | TERMS & NAMES |
|---|---|---|
| Progressive reforms continued under William Howard Taft and Woodrow Wilson. | Constitutional amendments passed during this time affect Americans today. | William Howard Taft   Clayton Antitrust Act <br> Sixteenth Amendment <br> Seventeenth Amendment   Federal Reserve Act |

**CALIFORNIA STANDARDS**

**8.12.5** Examine the location and effects of urbanization, renewed immigration, and industrialization (e.g., the effects on social fabric of cities, wealth and economic opportunity, the conservation movement).

**REP4** Students assess the credibility of primary and secondary sources and draw sound conclusions from them.

**HI6** Students interpret basic indicators of economic performance and conduct cost-benefit analyses of economic and political issues.

## ONE AMERICAN'S STORY

During the Progressive Era, many Americans became disturbed by the problems caused by capitalism. Some even turned to socialism. This is a system in which business and industry are totally controlled by the state. Labor leader Eugene V. Debs became a socialist while serving time in prison for his role in an 1894 labor strike.

In the 1908 presidential election, Debs ran as the Socialist Party candidate. In his campaign, he urged American workers to consider what competition was like in a capitalist system.

### A VOICE FROM THE PAST

Competition was natural enough at one time, but do you think you are competing today? . . . Against whom? Against Rockefeller? About as I would if I had a wheelbarrow and competed with the Santa Fe [railroad] from here to Kansas City.

**Eugene V. Debs,** quoted in *The Annals of America*

The forceful speeches of Eugene V. Debs attracted large audiences.

Debs made a decent showing in the election, winning more than 420,000 votes. However, the Republican candidate Taft did better and was elected.

### Taking Notes

Use your chart to take notes about problems faced by Americans and how they were solved.

| PROBLEM |
|---|
| **Political:** patronage; limited suffrage and de[...] |
| **Social:** poverty; alcohol abuse |
| **Economic:** power of big corporations; unemploy[...] |
| **Environmental:** impure food and water; diminishing |

## Taft and Progressivism

In the 1908 election, Debs ran against Republican **William Howard Taft** and Democrat William Jennings Bryan. Neither Debs nor Bryan stood much of a chance against Taft. He was Roosevelt's handpicked successor. Roosevelt's popularity swayed many people to vote for Taft, who promised to follow Roosevelt's progressive policies.

Taft continued Roosevelt's attack on trusts. During his four years in office, Taft pursued almost twice as many antitrust suits as Roosevelt had in nearly eight years in office. But Taft received less credit for his progressivism because he became allied with conservative Republicans rather than Roosevelt's progressive Republicans. Nevertheless, Taft did move forward with progressive reforms. His reforms addressed the progressive goals of democracy, social welfare, and economic reform. Two of the major progressive achievements under President Taft were constitutional amendments.

## Two Progressive Amendments

The <u>**Sixteenth Amendment**</u> was passed in 1909 and ratified in 1913. It gave Congress the power to create income taxes. The Constitution previously did not allow direct taxes on an individual's income. This amendment was intended to provide a means of spreading the cost of running the government among more people. The income tax soon became the main source of federal revenue.

## Economics *in* History

# Types of Taxes

The Sixteenth Amendment, ratified in 1913, made it constitutional for the federal government to have an income tax. Congress quickly passed an income tax law the same year that taxed the top one percent of the population . The income tax provides revenue to the federal government by taxing profits and earnings. In a graduated income tax, larger incomes are taxed at higher rates than smaller incomes. The income tax is only one of several taxes that governments use to raise money.

### CONNECT TO HISTORY

1. **Making Inferences** How might a corporate income tax fit the goals of the Progressive Era?

S See Skillbuilder Handbook, page R12.

### CONNECT TO TODAY

2. **Drawing Conclusions** Some states that have a sales tax do not charge that tax on the purchase of goods like food or clothing. Why do you think they make an exception for these purchases?

For more about taxes . . .

RESEARCH LINKS
CLASSZONE.COM

### INCOME TAXES

1. **Individual:** You pay a percentage of what you earn at work or from investments. Under the payroll deduction plan, income taxes are deducted (taken out) from your wages or salary before you get your paycheck.
2. **Corporate:** Corporations pay a percentage of their profits in income tax.

### PROPERTY TAXES

People pay taxes on property they own, such as land or a house. Property taxes are often used to support public services such as schools.

### TYPES OF TAXES

### SALES TAXES

Sales tax is imposed on the retail price of merchandise and collected by the retailer. For example, when you buy a pair of jeans, you pay sales tax, which will be listed on your receipt.

### ESTATE TAXES

This tax is charged against the value of the property of a person who has died. It is also called the "death tax" because it is collected from the dead person's estate before the estate is passed on to the heirs.

The **Seventeenth Amendment** was ratified in 1913. It provided for the direct election of U.S. senators by voters in each state. Formerly, state legislatures had chosen U.S. senators. Under this system, many senators obtained their positions through corrupt bargains. Because of this, the Senate was called the "Millionaires' Club." The Seventeenth Amendment gave people a more direct voice in the government.

*Reading*History
**A. Drawing Conclusions** Why are the Sixteenth and Seventeenth amendments considered progressive?

## The Election of 1912

Taft achieved a number of progressive reforms. However, a deep split developed between him and progressive leaders in the Republican Party. Still, with the support of conservative Republicans, Taft won the party's nomination as its presidential candidate in 1912.

However, many progressive Republicans supported Theodore Roosevelt. He had entered the race and formed the Progressive Party, also known as the Bull Moose Party.

The Democrats chose Governor Woodrow Wilson of New Jersey as their presidential candidate. Eugene Debs again entered the race as the Socialist candidate. With the Republicans deeply divided, Wilson won the election.

## The Wilson Presidency

As president, Wilson established a progressive record. Wilson believed that "bigness" itself was dangerous. He wanted the government to use its powers to break up monopolies—groups that sought complete control over an industry. He also wanted the government to help workers in their struggles against business owners.

At Wilson's urging, Congress passed the **Clayton Antitrust Act** of 1914. The new law laid down rules forbidding business practices that lessened competition. A business, for example, could no longer buy the stock of a competitor. The Clayton Act gave the government more power to regulate trusts. In addition, the Clayton Act was also prolabor:

1. It said labor unions and farm organizations could merge and expand.
2. It limited the ability of the courts to force workers to end strikes.
3. It legalized such labor tactics as strikes, picketing, and boycotts.

During Wilson's two terms, reforms to the nation's financial system occurred. In 1913, the **Federal Reserve Act** was passed. This improved the nation's monetary and banking system. The law created the modern banking system, which resembles a pyramid. At the top is the Federal Reserve Board, which is appointed by the president. Next are 12 Federal Reserve Banks for different regions of the country. These are "bankers'

**Vocabulary**
**boycott:** an attempt to pressure a business by refusing to buy a product or use a service

banks." They serve the bottom level—the member banks.

The Federal Reserve Act created a more flexible currency system by allowing banks to control the money supply. To raise money, for example, the Federal Reserve Board, or "Fed," lowers the interest rate that it charges member banks. These banks then borrow more from the Fed and thus have more money to lend to people and businesses.

President Wilson throws out a baseball at the opening game of the 1916 season.

*Reading*History
B. Summarizing
What were some of Wilson's achievements as a progressive president?

Wilson did no more to advance civil rights for African Americans than Roosevelt did. In fact, Wilson approved the segregation, or separation, of African-American and white employees in the federal government. Throughout the Progressive Era, presidents Roosevelt, Taft, and Wilson did not actively promote civil rights for African Americans.

## The Eighteenth Amendment

Another amendment passed during the Progressive Era was the Eighteenth Amendment. This is also called the Prohibition Amendment. During Wilson's administration, supporters of prohibition gained strength. Reformers thought an alcohol ban would reduce poverty. They argued that liquor added to unemployment and violence. Business leaders saw that alcohol made workers less efficient. Finally, in 1917, Congress passed a constitutional amendment. The Eighteenth Amendment prohibited the manufacture and sale of alcoholic beverages. The states ratified the amendment in 1919.

In the next section, you will read about the most important amendment of the era—the Nineteenth Amendment, which gave women the vote.

---

Section **2** Assessment

### 1. Terms & Names

**Explain the significance of:**

- William Howard Taft
- Sixteenth Amendment
- Seventeenth Amendment
- Clayton Antitrust Act
- Federal Reserve Act

### 2. Using Graphics

Complete the chart to review some of the major reforms of both the Taft and Wilson administrations. (HI1)

| Law | Description |
|---|---|
| Sixteenth Amendment | |
| Clayton Antitrust Act | |
| Federal Reserve Act | |

### 3. Main Ideas

**a.** What caused the Republican Party to split in 1912? (HI2)

**b.** What were the major progressive accomplishments of Wilson's presidency? (HI1)

**c.** What did the Federal Reserve Act do? (REP3)

### 4. Critical Thinking

**Making Inferences** Why did progressive presidents do little to advance civil rights for African Americans? (HI2)

**THINK ABOUT**

- the goals of progressivism
- the groups of people that progressivism aimed to help

**ACTIVITY OPTIONS**

**LANGUAGE ARTS**
**TECHNOLOGY**

Research one of the people mentioned in this section. Then write the **script** for the first 10 minutes of his documentary or design his **Web page**. (HI1)

# Women Win New Rights

| MAIN IDEA | WHY IT MATTERS NOW | TERMS & NAMES |
|---|---|---|
| Women became leaders in social reform movements and won the right to vote during the Progressive Era. | Today, American women enjoy the right to vote because of women reformers in the Progressive Era. | Susan B. Anthony    Nineteenth Amendment <br> Carrie Chapman Catt |

## ONE AMERICAN'S STORY

In the 1890s, Lillian Wald was teaching a home nursing class at a school for immigrants in New York City. One day a child asked Wald to help her sick mother. Following the child home, Wald was shocked by what she saw.

Lillian Wald

### A VOICE FROM THE PAST

Over broken asphalt, over dirty mattresses and heaps of refuse we went. The tall houses reeked with rubbish. . . . There were two rooms and a family of seven not only lived here but shared their quarters with boarders.

**Lillian Wald,** quoted in *Always a Sister*

Inspired to help such poor immigrants, Wald founded the Nurses' Settlement. This was later called the Henry Street Settlement. The program mainly helped poor women and children. In this section, you will read about others like Wald who worked to make life better for all women.

## New Roles for Women

The social reform movements of the Progressive Era were led by educated, middle-class women. At the turn of the century, women like Wald were looking for new roles outside the home. The growth of industry had changed many urban, middle-class homes. These homes now had indoor running water and electric power for lamps and vacuum cleaners.

In addition, factories produced the products that women once made in the home, such as soap, clothing, and canned goods. Such technological advances reduced some of the unpleasant work of homemaking. At the same time, families were becoming smaller as women had fewer children.

As a result, the homemaker's role began to change. High schools, colleges, and women's clubs offered courses in home economics and domestic science. In these courses, women were encouraged to apply the latest methods to running their homes.

Other women responded to changes in the home by taking jobs in factories, offices, and stores. Women worked as telephone operators, store clerks, and typists. Those who gained a college education could pursue a profession. The choices were limited to such fields as teaching and nursing. Women who could afford to were expected to quit their jobs when they married. In 1890, approximately 30 percent of women between the ages of 20 and 24 worked outside the home. However, only about 15 percent between the ages of 25 and 44 did so.

*Reading*History
**A. Finding Main Ideas** How and why did women's roles begin to change around the turn of the century?

## Women Progressives

The social reform movements that many middle-class, college-educated women took part in were focused on helping people. These included the settlement house and prohibition movements. A settlement house is a community center providing assistance to residents—particularly immigrants—in a slum neighborhood.

Jane Addams was a good example of the progressive female leader. After graduating from college, Addams sought a meaningful way to participate in society. She was financially independent. A visit to a settlement house in a London slum inspired her to start a similar program in Chicago. She was helped by her friend Ellen Starr.

With donations from wealthy Chicagoans, Addams and Starr rented an old mansion. Hull House was located in a poor, immigrant neighborhood. Within just a few years, they organized a full program of services, classes, and clubs. These were run by a group of young women residents and over 90 volunteers. Hull House served as an information bureau for new immigrants. It also helped the unemployed find jobs. It offered a kindergarten, a day nursery, after-school youth clubs, nutrition classes, and a concert program. Workers also pressured politicians for improved city services for the neighborhood.

### Connections TO LITERATURE

**WOMEN OUTSIDE THE HOME**
Charlotte Perkins Gilman (shown below) was an influential writer on women's rights. She wanted to free women from housework to pursue careers. In *Women and Economics* (1898), Gilman argued that a wife's dependency on her husband limited her personal development.

In *Concerning Children* (1900) and *The Home* (1903), she proposed that families live in large apartments. These would have centralized nurseries and a staff devoted to cooking, cleaning, and child-care. This support would free women to work outside the home.

---

*A VOICE FROM THE PAST*

One function of the settlement to its neighborhood somewhat resembled that of the big brother whose mere presence in the playground protected the little ones from bullies.

**Jane Addams,** quoted in *Women and the American Experience*

---

The young women residents of Hull House received no salary and had to pay for their room and board. This meant that they had to be financially independent. For some, Hull House provided training for other public service. Florence Kelley, for example, worked at Hull House from 1891 to 1898. She later became secretary of the National Consumers' League. This group promoted better working conditions in factories and stores.

Another prominent but controversial progressive leader was Carry Nation. She campaigned for prohibition. Nation had once been married to an alcoholic. Tall and strong, she adopted dramatic methods in her opposition to alcoholic beverages. In the 1890s, she smashed saloons with a hatchet. This caused law enforcement officials to arrest her for disturbing the peace. Although some people criticized Nation, her efforts helped bring about passage of the Eighteenth Amendment in 1919.

## Suffrage for Women

Many women progressives were active in the struggle for woman suffrage, or the right to vote. American women fought longer for the right to vote than they did for any other reform. Some leaders in the fight died before realizing their goal.

In 1890, two separate woman suffrage groups merged to form the National American Woman Suffrage Association (NAWSA). Elizabeth Cady Stanton served as its first president. Two years later, in 1892, **Susan B. Anthony** became president. She held the position until 1900. Expressing their frustration over the difficulty of gaining suffrage, Elizabeth Cady Stanton and Susan B. Anthony wrote, "Words can not describe the indignation, the humiliation a proud woman feels for her sex in disfranchisement [being deprived of the right to vote]."

NAWSA at first focused on state campaigns to win the right to vote, since earlier efforts at passing a federal amendment had failed. But by 1896, only four states allowed women to vote. These were Wyoming, Utah, Idaho, and Colorado. Between 1896 and 1910, women did not gain the right to vote in a single state. Then, between 1910 and 1914, seven more Western states approved full suffrage for women.

**Background**
Because she helped organize the woman suffrage movement, Susan B. Anthony became the first woman to be pictured on a U.S. coin.

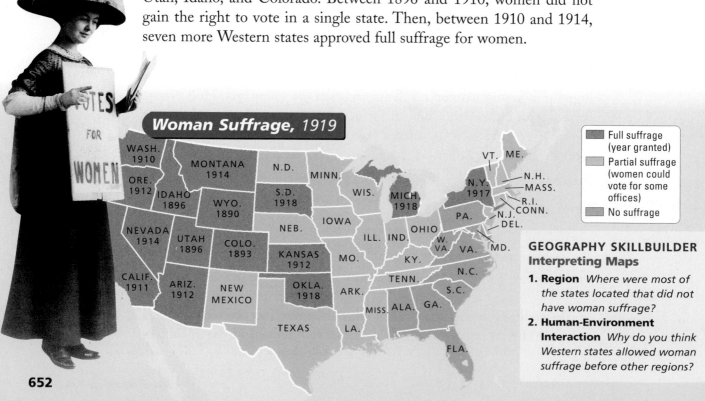

**Woman Suffrage, *1919***

WASH. 1910
MONTANA 1914
N.D.
MINN.
VT. ME.
N.H.
MASS.
ORE. 1912
IDAHO 1896
WYO. 1890
S.D. 1918
WIS.
MICH. 1918
N.Y. 1917
R.I.
CONN.
PA.
N.J.
DEL.
NEVADA 1914
UTAH 1896
NEB.
IOWA
ILL. IND.
OHIO
W. VA.
VA.
MD.
COLO. 1893
KANSAS 1912
MO.
KY.
N.C.
CALIF. 1911
ARIZ. 1912
NEW MEXICO
OKLA. 1918
ARK.
TENN.
S.C.
MISS. ALA. GA.
TEXAS
LA.
FLA.

Legend:
- Full suffrage (year granted)
- Partial suffrage (women could vote for some offices)
- No suffrage

**GEOGRAPHY SKILLBUILDER**
**Interpreting Maps**

1. **Region** Where were most of the states located that did not have woman suffrage?

2. **Human-Environment Interaction** Why do you think Western states allowed woman suffrage before other regions?

652

## The Progressive Amendments, 1909–1920

| Number | Description | Passed by Congress | Ratified by States |
|--------|-------------|--------------------|--------------------|
| 16th | Federal income tax | 1909 | 1913 |
| 17th | Senators elected by people rather than state legislatures | 1912 | 1913 |
| 18th | Manufacture, sale, or transport of alcohol prohibited | 1917 | 1919 |
| 19th | Woman suffrage | 1919 | 1920 |

**SKILLBUILDER Interpreting Charts**

**1.** For which amendment was there the longest gap between passage by Congress and ratification by states?

**2.** What do the dates 1909 and 1920 represent in this chart?

# The Nineteenth Amendment

The Western successes turned the tide in favor of woman suffrage. The United States' entry into World War I in 1917 made the final difference. During the war, membership in NAWSA reached 2 million. **Carrie Chapman Catt,** president of NAWSA, argued that the nation could no longer deny the right to vote to women, who were supporting the war effort by selling war bonds and organizing benefits. President Wilson urged the Senate to pass a women's suffrage amendment. He called passage "vital to the winning of the war."

In 1918, the House passed the **Nineteenth Amendment,** which gave women full voting rights. The Senate approved the amendment in 1919. In 1920, the states ratified it. In the final state campaigns, women staged marches, parades, and rallies around the country. Charlotte Woodard had attended the first women's rights convention in 1848 at Seneca Falls as a teenager. In 1920, the 91-year-old Woodard voted in a presidential election for the first time.

*Reading***History**

**B. Recognizing Effects** What factors helped women gain the right to vote?

---

**Section 3 Assessment**

### 1. Terms & Names

**Explain the significance of:**
- Susan B. Anthony
- Carrie Chapman Catt
- Nineteenth Amendment

### 2. Using Graphics

Use a chart to record the achievements of some women leaders of the era.

| Progressive Achievements | |
|--------------------------|--|
| Lillian Wald | |
| Jane Addams | |
| Florence Kelley | |

Which achievement seems greatest and why? (REP3)

### 3. Main Ideas

**a.** How did women's roles expand near the turn of the century? (HI3)

**b.** What was the background of many women who became leaders in social reform movements? (HI1)

**c.** How did World War I influence the passage of the Nineteenth Amendment? (HI2)

### 4. Critical Thinking

**Comparing and Contrasting** In what ways was the struggle for woman suffrage similar to and different from African Americans' struggle for equal rights? (HI3)

**THINK ABOUT**
- the restrictions that both groups faced
- how long they struggled for basic rights

**ACTIVITY OPTIONS**

**LANGUAGE ARTS**

**TECHNOLOGY**

Research one of the women reformers discussed in this chapter. Then write the **script** for the first 10 minutes of her documentary or design her **Web page.** (HI1)

## TERMS & NAMES

Briefly explain the significance of each of the following.

1. progressivism
2. muckrakers
3. referendum
4. Theodore Roosevelt
5. William Howard Taft
6. Sixteenth Amendment
7. Seventeenth Amendment
8. Susan B. Anthony
9. Carrie Chapman Catt
10. Nineteenth Amendment

## REVIEW QUESTIONS

### Roosevelt and Progressivism (pages 639–645)

1. What problems did progressivism address? (HI1)
2. How did progressive reformers expand democracy in the states? (HI1)
3. What was Roosevelt's "square deal"? (HI1)
4. What were Roosevelt's achievements in the area of conservation? (HI1)

### Taft and Wilson as Progressives (pages 646–649)

5. In what area did Taft achieve a more impressive progressive record than Roosevelt? (HI1)
6. What progressive goals did the Sixteenth and Seventeenth amendments address? (HI1)
7. How did Wilson's position on big business differ from Roosevelt's? (HI1)

### Women Win New Rights (pages 650–653)

8. How did women's lives change around 1900? (HI1)
9. What was the background of many women progressives? (HI1)
10. What helped further the passage of the Nineteenth Amendment in 1918? (HI2)

## CRITICAL THINKING

### 1. USING YOUR NOTES: IDENTIFYING AND SOLVING PROBLEMS

| PROBLEM | SOLUTION |
|---|---|
| **Political:** patronage; limited suffrage and democracy | |
| **Social:** poverty; alcohol abuse | |
| **Economic:** power of big corporations; unemployment | |
| **Environmental:** impure food and water; diminishing natural resources | |

Use your completed chart from the beginning of this chapter to answer these questions. (HI2)

a. Which solution to a problem do you think was most effective? Why?

b. Which solution was least effective and why?

c. To which problem on the chart might you offer a different solution, and what is your solution?

### 2. ANALYZING LEADERSHIP

Based on their domestic record, which president—Roosevelt, Taft, or Wilson—was most effective? Why? (HI1)

### 3. APPLYING CITIZENSHIP SKILLS

Why might women at the turn of the century consider the right to vote important enough to devote their lives to fighting for it? (HI1)

### 4. THEME: IMPACT OF THE INDIVIDUAL

In what ways did individuals affect the political, social, and economic life of the country during the Progressive Era? (HI2)

### Interact *with* History

How did your solution to one of the social problems of the Progressive Era compare to the solutions proposed by reformers?

## VISUAL SUMMARY

# The Progressive Era (HI2)

Corruption plagues the government.

Congress passes the Pendleton Civil Service Act (1883).

Theodore Roosevelt becomes president.

Roosevelt breaks up trusts, establishes "square deal," and advocates national parks.

Abuses in industry, politics, business, and labor are widespread.

Congress passes the Pure Food and Drug Act (1906), progressive amendments, Federal Reserve Act (1913), and the Clayton Antitrust Act (1914).

Women lack social justice and equality.

Vote for WOMEN

Women work to establish settlement houses, fight for woman suffrage, and gain 19th Amendment (1920).

Use the chart and your knowledge of U.S. history to answer questions 1 and 2.

Additional Test Practice, pp. S1–S33.

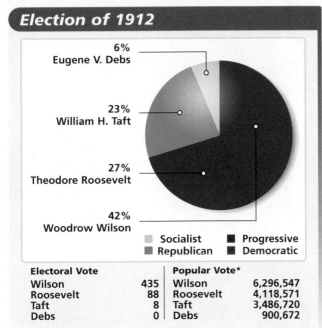

### Election of 1912

6%
**Eugene V. Debs**

23%
**William H. Taft**

27%
**Theodore Roosevelt**

42%
**Woodrow Wilson**

■ Socialist ■ Progressive
■ Republican ■ Democratic

| Electoral Vote | | Popular Vote* | |
|---|---|---|---|
| Wilson | 435 | Wilson | 6,296,547 |
| Roosevelt | 88 | Roosevelt | 4,118,571 |
| Taft | 8 | Taft | 3,486,720 |
| Debs | 0 | Debs | 900,672 |

*Other candidates received about 2% of the popular vote.

**1.** To which political party did Theodore Roosevelt belong? (8.12)

A. Democratic

B. Progressive

C. Republican

D. Socialist

**2.** How many electoral votes did Eugene Debs receive? (8.12)

A. 0

B. 6

C. 8

D. 88

This quotation from Eugene V. Debs describes his feelings about capitalism. Use the quotation and your knowledge of U.S. history to answer question 3.

#### PRIMARY SOURCE

Competition was natural enough at one time, but do you think you are competing today? . . . Against whom? Against Rockefeller? About as I would if I had a wheelbarrow and competed with the Santa Fe [railroad] from here to Kansas City.

**Eugene V. Debs,** quoted in *The Annals of America*

**3.** Which of the following best summarizes Debs' opinion of capitalism? (8.12.6)

A. Capitalism creates fair markets.

B. Capitalism creates unfair markets.

C. Capitalism creates competitive railroads.

D. Capitalism creates competitive farms.

**TEST PRACTICE**
CLASSZONE.COM

## ALTERNATIVE ASSESSMENT

**1.** ✎ **WRITING ABOUT HISTORY**

Jane Addams established Hull House with the help of donations from wealthy Chicago residents. Write a **letter** that Jane Addams might have written to people asking them to donate money to her project. (HI1)

- Research your letter by reading books about Jane Addams or about Hull House.
- Explain why people should donate money.

**2. COOPERATIVE LEARNING**

Working in a group, research the problems that African Americans faced during the Progressive Era and investigate President Wilson's attitudes toward civil rights. Write a script for a meeting in which African-American leaders confront Wilson about his voting record regarding civil rights. (REP4)

## INTEGRATED TECHNOLOGY

**DOING INTERNET RESEARCH**

Use the Internet to find information about national parks that interest you. Then choose one of these as the subject of a classroom presentation. (REP3)

- Begin your research on <u>nationalparks.com</u> where you can find information about all the parks. Use that information to decide on one park to research.
- Each national park has its own Web site. Use these sites to gather information.
- Include a map, a description of park features and recreational activities, photographs, and a database of facts in your presentation.

For more about national parks . . .

**INTERNET ACTIVITY**
CLASSZONE.COM

# Becoming a World Power 1880–1917

The "Great White Fleet" of the United States symbolized the nation's presence as a global power at the beginning of the 20th century.

**1893**
Planters overthrow the Hawaiian queen, Liliuokalani.

**1887**
Hawaii grants United States exclusive use of Pearl Harbor.

**1892**
Grover Cleveland is elected president.

**1896**
William McKinley is elected president.

USA
World 1880

**1884**
European nations meet at the Berlin Conference to divide Africa.

**1895**
Sino-Japanese War ends with Japanese victory over China.

The fleet was made up of 16 new battleships of the Atlantic Fleet that sailed around the world between 1907 and 1909.

The ships were manned by 14,000 sailors and covered 43,000 miles.

In 1907, the United States launches one of the greatest naval fleets in history—the Great White Fleet. With this fleet, the United States has the military might to enforce political decisions involving foreign countries. Now you, the U.S. president, need to decide where and how to best use this fleet.

# When should you get involved in the affairs of another country?

## What Do You Think?

- What interests does the United States have in other countries?
- How important is protecting those interests?

### RESEARCH LINKS
### CLASSZONE.COM
Visit the Chapter 23 links for more information about the growth of the United States.

**1898**
Spanish-American War takes place.

**1901**
Theodore Roosevelt becomes president after McKinley is assassinated.

**1904**
Roosevelt is elected president.

**1908**
William Howard Taft is elected president.

**1912**
Woodrow Wilson is elected president.

**1914**
Panama Canal opens.

**1917**

**•00**
ɔxer
ʈion
s in
ina.

**1903**
Republic of Panama established.

**1904**
Russo-Japanese War begins.

**1910**
Mexican Revolution begins.

**1916**
Pancho Villa makes a raid in the United States.

# Reading Strategy: Finding Main Ideas

## What Do You Know?

Was expansion something new, or was it a force that you have seen before in the history of the United States?

### Think About

- the idea of Manifest Destiny
- the Louisiana Purchase
- the War with Mexico
- your responses to the Interact with History about getting involved in the affairs of another country (see page 657)

## What Do You Want to Know?

What do you think might have caused the United States to expand overseas at the end of the 1800s? Make a list of the possible reasons before you read the chapter.

**CALIFORNIA STANDARDS**

**Reading 2.0** Students read and understand grade-level-appropriate material. They describe and connect the essential ideas, arguments, and perspectives of the text by using their knowledge of text structure, organization, and purpose.

The American eagle spreads its wings over Asia and Latin America in this political cartoon from 1904.

## Finding Main Ideas

An important skill for reading history is the ability to find main ideas. Identifying main ideas helps you to organize and understand the variety of details and examples that support those ideas. Use a chart like the one below to write main ideas about U.S. expansion overseas.

See Skillbuilder Handbook, page R5.

 Taking Notes

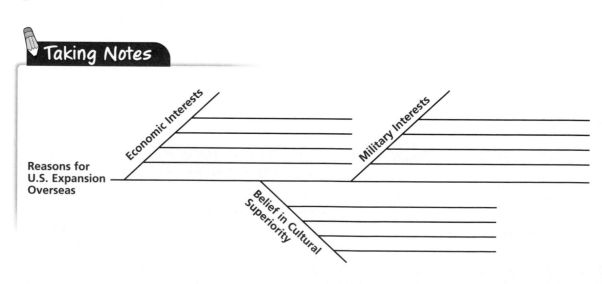

# The United States Continues to Expand

| MAIN IDEA | WHY IT MATTERS NOW | TERMS & NAMES |
|---|---|---|
| The United States expanded its interest in world affairs and acquired new territories. | During this period, the United States acquired Alaska and Hawaii as territories. | imperialism  Queen Liliuokalani<br>William Seward |

## ONE AMERICAN'S STORY

Alfred T. Mahan served in the U.S. Navy for nearly 40 years. In the 1890s, he wrote several books on the historical importance of sea power, trading stations, and colonies.

### A VOICE FROM THE PAST

The trading-station . . . [was] the same as the . . . colony. In both cases the mother-country had won a foothold in a foreign land, seeking a new outlet for what it had to sell, a new sphere for its shipping, more employment for its people, and more comfort and wealth for itself.

**A. T. Mahan,** *The Influence of Sea Power upon History, 1660–1805*

Naval historian Alfred Thayer Mahan at the turn of the century

CALIFORNIA STANDARDS

**CST3** Students use a variety of maps and documents to identify physical and cultural features of neighborhoods, cities, states, and countries and to explain the historical migration of people, expansion and disintegration of empires, and the growth of economic systems.

**REP3** Students distinguish relevant information, essential from incidental information, and verifiable from unverifiable information in historical narratives and stories.

**HI2** Students understand and distinguish cause, effect, sequence, and correlation in historical events, including the long- and short-term causal relations.

Mahan encouraged government officials to build up American naval forces. In this section you will learn how the United States began to extend its influence beyond the national boundaries.

## Reasons for U.S. Expansion

Americans had always sought to expand the size of their nation. Throughout the 19th century, they extended their control toward the Pacific Coast. By the 1880s, however, many leaders became convinced that the United States should join the imperialist powers of Europe and establish colonies overseas. **Imperialism**—the policy by which stronger nations extend their economic, political, or military control over weaker territories—was a trend around the world.

European nations had been establishing colonies for centuries. In the late 19th century, Africa became a major area of European expansion. By the early 20th century, only two countries in Africa—Ethiopia and Liberia—remained independent.

Imperialist countries also competed for territory in Asia, especially in China. There, European nations had to compete with Japan, which had also become a world power by the end of the 1800s.

✏️ **Taking Notes**

Use your chart to take notes about the reasons for U.S. expansion overseas.

Reasons for U.S. Expansion Overseas

*Becoming a World Power* **659**

Most Americans gradually came to approve of the idea of expansion overseas. Three factors helped to fuel the development of American imperialism.

1. **Economic Interests.** Economic leaders argued that expansion would increase U.S. financial prosperity. Industry had greatly expanded after the Civil War. Many industrialists saw new colonies as a potential source of cheap raw materials. Agriculture had also expanded. Farmers pointed out that colonies would mean new markets for their products.

2. **Military Interests.** In his books, Alfred T. Mahan had argued that economic interests went hand-in-hand with military interests. Foreign policy experts agreed. They urged U.S. leaders to follow the European example and establish a military presence overseas.

3. **Belief in Cultural Superiority.** Many Americans believed that their government, religion, and even race were superior to those of other societies. Some people hoped to spread democratic ideas overseas. Others saw a chance to advance Christianity. Racist ideas about the inferiority of the nonwhite populations in many foreign countries were also used to justify American imperialism.

Each of these developments—economic interests, military interests, and a belief in cultural superiority—led the United States to a larger role on the world stage.

*Reading***History**
**A. Making Inferences** Why might economic and military interests go hand in hand?

## Seward and Alaska

A strong backer of expansion was **William Seward,** Secretary of State under presidents Abraham Lincoln and Andrew Johnson. Seward made his biggest move in 1867, when he arranged the purchase of Alaska from Russia.

Not everyone was pleased by Seward's move, though. At the time, the $7.2-million deal was widely criticized. Newspapers called Alaska a "Polar Bear Garden" and "Seward's Icebox." Even so, the purchase of the resource-rich territory turned out to be a great bargain for the United States.

Throughout his career, Seward continued to pursue new territory. Before he retired in 1869, he considered acquiring the Hawaiian Islands, a group of volcanic and coral islands in the central Pacific Ocean. That would not happen, however, for almost 30 more years.

**Background**
In the late 1800s, large gold fields were discovered in Alaska. The territory was also rich in fur-bearing animals, timber, copper, coal, and oil.

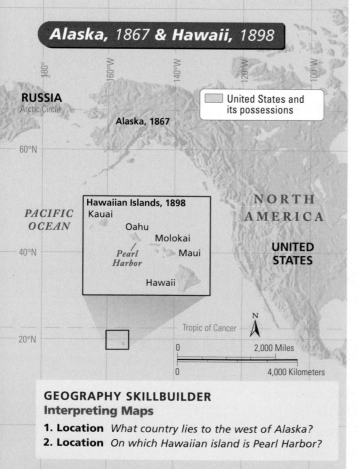

**Alaska, 1867 & Hawaii, 1898**

RUSSIA
Arctic Circle

Alaska, 1867

United States and its possessions

60°N

PACIFIC OCEAN

Hawaiian Islands, 1898
Kauai
Oahu
Molokai
*Pearl Harbor*  Maui
Hawaii

NORTH AMERICA

UNITED STATES

40°N

Tropic of Cancer

20°N

0    2,000 Miles
0    4,000 Kilometers

**GEOGRAPHY SKILLBUILDER**
**Interpreting Maps**

1. **Location** *What country lies to the west of Alaska?*
2. **Location** *On which Hawaiian island is Pearl Harbor?*

# The Annexation of Hawaii

*Reading*History
**B. Reading a Map**
Locate the Hawaiian Islands on the map on page 660.

In the early 1800s, Christian missionaries from the United States had moved to the Kingdom of Hawaii to convert the local population. Some of the missionaries' descendants started sugar plantations. By the late 1800s, wealthy planters dominated Hawaii's economy.

In 1891, **Queen Liliuokalani** (lee•LEE•oo•oh•kah•LAH•nee) became the leader of Hawaii. Believing that planters had too much influence, she wanted to limit their power. Around the same time, U.S. trade laws changed to favor sugar grown exclusively in American states.

American planters in Hawaii were upset by these threats to their political and economic interests. In January 1893, they staged a revolt. With the help of U.S. Marines, they overthrew the queen and set up their own government. They then asked to be annexed by the United States.

**Vocabulary**
**annex:** to add

U.S. leaders already understood the value of the islands. In 1887, they had pressured Hawaii to allow a U.S. naval base at Pearl Harbor, the kingdom's best port. The base became an important refueling station for American merchant and military ships bound for Asia.

Thus, when President Benjamin Harrison received the planters' request in 1893, he gave his approval and sent a treaty to the Senate. But before the Senate could act, Grover Cleveland became president. He did not approve of the planters' actions and withdrew the treaty. Hawaii would not be annexed until 1898, during the Spanish-American War. In the next section, you will read about the events that led to that war.

# AMERICA'S HISTORY MAKERS

**QUEEN LILIUOKALANI**
**1838–1917**

As a young princess, Liliuokalani received a Western education and toured the world. Although she learned about many cultures, she remained committed to Hawaii. An excellent musician, she wrote the famous Hawaiian song "Aloha Oe [Farewell to Thee]."

She was the first queen of Hawaii and proved to be a good leader. She resisted the foreign takeover of Hawaii and inspired a revolt against the planters. Only in 1895, when the safety of her supporters was threatened, did she agree to give up her throne.

**How did Queen Liliuokalani protect her followers after planters seized power?**

---

## Section 1 Assessment

### 1. Terms & Names

**Explain the significance of:**
• imperialism
• William Seward
• Queen Liliuokalani

### 2. Using Graphics

Use a chart like the one shown to record causes of U.S. expansion overseas in the late 1800s.

Causes → Effect: United States expansion

Which was the most important cause? (HI2)

### 3. Main Ideas

**a.** Where was the focus of U.S. expansion before the late 1800s? (HI1)

**b.** How did William Seward contribute to U.S. expansion? (HI1)

**c.** Why did the American planters' request for the annexation of Hawaii fail in the early 1890s? (HI1)

### 4. Critical Thinking

**Making Inferences** What benefits were American planters looking for when they staged a revolt in 1893? (REP5)

**THINK ABOUT**
• the new policies of Queen Liliuokalani
• changes in U.S. trade laws

**ACTIVITY OPTIONS**

**TECHNOLOGY**

**ART**

Read more about Hawaii's Queen Liliuokalani. Outline a **video presentation** on the overthrow of the queen or plan a **mural** that depicts the event. (HI1)

# The Spanish-American War

| MAIN IDEA | WHY IT MATTERS NOW | TERMS & NAMES |
|---|---|---|
| Independence movements in Spanish colonies led to the Spanish-American War in 1898. | U.S. involvement in Latin America and Asia expanded greatly after the Spanish-American War. | yellow journalism  Rough Riders<br>U.S.S. *Maine*  Platt Amendment<br>Spanish-American  Anti-Imperialist League<br>War  Luis Muñoz Rivera |

**CALIFORNIA STANDARDS**

**8.3.7** Understand the functions and responsibilities of a free press.

**CST3** Students use a variety of maps and documents to identify physical and cultural features of neighborhoods, cities, states, and countries and to explain the historical migration of people, expansion and disintegration of empires, and the growth of economic systems.

**REP3** Students distinguish relevant information, essential from incidental information, and verifiable from unverifiable information in historical narratives and stories.

**REP4** Students assess the credibility of primary and secondary sources and draw sound conclusions from them.

## ONE AMERICAN'S STORY

José Martí was forced to leave Cuba in the 1870s. In those years, Cuba was a Spanish colony, and he had spoken out for independence. Martí later described the terrible conditions suffered under Spanish rule.

### A VOICE FROM THE PAST

Cuba's children . . . suffer in indescribable bitterness as they see their fertile nation enchained and also their human dignity stifled . . . all for the necessities and vices of the [Spanish] monarchy.

**José Martí,** quoted in *José Martí, Mentor of the Cuban Nation*

José Martí dedicated his life to the Cuban struggle for independence from Spain.

In New York City, Martí began to plan a revolt against Spain that began in 1895. Martí's lifelong struggle for Cuban independence made him a symbol of liberty throughout Latin America. In this section, you will read how U.S. disapproval of Spain's treatment of Cubans led to the Spanish-American War.

## Rebellion Against Spain

The Spanish empire was crumbling at the end of the 19th century. Spain had once controlled most of the Americas, including land that became part of the United States. By the 1890s, however, it owned only a few colonies. Among them were the Philippine Islands in the Pacific and the Caribbean islands of Cuba and Puerto Rico. (See the maps on page 665.) Many of the inhabitants of these colonies had begun to demand independence.

Cubans had revolted against Spain several times in the second half of the nineteenth century. Each time, Spanish soldiers defeated the rebels. In 1895, an ongoing economic depression had increased Cubans' anger over Spanish rule, and they rebelled again. José Martí, who had helped to organize the rebellion from New York, returned to Cuba. He was killed in a skirmish with Spanish troops shortly after, but the revolt continued.

**Taking Notes**

Use your chart to take notes about the reasons for U.S. expansion overseas.

Reasons
for U.S.
Expansion
Overseas

Spain sent General Valeriano "the Butcher" Weyler to crush the rebels. Weyler's methods were harsh. He forced many Cubans from their homes and placed them in camps guarded by Spanish troops. Thousands died of starvation and disease in the camps.

The revolt in Cuba caused alarm in the United States. Business leaders were concerned because the fighting disrupted U.S. trade with Cuba. Most Americans, however, became outraged when the press began to describe the brutality of Spanish officials. Two New York City newspapers, in particular, stirred up people's emotions.

*Reading*History

A. Forming Opinions How can newspapers affect public opinion?

The *World*, owned by Joseph Pulitzer, and the *New York Journal*, owned by William Randolph Hearst, were battling for customers. Both owners were able to attract readers by printing stories that described—and often exaggerated—news about Spanish cruelty. This sensational style of writing was known as **yellow journalism**. It was named after "The Yellow Kid," a popular comic strip that ran in the two New York papers.

## The United States Goes to War

William McKinley, the U.S. president in 1898, did not want war. "I have been through [the Civil War]," he told a friend. "I have seen the dead piled up, and I do not want to see another."

Even so, public opinion—stirred up by sensational newspaper reports—forced McKinley to take action. He demanded that Spain halt its harsh treatment of Cubans. Spain did bring General Weyler home, but conditions remained severe.

In January 1898, McKinley sent the **U.S.S. *Maine*** to Cuba. Riots had broken out in the capital, Havana, and the battleship was dispatched to protect U.S. citizens. Then, the following month, the *Maine* exploded and sank in Havana's harbor, killing 260 sailors.

The explosion of the *Maine* and accounts of the event by yellow journalists led many Americans to favor war against Spain.

No one knows what caused the explosion. Most historians today believe that it was an accident. For example, a spark might have set off an explosion in the ship's coal bunker. Even so, Americans blamed Spain.

## Detecting Bias in the Media

Modern journalists try to report the news without bias—that is, without letting their personal opinions or those of their employer influence what they write. Unbiased reporting is one of the responsibilities of a free press. It allows citizens to weigh the facts and come to their own understanding of issues and events.

As you have read, journalists and their employers do not always avoid bias. In fact, in the 1890s, journalists were not concerned with bias. Before the United States declared war on Spain in 1898, 'yellow journalists' exaggerated stories to help sell newspapers. These stories helped turn U.S. public opinion in favor of war against Spain. They used words and images to reflect their bias that the United States should declare war on Spain—and sell more papers along the way.

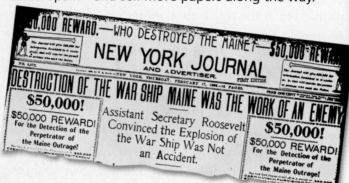

**William Randolph Hearst ran this headline in his *New York Journal* before authorities had a chance to determine the cause of the *Maine*'s explosion.**

### Can You Find Bias in the Media?

1. With a small group, collect news stories from different sources that cover the same issue or event.

2. Record any differences in the way a specific issue or event is covered by the oral, written, or visual sources you have selected.

3. Review the differences and decide whether any of the authors of the sources showed bias in their coverage.

4. Write a report that describes any bias you might detect. Explain why the biased source might have reported the story the way it did.

 See Citizenship Handbook, page 284.

For more about the news media . . .

 **RESEARCH LINKS** CLASSZONE.COM

---

"Remember the Maine!" became a call to arms. On April 20, 1898, President McKinley signed a congressional resolution that called for Cuba's independence and demanded a withdrawal of Spanish forces. He gave Spain three days to respond. Spain refused, and the **Spanish-American War** began.

## The War in the Philippines

The United States went to war to fight for Cuban freedom. But the first major battle of the Spanish-American War took place in a Spanish colony on the other side of the world—the Philippine Islands. Many Filipinos, as the inhabitants of the islands were called, had also revolted against Spanish rule in the 1890s.

Before the war began, the Filipino independence movement had attracted the attention of Theodore Roosevelt. At that time, Roosevelt was assistant secretary of the navy. He put a fleet of American ships in Hong Kong on alert. Their leader, Commodore George Dewey, prepared his forces and made contact with the head of the Filipino rebel forces, Emilio Aguinaldo (eh•MEE•lyoh AH•gee•NAHL•doh).

When the war began, Dewey set out for Manila, the Philippine capital, where part of the Spanish fleet was located. The battle in Manila Bay began early on the morning of May 1, 1898. By a little past noon,

*Reading*History
**B. Making Inferences** Why did Theodore Roosevelt put the U.S. fleet in Hong Kong on alert?

Dewey's forces had destroyed the Spanish fleet. About 380 Spanish sailors were dead or wounded. No Americans died. U.S. troops, aided by Filipino rebels, took control of Manila in August.

Dewey became an instant hero in the United States. Thousands of babies born at the time of the victory in Manila Bay were named for him, and a chewing gum called "Dewey's Chewies" became popular.

## The War in the Caribbean

When the Spanish-American War began, the U.S. Army had only 28,000 men. Within four months, over 200,000 more joined up. Among the new recruits was Theodore Roosevelt, who had resigned from the Navy Department to volunteer.

Roosevelt helped to organize the First United States Volunteer Cavalry. This unit was nicknamed the **Rough Riders.** Its recruits included cowboys, miners, college students, New York policemen, athletes, and Native Americans.

In June, the Rough Riders and about 16,000 other soldiers—nearly a quarter of them African American—gathered in Tampa, Florida. They then set out for Santiago, a Spanish stronghold in southern Cuba. When the Rough Riders arrived, their dark-blue wool uniforms were too hot for the Cuban climate. Also, many of the soldiers came down with tropical diseases. Even so, they fought their way toward Santiago.

In order to gain control of Santiago's port, American troops had to capture San Juan Hill. They attacked the Spanish on July 1.

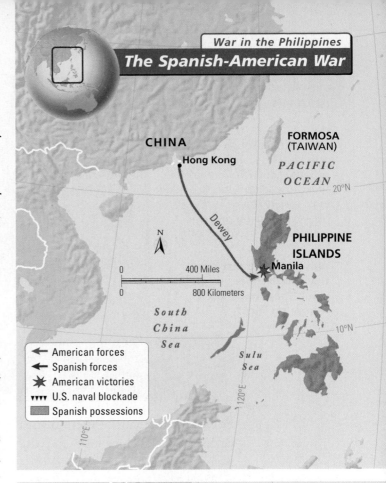

War in the Philippines
*The Spanish-American War*

← American forces
← Spanish forces
✴ American victories
▼▼▼▼ U.S. naval blockade
▨ Spanish possessions

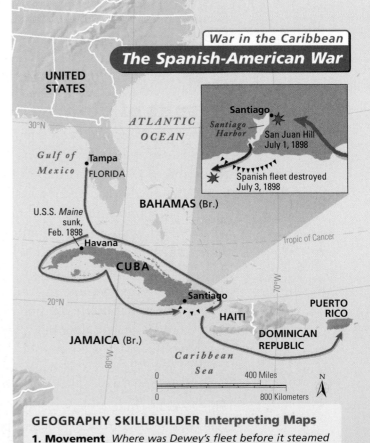

War in the Caribbean
*The Spanish-American War*

### GEOGRAPHY SKILLBUILDER Interpreting Maps

1. **Movement** Where was Dewey's fleet before it steamed toward the Philippines?
2. **Location** About how far is Havana from the tip of southern Florida?

**665**

**HISTORY through ART**

On July 1, 1898, U.S. troops, including the Rough Riders, attacked San Juan Hill outside of Santiago, Cuba. This painting shows Theodore Roosevelt leading a cavalry charge up the hill—even though the regiment's horses had been left behind in Florida.

**Why did the artist show the Rough Riders on horses when they made their charge on foot?**

African-American soldiers from the Tenth Cavalry began to drive the Spanish back. Roosevelt and the Rough Riders joined them as they rushed forward and captured the hill.

Two days later, American ships destroyed Spain's fleet as it tried to escape Santiago Harbor. On July 17, the city surrendered. A week later, U.S. forces took Puerto Rico. Finally, on August 12, 1898, Spain signed a truce. To U.S. Secretary of State John Hay, it had been "a splendid little war." For Spain, four centuries of glory had come to an end.

## Results of the War

Although the war had been fought over Cuba, U.S. leaders demanded that Spain give up other colonies after the war—including Puerto Rico, the island of Guam, and the Philippines. Spain had no choice but to agree. The final peace treaty was signed in Paris in December 1898.

One of the most difficult questions for U.S. leaders after the war was what to do with the Philippines. Filipinos had fought alongside Americans during the war and believed that Spain's defeat would bring them independence. But President McKinley eventually decided that the Philippines should become an American colony.

Filipinos were bitterly disappointed. Led by Emilio Aguinaldo, they began to fight against their new colonial rulers. American troops sent to put down the resistance were not able to restore order until 1902.

The United States was also reluctant to grant Cuba complete independence. First, Cuba had to add the **Platt Amendment** to its constitution. This gave the United States the right to intervene in Cuban affairs anytime there was a threat to "life, property, and individual liberty." Cuba also had to allow a U.S. naval base at Guantánamo Bay.

Puerto Rico became an American territory. The United States set up a government and appointed the top officials. Puerto Ricans had little to

*Reading* **History**

**C. Making Inferences** Why did the United States demand that Spain give up territories in addition to Cuba?

say in their own affairs. Only in 1917 would the United States agree to make Puerto Rico a self-governing territory and grant U.S. citizenship to all Puerto Ricans.

## The Anti-Imperialist League

U.S. treatment of Spain's former colonies after the Spanish-American War disappointed many people in the United States.

Several well-known Americans, including businessman Andrew Carnegie, reformer Jane Addams, and writer Mark Twain, joined with others to form the **Anti-Imperialist League.** Members of the League believed that Americans should not deny other people the right to govern themselves.

*Reading* **History**

**D. Finding Main Ideas** Why did the Anti-Imperialist League oppose U.S. efforts to collect colonies?

### A VOICE FROM THE PAST

We hold that the policy known as imperialism is hostile to liberty. . . . We regret that it has become necessary in the land of Washington and Lincoln to reaffirm that all men, of whatever race or color, are entitled to life, liberty, and the pursuit of happiness.

From the *Platform of the American Anti-Imperialist League*

The voice of the Anti-Imperialist League was lost, however, in the roar of popular approval of the Spanish-American War.

Many Americans hoped that their nation would surpass the glory of the old Spanish empire. In the next section, you will read more about how the United States continued its involvement overseas.

**AMERICA'S HISTORY MAKERS**

**LUIS MUÑOZ RIVERA**
**1859–1916**

**Luis Muñoz Rivera** devoted his life to obtaining self-government for Puerto Rico—first from Spain and then from the United States.

After Spain granted Puerto Rico self-rule in 1897, Muñoz Rivera joined the government. He resigned and renewed his struggle when Puerto Rico became a U.S. territory.

Muñoz Rivera died just before the United States granted Puerto Ricans U.S. citizenship and a large measure of self-government.

**In what ways did Muñoz Rivera use his leadership skills to help his country?**

---

Section **2** Assessment

### 1. Terms & Names

**Explain the significance of:**
- yellow journalism
- U.S.S. *Maine*
- Spanish-American War
- Rough Riders
- Platt Amendment
- Anti-Imperialist League
- Luis Muñoz Rivera

### 2. Using Graphics

Use a time line to record the major events of the Spanish-American War.

**Spanish-American War, 1898**

About how long did the Spanish-American War last? (CST2)

### 3. Main Ideas

**a.** What led to the Cuban rebellion against Spain in 1895? (HI2)

**b.** What was the first major military event of the Spanish-American War? (HI2)

**c.** What happened in the Philippines after the war? (HI2)

### 4. Critical Thinking

**Forming Opinions** Did the United States betray its democratic principles when it made the Philippines a colony? (REP4)

**THINK ABOUT**
- the public's response to yellow journalists and U.S. military victories
- the work of the Anti-Imperialist League

---

**ACTIVITY OPTIONS**

**LANGUAGE ARTS**
**MATH**

Research the Spanish-American War. Write a **television news script** covering a major battle or create a **database** of wartime casualties. (HI1)

# U.S. Involvement Overseas

| **MAIN IDEA** | **WHY IT MATTERS NOW** | **TERMS & NAMES** |
|---|---|---|
| In the early 1900s, the United States expanded its involvement in Asia and Latin America. | The United States still trades extensively with Asian and Latin American countries. | sphere of influence<br>Open Door Policy<br>Boxer Rebellion<br><br>Panama Canal<br>Roosevelt Corollary |

## ONE AMERICAN'S STORY

In 1852, President Millard Fillmore sent Commodore Matthew Perry on a mission to open Japan to U.S. trade. For over two centuries, Japan's rulers had kept the country closed to most foreigners. Perry wanted to break Japan's traditional policy.

### A VOICE FROM THE PAST

[I was determined] to adopt an entirely contrary plan of proceedings from that of all others who had . . . visited Japan on the same errand [to open up trade]: to demand as a right and not to [ask] as a favor those acts of courtesy which are due from one civilized nation to another.

**Commodore Matthew Perry,** *Personal Journal*

Commodore Matthew Perry meets with Japanese officials in 1853.

Under the threat of force, Japan signed a treaty in 1854 giving American ships access to its ports. In this section, you will read more about U.S. involvement in Asia, as well as in Latin America.

## A Power in the Pacific

Throughout the 1800s, the United States continued to expand its involvement in Asia. Toward the end of the century, the United States acquired a chain of islands—including Hawaii and Guam—that stretched across the Pacific Ocean to Asia.

During the Spanish-American War, Americans fought in the Philippine Islands, a Spanish colony in eastern Asia. After the war, the United States annexed the islands and put down the Filipino independence movement.

Some Americans objected to the annexation of the Philippines. However, supporters of imperialism, such as Indiana senator Albert Beveridge, applauded U.S. actions. Beveridge boasted, "The Philippines

**Taking Notes**

Use your chart to take notes about the reasons for U.S. expansion overseas.

Reasons for U.S. Expansion Overseas

are ours forever. And just beyond the Philippines are China's [unlimited] markets. We will not retreat from either. . . . The power that rules the Pacific is the power that rules the world."

*"The power that rules the Pacific . . . rules the world."*

**Albert Beveridge**

Many Americans looked forward to the profits promised by Asian markets and resources. Others saw a chance to extend U.S. democracy and culture in the region. The Philippines would provide a base for these activities.

## The United States in China

As Senator Beveridge noted, control of the Philippines gave Americans greater access to China. However, by the time the United States acquired the islands, other imperialist nations, including Japan, were already deeply involved in China.

When Commodore Perry opened Japan to U.S. trade in the 1850s, he also opened the nation to Western ideas. After Perry's voyages, Japan began to modernize and soon emerged as a world power. In the 1890s, Japan demonstrated its strength in a successful war against China.

After the war, both Japan and the major European powers expanded their **spheres of influence** in China. These were areas where foreign nations claimed special rights and economic privileges. By the late 1890s, France, Germany, Britain, Japan, and Russia had established prosperous settlements along the coast of China. They also claimed exclusive rights to railroad construction and mining development in the nation's interior.

The competition for spheres of influence worried U.S. leaders who wanted access to China's markets and resources. In 1899, Secretary of State John Hay asked nations involved in the region to follow an **Open Door Policy.** This meant that no single country should have a monopoly on trade with China. Eventually, most of the nations accepted Hay's proposal.

*Reading*History

**A. Analyzing Causes** Why did John Hay propose the Open Door Policy?

Many Chinese people were not pleased by the presence of foreigners. One group, called the "Boxers," was angered by the privileges given to foreigners and the disrespect they showed toward Chinese traditions. In 1900, Chinese resentment toward foreigners' attitude of cultural superiority led to a violent uprising known as the **Boxer Rebellion.** Many foreigners were killed before the uprising was put down by an international force.

## Imperialism in Asia, 1900

MANCHURIA

MONGOLIA

Beijing (Peking)

JAPAN

KOREA

CHINA

Shanghai

PACIFIC OCEAN

30°N

Macao (Portuguese)

Hong Kong (Br.)

FORMOSA (TAIWAN)

PHILIPPINE ISLANDS (U.S.)

0 ___ 1,000 Miles
0 ___ 2,000 Kilometers

■ Russian sphere
■ German sphere
■ British sphere
□ French sphere
■ Japanese sphere

**GEOGRAPHY SKILLBUILDER Interpreting Maps**

1. **Place** *What country controlled the port of Macao?*
2. **Region** *What country had the largest sphere of influence in the coastal region of China?*

# The Panama Canal

As American interests in the Pacific expanded, easy access to the region became vital. For that reason, U.S. leaders proposed a canal to connect the Atlantic and Pacific oceans. A canal would mean that U.S. ships would not have to travel around South America. The Spanish-American War, fought in both oceans, also made clear the need for such a shortcut.

The South American nation of Colombia controlled the best spot for the canal—the Isthmus of Panama. But Colombia was unwilling to give up this land. Ignoring Colombia's right to control its territory, President Roosevelt sent the U.S. Navy to support a revolution on the isthmus. Out of this revolution, the new nation of Panama was created in 1903.

The new Panamanian leaders granted the U.S. government rights to a ten-mile-wide strip of land called the Canal Zone. In return, the United States paid Panama $10 million and an annual fee of $250,000. There, the United States would build the **Panama Canal,** the shortcut that would connect the Atlantic and Pacific oceans.

Some people in Latin America and the United States opposed Roosevelt's actions. They believed that he had interfered in Colombia's affairs in order to cheat it out of land. In 1921, the United States finally paid Colombia $25 million for the loss of Panama.

**Vocabulary**
isthmus: a narrow strip of land connecting two larger masses of land

*Reading* **History**
**B. Summarizing** What political difficulty faced U.S. leaders who wanted to build the Panama Canal?

## Building the Canal

Building the canal was extremely difficult. The land was swampy and full of mosquitoes that carried the organism that causes malaria. In spite of the difficulties, the project moved forward. When Roosevelt visited Panama in 1906, he wrote a letter describing the work.

**Panama Canal**

ATLANTIC OCEAN

N

Canal route
Canal Zone

Colón
Cristóbal
Gatún Locks
*Chagres R.*
Madden Lake
*Chagres R.*
Madden Dam
Gatún Dam
*Gatún Lake*
Gaillard (Culebra) Cut
Pedro Miguel Locks
Miraflores Locks
*Miraflores Lake*
Panama City
Balboa

0    10 Miles
0    10 Kilometers

**GEOGRAPHY SKILLBUILDER Interpreting Maps**
1. **Location** *Which locks are closest to Panama City?*
2. **Movement** *In which direction do ships move through the canal from the Atlantic Ocean to the Pacific Ocean?*

### A VOICE FROM THE PAST

Steam shovels are hard at it; scooping huge masses of rock and gravel and dirt previously loosened by the drillers and dynamite blasters, loading it on trains which take it away. . . . They are eating steadily into the mountain cutting it down and down. . . . It is an epic feat.

**Theodore Roosevelt,** from a letter sent to his son

More than 45,000 workers, including many black West Indians, labored for years on the canal. They did not finish the work until 1914. The canal cost $352 million, the most expensive project up to that time. It was expensive in human terms, too. More than 5,000 workers died from diseases or accidents.

**Background**
In 1977, the United States signed a treaty that transferred ownership of the canal to Panama on December 31, 1999.

# How the Panama Canal Works

Engineers faced a problem in building the Panama Canal. Because of the region's different landscape elevations, no waterway would remain level. They solved this dilemma by building three sets of *locks*—water-filled chambers that raise or lower ships to match a canal's different water levels.

**1** The lock gates open on one end to allow the ship to enter.

**2** The gates close, and water is pumped in or out depending on whether the ship is moving up or down.

**3** Once the water in the chamber and the canal ahead is level, the second gate opens and the ship moves on.

The locks, whose steel gates rise six stories high, can hold as much as 26 million gallons of water—enough to supply a major U.S. city for one day.

**CALIFORNIA STANDARDS**

**8.12.1** Trace patterns of agricultural and industrial development as they relate to climate, use of natural resources, markets, and trade and locate such development on a map.

Gatún Locks — Culebra Cut — Pedro Miguel Locks
Gatún Lake — Miraflores Lake — Miraflores Locks
Atlantic Ocean — Pacific Ocean
◄— 51 miles —►

This cross-section shows the different elevations and locks that a ship moves through on the 8–9 hour trip through the canal. Before the canal was built, a trip around South America could take two months.

## CONNECT TO HISTORY
1. **Drawing Conclusions** Why did the United States want a shorter route between the Atlantic and Pacific oceans?

## CONNECT TO TODAY
2. **Researching** What is the economic and political status of the Panama Canal today?

For more about the Panama Canal . . .

**RESEARCH LINKS**
CLASSZONE.COM

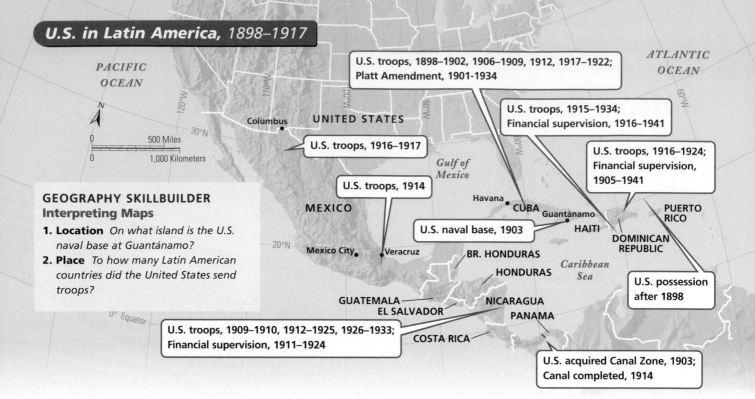

**U.S. in Latin America,** *1898–1917*

*PACIFIC OCEAN*

*ATLANTIC OCEAN*

U.S. troops, 1898–1902, 1906–1909, 1912, 1917–1922; Platt Amendment, 1901-1934

U.S. troops, 1915–1934; Financial supervision, 1916–1941

U.S. troops, 1916–1917

U.S. troops, 1916–1924; Financial supervision, 1905–1941

Columbus

UNITED STATES

U.S. troops, 1914

*Gulf of Mexico*

Havana

CUBA Guantánamo

PUERTO RICO

**GEOGRAPHY SKILLBUILDER**
**Interpreting Maps**

1. **Location** *On what island is the U.S. naval base at Guantánamo?*
2. **Place** *To how many Latin American countries did the United States send troops?*

MEXICO

U.S. naval base, 1903

HAITI

DOMINICAN REPUBLIC

Mexico City

Veracruz

BR. HONDURAS

*Caribbean Sea*

HONDURAS

U.S. possession after 1898

*Equator*

GUATEMALA
EL SALVADOR

NICARAGUA

PANAMA

U.S. troops, 1909–1910, 1912–1925, 1926–1933; Financial supervision, 1911–1924

COSTA RICA

U.S. acquired Canal Zone, 1903; Canal completed, 1914

## U.S. Involvement in Latin America

The Panama Canal was only one sign of U.S. involvement in Latin America. As the U.S. economy continued to grow, so did Americans' interest in the resources of their southern neighbors.

Businesses in the United States found that they could cheaply buy food and raw materials—for example, bananas, coffee, and copper—from Latin America. They shipped these goods to the United States and sold them for higher prices. U.S. companies also bought large amounts of land in the region for farming and mining.

As economic interests drew the United States deeper into Latin American affairs, U.S. leaders became concerned about political stability in the region. They were especially worried that instability might tempt European nations to intervene in the region.

*Reading* **History**

**C. Making Inferences** Why was the United States interested in the political stability of Latin America?

## Policing the Hemisphere

During his presidency, Theodore Roosevelt made it clear that the United States would remain the dominant power in the Western Hemisphere. He summed up his foreign policy toward the region with an African saying: "Speak softly, but carry a big stick." Roosevelt, however, rarely spoke softly. He made sure that everyone knew the United States would use military force if its interests were threatened.

Roosevelt reminded European powers of the Monroe Doctrine—the policy that prevented other nations from intervening in Latin America. In 1904, he added the **Roosevelt Corollary**. Now, the doctrine would not only prevent European intervention in Latin America; it also authorized the United States to act as a "policeman" in the region. That is, U.S. leaders would now intervene in Latin America's domestic affairs

Vocabulary
**corollary:** a statement that follows logically from an earlier statement

when they believed that such action was necessary to maintain stability.

In 1905, the United States used the Roosevelt Corollary to take control of the Dominican Republic's finances after the country failed to pay its foreign debts. A year later, when a revolt threatened Cuba's government, the policy was used to send troops there.

Later presidents expanded on Roosevelt's "big stick diplomacy." William Howard Taft urged American businesses to invest in Latin America, promising military action if anything threatened these investments. He kept his word. In 1912, Taft sent marines to Nicaragua to restore order.

**Background**
Taft's policy was known as "dollar diplomacy."

President Taft's successor, Woodrow Wilson, also intervened in Latin America. When a revolution in Mexico began to threaten U.S. interests, Wilson took action. In 1914, he sent a fleet to Veracruz after U.S. sailors were arrested. Two years later, he sent troops into Mexico after a Mexican revolutionary named Pancho Villa (PAHN•choh VEE•yah) raided New Mexico and killed 19 Americans in the town of Columbus.

Americans rarely questioned U.S. actions in Latin America. They saw their nation as a good police officer, maintaining peace and preventing disorder. But many Latin Americans saw the United States as an imperial power that cared only about its own interests. This mistrust continues to trouble U.S. relations with its neighbors. In the next chapter, you will read about U.S. involvement in another part of the world—Europe.

## Now and then

**GLOBO COP?**

In the early 1900s, the United States used its "police powers" in the Western Hemisphere. Today, U.S. forces participate in police actions all over the globe. This fact has led some journalists to call the United States the "Globo Cop."

In the 1990s, U.S. forces helped lead international police actions in Somalia (see photo below), Yugoslavia, and other areas in crisis. The United States also led the Gulf War forces that liberated Kuwait after it was seized by Iraq.

The United States continues to patrol its own hemisphere, too. In 1989, U.S. troops invaded Panama to overthrow dictator Manuel Noriega.

## Section 3 Assessment

### 1. Terms & Names

**Explain the significance of:**
• sphere of influence
• Open Door Policy
• Boxer Rebellion
• Panama Canal
• Roosevelt Corollary

### 2. Using Graphics

Use a chart like the one below to record details about U.S. involvement in Asia and Latin America.

| Asia | Latin America |
|------|---------------|
|      |               |

How was U.S. involvement in Asia different from that in Latin America? (REP3)

### 3. Main Ideas

**a.** Why was the United States interested in the Philippines? (HI2)

**b.** Why was the nation of Panama created in 1903? (HI2)

**c.** How did the Roosevelt Corollary change U.S. foreign policy? (HI2)

### 4. Critical Thinking

**Drawing Conclusions**
Why did the United States become so heavily involved in Asia and Latin America? (HI2)

**THINK ABOUT**
• U.S. economic growth
• American military interests

**ACTIVITY OPTIONS**

**SCIENCE**

**MATH**

Research the Panama Canal. Build a simple **model** of the canal or create a **graph** that shows how many ships use the canal each year. (CST3)

## Becoming a World Power (CST1)

### The United States Continues to Expand

In the late 1800s, the United States began to expand overseas.
- Alaska was purchased from Russia.
- Planters took over Hawaii's government.

### The Spanish-American War

Events in Cuba, a Spanish colony in the Caribbean, led to the Spanish-American War.
- U.S. forces won victories in the Caribbean and in Asia.
- Spain gave up its colonies in Cuba, Puerto Rico, the Philippines, and Guam.

### U.S. Involvement Overseas

In both Asia and Latin America, the United States began to play a larger role.
- U.S. leaders insisted on an Open Door Policy in China.
- The United States built the Panama Canal.

## TERMS & NAMES

Briefly explain the significance of each of the following.

1. imperialism
2. Queen Liliuokalani
3. yellow journalism
4. Spanish-American War
5. Rough Riders
6. Anti-Imperialist League
7. Open Door Policy
8. Boxer Rebellion
9. Panama Canal
10. Roosevelt Corollary

## REVIEW QUESTIONS

### The United States Continues to Expand (pages 659–661)

1. Why did Americans become interested in overseas expansion in the late 1800s? (HI2)
2. How did the public react when William Seward negotiated the purchase of Alaska in 1867? (HI2)
3. Why did the United States take an interest in Hawaii? (HI2)
4. Why might President Cleveland have wanted to restore Liliuokalani to the Hawaiian throne? (HI1)

### The Spanish-American War (pages 662–667)

5. How did the Spanish-American War begin? (HI2)
6. What were the most important battles of the war? (HI1)
7. What territories did the United States take control of as a result of its victory over the Spanish? (HI2)

### U.S. Involvement Overseas (pages 668–673)

8. Why did U.S. leaders want access to China's markets after the Spanish-American War? (HI1)
9. Why was there an interest in building a canal across Latin America? (HI1)
10. How were the Latin American policies of Roosevelt, Taft, and Wilson similar? (HI1)

## CRITICAL THINKING

### 1. USING YOUR NOTES: FINDING MAIN IDEAS

Using your completed chart, answer the questions below. (HI2)

a. How did U.S. economic interests in Latin America influence the foreign policy of the United States?

b. In what ways was the Boxer Rebellion a reaction to the attitude of foreigners in China?

### 2. ANALYZING LEADERSHIP

What qualities made Theodore Roosevelt an effective leader? (HI1)

### 3. THEME: EXPANSION

How did U.S. expansion at the end of the 19th century compare with expansion that occurred earlier? Discuss both similarities and differences. (CST1)

### 4. APPLYING CITIZENSHIP SKILLS

How might the activities of the Anti-Imperialist League have helped to remind citizens of their democratic responsibilities? (HI1)

### 5. FORMING OPINIONS

The "yellow journalism" of major newspapers influenced U.S. foreign policy at the turn of the century. How does modern media, such as television, shape public opinion today? (CST1)

### Interact *with* History

How has your study of U.S. involvement overseas at the turn of the century influenced your opinion about getting involved in the affairs of another country?

Use the graph and your knowledge of U.S. history to answer questions 1 and 2.

Additional Test Practice, pp. S1–S33.

**U.S. Trade Expansion,** *1865–1915*

Dollars (in millions)

Exports ■ Imports

Source: *Historical Statistics of the United States*

**1.** In what year was the value of U.S. imports approximately $1,500,000,000? (8.12.1)

**A.** 1885

**B.** 1895

**C.** 1905

**D.** 1915

**2.** In what time period did the value of U.S. exports remain nearly the same? (8.12.1)

**A.** 1875–1885

**B.** 1885–1895

**C.** 1895–1905

**D.** 1905–1915

**This quotation from the Anti-Imperialist League is about imperialism. Use the quotation and your knowledge of U.S. history to answer question 3.**

*PRIMARY SOURCE*

We hold that the policy known as imperialism is hostile to liberty. . . . We regret that it has become necessary in the land of Washington and Lincoln to reaffirm that all men, of whatever race or color, are entitled to life, liberty, and the pursuit of happiness.

From the *Platform of the American Anti-Imperialist League*

**3.** Which conclusion best sums up this passage? (8.12.5)

**A.** The League believed people of all nations should be free to make their own choices.

**B.** The League believed American freedoms should be brought to the world.

**C.** The League believed imperialism was more important than liberty.

**D.** The League believed all nations of the world wanted American help to become free.

**TEST PRACTICE**
CLASSZONE.COM

## ALTERNATIVE ASSESSMENT

**1.** 📝 **WRITING ABOUT HISTORY**

Suppose that you are a construction worker building the Panama Canal. Write a **letter** home that describes your work and living conditions. (REP3)

- Research your letter using library resources.

- Include a map or a diagram in your letter.

- Decide if you believe the canal is a good or a bad project and make your letter reflect your opinion.

## 2. COOPERATIVE LEARNING

Work with three or four other students to help to plan, write, and illustrate a news story that features an important event from the Spanish-American War. Remember to use a journalistic style, presenting information in an unbiased manner. (REP3)

## INTEGRATED TECHNOLOGY

### DOING INTERNET RESEARCH

When the United States annexed the Philippines after the Spanish-American War, Filipinos rose in rebellion. Prepare a multimedia presentation on the Philippine-American War that resulted from that rebellion. (REP5)

- Find quotes that express views of the Filipino and American soldiers, including African-American troops. Use online encyclopedias in your research.

- Use presentation software to show descriptions or images of the battle. Record any quotes you've found and play them along with your presentation.

- Prepare a datasheet or a chart indicating casualties on both sides during the conflict.

**For more about the Philippine-American war . . .**

**INTERNET ACTIVITY**
CLASSZONE.COM

# World War I
## 1914–1920

This photograph shows a battlefield view of trench warfare during World War I.

The soldiers "go over the top" and charge the enemy lines.

**August 15, 1914**
U.S.-built Panama Canal officially opens.

**May 7, 1915**
Many Americans die as a German U-boat sinks *Lusitania.*

**November 7, 1916**
Woodrow Wilson is reelected president.

USA
World 1914

**June 28, 1914**
Austria-Hungary's Archduke Franz Ferdinand is assassinated, starting World War I.

COME AND DO YOUR BIT

JOIN NOW

**February–December, 1915**
Allies and Central Powers clash at Gallipoli in the Ottoman Empire.

**July–November, 1916**
French, British, and Germans suffer huge losses at the Battle of the Somme.

The year is 1917, and the United States has been drawn into World War I. Each citizen is called upon to help the war effort. Some will join the American armed forces and go to fight in Europe. Others will work in factories at home, producing weapons and supplies. Even children will do their part.

# How will you support the war effort?

## What Do You Think?

- How can Americans at home help win the war?
- What might U.S. soldiers experience in Europe?
- How might being at war affect the country?

**RESEARCH LINKS**
CLASSZONE.COM

Visit the Chapter 24 links for more information about World War I.

Artillery shells pound the battlefield, killing soldiers and leaving great destruction behind.

**April 2, 1917**
Wilson asks Congress to declare war on Germany.

**January 8, 1918**
President Wilson proposes League of Nations.

**November 2, 1920**
Warren G. Harding is elected president.

1920

**March 3, 1918**
Russia withdraws from the war.

**November 11, 1918**
The Allies defeat the Central Powers, ending World War I.

**June 28, 1919**
The Allies and Germany sign the Treaty of Versailles.

*World War I* **677**

# Reading Strategy: Recognizing Effects

## What Do You Know?

What do you think of when you hear the phrase "world war"?
What were the major countries in the war? Where did most
of the fighting take place?

**Think About**
- what you've learned about World War I from
  movies or television
- reasons that millions of people might choose
  to risk their lives in a global conflict
- your responses to the Interact with History about
  supporting the war effort (see page 677)

**CALIFORNIA STANDARDS**

**Reading 2.0** Students read
and understand grade-level-
appropriate material. They
describe and connect the
essential ideas, arguments,
and perspectives of the text
by using their knowledge of
text structure, organization,
and purpose.

## What Do You Want to Know?

 What details do you need to help you understand what is involved in waging
a world war? Make a list of these details in your notebook before you read
the chapter.

## Recognizing Effects

To help you make sense of what you read, learn to analyze the effects of important
historical events. The chart below will help you analyze some of the effects of World War I,
both on the world and on the United States. In each box, fill in a different effect. Add more
boxes if you need to.

**S** See Skillbuilder Handbook, page R11.

### ✏ Taking Notes

EFFECTS ON THE WORLD

EFFECTS ON THE UNITED STATES

World War I

# War Breaks Out in Europe

| **MAIN IDEA** | **WHY IT MATTERS NOW** | **TERMS & NAMES** |
|---|---|---|
| After World War I broke out, the United States eventually joined the Allied side. | This was the first time that the United States was involved in a European conflict. | militarism      U-boat<br>Central Powers      Woodrow Wilson<br>Allies      neutrality<br>trench warfare      Zimmermann telegram |

## ONE AMERICAN'S STORY

In the late 1800s and early 1900s, European nations competed to expand their empires. Rivalry caused tension among these nations. In 1914, President Woodrow Wilson sent Colonel Edward M. House to study the situation.

House gave the president a troubling report. He compared Europe to an open keg of gunpowder that only needed a spark to explode. He was right. On June 28, 1914, a Serbian shot and killed Archduke Franz Ferdinand, the heir to the throne of Austria-Hungary. Soon Austria declared war on Serbia. The nations of Europe chose sides and the Great War, later called World War I, began.

*Archduke Franz Ferdinand and his wife are murdered at Sarajevo on June 28, 1914.*

**CALIFORNIA STANDARDS**

**CST1** Students explain how major events are related to one another in time.

**CST3** Students use a variety of maps and documents to identify physical and cultural features of neighborhoods, cities, states, and countries and to explain the historical migration of people, expansion and disintegration of empires, and the growth of economic systems.

**HI2** Students understand and distinguish cause, effect, sequence, and correlation in historical events, including the long- and short-term causal relations.

**HI4** Students recognize the role of chance, foresight, and error in history.

## Causes of World War I

A single action, the assassination of the archduke, started World War I. But the conflict had many underlying causes.

1. **Imperialism.** Britain, France, Germany, and Italy competed for colonies in Africa and Asia. Because it had fewer colonies than Britain and France, Germany felt it deserved more colonies to provide it with resources and buy its goods.

2. **Nationalism.** Europeans were very nationalistic, meaning that they had strong feelings of pride, loyalty, and protectiveness toward their own countries. They wanted to prove their nations were the best. They placed their countries' interests above all other concerns. In addition, some ethnic groups hoped to form their own separate nations and were willing to fight for such a cause.

3. **Militarism.** The belief that a nation needs a large military force is **militarism**. In the decades before the war, the major powers built up their armies and navies.

**Taking Notes**

Use your chart to take notes about the effects of World War I.

**A Divided Europe,** *Summer 1914*

Allies
Central Powers
Neutral Nations

NORWAY
SWEDEN
*North Sea*
DENMARK
*Baltic Sea*
GREAT BRITAIN
London
NETH.
BELG.
Berlin
GERMANY
RUSSIA
Paris
LUXEMBOURG
Vienna
FRANCE
SWITZ.
AUSTRIA-HUNGARY
*ATLANTIC OCEAN*
PORTUGAL
Madrid
SPAIN
Sarajevo
ITALY
MONTENEGRO
Rome
SERBIA
ALBANIA
ROMANIA
*Black Sea*
BULGARIA
GREECE
OTTOMAN EMPIRE
*Mediterranean Sea*
SP. MOROCCO

0    300 Miles
0    600 Kilometers

**STEPS TO WORLD WAR I**

1. **June 28** Archduke Franz Ferdinand is assassinated.

2. **July 28** Austria-Hungary declares war on Serbia.

3. **July 30** Russia (Serbia's ally) mobilizes armed forces.

4. **August 1** Germany (Austria-Hungary's ally) declares war on Russia.

5. **August 3** Germany declares war on France (Russia's ally); prepares to invade Belgium.

6. **August 4** Britain, having pledged to protect Belgium, declares war on Germany.

7. **August 6** Austria-Hungary declares war on Russia.

8. **August 12** France and Britain declare war on Austria-Hungary.

**GEOGRAPHY SKILLBUILDER Interpreting Maps**
1. **Location** *What neutral countries were landlocked in the heart of Europe?*
2. **Region** *Which country covered the greatest amount of land, including territory in both Europe and Asia?*

4. **Alliances** In 1914, a tangled network of competing alliances bound European nations together. An attack on one nation forced all its allies to come to its aid. Any small conflict could become a larger war. European nations had divided into two opposing alliances. The **Central Powers** were made up of Austria-Hungary, Germany, the Ottoman Empire, and Bulgaria. They faced the Allied Powers, or **Allies,** consisting of Serbia, Russia, France, Great Britain, Italy, and seven other countries.

## Stalemate in the Trenches

When the war began in August, most people on both sides assumed it would be over within a few months. With France as its goal, the German army invaded Belgium on August 4, 1914. Despite stiff resistance, the Germans fought their way west into France. They reached the Marne River about 40 miles from Paris. There the French, supported by the British, rallied and prepared to fight back. The First Battle of the Marne, in September 1914, stopped the German advance.

Instead of one side quickly defeating the other, the two sides stayed stuck in the mud for more than three years. The soldiers were fighting a new kind of battle, **trench warfare.** Troops huddled at the bottom of rat-infested trenches. They fired artillery and machine guns at each other. Lines of trenches stretched across France from the English Channel to the border with Switzerland. (See pages 684–685 for an

**Background**
The Ottoman Empire included modern-day Turkey and Syria.

*Reading* **History**
A. **Reading a Map** On the map on page 688, find the site of the first Battle of the Marne.

**Vocabulary**
trench: a long, deep ditch dug for protection

illustration of the trenches.) For more than three years, the battle lines remained almost unchanged. Neither side could win a clear victory.

In the trenches, soldiers faced the constant threat of sniper fire. Artillery shelling turned the area between the two opposing armies into a "no man's land" too dangerous to occupy. When soldiers left their trenches to attack enemy lines, they rushed into a hail of bullets and clouds of poison gas.

*Reading* **History**
**B. Reading a Map** Find the site of the Battle of the Somme on the map on page 688.

When battles did take place, they cost many thousands of lives, often without gaining an inch for either side. The Battle of the Somme (SAHM), between July and November 1916, resulted in more than 1.2 million casualties. British dead or wounded numbered over 400,000. German losses totaled over 600,000, and French nearly 200,000. Despite this, the Allies gained only about seven miles.

## A War of New Technology

New technology raised the death toll. The tank, a British invention, smashed through barbed wire, crossed trenches, and cleared paths through no man's land. Soldiers also had machine guns that fired 600 bullets a minute. Poison gas, used by both sides, burned and blinded soldiers.

World War I was the first major conflict in which airplanes were used in combat. By 1917, fighter planes fought each other far above the clouds. Manfred von Richthofen, known as the Red Baron, was Germany's top ace. An ace was an aviator who had downed five or more enemy aircraft. Von Richthofen shot down over 80 enemy planes.

**Background** U-boat was short for "undersea boat."

At sea, the Germans used submarines, which they called **U-boats,** to block trade. They were equipped with both guns and torpedoes. German U-boats sank over 11 million tons of Allied shipping.

**New Technology of War**

First used effectively during World War I, these new weapons caused high casualties.

Airplane

Poison Gas

Machine Gun

Tank

The British liner *Lusitania* is sunk off the Irish coast by a German submarine on May 7, 1915.

# America's Path to War

When the war started in 1914, President **Woodrow Wilson** announced a policy of **neutrality,** refusing to take sides in the war. A popular song, "I Didn't Raise My Boy to Be a Soldier," expressed the antiwar sentiment of many Americans.

Over time, however, German attacks shifted public opinion to the Allied cause. In the fall of 1914, Britain set up a naval blockade of German ports, seizing all goods bound for Germany. In response, German submarines sank all Allied merchant ships they found off the British coast. In May 1915, a German U-boat torpedoed the British passenger ship *Lusitania,* killing 1,198 people, including 128 Americans. The sinking turned many Americans against Germany.

But President Wilson kept the United States neutral. He demanded that the German government halt unrestricted submarine warfare, and it agreed. In the election of 1916, the Democratic Party's campaign slogan, "He kept us out of war," appealed to voters. Wilson won reelection.

Desperate to defeat Britain, Germany resumed unrestricted submarine warfare at the end of January 1917. Its military leaders knew this action would bring the United States into the war. However, they hoped to win the war before the Americans arrived.

The next month, another blow to German-American relations came from the **Zimmermann telegram.** The telegram was discovered by the British, who passed it on to the Americans. In it, Arthur Zimmermann, the German foreign minister, told the German ambassador in Mexico to propose that Mexico join the Germans. In exchange, Germany would help Mexico get back its "lost" territories of Texas, New Mexico, and Arizona. Americans were furious.

*Reading*History

**C. Making Inferences** Why did the sinking of the *Lusitania* turn Americans against Germany?

In March, German submarines sank three American ships. President Wilson asked for a declaration of war.

**A VOICE FROM THE PAST**

The world must be made safe for democracy. . . . We desire no conquest. . . . We are but one of the champions of the rights of mankind. We shall be satisfied when those rights have been made . . . secure.

**Woodrow Wilson,** message to Congress, April 2, 1917

*"The world must be made safe for democracy."*
**Woodrow Wilson**

Six senators and 50 representatives, including the first woman in Congress, Jeannette Rankin of Montana, voted against going to war. But the majority shared the president's commitment to join the Allies.

## Revolution in Russia

Events in Russia made U.S. entry into the war more urgent for the Allies. By early 1915, the huge Russian army had been outfought by a smaller German army led by better-trained officers. In August 1915, Czar Nicholas II insisted on taking control of the troops himself. His poor leadership was blamed for more deaths. By 1917, food shortages led to riots, and soaring inflation led to strikes by angry workers in Russia.

In March 1917, Czar Nicholas II was forced to step down. A temporary government continued the unpopular war until November. In that month the Bolsheviks, a communist group led by Vladimir Ilich Lenin, took power. Communism is a political system in which the government owns key parts of the economy, and there is no private property.

*Reading*History
**D. Analyzing Causes** What led Russia to pull out of the war?

Because the war had devastated Russia, Lenin at once began peace talks with Germany. In March 1918, Russia withdrew from the war by signing the Treaty of Brest-Litovsk. German troops could now turn from Russia to the Western front. The Allies urged American troops to come quickly, as you will read in the next section.

---

Section **1** Assessment

### 1. Terms & Names

**Explain the significance of:**
• militarism
• Central Powers
• Allies
• trench warfare
• U-boat
• Woodrow Wilson
• neutrality
• Zimmermann telegram

### 2. Using Graphics

Write at least four events that brought the United States into World War I.

Which of these events was most important? Why? (CST2)

### 3. Main Ideas

**a.** What were the long-term causes of World War I? (HI2)

**b.** Why were Americans divided over the issue of remaining neutral? (HI2)

**c.** Why was Russia's withdrawal from the war in 1917 a blow to Allies? (HI2)

### 4. Critical Thinking

**Analyzing Causes** How did imperialism, nationalism, and militarism work to reinforce each other? (CST1)

**THINK ABOUT**
• the goals of each
• how nationalism might encourage military buildup
• how nationalism contributed to the race for colonies

**ACTIVITY OPTIONS**

**SCIENCE**

**ART**

Research one of the new weapons of World War I. Explain how it works using a **model,** or draw an illustrated **diagram** of a defense against the weapon. (HI2)

# Survive Trench Warfare

You are a platoon leader assigned to a section of the front in central France. You have 60 men under your command. Day and night, through constant rain, earthen trenches full of sticky mud serve as your only protection. Sometimes, you think, the cold, rain, mud, rats, and fatigue are tougher to endure than a German bombardment.

**COOPERATIVE LEARNING** On this page are two challenges you face as a soldier during World War I. Working with a small group, decide how to deal with each challenge. Choose an option, assign a task to each group member, and do the activity. You will find useful information in the Data File. Be prepared to present your solutions to the class.

**CALIFORNIA STANDARDS**

**HI1** Students explain the central issues and problems from the past, placing people and events in a matrix of time and place.

**HI4** Students recognize the role of chance, foresight, and error in history.

**Reading 2.6** Use information from a variety of consumer, workplace, and public documents to explain a situation or decision and to solve a problem.

## PHYSICAL EDUCATION CHALLENGE

### *"They must have 20 or 30 pounds of mud on them."*

Until now, no one thought the trenches would be a permanent part of this war. So you, like the other soldiers along the front, weren't trained to cope with heavy, thick mud, 70-pound backpacks, and the other demands of living and fighting in these conditions. You learned on the job. Now you've been ordered to contribute ideas for a training program that will prepare recruits for the trenches. Look at the Data File for help. Then present your ideas using one of these options:

• Design an exercise regimen to strengthen troops for the trenches.

• Write a booklet of survival tips based on your platoon's experiences.

## THE TRENCHES

- Trenches covered about 450 miles between the North Sea and the Swiss border.

- In France, ten-foot-deep trenches were dug into the ground and topped with sandbag parapets.

- Inside was a fire step, a ledge two or three feet up from bottom of the trench, used by sentries or troops firing.

- The sides were held up by sandbags and timber.

## A SOLDIER'S GEAR

60–75 pounds of gear, including blankets, waterproof ground-sheet, extra boots and occasionally waterproof gum boots, quilted coat, shovel for digging trenches, helmet, wire clippers, pail for rations, 2 quarts of water, 4 days' food, 200 cartridges, 6 hand grenades, gas mask, 3 pairs of socks, soap, toothbrush, bottle of whale oil, towel, rifle, bayonet

## TRENCH FOOD

beef stew, corned beef, bread, hard biscuits, pork and beans, tins of jam, butter, sugar, tea

## PROBLEMS

- **trench foot:** condition caused by feet staying wet 24 hours a day; feet swell, turn numb and blue; if not treated, gangrene sets in and feet must be amputated; helped by rubbing whale oil on feet, changing to dry socks three times daily

- **mud:** mud traps the wounded until some drown, clogs rifles and gear, weighs men down, causes trench walls to fall in

- **rats:** huge rats, as big as rabbits, infest the trenches

For more about trench warfare . . .

**RESEARCH LINKS**
CLASSZONE.COM

## HEALTH CHALLENGE

### *"Your feet swell to two or three times . . . normal size."*

You're worried about your men getting trench foot. You've heard horror stories about men whose feet swelled so much they couldn't pull off their boots. Some of these men developed gangrene and had their feet amputated. The key to preventing trench foot is staying dry. What will you do? Use the Data File for help. Then present your solution using one of these options:

- Come up with a way to keep the men's feet dry.
- Role-play a conversation with veteran soldiers about preventing trench foot.

## ACTIVITY WRAP-UP

**Present to the Class** As a group, review your methods of surviving the trenches. Pick the most creative solution for each challenge, and present these solutions to the class.

# America Joins the Fight

**CALIFORNIA STANDARDS**

**CST3** Students use a variety of maps and documents to identify physical and cultural features of neighborhoods, cities, states, and countries and to explain the historical migration of people, expansion and disintegration of empires, and the growth of economic systems.

**HI4** Students recognize the role of chance, foresight, and error in history.

## ONE AMERICAN'S STORY

Eddie Rickenbacker was America's most famous flying ace. He was one of the first Americans to get a look at the trenches from the cockpit of an airplane.

### A VOICE FROM THE PAST

[T]here appeared to be nothing below but these old battered ditches . . . and billions of shell holes. . . . [N]ot a tree, a fence . . . nothing but . . . ruin and desolation. The whole scene was appalling.

**Eddie Rickenbacker,** *Fighting the Flying Circus*

An American gun crew advances against German positions in 1918.

As you will read in this section, Rickenbacker and other U.S. soldiers helped the Allies win the war.

### Taking Notes

Use your chart to take notes about the effects of America's entrance into World War I.

EFFECTS ON THE WORLD

EFFECTS ON THE UNITED STATES

World War I

## Raising an Army and a Navy

The U.S. Army was not ready for war. American fighting forces consisted of fewer than 200,000 soldiers, many of them recent recruits. To meet its need for troops, the government began a draft. This system of choosing people for forced military service was first used during the Civil War. In May 1917, Congress passed the Selective Service Act. This act required all males between the ages of 21 and 30 to sign up for military service. By the end of 1918, nearly 3 million men had been drafted.

About 2 million American soldiers went to France. They served under General **John J. Pershing** as the **American Expeditionary Force,** or AEF. British commanders asked the U.S. government to have AEF troops join existing French and British combat units. Wilson refused. He believed that having "distinct and separate" American combat units would guarantee the United States a major role in the peace talks at war's end. Most U.S. troops fought separately, but some fought under Allied command.

*Reading* **History**
**A. Finding Main Ideas** How did women serve in the U.S. armed forces?

Close to 50,000 American women also served in World War I. Some volunteered for overseas duty with the American Red Cross. However, for the first time in American history, women also served in the military. The Navy, desperate for clerical workers, took about 12,000 female volunteers. The Marine Corps accepted 305 female recruits, known as Marinettes. Over 1,000 women went overseas for the Army. Nurses made up the largest group of females in the armed forces. However, women also acted as interpreters, operated switchboards, entertained troops, and drove ambulances for the AEF.

Around 400,000 African Americans served in the armed forces. More than half of them served in France. As they had at home, African-American troops overseas faced discrimination. However, it came from white American soldiers rather than from their European allies. At first, the Army refused to take black draftees. However, responding to pressure from African-American groups, the military eventually created two African-American combat divisions.

## American Ships Make a Difference

In the first years of the war, German U-boat attacks on supply ships were a serious threat to the Allied war effort. American Rear Admiral William S. Sims convinced the Allies to adopt a system of protection. In a **convoy system,** a heavy guard of destroyers escorted merchant ships across the Atlantic in groups. Begun in May 1917, this strategy quickly reduced the loss rate.

**Vocabulary**
**mines:** hidden explosive devices

Another American tactic gave the Allies added protection from the U-boat menace. Beginning in June 1918, the Allies laid a barrier of 70,000 mines in the North Sea. The 180-mile-long minefield made U-boat access to the North Atlantic almost impossible. Admiral Sims called the North Sea minefield "one of the wonders of the war."

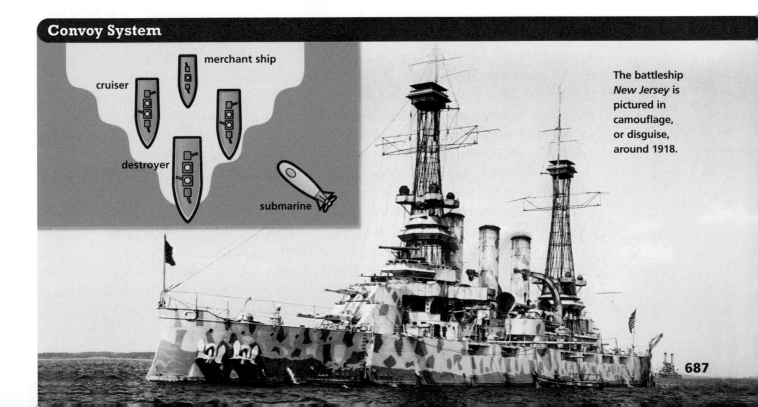

**Convoy System**

merchant ship
cruiser
destroyer
submarine

The battleship *New Jersey* is pictured in camouflage, or disguise, around 1918.

## The Western Front, 1914–1918

- Deepest German advance, July 18, 1918
- Allied drive, late summer and autumn 1918
- Armistice line, November 1918
- Major battle sites, 1914–1918

Ypres, 1st battle, 1914
2nd battle, 1915
3rd battle, 1917

Brussels

English Channel

Lille

BELGIUM

GERMANY

Somme R.

Somme, 1916

Amiens

Cantigny, 1918

Meuse R.

LUXEMBOURG

Moselle R.

Rhine R.

Seine R.

FRANCE

Aisne R.

Meuse-Argonne, 1918

Marne, 2nd battle, 1918

ARGONNE FOREST

Verdun, 1916

Metz

Belleau Wood, 1918

St. Mihiel, 1918

Château-Thierry, 1918

Marne R.

Marne, 1st battle, 1914

Paris

0    50 Miles
0    100 Kilometers

**GEOGRAPHY SKILLBUILDER** Interpreting Maps
1. **Location** What three battles occurred closest to the Armistice line?
2. **Movement** In what two directions did the Allied drives move?

## American Troops Enter the War

By the time the first American troops arrived in France in June 1917, the Allies had been at war for almost three years. The small force of 14,000 Yanks boosted the morale of the battle-weary Allies. However, almost a year would pass before the bulk of the American troops landed in Europe.

After their Russian opponents withdrew from the war, the Germans and the other Central Powers prepared to finish the fight in France. In March 1918, the Germans launched an offensive to end the war before the Americans arrived in force. Within two months, they had smashed through the French lines, reaching the Marne River only 50 miles from Paris. Just in time, in May 1918, one million fresh American troops arrived ready for action.

On May 28, American soldiers attacked the French town of Cantigny (kahn•tee•NYEE), which was occupied by the Germans. The soldiers advanced into the town, blasting enemy soldiers out of trenches and dragging them from cellars. Within two hours, the Yanks had taken control of Cantigny. The American victory lifted Allied morale.

When the Germans moved against the town of Château-Thierry (shah•toh•tyeh•REE), the Americans held their ground. They helped the French stop the German advance. Encouraged by these successes, French General Ferdinand Foch, commander of the Allied forces, ordered General Pershing's American forces to retake Belleau (beh•LOH) Wood.

**Background**
American soldiers were also called *doughboys*. This term was used even during the Civil War.

This was a forest near the Marne River well defended by German troops. American soldiers succeeded, but at a fearful cost. One unit lost 380 of its 400 men. However, the Americans had proved themselves in combat.

## Pushing the Germans Back

The **Second Battle of the Marne** in the summer of 1918 was the turning point of the war. It began with a German drive against the French line. During three days of heavy fighting, about 85,000 Americans helped the Allies halt the German advance. The Allies then took the initiative. They cut the enemy off from its supply lines and forced the Germans back.

For the rest of the war, the Allies advanced steadily. By early September, the Germans had lost all the territory they had gained since the spring. September 26, 1918, marked the beginning of the final Meuse-Argonne (myooz•ahr•GAHN) offensive. Around 1.2 million U.S. soldiers took part in a massive drive to push back the German line between the Argonne Forest and the Meuse River. The war's final battle left 26,000 Americans dead. But by November, the Germans were retreating.

*Reading*History
**B. Recognizing Effects** What was the effect of the Meuse-Argonne offensive?

The Meuse-Argonne offensive made a hero of American soldier **Alvin York.** At first, Tennessee-born Sergeant York seemed an unlikely candidate for military fame. Because of his religious beliefs, he tried unsuccessfully to avoid the draft. He refused to bear arms on religious grounds. An army captain convinced him to change his mind. In October 1918, in the Argonne Forest, York attacked German machine gunners, killing 25 of them. Other German soldiers surrendered, and York returned to the American lines with 132 captives.

*Reading*History
**C. Evaluating** What was heroic about Sergeant York?

Another American hero was pilot Eddie Rickenbacker. He won fame as the U.S. "ace of aces" for shooting down a total of 26 enemy planes. Just before the Meuse-Argonne offensive, he attacked seven German planes, sending two of them crashing to the ground. This action won him the Medal of Honor.

Four African-American combat units also received recognition for their battlefield valor. Fighting under French commanders, the 369th, 371st, and 372nd regiments (and part of the 370th) were awarded France's highest honor, the Croix de Guerre. The 369th spent more continuous time on the front lines than any other American unit. Although under intense fire for 191 days, it never lost a foot of ground.

## Connections TO LITERATURE

**LITERATURE OF WORLD WAR I**

Several notable American writers served in World War I. They included Ernest Hemingway, the poet E. E. Cummings, and John Dos Passos. Hemingway drove an ambulance for the Italian army. He put this experience into his war novel *A Farewell to Arms.* Cummings wrote of his time in France in *The Enormous Room.*

Dos Passos, who also worked as an ambulance driver, once explained what attracted him to the battlefront: "What was war like, we wanted to see with our own eyes. I wanted to see the show."

E. E. CUMMINGS
*The Enormous Room*

Ernest Hemingway

A FAREWELL to ARMS

Americans were proud of the contribution their troops made to the war effort. They helped shift the balance in favor of the Allies.

## Germany Stops Fighting

After the defeat of the Meuse-Argonne, General Erich Ludendorff advised the German government to seek peace. In early November, Germany's navy mutinied and its allies dropped out. On November 9, the Kaiser stepped down. Two days later Germany agreed to an **armistice,** an end to fighting. On November 11, 1918, at 11:00 A.M.—the 11th hour of the 11th day of the 11th month—all fighting ceased.

About 8.5 million soldiers died in the war, and about 21 million were wounded. Before he was killed in battle, one British soldier summed up the war's tragic costs.

**Background**
For many years after the war, Americans celebrated Armistice Day as a national holiday.

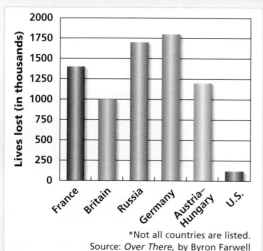

**CONNECTIONS TO MATH**
**Military Deaths in World War I***

Lives lost (in thousands)

France, Britain, Russia, Germany, Austria-Hungary, U.S.

*Not all countries are listed.
Source: *Over There,* by Byron Farwell

**SKILLBUILDER**
**Interpreting Graphs**
1. *Which two nations on the chart suffered the most deaths?*
2. *U.S. deaths were about what percentage of combined French and British deaths?*

### A VOICE FROM THE PAST

The sufferings of the men at the Front, of the wounded whose flesh and bodies are torn in a way you cannot conceive; the sorrow of those at home. . . . What a cruel and mad diversion of human activity!

**William John Mason,** quoted in *The Lost Generation of 1914*

Millions of civilians in Europe, Asia, and Africa also died in the war—from starvation and disease. In the next section, you will learn how the war affected U.S. civilians.

---

**Section 2 Assessment**

**1. Terms & Names**

**Explain the significance of:**
- John J. Pershing
- American Expeditionary Force
- convoy system
- Second Battle of the Marne
- Alvin York
- armistice

**2. Using Graphics**

Create a web to show how American groups or individuals helped fight the war.

Contributions

Whose contribution was most surprising? (REP3)

**3. Main Ideas**

**a.** Why did Wilson want U.S. forces to fight as a separate American combat unit? (HI1)

**b.** What were two ways the U.S. Navy countered the U-boat threat? (HI1)

**c.** Why was the Meuse-Argonne offensive a turning point in the war? (HI1)

**4. Critical Thinking**

**Recognizing Effects** How important was America's entry into the war to the Allied cause? (HI2)

**THINK ABOUT**
- the morale of Allied troops
- troop strength
- performance in battle

**ACTIVITY OPTIONS**

**MUSIC**
**LANGUAGE ARTS**

Make an **audiotape** of music or sounds that suggest the stages of the war, or write a **letter** in the voice of a soldier in the war. (REP5)

# Life on the Home Front

| MAIN IDEA | WHY IT MATTERS NOW | TERMS & NAMES |
|---|---|---|
| The war required sacrifice for Americans at home and changed life in other ways. | Some wartime changes were permanent, such as black migration to Northern cities. | war bonds **·** Sedition Act<br>propaganda **·** Oliver Wendell Holmes<br>Espionage Act **·** Great Migration |

## ONE AMERICAN'S STORY

On the home front, the war opened up new jobs for women. But when the war ended, female workers were laid off. Carrie Fearing wrote to her boss, hoping to keep her job.

### A VOICE FROM THE PAST

We never took a soldier's place, a soldier would not do the work we did . . . such as sweeping, picking up waste and paper. . . . We . . . like our job very much and I hope you will . . . place us back at the shop.

**Carrie Fearing,** quoted in *Women, War, and Work*

In May 1918, these women worked in the Union Pacific Railroad freight yard in Cheyenne, Wyoming.

**CALIFORNIA STANDARDS**

**REP4** Students assess the credibility of primary and secondary sources and draw sound conclusions from them.

**HI3** Students explain the sources of historical continuity and how the combination of ideas and events explains the emergence of new patterns.

**HI4** Students recognize the role of chance, foresight, and error in history.

Like Fearing, many women were proud of the part they played in getting the country ready for war. In this section, you will learn more about wartime life at home.

## Mobilizing for War

To prepare for war, the government needed money. World War I cost the United States $35.5 billion. Americans helped pay almost two-thirds of that amount by buying government war bonds. **War bonds** were low-interest loans by civilians to the government, meant to be repaid in a number of years. To sell the bonds, officials held Liberty Loan drives. Posters urged citizens to "Come Across or the Kaiser Will." Hollywood actors like Charlie Chaplin toured the country selling bonds to starstruck audiences.

Schoolchildren rolled bandages and collected tin cans, paper, toothpaste tubes, and apricot pits. The pits were burned and made into charcoal for gas mask filters. Some Boy Scout troops even sold war bonds. So that more food could be sent to soldiers, people planted "victory gardens" in backyards and vacant lots. Women's groups came together in homes and churches to knit socks and sweaters and sew hospital gowns.

**Taking Notes**

Use your chart to take notes about the effects of World War I on the home front.

EFFECTS ON THE WORLD | EFFECTS ON THE UNITED STATES

World War I

To persuade women to buy war bonds, this poster appealed to their love of family.

Patriotic citizens also saved food by observing wheatless Mondays and Wednesdays, when they ate no bread, and meatless Tuesdays. To save gas, they stopped their Sunday pleasure drives. The government limited civilian use of steel and other metals. Women donated their corsets with metal stays to scrap drives. Manufacturers stopped making tin toys for children and removed metal from caskets.

The war brought more government control of the economy. To produce needed war supplies, in 1917 President Wilson set up the War Industries Board. The board had great power. It managed the buying and distributing of war materials. It also set production goals and ordered construction of new factories. With the president's approval, the board also set prices. Another government agency, the National War Labor Board, settled conflicts between workers and factory owners.

To rally citizen support, Wilson created the Committee on Public Information. The committee's writers, artists, photographers, and film-makers produced **propaganda,** opinions expressed for the purpose of influencing the actions of others. The committee sold the war through posters, pamphlets, and movies. One popular pamphlet, "How the War Came to America," came out in Polish, German, Swedish, Bohemian, and Spanish. In movie houses, audiences watched such patriotic films as *Under Four Flags* and *Pershing's Crusaders.*

*Reading*History

A. Finding Main Ideas What were civilians asked to do for the war effort?

## Intolerance and Suspicion

Patriotic propaganda did much to win support for the war. But its anti-German, anti-foreign focus also fueled prejudice. Suddenly people distrusted anything German. A number of towns with German names changed their names. Berlin, Maryland, became Brunswick. People called sauerkraut "liberty cabbage," and hamburger became "Salisbury steak." Owners of German shepherds took to calling their pets "police dogs."

On June 15, 1917, Congress passed the **Espionage Act.** The **Sedition Act** followed in May 1918. These laws set heavy fines and long prison terms for such antiwar activities as encouraging draft resisters. The laws made it illegal to criticize the war. U.S. courts tried more than 1,500 pacifists, socialists, and other war critics. Hundreds went to jail. Socialist Party leader Eugene Debs gave a speech arguing that the war was fought by poor workingmen for the profit of wealthy business owners. For this talk, a judge sentenced him to ten years in prison.

The government ignored complaints that the rights of Americans were being trampled. In the 1919 decision in *Schenck* v. *United States,* the Supreme Court upheld the Espionage Act. Schenck, convicted of

*Reading*History

B. Recognizing Effects How did war propaganda fuel prejudice?

distributing pamphlets against the draft, had argued that the Espionage Act violated his right to free speech. Justice **Oliver Wendell Holmes, Jr.,** wrote the court's opinion.

### A VOICE FROM THE PAST

The most stringent [strict] protection of free speech would not protect a man in falsely shouting fire in a theater and causing a panic. . . . The question in every case is whether the words used . . . are of such a nature as to create a clear and present danger that they will bring about . . . evils that Congress has a right to prevent.

**Oliver Wendell Holmes, Jr.,** *Schenck* v. *United States,* 1919

*Reading*History

**C. Analyzing Points of View**
Why did Justice Holmes believe that free speech could be limited?

Justice Holmes argued that free speech, guaranteed by the First Amendment, could be limited, especially in wartime.

# New Jobs and the Great Migration

As soldiers went off to battle, the United States faced a labor shortage. Northern factories gearing up for war were suddenly willing to hire workers they had once rejected. Throughout the South, African Americans heeded the call. Between 1910 and 1920, about 500,000 African Americans moved north to such cities as New York, Chicago, Detroit, Cleveland, and St. Louis. This movement became known as the **Great Migration**. African Americans left to escape the bigotry, poverty, and racial violence of the South. They hoped for a better life in the North.

## HISTORY *through* ART

*The Migration of the Negro,* Panel No. 1 (1940–41), by Jacob Lawrence, shows three of the most common destinations for African Americans leaving the South.

**How does Lawrence's painting reflect continuity and change in American life?**

New jobs were opening up in the American Southwest. These jobs were fueled by the growth of railroads and irrigated farming. A revolution was under way in Mexico, and the chaos led many Mexicans to flee across the border after 1910. Many immigrants settled in Texas, Arizona, Colorado, and California. Most became farm workers. During the war years, some went to Northern cities to take better-paying factory jobs.

The wartime labor shortage also meant new job choices for women. Women replaced male workers in steel mills, ammunition factories, and assembly lines. Women served as streetcar conductors and elevator operators. The war created few permanent openings for women, but their presence in these jobs gave the public a wider view of their abilities. Women's contributions during the war helped them win the vote.

*Reading*History

**D. Recognizing Effects** What groups gained new jobs as a result of the war?

## Now *and* then

**THE FLU EPIDEMIC**

In 1918, flu victims often came down with pneumonia and died within a week. Today, bacterial infections such as pneumonia resulting from the flu can be controlled with antibiotics.

The 1998 discovery of the frozen remains of a 1918 flu victim in an Alaskan cemetery may one day lead to a better understanding of the virus. Scientists have found a genetic link between the 1918 flu virus and swine flu, a virus first found in pigs. The Alaskan find may help scientists develop vaccines to protect against future flu outbreaks.

## The Flu Epidemic of 1918

Another result of the war was a deadly flu epidemic that swept the globe in 1918. It killed more than 20 million people on six continents by the time it disappeared in 1919. It had no known cure. Spread around the world by soldiers, the virus took some 500,000 American lives. People tried desperately to protect themselves. Everywhere, schools and other public places shut down to limit the flu's spread.

In the army, more than a quarter of the soldiers caught the disease. In some AEF units, one-third of the troops died. Germans fell victim in even larger numbers than the Allies. World War I brought death and disease to millions. It would also have longer-term effects, as you will read in Section 4.

---

## Section 3 Assessment

### 1. Terms & Names

**Explain the significance of:**
- war bonds
- propaganda
- Espionage Act
- Sedition Act
- Oliver Wendell Holmes
- Great Migration

### 2. Using Graphics

Make a chart like the one below to show reasons for wartime shifts in population.

|  | Shift | Reason(s) |
|---|---|---|
| African Americans |  |  |
| Mexicans |  |  |

How similar were the two groups' reasons for moving? (HI2)

### 3. Main Ideas

**a.** What were three ways American families could contribute to the war effort? (HI1)

**b.** What was the purpose of the Espionage and Sedition Acts? What groups were most affected by them? (HI2)

**c.** What kinds of new job opportunities did the war create for women and minorities? (HI2)

### 4. Critical Thinking

**Making Inferences** What were the positive and the negative consequences of American wartime propaganda? (REP5)

**THINK ABOUT**
- contributions to war effort
- effect on opponents of war and on German-Americans

**ACTIVITY OPTIONS**

**SPEECH**
**MATH**

Deliver a **radio broadcast** on the importance of conserving food, or make a **calculation** of the amount of food your class wastes monthly. (HI6)

# The Legacy of World War I

| MAIN IDEA | WHY IT MATTERS NOW | TERMS & NAMES |
|---|---|---|
| After the war, Americans were divided over foreign policy and domestic issues. | The war affected the role the United States played in the world during the rest of the century. | League of Nations  reparations<br>Fourteen Points  Red Scare<br>Treaty of Versailles  Palmer raids |

## ONE AMERICAN'S STORY

Senator Henry Cabot Lodge opposed President Wilson's idea that the United States join the **League of Nations**—an organization set up to settle conflicts through negotiation. Lodge felt that joining such an alliance would require the United States to guarantee the freedom of other nations.

*A VOICE FROM THE PAST*

If we guarantee any country . . . its independence . . . we must [keep] at any cost . . . our word. . . . I wish [the American people] carefully to consider . . . whether they are willing to have the youth of America ordered to war by other nations.

**Henry Cabot Lodge,** speech to the Senate, February 28, 1919

Senator Henry Cabot Lodge (1850–1924) opposed U.S. entry into the League of Nations.

**CALIFORNIA STANDARDS**

**CST3** Students use a variety of maps and documents to identify physical and cultural features of neighborhoods, cities, states, and countries and to explain the historical migration of people, expansion and disintegration of empires, and the growth of economic systems.

**REP3** Students distinguish relevant information, essential from incidental information, and verifiable from unverifiable information in historical narratives and stories.

Lodge's speech helped turn the public against the League. In this section, you will learn how the United States and Europe adjusted to the end of the war.

## Wilson's Fourteen Points

In January 1918, ten months before the war ended, President Wilson told Congress his goals for peace. His speech became known as the **Fourteen Points** (see page 699). It called for smaller military forces, an end to secret treaties, freedom of the seas, free trade, and changes in national boundaries. Most of these changes gave independence to peoples that Austria-Hungary or the Ottoman Empire had ruled.

For Wilson, the fourteenth point mattered most. He called for an association of nations to peacefully settle disputes. This association was to become the League of Nations, which Republicans like Lodge opposed. Wilson firmly believed that acceptance of his Fourteen Points by the warring parties would bring about what he called a "peace without victory."

*Taking Notes*

Use your chart to take notes about the effects of World War I.

EFFECTS ON THE WORLD | EFFECTS ON THE UNITED STATES

World War I

## Treaty of Versailles

Wilson led the U.S. delegation to the peace conference in France. Though many Europeans considered him a hero, conference leaders did not. The leaders of Britain, France, and Italy did not share Wilson's vision of "peace without victory." They wanted Germany to pay heavily for its part in the war.

The **Treaty of Versailles** (vuhr•SY) forced Germany to accept full blame for the war. Germany was stripped of its colonies and most of its armed forces. It was also burdened with $33 billion in **reparations**—money that a defeated nation pays for the destruction caused by a war. The treaty divided up the empires of Austria-Hungary and the Ottomans. It created Yugoslavia and Czechoslovakia and recognized Poland's independence.

Wilson managed to include the League of Nations in the treaty. He firmly believed the League would help to keep the peace. He returned home to seek Senate approval for the treaty. But the Republican-run Senate was dead set against it. Senator Henry Cabot Lodge kept delaying a vote on the treaty.

After weeks of delay, Wilson decided to make his case to the public. In September of 1919, he began a cross-country speaking trip to build support for the League. In about 21 days, he traveled almost 10,000 miles and gave over 30 speeches.

*Reading*History
A. Recognizing Effects How were the Central Powers punished by the Treaty of Versailles?

### A VOICE FROM THE PAST

In the covenant [agreement] of the League of Nations, the moral forces of the world are mobilized . . . . They consent . . . to submit every matter of difference between them to the judgment of mankind, and just so certainly as they do that, . . . war will be pushed out of the foreground of terror in which it has kept the world.

**Woodrow Wilson,** speech in Pueblo, Colorado, on September 25, 1919

Shortly after giving this speech, Wilson collapsed from strain. Later, he suffered a stroke from which he never fully recovered.

Negotiations to get the treaty through Congress continued, but Americans were not eager for more foreign commitments. Lodge and his supporters offered to accept the treaty if major changes were made in the League. Wilson refused to compromise. As a result, the United States did not ratify the treaty. The League of Nations was formed without the United States.

The war and the Treaty of Versailles failed to make Europe "safe for democracy." In the next decades, Germany's resentment of the treaty grew. The treaty planted the seeds of World War II, an even more deadly conflict to come.

*Reading*History
B. Analyzing Causes Why didn't the United States ratify the Treaty of Versailles?

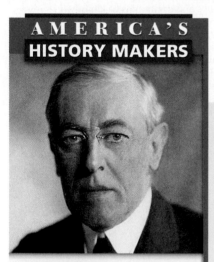

### AMERICA'S HISTORY MAKERS

**WOODROW WILSON**
**1856–1924**

A gifted speaker, Woodrow Wilson had a strong sense of duty, and he inspired great loyalty. Yet he could be a harsh judge of others, stiff and unbending in his relations with people. Sculptor Jo Davidson remarked that "He invoked fear and respect . . . but not affection." Though not America's best-loved president, he still commands respect. When historians list the nation's best presidents, Wilson often ranks in the top ten.

**How might Wilson's character have worked against approval of the Treaty of Versailles?**

## Postwar Europe, 1919

New nations

0 400 Miles
0 800 Kilometers

NORWAY  FINLAND
SWEDEN  ESTONIA  SOVIET RUSSIA
IRELAND  North Sea  DENMARK  LATVIA
  Baltic Sea  LITHUANIA
GREAT BRITAIN  NETH.
  GERMANY
ATLANTIC OCEAN  BELGIUM  POLAND
  LUX.  CZECHOSLOVAKIA
  FRANCE  SWITZ.  AUSTRIA
  HUNGARY
  YUGOSLAVIA  ROMANIA
PORTUGAL  Black Sea
  SPAIN  ITALY  BULGARIA
  Mediterranean Sea  ALBANIA  GREECE

### EFFECTS OF WORLD WAR I ON EUROPE

| IMMEDIATE EFFECTS | LONG-TERM EFFECTS |
| --- | --- |
| Revolution in Russia | Breakup of empires |
| Allied victory | Formation of League of Nations |
| Destruction in Europe | Resentments leading to World War II |

**GEOGRAPHY SKILLBUILDER Interpreting Maps**
1. **Region** *What new nations were created after the war?*
2. **Region** *In what part of Europe were most of the new nations located?*

# Strikes and the Red Scare

**Background**
In 1919, police, steelworkers, and coal miners also went on strike.

The Treaty of Versailles was not the only issue that divided Americans after the war. Shortly after the war ended, the United States experienced a number of labor strikes. For example, in Seattle, Washington, in February 1919, more than 55,000 workers took part in a peaceful general strike. The shutdown paralyzed the city.

Some Americans saw efforts to organize labor unions as the work of radicals, people who favor extreme measures to bring about change. The strikes sparked fears of a communist revolution like the one that toppled the Russian czar. In 1919–1920, this fear created a wave of panic called the **Red Scare** (communists were called *reds*). Public fear was heightened by the discovery of mail bombs sent to government officials. Many believed the bombs were the work of anarchists. Anarchists are radicals who do not believe in any form of government.

*Reading* **History**
C. **Recognizing Effects** What resulted from the Red Scare?

In January 1920, Attorney General A. Mitchell Palmer took action. He ordered federal agents and local police to raid the homes and headquarters of suspected radicals. His agents arrested at least 6,000 people in the **Palmer raids.** Without search warrants, agents burst into homes and offices and dragged citizens off to jail.

The Red Scare was not only antiradical but also antiforeign. During the Red Scare, two Italian-born anarchists, Nicola Sacco and Bartolomeo Vanzetti, were arrested for killing two men in an armed robbery in

Massachusetts. They claimed they were innocent, but both were found guilty and executed. Their trial attracted worldwide attention.

## Racial Tensions Increase

Americans also saw a rise in racial tensions after the war. Between 1910 and 1920, the Great Migration brought a half million African Americans to Northern cities. In the cities where African Americans had settled in large numbers, whites and blacks competed for factory jobs and housing.

On July 2, 1917, tensions erupted into a race riot in East St. Louis, Illinois. The trouble began when blacks were brought in to take the jobs of white union members who had gone on strike. A shooting incident touched off a full-scale riot.

Two years later, African-American soldiers returning from the war found their social plight unchanged. They had fought to make the world "safe for democracy." At home, though, they were still second-class citizens.

Simmering resentments over housing, job competition, and segregation exploded during the summer of 1919. In 25 cities around the country, race riots flared. In Chicago, a black man swimming in Lake Michigan drifted into the white section of a beach. Whites stoned him until he drowned. Thirteen days of rioting followed. Before it ended, 38 people were dead.

*Reading*History

**D. Analyzing Causes** How did the war contribute to racial tensions?

## Longing for "Normalcy"

By the time campaigning began for the 1920 election, Americans felt drained. Labor strikes, race riots, the Red Scare, and the fight over the Treaty of Versailles and the League of Nations had worn them out. Voters were ready for a break. Republican candidate Warren G. Harding of Ohio offered them one. His promise to "return to normalcy" appealed to voters. Harding won a landslide victory. In the next chapter, you will learn about American life after his election.

---

**Section**  **Assessment**

### 1. Terms & Names

**Explain the significance of:**
- League of Nations
- Fourteen Points
- Treaty of Versailles
- reparations
- Red Scare
- Palmer raids

### 2. Using Graphics

Create a diagram to examine the war's effects on Europe and America.

| Effects of World War I | |
|---|---|
| Europe | United States |
| | |

Which effects were positive and which were negative? (HI2)

### 3. Main Ideas

**a.** Why did Germany resent the Treaty of Versailles? (HI2)

**b.** Why did Lodge and other Republicans oppose joining the League of Nations? (HI2)

**c.** What caused the Red Scare? Who was most affected by it? (HI2)

### 4. Critical Thinking

**Analyzing Points of View** Why was Wilson unable to get other powers to accept his goals for the peace conference? (HI1)

**THINK ABOUT**
- conflicting goals
- practicality of Wilson's aims
- attitudes of other nations toward U.S. contributions during the war

**ACTIVITY OPTIONS**

**LANGUAGE ARTS**

**ART**

Imagine that you work for a newspaper. Write an **editorial** about the Palmer raids, or draw a political **cartoon** about the raids. (REP5)

# The Fourteen Points

**Setting the Stage** Nine months after the United States entered World War I, President Wilson delivered to Congress a statement of war aims. This statement became known as the "Fourteen Points." In the speech, President Wilson set forth 14 proposals for reducing the risk of war in the future. Numbers have been inserted to help identify the main points, as well as those omitted. **See Primary Source Explorer**

**CALIFORNIA STANDARDS**

**REP4** Students assess the credibility of primary and secondary sources and draw sound conclusions from them.

**Reading 2.2** Analyze text that uses proposition and support patterns.

All the peoples of the world are in effect partners . . . , and for our own part we see very clearly that unless justice be done to others it will not be done to us. The program of the world's peace, therefore, is our program; and that program, . . . as we see it, is this:

[1] Open **covenants**[1] of peace, openly arrived at, after which there shall be no private international understandings of any kind but diplomacy shall proceed always frankly and in the public view.

[2] Absolute freedom of navigation upon the seas . . . in peace and in war. . . .

[3] The removal, so far as possible, of all economic barriers and the establishment of an equality of trade conditions among all the nations. . . .

[4] Adequate guarantees given and taken that national **armaments**[2] will be reduced. . . .

[5] A free, open-minded, and absolutely impartial adjustment of all colonial claims, based upon . . . the principle that . . . the interests of the populations concerned must have equal weight with the . . . claims of the government whose title is to be determined.

[6–13: These eight points deal with specific boundary changes.]

[14] A general association of nations must be formed under specific covenants for the purpose of affording mutual guarantees of political independence and territorial **integrity**[3] to great and small states alike.

—*Woodrow Wilson*

1. **covenants:** binding agreements.
2. **armaments:** weapons and supplies of war.
3. **integrity:** the condition of being whole or undivided; completeness.

## A CLOSER LOOK

**THE VALUE OF OPENNESS**

The first of Wilson's points attempts to solve one of the problems that caused the outbreak of World War I—agreements between nations arrived at in secret.

**1. How might agreements arrived at in public prevent another world war?**

## A CLOSER LOOK

**BALANCING CLAIMS**

Wilson frequently appeals to fairness, balance, and impartiality in settling competing claims.

**2. What might be unusual about a leader such as Wilson calling for an impartial adjustment of colonial claims?**

## A CLOSER LOOK

**LEAGUE OF NATIONS**

Wilson proposes that nations join a formal organization to protect one another.

**3. Why did Wilson believe that such an organization would benefit the world?**

## Interactive Primary Source Assessment

### 1. Main Ideas

**a.** Why should diplomacy avoid private dealings and proceed in public view? (REP4)

**b.** How might equality of trade be important to keeping the peace? (REP4)

**c.** What must nations join together to guarantee? (REP4)

### 2. Critical Thinking

**Evaluating** The first five points address issues that Wilson believed had caused the war. How successful do you think Wilson's ideas have been in the rest of the 20th century? (REP4)

**THINK ABOUT**

• other conflicts since World War I

• peacekeeping efforts around the world

## TERMS & NAMES

Briefly explain the significance of each of the following.

1. militarism
2. Allies
3. trench warfare
4. Zimmermann telegram
5. American Expeditionary Force
6. convoy system
7. propaganda
8. Great Migration
9. Treaty of Versailles
10. Red Scare

## REVIEW QUESTIONS

### War Breaks Out in Europe (pages 679–685)

1. What were the sources of tension between the European powers that led to war? (HI2)
2. Why did the United States at first remain neutral in the war? (HI1)
3. What brought the United States into the war on the Allied side? (HI2)

### America Joins the Fight (pages 686–690)

4. How did the Allies fight the German U-boat threat? (HI1)
5. How did U.S. entry into the war affect the Allies? (HI2)
6. What led Germany to agree to an armistice? (HI2)

### Life on the Home Front (pages 691–694)

7. How did U.S. civilians aid the war effort? (HI1)
8. How did Congress contribute to increased prejudice and intolerance on the home front? (HI1)

### The Legacy of World War I (pages 695–699)

9. How did Wilson's goals for the peace conference differ from those of his European allies? (HI1)
10. Why did the Senate reject the Treaty of Versailles? (HI2)

## CRITICAL THINKING

### 1. USING YOUR NOTES: RECOGNIZING EFFECTS

Using your chart, answer the questions below. (HI2)

EFFECTS ON THE WORLD          World War I          EFFECTS ON THE UNITED STATES

a. Were the effects of the war greater in Europe or the United States?
b. What political effects did the war have on the United States?
c. How did the war affect African-American civilians?

### 2. APPLYING CITIZENSHIP SKILLS

Are limitations on freedom of speech justified by war? Explain your opinion. (HI5)

### 3. THEME: AMERICA IN THE WORLD

How did Wilson's view of the role the United States should play in world affairs compare with Theodore Roosevelt's view of America's role? (REP5)

### 4. ANALYZING LEADERSHIP

Do you think Wilson's refusal to compromise to get the Treaty of Versailles through Congress was a good decision? Why? (HI1)

### Interact *with* History

How accurately did you predict the ways in which American citizens might support the war effort?

## VISUAL SUMMARY

### World War I (CST2)

**War Breaks Out in Europe**
When the Allies and the Central Powers went to war in Europe, the United States reluctantly joined the Allies.

**America Joins the Fight**
Millions of U.S. soldiers and civilian volunteers went abroad and helped the Allies win the war.

**Life on the Home Front**
The war required Americans to sacrifice many things, even political freedoms. The war also brought new jobs.

**The Legacy of World War I**
The war broke up European empires and left lasting social changes in the United States.

Use the map and your knowledge of U.S. history to answer questions 1 and 2.

Additional Test Practice, pp. S1–S33.

**Great Migration, 1910–1920**

Northeast
201,000

Midwest
233,000

West Coast
16,000

← Movement of African Americans
**201,000** Number of migrants

Source: *Historical Statistics of the United States*

1. How many African Americans migrated to the Northeast? (8.11.2)
   A. 16,000
   B. 201,000
   C. 233,000
   D. 450,000

2. To which region did the fewest number of African Americans move? (8.11.2)
   A. Northwest
   B. Northeast
   C. Midwest
   D. West Coast

This quotation from Senator Henry Cabot Lodge supports his opposition to the United States entering the League of Nations. Use the quotation and your knowledge of U.S. history to answer question 3.

**PRIMARY SOURCE**

If we guarantee any country . . . its independence . . . we must [keep] at any cost . . . our word. I wish [the American people] carefully to consider . . . whether they are willing to have the youth of America ordered to war by other nations.

**Henry Cabot Lodge,** speech to the Senate, February 28, 1919

3. What was Lodge's major opposition to U.S. entry into the League of Nations? (8.12)
   A. The U.S. would have to pay the expenses.
   B. U.S. soldiers would have to fight foreign wars.
   C. The League of Nations would not be effective.
   D. Deals with a foreign country would lead to war.

**TEST PRACTICE**
CLASSZONE.COM

## ALTERNATIVE ASSESSMENT

### 1. ✎ WRITING ABOUT HISTORY

Write a **newspaper article** on the new technologies being used in World War I. Choose one type of technology, such as airplanes, submarines, or tanks, and explain its use, advantages, and disadvantages. (REP4)

- Look for and include primary sources from soldiers.
- Include a section on why you believe or do not believe that these new weapons are necessary.

### 2. COOPERATIVE LEARNING

Working in one of seven groups, research the conference that created the Treaty of Versailles. Your group will represent one of these nations: Germany, France, Britain, the United States, Italy, Japan, or Poland. Make a list of goals and issues you want discussed. Then choose a spokesperson to represent your group in a mock conference. (REP5)

## INTEGRATED TECHNOLOGY

### DOING INTERNET RESEARCH

Research the posters that were used to influence public opinion during World War I. Use a search engine to find pictures of these posters on the Internet. (REP4)

- View as many posters as possible.
- Print images of the two posters you find most interesting. Try to find some background information about the purpose and audience for each poster.
- Write your reactions to the posters including what actions you think the posters were trying to promote, how the posters made you feel, and how effective you think they were.

**For more about World War I posters . . .**

**INTERNET ACTIVITY**
CLASSZONE.COM

# Campaign for Liberty Bonds

To rally Americans to support World War I, the government set up the Committee on Public Information (CPI). This agency called on creative individuals to join "the world's greatest adventure in advertising." Speakers gave patriotic speeches in theaters, hotels, and restaurants. Artists designed posters persuading Americans to buy Liberty Bonds. These loans to the government helped fund the war effort. Liberty Bonds were actually sold through four Liberty Loan drives in 1917 and 1918.

**ACTIVITY** Create a poster to help the government raise money for World War I. In addition, write and present a patriotic speech that wins public support of the war.

**CALIFORNIA STANDARDS**

**REP1** Students frame questions that can be answered by historical study and research.

**Listening and Speaking 2.4** Deliver persuasive presentations.

## TOOLBOX

Each group will need:

| | |
|---|---|
| poster board | drawing paper |
| colored markers | glue |
| pencils | scissors |

Posters such as this one appealed to patriotism and love of family to sell Liberty Bonds.

## STEP BY STEP

**1** **Form an imaginary ad agency.** Meet with three or four other students to discuss your latest contract: The CPI has hired your agency to create a poster as part of a nationwide campaign to sell Liberty Bonds and promote World War I. Your group will:

- do research on Liberty Bonds
- design and create a poster advertising Liberty Bonds
- write and deliver a "pep talk" persuading people to buy Liberty Bonds

**2** **Research Liberty Bonds.** Look on the Internet, in this chapter, or in books about World War I to find out more about Liberty Bonds and to see actual posters. As you look over the posters, think about the feelings the posters bring out. What images and words seem most powerful or persuasive?

**3** **Choose a theme for your poster.** Persuading people to buy Liberty Bonds means that you need to show that winning World War I is important. One way is to appeal to people's emotions. For example, the poster can appeal to their sense of fear, pride, or love of family.

**4** **Sketch out your idea.** Write out a slogan and choose images based on the theme of your poster. Make sure your words and pictures communicate the same feeling and message. Draw an outline of the images and the letters. Then cut both the letters and images out. Be sure that they're large enough to be seen from several yards away.

**5** **Create the poster.** Decide where the art and writing will appear. Experiment with the arrangement of the art and the writing. Move them around. Do not overwhelm your viewers with too many images or too many words. Use vivid, patriotic colors for your poster.

**6** **Create a bulletin board display.**
Pin or tape your poster on the wall, along with the posters of the other groups. As you examine the other posters, compare and contrast your poster with the others.

## WRITE AND SPEAK

**Write a patriotic speech.** As a group, write a two-minute "pep talk" persuading people to buy Liberty Bonds and to support the soldiers fighting overseas. Include reasons why the war is worth fighting. Each group member should be prepared to deliver the speech, using the poster you made as a visual aid.

## HELP DESK

For related information, see pages 691–692 in Chapter 24.

### Researching Your Project
• *World War I* by Gail Stewart
• *Causes and Consequences of World War I* by Stewart Ross

**For more about World War I . . .**

**RESEARCH LINKS**
CLASSZONE.COM

### Did You Know?
The CPI used about 75,000 lecturers. They gave around 755,190 speeches to about 300 million people in 5,000 towns.

Even children were moved by advertising slogans to help fund the war: "Lick a stamp and lick the kaiser." Children filled books with war stamps, each worth 25 cents. These stamps were then converted into government bonds.

Even President Wilson helped to raise money for the war effort. He sold wool from sheep raised on the White House lawn.

### REFLECT & ASSESS
• What aspects of your poster do you think will inspire people to buy Liberty Bonds?

• How well does your speech inspire patriotic feeling about the war?

• Which do you think is a more powerful means of persuasion—your poster or your speech?

CHAPTER
25
EPILOGUE

# The United States Since 1919

**1920**
Warren G. Harding is elected president.

**1929**
Stock market crash marks beginning of Great Depression.

**1932**
Franklin D. Roosevelt is elected president.

**1941**
Japanese bomb Pearl Harbor, and U.S. enters World War II.

**1945**
Germany and Japan surrender, ending World War II.

**1950**
Korean War begins.

USA
World    **1919**

**1922**
Benito Mussolini becomes prime minister of Italy.

**1933**
Adolf Hitler is appointed chancellor of Germany.

**1937**
Japan invades China.

**1939**
Germany invades Poland, setting off World War II.

**1948**
Gandhi is assassinated in India.

**704**

During the 20th century, the United States has experienced many challenges. These include war, economic depression, and the struggle for equal rights. New challenges await you in the 21st century. You must decide what they are and how you will respond.

# How do you think the 21st century will differ from the 20th century?

## What Do You Think?

- How will technology play a part in your life?
- What are your talents, and how could you use them to benefit yourself and society?

**RESEARCH LINKS**
CLASSZONE.COM

Visit the Chapter 6 links for more information about the American Revolution.

**1963**
President Kennedy is assassinated.

**1972**
President Nixon travels to China.

**1980**
Ronald Reagan is elected president.

**2000**
George W. Bush is elected president.

**2001**
The World Trade Center in New York City is attacked by terrorists.

**1959**
Fidel Castro overthrows Batista in Cuba.

**1973**
Arab nations and Israel fight in Yom Kippur War.

**1989**
Berlin Wall is torn down.

**1991**
The Soviet Union collapses.

present

# Reading Strategy: Categorizing Information

## What Do You know?

What do you think of when you hear the phrase "the Great Depression"? Who do you think fought in World War II? How can a war be a "Cold War"?

### Think About

- what you've learned about any of these topics from movies, television, or travel
- how great events shape the lives of individuals
- your responses to the Interact with History about what the future holds (see page 705)

## What Do You Want to Know?

What questions do you have about great events of the 20th century? Record these questions in your notebook before you read the chapter.

## Categorizing Information

To help you make sense of what you read, learn to categorize. Categorizing means sorting information into groups. The chart below will help you to categorize the information in this chapter. Use the chart to take notes on important political, economic, and social events of selected decades of this century.

S See Skillbuilder Handbook, page R6.

 **Taking Notes**

| The 20th Century | Political Events | Economic Events | Social Events |
| --- | --- | --- | --- |
| 1920–1939 | | | |
| 1940–1959 | | | |
| 1960–1979 | | | |
| 1980–1999 | | | |

# Prosperity and the Great Depression

| MAIN IDEA | WHY IT MATTERS NOW | TERMS & NAMES |
|---|---|---|
| The stock market crash of 1929 and the Great Depression led to Franklin D. Roosevelt's New Deal. | The New Deal increased the role of the federal government. | Warren G. Harding    Great Depression<br>Calvin Coolidge    Franklin D. Roosevelt<br>jazz    New Deal<br>Harlem Renaissance |

**Louis Armstrong**

## ONE AMERICAN'S STORY

Louis Armstrong grew up in New Orleans. Armstrong often listened to jazz music played at funeral processions, dance halls, saloons, and lawn parties. He became a great jazz musician. In 1922, he accepted a job offer to play jazz with a Chicago band.

*A VOICE FROM THE PAST*

When I left New Orleans to go up North in 1922 the toughest Negro . . . his name is Slippers . . . he gave me a pep talk. . . . He loved the way I played those Blues. . . . When he found out that I was leaving to go to Chicago, he was the first one to congratulate me. . . . He said, "I love the way you blow that Quail." Of course he meant the cornet.

**Louis Armstrong,** quoted in *Louis: The Louis Armstrong Story*

In this section, you will read about popular culture, the Harlem Renaissance, and the stock market crash of 1929.

> **CALIFORNIA STANDARDS**
>
> **CST1** Students explain how major events are related to one another in time.
>
> **REP4** Students assess the credibility of primary and secondary sources and draw sound conclusions from them.
>
> **HI2** Students understand and distinguish cause, effect, sequence, and correlation in historical events, including the long- and short-term causal relations.

## The Roaring Twenties' Business Boom

By the start of the 1920s, Americans were turning away from progressive reforms. World War I was over. Americans were disappointed with the Treaty of Versailles. This, and the terrible human cost of the war, made them unwilling to fight "other people's wars." Now they wanted to help themselves. Americans were ready for a decade-long buying spree.

Earlier in the century, presidents like Roosevelt and Taft had sought to place tighter controls on business. Under presidents **Warren G. Harding** and **Calvin Coolidge,** the government put into practice pro-business policies. These policies made business growth easier and more profitable. President Coolidge came into office in 1923. He spoke for many when he said, "the chief business of the American people is business."

> ✏️ **Taking Notes**
>
> Use your chart to take notes about events in the 1920s and 1930s.
>
> | The 20th Century | Political Events |
> |---|---|
> | 1920–1939 | |
> | 1940–1959 | |
> | 1960–1979 | |
> | 1980–1999 | |

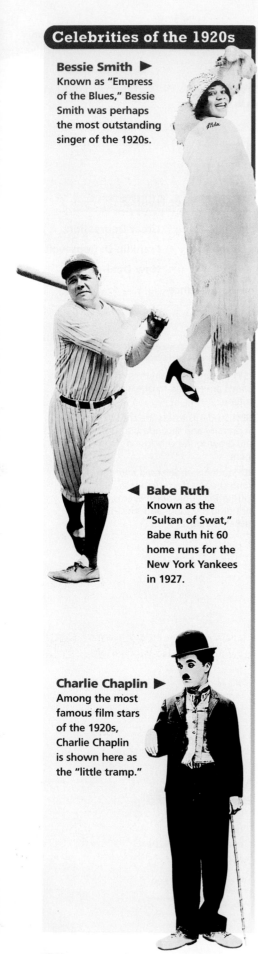

Giant business empires, such as the automobile industry, made the economy boom. Between 1920 and 1930, the number of cars in the United States almost tripled from about 8 million to 23 million. Car sales fueled demand for steel, oil, rubber, gasoline, and glass. Tourism thrived as more people took vacations by car. Improvements in methods of mass production made it possible to turn out products faster and more cheaply. As a result, prices fell for such goods as washing machines and refrigerators. At the same time, the nation's wealth grew. During the 1920s, the income of the average American rose by almost 40 percent. People had both more money to spend and more goods to buy.

## The Rise of Popular Entertainment

After the sacrifices of World War I, Americans wanted to enjoy themselves. Radio, movies, and sports gained in popularity. Big-city dwellers flocked to nightclubs where they learned hot new dances like the Charleston and the shimmy. The 1920s also introduced more Americans to a musical form called **jazz**. The new jazz music sprang up in cities such as New Orleans and Chicago. It blended African and European musical traditions. Trumpeter Louis Armstrong and composer and bandleader Duke Ellington drew crowds to jazz clubs and speakeasies. Singer Bessie Smith, known as "Empress of the Blues," thrilled audiences wherever she performed.

Audiences for movies grew throughout the decade. Even small towns had a movie theater. In 1922, people bought tickets to see such stars as Clara Bow and Charlie Chaplin on the silent screen. In 1925, Chaplin charmed audiences with his portrayal of the "little tramp" in silent films such as *The Gold Rush*. Two years later, Al Jolson's *The Jazz Singer* became the first talking picture. By the end of the decade, more than 100 million people a year were packing movie theaters for talking pictures.

The growing popularity of radio helped put sports in the spotlight. Radio spread the fame of such teams as the New York Yankees and the Chicago Cubs. It made national heroes out of sports figures like Babe Ruth, who was baseball's home-run king. Baseball, boxing, and football all gained wider audiences.

In literature, such writers as Ernest Hemingway, F. Scott Fitzgerald, and Edna St. Vincent Millay were

**Vocabulary**
**speakeasies:** places for illegal sale and consumption of alcoholic drinks during the 1920s

able to capture the feelings of disillusionment and rebellion that some young people felt at the end of World War I. In the Harlem section of New York City, the 1920s were a time of great creativity for African-American artists. Writers such as Langston Hughes, Countée Cullen, and Zora Neale Hurston belonged to the cultural movement known as the **Harlem Renaissance.** Hughes used jazz rhythms and dialect in his writings to celebrate black urban life and to call for social change.

## Stock Market Crash and Great Depression

During the 1920s, the stock market soared. Ordinary people saw buying stocks as a safe, quick way to get rich. Many ordinary people invested their life savings. Most did not understand the risks of investing. Many investors even borrowed money to buy shares. Then, in October 1929, the stock market crashed.

*"The chief business of the American people is business."*
**President Coolidge**

**Background**
The stock market crash came on October 29, 1929. On that day, the prices of stocks fell dramatically.

The crash sparked a chain reaction. First, banks demanded that customers pay back the money they had borrowed to buy stock. When people could not repay these loans, the banks ran short of money. Fearing that banks would close, customers lined up to withdraw their money. Since banks rarely keep enough cash on hand to pay all their customers at once, many banks shut down. The **Great Depression,** a time of great economic hardship, had begun.

*Reading* **History**
A. Analyzing Causes Why did some banks shut down during the Depression?

As banks failed or cut back on loans to businesses, factories produced fewer goods and therefore laid off workers. With more people out of work, spending declined. Businesses let more workers go and factories closed. By 1932, almost one-fourth of the nation's workers were jobless.

Everywhere, sales of farm products fell sharply. In the Midwest and Great Plains, farmers not only faced economic losses but also suffered a terrible drought that lasted for years. Poor farming methods and over-farming of the land led to massive soil erosion, making it impossible to grow crops. Winds carried away dry soil over millions of acres, creating the Dust Bowl. Thousands were forced to abandon their farms and leave the Great Plains.

Republican President Herbert Hoover took office early in 1929. When the stock market crashed in October 1929, he urged Americans to be patient. He warned that government programs would only make things worse. Relief, or government aid to the hungry and homeless, would make Americans dependent on government handouts. In the 1932 election, they voted for a leader who promised another way.

*Reading* **History**
B. Summarizing What was Hoover's attitude toward government action?

**Stock Prices,** *1925–1933*

Source: *Historical Statistics of the United States*

**SKILLBUILDER Interpreting Charts**
1. *In what year did stock prices begin their decline?*
2. *In what year did prices begin to rise again after the crash?*

The Federal Arts Project was part of the New Deal. It commissioned murals for post offices and other public buildings. This mural, titled *Construction of a Dam*, was painted by William Gropper (1897–1977). It was painted in the Department of the Interior building in Washington, D.C.

**What does the painting reveal about the value of work in a time of both economic depression and unemployment?**

# Roosevelt's New Deal

When Democrat **Franklin D. Roosevelt,** also known as FDR, took over as president, millions of families lacked food or shelter. People searched in garbage dumps for food or stood for hours in long lines for soup. Former business executives sold apples on streetcorners. Blaming Hoover for the hard times, the homeless called their camps consisting of tin-and-cardboard shacks "Hoovervilles." Roosevelt set out to restore hope and confidence both in government and in the American economy. His inaugural address expressed his optimism.

### A VOICE FROM THE PAST

This great nation will endure as it has endured, will revive and will prosper. So, first of all, let me assert my firm belief that the only thing we have to fear is fear itself.

**Franklin D. Roosevelt,** First Inaugural Address, March 4, 1933

Roosevelt promised immediate action, and he kept his word. His first target was the bank crisis. Calling for a "bank holiday," he ordered a brief shutdown of all banks. Federal officials went to work examining bank records. They decided which ones could reopen at once and which needed government help to do so. FDR's confidence persuaded Americans to put their money back into the banks.

With the public and Congress firmly supporting him, Roosevelt began a bold new program to end the Great Depression. It was called the **New Deal.** During a period known as the "Hundred Days," Congress passed with little debate almost all the bills the White House sent over. Even Republican lawmakers admired FDR's decisiveness.

Roosevelt's New Deal had three major goals, known as the "three R's":

1. **Relief programs** to help the hungry and jobless
2. **Recovery programs** to help agriculture and industry
3. **Reform of the economy** to ensure that a crisis like the Great Depression did not happen again

Not all of FDR's policies worked, and many angered business leaders because they led to higher taxes. Still, most Americans believed his policies were effective, and they reelected him to office in 1936.

## Lasting New Deal Changes

The New Deal made lasting changes in American society and government. It increased the power of the federal government. It encouraged presidents and Congress to practice deficit spending during economic hard times. This means spending more money than the government raises in taxes. Many New Deal programs were financed by deficit spending. The New Deal created Social Security, unemployment insurance, and other federal programs to care for the elderly, jobless, and needy. Roosevelt believed in using the power of government to help those in need. Government-supported social programs were the centerpiece of the New Deal.

Full economic prosperity did not return until the United States entered World War II in 1941. Even so, the New Deal restored Americans' faith in democracy. In the decade ahead, Americans put their lives on the line to preserve democracy abroad.

*Reading*History

**C. Summarizing**
What were some of the accomplishments of the New Deal?

**FRANKLIN DELANO ROOSEVELT**

**1882–1945**

A distant cousin of Theodore Roosevelt, Franklin D. Roosevelt became a New York state senator when he was 29. Later, he served as assistant secretary of the navy.

At the age of 39, FDR caught polio. For the rest of his life, he walked with braces or rode in a wheelchair (see below). Despite this, he continued in politics and was elected New York governor in 1928.

The public rarely saw photos revealing FDR's disability. Even so, many Americans sensed that he understood trouble. This quality helped him as a leader during the Depression.

**How would an understanding of trouble help FDR to lead?**

---

Section **1** Assessment

### 1. Terms & Names

**Explain the significance of:**
- Warren G. Harding
- Calvin Coolidge
- jazz
- Harlem Renaissance
- Great Depression
- Franklin D. Roosevelt
- New Deal

### 2. Using Graphics

Fill in the diagram with some causes of the Depression.

Which cause was most important? Why? (HI2)

### 3. Main Ideas

**a.** How did the boom times of the 1920s lead to the stock market crash? (HI2)

**b.** What happened to farm prices during the Great Depression? (HI2)

**c.** What were the three goals of FDR's New Deal? (REP3)

### 4. Critical Thinking

**Making Inferences** Why might the Great Depression have caused people to consider changes in the role of government? (HI1)

**THINK ABOUT**
- aims of democracy
- fears sparked by the Depression
- attitudes toward government

**ACTIVITY OPTIONS**

**LANGUAGE ARTS**

**MUSIC**

Prepare a short **essay** on a writer of the Harlem Renaissance or make a **class presentation** about jazz of the 1920s in which you play recordings of the music. (HI1)

# The Rise of Dictators and World War II

| MAIN IDEA | WHY IT MATTERS NOW | TERMS & NAMES |
|---|---|---|
| In the 1930s, the rise of dictators and their military aggression led to World War II. | Lessons learned in fighting aggression in World War II continue to influence American foreign policy. | Benito Mussolini fascism Adolf Hitler Nazi | World War II Dwight D. Eisenhower Holocaust |

**CALIFORNIA STANDARDS**

**CST1** Students explain how major events are related to one another in time.

**CST3** Students use a variety of maps and documents to identify physical and cultural features of neighborhoods, cities, states, and countries and to explain the historical migration of people, expansion and disintegration of empires, and the growth of economic systems.

**HI1** Students explain the central issues and problems from the past, placing people and events in a matrix of time and place.

**HI3** Students explain the sources of historical continuity and how the combination of ideas and events explains the emergence of new patterns.

**Taking Notes**

Use your chart to take notes about events during World War II.

| The 20th Century | Political Events |
|---|---|
| 1920–1939 | |
| 1940–1959 | |
| 1960–1979 | |
| 1980–1999 | |

## ONE AMERICAN'S STORY

Margaret Bourke-White was a photographer. Beginning in the 1930s, her powerful pictures in magazines and books helped Americans understand the events of their time. She was one of *Life* magazine's first photographers.

As you will read in this section, during the 1940s the United States joined Britain in fighting a war against Nazi Germany. As the first female photographer attached to U.S. forces, Bourke-White risked her life to send home vivid images of combat. She joined stunned soldiers entering Nazi concentration camps and was one of the first photographers to record the horrors they saw there.

## Dictators Take Power

The Great Depression spread around the world. In Germany and Italy, dictators appealed to desperate citizens by promising to restore prosperity. In Italy, **Benito Mussolini** built a political movement called **fascism**—a system under which the government rules through terror and by appealing to racism and nationalism. Using black-shirted followers to enforce his rule, Mussolini became prime minister in 1922. He won over nationalists by promising to turn Italy into a new Roman Empire. In 1935 his fascist troops invaded Ethiopia in Africa. The League of Nations had been formed to halt such aggression. However, it had little success.

In Germany, **Adolf Hitler** joined the National Socialist German Workers', or **Nazi,** Party. He tapped the bitter anger many Germans felt about the unfairness of the peace agreement ending World War I. The treaty required Germany to pay millions for war damages. Hitler skillfully blamed the nation's economic woes on Jews and other groups. After coming to power in 1933, he jailed critics. His expansion of German territory began with a violation of the World War I peace agreement. He sent troops into the Rhineland, a part of Germany near the French border. In

1938, he invaded Austria and attached it to Germany. Prime Minister Neville Chamberlain of Britain met with Hitler in Munich, Germany, in September 1938. Chamberlain agreed to allow Germany to take parts of Czechoslovakia. In return, Hitler promised not to demand any more land.

During this same period, dictator Joseph Stalin controlled the Soviet Union. Communist parties loyal to the Soviet Union had followers throughout Europe. Both Nazis and Fascists won many supporters by opposing the Communists. People feared Communist governments would seize their businesses and outlaw private property.

In Japan, military leaders held a powerful position in the government. In 1931, Japan invaded Manchuria, a province of China. This signaled the beginning of a planned Asian expansion. The League of Nations did little. In 1940, Japan, Italy, and Germany formed the Axis Powers.

## War Breaks Out in Europe

On September 1, 1939, the Nazis invaded Poland. Germany's massive air and ground attack finally made Britain and France understand that Hitler could only be stopped by force. Two days later, Britain and France declared war on Germany. **World War II** had begun.

The early war years were dark ones for the Allies, which included Britain, France, and the Soviet Union, among others. The German military seemed unstoppable. In the spring of 1940, German troops conquered Norway, Denmark, the Netherlands, and Belgium. Paris and much of France fell to the Germans in June.

In 1941, German forces smashed through Eastern Europe and invaded the Soviet Union. Great Britain now stood alone against Hitler. Despite nightly bombings of London and other cities by the Germans, Britain's prime minister, Winston Churchill, inspired Britons to hold on. In the United States, isolationists still urged Americans to stay out of European affairs and avoid war.

*Reading*History
**A. Interpreting Time Lines**
Which of the steps leading to World War II took place in Asia?

## Surprise Attack on Pearl Harbor

Roosevelt began his third term in 1941. He was the first and only president to serve more than two terms. He believed that failure to stop the

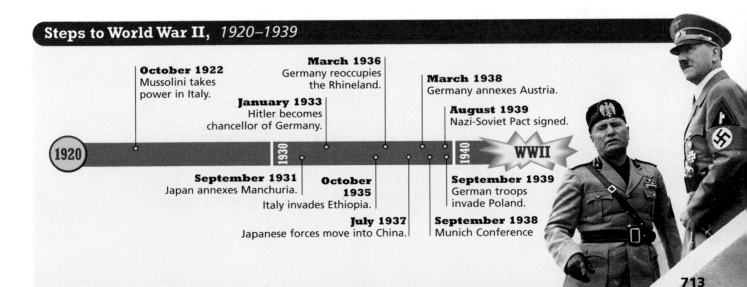

**Steps to World War II,** *1920–1939*

**October 1922**
Mussolini takes power in Italy.

**March 1936**
Germany reoccupies the Rhineland.

**March 1938**
Germany annexes Austria.

**January 1933**
Hitler becomes chancellor of Germany.

**August 1939**
Nazi-Soviet Pact signed.

1920 — 1930 — 1940 — **WWII**

**September 1931**
Japan annexes Manchuria.

**October 1935**
Italy invades Ethiopia.

**September 1939**
German troops invade Poland.

**July 1937**
Japanese forces move into China.

**September 1938**
Munich Conference

713

**U.S.S. ARIZONA MEMORIAL**

The U.S.S. *Arizona* suffered extensive damage during the attack on Pearl Harbor. The ship sank, and 1,177 of its crew died. The nation chose not to raise the battleship. Instead, officials created a memorial that sits above the sunken hull (see below). The names of all the crewmen who perished are carved on the memorial.

To commemorate the 50th anniversary of the attack against the U.S. naval base at Pearl Harbor, President George Bush visited the site in 1991.

Nazis and Fascists would endanger the United States. In early 1941, he gave a speech to Congress to prepare the public to aid the Allies.

### A VOICE FROM THE PAST

We look forward to a world founded upon four . . . human freedoms. The first is freedom of speech and expression—everywhere in the world. The second is freedom of every person to worship God in his own way. . . . The third is freedom from want. . . . The fourth is freedom from fear . . . anywhere in the world.

**Franklin D. Roosevelt,** State of the Union speech, January 6, 1941

Freedom required arms for its defense. Congress enacted the Lend-Lease Act in 1941. This law allowed the United States to ship arms and supplies, without immediate payment, to Britain and its allies.

On December 7, 1941, Japan launched an attack against the U.S. naval base in Pearl Harbor, Hawaii. Calling December 7 "a date which will live in infamy," FDR requested and Congress passed a declaration of war against Japan. Japan's allies—Italy and Germany—then declared war on the United States.

In 1942, the Axis Powers (Germany, Italy, Japan) seemed close to victory. By this time, the Soviet Union had joined the Allied Powers, following Germany's invasion of its territory in June 1941.

## The Home Front in America

Once the United States entered the war, its automobile plants and other factories were turned into defense plants. Airplanes, ships, weapons, and other supplies rolled off production lines at a rapid pace. By 1944, American assembly lines were producing 50 percent more armaments than those in the Axis nations combined.

Americans put up with wartime shortages so that resources such as steel, tin, and rubber could be redirected to military uses. Gasoline was in short supply. So were meat, butter, coffee, cheese, and sugar. Every family received ration books of stamps to buy goods.

With millions of men at war, women went to work in factories, shipyards, and offices. At first, heavy industries resisted hiring female workers, but by 1944 some 3.5 million worked on assembly lines turning out cargo ships and bombers.

As they had during World War I, hundreds of thousands of African Americans left the South for such cities as Cleveland, Chicago, and Detroit. More than 2 million took jobs in the defense industry. Roosevelt outlawed discrimination in industries with federal contracts.

Poster of factory worker during World War II

We Can Do It!

**Reading History**

**B. Summarizing**
What were some of the activities and challenges faced by women and minorities on the home front?

On the home front, Japanese Americans on the West Coast faced harsh treatment. By executive order, more than 100,000 loyal Japanese Americans were forced to leave their jobs, businesses, and homes. They were sent to internment camps throughout the West.

## War Continues in Europe and Asia

The invasion of Italy got under way with an attack on the island of Sicily in July 1943. The Allies forced the Germans out of Sicily and then swept into Italy. By this time, the Italians had imprisoned Mussolini. The new Italian government surrendered to the Allies in September 1943.

Meanwhile, in August 1942, German forces attacked the Russian city of Stalingrad, an important industrial center. A brutal battle took place. Soviet forces encircled and trapped the German army. As winter approached, the German commander begged Hitler to let him retreat. The *Führer* (or "leader") refused. The trapped Germans had no food or supplies. Each day, thousands of Nazi soldiers froze or starved to death. In late January 1943, the German troops surrendered. Each side had suffered staggering losses. With its defeat at Stalingrad, Germany's hopes of conquering the Soviet Union ended.

Another turning point in World War II came on June 6, 1944, known as D-Day. About 156,000 Allied troops crossed the English Channel and landed on the beaches of Normandy in northern France. They were

**World War II in Europe and Asia,** *1942–1945*

**Axis Powers**
**Axis-controlled**
**Allied Powers**
**Neutral nations**
**Allied advances**
**Allied victories**

**GEOGRAPHY SKILLBUILDER Interpreting Maps**

1. **Region** *Which three countries on the western fringes of Europe remained neutral?*
2. **Movement** *Which battle was fought closest to Japan?*

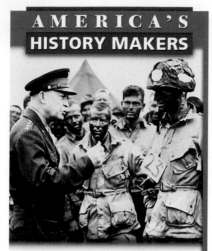

**DWIGHT D. EISENHOWER**
**1890–1969**

If ever there was a general who cared about his troops, it was General Dwight D. Eisenhower (at left, above). As Allied forces battled in Italy, Ike learned that he and another general were scheduled to stay in two large villas. "That's *not* my villa!" he exploded. "And that's not General Spaatz's villa! None of those will belong to any general as long as I'm Boss around here. This is supposed to be a rest center—for combat men—not a playground for the Brass [officers]!"

**How might Eisenhower's concern for the common man have affected his standing with the troops?**

part of a vast Allied invasion under the command of American General <u>**Dwight D. Eisenhower**</u>. British and American forces advanced on Germany from the west. The Soviets closed in from the east. In early May of 1945, Germany surrendered.

In the Pacific, the Japanese fought on. After 12 years as president, FDR died suddenly in April 1945, making Harry S. Truman the president. Truman decided to end the war before an invasion of Japan caused huge losses. In August 1945, American bombers dropped atomic bombs on Hiroshima and Nagasaki. In Hiroshima about 70,000 people died instantly. On September 2, 1945, Japan surrendered.

*Reading* **History**

**C. Reading a Map**
Use the map on page 715 to point out the locations of Hiroshima and Nagasaki on the Japanese mainland.

## The War Is Over

World War II had been the costliest and most destructive war in history. Approximately 55 million people died. Among them were some 6 million Jews, or almost two-thirds of Europe's Jews. Victims were shot, gassed, and worked to death in Nazi concentration camps, death camps, and slave labor camps. This systematic mass murder of 6 million Jews and other ethnic minorities by the Nazis became known as the **Holocaust.**

At war's end, the United States joined the United Nations, the international peacekeeping organization that replaced the League of Nations. New York City became its headquarters. The Soviet Union joined as well. Nevertheless, conflict between the former allies would lead to a new era of tension, as you will read in the next section.

---

*Section* **2** *Assessment*

### 1. Terms & Names

**Explain the significance of:**
• Benito Mussolini
• fascism
• Adolf Hitler
• Nazi
• World War II
• Dwight D. Eisenhower
• Holocaust

### 2. Using Graphics

Arrange these events with their dates on a time line: (CST2)

    event 2    event 4

event 1   event 3   event 5

• Normandy Invasion
• U.S. bombs Hiroshima
• Germany invades Russia
• Pearl Harbor bombed
• Germany invades Poland

### 3. Main Ideas

**a.** What events following World War I led to the rise of Hitler and Mussolini? (HI2)

**b.** Why were Americans reluctant to go to war? What made them change their minds? (HI2)

**c.** What ended the war in the Pacific? (HI2)

### 4. Critical Thinking

**Analyzing Causes** What elements in Nazi thinking might have contributed to the Holocaust? (HI2)

**THINK ABOUT**
• wartime fears
• attitudes toward minorities
• prejudice

**ACTIVITY OPTIONS**

**LANGUAGE ARTS**
**TECHNOLOGY**

Research women working in wartime factories. Write a **diary entry** of one woman's experiences or plan the contents of a **Web page** about women in World War II. (REP4)

# 3

# The Cold War

| MAIN IDEA | WHY IT MATTERS NOW | TERMS & NAMES |
|---|---|---|
| After World War II, the United States and the Soviet Union entered into a deadly struggle for world power. | This struggle affected American foreign policy for almost half a century. | Harry S. Truman    Lyndon B. Johnson<br>Cold War    Vietnam War<br>containment    Richard M. Nixon<br>John F. Kennedy    Watergate scandal |

## ONE AMERICAN'S STORY

World War II had destroyed European roads, bridges, mines, and railroads. Factories were shut down. U.S. leaders wanted to help the European economies and stop Communist expansion. George C. Marshall, secretary of state under President **Harry S. Truman**, came up with a plan to put Europe back on its feet.

### A VOICE FROM THE PAST

[The] United States should do whatever it [can] to assist in the return of . . . economic health in the world, without which there can be no political stability and no. . . peace. Our policy is directed . . . against hunger, poverty, desperation, . . . chaos.

**George C. Marshall,** speech at Harvard University, June 5, 1947

As you will read in this section, the Marshall Plan helped make Western and Southern Europe stable again.

**CALIFORNIA STANDARDS**

**REP4** Students assess the credibility of primary and secondary sources and draw sound conclusions from them.

**HI1** Students explain the central issues and problems from the past, placing people and events in a matrix of time and place.

**HI2** Students understand and distinguish cause, effect, sequence, and correlation in historical events, including the long- and short-term causal relations.

## The Cold War Begins

After World War II, fear and mistrust between the superpowers grew. The United States had hoped Eastern European nations would become democracies. Stalin feared that Eastern Europe could again become an invasion route into his country. For this reason, Stalin and the Soviets helped Communist governments come to power throughout Eastern Europe in the late 1940s.

President Truman and his advisers feared the spread of communism and looked for ways to stop it. This struggle marked the start of the **Cold War** between the superpowers. It was called a Cold War because there was no actual, direct fighting between the superpowers. This conflict was waged mainly with threats, spying, propaganda, and war in other countries.

**Taking Notes**

Use your chart to take notes about events after World War II.

| The 20th Century | Political Events |
|---|---|
| 1920–1939 | |
| 1940–1959 | |
| 1960–1979 | |
| 1980–1999 | |

Truman's anti-Soviet policy was called **containment**. It sought to contain, or stop, the Soviet Union from gaining influence outside its borders. Containment became the foundation of American foreign policy.

The Marshall Plan and the North Atlantic Treaty Organization (NATO) were key elements of containment. The Marshall Plan helped pay for Western and Southern Europe's recovery. Under the NATO agreement, Western allies formed a defense pact. The members pledged to protect one another in case of attack. The Soviet Union and its allies formed the Warsaw Pact.

## The Korean War and McCarthyism

In 1949, the Communists led by Mao Zedong took power in China. In 1950, troops from Communist North Korea, supplied by the Soviet Union, invaded American-backed South Korea. U.S. troops made up most of a UN force commanded by General Douglas MacArthur. The UN force drove the North Koreans out of the South and back into North Korea.

Fighting continued after General Dwight D. Eisenhower became the new U.S. president in 1953. He soon arranged a truce that ended the three-year war. The national boundaries of the two Koreas had changed very little. However, the United States had shown that the free world would fight Communist aggression.

In the postwar United States, public fears of communism allowed Senator Joseph McCarthy of Wisconsin to gain great power. He claimed that hundreds of government workers were Communists or Communist supporters. His hunt for Communists ruined many lives. A new word—McCarthyism—described the use of unproven charges against opponents and innocent citizens. By 1954, however, the public had turned away in disgust from McCarthy. His power quickly faded.

*Reading* **History**

**A. Recognizing Effects** What effect did the Communist takeover in China and Communist aggression in Korea have on American political life?

## Nuclear Threat and Superpower Conflicts

In 1945, the United States had dropped two atomic bombs on Japan to end World War II. Four years later, the Soviets built their own atomic bomb. A deadly arms race had begun. Both superpowers stockpiled nuclear weapons. By the end of the decade, both sides were developing missiles to carry bombs to each other's doorsteps.

**Vocabulary**
stockpiled: maintained a supply for future use

Neither superpower wanted to risk an all-out war. Instead, they pursued their rivalry indirectly by supporting opposite sides in conflicts in the Third World. These were the poorer nations of Latin America, Asia, and Africa. One such conflict brought the superpowers to the brink of war. In Cuba, Fidel Castro led a revolution that brought a Communist government to power in 1959. Attempts by the United States to topple Castro failed.

**This photograph shows a Soviet ship thought to be carrying nuclear missiles to Cuba.**

Then, in 1962, President **John F. Kennedy** learned that the Soviets were supplying Cuba with missiles. U.S. navy ships blockaded the island. The threat of nuclear war seemed very real. The world waited to see if the Soviets would remove all missiles and missile bases from Cuba. Finally, the Soviet Union agreed to remove them.

*Reading*History
B. Summarizing
What are some examples of superpower rivalry?

By the 1960s, the superpowers were in a space race as well as an arms race. Americans were stunned in 1957 when the Soviets sent *Sputnik,* a man-made satellite, into orbit around the earth. Alarm deepened as a Soviet cosmonaut took the first manned space flight. Throughout the 1960s, the two nations raced to see who would be first to put a person on the moon. Americans cheered as Neil Armstrong and Buzz Aldrin made the first lunar landing in 1969.

**The U.S. flag is planted on the surface of the moon in July 1969.**

In 1963, Kennedy was assassinated in Dallas, Texas. Kennedy's vice-president, **Lyndon B. Johnson,** succeeded him as president. Under Johnson, the United States became more deeply involved in conflict in the Southeast Asian countries of North and South Vietnam.

## War in Vietnam

In 1954, Vietnam was divided. Communists controlled North Vietnam and non-Communists controlled South Vietnam. The **Vietnam War** began in 1957 when Vietnamese citizens protested against the South Vietnamese government. Communists moved quickly into leadership of the protest movement. Eisenhower, Kennedy, and Johnson all feared a Communist victory. Experts argued that if South Vietnam became Communist, other Southeast Asian nations would also.

**Background**
The idea that if one nation fell to the Communists, others would soon follow, was called the "domino theory."

By 1968, more than 500,000 American troops were serving in Vietnam. U.S. planes dropped thousands of tons of bombs on North Vietnam. The large, well-equipped U.S. military faced a disciplined North Vietnamese force. Communist soldiers used hit-and-run guerrilla tactics. They sometimes relied on civilians for shelter and supplies. American soldiers won many battles, but they were stuck in an unwinnable war.

By 1968, the war had divided the United States. Strong criticism of Johnson's Vietnam policy contributed to his decision not to run for reelection. **Richard M. Nixon,** who was elected president in 1968, pledged to end the war. Over the next four years, he expanded the air war into neighboring Cambodia and Laos. At the same time, Nixon withdrew U.S. ground troops from South Vietnam. A 1973 ceasefire brought American troops home. Two years later, South Vietnam fell to the Communists. In 1976, the two Vietnams were united under Communist rule.

### daily *life*

**THE "TELEVISION WAR"**
The Vietnam War was the first "television war," broadcast each night on the evening news. Reports rarely showed actual battles, partly because much of the fighting occurred off and on and at night between small units.

Networks also tried to avoid gruesome scenes because they did not want to offend viewers. In addition, the networks agreed not to show any American dead or wounded so that their families would not recognize them on screen. Still, the images of war shocked viewers.

## CAUSE AND EFFECT: The Cold War, 1945–1991

| CAUSES | | IMMEDIATE EFFECTS | LONG-TERM EFFECTS |
|---|---|---|---|
| Soviet domination of Eastern Europe | THE COLD WAR | Truman Doctrine and Marshall Plan | Arms race between United States and Soviet Union |
| Communist victory in China | | East-West tension | Rivalry between United States and Soviet Union for world power |
| Distrust between United States and Soviet Union | | Founding of NATO and Warsaw Pact | |

**SKILLBUILDER Interpreting Charts**
1. Which of the causes was not centered in Europe?
2. Which alliance was founded by the Soviet Union and its allies?

## Nixon as President

In the early 1970s, President Nixon took steps to improve relations with the Soviet Union and Communist China. In 1972, Nixon visited China. He reopened direct communication between the two nations after a 21-year break. After Nixon's visit to the Soviet Union, the superpowers signed an agreement limiting nuclear arms.

The **Watergate scandal** took up much of Nixon's second term as president. People who worked for Nixon carried out illegal activities. These included wiretapping telephones and breaking into the Democratic Party headquarters in the Watergate building in Washington, D.C. An investigation showed that Nixon had ordered his staff to cover up White House involvement in these crimes.

In 1974, a congressional committee wanted to impeach Nixon. Rather than face impeachment, Nixon resigned. He became the only U.S. president to do so. Gerald Ford succeeded Nixon as president and eventually pardoned him.

## Foreign Policy of the 1970s and 1980s

Jimmy Carter won the 1976 presidential election, defeating Gerald Ford. He made human rights a cornerstone of his foreign policy. In 1977, Carter signed a treaty to turn the Panama Canal over to Panama in 2000. Carter also negotiated the Camp David Accords—a peace agreement between Egypt and Israel.

In 1979, the Soviet Union invaded Afghanistan to prop up a pro-Communist government. Ronald Reagan, who became president in 1980, took a tough stance toward the Soviet Union. Reagan increased U.S. defense spending and pledged to oppose communism in Central America. For several years, U.S.-Soviet relations became more tense.

By the late 1980s, however, U.S.-Soviet relations improved. A new Soviet leader, Mikhail Gorbachev, tried to reform the Soviet government and economy. Reagan and Gorbachev signed treaties agreeing to destroy some of their own nations' nuclear weapons.

*Reading* **History**
C. Summarizing
What were Reagan's policies toward the Soviet Union?

Meanwhile, many people in Communist nations wanted more freedom. They overthrew Communist rulers and formed democratic governments. In 1991, Communist leaders also lost power in the Soviet Union. The country split into independent states. Russia remained the largest of these states. The collapse of the Soviet Union ended the Cold War.

## New Threats to the United States

As the Soviet Union fell apart, the United States stood as the world's only superpower. But major issues still challenged the nation. In 1990, Iraq invaded Kuwait. President George H. W. Bush organized a coalition of nations to drive Iraq out of Kuwait. In 1991, the coalition defeated Iraq in the Persian Gulf War and freed Kuwait of Iraqi control.

Then, in 2001, Americans faced a more direct threat. On September 11, 2001, terrorists hijacked commercial airplanes and crashed them into the World Trade Center in New York City, the Pentagon, and in a Pennsylvania field. Within hours, both World Trade Center towers collapsed. In these attacks, nearly 3,000 people died.

President George W. Bush (George H. W. Bush's son) began a war against terrorism. In October 2001, the United States led a coalition attack on Afghanistan. The goal of the attack on Afghanistan was to break up the al-Qaeda terrorist network believed responsible for the September 11 attacks. And in March 2003, U.S. and British forces invaded Iraq. The goal of the war in Iraq was to prevent Iraq from supplying terrorists with weapons of mass destruction (WMD). (For more information on terrorism and the war in Iraq, see pages 732-737.)

Smoke billows from the World Trade Center buildings after the terrorist attack of September 11, 2001.

---

### Section 3 Assessment

#### 1. Terms & Names

**Explain the significance of:**
- Harry S. Truman
- Cold War
- containment
- John F. Kennedy
- Lyndon B. Johnson
- Vietnam War
- Richard M. Nixon
- Watergate scandal

#### 2. Using Graphics

Use a diagram to summarize America's Cold War policy. (HI1)

COLD WAR Containment

#### 3. Main Ideas

**a.** How did the goals of the Soviet Union and the United States for Eastern Europe differ after World War II? (HI1)

**b.** What were the space race and the arms race? (HI1)

**c.** How did the breakup of the Soviet Union change U.S.-Soviet relations? (HI2)

#### 4. Critical Thinking

**Comparing** How were the Korean War and the Vietnam War similar and different? (CST1)

**THINK ABOUT**
- American goals
- those who fought on each side
- the outcome of each struggle

---

**ACTIVITY OPTIONS**

**SPEECH**

**SCIENCE**

Give an **oral presentation** on one scientific challenge of landing on the moon or create a **diagram** of the lunar module. (HI1)

# Life in America Since 1945

**4**

| MAIN IDEA | WHY IT MATTERS NOW | TERMS & NAMES |

## MAIN IDEA

Since World War II, civil rights, economic growth, and social change have dominated American life.

## WHY IT MATTERS NOW

Prosperity, equality, and rapid change will remain important issues in the 21st century.

## TERMS & NAMES

baby boom

Dr. Martin Luther King, Jr.

Great Society

counterculture

---

**CALIFORNIA STANDARDS**

**REP4** Students assess the credibility of primary and secondary sources and draw sound conclusions from them.

**HI6** Students interpret basic indicators of economic performance and conduct cost-benefit analyses of economic and political issues.

## ONE AMERICAN'S STORY

When World War II ended, Americans were eager to return to normal life. Newlyweds and young families were looking for a way out of crowded city apartments. Builder William J. Levitt had the answer. He built cheap houses using assembly-line methods. On New York's Long Island, Levitt built more than 17,000 homes in Levittown. It was America's first suburban housing development. Levitt liked to brag that his home building was

Levittown, New York

helping to win the war against Communism. "No man who owns his own house and lot," he said, "can be a Communist. He has too much to do." As you will read, in the 1950s a home in the suburbs became a part of the American dream.

## Economic Boom and Baby Boom

After World War II, the U.S. economy boomed. The GI Bill offered returning soldiers schooling and job training. The Veterans Administration provided low-interest mortgages to home buyers. Rising demand for homes made possible the rapid growth of the suburbs. Other home builders were soon copying the building methods pioneered by Levitt. Car sales soared, too. Suburban families needed cars. They drove to work, to shopping centers, to movie theaters, and to restaurants.

During the late 1940s and the 1950s, the population grew rapidly. Americans were having more children, a trend known as the **baby boom**. Many people moved from the cities to the suburbs. They also moved from the Northeast to the sunbelt—the states of the South and the Southwest.

As Americans earned more, they spent more. Television appeared in almost every home. Americans eagerly bought the cars, electrical appliances, and other goods advertised on television and in magazines.

### Taking Notes

Use your chart to take notes about events in America after World War II.

| The 20th Century | Political Events |
| --- | --- |
| 1920–1939 | |
| 1940–1959 | |
| 1960–1979 | |
| 1980–1999 | |

Not all Americans shared in the new prosperity, however. In the 1950s, African Americans and other minorities continued to face discrimination, as did working women. In rural areas and inner cities, many people struggled to survive.

## The Civil Rights Movement

**HISTORIC DECISIONS**
*OF THE SUPREME COURT*
For more information on *Brown* v. *Board of Education of Topeka*, see pp. 752–753.

In the 1950s, reformers began to win legal victories to end segregation in the South. In 1954, in *Brown* v. *Board of Education of Topeka*, the Supreme Court ruled that segregated public schools were illegal. Two years later, after a black-led boycott of the Montgomery, Alabama, bus system, the Court ruled that segregated public transportation was against the law.

By the early 1960s, a young minister named **Dr. Martin Luther King, Jr.,** led a strong civil rights movement. Despite attacks by whites, the movement for equal rights remained largely nonviolent. At the 1963 March on Washington, King inspired more than 200,000 supporters with his words.

> *A VOICE FROM THE PAST*
>
> I have a dream that my four little children will one day live in a nation where they will not be judged by the color of their skin but by the content of their character. I have a dream today.
>
> **Martin Luther King, Jr., "I Have a Dream," August 28, 1963**

*Reading* **History**
**A. Recognizing Effects** What goals did Dr. Martin Luther King, Jr., help to achieve in civil rights?

In 1964, President Johnson pushed a Civil Rights Act through Congress. It banned discrimination in employment and voter registration. It also banned discrimination in public places such as restaurants, motels, and gas stations. Four years later, the Fair Housing Act outlawed discrimination in housing. Many of these changes were inspired by the leadership of Dr. King. King's assassination in Memphis, Tennessee, on April 4, 1968, stunned the nation.

Laws now guarantee African Americans and other minority groups equal treatment. With a growing number of African Americans elected to local, state, and federal offices, they have a greater voice in government.

## The Great Society

In 1964, President Lyndon B. Johnson convinced Congress to fund his War on Poverty. This effort created many government and private agencies to fight poverty. Some agencies provided job training. Others sent volunteers to teach in poor rural communities and rundown urban neighborhoods. Some programs funded part-time jobs for needy college students. Others offered preschool classes to give poor children a head

### AMERICA'S HISTORY MAKERS

**DR. MARTIN LUTHER KING, JR.**
**1929–1968**

Dr. King (shown below) became leader of the Montgomery bus boycott. Fresh out of school, he had been in Montgomery about a year. But his courage and eloquence made him the perfect person to lead the movement.

King learned about nonviolence by studying religious writers and thinkers. He came to believe that only love could convert people to the side of justice. He described the power of nonviolent resisters: "We will soon wear you down by our capacity to suffer. So in winning . . . freedom . . . you will be changed also."

**How might King's beliefs have supported his leadership of a nonviolent protest?**

start on learning. In 1965, Johnson got Congress to set aside millions for health care for poor, elderly, and disabled people. These health-care programs were called Medicare and Medicaid.

Reducing poverty, extending civil rights, and expanding medical care were all parts of Johnson's plan for a better America. He called it the **Great Society**. Like FDR's New Deal, the Great Society reflected Johnson's belief that government can improve people's lives. Johnson's social programs were costly. However, they attempted to reduce the poverty rate during the 1960s. As the U.S. role in the Vietnam War grew, though, fewer dollars were directed to Great Society programs.

## Rights for All

In the 1960s, minorities and women struggled for equal rights. Native Americans turned to the courts to fight for their land rights. They held protests highlighting the federal government's failure to honor treaties. One of the most outspoken Native American groups was the American Indian Movement (AIM).

In the early 1960s, César Chávez began organizing poorly paid Mexican-American farm workers in California. He led a five-year-long strike by grape pickers. Then Chávez formed the nation's first successful union of farm workers. It later became the United Farm Workers of America. Chávez's success inspired other Mexican Americans to work for change. In 1969–1970, they formed La Raza Unida—"the united people." This group worked to improve the lives of Mexican Americans and others.

In 1963, Betty Friedan wrote a best-selling book called *The Feminine Mystique*. This book led many women to rethink their roles. In 1966, Friedan and other activists founded the National Organization for Women (NOW). NOW and other women's groups such as Working Women and The American Association of University Women have worked to change laws that discriminate against women. They have helped to reform property rights and hiring. They continue working for equal pay and fair treatment in the workplace.

César Chávez organized the United Farm Workers of America during the 1960s.

*Reading* **History**

**B. Comparing and Contrasting** What was similar and different about the struggles of various groups for their rights?

## Youth Protests and the Counterculture

No controversy was more heated than that over the Vietnam War. Opponents of the war argued that it was a civil war between Communists and non-Communists for control of Vietnam. They stated that the United States had no right to interfere. The war's supporters considered these opponents to be traitors who were undermining the war effort. Antiwar protests brought millions of Americans into the streets. Shouting matches and flag burnings followed. Some protests turned violent. Antiwar activists clashed with supporters of the war. At Ohio's Kent State University in 1970, National Guardsmen fired their weapons and killed four students.

Vietnam widened the gap between younger and older Americans. Differences in beliefs and values between generations eventually gave rise to the **counterculture.** These were groups of people seeking new ways of living. One of the central values for members of the counterculture was a concern for the environment. Environmentalists sought to protect the environment by fighting pollution of the country's natural resources. Some younger Americans had different values from those of the mainstream. Many critics spoke out against the way young people questioned American values. Despite such concerns, in 1971 the Twenty-Sixth Amendment lowered the voting age to 18.

## Reagan, Bush, and Conservatism

Throughout the 1960s and 1970s, Democratic presidents such as Jimmy Carter had favored a strong role for government in the economy. They favored regulation of big business, support for organized labor, and public spending on the poor.

Ronald Reagan, a former movie actor and governor of California, was elected president in 1980, defeating Jimmy Carter. Reagan, a conservative Republican, wanted to reduce the role of government in American life. He sharply cut taxes and slashed spending on social programs for the poor. At the same time, he greatly increased military spending.

The tax cuts, coupled with heavy defense spending, caused the national debt to skyrocket. The government was borrowing more money to pay for spending than it was taking in through taxes. As a result, the national debt doubled in size from 1981 through 1986. Reagan pushed pro-business economic policies. He abolished thousands of government regulations on business. After a recession in 1982, the economy sharply improved.

Reagan's successor, George Bush, shared his conservative outlook. In the early 1990s, after his successful management of the Persian Gulf War, Bush's popularity surged. However, when the country headed into a recession, Bush's approval ratings fell sharply. In 1992, Bush lost his reelection bid to Democrat Bill Clinton, the governor of Arkansas.

## The Clinton Presidency

During his first term, Bill Clinton focused on domestic issues. To reduce the deficit, he supported tax increases and spending cuts. To fight crime, he pushed gun-control laws through Congress.

In 1994, the Democrats lost control of Congress to the Republicans. The new Congress pushed for deeper cuts in taxes and social programs than Clinton would support. A compromise led to deep cuts in some government social programs but protected some spending for education, welfare, and health care programs for the needy. The nation's strong economy helped Clinton win reelection in 1996.

*Reading***History**
**C. Summarizing**
What are some examples of how Reagan limited the role of government in economic affairs?

Protesters march in 1969 in opposition to the war in Vietnam.

Clinton's second term in office was marred by scandal. An investigation into Clinton's finances revealed that he had had an improper relationship with a White House intern. And he allegedly had lied about it under oath. The charges led to his impeachment in 1998. The Senate opened its trial of President Clinton in January 1999. Nearly a month later, the Senate acquitted him and Clinton remained in office.

*Reading***History**

**D. Contrasting**
What effect did the economy have on the elections of 1992 and 1996?

## The Bush Presidency

In 2000, the nation held a presidential election to choose Clinton's successor. The Democrats nominated Vice-President Al Gore as their candidate. The Republicans chose Texas governor George W. Bush, the son of the former president.

The 2000 election was one of the closest in U.S. history. By the morning after Election Day, Gore held a narrow lead in the popular vote. However, he did not have enough electoral votes to claim the presidency. Bush led in Florida by a few hundred votes, which promised to give him enough electoral votes to win the election. For five weeks, the two campaigns fought legal battles over recounts of the Florida ballots. Finally, on December 12, the U.S. Supreme Court voted 5 to 4 to stop the recounts, ensuring that Bush would win the presidency.

The election controversy widened the country's political divide. Critics wondered how Bush could govern effectively without winning the popular vote. Bush began his term working on domestic policies, such as educational reform. After the terrorist attacks of September 11, 2001, he focused on fighting terrorism at home and overseas. (See the Special Report beginning on page 732.)

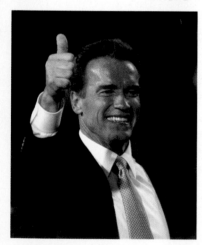

**Arnold Schwarzenegger became California's governor after winning the 2003 recall election.**

Political differences in California led to a historic recall election in 2003. A number of economic problems in 2000 and 2001, including a statewide electricity crisis, led many Californians to lose confidence in Democratic governor Gray Davis. Despite faltering support, Davis won reelection in 2002 by a slim margin. Shortly thereafter, Davis opponents began petitioning for a recall vote under state law, eventually gathering more than 1.3 million signatures. On October 7, 2003, more than 55 percent of voters chose to recall Davis. Actor Arnold Schwarzenegger was elected the new governor, receiving over 48 percent of the vote against 134 candidates.

While Bush's antiterrorism policies gained initial support, many Americans began to question his handling of the invasion of Iraq. In 2004, Massachusetts senator John Kerry challenged Bush. After both sides waged one of the most expensive campaigns in history, Bush was able to win a majority of the popular vote. However, once again the electoral vote came down to one state. In Ohio, Bush held a lead of more than 130,000 votes, which would give him the state's 20 electoral votes and the presidency. After deciding that the uncounted absentee and paper ballots would not be enough to take the lead, Kerry conceded the race to Bush the day after the election.

## Immigrants and the New Millennium

From 1981 to 1996, nearly 13.5 million legal immigrants came to the United States. These new immigrants increased U.S. diversity. Most of the immigrants who arrived in America during earlier periods had come from Europe. Nearly 85 percent of the most recent arrivals came from Latin America or Asia. The Census Bureau predicts that by 2020 the U.S. Hispanic population will increase from 12.5 percent to 17 percent. At the same time, the Asian population is expected to climb from 3.6 percent to nearly 6 percent.

While immigrants bring their culture to America, they also have embraced many American traditions. Most wear American clothes, adopt American customs, and learn English. Furthermore, they share with other Americans a belief in democracy and freedom.

Citizens of all races and backgrounds will play a vital role in shaping America. So will today's students. You have a part to play in helping the United States embrace people from every culture and land. You are the generation that will create the America of the future.

### The American People

| Origins of Immigrants, 1981–1996 | Numbers of Immigrants* |
|---|---|
| 1. Mexico | 3,300,000 |
| 2. Philippines | 840,000 |
| 3. China° | 730,000 |
| 4. Vietnam | 720,000 |
| 5. Dominican Republic | 510,000 |
| 6. India | 500,000 |
| 7. Korea | 450,000 |
| 8. Soviet Union† | 420,000 |
| 9. El Salvador | 360,000 |
| 10. Jamaica | 320,000 |

\* Numbers rounded to nearest 10,000.
° China includes Taiwan.
† The Soviet Union broke apart in 1991. This figure includes the former Soviet republics.

Source: *U.S. Bureau of the Census*

**SKILLBUILDER Interpreting Charts**

1. *From which European countries were there still substantial numbers of immigrants in the 1980s and 1990s?*
2. *From what regions of the world do most recent immigrants come?*

---

## Section 4 Assessment

### 1. Terms & Names

**Explain the significance of:**
- baby boom
- Dr. Martin Luther King, Jr.
- Great Society
- counterculture

### 2. Using Graphics

Use the chart to examine the aims of groups that protested in the 1960s. (HI1)

| | Goal | Success |
|---|---|---|
| African Americans | | |
| Mexican Americans | | |
| Native Americans | | |
| Women | | |

### 3. Main Ideas

**a.** How did the civil rights movement of the 1960s lessen discrimination against African Americans? (HI2)

**b.** What were the goals of President Johnson's Great Society programs? (HI3)

**c.** How did Reagan attempt to reduce the role of government in American life? (HI1)

### 4. Critical Thinking

**Supporting Opinions** Do any youth countercultures exist today? Why or why not? (HI1)

**THINK ABOUT**
- music and the arts
- politics
- religion
- values

**ACTIVITY OPTIONS**

**LANGUAGE ARTS**

**MATH**

Find out about voters' attitudes toward politicians. Create a survey, conduct a poll, and either write a **report** or display your results in a **graph.** (REP3)

# Protecting the Environment

The nation has made great strides over the past several decades in taking better care of the environment. However, much work remains to be done. As the United States embarks on a new century, the country continues to face such controversial issues as global warming and the problems of water pollution and a growing amount of waste.

**COOPERATIVE LEARNING** You have recently joined a local organization whose goal is to find solutions to the environmental challenges that affect your community. On these pages are three challenges you face as a member of the organization. Working with a small group, decide how to deal with each challenge. Choose an option, assign a task to each group member, and do the activity. You will find useful information in the Data File. Present your solutions to the class.

## ECONOMICS CHALLENGE

### *"from a feel-good issue to a bottom-line issue"*

**A growing number of businesses have begun taking steps to curb the amount of trash they produce. These companies have found that scaling back on waste helps to save money. How can you convince businesses in your community to follow this trend? Use the Data File for help. Use one of these options:**

- **Create an economic report showing companies ways they can cut back on waste while saving money.**

- **Write a proposal outlining further ways companies can reduce waste.**

## ART CHALLENGE

### *"very troubled waters"*

**In the decades after the Clean Water Act of 1972, many U.S. rivers became cleaner. Recently, however, the government has had to name more waterways as unsuitable for fishing or swimming.**

**The main pollutants include pesticide and sewage runoff from large farms, runoff from city and suburban sewer systems, and chemical waste from mining. How can you alert people in your community to these problems? Use the Data File for help. Present your information using one of these options:**

- **Design a poster showing one or more types of pollutants reaching a river.**

- **Create a graphic for town officials that depicts the Data File information about contaminated rivers.**

### CALIFORNIA STANDARDS

**HI6** Students interpret basic indicators of economic performance and conduct cost-benefit analyses of economic and political issues.

**Reading 2.6** Use information from a variety of consumer, workplace, and public documents to explain a situation or decision and to solve a problem.

**Listening and Speaking 2.3** Deliver research presentations

## MATH CHALLENGE

# "the seas would rise . . . and whole forest types could disappear"

Global warming remains a pressing environmental problem. Many scientists believe that air pollutants create a ceiling that traps heat near the earth's surface. Foremost among the pollutants is carbon dioxide—which is generated by factories, automobiles, and common household appliances. Encourage families to cut back on their carbon dioxide output. Use the Data File for help. Present your information using one of these options:

• Make a graph showing the yearly carbon dioxide output of various household items.

• Write a report detailing ways in which a family could reduce its carbon dioxide output by 25 percent.

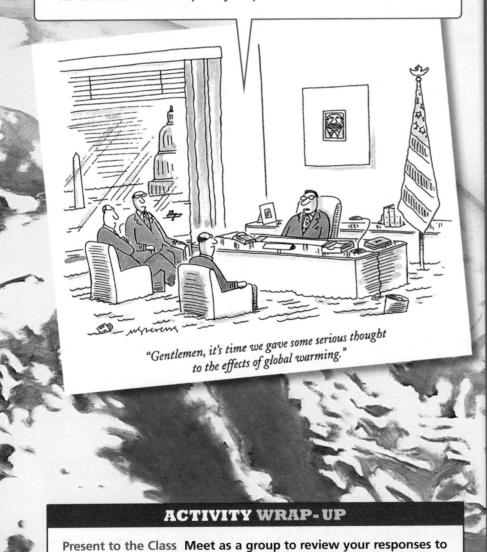

"Gentlemen, it's time we gave some serious thought to the effects of global warming."

## ACTIVITY WRAP-UP

**Present to the Class** Meet as a group to review your responses to various environmental challenges. Pick the most creative solution for each challenge and present these solutions to the class.

## Global Warming

Average U.S. Household's Yearly Output of Carbon Dioxide (in pounds):

Human respiration (2-6 persons)—1,950
Television—510
Range—933
Dishwasher—1,038
Lighting—1,045
Refrigerator—1,136
Dryer—1,177
Washer—1,199
Oil-fired water heater—4,476
Oil-fired space heater—12,958
Car—20,956

## What's in Our Dirty Rivers

From a 1998 study: 36 percent of U.S. rivers are contaminated. Percentage of contaminated rivers affected by the following pollutants:

• Toxic chemicals—9%

• Waste and chemicals from mining—13%

• City/suburban run-off (trash, chemical fertilizers)—13%

• Treated sewage (nitrogen and phosphorus)—14%

• Silt and sediment (from construction projects)—37%

• Agriculture runoff (dirt, manure, chemical fertilizers)—70%

## Corporate Conservation

• Colonial Pacific Leasing Corp. in Oregon cut $5,200 from its yearly electrical bill by using energy-efficient light bulbs.

• Stonyfield Farm Inc. in New Hampshire saved $60,000 one year by reducing the amount of plastic packaging on products.

• Mercer Color Corp. in Ohio made $8,000 one year by selling its waste for recycling.

• Xerox saves more than $200 million a year by reusing print and toner cartridges.

For more about conservation . . .

RESEARCH LINKS
CLASSZONE.COM

## VISUAL SUMMARY

## The United States Since 1919 (CST2)

**1920s:**
Prosperity; increased income and leisure

**1930s:**
Great Depression; New Deal; rise of dictators

**1940s:**
World War II; beginning of Cold War

**1950s:**
Prosperity; growth of suburbs; baby boom

**1960s:**
Civil rights movement; Vietnam War

**1970s:**
Détente; Vietnam War ends; Nixon resigns

**1980s:**
Soaring federal deficit; U.S.-Soviet relations improved

**1990s:**
Collapse of Soviet Union; prosperity

## TERMS & NAMES

Briefly explain the significance of each of the following.

1. Great Depression
2. New Deal
3. fascism
4. World War II
5. Holocaust
6. Harry S. Truman
7. Cold War
8. containment
9. baby boom
10. Great Society

## REVIEW QUESTIONS

### Prosperity and the Great Depression (pages 707–711)

1. What role did the market crash play in the Great Depression? (HI2)
2. What was the purpose of Roosevelt's bank holiday? (HI1)
3. What problems did FDR's New Deal address? (HI1)

### The Rise of Dictators and World War II (pages 712–716)

4. How did Hitler and the Nazi Party gain the support of Germans in the 1930s? (HI2)
5. How did the role of the United States in World War II change between 1939 and 1945? (HI1)

### The Cold War (pages 717–721)

6. What differences between the Soviet Union and the United States fueled the Cold War? (HI2)
7. What strategies did the United States use to carry out its containment policy? (HI1)
8. How did the end of the Cold War change the United States' role in world affairs? (HI3)

### Life in America Since 1945 (pages 722–729)

9. What methods did civil rights activists use? (HI1)
10. How did the views of presidents Johnson and Reagan differ on the role of government? (HI1)

## CRITICAL THINKING

### 1. USING YOUR NOTES: CATEGORIZING INFORMATION

| The 20th Century | Political Events | Economic Events | Social Events |
|---|---|---|---|
| 1920–1939 | | | |
| 1940–1959 | | | |
| 1960–1979 | | | |
| 1980–1999 | | | |

Using your completed chart, answer the questions below. (CST1)

a. What was an important political event in the period 1940–1950?

b. What was an important social event in the period 1960–1970?

c. What was an important economic event in the period 1980–1990?

### 2. APPLYING CITIZENSHIP SKILLS

How has the African-American struggle for civil rights changed since the 1960s? (HI1)

### 3. THEME: AMERICA IN THE WORLD

As the world's most powerful nation, does the United States have a special responsibility to intervene in conflicts around the world? Why or why not? (HI1)

### 4. ANALYZING LEADERSHIP

How do the leadership skills of a president differ in times of war and in times of peace and prosperity? Explain your answer. (HI1)

### 5. FORMING AND SUPPORTING OPINIONS

Should the government's focus today be on domestic issues or on foreign affairs? Explain your answer. (HI1)

### Interact with History

Now that you've read the chapter, what are some ways the 21st century may be the same as and different from the 20th century? Explain your ideas.

Use the map and your knowledge of U.S. history to answer questions 1 and 2.

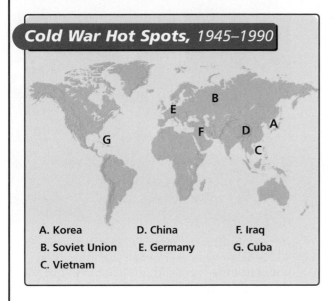

**Cold War Hot Spots,** *1945–1990*

| | | |
|---|---|---|
| A. Korea | D. China | F. Iraq |
| B. Soviet Union | E. Germany | G. Cuba |
| C. Vietnam | | |

Additional Test Practice, pp. S1–S33.

**1.** Which Cold War hot spot was located in Europe? (HI1)

**A.** Cuba

**B.** Germany

**C.** Korea

**D.** Iraq

**2.** What is the subject of this map? (HI1)

**A.** volcanic activity during the Cold War

**B.** popular travel spots during the Cold War

**C.** points of conflict during the Cold War

**D.** places occupied by foreign armies during the Cold War

This quotation is from President Franklin D. Roosevelt's first inaugural address. It was delivered in 1933, during the Great Depression. Use the quotation and your knowledge of U.S. History to answer question 3.

### PRIMARY SOURCE

This great nation will endure as it has endured, will revive and will prosper. So, first of all, let me assert my firm belief that the only thing we have to fear is fear itself.

**Franklin D. Roosevelt,** First Inaugural Address, March 4, 1933

**3.** What was Roosevelt trying to convey to Americans with this speech? (REP4)

**A.** a sense of reassurance

**B.** a growing feeling of fear

**C.** the worsening situation

**D.** the humor of the situation

**TEST PRACTICE**
CLASSZONE.COM

## ALTERNATIVE ASSESSMENT

### 1. ✍ WRITING ABOUT HISTORY

It is sometimes said that the 20th century will be remembered as the century of war. In other words, the thing that will be remembered most about the 20th century is the wars that were fought. Write a persuasive **essay** supporting or opposing this position. (REP5)

• Editorials in newspapers and magazines from 1999 and 2000 discussing the past century might be helpful.

• Remember to use specific examples to support your case and persuade your reader of your position.

### 2. COOPERATIVE LEARNING

Working in groups, make a list of social issues that concern Americans today, such as education, pollution, crime, or terrorism. Have each person research one issue and debate which is most important in front of the class. (REP4)

## INTEGRATED TECHNOLOGY

### DOING INTERNET RESEARCH

During the 1920s, there was a dramatic rise in popular entertainment. Using library resources and the Internet, find information about important celebrities of the time, such as Babe Ruth, Bessie Smith, or Charlie Chaplin. (REP4)

• Find images of the celebrities and perhaps film clips or recordings of the celebrities.

• Include short biographies of the celebrities.

• Present your research to the class.

For more about celebrities of the 1920s . . .

**INTERNET ACTIVITY**
CLASSZONE.COM

## Research Reports:
### Patterns of Immigration

**Writing Model**
ClassZone.com

**CALIFORNIA STANDARDS**
**Writing 2.3** Write research reports.

**PURPOSE:** To write a research report explaining the main reasons people have immigrated to this country

**AUDIENCE:** Your classmates

People have shaped America. Most of these people were immigrants, people who settled here from other lands. And America continues to be formed by its immigrants today. But these facts raise important questions. Why did these people leave their homes? What did they hope to find in America? These questions can be answered through research. As you may remember, a **research report** is a composition that pulls together information from several primary and secondary sources.

As this photograph shows, immigrants from the 1800s often lived in crowded conditions and endured other hardships in their pursuit of the American dream.

## Organization & Focus

Your assignment is to write a 500–700 word research report explaining why immigrants have come to the United States throughout its history. Review the history of immigration and find two or three broad reasons for immigration. You should also connect what you discover to your own family history.

Define your **thesis,** or controlling main idea, in the introduction of your report. Support the thesis in the body of your report. Draw meaning about America's history and your own family history in your report's conclusion. Finally, include a **bibliography** in your research report, listing your sources.

**IDENTIFYING PURPOSE AND AUDIENCE** As you learn about immigration and how it has shaped America, you will understand the impact immigration has had on your own life. Your audience is your classmates, and your purpose is to explain to them why people have immigrated— and continue to immigrate—to America.

## Research & Technology

Begin your search for information by reviewing this book. Look in each chapter for headings that signal information about the arrival of immigrants to this land. Extend your research by consulting library and Internet sources.

 **Technology Tip** Search for census information on the Internet. *U.S. Census information online* is one possible term to use for the search. You should be able to find census information dating back to 1790.

**ORGANIZING YOUR NOTES** Take notes from your sources. Record important ideas, concepts, and direct quotations. Paraphrase and summarize key ideas in your own words. Be sure to keep track of each source, including title, author, publisher, date, page number, or Web address. You will need these for your bibliography.

After you have taken notes from a variety of primary and secondary sources, look them over carefully. Identify three broad reasons for immigration and arrange your notes within those categories. After you have organized your notes, you should be able to answer the questions in the chart below.

| Reason 1 | Reason 2 | Reason 3 |
|---|---|---|
| Who immigrated for this reason? | Who immigrated for this reason? | Who immigrated for this reason? |
| When did they immigrate? | When did they immigrate? | When did they immigrate? |
| What was their experience in America? | What was their experience in America? | What was their experience in America? |

**OUTLINING AND DRAFTING** Use your organized note cards and your answers to the questions above to outline your research report. As you write your report, indicate with a footnote any fact or quotation you use from a source. Your word processor can place your footnotes automatically. Use visuals to illustrate your report. Display information on charts, maps, and graphs.

## Evaluation & Revision

Share your first draft with a reader for feedback. Can your reader identify the three reasons for immigration that you have cited? Can your reader see a clear connection between what you have learned about immigration and your own family history? If your reader cannot answer these questions, you should make those parts of your draft clearer.

**Self-Check**

Does my report have . . .

- ☐ a clearly defined thesis?
- ☐ supporting details drawn from a variety of sources?
- ☐ quotation marks to show borrowed words and ideas?
- ☐ footnotes in the proper form?
- ☐ a strong conclusion?
- ☐ a bibliography in the proper form?

## Publish & Present

Prepare a final copy of your report and present it to the class. Use the report as a springboard for a discussion of immigration in the United States today.

# The Attack: September 11, 2001

**CALIFORNIA STANDARDS**

**HI1** Students explain the central issues and problems from the past, placing people and events in a matrix of time and place.

Terrorism is the use of violence against people or property to force changes in societies or governments. Acts of terrorism are not new. Throughout history, individuals and groups have used terror tactics to achieve political or social goals.

In recent decades, however, terrorist groups have carried out increasingly destructive and high-profile attacks. The growing threat of terrorism has caused many people to feel vulnerable and afraid. However, it also has prompted action from many nations, including the United States.

Many of the terrorist activities of the late 20th century occurred far from U.S. soil. As a result, most Americans felt safe from such violence. All that changed, however, on the morning of September 11, 2001.

## A Surprise Strike

As the nation began another workday, 19 terrorists hijacked four airplanes heading from East Coast airports to California. The hijackers crashed two of the jets into the twin towers of the World Trade Center in New York City. They slammed a third plane into the Pentagon outside Washington, D.C. The fourth plane crashed into an empty field in Pennsylvania after passengers apparently fought the hijackers.

The attacks destroyed the World Trade Center and badly damaged a section of the Pentagon. In all, some 3,000 people died. Life for Americans would never be the same after that day. Before, most U.S. citizens viewed terrorism as something that happened in other countries. Now they knew it could happen on their soil as well.

Officials soon learned that those responsible for the attacks were part of a largely Islamic terrorist network known as al-Qaeda. Observers, including many Muslims, accuse al-Qaeda of preaching a false and extreme form of Islam. Its members believe, among other things, that the United States and other Western nations are evil.

U.S. president George W. Bush vowed to hunt down all those responsible for the attacks. In addition, he called for a greater international effort to combat global terrorism. "This battle will take time and resolve," the president declared. "But make no mistake about it: we will win."

## Securing the Nation

As the Bush Administration began its campaign against terrorism, it

### Flight Path of the Hijacked Airliners, September 11, 2001

also sought to prevent any further attacks on America. In October 2001, the president signed into law the USA Patriot Act. The law gave the federal government a broad range of new powers to strengthen national security.

The new law enabled officials to detain foreigners suspected of terrorism for up to seven days without charging them with a crime. Officials could also monitor all phone and Internet use by suspects, and prosecute terrorist crimes without any time restrictions or limitations.

In addition, the government created a new cabinet position, the Department of Homeland Security, to coordinate national efforts against terrorism. President Bush named former Pennsylvania governor Tom Ridge as the first Secretary of Homeland Security.

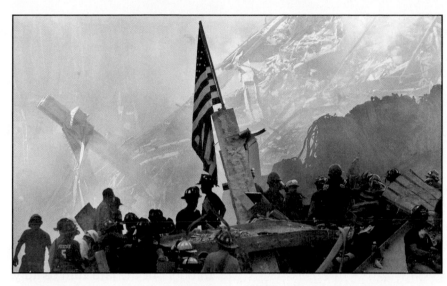

Underneath a U.S. flag posted amid the rubble of the World Trade Center, rescue workers search for survivors of the attack.

Some critics charged that a number of the government's new anti-terrorism measures violated people's civil rights. Supporters countered that occasionally limiting some civil liberties was justified in the name of greater national security.

The federal government also stepped in to ensure greater security at the nation's airports. The September 11 attacks had originated at several airports, with four hijackings occurring at nearly the same time. In November 2001, President Bush signed the Aviation and Transportation Security Act into law. The law put the federal government in charge of airport security. Before, individual airports had been responsible for security. The new law created a federal security force to inspect passengers and carry-on bags. It also required the screening of checked baggage.

While the September 11 attacks shook the United States, they also strengthened the nation's unity and resolve. In 2003, officials approved plans to rebuild on the World Trade Center site and construct a memorial. Meanwhile, the country has grown more unified as Americans recognize the need to stand together against terrorism.

Stunned bystanders look on as smoke billows from the twin towers of the World Trade Center moments after an airplane slammed into each one.

# Fighting Back

**The attack against the United States on September 11, 2001, represented the single most deadly act of terrorism in modern history. By that time, however, few regions of the world had been spared from terrorist attacks. Today, America and other nations are responding to terrorism in a variety of ways.**

## The Rise of Terrorism

The problem of modern international terrorism first gained world attention during the 1972 Summer Olympic Games in Munich, Germany. Members of a Palestinian terrorist group killed two Israeli athletes and took nine others hostage. Five of the terrorists, all the hostages, and a police officer were later killed in a bloody gun battle.

Since then, terrorist activities have occurred across the globe. In Europe, the Irish Republican Army (IRA) used terrorist tactics for decades against Britain. The IRA has long opposed British control of Northern Ireland. Since 1998, the two sides have been working toward a peaceful solution to their conflict. In South America, a group known as the Shining Path terrorized the residents of Peru throughout the late 20th century. The group sought to overthrow the government and establish a Communist state.

Africa, too, has seen its share of terrorism. Groups belonging to the al-Qaeda terrorist organization operated in many African countries. Indeed, officials have linked several major attacks against U.S. facilities in Africa to al-Qaeda. In 1998, for example, bombings at the U.S. embassies in Kenya and Tanzania left more than 200 dead and 5,000 injured.

Most terrorists work in a similar way: targeting high profile events or crowded places where people normally feel safe. They include such places as subway stations, bus stops, restaurants, or shopping malls. Terrorists choose these spots carefully in order to gain the most attention and to achieve the highest level of intimidation.

Terrorists use bullets and bombs as their main weapons. In recent years, however, some terrorist groups have used biological and chemical agents in their attacks. These actions involve the release of bacteria or poisonous gas into the air. Gas was the weapon of choice for a radical Japanese religious cult, Aum Shinrikyo. In 1995, cult members released sarin, a deadly nerve gas, in subway stations in Tokyo. Twelve people were killed and more than 5,700 injured. The possibility of this type of terrorism is particularly worrisome, because biochemical agents are relatively easy to acquire.

## Terrorism: A Global Problem

| PLACE | YEAR | EVENT |
|-------|------|-------|
| Munich, Germany | 1972 | Palestinians take Israeli hostages at Summer Olympics; hostages and terrorists die in gun battle with police |
| Beirut, Lebanon | 1983 | Terrorists detonate truck bomb at U.S. marine barracks, killing 241 |
| Tokyo, Japan | 1995 | Religious extremists release lethal gas into subway stations, killing 12 and injuring thousands |
| Omagh, Northern Ireland | 1998 | Faction of Irish Republican Army sets off car bomb, killing 29 |
| Moscow, Russia | 2002 | Rebels from Chechnya seize a crowded theater; rescue effort leaves more than 100 hostages and all the terrorists dead |

## Hunting Down Terrorists

Most governments have adopted an aggressive approach to tracking down and punishing terrorist groups. This approach includes spying on the groups to gather information on membership and future plans. It also includes striking back harshly after a terrorist attack, even to the point of assassinating known terrorist leaders.

Another approach that governments use is to make it more difficult for terrorists to act. This involves eliminating a terrorist group's source of funding. President Bush issued an executive order freezing the U.S. assets of alleged terrorist organizations as well as various groups accused of supporting terrorism. President Bush asked other nations to freeze such assets as well. By the spring of 2002, the White House reported, the United States and other countries had blocked nearly $80 million in alleged terrorist assets.

## Battling al-Qaeda

In one of the more aggressive responses to terrorism, the United States quickly took military action against those it held responsible for the September 11 attacks.

U.S. officials had determined that members of the al-Qaeda terrorist group had carried out the assault under the direction of the group's leader, Osama bin Laden. Bin Laden was a Saudi Arabian millionaire who lived in Afghanistan. He directed his terrorist activities under the protection of the country's extreme Islamic government, known as the Taliban.

The United States demanded that the Taliban turn over bin Laden. The Taliban refused. In October 2001, U.S. forces began bombing Taliban air defenses, airfields, and command centers. They also struck numerous al-Qaeda training camps. On the ground, the United States provided assistance to rebel groups opposed to the Taliban. By December, the United States had driven the Taliban from power and severely weakened the al-Qaeda network. However, as of September 2004, Osama bin Laden was still believed to be at large.

Osama bin Laden delivers a videotaped message from a hidden location shortly after the U.S.-led strikes against Afghanistan began.

Troops battling the Taliban in Afghanistan await transport by helicopter.

# The War in Iraq

In the ongoing battle against terrorism, the United States confronted the leader of Iraq, Saddam Hussein. The longtime dictator had concerned the world community for years. During the 1980s, Hussein had used chemical weapons to put down a rebellion in his own country. In 1990, he had invaded neighboring Kuwait—only to be pushed back by a U.S.-led military effort. In light of such history, many viewed Hussein as an increasing threat to peace and stability in the world. As a result, the Bush Administration led an effort in early 2003 to remove Hussein from power.

## The Path to War

One of the main concerns about Saddam Hussein was his possible development of so-called weapons of mass destruction. These are weapons that can kill large numbers of people. They include chemical and biological agents as well as nuclear devices.

Bowing to world pressure, Hussein allowed inspectors from the United Nations to search Iraq for such outlawed weapons. Some investigators, however, insisted that the Iraqis were not fully cooperating with the inspections.

U.S. and British officials soon threatened to use force to disarm Iraq. During his State of the Union address in January 2003, President Bush declared Hussein too great a threat to ignore in an age of increased terrorism. Reminding Americans of the September 11 attacks, Bush stated, "Imagine those 19 hijackers with other weapons and other plans—this time armed by Saddam Hussein. It would take one vial, one canister, one crate slipped into this country to bring a day of horror like none we have ever known. We will do every-thing in our power to make sure that day never comes."

## Operation Iraqi Freedom

In the months that followed, the UN Security Council debated what action to take. Some countries, such as France and Germany, called for letting the inspectors continue searching for weapons. British prime minister Tony Blair, however, accused the Iraqis of "deception and evasion" and insisted inspections would never work.

On March 17, President Bush gave Saddam Hussein and his top aides 48 hours to leave the country or face a military strike. The Iraqi leader refused. On March 19, a coalition led by the United States and Britain launched air strikes in and around the Iraqi capital, Baghdad. The next day, coalition forces marched into Iraq though Kuwait. The invasion of Iraq to remove Saddam Hussein, known as Operation Iraqi Freedom, had begun.

The military operation met with strong opposition from numerous countries. Russian president Vladimir Putin claimed the invasion could "in no way be justified." He and others criticized the policy of attacking a nation to prevent it from future misdeeds. U.S. and British officials, however, argued that they would not wait for Hussein to strike first.

As coalition troops marched north to Baghdad, they met pockets of stiff resistance and engaged in fierce fighting in several southern cities. Meanwhile, coalition forces parachuted into northern Iraq and began moving south toward the capital city. By early April, Baghdad had fallen and the regime of Saddam Hussein had collapsed. After less than four weeks of fighting, the coalition had won the war.

U.S. Army Specialist Shoshana Johnson was one of several Americans held prisoner and eventually released during the war in Iraq.

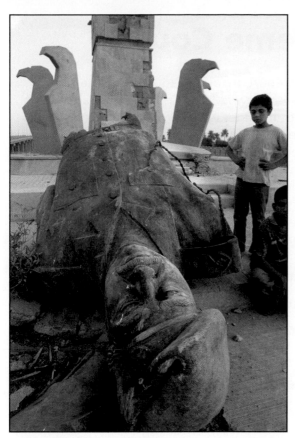

As the regime of Saddam Hussein collapsed, statues of the dictator toppled.

established their own interim government several months after the war. The new governing body went to work creating a constitution and planning democratic elections.

Meanwhile, intelligence officials searched for clues of Saddam Hussein's whereabouts. The defeated dictator was captured near his hometown of Tikrit on December 13, 2003. Despite Hussein's capture, numerous U.S. troops had to remain behind to help maintain order and battle pockets of Iraqi insurgents—different groups made up of Hussein loyalists, followers of rebel Islamic clerics, and terrorists with links to al-Qaeda.

Finally, weapons inspectors were not able to find any weapons of mass distruction in the months after major combat had ended. The governments of the United States and Britain issued reports in 2004

saying that pre-war intelligence regarding such weapons was flawed.

Despite the unresolved issues, coalition leaders declared the defeat of Saddam Hussein to be a victory for global security. In a post-war speech to U.S. troops aboard the aircraft carrier *USS Abraham Lincoln*, President Bush urged the world community to keep moving forward in its battle against terrorism. "We do not know the day of final victory, but we have seen the turning of the tide," declared the president. "No act of the terrorists will change our purpose, or weaken our resolve, or alter their fate. Their cause is lost. Free nations will press on to victory."

President George W. Bush and British prime minister Tony Blair stood together throughout the war.

## The Struggle Continues

Despite the coalition victory, much work remained in Iraq. The United States installed a civil administrator, retired diplomat L. Paul Bremer, to help oversee the rebuilding of the nation. With the help of Bremer and others, the Iraqis

---

### Special Report Assessment

#### 1. Main Ideas

**a.** What steps did the U.S. government take to make the nation more secure after the attacks on September 11, 2001? (HI2)

**b.** Why did the United States take military action against the Taliban in Afghanistan? (HI2)

**c.** What was the result of Operation Iraqi Freedom? (HI2)

#### 2. Critical Thinking

**Analyzing Issues** Is it important for the U.S. government to respect people's civil rights as it wages a war against terrorism? Why or why not? (REP4)

**THINK ABOUT**
• what steps are necessary to protect the nation
• a government that grows too powerful

# The Supreme Court

The task of the Supreme Court, according to Chief Justice John Marshall, is "to say what the law is." The Court reviews appeals of decisions by lower courts. It judges whether federal laws or government actions violate the Constitution. And it settles conflicts between state and federal laws.

By interpreting the law, the Supreme Court wields great power, for its decisions affect practically every aspect of life in the United States. In the following pages, you'll learn about some of the Supreme Court's landmark cases—decisions that altered the course of history or brought major changes to American life.

*"When we have examined . . . the Supreme Court and the [rights] which it exercises, we shall readily admit that a more imposing judicial power was never constituted by any people."*

— ALEXIS DE TOCQUEVILLE, *DEMOCRACY IN AMERICA* (1835)

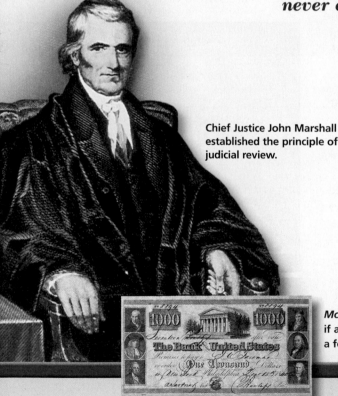

Chief Justice John Marshall established the principle of judicial review.

The development of steamships led to Supreme Court decisions on interstate commerce.

*McCulloch* v. *Maryland* decided if a state had the power to tax a federal agency.

**1803**
*Marbury* v. *Madison*
Judicial Review

**1819**
*McCulloch* v. *Maryland*
Powers of Congress and States' Rights

**1824**
*Gibbons* v. *Ogden*
State Versus Federal Authority

**1857**
*Dred Scott* v. *Sandford*
Citizenship

**1896**
*Plessy* v. *Ferguson*
Segregation

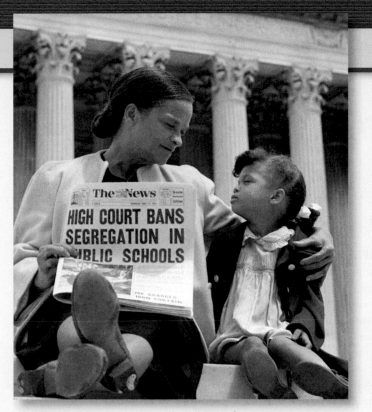

Landmark decisions on school desegregation helped give rise to the civil rights movement.

## TABLE OF CONTENTS

## BEFORE YOU READ

**Think About It** Why is there a need for a judicial authority "to say what the law is"? How might the history of the United States have been different if the Supreme Court had not taken on this role?

**Find Out About It** Use library resources or the Internet to find out what issues the Supreme Court is presently reviewing. How might the Court's decisions on these issues affect you?

For more information on the Supreme Court . . .

**RESEARCH LINKS**
CLASSZONE.COM

Opinions written by Justice Oliver Wendell Holmes, Jr., helped to set standards for free speech.

The Supreme Court has reviewed several affirmative-action cases in recent years.

**1919**
*Schenck* v. *United States*
Freedom of Speech

**1954**
*Brown* v. *Board of Education of Topeka*
School Desegregation

**1964**
*Reynolds* v. *Sims*
One Person, One Vote

**1978**
*Regents of the University of California* v. *Bakke*
Affirmative Action

# Marbury v. Madison (1803)

**THE ISSUE** Judicial Review

**ORIGINS OF THE CASE** In 1801, just before he left office, President John Adams appointed dozens of Federalists as judges. Most of these "midnight justices" took their posts before Thomas Jefferson, Adams's Democratic-Republican successor, took office. Jefferson ordered his secretary of state, James Madison, to block the remaining appointees from taking their posts. One of these appointees, William Marbury, asked the Supreme Court to issue an order forcing Madison to recognize the appointments.

**THE RULING** The Court ruled that the law under which Marbury had asked the Supreme Court to act was unconstitutional.

## The Legal Arguments

Chief Justice John Marshall wrote the Court's opinion, stating that Marbury had every right to receive his appointment. Further, Marshall noted, the Judiciary Act of 1789 gave Marbury the right to file his claim directly with the Supreme Court. But Marshall questioned whether the Court had the power to act. The answer, he argued, rested on the kinds of cases that could be argued directly in the Supreme Court without first being heard by a lower court.

Article 3 of the Constitution clearly identified those cases that the Court could hear directly. A case like Marbury's was not one of them. The Judiciary Act, therefore, was at odds with the Constitution. Which one should be upheld? Marshall's response was clear:

> . . . [T]he particular phraseology of the Constitution of the United States confirms and strengthens the principle . . . that a law repugnant to the Constitution is void; and that *courts* . . . are bound by that instrument.

Since Section 13 of the Judiciary Act violated the Constitution, Marshall concluded, it could not be enforced. The Court, therefore, could not issue the order. With this decision, Marshall appeared to limit the powers of the Supreme Court. In fact, the decision increased the Court's power because it established the principle of judicial review. This holds that the courts—most notably the Supreme Court—have the power to decide if laws are unconstitutional.

William Marbury received his appointment as a reward for his loyal support of John Adams in the 1800 presidential election.

## LEGAL *Sources*

### U.S. CONSTITUTION/LEGISLATION

**Article 3, Section 2 (1789)**
"In all cases affecting ambassadors, other public ministers and consuls, and those in which a state shall be party, the Supreme Court shall have original jurisdiction. In all the other cases . . . the Supreme Court shall have appellate jurisdiction."

**Judiciary Act, Section 13 (1789)**
"The Supreme Court shall . . . have power to issue . . . writs of *mandamus,* in cases warranted by the principles and usages of law."

### RELATED CASES

**Fletcher v. Peck (1810)**
For the first time, the Supreme Court ruled a state law unconstitutional.

**Cohens v. Virginia (1821)**
For the first time, the Court overturned a state court decision.

## Why Did It Matter Then?

The principle of judicial review had been set down in earlier state and lower federal court decisions. However, Marshall did not refer to those cases in *Marbury.* Rather, he based his argument on logic.

For a written constitution to have any value, Marshall stated, it is logical that any "legislative act [that is] contrary to the Constitution is not law." Only then could the Constitution be—as Article VI calls it—"the supreme law of the land." Who, then, decides that a law is invalid? Marshall declared that this power rests only with the courts:

> It is, emphatically, the province and duty of the judicial department to say what the law is. Those who apply the rule to particular cases must of necessity expound and interpret that rule. If [the Constitution and a law] conflict with each other, the courts must decide on the operation of each.

Not only did the courts have this power, Marshall said, it was "the very essence of judicial duty" for them to exercise it.

## Why Does It Matter Now?

Over the years, judicial review has become a cornerstone of American government. The principle plays a vital role in the system of checks and balances that limits the powers of each branch of the federal government. For example, since 1803 the Court has struck down more than 125 acts of Congress as unconstitutional.

The Court has cited *Marbury* more than 250 times to justify its decisions. In *Clinton* v. *Jones* (1997), for example, the Court found that presidents are not protected by the Constitution from lawsuits involving actions in their private lives. The Court supported this finding by pointing to its power "to say what the law is." More recently, in *United States* v. *Morrison* (2000), the Court ruled that Congress went beyond its constitutional bounds by basing a federal law banning violence against women on the Fourteenth Amendment and the Commerce Clause of the Constitution. The opinion pointed out that "ever since *Marbury* this Court has remained the ultimate [explainer] of the constitutional text."

John Marshall, a Federalist, was practically a "midnight justice." John Adams appointed him chief justice in January 1801, just two months before Thomas Jefferson took office.

## CONNECT TO HISTORY

1. **Making Decisions** Marshall was a Federalist, and many people expected him to act quickly on Marbury's case. What do you think might have been the consequences if Marshall had found for Marbury?

 See Skillbuilder Handbook, page R14.

## CONNECT TO TODAY

2. **Researching** Find a recent instance of a law or administrative action that was ruled unconstitutional by the Supreme Court. What were the Court's reasons for the ruling, and what impact did the decision have? Prepare a summary of your findings.

For more information on judicial review . . .

RESEARCH LINKS
CLASSZONE.COM

# McCulloch v. Maryland
## (1819)

**THE ISSUES**  Balance of power between the federal and state governments

**ORIGINS OF THE CASE**  The second Bank of the United States (BUS) was established by an act of Congress in 1816. It set up branches nationwide. But many states objected to the bank's policies and wanted to limit its operations. In fact, Maryland set a tax on the currency issued by the Baltimore branch. The bank could avoid the tax by paying an annual fee of $15,000. However, James McCulloch, the branch cashier, refused to pay either the tax or the fee. The state sued McCulloch, and the Maryland courts ordered him to pay. McCulloch appealed the case to the Supreme Court.

**THE RULING**  The Court ruled that Congress had the power to establish a national bank and that the Maryland tax on that bank was unconstitutional.

## The Legal Arguments

The Court first addressed Maryland's argument that the act establishing the BUS was unconstitutional. Chief Justice John Marshall wrote that the Constitution listed the specific powers of Congress. These included collecting taxes, borrowing money, and regulating commerce. In addition, the Elastic Clause gave Congress the authority to make all "necessary and proper" laws needed to exercise those powers. Establishing a bank, he concluded, was necessary for Congress to carry out its powers. The BUS, then, was constitutional.

Next, Marshall addressed whether Maryland had the power to tax the BUS. Marshall acknowledged that the states had the power of taxation. But he said:

> [T]he constitution and the laws made in pursuance thereof are supreme . . . they control the constitution and laws of the respective states, and cannot be controlled by them.

So, to give a state the power to tax a federal agency created under the Constitution would turn the Supremacy Clause, Article 6, Section 2, on its head. Further, Marshall observed, "the power to tax involves the power to destroy." If a state could tax one federal agency, it might tax others. This eventually "would defeat all the ends of government." He added that the framers of the Constitution certainly did not intend to make the national government subject to the states:

> [T]he States have no power, by taxation or otherwise, to retard, impede, burden, or in any manner control, the operations of the constitutional laws enacted by Congress to carry [out its] powers.

The Maryland tax, therefore, was unconstitutional.

## LEGAL *Sources*

### U.S. CONSTITUTION/LEGISLATION

**Article 1, Section 8 (1789)**
"The Congress shall have the power to . . . make all laws which shall be necessary and proper for carrying into execution the [specific powers given to Congress]."

**Article 6, Section 2 (1789)**
"This Constitution, and the laws of the United States . . . shall be the supreme law of the land; . . . anything in the Constitution or laws of any state to the contrary notwithstanding."

### RELATED CASES

**Fletcher v. Peck (1810)**
Noting that the Constitution was the supreme law of the land, the Supreme Court ruled a state law unconstitutional.

**Gibbons v. Ogden (1824)**
The Court ruled that the federal Congress—not the states—had the power to regulate interstate commerce.

## Why Did It Matter Then?

At the time of the *McCulloch* case, there was considerable debate over what powers Congress held. Some people took a very limited view. They suggested that Congress's powers should be restricted to those named in the Constitution. Others pointed out that the Elastic Clause implied that Congress had much broader powers.

The *McCulloch* opinion followed this second view. Marshall wrote:

> **Let the end be [lawful], let it be within the scope of the Constitution, and all means which are appropriate, which are plainly adapted to that end, which are not prohibited, but consist with the letter and spirit of the Constitution, are constitutional.**

In other words, Congress could exercise the powers it considered appropriate to achieve its lawful goals.

Marshall's broad view of congressional power strengthened the federal government. And this stronger government reflected and encouraged the growing nationalist spirit in the early 1800s.

## Why Does It Matter Now?

Since Marshall's time, the United States has undergone many changes. Over the course of the 19th and 20th centuries, the country has grown dramatically. The population has increased and moved. In Marshall's day, the United States was predominantly rural. Today, most people live in urban areas, where economic and leisure activities abound.

The economy of the United States, too, has changed. The country has moved from an agricultural economy to one based on industry and, later, service and information.

During this time, the federal government has stretched its powers to meet the needs of the ever-changing American society. Programs like Franklin Roosevelt's New Deal and Lyndon Johnson's Great Society came about through this expanding of powers. Marshall's broad reading of the Elastic Clause in the *McCulloch* opinion, in large part, laid the groundwork for this growth in the size and power of the federal government.

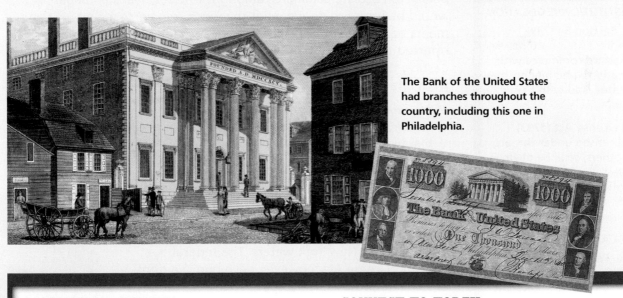

The Bank of the United States had branches throughout the country, including this one in Philadelphia.

---

### CONNECT TO HISTORY

1. **Forming and Supporting Opinions** Chief Justice John Marshall considered the *McCulloch* decision the most important that he made. Why do you think he considered it such an important decision? Give reasons for your answer.

    See Skillbuilder Handbook, page R17.

### CONNECT TO TODAY

2. **Researching** One issue addressed in *McCulloch* was states' rights and federal authority. Do research to find a recent Supreme Court case that has dealt with this issue. Write a paragraph describing the basis of the case and the Court's decision.

   For more information on states' rights and federal authority . . .

   **RESEARCH LINKS**
   CLASSZONE.COM

# Gibbons v. Ogden (1824)

**THE ISSUE** Federal power to regulate interstate commerce

**ORIGINS OF THE CASE** Aaron Ogden ran steamboats between New York City and New Jersey. The New York state legislature granted him a monopoly—the right to operate this service without any competition. However, Thomas Gibbons ran a competing service. He had a license to sail under the federal Coasting License Act of 1793. Ogden sued Gibbons for violating his monopoly. When the New York state courts found in Ogden's favor, Gibbons appealed to the United States Supreme Court.

**THE RULING** In a unanimous decision, the Court ruled that when state and federal laws on interstate commerce conflict, federal laws are superior.

## LEGAL *Sources*

### U.S. CONSTITUTION/LEGISLATION

**Article 1, Section 8 (1789)**
"The Congress shall have power to . . . regulate commerce with foreign nations, and among the several states, and with the Indian tribes."

**Coasting License Act (1793)**
All ships licensed under this act, "and no others, shall be deemed ships or vessels of the United States, entitled to the privileges of ships or vessels employed in the coasting trade or fisheries."

### RELATED CASES

**Fletcher v. Peck (1810)**
Citing the Supremacy Clause, the Court ruled that a state law was unconstitutional.

**McCulloch v. Maryland (1819)**
The Court established that states had no authority to tax federal agencies.

## The Legal Arguments

Chief Justice John Marshall wrote the Court's unanimous opinion, which found for Gibbons. Since the Constitution gave Congress the power to regulate commerce among the states, Marshall began, it would be useful to decide what the word *commerce* meant. In arguments before the Court, Ogden's lawyers had said that it simply referred to the buying and selling of goods. Marshall disagreed, suggesting that it also included the navigation necessary to move goods from one place to another. He wrote:

> The word used in the constitution comprehends . . . navigation within its meaning; and a power to regulate navigation is as expressly granted as if that term had been added to the word "commerce."

Marshall then pointed to the Supremacy Clause of the Constitution. This is Article 6, Section 2, which states, "This Constitution, and the laws of the United States . . . shall be the supreme law of the land."

The New York monopoly law denied Gibbons the right to sail in New York waters. The federal Coasting License Act, however, gave him the right to sail *all* U.S. waters. According to the Supremacy Clause, the Constitution and federal laws were the supreme law of the land. So, Marshall concluded, the Coasting License Act was "the supreme law of the land," and the New York monopoly was void.

Aaron Ogden obtained a monopoly on steamship operation between New York and New Jersey in 1815.

## Why Did It Matter Then?

At the time of the *Gibbons* case, navigation of the waters around New York was difficult. To encourage companies to provide water transportation, New York granted monopolies to the companies. Some states set up their own. Other states passed laws preventing New York steamboats from entering their waters. Obviously, such a situation was not good for trade among the states. By making it clear that the federal government regulated commerce among the states, the *Gibbons* decision brought order to interstate commerce. And this helped the national economy to grow.

Unlike other decisions of the Marshall Court that strengthened the federal government, *Gibbons* proved popular. Most Americans—even New Yorkers—were opposed to the New York steamboat monopoly. They saw any kind of monopoly as a limit to economic competition. As a result, the *Gibbons* decision was well received throughout the country. One newspaper reported the following incident:

> **Yesterday the Steamboat *United States*, [commanded by] Capt. Bunker, from New Haven, entered New York in triumph, with streamers flying and a large company of passengers [celebrating] the decision of the United States Supreme Court against the New York monopoly. She fired a salute which was loudly returned by [cheers] from the wharves.**

After the first voyage of Robert Fulton's *Clermont* in 1807, it soon became clear that operating steamships could be a profitable business.

## Why Does It Matter Now?

Marshall defined "commerce" very broadly in the *Gibbons* decision. Over the years, Congress has used Marshall's definition to expand its authority over interstate commerce. Today, Congress regulates practically every activity that affects or is connected to commerce.

In 1964, for example, Congress used the Commerce Clause to justify the passage of the Civil Rights Act. This law banned racial discrimination in hotels, restaurants, theaters, and other public places.

The Supreme Court rejected two challenges to the Civil Rights Act—in *Heart of Atlanta Motel, Inc.* v. *United States* (1964) and *Katzenbach* v. *McClung* (1964). In both cases, the Court noted that racial discrimination could harm interstate commerce.

---

### CONNECT TO HISTORY

1. **Drawing Conclusions** Many of Chief Justice John Marshall's opinions contributed to the growth of the nationalist spirit in the early 1800s. How do you think the *Gibbons* v. *Ogden* decision might have helped to build national unity?

   **S** See Skillbuilder Handbook, page R13.

### CONNECT TO TODAY

2. **Researching** Use library resources and the Internet to find recent Supreme Court cases that involved interstate commerce. Write a brief summary of one of these cases, noting whether it expanded or contracted Congress's power to regulate commerce.

   For more information on interstate commerce . . .

   **RESEARCH LINKS**
   CLASSZONE.COM

# Dred Scott v. Sandford (1857)

**THE ISSUE** The definition of citizenship

**ORIGINS OF THE CASE** Dred Scott was an enslaved African American who had lived for a while in Illinois and in the Wisconsin Territory, both of which banned slavery. Scott sued for his freedom, arguing that since he had lived in a free state and a free territory, he was a free man. In 1854, a federal court found against Scott, ruling that he was still a slave. Scott's lawyers appealed to the Supreme Court, which heard arguments in 1856 and delivered its decision the following year.

**THE RULING** The Court ruled that no African American could be a citizen and that Dred Scott was still a slave. The Court also ruled that the Missouri Compromise of 1820 was unconstitutional.

## The Legal Arguments

Chief Justice Roger Taney wrote the majority opinion for the Court. He began by addressing the issue of citizenship. He pointed out that since colonial times African Americans had been looked on as inferior and "had no rights which the white man was bound to respect." Taney added that where African Americans were mentioned in the Constitution, they were referred to as property—slaves. African Americans, whether enslaved or free, he continued:

> . . . are not included, and were not intended to be included, under the word 'citizens' in the Constitution, and can therefore claim none of the rights and privileges which that instrument provides for and secures to citizens of the United States.

Since Scott was not a citizen, Taney concluded, he had no right to use the courts to sue for his freedom.

Taney then went further, claiming Scott was still a slave because he had never been free. Congress had gone beyond its power when it passed the Missouri Compromise, he argued. The Constitution guaranteed the right to own property, and slaves were property. By banning slavery from the territories, Congress was, in effect, taking away private property without due process of the law. This action violated the Fifth Amendment. The Missouri Compromise was, Taney charged, "not warranted by the Constitution, and . . . therefore void." As a result, Scott remained a slave, regardless of where he lived.

Two justices disagreed with the majority on both grounds. They pointed to precedents—earlier legal rulings—that indicated that African Americans could, indeed, be citizens. They also argued that the Constitution gave Congress the power to establish rules and regulations for the territories.

## LEGAL Sources

### U.S. CONSTITUTION/LEGISLATION

**Article 4, Section 3 (1789)**
"No person held to service or labor in one state, . . . escaping into another, shall, in consequence of any law or regulation therein, be discharged from such service or labor. . . ."

**Fifth Amendment (1791)**
"No person shall be . . . deprived of life, liberty, or property, without due process of law."

**Missouri Enabling Act (1820)**
"[I]n all that territory . . . north of 36° 30' N latitude, . . . slavery . . . shall be . . . forever prohibited." Also known as the Missouri Compromise.

### RELATED CASE

**Ableman v. Booth (1858)**
The Court ruled that laws passed in Northern states that prohibited the return of fugitive slaves were unconstitutional.

## Why Did It Matter Then?

*Dred Scott* contributed to the growing dispute over slavery that led to the Civil War. White Southerners praised the ruling, seeing it as a spirited defense of their right to own slaves. Many Northerners, however, viewed it with alarm. They feared that if Congress could not ban slavery in the territories, slavery would spread. If this happened, slave states eventually would outnumber free states and would control Congress.

Stephen A. Douglas, a Northern Democrat, disagreed with the Court's finding. He favored leaving the issue of slavery to the voters in each territory. Most Southern Democrats, however, did not agree with him. As a result, the Democratic Party divided along sectional lines in the 1860 presidential election. Northern Democrats supported Douglas, while Southern Democrats backed a proslavery candidate. Because of this split, Abraham Lincoln of the anti-slavery Republican Party won the election. Soon after, many slave states seceded, and the Civil War began.

Northern abolitionists held meetings to show their support for Scott (shown here) and their opposition to the Supreme Court decision.

## Why Does It Matter Now?

The issues addressed by *Dred Scott* were resolved by the Thirteenth and Fourteenth amendments to the Constitution. The Thirteenth Amendment, which was ratified in 1865, abolished slavery in the United States. The Fourteenth Amendment, ratified three years later, made it very clear who was a citizen:

> All persons born or naturalized in the United States, and subject to the jurisdiction thereof, are citizens of the United States and of the state wherein they reside.

This amendment went on to guarantee all citizens "equal protection of the laws" and the right to due process. These amendments meant the rulings in *Dred Scott* no longer had the force of law.

Today, *Dred Scott* is not used as a precedent. Instead, it is pointed to as an example of how the Supreme Court can make mistakes. In fact, many legal scholars think it is the worst decision the Court has ever handed down.

## CONNECT TO HISTORY

1. **Forming and Supporting Opinions** The *Dred Scott* decision was just one in a long line of events that led to the Civil War. Write an editorial about the case in which you evaluate its importance in bringing about the war.

 See Skillbuilder Handbook, page R17.

## CONNECT TO TODAY

2. **Researching** Use library sources and the Internet to research a contemporary Court decision that affects civil rights. Use newspaper indices, periodical guides, and library catalogs, for example, to locate sources of this information. Create a public service brochure to report your findings.

For more information on citizenship . . .

 **RESEARCH LINKS** CLASSZONE.COM

# Plessy v. Ferguson (1896)

**THE ISSUE** Segregation

**ORIGINS OF THE CASE** By the 1890s, most Southern states had begun to pass laws enforcing segregation—the separation of the races—in public places. One Louisiana law called for "equal but separate accommodations for the white and colored races" on trains. On June 7, 1892, Homer Plessy, who was part African American, took a seat in a train car reserved for whites. When a conductor told him to move, Plessy refused. Plessy was convicted of breaking the "separate car" law. He appealed the case, saying that the law violated his rights under the Thirteenth and Fourteenth amendments.

**THE RULING** The Court ruled that "separate but equal" facilities for blacks and whites did not violate the Constitution.

## LEGAL Sources

### U.S. CONSTITUTION/LEGISLATION

**Thirteenth Amendment (1865)**
"Neither slavery nor involuntary servitude . . . shall exist within the United States, or any place subject to their jurisdiction."

**Fourteenth Amendment (1868)**
"No state shall make or enforce any law which shall abridge the privileges or immunities of citizens of the United States; nor shall any state deprive any person of life, liberty, or property, without due process of law; nor deny to any person within its jurisdiction the equal protection of the laws."

### RELATED CASE

**Cumming v. Board of Education of Richmond County (1899)**
The Court ruled that because education is a local issue, the federal government could not stop school districts from having separate facilities for black and white students.

## The Legal Arguments

The Court's opinion, written by Justice Henry Billings Brown, rejected Plessy's appeal. Brown first answered Plessy's claim that the separate car law created a relationship between whites and blacks similar to that which existed under slavery. The Thirteenth Amendment simply ended the ownership of one person by another, Brown wrote. Louisiana's law did not reestablish this system of ownership.

Brown then turned to Plessy's claim that the Fourteenth Amendment was designed to ensure the equality of the races before the law. Brown wrote that the amendment "could not have been intended to abolish distinctions based on color." A law that treated the races differently did not brand one race as inferior. If a law made people feel inferior, it was because they chose to see it that way. Summing up, Brown stated:

> A [law] which implies merely a legal distinction between the white and colored races . . . has no tendency to destroy the legal equality of the two races.

Justice John Marshall Harlan strongly disagreed with the majority view. In a bitter dissent, he wrote that the "thin disguise" of separate but equal facilities would fool no one, "nor atone for the wrong this day done."

In his dissent, Justice Harlan stated that "our constitution is color-blind, and neither knows nor tolerates classes among citizens."

## Why Did It Matter Then?

*Plessy* was one of several cases in the late 1800s involving the civil rights of African Americans. In these cases, the Court misread the Fourteenth Amendment and let stand state laws that denied African Americans their rights. *Plessy* has come to stand for all of these decisions because it said that "separate but equal" facilities for blacks and whites did not violate the Constitution.

Although the *Plessy* decision dealt only with public transportation, state governments across the South applied it to all areas of life. In time, "Jim Crow" laws forced African Americans to use separate restaurants, hotels, train cars, parks, schools, and hospitals. Signs reading "For Colored Only" and "Whites Only" ruled everyday life in the South for years to come.

## Why Does It Matter Now?

After *Plessy,* many African Americans and some whites looked for ways to fight segregation. Some of these people helped to found the National Association for the Advancement of Colored People (NAACP).

Throughout the first half of the 20th century, lawyers working for the NAACP chipped away at segregation laws. Their greatest victory came in 1954, in *Brown* v. *Board of Education of Topeka.* In this decision, the Supreme Court ruled that separate educational facilities were "inherently unequal" and, therefore, unconstitutional. Southern state and local governments had used the *Plessy* decision to build a system of legal segregation. In the same way, civil rights workers used the *Brown* ruling to dismantle it.

After the *Plessy* decision, signs designating separate facilities for whites and African Americans became a common sight throughout the South.

## CONNECT TO HISTORY

1. **Drawing Conclusions** Read the section of the Fourteenth Amendment reprinted in the "Legal Sources" section on page 748. Based on that passage, what do you think "equal protection of the laws" means? How does it apply to the *Plessy* case?

**S** See Skillbuilder Handbook, page R13.

## CONNECT TO TODAY

2. **Researching** Use library resources and the Internet to find information on Supreme Court cases that dealt with segregation. Present your findings in a three-column chart. Use "Case," "Brief Description of Issues Involved," and "Decision" as column headings.

For more information on segregation and the law . . .

RESEARCH LINKS
CLASSZONE.COM

# Schenck v. United States
# (1919)

**THE ISSUE** Freedom of Speech

**ORIGINS OF THE CASE** In August 1917, Charles Schenck, a Socialist Party official, distributed several thousand antiwar leaflets throughout the city of Philadelphia. The leaflets called the draft a crime and urged people to work for the repeal of the Selective Service Act. Schenck was found guilty of violating the Espionage Act of 1917 and sentenced to prison. He appealed his conviction, arguing that the language in the leaflets was protected by the First Amendment.

**THE RULING** The Court upheld the verdict against Schenck, noting that the leaflets presented "a clear and present danger" to the country during wartime.

## LEGAL *Sources*

### U.S. CONSTITUTION/LEGISLATION

**First Amendment (1791)**
"Congress shall make no law . . . abridging the freedom of speech, or of the press."

**The Espionage Act (1917)**
"[Anyone who] shall wilfully obstruct . . . the recruiting or enlistment service of the United States . . . shall be punished by . . . fine . . . or imprisonment . . . or both."

### RELATED CASES

**Debs v. United States (1919)**
Upheld the conviction of Socialist Party leader Eugene V. Debs for violating the Espionage Act.

**Frohwerk v. United States (1919)**
Confirmed the guilty verdict against a newspaper publisher for printing articles opposing U. S. involvement in World War I.

**Abrams v. United States (1919)**
Upheld convictions of five people under the Espionage Act. Holmes dissented, arguing that their action did not present "a clear and imminent danger."

## The Legal Arguments

Justice Oliver Wendell Holmes, Jr., wrote the Court's unanimous opinion. In ordinary times, Holmes noted, Schenck's claim of First Amendment rights might well be valid. "But the character of every act depends upon the circumstances in which it is done," Holmes added. Schenck distributed the leaflets during wartime, when "many things that might be said in time of peace . . . will not be endured." Holmes suggested that Schenck's "impassioned" appeal for people to oppose the draft was just like someone "falsely shouting fire in a theatre and causing a panic." The First Amendment certainly did not protect such behavior.

Holmes then went on to offer a guide for judging when speech is protected by the First Amendment:

> The question in every case is whether the words used are used in such circumstances and are of such a nature as to create a clear and present danger that they will bring about the . . . evils that Congress has a right to prevent.

Schenck's words, Holmes charged, did pose "a clear and present danger" to the United States war effort. Therefore, they did not merit protection under the First Amendment.

Justice Holmes's opinions in the Espionage Act cases set the standard for free speech.

## Why Did It Matter Then?

The Supreme Court decisions in *Schenck* and other Espionage Act cases considered the limits of free speech during wartime. In *Schenck,* Justice Holmes stated that speech that presented "a clear and present danger" to the country's well being was not protected. As he looked at other cases, however, Holmes began to refine this view.

In *Frohwerk* v. *United States* (1919), decided just a week after *Schenck,* the Court again upheld a conviction under the Espionage Act. However, Holmes noted that anti-government speech uttered during wartime is not always a crime. "We do not lose our right to condemn either measures or men because the country is at war," he wrote.

Holmes broadened this statement in his dissent to the majority opinion in *Abrams* v. *United States* (1919). The government's power to limit speech during wartime undoubtedly is greater, he noted, "because war opens dangers that do not exist at other times." However, the basic principles of free speech are the same in war as in peace:

> **It is only the present danger of immediate evil or an intent to bring it about that warrants Congress in setting a limit to the expression of opinion.**

All opinions, even ones we find hateful, should be heard, Holmes concluded.

During the Vietnam War, some Americans vigorously challenged government policies.

## Why Does It Matter Now?

The Supreme Court has been asked to decide on free speech issues dozens of times since *Schenck.* In making these decisions, the Court has attempted to heed Justice Holmes's words and strike a balance between protecting free speech and maintaining political and social order.

Over the years, the Court has applied this balance test to free speech questions in many settings, including schools. In *Tinker* v. *Des Moines Independent Community School District* (1969), the Court upheld students' right to protest in school. However, the Court added that in certain circumstances school officials might limit the exercise of such rights—if the students' actions disrupt the work of the school, for example.

In two later cases, *Bethel School District No. 403* v. *Fraser* (1986) and *Hazelwood School District* v. *Kuhlmeier* (1988), the Court felt that such circumstances existed. In *Bethel,* the Court upheld the suspension of a student who, during a school assembly, gave a speech that included inappropriate language. The Court ruled that the school could punish behavior that "interferes with the educational process." In *Hazelwood,* the Court ruled that school officials could censor the content of a student newspaper if it was "inconsistent with [the school's] educational mission."

---

## CONNECT TO HISTORY

1. **Making Inferences** The Supreme Court decided *Schenck* and other Espionage Act cases during the Red Scare. Do you think the timing of the cases influenced the Court's decisions? Why or why not?

 See Skillbuilder Handbook, page R12.

## CONNECT TO TODAY

2. **Researching** Working with a group of two or three other students, identify and research recent court cases involving free speech issues. Present your findings in a brief oral report to the class.

For more information on free speech . . .

RESEARCH LINKS
CLASSZONE.COM

# Brown v. Board of Education of Topeka (1954)

**THE ISSUE** School desegregation

**ORIGINS OF THE CASE** In September 1950, Oliver Brown tried to enroll his seven-year-old daughter, Linda, at the neighborhood grade school. The school principal rejected Brown's request because Linda was an African American. The school was for white students only. Linda ended up attending a school farther away from her home. Brown filed suit against the school board, demanding that Linda be allowed to go to the neighborhood school. The Supreme Court heard arguments in the *Brown* case in 1952 and 1953.

**THE RULING** A unanimous court ruled that segregation in education was unconstitutional.

## LEGAL *Sources*

### U.S. CONSTITUTION/LEGISLATION

**Fourteenth Amendment (1868)**
"No state shall . . . deprive any person of life, liberty, or property, without due process of law; nor deny to any person within its jurisdiction the equal protection of the laws."

### RELATED CASES

***Plessy* v. *Ferguson* (1896)**
Upheld Louisiana laws that segregated railroad passenger cars according to race. Established the doctrine of "separate but equal."

***Brown* v. *Board of Education of Topeka* (May, 1955)**
Ordered that desegregation take place "with all deliberate speed." Often called "*Brown II.*"

## The Legal Arguments

Chief Justice Earl Warren wrote the Court's decision. He began by reviewing the history of the Fourteenth Amendment. Its equal protection clause was the basis for the decision. The Court had ruled in *Plessy* v. *Ferguson* (1896) that "separate but equal" facilities for blacks and whites did not violate this amendment. However, Warren pointed out that *Plessy* involved transportation, not education. He then stressed the importance of education for society:

> It is doubtful that any child may reasonably be expected to succeed in life if he is denied the opportunity of an education.

Warren went on to suggest that segregation denied African-American children that opportunity. He concluded with *Brown's* most famous statement:

> . . . [I]n the field of public education the doctrine of "separate but equal" has no place. Separate educational facilities are inherently unequal.

The Court expected whites in the South, where segregation was dominant, to resist the ruling. Therefore, it delayed orders on how to put the decision into action for several months.

Thurgood Marshall was one of the team of lawyers that represented Oliver Brown. In 1967, Marshall became the first African American appointed as a Supreme Court justice.

## Why Did It Matter Then?

The Fourteenth Amendment had guaranteed African Americans equal rights as citizens. In the late 1800s, however, many Southern states passed "Jim Crow" laws, which enforced separation of the races in public places. In 1896, the Supreme Court upheld a "Jim Crow" law in *Plessy* v. *Ferguson.* In the Court's view, "separate but equal" rail cars did not violate the Fourteenth Amendment.

*Brown,* however, stated that segregated schools denied African Americans the "equal protection of the laws" guaranteed by the Fourteenth Amendment. Segregation, therefore, had no place in school systems.

As the Court expected, the decision met opposition. One Southern politician accused the Court of "a flagrant abuse of judicial power." Even after *Brown II,* many school districts, particularly in the South, dragged their feet on desegregation. Some 10 years later, segregation was still the rule in most Southern school districts. Even so, the impact of the *Brown* decision on American society was immense. It marked the beginning of the civil rights movement, which you read about in Chapter 29.

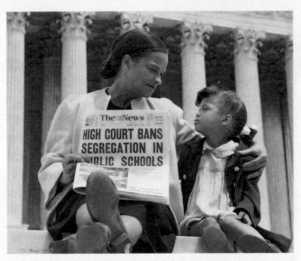

The *Brown* decision was a front-page story in newspapers across the United States.

## Why Does It Matter Now?

Throughout the 1960s and 1970s, the Supreme Court continued to review the issue of school segregation. In *Green* v. *New Kent County* (1968), the Court called for the end of the dual school system—one white and one black. This involved integrating not only students, but also teachers, support staff, and services.

In *Swann* v. *Charlotte-Mecklenburg Board of Education* (1971), the Court ruled that busing could be used to achieve school desegregation. Later, in *Milliken* v. *Bradley* (1974), the Court ruled that students might be bused between school districts to achieve this goal. However, this step could be taken only in very exceptional circumstances.

In recent years, the Court has moved away from enforcing desegregation. Still, the *Brown* decision brought about far-reaching changes. The statement that separate facilities are "inherently unequal" proved a powerful weapon against segregation in all areas of American life. Indeed, the Court's opinion in *Brown* provided the basis for most of the civil rights laws passed in the late 1950s and 1960s.

## CONNECT TO HISTORY

1. **Analyzing Points of View** Chief Justice Earl Warren wanted the *Brown* opinion to be unanimous. He even pressured Justice Stanley Reed, a southerner, not to file a dissenting opinion. Why do you think Warren insisted that all the justices agree to the *Brown* decision?

 See Skillbuilder Handbook, page R9.

## CONNECT TO TODAY

2. **Researching** Working with a group of two or three other students, conduct research to find out about efforts to desegregate another part of American society, such as the military, the workplace, or colleges. Report your findings to the class.

For more information on civil rights today . . .

**RESEARCH LINKS**
CLASSZONE.COM

# Reynolds v. Sims (1964)

**THE ISSUE** One Person, One Vote

**ORIGINS OF THE CASE** Most state constitutions require a redrawing of legislative districts every 10 years, based on the latest U.S. Census figures. By the 1960s, however, many states had not redrawn their districts for decades. For example, Alabama's last redrawing—in 1901—did not reflect the great population changes that had taken place. In 1962, a group of Alabama voters sued to have their legislative map redrawn. When a federal court found for the voters, the Alabama state legislature appealed to the Supreme Court.

**THE RULING** The Court firmly established the principle of "one person, one vote." It ruled that Alabama must redraw its legislative districts so that each district had about the same number of people.

## LEGAL Sources

### U.S. CONSTITUTION/LEGISLATION

**Fourteenth Amendment (1868)**
"No state shall . . . deprive any person of life, liberty, or property, without due process of law; nor deny to any person within its jurisdiction the equal protection of the laws."

**Alabama Constitution, Article 9, Section 198 (1901)**
"The members of the house of representatives shall be apportioned by the legislature among the several counties of the state, according to the number of inhabitants in them, respectively, as ascertained by the decennial census of the United States."

### RELATED CASES

**Baker v. Carr (1962)**
Ruled that federal courts could intervene in state legislative districting issues.

**Gray v. Sanders (1963)**
Ruled that when counting votes in primary elections, states should follow the principle of "one person, one vote."

## The Legal Arguments

The Court's ruling, written by Chief Justice Earl Warren, clearly stated the issue:

> The right to vote freely for the candidate of one's choice is of the essence of a democratic society, and any restrictions on that right strike at the heart of representative government.

Weakening the power of an individual's vote, Warren added, was as much a restriction as preventing that individual from voting.

"Legislators represent people, not trees or acres," Warren continued. Population, therefore, had to be the determining factor in redrawing legislative districts. Warren based his argument squarely on the Fourteenth Amendment:

Chief Justice Earl Warren considered *Reynolds* v. *Sims* one of the most important opinions he had written.

> We hold that as a basic constitutional standard, the Equal Protection Clause requires that seats in . . . a . . . state legislature must be apportioned on a population basis. . . . [T]he Equal Protection Clause requires that a State make an honest and good faith effort to construct districts . . . as nearly of equal population as is practicable.

John Marshall Harlan—the grandson of the justice who wrote the famous dissent to *Plessy* v. *Ferguson*—dissented. He claimed that the Constitution did not give the Court the power to interfere in how states decide on their legislative districts.

## Why Did It Matter Then?

*Reynolds* was one of several voting rights cases that the Court heard in the 1960s. In the first, *Baker* v. *Carr* (1962), the Court broke with past decisions and said that federal courts had the power to make sure that states drew legislative districts fairly. A year later, in *Gray* v. *Sanders* (1963), the Court applied the principle of "one person, one vote" for the first time. The Court observed that the vote of someone living in one part of a state should count as much as that of someone living in another part.

In *Reynolds,* the court extended the "one person, one vote" principle to the drawing of state legislative districts. In time, the *Reynolds* ruling forced most states to draw new district boundaries. As a result, there was a shift in political power in state legislatures. The number of state representatives from cities, which had larger populations, increased. In contrast, the number from rural areas, where fewer people lived, declined.

## Why Does It Matter Now?

During the 1990s, the Court faced a new redistricting issue. The Voting Rights Act of 1965 urged states to increase minority representation in the legislatures. To do so, many states created districts where minorities made up a voting majority. However, some white voters challenged these districts under the Fourteenth Amendment.

In several cases—*Bush* v. *Vera* (1996), for example—the Court ruled that such districts were unconstitutional. Since these districts were drawn *solely* based on race, the Court said, they violated the Fourteenth Amendment's equal protection clause. In *Lawyer* v. *Department of Justice* (1997), the Court upheld a Florida district drawn to include several African-American communities. The Court found that in this case, race was only one of several factors used to draw district boundary lines.

After the U.S. Census of 2000, the states began a new round of redistricting. As a result, the Supreme Court probably will revisit this issue over the next few years.

| Representation in the Alabama State Legislature, 1962 | | |
|---|---|---|
| COUNTY | POPULATION | NUMBER OF HOUSE REPRESENTATIVES |
| Bullock | 13,462 | 2 |
| Henry | 15,286 | 2 |
| Mobile | 314,301 | 3 |
| Jefferson | 634,864 | 7 |

Source: *U.S. Supreme Court,* Reynolds v. Sims, 377 U.S. 533 (1964)

In 1962, the rural counties of Bullock and Henry had less than one-thirtieth of the population of the urban counties of Mobile and Jefferson. Even so, they returned close to half as many state representatives as did the two urban counties.

## CONNECT TO HISTORY

1. **Finding Main Ideas** Use library or Internet resources to locate a copy of the majority opinion in *Reynolds* v. *Sims.* Make a chart listing the main idea and details for each part of the opinion. Make a similar chart for Harlan's dissenting opinion in this case.

 See Skillbuilder Handbook, page R5.

## CONNECT TO TODAY

2. **Researching** Conduct research to find news stories about a recent Supreme Court decision on the issue of redistricting. Write a summary of the background of the case, the ruling the Court made, and the legal reasoning behind that ruling.

For more information on the Supreme Court and redistricting . . .

RESEARCH LINKS
CLASSZONE.COM

# Regents of the University of California v. Bakke (1978)

**THE ISSUE** Affirmative action

**ORIGINS OF THE CASE** In 1970, the medical school of the University of California at Davis adopted an "affirmative action" admissions policy. The policy set a quota calling for 16 percent of each year's incoming students to be minority students. Allan Bakke, a white applicant, had better test scores and grades than most of the students accepted under the affirmative-action plan. However, he was not admitted. Bakke sued, arguing that he had been rejected because of his race. The California Supreme Court ordered the school to admit Bakke. The school appealed the case to the U.S. Supreme Court.

**THE RULING** The Court ruled that the school could use race as one of several factors in making admissions decisions but that setting racial quotas was unconstitutional.

## LEGAL *Sources*

### U.S. CONSTITUTION/LEGISLATION

**Fourteenth Amendment (1868)**
"No state shall . . . deprive any person of life, liberty, or property, without due process of law; nor deny to any person within its jurisdiction the equal protection of the laws."

**Civil Rights Act, Title VI (1964)**
"No person in the United States shall, on the ground of race, color, or national origin, be excluded from participation in . . . any program or activity receiving Federal financial assistance."

### RELATED CASE

**Fullilove v. Klutznick (1980)**
The Court upheld the Public Works Employment Act of 1977, which required that minority-owned businesses receive 10 percent of all federal funds for public works projects.

## The Legal Arguments

The Court upheld the California Supreme Court decision in a 5–4 vote. Four of the five majority justices maintained that holding a set number of admission slots for minority students violated the Civil Rights Act of 1964. The fifth justice, Justice Lewis Powell, noted that racial quotas violated the Fourteenth Amendment. Powell wrote:

> The guarantee of equal protection cannot mean one thing when applied to one individual and something else when applied to a person of another color. If both are not accorded the same protection, then it is not equal.

However, the Court did not reject affirmative action completely. By a different 5-4 majority, the Court ruled that race could be used as one of several factors in college admissions. Powell, who again provided the deciding vote, thought that race should be considered in order to promote a "diverse student body."

Allan Bakke graduated from the University of California at Davis with a medical degree in 1982.

## Why Did It Matter Then?

African Americans made many gains in civil rights during the 1950s and 1960s. President Lyndon Johnson, however, thought more needed to be done. He explained why:

> You do not take a person who for years has been hobbled by chains and . . . bring him up to the starting line of a race and then say, "you are free to compete with all the others" and still justly believe that you have been completely fair.

In 1965, Johnson urged companies to increase the hiring and promoting of minorities.

In time, many businesses, colleges, and other organizations set up affirmative-action programs. Not everyone was happy with this development, however. Some whites felt that affirmative action amounted to little more than "reverse discrimination." That is, they felt that they would be denied jobs or college places because of their race.

With the Bakke ruling, the Supreme Court took a compromise position on affirmative-action programs. They were acceptable, the Court said, as long as they did not use strict racial quotas.

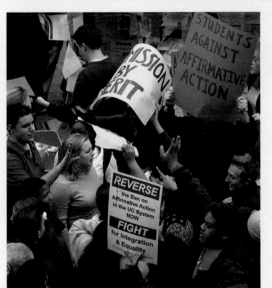

## Why Does It Matter Now?

Since *Bakke,* the Court has ruled on several affirmative-action cases. In *Metro Broadcasting* v. *Federal Communications Commission* (1990), for example, the Court upheld a policy that gave preference to minority broadcasters. However, in *Adarand Constructors, Inc.* v. *Peña* (1995), the Court struck down a similar affirmative-action program.

The standing of affirmative action in college admissions is somewhat clearer, however. Some states have abandoned the policy altogether. In California, for example, voters approved a 1996 referendum banning the state's universities from using affirmative action in admissions.

Washington voters passed a similar measure in 1998. These and other states are looking for new ways to help minority students attend college. One method—adopted by California, Florida, and Texas—guarantees admission to state universities for the top students from each high school graduating class.

The affirmative-action debate, at times, has been quite bitter. Here, supporters and opponents of affirmative action confront each other at a demonstration on the campus of the University of California at Berkeley.

---

## CONNECT TO HISTORY

1. **Making Inferences** In the *Bakke* case, the Supreme Court issued six separate opinions. Also, the voting on the two issues in the case was 5-4. From this information, what inferences can you draw on the Court's attitudes on affirmative action?

 See Skillbuilder Handbook, page R12.

## CONNECT TO TODAY

2. **Researching** The state university system of Michigan recently has faced court challenges to its affirmative-action program. Track the progress of these challenges and write a few paragraphs comparing the arguments and court findings in Michigan to those in the *Bakke* case.

For more information on affirmative action . . .

RESEARCH LINKS
CLASSZONE.COM

# Creating America

### A History of the United States
### Beginning through World War I

# Skillbuilder HANDBOOK

## Table of Contents

# 1.1 Summarizing

## Defining the Skill

When you **summarize,** you restate a paragraph, passage, or chapter in fewer words. You include only the main ideas and most important details. It is important to use your own words when summarizing.

## Applying the Skill

The passage below tells about Harriet Tubman, a prominent member of the Underground Railroad. She helped runaway slaves to freedom. Use the strategies listed below to help you summarize the passage.

### How to Summarize

**Strategy** ❶ Look for topic sentences stating the main idea. These are often at the beginning of a section or paragraph. Briefly restate each main idea—in your own words.

**Strategy** ❷ Include key facts and any numbers, dates, amounts, or percentages from the text.

**Strategy** ❸ After writing your summary, review it to see that you have included only the most important details.

---

**HARRIET TUBMAN**

❶ One of the most famous conductors on the Underground Railroad was Harriet Tubman. ❷ Born into slavery in Maryland, the 13-year-old Tubman once tried to save another slave from punishment. The angry overseer fractured Tubman's skull with a two-pound weight. She suffered fainting spells for the rest of her life but did not let that stop her from working for freedom. When she was 25, Tubman learned that her owner was about to sell her. Instead, ❷ she escaped.

After her escape, ❷ Harriet Tubman made 19 dangerous journeys to free enslaved persons. The tiny woman carried a pistol to frighten off slave hunters and medicine to quiet crying babies. Her enemies offered $40,000 for her capture, but ❷ no one caught her. "I never run my train off the track and I never lost a passenger," she proudly declared. Among the people she saved were her parents.

---

## Write a Summary

You can write your summary in a paragraph. The paragraph at right summarizes the passage you just read.

## Practicing the Skill

Turn to Chapter 6, Section 2, "Colonial Resistance Grows." Read "The Boston Tea Party" and write a paragraph summarizing the passage.

❸ *Harriet Tubman was one of the most famous conductors on the Underground Railroad. She had been a slave, but she escaped. She later made 19 dangerous journeys to free other slaves. She was never captured.*

# 1.2 Taking Notes

## Defining the Skill

When you **take notes,** you write down the important ideas and details of a paragraph, passage, or chapter. A chart or an outline can help you organize your notes to use in the future.

## Applying the Skill

The following passage describes President Washington's cabinet. Use the strategies listed below to help you take notes on the passage.

### How to Take and Organize Notes

**Strategy ❶** Look at the title to find the main topic of the passage.

**Strategy ❷** Identify the main ideas and details of the passage. Then summarize the main idea and details in your notes.

**Strategy ❸** Identify key terms and define them. The term *cabinet* is shown in boldface type and underlined; both techniques signal that it is a key term.

**Strategy ❹** In your notes, use abbreviations to save time and space. You can abbreviate words such as *department (dept.), secretary (sec.), United States (U.S.),* and *president (pres.)* to save time and space.

---

**❶ WASHINGTON'S CABINET**

**❷** The Constitution gave Congress the task of creating departments to help the president lead the nation. The **❷** president had the power to appoint the heads of these departments, which became his **❸** <u>cabinet</u>.

Congress created three departments. Washington chose talented people to run them. **❷** For secretary of war, he picked Henry Knox, a trusted general during the Revolution. **❷** For secretary of state, Washington chose Thomas Jefferson. He had been serving as ambassador to France. The State Department oversaw U.S. foreign relations. For secretary of the treasury, Washington turned to the brilliant **❷** Alexander Hamilton.

---

## Make a Chart

Making a chart can help you take notes on a passage. The chart below contains notes from the passage you just read.

| **❷** *Item* | *Notes* |
|---|---|
| *1.* **❸** *cabinet* | *heads of* **❹** *depts;* **❹** *pres. appoints heads* |
| *a. War Dept.* | *Henry Knox;* **❹** *sec. of war; former Revolutionary War general* |
| *b. State Dept.* | *Thomas Jefferson; sec. of state; oversees relations between* **❹** *U.S. and other countries* |
| *c. Treasury Dept.* | *Alexander Hamilton; sec. of the treasury* |

## Practicing the Skill

Turn to Chapter 3, Section 3, "Founding the Middle and Southern Colonies." Read "Maryland and the Carolinas" and use a chart to take notes on the passage.

# 1.3 Sequencing Events

## Defining the Skill

**Sequence** is the order in which events follow one another. By being able to follow the sequence of events through history, you can get an accurate sense of the relationship among events.

## Applying the Skill

The following passage describes the sequence of events involved in Britain's plan to capture the Hudson River Valley during the American Revolution. Use the strategies listed below to help you follow the sequence of events.

### How to Find the Sequence of Events

**Strategy ❶** Look for specific dates provided in the text. If several months within a year are included, the year is usually not repeated.

**Strategy ❷** Look for clues about time that allow you to order events according to sequence. Words such as *day, week, month,* or *year* may help to sequence the events.

> **BRITAIN'S STRATEGY**
>
> Burgoyne captured Fort Ticonderoga in ❶ July 1777. From there, it was 25 miles to the Hudson River, which ran to Albany. ❷ Burgoyne took three weeks to reach the Hudson. On ❶ August 3, Burgoyne received a message from Howe. He would not be coming north, Howe wrote, because he had decided to invade Pennsylvania to try to capture Philadelphia and General Washington. "Success be ever with you," Howe's message said. But General Burgoyne needed Howe's soldiers, not his good wishes. Howe did invade Pennsylvania. In ❶ September 1777, he defeated —but did not capture—Washington at the Battle of Brandywine.

## Make a Time Line

Making a time line can help you sequence events. The time line below shows the sequence of events in the passage you just read.

July 1777: Burgoyne captures Fort Ticonderoga.

August 3, 1777: Howe writes that he will not join Burgoyne.

Three weeks after the capture of Fort Ticonderoga: Burgoyne reaches the Hudson.

September 1777: Howe defeats Washington at Brandywine.

## Practicing the Skill

Turn to Chapter 2, Section 1, "Spain Claims an Empire." Read "Europeans Explore Foreign Lands" and make a time line showing the sequence of events in that passage.

# 1.4 Finding Main Ideas

## Defining the Skill

The **main idea** is a statement that summarizes the main point of a speech, an article, a section of a book, or a paragraph. Main ideas can be stated or unstated. The main idea of a paragraph is often stated in the first or last sentence. If it is the first sentence, it is followed by sentences that support that main idea. If it is the last sentence, the details build up to the main idea. To find an unstated idea, you must use the details of the paragraph as clues.

## Applying the Skill

The following paragraph describes the role of women in the American Revolution. Use the strategies listed below to help you identify the main idea.

### How to Find the Main Idea

**Strategy ❶** Identify what you think may be the stated main idea. Check the first and last sentences of the paragraph to see if either could be the stated main idea.

**Strategy ❷** Identify details that support that idea. Some details explain the main idea. Others give examples of what is stated in the main idea.

> **WOMEN IN THE REVOLUTION**
>
> ❶ Many women tried to help the army. Martha Washington and other wives followed their husbands to army camps. ❷ The wives cooked, did laundry, and nursed sick or wounded soldiers. ❷ A few women even helped to fight. ❷ Mary Hays earned the nickname "Molly Pitcher" by carrying water to tired soldiers during a battle. ❷ Deborah Sampson dressed as a man, enlisted, and fought in several engagements.

## Make a Chart

Making a chart can help you identify the main idea and details in a passage or paragraph. The chart below identifies the main idea and details in the paragraph you just read.

*Main Idea:* Women helped the army during the Revolution.

*Detail:* They cooked and did laundry.
*Detail:* They nursed the wounded and sick soldiers.
*Detail:* They helped to fight.
*Detail:* One woman, Molly Pitcher, carried water to soldiers during battles.

## Practicing the Skill

Turn to Chapter 5, Section 1, "Early American Culture." Read "Women and the Economy" and create a chart that identifies the main idea and the supporting details.

# 1.5 Categorizing

## Defining the Skill

To **categorize** is to sort people, objects, ideas, or other information into groups, called categories. Historians categorize information to help them identify and understand patterns in historical events.

## Applying the Skill

The following passage contains information about the reasons people went west during the mid-1800s. Use the strategies listed below to help you categorize information.

### How to Categorize

**Strategy** ① First, decide what kind of information needs to be categorized. Decide what the passage is about and how that information can be sorted into categories.

For example, find the different motives people had for moving west.

**Strategy** ② Then find out what the categories will be. To find why many different groups of people moved west, look for clue words such as *some, other,* and *another.*

**Strategy** ③ Once you have chosen the categories, sort information into them. Of the people who went west, which ones had which motives?

---

**THE LURE OF THE WEST**

① People had many different motives for going west. ② One motive was to make money. ② *Some* people called speculators bought huge areas of land and made great profits by selling it to thousands of settlers. ② *Other* settlers included farmers who dreamed of owning their own farms in the West because land was difficult to acquire in the East. ② *Another* group to move west was merchants. They hoped to earn money by selling items that farmers needed. Finally, ② *some* people went west for religious reasons. These people included ② missionaries, who wanted to convert the Native Americans to Christianity, and Mormons, who wanted a place where they could practice their faith without interference.

---

## Make a Chart

Making a chart can help you categorize information. You should have as many columns as you have categories. The chart below shows how the information from the passage you just read can be categorized.

③

| Motives | Money | Land | Religion |
|---------|-------|------|----------|
| Groups | • speculators<br>• merchants | • farmers | • missionaries<br>• Mormons |

## Practicing the Skill

Turn to Chapter 14, Section 3, "Reforming American Society." Read "Improving Education" and make a chart in which you categorize the changes happening in elementary, high school, and college education.

# 1.6 Making Public Speeches

## Defining the Skill

A speech is a talk given in public to an audience. Some speeches are given to persuade the audience to think or act in a certain way, or to support a cause. You can learn how to **make public speeches** effectively by analyzing great speeches in history.

## Applying the Skill

The following is an excerpt from the "I Have a Dream" speech delivered by Martin Luther King, Jr., in 1963 in Washington, D.C. Use the strategies listed below to help you analyze King's speech and prepare a speech of your own.

### How to Analyze and Prepare a Speech

**Strategy ❶** Choose one central idea or theme and organize your speech to support it. King organized his speech around his dream of equality.

**Strategy ❷** Use words or images that will win over your audience. King referred to the Declaration of Independence when he used the words "all men are created equal."

**Strategy ❸** Repeat words or images to drive home your main point—as if it is the "hook" of a pop song. King repeats the phrase "I have a dream."

---

### I HAVE A DREAM

❶ I have a dream that one day this nation will rise up and live out the true meaning of its creed—we hold these truths to be ❷ self-evident that all men are created equal.

❸ I have a dream that one day on the red hills of Georgia the sons of former slaves and the sons of former slave owners will be able to sit down together at the table of brotherhood.

❸ I have a dream that my four little children will one day live in a nation where they will not be judged by the color of their skin but by the content of their character.

❸ I have a dream today!

---

## Make an Outline

Making an outline like the one to the right will help you make an effective public speech.

## Practicing the Skill

Turn to Chapter 12, Section 2, "Jackson's Policy Toward Native Americans." Read the section and choose a topic for a speech. First, make an outline like the one to the right to organize your ideas. Then write your speech. Next, practice giving your speech. Make it a three-minute speech.

**Title:** I Have a Dream

I. **Introduce Theme:** I have a dream
  A. This nation will live up to its creed
  B. Quote from the Declaration of Independence: that all men are created equal

II. **Repeat theme:** I have a dream
  A. Sons of former slaves and slave owners will sit together in brotherhood
  B. My four children will be judged by their character, not by their skin color

III. **Conclude:** I have a dream

# 1.7 Writing for Social Studies

## Defining the Skill

**Writing for social studies** requires you to describe an idea, situation, or event. Often, social studies writing takes a stand on a particular issue or tries to make a specific point. To successfully describe an event or make a point, your writing needs to be clear, concise, and factually accurate.

## Applying the Skill

The following passage describes Stephen A. Douglas. Notice how the strategies below helped the writer explain Douglas's historical importance.

### How to Write for Social Studies

**Strategy ❶** Focus on your topic. Be sure that you clearly state the main idea of your piece so that your readers know what you intend to say.

**Strategy ❷** Collect and organize your facts. Collect accurate information about your topic to support the main idea you are trying to make. Use your information to build a logical case to prove your point.

**Strategy ❸** To express your ideas clearly, use standard grammar, spelling, sentence structure, and punctuation when writing for social studies. Proofread your work to make sure it is well organized and grammatically correct.

> ### STEPHEN A. DOUGLAS, 1813–1861
>
> ❶ Stephen A. Douglas was one of the most powerful members of Congress in the 1850s. In fact, ❷ he was called the "Little Giant" because he commanded great respect even though he was only five feet four inches tall. The most important issue that Douglas faced in his career was slavery in the territories. ❷ He played a key role in the passage of the Compromise of 1850 as well as the Kansas–Nebraska Act, which addressed this issue. In 1858, his famous debates with Abraham Lincoln also focused on slavery in the territories. ❷ When Douglas ran for president in 1860, his position on slavery was critical to his defeat.

## Practicing the Skill

Turn to Chapter 15, Section 1, "Growing Tensions Between North and South." Read the section and use the strategies above to write your answer to Question 4 on page 461.

# 2.1 Analyzing Points of View

## Defining the Skill

**Analyzing points of view** means looking closely at a person's arguments to understand the reasons behind that person's beliefs. The goal of analyzing a point of view is to understand a historical figure's thoughts, opinions, and biases about a topic.

## Applying the Skill

The following passage describes the Panic of 1837 and two politicians' points of view about it. Use the strategies listed below to help you analyze their points of view.

### How to Analyze Points of View

**Strategy 1** Look for statements that show you a person's view on an issue. For example, Van Buren said he believed the economy would improve if he took no action. Clay thought the government should do something to help the people.

**Strategy 2** Use information about people to validate them as sources and understand why they might disagree. What do you know about Clay and Van Buren that might explain their own biases and disagreements with each other?

**Strategy 3** Write a summary that explains why different people took different positions on the issue.

---

### THE PANIC OF 1837

The Panic of 1837 caused severe hardship. People had little money, so manufacturers had few customers for their goods. Almost 90 percent of factories in the East closed. Jobless workers could not afford food or rent. Many people went hungry.

**1** Whig senator Henry Clay wanted the government to do something to help the people. **1** President Van Buren, a Democrat, disagreed. He believed that the economy would improve if left alone. He argued that "the less government interferes with private pursuits the better for the general prosperity." Many Americans blamed Van Buren for the Panic, though he had taken office only weeks before it started. The continuing depression made it difficult for him to win reelection in 1840.

---

## Make a Diagram

Using a diagram can help you analyze points of view. The diagram below analyzes the views of Clay and Van Buren in the passage you just read.

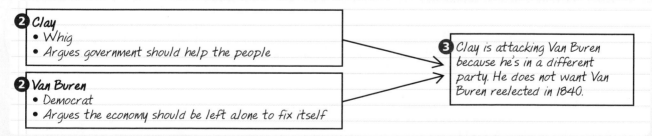

**2** Clay
- Whig
- Argues government should help the people

**2** Van Buren
- Democrat
- Argues the economy should be left alone to fix itself

**3** Clay is attacking Van Buren because he's in a different party. He does not want Van Buren reelected in 1840.

## Practicing the Skill

Turn to the Interactive Primary Sources on pages 238 and 239. Read the selections by James Madison and George Mason. Use their language, information from other sources, and information about each man to validate them as sources. Then make a chart to analyze their different points of view on the Constitution.

## 2.2 Comparing and Contrasting

### Defining the Skill

**Comparing** means looking at the similarities and differences between two or more things. **Contrasting** means examining only the differences between them. Historians compare and contrast events, personalities, behaviors, beliefs, and situations in order to understand them.

### Applying the Skill

The following paragraph describes the American and British troops during the Revolutionary War. Use the strategies listed below to help you compare and contrast these two armies.

### How to Compare and Contrast

**Strategy ① Look for two** aspects of the subject that may be compared and contrasted. This passage compares the British and American troops to show why the Americans won the war.

**Strategy ② To contrast, look** for clue words that show how two things differ. Clue words include *by contrast, however, except,* and *yet.*

**Strategy ③ To find similarities,** look for clue words indicating that two things are alike. Clue words include *both, like, as,* and *similarly.*

---

**WHY THE AMERICANS WON**

① By their persistence, the Americans defeated the British even though they faced many obstacles. The Americans lacked training and experience. They were often short of supplies and weapons. ② *By contrast*, the British forces ranked among the best trained in the world. They were experienced and well-supplied professional soldiers. ② *Yet*, the Americans also had advantages that enabled them to win. These advantages over the British were better leadership, foreign aid, a knowledge of the land, and motivation. Although ③ *both* the British and the Americans were fighting for their lives, ② the Americans were also fighting for their property and their dream of liberty.

---

### Make a Venn Diagram

Making a Venn diagram will help you identify similarities and differences between two things. In the overlapping area, list characteristics shared by both subjects. Then, in the separate ovals, list the characteristics of each subject not shared by the other. This Venn diagram compares and contrasts the British and American soldiers.

**American Soldiers:**
- lacked experience and training
- short of supplies and weapons
- had better leadership
- received foreign aid
- had knowledge of the land
- fought for liberty and property

**Both:** fought for their lives

**British Soldiers:**
- best trained in the world
- experienced
- well-supplied

### Practicing the Skill

Turn to Chapter 5, Section 1, "Early American Culture." Read "Young People at Work" and make a Venn diagram showing the similarities and differences between the roles of boys and girls in colonial America.

# 2.3 Analyzing Causes; Recognizing Effects

## Defining the Skill

A **cause** is an action in history that makes something happen. An **effect** is the historical event that is the result of the cause. A single event may have several causes. It is also possible for one cause to result in several effects. Historians identify cause-and-effect relationships to help them understand why historical events took place.

## Applying the Skill

The following paragraph describes events that caused changes in Puritan New England. Use the strategies listed below to help you identify the cause-and-effect relationships.

## How to Analyze Causes and Recognize Effects

**Strategy** ❶ Ask why an action took place. Ask yourself a question about the title and topic sentence, such as, "What caused changes in Puritan society?"

**Strategy** ❷ Look for effects. Ask yourself, "What happened?" (the effect). Then ask, "Why did it happen?" (the cause). For example, What caused the decline of Puritan religion in New England?

**Strategy** ❸ Look for clue words that signal causes, such as *cause* and *led to*.

**Strategy** ❹ One way to practice recognizing effects is to make predictions about the consequences that will result from particular actions. Then, as you read, look to see if your predictions were accurate.

---

❶ **CHANGES IN PURITAN SOCIETY**

❶ The early 1700s saw many changes in New England society.

❷ One of the most important changes was the gradual decline of the Puritan religion in New England. There were a number of reasons for that decline.

❸ One *cause* of this decline was the increasing competition from other religious groups. Baptists and Anglicans established churches in Massachusetts and Connecticut, where Puritans had once been the most powerful group. ❸ Political changes also *led to* a weakening of the Puritan community. In 1691, a new royal charter for Massachusetts granted the vote based on property ownership instead of church membership.

---

## Make a Diagram

Using a diagram can help you understand causes and effects. The diagram below shows two causes and an effect for the passage you just read.

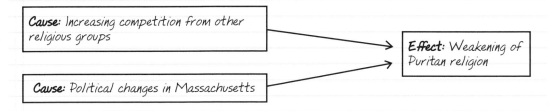

**Cause:** Increasing competition from other religious groups

**Cause:** Political changes in Massachusetts

**Effect:** Weakening of Puritan religion

## Practicing the Skill

Turn to Chapter 2, Section 1, "Spain Claims an Empire." Read "Reasons for Spanish Victories" and make a diagram about the causes and effects of the Spanish conquest of the Americas.

# 2.4 Making Inferences

## Defining the Skill

Inferences are ideas that the author has not directly stated. **Making inferences** involves reading between the lines to interpret the information you read. You can make inferences by studying what is stated and using your common sense and previous knowledge.

## Applying the Skill

The passage below describes the strengths and weaknesses of the North and the South as the Civil War began. Use the strategies listed below to help you make inferences from the passage.

### How to Make Inferences

**Strategy ① Read to find statements of facts and ideas. Knowing the facts will give you a good basis for making inferences.

**Strategy ② Use your knowledge, logic, and common sense to make inferences that are based on facts. Ask yourself, "What does the author want me to understand?" For example, from the facts about population, you can make the inference that the North would have a larger army than the South. See other inferences in the chart below.

> ### ADVANTAGES OF THE NORTH AND THE SOUTH
>
> The North had more people and resources than the South. ① The North had about 22 million people. ① The South had roughly 9 million, of whom about 3.5 million were slaves. In addition, ① the North had more than 80 percent of the nation's factories and almost all of the shipyards and naval power. The South had some advantages, too. ① It had able generals, such as Robert E. Lee. ① It also had the advantage of fighting a defensive war. Soldiers defending their homes have more will to fight than invaders do.

### Make a Chart

Making a chart will help you organize information and make logical inferences. The chart below organizes information from the passage you just read.

| ① Stated Facts and Ideas | ② Inferences |
|---|---|
| The North had about 22 million people. The Confederacy had about 9 million. | The North would have a larger army than the South. |
| The North had more factories, naval power, and shipyards. | The North could provide more weapons, ammunition, and ships for the war. |
| The Confederacy had excellent generals. | The Confederacy had better generals, which would help it overcome other disadvantages. |
| The Confederacy was fighting a defensive war. | Confederate soldiers would fight harder because they were defending their homes and families. |

## Practicing the Skill

Turn to Chapter 11, Section 1, "Early Industry and Inventions." Read "Free Enterprise and Factories" and use a chart like the one above to make inferences about early industry.

# 2.5 Drawing Conclusions

## Defining the Skill

**Drawing conclusions** means analyzing what you have read and forming an opinion about its meaning. To draw conclusions, look at the facts and then use your own common sense and experience to decide what the facts mean.

## Applying the Skill

The following passage presents information about the Intolerable Acts and the colonists' reactions to them. Use the strategies listed below to help you draw conclusions about those acts.

## How to Draw Conclusions

**Strategy ❶** Read carefully to identify and understand all the facts, or statements, that can be proven true.

**Strategy ❷** List the facts in a diagram and review them. Use your own experiences and common sense to understand how the facts relate to each other.

**Strategy ❸** After reviewing the facts, write down the conclusion you have drawn about them.

---

### THE INTOLERABLE ACTS

❶ In 1774, Parliament passed a series of laws to punish the Massachusetts colony and serve as a warning to other colonies.

❶ These laws were so harsh that colonists called them the **Intolerable Acts.** One of the acts closed the port of Boston. Others banned committees of correspondence and allowed Britain to house troops wherever necessary.

In 1773, Sam Adams had written, "I wish we could arouse the continent." ❶ The Intolerable Acts answered his wish. Other colonies immediately offered Massachusetts their support.

---

## Make a Diagram

Making a diagram can help you draw conclusions. The diagram below shows how to organize facts and inferences to draw a conclusion about the passage you just read.

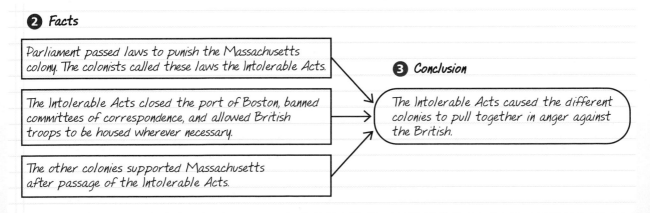

❷ Facts

| Parliament passed laws to punish the Massachusetts colony. The colonists called these laws the Intolerable Acts. |

❸ Conclusion

The Intolerable Acts caused the different colonies to pull together in anger against the British.

| The Intolerable Acts closed the port of Boston, banned committees of correspondence, and allowed British troops to be housed wherever necessary. |

| The other colonies supported Massachusetts after passage of the Intolerable Acts. |

## Practicing the Skill

Turn to Chapter 3, Section 2, "New England Colonies." Read "The Salem Witchcraft Trials" and use the diagram above as a model to draw conclusions about the trials.

# 2.6 Making Decisions

## Defining the Skill

**Making decisions** involves choosing between two or more options, or courses of action. In most cases, decisions have consequences, or results. Sometimes decisions may lead to new problems. By understanding how historical figures made decisions, you can learn how to improve your decision-making skills.

## Applying the Skill

The following passage describes Lincoln's decisions regarding federal forts after the Southern states seceded. Use the strategies listed below to help you analyze his decisions.

### How to Make Decisions

**Strategy 1** Identify a decision that needs to be made. Think about what factors make the decision difficult.

**Strategy 2** Identify possible consequences of the decision. Remember that there can be more than one consequence to a decision.

**Strategy 3** Identify the decision that was made.

**Strategy 4** Identify actual consequences that resulted from the decision.

> ## FIRST SHOTS AT FORT SUMTER
>
> **1** Lincoln had to decide what to do about the forts in the South that remained under federal control. A Union garrison still held **Fort Sumter**, but it was running out of supplies. **2** If Lincoln supplied the garrison, he risked war. **2** If he withdrew the garrison, he would be giving in to the rebels. **3** Lincoln informed South Carolina that he was sending supply ships to Fort Sumter. **4** Confederate leaders decided to prevent the federal government from holding on to the fort by attacking before the supply ships arrived. No one was killed, but **4** the South's attack on Fort Sumter signaled the beginning of the Civil War.

## Make a Flow Chart

A flow chart can help you identify the process of making a decision. The flow chart below shows the decision-making process in the passage you just read.

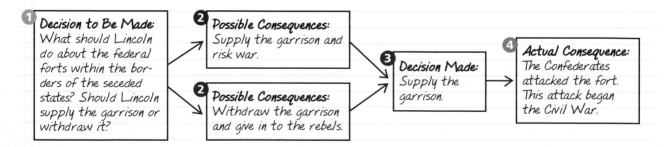

**1 Decision to Be Made:** What should Lincoln do about the federal forts within the borders of the seceded states? Should Lincoln supply the garrison or withdraw it?

**2 Possible Consequences:** Supply the garrison and risk war.

**2 Possible Consequences:** Withdraw the garrison and give in to the rebels.

**3 Decision Made:** Supply the garrison.

**4 Actual Consequence:** The Confederates attacked the fort. This attack began the Civil War.

## Practicing the Skill

Turn to Chapter 6, Section 1, "Tighter British Control." Read "The Colonies Protest the Stamp Act" and make a flow chart to identify a decision and its consequences described in that section.

# 2.7 Recognizing Propaganda

## Defining the Skill

**Propaganda** is communication that aims to influence people's opinions, emotions, or actions. Propaganda is not always factual. Rather, it uses one-sided language or striking symbols to sway people's emotions. Modern advertising often uses propaganda. By thinking critically, you will avoid being swayed by propaganda.

## Applying the Skill

The following political cartoon shows Andrew Jackson dressed as a king. Use the strategies listed below to help you understand how it works as propaganda.

### How to Recognize Propaganda

**Strategy ❶** Identify the aim, or purpose, of the cartoon. Point out the subject and explain the point of view.

**Strategy ❷** Identify those images on the cartoon that viewers might respond to emotionally and identify the emotions.

**Strategy ❸** Think critically about the cartoon. What facts has the cartoon ignored?

## Make a Chart

Making a chart will help you think critically about a piece of propaganda. The chart below summarizes the information from the anti-Jackson cartoon.

| ❶ | Identify Purpose | The cartoon portrays Jackson negatively by showing him as a king. |
|---|---|---|
| ❷ | Identify Emotions | The cartoonist knows that Americans like democracy. So he portrays Jackson as a king because kings are not usually supporters of democracy. He also shows Jackson standing on a torn U.S. Constitution—another thing that Americans love. |
| ❸ | Think Critically | The cartoon shows Jackson vetoing laws. But it ignores the fact that those actions were not against the Constitution. The president has the power to veto legislation. In this case, Jackson was exercising the power of the presidency, not acting like a king. |

## Practicing the Skill

Turn to Chapter 6, Section 2, "Colonial Resistance Grows," and look at the engraving *The Bloody Massacre* on page 165. Use a chart like the one above to think critically about the engraving as an example of propaganda.

# 2.8 Identifying Facts and Opinions

## Defining the Skill

**Facts** are events, dates, statistics, or statements that can be proved to be true. **Opinions** are the judgments, beliefs, and feelings of a writer or speaker. By identifying facts and opinions, you will be able to think critically when a person is trying to influence your own opinion.

## Applying the Skill

The following passage tells about the Virginia Plan for legislative representation offered at the Constitutional Convention of 1787. Use the strategies listed below to help you distinguish facts from opinions.

### How to Recognize Facts and Opinions

**Strategy ❶** Look for specific information that can be proved or checked for accuracy.

**Strategy ❷** Look for assertions, claims, and judgments that express opinions. In this case, one speaker's opinion is expressed in a direct quote.

**Strategy ❸** Think about whether statements can be checked for accuracy. Then, identify the facts and opinions in a chart.

> ### ANTIFEDERALIST VIEWS
>
> ❶ Antifederalists published their views about the Constitution in newspapers and pamphlets. ❶ They thought the Constitution took too much power away from the states and did not protect the rights of the people. They charged that the Constitution would destroy American liberties. As one Antifederalist wrote, ❷ "It is truly astonishing that a set of men among ourselves should have had the [nerve] to attempt the destruction of our liberties."

## Make a Chart

The chart below analyzes the facts and opinions from the passage above.

| Statement | ❸ Can It Be Proved? | ❸ Fact or Opinion |
|---|---|---|
| Antifederalists published their views in newspapers and pamphlets. | Yes. Check newspapers and other historical documents. | Fact |
| They thought the Constitution took too much power away from the states. | Yes. Check newspapers and other historical documents. | Fact |
| It is astonishing that some Americans would try to destroy American liberties. | No. This cannot be proved. It is what one speaker believes. | Opinion |

## Practicing the Skill

Turn to Chapter 11, Section 3, and read the section entitled "The Missouri Compromise." Make a chart in which you analyze key statements to determine whether they are facts or opinions.

# 2.9 Forming and Supporting Opinions

## Defining the Skill

When you **form opinions,** you interpret and judge the importance of events and people in history. You should always **support your opinions** with facts, examples, and quotes.

## Applying the Skill

The following passage describes events that followed the gold rush. Use the strategies listed below to form and support your opinions about the events.

### How to Form and Support Opinions

**Strategy ❶** Look for important information about the events. Information can include facts, quotations, and examples.

**Strategy ❷** Form an opinion about the event by asking yourself questions about the information. For example, How important was the event? What were its effects?

**Strategy ❸** Support your opinions with facts, quotations, and examples. If the facts do not support the opinion, then rewrite your opinion so it is supported by the facts.

---

### THE IMPACT OF THE GOLD RUSH

By 1852, the gold rush was over. ❶ While it lasted, about 250,000 people flooded into California. ❶ This huge migration caused economic growth that changed California. ❶ The port city San Francisco grew to become a center of banking, manufacturing, shipping, and trade. ❶ However, the gold rush ruined many *Californios. Californios* are the Hispanic people of California. The newcomers did not respect *Californios,* their customs, or their legal rights. ❶ In many cases, Americans seized their property.

Native Americans suffered even more. ❶ Thousands died from diseases brought by the newcomers. ❶ Miners hunted down and killed thousands more. ❶ By 1870, California's Native American population had fallen from 150,000 to only about 30,000.

---

## Make a Chart

Making a chart can help you organize your opinions and supporting facts. The following chart summarizes one possible opinion about the impact of the gold rush.

| ❷ Opinion | The effects of the gold rush were more negative than positive. |
|---|---|
| ❸ Facts | Californios were not respected, and their land was stolen. |
| | Many Native Americans died from diseases, and others were killed by miners. Their population dropped from 150,000 to about 30,000. |

## Practicing the Skill

Turn to Chapter 11, Section 3, "Nationalism and Sectionalism." Read "The Missouri Compromise" and form your own opinion about the compromise and its impact. Make a chart like the one above to summarize your opinion and the supporting facts and examples.

# 2.10 Identifying and Solving Problems

## Defining the Skill

**Identifying problems** means finding and understanding the difficulties faced by a particular group of people during a certain time. **Solving problems** means understanding how people tried to remedy those problems. By studying how people solved problems in the past, you can learn ways to solve problems today.

## Applying the Skill

The following paragraph describes problems that the Constitutional Convention faced on the issues of taxation, representation, and slavery. Use the strategies listed below to help you see how the Founders tried to solve these problems.

### How to Identify Problems and Solutions

**Strategy ①** Look for the difficulties, or problems, people faced.

**Strategy ②** Consider how the problem affected people with different points of view. For example, the main problem described here was how to count the population of each state.

**Strategy ③** Look for solutions people tried to deal with each problem. Think about whether the solution was a good one for people with differing points of view.

> **SLAVERY AND THE CONSTITUTION**
>
> Because the House of Representatives would have members according to the population of each state, ① the delegates had to decide who would be counted in the population of each state. The Southern states had many more slaves than the Northern states had. ② Southerners wanted the slaves to be counted as part of the general population for representation but not for taxation. ② Northerners argued that slaves were not citizens and should not be counted for representation, but that slaves should be counted for taxation. ③ The delegates decided that three-fifths of the slave population would be counted in the population to determine both representation and taxes.

## Make a Chart

Making a chart will help you identify and organize information about problems and solutions. The chart below shows problems and solutions included in the passage you just read.

| ① Problem | ② Differing Points of View | ③ Solution |
|---|---|---|
| Northerners and Southerners couldn't agree on how to count population because of slavery in the South. | Southerners wanted slaves counted for representation but not for taxation. Northerners wanted slaves counted for taxation but not for representation. | Delegates decided that three-fifths of the slave population should be counted. |

## Practicing the Skill

Turn to Chapter 8, Section 2, "Creating the Constitution." Read "The Delegates Assemble" and "The Virginia Plan." Then make a chart that summarizes the problems faced by the delegates at the Constitutional Convention and the solutions they agreed on.

# 2.11 Evaluating

## Defining the Skill

To **evaluate** is to make a judgment about something. Historians evaluate the actions of people in history. One way to do this is to examine both the positives and negatives of a historical action, then decide which is stronger—the positive or the negative.

## Applying the Skill

The following passage describes Susan B. Anthony's fight for women's rights. Use the strategies listed below to evaluate how successful she was.

## How to Evaluate

**Strategy** ① Before you evaluate a person's actions, first determine what that person was trying to do. In this case, think about what Anthony wanted to accomplish.

**Strategy** ② Look for statements that show the positive, or successful, results of her actions. For example, Did she achieve her goals?

**Strategy** ③ Also look for statements that show the negative, or unsuccessful, results of her actions. Did she fail to achieve something she tried to do?

**Strategy** ④ Write an overall evaluation of the person's actions.

### SUSAN B. ANTHONY

① Susan B. Anthony was a skilled organizer who fought for women's rights. ② She successfully built the women's movement into a national organization. Anthony believed that a woman must have money of her own. To this end, she supported laws that would give married women rights to control their own property and wages. ② Mississippi passed the first such law in 1839. New York passed a property law in 1848 and a wages law in 1860. ③ Anthony also wanted to win the vote for women but failed to convince lawmakers to pass this reform in her lifetime. This reform did go through in 1920, 14 years after her death.

## Make a Diagram for Evaluating

Using a diagram can help you evaluate. List the positives and negatives of the historical person's actions and decisions. Then make an overall judgment. The diagram below shows how the information from the passage you just read can be diagrammed.

② **Positive Results:**
- women's movement became a national organization
- Mississippi and New York passed property and wage laws

③ **Negative Results:**
- failed to win vote for women in her lifetime

④ **Evaluation:**
She was a successful reformer. Even the one reform she failed to achieve in her life did pass shortly after her death.

## Practicing the Skill

Turn to Chapter 2, Section 3, "The Spanish and Native Americans." Read "The Columbian Exchange" and make a diagram in which you evaluate whether the Columbian Exchange had mainly a positive or negative impact on the world.

# 2.12 Making Generalizations

## Defining the Skill

To **make generalizations** means to make broad judgments based on information. When you make generalizations, you should gather information from several sources.

## Applying the Skill

The following three passages contain different views on George Washington. Use the strategies listed below to make a generalization about these views.

### How to Make Generalizations

**Strategy ①** Look for information that the sources have in common. These three sources all discuss George Washington's ability as a military leader.

**Strategy ②** Form a generalization that describes Washington in a way that all three sources would agree with. State your generalization in a sentence.

---

### WASHINGTON'S LEADERSHIP

① Washington learned from his mistakes. After early defeats, he developed the strategy of dragging out the war to wear down the British. ① Despite difficulties, he never gave up.

—*Creating America*

① [Washington] was no military genius. . . . But he was a great war leader. Creating an army out of unpromising material, he kept it in being against great odds.

—*The Limits of Liberty*

① [Washington] certainly deserves some merit as a general, that he . . . can keep General Howe dancing from one town to another for two years together, with such an army as he has.

—*The Journal of Nicholas Cresswell, July 13, 1777*

---

## Make a Chart

Using a chart can help you make generalizations. The chart below shows how the information you just read can be used to generalize about people's views of Washington.

① Washington kept the army together against great odds.

① Washington kept the enemy guessing by moving his army quickly.

② Generalization: Although Washington made mistakes, he was a good military leader.

① Washington learned from his mistakes and never gave up.

## Practicing the Skill

Turn to Chapter 16, Section 1, "War Erupts." Read "Choosing Sides." Also read the excerpt from *Across Five Aprils* on pages 486–487. Then use a chart like the one above to make a generalization about how the outbreak of the Civil War affected Americans.

# 3.1 Using Primary and Secondary Sources

## Defining the Skill

**Primary sources** are materials written or made by people who lived during historical events and witnessed them. Primary sources can be letters, journal entries, speeches, autobiographies, or artwork. Other kinds of primary sources are government documents, census surveys, and financial records. **Secondary sources** are materials written by people who did not participate in an event. History books are secondary sources.

## Applying the Skill

The following passage contains both a primary source and a secondary source. Use the strategies listed below to help you read them.

### How to Read Primary and Secondary Sources

**Strategy ❶** Distinguish secondary sources from primary sources. The first paragraph is a secondary source. The Declaration of Independence is a primary source. The secondary source explains something about the primary source.

**Strategy ❷** Analyze the primary source and consider why the author produced it. Consider what the document was supposed to achieve and who would read it.

**Strategy ❸** Identify the author of the primary source and note when and where it was written.

> ❶ The core idea of the Declaration is based on the philosophy of John Locke. This idea is that people have unalienable rights, or rights that government cannot take away. Jefferson stated this belief in what was to become the Declaration's best-known passage.
>
> ❷ We hold these truths to be self-evident, that all men are created equal, that they are endowed by their Creator with certain unalienable Rights, that among these are Life, Liberty and the pursuit of Happiness.
>
> ❸ —Thomas Jefferson, *The Declaration of Independence*, 1776

## Make a Chart

Making a chart will help you summarize information from primary sources and secondary sources. The chart below summarizes the information from the passage you just read.

| Author | Thomas Jefferson |
|---|---|
| Document | The Declaration of Independence |
| Notes on Primary Source | The Declaration says that "all men are created equal." It also says that people have "unalienable rights." These rights include the right to life and the right to liberty, as well as a right to pursue happiness. |
| Notes on Secondary Source | Jefferson based his ideas on those of John Locke. Locke had written about rights that governments could not take away from the people. |

## Practicing the Skill

Turn to Chapter 6, Section 3, "The Road to Lexington and Concord." Read "Between War and Peace" and make a chart like the one above to summarize the information in the primary source and the secondary source.

# 3.2 Interpreting Graphs

## Defining the Skill

**Graphs** use pictures and symbols, instead of words, to show information. Graphs are created by taking information and presenting it visually. The graph on this page takes numerical information on immigration and presents it as a bar graph. There are many different kinds of graphs. Bar graphs, line graphs, and pie graphs are the most common. Bar graphs compare numbers or sets of numbers. The length of each bar shows a quantity. It is easy to see how different categories compare on a bar graph.

## Applying the Skill

The bar graph below shows numbers of immigrants coming to the United States between 1821 and 1860. Use the strategies listed below to help you interpret the graph.

### How to Interpret a Graph

**Strategy ①** Read the title to identify the main idea of the graph. Ask yourself what kinds of information the graph shows. For example, does it show chronological information, geographic patterns and distributions, or something else?

**Strategy ②** Read the vertical axis (the one that goes up and down) on the left side of the graph. This one shows the number of immigrants in thousands. Each bar represents the number of immigrants during a particular decade.

**Strategy ③** Read the horizontal axis (the one that runs across the bottom of the graph). This one shows the four decades from 1821 to 1860.

**Strategy ④** Summarize the information shown in each part of the graph. Use the title to help you focus on what information the graph is presenting.

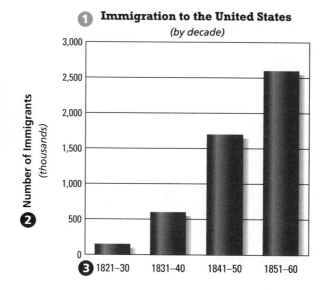

① **Immigration to the United States**
(by decade)

② Number of Immigrants (thousands)

③ 1821–30    1831–40    1841–50    1851–60

## Write a Summary

Writing a summary will help you understand the information in the graph. The paragraph to the right summarizes the information from the bar graph.

## Practicing the Skill

Turn to Chapter 2, Section 4, "Beginnings of Slavery in the Americas." Look at the graph entitled "Slaves Imported to the Americas, 1493–1810" and write a paragraph in which you summarize what you learned from it.

④ *Immigration to the United States increased between 1821 and 1860. Between 1821 and 1830, fewer than 200,000 immigrants arrived. In the next decade, more than 500,000 immigrants came. During the 1840s, more than 1.5 million immigrants arrived, and that number increased to more than 2.5 million in the 1850s.*

# 3.3 Interpreting Charts

## Defining the Skill

**Charts**, like graphs, present information in a visual form. Charts are created by organizing, summarizing, and simplifying information and presenting it in a format that makes it easy to understand. Tables and diagrams are examples of commonly used charts.

## Applying the Skill

The chart below shows the number of slaves who were imported to the Americas between 1601 and 1810. Use the strategies listed below to help you interpret the information in the chart.

### How to Interpret a Chart

**Strategy ❶** Read the title. It will tell you what the chart is about. Ask yourself what kinds of information the chart shows. For example, does it show chronological information, geographic patterns and distributions, or something else?

**Strategy ❷** Read the labels to see how the information in the chart is organized. In this chart, it is organized by region and years.

**Strategy ❸** Study the data in the chart to understand the facts that the chart intends to show.

**Strategy ❹** Summarize the information shown in each part of the chart. Use the title to help you focus on what information the chart is presenting.

**1601–1810**

❶ **Slaves Imported to the Americas** (*in thousands*)

| ❷ REGION/COUNTRY | 1601–1700 | 1701–1810 |
|---|---|---|
| ❸ British N. America | * | 348 |
| British Caribbean | 263.7 | 1,401.3 |
| French Caribbean | 155.8 | 1,348.4 |
| Spanish America | 292.5 | 578.6 |
| Dutch Caribbean | 40 | 460 |
| Danish Caribbean | 4 | 24 |
| Brazil (Portugal) | 560 | 1,891.4 |

*= less than 1,000

Source: Philip D. Curtin, *The Atlantic Slave Trade*

### Write a Summary

Writing a summary can help you understand the information given in a chart. The paragraph to the right summarizes the information in the chart "Slaves Imported to the Americas, 1601–1810."

### Practicing the Skill

Turn to Chapter 27, Section 5, and look at the chart entitled "World War II Military Casualties, 1939–1945." Study the chart and ask yourself what geographic patterns and distributions are shown in it. Then write a paragraph in which you summarize what you learned from the chart.

❹ The chart shows how many slaves were imported to the Americas between 1601 and 1810. It divides the Americas into seven regions. It also divides the time period into two parts: 1601–1700 and 1701–1810. The number of slaves imported increased greatly from the 1600s to the 1700s. More slaves were imported to Brazil than to any other region.

# 3.4 Interpreting Time Lines

## Defining the Skill

A **time line** is a visual list of events and dates shown in the order in which they occurred. Time lines can be horizontal or vertical. On horizontal time lines, the earliest date is on the left. On vertical time lines, the earliest date is often at the top.

## Applying the Skill

The time line below lists dates and events during the presidencies of John Adams, Andrew Jackson, and Martin Van Buren. Use the strategies listed below to help you interpret the information.

## How to Read a Time Line

**Strategy ❶** Read the dates at the beginning and end of the time line. These will show the period of history that is covered. The time line below is a dual time line. It includes items related to two topics. The labels show that the information covers U.S. events and world events.

**Strategy ❷** Read the dates and events in sequential order, beginning with the earliest one. Pay particular attention to how the entries relate to each other. Think about which events caused later events.

**Strategy ❸** Summarize the focus, or main idea, of the time line. Try to write a main idea sentence that describes the time line.

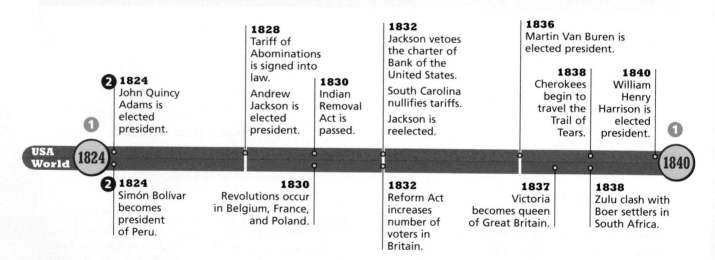

## Write a Summary

Writing a summary can help you understand information shown on a time line. The summary to the right states the main idea of the time line and tells how the events are related.

## Practicing the Skill

Turn to Chapter 15, page 455, and write a summary of the information shown on the time line.

❸ The time line covers the period between 1824, when John Quincy Adams was elected president, and 1840, when William Henry Harrison was elected president. During that period of time, Andrew Jackson and Martin Van Buren also served as president. The time line shows that the important issues in the United States were tariffs, banking, and relations with Native Americans.

# 3.5 Reading a Map

## Defining the Skill

**Maps** are representations of features on the earth's surface. Some maps show political features, such as national borders. Other maps show physical features, such as mountains and bodies of water. By learning to use map elements and math skills, you can better understand how to read maps.

## Applying the Skill

The following map shows the Battle of Yorktown during the Revolution. Use the strategies listed below to help you identify the elements common to most maps.

### How to Read a Map

**Strategy ❶** Read the title. This identifies the main idea of the map.

**Strategy ❷** Look for the grid of lines that form a pattern of squares over the map. These numbered lines are the lines of latitude (horizontal) and longitude (vertical). They indicate the location of the area on the earth.

**Strategy ❸** Read the map key. It is usually in a box. This will give you the information you need to interpret the symbols or colors on the map.

**Strategy ❹** Use the scale and the pointer, or compass rose, to determine distance and direction.

**❶ Battle of Yorktown, 1781**

## Make a Chart

A chart can help you organize information given on maps. The chart below summarizes information about the map you just studied.

| Title | Battle of Yorktown, 1781 |
|---|---|
| Location | between latitude 40° N and 35° N, just east of longitude 80° W |
| Map Key Information | blue = American and allied forces, red = British forces |
| Scale | 7/16 in. = 100 miles, 9/16 in. = 200 km |
| Summary | British commanders Graves and Hood sailed south from New York. They were defeated by De Grasse at the Battle of the Capes. British commander Cornwallis marched north from Wilmington, North Carolina, to Virginia, where he was defeated by American forces. |

## Practicing the Skill

Turn to Chapter 1, Section 5, "Early European Explorers." Read the map entitled "Exploration Leads to New Sea Routes" and make a chart to identify information on the map.

# 3.6 Reading a Special-Purpose Map

## Defining the Skill

**Special-purpose maps** help people focus on a particular aspect of a region, such as economic development in the South. These kinds of maps often use symbols to indicate information.

## Applying the Skill

The following special-purpose map indicates the products of the Southern colonies. Use the strategies listed below to help you identify the information shown on the map.

### How to Read a Special-Purpose Map

**Strategy ① Read the title.** It tells you what the map is intended to show.

**Strategy ② Read the legend.** This tells you what each symbol stands for. This legend shows the crops that were grown in various Southern colonies.

**Strategy ③ Look for the places** on the map where the symbol appears. These tell you the places where each crop was grown.

**① The Southern Colonies, 1750**

**②** Corn
Indigo
Naval stores
Pigs
Rice
Tobacco

## Make a Chart

A chart can help you understand special-purpose maps. The chart below shows information about the special-purpose map you just studied.

|  | Corn | Indigo | Naval stores | Pigs | Rice | Tobacco |
|---|---|---|---|---|---|---|
| Maryland |  |  |  |  |  | x |
| Virginia | x |  |  | x |  | x |
| North Carolina | x |  | x | x | x | x |
| South Carolina | x | x | x | x | x |  |
| Georgia |  | x |  | x | x |  |

## Practicing the Skill

Turn to Chapter 4, Section 1, "New England: Commerce and Religion." Look at the special-purpose map entitled "The New England Colonies" and make a chart that shows information about products from New England.

# 3.7 Creating a Map

## Defining the Skill

**Creating a map** involves representing geographical information. When you draw a map, it is easiest to use an existing map as a guide. On the map you draw, you can show geographical information. You can also show other kinds of information, such as data on climates, population trends, resources, or routes. Often, this data comes from a graph or a chart.

## Applying the Skill

Below is a map that a student created to show information about the number of slaves in 1750. Read the strategies listed below to see how the map was created.

### How to Create a Map

**Strategy** ❶ Select a title that identifies the geographical area and the map's purpose. Include a date in your title.

**Strategy** ❷ Draw the lines of latitude and longitude using short dashes.

**Strategy** ❸ Create a key that shows the colors.

**Strategy** ❹ Draw the colors on the map to show information.

**Strategy** ❺ Draw a compass rose and scale.

❶ Slave Population of the Southern Colonies, 1750

❸
- less than 300,000
- 300,000–400,000
- 400,000–450,000
- Over 450,000

❺ 0 — 100 Miles / 0 — 200 Kilometers

## Practicing the Skill

Make your own map. Turn to page 104 in Chapter 3 and study the graph entitled "The 13 Colonies." Use the strategies described above to create a map that shows the 13 colonies and the dates that they were founded. You can use the map on page 102 of that chapter as a guide.

# 3.8 Interpreting Political Cartoons

## Defining the Skill

**Political cartoons** are cartoons that use humor to make a serious point. Political cartoons often express a point of view on an issue better than words do. Understanding signs and symbols will help you to interpret political cartoons.

## Applying the Skill

The cartoon below shows Abraham Lincoln and the other candidates running for the presidency in 1860. Use the strategies listed below to help you understand the cartoon.

### How to Interpret a Political Cartoon

**Strategy ❶** Identify the subject by reading the title of the cartoon and looking at the cartoon as a whole.

**Strategy ❷** Identify important symbols and details. The cartoonist uses the image of a running race to discuss a political campaign. The White House is the finish line.

**Strategy ❸** Interpret the message. Why is Lincoln drawn so much taller than the other candidates? How does that make him the fittest candidate?

## Make a Chart

Making a chart will help you summarize information from a political cartoon. The chart below summarizes the information from the cartoon above.

| Subject | "A Political Race" (The Election of 1860) |
|---|---|
| Symbols and Details | Running is a symbol for a political campaign. Lincoln is the tallest and fastest candidate. |
| Message | ❸ Lincoln is pulling ahead of the other candidates in the campaign for the presidency. |

## Practicing the Skill

Turn to Chapter 18, Section 3, "End of Reconstruction." Look at the political cartoon on page 547. It shows a cartoonist's view of corruption in President Grant's administration. Use a chart like the one above and the strategies outlined to interpret the cartoon.

# 3.9 Creating a Model

## Defining the Skill

When you **create a model,** you use information and ideas to show an event or a situation in a visual way. A model might be a poster or a diagram that explains how something happened. Or, it might be a three-dimensional model, such as a diorama, that depicts an important scene or situation.

## Applying the Skill

The following sketch shows the early stages of a model of three ways that people could have traveled from the eastern United States to California during the gold rush. Use the strategies listed below to help you create your own model.

### How to Create a Model

**Strategy ❶** Gather the information you need to understand the situation or event. In this case, you need to be able to show the three routes and their dangers.

**Strategy ❷** Visualize and sketch an idea for your model. Once you have created a picture in your mind, make an actual sketch to plan how it might look.

**Strategy ❸** Think of symbols you may want to use. Since the model should give information in a visual way, think about ways you can use color, pictures, or other visuals to tell the story.

**Strategy ❹** Gather the supplies you will need and create the model. For example, you will need a globe and art supplies, such as yarn, for this model.

**The California Gold Rush**
Dangerous Routes West

**Wagon:**
Dangers from hardships of the trail, mountains, rivers

**Boat/overland:**
Dangers from tropical sickness

**Boat:**
Dangers from sickness, storms, spoiled food

## Practicing the Skill

Read the History Workshop called "Pack Your Trunk" on pages 450–451. Follow the step-by-step directions to create a model of a trunk that shows what immigrants might have decided to bring with them when they came to America.

# 4.1 Using an Electronic Card Catalog

## Defining the Skill

An **electronic card catalog** is a library's computerized search program that will help you find information about the books and other materials in the library. You can search the catalog by entering a book title, an author's name, or a subject of interest to you. The electronic card catalog will give you information about the materials in the library. This information is called bibliographic information. You can use an electronic card catalog to create a bibliography (a list of books) on any topic you are interested in.

## Applying the Skill

The screen shown below is from an electronic search for information about Thomas Jefferson. Use the strategies listed below to help you use the information on the screen.

### How to Use an Electronic Card Catalog

**Strategy ❶** Begin searching by choosing either subject, title, or author, depending on the topic of your search. For this search, the user chose "Subject" and typed in the words "Jefferson, Thomas."

**Strategy ❷** Once you have selected a book from the results of your search, identify the author, title, city, publisher, and date of publication.

**Strategy ❸** Look for any special features in the book. This book is illustrated, and it includes bibliographical references and an index.

**Strategy ❹** Locate the call number for the book. The call number indicates the section in the library where you will find the book. You can also find out if the book is available in the library you are using. If not, it may be in another library in the network.

```
Search Request:
❶ Subject          Title          Author
   ─────────────────────────────────────────
   Find  Options  Locations  Backup  Startover  Help

❷ Miller, Douglas T. Thomas Jefferson and the
   creation of America. New York: Facts on File,
   1997.
        ❷ AUTHOR:  Miller, Douglas T.
           TITLE:  Thomas Jefferson and the
                   creation of America/Douglas T.
                   Miller.
   ❷ PUBLISHED:    New York: Facts on File, ©1997.
      ❸ PAGING:    vi, 122p. : ill ; 24 cm.
         SERIES:   Makers of America.
       ❸ NOTES:    Includes bibliographical
                   references (p. 117-118) and index.
   ❹ CALL NUMBER:  1. 973.46 N61T 1997—Book Available—
```

## Practicing the Skill

Turn to Chapter 10, "The Jefferson Era," and find a topic that interests you, such as the Federalists, the Louisiana Purchase, the Lewis and Clark expedition, or the War of 1812. Use the SUBJECT search on an electronic card catalog to find information about your topic. Make a bibliography of books about the subject. Be sure to include the author, title, city, publisher, and date of publication for all the books included.

# 4.2 Creating a Database

## Defining the Skill

A **database** is a collection of data, or information, that is organized so that you can find and retrieve information on a specific topic quickly and easily. Once a computerized database is set up, you can search it to find specific information without going through the entire database. The database will provide a list of all information in the database related to your topic. Learning how to use a database will help you learn how to create one.

## Applying the Skill

The chart below is a database for the significant battles of the Civil War. Use the strategies listed below to help you understand and use the database.

### How to Create a Database

**Strategy 1** Identify the topic of the database. The keywords, or most important words, in this title are *Civil War* and *Battles.* These words were used to begin the research for this database.

**Strategy 2** Ask yourself what kind of data you need to include. For example, what geographic patterns and distributions will be shown? Your choice of data will provide the column headings for your database. The key words *Battle, Date, Location,* and *Significance* were chosen to focus the research.

**Strategy 3** Identify the entries included under each heading.

**Strategy 4** Use the database to help you find information quickly. For example, in this database you could search for "Union victories" to find a list of significant battles won by the North.

**① LOCATION OF SIGNIFICANT CIVIL WAR BATTLES**

| **② BATTLE** | **DATE** | **② LOCATION** | **SIGNIFICANCE** |
|---|---|---|---|
| **③** Fort Sumter | April 12, 1861 | Charleston, SC | Beginning of the Civil War |
| First Battle of Bull Run (Manassas) | July 21, 1861 | Virginia | Confederate victory |
| Shiloh | April 6–7, 1862 | Tennessee (near Shiloh Church) | **④** Union victory |
| Antietam | September 17, 1862 | Sharpsburg, MD | No clear victory; considered bloodiest battle of war |
| Gettysburg | July 1–3, 1863 | Gettysburg, PA | Retreat of Confederacy |
| Vicksburg | Three-month siege ending July 3, 1863 | Vicksburg, MS | Union gained control of Mississippi River |
| Chattanooga | November 23–25, 1863 | Chattanooga, TN | **④** Union victory |
| Atlanta | September 2, 1864 | Atlanta, GA | **④** Union victory; helped convince Confederacy of defeat |

## Practicing the Skill

Create a database for U.S. presidents through the Civil War that shows each president's home state, political party, and years served as president. Use the information in "Presidents of the United States" on pages R36–R38 to provide the data. Use a format like the one above for your database.

# 4.3 Using the Internet

## Defining the Skill

The Internet is a computer network that connects to universities, libraries, news organizations, government agencies, businesses, and private individuals throughout the world. Each location on the Internet has a home page with its own address, or URL (universal resource locator). With a computer connected to the Internet, you can reach the home pages of many organizations and services. The international collection of home pages, known as the World Wide Web, is a good source of up-to-date information about current events as well as research on subjects in history.

## Applying the Skill

The Web page below shows the links for Chapter 6 of *Creating America.* Use the strategies listed below to help you understand how to use the Web page.

### How to Use the Internet

**Strategy ① Go directly to** a Web page. For example, type http://www.mcdougallittell.com in the box at the top of the screen and press ENTER (or RETURN). The Web page will appear on your screen. Then click on ClassZone and find the link to *Creating America.*

**Strategy ② Explore the** *Creating America* links. Click on any one of the links to find out more about a specific subject. These links take you to other pages at this Web site. Some pages include links to related information that can be found at other places on the Internet.

**Strategy ③ When using the** Internet for research, you should confirm the information you find. Web sites set up by universities, government agencies, and reputable news sources are more reliable than other sources. You can often find information about the creator of a site by looking for copyright information.

## Practicing the Skill

Turn to Chapter 14, Section 2, "American Literature and Art." Read the section and make a list of topics you would like to research. If you have Internet access, go to the McDougal Littell home page at http://www.mcdougallittell.com and click on ClassZone. There you will find links that provide more information about the topics in the section.

# 4.4 Creating a Multimedia Presentation

## Defining the Skill

Movies, CD-ROMs, television, and computer software are different kinds of media. To **create a multimedia presentation,** you need to collect information in different media and organize them into one presentation.

## Applying the Skill

The scene below shows students using computers to create a multimedia presentation. Use the strategies listed below to help you create your own multimedia presentation.

### How to Create a Multimedia Presentation

**Strategy ❶** Identify the topic of your presentation and decide which media are best for an effective presentation. For example, you may want to use slides or posters to show visual images of your topic. Or, you may want to use CDs or audiotapes to provide music or spoken words.

**Strategy ❷** Research the topic in a variety of sources. Images, text, props, and background music should reflect the historical period of the event you choose.

**Strategy ❸** Write the script for the oral portion of the presentation. You could use a narrator and characters' voices to tell the story. Primary sources are an excellent source for script material. Make sure the recording is clear so that the audience will be able to understand the oral part of the presentation.

**Strategy ❹** Videotape the presentation. Videotaping the presentation will preserve it for future viewing and allow you to show it to different groups of people.

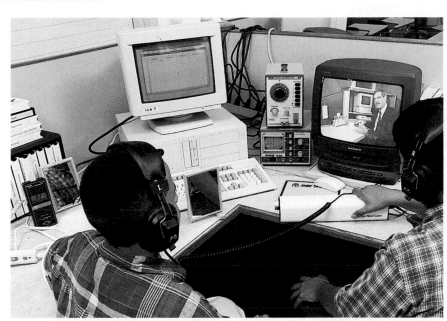

## Practicing the Skill

Turn to Chapter 24, "World War I." Choose a topic from the chapter and use the strategies listed above to create a multimedia presentation about it.

**Alabama**
4,486,508 people
52,218 sq. mi.
Rank in area: 30
Entered Union in 1819

**Alaska**
643,786 people
616,240 sq. mi.
Rank in area: 1
Entered Union in 1959

**Arizona**
5,456,453 people
113,998 sq. mi.
Rank in area: 6
Entered Union in 1912

**Arkansas**
2,710,079 people
53,178 sq. mi.
Rank in area: 28
Entered Union in 1836

**California**
35,116,033 people
158,854 sq. mi.
Rank in area: 3
Entered Union in 1850

**Colorado**
4,506,542 people
104,093 sq. mi.
Rank in area: 8
Entered Union in 1876

**Connecticut**
3,460,503 people
5,543 sq. mi.
Rank in area: 48
Entered Union in 1788

**Delaware**
807,385 people
2,396 sq. mi.
Rank in area: 49
Entered Union in 1787

**District of Columbia**
570,898 people
68 sq. mi.

**Florida**
16,713,149 people
59,909 sq. mi.
Rank in area: 23
Entered Union in 1845

**Georgia**
8,560,310 people
58,970 sq. mi.
Rank in area: 24
Entered Union in 1788

**Hawaii**
1,244,898 people
6,641 sq. mi.
Rank in area: 47
Entered Union in 1959

**Idaho**
1,341,131 people
83,570 sq. mi.
Rank in area: 14
Entered Union in 1890

**Illinois**
12,600,620 people
57,914 sq. mi.
Rank in area: 25
Entered Union in 1818

**Indiana**
6,159,068 people
36,418 sq. mi.
Rank in area: 38
Entered Union in 1816

**Iowa**
2,936,760 people
56,271 sq. mi.
Rank in area: 26
Entered Union in 1846

**Kansas**
2,715,884 people
82,276 sq. mi.
Rank in area: 15
Entered Union in 1861

**Kentucky**
4,092,891 people
40,409 sq. mi.
Rank in area: 37
Entered Union in 1792

**Louisiana**
4,482,646 people
49,650 sq. mi.
Rank in area: 31
Entered Union in 1812

**Maine**
1,294,464 people
33,738 sq. mi.
Rank in area: 39
Entered Union in 1820

**Maryland**
5,458,137 people
12,297 sq. mi.
Rank in area: 42
Entered Union in 1788

**Massachusetts**
6,427,801 people
9,240 sq. mi.
Rank in area: 45
Entered Union in 1788

**Michigan**
10,050,446 people
96,716 sq. mi.
Rank in area: 11
Entered Union in 1837

**Minnesota**
5,019,720 people
86,938 sq. mi.
Rank in area: 12
Entered Union in 1858

**Mississippi**
2,871,782 people
48,282 sq. mi.
Rank in area: 32
Entered Union in 1817

**Missouri**
5,672,579 people
69,704 sq. mi.
Rank in area: 21
Entered Union in 1821

**Montana**
909,453 people
147,042 sq. mi.
Rank in area: 4
Entered Union in 1889

Sources: U.S. Bureau of the Census, July 1 2002 population estimates.
*World Almanac and Book of Facts,* 2003
*Statistical Abstract of the United States,* 2002

**Nebraska**
1,729,180 people
77,353 sq. mi.
Rank in area: 16
Entered Union in 1867

**Ohio**
11,421,267 people
44,825 sq. mi.
Rank in area: 34
Entered Union in 1803

**Texas**
21,779,893 people
267,256 sq. mi.
Rank in area: 2
Entered Union in 1845

**Nevada**
2,173,491 people
110,560 sq. mi.
Rank in area: 7
Entered Union in 1864

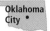
**Oklahoma**
3,493,714 people
69,898 sq. mi.
Rank in area: 20
Entered Union in 1907

**Utah**
2,316,256 people
84,898 sq. mi.
Rank in area: 13
Entered Union in 1896

**New Hampshire**
1,275,056 people
9,282 sq. mi.
Rank in area: 44
Entered Union in 1788

**Oregon**
3,521,515 people
97,126 sq. mi.
Rank in area: 10
Entered Union in 1859

**Vermont**
616,592 people
9,614 sq. mi.
Rank in area: 43
Entered Union in 1791

**New Jersey**
8,590,300 people
8,214 sq. mi.
Rank in area: 46
Entered Union in 1787

**Pennsylvania**
12,335,091 people
46,055 sq. mi.
Rank in area: 33
Entered Union in 1787

**Virginia**
7,293,542 people
42,328 sq. mi.
Rank in area: 35
Entered Union in 1788

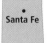
**New Mexico**
1,855,059 people
121,589 sq. mi.
Rank in area: 5
Entered Union in 1912

**Rhode Island**
1,069,725 people
1,231 sq. mi.
Rank in area: 50
Entered Union in 1790

**Washington**
6,068,996 people
70,634 sq. mi.
Rank in area: 19
Entered Union in 1889

**New York**
19,157,532 people
54,077 sq. mi.
Rank in area: 27
Entered Union in 1788

**South Carolina**
4,107,183 people
31,190 sq. mi.
Rank in area: 40
Entered Union in 1788

**West Virginia**
1,801,873 people
24,230 sq. mi.
Rank in area: 41
Entered Union in 1863

**North Carolina**
8,320,146 people
52,670 sq. mi.
Rank in area: 29
Entered Union in 1789

**South Dakota**
761,063 people
77,116 sq. mi.
Rank in area: 17
Entered Union in 1889

**Wisconsin**
5,441,196 people
65,498 sq. mi.
Rank in area: 22
Entered Union in 1848

**North Dakota**
634,110 people
70,699 sq. mi.
Rank in area: 18
Entered Union in 1889

**Tennessee**
5,797,289 people
42,143 sq. mi.
Rank in area: 36
Entered Union in 1796

**Wyoming**
498,703 people
97,813 sq. mi.
Rank in area: 9
Entered Union in 1890

## United States: *Major Dependencies*

- American Samoa—68,688 people; 90 sq. mi.
- Guam—160,796 people; 217 sq. mi.
- Commonwealth of Puerto Rico—3,957,988 people; 5,324 sq. mi.
- Virgin Islands of the United States—123,498 people; 171 sq. mi.
- Midway Atoll—no indigenous inhabitants; 2 sq. mi.
- Wake Atoll—no indigenous inhabitants; 3 sq. mi.

# PRESIDENTS of the UNITED STATES

Here are some little-known facts about the presidents of the United States:

- Only former president to serve in Congress: John Quincy Adams
- First president born in the new United States: Martin Van Buren (eighth president)
- Only president who was a bachelor: James Buchanan
- First left-handed president: James A. Garfield
- Largest president: William H. Taft (6 feet 2 inches, 326 pounds)
- Youngest president: Theodore Roosevelt (42 years old)
- Oldest president: Ronald Reagan (77 years old when he left office in 1989)
- First president born west of the Mississippi River: Herbert Hoover (born in West Branch, Iowa)
- First president born in the 20th century: John F. Kennedy (born May 29, 1917)

**1  George Washington**
**1789–1797**
No Political Party
Birthplace: Virginia
Born: February 22, 1732
Died: December 14, 1799

**2  John Adams**
**1797–1801**
Federalist
Birthplace: Massachusetts
Born: October 30, 1735
Died: July 4, 1826

**3  Thomas Jefferson**
**1801–1809**
Democratic-Republican
Birthplace: Virginia
Born: April 13, 1743
Died: July 4, 1826

**4  James Madison**
**1809–1817**
Democratic-Republican
Birthplace: Virginia
Born: March 16, 1751
Died: June 28, 1836

**5  James Monroe**
**1817–1825**
Democratic-Republican
Birthplace: Virginia
Born: April 28, 1758
Died: July 4, 1831

**6  John Quincy Adams**
**1825–1829**
Democratic-Republican
Birthplace: Massachusetts
Born: July 11, 1767
Died: February 23, 1848

**7  Andrew Jackson**
**1829–1837**
Democrat
Birthplace: South Carolina
Born: March 15, 1767
Died: June 8, 1845

**8  Martin Van Buren**
**1837–1841**
Democrat
Birthplace: New York
Born: December 5, 1782
Died: July 24, 1862

**9  William H. Harrison**
**1841**
Whig
Birthplace: Virginia
Born: February 9, 1773
Died: April 4, 1841

**10  John Tyler**
**1841–1845**
Whig
Birthplace: Virginia
Born: March 29, 1790
Died: January 18, 1862

**11  James K. Polk**
**1845–1849**
Democrat
Birthplace: North Carolina
Born: November 2, 1795
Died: June 15, 1849

**12  Zachary Taylor**
**1849–1850**
Whig
Birthplace: Virginia
Born: November 24, 1784
Died: July 9, 1850

**13 Millard Fillmore**
**1850–1853**
Whig
Birthplace: New York
Born: January 7, 1800
Died: March 8, 1874

**14 Franklin Pierce**
**1853–1857**
Democrat
Birthplace: New Hampshire
Born: November 23, 1804
Died: October 8, 1869

**15 James Buchanan**
**1857–1861**
Democrat
Birthplace: Pennsylvania
Born: April 23, 1791
Died: June 1, 1868

**16 Abraham Lincoln**
**1861–1865**
Republican
Birthplace: Kentucky
Born: February 12, 1809
Died: April 15, 1865

**17 Andrew Johnson**
**1865–1869**
National Union
Birthplace: North Carolina
Born: December 29, 1808
Died: July 31, 1875

**18 Ulysses S. Grant**
**1869–1877**
Republican
Birthplace: Ohio
Born: April 27, 1822
Died: July 23, 1885

**19 Rutherford B. Hayes**
**1877–1881**
Republican
Birthplace: Ohio
Born: October 4, 1822
Died: January 17, 1893

**20 James A. Garfield**
**1881**
Republican
Birthplace: Ohio
Born: November 19, 1831
Died: September 19, 1881

**21 Chester A. Arthur**
**1881–1885**
Republican
Birthplace: Vermont
Born: October 5, 1829
Died: November 18, 1886

**22 24 Grover Cleveland**
**1885–1889, 1893–1897**
Democrat
Birthplace: New Jersey
Born: March 18, 1837
Died: June 24, 1908

**23 Benjamin Harrison**
**1889–1893**
Republican
Birthplace: Ohio
Born: August 20, 1833
Died: March 13, 1901

**25 William McKinley**
**1897–1901**
Republican
Birthplace: Ohio
Born: January 29, 1843
Died: September 14, 1901

**26 Theodore Roosevelt**
**1901–1909**
Republican
Birthplace: New York
Born: October 27, 1858
Died: January 6, 1919

**27 William H. Taft**
**1909–1913**
Republican
Birthplace: Ohio
Born: September 15, 1857
Died: March 8, 1930

**28 Woodrow Wilson**
**1913–1921**
Democrat
Birthplace: Virginia
Born: December 28, 1856
Died: February 3, 1924

**29 Warren G. Harding**
**1921–1923**
Republican
Birthplace: Ohio
Born: November 2, 1865
Died: August 2, 1923

# PRESIDENTS of the UNITED STATES

**30** **Calvin Coolidge**
**1923–1929**
Republican
Birthplace: Vermont
Born: July 4, 1872
Died: January 5, 1933

**31** **Herbert C. Hoover**
**1929–1933**
Republican
Birthplace: Iowa
Born: August 10, 1874
Died: October 20, 1964

**32** **Franklin D. Roosevelt**
**1933–1945**
Democrat
Birthplace: New York
Born: January 30, 1882
Died: April 12, 1945

**33** **Harry S. Truman**
**1945–1953**
Democrat
Birthplace: Missouri
Born: May 8, 1884
Died: December 26, 1972

**34** **Dwight D. Eisenhower**
**1953–1961**
Republican
Birthplace: Texas
Born: October 14, 1890
Died: March 28, 1969

**35** **John F. Kennedy**
**1961–1963**
Democrat
Birthplace: Massachusetts
Born: May 29, 1917
Died: November 22, 1963

**36** **Lyndon B. Johnson**
**1963–1969**
Democrat
Birthplace: Texas
Born: August 27, 1908
Died: January 22, 1973

**37** **Richard M. Nixon**
**1969–1974**
Republican
Birthplace: California
Born: January 9, 1913
Died: April 22, 1994

**38** **Gerald R. Ford**
**1974–1977**
Republican
Birthplace: Nebraska
Born: July 14, 1913

**39** **James E. Carter, Jr.**
**1977–1981**
Democrat
Birthplace: Georgia
Born: October 1, 1924

**40** **Ronald W. Reagan**
**1981–1989**
Republican
Birthplace: Illinois
Born: February 6, 1911
Died: June 5, 2004

**41** **George H. W. Bush**
**1989–1993**
Republican
Birthplace: Massachusetts
Born: June 12, 1924

**42** **William J. Clinton**
**1993–2001**
Democrat
Birthplace: Arkansas
Born: August 19, 1946

**43** **George W. Bush**
**2001–**
Republican
Birthplace: Connecticut
Born: July 6, 1946

The Gazetteer identifies important places and geographical features in this book. Entries include a short description, often followed by two page numbers. The first number refers to a text page on which the entry is discussed, and the second, in italics, refers to a map where the place appears. (The reference *Atlas* is to the section of U.S. and world maps on pages A2–A39.) In addition, some entries include rounded-off geographical coordinates. There are entries for all U.S. states (with capital cities).

**Africa** world's second largest continent. *Atlas*

**Alabama** 22nd state. Capital: Montgomery. *Atlas*

**Alamo** Texas mission in San Antonio captured by Mexico in 1836. (29°N 98°W), 402, *m405*

**Alaska** 49th state. Capital: Juneau. *Atlas*

**Antarctica** continent at the South Pole. *Atlas*

**Antietam** Maryland creek; site of bloodiest day's fighting in the Civil War. (39°N 77°W), 497, *m495*

**Appalachian Mountains** mountain range running from Alabama into Canada. 126, *m127*

**Appomattox Court House** town near Appomattox, Virginia, where Lee surrendered to Grant on April 9, 1865. (37°N 79°W), 519, *m517*

**Arizona** 48th state. Capital: Phoenix. *Atlas*

**Arkansas** 25th state. Capital: Little Rock. *Atlas*

**Asia** world's largest continent. *Atlas*

**Atlantic Ocean** ocean forming east boundary of the United States. *Atlas*

**Australia** island country between Indian and Pacific oceans; also the world's smallest continent. *Atlas*

**Austria-Hungary** one of the Central Powers in World War I; after the war, divided into smaller countries. 680, *m680*

**Aztec Empire** former region of Mexico once under Aztec control. 63, *m63*

**Backcountry** identification for former undeveloped region beginning in the Appalachian Mountains and extending west. 126, *m127*

**Baltimore** Maryland city on Chesapeake Bay. (39°N 77°W), 332, *m331*

**Beringia** former land bridge connecting Asia with North America and now under waters of Bering Strait. (66°N 169°W), 27, *m28*

**Boston** capital of Massachusetts; site of early colonial unrest and conflict. (42°N 71°W), 165, *m172*

**Bull Run** stream 30 miles southwest of Washington, D.C.; site of first land battle of Civil War. (39°N 78°W), 485, *m495*

**Bunker Hill** hill now part of Boston; its name misidentifies Revolutionary War battle fought at nearby Breed's Hill. (42°N 71°W), 177

**Cahokia** Illinois Mound Builders site; village taken from British by Clark in 1778. (39°N 90°W), 31, *m203*

**California** 31st state. Capital: Sacramento. *Atlas*

**Canada** nation sharing northern U.S. border. *Atlas*

**Caribbean Sea** expanse of the Atlantic Ocean between the Gulf of Mexico and South America. *Atlas*

**Central America** area of North America between Mexico and South America. *m72*, *Atlas*

**Charleston** as Charles Town, largest Southern colonial city; South Carolina site of first Civil War shots, at offshore Fort Sumter. (33°N 80°W), 481, *m483*

**Charlestown** former town, now part of Boston; site of both Bunker and Breed's hills. (42°N 71°W ), 177, *m172*

**Chicago** large Illinois city on Lake Michigan. (42°N 88°W), 602, *Atlas*

**China** large nation in Asia. *Atlas*

**Colorado** 38th state. Capital: Denver. *Atlas*

**Concord** Massachusetts city and site of second battle of the Revolutionary War. (42°N 71°W), 172, *m172*

**Confederate States of America** nation formed by 11 Southern states during the Civil War. Capital: Richmond, Virginia. 473 and 482, *m483*

**Connecticut** 5th state. Capital: Hartford. *Atlas*

**Cuba** Caribbean island south of Florida. 662, *m665*

**Delaware** 1st state. Capital: Dover. *Atlas*

**District of Columbia (D.C.)** self-governing federal district between Virginia and Maryland, made up entirely of the city of Washington, the U.S. capital. (39°N 77°W), 305, *Atlas*

**Dominican Republic** nation sharing the island of Hispaniola with Haiti. 673, *m672*

**England** southern part of Great Britain. *Atlas*

**English Channel** narrow waterway separating Great Britain from France. 69, *m764*

**Erie Canal** all-water channel dug out to connect the Hudson River with Lake Erie. 355, *m355*

**Europe** second smallest continent, actually a peninsula of the Eurasian landmass. *Atlas*

**Florida** 27th state. Capital: Tallahassee. *Atlas*

**Fort McHenry** fort in Baltimore harbor where 1814 British attack inspired U.S. national anthem. (39°N 77°N), 332, *m331*

**Fort Sumter** fort in Charleston, South Carolina, harbor where 1861 attack by Confederates began the Civil War. (33°N 80°W), 481, *m483*

**France** nation in western Europe; it aided America in the Revolutionary War. *Atlas*

**Gadsden Purchase** last territory (from Mexico, 1853) added to continental United States. 411, *m410*

**Georgia** 4th state. Capital: Atlanta. *Atlas*

**Germany** nation in central Europe; once divided into West and East Germany, 1949–1990. *Atlas*

**Gettysburg** Pennsylvania town and site of 1863 Civil War victory for the North that is considered war's turning point. (40°N 77°W), 513, *m514*

**Ghana** first powerful West African trading empire. 40, *m40*

**Great Britain** European island nation across from France; it consists of England, Scotland, and Wales. *Atlas*

**Great Lakes** five connected lakes—Ontario, Erie, Huron, Michigan, and Superior—on the U.S. border with Canada. 355, *m355*

**Great Plains** vast grassland region in the central United States. 393, *m395*

**Gulf of Mexico** body of water forming southern U.S. boundary from east Texas to west Florida. *Atlas*

**Haiti** nation sharing the island of Hispaniola with Dominican Republic. *Atlas*

**Harpers Ferry** village today in extreme eastern West Virginia where John Brown raided stored U.S. weapons in 1859. (39°N 78°W), 469, *m495*

**Hawaii** 50th state. Capital: Honolulu. *Atlas*

**Hispaniola** West Indies island (shared today by Dominican Republic and Haiti) that Columbus mistook for Asia. 52, *m51*

**Hudson River** large river in eastern New York. 100, *m95*

**Idaho** 43rd state. Capital: Boise. *Atlas*

**Illinois** 21st state. Capital: Springfield. *Atlas*

**Indiana** 19th state. Capital: Indianapolis. *Atlas*

**Indian Territory** area, mainly of present-day Oklahoma, that in the 1800s became land for relocated Native Americans. 376, *m376*

**Iowa** 29th state. Capital: Des Moines. *Atlas*

**Ireland** island country west of England whose mid-1800s famine caused more than one million people to emigrate to America. 426, *Atlas*

**Israel** Jewish nation in the Middle East. *Atlas*

**Italy** nation in southern Europe. *Atlas*

**Jamestown** community in Virginia that was the first permanent English settlement in North America. 87, *m87*

**Japan** island nation in east Asia. *Atlas*

**Kansas** 34th state. Capital: Topeka. *Atlas*

**Kentucky** 15th state. Capital: Frankfort. *Atlas*

**Latin America** region made up of Mexico, Caribbean Islands, and Central and South America, where Latin-based languages of Spanish, French, or Portuguese are spoken. 359, *m672*

**Lexington** Massachusetts city and site of first Revolutionary War battle in 1775. (42°N 71°W), 173, *m172*

**Little Bighorn River** Montana site of Sioux and Cheyenne victory over Custer. (46°N 108°W), 565, *m563*

**Louisiana** 18th state. Capital: Baton Rouge. *Atlas*

**Louisiana Purchase** land west of the Mississippi River purchased from France in 1803. 319, *m320*

**Lowell** Massachusetts city built in early 1800s as planned factory town. (43°N 71°W), 342

**Maine** 23rd state. Capital: Augusta. *Atlas*

**Mali** early West African trading empire succeeding Ghana empire. 41, *m40*

**Maryland** 7th state. Capital: Annapolis. *Atlas*

**Massachusetts** 6th state. Capital: Boston. *Atlas*

**Mexico** nation sharing U.S. southern border. *Atlas*

**Michigan** 26th state. Capital: Lansing. *Atlas*

**Minnesota** 32nd state. Capital: St. Paul. *Atlas*

**Mississippi** 20th state. Capital: Jackson. *Atlas*

**Mississippi River** second longest U.S. river, south from Minnesota to the Gulf of Mexico. 146, *m153*

**Missouri** 24th state. Capital: Jefferson City. *Atlas*

**Missouri River** longest U.S. river, east from the Rockies to the Mississippi River. 321, *m320*

**Montana** 41st state. Capital: Helena. *Atlas*

**Montgomery** Alabama capital and site of 1955 African-American bus boycott. (32°N 86°W), 813, *m350*

**Nebraska** 37th state. Capital: Lincoln. *Atlas*

**Nevada** 36th state. Capital: Carson City. *Atlas*

**New England** northeast U.S. region made up of Maine, New Hampshire, Vermont, Massachusetts, Rhode Island, and Connecticut. 109, *m110*

**New France** first permanent French colony in North America. 70, *m148*

**New Hampshire** 9th state. Capital: Concord. *Atlas*

**New Jersey** 3rd state. Capital: Trenton. *Atlas*

**New Mexico** 47th state. Capital: Santa Fe. *Atlas*

**New Netherland** early Dutch colony that became New York in 1664. 70

**New Orleans** Louisiana port city at mouth of the Mississippi River. *Atlas*

**New Spain** former North American province of the Spanish Empire, made up mostly of present-day Mexico and the southwest United States. 71, *m72*

**New York** 11th state. Capital: Albany. *Atlas*

**New York City** largest U.S. city, at the mouth of the Hudson River; temporary U.S. capital, 1785–1790. *Atlas*

**Normandy** region of northern France where Allied invasion in 1944 turned tide of World War II. 766, *m766*

**North America** continent of Western Hemisphere north of Panama-Colombia border. *Atlas*

**North Carolina** 12th state. Capital: Raleigh. *Atlas*

**North Dakota** 39th state. Capital: Bismarck. *Atlas*

**Northwest Territory** U.S. land north of the Ohio River to the Great Lakes and west to the Mississippi River; acquired in 1783. 223, *m226*

**Ohio** 17th state. Capital: Columbus. *Atlas*

**Ohio River** river that flows from western Pennsylvania to the Mississippi River. *Atlas*

**Oklahoma** 46th state. Capital: Oklahoma City. *Atlas*

**Oregon** 33rd state. Capital: Salem. *Atlas*

**Oregon Country** former region of northwest North America claimed jointly by Britain and the United States until 1846. 318, *m320*

**Oregon Trail** pioneer wagon route from Missouri to the Oregon Territory in the 1840s and 1850s. *m395, 396*

**Pacific Ocean** world's largest ocean, on the west coast of the United States. *Atlas*

**Panama Canal** ship passageway cut through Panama in Central America, linking Atlantic and Pacific oceans. (8°N 80°W), 670, *m670*

**Pearl Harbor** naval base in Hawaii; site of surprise Japanese aerial attack in 1941. (21°N 158°W), 661 *m660*

**Pennsylvania** 2nd state. Capital: Harrisburg. *Atlas*

**Persian Gulf** waterway between Saudi Arabia and Iran, leading to Kuwait and Iraq. 875, *m865*

**Philadelphia** large port city in Pennsylvania; U.S. capital, 1790–1800. (40°N 76°W), 229, *Atlas*

**Philippine Islands** Pacific island country off the southeast coast of China. 662, *m665*

**Plymouth** town on Massachusetts coast and site of Pilgrim landing and colony. (42°N 71°W), 93, *m95*

**Portugal** nation in southwestern Europe; leader in early oceanic explorations. 49, *m51*

**Potomac River** historic river separating Virginia from Maryland and Washington, D.C. 496, *m495*

**Puerto Rico** Caribbean island that has been U.S. territory since 1898. 667, *m665*

**Quebec** major early Canadian city; also a province of eastern Canada. 146, *m148*

**Rhode Island** 13th state. Capital: Providence. *Atlas*

**Richmond** Virginia capital that was also the capital of the Confederacy. (38°N 77°W), 482, *m483*

**Rio Grande** river that forms part of the border between the United States and Mexico. *Atlas*

**Roanoke Island** island off the coast of North Carolina; 1585 site of the first English colony in the Americas. (36°N 76°W), 85, *m87*

**Rocky Mountains** mountain range in the western United States and Canada. *Atlas*

**Russia** large Eurasian country, the major republic of the former Soviet Union (1922–1991). 680, *m680*

**St. Augustine** oldest permanent European settlement (1565) in the United States, on Florida's northeast coast. (30°N 81°W), 68, *m63*

**St. Lawrence River** Atlantic-to-Great Lakes waterway used by early explorers of mid-North America. 146, *m148*

**St. Louis** Missouri city at the junction of the Missouri and Mississippi rivers. (39°N 90°W), 320, *Atlas*

**San Antonio** Texas city and site of the Alamo. (29°N 99°W), 402, *m405*

**San Francisco** major port city in northern California. (38°N 123°W), 416, *m592*

**San Salvador** West Indies island near the Bahamas where Columbus first landed in the Americas. (24°N 74°W), 52, *m51*

**Santa Fe Trail** old wagon route from Missouri to Santa Fe in Mexican province of New Mexico. 395, *m395*

**Songhai** early West African trading empire succeeding Mali empire. 42, *m40*

**South America** continent of Western Hemisphere south of Panama-Colombia border. *Atlas*

**South Carolina** 8th state. Capital: Columbia. *Atlas*

**South Dakota** 40th state. Capital: Pierre. *Atlas*

**Spain** nation in southwestern Europe; early empire builder in the Americas. 50, *m51*

**Tennessee** 16th state. Capital: Nashville. *Atlas*

**Tenochtitlán** Aztec Empire capital; now site of Mexico City. 64, *m63*

**Texas** 28th state. Capital: Austin. *Atlas*

**Utah** 45th state. Capital: Salt Lake City. *Atlas*

**Valley Forge** village in southeast Pennsylvania and site of Washington's army camp during winter of 1777–1778. (40°N 75°W), 202, *m209*

**Vermont** 14th state. Capital: Montpelier. *Atlas*

**Vicksburg** Mississippi River site of major Union victory (1863) in Civil War. (32°N 91°W), 516, *m517*

**Virginia** 10th state. Capital: Richmond. *Atlas*

**Washington** 42nd state. Capital: Olympia. *Atlas*

**Washington, D.C.** capital of the United States since 1800; makes up whole of District of Columbia (D.C.). (39°N 77°W), 305, *Atlas*

**West Africa** region from which most Africans were brought to the Americas. 39, *m40*

**Western Hemisphere** the half of the world that includes the Americas. 75, *m74*

**West Indies** numerous islands in the Caribbean Sea, between Florida and South America. 111, *m111*

**West Virginia** 35th state. Capital: Charleston. *Atlas*

**Wisconsin** 30th state. Capital: Madison. *Atlas*

**Wounded Knee** South Dakota site that was scene of 1890 massacre of Sioux. (43°N 102°W), 566, *m563*

**Wyoming** 44th state. Capital: Cheyenne. *Atlas*

**Yorktown** Virginia village and site of American victory that sealed British defeat in Revolutionary War. (37°N 77°W), 209, *m209*

## A

**abolition** (AB uh LIHSH uhn) *n.* the movement to end slavery. (p. 440)

**abridge** (uh BRIHJ) *v.* to reduce. (p. 266)

**AEF** *n.* the American Expeditionary Force, U.S. forces during World War I. (p. 686)

**affirmation** (AF uhr MAY shuhn) *n.* a statement declaring that something is true. (p. 257)

**African Diaspora** (AF rih kuhn  dy AS puhr uh) *n.* the forced removal of Africans from their homelands to serve as slave labor in the Americas. (p. 78)

**Albany Plan of Union** *n.* the first formal proposal to unite the American colonies, put forth by Benjamin Franklin. (p. 149)

**Alien and Sedition** (si DISH uhn) **Acts** *n.* a series of four laws enacted in 1798 to reduce the political power of recent immigrants to the United States. (p. 306)

**Allies** (AL yz) *n.* an alliance of Serbia, Russia, France, Great Britain, Italy, and seven other countries during World War I. (p. 680)

**ally** (AL eye) *n.* a country that agrees to help another country achieve a common goal. (p. 200)

**American Federation of Labor (AFL)** *n.* a national organization of labor unions founded in 1886. (p. 603)

**American System** *n.* a plan introduced in 1815 to make the United States economically self-sufficient. (p. 354)

**Anaconda** (AN uh KAHN duh) **Plan** *n.* a  strategy by which the Union proposed to defeat the Confederacy in the Civil War. (p. 484)

**Angel Island** *n.* the first stop in the United States for most immigrants coming from Asia. (p. 615)

**Antifederalist** (AN tee FED uhr uh list) *n.* a person who opposed the ratification of the U.S. Constitution. (p. 234)

**Anti-Imperialist** (AN tee im PEER y uh LIZT) **League** *n.* a group of well-known Americans that believed the United States should not deny other people the right to govern themselves. (p. 667)

**Appalachian** (AP uh LAY chee uhn) **Mountains** *n.* a mountain range that stretches from eastern Canada south to Alabama. (p. 126)

**appellate** (uh PEL it) *adj.* having power to review court decisions. (p. 260)

**Appomattox** (AP uh MAT uhks) **Court House** *n.* the Virginia town where Robert E. Lee surrendered to Ulysses S. Grant in 1865, ending the Civil War. (p. 519)

**apprentice** (uh PREN tis) *n.* a beginner who learns a trade or a craft from an experienced master. (p. 137)

**appropriation** (uh PROH pree AY shuhn) *n.* public funds set aside for a specific purpose. (p. 253)

**archaeologist** (AHR kee AHL uh jist) *n.* a scientist who studies the human past by examining the things people left behind. (p. 27)

**armistice** (AHR mi stis) *n.* an end to fighting. (p. 690)

**Articles of Confederation** *n.* a document, adopted by the Continental Congress in 1777 and finally approved by the states in 1781, that outlined the form of government of the new United States. (p. 222)

**artifact** (AHR tuh FAKT) *n.* a tool or other object made by  humans. (p. 27)

**artillery** (ahr TIL uhr ee) *n.* a cannon or large gun. (p. 177)

**artisan** (AHR ti zuhn) *n.* a skilled worker, such as a weaver or a potter, who makes goods by hand; a craftsperson. (p. 117)

**assimilation** (uh SIM uh LAY shuhn) *n.* the process of blending into society. (p. 616)

## B

**baby boom** *n.* the term for the generation born between 1946 and 1961, when the U.S. birthrate sharply increased following World War II. (p. 801)

**Backcountry** *n.* a colonial region that ran along the Appalachian Mountains through the far western part of the New England, Middle, and Southern colonies. (p. 109)

**Bacon's Rebellion** *n.* a revolt against powerful colonial authority in Jamestown by Nathaniel Bacon and a group of landless frontier settlers that resulted in the burning of Jamestown in 1676. (p. 89)

**bail** (bayl) *n.* money paid as security by arrested persons to guarantee they will return for trial. (p. 268)

**Battle of Antietam** (an TEE tuhm) *n.* a Civil War battle in 1862 in which 25,000 men were killed or wounded. (p. 497)

**Battle of Fallen Timbers** *n.* in 1794, an American army defeated 2,000 Native Americans in a clash over control of the Northwest Territory. (p. 299)

**Battle of Gettysburg** (GET eez BURG) *n.* an 1863 battle in the Civil War in which the Union defeated the Confederacy, ending hopes for a Confederate victory in the North. (p. 513)

**Battle of Quebec** (kwi BEK) *n.* a battle won by the British over the French, and the turning point in the French and Indian War. (p. 150)

**Battle of Shiloh** (SHY loh) *n.* an 1862 battle in which the Union forced the Confederacy to retreat in some of the fiercest fighting in the Civil War. (p. 494)

**Battle of Yorktown** *n.* the last major battle of the Revolutionary War, which resulted in the surrender of British forces in 1781. (p. 210)

**Battle of the Alamo** (AL uh MOH) *n.* in 1836, Texans defended a church called the Alamo against the Mexican army; all but five Texans were killed. (p. 403)

**Battle of the Little Bighorn** *n.* an 1876 battle in which the Sioux and the Cheyenne wiped out an entire force of U.S. troops. (p. 565)

**Battle of the Thames** (temz) *n.* an American victory over the British in the War of 1812, which ended the British threat to the Northwest Territory. (p. 332)

**Battles of Saratoga** (SAR uh TOH guh) *n.* a series of conflicts between British soldiers and the Continental Army in 1777 that proved to be a turning point in the Revolutionary War. (p. 199)

**bayonet** (BAY uh net) *n.* a long steel knife attached to the end of a gun. (p. 202)

**Bear Flag Revolt** *n.* the 1846 rebellion by Americans against Mexican rule in California. (p. 409)

**Benin** (buh NIN) *n.* a West African kingdom that arose near the Niger River delta in the 1300s. (p. 43)

**Bessemer** (BES uh muhr) **steel process** *n.* a new way of making steel that was developed in the 1850s and caused steel production to soar. (p. 587)

**bill of attainder** (uh TAYN duhr) *n.* a law that condemns a person without a trial in court. (p. 255)

**Bill of Rights** *n.* the first ten amendments to the U.S. Constitution, added in 1791, and consisting of a formal list of citizens' rights and freedoms. (p. 237)

**black code** *n.* a law passed by Southern states that limited the freedom of former slaves. (p. 534)

**blockade** *n.* when armed forces prevent the transportation of goods or people into or out of an area. (p. 484)

**boomtown** *n.* a town that has a sudden burst of economic or population growth. (p. 558)

**border state** *n.* a slave state that bordered states in which slavery was illegal. (p. 482)

**Boston Massacre** (MAS uh kuhr) *n.* a clash between British soldiers and Boston colonists in 1770, in which five of the colonists, including Crispus Attucks, were killed. (p. 165)

**Boston Tea Party** *n.* the dumping of 342 chests of tea into Boston Harbor by colonists in 1773 to protest the Tea Act. (p. 167)

**bounty** (BOWN tee) *n.* a reward or cash payment given by a government. (pp. 271, 508)

**Boxer Rebellion** *n.* in 1900, Chinese resentment toward foreigners' attitude of cultural superiority resulted in this violent uprising. (p. 669)

**boycott** (BOI KOT) *n.* a refusal to buy certain goods. (p. 161)

**buck** *n.* a buckskin from an adult male deer was a unit of money for settlers. (p. 127)

**buffalo soldier** *n.* a name given by Native Americans to African Americans serving in the U.S. army in the West. (p. 570)

**business cycle** *n.* the pattern of good times and bad times in the economy. (p. 586)

## C

**cabinet** *n.* a group of department heads who serve as the president's chief advisers. (p. 294)

**California gold rush** *n.* in 1849, large numbers of people moved to California because gold had been discovered there. (p. 413)

**caravel** (KAR uh VEL) *n.* a ship with triangular sails that allowed it to sail into the wind and with square sails that carried it forward when the wind was at its back. (p. 49)

**cash crop** *n.* a crop grown by a farmer to be sold for money rather than for personal use. (p. 115)

**cavalry** *n.* soldiers on horseback. (p. 496)

**Centennial** (sen TEN ee uhl) **Exhibition** *n.* an exhibition in Philadelphia in 1876 that celebrated America's 100th birthday. (p. 588)

**Central Powers** *n.* an alliance of Austria-Hungary, Germany, the Ottoman Empire, and Bulgaria during World War I. (p. 680)

**charter** *n.* a written contract issued by a government giving the holder the right to establish a colony. (p. 87)

**checks and balances** *n.* the ability of each branch of government to exercise checks, or controls, over the other branches. (p. 246)

**Chinese Exclusion Act** *n.* enacted in 1882, this law banned Chinese immigration for ten years. (p. 617)

**civil disobedience** (DIS uh BEE dee uhns) *n.* peacefully refusing to obey laws one considers unjust. (p. 431)

**civilization** (SIV uh li ZAY shuhn) *n.* a form of culture characterized by city trade centers, specialized workers, organized forms of government and religion, systems of record keeping, and advanced tools. (p. 29)

**civil rights** *n.* rights granted to all citizens. (p. 535)

**clan** *n.* a large group of families that claim a common ancestor. (p. 127)

**Clayton Antitrust Act** *n.* a law passed in 1914 that laid down rules forbidding business practices that lessened competition; it gave the government more power to regulate trusts. (p. 648)

**Cold War** *n.* the state of hostility, without direct military conflict, that developed between the United States and the Soviet Union after World War II. (p. 717)

**Columbian** (kuh LUM bee uhn) **Exchange** *n.* the transfer of plants, animals, and diseases between the Western and the Eastern hemispheres. (p. 74)

**committee of correspondence** *n.* a group of people in the colonies who exchanged letters on colonial affairs. (p. 166)

**common law** *n.* a system of law developed in England, based on customs and previous court decisions. (p. 268)

**Compromise of 1850** *n.* a series of Congressional laws intended to settle the major disagreements between free states and slave states. (p. 461)

**Compromise of 1877** *n.* the agreement that resolved an 1876 election dispute: Rutherford B. Hayes became president and then removed the last federal troops from the South. (p. 548)

**compulsory process** *n.* a required procedure. (p. 267)

**Conestoga** (KON i STOW guh) **wagon** *n.* a vehicle with wide wheels, a curved bed, and a canvas cover used by American pioneers traveling west. (p. 117)

**Confederate States of America** *n.* the confederation formed in 1861 by the Southern states after their secession from the Union. (p. 473)

**conquistador** (kon KWIS tuh DAWR) *n.* a Spaniard who traveled to the Americas as an explorer and a conqueror in the 16th century. (p. 63)

**conscription** (kuhn SKRIP shuhn) *n.* a law that required men to serve in the military or be drafted. (p. 508)

**Constitutional Convention** *n.* a meeting held in 1787 to consider changes to the Articles of Confederation; resulted in the drafting of the Constitution. (p. 229)

**containment** (kuhn TAYN muhnt) *n.* the blocking by one nation of another nation's attempts to spread influence—especially the efforts of the United States to block the spread of Soviet Communism during the late 1940s and early 1950s. (p. 793)

**Continental Army** *n.* a colonial force authorized by the Second Continental Congress in 1775, with George Washington as its commanding general. (p. 177)

**convene** (kuhn VEEN) *v.* to call together. (p. 259)

**convoy system** *n.* a heavy guard of destroyers that escorts merchant ships during wartime. (p. 687)

**cooperative** (koh OP uhr uh tiv) *n.* an organization owned and run by its members. (p. 577)

**Copperheads** *n.* Abraham Lincoln's main political opponents; they favored peace with the South. (p. 508)

**corporation** *n.* a business owned by investors who buy part of the company through shares of stock. (p. 594)

**cotton gin** *n.* a machine invented in 1793 that cleaned cotton much faster and far more efficiently than human workers. (p. 348)

**counterculture** (KOWN tuhr KUL chur) *n.* a group of young people with values and lifestyles in opposition to those of the established culture. (p. 725)

**Crittenden** (KRIT uhn duhn) **Plan** *n.* a compromise introduced in 1861 that might have prevented secession. (p. 475)

**Crusades** (kroo SAYDZ) *n.* a series of wars to capture the Holy Land, launched in 1096 by European Christians. (p. 45)

**culture** (KUL chuhr) *n.* a way of life shared by people with similar arts, beliefs, and customs. (p. 28)

**D**

**Dawes** (dawz) **Act** *n.* a law, enacted in 1887, that distributed reservation land to individual owners. (p. 567)

**Declaration of Independence** *n.* the document, written in 1776, in which the colonies declared independence from Britain. (p. 180)

**department store** *n.* a store that sells everything from clothing to furniture to hardware. (p. 627)

**depression** *n.* a severe economic slump. (p. 386)

**desert** (di ZURT) *v.* to leave military duty without intending to return. (p. 203)

**direct primary** *n.* voters, rather than party conventions, choose candidates to run for public office. (p. 640)

**diversity** (di VUR si tee) *n.* a variety of people. (p. 117)

**doctrine of nullification** (NUL uh fi KAY shuhn) *n.* a right of a state to reject a federal law that it considers unconstitutional. (p. 381)

**domestication** (doh MES ti KAY shuhn) *n.* the practice of breeding plants or taming animals to meet human needs. (p. 28)

***Dred Scott* v. *Sandford*** *n.* an 1856 Supreme Court case in which a slave, Dred Scott, sued for his freedom because he had been taken to live in territories where slavery was illegal; the Court ruled against Scott. (p. 467)

**due process of law** *n.* fair treatment under the law. (p. 267)

**elector** *n.* a voter. (p. 249)

**Ellis Island** *n.* the first stop in the United States for most immigrants coming from Europe. (p. 614)

**Emancipation** (i MAN suh PAY shuhn) **Proclamation** *n.* an executive order issued by Abraham Lincoln on January 1, 1863, freeing the slaves in all regions in rebellion against the Union. (p. 504)

**Embargo** (em BAHR goh) **Act of 1807** *n.* an act that stated that American ships were no longer allowed to sail to foreign ports, and it also closed American ports to British ships. (p. 328)

**emigrant** (EM i gruhnt) *n.* a person who leaves a country. (p. 423)

***encomienda*** (en koh mee YEN duh) *n.* a grant of Native American labor. (p. 72)

**English Bill of Rights** *n.* an agreement signed by William and Mary to respect the rights of English citizens and of Parliament, including the right to free elections. (p. 144)

**enlightenment** (en LYT n muhnt) *n.* an 18th-century movement that emphasized the use of reason and the scientific method to obtain knowledge. (p. 140)

**enumeration** (i NOO muh RAY shuhn) *n.* an official count, such as a census. (p. 249)

**equity** (EK wi tee) *n.* a system of justice not covered under common law. (p. 269)

**Erie** (EER ee) **Canal** *n.* completed in 1825, this waterway connected New York City and Buffalo, New York. (p. 355)

**Espionage** (ES pee uh NAHZH) **Act** *n.* passed in 1917, this law set heavy fines and long prison terms for antiwar activities and for encouraging draft resisters. (p. 692)

**European Middle Ages** *n.* a period from the late 400s to about the 1300s, during which Europeans turned to feudalism and the manor system. (p. 44)

**exoduster** (EKS suh duhs tuhr) *n.* an African American who left the South for the West and compared himself or herself to Biblical Hebrews who left slavery in Egypt. (p. 575)

**ex post facto** (EKS pohst FAK toh) **law** *n.* a law that would make an act a criminal offense after it was committed. (p. 255)

**factory system** *n.* a method of production that brought many workers and machines together into one building. (p. 341)

**fall line** *n.* the point at which a waterfall prevents large boats from moving farther upriver. (p. 126)

**famine** (FAM in) *n.* a severe food shortage. (p. 426)

**fascism** (FASH iz uhm) *n.* a political philosophy that advocates a strong, centralized, nationalistic government headed by a powerful dictator. (p. 756)

**federalism** *n.* a system of government where power is shared among the central (or federal) government and the states. (pp. 234, 245)

**Federalists** *n.* supporters of the Constitution. (p. 234)

***Federalist Papers*** *n.* a series of essays defending and explaining the Constitution. (p. 235)

**Federal Judiciary** (joo DISH ee ER ee) **Act** *n.* it helped create a court system and gave the Supreme Court six members. (p. 294)

**Federal Reserve Act** *n.* a law passed in 1913 that "created" the nation's banking system and instituted a flexible currency system. (p. 648)

**felony** (FEL uh nee) *n.* a serious crime. (p. 253)

**feudalism** (FYOOD l iz uhm) *n.* a political system in which the king allows nobles the use of his land in exchange for their military service and their protection of people living on the land. (p. 44)

**Fifteenth Amendment** *n.* passed in 1870, this amendment to the U.S. Constitution stated that citizens could not be stopped from voting "on account of race, color, or previous condition of servitude." (p. 546)

**54th Massachusetts Regiment** *n.* one of the first African-American regiments organized to fight for the Union in the Civil War. (p. 506)

**First Battle of Bull Run** *n.* an 1861 battle of the Civil War in which the South shocked the North with a victory. (p. 485)

**foreign** (FAWR in) **policy** *n.* relations with the governments of other countries. (p. 304)

**Fort Sumter** *n.* a federal fort located in the harbor of Charleston, South Carolina; the Southern attack on Fort Sumter marked the beginning of the Civil War. (p. 481)

**forty-niner** *n.* a person who went to California to find gold, starting in 1849. (p. 412)

**Fourteen Points** *n.* President Woodrow Wilson's goals for peace after World War I. (p. 695)

**Fourteenth Amendment** *n.* an amendment to the U.S. Constitution, passed in 1868, that made all persons born or naturalized in the United States— including former slaves—citizens of the country. (p. 535)

**First Continental Congress** *n.* a meeting of delegates in 1774 from all the colonies except Georgia to uphold colonial rights. (p. 171)

**Freedmen's Bureau** *n.* a federal agency set up to help former slaves after the Civil War. (p. 533)

**freedmen's school** *n.* a school set up to educate newly freed African Americans. (p. 541)

**Free Soil Party** *n.* a political party dedicated to stopping the expansion of slavery. (p. 459)

**French and Indian War** *n.* a conflict in North America from 1754 to 1763 that was part of a worldwide struggle between France and Britain; Britain defeated France and gained French Canada. (p. 147)

**frontier** (frun TEER) *n.* unsettled or sparsely settled area occupied largely by Native Americans. (p. 557)

**Fugitive Slave Act** *n.* an 1850 law to help slaveholders recapture runaway slaves. (p. 462)

**French Revolution** *n.* in 1789, the French launched a movement for liberty and equality. (p. 301)

**Fundamental Orders of Connecticut** *n.* a set of laws that were established in 1639 by a Puritan congregation who had settled in the Connecticut Valley and that expanded the idea of representative government. (p. 95)

G

**generator** *n.* a machine that produces electric current. (p. 587)

**Ghana** (GAH nuh) *n.* a West African empire in the 8th–11th centuries A.D. (p. 39)

**Gilded** (gil did) **Age** *n.* an era during the late 1800s of fabulous wealth. (p. 596)

**"Glorious Revolution"** *n.* the overthrow of English King James II in 1688 and his replacement by William and Mary. (p. 144)

**gold standard** *n.* a policy under which the government backs every dollar with a certain amount of gold. (p. 577)

**Grange** (graynj) *n.* formed in 1867, the Patrons of Husbandry tried to meet the social needs of farm families. (p. 577)

**Great Awakening** *n.* a revival of religious feeling in the American colonies during the 1730s and 1740s. (p. 139)

**Great Compromise** *n.* the Constitutional Convention's agreement to establish a two-house national legislature, with all states having equal representation in one house and each state having representation based on its population in the other house. (p. 232)

**Great Depression** *n.* a period, lasting from 1929 to 1941, in which the U.S. economy was in severe decline and millions of Americans were unemployed. (p. 709)

**Great Migration** *n.* the movement of Puritans from England to establish settlements around the world, including 20,000 who sailed for America (p. 94); the movement of African Americans between 1910 and 1920 to northern cities from the South. (p. 693)

**Great Plains** *n.* the area from the Missouri River to the Rocky Mountains. (p. 557)

**Great Society** *n.* a program started by President Lyndon Johnson that provided help to the poor, the elderly, and women, and also promoted education and outlawed discrimination. (p. 724)

**greenback** *n.* paper currency issued by the federal government during the Civil War. (p. 509)

**gristmill** (GRIST MIL) *n.* a mill in which grain is ground to produce flour or meal. (p. 115)

**guerrilla** (guh RIL uh) *n.* a soldier who weakens the enemy with surprise raids and hit-and-run attacks. (p. 207)

**H**

**hacienda** (HAH see EN duh) *n.* a large farm or estate. (p. 72)

**Harlem Renaissance** *n.* a flowering of African-American artistic creativity during the 1920s, centered in the Harlem community of New York City. (p. 709)

**Harpers Ferry** *n.* a federal arsenal in Virginia that was captured in 1859 during a slave revolt. (p. 469)

**Hausa** (HOW suh) *n.* a West African people who lived in what is now northern Nigeria after A.D. 1000. (p. 42)

**hawk** *n.* a person who supports war. (p. 847)

**Haymarket affair** *n.* in 1886, a union protest resulted in about 100 dead after an unknown person threw a bomb, and police opened fire on the crowd. (p. 602)

**Holocaust** ( HOL uh KAWST) *n.* the systematic killing by Germany during World War II of about six million Jews as well as millions from other ethnic groups. (p. 716)

**homestead** *n.* land to settle on and farm. (p. 568)

**Homestead Act** *n.* passed in 1862, this law offered 160 acres of land free to anyone who agreed to live on and improve the land for five years. (p. 574)

**House of Burgesses** *n.* created in 1619, the first representative assembly in the American colonies. (p. 88)

**Hudson River school** *n.* a group of artists living in the Hudson River Valley in New York. (p. 430)

**Hull House** *n.* founded in 1889, a model for other settlement houses of the time. (p. 613)

**hygiene** (HY JEEN) *n.* conditions and practices that promote health. (p. 490)

**I**

**immigrant** *n.* a person who settles in a new country. (p. 423)

**immunity** *n.* legal protection. (p. 262)

**impeachment** *n.* the process of accusing a public official of wrongdoing. (p. 249)

**imperialism** *n.* the policy by which stronger nations extend their economic, political, or military control over weaker nations or territories. (p. 659)

**impressment** *n.* the act of seizing by force. (p. 327)

**inaugurate** (in AW gyuh RAYT) *v.* to swear in or induct into office in a formal ceremony. (p. 293)

**income tax** *n.* a tax on earnings. (p. 509)

**indentured servant** *n.* a person who sold his or her labor in exchange for passage to America. (p.88)

**Indian Removal Act** *n.* this 1830 act called for the government to negotiate treaties that would require Native Americans to relocate west. (p. 376)

**Indian Territory** *n.* present-day Oklahoma and parts of Kansas and Nebraska to which Native Americans were moved under the Indian Removal Act of 1830. (p. 376)

**indictment** (in DYT muhnt) *n.* a written statement issued by a grand jury charging a person with a crime. (p. 250)

**indigo** *n.* a plant grown in the Southern colonies that yields a deep blue dye. (p. 121)

**individual right** *n.* a personal liberty and privilege guaranteed to U.S. citizens by the Bill of Rights. (p. 247)

**Industrial Revolution** *n.* in late 18th-century Britain, factory machines began replacing hand tools and manufacturing replaced farming as the main form of work. (p. 341)

**inferior court** *n.* a court with less authority than the Supreme Court. (p. 260)

**inflation** *n.* an increase in the price of goods and services and a decrease in the value of money. (p. 386)

**initiative** (i NISH uh tiv) *n.* the procedure that allows voters to propose a law directly. (p. 640)

**inoperative** *adj.* no longer in force. (p. 274)

**insurrection** (IN suh REK shuhn) *n.* open revolt against a government. (p. 271)

**interchangeable part** *n.* a part that is exactly like another part. (p. 343)

**Intolerable Acts** *n.* a series of laws enacted by Parliament in 1774 to punish Massachusetts colonists for the Boston Tea Party. (p. 170)

**ironclad** *n.* a warship covered with iron. (p. 491)

**Iroquois** (IR uh KWOH) **League** *n.* a 16th-century alliance of the Cayuga, Mohawk, Oneida, Onondaga, and Seneca Native American groups living in the eastern Great Lakes region. (p. 37)

**irrigation** *n.* the practice of bringing water to crops. (p. 29)

**Islam** (is LAHM) *n.* a religion founded by the prophet Muhammad in the 600s, which teaches that there is one God, named Allah. (p. 41)

**J**

**Jacksonian Democracy** *n.* the idea of spreading political power to all the people, thereby ensuring majority rule. (p. 370)

**Jamestown** *n.* the first permanent English settlement in North America. (p. 87)

**Jay's Treaty** *n.* the agreement that ended dispute over American shipping during the French Revolution. (p. 302)

**jazz** *n.* a new kind of music in the 1920s that captured the carefree spirit of the times. (p. 717)

**Jim Crow** *n.* laws meant to enforce separation of white and black people in public places in the South. (p. 621)

**joint-stock company** *n.* a business in which investors pool their wealth in order to turn a profit. (p. 86)

**judicial** (joo DISH uhl) **review** *n.* the principle that the Supreme Court has the final say in interpreting the Constitution. (p. 317)

**Judiciary** (joo DISH ee ER ee) **Act of 1801** *n.* a law that increased the number of federal judges, allowing President John Adams to fill most of the new spots with Federalists. (p. 316)

**K**

**Kansas-Nebraska Act** *n.* an 1854 law that established the territories of Kansas and Nebraska and gave their residents the right to decide whether to allow slavery. (p. 464)

**kayak** (KY AK) *n.* a small boat made of animal skins. (p. 33)

**King Cotton** *n.* cotton was called king because cotton was important to the world market, and the South grew most of the cotton for Europe's mills. (p. 484)

**King Philip's War** *n.* a war between the Puritan colonies and Native Americans in 1675–1676. (p. 96)

**Knights of Labor** *n.* an organization of workers from all different trades formed after the Civil War. (p. 601)

**Ku Klux Klan** *n.* a group formed in 1866 that wanted to restore Democratic control of the South and to keep former slaves powerless; the group called for a "racially and morally pure" America. (pp. 544)

**L**

**labor union** *n.* a group of workers who band together to seek better working conditions. (p. 434)

**Land Ordinance of 1785** *n.* a law that established a plan for surveying and selling the federally owned lands west of the Appalachian Mountains. (p. 223)

**land speculator** *n.* a person who buys huge areas of land for a low price and then sells off small sections of it at high prices. (p. 394)

**League of Nations** *n.* an organization set up after World War I to settle international conflicts. (p. 695)

**leisure** (LEE zhuhr) *n.* free time. (p. 627)

**Lewis and Clark expedition** *n.* a group led by Meriwether Lewis and William Clark who explored the lands of the Louisiana Purchase beginning in 1803. (p. 320)

**Lexington and Concord** *n.* sites in Massachusetts of the first battles of the American Revolution. (p. 173)

**limited government** *n.* the principle that requires all U.S. citizens, including government leaders, to obey the law. (p. 247)

**lode** *n.* a deposit of mineral buried in rock. (p. 558)

**Lone Star Republic** *n.* the nickname of the republic of Texas, given in 1836. (p. 405)

**long drive** *n.* taking cattle by foot to a railway. (p. 560)

**Louisiana** (loo EE zee AN uh) **Purchase** *n.* the 1803 purchase of the Louisiana Territory from France. (p. 319)

**Lowell mills** *n.* textile mills located in the factory town of Lowell, Massachusetts, founded in 1826. (p. 342)

**Loyalist** *n.* an American colonist who supported the British in the American Revolution. (p. 173)

# M

**mail-order catalog** *n.* a publication that contains pictures and descriptions of items so that people can order by mail. (p. 627)

**Magna Carta** *n.* "Great Charter;" a document guaranteeing basic political rights in England, approved by King John in 1215. (p. 141)

**Mali** (MAH lee) *n.* a West African empire from the 13th–15th centuries that grew rich from trade. (p. 41)

**manifest destiny** *n.* the belief that the United States was destined to stretch across the continent from the Atlantic Ocean to the Pacific Ocean. (p. 407)

**manor system** *n.* a system in which lords divided their lands into estates, which were farmed mostly by serfs who received protection from the lord in return. (p. 45)

**Marbury v. Madison** *n.* an 1803 case in which the Supreme Court ruled that it had the power to abolish laws by declaring them unconstitutional. (p. 317)

**mass culture** *n.* a common culture experienced by large numbers of people. (p. 626)

**matrilineal** (MAT ruh LIN ee uhl) *adj.* a society in which ancestry is traced through the mother. (p. 36)

**Mayflower Compact** *n.* an agreement established by the men who sailed to America on the *Mayflower,* which called for laws for the good of the colony and set forth the idea of self-government. (p. 93)

**melting pot** *n.* a place where cultures blend. (p. 616)

**mercantilism** (MUHR kuhn tee LIZ uhm) *n.* an economic system in which nations increase their wealth and power by obtaining gold and silver and by establishing a favorable balance of trade. (p. 61)

**mercenary** (MUR suh NER ee) *n.* a professional soldier hired to fight for a foreign country. (p. 195)

**Mexican Cession** (sesh uhn) *n.* a vast region given up by Mexico after the War with Mexico; it included the present-day states of California, Nevada, Utah, most of Arizona, and parts of New Mexico, Colorado, and Wyoming. (p. 411)

**Mexicano** (may hi KAH noh) *n.* a person of Spanish descent whose ancestors had come from Mexico and settled in the Southwest. (p. 570)

**Middle Passage** *n.* the middle leg of the triangular trade route—the voyage from Africa to the Americas—that brought captured Africans into slavery. (p. 78)

**migrate** *v.* to move from one location to another. (p. 27)

**militarism** *n.* the belief that a nation needs a large military force. (p. 679)

**militia** (muh LISH uh) *n.* a force of armed civilians pledged to defend their community during the American Revolution. (p. 170); an emergency military force that is not part of the regular army. (p. 254)

**minié** (MIN ee) **ball** *n.* a bullet with a hollow base. (p. 491)

**Minuteman** *n.* a member of the colonial militia who was trained to respond "at a minute's warning." (p. 170)

**misdemeanor** (mis di MEE nuhr) *n.* a violation of the law. (p. 259)

**mission** *n.* a settlement created by the Church in order to convert Native Americans to Christianity. (p. 72)

**missionary** *n.* a person sent by the Church to preach, teach, and convert native peoples to Christianity. (p. 61)

**Missouri Compromise** *n.* a series of laws enacted in 1820 to maintain the balance of power between slave states and free states. (p. 358)

**monopoly** *n.* a company that eliminates its competitors and controls an industry. (p. 595)

**Monroe Doctrine** *n.* a policy of U.S. opposition to any European interference in the Western Hemisphere, announced by President Monroe in 1823. (p. 359)

**Mormon** *n.* a member of a church founded by Joseph Smith in 1830. (p. 397)

**Mound Builder** *n.* an early Native American who built large earthen structures. (p. 31)

**mountain man** *n.* a fur trapper or explorer who opened up the West by finding the best trails through the Rocky Mountains. (p. 393)

**muckraker** *n.* around 1900, the term for a journalist who exposed corruption in American society. (p. 640)

**Muslim** (MUZ luhm) *n.* a follower of Islam. (p. 41)

# N

**nationalism** *n.* a feeling of pride, loyalty, and protectiveness toward one's country. (p. 354)

**nativist** *n.* a native-born American who wanted to eliminate foreign influence. (p. 428)

**natural-born citizen** *n.* a citizen born in the United States or a commonwealth of the United States or to parents who are U.S. citizens living outside the country. (p. 257)

**naturalization** *n.* a way to give full citizenship to a person born in another country. (pp. 253, 270)

**Navigation Acts** *n.* a series of laws passed by Parliament, beginning in 1651, to ensure that England made money from its colonies' trade. (p. 112)

**navigator** *n.* a person who plans the course of a ship while at sea. (p. 49)

**Nazi** (NAHT see) **Party** *n.* the National Socialist German Workers' Party; came to power under Adolf Hitler in the 1930s. (p. 712)

**neutral** (NOO truhl) *adj.* not siding with one country or the other. (p. 302)

**neutrality** (noo TRAL i tee) *n.* refusing to take sides in a war. (p. 682)

**New Deal** *n.* President Franklin Roosevelt's programs to fight the Great Depression. (p. 710)

**New France** *n.* a fur-trading post established in 1608 that became the first permanent French settlement in North America. (p. 70)

**new immigrant** *n.* a person from southern or eastern Europe who entered the United States after 1900. (p. 614)

**New Jersey Plan** *n.* a plan of government proposed at the Constitutional Convention in 1787 that called for a one-house legislature in which each state would have one vote. (p. 231)

**Nineteenth Amendment** *n.* an amendment to the U.S. Constitution, ratified in 1920, which gave women full voting rights. (p. 653)

**Northwest Ordinance** *n.* it described how the Northwest Territory was to be governed and set conditions for settlement and settlers' rights. (p. 223)

**Northwest Territory** *n.* territory covered by the Land Ordinance of 1785, which included land that formed the states of Ohio, Indiana, Michigan, Illinois, Wisconsin, and part of Minnesota. (p. 223)

**Open Door Policy** *n.* in 1899, the United States asked nations involved in Asia to follow a policy in which no one country controlled trade with China. (p. 669)

**Oregon Trail** *n.* a trail that ran westward from Independence, Missouri, to the Oregon Territory. (p. 396)

**overseer** *n.* a worker hired by a planter to watch over and direct the work of slaves. (p. 122)

**pacifist** (PAS uh fist) *n.* a person morally opposed to war. (p. 209)

**Palmer raids** *n.* in 1920, federal agents and police raided the homes of suspected radicals. (p. 697)

**Panama** (PAN uh MAH) **Canal** *n.* a shortcut through Panama that connects the Atlantic and the Pacific oceans. (p. 670)

**Panic of 1837** *n.* a financial crisis in which banks closed and the credit system collapsed. (p. 386)

**Panic of 1873** *n.* a financial crisis in which banks closed and the stock market collapsed. (p. 547)

**Parliament** (PAHR luh muhnt) *n.* England's chief law-making body. (p. 142)

**patent** *n.* a government document giving an inventor the exclusive right to make or sell his or her invention for a specific number of years. (p. 586)

**Patriot** *n.* an American colonist who sided with the rebels in the American Revolution. (p. 173)

**patroon** (puh TROON) *n.* a person who brought 50 settlers to New Netherland and in return received a large land grant and other special privileges. (p. 101)

**petroleum** *n.* an oily, flammable liquid. (p. 585)

**philanthropist** (fil LAN thruh pist) *n.* a person who gives large sums of money to charities. (p. 596)

**Pickett's Charge** *n.* General George Pickett led a direct attack on Union troops during the 1863 Civil War battle at Gettysburg; the attack failed. (p. 513)

**piedmont** *n.* a broad plateau that leads to the foot of a mountain range. (p. 126)

**Pilgrim** *n.* a member of the group that rejected the Church of England, sailed to America, and founded the Plymouth Colony in 1620. (p. 92)

**Pinckney's** (PINGK neez) **Treaty** *n.* a 1795 treaty with Spain that allowed Americans to use the Mississippi River and to store goods in New Orleans; made the 31st parallel the southern U.S. border. (p. 302)

**plantation** *n.* a large farm that raises cash crops. (p. 73)

**platform** *n.* a statement of beliefs. (p. 471)

**Platt Amendment** *n.* a result of the Spanish-American War, which gave the United States the right to intervene in Cuban affairs when there was a threat to "life, property, and individual liberty." (p. 666)

**Plessy v. Ferguson** *n.* an 1896 case in which the Supreme Court ruled that separation of the races in public accommodations was legal. (p. 621)

**political machine** *n.* an organization that influences enough votes to control a local government. (p. 613)

**political party** *n.* a group of people that tries to promote its ideas and influence government, and also backs candidates for office. (p. 304)

**Pontiac's** (PON tee AKS) **Rebellion** *n.* a revolt against British forts and American settlers in 1763, led in part by Ottawa war leader Pontiac, in response to settlers' claims of Native American lands and to harsh treatment by British soldiers. (p. 151)

**popular sovereignty** (SOV uhr in tee) *n.* a government in which the people rule (p. 244); a system in which the residents vote to decide an issue. (p. 463)

**Populist Party** *n.* also known as the People's Party and formed in the 1890s, this group wanted a policy that would raise crop prices. (p. 577)

**prejudice** (PREJ uh dis) *n.* a negative opinion that is not based on facts. (p. 427)

**printing press** *n.* a machine invented about 1455 by Johannes Gutenberg. (p. 47)

**privateer** (PRY vuh TEER) *n.* a privately owned ship that has government permission during wartime to attack an enemy's merchant ships. (p. 204)

**Proclamation** (PRAHK luh MAY shuhn) **of 1763** *n.* an order in which Britain prohibited its American colonists from settling west of the Appalachian Mountains. (p. 151)

**profit** *n.* money a business makes, after subtracting the costs of doing business from the income. (p. 48)

**progressivism** (pruh GREHS ih VIHZ uhm) *n.* an early 20th-century reform movement seeking to return control of the government to the people, to restore economic opportunities, and to correct injustices in American life. (p. 639)

**propaganda** (PRAHP uh GAN duh) *n.* an opinion expressed for the purpose of influencing the actions of others. (p. 692)

**proprietary** (pruh PRY ih TEHR ee) **colony** *n.* a colony with a single owner. (p. 101)

**pro tempore** (proh TEHM puh ree) *adv.* Latin phrase meaning "for the time being." (p. 250)

**Pullman Strike** *n.* a nationwide railway strike that spread throughout the rail industry in 1894. (p. 603)

**Puritan** *n.* a member of a group from England that settled the Massachusetts Bay Colony in 1630 and sought to reform the practices of the Church of England. (p. 94)

**push-pull factor** *n.* a factor that pushes people out of their native lands and pulls them toward a new place. (p. 424)

**Quaker** (KWAY kuhr) *n.* a person who believed all people should live in peace and harmony; accepted different religions and ethnic groups. (p. 101)

**quarter** *v.* to give a place to stay. (p. 267)

**Quartering Act** *n.* a law passed by Parliament in 1765 that required the colonies to house and supply British soldiers. (p. 160)

**quorum** (KWAWR uhm) *n.* the minimum number of members that must be present for official business to take place. (p. 251)

**racial** (RAY shuhl) **discrimination** (dih SKRIHM uh NAY shuhn) *n.* different treatment based on a person's race. (p. 620)

**racism** (RAY SIHZ uhm) *n.* the belief that some people are inferior because of their race. (p. 79)

**radical** (RAD ih kuhl) *n.* a person who takes extreme political positions. (p. 313)

**Radical Republican** (rih PUHB lih kuhn) *n.* a congressman who, after the Civil War, favored using the government to create a new order in the South and to give African Americans full citizenship and the right to vote. (p. 533)

**ragtime** *n.* a blend of African-American songs and European musical forms. (p. 629)

**ratification** (RAT uh fih KAY shuhn) *n.* official approval. (p. 264)

**recall** *v.* to vote an official out of office. (p. 640)

**Reconstruction** *n.* the process the U.S. government used to readmit the Confederate states to the Union after the Civil War. (p. 533)

**Red Scare** *n.* in 1919–1920, a wave of panic from fear of a Communist revolution. (p. 697)

**referendum** (REHF uh REHN duhm) *n.* when a proposed law is submitted to a vote of the people. (p. 640)

**Reformation** *n.* a 16th-century religious movement to correct problems in the Roman Catholic Church. (p. 47)

**Renaissance** (REHN ih SAHNS) *n.* a period of European history, lasting from the 1300s to 1600, that brought increased interest in art and learning. (p. 46)

**rendezvous** (RAHN day VOO) *n.* a meeting. (p. 197)

**reprieve** (rih PREEV) *n.* a delay or cancellation of punishment. (p. 259)

**republic** (rih PUHB lihk) *n.* a government in which people elect representatives to govern for them. (p. 222)

**republicanism** (rih PUHB lih keh NIHZ uhm) *n.* the belief that government should be based on the consent of the people; people exercise their power by voting for political representatives. (pp. 214, 245)

**Republican Party** *n.* the political party formed in 1854 by opponents of slavery in the territories. (p. 466)

**reservation** *n.* land set aside by the U.S. government for Native American tribes. (p. 562)

**revenue** (REHV uh noo) *n.* income a government collects to cover expenses. (pp. 160, 252)

**revival** (rih VY vuhl) *n.* a meeting designed to reawaken religious faith. (p. 433)

**rifle** *n.* a gun with a grooved barrel that causes a bullet to spin through the air. (p. 491)

**robber baron** *n.* a business leader who became wealthy through dishonest methods. (p. 594)

**romanticism** (roh MAN tih SIHZ uhm) *n.* a European artistic movement that stressed the individual, imagination, creativity, and emotion. (p. 429)

**Roosevelt Corollary** (KAWR uh lehr ee) *n.* a 1904 addition to the Monroe Doctrine allowing the United States to be the "policeman" in Latin America. (p. 672)

**Rough Rider** *n.* a member of the First United States Volunteer Cavalry, organized by Theodore Roosevelt during the Spanish-American War. (p. 665)

**royal colony** *n.* a colony ruled by governors appointed by a king. (p. 103)

**salutary** (SAL yuh TEHR ee) **neglect** *n.* a hands-off policy of England toward its American colonies during the first half of the 1700s. (p. 144)

**Sand Creek Massacre** (MAS uh kuhr) *n.* an 1864 attack in which more than 150 Cheyenne men, women, and children were killed by the Colorado militia. (p. 564)

**Santa Fe** (SAN tuh FAY) **Trail** *n.* a trail that began in Missouri and ended in Santa Fe, New Mexico. (p. 395)

**secede** (sih SEED) *v.* to withdraw. (p. 473)

**secession** (sih SEHSH uhn) *n.* withdrawal. (p. 383)

**Second Battle of the Marne** (mahrn) *n.* a 1918 battle during World War I that marked the turning point in the war; allied troops along with Americans halted the German advance into France. (p. 689)

**Second Continental Congress** *n.* a governing body whose delegates agreed, in May 1775, to form the Continental Army and to approve the Declaration of Independence. (p. 177)

**Second Great Awakening** *n.* the renewal of religious faith in the 1790s and early 1800s. (p. 433)

**sectionalism** (SEHK shuh nuh LIHZ uhm) *n.* the placing of the interests of one's own region ahead of the interests of the nation as a whole. (p. 357)

**Sedition** (sih DIHSH uhn) **Act** *n.* a 1918 law that made it illegal to criticize the war; it set heavy fines and long prison terms for those who engaged in antiwar activities. (p. 692)

**segregation** (SEHG rih GAY shuhn) *n.* separation, especially of races. (p. 621)

**Seneca** (SEHN ih kuh) **Falls Convention** *n.* a women's rights convention held in Seneca Falls, New York, in 1848. (p. 444)

**separation of powers** *n.* the division of basic government roles into branches. (p. 246)

**servitude** (SUR vih TOOD) *n.* a state of belonging to an owner or master. (p. 270)

**Seven Days' Battles** *n.* an 1862 Civil War battle in which the Confederacy forced the Union to retreat before it could capture the Southern capital of Richmond. (p. 496)

**Seventeenth Amendment** *n.* an amendment to the U.S. Constitution, ratified in 1913, that provided for the direct election of U.S. senators. (p. 648)

**sharecropping** *n.* a system in which landowners gave farm workers land, seed, and tools in return for a part of the crops they raised. (p. 543)

**Shays's** (SHAY zuhz) **Rebellion** *n.* an uprising of debt-ridden Massachusetts farmers in 1787. (p. 225)

**Sherman Antitrust Act** *n.* a law passed in 1890 that made it illegal for corporations to gain control of industries by forming trusts. (p. 641)

**Siege** (seej) **of Vicksburg** *n.* an 1863 Union victory in the Civil War that enabled the Union to control the entire Mississippi River. (p. 516)

**Sixteenth Amendment** *n.* an amendment to the U.S. Constitution, ratified in 1913, that gave Congress the power to create income taxes. (p. 647)

**slash-and-burn agriculture** (ag rih kuhl chuhr) *n.* a farming method in which people clear fields by cutting and burning trees and grasses, the ashes of which fertilize the soil. (p. 37)

**slave code** *n.* a law passed to regulate the treatment of slaves. (p. 79)

**slavery** *n.* the practice of holding a person in bondage for labor. (p. 76)

**slum** *n.* a neighborhood with overcrowded and dangerous housing. (p. 612)

**smuggle** *v.* to illegally import or export goods. (p. 112)

**social gospel** (GAHS puhl) *n.* a movement aimed at improving the lives of the poor. (p. 612)

**socialism** *n.* an economic system in which all members of a society are equal owners of all businesses; members share the work and the profits. (p. 602)

**sodbuster** *n.* a farmer on the frontier. (p. 575)

**Songhai** (SAWNG HY) *n.* a West African empire that succeeded Mali and controlled trade from the 1400s to 1591. (p. 42)

**Sons of Liberty** *n.* a group of colonists who formed a secret society to oppose British policies at the time of the American Revolution. (p. 161)

**Spanish-American War** *n.* a war in 1898 that began when the United States demanded Cuba's independence from Spain. (p. 664)

**Spanish Armada** (ahr MAH duh) *n.* a fleet of ships sent in 1588 by Philip II, the Spanish king, to invade England and restore Roman Catholicism. (p. 69)

**sphere of influence** *n.* an area where foreign nations claim special rights and economic privileges. (p. 669)

**spiritual** *n.* a religious folk song. (p. 351)

**spoils system** *n.* the practice of winning candidates giving government jobs to political backers or supporters. (p. 373)

**Stamp Act** *n.* a 1765 law passed by Parliament that required all legal and commercial documents to carry an official stamp showing a tax had been paid. (p. 160)

**standard time** *n.* a system adopted in 1918 that divided the United States into four time zones. (p. 592)

**states' rights** *n.* theory that said that states had the right to judge when the federal government had passed an unconstitutional law. (p. 307)

**steerage** *n.* the cheapest deck or place on a ship. (p. 423)

**Stono** (STOH noh) **Rebellion** *n.* a 1739 uprising of slaves in South Carolina, leading to the tightening of already harsh slave laws. (p. 123)

**strategy** *n.* an overall plan of action. (p. 196)

**strike** *v.* to stop work to demand better working conditions. (p. 434)

**subsistence farm** *n.* a farm that produces enough food for the family with a small additional amount for trade. (p. 110)

**suffrage** *n.* the right to vote. (pp. 262, 444)

**Sugar Act** *n.* a law passed by Parliament in 1764 that placed a tax on sugar, molasses, and other products shipped to the colonies; also called for harsh punishment of smugglers. (p. 160)

**sweatshop** *n.* a place where workers labored long hours under poor conditions for low wages. (p. 600)

**T**

**Tammany** (TAM uh nee) **Hall** *n.* a famous political machine, located in New York City in the late 19th century. (p. 613)

**tariff** *n.* a tax on imported goods. (p. 296)

**Tariff of Abominations** *n.* an 1828 law that raised the tariffs on raw materials and manufactured goods; it upset Southerners who felt that economic interests of the Northeast were determining national economic policy. (p. 381)

**technology** *n.* the use of tools and knowledge to meet human needs. (p. 32)

**Tejano** (tuh HAH noh) *n.* a person of Spanish heritage who considered Texas to be home. (p. 400)

**temperance movement** *n.* a campaign to stop the drinking of alcohol. (p. 434)

**tender** *n.* money. (p. 255)

**tenement** *n.* an apartment building that is usually run-down and overcrowded. (p. 611)

**Thirteenth Amendment** *n.* an amendment to the U.S. Constitution, adopted in 1865, banning slavery and involuntary servitude in the United States. (p. 521)

**Three-Fifths Compromise** *n.* the Constitutional Convention's agreement to count three-fifths of a state's slaves as population for purposes of representation and taxation. (p. 232)

**Townshend** (TOWN zuhnd) **Acts** *n.* a series of laws passed by Parliament in 1767 that suspended New York's assembly and established taxes on goods brought into the British colonies. (p. 163)

**Trail of Tears** *n.* the tragic journey of the Cherokee people from their homeland to Indian Territory between 1838 and 1839; thousands of Cherokee died. (p. 377)

**transcendentalism** (TRAN sen DEN tl IZ uhm) *n.* a 19th-century philosophy that taught the spiritual world is more important than the physical world and that people can find truth within themselves through feeling and intuition. (p. 431)

**transcontinental** (TRANS kon tuh NEN tl) **railroad** *n.* a railroad that spanned the entire continent. (p. 590)

**Treaty of Ghent** (gent) *n.* treaty, signed in 1814, which ended the War of 1812; no territory exchanged hands and trade disputes were not resolved. (p. 333)

**Treaty of Greenville** *n.* a 1795 agreement in which 12 Native American tribes surrendered much of present-day Ohio and Indiana to the U.S. government. (p. 300)

**Treaty of Guadalupe Hidalgo** (GWAHD loop hi DAH goh) *n.* the 1848 treaty ending the U.S. war with Mexico; Mexico ceded nearly one-half of its land to the United States. (p. 410)

**Treaty of Paris** *n.* the 1763 treaty that ended the French and Indian War; Britain gave up all of North America east of the Mississippi River. (p. 150)

**Treaty of Paris of 1783** *n.* the treaty that ended the Revolutionary War, confirming the independence of the United States and setting the boundaries of the new nation. (p. 212)

**Treaty of Tordesillas** (TAWR duh SEE uhs) *n.* the 1494 treaty in which Spain and Portugal agreed to divide the lands of the Western Hemisphere between them and moved the Line of Demarcation to the west. (p. 61)

**Treaty of Versailles** (vuhr SY) *n.* the 1919 treaty that ended World War I. (p. 696)

**trench warfare** *n.* a kind of warfare during World War I in which troops huddled at the bottom of trenches and fired artillery and machine guns at each other. (p. 680)

**triangular trade** *n.* the transatlantic system of trade in which goods, including slaves, were exchanged between Africa, England, Europe, the West Indies, and the colonies in North America. (p. 111)

**tribunal** (try BYOO nuhl) *n.* a court. (p. 253)

**trust** *n.* a legal body created to hold stock in many companies, often in the same industry. (p. 595)

**tundra** (TUN druh) *n.* a treeless plain that remains frozen under its top layer of soil. (p. 33)

## U

**unanimous** (yoo NAN uh muhs) **consent** *n.* complete agreement. (p. 264)

**Uncle Tom's Cabin** *n.* a novel published by Harriet Beecher Stowe in 1852 that portrayed slavery as brutal and immoral. (p. 462)

**unconstitutional** *n.* something that contradicts the law of the Constitution. (p. 317)

**Underground Railroad** *n.* a series of escape routes used by slaves escaping the South. (p. 442)

**urbanization** *n.* growth of cities resulting from industrialization. (p. 609)

**U.S.S. *Maine*** *n.* a U.S. warship that mysteriously exploded and sank in the harbor of Havana, Cuba, on February 15, 1898. (p. 663)

## V

**vaquero** (vah KAIR oh) *n.* a cowhand that came from Mexico with the Spaniards in the 1500s. (p. 560)

**vaudeville** (VAWD vil) *n.* a form of live stage entertainment with a mixture of songs, dance, and comedy. (p. 629)

**viceroyalty** (VYS ROI uhl tee) *n.* a province ruled by a viceroy, who ruled in the king's name. (p. 71)

**Vietnam War** (vee ET NAHM) *n.* a military conflict from 1957 to 1975 between the North Vietnam Communists and the non-Communist forces of South Vietnam supported by the United States. (p. 719)

**vigilante** (vij uh LAN tee) *n.* a person willing to take the law into his or her own hands. (p. 561)

**Virginia Plan** *n.* a plan proposed by Edmund Randolph, a delegate to the Constitutional Convention in 1787, that proposed a government with three branches and a two-house legislature in which representation would be based on a state's population or wealth. (p. 231)

## W

**war bond** *n.* a low-interest loan by civilians to the government, meant to be repaid in a number of years. (p. 691)

**War Hawk** *n.* a westerner who supported the War of 1812. (p. 329)

**Watergate scandal** *n.* a scandal resulting from the Nixon administration's attempt to cover up its involvement in the 1972 break-in at the Democratic National Committee headquarters in the Watergate apartment complex in Washington, D.C. (p. 720)

**Webster-Hayne debate** *n.* an 1830 debate between Daniel Webster and Robert Hayne over the doctrine of nullification. (p. 382)

**Whig** (hwig) **Party** *n.* a political party organized in 1834 to oppose the policies of Andrew Jackson. (p. 387)

**Whiskey Rebellion** *n.* a 1794 protest against the government's tax on whiskey, which was valuable to the livelihood of backcountry farmers. (p. 301)

**Wilderness Road** *n.* the trail into Kentucky that woodsman Daniel Boone helped to build. (p. 221)

**Wilmot** (WIL muht) **Proviso** (pruh VY zoh) *n.* an 1846 proposal that outlawed slavery in any territory gained from the War with Mexico. (p. 459)

**World War II** *n.* a war fought from 1939 to 1945, in which Great Britain, France, the Soviet Union, the United States, and other allies defeated Germany, Italy, and Japan. (p. 713)

**Wounded Knee Massacre** *n.* the massacre by U.S. soldiers of 300 unarmed Native Americans at Wounded Knee Creek, South Dakota, in 1890. (p. 566)

**writ** (rit) **of assistance** *n.* a search warrant that allowed British officers to enter colonial homes or businesses to search for smuggled goods. (p. 164)

## X

**XYZ Affair** *n.* a 1797 incident in which French officials demanded a bribe from U.S. diplomats. (p. 306)

## Y

**yellow journalism** *n.* a style of journalism that exaggerates and sensationalizes the news. (p. 663)

**Yoruba** (YOH roo bah) *n.* a West African people who formed several states southwest of the Niger River. (p. 42)

## Z

**Zimmermann telegram** *n.* a message sent in 1917 by the German foreign minister to the German ambassador in Mexico, proposing a German-Mexican alliance and promising to help Mexico regain Texas, New Mexico, and Arizona if the United States entered World War I. (p. 682)

**abolition** [abolición] *s.* movimiento para eliminar la esclavitud. (p. 440)

**abridge** [abreviar] *v.* reducir. (p. 266)

**AEF** *s.* Fuerza Expedicionaria Estadounidense, fuerzas de EE. UU. durante la primera guerra mundial. (p. 686)

**affirmation** [afirmación] *s.* declaración de que algo es cierto. (p. 257)

**African Diaspora** [diáspora africana] *s.* traslado forzado de los africanos, desde su patria a las Américas para trabajar allí como esclavos. (p. 78)

**Albany Plan of Union** [Plan de la Unión de Albany] *s.* primera propuesta formal para unir las colonias norteamericanas, presentado por Benjamín Franklin. (p. 149)

**Alien and Sedition Acts** [leyes de Extranjeros y Sedición] *s.* serie de cuatro leyes promulgadas en 1798 para reducir el poder político de inmigrantes recién llegados a Estados Unidos. (p. 306)

**allies** [aliados] *s.* alianza de Serbia, Rusia, Francia, Gran Bretaña, Italia y otros siete países durante la primera guerra mundial. (p. 680)

**ally** [aliado] *s.* país que acuerda ayudar a otro país a alcanzar un objetivo común. (p. 200)

**American Federation of Labor (AFL)** [Federación Norteamericana del Trabajo] *s.* organización nacional de sindicatos obreros fundada en 1886. (p. 603)

**American System** [Sistema Americano] *s.* plan presentado en 1815 para hacer autosuficiente a Estados Unidos. (p. 354)

**Anaconda Plan** [Plan Anaconda] *s.* estrategia de tres pasos mediante la cual la Unión se proponía derrotar a la Confederación durante la guerra civil estadounidense. (p. 484)

**Angel Island** [isla del Ángel] *s.* primera parada en Estados Unidos para la mayoría de los inmigrantes que venían de Asia. (p. 615)

**Antifederalist** [antifederalista] *s.* persona que se oponía a la ratificación de la Constitución de los Estados Unidos. (p. 234)

**Anti-Imperialist League** [Liga Antiimperialista] *s.* grupo de estadounidenses importantes que creían que Estados Unidos no debía negarle a otras personas el derecho de gobernarse a sí mismas. (p. 667)

**Appalachian Mountains** [montes Apalaches] *s.* cadena de montañas que se extiende desde el este de Canadá hacia el sur, hasta Alabama. (p. 126)

**appellate** [de apelación] *adj.* que tiene el poder de reexaminar decisiones de las cortes. (p. 260)

**Appomattox Court House** [Appomattox] *s.* pueblo de Virginia donde Robert E. Lee se rindió a Ulysses s. Grant en 1865, finalizando así la guerra civil. (p. 519)

**apprentice** [aprendiz] *s.* joven que aprende un oficio o una artesanía de un maestro experto. (p. 137)

**appropiation** [apropiación] *s.* fondos públicos que se reservan para un propósito específico. (p. 253)

**archaeologist** [arqueólogo] *s.* científico que estudia el pasado humano examinando artículos que dejó la gente. (p. 27)

**armistice** [armisticio] *s.* suspención de la lucha en una guerra. (p. 690)

**Articles of Confederation** [Artículos de Confederación] *s.* documento, adoptado por el Congreso Continental en 1777 y finalmente aprobado por los estados en 1781, que delineaba la forma de gobierno de los nuevos Estados Unidos. (p. 222)

**artifact** [artefacto] *s.* herramienta u otro artículo hecho por seres humanos. (p. 27)

**artillery** [artillería] *s.* cañon o arma grande. (p. 177)

**artisan** [artesano] *s.* obrero especializado, como un tejedor a telar o un alfarero, que hace artículos a mano; artífice. (p. 117)

**assimilation** [asimilación] *s.* proceso de integrarse a una sociedad. (p. 616)

**baby boom** *s.* término para la generación que nació en Estados Unidos entre 1946 y 1961, cuando el índice de natalidad aumentó marcadamente después de la segunda guerra mundial. (p. 722)

**Backcountry** [tierras fronterizas] *s.* región colonial que se extendía a lo largo de los montes Apalaches a través de la sección oeste de Nueva Inglaterra y las colonias del centro y del sur. (p. 109)

**Bacon's Rebellion** [Rebelión de Bacon] *s.* levantamiento contra la poderosa autoridad colonial de Jamestown por Nathaniel Bacon y un grupo de habitantes de la frontera que resultó en la quema de Jamestown en 1676. (p. 89)

**bail** [fianza] *s.* dinero que pagan como fianza las personas arrestadas para garantizar que van a regresar para el juicio. (p. 268)

**Battle of Antietam** [batalla de Antietam] *s.* batalla de la guerra civil, en 1862, en que murieron o resultaron heridos 25,000 hombres. (p. 497)

**Battle of Fallen Timbers** *s.* en 1794 el ejército estadounidense derrotó a 2,000 amerindios en un enfrentamiento por el control del territorio del Noroeste. (p. 299)

**Battle of Gettysburg** [batalla de Gettysburg) *s.* batalla de 1863 de la guerra civil en que la Unión derrotó a la Confederación, poniendo fin a la esperanza de una victoria confederada en el Norte. (p. 513)

**Battle of Quebec** [batalla de Quebec] *s.* batalla en la que los británicos derrotaron a los franceses y cambio decisivo en la guerra Francesa y Amerindia. (p. 150)

**Battle of Shiloh** [batalla de Shiloh] *s.* batalla de 1862 en que la Unión obligó a la Confederación a retroceder; fue una de las batallas más encarnizadas de la guerra civil. (p. 494)

**Battle of Yorktown** [batalla de Yorktown] *s.* última batalla importante de la guerra Revolucionaria que resultó en la capitulación de las fuerzas británicas en 1781. (p. 210)

**Battle of the Alamo** [batalla de El Álamo] *s.* en 1836 los texanos defendieron contra el ejército mexicano una misión llamada El Álamo; sobrevivieron sólo cinco texanos (p. 403)

**Battle of the Little Bighorn** [batalla del Little Bighorn] *s.* batalla de 1876 en que los sioux y los cheyennes aniquilaron toda una partida militar estadounidense. (p. 565)

**Battle of the Thames** [batalla de Thames] *s.* victoria estadounidense sobre los británicos en la guerra de 1812 que puso fin a la amenaza británica en el Territorio del Noroeste. (p. 332)

**Battles of Saratoga** [batallas de Saratoga] *s.* serie de conflictos en 1777, entre soldados británicos y el Ejército Continental que resultó en un cambio decisivo en la guerra Revolucionaria. (p. 199)

**bayonet** [bayoneta] *s.* largo cuchillo de acero colocado en el extremo de un arma de fuego. (p. 202)

**Bear Flag Revolt** [revuelta de la Bandera del Oso] *s.* rebelión de 1846 por los estadounidenses contra el dominio mexicano en California. (p. 409)

**Benin** [Benín] *s.* reino de África Occidental que se estableció cerca del delta del río Níger en el siglo XIV y se transformó en un estado importante en el siglo XV. (p. 43)

**Bessemer steel process** [proceso siderúrgico Bessemer] *s.* manera nueva de producir acero desarrollada hacia 1850 que causó un gran incremento en la producción side rúrgica. (p. 587)

**bill of attainder** [decreto de proscripción] *s.* ley que condena a una persona sin juicio ante un tribunal. (p. 255)

**Bill of Rights** [Carta de Derechos] *s.* diez primeras enmiendas a la Constitución de Estados Unidos, adoptadas en 1791, que consisten en una lista formal de los derechos y libertades de los ciudadanos. (p. 237)

**black code** [código negro] *s.* ley pasada por los estados sureños que limitaba la libertad de los antiguos esclavos. (p. 534)

**blockade** [bloqueo] *s.* acción de las fuerzas armadas que impide la entrada o salida de mercaderías o personas. (p.484)

**boomtown** [pueblo en auge] *s.* pueblo que tiene una explosión repentina de crecimiento económico o demográfico. (p. 558)

**border state** [estado fronterizo] *s.* estados esclavistas fronterizos a estados en que la esclavitud era ilegal. (p. 482)

**Boston Massacre** [Matanza de Boston] *s.* choque en 1770 entre soldados británicos y colonos de Boston en que perecieron cinco de los colonistas, incluso Crispus Attucks. (p. 165)

**Boston Tea Party** [Motín del Té de Boston] *s.* como protesta contra el Acta del té, en 1773 los colonos arrojaron al puerto de Boston 342 cajones de té. (p. 167)

**bounty** [gratificación] *s.* recompensa o pago en dinero que da un gobierno. (pp. 271, 508)

**Boxer Rebellion** [Rebelión bóxer] *s.* en 1900 el resentimiento chino contra la actitud de superioridad cultural de los extranjeros resultó en este violento levantamiento. (p. 669)

**boycott** [boicot] *v.* negarse a comprar ciertos productos. (p. 161)

**buck** [ciervo] gamuza obtenida de la piel de un ciervo adulto, o unidad de dinero de los colonos. (p. 127)

**buffalo soldier** [soldado búfalo] *s.* apodo que los amerindios les dieron a los afroamericanos que servían en el ejército estadounidense del oeste. (p. 570)

**business cycle** [ciclo económico] *s.* serie de períodos de la economía buenos y malos. (p. 586)

**cabinet** [gabinete ministerial] *s.* grupo de ministros que actúan como los asesores princpales del presidente. (p. 294)

**California gold rush** [fiebre del oro de California] *s.* en 1849 gran cantidad de gente se fue a California porque allí se había descubierto oro. (p. 413)

**caravel** [carabela] *s.* barco con velas triangulares que le permitían navegar hacia el viento y con velas cuadradas que lo llevaban hacia delante cuando soplaba viento en popa. (p. 49)

**cash crop** [cultivo comercial] *s.* cultivo que produce un agricultor para venderlo por dinero y no para su uso personal. (p. 115)

**cavalry** [caballería] *s.* soldados montados a caballo. (p. 496)

**Centennial Exhibition** [Exposición del Centenario] *s.* exposición de 1876 en Filadelfia que celebró el centésimo cumpleaños de Estados Unidos. (p. 588)

**Central Powers** [Potencias Centrales] *s.* alianza de Austria-Hungría, Alemania, el Imperio otomano y Bulgaria durante la primera guerra mundial. (p. 680)

**charter** [cédula] *s.* contrato escrito que concede un gobierno otorgando al que lo recibe el derecho a establecer una colonia. (p. 87)

**checks and balances** [frenos y cortapisas] *s.* capacidad de cada rama del gobierno de usar frenos o controles sobre las otras ramas. (p. 246)

**Chinese Exclusion Act** [ley de Exclusión para chinos] *s.* aprobada en 1882, esta ley prohibía la inmigración china por diez años. (p. 617)

**civil disobedience** [desobediencia civil] *s.* negarse pacíficamente a obedecer leyes que uno considera injustas. (p. 431)

**civilization** [civilización] *s.* forma de cultura caracterizada por ciudades con centros de comercio, trabajadores especializados, formas de gobierno y religión organizadas, sistemas de mantener registros, y herramientas avanzadas. (p. 29)

**civil rights** [derechos civiles] *s.* derecho otorgado a todos los ciudadanos. (p. 535)

**clan** [clan] *s.* grupo grande de familias procedentes de un antepasado común. (p. 127)

**Clayton Antitrust Act** [ley Anti-trust Clayton] *s.* ley aprobada en 1914 que establecía reglas que prohibían prácticas comerciales que disminuyeran la competencia y le daba al gobierno más poder para reglamentar los trusts. (p. 648)

**Cold War** [guerra fría] *s.* estado de hostilidad, sin conflicto militar directo, que se desarrolló entre Estados Unidos y la Unión Soviética después de la segunda guerra mundial. (p. 717)

**Columbian Exchange** [transferencia colombina] *s.* transferencia de plantas, animales y enfermedades entre el hemisferio occidental y el oriental. (p. 74)

**committee of correspondence** [comité de correspondencia] *s.* grupo de personas de las colonias que se intercambiaban cartas sobre asuntos coloniales. (p. 166)

**Committee to Reelect the President** [Comité de Reelección del Presidente] *s.* organización cuya conexión con el allanamiento de la Sede Central del Partido Demócrata hizo estallar el escándalo Watergate. (p. 860)

**common law** [derecho consuetudinario] *s.* sistema de leyes desarrollado en Inglaterra, basado en costumbres y decisiones jurídicas anteriores. (p. 268)

**Compromise of 1850** [Acuerdo de 1850] *s.* serie de medidas del Congreso para resolver los desacuerdos principales entre los estados libres y los esclavistas. (p. 461)

**Compromise of 1877** [Acuerdo de 1877] *s.* acuerdo que resolvió la disputa sobre las elecciones de 1876: se declaró presidente a Rutherford B. Hayes, quien entonces retiró las tropas federales que quedaban en el Sur. (p. 548)

**compulsory process** [proceso obligatorio] *s.* procedimiento requerido. (p. 267)

**Conestoga wagon** [carreta conestoga] *s.* vehículo que tenía ruedas anchas, caja de carro curvada y capota de lona y se usaba para transportar gente y artículos. (p. 117)

**Confederate States of America** [Estados Confederados de América] *s.* confederación constituida en 1861 por los estados sureños después de separarse de la Unión. (p. 473)

**conquistador** [conquistador] *s.* español que en el siglo XVI viajó a las Américas para explorar y conquistar. (p. 63)

**conscription** [conscripción] *s.* ley que requería que los hombres sirvieran en las fuerzas armadas o que fueran reclutados. (p. 508)

**Constitutional Convention** [Convención Constitucional] *s.* reunión realizada en 1787 para considerar cambios a los Artículos de Confederación, que resultó en la redacción de la Constitución. (p. 229)

**containment** [contención] *s.* bloqueo de una nación en la expansión de la influencia de otras naciones, especialmente los esfuerzos de Estados Unidos por bloquear la expansión de la influencia soviética hacia fines de los años cuarenta y comienzos de los cincuenta. (p. 718)

**Continental Army** [Ejército Continental] *s.* fuerzas coloniales autorizadas en 1775 por el segundo Congreso Continental, con George Washington como su comandante en jefe. (p. 177)

**convene** [convocar] *v.* llamar a reunión. (p. 259)

**convoy system** [sistema de convoyes] *s.* fuerte flotilla de destructores que escolta a los barcos mercantes durante épocas de guerra. (p. 687)

**cooperative** [cooperativa] *s.* organización propiedad de los asociados que la dirigen. (p. 577)

**Copperheads** [víboras cobrizas] *s.* los principales adversarios políticos de Abraham Lincoln; abogaban por la paz con el Sur. (p. 508)

**corporation** [corporación] *s.* empresa propiedad de inversionistas que compran parte de la compañía mediante acciones. (p. 594)

**cotton gin** [desmontadora de algodón] *s.* máquina inventada en 1793 que limpiaba el algodón con mucha más rapidez y eficiencia que los obreros humanos. (p. 348)

**counterculture** [contracultura] *s.* grupo de jóvenes con valores morales y modos de vida contrarios a los de la cultura establecida. (p. 725)

**Crittenden Plan** [Plan de Crittenden] *s.* acuerdo presentado en 1861 que podría haber evitado la secesión. (p. 475)

**Crusades** [cruzadas] *s.* serie de guerras para capturar la Tierra Santa, iniciada en 1096 por cristianos europeos. (p. 45)

**culture** [cultura] *s.* manera de vida compartida por gente que tiene artes, creencias y costumbres semejantes. (p. 28)

**Dawes Act** [ley Dawes] *s.* ley, aprobada en 1887, que distribuía la tierra de las reservas amerindias a dueños individuales. (p. 567)

**Declaration of Independence** [Declaración de Independencia] *s.* documento, escrito en 1776, en que las colonias declararon su independendia de Gran Bretaña. (p. 180)

**department store** [almacén departamental] *s.* tienda que vende de todo, desde ropa a muebles a artículos de ferretería. (p. 627)

**depression** [depresión] *s.* aguda crisis económica. (p. 386)

**desert** [desertar] *v.* abandonar el servicio militar sin intenciones de regresar. (p. 203)

**direct primary** [elecciones primarias directas] *s.* el electorado, y no las convenciones de partido, eligen a los candidatos para los cargos públicos. (p. 640)

**diversity** [diversidad] *s.* variedad de gente. (p. 117)

**doctrine of nullification** [doctrina de la invalidación] *s.* derecho de un estado a rechazar una ley federal que considerase inconstitucional. (p. 381)

**domestication** [domesticación] *s.* práctica de criar plantas o amansar animales para satisfacer las necesidades humanas. (p. 28)

***Dred Scott* v. *Sandford*** [Dred Scott contra Sandford] *s.* caso de 1865 de la Corte Suprema en que un esclavo, Dred Scott, entabló juicio por su libertad porque su amo lo había llevado a vivir en territorios donde la esclavitud era ilegal; la Corte dictaminó contra Scott. (p. 467)

**due process of law** [proceso legal debido] *s.* tratamiento justo bajo la ley. (p. 267)

**elector** [elector] *s.* votante. (p. 249)

**Ellis Island** [isla Ellis] *s.* para la mayoría de los inmigrantes que vienen de Europa, la primera parada en Estados Unidos. (p. 614)

**Emancipation Proclamation** [Proclama de Emancipación] *s.* orden ejecutiva dictada por Abraham Lincoln el 1.° de enero de 1863, que liberaba a los esclavos de todas las regiones insurgentes contra la Unión. (p. 504)

**Embargo Act of 1807** [ley de Embargo de 1807] *s.* ley que dictaminaba que los barcos estadounidenses ya no estaban autorizados para ir a puertos extranjeros y que también cerraba los puertos de Estados Unidos a los barcos británicos. (p. 328)

**emigrant** [emigrante] *s.* persona que abandona un país. (p. 423)

***encomienda*** [encomienda] *s.* concesión del trabajo de los amerindios. (p. 72)

**English Bill of Rights** [Carta de Derechos Ingleses] *s.* acuerdo firmado por Guillermo y María por el que prometían respetar los derechos del Parlamento y los ciudadanos ingleses, incluso el derecho a elecciones libres. (p. 144)

**enlightenment** [Ilustración] *s.* movimiento del siglo XVIII que enfatizaba el uso de la razón y el método científico para obtener conocimiento. (p. 140)

**enumeration** [enumeración] *s.* recuento oficial, como un censo. (p. 249)

**equity** [equidad] *s.* sistema de justicia no cubierto bajo la ley común. (p. 269)

**Erie Canal** [canal de Erie] *s.* completado en 1825, esta vía navegable conectaba a la ciudad de Nueva York con Buffalo, New York. (p. 355)

**Espionage Act** [ley sobre el Espionaje] *s.* aprobada en 1917, esta ley establecía multas severas y muchos años de prisión para quienes participaran en actividades contra la guerra o alentaran a los que resistían la conscripción. (p. 692)

**European Middle Ages** [Edad Media europea] *s.* período desde fines del siglo V hasta aproximadamente el siglo XIV, durante el cual los europeos adoptaron el feudalismo y el sistema señorial. (p. 44)

**exodusters** *s.* afroamericanos que abandonaron el Sur para irse al Oeste y se comparaban a los hebreos bíblicos que habían escapado la esclavitud de Egipto. (p. 575)

**ex post facto law** [ley ex post facto] *s.* ley que hace que un acto sea una ofensa criminal aprobada después de cometido el acto. (p. 255)

**factory system** [sistema fabril] *s.* un método de producción que juntó a obreros y máquinas en el mismo edificio. (p. 341)

**fall line** *s.* punto a partir del cual una catarata impide que los barcos grandes continúen río arriba. (p. 126)

**famine** [hambruna] *s.* severa escasez de alimentos. (p. 426)

**fascism** [fascismo] *s.* filosofía política que propugna un fuerte gobierno nacionalista centralizado, con un dictador poderoso a la cabeza. (p. 712)

**federalism** [federalismo] *s.* sistema de gobierno en que el poder está dividido entre el gobierno central (o federal) y los estados. (pp. 234, 245)

**Federalists** [federalistas] *s.* partidarios de la Constitución. (p. 234)

**Federalist Papers** [*El federalista*] *s.* serie de ensayos que defienden y explican la Constitución, escritos por Alexander Hamilton, James Madison y John Jay. (p. 235)

**Federal Judiciary Act** [ley de la Judicatura Federal] *s.* ayudó a establecer un sistema de tribunales; le dio al Tribunal Supremo seis miembros. (p. 294)

**Federal Reserve Act** [ley de la Reserva Federal] *s.* ley aprobada en 1913 que creó el sistema bancario de la nación e instituyó un sistema monetario flexible. (p. 648)

**felony** [felonía] *s.* delito grave. (p. 253)

**feudalism** [feudalismo] *s.* sistema político en que el rey concedía a sus nobles el uso de sus tierras a cambio de su prestación militar y la protección de la gente que vivía en esas tierras. (p. 44)

**Fifteenth Amendment** [Enmienda Decimoquinta] *s.* aprobada en 1870, esta enmienda a la Constitución de Estados Unidos declaraba que a los ciudadanos no se les podía impedir que votaran "por motivo de raza, color ni condición anterior de esclavitud". (p. 546)

**54th Massachusetts Regiment** [54.° Regimiento de Massachusetts] *s.* regimientos afroamericano organizado para luchar por la Unión en la guerra civil. (p. 506)

**First Battle of Bull Run** [primera batalla de Bull Run] *s.* una batalla de la guerra civil, de 1861, en que el Sur horrorizó al Norte con una victoria. (p. 485)

**foreign policy** [política exterior] *s.* relaciones con los gobiernos de otros países. (p. 304)

**Fort Sumter** [fuerte Sumter] *s.* fuerte federal ubicado en el puerto de Charleston, Carolina del Sur; el ataque sureño al fuerte Sumter marcó el comienzo de la guerra civil. (p. 481)

**forty-niner** [buscador de ventura del 49] *s.* persona que fue a California en búsqueda de oro, empezando en 1849. (p. 412)

**Fourteen Points** [Catorce puntos] *s.* los objetivos del presidente Woodrow Wilson para la paz que siguió a la primera guerra mundial. (p. 695)

**Fourteenth Amendment** [Enmienda Decimocuarta] *s.* enmienda a la Constitución de Estados Unidos, aprobada en 1868, que hizo ciudadanos del país a todas las personas nacidas en Estados Unidos o naturalizadas, incluso a los antiguos esclavos. (p. 535)

**First Continental Congress** [primer Congreso Continental] *s.* reunión en 1774 de delegados de todas las colonias, excepto Georgia, para defender los derechos coloniales. (p. 171)

**Freedmen's Bureau** [Agencia de Manumisos] *s.* agencia federal establecida para ayudar a los antiguos esclavos después de la guerra civil. (p. 533)

**freedmen's school** [escuela para los manumisos] *s.* escuela establecida por la Agencia de Manumisos para educar a los recientes libertos afroamericanos. (p. 541)

**Free Soil Party** [Partido del Suelo Libre] *s.* partido político dedicado a parar la expansión de la esclavitud. (p. 459)

**French and Indian War** [guerra Francesa y Amerindia] *s.* conflicto en Norteamérica, entre 1754 y 1763, que fue parte de una lucha mundial entre Francia y Gran Bretaña y que terminó con la derrota de Francia y el traspaso del Canadá francés a Gran Bretaña. (p. 147)

**frontier** [frontera] *s.* región sin o con muy pocos asentamientos ocupada mayormente por amerindios. (p. 557)

**Fugitive Slave Act** [ley de los Esclavos Fugitivos] *s.* ley de 1850 para ayudar a los dueños de esclavos a recapturar los esclavos fugados. (p. 462)

**French Revolution** [Revolución francesa] *s.* en 1789 los franceses iniciaron un movimiento por la libertad y la igualdad. (p. 301)

**Fundamental Orders of Connecticut** [Órdenes Fundamentales de Connecticut] *s.* conjunto de leyes establecidas en 1639 por una congregación puritana que se había asentado en el valle del río Connecticut y que ampliaban la idea de un gobierno representativo. (p. 95)

## G

**generator** [generador] *s.* máquina que produce corriente eléctrica. (p. 587)

**Ghana** [Ghana] *s.* imperio del África Occidental entre los siglos VIII y XI d.de C. (p. 39)

**Gilded Age** [Edad Dorada] *s.* época de fines del siglo XIX de fabulosa riqueza. (p. 596)

**"Glorious Revolution"** [Revolución gloriosa] *s.* derrocamiento, en 1688, del rey inglés Jacobo II y su substitución por Guillermo y María. (p. 144)

**gold standard** [patrón oro] *s.* sistema en que el gobierno garantiza cada dólar con una cierta cantidad de oro. (p. 577)

**Grange** [La Quinta] *s.* creada en 1867 por un grupo de agricultores para tratar de satisfacer las necesidades sociales de las familias granjeras. (p. 577)

**Great Awakening** [Gran Despertar] *s.* renovación del sentimiento religioso en las colonias norteamericanas durante las décadas de 1730 a 1750. (p. 139)

**Great Compromise** [Gran Compromiso] *s.* acuerdo en la Convención Constitucional que estableció una legislatura nacional de dos cámaras; en una de estas cámaras, todos los estados tendrían representación igual, en la otra, cada estado tendría representación basada en su población. (p. 232)

**Great Depression** [gran depresión] *s.* período que duró desde 1929 hasta 1941, en que la economía de Estados Unidos declinó severamente y millones de estadounidenses estaban sin empleo. (p. 709)

**Great Migration** [Gran Emigración] *s.* movimiento de puritanos que salieron de Inglaterra para establecer asentamientos por todo el mundo, incluyendo a 20,000 que partieron para América (p. 94); el movimiento de afroamericanos entre 1910 y 1920 del Sur hacia las ciudades del Norte. (p. 693)

**Great Plains** [Grandes Llanuras] *s.* región desde el río Missouri hasta las montañas Rocosas. (p. 557)

**Great Society** [gran sociedad] *s.* programa iniciado por Lyndon Johnson para ayudan a los pobres, los ancianos y las mujeres y también promovía la educación, prohibía la discriminación racial y protegía el medio ambiente. (p. 724)

**greenback** [billete verde] *s.* papel moneda emitido por el gobierno federal durante la guerra civil. (p. 509)

**gristmill** [molino harinero] *s.* molino en que el grano se muele para producir cualquier tipo de harina. (p. 115)

**guerrilla** [guerrillero] *s.* soldado que debilita al enemigo con asaltos inesperados y ataques relámpagos. (p. 207)

**H**

*hacienda* [hacienda] *s.* granja grande o finca. (p. 72)

**Harlem Renaissance** [renacimiento de Harlem] *s.* florecimiento de la creatividad artística afroamericana durante los años veinte, centrada en la comunidad de Harlem de la ciudad de Nueva York. (p. 709)

**Harpers Ferry** *s.* arsenal federal en Virginia, capturado en 1859 durante un levantamiento de esclavos. (p. 469)

**Hausa** [hausa] *s.* gente de África Occidental que después del año 1000 d.C. vivió en lo que ahora es la región norte de Nigeria. (p. 42)

**Haymarket affair** [asunto Haymarket] *s.* mitín de protesta sindicalista que resultó aproximadamente en un centenar de muertes después de que un desconocido tiró una bomba y la policía abrió fuego contra la multitud. (p. 602)

**Holocaust** [Holocausto] *s.* matanza sistemática en Alemania, durante la segunda guerra mundial, de unos seis millones de judíos así como millones de otros grupos étnicos. (p. 716)

**homestead** [residencia] *s.* tierra para asentarse y construir una casa. (p. 568)

**Homestead Act** [ley de Residencia] *s.* aprobada en 1862, esta ley ofrecía 160 acres de tierra gratis a cualquiera que acordara ocuparla y trabajarla por cinco años. (p. 574)

**House of Burgesses** [Cámara de los Burgueses] *s.* creada en 1619, la primera asamblea representativa de las colonias norteamericanas. (p. 88)

**Hudson River School** [Escuela del río Hudson] *s.* grupo de artistas que vivían en el valle del río Hudson del estado de New York. (p. 430)

**Hull House** [Casa Hull] *s.* fundada en 1889, fue modelo para otras casas de acogida de la época. (p. 613)

**hygiene** [higiene] *s.* condiciones y prácticas que fomentan la buena salud. (p. 490)

**I**

**immigrant** [inmigrante] *s.* persona que se establece en un país nuevo. (p. 423)

**immunity** [inmunidad] *s.* protección legal. (p. 262)

**impeachment** [imputación] *s.* proceso de acusar a un funcionario público de un delito en el desempeño de sus funciones. (p. 249)

**imperialism** [imperialismo] *s.* política por la cual las naciones más poderosas extienden su control económico, político o militar sobre territorios o naciones más débiles. (p. 659)

**impressment** [secuestro] *s.* el acto de capturar personas a la fuerza. (p. 327)

**inaugurate** [investir] *v.* conferir un cargo oficial en una ceremonia formal. (p. 293)

**income tax** [impuesto sobre la renta] *s.* impuesto sobre los ingresos. (p. 509)

**indentured servant** [siervo escriturado] *s.* persona que vendía su trabajo a cambio de pasaje a Norteamérica. (p. 88)

**Indian Removal Act** [ley del Traslado de los Indígenas] *s.* esta ley de 1830 requería que el gobierno negociara tratados para el traslado de los amerindios al oeste. (p. 376)

**Indian Territory** [territorio Indio] *s.* lo que hoy son Oklahoma y partes de Kansas y Nebraska a la cual se trasladó a los amerindios bajo la ley del Traslado de los Indígenas de 1830. (p. 376)

**indictment** [acusación] *s.* declaración escrita dictada por un jurado de acusación que inculpa a una persona de un delito. (p. 250)

**indigo** [añil] *s.* planta que cultivaban las colonias sureñas de la cual se obtiene un colorante azul oscuro. (p. 121)

**individual right** [derecho individual] *s.* libertad y privilegio personal que garantiza a los ciudadanos estadounidenses la Carta de Derechos. (p. 247)

**Industrial Revolution** [revolución industrial] *s.* en la Inglaterra de fines del siglo XVIII, las maquinarias de fábrica empezaron a reemplazar las herramientas manuales, y la producción de bienes manufacturados reemplazó la agricultura como el principal modo de trabajo. (p. 341)

**inferior court** [tribunal inferior] *s.* corte con autoridad menor que la del Tribunal Supremo. (p. 260)

**inflation** [inflación] *s.* subida en el precio de los productos y los servicios y disminución del valor del dinero. (p. 386)

**initiative** [iniciativa] *s.* el procedimiento que permite a los votantes proponer una ley directamente. (p. 640)

**inoperative** [inoperante] *adj.* que no está vigente. (p. 274)

**insurrection** [insurrección] *s.* levantamiento abierto contra un gobierno. (p. 271)

**interchangeable part** [parte intercambiable] *s.* parte que es exactamente igual a otra parte. (p. 343)

**Intolerable Acts** [leyes Intolerables] *s.* serie de leyes aprobadas en 1774 por el Parlamento para castigar a Massachusetts por el Motín del Té de Boston. (p. 170)

**ironclad** [acorazado] *s.* buque de guerra cubierto de hierro. (p. 491)

**Iroquois League** [Liga Iroquesa] *s.* alianza del siglo XVI entre los pueblos amerindios cayuga, mohawk, oneida, onondaga y seneca, que vivían en la región oriental de los Grandes lagos. (p. 37)

**irrigation** [irrigación] *s.* práctica de llevar agua a los cultivos. (p. 29)

**Islam** [islam] *s.* religión fundada por el profeta Mahoma en el siglo VII, que enseña que hay un solo Dios: Alá. (p. 41)

**J**

**Jacksonian Democracy** [democracia jacksoniana] *s.* idea de extender el poder político a toda la gente asegurando de ese modo el gobierno de la mayoría. (p. 370)

**Jamestown.** *s.* primer asentamiento inglés permanente en Norteamérica. (p. 87)

**Jay's Treaty** [Tratado de Jay] *s.* el acuerdo que puso fin a la disputa sobre los derechos marítimos estadounidenses durante la Revolución francesa. (p. 302)

**jazz** [jazz] *s.* tipo nuevo de música en los años veinte que capturó el despreocupado espíritu de la época. (p. 708)

**Jim Crow** [ley Jim Crow] *s.* ley que imponía la separación entre la gente blanca y la de piel negra en los lugares públicos del Sur. (p. 621)

**joint-stock company** [sociedad por acciones] *s.* empresa en que los inversionistas colocan su dinero en un fondo común con la intención de sacar ganancias. (p. 86)

**judicial review** [revisión judicial] *s.* principio de que el Tribunal Supremo tiene la última palabra en la interpretación de la Constitución. (p. 317)

**Judiciary Act of 1801** [ley Judicial de 1801] *s.* ley que aumentó el número de jueces federales, permitiéndole al presidente John Adams cubrir la mayoría de los puestos nuevos con federalistas. (p. 316)

**K**

**Kansas-Nebraska Act** [ley de Kansas-Nebraska] *s.* ley de 1854 que estableció los territorios de Kansas y Nebraska y otorgó a sus habitantes el derecho a decidir si querían o no permitir la esclavitud. (p. 464)

**kayak** [kayak] *s.* embarcación pequeña hecha de piel de animales. (p. 33)

**King Cotton** [rey Algodón] *s.* al algodón se lo llamaba rey porque era importante en el mercado mundial y el Sur cultivaba la mayor parte del algodón que usaban las fábricas textiles de Europa. (p. 484)

**King Philip's War** [guerra del rey Felipe] *s.* guerra entre las colonias puritanas y los amerindios que se libró entre 1675 y 1676. (p. 96)

**Knights of Labor** [Caballeros del Trabajo] *s.* organización de obreros de oficios diferentes formada después de la guerra civil. (p. 601)

**Ku Klux Klan** *s.* grupo constituido en 1866 que quería restaurar el control del Sur a los demócratas y mantener sumisos a los antiguos esclavos. (p. 544)

**L**

**labor union** [sindicato laboral] *s.* obreros que se unen para tratar de conseguir mejores condiciones de trabajo. (p. 434)

**Land Ordinance of 1785** [Ordenanza de Tierras de 1785] *s.* ley que establecía un plan para la agrimensura y venta de las tierras públicas al oeste de los montes Apalaches. (p. 223)

**land speculator** [especulador en tierras] *s.* persona que compra grandes extensiones de terreno a precio bajo y luego vende secciones pequeñas a precios altos. (p. 394)

**League of Nations** [Sociedad de Naciones] *s.* organización establecida después de la primera guerra mundial para resolver conflictos internacionales. (p. 695)

**leisure** *s.* tiempo libre. (p. 627)

**Lewis and Clark expedition** [expedición de Lewis y Clark] *s.* grupo dirigido por Meriwether Lewis y William Clark que exploró las tierras de la Compra de Luisiana empezando en 1803. (p. 320)

**Lexington and Concord** *s.* escenarios, en Massachusetts, de las primeras batallas de la Revolución norteamericana. (p. 173)

**limited government** [gobierno limitado] *s.* principio que requiere que todos los ciudadanos estadounidenses, incluso los líderes gubernamentales, obedezcan la ley. (p. 247)

**lode** [veta] *s.* mineral enterrado entre capas de roca. (p. 558)

**Lone Star Republic** [República de la Estrella Solitaria] *s.* apodo de la República de Texas, que se le dio en 1836. (p. 405)

**long drive** [largo arreo] *s.* arreo de ganado al ferrocarril. (p. 560)

**Louisiana Purchase** [Compra de Luisiana] *s.* en 1803, la compra a Francia del Territorio de Luisiana. (p. 319)

**Lowell mills** [fábricas de Lowell] *s.* fábricas textiles ubicadas en el pueblo manufacturero de Lowell, Massachusetts, fundado en 1826. (p. 342)

**Loyalist** [realista]. *s.* colono norteamericano que apoyaba a los británicos durante la Revolución norteamericana. (p. 173)

# M

**mail-order catalog** [catálogo de venta por correo] *s.* publicación que contenía fotografías y la descripción de los artículos para que la gente encargara por correo. (p. 627)

**Magna Carta** [Carta Magna] *s.* "Gran Cédula Real"; documento que garantizaba los derechos políticos básicos en Inglaterra, aprobada por el rey Juan en el año 1215. (p. 141)

**Mali** [Malí] *s.* imperio del África Occidental desde el siglo XIII hasta el siglo XVI y que se enriqueció gracias al comercio. (p. 41)

**manifest destiny** [destino manifiesto] *s.* creencia de que era el destino de Estados Unidos extenderse por todo el continente, desde el océano Atlántico al océano Pacífico. (p. 407)

**manor system** [sistema señorial] *s.* sistema en que los nobles dividían sus tierras en propiedades, cultivadas mayormente por los siervos, quienes recibían la protección del noble. (p. 45)

**Marbury v. Madison** [Marbury contra Madison] *s.* caso de 1803 en que el Tribunal Supremo dictaminó que tenía el poder de invalidar leyes declarándolas inconstitucionales. (p. 317)

**mass culture** [cultura de masas] *s.* cultura común compartida por grandes números de personas. (p. 626)

**matrilineal** [por línea materna] *adj.* sociedad en que la ascendencia se determina mediante la madre. (p. 36)

**Mayflower Compact** [Pacto del Mayflower] *s.* acuerdo firmado por los hombres que viajaron a América en el Mayflower, que requería leyes para el bien de la colonia y establecía el concepto de autogobierno. (p. 93)

**melting pot** [crisol de culturas] *s.* lugar donde las culturas se amalgaman. (p. 616)

**mercantilism** [mercantilismo] *s.* sistema económico en que las naciones tratan de aumentar su riqueza y poder obteniendo oro y plata y estableciendo una balanza comercial favorable. (p. 61)

**mercenary** [mercenario] *s.* soldado profesional contratado para luchar por un país extranjero. (p. 195)

**Mexican Cession** [Cesión mexicana] *s.* extensa región cedida por México después de la guerra con México; incluía los actuales estados de California, Nevada, Utah, la mayor parte de Arizona y partes de Nuevo México, Colorado y Wyoming. (p. 411)

**Mexicano** [mexicano] *s.* persona de ascendencia española cuyos antepasados habían venido de México y se habían establecido en el sudoeste. (p. 570)

**middle passage** [travesía intermedia] *s.* parte intermedia de la ruta del comercio triangular (el viaje de África a las Américas) que traía africanos capturados a la esclavitud. (p. 78)

**migrate** [migrar] *v.* mudarse de un lugar a otro. (p. 27)

**militarism** [militarismo] *s.* creencia de que una nación necesita una fuerza militar grande. (p. 679)

**militia** [milicia] *s.* fuerza de civiles armados comprometidos a defender su comunidad durante la Revolución norteamericana. (p. 170); fuerza militar de emergencia, que no es parte del ejército profesional. (p. 254)

**minié ball** [bala minié] *s.* bala con base hueca. (p. 491)

**Minuteman** [minutero] *s.* miembro de la milicia colonial entrenado para responder "con un minuto de aviso". (p. 170)

**misdemeanor** [fechoría] *s.* violación de la ley. (p. 259)

**mission** [misión] *s.* asentamiento creado por la Iglesia con el propósito de convertir a los amerindios al cristianismo. (p. 72)

**missionary** [misionero] *s.* persona enviada por la Iglesia para predicar, enseñar y convertir a los indígenas al cristianismo. (p. 61)

**Missouri Compromise** [Acuerdo de Missouri] *s.* serie de leyes aprobadas en 1820 para mantener el equilibrio del poder político entre los estados esclavistas y los libres. (p. 358)

**monopoly** [monopolio] *s.* compañía que elimina a sus competidores y controla una industria. (p. 595)

**Monroe Doctrine** [Doctrina Monroe] *s.* política de oposición estadounidense a cualquier interferencia europea en el hemisferio occidental, proclamada por el presidente Monroe en 1823. (p. 359)

**Mormon** [mormón] *s.* miembro de una iglesia fundada por Joseph Smith en 1830. (p. 397)

**Mound Builder** [constructor de túmulos] *s.* amerindio primitivo que construía grandes estructuras de tierra. (p. 31)

**mountain man** [hombre de las montañas] *s.* trampero o explorador que abrió el oeste hallando sendas a través de las montañas Rocosas. (p. 393)

**muckraker** [revuelve estiércol] *s.* hacia comienzos del siglo XX, periodista que exponía la corrupción dentro de la sociedad estadounidense. (p. 640)

**Muslim** [musulmán] *s.* adherente del islam. (p. 41)

**N**

**nationalism** [nacionalismo] *s.* sentido de orgullo, lealtad y protección hacia el país de uno. (p. 354)

**nativist** [nativista] *s.* estadounidense nativo que quería eliminar toda influencia extranjera. (p. 428)

**natural-born citizen** [ciudadano nato] *s.* ciudadano nacido en Estados Unidos o en un estado asociado o dependencia de Estados Unidos, o a padres que son ciudadanos estadounidenses que viven fuera del país. (p. 257)

**naturalization** [naturalización] *s.* manera de darle ciudadanía completa a una persona nacida en otro país. (pp. 253, 270)

**Navigation Acts** [Actas de Navegación] *s.* serie de leyes aprobadas por el Parlamento, empezando en 1651, para asegurarse Inglaterra de que el comercio de sus colonias le rindiera ganancias económicas. (p. 112)

**navigator** [oficial de derrota] *s.* persona que planea el rumbo de un barco mientras está en el mar. (p. 49)

**Nazi Party** [Partido Nazi] *s.* partido Alemán Nacionalsocialista de los Trabajadores, llegó al poder bajo Adolfo Hitler en 1930. (p. 712)

**neutral** [neutral] *adj.* que no apoya ni a un país ni al otro. (p. 302)

**neutrality** [neutralidad] *s.* rechazo de la idea de apoyar a un país u otro durante una guerra. (p. 682)

**New Deal** [Nuevo Trato] *s.* programas de Franklin Roosevelt para luchar contra la depresión. (p. 710)

**New France** [Nueva Francia] *s.* puesto para el comercio de las pieles establecido en 1608 que se convirtió en el primer asentamiento francés permanente en Norteamérica. (p. 70)

**new immigrant** [inmigrante nuevo] *s.* persona del sur y el este de Europa que entró a Estados Unidos después de 1900. (p. 614)

**New Jersey Plan** [Plan de Nueva Jersey] *s.* plan de gobierno propuesto en 1787 en la Convención Constitucional que proponía una cámara legislativa única en que cada estado tendría un solo voto. (p. 231)

**Nineteenth Amendment** [Enmienda Decimonovena] *s.* enmienda a la Constitución de Estados Unidos ratificada en 1920 que dio a las mujeres el derecho absoluto a votar. (p. 653)

**Northwest Ordinance** [Ordenanza del Noroeste] *s.* describe cómo se iba a gobernar el territorio del Noroeste y establecía las condiciones para el asentamiento, así como los derechos de los colonos. (p. 223)

**Northwest Territory** [territorio del Noroeste] *s.* territorio organizado por la Ordenanza de Tierras de 1785, que incluía tierras que formaron los estados de Ohio, Indiana, Michigan, Illinois, Wisconsin y parte de Minnesota. (p. 223)

**O**

**Open Door Policy** [política de puertas abiertas] *s.* en 1899 Estados Unidos instó a las naciones que tenían intereses en China a que siguieran una política según la cual ningún país controlaría el comercio con China. (p. 669)

**Oregon Trail** [Camino de Oregón] *s.* camino hacia el oeste que iba de Independence, Missouri, al territorio de Oregón. (p. 396)

**overseer** [capataz] *s.* persona contratada por el dueño de una plantación para vigilar a los esclavos y dirigir su trabajo. (p. 122)

**P**

**pacifist** [pacifista] *s.* persona moralmente opuesta a la guerra. (p. 209)

**Palmer raids** [allanamientos de Palmer] *s.* en 1920 agentes federales y la policía allanaron los hogares de personas que se sospechaba que eran radicales. (p. 697)

**Panama Canal** [canal de Panamá] *s.* atajo a través de Panamá que conecta los océanos Atlántico y Pacífico. (p. 670)

**Panic of 1837** [pánico de 1837] *s.* crisis financiera con clausura de bancos y colapso del sistema crediticio, que resultó en muchas quiebras y serio desempleo. (p. 386)

**Panic of 1873** [pánico de 1873] *s.* crisis financiera en que los bancos se clausuraron y la bolsa de comercio se derrumbó. (p. 547)

**Parliament** [Parlamento] *s.* el cuerpo legislativo principal de Inglaterra. (p. 142)

**patent** [patente] *s.* documento del gobierno que otorga a un inventor el derecho exclusivo a hacer o vender su invención durante un determinado número de años. (p. 586)

**Patriot** [patriota] *s.* colono norteamericano que durante la Revolución norteamericana estaba a favor de los rebeldes. (p. 173)

**patroon** [patrono] *s.* persona que traía 50 colonos a Nueva Holanda y a cambio recibía una gran concesión de tierras y otros privilegios especiales. (p. 101)

**petroleum** [petróleo] *s.* líquido aceitoso e inflamable. (p. 585)

**philanthropist** [filántropo] *s.* persona que da grandes sumas de dinero a las organizaciones benéficas. (p. 596)

**Pickett's Charge** [carga de Pickett] *s.* en 1863 el general George Pickett dirigió una carga frontal contra las fuerzas de la Unión durante la batalla de la guerra civil en Gettysburg; el ataque fracasó. (p. 513)

**piedmont** [tierras bajas] *s.* ancha extensión de tierra llana al pie de una cadena de montañas. (p. 126)

**Pilgrim** [peregrino] *s.* miembros del grupo que rechazó la Iglesia de Inglaterra, viajó a América y fundó la colonia de Plymouth en 1620. (p. 92)

**Pinckney's Treaty** [Tratado de Pinckney] *s.* tratado de 1795 con España que otorgaba a Estados Unidos el uso del río Mississippi y el derecho a depositar bienes en Nueva Orleans; creó el paralelo 31 como el límite sur de Estados Unidos. (p. 302)

**plantation** [plantación] *s.* finca grande para cultivos comerciales. (p. 73)

**platform** [plataforma] *s.* declaración de creencias. (p. 471)

**Platt Amendment** [Enmienda Platt] *s.* resultado de la guerra entre Estados Unidos y España, dio a Estados Unidos el derecho a intervenir en los asuntos de Cuba cuando existiera amenaza a la "vida, propiedad y libertad individual". (p. 666)

**Plessy v. Ferguson** [Plessy contra Ferguson] *s.* caso de 1896 en que el Tribunal Supremo dictaminó que la separación de las razas en las instalaciones públicas era legal. (p. 621)

**political machine** [maquinaria política] *s.* organización que logra votos suficientes para controlar un gobierno local. (p. 613)

**political party** [partido político] *s.* grupo de personas que trata de promover sus ideas y ejercer su influencia sobre el gobierno, y que también apoya a candidatos a los cargos públicos. (p. 304)

**Pontiac's Rebellion** [rebelión de Pontiac] *s.* rebelión de 1763 contra los fuertes británicos y los colonos norteamericanos, dirigida en parte por el líder ottawa Pontiac, en reacción a los colonos que demandaban las tierras de los amerindios, así como a la severidad con que trataban a éstos los soldados británicos. (p. 151)

**popular sovereignty** [soberanía popular] *s.* gobierno en que gobierna la gente (p. 244); sistema en que los ciudadanos votan para decidir un asunto. (p. 463)

**Populist Party** [Partido Populista] *s.* también conocido como el Partido del Pueblo y constituido en 1890, este grupo quería una política que aumentara el precio de lo que cultivaban los granjeros. (p. 577)

**prejudice** [prejuicio] *s.* opinión negativa no basada en los hechos. (p. 427)

**printing press** [imprenta] *s.* máquina inventada por Johannes Gutenberg alrededor de 1455. (p. 47)

**privateer** [corsario] *s.* barco de propiedad particular autorizado por un gobierno que está en guerra a atacar los barcos de la marina mercante enemiga. (p. 204)

**Proclamation of 1763** [Proclama de 1763] *s.* orden por la cual Gran Bretaña les prohibía a los colonos norteamericanos establecer asentamientos al oeste de los montes Apalaches. (p. 151)

**profit** [ganancia] *s.* cantidad de dinero que saca una empresa después de descontar a las entradas los gastos empresariales. (p. 48)

**progressivism** [progresismo] *s.* movimiento reformista de principios del siglo XX que buscaba devolver el control del gobierno al pueblo, restablecer oportunidades económicas y corregir las injusticias de la vida estadounidense. (p. 639)

**propaganda** [propaganda] *s.* opinión expresada con el propósito de influir en las acciones de otras personas. (p. 692)

**proprietary colony** [colonia de proprietario] *s.* colonia de un único dueño. (p. 101)

**pro tempore** *adv.* latín para "por el momento". (p. 250)

**Pullman Strike** [huelga de Pullman] *s.* huelga nacional de ferrocarriles que se extendió por toda la industria ferroviaria en 1894. (p. 603)

**Puritan** [puritano] *s.* miembro de un grupo de Inglaterra que se asentó en la Colonia de la bahía de Massachusetts en 1630 y trató de reformar las prácticas de la Iglesia de Inglaterra. (p. 94)

**push-pull factor** *s.* factor que empuja a la gente a irse de su tierra natal y las atrae a un lugar nuevo. (p. 424)

## Q

**Quaker** [cuáquero] *s.* persona que creía que todas las personas debieran vivir en paz y armonía; aceptaba a religiones y grupos étnicos diferentes. (p. 101)

**quarter** [acuartelar] *v.* dar alojamiento. (p. 267)

**Quartering Act** [ley de Acuartelamiento] *s.* ley aprobada por el Parlamento en 1765 que requería que las colonias alojaran a los soldados británicos y los aprovisionaran. (p. 160)

**quorum** [quórum] *s.* número mínimo de miembros que deben estar presentes para que pueda empezar a deliberar oficialmente una asamblea. (p. 251)

## R

**racial discrimination** [discriminación racial] *s.* tratamiento diferente por motivos de raza. (p. 620)

**racism** [racismo] *s.* creencia de que alguna gente es inferior a causa de su raza. (p. 79)

**radical** [radical] *s.* persona que adopta posiciones políticas extremas. (p. 313)

**Radical Republican** [republicano radical] *s.* diputado que después de la guerra civil estaba a favor de usar el gobierno para crear un nuevo orden en el Sur y dar la ciudadanía total y derecho al voto a los afroamericanos. (p. 533)

**ragtime** *s.* mezcla de canciones afroamericanas y formas musicales europeas. (p. 629)

**ratification** [ratificación] *s.* aprobación oficial. (p. 264)

**recall** [destituir] *v.* votar para sacar a un funcionario de su cargo. (p. 640)

**Reconstruction** [Reconstrucción] *s.* proceso que usó el gobierno de Estados Unidos para readmitir a los estados confederados a la Unión después de la guerra civil. (p. 533)

**Red Scare** [Terror Rojo] *s.* entre 1919 y 1920, ola de pánico sobre una posible revolución comunista. (p. 697)

**referendum** [referéndum] *s.* cuando una ley que se ha propuesto se somete al voto del pueblo. (p. 640)

**Reformation** [Reforma] *s.* movimiento religioso del siglo XVI para corregir los problemas de la Iglesia Católica Romana. (p. 47)

**Renaissance** [Renacimiento] *s.* período de la historia europea que duró desde el siglo XIV hasta comienzos del XVII y que acrecentó el interés por el arte y el saber. (p. 46)

**rendezvous** [encuentro] *s.* reunión. (p. 197)

**reprieve** [indultar] *n.* cancelación de un castigo. (p. 259)

**republic** [república] *s.* gobierno en que el pueblo elige representantes para que lo gobiernen. (p. 222)

**republicanism** [republicanismo] *s.* creencia de que el gobierno se debe basar en el consentimiento del pueblo; el pueblo ejercita su poder votando por representantes políticos. (pp. 214, 245)

**Republican Party** [Partido Republicano] *s.* el partido político constituído en 1854 por los que se oponían a la esclavitud en los territorios. (p. 466)

**reservation** [reserva] *s.* tierras destinadas por el gobierno de Estados Unidos para las tribus amerindias. (p. 562)

**revenue** [rentas públicas] *s.* entradas que recibe un gobierno para cubrir sus gastos. (pp. 160, 252)

**revival** [renacimiento religioso] *s.* reunión diseñada para revivir la fe religiosa. (p. 433)

**rifle** [rifle] *s.* arma de barril estriado que hace que la bala vaya girando por el aire. (p. 491)

**robber baron** [capitalista inescrupuloso] *s.* líder industrial que se hizo acaudalado usando medios deshonestos. (p. 594)

**romanticism** [romanticismo] *s.* movimiento artístico europeo que acentuaba al individuo, la imaginación, la creatividad y la emoción. (p. 429)

**Roosevelt Corollary** [Corolario de Roosevelt] *s.* la adición en 1904 a la Doctrina Monroe permitiendo a los Estados Unidos a actuar de "policía" en Latinoamérica. (p. 672)

**Rough Rider** *s.* miembro del Primer Regimiento Estadounidense de Voluntarios de Caballería que organizó Theodore Roosevelt y que luchó en la guerra entre España y Estados Unidos. (p. 665)

**royal colony** [colonia real] *s.* colonia regida por gobernadores nombrados por un rey. (p. 103)

**S**

**salutary neglect** [indiferencia beneficiosa] *s.* política de no interferir Inglaterra en los asuntos de sus colonias norteamericanas durante la primera mitad del siglo XVIII. (p. 144)

**Sand Creek Massacre** [masacre de Sand Creek] *s.* un ataque en 1864, en el que más de 150 hombres, mujeres y niños del pueblo cheyene murieron a manos de la milicia de Colorado. (p. 564)

**Santa Fe Trail** [Camino de Santa Fe] *s.* camino hacia el oeste que iba de Missouri a Santa Fe, New Mexico. (p. 395)

**secede** [separarse] *v.* retirarse. (p. 473)

**secession** [secesión] *s.* separarse como parte de Estados Unidos. (p. 383)

**Second Battle of the Marne** [segunda batalla del Marne] *s.* en 1918 esta batalla de la primera guerra mundial marcó el cambio decisivo en el curso de la guerra; las tropas aliadas junto con las estadounidenses detuvieron el avance alemán hacia el interior de Francia. (p. 689)

**Second Continental Congress** [segundo Congreso Continental] *s.* organismo de gobierno cuyos delegados acordaron en mayo de 1775 organizar el Ejército Continental y aprobar la Declaración de Independencia. (p. 177)

**Second Great Awakening** [segundo Gran Despertar] *s.* renovación de la fe religiosa durante fines del siglo XVIII y comienzos del XIX. (p. 433)

**sectionalism** [seccionalismo] *s.* colocar los intereses de la región propia por encima de los de la nación como unidad. (p. 357)

**Sedition Act** [ley de Sedición] *s.* ley aprobada en 1918 que hacía ilegal la crítica de la guerra. Imponía fuertes multas y largos períodos de encarcelamiento para los que participaran en actividades contra la guerra. (p. 692)

**segregation** [segregación] *s.* separación. (p. 621)

**Seneca Falls Convention** [convención de Seneca Falls] *s.* convención sobre los derechos de la mujer llevada a cabo en Seneca Falls, New York, en 1848. (p. 444)

**separation of powers** [separación de poderes] *s.* división de las funciones básicas del gobierno en tres ramas. (p. 246)

**servitude** [servitud] *s.* práctica de pertenecer a un dueño o amo. (p. 270)

**Seven Days' Battles** [batallas de los Siete Días] *s.* batalla de 1862 de la guerra civil en que la Confederación forzó a la Unión a retroceder después de un intento fracasado de capturar la capital sureña de Richmond. (p. 496)

**Seventeenth Amendment** [Enmienda Decimoséptima] *s.* enmienda a la Constitución estadounidense, ratificada en 1913, que autorizaba la elección directa de los senadores estadounidenses por el electorado de cada estado. (p. 648)

**sharecropping** [aparcería] *s.* sistema en que los terratenientes daban a los agricultores tierra, semilla y herramientas a cambio de parte de la cosecha. (p. 543)

**Shays's Rebellion** [revuelta de Shay] *s.* sublevación de granjeros adeudados de Massachusetts en 1787. (p. 225)

**Sherman Antitrust Act** [ley Antitrust Sherman] *s.* ley aprobada en 1890 que declaró ilegal que las corporaciones obtuvieran control de las industrias formandos trusts. (p. 641)

**Siege of Vicksburg** [sitio de Vicksburg] *s.* victoria unionista de 1863, durante la guerra civil que le permitió a la Unión controlar todo el río Misisipí. (p. 516)

**sit-down strike** *s.* [huelga de brazos caídos] huelga en que los obreros permanecen dentro de la fábrica pero se niegan a trabajar. (p. 743)

**Sixteenth Amendment** [Enmienda Decimosexta] *s.* enmienda a la Constitución de Estados Unidos, ratificada en 1913, que dio al Congreso el poder de crear impuestos a las rentas. (p. 647)

**slash-and-burn agriculture** [agricultura de corte y quema] *s.* método agrícola en que la gente preparaba los campos cortando y quemando árboles y pastos, cuyas cenizas fertilizaban la tierra. (p. 37)

**slave code** [código de los esclavos] *s.* ley pasada para reglamentar el tratamiento de los esclavos. (p. 79)

**slavery** [esclavitud] *s.* sistema de servidumbre humana involuntaria. (p. 76)

**slum** [barrio bajo] *s.* barrio de casas abarrotadas de gente y peligrosas. (p. 612)

**smuggle** [contrabandear] *v.* importar o exportar mercancías ilegalmente. (p. 112)

**social gospel** [evangelio social] *s.* movimiento cuyo objetivo era mejorar la vida de los pobres. (p. 612)

**socialism** [socialismo] *s.* sistema económico en que todos los miembros de una sociedad son propietarios por igual de todas las empresas; los miembros comparten el trabajo y las ganancias (p. 602)

**sodbuster** *s.* granjero de la frontera. (p. 575)

**Songhai** *s.* imperio de África Occidental que sucedió a Malí y controló el comercio desde el siglo XV hasta fines del XVI. (p. 42)

**Sons of Liberty** [Hijos de la Libertad] *s.* grupo de colonos que formaron una sociedad secreta para oponerse a las políticas británicas en los tiempos de la revolución norteamericana. (p. 161)

**Spanish-American War** *s.* guerra de 1898 que comenzó cuando Estados Unidos demandó que España le concediera la independencia a Cuba. (p. 664)

**Spanish Armada** [Armada española] *s.* flota de buques enviada en 1588 por el rey español Felipe Segundo para invadir a Inglaterra y restaurar allí el catolicismo romano. (p. 69)

**sphere of influence** [esfera de influencia] *s.* región donde las naciones extranjeras demandan derechos especiales y privilegios económicos. (p. 669)

**spiritual** [canción espiritual] *s.* canción folklórica religiosa. (p. 351)

**spoils system** [sistema de prebendas] *s.* práctica de otorgar los candidatos elegidos empleos gubernamentales a los simpatizantes políticos. (p. 373)

**Stamp Act** [ley del Timbre] *s.* ley aprobada por el Parlamento en 1765 que requería que todos los documentos comerciales y legales llevaran un timbre oficial que indicaba que se había pagado un impuesto. (p. 160)

**standard time** [hora oficial] *s.* sistema adoptado en 1918 que dividió a Estados Unidos en cuatro zonas horarias. (p. 592)

**states' rights** [derechos estatales] *s.* teoría que sostenía que los estados tenían el derecho a decidir cuándo el gobierno federal había pasado una ley inconstitucional. (p. 307)

**steerage** [tercera clase] *s.* nivel o lugar más barato de un barco. (p. 423)

**Stono Rebellion** [Rebelión de Stono] *s.* sublevación de esclavos de 1739, en Carolina del Sur, que resultó en que se hicieran aún más estrictas las leyes que controlaban a los esclavos. (p. 123)

**strategy** [estrategia] *s.* plan general de acción. (p. 196)

**strike** [declararse en huelga] *v.* suspender los obreros el trabajo para tratar de conseguir condiciones de trabajo mejores. (p. 434)

**subsistence farm** *v.* una granja que produce bastante alimento para la familia con sólo una pequeña cantidad para vender. (p. 110)

**suffrage** [sufragio] *s.* derecho a votar. (pp. 262, 444)

**Sugar Act** [ley del Azúcar] *s.* ley aprobada por el Parlamento en 1764 que impuso impuestos al azúcar, la melaza y otros productos que llegaban a las colonias; también establecía severos castigos para los contrabandistas. (p. 160)

**sweatshop** *s.* lugar donde los obreros trabajaban largas horas en condiciones muy malas por salarios muy bajos. (p. 600)

**T**

**Tammany Hall** *s.* famosa maquinaria política de la ciudad de Nueva York de fines del siglo XIX. (p. 613)

**tariff** [arance aduanero] *s.* impuesto a las mercancías importadas. (p. 296)

**Tariff of Abominations** [arancel de las Abominaciones] *s.* ley de 1828 que subió los aranceles de las materias primas y las manufacturas; alteró a los sureños, quienes sentían que la política económica nacional la estaban determinando los intereses económicos del noreste. (p. 381)

**technology** [tecnología] *s.* uso de herramientas y conocimiento para satisfacer las necesidades humanas. (p. 32)

*Tejano* [tejano] *s.* persona de ascendencia española que consideraba a Texas su hogar. (p. 400)

**temperance movement** [movimiento de la templanza] *s.* campaña para acabar con el consumo de las bebidas alcohólicas. (p. 434)

**tender** *s.* dinero (p. 255)

**tenement** [casa de vecindad] *s.* edificio de apartamentos generalmente en muy malas condiciones y atestado. (p. 611)

**Thirteenth Amendment** [Enmienda Decimotercera] *s.* enmienda a la Constitución de Estados Unidos adoptada en 1865 que abolía la esclavitud y la servidumbre involuntaria en Estados Unidos. (p. 521)

**Three-Fifths Compromise** [Acuerdo de los Tres Quintos] *s.* acuerdo de la Convención Constitucional que establecía que, para efectos de la representación y del cobro de impuestos, se contarían como parte de la población tres quintos de los esclavos de un estado. (p. 232)

**Townshend Acts** [leyes de Townshend] *s.* serie de leyes aprobadas por el Parlamento en 1767 que suspendieron la Asamblea de Nueva York y establecieron impuestos a las mercancías importadas a las colonias británicas. (p. 163)

**Trail of Tears** [Sendero de las Lágrimas] *s.* trágica marcha del pueblo cherokee desde sus tierras hasta el Territorio Indio, entre 1838 y 1839; miles de cherokees murieron. (p. 377)

**transcendentalism** [trascendentalismo] *s.* filosofía del siglo XIX que enseñaba que el mundo espiritual es más importante que el mundo físico y que las personas pueden hallar la verdad dentro de sí mismas mediante los sentimientos y la intuición. (p. 431)

**transcontinental railroad** [ferrocarril transcontinental] *s.* ferrocarril que se extendía por todo el continente. (p. 590)

**Treaty of Ghent** [Tratado de Gante] *s.* tratado firmado en 1814 que puso fin a la guerra de 1812; no cambió de dueño ningún territorio ni se resolvieron los conflictos comerciales. (p. 333)

**Treaty of Greenville** [Tratado de Greenville] *s.* acuerdo de 1795 por el cual 12 tribus amerindias cedieron al gobierno de Estados Unidos gran parte de lo que hoy son los estados de Ohio e Indiana. (p. 300)

**Treaty of Guadalupe Hidalgo** [Tratado de Guadalupe Hidalgo] *s.* tratado de 1848 que puso fin a la guerra estadounidense con México; México cedió California y Nuevo México a los Estados Unidos. (p. 410)

**Treaty of Paris** [Tratado de París] *s.* tratado de 1763 que puso fin a la guerra Francesa y Amerindia; Inglaterra entregó toda norteamérica del este del río Mississippi. (p. 150)

**Treaty of Paris of 1783** [Tratado de París de 1783] *s.* tratado que puso fin a la guerra Revolucionaria, confirmó la independencia de Estados Unidos y estableció los límites de la nueva nación. (p. 212)

**Treaty of Tordesillas** [Tratado de Tordesillas] *s.* tratado de 1494 por el cual España y Portugal acordaron repartirse las tierras del hemisferio occidental y movieron la línea de demarcación hacia el oeste. (p. 61)

**Treaty of Versailles** [Tratado de Versailles] *s.* tratado de 1919 que puso fin a la primera guerra mundial. (p. 696)

**trench warfare** [guerra de trincheras] *s.* clase de guerra durante la primera guerra mundial en que los combatientes se apiñaban en zanjas fortificadas y se disparaban artillería y fuego de ametralladora. (p. 680)

**triangular trade** [comercio triangular] *s.* sistema de comercio transatlántico en que se intercambiaban mercancías, incluso esclavos, entre África, Inglaterra, Europa, las Antillas y las colonias de Norte América. (p. 111)

**tribunal** [tribunal] *s.* corte. (p. 253)

**trust** *s.* cuerpo legal creado para tener una cartera de acciones de varias empresas, con frecuencia en la misma industria. (p. 595)

**tundra** [tundra] *s.* pradera sin árboles que está permanentemente helada debajo de su capa de superior de tierra. (p. 33)

**U**

**unanimous consent** [consentimiento unánime] *s.* acuerdo completo. (p. 264)

*Uncle Tom's Cabin* [*La cabaña del tío Tom*] *s.* novela publicada por Harriet Beecher Stowe en 1852, que mostraba la esclavitud como brutal e inmoral. (p. 462)

**unconstitutional** [inconstitucional] *adj.* que contradice la ley de la constitución. (p. 317)

**Underground Railroad** [ferrocarril clandestino] *s.* serie de rutas de escape que usaban los esclavos para escaparse del Sur. (p. 442)

**urbanization** [urbanización] *s.* crecimiento de las ciudades como resultado de la industrialización. (p. 609)

**U.S.S. *Maine*** s. barco de guerra estadounidense que explotó misteriosamente y se hundió en el puerto de La Habana, Cuba, el 15 de febrero de 1898. (p. 663)

## V

**vaquero** [vaquero] s. peón de ganado que vino de México con los españoles en el siglo XVI. (p. 560)

**vaudeville** [vodevil] s. tipo de espectáculo teatral en vivo con mezcla de canciones, baile y comedia. (p. 629)

**viceroyalty** [virreinato] s. provincia regida por un virrey, que gobernaba en nombre del rey. (p. 71)

**Vietnam War** [guerra de Vietnam] s. conflicto militar que duró desde 1954 hasta 1975, entre el Vietnam del Norte comunista, apoyado por China y la Unión Soviética y las fuerzas no comunistas de Vietnam del Sur, apoyados por Estados Unidos. (p.719).

**vigilante** [vigilante] s. persona dispuesta a tomar la ley en sus propias manos. (p. 561)

**Virginia Plan** s. plan presentado por Edmund Randolph, delegado a la Convención Constitucional de 1787, que proponía un gobierno de tres ramas y una legislatura bicameral en la que la representación se basaría en la población o la riqueza de un estado. (p. 231)

## W

**war bond** [bono de guerra] s. préstamo de interés bajo de la población civil al gobierno, que se pagaría dentro de un número de años. (p. 691)

**War Hawk** s. habitante de las regiones del oeste que apoyaba la guerra de 1812. (p. 329)

**Webster-Hayne debate** [debate Webster-Hayne] s. debate de 1830 entre Daniel Webster y Robert Hayne sobre la doctrina de la invalidación. (p. 382)

**Whig Party** [Partido Whig] s. partido político organizado en 1834 en oposición a las políticas de Andrew Jackson. (p. 387)

**Whiskey Rebellion** [rebelión del Whisky] s. protesta de 1794 contra el impuesto que impuso el gobierno al whisky, valioso medio económico de los granjeros de la frontera. (p. 301)

**Wilderness Road** [Camino al Desierto] s. sendero a Kentucky que ayudó a construir el pionero Daniel Boone. (p. 221)

**Wilmot Proviso** [Claúsula de Wilmot] s. propuesta de 1846 que excluía la esclavitud de cualquier territorio adquirido como resultado de la guerra con México. (p. 459)

**World War II** [segunda guerra mundial] s. guerra que se libró entre 1939 y 1945, en que Gran Betaña, Francia, la Unión Soviética, Estados Unidos, China y otros aliados derrotaron a Alemania, Italia y Japón. (p.713)

**Wounded Knee Massacre** [masacre de Wounded Knee] s. masacre de 1890 por soldados estadounidenses de 300 amerindios desarmados, en Wounded Knee Creek, Dakota del Sur. (p. 566)

**writ of assistance** [mandato judicial de transferencia] s. orden de registro que permitía a los oficiales británicos entrar en los hogares o comercios coloniales en busca de contrabando. (p. 164)

## X

**XYZ Affair** [asunto XYZ] s. incidente de 1797 en que funcionarios franceses demandaron que los diplomáticos estadounidenses les pagaran un soborno. (p. 306)

## Y

**yellow journalism** [periodismo amarillo] s. estilo de periodismo que usa la exageración y el sensacionalismo para presentar las noticias. (p. 663)

**Yoruba** [Yoruba] s. gente de África Occidental que constituyó varios estados al sudoeste del río Níger. (p. 42)

## Z

**Zimmermann telegram** [telegrama de Zimmerman] s. mensaje enviado en 1917 por el ministro de Relaciones Exteriores alemán al embajador alemán en México proponiendo una alianza entre México y Alemania y prometiendo ayudar a México a recuperar Texas, New Mexico y Arizona si Estados Unidos entraba en la guerra. (p. 682)

**evaluating information,** 56, 81, 171, 197, 347, 373, 528, 551, 664, 694. See also under Reading and Critical Thinking.

**forming and supporting opinions,** 97, 98-99, 101, 118, 173, 202, 309, 360, 389, 491, 551, 579, 624-625, 701, 731. See also under Historical Interpretation; and Reading and Critical Thinking.

**framing historical questions,** 43, 48, 79, 80, 91, 188, 208, 360, 450, 477, 593, 605, 630, 631, 632, 655, 675, 699, 702-703, 737. See also under Reading and Critical Thinking.

**internet research,** 21, 55, 62, 81, 91, 105, 125, 131, 142, 151, 153, 175, 187, 188, 189, 191, 208, 215, 241, 309, 311, 325, 335, 347, 363, 372, 389, 391, 398, 415, 419, 427, 447, 449, 455, 458, 476, 477, 487, 492, 499, 515, 519, 527, 529, 531, 537-539, 549, 551, 581, 583, 589, 599, 605, 612, 619, 623, 629, 631, 643, 645, 647, 655, 657, 664, 667, 671, 673, 675, 677, 683, 684, 685, 701, 703, 705, 728, 731, 739

**library research,** 81, 105, 131, 153, 173, 188, 189, 208, 215, 217, 309, 329, 335, 336, 363, 383, 389, 398, 419, 449, 469, 470, 477, 492, 499, 519, 529, 549, 551, 581, 605, 619, 629, 631, 643, 667, 671, 673, 675, 683, 684-685, 702-703, 739

**point of view / perspective,** 38, 55, 91, 127, 131, 151, 203, 205, 309, 360, 469, 486, 499, 551, 604, 605, 624-625, 655, 668, 675, 703

**primary sources,** 21, 27, 29, 32, 33, 38, 39, 43, 47, 52, 55, 63, 67, 71, 75, 78, 81, 85, 92, 94, 97, 98, 99, 100, 105, 109, 114, 116, 118, 119, 122, 124, 126, 128, 129, 131, 134, 135, 139, 141, 142, 148, 151, 153, 159, 160, 162, 164, 165, 167, 172, 182-185, 187, 196, 200, 202, 209, 215, 217, 221, 230, 231, 234, 238, 239, 241, 242, 247, 248-275, 293, 298, 301, 303, 309, 313, 315, 322, 324, 330, 335, 342, 344, 348, 351, 352, 353, 354, 356, 359, 360-361, 363, 369, 372, 374, 377, 379, 382, 384, 385, 389, 393, 396, 409, 419, 423, 433, 438-439, 440, 444, 449, 457, 477, 481, 488, 504, 519, 524, 525, 527, 538, 545, 547, 548, 551, 557, 567, 568, 581, 620, 624-625, 631, 641, 655, 670, 675, 696, 699, 701, 731

**secondary sources,** 14, 91, 104, 105, 169, 217, 347, 451, 477, 484, 538-539, 551, 569, 573, 661, 684-685. See also library research under Research, Evidence, and Point of View.

**solving problems,** 215, 285, 465, 685, 738. See also under Historical Interpretation; and Reading and Critical Thinking.

**summarizing,** 258, 315, 334, 715, 720, 725. See also under Historical Interpretation; and Reading and Critical Thinking.

**using notes,** 186, 292, 308, 334, 418, 448, 498, 502, 526, 550, 580, 630, 654, 674, 700, 730. See also taking notes under Writing and Speaking.

## Historical Interpretation

**analyzing causes,** 20, 36, 40, 46, 48, 52, 79, 88, 104, 108, 112, 121, 125, 152, 194, 210, 213, 214, 224, 316, 327, 357, 370, 397, 402, 405, 408, 414, 416, 444, 534, 541, 561, 575, 599, 601, 602, 623, 645, 649, 661, 668, 669, 709, 737. See also under Reading and Critical Thinking.

**analyzing points of view,** 296, 314, 350, 358, 383, 385, 463, 469, 542, 567, 578, 588, 595, 693, 698

**asking questions,** 575

**biography,** 37, 50, 64, 86, 88, 112, 121, 140, 166, 181, 193, 194, 205, 210, 228, 230, 293, 295, 315, 316, 319, 321, 324-325, 353, 370, 375, 394, 404, 435, 441, 443, 444, 449, 461, 482, 496, 510, 516, 519, 522, 534, 565, 570, 571, 578, 588, 595, 613, 622, 643, 648, 661, 667, 696, 711, 716, 723

**causal relationships,** 17, 25, 31, 36, 37, 46, 54, 171, 174, 182, 329, 333, 711, 737

**cause and effect,** 96, 323, 340, 523, 661, 720

**comparing,** 31, 50, 81, 102, 142, 180, 214, 235, 336, 430, 441, 458, 482, 502, 571, 576, 629, 653, 724, 738

**contrasting,** 48, 137, 138, 209, 235, 297, 343, 351, 404, 494, 502, 521, 596, 629, 653, 673, 724

**cost-benefit analysis,** 309, 728

**decision-making,** 204, 285

**drawing conclusions,** 29, 30, 35, 65, 69, 77, 80, 145, 149, 162, 166, 173, 185, 207, 302, 206, 332, 373, 397, 415, 447, 517, 571, 587, 591, 604, 643, 618, 654, 671, 673, 737. See also under Reading and Critical Thinking.

**economic and political issues,** 48, 62, 214, 296, 309, 380, 387, 388, 424, 458, 509, 521, 571, 576, 586, 593, 603, 604, 640, 647, 671, 706, 728

**economic performance,** 20, 62, 124, 296, 335, 350, 380, 458, 573, 595

**evaluating,** 197, 207, 212, 229, 248, 291, 438, 451, 613, 624-625, 630, 643. See also under Reading and Critical Thinking.

**finding main ideas,** 62, 75, 79, 80, 88, 89, 97, 99, 103, 122, 134, 136, 150, 152, 185, 223, 322, 356, 397, 411, 448, 525, 541, 587, 619, 651, 658, 674, 684, 687, 738. See also under Reading and Critical Thinking.

**forming and supporting opinions,** 5, 20, 53, 59, 96, 107, 118, 157, 199, 233, 325, 328, 428, 451, 549, 579, 604, 613, 663, 684, 727, 730. See also under Reading and Critical Thinking.

**historical continuity,** 113, 120, 141, 150, 186, 242, 300, 304, 317, 375, 386, 410, 446, 464, 538, 549, 593, 671

**identifying problems,** 45, 83, 104, 129, 133, 427, 550, 603, 615, 621, 631, 671, 684, 729, 737

**influence of geographic patterns / factors,** 18, 28, 52, 83, 124, 149, 324, 424, 446, 593, 671

## Reading and Critical Thinking

## Writing and Speaking

An *i* preceding a page reference in italics indicates that there is an illustration, and usually text information as well, on that page. An *m* or a *c* preceding an italic page reference indicates a map or a chart, as well as text information on that page.

petroleum, 585, 595, *m599*
Philadelphia, Pa., 116
  Constitutional Convention in, 228, *i229*
  introduction of telephone in, 588
  religious riot in, *i428*
  world's fair in, 628
philanthropists, 596
Philip II (Spanish monarch), 69
Philippines
  imperialism and, *m669*
  in Spanish-American War, 664, *m665*, 666, 668–669
Phillips, Wendell, 548
Phoenix, Ariz., *m18*
photography, *i518*
physical geography, 6, 10–13
Pickett, George, 513
Pickett's Charge, *i514, m514*
piedmont, 126
Pierce, Franklin, R37
Pike, Zebulon, *m320*, 322–323
Pikes Peak, *m320*, 322, 569
Pilgrims, 92, 93
Pinckney, Charles, 305–306
Pinckney, Thomas, 302
Pinckney's Treaty, 302
*Pinta*, 51
pioneers, *i390*
pirates, 326
Pitcher, Molly, 195
Pitt, William, 149, 162
Pittsburgh, Pa., 148
Pizarro, Francisco, 65
place, 4
plantations, *i120*
  after Civil War, 523, 542–543
  cotton farming on, 349–351
  economy of, 119–123
  in Southern economy, 457
  sugar cultivation on, 72, 76, *i657*
plateau, *i15*
Platt Amendment, 666, *m672*
Plessy, Homer, 742
*Plessy* v. *Ferguson*, 621, 742–743, 746
plow, 342, *i345*, 576
Plymouth, Mass., 93
Pocahontas, 88
Poe, Edgar Allan, 432
points of view, analyzing *c456*, 469, R9
poison gas, *i681*
Poland, 696, 713

police, 267
political cartoon
  on Copperheads, *i508*
  on 1860 election, *i472*
  on Grant's presidency, *i547*
  interpreting, R28
  on isolationism, *i706*
  on Jackson's opposition to Second Bank of the United States, *i385*
  on ratification of U.S. Constitution, *i265*
  on Roosevelt's foreign policy, *i675*
  on Stamp Act, *i162*
  on XYZ Affair, *i306*
political machines, 613, 615
political maps, 6, *mR34–R35*
political parties. *See also* Democratic Party; Republican Party.
  Constitutional Union Party, 472
  development of, 295–297, 301–302, 303–307, *i386*
  Federalists, 145, *c304*, 305, 307, 313–314, 316
  Know-Nothing Party, 428
  Populist Party, 577–578
  progressive reforms and, 648
  Radical Republicans, 534–536, 542
  Whig Party, 386–387
Polk, James K., 406, 408, R36
poll tax, 275, 548, 621
pollution, 17, 728–729
Polo, Marco, 50
Pomeiock, *i85*
Pomo people, 34
Pontiac, *i151*
Pontiac's Rebellion, 151
*Poor Richard's Almanack*, 138
Popé, 72
popular sovereignty, 244, 463–464, 469
population
  colonial, *c105*
  growth of industry and, 585
  slave, *c120*
  of Western cities in 1860 and 1890, *c569*
Populism, 577–578
Portland, Ore., *c569*
Portugal
  exploration by, 49, 61
  Monroe Doctrine and, 360–361
  and slave trade, 43, 77

potatoes, 75, 426
potlatch, 34
Pottawatomie Massacre, 465
poverty
  and Irish immigration, 426
  Progressive Era and, 636
  reform movements and, 639
  urbanization and, 611, 612
Powell, Colin, *i506*
Powell, Lewis, 750
Powhatan, 88
prairie, *i15*
prairie schooners, 395
prejudice, 427
president. *See also names of individual presidents.*
  Antifederalist view of, 239
  cabinet of, 294
  constitutional provisions for, 269, 275–276
  lame duck sessions and, 273
  lawmaking process and, 252, *c253*
  oath of, 257
  roles of, *i258*
  salary of, 257
  term of office of, *c250*, 274
primary sources
  Constitution, 248–277
  *Crusade for Justice*, 624
  Declaration of Independence, 182–185
  Dix's report on treatment of the mentally ill, 438–439
  early map of North and South America, *m55*
  *Federalist Papers*, 238
  Fourteen Points, *i699*
  Fundamental Orders of Connecticut, 98–99
  Gettysburg Address, 524
  Iroquois Great Law of Peace, 38
  Kee Low interview, 625
  Lincoln's Second Inaugural Address, 525
  Mayflower Compact, 98
  Monroe Doctrine, 360–361
  "Objections to the Constitution of Government Formed by the Convention," 239
  using, R21
prime meridian, *i8*
printing press, 47
prison camps, 511

# ACKNOWLEDGMENTS

## TEXT ACKNOWLEDGMENTS

**Chapter 1,** page 28: map, "New Paths to the Americas," *U.S. News & World Report,* October 12, 1998, page 62. Copyright © October 12, 1998, U.S. News and World Report. Visit us at our Web site at www.usnews.com for additional information. Adapted by permission of U.S. News & World Report.

page 33: Excerpt from "Navajo Blessing Way," from *Language and Art in the Navajo Universe* by Gary Witherspoon, page 26 (Ann Arbor: The University of Michigan Press, 1977). Reprinted by permission of The University of Michigan Press.

**Chapter 6,** pages 174–175: Excerpt from *Johnny Tremain* by Esther Forbes. Copyright © 1943 by Esther Forbes Hoskins, copyright renewed by Linwood M. Erskine, Jr., executor of the Estate of Esther Forbes Hoskins. Reprinted by permission of Houghton Mifflin Company. All rights reserved.

**Chapter 9,** page 300: "Obeying Rules and Laws," from *Government in America* by Richard J. Hardy. Copyright © 1995 by Houghton Mifflin Company. All rights reserved. Reprinted by permission.

**Chapter 16,** pages 486–487: Excerpt from *Across Five Aprils* by Irene Hunt. Copyright © 1964 by Irene Hunt. All rights reserved. Reprinted by permission of Shirley Beem on behalf of the author.

**Chapter 17,** pages 508, 509, 510, 512, 513, 516, 518, 519: Excerpts from *The Civil War* by Kenneth Burns, Ric Burns, and Geoffrey Ward. Copyright © 1990 by American Documentaries, Inc. Reprinted by permission of Alfred A. Knopf, a division of Random House, Inc.

**Chapter 19,** page 562: Excerpt from "Wahenee: An Indian Girl's Story Told by Herself to Gilbert L. Wilson," *North Dakota History,* Vol. 38, Nos. 1 & 2. Copyright © 1971 State Historical Society of North Dakota. Used by permission.

**Chapter 21,** pages 618–619: Excerpt from *Dragonwings* by Laurence Yep. Copyright © 1975 by Laurence Yep. Used by permission of HarperCollins Publishers.

pages 624–625: Excerpt from *Crusade for Justice: The Autobiography of Ida B. Wells,* edited by Alfreda M. Duster. Copyright © 1970 by The University of Chicago. All rights reserved. Reprinted by permission of The University of Chicago Press.

**Epilogue,** page 723: Excerpt from "I Have a Dream" by Martin Luther King, Jr. Copyright © 1963 by Martin Luther King, Jr., copyright renewed 1991 by Coretta Scott King. Reprinted by arrangement with The Heirs to the Estate of Martin Luther King, Jr., c/o Writers House, Inc., as agent for the proprietor.

page 731: Quote by Ken Burns from "Of documentaries and storytelling, historical awareness and arrogance, heroes and villains . . . a conversation with Ken Burns" by Sam Stall, *America West Airlines Magazine,* November 1997. Reprinted by permission of America West Airlines Magazine and Sam Stall.

## ART CREDITS

### Cover and Frontispiece

*cover background* Copyright © Bob Gelberg/SharpShooters.
*frontispiece background* The Granger Collection, New York.

**Abraham Lincoln:** The Library of Congress.

**Ida Bell Wells:** The Granger Collection, New York.

**Juan Seguín:** Detail of *Juan Seguín* (1838), Jefferson Wright. Texas State Library and Archives Commission.

**Abigail Adams:** *Portrait traditionally said to be Abigail Adams* (about 1795), artist unknown. Oil on canvas, 30 1/4" × 26 1/2", N-150.55. Photo by Richard Walker. Copyright © New York State Historical Association, Cooperstown, New York.

**Andrew Jackson:** *Andrew Jackson* (1845), Thomas Sully. The Granger Collection, New York.

**Zitkala-Sǎ:** Negative no. Mss 299, Tom Perry Special Collections, Harold B. Lee Library, Brigham Young University, Provo, Utah.

**Elizabeth Cady Stanton:** The Granger Collection, New York.

**Crispus Attucks:** Copyright © Stock Montage.

**Queen Liliuokalani:** *Portrait of Queen Liliuokalani,* date and artist unknown. Bishop Museum.

**George Washington:** Corbis.

### Table of Contents

viii–xvii *background* The Granger Collection, New York; **viii** *top* The Metropolitan Museum of Art, The Michael C. Rockefeller Memorial Collection, Gift of Nelson A. Rockefeller, 1972 (1978.412.310). Photograph copyright © 1983 The Metropolitan Museum of Art; *bottom* The Granger Collection, New York; **ix** *top* Copyright © Michael Gadomski/Photo Researchers, Inc.; *center* The Granger Collection, New York; *bottom* Library of Congress; **x** *top* Copyright © R. Kord/H. Armstrong Roberts; *center George Washington in the Uniform of a British Colonial Colonel,* 1772, by Charles Willson Peale. Washington-Custis-Lee Collection, Washington and Lee University, Lexington, VA; *bottom* Illustration by Bill Cigliano; **xi** *bottom right* Copyright © John E. Fletcher & Arlan R. Wiler/NGS Image Collection; *bottom* Corbis; **xii** *top* Copyright © 1998 North Wind Pictures; *center* National Museum of American History, Smithsonian Institution; *bottom* Illustration by Patrick Whelan; **xiii** *top* From the collections of the Minnesota Historical Society; *bottom left* Copyright © 1998 Louis Psihoyos/Matrix; *bottom right* The Granger Collection, New York; **xiv** *top* Copyright © George Peter Alexandre Healy/Wood River Gallery/PNI; *center* Courtesy; *Soldier* magazine, U.S. Army; *bottom* The Granger Collection, New York; **xv** top, *Northern Pacific Railroad. The Pioneer Route to Fargo Moorhead Town Bismark Dakota and Montana and the Famous Valley of the Yellowstone* (about 1885), Creator–Poole Brothers, Printers. Broadside. Chicago Historical Society; *bottom* The Granger Collection, New York; **xvi** *top* Doubleday, Page and Company, New York, 1906, second issue; *center, Portrait of Queen Liliuokalani,* date and artist unknown. Bishop Museum; *bottom left* Culver Pictures; *bottom right* The Granger Collection, New York; **xvii** *bottom left* NASA; *bottom right* From the Collection of David J. and Janice L. Frent.

### Voices from the Past

xxi *left The Last Voyage of Henry Hudson,* (1881) John Collier. Tate Gallery, London/Art Resource, NY; *right* The Granger Collection, New York; **xxii** Corbis; **xxiii** *left* Illustration from *The Headless Horseman* by Natalie Standiford. Illustration Copyright © 1992 by Donald Cook, Reprinted by permission of Random House, Inc.; *right* Corbis/Bettmann; **xxiv** *top left* Courtesy of the U.S. Naval Academy Museum; *center right* Copyright © 1963 Bob Adelman/Magnum Photos; *bottom right* Survey Compass, accession number 1982–145. Colonial Williamsburg Foundation.

## Themes of American History

**xxviii** *top* Copyright © 1999 PhotoDisc, Inc.; *center* Photo by Howard Sochrer/*Life* Magazine, Copyright © Time Inc.; *bottom* Michael S. Yamashita/Corbis; **xxix** *top* Library of Congress; *bottom* National Museum of American History/Smithsonian Institution.

## Geography Handbook

**2** *top right* Copyright © H. Abernathy/H. Armstrong Roberts; *center left* Copyright © Warren Morgan/H. Armstrong Roberts; *bottom* Copyright © 1996 Denver A. Bryan; **3** *top* Copyright © Nathan Benn/Stock Boston; *bottom right* Copyright © Andy Sacks/Tony Stone Images; **4–5** The Granger Collection, New York; **4** *top* Copyright © 1997 David Noble/FPG International; **5** *top* Copyright © John Coletti/Stock Boston; *center* Copyright © Bill Horsman/Stock Boston; **6** *top* Copyright © George Mobley/NGS Image Collection; *center* Copyright © Lowell Georgia/NGS Image Collection; *bottom left* The Granger Collection, New York; **10** *top* Copyright © T. Algire/H. Armstrong Roberts; *bottom* Copyright © Ken Graham/Tony Stone Images; **11** *top* Copyright © SuperStock; *bottom* Copyright © Tom Dietrich/Tony Stone Images; **12** *top* Copyright © Zane Williams/Tony Stone Images; *bottom* Copyright © Eastcott/Momatiuk/Tony Stone Images; **13** *top* Copyright © SuperStock; *bottom* Copyright © F. Sieb/H. Armstrong Roberts; **14–15** Illustration by Ken Goldammer; **16** *top* Copyright © M. Schneiders/H. Armstrong Roberts; *bottom* Copyright © D. Frazier/H. Armstrong Roberts; **17** *top left* Copyright © Ron Levy/Liaison Agency; *top right, center right, bottom right* Copyright © Steve Adams/NGS Image Collection; *bottom left* Copyright © Cathlyn Melloan/Tony Stone Images; **18** *bottom* Copyright © J. Marshall/The Image Works; **19** *left* Culver Pictures; *right* Copyright © Santi Visalli/The Image Bank.

## Unit 1

**22–23** Copyright © R. Kord/H. Armstrong Roberts.

**Chapter 1, 24–25** The Granger Collection, New York; **24** *left* Courtesy of the Ohio Historical Society; *right* Roman horseman (A.D. first–third century). Bronze figurine from Orange, France. Musée des Antiquites Nationales, Saint-Germain-en-Laye, France. Photo © Erich Lessing/Art Resource, New York; **25** *left* © Leonard de Selva/Corbis; *right* The Granger Collection, New York; **28** *center left* Courtesy Arizona State Museum, University of Arizona, Tucson, Arizona. Photo copyright © 1996 Jerry Jacka; **29** Copyright © Francois Gohier/Photo Researchers, Inc.; **30** Copyright © SuperStock; **34** National Museum of Anthropology, Mexico City, Mexico/Werner Forman Archive/Art Resource, New York; **35** Smithsonian Institution, Washington, D.C.; **36** *background* Copyright © Richard Saker/AllSport; *bottom left* Copyright © Salamander Picture Library; **40** *left* Copyright © Aldona Sabalis/Photo Researchers, Inc.; **41** The Granger Collection, New York; **42** PNI; **43** The Metropolitan Museum of Art, The Michael C. Rockefeller Memorial Collection, gift of Nelson A. Rockefeller, 1972 (1978.412.310). Photograph copyright © 1983 The Metropolitan Museum of Art; **45** Illustration by Alexander Verbitsky; **47** *School of Athens* (1508), Raphael (Raffaello Santi). Stanza della Segnatura, Vatican City, Vatican. Photo copyright © Erich Lessing/Art Resource, New York; **49** Detail of *St. Vincent Polyptych* (date unknown), Nuno Gonçalves. Museu Nacional de Arte Antiga, Lisbon, Portugal. Copyright © Scala/Art Resource, New York; **50** *Portrait of a Man, Called Christopher Columbus* (1519), Sebastiano del Piombo. Oil on canvas, 42" x 34 3/4". The Metropolitan Museum of Art, gift of J. Pierpont Morgan, 1900; **52** Archivio Fotografico del Museo Preistorico Etnografico L. Pigorini, Rome. Photo by Lorenzo de Masi; **53** Cliché Bibliothèque nationale de France, Paris; **56** Copyright © Francois Gohier/Photo Researchers, Inc.; **57** Photos by Sharon Hoogstraten.

**Chapter 2, 58–59** The Granger Collection, New York; **58** *top left* Mask, representing the god Quetzalcoatl or Tonatiuh (about 1500), Aztec. Museum of Mankind, London. Photo © Bridgeman Art Library; *bottom left* © Gianni Dagli Orti/Corbis; *right* © Bettmann/Corbis; **59** The Granger Collection, New York; **61** Detail of *Pope Alexander VI Borgia Kneeling in Prayer* (date unknown), Bernardino Pinturicchio. Sala die Misteri della Fede, Appartamento Borgia, Vatican Palace, Vatican State/Scala/Art Resource, New York; **64** Corbis; **65** Aztec mask (early 16th century), artist unknown. Turquoise, pearl shell. Werner Forman Archive/British Museum, London/Art Resource, New York; **66** The Granger Collection, New York; **68** PNI; **69** *Sea Battle between the Spanish Armada and English Naval Forces* (about 1600), Hendrik Corneliez Vroom. Oil on canvas, 91 cm x 153 cm. Landesmuseum Ferdinandeum, Innsbruck, Austria. Photo copyright © Erich Lessing/Art Resource, New York; **71** The Granger Collection, New York; **73** The British Library; **75** PNI; **76** Copyright © The Fotomas Index; **77** Corbis; **78** *left* The Newberry Library, Chicago; *right, Slaves Below Deck of Albanez* (date unknown), Francis Meynell. Copyright © National Maritime Museum Picture Library, London.

**Chapter 3, 82–83** Colonial Williamsburg Foundation, Virginia; **82** *top Captain John Smith, 1st Governor of Virginia* (about 1616), English School. Private collection. Photo © Bridgeman Art Library; *bottom Portrait of Akbar and Prince Salim* (19th century), Indian, Mughal dynasty. The Newark Museum, Newark, New Jersey. Photo © The Newark Museum/Art Resource, New York; **83** *left* © Bettmann/Corbis; *right* The Granger Collection, New York; **84** The Granger Collection, New York; **85** British Museum; **87** AP/Wide World Photos; **88** *Pocahontas* (1616), Simon van de Passe. Engraving, 6 7/8" x 4 3/4" (17.5 cm x 12 cm). Published in the *Baziliologia,* London, 1618. National Portrait Gallery, Smithsonian Institution/Art Resource, New York; **89** The Granger Collection, New York; **90–91** Illustration by Ivan Lapper. Copyright © The Reader's Digest Association; **92** The Granger Collection, New York; **93** *The Mayflower in Plymouth Harbor* (1882), William Halsall. Courtesy of the Pilgrim Society, Plymouth, Massachusetts; **94** *top* Copyright © SuperStock; *bottom* Copyright © Andrew J. Martinez/Photo Researchers, Inc.; **95** *bottom* The Granger Collection, New York; **96** *left* Courtesy of American Antiquarian Society; *right* The New York Public Library; **97** *Trial of George Jacobs for Witchcraft, 1692* (1855), T. H. Matteson. Oil on canvas, acc. #1246. Peabody Essex Museum, Salem, Massachusetts. Photo by Mark Sexton; **100** Detail of *Peter Stuyvesant and the Trumpeter (The Wrath of Peter Stuyvesant)* (1835), Asher B. Durand. Oil on canvas, 24 1/4" x 30 1/4", accession no. 1858.28. Copyright © Collection of The New-York Historical Society; **101** Copyright © Tom Dietrich/Tony Stone Images; **103** Brown Brothers.

**Chapter 4, 106–107** The Granger Collection, New York; **106** *top* © Joseph Sohm; ChromoSohm Inc./Corbis; *bottom* The Granger Collection, New York; **107** *left* © Bettmann/Corbis; *right Portrait of Nadir Shah Afshar of Persia* (1700–1725), Mughal School. Victoria & Albert Museum, London. Photo © The Stapleton Collection/Bridgeman Art Library; **109** *Sperm Whaling: No. 2, The Capture* (1862), A. Van Best and R. S. Gifford. Lithograph by Endicott and Company, corrected by Benjamin Russell, 16 3/4" x 25 3/4" (43 cm x 65 cm). N.M.A.H., Harry Peters "America on Stone" Lithography Collection; **110** *right* Copyright © Thomas Neill; **112** North Carolina Collection, University of North Carolina Library at Chapel Hill; **114** Detail of *Quaker Meeting* (date unknown), Egbert Van Heemskerk. The Quaker Collection, Haverford (Pennsylvania) College Library; **115** *right* Historic

Hudson Valley, Tarrytown, New York; **116** The Granger Collection, New York; **118** Library of Congress; **119** Detail of *George Mason* (1811), Dominic W. Boudet. Oil on canvas, 30" x 25" (76.2 cm x 63.5 cm). Virginia Museum of Fine Arts, Richmond. Gift of David K. E. Bruce. Photo by Ron Jennings. Copyright © Virginia Museum of Fine Arts; **120** *right* Copyright © Chip Henderson/Tony Stone Images; **121** Virginia Historical Society, Richmond, Virginia; **122** The Granger Collection, New York; **124** *bottom left* Smithsonian Institution, Washington, D.C.; *bottom right background* Photo copyright © Dorothy Miller; *bottom right foreground* Copyright © The New York Botanical Garden; **125** *bottom center* Copyright © Old Dartmouth Historical Society, New Bedford (Massachusetts) Whaling Museum; **126** The Granger Collection, New York; **127** *right* Copyright © Michael P. Gadomski/Photo Researchers, Inc.; **128** Copyright © Mark McGehearty/AllSport; **129** *Catching the Wild Horse* (date unknown), George Catlin. Oil on canvas, 12 1/4" x 16 1/4". The Thomas Gilcrease Institute of American History and Art, Tulsa, Oklahoma.

**Chapter 5, 132–133** The Granger Collection, New York; **132** *top* The Granger Collection, New York; *bottom left King William III* (18th century), English School. Photo © Derrick E. Witty/National Trust Photographic Library/Bridgeman Art Library; *bottom right Mary Stewart, Consort of William III* (17th century), William Wissing or Wissmig. Photo © Derrick E. Witty/National Trust Photographic Library/The Bridgeman Art Library; **133** *left King George II* (about 1743–1745), Joseph Highmore. Tate Gallery, London. Photo © Tate Gallery, London/Art Resource, New York; *right* The Granger Collection, New York; **134** Library of Congress; **137, 139** The Granger Collection, New York; **140** Corbis; **142** Courtesy of Knox County, Illinois Teen Court; **143** The Granger Collection, New York; **145** *left* Corbis; *right* The Newberry Library, Chicago; **146** Detail of *Braddock's Defeat* (1903), Edward Deming. State Historical Society of Wisconsin Museum Collection; **147** Library of Congress; **149, 151** The Granger Collection, New York; **153A** Detail of *Quaker Meeting* (date unknown), Egbert Van Heemskerk. The Quaker Collection, Haverford (Pennsylvania) College Library.

## Unit 2

**154–155** Copyright © William Johnson/Stock Boston.

**Chapter 6, 156–157** The Granger Collection, New York; **156** *left* Rare Books and Manuscript Division of the New York Public Library, Astor, Lenox, and Tilden Foundations; *right* © Dorling Kindersley; **157** *left The Boston Massacre (The Bloody Massacre)* (1770), Paul Revere. The Granger Collection, New York; *right Louis XVI, King of France* (1770s), Joseph-Siffrède Duplessis. Musée du Château de Versailles, Paris. Photo © Dagli Orti/The Art Archive; **158** The Granger Collection, New York; **159** *James Otis Arguing Against the Writs of Assistance in the Old Towne House* (1901), Robert Reid. Courtesy Commonwealth of Massachusetts Art Commission; **160** *top* Rare Books Division, The New York Public Library. Astor, Lenox, and Tilden Foundations; *bottom* Emmet Collection, Manuscripts and Archives Division, The New York Public Library. Astor, Lenox, and Tilden Foundations; **161, 162** The Granger Collection, New York; **164** Copyright © Collection of The New-York Historical Society; **165** The Granger Collection, New York; **166** *left* The Granger Collection, New York; *right, John Adams* (date unknown), John Trumbull. National Portrait Gallery, Smithsonian Institution/Art Resource, New York; **167** The Granger Collection, New York; **168–169** Copyright © McDougal Littell Inc.; **170** Copyright © Paul Mozell/Stock Boston; **173** Copyright © Charles Winters/Stock Boston; **174** Copyright © McDougal Littell Inc.; **175** The Granger Collection, New York; **176** *Portrait traditionally said to be*

*Abigail Adams* (about 1795), artist unknown. Oil on canvas, 30 1/4" x 26 1/2", N-150.55. Photo by Richard Walker. Copyright © New York State Historical Association, Cooperstown, New York; **177** Detail of *The Death of General Warren at the Battle of Bunker's Hill, 17 June 1775* (date unknown), John Trumbull. Oil on canvas. Yale University Art Gallery, Trumbull Collection; **178** Library of Congress; **179** *top* The Granger Collection, New York; *bottom* Library of Congress; **180** *top* Detail of *The Declaration of Independence, 4 July 1776* (date unknown), John Trumbull. Oil on canvas. Yale University Art Gallery, Trumbull Collection; *bottom* Copyright © R. Kord/H. Armstrong Roberts; **181, 182** The Granger Collection, New York; **188** The Granger Collection, New York; **189** Photos by Sharon Hoogstraten.

**Chapter 7, 190–191** The Granger Collection, New York; **190** *bottom left* © Bettmann/Corbis; *bottom right* ©Archivo Iconografico, S.A./Corbis; **191** *top* © Getty Images; *bottom* © Bettmann/Corbis; **193** Haym Salomon Home for nursing and Rehabilitation, Brooklyn, N.Y. Courtesy of American Jewish Historical Society, Waltham, Massachusetts and New York, New York; **194** *George Washington in the Uniform of a British Colonial Colonel* (1772), Charles Willson Peale. Washington-Custis-Lee Collection. Washington and Lee University, Lexington, Virginia; **195** *top* From *American Story: The Revolutionaries.* Courtesy of the Jamestown-Yorktown Educational Trust. Photo by Katherine Wetzel. Copyright © 1996 Time-Life Books Inc.; **196** *Washington Crossing the Delaware* (1851), Emanuel Gottlieb Leutze. Oil on canvas, 149" x 255". The Metropolitan Museum of Art, gift of John S. Kennedy, 1897; **197** *bottom* The Granger Collection, New York; **198** Copyright © Michael Newman/PhotoEdit/PNI; **199** *Two American Flags Flown by John Paul Jones in 1779* (date unknown), unknown Dutch artist. Watercolor. Chicago Historical Society; **200, 201** The Granger Collection, New York; **202** From *American Story: The Revolutionaries.* Courtesy of the Jamestown-Yorktown Educational Trust. Photo by Katherine Wetzel. Copyright © 1996 Time-Life Books Inc.; **205** The Granger Collection, New York; **206** Library of Congress; **207** Defense Visual Information Center, Linda Delatorre, Researcher; **208** Illustration by Bill Cigliano; **210** *Surrender of Lord Cornwallis at Yorktown* (date unknown), John Trumbull. Yale University Art Gallery, Trumbull Collection; **211** Private collection; **212** The Granger Collection, New York; **215** Courtesy of the Massachusetts Historical Society; **216** Private collection.

**Chapter 8, 218–219** *The Signing of the Constitution* (about 1940), Howard Chandler Christy. Private collection. Photo © Art Resource, New York; **218** *left* The Granger Collection, New York; *right* © Archivo Iconografico, S.A./Corbis; **219** *left* © Getty Images; *right* © Christie's Images/Corbis; **221** Detail of *Daniel Boone Escorting Settlers Through the Cumberland Gap* (1851–1852), George Caleb Bingham. Oil on canvas, 36 1/2" x 50 1/4". Washington University Gallery of Art, St. Louis (Missouri). Gift of Nathaniel Phillips, 1890; **225** *top* The Granger Collection, New York; **225** *bottom* Copyright © Thad Samuels Abell II/NGS Image Collection; **226** *bottom left* Copyright © John E. Fletcher & Arlan R. Wiler/NGS Image Collection; *bottom right* William L. Clements Library, Map Division, University of Michigan; **227** *top* The Granger Collection, New York; *bottom* Courtesy of the Shelby County (Ohio) Historical Society; **228** Library of Congress; **229** Copyright © Joseph Nettis/Tony Stone Images; **230** The Granger Collection, New York; **231** PNI; **234** The Granger Collection, New York; **235** *left, Portrait of John Jay* (c. 1783, 1804–1808), Gilbert Stuart, believed to have been begun by and finished by John Trumbull. National Portrait Gallery, Smithsonian Institution/Art Resource, New York; **235** *right*, **236** The Granger Collection, New York.

## Constitution Handbook

**242** *left* The Granger Collection, New York; *right* Copyright © Ivan Massar/Black Star; **243** *top* Copyright © Bob Daemmrich/The Image Works; *center* Copyright © Topham/The Image Works; *bottom* Courtesy of The New York *Times;* **244** *bottom* Copyright © J. L. Atlan/Sygma; **245** *top* Copyright © Robert E. Daemmrich/Tony Stone Images; **247** *top* Copyright © 1973 Engelhardt in the *St. Louis Post-Dispatch*/Reprinted with permission; *bottom* Copyright © Patrick Forden/Sygma; **248** *background* The Granger Collection, New York; **248** *inset,* **257** AP/Wide World Photos; **258** *top right* Copyright © Archive Photos; *top left* Culver Pictures; *center right* Copyright © 1972 Magnum Photos, Inc.; *center left* AP/Wide World Photos; *bottom right* Courtesy Ronald Reagan Library; **264** AP/Wide World Photos; **265** Copyright © Collection of The New-York Historical Society; **267** Copyright © Baron Wolman/Tony Stone Images; **268** *left* Copyright © Jean-Marc Giboux/Liaison Agency; *right* Copyright © Bob Daemmrich/Sygma; **270** Copyright © 1993 Ron Rovtar/FPG International; **272** The Granger Collection, New York; **273** *left* Copyright © 1998 FPG International; *right* Copyright © Cynthia Johnson/Liaison Agency; **274** Franklin D. Roosevelt Library; **277** Copyright © Rock the Vote Inc.

## Citizenship Handbook

**280** AP/Wide World Photos; **281** *background* Copyright © Bob Daemmrich; *foreground* Copyright © 1994 Mark Harmel/FPG International; **284** Copyright © Bob Daemmrich/The Image Works; **285** Copyright © David Young-Wolff/Tony Stone Images; **286** AP/Wide World Photos; **287A** Copyright © Collection of The New-York Historical Society.

## Unit 3

**288–289** Copyright © Marvin E. Newman/The Image Bank.

**Chapter 9, 290–291** The Granger Collection, New York; **290** *left* © Lee Snider; Lee Snider/Corbis; *right* © Leonard de Selva/Corbis; **291** *left* © Getty Images; *right* © Charles & Josette Lenars/Corbis; **292** © Joseph Sohm; Visions of America/Corbis; **294** AP/Wide World Photos; **295** *Portrait of Alexander Hamilton* (about 1796), James Sharples (the Elder). National Portrait Gallery, Smithsonian Institution/Art Resource, New York; **297** Copyright © Larry Stevens/Nawrocki Stock Photo Inc.; **299** *right* Ohio Historical Society; **301** *Execution of Louis XVI* (18th century), anonymous. Colored engraving. Musée de la Ville de Paris, Musée Carnavalet, Paris, France/Giraudon/Art Resource, NY; **303** Mount Vernon Ladies Association; **305** *top* The Granger Collection, New York; *center right* Maryland Historical Society; **306** The Granger Collection, New York.

**Chapter 10, 310–311** © Historical Picture Archive/Corbis; **310** © Bettmann/Corbis; **311** *top* © Francis G. Mayer/Corbis; *bottom left* Miguel Hidalgo y Costilla (1895). Engraving from Mexican publication *Patria e Independencia,* Illustrated folio. Antochiw Collection, Mexico. Photo by Mireille Vautier/The Art Archive; *bottom right* © Archivo Iconografico, S.A./Corbis; **314** The Granger Collection, New York; **315** *center right* Kirby Collection of Historical Paintings, Lafayette College; *bottom background* Monticello/Thomas Jefferson Memorial Foundation, Inc.; *bottom center* Polygraph, 1806. John Isaac Hawkins, Charles Willson Peale. University of Virginia. Photo courtesy of Monticello/Thomas Jefferson Memorial Foundation, Inc.; **316** Boston Athenaeum; **317** Copyright © James Blair/NGS Image Collection; **318, 319** The Granger Collection, New York; **320** *inset* Copyright © Addison Geary/Stock Boston/PNI; **321** *Lewis and Clark at Three Forks* (date unknown), E. S. Paxson. Mural in the Montana State Capitol. Courtesy of the Montana Historical Society. Photo by John Reddy; **322** Copyright © 1998 North Wind Pictures; **323** National Museum of American History, Smithsonian Institution; **324** *center left* Copyright © Stock Montage; *center right, The Surrounder, Chief of the Tribe* (1833), George Catlin. Oto tribe. National Museum of American Art, Smithsonian Institution/Art Resource, New York; *bottom center, bottom right* Peabody Museum, Harvard University. Copyright © President and Fellows of Harvard College. Photo by Hillel Burger; **325** *center left, Mink, a Pretty Girl* (1832), George Catlin. National Museum of American Art, Smithsonian Institution/Art Resource, New York; *center right, Steep Wing, a Brave of the Bad Arrow Points Band* (1832), George Catlin. Teton Dakota (Western Sioux). National Museum of American Art, Smithsonian Institution/Art Resource, New York; *bottom* Whaling Chief's Hat, Makah or Nootka. Cedar bark, bear grass, unidentified mammal hair, remnant feathers, leather thong. H 22 cm, D 27 cm. PM# 99-12-10/53080. Peabody Museum of Archeology and Ethnology, Harvard University. Copyright © President and Fellows of Harvard College. Photo by Hillel Burger; **326** Detail of *Decatur Boarding the Tripolitan Gunboat* (date unknown), Dennis Malone Carter. Oil on canvas. Courtesy of the Naval Historical Foundation; **327** Library of Congress; **328** The Granger Collection, New York; **330** *left* White House Collection. Copyright © White House Historical Association; *right* The Granger Collection, New York; **332** National Museum of American History, Smithsonian Institution; **334** *top, Thomas Jefferson* (date unknown), Rembrandt Peale. Copyright © Collection of the New-York Historical Society; *bottom* National Museum of American History, Smithsonian Institution; **336** *top left* Elk skin bound journal (1805), William Clark. Ink on paper. Missouri Historical Society; *right, bottom* Copyright © 1998 North Wind Pictures; **337** Photos by Sharon Hoogstraten.

**Chapter 11, 338–339** © Bettmann/Corbis; **338** *left* © Bettmann/Corbis; *right* © Archivo Iconografico, S.A./Corbis; **339** *top* Library of Congress; *bottom* © Paul Almasy/Corbis; **341** Corbis-Bettmann; **342** The Granger Collection, New York; **343** Illustration by Patrick Whelan; **344** Corbis-Bettmann; **345** Copyright © Stock Montage; **346–347** Illustrations by Randal Birkey; **348** The Granger Collection, New York; **349** Illustration by Patrick Whelan; **351** Detail of *Plantation Burial* (1860), John Antrobus. Williams Research Center, The Historic New Orleans Collection. Photo copyright © Jan White Brantley; **352** Corbis-Bettmann; **353** The Granger Collection, New York; **354** Corbis-Bettmann; **355** *right inset* The Granger Collection, New York; **356, 357** *right inset* Corbis-Bettmann; **363A** The Granger Collection, New York.

## Unit 4

**364–365** Layne Kennedy/Corbis.

**Chapter 12, 366–367** The Granger Collection, New York; **366** © Archivo Iconografico, S.A./Corbis; **367** The Granger Collection, New York; **369** Redwood Library and Athenaeum, Newport, Rhode Island; **370** *left, John Quincy Adams* (1858), George Healy. Oil on canvas, 62" x 47". White House Collection. Copyright © White House Historical Association; *right, Andrew Jackson* (1845), Thomas Sully, The Granger Collection, New York; **371** The Hermitage: Home of President Andrew Jackson, Nashville, Tennessee. Photo of ribbon by Sharon Hoogstraten; **372** Copyright © The *News-Sentinel,* Fort Wayne, Indiana; **373** *left* The Granger Collection, New York; *right* Culver Pictures; **374** *Sequoyah, Indian Statesman* (date unknown), anonymous, after Charles Bird King. Hand-colored lithograph, J. T. Bowen lithography company. National Portrait Gallery, Smithsonian Institution/Art Resource, New York; **375** Copyright © J. Pat Carter/Liaison Agency; **377** *The Trail of Tears* (date unknown),

Robert Lindneux. Woolaroc Museum, Bartlesville, Oklahoma; **378** The Granger Collection, New York; **381** *top* The Granger Collection, New York; **381** *bottom* The Museum of the Confederacy, Richmond, Virginia. Photo by Katherine Wetzel; **382** Detail of *Webster's Reply to Hayne* (date unknown), George Healy. Courtesy Boston Art Commission; **384** *Nicholas Biddle* (1839), Henry Inman. Oil on canvas [1978.2]. The Historical Society of Pennsylvania; **385** The Granger Collection, New York; **386** Copyright © Collection of The New-York Historical Society; **389** Library of Congress.

**Chapter 13, 390–391** National Archives; **390** *left* The Granger Collection, New York; *right* The Granger Collection, New York; **391** *left* © Bettmann/Corbis; *right* © Archivo Iconografico, S.A./Corbis; **393** *Jedediah Smith in the Badlands* (date unknown), Harvey Dunn. The South Dakota Art Museum Collection; **394** Copyright © United States Postal Service; **395** *inset* Copyright © Ric Ergenbright; **396** Skillet, negative no. OrHi 97119. Oregon Historical Society; **401** *top* Broadsides Collection, The Center for American History, The University of Texas at Austin; **402** Copyright © Bob Daemmrich/Stock Boston/PNI; **403** *The Battle of the Alamo* (about 1913), Frederick C. Yohn. Courtesy Continental Insurance; **404** *left* Texas State Library and Archives Commission; **404** *right*, **406** The Granger Collection, New York; **408** *inset*, **412** Courtesy of the California History Room, California State Library, Sacramento, California; **413** Copyright © Collection of The New-York Historical Society; **414** Courtesy of Levi Strauss Company; **415, 417** Courtesy of the California History Room, California State Library, Sacramento, California.

**Chapter 14, 420–421** © Getty Images; **420** *left* © Archivo Iconografico, S.A./Corbis; *right* The Granger Collection, New York; **421** *left, right* The Granger Collection, New York; **422** The New York Public Library; **423** *background* From the collections of the Minnesota Historical Society; *foreground* Copyright © Collection of The New-York Historical Society; **424** *center* The Granger Collection, New York; **427** Michael S. Yamashita/Corbis; **428** The Granger Collection, New York; **429** From *The Headless Horseman* by Natalie Standiford, illustrated by Donald Cook. Illustration copyright © 1992 Donald Cook. Reprinted by permission of Random House, Inc.; **430** The Granger Collection, New York; **432** *background* Photo by Simon Marsden/The Marsden Archive; **433** The Granger Collection, New York; **434** Copyright © Archive Photos; **435** Department of Archives, Oberlin (Ohio) College; **436, 440** The Granger Collection, New York; **441** Chester County Historical Society, West Chester, Pennsylvania; **443** *from left to right* The Granger Collection, New York; The Granger Collection, New York; The Granger Collection, New York; The Granger Collection, New York; Corbis-Bettmann; **444** The Granger Collection, New York; **445** *The Discord* (1885), F. Heppenheimer. Color lithograph, negative no. 51038. Copyright © Collection of The New-York Historical Society; **446** *center* Sophia Smith Collection, Smith College; *bottom right, bottom left* Copyright © 1998 Louis Psihoyos/Matrix; **447** *bottom* From the Collections of the National Underground Railroad Freedom Center, Cincinnati, Ohio; **450** From the collections of the Minnesota Historical Society; **451** Photos by Sharon Hoogstraten; **451A** The Granger Collection, New York.

**Unit 5**

**452–453** Corbis.

**Chapter 15, 454–455** The Granger Collection, New York; **454** *top, bottom* The Granger Collection, New York; **455** *left* © Bettmann/Corbis; *right* © Hulton-Deutsch Collection/Corbis; **456** The Granger Collection, New York; **457, 460** The Granger Collection, New York; **461** Corbis; **462** Hulton-Deutsch Collection/Corbis; **463** *left* The Granger Collection, New York; *right* Corbis-Bettmann; **466** From the Collection of David J. and Janice L. Frent; **467** AFP/Corbis; **468, 470** *Tragic Prelude—John Brown*, *(1937–42)*, John Steuart Curry. Kansas State House, Topeka, Kansas. Photo courtesy Photo One, Topeka, Kansas; **471** The Granger Collection, New York; **472** Lloyd Ostendorf Collection; **474** *background* Hulton-Deutsch Collection/Corbis; *inset* Copyright © George Peter Alexandre Healy/Wood River Gallery/PNI.

**Chapter 16, 478–479** The Granger Collection, New York; **478** *left* © Massimo Listri/Corbis; *right* © Museum of the City of New York/Corbis; **479** © Bettmann/Corbis; **482** The Lincoln Museum, Fort Wayne, Indiana. #0-43; **485** Copyright © H. Armstrong Roberts; **486** Copyright © McDougal Littell Inc.; **487** *left* Courtesy of Brian C. Pohanka; *right* Massachusetts Commandery Military Order of the Loyal Legion and the U.S. Army Military History Institute; **488** Bureau of Archives and History, New Jersey State Library; **489** Corbis-Bettmann; **490** Culver Pictures; **491** The Granger Collection, New York; **492** Illustration by Alexander Verbitsky; **496** U.S. Signal Corps photo no. 111-B-4146 (Brady Collection) in the National Archives; **497** Chicago Historical Society; **498** *left, center* Photos by Larry Sherer. Copyright © Time-Life Books Inc.; *bottom right* Fort Sumter National Park.

**Chapter 17, 500–501** Detail of *Cavalry Charge at Yellow Tavern, VA, May 11, 1864* (1871), H.W. Chaloner. West Point Museum Art Collection, United States Military Academy; **500** *left* The Granger Collection, New York; *right* © Paul Almasy/Corbis; **501** *left* The Granger Collection, New York; *right* Library of Congress; **503** Corbis; **504** The Granger Collection, New York; **505** *top* Copyright © Archive Photos; *bottom* Library of Congress; **506** Defense Visual Information Center, Linda Delatorre, Researcher; **507** Culver Pictures; **508** The Granger Collection, New York; **510** American Red Cross; **511** *background* Corbis; *foreground* Massachusetts Commandery Military Order of the Loyal Legion and the U.S. Army Military History Institute; **513** Copyright © 1994 Kunio Owaki/The Stock Market; **514–515** *background* Illustration by Ken Goldammer; **514** *center* Library of Congress; *bottom left* From *Echoes of Glory: Arms & Equipment of The Union*. Photo by Larry Sherer. Copyright © 1991 Time-Life Books Inc.; *bottom right* The Museum of the Confederacy, Richmond, Virginia. Photo by Katherine Wetzel; **515** *bottom* From *Echoes of Glory: Arms & Equipment of The Union*. Photo by Larry Sherer. Copyright © 1991 Time-Life Books Inc.; **516** Library of Congress; **518** *top left* Courtesy of Stamatelos Brothers Collection. Photo by Larry Sherer. Copyright © 1991 Time-Life Books Inc.; *bottom* Courtesy Meserve-Kunhardt Collection, Mount Kisco, New York; **520** Copyright © Robert M. Anderson/Uniphoto, Inc.; **522** National Archives; **526** *top right* Manassas National Battlefield Park, National Park Service. Photo by Larry Sherer; *bottom right* Collection of Old Capitol Museum of Mississippi History; **528** *center left, center* High Impact Photography/Copyright © Time-Life Books Inc.; *center right* Courtesy of Stamatelos Brothers Collection. Photo by Larry Sherer. Copyright © 1991 Time-Life Books Inc.; **529** Photos by Sharon Hoogstraten.

**Chapter 18, 530–531** National Archives; **530** © Bettmann/Corbis; **531** *top left* © Bettmann/Corbis; *bottom left* © Corbis; *right* Library of Congress; **533, 534** The Granger Collection, New York; **535** Corbis; **536** *His First Vote* (1868), Thomas Waterman Wood. Oil on board. Cheekwood Museum of Art, Nashville, Tennessee; **537, 538–539** *background* The Granger Collection, New York; **538** *top right*, **540, 541** Corbis; **542** Library of Congress; **544** The Granger Collection, New York; **545** Library of Congress; **546, 547** The Granger Collection, New York; **548** Library of Congress; **551A** Culver Pictures.

## Unit 6

552–553 The Granger Collection, New York.

Chapter 19, 554–555 © Corbis; 554 *left* The Granger Collection, New York; *right* © Corbis; 555 *left* © Bettmann/Corbis; *right* © Bettmann/Corbis; 557 Denver Public Library; 559 *top* The Granger Collection, New York; *bottom* Copyright © Dan Suzio/Photo Researchers, Inc.; 560 *California Vaqueros* (1875), James Walker. Oil on canvas, 31" x 46". Courtesy of The Anschutz Collection. Photo by William J. O'Connor; 562 State Historical Society of North Dakota; 564 *Custer's Last Stand* (1899), Edgar S. Paxson. Oil on canvas, 70 1/2" x 106". Buffalo Bill Historical Center, Cody, Wyoming; 565 *top* The Granger Collection, New York; *center* Culver Pictures; *bottom* Library of Congress; 566 Western History Collections, University of Oklahoma Libraries; 567 Library of Congress; 568 The Kansas State Historical Society, Topeka, Kansas; 569 *top, View of San Francisco [Formerly Yerba Buena]* (1847), attributed to Victor Prevost. Oil on canvas, 25" x 30". California Historical Society, gift of the Ohio Historical Society; *bottom* The Bancroft Library, University of California, Berkeley; 570 *top* The Granger Collection, New York; *center* Courtesy of the Arizona Historical Society/Tucson; *bottom* The Granger Collection, New York; 572–573 Wyoming Division of Cultural Resources; 573 *top* Library of Congress; 575 Solomon D. Butcher Collection, Nebraska State Historical Society; 577 The Granger Collection, New York; 578 Culver Pictures; 579 *Rush for the Oklahoma Land* (1894), John Steuart Curry. Department of the Interior.

Chapter 20, 582–583 The Granger Collection, New York; 582 *top* National Museum of American History/Smithsonian Institution; *bottom* © Hulton-Deutsch Collection/Corbis; 583 *left* © Michael Maslan Historic Photographs/Corbis; *right* © Bettmann/Corbis; 585 Corbis-Bettmann; 587 Library of Congress; 588 *background* U.S. Dept. of Commerce—Patent & Trademark Office, Washington, D.C.; *left foreground* The Granger Collection, New York; *right foreground* Courtesy of AT&T; 589 *left background* U.S. Dept. of Commerce—Patent & Trademark Office, Washington, D.C.; *left foreground* First Church of Christ, Lynn, Massachusetts; 590 Special Collections Division, University of Washington Libraries. Negative no. 2315; 591 *top* Courtesy Colorado Historical Society; *bottom, The Last Spike* (1869). William T. Garrett Foundry, San Francisco. 17 6/10 carat gold, alloyed with copper. 5 9/16" x 7/16" x 1/2" (shaft including head), 1/2" x 1 3/8" x 1 1/4". Iris & B. Gerald Cantor Center for Visual Arts at Stanford University. Gift of David Hewes, 1998.115; 593 Stamp Designs © United States Postal Service. Displayed with permission. All rights reserved. Written authorization from the Postal Service is required to use, reproduce, post, transmit,, distribute, or publicly display these images; 594 Corbis-Bettmann; 595 *left, John Davison Rockefeller* (1967), Adrian Lamb, after the 1917 oil by John Singer Sargent. Oil on canvas, 58 3/4" x 45 3/4". National Portrait Gallery, Smithsonian Institution/Art Resource, New York; *right* National Portrait Gallery, Smithsonian Institution/Art Resource, New York; 596 *left The Hatch Family* (1871), Eastman Johnson. Oil on canvas, 48 x 73 3/8". The Metropolitan Museum of Art, Gift of Frederic H. Hatch, 1926 (26.97). Photograph copyright © 1999 The Metropolitan Museum of Art. *right, Room in a Tenement Flat* (about 1910), photo by Jessie Tarbox Beals. The Jacob A. Riis Collection, Museum of the City of New York; 598 *top right* Library of Congress; *center left* Chicago Historical Society; *bottom right* Library of Congress; 598 *bottom left,* 599 *center left* Corbis-Bettmann; 599 *bottom* Chicago Historical Society; 601 Corbis-Bettmann; 602 Brown Brothers.

Chapter 21, 606–607 The Granger Collection, New York; 606 *left* The Granger Collection, New York; *right* © Corbis; 607 *top* © Corbis; *bottom* The Granger Collection, New York; 609 Copyright © Collection of The New-York Historical Society; 610 Illustration by Patrick Gnan; 611 The Granger Collection, New York; 613 Corbis-Bettmann; 614 The Granger Collection, New York; 616 Brown Brothers; 617 Michael S. Yamashita/Corbis; 618 Illustration by Ronald Himler. Copyright © 1995 HarperCollins Publishers. Bottom background copyright © Bill Pogue; 619 Corbis; 620 Copyright © Jacques Chenet/Liaison Agency; 621 *top* Joseph Schwartz Collection/Corbis; *bottom* Corbis; 622 Library of Congress; 623 The Granger Collection, New York; 626, 627 Corbis-Bettmann; 628 *top* Lake County Museum/Corbis; *center, bottom* The Granger Collection, New York; 629 Corbis-Bettmann; 632 *top right* The Granger Collection, New York; 632 *bottom left* Culver Pictures; 633 Photos by Sharon Hoogstraten; 633A Corbis-Bettmann.

## Unit 7

634–635 Brown Brothers.

Chapter 22, 636 *top* Family Making Artificial Flowers (about 1910), photo by Jessie Tarbox Beals. The Jacob A. Riis Collection, Museum of the City of New York; *center* © Bettmann/Corbis; *bottom* © Bettmann/Corbis; 637 *top* Library of Congress; *center* © Corbis; *bottom* © Bettmann/Corbis; 638 Brown Brothers; 640, 641 Library of Congress; 642 *bottom* Brown Brothers; *left inset* Doubleday, Page and Company, New York, 1906, second issue; 643 *Theodore Roosevelt* (date unknown), John Singer Sargent. White House Collection. Copyright © 1992 White House Historical Association; 644 *center* Culver Pictures; *bottom left* Copyright © F. Sieb/H. Armstrong Roberts; *bottom right* Copyright © W. Bertsch/H. Armstrong Roberts; 645 *bottom* Copyright © J. Blank/H. Armstrong Roberts; 646 Eugene V. Debs Collection/Tamiment Institute Library, New York University; 648, 649 Culver Pictures; 650 *Lillian Wald* 1867-1940, public health nurse, social worker. William Valentine Schevill, 1864-1951. Oil on cardboard, 71.7 x 71.7 cm (28 1/4 x 28 1/4 in.) feigned circle, 1919. NPG. 76.37 National Portrait Gallery, Smithsonian Institution. Gift of the Visiting Nurse Service of New York/Art Resource, NY; 651 The Granger Collection, New York; 652 *left* Copyright © 1994 FPG International.

Chapter 23, 656–657 *Great White Fleet,* Harry Reuterdahl. Courtesy of the U.S. Naval Academy Museum; 656 *left* The Granger Collection, New York; *right* © Bettmann/Corbis; 657 *left The Mexican Revolution,* Diego Rivera © 2004 Banco de México Diego Rivera and Frida Kahlo Museums Trust Av. Cinco de Mayo No. 2, Col. Centro, Del Cuauhtémoc 06059, México D.F./Charles & Josette Lenars/Corbis; *right* © Lake County Museum/Corbis; 658 The Granger Collection, New York; 659 Corbis; 661 *Portrait of Queen Liliuokalani,* date and artist unknown. Bishop Museum; 662 The Granger Collection, New York; 663 Chicago Historical Society; 664, 666 The Granger Collection, New York; 667 From *Puerto Rico: A Political and Cultural History,* Arturo Morales Carrion; 668 U.S. Naval Academy Museum; 671 Illustration by Nick Rotondo; *center left* Corbis-Bettmann; 673 Copyright © Caren Firouz/Black Star/PNI; 674, The Granger Collection, New York.

### Chapter 24

Chapter 24, 676–677 The Granger Collection, New York; 676 *top* © Bettmann/Corbis; *bottom* © Swim Ink/Corbis; 677 *left* Library of Congress; *right* © Bettmann/Corbis; 679 The Granger Collection, New York; 681 *top center* Copyright © Mike Fizer/Check Six; *top right* Copyright © Hulton Getty/Tony

Stone Images; *bottom left* Hulton-Deutsch Collection/Corbis; *bottom right* Copyright © Hulton Getty/Tony Stone Images; **682** The Granger Collection, New York; **684–685** Illustration by Patrick Whelan; **684** *top right,* **686, 687** Corbis; **689** *left* From *The Enormous Room* by E. E. Cummings, Penguin Twentieth Century Classics Edition. Cover painting *Prisoner's Round* (1890), Vincent Van Gogh, after Dore. Pushkin Museum of Fine Arts, Moscow. Photo courtesy Scala/Art Resource, New York; *right* Book cover from *A Farewell to Arms* by Ernest Hemingway. Cover illustration by Cathie Bleck. Reprinted by permission of Scribner, a Division of Simon & Schuster (New York: Scribner/Simon & Schuster, 1995); **691** Wyoming Division of Cultural Resources; **692** Culver Pictures; **693** Panel no. 1: "During the World War There Was a Great Migration North by Southern Negroes" from *The Migration of the Negro* mural series (1940–41), Jacob Lawrence. Tempera on masonite, 12″ × 18″. Acquired through Downtown Gallery, 1942. The Phillips Collection, Washington, D.C.; **695** Corbis; **696** The Granger Collection, New York; **697** The Granger Collection, New York; **702** Culver Pictures; **703** Photos by Sharon Hoogstraten.

### Epilogue

**704–705** *top, left to right* LIFE cover (July 1, 1926) Fred Cooper; The Granger Collection, New York; National Archives; U.S. Air Force; *bottom, left to right* Used by permission, Elvis Presley Enterprises, Inc.; James P. Blair/National Geographic Image Collection; Larry Burrows/TimePix; © R. Ian Lloyd/Masterfile; **704** *left* © Getty Images; **705** *left* Courtesy Ronald Reagan Library; *right* © Owen Franken/Corbis. **707** Brown Brothers; **708** *top* Culver Pictures; *center* Copyright © Blank Archives/Archive Photos; *bottom* Movie Still Archives; **710** National Museum of American Art, Smithsonian Institution/Art Resource, New York; **711** Photo by Margaret Suckley/Franklin D. Roosevelt Library; **713** Copyright © Hulton Getty/Liaison Agency; **714** *top* Copyright © 1999 Owen H. K./Black Star; *bottom* The Granger Collection, New York; **716** UPI/Corbis-Bettmann; **718** U.S. Air Force Photo; **719** *top* NASA; *bottom* UPI/Corbis-Bettmann; **721** Copyright © Dirck Halstead/Liaison Agency; **722** Copyright © 1970 Elliott Erwitt/Magnum Photos, Inc.; **723** Copyright © 1963 Bob Adelman/Magnum Photos, Inc.; **724** Copyright © 1978 George Ballis/Take Stock; **725** *top* Wally McNamee/Corbis; *bottom* From the Collection of David J. and Janice L. Frent; **726** Copyright © Kenneth James/Corbis; **727** Copyright © Robert Brenner/PhotoEdit/PNI; **728–729** *background* NASA; **728** *top right* Copyright © 1996 Tom Stewart/The Stock Market; *bottom left* Copyright © Scott McKlernan/Zuna Images/The Stock Market; **729** *center* Copyright © The New Yorker Collection 1999 Mick Stevens from cartoonbank.com. All rights reserved; **731A** Library of Congress.

### Special Report

**733** *top, bottom* AP/Wide World Photos; **735** *top, bottom* AP/Wide World Photos; **736** AP/Wide World Photos; **737** *left* © Mario Tama/Getty Images; *right* © Reuters NewMedia Inc./Corbis.

### Historic Decisions of the Supreme Court

**738** *top left* Corbis; *bottom left* Copyright © 1994 North Wind Pictures; *bottom center* The Granger Collection, New York; *bottom right* Copyright © 1999 North Wind Pictures; **739** *top* Corbis; *bottom left* Corbis-Bettmann; *bottom right* AP/Wide World Photos; **740** *top left* Corbis; *bottom right* The Granger

Collection, New York; **741** Copyright © 1994 North Wind Pictures; **742** Corbis; **743** *left* Culver Pictures; *right* The Granger Collection, New York; **744** Corbis; *bottom right* The Granger Collection, New York; **745** Copyright © 1999 North Wind Pictures; **746** Corbis; **747** *left* The Granger Collection, New York; *right* Lincoln University Archives, Langston Hughes Memorial Library, Lincoln University, Penn.; **748** *top left* Corbis; *bottom right* The Granger Collection, New York; **749** AP/Wide World Photos; **750** *top left* Corbis; **751** Wally Mcnamee/Corbis; **752** *top left* Corbis; *bottom right* AP/Wide World Photos; **753** Corbis; **754** *top left* Corbis; *bottom right* Corbis-Bettmann; **756** *top left* Owen Franken/Corbis; *bottom right,* **757** AP/Wide World Photos.

### SkillBuilder Handbook

**R15** Library of Congress; **R28** Courtesy of the Lloyd Ostendorf Collection.

### Presidents of the United States

**R36-R38** The Oval Office Collection™ *except Clinton and George W. Bush;* **R38** *Clinton* AP/Wide World Photos; *George W. Bush* Bush-Cheney 2000, Inc.

Maps created by Mapping Specialists

McDougal Littell has made every effort to locate the copyright holders of all copyrighted material in this book and to make full acknowledgment for its use.